FINANCIAL ACCOUNTING

THE IMPACT ON DECISION MAKERS

SECOND EDITION

FINANCIAL ACCOUNTING
THE IMPACT ON DECISION MAKERS

SECOND EDITION

GARY A. PORTER
Loyola University Chicago

CURTIS L. NORTON
Northern Illinois University

The Dryden Press
Harcourt Brace College Publishers

Fort Worth   Philadelphia   San Diego   New York   Orlando   Austin   San Antonio
Toronto   Montreal   London   Sydney   Tokyo

Publisher	George Provol
Executive Editor	Mike Reynolds
Acquisitions Editor	Sara Tenney
Product Manager	Craig Johnson
Developmental Editor	Craig Avery
Project Editor	Jim Patterson
Art Director	Jeanette Barber
Production Manager	Lois West

Credits appear on page C-1, which constitutes a continuation of the copyright page.
Cover illustration: Andrew Judd/Masterfile

ISBN: 0-03-020483-6
Library of Congress Catalog Card Number: 97-65089

Address for orders:
The Dryden Press
6277 Sea Harbor Drive
Orlando, FL 32887-6777
1-800-782-4479

Address for editorial correspondence:
The Dryden Press
301 Commerce Street, Suite 3700
Fort Worth, TX 76102

Web site address:
http://www.hbcollege.com

The Dryden Press
Harcourt Brace College Publishers

To those who really "count":
Melissa
Kathy, Amy, Andrew

THE DRYDEN PRESS SERIES IN ACCOUNTING

Introductory

Bischoff
Introduction to College Accounting
Third Edition

Computerized

Wanlass
Computer Resource Guide: Principles of Accounting
Fourth Edition

Financial

Hanson and Hamre
Financial Accounting
Eighth Edition

Porter and Norton
Financial Accounting: The Impact on Decision Makers
Second Edition

Porter and Norton
Financial Accounting: The Impact on Decision Makers
Alternate Edition

Stickney and Weil
Financial Accounting: An Introduction to Concepts, Methods, and Uses
Eighth Edition

Managerial

Maher, Stickney, and Weil
Managerial Accounting: An Introduction to Concepts, Methods, and Uses
Sixth Edition

Intermediate

Williams, Stanga, and Holder
Intermediate Accounting
Fifth Edition

Advanced

Pahler and Mori
Advanced Accounting
Sixth Edition

Financial Statement Analysis

Stickney
Financial Statement Analysis: A Strategic Perspective
Third Edition

Auditing

Guy, Alderman, and Winters
Auditing
Fourth Edition

Rittenberg and Schwieger
Auditing: Concepts for a Changing Environment
Second Edition

Theory

Bloom and Elgers
Foundations of Accounting Theory and Policy: A Reader

Bloom and Elgers
Issues in Accounting Policy: A Reader

Reference

Bailey and Miller
Miller Comprehensive GAAS Guide
College Edition

Williams and Miller
Miller Comprehensive GAAP Guide
College Edition

Governmental and Not-For-Profit

Douglas
Governmental and Nonprofit Accounting:Theory and Practice
Second Edition

ABOUT THE AUTHORS

The Porter/Norton Story

When the first edition of *Financial Accounting: The Impact on Decision Makers* was published in 1995, an unparalleled success story was created. The authors' own teaching experiences and observations, combined with extensive research by The Dryden Press, culminated in a new entry into the accounting market and a fresh approach to teaching. This approach was simple: deemphasize procedures, focus on introductory accounting concepts, and teach financial accounting from a financial statement user—rather than preparer—perspective. The Porter/Norton story was born.

Now, with the second edition, a great book has been made even better. Gary Porter and Curt Norton listened to users of the first edition who suggested three things: emphasize key concepts, eliminate unnecessary procedural detail, and engage the student even more in subject material.

The changes have resulted in a more streamlined, less procedural, and more student-friendly textbook—a book based on four guiding philosophies: (1) today's introductory accounting students must learn how to interpret and use financial statements; (2) students need practice relating the fundamental accounting concepts to real-world statements; (3) students should focus on the "why" instead of the "how" in using accounting information to make decisions; and (4) students do not all learn the same, nor do professors teach in the same way.

The authors invite you to share these philosophies in the second edition, as they have in their own classrooms and professional lives.

Gary A. Porter, CPA, is Professor of Accounting at Loyola University Chicago. He earned Ph.D. and M.B.A. degrees from the University of Colorado and his B.S.B.A. from Drake University. He has published in the *Journal of Accounting Education, Journal of Accounting, Auditing & Finance,* and *Journal of Accountancy,* among others and has conducted numerous workshops on the subject of introductory accounting education.

Dr. Porter's professional activities include membership on the Illinois CPA Society's Innovations in Accounting Education Grants Committee, experience as a staff accountant with Deloitte & Touche in Denver, and a participant in KPMG Peat Marwick Foundation's Faculty Development Program.

He has won an Excellence in Teaching award from the University of Colorado and an Outstanding Professor award from San Diego State University. Dr. Porter has served on the steering committee of the midwest region of the American Accounting Association and is currently on the board of directors of the Chicago chapter of the Financial Executives Institute.

Curtis L. Norton is Deloitte & Touche Professor of Accountancy at Northern Illinois University in DeKalb, Illinois. He earned his Ph.D. from Arizona State University, his M.B.A. from the University of South Dakota, and his B.S. from Jamestown College, North Dakota. His extensive list of publications includes articles in *Accounting Horizons, The Journal of Accounting Education, Journal of Accountancy, Journal of Corporate Accounting, Journal of the American Taxation Association, Real Estate Review, The Accounting Review, CPA Journal,* and many others. In 1988–89, Dr. Norton received the University Excellence in Teaching Award, the highest university-wide teaching recognition at NIU. He is also a consultant and has conducted training programs for governmental authorities, banks, utilities, and other entities.

Dr. Norton is a member of the American Accounting Association and a member and officer of the Financial Executives Institute.

PREFACE

To the Instructor

It is our goal in writing this textbook that students gain a thorough understanding of introductory concepts in accounting as well as the powerful ability to make the transition from textbook concepts to the real world, an ability that is important in any business career. This textbook offers the flexibility of teaching a conceptual and real-world approach to financial accounting.

Throughout the development of the second edition, we were continually reminded by adopters and reviewers of the demands in accomplishing the above goal in the classroom. We were also reminded of the need to emphasize key concepts, eliminate unnecessary procedural details, and find ways to engage students in the material. In writing the second edition, we have responded to such feedback while utilizing four guiding philosophies:

1. **Today's introductory accounting students must learn to interpret and use financial statements.** Our original two introductory chapters, "Accounting as a Form of Communication" and "Financial Statements and the Annual Report," have been retained, given their great success in launching a financial statement focus in the course. We have taken greater steps to incorporate information that will allow students to gain the necessary knowledge of the uses and interrelationships of financial statements:

   ■ To increase our emphasis on how to read and understand financial statements, we have **reduced the number of preparer-oriented topics.** We continue to link transactions and journal entries to the financial statements by way of the accounting equation.

   ■ A **new cash flows exhibit** found in Chapters 6 through 12 relates the material presented in each chapter to the statement of cash flows.

   ■ Our **end-of-chapter problems and cases** have been revised to add **more thought-provoking questions and more practice** in interpreting financial statements.

   Our approach to accounting topics is to provide very clear concepts, examples, and terminology for students. As in the first edition, we have taken great efforts to ensure we clearly explain difficult concepts. Additionally,

   ■ **Chapter 2, "Financial Statements and the Annual Report," is considerably streamlined** by substituting the statements of only one company, Starbucks, for numerous companies' statements found in the first edition. We retained the parallel coverage of simple statements of our hypothetical company, Dixon Sporting Goods, with that of Starbucks.

   ■ **ALTERNATE TERMS** in every chapter have been **expanded** to address the varying use of terminology that can roadblock a student's learning. We have also made

FOCUS ON FINANCIAL STATEMENTS

certain that new terms are defined as they are introduced and that the vocabulary in each chapter is not overwhelming.

- **End-of-chapter exercises, problems, and cases** have been carefully checked to ensure that they fully conform to and adequately test the content of the chapter. Further, the test bank has also been developed in parallel with the end-of-chapter material to ensure maximum pedagogical value.

REAL-COMPANY FOCUS

2. **Students need practice relating fundamental accounting concepts to real-world statements.**

- We continue to use **Ben & Jerry's** as a "flagship company." Its straightforward and entertaining annual report is packaged with new copies of the textbook, and its financial statements and notes are reprinted in an appendix at the back of the book.

- Each **chapter-opening company** has been **more fully integrated into the chapter text** and additionally as sidebars, in the chapter-ending statement of cash flows exhibit, in end-of-chapter materials, and onto our Web site. In many instances, financial statement items are compared and contrasted with other companies. Integrating the chapter-opening company into the chapter allows students to gain more familiarity with the company and its numbers, allowing them to more fully analyze the company, its industry conditions, and business strategies.

- A number of **new companies** have been added to this edition—both in the text and in the end-of-chapter materials—to stimulate student interest and identification with the topic. Companies with a similar appeal to Ben & Jerry's, such as Ride, Inc., a snowboard manufacturer, are used to illustrate key concepts.

DECISION EMPHASIS

3. **If students have a concrete understanding of the "why" instead of the "how," they will be much better able to use accounting information to make decisions.** As in the first edition, we continue to incorporate a decision-making emphasis, adding new material such as the uses of **time-value of money** concepts and the **choice of stock versus bond financing alternatives.** Additionally,

- **ACCOUNTING FOR YOUR DECISIONS** boxes were a unique feature of the first edition that placed the student in a role-playing situation as a user of financial information. In the second edition, we have **significantly increased** the number of these in-text, role-playing scenarios (from two to four in most chapters), so they can also be used as a form of **self-study problem.** We have also **broadened their focus** to include both business decisions and financial decisions students might make.

- The **end-of-chapter material** has been expanded to include more questions that **ask the student to analyze, evaluate, and make decisions or recommendations** regarding specific material.

- The accompanying **Interactive Decision Cases for Financial Accounting CD-ROM** additionally reinforces practice in making decisions based on real company information.

PEDAGOGY AND STUDENT APPEAL

4. **Not all students learn in the same way, nor do their professors teach in the same way.** For the *professor,*

- Our textbook provides instructors with flexibility, allowing them to emphasize either journal entries or the accounting equation as a way to understand transactions.

- We have retained the organization of the first edition in which the first two chapters give a big picture overview, followed by an introduction to the accounting model and sections on assets, liabilities, and owners' equity items. We believe this **transactions-based approach to financial accounting** provides a highly logical, structured approach to understanding the composition of financial statements and how they can be used in making decisions.

- We have also retained the 15-chapter organization of the first edition, which gives instructors the option of covering later chapters if desired.

- We **eliminated unnecessary procedural details,** and you will find such changes worth noting in the "Content Changes" section below.

For the *student,* we have added an **international perspective** throughout the text, serving the increasing need for students to have global business awareness and out-lining conceptually interesting aspects of international accounting. Also, throughout the book we have attempted to engage the student in a variety of ways to learn other than simply the printed word:

- **STUDY LINKS** at the beginning of each chapter review the previous chapter, introduce the current chapter, and look forward to the following chapter. This gives the student an integrated perspective on the text.

- **Photos and captions** have been revised and expanded to **better explain or eluci-date** text material.

- **Exhibits** have been enhanced and added wherever possible to be more visually ap-pealing to students and make it **easier to learn.**

- **Captions are used in selected real financial statements** to allow students to focus their attention on a specific reporting issue and not become bogged down with the complexities of the statements. Wherever financial statement information appears in text, it has been highlighted with a green border to distinguish it from other tabular material.

Content Changes

In **Chapter 1,** "Accounting as a Form of Communication," we have revised the exhibit that explains articulation of the financial statements to make it easier to understand. A new section was added to interest students in accounting as a career, focusing on both the opportunities and salaries in the profession. The section in the chapter on standard setting is enhanced with a discussion of the role of the International Accounting Stan-dards Committee (IASC).

Chapter 2, "Financial Statements and the Annual Report," serves as an overview of the various elements in the annual report by comparing the statements of a hypothetical company, Dixon Sporting Goods, with those of a real company. The coverage in this chapter has been streamlined considerably from the first edition, most noticeably by substituting the statements of only one company, Starbucks, for the numerous company statements presented in the first edition. An international perspective has been added following the conceptual framework section of the chapter by introducing the efforts of the IASC in this area.

We have streamlined the coverage of the accounting cycle in **Chapter 3,** "Processing Accounting Information" and **Chapter 4,** "Income Measurement and Accrual Account-ing," by eliminating procedural topics such as reversing entries, finding errors in the trial balance, and post-closing trial balances. The emphasis of the chapters is on ac-counting as an information system; therefore, topics such as posting from the journal to the ledger are still covered, but not in as much procedural detail as in the first edition.

We have made similar changes in **Chapter 5,** "Merchandise Accounting and Internal Control." Only the gross method of accounting for sales and purchases discounts is cov-ered, and the appendix on worksheets and closing entries for a merchandiser has been eliminated. The coverage of internal control in the body of the chapter focuses on the fundamental concepts, with the material on document flow for a merchandiser moved to an appendix.

Chapter 6, "Inventories and Costs of Goods Sold," has been enhanced with a discus-sion of how companies in other countries account for inventory and the stance of the IASC. The section on analyzing the management of inventory turnover has been en-hanced, and a new exhibit has been added to compare inventory turnover for Circuit

City and Safeway. Coverage of both the retail inventory method and the lower-of-cost-or-market rule have been streamlined. As mentioned earlier, beginning in this chapter and continuing through Chapter 12, two new exhibits have been added to each chapter to illustrate how key financial statement items are reported on the statement of cash flows.

Chapter 7, "Cash and Receivables," has been revised to focus sharper attention on the key reporting and control issues for cash and receivables. To do this, we have eliminated the coverage of bad debt recoveries and significantly shortened the discussion of discounting notes receivable.

Chapter 8, "Operating Assets: Property, Plant, and Equipment, Natural Resources, and Intangibles," has been simplified by eliminating much of the discussion of the capitalization of interest and by deleting the sum-of-years' digits depreciation method. The chapter has been enhanced by a new exhibit and explanation of the factors that management should consider in choosing a depreciation method. The cash flow consequences of depreciation and other transactions affecting long-term assets is illustrated for the opening vignette company.

A new exhibit has been added to **Chapter 9,** "Current Liabilities, Contingent Liabilities, and the Time Value of Money," to compare the current and quick ratios of six real-world companies. A new section has been added to explain more fully why the time value of money is important in both personal and accounting decisions. The discussion of contingent liabilities has been revised, and an exhibit illustrating the cash-flow impacts of current liabilities has been added.

Chapter 10, "Long-Term Liabilities," has been simplified by reducing the discussion of amortization of bond discounts and premiums to one method, the effective interest method. A new exhibit has been added to illustrate how to read bond listings in *The Wall Street Journal*. The chapter utilizes the real-world statements of both Coca-Cola and PepsiCo to allow instructors to compare two companies within the same industry. Finally, the section on analysis of long-term liabilities has been moved toward the end of the chapter.

Chapter 11, "Stockholders' Equity," contains a new section on comparing stock and debt as financing alternatives. Detail has been removed by eliminating the topic of stock subscriptions, much of the material on retirement of stock, and a portion of the material on treasury stock. The chapter introduces the real-world financial statements of both Ford and Chrysler and presents a new exhibit on the dividend payout ratios of the companies in the auto industry.

The focus of **Chapter 12,** "Analysis of Retained Earnings and Stockholders' Equity," has been altered to emphasize additional aspects of retained earnings and stockholders' equity, and the chapter title reflects the new focus. A section was added to stress the role of retained earnings as a link between the income statement and balance sheet, and a new exhibit illustrates this important concept graphically. Much of the discussion of appropriations of retained earnings has been eliminated, and the section on the statement of stockholders' equity has been reduced.

In **Chapter 13,** "Additional Reporting Issues: Intercompany Investments and Foreign Currency," we have added a new exhibit on foreign exchange rates to help students understand how to read foreign currency quotes in the newspaper. We have also added an excerpt from the statement of cash flows of Intel to augment the section on how companies reflect investments in their cash flows statement.

Chapter 14, "The Statement of Cash Flows," and **Chapter 15,** "Financial Statement Analysis," allow the instructor the maximum flexibility. In Chapter 14, instructors can emphasize either the concepts of cash flows or the preparation of the cash flows statement, or both, or they can defer the chapter to a later course. Chapter 15 consolidates the coverage of ratios that was integrated into the chapters, allowing instructors to teach financial statement analysis throughout the course, only in this chapter, or in another course. Thus we have made only minimal changes to these well-received chapters.

An extensive listing of chapter-by-chapter changes can be found on our Web site.

Supplements and Teaching Materials

A key contributor to the success of the first edition was a supplements package that was flexible, functional, innovative, and fully integrated with the goals and pedagogy of the text. For the second edition, we have once again listened to instructors' and students' needs in the new classroom and study environment and created a teaching and learning package to meet those needs.

For the Instructor

Solutions Manual (by the text authors), contains solutions to questions, exercises, problems, cases, and "From Concept to Practice" boxes for each chapter. (Suggested solutions for research cases appear on the book's Web site.) End-of-chapter items have been independently solved by two instructors (David Malone of Texas Tech University and Michael Claire of the College of San Mateo) to assure solution accuracy. *Also available in Word 6.0 for Windows files*.

Instructor's Resource Kit (by Patricia Doherty, Boston University) is a complete toolbox for instructors who teach a more financial statement user–oriented, interactive course. Containing chapter outlines, projects and activities, and a bibliography of readings, the Instructor's Resource Kit will provide ideas, suggestions, and resources for a variety of classroom styles. Numerous activities throughout are based on annual report exhibits, supporting the approach taken in the text. *Also available in Word 6.0 for Windows files*.

Test Bank (by Diane L. Tanner, University of North Florida, and Kevin Feeney, Southern Connecticut State University) has been thoroughly revised to increase its flexibility. Now containing more test items (approximately 150 questions per chapter), the Test Bank for the second edition has a greater variety of types of problem material to choose from, including multiple choice, short problems, matching, fill in the blanks, new cross-out the incorrect answer, new true-or-false questions, and new essay questions. It has been thoroughly error-checked and compared with the end-of-chapter material in the textbook for maximum pedagogical value.

EXAMASTER+ Computerized Test Bank (Windows) allows instructors to customize their tests by selecting items according to their individual teaching preferences. In addition, RequesTest service allows instructors to call a toll-free number to order custom test masters. A fax service is also available. RequesTest service is available Monday through Friday from 9 A.M. to 4 P.M. (Central Standard Time). Your sales representative can supply details.

Solutions Transparencies for selected exercises, problems, and cases are available in large type in acetate form. Transparency masters are available for all remaining solutions.

Teaching Transparencies contain a variety of visual tools for lecture enhancement taken largely from the text and based on the Lectures in PowerPoint. Includes text charts and graphs, reproductions of selected financial statements, lecture outlines, and additional lecture aids.

Lectures in PowerPoint (by Sandra Devona, Northern Illinois University) have been extensively revised for easier use for the second edition. More concise and focused on key topics and visual learning styles, Lectures in PowerPoint slides feature charts and graphs from the text as well as real-world financial statements.

Lecture Launching Videos provide a fuller view of selected chapter-opening companies, their strategic concerns, and recent financial decisions.

Classroom Guide to the Interactive CD-ROM (by Karen Walton, John Carroll University) contains classroom suggestions on the use of the student Interactive Decisions CD-ROM.

Software Support is available by calling 1-800-447-9457 Monday–Friday from 7 A.M. to 6 P.M. (Central Standard Time). Technical support is available twenty-four hours every day by fax or Internet. Users may access the fax-on-demand service at 1-800-352-1680. Users may contact the Technical Support Center at http://www.hbtechsupport.com

For the Student

Study Guide (by Mary Nisbet, University of California at Santa Barbara) contains study aids that let students better review chapter topics on their own, including a review of key concepts by learning objective with integrated Test Your Understanding questions and answers and a greater variety of self-test items.

Student Lecture Mate (by Sandy Devona, Northern Illinois University) contain printed versions of all the Lectures in PowerPoint slides in one handy booklet so that students can follow along during PowerPoint lectures and concentrate on the lecture rather than on taking notes.

Working Papers for every end-of-chapter exercise, problem, and case allow students to complete their assignments with a minimum of scratch work. Where possible, given data and repetitive or nonessential information has been pre-completed so that students can better concentrate on developing their problem-solving skills.

Guide to Understanding and Using Annual Reports (by Angela Bell, Floyd W. Kirby, and Elise M. Gantt, all of Jacksonville State University) contains a series of structured assignments in financial statement analysis, using World Wide Web and traditional research techniques outlined in the case, culminating in groupwork, decision-making scenarios, and writing exercises. The case is designed to foster business skills in systematic data gathering, understanding, analyzing, presenting, and making decisions using financial information. It is available with an Excel/Lotus spreadsheet disk.

Interactive Decision Cases for Financial Accounting CD-ROM (by Guided Explorations LLC) consist of eight cases linked to important financial accounting topics. This CD-ROM allows the student to play the role of an internal or external user of accounting information. Actual company financial statements as well as video and news clips, internal corporate correspondence, and other critical information are available to aid the student in making financial accounting decisions. Each case uses information pertaining to real-life companies such as Whirlpool, Kmart, or Dell Computer.

Bridge Software is tutorial software covering procedures no longer included in many user-oriented introductory accounting courses.

Tax Supplement (by Anita Feller, University of Illinois) contains essential coverage of corporate and individual taxation issues, complete with assignment material. (Instructor's solutions to assignment material are available free to adopters.)

Computerized Practice Set is a brief practice set containing reduced procedures and flexible, user-friendly general ledger software.

Procedural Review Software is based on the first edition's printed Procedural Review supplement. This software is designed to provide extra practice for procedures covered in the text, freeing class time for other activities.

Key Figures contain check figures for selected end-of-chapter assignments. It is available to adopters individually or in class bundles of 30.

Porter/Norton Web site. The Dryden Press has developed a Web site (http://www.dryden.com) to help instructors and students use the wealth of financial information available on the World Wide Web. The student can obtain financial statements, current news, SEC filings, and stock quotes for every company found in the text. The instructor can obtain all the above plus view and download many of the ancillaries to the text. As a special feature, the Porter/Norton Web site presents an Online Case Company to parallel the use of Ben & Jerry's annual report in the text. We have selected IBM's online annual report for its ease of use and instructional value. The student is challenged to read and interpret IBM's annual report by our **online "FROM CONCEPT TO PRACTICE"** exercises and **online chapter cases.**

http://www.dryden.com/account/porter

Acknowledgments

To develop, write, and publish a book to meet the changing needs of students and instructors truly requires a team effort. We appreciate the sincere and devoted work of all those who have contributed to our book.

Reviewers and Focus Group Participants for the First Edition:

Diana Adcox
University of North Florida
Saul Ahiaria
SUNY at Buffalo
Mike Akers
Marquette University
Marcia Anderson
University of Cincinnati
David Angelovich
San Francisco State University
Alana Baier
Marquette University
Amelia A. Baldwin-Morgan
Eastern Michigan University
Bobbe M. Barnes
University of Colorado at Denver
Maj. Curt Barry
U.S. Military Academy
Peter Battell
University of Vermont
Paul Bayes
East Tennessee State University
Mark Bettner
Bucknell University
Frank Biegbeder
Rancho Santiago Community College
Francis Bird
University of Richmond
Karen Bird
University of Michigan
Eddy Birrer
Gonzaga University
Michelle Bissonnette
California State University–Fresno
John Blahnik
Lorain County Community College
Ed Bresnahan
American River College
Sarah Brown
University of North Alabama
Philip Buchanan
George Washington University
Rosie Bukics
Lafayette College

Carolyn Callahan
University of Notre Dame
Linda Campbell
University of Toledo
Jim Cashell
Miami University
Charles Caufield
Loyola University Chicago
Gyan Chandra
Miami University
Mayer Chapman
California State University at Long Beach
Alan Cherry
Loyola Marymount University
Mike Claire
College of San Mateo
David C. Coffee
Western Carolina University
David Collins
Eastern Kentucky University
Judith Cook
Grossmont College
John C. Corless
California State University–Sacramento
Dean Crawford
University of Toledo
Shirley J. Daniel
University of Hawaii at Manoa
Alan Davis
Community College of Philadelphia
Henry H. Davis
Eastern Illinois University
Lyle E. Dehning
Metropolitan State College–Denver
Patricia Doherty
Boston University
Margaret Douglas
University of Arkansas
Kathy Dunne
Rider College
Kenneth Elvik
Iowa State University
Anette Estrada
Grand Valley State University

Ed Etter
Syracuse University
Alan Falcon
Loyola Marymount University
Charles Fazzi
Robert Morris College
Anita Feller
University of Illinois
Howard Felt
Temple University
David Fetyko
Kent State University
Richard File
University of Nebraska–Omaha
Ed Finkhauser
University of Utah
Jeannie M. Folk
College of DuPage
J. Patrick Forrest
Western Michigan University
Patrick Fort
University of Alaska–Fairbanks
Diana Franz
University of Toledo
Tom Frecka
University of Notre Dame
Gary Freeman
University of Tulsa
Veronique Frucot
Rutgers University–Camden
Joe Gallo
Cuyahoga Community College
Michelle Gannon
Western Connecticut State University
Will Garland
Coastal Carolina University
John Gartska
Loyola Marymount University
Roger Gee
San Diego Mesa College
Cynthia Van Gelderen
Aquinas College
Linda Genduso
Nova University

Don E. Giacomino
Marquette University
Claudia Gilbertston
Anoka Ramsey Community College
Lorraine Glascock
University of Alabama
Larry Godwin
University of Montana
Lynn Grace
Edison Community College
Marilyn Greenstein
Lehigh University
Paul Griffin
University of California–Davis
Leon Hanouille
Syracuse University
Joseph Hargadon
Widener University
Robert Hartwig
Worcester State College
Jean Hatcher
University of South Carolina at Sumner
Donna Sue Hetzel
Western Michigan University
Thomas F. Hilgeman
St. Louis Community College–Meramec
Robert E. Holtfreter
Ft. Hays State University
Kathy Horton
University of Illinois, Chicago
Bruce Ikawa
Loyola Marymount University
Danny Ivancevich
University of Nevada–Las Vegas
Janet Jackson
Wichita State University
Sharon Jackson
Auburn University at Montgomery
Randy Johnston
Pennsylvania State University
William Jones
Seton Hall University
Naida Kaen
University of New Hampshire
Manu Kai'ama
University of Hawaii at Manoa
Jane Kapral
Clark University
Marcia Kertz
San Jose State University
Jean Killey
Midlands Technical College
Ronald King
Washington University
William Kinsella
Loyola Marymount University
Jay LaGregs
Tyler Junior College
Michael Lagrone
Clemson University
Lucille E. Lammers
Illinois State University
Ellen Landgraf
Loyola University Chicago
Horace Landry
Syracuse University
Kristine Lawyer
North Carolina State University

Terry Lease
Loyola Marymount University
Susan Lightle
Wright State University
Tom Linsmeier
University of Iowa
Chao-Shin Liu
University of Notre Dame
Bruce Lubich
Syracuse University
Catherine Lumbattis
Southern Illinois University
Patsy Lund
Lakewood Community College
Raymond D. MacFee, Jr.
University of Colorado
David Malone
University of Idaho
Janice Mardon
Green River Community College
Mary D. Maury
St. John's University
Al Maypers
University of North Texas
John C. McCabe
Ball State University
Nancy McClure
Lock Haven University
Margaret McCrory
Marist College
Christine McKeag
University of Evansville
Thomas D. McLaughlin
Monmouth College
Laura McNally
Black Hills State College
Mallory McWilliams
San Jose State University
E. James Meddaugh
Ohio University
Cynthia Miller
GM Institute
William Mister
Colorado State University
Tami Mittelstaedt
University of Notre Dame
Perry Moore
David Lipscomb University
Barbara Morris
Angelo State University
Mike Morris
University of Notre Dame
Theodore D. Morrison
Valparaiso University
Howard E. Mount
Seattle Pacific University
Rafael Munoz
University of Notre Dame
Mary J. Nisbet
University of California–Santa Barbara
Curtis L. Norton
Northern Illinois University
Priscilla O'Clock
Xavier University
Phil Olds
Virginia Commonwealth University
Michael O'Neill
Gannon University

Janet O'tousa
University of Notre Dame
Rimona Palas
William Paterson College of New Jersey
Beau Parent
Tulane University
Paul Parkison
Ball State University
Sue Pattillo
University of Notre Dame
Ron Pawliczek
Boston College
Donna Philbrick
Portland State University
Gary A. Porter
Loyola University Chicago
Harry V. Poynter
Central Missouri State University
Joseph Ragan
St. Joseph's University
Mitchell Raiborn
Bradley University
Ann Riley
American University
Mary Rolfes
Mankato State University
Leo A. Ruggle
Mankato State University
Victoria Rymer
University of Maryland
George Sanderson
Moorhead State University
Karen Saurlander
University of Toledo
Warren Schlesinger
Ithaca College
Edward S. Schwan
Susquehanna University
Don Schwartz
National University
Richard Scott
University of Virginia
Richard Sherman
St. Joseph's University
Ray Slager
Calvin College
Amy Spielbauer
St. Norbert College
Charles Stanley
Baylor University
Catherine Staples
Virginia Commonwealth University
Anita Stellenwerf
Ramapo College
Stephen Strange
Indiana University at Kokomo
Linda Sugarman
University of Akron
Kathy Sullivan
George Washington University
Jeanie Sumner
Pacific Lutheran University
Judy Swingen
Rochester Institute of Technology
Tim Tancy
University of Notre Dame
Bente Villadsen
Washington University

Alan K. Vogel
Cuyahoga Community College–Western
Vicki Vorell
Cuyahoga Community College–Western
Phil Walter
Bellevue Community College
Ann Watkins
Louisiana State University
Judy Wenzel
Gustavus Adolphus College
Charles Werner
Loyola University Chicago

Michael Werner
University of Miami
Paul Wertheim
Pepperdine University
Shari Wescott
Houston Baptist University
T. Sterling Wetzel
Oklahoma State University
Steven D. White
Western Kentucky University
Samuel Wild
Loyola Marymount University

Jack Wilkerson
Wake Forest University
Lyle Wimmergren
Worcester Polytechnic Institute
Carol Wolk
University of Tennessee
Steve Wong
San Jose City College
Robert Zahary
California State University at Los Angeles
Thomas L. Zeller
Loyola University Chicago

Survey Respondents for the Second Edition:

Ray Bainbridge
Lehigh University
Dorcas Berg
Wingate University
Bruce Bolick
University of Mary Hardin Baylor
Frank Bouchlers
North Carolina State University
Thomas Brady
University of Dayton
Bob Brill
St. Bonaventure University
Sarah Brown
University of North Alabama
David Brunn
Carthage College
Gary Bulmash
American University
Brian Burks
Harding University
Judith Cadle
Tarleton State University
John E. Coleman
University of Massachusetts at Boston
Carrie Cristea
Augustana College, South Dakota
Fred Current
Furman University
Jim Davis
Clemson University
Les Dlabay
Lake Forest College
Patricia Douglas
Loyola Marymount University
Joan Friedman
Illinois Wesleyan University
Sharon Garvin
Wayne State College
Art Goldman
University of Kentucky
Bud Granger
Mankato State University
Jack Grinnell
University of Vermont
Al Hannan
College of Notre Dame
Suzanne Hartley
Franklin University

Donna Hetzel
Western Michigan University
Nathan Hindi
Shippensburgh University of Pennsylvania
Betty Horn
Southern Connecticut State University
Fred Ihrke
Winona State University
Patricia Johnson
Canisius College
Becky Jones
Baylor University
Don Kellogg
Rock Valley College
Rita Kiugery
University of Delaware
Paul Kleichman
University of Richmond
George Klersey
Birmingham Southern College
Lynn Koshiyama
University of Alaska
Bobby Kuhlmann
Chaffey College
James Kurtenbach
Iowa State University
Jay LaGregs
Tyler Junior College
Laurie Larson
Valencia Community College
Chao Liu
Tarleton State University
Gina Lord
Santa Rosa Junior College
George Macklin
Susquehanna University
Jim Martin
University of Montevallo
Laurie McWhorter
University of Kentucky
Paul Mihalek
University of Hartford
Charles Milliner
Glendale Community College
Marcia Niles
University of Idaho
Mary Ellen O'Grady
Ramapo College

Bruce Oliver
Rochester Institute of Technology
Paul Parkison
Ball State University
Victor Pastena
SUNY Buffalo
Charles A. Pauley
Gannon University
Chris Pew
Galivan College
Al Rainford
Greenfield Community College
Keith Richardson
Indiana State University
Joseph Rue
Syracuse University
Rick Samuelson
San Diego State University
Gail Sanderson
Lebanon Valley College
Richard Sathe
University of St. Thomas
Ron Singer
University of Wisconsin–Parkside
David Smith
Metropolitan State University
David Smith
University of Dayton
Kim Sorenson
Eastern Oregon State University
Jens Stephan
University of Cincinnati
David Strupeck
Indiana University NW
Larry Tartaligno
Cabrillo College
Dewey Ward
Michigan State University
Jennifer Wells
University of San Francisco
Paul Wertheim
Pepperdine University
Jill Whitley
Sioux Falls College
Jane Wiese
Valencia Community College
David Willis
Illinois Wesleyan University

Reviewers and Focus Group Participants for the Second Edition:

Angela Bell
Jacksonville University
Bryan Burks
Harding University
Judith Cook
Grossmont Community College
Rosalind Cranor
Virginia Polytechnic Institute
Les Dlabay
Lake Forest College
Jaime Doran
Muhlenberg College
Alan Doyle
Pima Community College East
Alan Drebin
Northwestern University
Dean Edmiston
Emporia State University
Leo Gabriel
Bethel College
Lorraine Glasscock
University of North Alabama
Bonnie Hairrell
Birmingham Southern
Sharon Jackson
Auburn University, Montgomery
Stanley Jenne
University of Montana

Mary Keim
California State University–Bakersfield
Anne Marie Keinath
Indiana University Northwest
Robert Kelly
Corning Community College
Charles Konkol
University of Wisconsin–Milwaukee
Frank Korman
Mountain View College
James Kurtenbach
Iowa State University
Tom Lee
Winona State University
Alan Lord
Bowling Green State University
Bruce Lubich
American University
Jim Martin
University of Montevallo
Daniel O'Mara
Quinnipiac College
John Osborn
California State University–Fresno
Prakash Pai
Kent State University
John Rhode
University of San Francisco

Marilyn Sagrillo
University of Wisconsin–Green Bay
Karen Sedatole
Stephen F. Austin
John Sherman
University of Texas, Dallas
Richard Silkoff
Quinnipiac College
Jill Smith
Idaho State University
Donna Street
James Madison University
Martha Turner
Bowling Green State University
Karen Walton
John Carroll University
Dewey Ward
Michigan State University
Michael Welker
Drexel University
Jane Wells
University of Kentucky
Betty Wolterman
St. John's University, MN
Steven Wong
San Jose City College
Gail Wright
Bryant College

We wish to thank Donna Street (James Madison University) for her suggestions leading to the inclusion of international accounting issues. Jeannie Folk (College of DuPage) and Donna Hetzel (Western Michigan University) provided invaluable help in revising end-of-chapter problem material and the Solutions Manual. We also wish to thank Sylvia Ong (Paradise Valley Community College), Les Dlabay (Lake Forest College), Stuart Weiss, and Karen Hill for their help in revising the features in the text.

The following supplement reviewers have aided us in the development of the package: Sarah Brown (University of North Alabama), Jennifer Wells (University of San Francisco), Laurie Larson, (Valencia Community College), Richard Silkoff (Quinnipiac College), Mary Houser (Western Michigan University) Steven Wong (San Jose City College), Suzanne Hartley (Franklin University).

We wish to thank O'Donnell and Associates, in particular Carrie O'Donnell and Karen Misler, for their many efforts in this project, its research, and its supplements. We also wish to thank Michael Mueller, our webmaster, as well as Archipelago Productions, for their initiatives on the book's Web site.

We are grateful to the editorial, marketing, and production team at The Dryden Press for their invaluable efforts: Mike Reynolds, Sara Tenney, Craig Avery, Laura Hayes, Craig Johnson, Jennifer Langer, Jim Patterson, Lois West, Jeanette Barber, and Annette Coolidge.

Gary A. Porter
Curtis L. Norton

BRIEF CONTENTS

CONTENTS

Ben & Jerry's Homemade Inc., like all companies in this book, uses its annual report to communicate the year's financial performance.

Each chapter contains the following material:
Review Problem, Solution to Review Problem, Chapter Highlights, Key Terms Quiz,
Alternate Terms, Questions, Exercises, Problems, Alternate Problems, Cases,
Solutions to Key Terms Quiz

Starbucks Corporation has an ambitious growth plan, and by reading and understanding its financial statements, users can see how that growth can be sustained in the future.

Ride Inc. had multimillion-dollar sales in snowboard equipment in its first year, and spectacular growth by year 3—due in part to the strength of an accounting system that lets its managers make smart decisions based on accurate and timely information.

McDonald's Corporation uses income from franchises as fuel for growth, and this chapter looks at the revenue recognition principles underlying how McDonald's earns those revenues.

The Gap Inc. creates value in its products, holds down costs of goods sold, and grows sales in a controlled environment outlined in a section of its annual report titled "Management's Report on Financial Information."

Circuit City focuses on the inventory valuation issues covered in this chapter, as inventories on a diverse mix of products comprise about half its investment in assets.

PepsiCo Inc. generates significant cash and receivables from its operations; CEO Wayne Calloway sees cash flows as contributing greatly to the "strength and vitality" of the company.

Time Warner relies on operating assets and intangible assets such as copyrights, trademarks, and franchises to market information and entertainment through its cable-TV systems, prime-time television programming, print media, and musical recordings.

PART III
Accounting for Liabilities and Owners' Equity   405

Chapter 9
Current Liabilities, Contingent Liabilities, and the Time Value of Money   406

JCPenney monitors its current liabilities carefully in order to maintain close supplier relationships and speed distribution of new products to meet the demands of consumers.

Coca-Cola's global presence has allowed it to issue long-term debt in U.S. dollars, Japanese yen, and German marks to minimize the overall costs of borrowing.

The value of Ford Motor Company's stock has grown dramatically as a result of cash dividends, stock splits, and the favorable earnings of the company.

Sprint's industry has undergone massive change because of telecommunications deregulation; as a result, Sprint reports its earnings in several different categories.

Whirpool employs a global strategy to market its home appliances in more than 140 countries, and its annual report reflects the impact of those international ventures.

IBM's statement of cash flows provides insights into why it is now the world's largest information technology service company.

Wrigley Company has been successful in the chewing gum business, and its financial statements and highlights of operations can be analyzed to provide insights into the history of that success.

FINANCIAL ACCOUNTING
THE IMPACT ON DECISION MAKERS

SECOND EDITION

A WORD TO STUDENTS ABOUT THIS COURSE

Knowing about accounting is just smart for everyone in today's job market. Whether you plan a career in marketing, management, or graphic arts, understanding how financial information affects you and your work is important. Granted, you'll crunch some numbers in this course, but you'll take it one guided step after another. You'll also learn how companies present themselves to the public in actual annual reports. You'll acquire the skills and tools to understand and analyze their numbers for yourself—even make financial decisions based on your analysis. And you'll learn to back up your numbers in writing. Along the way, you'll have the chance to play different decision-making roles as student and businessperson, and to meet successful users of financial information. **In short, this course will help you think, talk, and write more effectively, whatever your future occupation.**

The Accounting Model

Accounting as a Form of Communication

STUDY LINKS

A Look at This Chapter

We begin the study of accounting by considering why financial information is important in making decisions and who uses this information. This will require us to examine the various forms that organizations take and the types of activities in which they engage. We will see that accounting is an important form of communication and that financial statements are the medium that accountants use to communicate with those who in some way have an interest in the financial affairs of a company.

A Look at Upcoming Chapters

Chapter 1 introduces you to accounting and financial statements. In Chapter 2, we look in more detail at the composition of each of the statements and the conceptual framework that supports the work of the accountant. Chapter 3 steps back from financial statements, the end result, and examines how companies process economic events as a basis for preparing the statements. Chapter 4 completes our introduction to the accounting model by considering the importance of accrual accounting in this communication process.

FOCUS ON FINANCIAL RESULTS

Who cares about the financial performance of Ben & Jerry's Homemade? The company's managers. They track financial data to correct performance problems. Investors also care. The company's financial status affects the value of their investments. Financial performance might also influence decisions to work for the company, buy a franchise, or serve as a supplier. Ben & Jerry's can best fulfill its end of such arrangements if it is financially solid.

To communicate its financial performance, Ben & Jerry's uses the language of accounting. It publishes an annual report detailing the company's financial resources and obligations, as well as what it earned and spent that year. The five-year financial highlights shown here summarize key measures, including sales, income, assets, and

Ben & Jerry's

5-Year Financial Highlights

The following table contains selected financial information for the Company's fiscal years 1991 through 1995. (In thousands except per share data)

Summary of Operations:	12/30/95	12/31/94	Year Ended 12/25/93	12/26/92	12/28/91
Net sales	$ 155,333	$ 148,802	$ 140,328	$ 131,969	$ 96,997
Cost of sales	109,125	109,760	100,210	94,389	68,500
Gross profit	46,208	39,042	40,118	37,580	28,497
Selling, general and administrative expenses	36,362	36,253	28,270	26,243	21,264
Asset write-down		6,779			
Other income (expense)–net	(441)	228	197	(23)	(729)
Income (loss) before income taxes	9,405	(3,762)	12,045	11,314	6,504
Income tax expense (benefit)	3,457	(1,893)	4,844	4,639	2,765
Net income (loss)	5,948	(1,869)	7,201	6,675	3,739
Net income (loss) per common share[1]	$ 0.83	$ (0.26)	$ 1.01	$ 1.07	$ 0.67
Weighted average common and common equivalent shares outstanding[1]	7,222	7,148	7,138	6,254	5,572

Balance Sheet Data:	12/30/95	12/31/94	Year Ended 12/25/93	12/26/92	12/28/91
Working capital	$ 51,023	$ 37,456	$ 29,292	$ 18,053	$ 11,035
Total assets	131,074	120,296	106,361	88,207	43,056
Long-term debt	31,977	32,419	18,002	2,641	2,787
Stockholders' equity[2]	78,531	·72,502	74,262	66,760	26,269

[1] The per share amounts and average shares outstanding have been adjusted for the effects of all stock splits, including stock splits in the form of stock dividends.

[2] No cash dividends have been declared or paid by the Company on its capital stock since the Company's organization. The Company intends to reinvest earnings for use in its business and to finance future growth. Accordingly, the Board of Directors does not anticipate declaring any cash dividends in the foreseeable future.

debt. This information shows that the company's sales rose over each of the five years reported but at a declining rate. It shows that Ben & Jerry's long-term debt jumped in 1993 and 1994.

Such observations provoke further questions. Does Ben & Jerry's have ideas for boosting sales? Is the debt increase part of a strategy to build sales? To answer these questions, you will need to study other information in the annual report, including more detailed financial statements, the CEO's letter, and the marketing report.

If you were considering a marketing job with Ben & Jerry's, what financial information would you want to review? Use this chapter to help you identify and evaluate financial information.

SOURCE: Ben & Jerry's Homemade, Inc., Annual Report, 1995.

LEARNING OBJECTIVES

After studying this chapter, you should be able to

LO 1 Explain why financial information is important in making decisions.

LO 2 Distinguish among the forms of organization.

LO 3 Describe the various types of business activity.

LO 4 Identify the primary users of accounting information and their needs.

LO 5 Explain the purpose of each of the financial statements and the relationships among them and prepare a set of simple statements.

LO 6 Identify and explain the primary assumptions made in preparing financial statements.

LO 7 Describe the process of setting standards in financial accounting and the groups involved in the process.

LO 8 Describe the various roles played by accountants in organizations.

Ben & Jerry's: The Need to Make Financial Decisions

LO 1 Explain why financial information is important in making decisions.

Ben & Jerry's, Vermont's Finest All Natural Ice Cream & Frozen Yogurt, was founded in 1978 in a renovated gas station in Burlington, Vermont by childhood friends Ben Cohen and Jerry Greenfield with a $12,000 investment ($4,000 of which was borrowed). With the help of an old-fashioned rock salt ice cream maker and a then-$5 correspondence course in ice cream-making from Penn State under their belt, they soon became popular for their funky, chunky, flavors, made from fresh Vermont milk and cream. A year later they were delivering Ben & Jerry's ice cream to grocery stores and restaurants.[1]

Today Ben & Jerry's is a highly successful corporation. Sales in 1995 exceeded $155 million. Numerous reasons account for the company's phenomenal success. From its beginning, the company has taken an extremely active role in promoting social responsibility. It has some of the most far-reaching and liberal employment policies in U.S. business. However, any company owes a major part of its success to its ability to make *financial decisions*. Initially, Ben Cohen and Jerry Greenfield made the decision to invest $8,000 of their own money and to borrow $4,000 to start their ice cream–making business. Would *you* have been willing to risk your savings to start a new business? Would you have been willing to sign a note agreeing to repay a loan in the future? Both of these were financial decisions the two had to make.

In 1980, after two years in business, Ben and Jerry decided to rent space in an old mill and to begin packing ice cream in pints. Once again, they were faced with a financial decision: could they make enough money from selling pints of ice cream to pay the rent? More decisions, each one involving higher stakes, faced the young entrepreneurs during the 1980s. In 1984 Ben and Jerry decided to sell stock to the public for the first time (staying loyal to their adopted state, the stock was available only to Vermonters). What prompted them to make this financial decision? On the basis of record sales of $4 million in 1984, they realized that their current production facilities were inadequate to handle the increased volume. They needed money to build a new plant. The sale of stock that year netted the company about $700,000. The company made an even larger decision that same year, however: it borrowed more than $2 million. At that point, major financial decisions about the company were being made not only by the original owners but also by outsiders. Given the opportunity back then, would you have bought stock in this company? Would you have been willing to lend money to it that year, as many people and organizations did?

In 1985 the company borrowed more money and sold stock to people outside Vermont for the first time. It was the first year the stock of Ben & Jerry's was traded on an organized stock exchange. Then came more decisions for Ben & Jerry's and those who

From two guys making ice cream came today's Ben & Jerry's Homemade, Inc. Growing their business required skills in making and selling ice cream, in expanding their operation with new equipment and resources, and in working with managers and professionals who could understand the financial side of the business.

[1]*The History of Ben & Jerry's Homemade, Inc.,* Statement of Mission, 1988.

4

lent money to the company and bought stock in it. Construction on the new manufacturing plant and company headquarters began in 1985 and was completed the following year. Was it a wise decision to sell stock and borrow money to build the new facility? Sales in 1986 were double those of the prior year, reaching almost $20 million. By 1992 the company was so successful that it began construction on its *third* manufacturing plant. At the end of 1995, Ben & Jerry's had spent approximately $38.2 million in building and equipping the new plant.

All of us use financial information in making decisions. For example, when you were deciding whether to enroll at your present school, you needed information on the tuition and room-and-board costs at the different schools you were considering. When a stockbroker decides whether to recommend to a client the purchase of stock in a company, the broker needs information on the company's profits and whether it pays dividends. When trying to decide whether to lend money to a company, a banker must consider the company's current debts.

In this book, we explore how accounting can help all of us in making informed financial decisions. Before we turn to the role played by accounting in decision making, we need to explore business in more detail. What forms of organizations carry on business activity? In what types of business activity do those organizations engage?

Forms of Organization

There are many different types of organizations in our society. One convenient way to categorize the myriad types is to distinguish between those that are organized to earn money and those that exist for some other purpose. Although the lines can become blurred, business entities generally are organized to earn a profit, whereas nonbusiness entities generally exist to serve various segments of society. Both types are summarized in Exhibit 1-1.

LO 2 Distinguish among the forms of organization.

Business Entities

Business entities are organized to earn a profit. Legally, a profit-oriented company is one of three types: sole proprietorships, partnerships, and corporations.

Sole Proprietorships   This form of organization is characterized by a single owner. Many small businesses are organized as sole proprietorships. Very often the business is owned and operated by the same person. Because of the close relationship between the owner and the business, the affairs of the two must be kept separate. This is one example in accounting of the economic entity concept, which requires that a single, identifiable unit of organization be accounted for in all situations. For example, assume that Bernie Berg owns a neighborhood grocery store. In paying the monthly bills, such as utilities

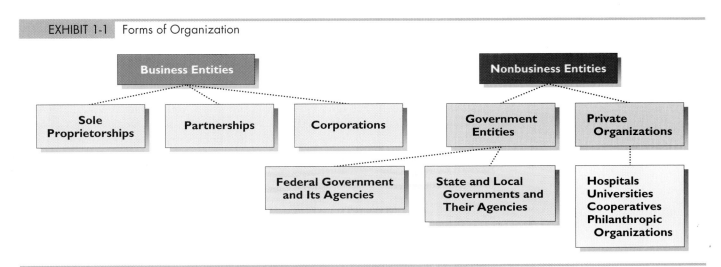

EXHIBIT 1-1   Forms of Organization

and supplies, Bernie must separate his personal costs from the costs associated with the grocery business. In turn, financial statements prepared for the business must not intermingle Bernie's personal affairs with the affairs of the company.

Unlike the distinction made for accounting purposes between an individual's personal and business affairs, the IRS does not recognize the separate existence of a proprietorship from its owner. That is, a sole proprietorship is not a taxable entity; any profits earned by the business are taxed on the return of the individual.

Partnerships A **partnership** is a business owned by two or more individuals. Ben & Jerry's began as a partnership. When the two partners started selling ice cream, they needed some sort of agreement as to how much each would contribute to the business and how they would divide any profits. In many small partnerships, the agreement is often just an oral understanding between the partners. In large businesses, the partnership agreement is formalized in a written document.

Although Ben & Jerry's involved just two owners, some partnerships have thousands of partners. Public accounting firms, law firms, and other types of service companies are often organized as partnerships. Like a sole proprietorship, a partnership is not a taxable entity. The individual partners pay taxes on their proportionate shares of the profits of the business.

Corporations Although sole proprietorships and partnerships dominate in sheer number, corporations control an overwhelming majority of the private resources in this country. A **corporation** is an entity organized under the laws of a particular state. Each of the 50 states is empowered to regulate the creation and operation of businesses organized as corporations in it.

To start a corporation, one must file articles of incorporation with the state. If the articles are approved by the state, a corporate charter is issued, and the corporation can begin to issue stock. A **share of stock** is a certificate that acts as evidence of ownership in a corporation. Although not always the case, stocks of many corporations are traded on organized stock exchanges, such as the New York and American Stock Exchanges.

What are the advantages of running a business as a corporation rather than a partnership? This was the question Ben and Jerry had to ask themselves. The company enjoyed early success in the market, and to capitalize on that success, it needed to grow. To grow meant that it would need a larger production facility, more equipment, and a larger staff. All of these things cost money. Where would the money come from?

One of the primary advantages of the corporate form of organization is the ability to raise large amounts of money in a relatively brief period of time. This is what prompted Ben & Jerry's to "go public" in 1984. To raise money, the company sold two different types of securities: stocks and bonds. As stated earlier, a share of stock is simply a certificate that evidences ownership in a corporation. A **bond** is similar in that it is a certificate or piece of paper issued to someone. However, it is different from a share of stock in that a bond represents a promise by the company selling it to repay a certain amount of money at a future date. In other words, if you were to buy a bond from Ben & Jerry's, you would be lending it money. Interest on the bond is usually paid semiannually. We will have more to say about stocks and bonds when we discuss financing activities later in the chapter.

The ease of transfer of ownership in a corporation is another advantage of this form of organization. If you hold shares of stock in a corporation whose stock is actively traded and you decide that you want out, you simply call your broker and put in an order to sell. Another distinct advantage is the limited liability of the stockholder. Generally speaking, a stockholder is liable only for the amount contributed to the business. That is, if a company goes out of business, the most the stockholder stands to lose is the amount invested. On the other hand, both proprietors and general partners usually can be held personally liable for the debts of the business.

Nonbusiness Entities

Most **nonbusiness entities** are organized for a purpose other than to earn a profit. They exist to serve the needs of various segments of society. For example, a hospital is

EXHIBIT 1-2 How Companies Meet Their Social Responsibilities

COMPANY	CAUSE SUPPORTED
Target	The Family
Ben & Jerry's	The Rainforest
Starbucks	Education in the Third World
Patagonia	The Environment
Body Shop	No Animal Testing
Levi Strauss & Co.	Human Rights
Sassaby	AIDS
American Express	Hunger
McDonald's	Children's Cancer
H.B. Fuller	Local Causes

SOURCE: *Potentials in Marketing,* "Angels in the Boardroom," June 1, 1996.

organized to provide health care to its patients. A municipal government is operated for the benefit of its citizens. A local school district exists to meet the educational needs of the youth in the community.

All of these entities are distinguished by the lack of an identifiable owner. The lack of an identifiable owner and of the profit motive changes to some extent the type of accounting used by nonbusiness entities. This type, called *fund accounting,* is discussed in advanced accounting courses. Regardless of the lack of a profit motive in nonbusiness entities, there is still a demand for the information provided by an accounting system. For example, a local government needs detailed cost breakdowns in order to levy taxes. A hospital may want to borrow money and will need financial statements to present to the prospective lender.

Organizations and Social Responsibility

Although nonbusiness entities are organized specifically to serve members of society, U.S. business entities also have become more sensitive to their broader social responsibilities. Because they touch the lives of so many members of society, most large corporations recognize the societal aspects of their overall mission. For example, Ben & Jerry's statement of mission consists of three parts: a product mission, a social mission, and an economic mission. Its social mission is as follows:

> To operate the company in a way that actively recognizes the central role that business plays in the structure of society by initiating innovative ways to improve the quality of life of a broad community: local, national, & international.[2]

Ben & Jerry's has done more than just pay lip service to its social mission. Each year it donates 7.5% of its pretax earnings to a foundation that in turn awards monies to charities. Most other large corporations have established similar charitable foundations to foster their goals in this area. Some companies focus their efforts on local charities while others donate to national or international causes. It is interesting to note the causes supported by some highly recognizable companies, including Ben & Jerry's, as shown in Exhibit 1-2.

Notice the inclusion in this list of the popular coffee retailer Starbucks and its interest in education in Third World countries. In Chapter 2 we will introduce you in greater detail to Starbucks, and you will have the opportunity to learn more about the company through its financial statements. For now we turn our attention back to Ben & Jerry's and the various types of business activities.

[2]*Ben & Jerry's 1995 Annual Report,* p. 1.

The Nature of Business Activity

LO 3 Describe the various types of business activity.

Because corporations dominate business activity in the United States, we will focus our attention in this book on this form of organization. Corporations engage in a multitude of different types of activities. It is possible to categorize all of them into one of three types, however: financing, investing, and operating.

Financing Activities

All businesses must start with financing. Simply put, money is needed to start a business. Ben and Jerry needed $12,000 to start their business. They came up with $8,000 of their own funds and borrowed the other $4,000. As described earlier, the company found itself in need of additional financing in 1984 when it started construction on the new manufacturing plant. At that point, it obtained approximately $2 million from the sale of bonds and another $700,000 from the sale of stock to citizens of Vermont. In 1985 the company continued to look for sources of financing. For the first time, it issued stock to investors outside the state of Vermont and raised more than $5 million. More recently, the company borrowed approximately $15 million in each of the years 1993 and 1994 on a long-term basis.

As you will see throughout this book, accounting has its own unique set of terminology. In fact, accounting is often referred to as *the language of business.* The discussion of financing activities brings up two important accounting terms: liabilities and capital stock. A liability is an obligation of a business; it can take many different forms. When a company borrows money at a bank, the liability is called a *note payable.* When a company sells bonds, the obligation is termed *bonds payable.* Amounts owed to the government for taxes are called *taxes payable.* Ben & Jerry's happens to buy the milk it needs to produce ice cream from the St. Albans Cooperative Creamery. Assume that St. Albans gives the company 30 days to pay for purchases. During this 30-day period, Ben & Jerry's has an obligation called *accounts payable.*

Capital stock is the term used by accountants to indicate the dollar amount of stock sold to the public. Capital stock differs from liabilities in one very important respect. Those who buy stock in a corporation are not lending money to the business, as are those who buy bonds in the company or make a loan in some other form to the company. Someone who buys stock in a company is called a stockholder, and that person is providing a *permanent* form of financing to the business. In other words, there is not a due date at which time the stockholder will be repaid. Normally, the only way for a stockholder to get back his or her original investment from buying stock is to sell it to someone else. Occasionally, a corporation buys back the stock of one of its stockholders. Someone who buys bonds in a company or in some other way makes a loan to it is called a creditor. A creditor does *not* provide a permanent form of financing to the business. That is, the creditor expects repayment of the amount loaned and, in many instances, payment of interest for the use of the money as well.

Investing Activities

There is a natural progression in a business from financing activities to investing activities. That is, once funds are generated from creditors and stockholders, money is available to invest. Ben & Jerry's used the cash obtained from selling stock and bonds to build its manufacturing plant and to add to its equipment, in particular its storage freezer.

An asset is a future economic benefit to a business. For example, cash is an asset to a company. Ben & Jerry's buildings are assets to it, as are its storage freezers and its other equipment. At any point in time, Ben & Jerry's has a supply of ice cream awaiting sale, as well as supplies of raw materials such as milk and other ingredients to be used in the production of ice cream. The finished products and the raw materials are called *inventory* and are another valuable asset of a company.

An asset represents the right to receive some sort of benefit in the future. The point is that not all assets are tangible in nature, as are inventories and plant and equipment.

For example, assume that Ben & Jerry's sells ice cream to one of its distributors and allows this customer to pay for its purchase at the end of 30 days. At the time of the sale, Ben & Jerry's doesn't have cash yet, but it has another valuable asset. The right to collect the amount due from the customer in 30 days is an asset called an *account receivable*. As a second example, assume that a company acquires from an inventor a patent that will allow the company the exclusive right to manufacture a certain product. The right to the future economic benefits from the patent is an asset. In summary, an asset is a valuable resource to the company that controls it.

At this point, you should notice the inherent tie between assets and liabilities. How does a company satisfy its liabilities, that is, its obligations? Although there are some exceptions, most liabilities are settled by transferring assets. The asset most often used to settle a liability is cash.

Operating Activities

Once funds are obtained from financing and investments are made in productive assets, a business is ready to begin operations. Every business is organized with a purpose in mind. The purpose of some businesses is to sell a *product*. Ben and Jerry organized their company to sell ice cream. Other companies provide *services*. Service-oriented businesses are becoming an increasingly important sector of the U.S. economy. Some of the largest corporations in this country, such as banks and airlines, sell services rather than products. Some companies sell both products and services.

Accountants have a name for the sale of products and services. Revenue is the inflow of assets resulting from the sale of products and services. When a company makes a cash sale, the asset it receives is cash. When a sale is made on credit, the asset received is an account receivable. For now, you should understand that *revenue is a representation*. That is, it represents the dollar amount of sales of products and services for a specific period of time.

We have thus far identified one important operating activity: the sale of products and services. However, costs must be incurred to operate a business. Employees must be paid salaries and wages. Suppliers must be paid for purchases of inventory, and the utility company has to be paid for heat and electricity. The government must be paid the taxes owed it. All of these are examples of important operating activities of a business. As you might expect by now, accountants use a specific name for the costs incurred in operating a business. An expense is the outflow of assets resulting from the sale of goods and services.

Exhibit 1-3 summarizes the three types of activities conducted by a business. Our discussion and the exhibit present a simplification of business activity, but actual businesses are in a constant state of motion with many different financing, investing, and operating activities going on at any one time. The model as portrayed in Exhibit 1-3 should be helpful as you begin the study of accounting, however. To summarize, a company obtains money from various types of financing activities, uses the money raised to invest in productive assets, and then provides goods and services to its customers.

What Is Accounting?

Many people have preconceived notions about what accounting is. They think of it as a highly procedural activity practiced by people who are "good in math." This notion of accounting is very narrow and focuses only on the *record-keeping* or *bookkeeping* aspects of the discipline. Accounting is in fact much broader than this in its scope. Specifically, accounting is "the process of identifying, measuring, and communicating economic information to permit informed judgments and decisions by users of the information."[3]

Each of the three activities in this definition—*identifying, measuring,* and *communicating*—requires the judgment of a trained professional. We will return later in this

[3]American Accounting Association, *A Statement of Basic Accounting Theory* (Evanston, Ill.: American Accounting Association, 1966), p. 1.

EXHIBIT 1-3   A Model of Business Activities

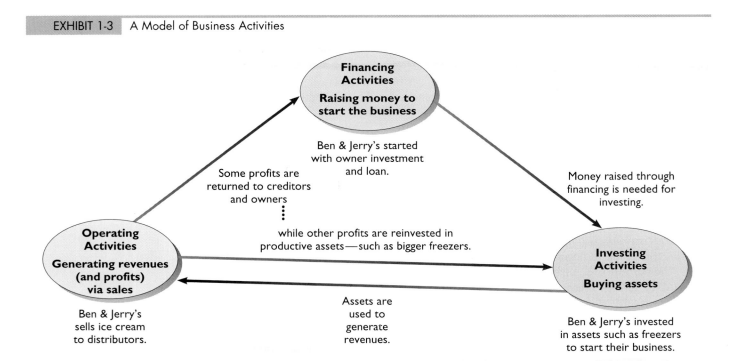

chapter to accounting as a profession and the various roles of accountants in our society. Note that the definition refers to the users of economic information and the decisions they make. Who *are* the users of accounting information? We turn our attention now to this important question.

Users of Accounting Information and Their Needs

LO 4 Identify the primary users of accounting information and their needs.

It is helpful to categorize users of accounting information on the basis of their relationship to the organization. Internal users, primarily the managers of a company, are involved in the daily affairs of the business. All other groups are external users.

Internal Users

The management of a company is in a position to obtain financial information in a way that best suits its needs. For example, if a production manager at Ben & Jerry's needs to know how much it costs to produce a pint of Chubby Hubby ice cream, this information exists in the accounting system and can be reported. If a department supervisor wants to find out if monthly expenditures are more or less than the budgeted amount, a report can be generated to provide the answer. Management accounting is the branch of accounting concerned with providing internal users (management) with information to facilitate the planning and control functions. The ability to produce management accounting reports is limited only by the extent of the data available and the cost involved in generating the relevant information.

External Users

External users, those not involved directly in the operations of a business, need information that differs from that needed by internal users. In addition, the ability of external users to obtain the information is more limited. Without the day-to-day contact with the affairs of the business, outsiders must rely on the information presented to them by the management of the company.

Certain external users, such as the Internal Revenue Service, require that information be presented in a very specific manner, and they have the authority of the law to ensure that they get the required information. Stockholders, bondholders, and other creditors must rely on general-purpose financial statements for their information.[4] **Financial accounting is the branch of accounting concerned with the preparation of general-purpose financial statements for use by both management and outsiders.**

Stockholders and Potential Stockholders   Both existing and potential stockholders need financial information about a business. If you currently own stock in a company, you need information that will aid in your decision either to continue to hold the stock or to sell it. If you are considering buying stock in a company, you need financial information that will help in choosing among competing alternative investments. What has been the recent performance of the company in the stock market? What were its profits for the most recent year? How do these profits compare with those of the prior year? How much did the company pay in dividends? One source for much of this information is the company's financial statements.

Bondholders, Bankers, and Other Creditors   Before buying a bond in a company (remember you are lending money to the company), you need to feel comfortable that the company will be able to pay you the amount owed at maturity and the periodic interest payments. Financial statements can help you to decide whether to purchase a bond. Similarly, before lending money, a bank needs information that will help it to determine the company's ability to repay both the amount of the loan and interest. Therefore, a set of financial statements is a key ingredient in a loan proposal.

Government Agencies   Numerous government agencies have information needs specified by law. For example, the Internal Revenue Service (IRS) is empowered to collect a tax on income from both individuals and corporations. Every year a company prepares a tax return to report to the IRS the amount of income it earned. Another government agency, the Securities and Exchange Commission (SEC), was created in the aftermath of the Great Depression. This regulatory agency is empowered to set the rules under which financial statements must be prepared for corporations that sell their stock to the public on organized stock exchanges. Similar to the IRS, the SEC has the authority to prescribe the manner in which financial information is presented to it. Companies operating in specialized industries submit financial reports to other regulatory agencies, such as the Interstate Commerce Commission and the Federal Trade Commission.

Other External Users   Many other individuals and groups rely on financial information given to them by businesses. A supplier of raw material needs to know the creditworthiness of a company before selling it a product on credit. To promote its industry, a trade association must gather financial information on the various companies in the industry. Other important users are financial intermediaries, such as stockbrokers and financial analysts. They use financial reports in advising their clients on investment decisions. In reaching their decisions, all of these users rely to a large extent on accounting information provided by management.

Financial Statements: How Accountants Communicate

The primary concern of this book is financial accounting. As we noted earlier, this branch of accounting is concerned with the preparation of general-purpose financial statements. We turn our attention now to the composition of each of the major statements: the balance sheet, the income statement, the statement of retained earnings, and the statement of cash flows.

LO 5 Explain the purpose of each of the financial statements and the relationships among them and prepare a set of simple statements.

[4]Technically, stockholders are insiders because they own stock in the business. In most large corporations, however, it is not practical for stockholders to be involved in the daily affairs of the business. Thus, they are better categorized here as external users because they normally rely on general-purpose financial statements, as do creditors.

The Accounting Equation and the Balance Sheet

The *accounting equation* is the foundation for the entire accounting system:

$$\text{Assets} = \text{Liabilities} + \text{Owners' Equity}$$

The left side of the accounting equation refers to the valuable economic resources controlled by a company—that is, its assets. The logic of the equation is that assets come from somewhere. In other words, what are the *sources* of these assets? Who has a *claim* on these assets? This is what the right side of the equation tells us. It tells us that some of the company's assets were provided by creditors. To them we have an obligation, or a liability. Other assets were provided by the owners of the business. Their claim to the assets of the business is represented by owners' equity in the accounting equation.

The term *stockholders' equity* is used to refer to the owners' equity of a corporation. Stockholders' equity is the mathematical difference between a corporation's assets and its obligations or liabilities. That is, after the amounts owed to bondholders, banks, suppliers, and other creditors are subtracted from the assets, the amount remaining is the stockholders' equity, the amount of interest or claim that the owners have on the assets of the business.

Stockholders' equity arises in two distinct ways. First, it is created when a company issues stock to an investor. As we noted earlier, capital stock is a representation of ownership in a corporation in the form of a certificate. It represents the amounts contributed by the owners to the company. Second, stockholders have a claim on the assets of a business when it is profitable. Retained earnings represents the owners' claims on the company's assets that result from its earnings that have not been paid out in dividends. It is the earnings retained by the company.

The balance sheet is the financial statement that summarizes the assets, liabilities, and owners' equity of a company. It is a "snapshot" of the business at a certain date. A balance sheet can be prepared on any day of the year, although it is most commonly prepared on the last day of a month, quarter, or year. At any point in time, the balance sheet must be "in balance." That is, assets must equal liabilities and owners' equity.

An alternative title for the balance sheet is the *statement of financial position*. Although this title is more descriptive than the *balance sheet,* it has not achieved widespread popularity. We will refer to the statement that summarizes assets, liabilities, and owners' equity as the balance sheet.

Comparative balance sheets for Ben & Jerry's at the end of two recent years are shown in Exhibit 1-4. When a balance sheet is presented, the balance sheet at the end of the prior period is usually presented as well. This allows the user to make comparisons between one period and the next. Note the date of each of the two balance sheets. Unlike many companies, Ben & Jerry's does not always end its fiscal or accounting year on December 31. The date on each of these balance sheets corresponds with the last Saturday in the calendar year.

Also note the description in parentheses at the top of the statement, telling you that all amounts are in thousands of dollars. This means that the company has rounded each of the amounts to the nearest thousand dollars. For example, cash and cash equivalents appears on the balance sheet at the end of 1995 at $35,406. This means that the actual amount of cash and cash equivalents is $35,406,000, rounded to the nearest thousand dollars. Ben & Jerry's is a relatively small corporation. Larger companies may present the amounts in their statements in millions of dollars.

One of the purposes of this book is to enhance your understanding of the balance sheet. Note for now the types of items that appear on the balance sheet. Property, Plant, and Equipment is Ben & Jerry's largest asset, which is typical for a company that produces a product. Because it sells a product, Inventories is another significant asset of the company. Accounts Receivable arises from selling ice cream products to distributors on credit. Similarly, Ben & Jerry's purchases supplies and other items on credit, as indicated by the significant balance in Accounts Payable and Accrued Expenses.

The Income Statement

An income statement, or statement of income, as it is sometimes called, summarizes the revenues and expenses of a company for a period of time. Comparative income

EXHIBIT 1-4   Ben & Jerry's Balance Sheet

Consolidated Balance Sheets

(In thousands except share data)

Assets	December 30, 1995	December 31,1994
Current assets:		
Cash and cash equivalents	$ 35,406	$ 20,778
Accounts receivable		
Trade (less allowance of $802 in 1995 and $504 in 1994		
for doubtful accounts)	11,660	9,902
Other	854	2,003
Inventories	12,616	13,463
Deferred income taxes	3,599	3,146
Income taxes receivable	2,831	2,098
Prepaid expenses	1,097	534
Total current assets	68,063	51,924
Property, plant and equipment, net	59,600	57,981
Investments	1,000	8,000
Other assets	2,411	2,391
	$ 131,074	$ 120,296

Liabilities & Stockholders' Equity		
Current liabilities:		
Accounts payable and accrued expenses	$ 16,592	$ 13,915
Current portion of long-term debt and		
capital lease obligations	448	553
Total current liabilities	17,040	14,468
Long-term debt and capital lease obligations	31,977	32,419
Deferred income taxes	3,526	907
Commitments and contingencies		
Stockholders' equity:		
$1.20 noncumulative Class A preferred stock -		
$1.00 par value, redeemable at the Company's option		
at $12.00 per share; 900 shares authorized,		
issued and outstanding, aggregate preference		
on voluntary or involuntary liquidation - $9	1	1
Class A common stock - $.033 par value; authorized		
20,000,000 shares; issued: 6,330,302 shares at		
December 30, 1995 and 6,290,580 shares at		
December 31, 1994	209	208
Class B common stock - $.033 par value; authorized		
3,000,000 shares; issued: 914,325 shares at		
December 30, 1995 and 932,448 shares at		
December 31, 1994	30	31
Additional paid-in capital	48,521	48,366
Retained earnings	31,264	25,316
Cumulative translation adjustment	(114)	
Treasury stock, at cost: 67,032 Class A and 1,092		
Class B shares at December 30, 1995 and 69,032		
Class A and 1,092 Class B shares at		
December 31, 1994	(1,380)	(1,420)
Total stockholders' equity	78,531	72,502
	$ 131,074	$ 120,296

See accompanying notes.

34

statements for Ben & Jerry's for three recent years are shown in Exhibit 1-5. Note that Ben & Jerry's uses the title *statements of operations* as an alternative to *income statements*. Unlike the balance sheet, an income statement is a *flow* statement. That is, it summarizes the flow of revenues and expenses for the year. As was the case for the balance sheet, you are not expected at this point to understand fully all of the complexities involved in preparing an income statement.

The Statement of Retained Earnings

As discussed earlier, Retained Earnings represents the accumulated earnings of a business less the amount paid in dividends to stockholders. **Dividends** are distributions of the net income or profits of a business to its stockholders. Not all businesses pay cash dividends. Ben & Jerry's rationale for not paying dividends to stockholders is stated in its annual report:

> The Company has never declared a cash dividend on its Class A Common Stock or the Class B Common Stock and the current policy of its Board of Directors is to retain earnings for expansion and development of the Company's business. Accordingly, the Board of Directors does not anticipate declaring any cash dividends on the Class A or Class B Common Stock in the foreseeable future.

A **statement of retained earnings** explains the change in retained earnings during the period. The basic format for the statement is as follows:

Beginning balance	$xxx,xxx
Add: Net income for the period	xxx,xxx
Deduct: Dividends for the period	xxx,xxx
Ending balance	$xxx,xxx

Revenues minus expenses, or net income, is an increase in retained earnings, and dividends are a decrease in the balance. Why are dividends shown on a statement of retained earnings instead of on an income statement? Dividends are not an expense and thus are *not a determinant of* net income, as are expenses. Instead, they are a *distribution of* the income of the business to its stockholders.

Recall that stockholders' equity consists of two parts: capital stock and retained earnings. Some corporations prepare a comprehensive statement to explain the changes both in the various capital stock accounts and in retained earnings during the period. A statement of stockholders' equity for Ben & Jerry's is presented in Exhibit 1-6. Note the way in which the statement is presented. The various elements of stockholders' equity are presented across the top of the statement in columns. The activity in each of the elements is described down the left side of the statement. For now, focus your attention on the fifth column only, in which the changes in retained earnings are presented. The activities described in the other columns involve complexities beyond our scope of attention at this time. For each of the three years presented in the statement, net

ACCOUNTING FOR YOUR DECISIONS
You Are a Potential Stockholder

You are deciding whether to invest in a company's stock. Which financial statement would you want to see, and which areas would you be most interested in?

ANS: All of them. The balance sheet will show the relative size of the assets and liabilities, and the stockholders' equity section should state how many shares of stock have been sold (outstanding shares) and how many more are available (authorized but not yet issued). The income statement's net sales, gross profit, operating income, and net income are important, not only for the most current year but also for previous years to determine trends. The statement of retained earnings will report if dividends were paid and, if so, the amount. (Ben & Jerry's does not pay any dividends.) The statement of cash flows will indicate if cash flows were provided or used for each of the three major activities.

EXHIBIT 1-5   Ben & Jerry's Income Statement

Consolidated Statements of Operations

(In thousands except per share data)

	Dec. 30, 1995	Years Ended Dec. 31, 1994	Dec.25,1993
Net sales	$ 155,333	$ 148,802	$ 140,328
Cost of sales	109,125	109,760	100,210
Gross profit	46,208	39,042	40,118
Selling, general and administrative expenses	36,362	36,253	28,270
Asset write-down		6,779	
Other income (expense):			
Interest income	1,681	1,034	757
Interest expense	(1,525)	(295)	(104)
Other	(597)	(511)	(456)
	(441)	228	197
Income (loss) before income taxes	9,405	(3,762)	12,045
Income tax expense (benefit)	3,457	(1,893)	4,844
Net income (loss)	$ 5,948	$ (1,869)	$ 7,201
Net income (loss) per common share	$ 0.83	$ (0.26)	$ 1.01
Weighted average common and common equivalent shares outstanding.	7,222	7,148	7,138

See accompanying notes.

EXHIBIT 1-6   Ben & Jerry's Statement of Stockholders' Equity

Consolidated Statements of

(In thousands except share data)

	Preferred Stock Par Value	Common Stock Class A Par Value	Common Stock Class B Par Value	Additional Paid-in Capital
Balance at December 26, 1992	$1	$ 206	$ 33	$47,941
Net income				
Common stock issued under stock purchase plan (12,826 Class A shares)				280
Common stock issued under restricted stock plan (100 Class A shares)				1
Conversion of Class B shares to Class A shares (14,371 shares)		1	(1)	
Amortization of unearned compensation				
Balance at December 25, 1993	1	207	32	48,222
Net income (loss)				
Common stock issued under stock purchase plan (8,619 Class A shares)				139
Conversion of Class B shares to Class A shares (15,189 shares)		1	(1)	
Termination of stock award (Class A shares)				5
Balance at December 31, 1994	1	208	31	48,366
Net income				
Common stock issued under stock purchase plan (21,599 Class A shares)				174
Conversion of Class B shares to Class A shares (18,123 shares)		1	(1)	
Common stock issued under restricted stock plan (2,000 Class A shares)				(19)
Foreign currency translation adjustment				
Balance at December 30, 1995	$1	$ 209	$30	$ 48,521

See accompanying notes.

36

EXHIBIT 1-6   continued

Stockholders' Equity

For now, focus on this column to see changes in retained earnings

			Treasury Stock	
			Class A	**Class B**
Retained Earnings	**Unearned Compensation**	**Cumulative Translation Adjustment**	**Cost**	**Cost**
$19,984	$ (38)	$0	$(1,362)	$(5)
7,201				
			2	
	18			
27,185	(20)	0	(1,360)	(5)
(1,869)				
	20		(55)	
25,316	0	0	(1,415)	(5)
5,948				
			40	
		(114)		
$ 31,264	$0	$ (114)	$ (1,375)	$(5)

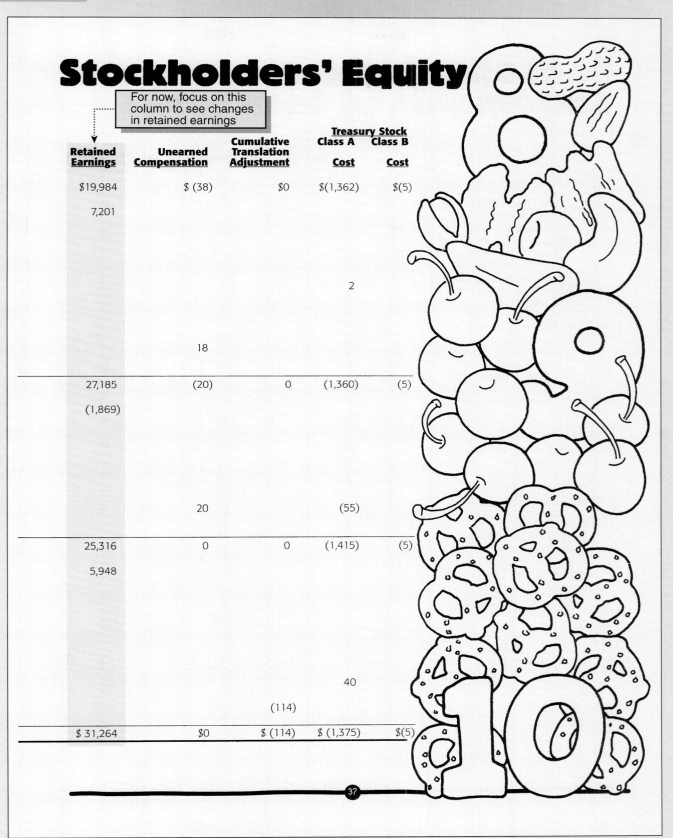

37

EXHIBIT 1-7 Ben & Jerry's Statement of Cash Flows

Consolidated Statements of Cash Flows

(In thousands)

	December 30, 1995	December 31, 1994	December 25, 1993
		Years Ended	
Cash flows from operating activities:			
Net income (loss)	$ 5,948	$ (1,869)	$ 7,201
Adjustments to reconcile net income (loss) to net cash provided by operating activities:			
Depreciation and amortization	5,928	4,707	4,303
Deferred income taxes	2,166	(1,564)	(264)
Provision for doubtful accounts	400	311	58
Amortization of unearned compensation			18
Loss on asset write-down		6,779	
Loss (gain) on disposition of assets	171	69	(10)
Stock awards	21		3
Changes in assets and liabilities			
Accounts receivable	(1,009)	(536)	(2,888)
Income taxes receivable/payable	(733)	(2,442)	650
Inventories	847	(10)	3,637
Prepaid expenses and other assets	(563)	313	(639)
Accounts payable and accrued expenses	2,677	(1,159)	(4,790)
Net cash provided by operating activities	15,853	4,599	7,279
Cash flows from investing activities:			
Additions to property, plant and equipment	(7,532)	(26,213)	(17,796)
Proceeds from sale of property, plant and equipment	96	194	48
Decrease in investments	7,000	14,000	3,200
Changes in other assets	(303)	(882)	(57)
Net cash used for investing activities	(739)	(12,901)	(14,605)
Cash flows from financing activities:			
Net proceeds from long-term debt		14,936	15,145
Repayments of long-term debt and capital leases	(547)	(700)	(751)
Net proceeds from issuance of common stock	174	139	281
Net cash (used for) provided by financing activities	(373)	14,375	14,675
Effect of exchange rate changes on cash	(113)		
Increase in cash and cash equivalents	14,628	6,073	7,349
Cash and cash equivalents at beginning of year	20,778	14,705	7,356
Cash and cash equivalents at end of year	$ 35,406	$ 20,778	$ 14,705

See accompanying notes.

income is added (or net loss is deducted) in the Retained Earnings column. If dividends had been paid, they would be reflected as a deduction in this column.

The Statement of Cash Flows

We talked earlier in the chapter about the types of business activities conducted by organizations. The purpose of the statement of cash flows is to summarize the cash effects of a company's operating, investing, and financing activities for a period of time. Because it summarizes flows for a period of time, the statement of cash flows is similar to the income statement. It differs from the income statement in two important respects, however. First, the income statement reports only on the operating activities during the period. The statement of cash flows is broader in that it reports financing and investing activities as well as operating activities. Second, an income statement is prepared on an *accrual* basis. This means that revenues are recognized when they are earned and expenses when they are incurred, regardless of when cash is received or paid. Alternatively, a statement of cash flows reflects the *cash* effects from buying and selling products and services.

A statement of cash flows for Ben & Jerry's is shown in Exhibit 1-7. Note the three major categories on the statement: operating, investing, and financing. We will return to the preparation of this important statement later in the book. For now, note that net income (or net loss, as was the case for 1994) is the first item in the operating activities section of the statement. Adjustments are made to this number to convert it to net cash provided by operating activities.

A comparison of the statements of cash flows for the three years gives the reader a sense of where Ben & Jerry's has placed the most emphasis, at least from a financial point of view. For example, both 1993 and 1994 were busy years in terms of adding to Property, Plant, and Equipment: approximately $18 million was spent on additions in 1993 and another $26 million in 1994. Much of the funding for these additions came from borrowing about $15 million in each of these years on a long-term basis, as noted in the financing activities section of the report. By contrast, 1995 was relatively quiet as the company began to focus its attention on producing ice cream at its new plant. As shown on page 20, all of these statements are related to one another.

ACCOUNTING FOR YOUR DECISIONS

You Are the Banker

Assume Ben & Jerry's comes to your bank and wants to borrow $1 million for five years at 10% interest. What items on the balance sheet and statement of cash flows would immediately be of interest to you?

ANS: As a banker, you would be concerned with Ben & Jerry's ability to pay back the $1 million loan. Therefore, you would be very interested in what other obligations the company has. A good place to find those obligations is under the liability section of the balance sheet, where you can see what else is owed to other creditors. Another important number is the net cash provided by operations on the statement of cash flows. Since you require an annual interest payment of $100,000, you would be interested in knowing what kind of cushion Ben & Jerry's would have beyond the company's obligation to you. For instance, in 1995, Ben & Jerry's net cash provided from operating activities was $15.8 million, a large amount in relation to the annual interest payment.

How To Find Financial Information about a Company The next chapter introduces in more detail the various elements of a company's annual report. A set of financial statements is certainly an integral part of the annual report. In addition to the annual report, many companies also prepare quarterly financial statements, which they distribute to their stockholders. If you do not own stock in a company, how can you get access to its financial statements? One way is by either calling or writing to the company's investor relations department. A much more efficient and timely approach to gathering this type of information, however, is to use the World Wide Web on the Internet. Ben & Jerry's is one of a growing number of companies that post financial statements and other information on Web sites. Check out Ben & Jerry's home page at the following address: http://www.benjerry.com.

Internet

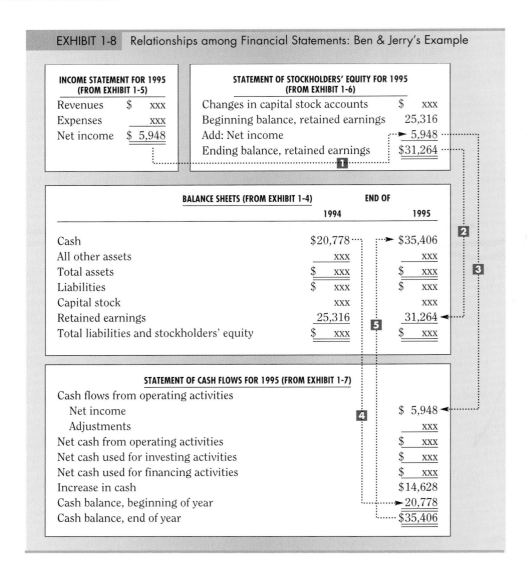

EXHIBIT 1-8   Relationships among Financial Statements: Ben & Jerry's Example

Relationships among Ben & Jerry's Financial Statements

Because the statements of a real-world company such as Ben & Jerry's are complex, it may not be easy at this point to see the important *links* among them. The relationships among the statements are summarized for you in Exhibit 1-8. Five important relationships are seen by examining the exhibit (the numbers that follow correspond to the highlighted numbers in the exhibit and are stated in thousands of dollars):

1 The 1995 income statement reports net income of $5,948. Net income increases retained earnings as reported on the statement of stockholders' equity.

2 The ending balance of $31,264 in retained earnings, as reported on the statement of stockholders' equity for 1995, is transferred to the balance sheet at the end of 1995.

3 Net income appears in the operating activities section of the statement of cash flows. Adjustments are made to convert net income to net cash from operating activities.

4 The cash balance on the balance sheet at the end of 1994 is $20,778. This amount appears at the bottom of the statement of cash flows for 1995. When this balance is added to the increase in cash of $14,628 for 1995, the result is the ending balance in cash of $35,406.

5 The ending cash balance of $35,406 appears as an asset on the balance sheet at the end of 1995.

The Conceptual Framework: Foundation for Financial Statements

The task of preparing financial statements for Ben & Jerry's or any other business may appear at first glance to be procedural in nature. As noted previously, many observers of the accounting profession perceive the work of an accountant as being routine. In reality, accounting is anything but routine and requires a great deal of judgment on the part of the accountant. The record-keeping aspect of accounting—what we normally think of as bookkeeping—is the routine part of the accountant's work and only a small part of it. Most of the job deals with communicating relevant information to financial statement users.

The accounting profession has worked in recent years to develop a *conceptual framework for accounting.* The purpose of the framework is to act as a foundation for the specific principles and standards needed by the profession. An important part of the conceptual framework is a set of assumptions we make in preparing financial statements. We will briefly consider these assumptions, returning to a more detailed discussion of them in later chapters.

The *economic entity concept,* as discussed earlier in the chapter relative to a sole proprietorship, has just as much relevance to a partnership or corporation. The economic entity concept or assumption requires that an identifiable, specific entity be the subject of a set of financial statements. For example, even though Ben Cohen and Jerry Greenfield are stockholders and therefore own part of Ben & Jerry's, their personal affairs must be kept separate from the business affairs. When we look at a balance sheet for the ice cream business, we need assurance that it shows the financial position of that entity only and does not intermingle the personal assets and liabilities of Ben, Jerry, or any of the other stockholders.

What is the basis for recording assets on a balance sheet? For example, what amount should appear on a balance sheet for inventory or for land? The **cost principle** requires that we record assets at the cost paid to acquire them and continue to show this amount on all balance sheets until we dispose of them. With a few exceptions, companies do not carry assets at their market value but at original cost. Accountants use the term *historical cost* to refer to the original cost of an asset. Why not show an asset such as land at market value? This might seem appropriate in certain instances, but the *subjectivity* inherent in determining market values supports the practice of carrying assets at their *historical cost.* The cost of an asset is subject to verification by an independent observer and is much more *objective* than market value.

We assume in accounting that the entity being accounted for is a **going concern.** That is, we assume that Ben & Jerry's is not in the process of liquidation and that it will continue indefinitely into the future. Another important justification for the use of historical cost rather than market value to report assets is the going concern assumption. If we assume that a business is *not* a going concern, then we assume that it is in the process of liquidation. If this is the case, market value might be more relevant than cost as a basis for recognizing the assets. But if we are able to assume that a business will continue indefinitely, cost can be more easily justified as a basis for valuation. The **monetary unit** used in preparing the statements of Ben & Jerry's was the dollar. The reason for using the dollar as the monetary unit is that it is the recognized medium of exchange in the United States. It provides a convenient yardstick to measure the position and earnings of the business. As a yardstick, however, the dollar, like the currencies of all other countries, is subject to instability. We are all well aware that a dollar will not buy as much today as it did 10 years ago.

Inflation is evidenced by a general rise in the level of prices in an economy. Its effect on the measuring unit used in preparing financial statements is an important concern to the accounting profession. Although accountants have experimented with financial statements adjusted for the changing value of the measuring unit, the financial statements now prepared by corporations are prepared under the assumption that the monetary unit is relatively stable. At various times in the past, this has been a reasonable assumption and at other times not so reasonable.

LO 6 Identify and explain the primary assumptions made in preparing financial statements.

One firm goes out of business, another thrives in the same location. The difference may lie simply in the natural abilities of the owner or manager. More often, success comes from setting goals, working hard to reach them, and making the best decisions possible based on high-quality financial information.

One final assumption made in preparing financial statements is the **time period** assumption. We assume that it is possible to prepare an income statement that accurately reflects net income or earnings for a specific time period. In the case of Ben & Jerry's, this time period was one year. It is somewhat artificial to measure the earnings of a business for a period of time indicated on a calendar, whether it be a month, a quarter, or a year. Of course, the most accurate point in time to measure the earnings of a business would be at the end of its life. We prepare periodic statements, however, because the users of the statements demand information about the entity on a regular basis. We will see in later chapters that the time period assumption requires the accountant to make a number of estimates.

An important concept regarding financial statements concerns **generally accepted accounting principles (GAAP).** This term refers to the various methods, rules, practices, and other procedures that have evolved over time in response to the need for some form of regulation over the preparation of financial statements. For example, the cost principle, mentioned earlier, is an important part of GAAP. As changes have taken place in the business environment over time, GAAP have developed in response to these changes.

Accounting as a Social Science

Accounting is a service activity. As we have seen, its purpose is to provide financial information to decision makers. Thus, accounting is a *social* science. Accounting principles are much different from the rules that govern the *physical* sciences. For example, it is a rule of nature that an object dropped from your hand will eventually hit the ground rather than be suspended in air. There are no rules comparable to this in accounting. The principles that govern financial reporting are not governed by nature but instead develop in response to changing business conditions. For example, consider the lease of an office building. Leasing has developed in response to the need to have access to valuable assets, such as office space, without spending the large sum necessary to buy the asset. As leasing has increased in popularity, it has been left to the accounting profession to develop guidelines, some of which are quite complex, to be followed in accounting for leases. Those guidelines are now part of generally accepted accounting principles.

Who Determines the Rules of the Game?

Who determines the rules to be followed in preparing an income statement or a balance sheet? We know that the government, through the Internal Revenue Service, dictates the requirements in preparing a tax return. However, neither the government nor any one group in the private sector is totally responsible for setting the standards or principles to be followed in preparing financial statements. The process is a joint effort. We will briefly consider the groups that have been involved in setting generally accepted accounting principles.

The Securities and Exchange Commission The federal government, through the **Securities and Exchange Commission (SEC),** has the ultimate authority to determine the rules to be followed in preparing financial statements by companies whose securities are sold to the general public. This authority was given to the commission when Congress established it in 1934. The SEC requires that companies file both annual and quarterly financial statements, as well as other types of reports, on a timely basis. Although the SEC has the authority to set accounting principles, the commission has to a large extent allowed the accounting profession to establish its own rules. The commission has on occasion intervened and dictated certain rules when it has believed that the profession was not responding quickly enough or in the correct manner.

The Financial Accounting Standards Board   The Financial Accounting Standards Board (FASB) currently has the authority to set accounting standards in the United States. Although the FASB receives funding from various sources, it exists as an independent group with seven full-time members supported by a large staff. The board has issued more than 130 financial accounting standards since its creation in the early 1970s. These standards deal with a variety of financial reporting issues, such as the proper accounting for lease arrangements and pension plans. In addition, the FASB has issued six statements of financial accounting concepts, which are used to guide the board in setting accounting standards.

American Institute of Certified Public Accountants   The American Institute of Certified Public Accountants (AICPA) has taken an active role in setting accounting standards. Prior to the establishment of the FASB, the AICPA had the primary responsibility for setting GAAP through its Accounting Principles Board. With the creation of the FASB, the AICPA has acted in a more advisory role. The AICPA does, however, set the *auditing* standards to be followed by public accounting firms. We will consider the work of public accounting firms in the next section.

The AICPA is the professional organization of certified public accountants. The title Certified Public Accountant (CPA) is the professional designation for an accountant who has passed a rigorous exam and met certain other requirements. Each of the 50 states regulates the requirements to become a CPA in a particular state. However, all candidates for the certificate take a uniform exam prepared and graded by the American Institute of Certified Public Accountants. Although many CPAs are in public practice, accountants with the professional certification are also employed in business and nonbusiness entities, as well as in the academic community.

International Accounting Standards Committee   What if you are considering buying stock in Porsche, the German-based car manufacturer? When you review its most recent set of financial statements, can you be sure that the rules Porsche followed in preparing the statements are similar to those the FASB requires for U.S. companies? Unfortunately, accounting standards are not uniform throughout the world and can differ considerably from one country to another.

The International Accounting Standards Committee (IASC) was formed in 1973 to develop worldwide accounting standards. More than 100 organizations from 80 different countries, including the FASB in this country, participate in the IASC's efforts to develop international reporting standards. Although the group has made considerable progress, compliance with the standards of the IASC is strictly voluntary, and much work remains to be done in developing international accounting standards.

The Accounting Profession

Accountants play many different roles in society. Understanding the various roles will help you to more fully appreciate the importance of accounting in organizations.

LO 8 Describe the various roles played by accountants in organizations.

Employment by Private Business

Many accountants work for business entities. Regardless of the types of activities a company engages in, accountants perform a number of important functions for them. A partial organization chart for a corporation is shown in Exhibit 1-9. The chart indicates

EXHIBIT 1-9 Partial Organization Chart

This partial organization chart does not show the other departments in the company—such as marketing, sales, production, and so on. That does not mean they are unimportant to the flow of accounting information. In fact, accounting information for internal decision making forms a complex system of reporting, responsibility, and control collectively known as management accounting.

that three individuals report directly to the chief financial officer: the controller, the treasurer, and the director of internal auditing.

The **controller** is the chief accounting officer for a company and typically has responsibility for the overall operation of the accounting system. Accountants working for the controller record the company's activities and prepare periodic financial statements. In this organization, the payroll function is assigned to the controller's office, as is responsibility for the preparation of budgets.

The **treasurer** of an organization is typically responsible for the safeguarding, as well as the efficient use, of the company's liquid resources, such as cash. Note that the director of the tax department in this corporation reports to the treasurer. Accountants in the tax department are responsible for both preparing the company's tax returns and planning transactions in such a way that the company pays the least amount of taxes possible within the laws of the Internal Revenue Code.

Internal auditing is the department in a company responsible for the review and appraisal of accounting and administrative controls. The department must determine whether the company's assets are properly accounted for and protected from losses. Recommendations are made periodically to management for improvements in the various controls.

Employment by Nonbusiness Entities

Nonbusiness organizations, such as hospitals, universities, and various branches of the government, have as much need for accountants as do companies organized to earn a profit. Although the profit motive is not paramount to nonbusiness entities, all organizations must have financial information to operate efficiently. A county government needs detailed cost information in determining the taxes to levy on its constituents. A university must pay close attention to its various operating costs in setting the annual tuition rates. Accountants working for nonbusiness entities perform most of the same tasks as their counterparts in the business sector. In fact, many of the job titles in business entities, such as controller and treasurer, are also used by nonbusiness entities.

Employment in Public Accounting

Public accounting firms provide valuable services in much the same way as do law firms or architectural firms. They provide a professional service for their clients in return for a fee. The usual services provided by public accounting firms include auditing and tax and management consulting services.

Auditing Services The auditing services rendered by public accountants are similar in certain respects to the work performed by internal auditors. However, there are key differences between the two types of auditing. Internal auditors are more concerned with the efficient operation of the various segments of the business, and therefore, the work they do is often called *operational auditing.* On the other hand, the primary objective of the external auditor, or public accountant, is to provide assurance to stockholders and other users that the statements are fairly presented. In this respect, auditing is the process of examining the financial statements and the underlying records of a company in order to render an opinion as to whether the statements are fairly presented.

As we discussed earlier, the financial statements are prepared by the company's accountants. The external auditor performs various tests and procedures to be able to render his or her opinion. The public accountant has a responsibility to the company's stockholders and any other users of the statements. Because most stockholders are not actively involved in the daily affairs of the business, they must rely on the auditors to ensure that management is fairly presenting the financial statements of the business.

Note that the auditors' report is an *opinion,* not a statement of fact. For example, one important procedure performed by the auditor to obtain assurance as to the validity of a company's inventory is to observe the year-end physical count of inventory by the company's employees. However, this is done on a sample basis. It would be too costly for the auditors to make an independent count of every single item of inventory.

The auditors' report on the financial statements for Ben & Jerry's is shown in Exhibit 1-10. Note first that the report is directed to the company's stockholders and board of directors. The company is audited by Ernst & Young, a large international accounting firm. Public accounting firms range in size from those with a single owner to others, such as Ernst & Young, that have thousands of partners. The opinion given by Ernst & Young on the company's financial statements is the *standard auditors' report.* The first paragraph indicates that the firm has examined the company's balance sheet and the related statements of income, stockholders' equity, and cash flows. Note that the second paragraph of the report indicates that evidence supporting the amounts and disclosures in the statements was examined on a *test* basis. The third paragraph states the firm's *opinion* that the financial statements are fairly presented in conformity with generally accepted accounting principles.

Tax Services In addition to auditing, public accounting firms provide a variety of tax services. Firms often prepare the tax return for the companies they audit. They also usually work throughout the year with management to plan acquisitions and other transactions to take full advantage of the tax laws. For example, if tax rates are scheduled to decline next year, a public accounting firm would advise its client to accelerate certain expenditures this year as much as possible to receive a higher tax deduction than would be possible by waiting until next year.

Management Consulting Services By working closely with management to provide auditing and tax services, a public accounting firm becomes very familiar with various aspects of a company's business. This vantage point allows the firm to provide expert advice to the company to improve its operations. The management consulting services rendered by public accounting firms to their clients take a variety of forms. For example, the firm might advise the company on the design and installation of a computer system to fill its needs. The services provided in this area have grown dramatically to include such diverse activities as advice on selection of a new plant site or an investment opportunity.

Accountants in Education

Some accountants choose a career in education. As the demand for accountants in business entities, nonbusiness organizations, and public accounting has increased, so has the need for qualified professors to teach this discipline. Accounting programs range from two years of study at community colleges to doctoral programs at some universities. All of these programs require the services of knowledgeable instructors. In addition

FROM CONCEPT TO PRACTICE 1.2
READING BEN & JERRY'S AUDITORS' REPORT Note the date at the bottom of the report. Why do you think it takes one month after the end of the year to release this report?

EXHIBIT 1-10 Ben & Jerry's Auditors' Report

Report of Ernst & Young LLP, Independent Auditors

The Board of Directors and Stockholders
Ben & Jerry's Homemade, Inc.

We have audited the accompanying consolidated balance sheets of Ben & Jerry's Homemade, Inc. as of December 30, 1995 and December 31, 1994, and the related consolidated statements of operations, stockholders' equity, and cash flows for each of the three years in the period ended December 30, 1995. These financial statements are the responsibility of the Company's management. Our responsibility is to express an opinion on these financial statements based on our audits.

We conducted our audits in accordance with generally accepted auditing standards. Those standards require that we plan and perform the audit to obtain reasonable assurance about whether the financial statements are free of material misstatement. An audit includes examining, on a test basis, evidence supporting the amounts and disclosures in the financial statements. An audit also includes assessing the accounting principles used and significant estimates made by management, as well as evaluating the overall financial statement presentation. We believe that our audits provide a reasonable basis for our opinion.

In our opinion, the consolidated financial statements referred to above present fairly, in all material respects, the consolidated financial position of Ben & Jerry's Homemade, Inc. at December 30, 1995 and December 31, 1994 and the consolidated results of its operations and its cash flows for each of the three years in the period ended December 30, 1995 in conformity with generally accepted accounting principles.

Boston, Massachusetts
January 26, 1996

Ernst + Young LLP

Standard Auditor's Report

First Paragraph	Second Paragraph	Third Paragraph
says that the auditor has examined the statements.	indicates that evidence was gathered on a test basis.	states the auditors opinion.

47

to their teaching duties, many accounting educators are actively involved in research. The **American Accounting Association** is a professional organization of accounting educators and others interested in the future of the profession. The group advances its ideas through its many committees and the publication of a number of journals.

Accounting as a Career

As the preceding paragraphs have pointed out, a number of different career paths in accounting are possible. The stereotypical view of the accountant as a "bean counter"

EXHIBIT 1-11	Salaries in the Accounting Profession	
POSITION	**SALARY RANGE**	
Public Accounting		
Staff Auditors (1–3 years' experience)	$26,000–$35,500	$
Managers	$53,000–$84,500	$$
Partners	$130,000+	$$$
Industry		
Staff Accountants (1–3 years' experience)	$26,000–$36,000	$
Corporate Controllers	$46,000–$134,000	$$–$$$
Chief Financial Officers	$60,000–$300,000	$$–$$$$
Government (entry-level)		
Federal	$27,700 average	$
State/local	$20,700 average	$

Accounting graduates start here.

wearing green eyeshades is a seriously outdated notion. Given the expanded role of accounting in today's business world, what is the demand for accountants? And what about salaries?

A 1994 report of the U.S. Department of Labor's Bureau of Labor Statistics predicts that accounting will be one of the 10 fastest-growing industries during the next 10 years.[5] A number of specialties are now emerging, including tax accounting, environmental accounting, forensic accounting, software development, and accounting in the entertainment and telecommunications industries. Some of these opportunities exist in both the business and the nonbusiness sectors. For example, forensic accounting has become an exciting career field as both corporations and various agencies of the federal government, such as the FBI, concern themselves with fraud and white-collar crime.

As in any profession, salaries in accounting vary considerably depending on numerous factors, including educational background and other credentials, number of years of experience, and size of the employer. For example, most employers pay a premium for candidates with a master's degree and professional certification, such as the CPA. Exhibit 1-11 indicates salaries for various positions within the accounting field.

ACCOUNTING FOR YOUR DECISIONS
You Are a Student

As a student, you decide to go into the accounting profession. However, you are not sure which area to focus on: private, nonbusiness, public, or education. What information would you seek to help you make this decision?

ANS: You may want to consider the following (not necessarily in this order): (1) both starting and potential increases in salaries; (2) education requirements; (3) advancement opportunities; (4) fringe benefits; and (5) challenging work.

Accountants and Ethical Judgments

Remember the primary goal of accounting: to provide useful information to aid in the decision-making process. As we discussed, the work of the accountant in providing useful information is anything but routine and requires the accountant to make subjective

[5]The information in this section regarding career opportunities and salaries was drawn primarily from *Room Zoom,* an innovative and entertaining CD-ROM product published by the AICPA.

FOCUS ON USERS

USING FINANCIAL DATA TO MAKE CAREER DECISIONS

As you make your way through college, you're constantly confronted with decisions based on financial data. Where to go to school. Whether to buy a computer. Whether to live in the dorm or live off campus. Whether to buy a car. And that's just the beginning. After you graduate, you have to decide where to live, what job or career path to take, whether to pay off your student loans over five years or ten . . .

During her years at UCLA, Minnie Bautista constantly had to make trade-offs. A resident of New York, she had to pay higher tuition as an out-of-state resident, but she decided it was worth it to attend such a fine school. To make ends meet, she took a part-time job, managing a computer database for the medical school's radiation safety department. Other students who didn't have to work had more time to concentrate on studies and extracurricular activities.

When she graduated from college in 1992, she returned home to New York where she had a series of jobs that used her math background and her part-time work experience. At Shearson Lehman Brothers, the big stock brokerage firm, she worked closely with the operations staff to solve client problems and also assisted financial consultants with client transactions. After that, she worked for Johnson & Higgins, an insurance brokerage firm, where she conducted productivity and efficiency analysis to determine company savings in terms of travel. Both of these jobs were in New York City, probably the nation's most expensive place to live.

After a few years of these types of jobs, Minnie was confronted with another career decision which would ultimately be based partly on financial data: Should she go back to graduate school, thus boosting her career prospects? And if so, should she go back

Name: Minnie Bautista
Profession: Business Consultant
College Major: Mathematics

to school at night while working during the day, or should she undertake a full-time program?

At UCLA, Minnie had taken some accounting courses, so she was comfortable looking at financial data. By carefully weighing the costs and benefits, she decided to enroll full-time at Boston College, where she received an MBA in 1996. By attending during the day, she gave up two years of salary—plus she had tuition and other expenses. That meant thousands of dollars in student loans. But if she had attended at night, it would have taken her about five years to complete the program.

When she graduated, another decision based partly on financial data confronted her: she had three technology consulting jobs in different cities offering virtually the same salary and similar career opportunities. One job was in Boston, one was in San Francisco, and the third was in Portland, Oregon. She chose Portland, because the cost of living was significantly lower.

Since her student debt is still substantial, she is very careful about her month-to-month budgeting. Using a spreadsheet computer program, she categorizes her expenses such as rent, utilities, food, and entertainment. Although she has ten years to pay off her loans, she has calculated that by paying off the loans sooner she would save thousands of dollars in interest charges. "I can save about ten thousand dollars in interest by paying the loan off over four years instead of ten," she says. It's just one of a series of personal decisions in life that arise from looking at the numbers.

judgments about what information to present and how to present it. The latitude given accountants in this respect is one of the major reasons accounting is a profession and its members are considered professionals. Along with this designation as a professional, however, comes a serious responsibility. As we noted, general-purpose financial statements are prepared for external parties who must rely on these statements to provide information on which to base important decisions.

At the end of each chapter are cases titled "Accounting and Ethics: What Would You Do?" The cases require you to evaluate difficult issues and make a decision. Judgment is needed in deciding which accounting method to select or how to report a certain item in the statements. As you are faced with these decisions, keep in mind the trust placed in the accountant by various financial statement users. This is central to reaching an ethical decision.

A Final Note About Ben & Jerry's

As you have seen in this chapter, accounting is a practical discipline. Financial statements of real companies, including Ben & Jerry's, are used throughout the remainder of the book to help you learn more about this practical discipline. For example, some of the From Concept to Practice sidebars in future chapters will require you to return to Ben & Jerry's financial statements, as will some of the cases at the end of the chapters. Because no two sets of financial statements look the same, however, you will be introduced to the financial statements of many other real companies as well. Use this opportunity to not only learn more about accounting, but also about each of these companies.

Review Problem

> **Note to the student:** At the end of each chapter is a problem to test your understanding of some of the major ideas presented in the chapter. Try to solve the problem before turning to the solution that follows it.

Greenway Corporation is organized on June 1, 1998. The company will provide lawn care and tree-trimming services on a contract basis. Following is an alphabetical list of the items that should appear on its income statement for the first month and on its balance sheet at the end of the first month (you will need to determine on *which* statement each should appear).

Accounts payable	$ 800
Accounts receivable	500
Building	2,000
Capital stock	5,000
Cash	3,300
Gas, utilities, and other expenses	300
Land	4,000
Lawn care revenue	1,500
Notes payable	6,000
Retained earnings (beginning balance)	–0–
Salaries and wages expense	900
Tools	800
Tree-trimming revenue	500
Truck	2,000

Required

1. Prepare an income statement for the month of June.
2. Prepare a balance sheet at June 30, 1998. *Note:* You will need to determine the balance in Retained Earnings at the end of the month.

Solution to Review Problem

1.

GREENWAY CORPORATION
INCOME STATEMENT
FOR THE MONTH ENDED JUNE 30, 1998

Revenues:		
Lawn care	$1,500	
Tree trimming	500	$2,000
Expenses:		
Salaries and wages	$ 900	
Gas, utilities, and other expenses	300	1,200
Net income		$ 800

2.

GREENWAY CORPORATION
BALANCE SHEET
AT JUNE 30, 1998

ASSETS		LIABILITIES AND OWNERS' EQUITY	
Cash	$ 3,300	Accounts payable	$ 800
Accounts receivable	500	Notes payable	6,000
Truck	2,000	Capital stock	5,000
Tools	800	Retained earnings	800
Building	2,000		
Land	4,000		
		Total Liabilities and	
Total Assets	$12,600	Owners' Equity	$12,600

Chapter Highlights

1. **LO 1** All organizations rely on financial information in making decisions. This is not the only type of information that must be considered in making decisions, but it is certainly one of the most important.

2. **LO 2** The information needed for making decisions depends on the organizational form of an entity. Business entities are organized to earn a profit, whereas nonbusiness organizations exist for some other purpose, such as providing health care or municipal services. Business entities are organized as either *sole proprietorships, partnerships,* or *corporations.*

3. **LO 3** All businesses carry on three basic types of activities: financing, investing, and operating activities. Financing activities are necessary to provide the funds to start a business and to expand in the future. Investing activities are needed to provide the valuable assets required to run the business. Operating activities focus on the sale of products and services.

4. **LO 4** Both individuals external to a business and those involved in the internal management of the company use accounting information. External users include present and potential stockholders, bankers and other creditors, government agencies, suppliers, trade associations, labor unions, and other interested groups.

5. **LO 5** The accounting equation is the basis for the entire accounting system: Assets = Liabilities + Owners' Equity.

Assets are future economic benefits. Liabilities are future sacrifices of economic benefits. Owners' equity is the residual interest that remains after deducting liabilities from assets.

6. **LO 5** A balance sheet summarizes the financial position of a company at a *specific point in time.* An income statement reports on its revenues and expenses for a *period of time.* The statement of cash flows summarizes the operating, financing, and investing activities of a company for a *period of time.* A statement of retained earnings explains the changes in retained earnings *during a particular period.*

7. **LO 6, 7** A number of assumptions are made in preparing financial statements. Accounting is not an exact science, and judgment must be used in deciding what to report on financial statements and how to report the information. Generally accepted accounting principles (GAAP) have evolved over time and are based on a conceptual framework. The *Securities and Exchange Commission* in the public sector and the *Financial Accounting Standards Board* in the private sector have the most responsibility for developing GAAP at the present time.

8. **LO 8** Accountants are employed by business entities, nonbusiness entities, public accounting firms, and educational institutions. Public accounting firms provide audit services for their clients, as well as tax and management consulting services.

Key Terms Quiz

Note to the student: We conclude each chapter with a quiz on the key terms, which are in color where they appear in the chapter. Because of the large number of terms introduced in this chapter, it has two key terms quizzes.

Read each definition below and then write the number of that definition in the blank beside the appropriate term it defines. The first one has been done for you. The solution appears at the end of the chapter. *Study tip:* When reviewing terminology, come back to your completed key terms quiz. Also check the glossary at the end of the book.

Quiz 1

___ Sole proprietorship
___ Partnership
___ Share of stock
___ Nonbusiness entity
___ Capital stock
___ Creditor
___ Revenue
___ Accounting
___ Financial accounting
___ Stockholders' equity
___ Balance sheet
___ Dividends
___ Statement of cash flows

___ Economic entity concept
___ Corporation
___ Bond
___ Liability
___ Stockholder
_1_ Asset
___ Expense
___ Management accounting
___ Owners' equity
___ Retained earnings
___ Income statement
___ Statement of retained earnings

1. **A future economic benefit.**
2. A statement that summarizes revenues and expenses.
3. The statement that summarizes the income earned and dividends paid over the life of a business.
4. The owners' equity in a corporation.
5. The process of identifying, measuring, and communicating economic information to various users.
6. A business owned by two or more individuals; organization form often used by accounting firms and law firms.
7. The branch of accounting concerned with the preparation of general-purpose financial statements for both management and outsider use.
8. The owners' claim on the assets of an entity.
9. The statement that summarizes the cash effects of the operating, investing, and financing activities for a period of time.
10. The financial statement that summarizes the assets, liabilities, and owners' equity at a specific point in time.
11. An inflow of assets resulting from the sale of goods and services.
12. A form of entity organized under the laws of a particular state; ownership evidenced by shares of stock.
13. Organization operated for some purpose other than to earn a profit.
14. The part of owners' equity that represents the income earned less dividends paid over the life of an entity.
15. An outflow of assets resulting from the sale of goods and services.
16. An obligation of a business.
17. The branch of accounting concerned with providing management with information to facilitate the planning and control functions.
18. A certificate that acts as ownership in a corporation.
19. A certificate that represents a corporation's promise to repay a certain amount of money and interest in the future.
20. One of the owners of a corporation.
21. Someone to whom a company has a debt.
22. The assumption that a single, identifiable unit must be accounted for in all situations.
23. Form of organization with a single owner.
24. A category on the balance sheet to indicate the owners' contributions to a corporation.
25. A distribution of the net income of a business to its owners.

Quiz 2

___ Cost principle
___ Monetary unit
___ Generally accepted accounting principles (GAAP)
___ Financial Accounting Standards Board (FASB)
___ American Institute of Certified Public Accountants (AICPA)
___ International Accounting Standards Committee (IASC)
___ Treasurer

___ American Accounting Association
___ Going concern
___ Time period
___ Securities and Exchange Commission (SEC)
___ Certified Public Accountant (CPA)
___ Controller
___ Internal auditing
___ Auditing
___ Auditors' report

1. The various methods, rules, practices, and other procedures that have evolved over time in response to the need to regulate the preparation of financial statements.

2. Assets recorded at the cost to acquire them.

3. The federal agency with ultimate authority to determine the rules in preparing statements for companies whose stock is sold to the public.

4. The professional designation for public accountants who have passed a rigorous exam and met certain requirements determined by the state.

5. The professional organization for accounting educators.

6. The officer of an organization responsible for the safeguarding and efficient use of a company's liquid assets.

7. The assumption that an entity is not in the process of liquidation and that it will continue indefinitely.

8. The group in the private sector with authority to set accounting standards.

9. The yardstick used to measure amounts in financial statements; the dollar in the United States.

10. The professional organization for certified public accountants.

11. The department in a company responsible for the review and appraisal of a company's accounting and administrative controls.

12. Artificial segment on the calendar used as the basis for preparing financial statements.

13. The chief accounting officer for a company.

14. The process of examining the financial statements and the underlying records of a company in order to render an opinion as to whether the statements are fairly presented.

15. The organization formed to develop worldwide accounting standards.

16. The opinion rendered by a public accounting firm concerning the fairness of the presentation of the financial statements.

Alternate Terms

Balance sheet   Statement of financial position.
Cost principle   Original cost; historical cost.
Creditor   Lender.
Income statement   Statement of income.

Net income   Profits or earnings.
Auditors' report   Report of independent accountants.
Stockholder   Shareholder.

Questions

1. What is accounting? Define it in terms understandable to someone without a business background.

2. How do financial accounting and management accounting differ?

3. What are five different groups of users of accounting information? Briefly describe the types of decisions each group must make.

4. What are the three forms of business organization? Briefly describe each form.

5. What is an asset? Give three examples.

6. What is a liability? How does the definition of *liability* relate to the definition of *asset?*

7. How does owners' equity fit in to the accounting equation?

8. What are the two distinct elements of owners' equity in a corporation? Define each element.

9. What is the purpose of a balance sheet?

10. How should a balance sheet be dated: as of a particular day or for a particular period of time? Explain your answer.

11. What does the term *cost principle* mean?

12. What is the purpose of an income statement?

13. How should an income statement be dated: as of a particular day or for a particular period of time? Explain your answer.

14. Rogers Corporation starts the year with a Retained Earnings balance of $55,000. Net income for the year is

$27,000. The ending balance in Retained Earnings is $70,000. What was the amount of dividends for the year?

15. What is the purpose of a statement of cash flows?

16. How do an income statement and a statement of cash flows differ? How are they similar?

17. How do the duties of the controller of a corporation typically differ from those of the treasurer?

18. What are the three basic types of services performed by public accounting firms?

19. How would you evaluate the following statement: "The auditors are in the best position to evaluate a company because they have prepared the financial statements"?

20. Why is the economic entity assumption important in preparing a set of financial statements?

21. What is the relationship between the cost principle and the going concern assumption?

22. Why does inflation present a challenge to the accountant? Relate your answer to the monetary unit assumption.

23. What is meant by the phrase *generally accepted accounting principles?*

24. What role has the Securities and Exchange Commission played in setting accounting standards? Contrast its role with that played by the Financial Accounting Standards Board.

Exercises

LO 1   **Exercise 1-1** Annual Report Information

Critics of financial reporting have said that accounting information, specifically an annual report, is not useful for decision making because it is published three or more months after the end of the company's fiscal year. Therefore, it does not contain any real news. Besides, *all* the information you need about a company can be found in the business section of newspapers or trade and news periodicals.

Look at the annual report for Ben & Jerry's. What information is usually available in detail *only* in the annual report? What advantages or disadvantages are involved in relying on annual reports for making financial decisions about investing in or lending to a company?

LO 2   **Exercise 1-2** Forms of Organization

A university is an entity that requires an accounting system. Is a university a business or nonbusiness entity? What type of accounting system do universities use? Within large entities, such as a university, are smaller entities. Food service is often a separate entity within a university, and it operates as a business entity. Identify some other entities that may exist within a university and therefore require separate accounting records. Identify each as a business or nonbusiness entity.

LO 4   **Exercise 1-3** Users of Accounting Information and Their Needs

Listed below are a number of the important users of accounting information. Below the list are descriptions of a major need of each of these various users. Fill in the blank with the one user group that is most likely to have the need described to the right of the blank.

Company management	**Banker**
Stockholder	**Supplier**
Securities and Exchange Commission	**Labor union**
Internal Revenue Service	

USER GROUP   **NEEDS INFORMATION ABOUT**

_____ **1.** The profitability of each division in the company.

_____ **2.** The prospects for future dividend payments.

_____ **3.** The profitability of the company since the last contract with the work force was signed.

_____ **4.** The financial status of a company issuing securities to the public for the first time.

_____ **5.** The prospects that a company will be able to meet its interest payments on time.

_____ **6.** The prospects that a company will be able to pay for its purchases on time.

_____ **7.** The profitability of the company based on the tax code.

LO 5   **Exercise 1-4** The Accounting Equation

For each of the following independent cases, fill in the blank with the appropriate dollar amount.

	ASSETS	=	LIABILITIES	+	OWNERS' EQUITY
Case 1	$125,000		$ 75,000		$_____
Case 2	400,000		_____		100,000
Case 3	_____		320,000		95,000

LO 5   **Exercise 1-5** The Accounting Equation

Ginger Enterprises began the year with total assets of $500,000 and total liabilities of $250,000. Using this information and the accounting equation, answer each of the following independent questions.

Required

1. What was the amount of Ginger's owners' equity at the beginning of the year?

2. If Ginger's total assets increased by $100,000 and its total liabilities increased by $77,000 during the year, what was the amount of Ginger's owners' equity at the end of the year?

3. If Ginger's total liabilities increased by $33,000 and its owners' equity decreased by $58,000 during the year, what was the amount of its total assets at the end of the year?

4. If Ginger's total assets doubled to $1,000,000 and its owners' equity remained the same during the year, what was the amount of its total liabilities at the end of the year?

LO 5 **Exercise 1-6** The Accounting Equation

Using the accounting equation, answer each of the following independent questions.

1. Burlin Company starts the year with $100,000 in assets and $80,000 in liabilities. Net income for the year is $25,000, and no dividends are paid. How much is owners' equity at the end of the year?

2. Chapman Inc. doubles the amount of its assets from the beginning to the end of the year. Liabilities at the end of the year amount to $40,000, and owners' equity is $20,000. What is the amount of Chapman's assets at the beginning of the year?

3. During the year, the liabilities of Dixon Enterprises triple in amount. Assets at the beginning of the year amount to $30,000, and owners' equity is $10,000. What is the amount of liabilities at the end of the year?

LO 5 **Exercise 1-7** Changes In Owners' Equity

The following amounts are available from the records of Coaches and Carriages Inc. at the end of the years indicated:

DECEMBER 31	TOTAL ASSETS	TOTAL LIABILITIES
1996	$ 25,000	$ 12,000
1997	79,000	67,000
1998	184,000	137,000

Required

1. Compute the changes in Coaches and Carriages' owners' equity during 1997 and 1998.

2. Compute the amount of Coaches and Carriages' net income (or loss) for 1997 assuming that no dividends were paid during the year.

3. Compute the amount of Coaches and Carriages' net income (or loss) for 1998 assuming that dividends paid during the year amounted to $10,000.

LO 5 **Exercise 1-8** The Accounting Equation

For each of the following independent cases, fill in the blank with the appropriate dollar amount.

	CASE 1	CASE 2	CASE 3	CASE 4
Total assets, end of period	$40,000	$_____	$75,000	$50,000
Total liabilities, end of period	_____	15,000	25,000	10,000
Capital stock, end of period	10,000	5,000	20,000	15,000
Retained earnings, beginning of period	15,000	8,000	10,000	20,000
Net income for the period	8,000	7,000	_____	9,000
Dividends for the period	2,000	1,000	3,000	_____

LO 5 **Exercise 1-9** Classification of Financial Statement Items

Classify each of the following items according to (1) whether it belongs on the income statement (IS) or balance sheet (BS) and (2) whether it is a revenue (R), expense (E), asset (A), liability (L), or owners' equity (OE) item.

ITEM	APPEARS ON THE	CLASSIFIED AS
Example: Cash	BS	A
1. Salaries expense	_____	_____
2. Equipment	_____	_____
3. Accounts payable	_____	_____
4. Membership fees earned	_____	_____
5. Common stock	_____	_____
6. Accounts receivable	_____	_____
7. Buildings	_____	_____
8. Advertising expense	_____	_____
9. Retained earnings	_____	_____

LO 5 **Exercise 1-10** Net Income (or Loss) and Retained Earnings

The following information is available from the records of Prestige Landscape Design Inc. at the end of the 1998 calendar year:

Accounts payable	$ 5,000	Office equipment	$ 7,500
Accounts receivable	4,000	Rent expense	6,500
Capital stock	8,000	Retained earnings,	
Cash	13,000	beginning of year	8,500
Dividends paid		Salary and wage expense	12,000
during the year	3,000	Supplies	500
Landscaping revenues	25,000		

Required

Use the information above to answer the following questions:

1. What was Prestige's net income for the year ended December 31, 1998?
2. What is Prestige's retained earnings balance at the end of the year?
3. What is the total amount of Prestige's assets at the end of the year?
4. What is the total amount of Prestige's liabilities at the end of the year?
5. How much owners' equity does Prestige have at the end of the year?
6. What is Prestige's accounting equation at December 31, 1998?

LO 5 **Exercise 1-11** Statement of Retained Earnings

Ace Corporation has been in business for many years. Retained earnings on January 1, 1998, is $235,800. The following information is available for the first two months of 1998:

	JANUARY	FEBRUARY
Revenues	$83,000	$96,000
Expenses	89,000	82,000
Dividends paid	–0–	5,000

Required

Prepare a statement of retained earnings for the month ended February 28, 1998.

LO 6 **Exercise 1-12** Accounting Principles and Assumptions

The following basic accounting principles and assumptions were discussed in the chapter:

Economic entity   **Going concern**
Monetary unit   **Time period**
Cost principle

Fill in each of the blanks with the accounting principle or assumption that is relevant to the situation described.

_____ 1. Genesis Corporation is now in its 30th year of business. The founder of the company is planning to retire at the end of the year and turn the business over to his daughter.

_____ 2. Nordic Company purchased a 20-acre parcel of property on which to build a new factory. The company recorded the property on the records at the amount of cash given to acquire it.

_____ 3. Jim Bailey enters into an agreement to operate a new law firm in partnership with a friend. Each partner will make an initial cash investment of $10,000. Jim opens a checking account in the name of the partnership and transfers $10,000 from his personal account into the new account.

_____ 4. Multinational Corp. has a division in Japan. Prior to preparing the financial statements for the company and all of its foreign divisions, Multinational translates the financial statements of its Japanese division from yen to U.S. dollars.

_____ 5. Camden Company has always prepared financial statements annually, with a year-end of June 30. Because the company is going to sell its stock to the public for the first time, quarterly financial reports will also be required by the Securities and Exchange Commission.

LO 7   **Exercise 1-13** Organizations and Accounting

Match each of the organizations listed below with the statement that most adequately describes the role of the group.

> **Securities and Exchange Commission**
>
> **International Accounting Standards Committee**
>
> **Financial Accounting Standards Board**
>
> **American Institute of Certified Public Accountants**
>
> **American Accounting Association**

_____ 1. Federal agency with ultimate authority to determine rules used in preparing financial statements for companies whose stock is sold to the public.

_____ 2. Professional organization for accounting educators.

_____ 3. Group in the private sector with authority to set accounting standards.

_____ 4. Professional organization for certified public accountants.

_____ 5. Organization formed to develop worldwide accounting standards.

Multi-Concept Exercises

LO 3, 5   **Exercise 1-14** Cash Flows

The operating activities of Springview Corporation generated $50,000 of cash during the year. Net income for the year was $75,000, and cash dividends of $45,000 were paid. Springview spent $35,000 to acquire a piece of real estate. The company borrowed $25,000 from the bank during the year. Springview had cash at the end of the year of $220,000.

Required

Was enough cash generated from operating activities to pay for Springview's acquisitions and its dividends? Where did the rest of the money come from? Compute the amount of cash at the beginning of the year.

LO 4, 8   **Exercise 1-15** Roles of Accountants

One day on campus, you overhear two nonbusiness majors discussing the reasons each did not major in accounting. "Accountants are bean counters. They just sit in a room and play with the books all day. They do not have people skills, but I suppose it really doesn't matter because no one ever looks at the statements they prepare," said the first student. The second student replied, "Oh, they are very intelligent, though, because they must know all about the tax laws, and that's too complicated for me."

Required

Comment on the students' perceptions of the roles of accountants in society. Do you agree that no one ever looks at the statements they prepare? If not, identify who the primary users are.

Problems

LO 1 **Problem 1-1** You Won the Lottery

You have won a lottery! You will receive $200,000, after taxes, each year for the next five years.

Required

Describe the process you will go through in determining how to invest your winnings. Consider at least two options and make a choice. You may consider the stock of a certain company, bonds, real estate investments, bank deposits, and so on. Be specific. Identify how much risk you are willing to take and why. What information did you need to make a final decision? How was your decision affected by the fact that you will receive the winnings over a five-year period rather than in one lump sum? Would you prefer one payment? Explain.

LO 2 **Problem 1-2** Effect of Forms of Organization on Accounting for the Entity

Entities can be organized as sole proprietorships, partnerships, or corporations. The following is a list of entities:

1. A snow cone stand, open for the summer only, in a leased space, owned and operated by a college student.
2. A chain of snow cone stands that owns portable kiosks, located throughout the state, owned and operated by two brothers.
3. An accounting firm that was organized by two accountants—one experienced, the other a new college graduate—and two bookkeepers and that operates in leased space.
4. A real estate office with one broker and five agents, operating in a small converted gas station owned by the broker.
5. A bridge and road construction company started by 10 investors and operated by a hired manager.

Required

For each of the entities, recommend the type of organization you believe suits it best. Write a sentence or two explaining your reason for the choice. The reason is just as important as the choice.

LO 3 **Problem 1-3** Cash Flows for McDonald's Corporation

McDonald's Corporation had cash and equivalents of $334.8 million on December 31, 1995. McDonald's reported revenues of $9,794.5 million, total operating costs and expenses of $7,193.2 million, and net income of $1,427.3 million for the year ended December 31, 1995. Cash provided by operations during 1995 amounted to $2,296.2 million. During 1995, McDonald's purchased property and equipment in the amount of $2,063.7 million. McDonald's also borrowed $1,250.2 million for long-term financing during 1995. Cash amounting to $45.3 million was used for various other investing activities, and cash used for other types of financing activities amounted to $1,282.5 million during the year.

Required

1. Prepare a simplified statement of cash flows for McDonald's for the year ended December 31, 1995.
2. What possible types of business activities might be included in the other investing and financing activities mentioned above?

LO 4 **Problem 1-4** Users of Accounting Information and Their Needs

Microsenses Company would like to buy a building and equipment to produce a new product line. Some information about Microsenses is more useful to some people involved in the project than to others.

Required

Complete the following chart by identifying the information listed on the right with the user's need to know the information. Identify the information as

a. *need* to know;

b. *helpful* to know; or

c. *not necessary* to know.

USER OF THE INFORMATION			
MANAGEMENT	**STOCKHOLDERS**	**BANKER**	**INFORMATION**

1. Amount of current debt, repayment schedule, and interest rate.
2. Fair market value of the building.
3. Condition of the roof and heating and cooling, electrical, and plumbing systems.
4. Total cost of the building, improvements, and equipment to set up production.
5. Expected sales from the new product, variable production costs, related selling costs.

LO 5 **Problem 1-5** Balance Sheet

The following items are available from records of Freescia Corporation at the end of the 1998 calendar year:

Accounts payable	$12,550
Accounts receivable	23,920
Advertising expense	2,100
Buildings	85,000
Capital stock	25,000
Cash	4,220
Notes payable	50,000
Office equipment	12,000
Retained earnings, end of year	37,590
Salary and wage expense	8,230
Sales revenue	14,220

Required

Prepare a balance sheet. *Hint:* Not all of the items listed should appear on a balance sheet. For each of these items, indicate where it should appear.

LO 5 **Problem 1-6** Corrected Balance Sheet

Dave is the president of Avon Consulting Inc. Avon began business on January 1, 1998. The company's controller is out of the country on business. Dave needs a copy of the company's balance sheet for a meeting tomorrow and asked his secretary to obtain the required information from the company's records. She presented Dave with the following balance sheet. He asks you to review it for accuracy.

AVON CONSULTING INC.
BALANCE SHEET
FOR THE YEAR ENDED DECEMBER 31, 1998

ASSETS		LIABILITIES AND OWNERS' EQUITY	
Accounts payable	$13,000	Accounts receivable	$16,000
Cash	21,000	Capital stock	20,000
Cash dividends paid	16,000	Net income for 1998	72,000
Furniture and equipment	43,000	Supplies	9,000

Required

1. Prepare a corrected balance sheet.

2. Draft a memo explaining the major differences between the balance sheet Dave's secretary prepared and the one you prepared.

LO 5 **Problem 1-7** Income Statement, Statement of Retained Earnings, and Balance Sheet

Shown below, in alphabetical order, is a list of the various items that regularly appear on the financial statements of Maple Park Theatres Corp. The amounts shown for balance sheet items are balances as of September 30, 1998 (with the exception of Retained Earnings, which is the balance on September 1, 1998), and the amounts shown for income statement items are balances for the month ended September 30, 1998:

Accounts payable	$17,600
Accounts receivable	6,410
Advertising expense	14,500
Buildings	60,000
Capital stock	50,000
Cash	15,230
Concessions revenue	60,300
Cost of concessions sold	23,450
Dividends paid during the month	8,400
Furniture and fixtures	34,000
Land	26,000
Notes payable	20,000
Projection equipment	25,000
Rent expense—movies	50,600
Retained earnings	73,780
Salaries and wages expense	46,490
Ticket sales	95,100
Water, gas, and electricity	6,700

Required

1. Prepare an income statement for the month ended September 30, 1998.

2. Prepare a statement of retained earnings for the month ended September 30, 1998.

3. Prepare a balance sheet at September 30, 1998.

4. You have $1,000 to invest. On the basis of the statements you prepared, would you use it to buy stock in Maple Park? What other information would you want before making a final decision?

LO 5 **Problem 1-8** Income Statement and Balance Sheet

Green Bay Corporation began business in July 1998 as a commercial fishing operation and passenger service between islands. Shares of stock were issued to the owners in exchange for cash. Boats were purchased by making a down payment in cash and signing a note payable for the balance. Fish are sold to local restaurants on open account, and customers are given 15 days to pay their account. Cash fares are collected for all passenger traffic. Rent for the dock facilities is paid at the beginning of each month. Salaries and wages are paid at the end of the month. The following amounts are from the records of Green Bay Corporation at the end of its first month of operations:

Accounts receivable	$18,500
Boats	80,000
Capital stock	40,000
Cash	7,730
Dividends	5,400
Fishing revenue	21,300
Notes payable	60,000
Passenger service revenue	12,560
Rent expense	4,000
Retained earnings	???
Salary and wage expense	18,230

Required

1. Prepare an income statement for the month ended July 31, 1998.
2. Prepare a balance sheet at July 31, 1998.
3. What information would you need about Notes Payable to fully assess Green Bay's long-term viability? Explain your answer.

LO 5 **Problem 1-9** Corrected Financial Statements

Hometown Cleaners Inc. operates a small dry-cleaning business. The company has always maintained a complete and accurate set of records. Unfortunately, the company's accountant left in a dispute with the president and took the 1998 financial statements with him. The balance sheet and the income statement shown below were prepared by the company's president.

HOMETOWN CLEANERS INC.
INCOME STATEMENT
FOR THE YEAR ENDED DECEMBER 31, 1998

Revenues:		
Accounts receivable	$15,200	
Cleaning revenue—cash sales	32,500	$47,700
Expenses:		
Dividends	$ 4,000	
Accounts payable	4,500	
Utilities	12,200	
Salaries and wages	17,100	37,800
Net income		$ 9,900

HOMETOWN CLEANERS INC.
BALANCE SHEET
DECEMBER 31, 1998

ASSETS		LIABILITIES AND OWNERS' EQUITY	
Cash	$ 7,400	Cleaning revenue—	
Building and equipment	80,000	credit sales	$26,200
Less: Notes payable	(50,000)	Capital stock	20,000
Land	40,000	Net income	9,900
		Retained earnings	21,300
		Total liabilities and	
Total assets	$77,400	owners' equity	$77,400

The president is very disappointed with the net income for the year because it has averaged $25,000 over the last 10 years. She has asked for your help in determining whether the reported net income accurately reflects the profitability of the company and whether the balance sheet is prepared correctly.

Required

1. Prepare a corrected income statement for the year ended December 31, 1998.
2. Prepare a statement of retained earnings for the year ended December 31, 1998. (The actual balance of retained earnings on January 1, 1998 was $42,700. Note that the December 31, 1998, balance shown above is incorrect. The president simply "plugged" this amount in to make the balance sheet balance.)
3. Prepare a corrected balance sheet at December 31, 1998.
4. Draft a memo to the president explaining the major differences between the income statement she prepared and the one you prepared.

LO 7 **Problem 1-10** Setting New Standards

Kmart Corporation reported a net loss of $571 million for the fiscal year ended January 31, 1996. In his letter to shareholders, dated March 19, 1996, the chairman, president, and chief executive officer of Kmart stated that Kmart "bit the bullet in 1995 and early 1996 in a number of ways." Kmart disposed of many noncore assets by selling its investments in the Border Group, OfficeMax, The Sports Authority, and Coles Myer and the assets of its 860 automotive service centers. Kmart closed 214 underperforming stores and disposed of $700 million in aged and discontinued inventory. The company is continuing its efforts to reduce its selling, general and administrative costs.[6]

In recent years, numerous other companies have been restructuring, "downsizing," and "rightsizing." Typically, these companies close locations, sell assets, and lay off employees. Companies taking such actions often pay costs to close locations, realize losses on the disposition of assets, and incur severance pay and retraining costs.

As the financial environment changes, so do accounting standards. Currently, costs associated with the actions described above are expensed in the year in which the changes take place.

Required

Write clear, concise answers to the following questions:

1. The actions taken by Kmart are expected to improve its bottom line. If Kmart will benefit from these changes in future years, do you think that the costs associated with these actions should be matched with future years when the benefits will be realized?

2. What could you do to have an accounting standard changed? Choose a position either for or against changing the way restructuring costs are handled and write a letter to the organization that you believe would be most effective in acting on your recommendation.

Multi-Concept Problems

LO 2, 8 **Problem 1-11** Role of the Accountant in Various Organizations
The following positions in various entities require a knowledge of accounting practices:

1. Chief financial officer for the subsidiary of a large company.
2. Tax adviser to a consolidated group of entities.
3. Independent computer consultant.
4. Financial planner in a bank.
5. Real estate broker in an independent office.
6. Production planner in a manufacturing facility.
7. Quality control adviser.
8. Superintendent of a school district.
9. Manager of one store in a retail clothing chain.
10. Salesperson for a company that offers subcontract services to hospitals, such as food service and maintenance.

Required

For each position listed above, identify the entity in which it occurs as business or non-business and describe the kind of accounting knowledge (such as financial, managerial, taxes, not-for-profit) required by each position.

LO 5, 6 **Problem 1-12** Primary Assumptions Made in Preparing Financial Statements
Joe Hale opened a machine repair business in leased retail space, paying the first month's rent of $300 and a $1,000 security deposit with a check on his personal account. He took the tools and equipment, worth about $7,500, from his garage to the shop. He also bought some more equipment to get started. The new equipment had a list price of $5,000, but Joe was able to purchase it on sale at Sears for only $4,200. He charged the new equipment on his personal Sears charge card. Joe's first customer paid

$400 for services rendered, so Joe opened a checking account for the company. He completed a second job, but the customer has not paid Joe the $2,500 for his work. At the end of the first month, Joe prepared the following balance sheet and income statement.

JOE'S MACHINE REPAIR SHOP
BALANCE SHEET
JULY 31, 1998

Cash	$ 400		
Tools	5,000	Equity	$5,400
Total	$5,400	Total	$5,400

JOE'S MACHINE REPAIR SHOP
INCOME STATEMENT
FOR MONTH ENDED JULY 31, 1998

Sales		$2,900
Rent	$ 300	
Tools	4,200	4,500
Loss		($1,600)

Joe believes that he should show a greater profit next month because he won't have large expenses for items such as tools.

Required

Identify the assumptions that Joe has violated and explain how each event should have been handled. Prepare a corrected balance sheet and income statement.

Alternate Problems

LO 1 **Problem 1-1A** What to do With a Million Dollars
You have inherited $1 million!

Required

Describe the process you will go through in determining how to invest your inheritance. Consider at least two options and choose one. You may consider the stock of a certain company, bonds, real estate investments, bank deposits, and so on. Be specific. Identify how much risk you are willing to take and why. What information did you need to make a final decision? Where did you find the information you needed? What additional information will you need to determine if you want to make a change in your investment?

LO 2 **Problem 1-2A** Effect of Forms of Organization on Accounting for the Entity
Entities can be organized as sole proprietorships, partnerships, or corporations. The following is a list of entities:

1. A landscaping service owned and operated by a college student.
2. A landscaping service owned and operated by two college roommates.
3. An advertising agency owned and operated by one executive with a staff of 25 employees.
4. A sporting goods store started by 10 investors and operated by a hired manager.

Required

For each of the entities, recommend the type of organization you believe suits it best. Write a sentence or two explaining your reason for the choice. The reason is just as important as the choice.

LO 3 **Problem 1-3A** Cash Flows for PepsiCo Inc.
PepsiCo Inc. and subsidiaries had cash and cash equivalents of $382 million on December 30, 1995. PepsiCo reported net sales (or revenues) of $30,421 million, total operating costs and expenses, net, of $27,434 million, and net income of $1,606 million for the year ended December 30, 1995. Cash provided by operations during 1995 amounted to

$3,742 million. During 1995, PepsiCo purchased property, plant, and equipment in the amount of $2,104 million. PepsiCo also received $2,030 million as the proceeds from issuances of long-term debt during 1995. Cash amounting to $346 million was used for various other investing activities, and cash used for other types of financing activities amounted to $3,263 million during the year. In addition, the effect of exchange rate changes during the year on PepsiCo's cash and cash equivalents was an outflow of $8 million.

Required

1. Prepare a simplified statement of cash flows for PepsiCo for the year ended December 30, 1995.

2. What possible types of business activities might be included in the other investing and financing activities mentioned above?

LO 4 **Problem 1-4A** Users of Accounting Information and Their Needs

McCormick Inc. would like to buy a franchise to provide a specialized service. Some information about McCormick is more useful to some people involved in the project than to others.

Required

Complete the following chart by identifying the information listed on the left with the user's need to know the information. Identify the information as

a. *need* to know;

b. *helpful* to know; or

c. *not necessary* to know.

INFORMATION	USER OF THE INFORMATION		
	MANAGER	STOCKHOLDERS	FRANCHISOR
1. Expected revenue from the new service.			
2. Cost of the franchise fee and recurring fees to be paid to the franchisor.			
3. Cash available to McCormick, the franchisee, to operate the business after the franchise is purchased.			
4. Expected overhead costs of the service outlet.			
5. McCormick's required return on its investment.			

LO 5 **Problem 1-5A** Balance Sheet

The following items are available from the records of Victor Corporation at the end of its fiscal year ended July 31, 1998:

Accounts payable	$16,900
Accounts receivable	5,700
Buildings	35,000
Butter and cheese inventory	12,100
Capital stock	25,000
Cash	21,800
Computerized mixers	25,800
Delivery expense	4,600
Notes payable	50,000
Office equipment	12,000
Retained earnings, end of year	26,300
Salary and wage expense	8,230
Sales revenue	14,220
Tools	5,800

Required

Prepare a balance sheet. *Hint:* Not all of the items listed should appear on a balance sheet. For each of these items, indicate where it should appear.

LO 5 **Problem 1-6A** Corrected Balance Sheet

Pete is the president of Island Enterprises. Island Enterprises began business on January 1, 1998. The company's controller is out of the country on business. Pete needs a copy of the company's balance sheet for a meeting tomorrow and asked his secretary to obtain the required information from the company's records. She presented Pete with the following balance sheet. He asks you to review it for accuracy.

ISLAND ENTERPRISES
BALANCE SHEET
FOR THE YEAR ENDED DECEMBER 31, 1998

ASSETS		LIABILITIES AND OWNERS' EQUITY	
Accounts payable	$ 29,600	Accounts receivable	$ 23,200
Cash	14,750	Capital stock	100,000
Cash dividends paid	16,000	Net income for 1998	113,850
Building and equipment	177,300	Supplies	12,200

Required

1. Prepare a corrected balance sheet.
2. Draft a memo explaining the major differences between the balance sheet Pete's secretary prepared and the one you prepared.

LO 5 **Problem 1-7A** Income Statement, Statement of Retained Earnings, and Balance Sheet

Shown below, in alphabetical order, is a list of the various items that regularly appear on the financial statements of Sterns Audio Book Rental Corp. The amounts shown for balance sheet items are balances as of December 31, 1998 (with the exception of retained earnings, which is the balance on January 1, 1998), and the amounts shown for income statement items are balances for the year ended December 31, 1998:

Accounts payable	$ 4,500
Accounts receivable	300
Advertising expense	14,500
Audio tape inventory	70,000
Capital stock	50,000
Cash	2,490
Display fixtures	45,000
Dividends paid during the year	12,000
Notes payable	10,000
Rental revenue	125,900
Rent paid on building	60,000
Retained earnings	35,390
Salaries and wages expense	17,900
Water, gas, and electricity	3,600

Required

1. Prepare an income statement for the year ended December 31, 1998.
2. Prepare a statement of retained earnings for the year ended December 31, 1998.
3. Prepare a balance sheet at December 31, 1998.
4. You have $1,000 to invest. On the basis of the statements you prepared, would you use it to buy stock in this company? What other information would you want before making a final decision?

LO 5 **Problem 1-8A** Income Statement and Balance Sheet

Fort Worth Corporation began business in January 1998 as a commercial carpet cleaning and drying service. Shares of stock were issued to the owners in exchange for cash. Equipment was purchased by making a down payment in cash and signing a note payable for the balance. Services are performed for local restaurants and office buildings on open account, and customers are given 15 days to pay their account. Rent for office and storage facilities is paid at the beginning of each month. Salaries and wages are paid at the end of the month. The following amounts are from the records of Fort Worth Corporation at the end of its first month of operations:

Accounts receivable	$24,750
Capital stock	80,000
Cash	51,650
Cleaning revenue	45,900
Dividends	5,500
Equipment	62,000
Notes payable	30,000
Rent expense	3,600
Retained earnings	???
Salary and wage expense	8,400

Required

1. Prepare an income statement for the month ended January 31, 1998.

2. Prepare a balance sheet at January 31, 1998.

3. What information would you need about Notes Payable to fully assess Fort Worth's long-term viability? Explain your answer.

LO 5 **Problem 1-9A** Corrected Financial Statements

Heidi's Bakery Inc. operates a small pastry business. The company has always maintained a complete and accurate set of records. Unfortunately, the company's accountant left in a dispute with the president and took the 1998 financial statements with her. The balance sheet and the income statement shown below were prepared by the company's president.

HEIDI'S BAKERY INC.
INCOME STATEMENT
FOR THE YEAR ENDED DECEMBER 31, 1998

Revenues:		
Accounts receivable	$15,500	
Pastry revenue—cash sales	23,700	$39,200
Expenses:		
Dividends	$ 5,600	
Accounts payable	6,800	
Utilities	9,500	
Salaries and wages	18,200	40,100
Net loss		$ (900)

HEIDI'S BAKERY INC.
BALANCE SHEET
DECEMBER 31, 1998

ASSETS		LIABILITIES AND OWNER'S EQUITY	
Cash	$ 3,700	Pastry revenue—	
Building and equipment	60,000	credit sales	$22,100
Less: Notes payable	(40,000)	Capital stock	30,000
Land	50,000	Net loss	(900)
		Retained earnings	22,500
		Total liabilities and	
Total assets	$73,700	owners' equity	$73,700

The president is very disappointed with the net loss for the year because net income has averaged $21,000 over the last 10 years. He has asked for your help in determining whether the reported net loss accurately reflects the profitability of the company and whether the balance sheet is prepared correctly.

Required

1. Prepare a corrected income statement for the year ended December 31, 1998.

2. Prepare a statement of retained earnings for the year ended December 31, 1998. (The actual amount of Retained Earnings on January 1, 1998, was $39,900. The December 31, 1998, balance shown above is incorrect. The president simply "plugged" this amount in to make the balance sheet balance.)

3. Prepare a corrected balance sheet at December 31, 1998.

4. Draft a memo to the president explaining the major differences between the income statement he prepared and the one you prepared.

LO 7 **Problem 1-10A** Setting New Standards

Coca-Cola is a global business that operates in approximately 200 countries. The majority of its operating income is generated outside the United States. In its 1995 annual report, the president and chief operating officer responded to questions about Coca-Cola's sales, marketing, and operations. Questions about Coca-Cola's Middle and Far East Group, Latin America Group, and Africa Group included references to the anti-multinational sentiment that exists in India, the economic difficulties of Mexico and Argentina, and the economic impact of an oil strike that crippled Nigeria's economy in 1994. In its "Management's Discussion and Analysis," Coca-Cola notes that it is "uniquely positioned to benefit from operating in a variety of currencies, as downturns in one region are often offset by strengths in others."[7]

In recent years, many other companies have been expanding their operations into underdeveloped countries. These countries may have unstable economies and governments. Many users of financial statements are concerned that the assets invested in these countries are commingled with other company assets.

Required

Write clear, concise answers to the following questions:

1. As a potential investor, why would you be concerned if Coca-Cola co-mingles its assets in foreign countries with those in the United States?

2. To which accounting assumption would you refer if you wanted the profession to consider a change in the way these assets are reported? Which organizations would you write? Write a letter to the organization that you believe would be most effective in acting on your recommendation to report assets invested in underdeveloped countries in a different manner.

Alternate Multi-Concept Problems

LO 2, 8 **Problem 1-11A** Role of the Accountant in Various Organizations

The following positions in various entities require a knowledge of accounting practices:

1. Chief financial officer for the subsidiary of a large company.

2. Tax adviser to a consolidated group of entities.

3. Accounts receivable computer analyst.

4. Financial planner in a bank.

5. Budget analyst in a real estate office.

6. Production planner in a manufacturing facility.

7. Quality control adviser.

8. Manager of the team conducting an audit on a state lottery.

9. Assistant superintendent of a school district.

10. Manager of one store in a retail clothing chain.

11. Controller in a company that offers subcontract services to hospitals, such as food service and maintenance.

12. Staff accountant in a large audit firm.

[7]Summarized from Coca-Cola's 1995 *Annual Report,* pp. 30–40, 47.

Required

For each position listed above, fill in the blank to classify the position as one of the general categories of accountants listed below.

Financial accountant

Managerial accountant

Tax accountant

Accountant for not-for-profit organization

Auditor

Not an accounting position

LO 5, 6 **Problem 1-12A** Primary Assumptions Made in Preparing Financial Statements

Millie Abrams opened a ceramic studio in leased retail space, paying the first month's rent of $300 and a $1,000 security deposit with a check on her personal account. She took molds and paint, worth about $7,500, from her home to the studio. She also bought a new firing kiln to start the business. The new kiln had a list price of $5,000, but Millie was able to trade in her old kiln, worth $500 at the time of trade, on the new kiln, and therefore she paid only $4,500 cash. She wrote a check on her personal checking account. Millie's first customers paid a total of $1,400 to attend classes for the next two months. She opened a checking account in the company's name with the $1,400. She has conducted classes for one month and has sold for $3,000 unfinished ceramic pieces called *greenware.* Greenware sales are all cash. Millie incurred $1,000 of personal cost in making the greenware. At the end of the first month, Millie prepared the following balance sheet and income statement.

MILLIE'S CERAMIC STUDIO
BALANCE SHEET
JULY 31, 1998

Cash	$1,400		
Kiln	5,000	Equity	$6,400
Total	$6,400	Total	$6,400

MILLIE'S CERAMIC STUDIO
INCOME STATEMENT
FOR THE MONTH ENDED JULY 31, 1998

Sales		$4,400
Rent	$300	
Supplies	600	900
Income		$3,500

Millie needs to earn at least $3,000 each month for the business to be worth her time. She is pleased with the results.

Required

Identify the assumptions that Millie has violated and explain how each event should have been handled. Prepare a corrected balance sheet and income statement.

Cases

Reading and Interpreting Financial Statements

LO 4 **Case 1-1** An Annual Report as Ready Reference

Refer to the Ben & Jerry's annual report, and identify where each of the following users of accounting information would first look to answer their respective questions about Ben & Jerry's:

1. Investors: How much did the company earn for each share of stock I own? How much of those earnings did I receive, and how much was reinvested in the company?

2. Potential Investors: What amount of earnings can I expect to see from Ben & Jerry's in the near future?

3. Bankers and creditors: Should I extend the short-term borrowing limit to Ben & Jerry's? Do they have sufficient cash or cash-like assets to repay short-term loans?

4. Internal Revenue Service: How much does Ben & Jerry's owe for taxes?

5. Employees: How much money did the president and vice-presidents earn? Should I ask for a raise?

LO 5 **Case 1-2** Reading and Interpreting Ben & Jerry's Financial Statements

Refer to the financial statements for Ben & Jerry's reproduced in the chapter and answer the following questions:

1. What was the company's net income for 1995?

2. What was the company's net cash provided by operating activities for 1995?

3. What are some of the reasons that the amounts in 1 and 2 above are different?

4. State Ben & Jerry's financial position on December 30, 1995, in terms of the accounting equation.

5. Explain the reason for the change in retained earnings from a balance of $25,316,000 on December 31, 1994, to a balance of $31,264,000 on December 30, 1995. Also, what amount of dividends did the company pay in 1995?

Making Financial Decisions

Decision Making

LO 1, 5 **Case 1-3** Preparation of Projected Statements for a New Business

Upon graduation from MegaState University, you and your roommate decide to start your respective careers in accounting and salmon fishing in Remote, Alaska. Your career as a CPA in Remote is going well, as is your roommate's job as a commercial fisher. After one year in Remote, he approaches you with a business opportunity.

As we are well aware, the video rental business has yet to reach Remote, and the nearest rental facility is 250 miles away. We each put up our first year's savings of $5,000 and file for articles of incorporation with the state of Alaska to do business as Remote Video World. In return for our investment of $5,000, we will each receive equal shares of capital stock in the corporation. Then we go to the Corner National Bank and apply for a $10,000 loan. We take the total cash of $20,000 we have now raised and buy 2,000 videos at $10 each from a mail-order supplier. We rent the movies for $3 per title and sell monthly memberships for $25, allowing a member to check out an unlimited number of movies during the month. Individual rentals would be a cash-and-carry business, but we would give customers until the 10th of the following month to pay for a monthly membership. My most conservative estimate is that during the first month alone, we will rent 800 movies and sell 200 memberships. As I see it, we will have only two expenses. First, we will hire two high school students to run the store for 30 hours each per week and pay them $5 per hour. Second, the landlord of a vacant store in town will rent us space in the building for $1,000 per month.

Required

1. Prepare a projected income statement for the first month of operations.

2. Prepare a balance sheet as it would appear at the end of the first month of operations.

3. Assume that the bank is willing to make the $10,000 loan. Would you be willing to join your roommate in this business? Explain your response. Also, indicate any information other than what he has provided that you would like to have before making a final decision.

Decision Making

LO 1 **Case 1-4** An Investment Opportunity

You have saved enough money to pay for your college tuition for the next three years when a high school friend comes to you with a deal. He is an artist who has spent most of the past two years drawing on the walls of old buildings. The buildings are about to be demolished and your friend thinks you should buy the walls before the buildings are demolished and open a gallery featuring his work. Of course, you are levelheaded and would normally say "No!" Recently, however, your friend has been featured on several local radio and television shows and is talking to some national networks about doing a feature on a well-known news show. To set up the gallery would take all of your savings, but your friend feels that you will be able to sell his artwork for 10 times the cost of your investment. Describe the relationship between risk and potential return as it relates to these two investments—college education and the art gallery. What kind of profit split would you suggest to your friend if you decide to open the gallery?

Accounting and Ethics: What Would You Do?

LO 1, 4, 5 **Case 1-5** Identification of Errors in Financial Statements and Preparation of Revised Statements

Lakeside Slammers Inc. is a minor-league baseball organization that has just completed its first season. You and three other investors organized the corporation; each put up $10,000 in cash for shares of capital stock. Because you live out of state, you have not been actively involved in the daily affairs of the club. However, you are thrilled to receive a dividend check for $10,000 at the end of the season—an amount equal to your original investment! Included with the check are the following financial statements, along with supporting explanations.

LAKESIDE SLAMMERS INC.
INCOME STATEMENT
FOR THE YEAR ENDED DECEMBER 31, 1998

Revenues:		
Single-game ticket revenue	$420,000	
Season-ticket revenue	140,000	
Concessions revenue	280,000	
Advertising revenue	100,000	$940,000
Expenses:		
Cost of concessions sold	$110,000	
Salary expense—players	225,000	
Salary and wage expense—staff	150,000	
Rent expense	210,000	695,000
Net Income		$245,000

LAKESIDE SLAMMERS INC.
STATEMENT OF RETAINED EARNINGS
FOR THE YEAR ENDED DECEMBER 31, 1998

Beginning balance, January 1, 1998	$ –0–
Add: Net income for 1998	245,000
Deduct: Cash dividends paid in 1998	(40,000)
Ending balance, December 31, 1998	$205,000

LAKESIDE SLAMMERS INC.
BALANCE SHEET
AT DECEMBER 31, 1998

ASSETS		LIABILITIES AND OWNERS' EQUITY	
Cash	$ 5,000	Notes payable	$ 50,000
Accounts receivable		Capital stock	40,000
Season tickets	140,000	Additional owners' capital	80,000
Advertisers	100,000	Parent club's equity	125,000
Auxiliary assets	80,000	Retained earnings	205,000
Equipment	50,000		
Player contracts	125,000	Total liabilities and	
Total assets	$500,000	owners' equity	$500,000

Additional information:

a. Single-game tickets sold for $4 per game. The team averaged 1,500 fans per game. With 70 home games × $4 per game × 1,500 fans, single-game ticket revenue amounted to $420,000.

b. No season tickets were sold during the first season. During the last three months of 1998, however, an aggressive sales campaign resulted in the sale of 500 season tickets for the 1999 season. Therefore, the controller (who is also one of the owners) chose to record an Account Receivable—Season Tickets and corresponding revenue for 500 tickets × $4 per game × 70 games, or $140,000.

c. Advertising revenue of $100,000 resulted from the sale of the 40 signs on the outfield wall at $2,500 each for the season. However, none of the advertisers have paid their bills yet (thus, an account receivable of $100,000 on the balance sheet) because the contract with Lakeside required them to pay only if the team averaged 2,000 fans per game during the 1998 season. The controller believes that the advertisers will be sympathetic to the difficulties of starting a new franchise and be willing to overlook the slight deficiency in the attendance requirement.

d. Lakeside has a working agreement with one of the major-league franchises. The minor-league team is required to pay $5,000 *every* year to the major-league team for each of the 25 players on its roster. The controller believes that each of the players is certainly an asset to the organization and has therefore recorded $5,000 × 25, or $125,000, as an asset called Player Contracts. The item on the right side of the balance sheet entitled Parent Club's Equity is the amount owed to the major league team by February 1, 1999, as payment for the players for the 1998 season.

e. In addition to the cost described in d, Lakeside directly pays each of its 25 players a $9,000 salary for the season. This amount—$225,000—has already been paid for the 1998 season and is reported on the income statement.

f. The items on the balance sheet entitled Auxiliary Assets on the left side and Additional Owners' Capital on the right side represent the value of the controller's personal residence. She has a mortgage with the bank for the full value of the house.

g. The $50,000 note payable resulted from a loan that was taken out at the beginning of the year to finance the purchase of bats, balls, uniforms, lawn mowers, and other miscellaneous supplies needed to operate the team (equipment is reported as an asset for the same amount). The loan, with interest, is due on January 15, 1999. Even though the team had a very successful first year, Lakeside is a little short of cash at the end of 1998 and has therefore asked the bank for a three-month extension of the loan. The controller reasons, "By the due date of April 15, 1999, the cash due from the new season ticket holders will be available, things will be cleared up with the advertisers, and the loan can be easily repaid."

Required

1. Identify any errors that you think the controller has made in preparing the financial statements.

2. On the basis of your answer in 1, prepare a revised income statement, statement of retained earnings, and balance sheet.

3. On the basis of your revised financial statements, identify any ethical dilemma you now face. Do you have a responsibility to share these revisions with the other three owners? What is your responsibility to the bank?

Research Case

Case 1-6 Ben & Jerry's

Imagine ice cream with ricotta cheese. Add candied pistachios and cocoa-coated cannoli pieces, and you have Ben & Jerry's "Holy Cannoli" flavor ice cream. This is just one of the many ice cream products the company has developed to attract customers. Every purchase of a Ben & Jerry's product influences company sales, net income, and other financial aspects.

Conduct a search of the World Wide Web, obtain Ben & Jerry's most recent annual report, or use library resources to obtain company financial data, and answer the following:

1. Locate Ben & Jerry's net sales and net income for the most recent year available. How do these numbers compare with the amounts for these items in the "Focus on Financial Results" in the opening vignette shown at the start of this chapter?

2. Based on the latest accounting year available, what is Ben & Jerry's long-term debt? How has this amount changed from the previous year? What may have caused this change?

3. As an observer of business activities and a consumer of ice cream, what actions would you recommend for Ben & Jerry's future financial success?

Optional Research. Develop a brief description of Ben & Jerry's competitors through in-store observations of ice cream products and a search of the World Wide Web for brands such as Haagen-Daz, Good Humor, and Bryer's.

Solutions to Key Terms Quiz

Quiz 1

23 Sole proprietorship (p. 5)
6 Partnership (p. 6)
18 Share of stock (p. 6)
13 Nonbusiness entity (p. 6)
24 Capital stock (p. 8)
21 Creditor (p. 8)
11 Revenue (p. 9)
5 Accounting (p. 9)
7 Financial accounting (p. 11)
4 Stockholders' equity (p. 12)
10 Balance sheet (p. 12)
25 Dividends (p. 14)
9 Statement of cash flows (p. 18)
22 Economic entity concept (p. 5)
12 Corporation (p. 6)
19 Bond (p. 6)
16 Liability (p. 8)
20 Stockholder (p. 8)
1 Asset (p. 8)
15 Expense (p. 9)
17 Management accounting (p. 10)
8 Owners' equity (p. 12)
14 Retained earnings (p. 12)
2 Income statement (p. 12)
3 Statement of retained earnings (p. 14)

Quiz 2

2 Cost principle (p. 21)
9 Monetary unit (p. 21)
1 Generally accepted accounting principles (GAAP) (p. 22)
8 Financial Accounting Standards Board (FASB) (p. 23)
10 American Institute of Certified Public Accountants (AICPA) (p. 23)
15 International Accounting Standards Committee (IASC) (p. 23)
6 Treasurer (p. 24)
5 American Accounting Association (p. 26)
7 Going concern (p. 21)
12 Time period (p. 22)
3 Securities and Exchange Commission (SEC) (p. 22)
4 Certified Public Accountant (CPA) (p. 23)
13 Controller (p. 24)
11 Internal auditing (p. 24)
14 Auditing (p. 25)
16 Auditors' report (p. 25)

STUDY LINKS

A Look at the Previous Chapter

Chapter 1 introduced the role of accounting in our society. We explored how investors, creditors, and others use accounting and the outputs of an accounting system, financial statements, in reaching informed decisions.

A Look at This Chapter

In this chapter, we take a closer look at the financial statements, as well as the other elements that make up an annual report. In the first part of the chapter, we explore the underlying *conceptual framework of accounting.* Every discipline has a set of interrelated concepts, principles, and conventions that guide daily practice. In the second part of the chapter, we will see how the concepts introduced in the first part of the chapter are used in the development of financial statements.

A Look at Upcoming Chapters

Chapter 2 focuses on the end result by examining the outputs of an accounting system, the financial statements. We will take a step back in Chapters 3 and 4 to consider how economic events are processed in an accounting system and are then summarized in the financial statements.

Financial Statements and the Annual Report

FOCUS ON FINANCIAL RESULTS

Every annual report tells a story; Starbucks Corporation's 1995 story told of nearly tenfold earnings growth over four years. That impressive growth resulted from savvy marketing. Starbucks also guards its reputation for quality, controlling each step in the marketing channel from purchases of green coffee beans through sales to consumers. Despite opening 253 new stores, the company improved its profit margin (net income as a percentage of net sales). To offset any slowdown in growth of coffee sales, Starbucks partners with other companies to launch products that support its image: Starbucks

.... $465.2

.... $284.9

.... $176.5

.... $103.2
.... $ 65.3

1991   1992   1993   1994   1995

Net Sales
(in millions)

.... $26,102

.... $10,206⁽¹⁾
.... $ 8,282

.... $ 4,454
.... $ 2,651

1991   1992   1993   1994   1995

Net Earnings
(in thousands)

⁽¹⁾1994 net earnings include merger costs of $3,867 ($2,940, net of taxes)

.... 676

.... 425

.... 272

.... 165
.... 116

1991   1992   1993   1994   1995

Retail Store Count At Year End
(including licensed airport stores)

.... 8.6%
.... 8.2%

.... 7.1%
.... 6.9%

.... 5.3%

1991   1992   1993   1994   1995

Operating Margin
(operating income as a percentage of net sales)

coffee ice cream (made by Dreyer's Grand Ice Cream), Double Black Stout (coffee-flavored beer from Redhook Ale Brewery), Mazagran (a coffee-based beverage developed with Pepsi-Cola), and a compact-disc recording of jazz classics (produced with Capitol Records under its Blue Note label) to support the launch of Blue Note Blend coffee.

Starbucks' annual report also announced goals to open more than 2,000 stores by the year 2000 and to go international, beginning in Tokyo. Against this onslaught, can other coffee retailers compete? If you ran a cafe in Tokyo, you might seek clues in Starbucks' annual report. Besides a statement of the company's mission and plans for growth, it provides standardized financial statements detailing Starbucks' resources and how it spends and earns money.

What are Starbucks' competitive advantages and potential pitfalls? When studying this chapter, identify elements of Starbucks' annual report that can help you answer this question.

SOURCE: Starbucks Corporation, *Annual Report,* 1995.

After studying this chapter, you should be able to

LO 1   Describe the objectives of financial reporting.

LO 2   Describe the qualitative characteristics of accounting information.

LO 3   Explain the concept and purpose of a classified balance sheet and prepare the statement.

LO 4   Use a classified balance sheet to analyze a company's financial position.

LO 5   Explain the difference between a single-step and a multiple-step income statement and prepare each type of income statement.

LO 6   Use a multiple-step income statement to analyze a company's operations.

LO 7   Identify the components of the statement of retained earnings and the statement of stockholders' equity and prepare each statement.

LO 8   Identify the components of the statement of cash flows and prepare the statement.

LO 9   Describe the various elements in the annual report of a publicly held company.

Objectives of Financial Reporting

LO 1   Describe the objectives of financial reporting.

Chapter 1 introduced Ben & Jerry's financial statements. Later in this chapter you will learn more about Starbucks through its financial statements. When the accountants for these companies prepare the statements they must keep in mind the objectives of financial reporting. Financial reporting has one overall objective and a set of related objectives that follow from it. We will first examine the primary objective and then turn our attention to the secondary ones.

The Primary Objective: Provide Information for Decision Making

The primary objective of financial reporting is to *provide economic information to permit users of the information to make informed decisions.* Users include both the management of a company (internal users) and others not involved in the daily operations of the business (external users). Without access to the detailed records of the business and without the benefit of daily involvement in the affairs of the company, external users make their decisions based on *general-purpose financial statements* prepared by management. According to the Financial Accounting Standards Board (FASB),

> Financial reporting should provide information that is useful to present and potential investors and creditors and other users in making rational investment, credit, and similar decisions.[1]

We see from this statement how closely the objective of financial reporting is tied to decision making. The purpose of financial reporting is to help the users reach their decisions in an informed manner.

Secondary Objective: Reflect Prospective Cash Receipts to Investors and Creditors

Present stockholders must decide whether to hold their stock in a company or sell it. For potential stockholders, the decision is whether to buy the stock in the first place. Bankers, suppliers, and other types of creditors must decide whether to lend money to a company. All of these groups rely *partially* on the information provided in financial statements in making their decisions. Other sources of information are sometimes as important, or more important, in reaching a decision. For example, the most recent income statement may report the highest profits in the history of a company. However, a potential investor may choose not to buy stock in a company if the *Wall Street Journal*

[1]*Statement of Financial Accounting Concepts [SFAC] No. 1,* "Objectives of Financial Reporting by Business Enterprises" (Stamford, Conn.: Financial Accounting Standards Board, November 1978), par. 34.

or *Business Week* reports that a strike is likely to shut down operations for an indeterminable period of time.

If you buy stock in a company, your primary concern is the *future cash to be received from the investment.* First, how much, if anything, will you periodically receive in *cash dividends?* Second, how much cash will you receive from the *sale of the stock?* The interests of a creditor, such as a banker, are similar. The banker is concerned with receiving the original amount of money lent and the interest on the loan. In summary, another objective of financial reporting is to

> Provide information to help present and potential investors and creditors and other users in assessing the amounts, timing, and uncertainty of prospective cash receipts from dividends or interest and the proceeds from the sale, redemption, or maturity of securities or loans.[2]

Secondary Objective: Reflect Prospective Cash Flows to the Enterprise

Thus, the two ultimate concerns of the investor or creditor are the cash received from sale of the stock, or maturity of the loan, and cash received from dividends, or interest. Note that your ultimate concern is not the *company's* cash flows but the cash *you* receive from an investment. It is generally acknowledged, however, that a relationship exists between the cash flows to the company and those to the investor:

> Thus, since an enterprise's ability to generate favorable cash flows affects both its ability to pay dividends and interest and the market prices of its securities, expected cash flows to investors and creditors are related to expected cash flows to the enterprise in which they have invested or to which they have loaned funds.[3]

Therefore, another objective of accounting is to provide information that will allow users to make decisions about the cash flows of a company. This does *not* mean, however, that a company should use a *cash basis* of accounting to attain this objective. Certainly, the cash flow statement provides useful information in making decisions about the cash flows of a company in the future. However, income statements and balance sheets prepared using the accrual basis of accounting are better indicators of the ability to generate favorable cash flows than are statements limited to the effects of cash inflows and outflows.

Secondary Objective: Reflect Resources and Claims to Resources

The FASB has emphasized the roles of the balance sheet and income statement in providing useful information:

> Financial reporting should provide information about the economic resources of an enterprise, the claims to those resources (obligations of the enterprise to transfer resources to other entities and owner's equity), and the effects of transactions, events, and circumstances that change resources and claims to those resources.[4]

Exhibit 2-1 summarizes the objectives of financial reporting as they pertain to the decision of a potential investor. The exhibit should help you to understand how something as abstract as a set of financial reporting objectives can be applied to a decision-making situation.

What Makes Accounting Information Useful? Qualitative Characteristics

Quantitative considerations, such as tuition costs, certainly were a concern when you chose your current school. In addition, your decision required you to make subjective judgments about the *qualitative characteristics* you were looking for in a college. Similarly, there are certain qualities that make accounting information useful.

LO 2 Describe the qualitative characteristics of accounting information.

[2]*SFAC No. 1,* par. 37.
[3]*SFAC No. 1,* par. 39.
[4]*SFAC No. 1,* par. 40.

EXHIBIT 2-1	The Application of Financial Reporting Objectives

FINANCIAL REPORTING OBJECTIVE	POTENTIAL INVESTOR'S QUESTIONS
1. Provide information useful to present and potential investors, creditors, and other users in making investment, credit, and similar decisions.	"Should I buy a share of stock in the ABC Corporation?"
2. Provide information to help present and potential investors, creditors, and other users in assessing the amounts, timing, and uncertainty of prospective cash receipts from dividends or interest and the proceeds from the sale, redemption, or maturity of securities or loans.	"How much cash will I receive in dividends each year and from the sale of the stock of ABC Corporation in the future?"
3. Provide information to help investors, creditors, and others assess the amounts, timing, and uncertainty of prospective net cash inflows to the related enterprise.	"What will be the prospective net cash inflows of the ABC Corporation during the time I hold the stock as an investment?"
4. Provide information about the economic resources, the claims to those resources, and the effects of transactions that change resources and the claims to those resources.	"How much has ABC Corporation invested in new plant and equipment?"

Understandability

For anything to be useful, it must be understandable. Usefulness and understandability go hand in hand. However, understandability of financial information varies considerably, depending on the background of the user. For example, should financial statements be prepared so that they are understandable by anyone with a college education? Or should it be assumed that all readers of financial statements have completed at least one accounting course? Is a background in business necessary for a good understanding of financial reports, regardless of one's formal training? As you might expect, there are no simple answers to these questions. However, the FASB believes that financial information should be comprehensible to *those who are willing to spend the time to understand it:*

> Financial information is a tool and, like most tools, cannot be of much direct help to those who are unable or unwilling to use it or who misuse it. Its use can be learned, however, and financial reporting should provide information that can be used by all—nonprofessionals as well as professionals—who are willing to learn to use it properly.[5]

ACCOUNTING FOR YOUR DECISIONS
You Are the Stockholder

ABC Technology produces a highly technical product used in the computer industry. You are a stockholder and are currently in the process of reading this year's annual report. You find that you can't understand the report because it contains so much accounting jargon. But the annual report contains a 1–800 number for shareholder inquiries. You call the number and complain about the annual report, but the corporate spokesman politely tells you that "that's the way people talk in accounting." Is your complaint valid?

ANS: One of the purposes of an annual report is to interest potential stockholders in the company. A small percentage of those potential investors are professional money managers who are familiar with the accounting terminology. However, most readers are individual investors who probably don't have a sophisticated accounting background. It is true that the report must assume a minimum level of formal education; accountants expect those who read the report to take the time to understand it. Technicalities aside, however, it is important to write an annual report for as broad an audience as possible.

Relevance

Understandability alone is certainly not enough to render information useful. To be useful, information must be relevant. Relevance is the capacity of information to make a

[5]*SFAC No. 1,* par. 36.

difference in a decision.[6] For example, assume that in your role as a banker, Parker Company has presented you with its most recent annual report as the basis for a loan. The comparative income statements show a very profitable company over the past several years, and the balance sheet indicates a sound financial position. According to a report you read in yesterday's newspaper, however, the company has been named as the defendant in a multimillion-dollar antitrust lawsuit filed by the federal government. Undoubtedly, this information will be relevant to your decision. Disclosure of the lawsuit in the financial statements will add to their relevancy.

Reliability

What makes accounting information reliable? According to the FASB,

> Accounting information is reliable to the extent that users can depend on it to represent the economic conditions or events that it purports to represent.[7]

Three individual characteristics are involved in the concept of reliability: verifiability, representational faithfulness, and neutrality. To understand these qualities, consider historical cost, which is often defended as a basis of measuring value because of its high degree of reliability. Assume that a company buys a parcel of land for $100,000. The historical cost, or amount paid, for the land is *verifiable,* or free from error, because we can simply look at the contract to determine cost. Information is a *faithful representation* when it is valid, that is, when there is agreement between the underlying data and the events represented. Again, the use of historical cost is defended on the basis that it provides a valid representation of the transaction that resulted in the acquisition of the land. Finally, accounting information is *neutral* when it is not slanted to portray a company's position in a light any worse or any better than the actual circumstances would dictate. Whether or not the historical cost of the land is a neutral measurement of its value today is questionable. For example, what if the land has a market value of $500,000? Is neutrality violated if the accountant continues to report the asset on the balance sheet at only $100,000? Does this portray the company's position in a worse light than circumstances would dictate? There are no easy answers to these questions, and the issue of whether historical cost or current market value is a better measuring unit remains unsettled.

It is interesting to note that other countries have experimented with the use of current values in reporting property, plant, and equipment. Although there is a strict prohibition in the United States against the valuation of long-term physical assets in an amount in excess of cost, the practice is acceptable for certain types of assets in the United Kingdom, Australia, Canada, and South Africa.

Comparability and Consistency

Comparability allows comparisons to be made *between or among companies.* Generally accepted accounting principles (GAAP) allow a certain amount of freedom in choosing among competing alternative treatments for certain transactions.

For example, one of the choices a company must make is the method of depreciation to use. Depreciation is the process of *allocating* the cost of a long-term tangible asset such as a building or equipment over its useful life. One approach to allocating the cost of an asset over its useful life is the straight-line method. *Straight-line depreciation* assigns an equal amount of expense to each year in the useful life of the asset. An alternative is the use of an accelerated method. *Accelerated depreciation* results in the assignment of more depreciation to the earlier years in the useful life of the asset and less depreciation to the later years. GAAP allow a company to choose between the straight-line method and one of the accelerated methods. How does this freedom of

---

[6]*Statement of Financial Accounting Concepts No. 2,* "Qualitative Characteristics of Accounting Information" (Stamford, Conn.: Financial Accounting Standards Board, May 1980), par. 47.
[7]*SFAC No. 2,* par. 62.

Companies produce annual reports like these as a way to summarize the past year's business activities, discuss the firm's performance, preview upcoming products and business trends, and give investors and other users of financial information a format for analyzing its financial information.

choice in selecting a depreciation method affect the ability of an investor to make comparisons between companies?

Assume that at the end of 1995, you were considering buying stock in one of three companies: General Electric (GE), Motorola, or Intel. According to the 1995 annual reports of these companies, General Electric and Motorola used accelerated methods of depreciation, whereas Intel used the straight-line method. Does this lack of a common depreciation method make it impossible for you to compare the performance of the three companies?

Obviously, comparisons among GE, Motorola, and Intel would be easier and more meaningful if all three used the same depreciation method. However, comparisons are not rendered impossible just because companies use different methods. The accounting profession continues to debate the relative merits of comparability and *uniformity*. Certainly, the more alike—that is, uniform—statements are in terms of the principles used to prepare them, the more comparable they will be. However, the profession has felt it necessary to allow a certain freedom of choice in selecting from among alternative generally accepted accounting principles.

To render statements of companies using different methods more meaningful, *disclosure* assumes a very important role. For example, we will see later in this chapter that the first footnote in the annual report of a publicly traded company is the disclosure of its accounting policies. The reader of this footnote for each of the three companies is made aware that the companies do not use the same depreciation method. Disclosure of accounting policies allows the reader to make some sort of subjective adjustment to the statements of one or more of the companies to compensate for the different depreciation method being used.

Consistency is closely related to the concept of comparability. Both involve the relationship between two numbers. *However, comparability allows for comparisons to be made between two or more companies, whereas consistency allows for comparisons to be made within a single company from one accounting period to the next.*

Occasionally, companies decide to change from one accounting method to another. For example, a company may decide to change from an accelerated method of depreciation to the straight-line method. Will it be possible to compare this company's earnings in the period in which it switches methods with earnings in prior years if the depreciation methods differ? Like the different methods used by different companies, changes in accounting methods from one period to the next do not make comparisons impossible, only more difficult. When a company makes an accounting change, accounting standards require various disclosures to help the reader evaluate the impact of the change. Accounting changes are covered in more detail in Chapter 12.

Materiality

We have concluded that to be useful, accounting information must be relevant to a decision. The concept of **materiality** is closely related to relevance and deals with the size of an error in accounting information. The issue is whether the error is large enough to affect the judgment of someone relying on the information. Consider the following example. A company pays cash for two separate purchases: one for a $5 pencil sharpener and the other for a $50,000 computer. Theoretically, each expenditure results in the acquisition of an asset that should be depreciated over its useful life. However, what if the company decides to account for the $5 as an expense of the period rather than treat it in the theoretically correct manner? *Will this error affect in any way the judgment of someone relying on the financial statements?* Because such a slight error will not affect any decisions, minor expenditures of this nature are considered *immaterial* and are accounted for as an expense of the period.

The *threshold* for determining materiality will vary from one company to the next, depending to a large extent on the size of the company. Many companies establish policies that *any* expenditure under a certain dollar amount should be accounted for as an expense of the period. The threshold might be $50 for the corner grocery store but $1,000 for a large corporation.

| EXHIBIT 2-2 | Qualitative Characteristics of Accounting Information |

SITUATION   A bank is trying to decide whether to extend a $1 million loan to Poston Corporation. Poston presents the bank with its most recent balance sheet, showing its financial position on a historical cost basis. Each quality of the information is summarized in the form of a question.

QUALITY	QUESTION
Understandability	Can the information be used by those willing to learn to use it properly?
Relevance	Would the information be useful in deciding whether or not to loan money to Poston?
Reliability	
Verifiability	Can the information be verified?
	Is the information free from error?
Representational faithfulness	Is there agreement between the information and the events represented?
Neutrality	Is the information slanted in any way to present the company more favorably than is warranted?
Comparability	Are the methods used in assigning amounts to assets the same as those used by other companies?
Consistency	Are the methods used in assigning amounts to assets the same as those used in prior years?
Materiality	Will a specific error affect in any way the judgment of someone relying on the financial statements?
Conservatism	If there is any uncertainty about any of the amounts assigned to items in the balance sheet, are they recognized using the least optimistic estimate?

Conservatism

The concept of **conservatism** is a holdover from earlier days when the primary financial statement was the balance sheet and the primary user of this statement was the banker. It was customary to deliberately understate assets in the balance sheet because this resulted in an even larger margin of safety that the assets being provided as collateral for a loan were sufficient.

Today the balance sheet is not the only financial statement, and deliberate understatement of assets is no longer considered desirable. The practice of conservatism is reserved for those situations in which there is *uncertainty* about how to account for a particular item or transaction:

> Thus, if two estimates of amounts to be received or paid in the future are about equally likely, conservatism dictates using the less optimistic estimate; however, if two amounts are not equally likely, conservatism does not necessarily dictate using the more pessimistic amount rather than the more likely one.[8]

Various accounting rules are based on the concept of conservatism. For example, inventory held for resale is reported on the balance sheet at *the lower of cost or market*. This rule requires a company to compare the cost of its inventory with the market price, or current cost to replace that inventory, and report the lower of the two amounts on the balance sheet at the end of the year. In Chapter 6 we will more fully explore the lower of cost or market rule as it pertains to inventory.

Exhibit 2-2 summarizes the qualities that make accounting information useful as these characteristics pertain to a banker's decision as to whether to lend money to a company.

Financial Reporting: An International Perspective

In Chapter 1 we introduced the International Accounting Standards Committee (IASC) and its efforts to improve the development of accounting standards around the world.

[8]*SFAC No. 2*, par. 95.

Interestingly, four of the most influential members of this group, representing the standard-setting bodies in the United States, the United Kingdom, Canada, and Australia, agree on the primary objective of financial reporting. All recognize that the primary objective is to provide information useful in making economic decisions.

The standard-setting body in the United Kingdom distinguishes between qualitative characteristics that relate to *content* of the information presented and those that relate to *presentation.* Similar to the FASB, this group recognizes relevance and reliability as the primary characteristics related to content. Comparability and understandability are the primary qualities related to the presentation of the information.

The concept of conservatism is also recognized in other countries. For example, both the IASC and the standard-setting body in the United Kingdom list "prudence" among their qualitative characteristics. Prudence requires the use of caution in making the various estimates required in accounting. Like the U.S. standard-setting body, these groups recognize that prudence does not justify the deliberate understatement of assets or revenues or the deliberate overstatement of liabilities or expenses.

The Classified Balance Sheet

LO 3 Explain the concept and purpose of a classified balance sheet and prepare the statement.

Now that we have learned about the conceptual framework of accounting, we turn our attention to the outputs of the system: the financial statements. First, we will consider the significance of a *classified balance sheet.* We will then examine the *income statement*, the *statement of stockholders' equity*, and the *statement of cash flows.* The chapter concludes with a brief look at other elements in an annual report.

What Are the Parts of the Balance Sheet? Understanding the Operating Cycle

In the first part of this chapter, we stressed the importance of *cash flow.* For a company that sells a product, the operating cycle begins when cash is invested in inventory and ends when cash is collected by the enterprise from its customers.

Assume that on August 1 a retailer, Laptop Computer Sales, buys a computer for $5,000 from the manufacturer, BIM Corp. At this point, Laptop has merely substituted one asset, cash, for another, inventory. On August 20, 20 days after buying the computer, Laptop sells it to an accounting firm, Arthur & Company, for $6,000. Under the purchase agreement, Arthur will pay for the computer within the next 30 days. At this point, both the form of the asset and the amount have changed. The form of the asset held by Laptop has changed from inventory to accounts receivable. Also, because the inventory has been sold for $1,000 more than its cost of $5,000, the size of the asset held, the account receivable, is now $6,000. Finally, on September 20, Arthur pays $6,000 to Laptop, and the operating cycle is complete. Laptop can now take the cash and buy another computer for resale.

Laptop's operating cycle is summarized in Exhibit 2-3. The length of the company's operating cycle was 50 days. The operating cycle consisted of two distinct parts. From the time Laptop purchased the inventory, 20 days elapsed before it sold the computer. Another 30 days passed before the account receivable was collected. The length of the operating cycle depends to a large extent on the nature of a company's business. For example, in our illustration, the manufacturer of the computer, BIM Corp., received cash immediately from Laptop and did not have to wait to collect a receivable. However, additional time is added to the operating cycle of BIM Corp. to *manufacture* the computer.

The operating cycle of the accounting firm in our example, Arthur & Company, differs from that of either the manufacturer or the retailer. Arthur sells a service rather than a product. Its operating cycle is determined by two factors: the length of time involved in providing a service to the client and the amount of time required to collect any account receivable.

EXHIBIT 2-3	The Operating Cycle for a Retailer	
DATE	**TRANSACTION**	**ASSET FORM**
		Cash of $5,000
August 1	Laptop Computer Sales buys a computer from the manufacturer, BIM Corp., for $5,000 in cash.	Inventory of $5,000
August 20	Laptop sells the computer to Arthur & Company for $6,000; customer has 30 days to pay.	Accounts Receivable of $6,000
September 20	Laptop collects $6,000 from Arthur.	Cash of $6,000

Current Assets

The basic distinction on a classified balance sheet is between current and noncurrent items. **Current assets** are

> cash and other assets that are reasonably expected to be realized in cash or sold or consumed during the normal operating cycle of a business or within one year if the operating cycle is shorter than one year.[9]

Most businesses have an operating cycle shorter than one year. The operating cycle for Laptop Computer Sales in our illustration was 50 days. Therefore, cash, accounts receivable, and inventory are classified as current assets because they either *are* cash, will be *realized* in (converted to) cash (accounts receivable), or will be *sold* (inventory) within one year.

Can you think of a situation in which a company's operating cycle is longer than one year? A construction company is a good example. A construction company essentially builds an item of inventory, such as an office building, to a customer's specifications. The entire process, including constructing the building and collecting the sales amount from the customer, may take three years to complete. According to our earlier definition, because the inventory will be sold and the account receivable will be collected within the operating cycle, they will still qualify as current assets.

In addition to cash, accounts receivable, and inventory, the two other most common types of current assets are marketable securities and prepaid expenses. Excess cash is often invested in the stocks and bonds of other companies, as well as in various government instruments. If the investments are made for the short term, they are classified as current and are typically called either *short-term investments* or *marketable securities*. Alternatively, some investments are made for the purpose of exercising influence over another company and thus are made for the long term. These investments are classified as noncurrent assets. Various prepayments, such as office supplies, rent, and insurance, are classified as *prepaid expenses* and thus are current assets. These assets qualify as current because they will usually be *consumed* within one year.

Noncurrent Assets

Any assets that do not meet the definition of a current asset are classified as *long-term* or *noncurrent assets*. Three common categories of long-term assets are (1) investments, (2) property, plant, and equipment, and (3) intangibles.

Compare the length of the operating cycle of a builder of an office building (or of communications equipment for the Internet) to that of a computer retailer. From the time a construction project "launches" to cash collection may be years, not weeks or months.

[9]Accounting Principles Board, *Statement of the Accounting Principles Board, No. 4,* "Basic Concepts and Accounting Principles Underlying Financial Statements of Business Enterprises" (New York: American Institute of Certified Public Accountants, 1970), par. 198.

Investments   Recall from the discussion of current assets that stocks and bonds expected to be sold within the next year are classified as current assets. Securities that are *not* expected to be sold within the next year are classified as *investments*. In many cases, the investment is in the common stock of another company. Sometimes companies invest in another company either to exercise some influence or actually to control the operation of the other company. Other types of assets classified as investments are land held for future use and buildings and equipment not currently used in operations. Finally, a special fund held for the retirement of debt or for the construction of new facilities is also classified as an investment.

Property, Plant, and Equipment   This category consists of the various *tangible, productive assets* used in the operation of a business. Land, buildings, equipment, machinery, furniture and fixtures, trucks, and tools are all examples of assets held for use in the *operation* of a business rather than for *resale*. The distinction between inventory and equipment, for example, depends on the company's *intent* in acquiring the asset. For example, IBM classifies a computer system as inventory because its intent in manufacturing the asset is to offer it for resale. However, this same computer in the hands of a law firm would be classified as equipment because its intent in buying the asset from IBM is to use it in the long-term operation of the business.

The relative size of property, plant, and equipment depends largely on a company's business. Consider Sprint, a telecommunications company with over $15 billion in total assets at the end of 1995. Almost 64% of the total assets was invested in property, plant, and equipment. On the other hand, property, plant, and equipment represented barely 17% of the total assets of Microsoft, the highly successful software company. Regardless of the relative size of property, plant, and equipment, all assets in this category are subject to depreciation, with the exception of land. A separate accumulated depreciation account is used to account for the depreciation recorded on each of these assets over its life.

Intangibles   Intangible assets are similar to property, plant, and equipment in that they provide benefits to the firm over the long term. The distinction, however, is in the *form* of the asset. *Intangible assets lack physical substance.* Trademarks, copyrights, franchise rights, patents, and goodwill are examples of intangible assets. The cost principle governs the accounting for intangibles, just as it does for tangible assets. For example, the amount paid to an inventor for the patent rights to a new product is recorded as an intangible asset. Similarly, the amount paid to a franchisor of a fast-food restaurant for the exclusive right to operate in a certain geographic area is recorded as an intangible asset. Like tangible assets, intangibles are written off to expense over their useful lives. *Depreciation* is the name given to the process of writing off tangible assets; the same process for intangible assets is called *amortization*. Depreciation and amortization are both explained more fully in Chapter 8.

ACCOUNTING FOR YOUR DECISIONS
You Are a Student
What types of current assets and noncurrent assets would you like to have after you graduate and land that high-paying job?

ANS: You might desire current assets such as cash, short-term marketable securities, and other short-term investments and noncurrent assets such as long-term marketable securities, large mansions, summer homes, and sports cars.

Current Liabilities

The definition of a current liability is closely tied to that of a current asset. A current liability is an obligation that will be satisfied within the next operating cycle or within one year if the cycle is shorter than one year. For example, the classification of a note payable on the balance sheet depends on its maturity date. If the note will be paid within the next year, it is classified as current; otherwise, it is classified as a long-term liability. On the other hand, by their nature, accounts payable, wages payable, and income taxes payable are all short-term or current liabilities.

Most liabilities, such as those for purchases of merchandise on credit, are satisfied by the payment of cash. However, certain liabilities are eliminated from the balance sheet when the company performs services. For example, the liability Subscriptions Received in Advance, which would appear on the balance sheet of a magazine publisher, is satisfied not by the payment of any cash but by the delivery of the magazine to the customers. Finally, it is possible to satisfy one liability by substituting another in its place. For example, a supplier might ask a customer to sign a written promissory note to replace an existing account payable if the customer is unable to pay at the present time.

Long-Term Liabilities

Any obligation that will not be paid or otherwise satisfied within the next year or the operating cycle, whichever is longer, is classified as a long-term liability. Notes payable and bonds payable, both promises to pay money in the future, are two common forms of long-term debt. Some bonds have a life as long as 25 or 30 years. Companies that enter into long-term leases for the use of various types of property are required in certain cases to recognize a liability for the future cash payments required by the contract.

Stockholders' Equity

Recall that stockholders' equity represents the owners' claims on the assets of the business. These claims arise from two sources: *contributed capital* and *earned capital*. Contributed capital appears on the balance sheet in the form of capital stock, and earned capital takes the form of retained earnings. *Capital stock* indicates the owners' investment in the business. *Retained earnings* represents the accumulated earnings, or net income, of the business since its inception less all dividends paid during that time.

Most companies have a single class of capital stock called *common stock*. This is the most basic form of ownership in a business. All other claims against the company, such as those of *creditors* and *preferred stockholders,* take priority. *Preferred stock* is a form of capital stock that, as the name implies, carries with it certain preferences. For example, the company must pay dividends on preferred stock before it makes any distribution of dividends on common stock. In the event of liquidation, preferred stockholders have priority over common stockholders in the distribution of the entity's assets.

Capital stock may appear as two separate items on the balance sheet: *Par Value* and *Paid-in Capital in Excess of Par Value.* The total of these two items tells us the amount that has been paid by the owners for the stock. We will take a closer look at these items in Chapter 11.

Using a Classified Balance Sheet

A classified balance sheet is different from the type of balance sheet presented in the previous chapter in that the line items are grouped under the various headings just discussed. An example of a classified balance sheet for a hypothetical company, Dixon Sporting Goods Inc., is shown in Exhibit 2-4. After examining Dixon's financial statements, we will compare each of them to the same statements for an actual company.

LO 4 Use a classified balance sheet to analyze a company's financial position.

Working Capital

One important use of a balance sheet is in evaluating the liquidity of a business. **Liquidity** is a relative term and deals with the ability of a company to pay its debts as they come due. As you might expect, bankers and other creditors are particularly interested in the liquidity of businesses to which they have lent money. A comparison of current assets and current liabilities is a starting point in evaluating the ability of a company to meet its

EXHIBIT 2-4   Balance Sheet for Dixon Sporting Goods Inc.

DIXON SPORTING GOODS INC.
BALANCE SHEET
AT DECEMBER 31, 1996

ASSETS

Current assets

Cash	$ 5,000	
Marketable securities	11,000	
Accounts receivable	23,000	
Merchandise inventory	73,500	
Prepaid insurance	4,800	
Store supplies	700	
Total current assets		$118,000

Investments

Land held for future office site		150,000

Property, plant, and equipment

Land		100,000	
Buildings	$150,000		
Less: Accumulated depreciation	60,000	90,000	
Store furniture and fixtures	$ 42,000		
Less: Accumulated depreciation	12,600	29,400	
Total property, plant, and equipment			219,400

Intangible assets

Franchise agreement	55,000
Total assets	$542,400

LIABILITIES

Current liabilities

Accounts payable	$ 15,700	
Salaries and wages payable	9,500	
Income taxes payable	7,200	
Interest payable	2,500	
Bank loan payable	25,000	
Total current liabilities		$ 59,900

Long-term debt

Notes payable, due December 31, 2006	120,000
Total liabilities	$179,900

STOCKHOLDERS' EQUITY

Contributed capital

Capital stock, $10 par, 5,000 shares issued and outstanding	$ 50,000	
Paid-in capital in excess of par value	25,000	
Total contributed capital	$ 75,000	
Retained earnings	287,500	
Total stockholders' equity		362,500
Total liabilities and stockholders' equity		$542,400

obligations. **Working capital** is the difference between current assets and current liabilities at a point in time. The working capital for Dixon Sporting Goods on December 31, 1996, is

WORKING CAPITAL

FORMULA	FOR DIXON SPORTING GOODS
Current Assets − Current Liabilities	$118,000 − $59,900 = $58,100

The management of working capital is an important task for any business. A company must continually strive for a *balance* in managing its working capital. For example, too little working capital—or in the extreme, negative working capital—may signal the inability to pay creditors on a timely basis. However, an overabundance of working capital could indicate that the company is not investing enough of its available funds in productive resources, such as new machinery and equipment.

Current Ratio

Because it is an absolute dollar amount, working capital is limited in its informational value. For example, $1 million may be an inadequate amount of working capital for a large corporation but far too much for a smaller company. In addition, a certain dollar amount of working capital may have been adequate for a company earlier in its life but is inadequate now. A related measure of liquidity, the current ratio, allows us to compare the liquidity of companies of different sizes and of a single company over time. The ratio is computed by dividing current assets by current liabilities. Dixon Sporting Goods has a current ratio of just under 2 to 1:

CURRENT RATIO

FORMULA	**FOR DIXON SPORTING GOODS**
$\dfrac{\text{Current Assets}}{\text{Current Liabilities}}$	$\dfrac{\$118,000}{\$59,900} = 1.97 \text{ to } 1$

Some analysts use a rule of thumb of 2 to 1 for the current ratio as a sign of short-term financial health. However, as is always the case, rules of thumb can be dangerous. Historically, companies in certain industries have operated quite efficiently with a current ratio of less than 2 to 1, whereas a ratio much higher than this is necessary to survive in other industries. Consider two popular clothing companies: Tommy Hilfiger and L.A. Gear. At the end of the fiscal year 1995, they had current ratios of 4.06 to 1 and 6.84 to 1, respectively. On the other hand, companies in the telephone communication business routinely have current ratios well under 1 to 1. Sprint's current ratio at the end of 1995 was only slightly over .70 to 1.

Unfortunately, neither the amount of working capital nor the current ratio tells us anything about the *composition* of current assets and current liabilities. For example, assume two companies both have total current assets equal to $100,000. Company A has cash of $10,000, accounts receivable of $50,000, and inventory of $40,000. Company B also has cash of $10,000 but accounts receivable of $20,000 and inventory of $70,000. All other things being equal, Company A is more liquid than Company B because more of its total current assets are in receivables than inventory. Receivables are only one step away from being cash, whereas inventory must be sold and then the receivable collected. Note that Dixon's inventory of $73,500 makes up a large portion of its total current assets of $118,000. An examination of the *relative* size of the various current assets for a company may reveal certain strengths and weaknesses not evident in the current ratio.

In addition to the composition of the current assets, the *frequency* with which they are "turned over" is important. For instance, how long does it take to sell an item of inventory? How long is required to collect an account receivable? Many companies could not exist with the current ratio of .53 reported by McDonald's Corporation at the end of 1995. However, think about the nature of the fast-food business. The frequency of its sales and thus the numerous operating cycles within a single year mean that it can operate with a much lower current ratio than a manufacturing company, for example.

Debt-to-Equity Ratio

Investors and creditors are interested in not only the short-run liquidity of a company but also its *solvency* or ability to remain in business over the long run. The *capital structure* of a company is the focal point in making this determination. This refers to the right side of the balance sheet and the mix between liabilities and stockholders' equity. All companies need a minimum investment by the owners to start a new business.

Many businesses benefit by incurring debt, however. Finding the right mix of debt and equity is as important to a business in the long run as managing working capital is in the short run. One common measure of long-run viability is the debt-to-equity ratio. Dixon's ratio at the end of the year is computed as follows:

DEBT-TO-EQUITY RATIO

FORMULA	FOR DIXON SPORTING GOODS
$\dfrac{\text{Total Liabilities}}{\text{Total Stockholders' Equity}}$	$\dfrac{\$179,900}{\$362,500} = \underline{\underline{.5 \text{ to } 1}}$

The debt-to-equity ratio tells us that for every $1 of stockholders' equity, Dixon has $.50 of liabilities or debt. Recall the accounting equation: Total Assets = Total Liabilities + Total Stockholders' Equity. An alternative way to assess the long-run solvency of a business is to compare debt to *total assets* rather than to stockholders' equity. Because Dixon has $.50 of liabilities for every $1 of stockholders' equity, we would expect to find that it has a debt-to-total-assets ratio of .50/(.50 + 1.00), or .33 to 1:

DEBT-TO-TOTAL-ASSETS RATIO

FORMULA	FOR DIXON SPORTING GOODS
$\dfrac{\text{Total Liabilities}}{\text{Total Assets}}$	$\dfrac{\$179,900}{\$542,400} = \underline{\underline{.33 \text{ to } 1}}$

Based on its debt-to-total-assets ratio, Dixon does not appear to be too reliant on creditors for funds. Two-thirds of the existing assets have been funded through stock and retained earnings. Whether Dixon could profit by borrowing additional money to invest in inventories and various types of plant and equipment is a question requiring much more analysis. Financial statement analysis is explored in more detail in Chapter 15.

The Balance Sheet for Starbucks Corporation

The balance sheet for our hypothetical company, Dixon Sporting Goods Inc., introduced the components of a classified balance sheet. We now turn our attention to the balance sheet of an actual company, Starbucks Corporation. This balance sheet is more complex and requires additional analysis and a better understanding of accounting to fully appreciate it. However, we will concentrate our attention on certain elements of the statement. At this stage in your study of accounting, you should look for the similarities rather than the differences between this balance sheet and that of Dixon.

You were introduced to Starbucks Corporation in Chapter 1. The company traces its roots to 1971, when some friends in Seattle began a search for the perfect roasting beans for coffee. The company has experienced tremendous growth, increasing from 17 stores at the end of fiscal 1987 to 676 stores at October 1, 1995. As we will see later in this chapter, the notes to a set of financial statements give the reader a variety of information about a company. Like the statements of many companies, Starbucks' financial statements include a note that describes its business:

> The Company purchases and roasts high-quality whole bean coffees and sells them, along with a variety of coffee beverages, pastries, confections, and coffee-related accessories and equipment, primarily through its retail stores. In addition to its retail operations, the Company sells primarily whole bean coffees through a specialty sales group and a national mail order operation.[10]

The balance sheets for Starbucks at the end of each of two years are shown in Exhibit 2-5. First, note Starbucks' choice for its accounting or *fiscal year*. Its fiscal year ends on the Sunday closest to September 30. Most companies choose an accounting year that corresponds to the calendar, that is, beginning on January 1 and ending on December 31. However, some companies choose a fiscal year that ends at a point when sales are at

[10]*Starbucks Corporation 1995 Annual Report*, p. 37.

EXHIBIT 2-5 Starbucks' Comparative Balance Sheets

[Consolidated Balance Sheets]
in thousands, except share data

	Oct 1, 1995	Oct 2, 1994
Assets		
Current Assets:		
Cash and cash equivalents	$ 20,944	$ 8,394
Short-term investments	41,507	7,527
Accounts receivable (net of allowance for doubtful accounts of $242 and $126)	10,157	5,394
Inventories	123,657	56,064
Prepaid expenses and other current assets	4,746	5,288
Deferred tax assets, net	4,644	1,913
Total current assets	205,655	84,580
Equity investments	11,628	300
Property, plant, and equipment, net	244,728	140,754
Deposits and other assets	6,167	5,787
Total	$468,178	$231,421
Liabilities and Shareholders' Equity		
Current Liabilities:		
Accounts payable	$ 28,668	$ 9,128
Checks drawn in excess of bank balances	13,138	11,965
Accrued compensation and related costs	12,786	9,075
Other accrued expenses	16,454	10,250
Total current liabilities	71,046	40,418
Deferred income taxes, net	3,490	605
Capital lease obligation	1,013	—
Convertible subordinated debentures	80,398	80,500
Commitments (notes 5 and 12)		
Shareholders' Equity:		
Common stock – Authorized, 100,000,000 shares;		
issued and outstanding, 70,956,990 and 57,936,988 shares	265,679	93,532
Less stock subscription notes receivable	—	(3,671)
	265,679	89,861
Retained earnings, including cumulative translation adjustment of $(435) and $(707) respectively,		
and net unrealized holding gain (loss) on investments of $34 and $(107), respectively	46,552	20,037
Total shareholders' equity	312,231	109,898
Total	$468,178	$231,421

See notes to consolidated financial statements.

their lowest in the annual cycle. For example, The Gap ended its 1995 fiscal year on February 3, 1996, after the busy holiday season.

Starbucks releases what are called *consolidated financial statements,* which reflect the position and results of all operations that are controlled by a single entity. Starbucks owns two other companies, The Coffee Connection Inc. and Starbucks New Venture Company. The former is a retailer of specialty coffee on the East Coast. One of the projects of the New Venture Company is a joint venture with PepsiCo Inc. to develop ready-to-drink coffee-based beverages. Both of these Starbucks companies are legally separate companies and are called *subsidiaries.* We will explore the concept of including the financial statements of subsidiaries controlled by another company in that company's financial statements in Chapter 13.

Starbucks presents comparative balance sheets to indicate its financial position at the end of each of the last two years. As a minimum standard, the Securities and Exchange

Commission requires that the annual report include balance sheets as of the two most recent years and income statements for each of the three most recent years. Note that all amounts on the balance sheet are stated in thousands of dollars. This type of rounding is a common practice in the financial statements of large corporations and is justified under the materiality concept. Knowing the exact dollar amount of each asset would not change a decision made by an investor.

The presentation of comparative balance sheets allows the reader to make comparisons between years. For example, Starbucks' *working capital* increased significantly between October 2, 1994, and October 1, 1995:

WORKING CAPITAL

	OCTOBER 1, 1995	OCTOBER 2, 1994
Current Assets − Current Liabilities	$205,655 − 71,046 = $134,609	$84,580 − 40,418 = $44,162

Starbucks' *current ratio* at each of the two dates follows:

CURRENT RATIO

	OCTOBER 1, 1995	OCTOBER 2, 1994
$\dfrac{\text{Current Assets}}{\text{Current Liabilities}}$	$\dfrac{\$205,655}{\$71,046} = 2.89 \text{ to } 1$	$\dfrac{\$84,580}{\$40,418} = 2.09 \text{ to } 1$

As you can now see, both the amount of working capital and the current ratio increased between 1994 and 1995. The largest change in the current assets is the increase in inventories, from just over $56 million to over $123 million.

On the liability side of its balance sheet, Starbucks lists three noncurrent liabilities: deferred income taxes, capital lease obligation, and convertible subordinated debentures. The last is a form of bonds payable. All three types of long-term debt will be discussed more fully in Chapter 10. Starbucks does not report an amount for total liabilities, so we need to add these three amounts to the total current liabilities to find total liabilities. Starbucks' total stockholders' (shareholders') equity consists of two elements, common stock and retained earnings.

Starbucks' *debt-to-equity ratio* at the end of each of the two years is as follows:

DEBT-TO-EQUITY RATIO

	OCTOBER 1, 1995	OCTOBER 2, 1994
$\dfrac{\text{Total Liabilities}}{\text{Total Shareholders' Equity}}$	$\dfrac{\$155,947}{\$312,231} = .50 \text{ to } 1$	$\dfrac{\$121,523}{\$109,898} = 1.11 \text{ to } 1$

The significant decrease in Starbucks' debt-to-equity ratio from 1994 to 1995 is attributable to the large increase in stockholders' equity during 1995. This sizable increase is due primarily to the large addition to common stock during 1995, an indication that Starbucks issued additional shares of stock during the year.

The Income Statement

The income statement is used to summarize the results of operations of an entity for a *period of time*. At a minimum, all companies prepare income statements at least once a year. Companies that must report to the Securities and Exchange Commission prepare financial statements, including an income statement, every three months. Monthly income statements are usually prepared for internal use by management.

What Appears on the Income Statement?

From an accounting perspective, it is important to understand what transactions of an entity should appear on the income statement. In general, the income statement reports the excess of *revenue over expense,* that is, the *net income,* or in the event of an excess

EXHIBIT 2-6 Income Statement (Single-Step Format) for Dixon Sporting Goods Inc.

DIXON SPORTING GOODS INC.
INCOME STATEMENT (SINGLE-STEP FORMAT)
FOR THE YEAR ENDED DECEMBER 31, 1996

Revenues		
Sales	$357,500	
Interest	1,500	
Total revenues		$359,000
Expenses		
Cost of goods sold	$218,300	
Depreciation on store furniture and fixtures	4,200	
Advertising	13,750	
Salaries and wages for sales staff	22,000	
Depreciation on buildings and		
amortization of trademark	6,000	
Salaries and wages for office staff	15,000	
Insurance	3,600	
Supplies	1,050	
Interest	16,900	
Income taxes	17,200	
Total expenses		318,000
Net income		**$ 41,000**
Earnings per share		**$ 8.20**

of *expense over revenue,* the *net loss* of the period. As a reference to the "bottom line" on an income statement, it is common to use the terms *profits* or *earnings* as synonyms for *net income.*

Certain special types of revenues, called *gains,* are sometimes reported on the income statement, as are certain special types of expenses, called *losses.* For example, assume that Sanders Company holds a parcel of land for a future building site. The company paid $50,000 for the land 10 years ago. The state pays Sanders $60,000 for the property to use in a new highway project. Sanders has a special type of revenue from the condemnation of its property. It will recognize a *gain* of $10,000: the excess of the cash received from the state, $60,000, over the cost of the land, $50,000.

Format of the Income Statement

Although we said earlier that the purpose of the income statement is to present the results of operations of the entity for a period of time, different formats are used by corporations to present their results. The major choice a company makes is whether to prepare the income statement in a single-step or a multiple-step form. Both forms are generally accepted. According to the AICPA's annual survey of 600 companies, more than twice as many use the multiple-step form as compared to the single-step form. Next, we'll explain the differences between the two forms and their variations.

Single-Step Format for the Income Statement In a single-step income statement, all expenses are added together and then are deducted *in a single step* from all revenues to arrive at net income. A single-step format for the income statement of Dixon Sporting Goods is presented in Exhibit 2-6. The primary advantage of the single-step form is its simplicity. No attempt is made to classify either revenues or expenses or to associate any of the expenses with any of the revenues.

Multiple-Step Format for the Income Statement The purpose of the multiple-step income statement is to subdivide the income statement into specific sections and provide the reader with important subtotals. This format is illustrated for Dixon Sporting Goods in Exhibit 2-7.

LO 5 Explain the difference between a single-step and a multiple-step income statement and prepare each type of income statement.

EXHIBIT 2-7 Income Statement (Multiple-Step Format) for Dixon Sporting Goods Inc.

DIXON SPORTING GOODS INC.
INCOME STATEMENT (MULTIPLE-STEP FORMAT)
FOR THE YEAR ENDED DECEMBER 31, 1996

Sales		$357,500	
Cost of goods sold		218,300	
Gross profit			$139,200
Operating expenses			
Selling expenses			
Depreciation on store			
furniture and fixtures	$ 4,200		
Advertising	13,750		
Salaries and wages	22,000		
Total selling expenses		$ 39,950	
General and administrative expenses			
Depreciation on buildings and			
amortization of trademark	$ 6,000		
Salaries and wages	15,000		
Insurance	3,600		
Supplies	1,050		
Total general and administrative expenses		25,650	
Total operating expenses			65,600
Income from operations			$ 73,600
Other revenues and expenses			
Interest revenue		$ 1,500	
Interest expense		16,900	
Excess of other expenses over other revenue			15,400
Income before taxes			$ 58,200
Income tax expense			17,200
Net income			$ 41,000
Earnings per share			$ 8.20

The multiple-step income statement for Dixon indicates three important subtotals. First, cost of goods sold is deducted from sales to arrive at **gross profit:**

Gross profit = Sales − Cost of goods sold

Sales	$357,500
Cost of goods sold	218,300
Gross profit	$139,200

Cost of goods sold, as the name implies, is the cost of the units of inventory sold during the year. It is logical to associate cost of goods sold with the sales revenue for the year because the latter represents the *selling price* of the inventory sold during the period.

The second important subtotal on Dixon's income statement is *income from operations* of $73,600. This is found by subtracting *total operating expenses* of $65,600 from the gross profit of $139,200. Operating expenses are further subdivided between *selling expenses* and *general and administrative expenses.* For example, note that two depreciation amounts are included in operating expenses. Depreciation on store furniture and fixtures is classified as a selling expense because the store is where sales take place. Alternatively, we will assume that the buildings are offices for the administrative staff and thus depreciation on the buildings is classified as a general and administrative expense.

The third important subtotal on the income statement is *income before taxes* of $58,200. Interest revenue and interest expense, neither of which is an operating item, are included in *other revenues and expenses.* The excess of interest expense of $16,900 over interest revenue of $1,500, which equals $15,400, is subtracted from income from operations to arrive at income before taxes. Finally, *income tax expense* of $17,200 is deducted to arrive at *net income* of $41,000.

Using a Multiple-Step Income Statement

The distinct advantage of the multiple-step income statement is that it provides additional information to the reader. Although all of the amounts needed to calculate certain ratios are available on a single-step statement, such calculations are easier to figure with a multiple-step statement. For example, the deduction of cost of goods sold from sales to arrive at gross profit allows us to quickly calculate the gross profit ratio. The ratio of Dixon's gross profit to its sales, rounded to the nearest percent, is as follows:

LO 6 Use a multiple-step income statement to analyze a company's operations.

GROSS PROFIT RATIO

FORMULA	FOR DIXON SPORTING GOODS
$\dfrac{\text{Gross Profit}}{\text{Sales}}$	$\dfrac{\$139,200}{\$357,500} = 39\%$

The gross profit ratio tells us that after paying for the product, for every dollar of sales, 39¢ is available to cover other expenses and earn a profit. The complement of the gross profit ratio is the ratio of cost of goods sold to sales. For Dixon, this ratio is $1 - .39 = .61$, or 61%. For every dollar of sales, Dixon spends $.61 on the cost of the product.

An important use of the income statement is to evaluate the *profitability* of a business. For example, a company's profit margin is the ratio of its net income to its sales. Dixon's profit margin is as follows:

PROFIT MARGIN

FORMULA	FOR DIXON SPORTING GOODS
$\dfrac{\text{Net Income}}{\text{Sales}}$	$\dfrac{\$41,000}{\$357,500} = 11\%$

For every dollar of sales, Dixon has $.11 in net income.

Two important factors should be kept in mind in evaluating any financial statement ratio. First, how does this year's ratio differ from ratios of prior years? For example, a decrease in the profit margin may indicate that the company is having trouble this year controlling certain costs. Second, how does the ratio compare with industry norms? It is always helpful to compare key ratios, such as the profit margin, with an industry average or with the same ratio for a close competitor of the company.

All publicly held companies are required to report earnings per share on the face of the income statement. This ratio translates an entity's net income from an absolute dollar amount to an amount per share of common stock:

EARNINGS PER SHARE

$$\dfrac{\text{Net Income}}{\text{Average Number of Common Shares Outstanding}}$$

Dixon's earnings per share of $8.20 was calculated by dividing its net income of $41,000 by the 5,000 shares of common stock, as indicated on the balance sheet in Exhibit 2-4.

DIXON'S EARNINGS PER SHARE

$$\dfrac{\$41,000}{5,000 \text{ shares}} = \$8.20$$

One important advantage of earnings per share over net income as a measure of profitability is that this ratio can be related to the market price of a company's stock. Many investors pay close attention to a company's *price-earnings ratio,* which is simply the ratio of market price per share of the stock to earnings per share. For example, a low price-earnings ratio may be an indication of an undervalued stock. That is, it can be bought at a low price, relative to its earnings.

Knowing a company's profit margin has limited informational value to investors. The ratio indicates profitability but does not relate it to the size of the investment. The

FROM CONCEPT TO PRACTICE 2.1

READING BEN & JERRY'S INCOME STATEMENT Which income statement format does Ben & Jerry's use: single-step or multiple-step? Calculate Ben & Jerry's 1995 and 1994 gross profit ratio. Explain what happened from 1994 to 1995.

return on stockholders' equity ratio measures the relationship between profitability and the investment made by the stockholders:

RETURN ON STOCKHOLDERS' EQUITY

$$\frac{\text{Net Income}}{\text{Average Stockholders' Equity}}$$

We will look in much more detail in Chapter 15 at the analysis of financial statements. For now, however, it is worth noting that because net income is a measure of profitability *for the year,* it is necessary to use *average* stockholders' equity in calculating return on equity. If we assume that Dixon's stockholders' equity at the beginning of the year was $346,500, its return on equity ratio is as follows:

DIXON'S RETURN ON STOCKHOLDERS' EQUITY

$$\frac{\$41,000}{(\$346,500 + \$362,500)/2} = \underline{\underline{12\%}}$$

The ratio indicates that for every dollar invested by the stockholders, the company has earned a return for them of $.12.

The Income Statement for Starbucks Corporation

We have examined two basic formats for the income statement: the single-step format and the multiple-step format. In practice, numerous variations on these two basic formats exist, depending to a large extent on the nature of a company's business. For example, the multiple-step form, with its presentation of gross profit, is not used by service businesses because they do not sell a product. (Remember that gross profit is sales less cost of goods sold.) As we will see in the following example, the form of the income statement is a reflection of a company's operations.

Multiple-step income statements for Starbucks for a three-year period are presented in Exhibit 2-8. A number of points should be noted about these statements. First, "statement of earnings" is an acceptable alternative to "income statement" as a title for the statement. Second, note that Starbucks does not report gross profit as a line item on its statement. Instead, "cost of sales and related occupancy costs" are deducted, along with the four other expenses, to arrive at operating income ("cost of sales" is an acceptable alternative name for cost of goods sold, and at this point we will not concern ourselves with what might be included in "related occupancy costs"). Finally, note the inclusion of net earnings per share at the bottom of the statement. This amount for 1995, $.36, was calculated by dividing the net earnings (another name for net income) of $26,102 by the weighted average number of shares outstanding of 71,909.

FROM CONCEPT TO PRACTICE 2.2

READING STARBUCKS' INCOME STATEMENT

Compute Starbucks' profit margin for the past two years. Did it go up or down from the prior year to the current year?

The Statements of Retained Earnings and Stockholders' Equity

LO 7 Identify the components of the statement of retained earnings and the statement of stockholders' equity and prepare each statement.

The purpose of a statement of stockholders' equity is to explain the changes in the components of owners' equity during the period. Retained earnings and capital stock are the two primary components of stockholders' equity. If there are no changes during the period in a company's capital stock, it may choose to present a statement of retained earnings instead of a statement of stockholders' equity.[11] A statement of retained earnings for Dixon Sporting Goods is shown in Exhibit 2-9.

The statement of retained earnings provides an important link between the income statement and the balance sheet. Dixon's net income of $41,000, as detailed on the income statement, is an *addition* to retained earnings. Note that the dividends declared and paid of $25,000 do not appear on the income statement because they are a payout,

---

[11]According to the AICPA's annual survey, most corporations (about 80%) present a statement of stockholders' equity. A separate statement of retained earnings, or a combined statement of income and retained earnings, is used by a small minority of companies.

EXHIBIT 2-8   Starbucks' Comparative Income Statements

[Consolidated Statements of Earnings]
in thousands, except earnings per share

Fiscal year ended:	Oct 1, 1995	Oct 2, 1994	Oct 3, 1993
Net sales	$465,213	$284,923	$176,541
Cost of sales and related occupancy costs	204,795	127,268	80,474
Store operating expenses	155,269	93,153	56,641
Other operating expenses	13,936	8,696	5,326
Depreciation and amortization	22,486	12,535	6,716
General and administrative expenses	28,611	19,973	14,766
Operating income	40,116	23,298	12,618
Interest income	6,792	2,130	1,680
Interest expense	(3,765)	(3,807)	(772)
Provision for merger costs	—	(3,867)	—
Earnings before income taxes	43,143	17,754	13,526
Income taxes	17,041	7,548	5,244
Net earnings	26,102	10,206	8,282
Preferred stock dividends	—	270	405
Net earnings available to common shareholders	$ 26,102	$ 9,936	$ 7,877
Net earnings per share	$ 0.36	$ 0.17	$ 0.14
Weighted average shares outstanding	71,909	59,757	59,692

See notes to consolidated financial statements.

or *distribution,* of net income to stockholders rather than one of the expenses deducted to arrive at net income. Accordingly, they appear as a direct deduction on the statement of retained earnings. The beginning balance in retained earnings is carried forward from last year's statement of retained earnings.

To emphasize the relationship between the two, some companies combine the statement of retained earnings with the income statement. The general format of a combined statement is as follows:

Revenues	$xxx
Less: Expenses	xxx
Net income	$xxx
Add: Retained earnings at beginning of year	xxx
Subtotal	$xxx
Less: Dividends declared during the year	xxx
Retained earnings at end of year	$xxx

EXHIBIT 2-9   Statement of Retained Earnings for Dixon Sporting Goods Inc.

DIXON SPORTING GOODS INC.
STATEMENT OF RETAINED EARNINGS
FOR THE YEAR ENDED DECEMBER 31, 1996

Retained earnings, January 1, 1996	$271,500
Add: Net income for 1996	41,000
	$312,500
Less: Dividends declared and paid in 1996	(25,000)
Retained earnings, December 31, 1996	$287,500

The Statement of Cash Flows

LO 8 Identify the components of the statement of cash flows and prepare the statement.

The statement of cash flows was introduced in Chapter 1, and we will return to a detailed discussion of how to prepare the statement in Chapter 14. For now, however, recall the purpose of the statement: to summarize the cash flow effects of a company's operating, investing, and financing activities for the period. All publicly held corporations are required to present a statement of cash flows in their annual reports.

The Cash Flow Statement for Dixon Sporting Goods

The statement for Dixon Sporting Goods is shown in Exhibit 2-10. The statement consists of three categories: operating activities, investing activities, and financing activities. Each of these three categories can result in a net inflow of cash or a net outflow of cash.

Dixon's *operating activities* generated $56,100 of cash during the period. As the name implies, operating activities concern the purchase and sale of a product, in this case the acquisition of sporting goods from distributors and the subsequent sale of those goods. An income statement summarizes a company's operations for the period; thus, net income is listed as the first item in this section of the statement. However, net income reflects revenues when they are earned, not necessarily when cash is received. Expenses are reflected when they are incurred, not necessarily when cash is paid. In Chapter 14, we will discuss the statement of cash flows in detail and the preparation of this section of the statement. For now, it is enough to know that adjustments are necessary to convert net income to a cash basis.

The one *investing activity,* the purchase of land for a future office site, required the use of cash and thus is shown as a net outflow of $150,000. Dixon had two *financing*

EXHIBIT 2-10   Statement of Cash Flows for Dixon Sporting Goods Inc.

DIXON SPORTING GOODS INC.
STATEMENT OF CASH FLOWS
FOR THE YEAR ENDED DECEMBER 31, 1996

CASH FLOWS FROM OPERATING ACTIVITIES		
Net income	$ 41,000	
Adjustments to reconcile net income to net cash provided by operations:		
Depreciation expense	10,200	
Decrease in accounts receivable	5,000	
Increase in inventory	(3,000)	
Increase in prepaid insurance	(1,200)	
Decrease in store supplies	200	
Increase in accounts payable	4,100	
Decrease in salaries and wages payable	(1,500)	
Increase in income taxes payable	1,300	
Net cash provided by operating activities		$ 56,100
CASH FLOWS FROM INVESTING ACTIVITIES		
Purchase of land for future office site		(150,000)
CASH FLOWS FROM FINANCING ACTIVITIES		
Dividends declared and paid	$ (25,000)	
Proceeds from issuance of long-term note	120,000	
Net cash provided by financing activities		95,000
Net increase in cash		$ 1,100
Cash at beginning of year		3,900
Cash at end of year		$ 5,000

activities: dividends of $25,000 required the use of cash, and the issuance of a long-term note generated cash of $120,000. The balance in cash on the bottom of the statement of $5,000 must agree with the balance for this item as shown on the balance sheet in Exhibit 2-4.

Other Elements of an Annual Report

No two annual reports look the same. The appearance of an annual report depends not only on the size of a company but also on the budget devoted to the preparation of the report. Some companies publish "bare-bones" annual reports, whereas others issue a glossy report complete with pictures of company products and employees. In recent years many companies, as a cost-cutting measure, have scaled back the amount spent on the annual report. For example, General Motors printed a recent annual report on plain paper. The creativity in annual reports varies as well. Batman graced the cover of the 1995 Time Warner annual report; Ben & Jerry's report for the same year came complete with crayons.

> **LO 9** Describe the various elements in the annual report of a publicly held company.

Privately held companies tend to distribute only financial statements, without the additional information normally included in the annual reports of public companies. For the annual reports of public companies, however, certain basic elements are considered standard. A letter to the stockholders from either the president or the chairman of the board of directors appears in the first few pages of most annual reports. A section describing the company's products and markets is usually included. At the heart of any annual report is the financial report or review, which consists of the financial statements accompanied by footnotes to explain various items on the statements. We will now consider these other elements as presented in the 1995 annual report of Starbucks.

Report of Management and Report of Independent Auditors

Two important reports that accompany Starbucks' financial statements are reproduced in Exhibits 2-11 and 2-12. These reports set out the responsibilities of the management and the auditors for the financial statements.

The first sentence in the management's report clearly states management's responsibility for the information in the annual report. The first paragraph also refers to generally accepted accounting principles. There are also references in the report to the company's independent auditors and to the audit committee of the board of directors.

Two key phrases should be noted in the first sentence of the last paragraph of the auditors' report: *in our opinion* and *present fairly*. The report indicates that responsibility for the statements rests with Starbucks and that the auditors' job is to *express an opinion* on the statements based on certain tests. It would be impossible for an auditing firm to spend the time or money to retrace and verify every single transaction entered into during the year by Starbucks. Instead, the auditing firm performs various tests of the accounting records to be able to assure itself that the statements are free of *material misstatement*. Auditors do not "certify" the total accuracy of a set of financial statements but render an opinion as to the reasonableness of those statements.

The Ethical Responsibility of Management and the Auditors

The management of a company and its auditors share a common purpose: to protect the interests of stockholders. In large corporations, the stockholders are normally removed from the daily affairs of the business. The need for a professional management team to run the business is a practical necessity, as is the need for a periodic audit of the company's records. Because stockholders cannot run the business themselves, they need assurances that the business is being operated effectively and efficiently and that the financial statements presented by management are a fair representation of the company's

EXHIBIT 2-11   Starbucks' Report of Management

[**Management's Responsibility for Financial Reporting**]
Starbucks Corporation

The management of Starbucks Corporation is responsible for the preparation and integrity of the financial statements included in this Annual Report to Shareholders. The financial statements have been prepared in conformity with generally accepted accounting principles and include amounts based on management's best judgment where necessary. Financial information included elsewhere in this Annual Report is consistent with these financial statements.

Management maintains a system of internal controls and procedures designed to provide reasonable assurance that transactions are executed in accordance with proper authorization, that transactions are properly recorded in the Company's records, that assets are safeguarded, and that accountability for assets is maintained. The concept of reasonable assurance is based on the recognition that the cost of maintaining our system of internal accounting controls should not exceed benefits expected to be derived from the system. Internal controls and procedures are periodically reviewed and revised, when appropriate, due to changing circumstances and requirements.

Independent auditors are appointed by the Company's Board of Directors and ratified by the Company's shareholders to audit the financial statements in accordance with generally accepted auditing standards and to independently assess the fair presentation of the Company's financial position, results of operations, and cash flows. Their report appears in this Annual Report.

The Audit Committee of the Board of Directors, a majority of whom are outside directors, is responsible for monitoring the Company's accounting and reporting practices. The Audit Committee meets periodically with management and the independent auditors to ensure that each is properly discharging its responsibilities. The independent auditors have full and free access to the Committee without the presence of management to discuss the results of their audits, the adequacy of internal accounting controls, and the quality of financial reporting.

Howard Schultz	Orin Smith	Michael Casey
chairman and	president and	senior vice president and
chief executive officer	chief operating officer	chief financial officer

operations and financial position. The management and the auditors have a very important ethical responsibility to their constituents, the stockholders of the company.

Management Discussion and Analysis

Preceding the financial statements is a section of Starbucks' annual report titled "Management's Discussion and Analysis of Financial Condition and Results of Operations." This report gives management the opportunity to discuss the financial statements and provide the stockholders with explanations for certain amounts reported in the statements. For example, management explains the increase in net sales as follows:

Net sales increased 63% to $465.2 million for fiscal 1995, compared to $284.9 million for fiscal 1994. Retail sales increased 62% to $402.7 million from $248.5 million. Comparable store sales increased 9% for the 52 weeks ended October 1, 1995 compared to the same 52-week period in fiscal 1994. Comparable store sales increases resulted from an increase

EXHIBIT 2-12   Starbucks' Report of Independent Auditors

[Starbucks Corporation]
Seattle, Washington

We have audited the accompanying consolidated balance sheets of Starbucks Corporation and subsidiaries (the Company) as of October 1, 1995, and October 2, 1994, and the related consolidated statements of earnings, shareholders' equity, and cash flows for each of the three years in the period ended October 1, 1995. These financial statements are the responsibility of the Company's management. Our responsibility is to express an opinion on these financial statements based on our audits.

We conducted our audits in accordance with generally accepted auditing standards. Those standards require that we plan and perform the audit to obtain reasonable assurance about whether the financial statements are free of material misstatement. An audit includes examining, on a test basis, evidence supporting the amounts and disclosures in the financial statements. An audit also includes assessing the accounting principles used and significant estimates made by management, as well as evaluating the overall financial statement presentation. We believe that our audits provide a reasonable basis for our opinion.

In our opinion, such consolidated financial statements present fairly, in all material respects, the financial position of Starbucks Corporation and subsidiaries as of October 1, 1995, and October 2, 1994, and the results of their operations and their cash flows for each of the three years in the period ended October 1, 1995, in conformity with generally accepted accounting principles.

DELOITTE & TOUCHE LLP
Seattle, Washington
November 22, 1995

in the number of transactions combined with an increase in the average dollar value per transaction. The increase in average dollar value per transaction included an increase in coffee beverage and whole bean prices which took place in July 1994.[12]

Notes to Consolidated Financial Statements

The sentence "See notes to consolidated financial statements" appears at the bottom of each of Starbucks' four financial statements. These comments, or *footnotes,* as they are commonly called, are necessary to satisfy the need for *full disclosure* of all the facts relevant to a company's results and financial position. The first footnote in all annual reports is a summary of *significant accounting policies.* A company's policies for valuing inventories, depreciating assets, and recognizing revenue are among the important items contained in this footnote. For example, Starbucks describes its policy for depreciating assets as follows:

Depreciation of property, plant, and equipment is provided on the straight-line method over estimated useful lives, generally ranging from three to seven years for equipment and 40 years for buildings.[13]

In addition to the summary of significant accounting policies, other footnotes discuss such topics as income taxes and employee benefit plans.

[12]*Starbucks Corporation 1995 Annual Report,* p. 25.
[13]*Starbucks Corporation 1995 Annual Report,* p. 38.

ACCOUNTING FOR YOUR DECISIONS
You Are the Customer

You love to visit Starbucks coffee houses. Not only do you love the flavor, but you enjoy the fact that the coffee is always served piping hot. Recently, you read that McDonald's was sued for millions of dollars by a customer because she burned herself by trying to hold the coffee cup while driving a car. You have become curious about whether Starbucks has had similar legal troubles. Where would you find out?

ANS: You would take a look at Starbucks' annual report, flipping to the back under the footnotes to the financial statements. Any significant legal issues are disclosed there. As of this writing, no one has sued Starbucks because the coffee was served too hot. But you can be sure that the McDonald's case got the attention of the top executives at Starbucks.

Summary of Selected Financial Data

It is common to include in an annual report a summary of selected data, such as revenue, net income, and total assets, for the current year and a number of prior years. Starbucks' report includes a five-year summary. These summaries allow the reader to look for trends in the data and, the company hopes, will aid him or her in predicting future sales and earnings for the company.

This completes our discussion of the makeup of the annual report. By now you should appreciate the flexibility companies have in assembling the report, aside from the need to follow generally accepted accounting principles in preparing the statements. The accounting standards followed in preparing the statements, as well as the appearance of the annual report itself, differ in other countries. As has been noted elsewhere, although many corporations operate internationally, accounting principles are far from being standardized.

The following review problem will give you the opportunity to apply what you have learned by preparing two of the financial statements for an actual company.

Review Problem

Recently companies have begun to publish *summary* annual reports. These reports present highly condensed financial statements and normally do not include management's discussion and analysis or the footnotes. The reader of one of these summary annual reports is referred to the company's *Form 10-K*, the annual report filed with the Securities and Exchange Commission, for complete financial statements and other elements normally included in the annual report.

The following review problem is based on Compaq Computer Corporation's *Summary Annual Report* for 1995. Shown below, in alphabetical order, are items taken from Compaq's 1995 condensed financial statements (all amounts are in millions of dollars). Use the items to prepare two statements. First, prepare an *income statement* for the year ended December 31, 1995. The income statement should be in *multiple-step* form. Second, prepare a *classified balance sheet* at December 31, 1995. The descriptions in parentheses are *not* part of the items but have been added to provide you with certain hints. The solution that follows is a reprint of the two actual statements published by Compaq. As you check your solution against the one provided, be sure to look only at the numbers for 1995.

Accounts payable	$ 1,379
Accounts receivable, net	3,141
Cash and cash equivalents	745
Common stock and capital in excess of $.01 par value	890
Cost of sales	11,367
Deferred income taxes (current asset)	365
Deferred income taxes (noncurrent liability)	224
Income taxes payable	190
Inventories	2,156
Long-term debt	300

Other assets (noncurrent)	$ 181
Other current liabilities	1,111
Other income and expense, net	95
Prepaid expenses and other current assets	120
Property, plant, and equipment, less accumulated depreciation	1,110
Provision for income taxes (another name for income tax expense)	399
Purchased in-process technology (expense item)	241
Research and development costs (expense item)	270
Retained earnings	3,724
Sales	14,755
Selling, general, and administrative expense	1,594

Solution to Review Problem

condensed consolidated statement of income
Compaq Computer Corporation

Year ended December 31, (in millions except per share amounts)	1995	1994	1993
Sales	$ 14,755	$ 10,866	$ 7,191
Cost of sales	11,367	8,139	5,493
	3,388	2,727	1,698
Selling, general, and administrative expense	1,594	1,235	837
Research and development costs	270	226	169
Purchased in-process technology[1]	241		
Other income and expense, net [2]	95	94	76
	2,200	1,555	1,082
Income before provision for income taxes	1,188	1,172	616
Provision for income taxes [3]	399	305	154
Net income	$ 789	$ 867	$ 462
Earnings per common and common equivalent share:			
Primary [4]	$ 2.88	$ 3.23	$ 1.82
Assuming full dilution [4]	$ 2.87	$ 3.21	$ 1.78
Shares used in computing earnings per common and common equivalent share:			
Primary [4]	273.6	268.6	254.1
Assuming full dilution [4]	275.0	270.1	258.9

Notes to Selected Financial Information

[1] Represents a non-recurring, non-tax deductible charge of $241 million ($.87 per share) in 1995 for purchased in-process technology in connection with the NetWorth and Thomas-Conrad acquisitions.

[2] Includes restructuring charges of $12 million, $87 million, and $139 million in 1993, 1992, and 1991, respectively, and a realized gain on investment in affiliated company of $86 million in 1992.

[3] The company's effective tax rate in 1995, 1994, and 1993 reflects the company's decision to reinvest indefinitely a portion of the undistributed earnings of its Singaporean manufacturing subsidiary.

[4] All share and per share data have been adjusted to reflect the company's three-for-one and two-for-one stock splits in 1994 and 1990, respectively.

Solution to Review Problem (continued)

condensed consolidated balance sheet
Compaq Computer Corporation

Year ended December 31, (dollars in millions except par value)	1995	1994
ASSETS		
Current assets:		
Cash and cash equivalents	$ 745	$ 471
Accounts receivable, net	3,141	2,287
Inventories	2,156	2,005
Deferred income taxes	365	303
Prepaid expenses and other current assets	120	92
Total current assets	6,527	5,158
Property, plant, and equipment, less accumulated depreciation	1,110	944
Other assets	181	64
	$ 7,818	$ 6,166
LIABILITIES AND STOCKHOLDERS' EQUITY		
Current liabilities:		
Accounts payable	$ 1,379	$ 888
Income taxes payable	190	246
Other current liabilities	1,111	879
Total current liabilities	2,680	2,013
Long-term debt	300	300
Deferred income taxes	224	179
Stockholders' equity:		
Preferred stock, $.01 par value: 10 million shares authorized; none outstanding		
Common stock and capital in excess of $.01 par value: 1 billion shares authorized; 267 and 261 million shares issued and outstanding	890	739
Retained earnings	3,724	2,935
Total stockholders' equity	4,614	3,674
	$ 7,818	$ 6,166

Chapter Highlights

1. **LO 1** The primary objective of financial reporting is to provide information that is useful in making investment, credit, and similar decisions.

2. **LO 1** Investors and creditors are ultimately interested in their own prospective cash receipts from dividends or interest and the proceeds from the sale, redemption, or maturity of loans. Because these expected cash flows are related to the expected cash flows to the company, its cash flows are of interest to investors and creditors. The entity's economic resources, claims to them, and the effects of transactions that change resources and claims to those resources are also of interest.

3. **LO 2** Financial information should be understandable to those who are willing to spend the time to under-

stand it. To be useful, the information should be relevant and reliable. Relevant information has the capacity to make a difference in a decision. Reliable information can be depended on to represent the economic events that it purports to represent.

4. **LO 2** Comparability is the quality that allows for comparisons to be made between two or more companies, whereas consistency is the quality that allows for comparisons to be made within a single company from one period to the next. These two qualities of useful accounting information are aided by full disclosure—in the footnotes to the financial statements—of all relevant information.

5. **LO 3** The operating cycle depends to a large extent on the nature of a company's business. For a retailer, it

encompasses the period of time from the investment of cash in inventory to the collection of any account receivable from sale of the product. The operating cycle for a manufacturer is expanded to include the period of time required to convert raw materials into finished products.

6. **LO 3** Current assets will be realized in cash or sold or consumed during the operating cycle or within one year if the cycle is shorter than one year. Because most businesses have numerous operating cycles within a year, the cutoff for classification as a current asset is usually one year. Cash, accounts receivable, inventory, and prepaid expenses are all examples of current assets.

7. **LO 3** The definition of *current liability* is related to that of *current asset*. A current liability is an obligation that will be satisfied within the operating cycle or within one year if the cycle is shorter than one year. Many liabilities are satisfied by making a cash payment. However, some obligations are settled by rendering a service.

8. **LO 4** A classified balance sheet is helpful in evaluating the liquidity of a business. Working capital, the difference between current assets and current liabilities, indicates the buffer of protection for creditors. The current ratio, current assets divided by current liabilities, provides the reader with a relative measure of liquidity. The debt-to-equity ratio is a useful measure of the long-run solvency of a company.

9. **LO 5** All expenses are added together and subtracted from all revenues in a single-step income statement. The multiple-step income statement provides the reader with classifications of revenues and expenses as well as with important subtotals. Cost of goods sold is subtracted from sales revenue on a multiple-step statement, with the result reported as gross profit.

10. **LO 6** Profitability analysis includes such measures as the gross profit ratio (the ratio of gross profit to sales) and the profit margin (the ratio of net income to sales). A combination of information from the balance sheet and the income statement is useful in assessing profitability. The return on stockholders' equity ratio indicates net income relative to the investment made by the stockholders.

11. **LO 7, 8** A statement of stockholders' equity summarizes the changes in owners' equity during the period. If there are no changes in the capital stock accounts, some companies present a statement of retained earnings or a combined statement of income and retained earnings. The statement of cash flows summarizes the operating, investing, and financing activities of an entity for the period.

12. **LO 9** No two annual reports are the same. However, certain basic elements are included in most of them. In addition to the financial statements, annual reports include the reports of management and the independent auditors, management's discussion of the amounts appearing in the statements, footnotes to the statements, and a summary of selected financial data over a period of years.

Key Terms Quiz

Read each definition below and then write the number of the definition in the blank beside the appropriate term it defines. The solution appears at the end of the chapter.

____ Understandability
____ Relevance
____ Reliability
____ Depreciation
____ Materiality
____ Operating cycle
____ Current liability
____ Working capital
____ Debt-to-equity ratio
____ Multiple-step income statement
____ Gross profit ratio
____ Earnings per share

____ Comparability
____ Consistency
____ Conservatism
____ Current asset
____ Liquidity
____ Current ratio
____ Debt-to-total-assets ratio
____ Single-step income statement
____ Gross profit
____ Profit margin
____ Return on stockholders' equity

1. An income statement in which all expenses are added together and subtracted from all revenues.
2. The magnitude of an omission or misstatement in accounting information that will affect the judgment of someone relying on the information.
3. The capacity of information to make a difference in a decision.
4. An income statement that provides the reader with classifications of revenues and expenses as well as with important subtotals.
5. The practice of using the least optimistic estimate when two estimates of amounts are about equally likely.
6. The quality of accounting information that makes it comprehensible to those willing to spend the necessary time.

7. Net income divided by number of common shares outstanding.

8. Gross profit divided by sales.

9. Current assets divided by current liabilities.

10. The quality of accounting information that makes it dependable in representing the events that it purports to represent.

11. An obligation that will be satisfied within the next operating cycle or within one year if the cycle is shorter than one year.

12. The period of time between the purchase of inventory and the collection of any receivable from the sale of the inventory.

13. Total liabilities divided by total stockholders' equity.

14. Current assets minus current liabilities.

15. Net income divided by sales.

16. The quality of accounting information that allows a user to analyze two or more companies and look for similarities and differences.

17. Total liabilities divided by total assets.

18. An asset that is expected to be realized in cash or sold or consumed during the operating cycle or within one year if the cycle is shorter than one year.

19. The ability of a company to pay its debts as they come due.

20. The quality of accounting information that allows a user to compare two or more accounting periods for a single company.

21. Sales less cost of goods sold.

22. Net income divided by average stockholders' equity.

23. The allocation of the cost of a tangible, long-term asset over its useful life.

Alternate Terms

Balance sheet Statement of financial position or condition.

Capital stock Contributed capital.

Cost of goods sold Cost of sales.

Gross profit Gross margin.

Income statement Statement of income.

Income tax expense Provision for income taxes.

Long-term assets Noncurrent assets.

Net income Profits or earnings.

Report of independent auditors Auditors' report.

Report of management Management's report.

Retained earnings Earned capital.

Stockholders' Equity Shareholders' equity.

Questions

1. How would you evaluate the following statement: "The cash flows to a company are irrelevant to an investor; all the investor cares about is the potential for receiving dividends on the investment"?

2. A key characteristic of useful financial information is understandability. How does this qualitative characteristic relate to the background of the user of the information?

3. What does *relevance* mean with regard to the use of accounting information?

4. What is the qualitative characteristic of comparability, and why is it important in preparing financial statements?

5. What is the difference between comparability and consistency as they relate to the use of accounting information?

6. How does the concept of materiality relate to the size of a company?

7. How does the operating cycle of a retailer differ from that of a service company?

8. How does the concept of the operating cycle relate to the definition of a current asset?

9. What are two examples of the way a company's intent in using an asset affect classification of the asset on the balance sheet?

10. How would you evaluate the following statement: "A note payable with an original maturity of five years will be classified on the balance sheet as a long-term liability until it matures"?

11. How do the two basic forms of owners' equity items for a corporation—capital stock and retained earnings—differ?

12. What are the limitations of working capital as a measure of the liquidity of a business as opposed to the current ratio?

13. What is meant by a company's capital structure?

14. How would you evaluate the following statement: "The debt-to-total-assets ratio is a better indicator of a company's solvency than is the debt-to-equity ratio"?

15. What is the major weakness of the single-step form for the income statement?

16. Why might a company's gross profit ratio increase from one year to the next but its profit margin ratio decrease?

17. What advantage does the return on stockholders' equity ratio have over the profit margin ratio as a measure of profitability?

18. Why should *average* stockholders' equity be used in calculating return on stockholders' equity?

19. How does a statement of retained earnings act as a link between an income statement and a balance sheet?

20. How would you evaluate the following statement: "A statement of cash flows is unnecessary, and actually

redundant, because the increase or decrease in cash for the period can be easily calculated by looking at the cash account on two successive balance sheets"?

21. In auditing the financial statements of a company, does a certified public accountant *certify* that the statements are totally accurate and without errors of any size or variety?

22. What is the first footnote in the annual report of all publicly held companies, and what is its purpose?

Exercises

LO 2 **Exercise 2-1** Characteristics of Useful Accounting Information

Fill in the blank with the qualitative characteristic for each of the following descriptions:

_____ 1. Information that users can depend on to represent the events that it purports to represent.

_____ 2. Information that has the capacity to make a difference in a decision.

_____ 3. Information that is valid, that indicates an agreement between the underlying data and the events represented.

_____ 4. Information that allows for comparisons to be made from one accounting period to the next.

_____ 5. Information that is free from error.

_____ 6. Information that is meaningful to those who are willing to learn to use it properly.

_____ 7. Information that is not slanted to portray a company's position any better or worse than the circumstances warrant.

_____ 8. Information that allows for comparisons to be made between or among companies.

LO 3 **Exercise 2-2** Classification of Assets and Liabilities

Indicate the appropriate classification of each of the following as a current asset (CA), noncurrent asset (NCA), current liability (CL), or long-term liability (LTL):

_____ 1. Inventory.

_____ 2. Accounts payable.

_____ 3. Cash.

_____ 4. Patents.

_____ 5. Notes payable, due in six months.

_____ 6. Taxes payable.

_____ 7. Prepaid rent (for the next nine months).

_____ 8. Bonds payable, due in 10 years.

_____ 9. Machinery.

LO 4 **Exercise 2-3** Relationship Between the Debt-To-Equity Ratio and the Debt-To-Total-Assets Ratio

Van Buren Corporation has a debt-to-total-assets ratio of .40 to 1. Total debt or liabilities amount to $64,000. What is the dollar amount of total assets? What is the company's debt-to-equity ratio? Is the *information* provided by these two ratios different? Explain your answer.

LO 5 **Exercise 2-4** Selling Expenses and General and Administrative Expenses

Operating expenses are subdivided between selling expenses and general and administrative expenses when a multiple-step income statement is prepared. From the following list, identify each item as a selling expense (S) or general and administrative expense (G&A):

_____ 1. Advertising expense.

_____ 2. Depreciation expense—store furniture and fixtures.

_____ 3. Office rent expense.

_____ 4. Office salaries expense.

_____ 5. Store rent expense.

_____ 6. Store salaries expense.

_____ 7. Insurance expense.

_____ **8.** Supplies expense.

_____ **9.** Utilities expense.

LO 5 **Exercise 2-5** Missing Income Statement Amounts

For each of the following independent cases, fill in the blank with the appropriate dollar amount:

	SARA'S COFFEE SHOP	AMY'S DELI	JANE'S BAGELS
Net sales	$35,000	$ _____	$78,000
Cost of goods sold	_____	45,000	
Gross profit	7,000	18,000	_____
Selling expenses	3,000	_____	9,000
General and administrative expenses	1,500	2,800	_____
Total operating expenses	_____	8,800	13,600
Net income	$ 2,500	$ 9,200	$25,400

LO 6 **Exercise 2-6** Income Statement Ratios

The 1998 income statement of Holly Enterprises shows net income of $45,000, comprising net sales of $134,800, cost of goods sold of $53,920, selling expenses of $18,310, general and administrative expenses of $16,990, and interest expense of $580. Holly's stockholders' equity was $280,000 at the beginning of the year and $320,000 at the end of the year. The company has 20,000 shares of stock outstanding at December 31, 1998.

Required

Compute Holly's (1) gross profit ratio, (2) profit margin, (3) earnings per share and (4) return on stockholders' equity. What other information would you need to be able to comment on whether these ratios are favorable?

LO 7 **Exercise 2-7** Statement of Retained Earnings

Landon Corporation was organized on January 2, 1996, with the investment of $100,000 by each of its two stockholders. Net income for its first year of business was $85,200. Net income increased during 1997 to $125,320 and to $145,480 during 1998. Landon paid $20,000 in dividends to each of the two stockholders in each of the three years.

Required

Prepare a statement of retained earnings for the year ended December 31, 1998.

LO 8 **Exercise 2-8** Components of the Statement of Cash Flows

From the following list, identify each item as operating (O), investing (I), financing (F), or not on the statement of cash flows (N):

_____ **1.** Paid for supplies.

_____ **2.** Sold products.

_____ **3.** Purchased land (held for resale).

_____ **4.** Purchased land (for construction of new building).

_____ **5.** Paid dividend.

_____ **6.** Issued stock.

_____ **7.** Purchased computers.

_____ **8.** Sold old equipment.

LO 9 **Exercise 2-9** Basic Elements of Financial Statements

Most financial reports contain the following list of basic elements. For each element, identify the person(s) who prepared the element and describe the information a user would expect to find in each element. Some information is verifiable; other information is subjectively chosen by management. Comment on the verifiability of information in each element.

1. Management's report.
2. Product/markets of company.
3. Financial statements.
4. Notes to financial statements.
5. Auditors' opinion.

Multi-Concept Exercises

LO 3, 5, 7 **Exercise 2-10** Financial Statement Analysis
Potential stockholders and lenders are interested in a company's financial statements. For the list below, identify the statement: balance sheet (BS), income statement (IS), retained earnings statement (RE) on which each item would appear.

_____ 1. Accounts payable.	_____ 2. Accounts receivable.
_____ 3. Advertising expense.	_____ 4. Bad debt expense.
_____ 5. Bonds payable.	_____ 6. Buildings.
_____ 7. Cash.	_____ 8. Common stock.
_____ 9. Deferred income taxes.	_____ 10. Depreciation expense.
_____ 11. Dividends.	_____ 12. Land held for future expansion.
_____ 13. Loss on the sale of equipment.	_____ 14. Office supplies.
_____ 15. Organizational costs.	_____ 16. Patent amortization expense.
_____ 17. Retained earnings.	_____ 18. Sales.
_____ 19. Unearned revenue.	_____ 20. Utilities expense.

LO 5, 6 **Exercise 2-11** Single- and Multiple-Step Income Statement
Some headings and/or items are used on either the single-step or the multiple-step income statement. Some are used on both. For the list below, indicate the following: single-step (S), multiple-step (M), both formats (B), or not used on either income statement (N).

_____ 1. Sales.
_____ 2. Cost of goods sold.
_____ 3. Selling expenses.
_____ 4. Total revenues.
_____ 5. Utilities expense.
_____ 6. Administrative expense.
_____ 7. Net loss.
_____ 8. Supplies on hand.
_____ 9. Accumulated depreciation.
_____ 10. Gross profit.

LO 5, 6 **Exercise 2-12** Multiple-Step Income Statement
Gaynor Corporation's partial income statement follows:

Sales	$1,200,000
Cost of sales	450,000
Selling expenses	60,800
General and administrative expenses	75,000

Required

Determine the gross profit ratio, profit margin, earnings per share (1,000,000 shares outstanding), and price-earnings ratio (the market price is $7.50). Would you consider investing in Gaynor Corporation? Explain your answer.

Problems

LO 2 **Problem 2-1** Materiality

Joseph Knapp, a newly hired accountant, wanted to impress his boss, so he stayed late one night to analyze the office supplies expense. He determined the cost by month, for the past 12 months, of each of the following: computer paper, copy paper, fax paper, pencils and pens, note pads, postage, corrections supplies, stationery, and miscellaneous items.

1. What did Joseph think his boss would learn from this information? What action might be taken as a result of knowing it?

2. Would this information be more relevant if Joseph worked for a hardware store or for a real estate company? Discuss.

LO 2 **Problem 2-2** Costs and Expenses

The following costs are incurred by a retailer:

1. Display fixtures in a retail store.

2. Advertising.

3. Merchandise for sale.

4. Incorporation (i.e., legal costs, stock issue costs).

5. Cost of a franchise.

6. Office supplies.

7. Wages in a restaurant.

8. Computer software.

9. Computer hardware.

Required

For each of these costs, explain whether all of the cost or only a portion of the cost would appear as an expense on the income statement for the period in which the cost was incurred. If not all of the cost would appear on the income statement for that period, explain why not.

LO 2 **Problem 2-3** Changes in Accounting Principles—Sara Lee

Your aunt is considering making an investment in the common stock of Sara Lee Corporation and asks for your advice. You obtain Sara Lee's annual report and note that the following paragraph is included in the footnotes to the company's consolidated financial statements:

> During 1994, the American Institute of Certified Public Accountants issued Statement of Position 93-7, "Reporting on Advertising Costs," which will be effective for the corporation's fiscal 1995 financial statements. The statement primarily requires that the cost of advertising be expensed no later than the first time the advertising takes place. The impact of adopting this statement is not expected to have a material impact upon the corporation's results of operations or financial condition.[14]

Required

Write your aunt a brief letter that addresses the following:

1. What impact does this change in accounting principle have on the comparability and consistency of the company's financial statements?

2. How will this change in accounting provide better matching of revenues and expenses?

LO 3 **Problem 2-4** Classified Balance Sheet

The following balance sheet items, listed in alphabetical order, are available from the records of Ruth Corporation at December 31, 1998:

Accounts payable	$ 18,255
Accounts receivable	23,450
Accumulated depreciation—automobiles	22,500
Accumulated depreciation—buildings	40,000

[14]*Sara Lee Corporation 1994 Annual Report.*

Automobiles	$112,500
Bonds payable, due December 31, 2002	160,000
Buildings	200,000
Capital stock, $10 par value	150,000
Cash	13,230
Income taxes payable	6,200
Interest payable	1,500
Inventory	45,730
Land	250,000
Long-term investments	85,000
Notes payable, due June 30, 1999	10,000
Office supplies	2,340
Paid-in capital in excess of par value	50,000
Patents	40,000
Prepaid rent	1,500
Retained earnings	311,095
Salaries and wages payable	4,200

Required

1. Prepare in good form a classified balance sheet as of December 31, 1998.
2. Compute Ruth's current ratio.
3. On the basis of your answer to requirement 2, does Ruth appear to be *liquid?* What other information do you need to fully answer this question?

LO 4 **Problem 2-5** Financial Statement Ratios

The following items, in alphabetical order, are available from the records of Walker Corporation as of December 31, 1998 and 1997:

	DECEMBER 31, 1998	DECEMBER 31, 1997
Accounts payable	$ 8,400	$ 5,200
Accounts receivable	13,230	19,570
Cash	10,200	9,450
Cleaning supplies	450	700
Interest payable	–0–	1,200
Inventory	24,600	26,200
Marketable securities	6,250	5,020
Note payable, due in six months	–0–	12,000
Prepaid rent	3,600	4,800
Taxes payable	1,450	1,230
Wages payable	1,200	1,600

Required

1. Calculate the following, as of December 31, 1998, and December 31, 1997:
   a. Working capital.
   b. Current ratio.
2. On the basis of your answers in 1, comment on the relative liquidity of the company at the beginning and the end of the year. As part of your answer, explain the change in the company's liquidity from the beginning to the end of 1998.

LO 4 **Problem 2-6** Working Capital and Current Ratio

The balance sheet of Stevenson Inc. includes the following items:

Cash	$ 23,000
Accounts receivable	13,000
Inventory	45,000
Prepaid insurance	800
Land	80,000

Accounts payable	$ 54,900
Salaries payable	1,200
Capital stock	100,000
Retained earnings	5,700

Required

1. Determine the current ratio and working capital.

2. Beyond the information provided in your answers to 1, what does the composition of the current assets tell you about Stevenson's liquidity?

3. What other information do you need to fully assess Stevenson's liquidity?

LO 4 **Problem 2-7** Effects of Transactions on Current and Debt-to-Equity Ratios

(Students: Consider completing Problem 2-8 after this problem to ensure that you obtain a clear understanding of the effect of various transactions on these measures of liquidity.)

Debra Corwin, the president of Global Technologies, is very concerned about the company's current ratio and debt-to-equity ratio. When the company negotiated a new lending agreement with its bank earlier this year, Debra agreed to maintain these ratios within certain ranges. Currently, the company has a current ratio of 2 to 1 (based on current assets of $250,000 and current liabilities of $125,000) and a debt-to-equity ratio of 2 to 1 (based on total liabilities of $600,000 and total stockholders' equity of $300,000). During the last few days of the company's fiscal year, various transactions are anticipated or being contemplated. Debra has asked you to determine the impact that each of these transactions will have on the company's ratios.

Required

Determine the impact of each individual transaction on the company's current ratio and debt-to-equity ratio by recalculating each of the ratios (round to the nearest hundredth). Then, describe the effect of each of these transactions on the company's current ratio and debt-to-equity ratio by indicating whether the transaction would increase, decrease, or have no effect on each of these measures of the company's liquidity.

DESCRIPTION OF TRANSACTION	CURRENT RATIO	EFFECT OF TRANSACTION	DEBT-TO-EQUITY RATIO	EFFECT OF TRANSACTION
Example: Purchase of office supplies for cash of $12,000.	2.00 to 1	No effect	2.00 to 1	No effect
1. Purchase of equipment for cash of $45,000.				
2. Cash collections from accounts receivable of $21,000.				
3. Cash payment of accounts payable of $75,000.				
4. Cash payment of dividends payable of $100,000.				
5. Repayment of a short-term loan of $60,000.				
6. Issuance of capital stock for cash of $150,000.				
7. Declaration of a cash dividend of $25,000 to be paid after the end of the year.				

LO 4 **Problem 2-8** Effects of Transactions on Current and Debt-to-Equity Ratios

(Students: Consider completing this problem after Problem 2-7 to ensure that you obtain a clear understanding of the effect of various transactions on these measures of liquidity.)

Refer to the information set forth in Problem 2-7. Assume instead that the company has a current ratio of .9 to 1 (based on current assets of $450,000 and current liabilities of

$500,000) and a debt-to-equity ratio of .9 to 1 (based on total liabilities of $1,080,000 and total stockholders' equity of $1,200,000).

Required

1. Determine the impact of each individual transaction on the company's current ratio and debt-to-equity ratio by recalculating each of the ratios (round to the nearest hundredth). Then, describe the effect of each of these transactions on the company's current ratio and debt-to-equity ratio by indicating whether the transaction would increase, decrease, or have no effect on each of these measures of the company's liquidity.

DESCRIPTION OF TRANSACTION	CURRENT RATIO	EFFECT OF TRANSACTION	DEBT-TO-EQUITY RATIO	EFFECT OF TRANSACTION
Example: Purchase of office supplies for cash of $12,000.	.90 to 1	No effect	.90 to 1	No effect
1. Purchase of equipment for cash of $45,000.				
2. Cash collections from accounts receivable of $21,000.				
3. Cash payment of accounts payable of $75,000.				
4. Cash payment of dividends payable of $100,000.				
5. Repayment of a short-term loan of $60,000.				
6. Issuance of capital stock for cash of $150,000.				
7. Declaration of a cash dividend of $25,000 to be paid after the end of the year.				

2. Note that the preexisting current ratio and debt-to-equity ratio assumed in Problem 2-7 both exceeded 1 to 1. The preexisting current ratio and debt-to-equity ratio assumed in this problem were both less than 1 to 1. Compare the "Effect of Transaction" columns completed for each of these problems. Which transactions actually have an indeterminable effect on the ratios (that is, the effect—increase or decrease—actually depends on whether the preexisting ratios are greater or less than 1 to 1)?

LO 5 **Problem 2-9** Single-Step Income Statement

The following income statement items, arranged in alphabetical order, are taken from the records of Shaw Corporation for the year ended December 31, 1998:

Advertising expense	$ 1,500
Commissions expense	2,415
Cost of goods sold	29,200
Depreciation expense—office building	2,900
Income tax expense	1,540
Insurance expense—salesperson's auto	2,250
Interest expense	1,400
Interest revenue	1,340
Rent revenue	6,700
Salaries and wages expense—office	12,560
Sales revenue	48,300
Supplies expense—office	890

Required

1. Prepare a single-step income statement for the year ended December 31, 1998.
2. What weaknesses do you see in this form for the income statement?

LO 5 **Problem 2-10** Multiple-Step Income Statement

Refer to the list of income statement items in Problem 2-9. Assume that Shaw Corporation classifies all operating expenses into two categories: (1) selling and (2) general and administrative.

1. Prepare a multiple-step income statement for the year ended December 31, 1998.
2. Compute Shaw's gross profit percentage.
3. What does this percentage tell you about Shaw's markup on its products?

LO 7 **Problem 2-11** Statement of Stockholders' Equity and Retained Earnings

Timeshare Inc. includes the changes in retained earnings in a statement that combines retained earnings and stockholders' equity. Use the following information to complete the statement for the years 1996, 1997, and 1998.

1996	Net income, $5,000,000
	Dividends, $1,000,000
1997	Net income, $12,000,000
	Dividends, $1,100,000
	Issued 100,000 shares of stock for $2 each
1998	Net income, $18,000,000
	Dividends, $1,650,000

	NUMBER OF SHARES	COMMON STOCK, PAR	PAID-IN CAPITAL IN EXCESS OF PAR VALUE	RETAINED EARNINGS	TOTAL
Jan. 1, 1996	1,000,000	$1,000,000	$500,000	$24,462,000	$25,962,000
Dec. 31, 1996					
Dec. 31, 1997					
Dec. 31, 1998					

LO 8 **Problem 2-12** Statement of Cash Flows

Colorado Corporation was organized on January 1, 1998, with the investment of $250,000 in cash by its stockholders. The company immediately purchased an office building for $300,000, paying $210,000 in cash and signing a three-year promissory note for the balance. Colorado signed a five-year, $60,000 promissory note at a local bank during 1998 and received cash in the same amount. During its first year, Colorado generated $4,870 in cash from operations and paid $5,600 in cash dividends.

1. Prepare a statement of cash flows for the year ended December 31, 1998.
2. What does this statement tell you that an income statement doesn't?

LO 9 **Problem 2-13** Basic Elements of Financial Reports

Comparative income statements for Grammar Inc. are presented below.

	1998	1997
Sales	$1,000,000	$500,000
Cost of sales	500,000	300,000
Gross margin	$ 500,000	$200,000
Operating expenses	120,000	100,000
Operating income	$ 380,000	$100,000
Loss on sale of subsidiary	(400,000)	—
Net income	$ (20,000)	$100,000

Required

The president and management believe that the company performed better in 1998 than it did in 1997. Write the letter from the president to be included in the 1998 annual report. Explain why the company is financially sound and shareholders should not be alarmed by the $20,000 loss in a year when sales have doubled.

Multi-Concept Problems

LO 2, 5 **Problem 2-14** Comparability and Consistency in Income Statements

The following income statements were provided by Gleeson Company, a retailer:

1998 INCOME STATEMENT		1997 INCOME STATEMENT	
Sales	$1,700,000	Sales	$1,500,000
Cost of sales	520,000	Cost of sales	450,000
Gross profit	$1,180,000	Sales salaries	398,000
Selling expense	702,000	Advertising	175,000
Administrative expense	95,000	Office supplies	54,000
Total selling and		Depreciation—building	40,000
administrative expense	$ 797,000	Delivery expense	20,000
		Total expenses	$1,137,000
Net income	$ 383,000	Net income	$ 363,000

Required

1. Identify each income statement as either single-step or multiple-step format.
2. Convert the 1997 income statement to the same format as the 1998 income statement.

LO 4, 5 **Problem 2-15** Classified Balance Sheet and Combined Multiple-Step Statement of Income and Retained Earnings for Kellogg's

Shown below, in alphabetical order, are items taken from Kellogg's 1995 consolidated financial statements:

	(IN MILLIONS)
Accounts payable	$ 370.8
Accounts receivable	590.1
Accrued liabilities (current liability)	704.7
Capital in excess of par value	105.2
Cash and cash equivalents	221.9
Common stock	77.8
Cost of goods sold	3,177.7
Currency translation adjustment (reduction of owners' equity listed after treasury stock)	(193.9)
Current maturities of long-term debt	1.9
Dividends paid	328.5
Income taxes (expense)	305.7
Interest expense	62.6
Inventories	376.7
Long-term debt	717.8
Net sales	7,003.7
Nonrecurring charges (operating expense)	421.8
Notes payable (current liability)	188.0
Other assets (long-term assets)	201.0
Other current assets	240.1
Other income (expense), net	21.1
Other liabilities (long-term liabilities)	840.5
Property, net	2,784.8
Retained earnings, beginning of year	3,801.2
Selling and administrative expense	2,566.7
Treasury stock (reduction of owners' equity listed after retained earnings)	(2,361.2)

(Note: The descriptions in parentheses are not part of the items but have been added to provide you with hints as you complete this problem.)

Required

1. Prepare a combined statement of income and retained earnings for Kellogg for the year ended December 31, 1995. Use a multiple-step approach for the income statement.

2. Prepare a classified balance sheet for Kellogg at December 31, 1995.

`LO 1, 4, 8` **Problem 2-16** Cash Flow

Franklin Co., a specialty retailer, has a history of paying quarterly dividends of $.50 per share. Management is trying to determine whether the company will have adequate cash on December 31, 1998, to pay a dividend if one is declared by the board of directors. The following additional information is available:

■ All sales are on account, and accounts receivable are collected one month after the sale. Sales volume has been increasing 5% each month.

■ All purchases of merchandise are on account, and accounts payable are paid one month after the purchase. Cost of sales is 40% of the sales price. Inventory levels are maintained at $75,000.

■ Operating expenses in addition to the mortgage are paid in cash. They amount to $3,000 per month and are paid as they are incurred.

FRANKLIN CO.
BALANCE SHEET
SEPTEMBER 30,1998

Cash	$ 5,000	Accounts payable	$ 5,000
Accounts receivable	12,500	Mortgage note†	150,000
Inventory	75,000	Common stock—$1 par	50,000
Note receivable*	10,000	Retained earnings	66,500
Building/Land	169,000	Total liabilities	
Total assets	$271,500	and stockholders' equity	$271,500

*Note receivable represents a one-year, 5% interest-bearing note, due November 1, 1998.
†Mortgage note is a 30-year, 7% note due in monthly installments of $1,200.

Required

Determine the cash that Franklin will have available to pay a dividend on December 31, 1998. Round all amounts to the nearest dollar. What can Franklin's management do to increase the cash available? Should management recommend that the board of directors declare a dividend?

Alternate Problems

`LO 2` **Problem 2-1A** Materiality

Jane Erving, a newly hired accountant, wanted to impress her boss, so she stayed late one night to analyze the long-distance calls by area code and time of day placed. She determined the monthly cost, for the past 12 months, by hour and area code called.

Required

1. What did Jane think her boss would learn from this information? What action might be taken as a result of knowing it?

2. Would this information be more relevant if Jane worked for a hardware store or for a real estate company? Discuss.

`LO 2` **Problem 2-2A** Costs and Expenses

The following costs are incurred by a retailer:

1. Point-of-sale systems in a retail store.

2. An ad in the yellow pages.

3. An inventory-control computer software system.

4. Shipping merchandise for resale to chain outlets.

For each of these costs, explain whether all of the cost or only a portion of the cost would appear as an expense on the income statement for the period in which the cost is incurred. If not all of the cost would appear on the income statement for that period, explain why not.

LO 2 **Problem 2-3A** Changes in Accounting Principles—Walt Disney

Your grandfather is considering making an investment in the common stock of Walt Disney Company and asks for your advice. You obtain Walt Disney's annual report and note that the following paragraph is included in the footnotes to the company's consolidated financial statements:

> As discussed in Note 1, during 1993 the Company changed its method of accounting for pre-opening costs. In years prior to 1993, project-related pre-opening costs were capitalized and amortized on a straight-line basis over periods of up to five years. Under the new method, project-related pre-opening costs are expensed as incurred. The cumulative effect of the change in method on prior years was a charge against income of $271.2 million, or $.50 per share, after related income tax benefit of $71.0 million, of which $233.0 million related to the impact of the accounting change on the Company's investment in EuroDisney. The effect of this change was to increase income in 1993 by $40.2 million after-tax, or $.07 per share.[15]

Required

Write your grandfather a brief letter that addresses the following:

1. What impact does this change in accounting principle have on the comparability and consistency of the company's financial statements?

2. How will this change in accounting provide better matching of revenues and expenses?

LO 3 **Problem 2-4A** Classified Balance Sheet

The following balance sheet items, listed in alphabetical order, are available from the records of Singer Company at December 31, 1998:

Accounts payable	$ 34,280
Accounts receivable	26,700
Accumulated depreciation—buildings	40,000
Accumulated depreciation—equipment	12,500
Bonds payable, due December 31, 2004	250,000
Buildings	150,000
Capital stock, $1 par value	200,000
Cash	60,790
Equipment	84,500
Income taxes payable	7,500
Interest payable	2,200
Land	250,000
Marketable securities	15,000
Merchandise inventory	112,900
Notes payable, due April 15, 1999	6,500
Office supplies	400
Paid-in capital in excess of par value	75,000
Patents	45,000
Prepaid rent	3,600
Retained earnings	113,510
Salaries payable	7,400

Required

1. Prepare a classified balance sheet as of December 31, 1998.

2. Compute Singer's current ratio.

3. On the basis of your answer to 2, does Singer appear to be *liquid?* What other information do you need to fully answer this question?

---

[15]*Walt Disney 1995 Annual Report,* p 64.

LO 4 **Problem 2-5A** Financial Statement Ratios

The following items, in alphabetical order, are available from the records of Quinn Corporation as of December 31, 1998 and 1997:

	DECEMBER 31, 1998	DECEMBER 31, 1997
Accounts payable	$10,500	$ 6,500
Accounts receivable	16,500	26,000
Cash	12,750	11,800
Interest receivable	200	–0–
Note receivable, due 12/31/2000	12,000	12,000
Office supplies	900	1,100
Prepaid insurance	400	250
Salaries payable	1,800	800
Taxes payable	10,000	5,800

Required

1. Calculate the following, as of December 31, 1998, and December 31, 1997:

   a. Working capital.

   b. Current ratio.

2. On the basis of your answers in 1, comment on the relative liquidity of the company at the beginning and the end of the year. As part of your answer, explain the change in the company's liquidity from the beginning to the end of 1998.

LO 4 **Problem 2-6A** Working Capital and Current Ratio

The balance sheet of Kapinski Inc. includes the following items:

Cash	$ 23,000
Accounts receivable	43,000
Inventory	75,000
Prepaid insurance	2,800
Land	80,000
Accounts payable	84,900
Salaries payable	3,200
Capital stock	100,000
Retained earnings	35,700

Required

1. Determine the current ratio and working capital.

2. Kapinski appears to have a positive current ratio and a large net working capital. Why would it have trouble paying bills as they come due?

3. Suggest three things that Kapinski can do to help it pay bills on time.

LO 4 **Problem 2-7A** Effects of Transactions on Current and Debt-to-Equity Ratios

(Students: Consider completing Problem 2-8A after this problem to ensure that you obtain a clear understanding of the effect of various transactions on these measures of liquidity.)

Robert Murdock, the president of Winston Sporting Goods, is very concerned about the company's current ratio and debt-to-equity ratio. When the company negotiated a new lending agreement with its bank earlier this year, Robert agreed to maintain these ratios within certain ranges. Currently, the company has a current ratio of 2 to 1 (based on current assets of $500,000 and current liabilities of $250,000) and a debt-to-equity ratio of 2 to 1 (based on total liabilities of $1,200,000 and total stockholders' equity of $600,000). During the last few days of the company's fiscal year, various transactions are anticipated or being contemplated. Robert has asked you to determine the impact that each of these transactions will have on the company's ratios.

Required

Determine the impact of each individual transaction on the company's current ratio and debt-to-equity ratio by recalculating each of the ratios (round to the nearest hundredth). Then, describe the effect of each of these transactions on the company's current ratio and debt-to-equity ratio by indicating whether the transaction would increase, decrease, or have no effect on each of these measures of the company's liquidity.

DESCRIPTION OF TRANSACTION	CURRENT RATIO	EFFECT OF TRANSACTION	DEBT-TO-EQUITY RATIO	EFFECT OF TRANSACTION
Example: Purchase of office supplies on credit for $80,000.	1.76 to 1	Decrease	2.13 to 1	Increase
1. Purchase of equipment on credit for $65,000.				
2. Cash collections from accounts receivable of $42,000.				
3. Cash payment of accounts payable of $150,000.				
4. Cash payment for salaries of company executives of $200,000.				
5. Repayment of a long-term loan of $120,000.				
6. Issuance of capital stock for cash of $300,000.				
7. Declaration and payment of a cash dividend of $50,000.				

LO 4 **Problem 2-8A** Effects of Transactions on Current and Debt-to-Equity Ratios
(Students: Consider completing this problem after Problem 2-7A to ensure that you obtain a clear understanding of the effect of various transactions on these measures of liquidity.)

Refer to the information set forth in Problem 2-7A. Assume instead that the company has a current ratio of .9 to 1 (based on current assets of $900,000 and current liabilities of $1,000,000) and a debt-to-equity ratio of .9 to 1 (based on total liabilities of $2,160,000 and total stockholders' equity of $2,400,000).

Required

1. Determine the impact of each individual transaction on the company's current ratio and debt-to-equity ratio by recalculating each of the ratios (round to the nearest hundredth). Then, describe the effect of each of these transactions on the company's current ratio and debt-to-equity ratio by indicating whether the transaction would increase, decrease, or have no effect on each of these measures of the company's liquidity.

DESCRIPTION OF TRANSACTION	CURRENT RATIO	EFFECT OF TRANSACTION	DEBT-TO-EQUITY RATIO	EFFECT OF TRANSACTION
Example: Purchase of office supplies on credit for $80,000.	.91 to 1	Increase	.93 to 1	Increase
1. Purchase of equipment on credit for $65,000.				
2. Cash collections from accounts receivable of $42,000.				
3. Cash payment of accounts payable of $150,000.				
4. Cash payment for salaries of company executives of $200,000.				

5. Repayment of a long-term loan
   of $120,000.
6. Issuance of capital stock for
   cash of $300,000.
7. Declaration and payment of a
   cash dividend of $50,000.

---

2. Note that the preexisting current ratio and debt-to-equity ratio assumed in Problem
2-7A both exceeded 1 to 1. The preexisting current ratio and debt-to-equity ratio assumed in this problem were both less than 1 to 1. Compare the "Effect of Transaction"
columns completed for each of these problems. Which transactions actually have an
indeterminable effect on the ratios (that is, the effect—increase or decrease—actually
depends on whether the preexisting ratios are greater or less than 1 to 1)?

LO 5 **Problem 2-9A** Single-Step Income Statement

The following income statement items, arranged in alphabetical order, are taken from the
records of Corbin Enterprises, a software sales firm, for the year ended December 31, 1998:

Advertising expense	$ 9,000
Cost of goods sold	150,000
Depreciation expense—computer	4,500
Dividend revenue	2,700
Income tax expense	30,700
Interest expense	1,900
Rent expense—office	26,400
Rent expense—salesperson's car	18,000
Sales revenue	350,000
Supplies expense—office	1,300
Utilities expense	6,750
Wages expense—office	45,600

Required

1. Prepare a single-step income statement for the year ended December 31, 1998.
2. What weaknesses do you see in this form for the income statement?

LO 5 **Problem 2-10A** Multiple-Step Income Statement

Refer to the list of income statement items in Problem 2-9A. Assume that Corbin Enterprises classifies all operating expenses into two categories: (1) selling and (2) general
and administrative.

Required

1. Prepare a multiple-step income statement for the year ended December 31, 1998.
2. Compute Corbin's gross profit percentage.
3. What does this percentage tell you about Corbin's markup on its products?

LO 7 **Problem 2-11A** Statement of Stockholders' Equity and Retained Earnings

Texas Two-Step Inc. includes the changes in retained earnings in a statement that combines retained earnings and stockholders' equity. Use the following information to complete the statement for the years 1996, 1997, and 1998.

1996	Net income, $45,000
	Dividends, $21,000
1997	Net loss, ($15,000)
	Dividends, $11,000
	Issued 100,000 shares of stock for $6 each
1998	Net income, $15,000
	Dividends, $11,650

TEXAS TWO-STEP INC.
STATEMENT OF STOCKHOLDERS' EQUITY AND RETAINED EARNINGS

	NUMBER OF SHARES	COMMON STOCK, PAR	PAID-IN CAPITAL IN EXCESS OF PAR VALUE	RETAINED EARNINGS	TOTAL
Jan. 1, 1996	7,000,000	$7,000,000	$900,000	$162,000	$8,062,000
Dec. 31, 1996					
Dec. 31, 1997					
Dec. 31, 1998					

LO 8 **Problem 2-12A** Statement of Cash Flows

Wisconsin Corporation was organized on January 1, 1998, with the investment of $400,000 in cash by its stockholders. The company immediately purchased a manufacturing facility for $300,000, paying $150,000 in cash and signing a five-year promissory note for the balance. Wisconsin signed another five-year note at the bank for $50,000 during 1998 and received cash for the same amount. During its first year, Wisconsin generated $54,900 in cash from operations and paid $4,000 in dividends.

Required

1. Prepare a statement of cash flows for the year ended December 31, 1998.
2. What does this statement tell you that an income statement doesn't?

LO 9 **Problem 2-13A** Basic Elements of Financial Reports

Comparative income statements for Thesaurus Inc. are presented below.

	1998	1997
Sales	$1,000,000	$500,000
Cost of sales	500,000	300,000
Gross margin	$ 500,000	$200,000
Operating expenses	120,000	100,000
Operating income	$ 380,000	$100,000
Gain on the sale of subsidiary	—	400,000
Net income	$ 380,000	$500,000

Required

The president and management believe that the company performed better in 1998 than it did in 1997. Write the letter from the president to be included in the 1998 annual report. Explain why the company is financially sound and shareholders should not be alarmed by the reduction in income in a year when sales have doubled.

Alternate Multi-Concept Problems

LO 2, 5 **Problem 2-14A** Comparability and Consistency in Income Statements

The following income statements were provided by Chisholm Company, a wholesale food distributor:

	1998	1997
Sales	$1,700,000	$1,500,000
Cost of sales	612,000	450,000
Sales salaries	427,000	398,000
Delivery expense	180,000	175,000
Office supplies	55,000	54,000
Depreciation—truck	40,000	40,000
Computer line expense	23,000	20,000
Total expenses	$1,337,000	$1,137,000
Net income	$363,000	$ 363,000

Required

1. Identify each income statement as either single-step or multiple-step format.
2. Restate each item in the income statements as a percentage of sales. Why did net income remain unchanged when sales increased?

LO 4, 5 **Problem 2-15A** Classified Balance Sheet and Multiple-Step Income Statement for Walgreen's
Shown below, in alphabetical order, are items taken from Walgreen's 1995 consolidated financial statements. Walgreen Co. has a fiscal year ending August 31.

	(IN THOUSANDS)
Accounts receivable	$ 246,086
Accrued expenses and other liabilities (current liability)	448,219
Cash and cash equivalents	22,245
Common stock	76,919
Cost of sales	7,482,344
Deferred income taxes (long-term liabilities)	142,278
Income taxes (current liability)	23,280
Income tax provision (expense)	202,950
Interest expense	1,190
Interest income	4,910
Inventories	1,453,881
Net sales	10,395,096
Other current assets	90,705
Other noncurrent assets	190,728
Other noncurrent liabilities	239,981
Property and equipment, net	1,248,962
Retained earnings, end of year	1,715,667
Selling, occupancy, and administration (expense)	2,392,731
Trade accounts payable	606,263

(Note: the descriptions in parentheses are not part of the items but have been added to provide you with hints as you complete this problem.)

Required

1. Prepare a multiple-step income statement for Walgreen's for the year ended August 31, 1995.
2. Prepare a classified balance sheet for Walgreen's at August 31, 1995.

LO 1, 4, 8 **Problem 2-16A** Cash Flow
Roosevelt Inc., a consulting service, has a history of paying annual dividends of $1 per share. Management is trying to determine whether the company will have adequate cash on December 31, 1998, to pay a dividend if one is declared by the board of directors. The following additional information is available:

- All sales are on account, and accounts receivable are collected one month after the sale. Sales volume has been decreasing 5% each month.
- Operating expenses are paid in cash in the month incurred. Average monthly expenses are $10,000 (exluding the biweekly payroll).
- Biweekly payroll is $4,500, and it will be paid December 15 and December 31.
- Unearned revenue is expected to be earned in December. This amount was taken into consideration in the expected sales volume.

ROOSEVELT INC.
BALANCE SHEET
DECEMBER 1, 1998

Cash	$ 15,000	Unearned revenue	$ 2,000
Accounts receivable	40,000	Note payable*	30,000
Computer equipment	120,000	Common stock—$2 par	50,000
		Retained earnings	$ 93,000
		Total liabilities and	
Total assets	$175,000	stockholders' equities	$175,000

*The note payable plus 3% interest for six months is due January 15, 1999.

Required

Determine the cash that Roosevelt will have available to pay a dividend on December 31, 1998. Round all amounts to the nearest dollar. Should management recommend that the board of directors declare a dividend?

Cases

Reading and Interpreting Financial Statements

LO 9   **Case 2-1** Interpretation of Walgreen's Auditors' Report

The following is an excerpt from a retailer's 1995 annual report. Explain the significance of each of the words or phrases in italics. Why does the board of directors contract with an accounting firm to perform an audit?

> We have *audited* the accompanying consolidated balance sheets . . . as of August 31, 1995 and 1994, and the related consolidated statements of earnings, retained earnings, and cash flows for each of the three years in the period ended August 31, 1995. These *financial statements are the responsibility of the Company's management.* Our responsibility is to *express an opinion* on these financial statements based on our audits.
> We conducted our audits in accordance with generally accepted auditing standards. Those standards require that we plan and perform the audit to *obtain reasonable assurance* about whether the financial statements are free of *material misstatement.*[16]

LO 5, 6   **Case 2-2** Profitability Analysis

The income statements for a specialty retailer are presented below in a condensed form, rounded to the nearest million except for the shares outstanding.

	1998	1997	1996
Sales	$629	$587	$563
Cost of sales	383	358	352
Selling expenses	180	173	170
Depreciation	15	15	14
Interest	15	16	12
Loss on sale of subsidiary	6	—	—
Taxes	9	9	5
Loss from subsidiary	4	4	2
Income	$ 17	$ 12	$ 8
Shares outstanding each year:			
37,500,000 shares			

Required

For each year, compute the gross profit ratio, profit margin, and earnings per share. Why did the income go up so much in 1998? To compare operating results from one year to the next, it is sometimes helpful to take out nonrecurring items and subsidiary

[16]*Walgreen 1995 Annual Report,* p. 29.

income (loss). After doing this, what statement can you make about 1998 that was not evident before? Would you recommend investing in this company? What other information would you want to know first?

Making Financial Decisions

Decision
Making

LO 8 **Case 2-3** Analysis of Cash Flow for a Small Business

Charles, a financial consultant, has been self-employed for two years. His list of clients has grown, and he is earning a reputation as a shrewd investor. Charles rents a small office, uses the pool secretarial services, and has purchased a car that he is depreciating over three years. The following income statements cover Charles's first two years of business:

	YEAR 1	YEAR 2
Commissions revenue	$ 25,000	$65,000
Rent	12,000	12,000
Secretarial services	3,000	9,000
Car expenses, gas, insurance	6,000	6,500
Depreciation	15,000	15,000
Net income	$(11,000)	$22,500

Charles believes that he should earn more than $11,500 for working very hard for two years. He is thinking about going to work for an investment firm where he can earn $40,000 per year. What would you advise Charles to do?

Decision
Making

LO 9 **Case 2-4** Factors Involved in an Investment Decision

As an investor, you are considering purchasing stock in a fast-food restaurant chain. The annual reports of several companies are available for comparison.

Required

Prepare an outline of the steps you would follow to make your comparison. Start by listing the first section that you would read in the financial reports. What would you expect to find there, and why did you choose that section to read first? Continue with the other sections of the financial report.

Many fast-food chains are owned by large conglomerates. What limitation does this create in your comparison? How would you solve it?

Accounting and Ethics: What Would You Do?

LO 4, 6 **Case 2-5** Barbara Applies For a Loan

Barbara Bites, owner of Bites of Bagels, a drive-through bagel shop, would like to expand her business from its current one location to a chain of bagel shops. Sales in the bagel shop have been increasing an average of 8% each quarter. Profits have been increasing accordingly. Barbara is conservative in spending and a very hard worker. She has an appointment with a banker to apply for a loan to expand the business. To prepare for the appointment, she instructs you, as the chief financial officer and payroll clerk, to copy the quarterly income statements for the past two years but not to include a balance sheet. Barbara already has a substantial loan from another bank on the books. In fact, she has very little of her own money invested in the business.

What should you do? Do you think the banker will lend Barbara more money?

LO 2 **Case 2-6** The Expenditure Approval Process

Roberto is the plant superintendent of a small manufacturing company that is owned by a large corporation. The corporation has a policy that any expenditure over $1,000 must be approved by the chief financial officer in the corporate headquarters. The approval process takes a minimum of three weeks. Roberto would like to order a new labeling machine that is expected to reduce costs and pay for itself in six months. The machine costs $2,200, but Roberto can buy the sales rep's demo for $1,800. Roberto has asked the sales rep to send two separate bills for $900 each.

What would you do if you were the sales rep? Do you agree or disagree with Roberto's actions? What do you think about the corporate policy?

Research Case

Case 2-7 Starbucks

Once it was just coffee. However, today Starbucks has expanded the types, flavors, and product variations. By using an intensive distribution strategy, Starbucks attempts to improve the company's revenues and profit margin in the retail ready-to-drink coffee industry.

Conduct a search of the World Wide Web, obtain Starbucks' most recent annual report, or use library resources to obtain company financial data, and answer the following:

1. For the most recent year available, what is Starbucks' net sales? How does this compare to the previous year?

2. Calculate Starbucks' profit margin based on the latest accounting year available. How does this compare to the previous year?

3. Obtain the past 52-week high, low, and most current prices for Starbucks' stock. How might the company's profit margin have affected the stock price? What other factors might affect fluctuations in Starbucks' stock price?

Optional Research. Conduct a survey of students and other consumers about coffee-drinking habits and coffee flavor preferences. If possible, visit a Starbucks store to observe available products. Do Starbucks' current product offerings match the needs of your survey respondents?

Solution to Key Terms Quiz

6 Understandability (p. 56)

3 Relevance (p. 56)

10 Reliability (p. 57)

23 Depreciation (p. 57)

2 Materiality (p. 58)

12 Operating cycle (p. 60)

11 Current liability (p. 62)

14 Working capital (p. 64)

13 Debt-to-equity ratio (p. 66)

4 Multiple-step income statement (p. 69)

8 Gross profit ratio (p. 71)

7 Earnings per share (p. 71)

16 Comparability (p. 57)

20 Consistency (p. 58)

5 Conservatism (p. 59)

18 Current asset (p. 61)

19 Liquidity (p. 63)

9 Current ratio (p. 65)

17 Debt-to-total-assets ratio (p. 66)

1 Single-step income statement (p. 69)

21 Gross profit (p. 70)

15 Profit margin (p. 71)

22 Return on stockholders' equity (p. 72)

Processing Accounting Information

STUDY LINKS

A Look at Previous Chapters

Up to this point, we have focused our attention on the role of accounting in decision making and the way accountants use financial statements to communicate useful information to the various users of the statements.

A Look at This Chapter

In this chapter, we consider how accounting information is *processed*. We begin by considering the *inputs* to an accounting system, that is, the transactions entered into by a business. We look at how transactions are analyzed, and then we turn to a number of accounting tools and procedures designed to facilitate the preparation of the *outputs* of the system, the financial statements. Ledger accounts, journal entries, and trial balances are tools that allow a company to process vast amounts of data efficiently.

A Look at Upcoming Chapters

Chapter 4 concludes our overview of the accounting model. We will examine the accrual basis of accounting and its effect on the measurement of income. Adjusting entries, which are the focus of the accrual basis, will be discussed in detail in Chapter 4, along with the other steps in the accounting cycle.

FOCUS ON FINANCIAL RESULTS

Imagine transforming your favorite sport into a multimillion-dollar business. That's what three young entrepreneurs did by founding Ride Inc., which sells snowboards and related equipment and clothing. In 1993, its first full year, Ride achieved sales of $5.9 million; fueled by a boom in the sport, third-year sales skyrocketed to $74.9 million.

An organization that serves the fastest-growing sport in the world (especially since snowboarding was made a full-medal sport in the 1998 Winter Olympics) requires agile management. Ride positioned itself to serve all market segments by offering several lines of

Ride Inc.

| | Year ended December 31, | | |
	1993	1994	1995
Net sales	$ 5,877	$25,349	$74,850
Cost of goods sold	3,879	18,398	54,988
Gross profit	1,998	6,951	19,862
Selling, general and administrative expenses	1,373	4,022	10,868
Operating income	625	2,929	8,994
Interest expense	(130)	(1)	(18)
Interest income	2	72	406
Income before income taxes and extraordinary item	497	3,000	9,382
Provision for income taxes (Note 7)	–	1,134	3,427
Income before extraordinary item	497	1,866	5,955
Extraordinary item – loss on extinguishment of debt (Note 6)	(83)	–	–
Net income	$ 414	$ 1,866	$ 5,955
Net income per share:			
Primary		$ 0.29	$ 0.60
Fully diluted		$ 0.27	$ 0.57

merchandise at high, moderate, and low price points. It added substantial capacity by acquiring Thermal Snowboards (a leading snowboard manufacturer), 5150 Snowboards Inc. (serving the performance-oriented market), and SMP Clothing (maker of an established year-round line of clothing). Ride also significantly increased hiring to maintain customer service.

These activities—and many others—generate revenues and expenses, which appear on Ride's income statement. As the pace has intensified, the numbers have soared. Ride's income statement documents a dramatic success story.

Income statements result from an accounting process and this chapter introduces that process. While learning its steps, consider why an accounting system is important. If you started a growing company like Ride, how would the accounting system help you? Which numbers would you watch most carefully?

SOURCE: *Ride Inc. Annual Report,* 1995.

After studying this chapter, you should be able to

LO 1 Explain the difference between an external and an internal event.

LO 2 Explain the role of source documents in an accounting system.

LO 3 Analyze the effects of transactions on the accounting equation.

LO 4 Define the concept of a general ledger and understand the use of the T account as a method for analyzing transactions.

LO 5 Explain the rules of debits and credits.

LO 6 Explain the purposes of a journal and the posting process.

LO 7 Explain the purpose of a trial balance.

Economic Events—The Basis for Recording Transactions

LO 1 Explain the difference between an external and an internal event.

Many different types of economic events affect an entity during the year. A sale is made to a customer. Inventory is purchased from a supplier. A loan is taken out at the bank. A fire destroys a warehouse. A new contract is signed with the union. In short, "An **event** is a happening of consequence to an entity."[1]

External and Internal Events

Two types of events affect an entity: internal and external. An **external event** "involves interaction between the entity and its environment."[2] For example, the *purchase* of raw material from a supplier is an external event, as is the *sale* of inventory to a customer. An **internal event** occurs entirely within the entity. The *transfer* of raw material into production is an internal event, as is the use of a piece of equipment. We will use the term **transaction** to refer to any event, external or internal, that is recognized in a set of financial statements.[3]

What is necessary to recognize an event in the records? Are all economic events recognized as transactions by the accountant? The answers to these questions involve the concept of *measurement*. An event must be measured to be recognized. Certain events are relatively easy to measure: the payroll for the week, the amount of inventory destroyed by an earthquake, or the sales for the day. Not all events that affect an entity can be measured *reliably,* however. For example, how does a manufacturer of breakfast cereal measure the effect of a drought on the price of wheat? A company hires a new chief executive. How can it reliably measure the value of the new officer to the company? There is no definitive answer to the measurement problem in accounting. It is a continuing challenge to the accounting profession and something we will return to throughout the text.

FROM CONCEPT TO PRACTICE 3.1

READING RIDE'S FINANCIAL STATEMENTS

Ride Inc. purchases wood to use in making snowboards. Is this an internal or an external event? The company subsequently uses the wood in the production process. Is this an internal or an external event?

The Role of Source Documents in Recording Transactions

LO 2 Explain the role of source documents in an accounting system.

The initial step in the recording process is *identification.* A business needs a systematic method for recognizing events as transactions. A **source document** provides the evidence needed in an accounting system to record a transaction. Source documents take many different forms. An invoice received from a supplier is the source document for a purchase of inventory on credit. A cash register tape is the source document used by a retailer to recognize a cash sale. The payroll department sends the accountant the time cards for the week as the necessary documentation to record wages.

---

[1]*Statement of Financial Accounting Concepts No. 3,* "Elements of Financial Statements of Business Enterprises" (Stamford, Conn.: Financial Accounting Standards Board, 1982), par. 65.

[2]*SFAC No. 3.*

[3]Technically, a transaction is defined by the Financial Accounting Standards Board as a special kind of external event in which the entity exchanges something of value with an outsider. Because the term *transaction* is used in practice to refer to any event that is recognized in the statements, we will use this broader definition.

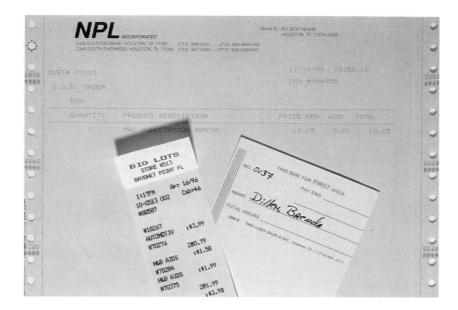

Source documents like these—such as contracts, lease agreements, invoices, delivery vouchers, check stubs, cash register tapes, and deposit slips—are records that document transactions the business engages in.

Not all recognizable events are supported by a standard source document. For certain events, some form of documentation must be generated. For example, no standard source document exists to recognize the financial consequences from a fire or the settlement of a lawsuit. Documentation is just as important for these types of events as it is for standard, recurring transactions.

Analyzing the Effects of Transactions on the Accounting Equation

Economic events are the basis for recording transactions in an accounting system. For every transaction it is essential to analyze its effect on the accounting equation

LO 3 Analyze the effects of transactions on the accounting equation.

$$\text{Assets} = \text{Liabilities} + \text{Owners' Equity}$$

We will now consider a series of events and their recognition as transactions for a hypothetical corporation, Glengarry Health Club.

(1) *Issuance of capital stock.* The company is started when Mary-Jo Kovach and Irene McGuinness file articles of incorporation with the state to obtain a charter. Each invests $50,000 in the business. In return, each receives 5,000 shares of capital stock. Thus, at this point, each of them owns 50 percent of the outstanding stock of the company and has a claim to 50 percent of its assets. The effect of this transaction on the accounting equation is to increase both assets and owners' equity:

		Assets				=	Liabilities	+	Owners' Equity	
NUMBER	CASH	ACCOUNTS RECEIVABLE	EQUIPMENT	BUILDING	LAND		ACCOUNTS PAYABLE	NOTES PAYABLE	CAPITAL STOCK	RETAINED EARNINGS
1	$100,000								$100,000	
Totals		$100,000							$100,000	

As you see, each side of the accounting equation increases by $100,000. Cash is increased, and because the owners contributed this amount, their claim to the assets is increased in the form of Capital Stock.

(2) *Acquisition of property in exchange for a note.* The company buys a piece of property for $200,000. The seller agrees to accept a five-year promissory note. The note is given by the health club to the seller and is a written promise to repay the principal amount of the loan at the end of five years. To the company, the promissory note is a liability. The property consists of land valued at $50,000 and a newly constructed building valued at $150,000. The effect of this transaction on the accounting equation is to increase both assets and liabilities by $200,000:

			Assets			=	Liabilities		+	Owners' Equity	
NUMBER	CASH	ACCOUNTS RECEIVABLE	EQUIPMENT	BUILDING	LAND		ACCOUNTS PAYABLE	NOTES PAYABLE		CAPITAL STOCK	RETAINED EARNINGS
Bal.	$100,000									$100,000	
2				$150,000	$50,000			$200,000			
Bal.	$100,000			$150,000	$50,000			$200,000		$100,000	
Totals			$300,000						$300,000		

(3) *Acquisition of equipment on an open account.* Mary-Jo and Irene contact an equipment supplier and buy $20,000 of exercise equipment: treadmills, barbells, and stationary bicycles. The supplier agrees to accept payment in full in 30 days. The health club has acquired an asset and at the same time incurred a liability:

			Assets			=	Liabilities		+	Owners' Equity	
NUMBER	CASH	ACCOUNTS RECEIVABLE	EQUIPMENT	BUILDING	LAND		ACCOUNTS PAYABLE	NOTES PAYABLE		CAPITAL STOCK	RETAINED EARNINGS
Bal.	$100,000			$150,000	$50,000			$200,000		$100,000	
3			$20,000				$20,000				
Bal.	$100,000		$20,000	$150,000	$50,000		$20,000	$200,000		$100,000	
Totals			$320,000						$320,000		

(4) *Sale of monthly memberships on account.* The owners open their doors for business. During the first month, they sold 300 monthly club memberships for $50 each, or a total of $15,000. The members have until the 10th of the following month to pay. Glengarry does not have cash from the new members but instead has a promise from each member to pay cash in the future. The promise from a customer to pay an amount owed is an asset called an *account receivable.* The other side of this transaction is an increase in the owners' equity (specifically retained earnings) in the business. In other words, the assets have increased by $15,000 without any increase in a liability or decrease in another asset. The increase in owners' equity indicates that the owners' residual interest in the assets of the business has increased by this amount. More specifically, an inflow of assets resulting from the sale of goods and services by a business is called *revenue.* The change in the accounting equation follows:

			Assets			=	Liabilities		+	Owners' Equity	
NUMBER	CASH	ACCOUNTS RECEIVABLE	EQUIPMENT	BUILDING	LAND		ACCOUNTS PAYABLE	NOTES PAYABLE		CAPITAL STOCK	RETAINED EARNINGS
Bal.	$100,000		$20,000	$150,000	$50,000		$20,000	$200,000		$100,000	
4		$15,000									$15,000
Bal.	$100,000	$15,000	$20,000	$150,000	$50,000		$20,000	$200,000		$100,000	$15,000
Totals			$335,000						$335,000		

(5) *Sale of court time for cash.* In addition to memberships, Glengarry sells court time. Court fees are paid at the time of use and amount to $5,000 for the first month:

			Assets			=	Liabilities		+	Owners' Equity	
NUMBER	CASH	ACCOUNTS RECEIVABLE	EQUIPMENT	BUILDING	LAND		ACCOUNTS PAYABLE	NOTES PAYABLE		CAPITAL STOCK	RETAINED EARNINGS
Bal.	$100,000	$15,000	$20,000	$150,000	$50,000		$20,000	$200,000		$100,000	$15,000
5	5,000										5,000
Bal.	$105,000	$15,000	$20,000	$150,000	$50,000		$20,000	$200,000		$100,000	$20,000
Totals			$340,000						$340,000		

The only difference between this transaction and (4) is that cash is received rather than a promise to pay at a later date. Both transactions result in an increase in an asset and an increase in the owners' claim to the assets. In both cases, there is an inflow of assets, in the form of either Accounts Receivable or Cash. Thus, in both cases, the company has earned revenue.

(6) *Payment of wages and salaries.* The wages and salaries for the first month amount to $10,000. The payment of this amount results in a decrease in cash and a decrease in the owners' claim on the assets, that is, a decrease in retained earnings. More specifically, an outflow of assets resulting from the sale of goods or services is called an *expense.* The effect of this transaction is to decrease both sides of the accounting equation:

		Assets				=	Liabilities	+	Owners' Equity	
NUMBER	CASH	ACCOUNTS RECEIVABLE	EQUIPMENT	BUILDING	LAND	ACCOUNTS PAYABLE	NOTES PAYABLE	CAPITAL STOCK	RETAINED EARNINGS
Bal.	$105,000	$15,000	$20,000	$150,000	$50,000	$20,000	$200,000	$100,000	$20,000
6	− 10,000								−10,000
Bal.	$ 95,000	$15,000	$20,000	$150,000	$50,000	$20,000	$200,000	$100,000	$10,000
Totals		$330,000					$330,000		

(7) *Payment of utilities.* The cost of utilities for the first month is $3,000. Glengarry pays this amount in cash. Both the utilities and the salaries and wages are expenses, and they have the same effect on the accounting equation. Cash is decreased, accompanied by a corresponding decrease in the owners' claim on the assets of the business:

		Assets				=	Liabilities	+	Owners' Equity	
NUMBER	CASH	ACCOUNTS RECEIVABLE	EQUIPMENT	BUILDING	LAND	ACCOUNTS PAYABLE	NOTES PAYABLE	CAPITAL STOCK	RETAINED EARNINGS
Bal.	$95,000	$15,000	$20,000	$150,000	$50,000	$20,000	$200,000	$100,000	$10,000
7	− 3,000								−3,000
Bal.	$92,000	$15,000	$20,000	$150,000	$50,000	$20,000	$200,000	$100,000	$ 7,000
Totals		$327,000					$327,000		

(8) *Collection of accounts receivable.* Even though the January monthly memberships are not due until the 10th of the following month, some of the members pay their bills by the end of January. The amount received from members in payment of their accounts is $4,000. The effect of the collection of an open account is to increase cash and decrease accounts receivable:

		Assets				=	Liabilities	+	Owners' Equity	
NUMBER	CASH	ACCOUNTS RECEIVABLE	EQUIPMENT	BUILDING	LAND	ACCOUNTS PAYABLE	NOTES PAYABLE	CAPITAL STOCK	RETAINED EARNINGS
Bal.	$92,000	$15,000	$20,000	$150,000	$50,000	$20,000	$200,000	$100,000	$7,000
8	4,000	− 4,000							
Bal.	$96,000	$11,000	$20,000	$150,000	$50,000	$20,000	$200,000	$100,000	$7,000
Totals		$327,000					$327,000		

This is the first transaction we have seen that affects only one side of the accounting equation. In fact, the company simply traded assets: accounts receivable for cash. Thus, note that the totals for the accounting equation remain at $327,000. Also note that retained earnings is not affected by this transaction because revenue was recognized earlier, in (4), when accounts receivable was increased.

(9) *Payment of dividends.* At the end of the month, Mary-Jo and Irene, acting on behalf of Glengarry Health Club, decide to pay a dividend of $1,000 on the shares of stock owned by each of them, or $2,000 in total. The effect of this dividend is to decrease both cash and retained earnings. That is, the company is returning cash to the owners, based on the profitable operations of the business for the first month. The transaction not only reduces cash but also decreases the owners' claims on the assets of the company. Dividends are not an expense but rather a direct reduction of retained earnings. The effect on the accounting equation follows:

		Assets				=	Liabilities		+	Owners' Equity	
NUMBER	CASH	ACCOUNTS RECEIVABLE	EQUIPMENT	BUILDING	LAND		ACCOUNTS PAYABLE	NOTES PAYABLE		CAPITAL STOCK	RETAINED EARNINGS
Bal.	$96,000	$11,000	$20,000	$150,000	$50,000		$20,000	$200,000		$100,000	$7,000
9	− 2,000										− 2,000
Bal.	$94,000	$11,000	$20,000	$150,000	$50,000		$20,000	$200,000		$100,000	$5,000
Totals			$325,000						$325,000		

The Cost Principle An important principle governed the accounting for both the exercise equipment in (3) and the building and land in (2). The cost principle requires that we record an asset at the cost to acquire it and continue to show this amount on all balance sheets until we dispose of the asset. With a few exceptions, an asset is not carried at its market value but at its original cost. Why not show the land on future balance sheets at its market value? Although this might seem more appropriate in certain instances, the *subjectivity* inherent in determining market values is a major reason behind the practice of carrying assets at their historical cost. The cost of an asset is subject to verification by an independent observer and is much more *objective* than market value.

Balance Sheet and Income Statement for the Health Club

To summarize, Exhibit 3-1 indicates the effect of each transaction on the accounting equation, specifically the individual items increased or decreased by each transaction. Note the *dual* effect of each transaction. At least two items were involved in each

---

EXHIBIT 3-1 Glengarry Health Club Transactions for the Month of January

		Assets				=	Liabilities		+	Owners' Equity	
NO.	CASH	ACCOUNTS RECEIVABLE	EQUIPMENT	BUILDING	LAND		ACCOUNTS PAYABLE	NOTES PAYABLE		CAPITAL STOCK	RETAINED EARNINGS
1	$100,000									$100,000	
2				$150,000	$50,000			$200,000			
Bal.	$100,000			$150,000	$50,000			$200,000		$100,000	
3			$20,000				$20,000				
Bal.	$100,000		$20,000	$150,000	$50,000		$20,000	$200,000		$100,000	
4		$15,000									$ 15,000
Bal.	$100,000	$15,000	$20,000	$150,000	$50,000		$20,000	$200,000		$100,000	$ 15,000
5	5,000										5,000
Bal.	$105,000	$15,000	$20,000	$150,000	$50,000		$20,000	$200,000		$100,000	$ 20,000
6	− 10,000										− 10,000
Bal.	$ 95,000	$15,000	$20,000	$150,000	$50,000		$20,000	$200,000		$100,000	$ 10,000
7	− 3,000										− 3,000
Bal.	$ 92,000	$15,000	$20,000	$150,000	$50,000		$20,000	$200,000		$100,000	$ 7,000
8	4,000	− 4,000									
Bal.	$ 96,000	$11,000	$20,000	$150,000	$50,000		$20,000	$200,000		$100,000	$ 7,000
9	− 2,000										− 2,000
Bal.	$ 94,000	$11,000	$20,000	$150,000	$50,000		$20,000	$200,000		$100,000	$ 5,000

Total assets: $325,000   Total liabilities and owners' equity: $325,000

EXHIBIT 3-2   Balance Sheet for Glengarry Health Club

GLENGARRY HEALTH CLUB
BALANCE SHEET
JANUARY 31, 1998

ASSETS		LIABILITIES AND OWNERS' EQUITY	
Cash	$ 94,000	Accounts payable	$ 20,000
Accounts receivable	11,000	Notes payable	200,000
Equipment	20,000	Capital stock	100,000
Building	150,000	Retained earnings	5,000
Land	50,000		
		Total liabilities	
Total assets	$325,000	and owners' equity	$325,000

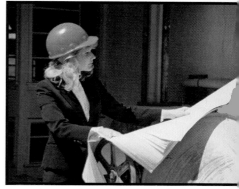

Planning the startup of a new business can be exhilarating, with decisions needed on hundreds or thousands of details: Finding and leasing the right retail space, the construction of a store interior, contracting with a design frim for a logo and signage, paying for an advertising campaign for the new store, ordering and accepting delivery of goods for resale, and depositing the first day's sales revenues are just the beginning. These details, if they are measurable, are *economic events* that must be accounted for in *transactions* identified by *source documents*.

transaction. For example, the initial investment by the owners resulted in an increase in an asset and an increase in capital stock. The payment of the utility bill caused a decrease in an asset and a decrease in retained earnings.

You can now see the central idea behind the accounting equation: even though individual transactions may change the amount and composition of the assets and liabilities, the *equation* must always balance *for* each transaction, and the *balance sheet* must balance *after* each transaction.

A balance sheet for Glengarry Health Club appears in Exhibit 3-2. All of the information needed to prepare this statement is available in Exhibit 3-1. The balances at the bottom of this exhibit are entered on the balance sheet, with assets on the left side and liabilities and owners' equity on the right side.

An income statement for Glengarry is shown in Exhibit 3-3. An income statement summarizes the revenues and expenses of a company for a period of time. In our example, the statement is for the month of January, as indicated on the third line of the heading of the statement. Glengarry earned revenues from two sources: (1) memberships and (2) court fees. Two types of expenses were incurred: (1) salaries and wages and (2) utilities. The difference between the total revenues of $20,000 and the total expenses of $13,000 is the net income for the month of $7,000. Finally, remember that dividends appear on a statement of retained earnings rather than on the income statement. They are a *distribution* of net income of the period, not a *determinant* of net income as are expenses.

We have seen how transactions are analyzed and how they affect the accounting equation and ultimately the financial statements. While the approach we took to analyzing the nine transactions of the Glengarry Health Club was manageable, can you

EXHIBIT 3-3   Income Statement for Glengarry Health Club

GLENGARRY HEALTH CLUB
INCOME STATEMENT
FOR THE MONTH ENDED JANUARY 31, 1998

Revenues:		
Memberships	$15,000	
Court fees	5,000	$20,000
Expenses:		
Salaries and wages	10,000	
Utilities	3,000	13,000
Net income		$ 7,000

imagine using this type of analysis for a company with *thousands* of transactions in any one month? We now turn our attention to various *tools* used by the accountant to process a large volume of transactions effectively and efficiently.

The Account: Basic Unit for Recording Transactions

An **account** is the record used to accumulate monetary amounts for each asset, liability, and component of owners' equity, such as capital stock, retained earnings, and dividends. It is the basic recording unit for each element in the financial statements. Each revenue and expense has its own account. In the Glengarry Health Club example, nine accounts were used: Cash, Accounts Receivable, Equipment, Building, Land, Accounts Payable, Notes Payable, Capital Stock, and Retained Earnings. (Recall that revenues, expenses, and dividends were recorded directly in the Retained Earnings account. Later in the chapter we will see that normally each revenue and expense is recorded in a separate account.) In the real world, a company might have hundreds, or even thousands, of individual accounts.

No two entities have exactly the same set of accounts. To a certain extent, the accounts used by a company depend on its business. For example, a manufacturer normally has three inventory accounts: Raw Materials, Work in Process, and Finished Goods. A retailer uses just one account for inventory, a Merchandise Inventory account. A service business has no need for an inventory account.

Chart of Accounts

Companies need a way to organize the large number of accounts they use to record transactions. A **chart of accounts** is a numerical list of all of the accounts an entity uses. The numbering system is a convenient way to identify accounts. For example, all asset accounts might be numbered from 100 to 199, liability accounts from 200 to 299, equity accounts from 300 to 399, revenues from 400 to 499, and expenses from 500 to 599. A chart of accounts for a hypothetical company, Widescreen Theaters Corporation, is shown in Exhibit 3-4. Note the division of account numbers within each of the financial statement categories. For example, within the asset category, the various cash accounts are numbered from 100 to 109, receivables from 110 to 119, and so forth. Not all of the

FROM CONCEPT TO PRACTICE 3.2

READING BEN & JERRY'S BALANCE SHEET AND FOOTNOTES How many liability accounts does the company report on its balance sheet? How are these liability accounts broken down in the accompanying notes?

EXHIBIT 3-4	Chart of Accounts for a Theater
100–199:	ASSETS
100–109:	Cash
101:	Cash, Checking, Second National Bank
102:	Cash, Savings, Third State Bank
103:	Cash, Change, or Petty Cash Fund (coin and currency)
110–119:	Receivables
111:	Accounts Receivable
112:	Due from Employees
113:	Notes Receivable
120–129:	Prepaid Assets
121:	Cleaning Supplies
122:	Prepaid Insurance
130–139:	Property, Plant, and Equipment
131:	Land
132:	Theater Buildings
133:	Projection Equipment
134:	Furniture and Fixtures

EXHIBIT 3-4	continued

200–299:	LIABILITIES
200–209:	Short-Term Liabilities
201:	Accounts Payable
202:	Wages and Salaries Payable
203:	Taxes Payable
203.1:	Income Taxes Payable
203.2:	Sales Taxes Payable
203.3:	Unemployment Taxes Payable
204:	Short-Term Notes Payable
204.1:	Six-Month Note Payable to First State Bank
210–219:	Long-Term Liabilities
211:	Bonds Payable, due in 2010
300–399:	STOCKHOLDERS' EQUITY
301:	Preferred Stock
302:	Common Stock
303:	Retained Earnings
400–499:	REVENUES
401:	Tickets
402:	Video Rentals
403:	Concessions
404:	Interest
500–599:	EXPENSES
500–509:	Rentals
501:	Films
502:	Videos
510–519:	Concessions
511:	Candy
512:	Soda
513:	Popcorn
520–529:	Wages and Salaries
521:	Hourly Employees
522:	Salaries
530–539:	Utilities
531:	Heat
532:	Electric
533:	Water
540–549:	Advertising
541:	Newspaper
542:	Radio
550–559:	Taxes
551:	Income Taxes
552:	Unemployment Taxes

numbers are currently assigned. For example, only three of the available nine numbers are currently utilized for cash accounts. This allows the company to add accounts as the need arises.

The General Ledger

Companies store their accounts in different ways, depending on their accounting system. In a manual system, a separate card or sheet is used to record the activity in each account. A general ledger is simply the file or book that contains the accounts.[4] For

LO 4 Define the concept of a general ledger and understand the use of the T account as a method for analyzing transactions.

[4]In addition to a general ledger, many companies maintain subsidiary ledgers. For example, an accounts receivable subsidiary ledger contains a separate account for each customer. The use of a subsidiary ledger for Accounts Receivable is discussed further in Chapter 7.

example, the general ledger for Widescreen Theaters Corporation might consist of a file of cards in a cabinet, with a card for each of the accounts listed in the chart of accounts.

In today's business world, most companies have an automated accounting system. The computer is ideally suited for the job of processing vast amounts of data rapidly. *All of the tools discussed in this chapter are as applicable to computerized systems as they are to manual systems. It is merely the appearance of the tools that differs between manual and computerized systems.* For example, the ledger in an automated system might be contained on a diskette rather than stored in a file cabinet. Throughout the book, we will use a manual system to explain the various tools, such as ledger accounts. The reason is that it is easier to illustrate and visualize the tools in a manual system. However, all of the ideas apply just as well to a computerized system of accounting.

ACCOUNTING FOR YOUR DECISIONS
You Are the Owner

After many years of working together as a family, your mother and father decide to retire and sell you their remaining stock in the family furniture store. For all these many years, they have handled the bookkeeping for the business manually, preferring not to automate this chore because they didn't feel comfortable in front of a computer. Now that you're in charge, the first thing you want to do is to computerize the company's accounting records. How would you go about doing this?

ANS: The first step is to analyze the reporting needs of your company. Because you took basic accounting, you understand the way financial transactions fit together to produce financial statements. After years of working in the family business, you are also aware of what information is needed by users of your company's financial statements. Once you've determined your information needs, the next step is to choose the appropriate accounting software.

The Double Entry System

The origin of the double entry system of accounting can be traced to Venice, Italy, in 1494. In that year, Fra Luca Pacioli, a Franciscan monk, wrote a mathematical treatise. Included in his book was the concept of debits and credits that is still used almost universally today.

The T Account

The form for a general ledger account will be illustrated later in the chapter. However, the form of account often used to analyze transactions is called the *T account*, so named because it resembles the capital letter T. The name of the account appears across the horizontal line. One side is used to record increases and the other side decreases, but as you will see, the same side is not used for increases for every account. As a matter of convention, the *left* side of an *asset* account is used to record *increases* and the *right* side to record *decreases*. To illustrate a T account, we will look at the Cash account for Glengarry Health Club. The transactions recorded in the account can be traced to Exhibit 3-1.

CASH

INCREASES		DECREASES	
Investment by owners	100,000	Wages and salaries	10,000
Court fees collected	5,000	Utilities	3,000
Accounts collected	4,000	Dividends	2,000
	109,000		15,000
Bal.	94,000		

The amounts $109,000 and $15,000 are called *footings*. They represent the totals of the amounts on each side of the account. Neither these amounts nor the balance of $94,000 represents transactions. They are simply shown to indicate the totals and the balance in the account.

Debits and Credits

Rather than refer to the left or right side of an account, accountants use specific labels for each side. The *left* side of any account is the debit side and the *right* side of any account is the **credit** side. We will also use the terms *debit* and *credit* as verbs. If we *debit* the Cash account, we enter an amount on the left side. Similarly, if we want to enter an amount on the right side of an account, we *credit* the account. To *charge* an account has the same meaning as to *debit* it. No such synonym exists for the act of crediting an account.

Note that *debit* and *credit* are *locational* terms. They simply refer to the left or right side of a T account. They do *not* represent increases or decreases. As we will see, when one type of account is increased (for example, the Cash account), the increase is on the left or *debit* side. When certain other types of accounts are increased, however, the entry will be on the right or *credit* side.

As you would expect from your understanding of the accounting equation, the conventions for using T accounts for assets and liabilities are opposite. Assets are future economic benefits, and liabilities are obligations to transfer economic benefits in the future. If an asset is *increased* with a *debit,* how do you think a liability would be increased? *Because assets and liabilities are opposites, if an asset is increased with a debit, a liability is increased with a credit.* Thus, the right side, or credit side, of a liability account is used to record an increase. Like liabilities, owners' equity accounts are on the opposite side of the accounting equation as are assets. *Thus, like a liability, an owners' equity account is increased with a credit.* We can summarize the logic of debits and credits, increases and decreases, and the accounting equation in the following way:

LO 5 Explain the rules of debits and credits.

ASSETS		=	LIABILITIES		+	OWNERS' EQUITY	
Debits	Credits		Debits	Credits		Debits	Credits
Increases	Decreases		Decreases	Increases		Decreases	Increases
+	−		−	+		−	+

Note again that debits and credits are location-oriented. Debits are always on the left side of an account and credits on the right side.

ACCOUNTING FOR YOUR DECISIONS
You Are a Student

A classmate comes to you with a question about the bank statement she has received. Why does the bank credit her account when she makes a deposit to her account, but accounting rules state that cash is increased with a debit?

ANS: The bank is looking at customer deposits from its perspective and not the customers'. Checking account deposits represent liabilities to the bank, such as "Deposits Payable." Thus, when customers make deposits, the bank has increased its liability to those customers, with a credit to its "Deposits Payable."

Debits and Credits for Revenues, Expenses, and Dividends

In our Glengarry Health Club example, revenues were an increase in Retained Earnings. The sale of memberships was not only an increase in the asset Accounts Receivable but also an increase in the owners' equity account Retained Earnings. The transaction resulted in an increase in the owners' claim on the assets of the business. Rather than being recorded directly in Retained Earnings, however, each revenue item is maintained in a separate account. The following logic is used to arrive at the rules for increasing and decreasing revenues:[5]

1. Retained Earnings is increased with a credit.
2. Revenue is an increase in Retained Earnings.

---

[5]We normally think of both revenues and expenses as being only increased, not decreased. Because we will need to decrease them as part of the closing procedure, it is important to know how to reduce these accounts as well as increase them.

3. Revenue is increased with a credit.

4. Because revenue is increased with a credit, it is decreased with a debit.

The same logic is applied to the rules for increasing and decreasing expense accounts:

1. Retained Earnings is decreased with a debit.

2. Expense is a decrease in Retained Earnings.

3. Expense is increased with a debit.

4. Because expense is increased with a debit, it is decreased with a credit.

Recall that dividends reduce cash. But they also reduce the owners' claim on the assets of the business. Earlier we recognized this decrease in the owners' claim as a reduction of Retained Earnings. As we do for revenue and expense accounts, we will use a separate Dividends account:

1. Retained Earnings is decreased with a debit.

2. Dividends are a decrease in Retained Earnings.

3. Dividends are increased with a debit.

4. Because dividends are increased with a debit, they are decreased with a credit.

Summary of the Rules for Increasing and Decreasing Accounts

The rules for increasing and decreasing the various types of accounts are summarized as follows:

TYPE OF ACCOUNT	DEBIT	CREDIT
Asset	Increase	Decrease
Liability	Decrease	Increase
Owners' equity	Decrease	Increase
Revenue	Decrease	Increase
Expense	Increase	Decrease
Dividends	Increase	Decrease

Normal Account Balances

Each account has a "normal" balance. For example, assets normally have debit balances. Would it be possible for an asset such as Cash to have a credit balance? Assume that a company has a checking account with a bank. A credit balance in the account would indicate that the decreases in the account, from checks written and other bank charges, were more than the deposits into the account. If this were the case, however, the company would no longer have an asset, Cash, but instead would have a liability to the bank. The normal balances for the accounts we have looked at are as follows:

TYPE OF ACCOUNT	NORMAL BALANCE
Asset	Debit
Liability	Credit
Owners' equity	Credit
Revenue	Credit
Expense	Debit
Dividends	Debit

Debits Aren't Bad and Credits Aren't Good

Students often approach their first encounter with debits and credits with preconceived notions. The use of the terms *debit* and *credit* in everyday language leads to many of these notions. "Joe is a real credit to his team." "Nancy should be *credited* with saving Mary's career." These both appear to be very positive statements. You must resist the temptation to associate the term *credit* with something good or positive and the term *debit* with something bad or negative. *In accounting, debit means one thing: an entry made on the left side of an account. A credit means an entry made on the right side of an account.*

Debits and Credits Applied to Transactions

Recall the first transaction recorded by Glengarry Health Club earlier in the chapter: the owners invested $100,000 cash in the business. The transaction resulted in an increase in the Cash account and an increase in the Capital Stock account. Applying the rules of debits and credits, we would *debit* the Cash account for $100,000 and *credit* the Capital Stock account for the same amount:[6]

CASH		CAPITAL STOCK	
(1) 100,000			100,000 (1)

You now can see why we refer to the **double entry system** of accounting. Every transaction is recorded so that the equality of debits and credits is maintained, and in the process, the accounting equation is kept in balance. *Every transaction is entered in at least two accounts on opposite sides of T accounts. Our first transaction resulted in an increase in an asset account and an increase in an owners' equity account. For every transaction, the debit side must equal the credit side. The debit of $100,000 to the Cash account equaled the credit of $100,000 to the Capital Stock account.* It naturally follows that if the debit side must equal the credit side for every transaction, at any point in time the total of all debits recorded must equal the total of all credits recorded. Thus, the fundamental accounting equation remains in balance.

Transactions for Glengarry Health Club

Three distinct steps are involved in recording a transaction in the accounts. First, we *analyze* the transaction. That is, we decide what accounts are increased or decreased and by how much. Second, we *recall* the rules of debits and credits as they apply to the transaction we are analyzing. Finally, we *record* the transaction using the rules of debits and credits.

We return to the transactions of the health club. We have already explained the logic for the debit to the Cash account and the credit to the Capital Stock account for the initial investment by the owners. We will now analyze the remaining eight transactions for the month. Refer to Exhibit 3-1 for a summary of the transactions.

(2) A building and land are exchanged for a promissory note.

　　(a) *Analyze:* Two asset accounts are increased: Building and Land. The liability account Notes Payable is also increased.

　　(b) *Recall the rules of debits and credits:* An asset is increased with a debit, and a liability is increased with a credit.

　　(c) *Record the transaction:*

BUILDING		NOTES PAYABLE	
(2) 150,000			200,000 (2)

LAND	
(2)　50,000	

(3) Exercise equipment is purchased from a supplier on open account. The purchase price is $20,000.

　　(a) *Analyze:* An asset account, Equipment, is increased. A liability account, Accounts Payable, is also increased. Thus, the transaction is identical to the last transaction in that an asset or assets are increased and a liability is increased.

---

[6]We will use the numbers of each transaction, as they were labeled earlier in the chapter, to identify the transactions. In practice, a formal ledger account is used, and transactions are entered according to their date.

(b) *Recall the rules of debits and credits:* An asset is increased with a debit, and a liability is increased with a credit.

(c) *Record the transaction:*

EQUIPMENT		ACCOUNTS PAYABLE	
(3) 20,000			20,000 (3)

(4) Three hundred club memberships are sold for $50 each. The members have until the 10th of the following month to pay.

    (a) *Analyze:* The asset account Accounts Receivable is increased by $15,000. This amount is an asset because the company has the right to collect it in the future. The owners' claim to the assets is increased by the same amount. Recall, however, that we do not record these claims—revenues—directly in an owners' equity account but instead use a separate revenue account. We will call the account Membership Revenue.

    (b) *Recall the rules of debits and credits:* An asset is increased with a debit. Owners' equity is increased with a credit. Because revenue is an increase in owners' equity, it is increased with a credit.

    (c) *Record the transaction:*

ACCOUNTS RECEIVABLE		MEMBERSHIP REVENUE	
(4) 15,000			15,000 (4)

(5) Court fees are paid at the time of use and amount to $5,000 for the first month.

    (a) *Analyze:* The asset account Cash is increased by $5,000. The owners' claim to the assets is increased by the same amount. The account used to record the increase in the owners' claim is Court Fee Revenue.

    (b) *Recall the rules of debits and credits:* An asset is increased with a debit. Owners' equity is increased with a credit. Because revenue is an increase in owners' equity, it is increased with a credit.

    (c) *Record the transaction:*

CASH		COURT FEE REVENUE	
(1) 100,000			5,000 (5)
(5) 5,000			

(6) Wages and salaries amount to $10,000, and they are paid in cash.

    (a) *Analyze:* The asset account, Cash, is decreased by $10,000. At the same time, the owners' claim to the assets is decreased by this amount. However, rather than record a decrease directly to Retained Earnings, we set up an expense account, Wage and Salary Expense.

    (b) *Recall the rules of debits and credits:* An asset is decreased with a credit. Owners' equity is decreased with a debit. Because expense is a decrease in owners' equity, it is increased with a debit.

    (c) *Record the transaction:*

CASH		WAGE AND SALARY EXPENSE	
(1) 100,000	10,000 (6)	(6) 10,000	
(5) 5,000			

(7) The utility bill of $3,000 for the first month is paid in cash.

    (a) *Analyze:* The asset account Cash is decreased by $3,000. At the same time, the owners' claim to the assets is decreased by this amount. However, rather than record a decrease directly to Retained Earnings, we set up an expense account, Utility Expense.

    (b) *Recall the rules of debits and credits:* An asset is decreased with a credit. Owners' equity is decreased with a debit. Because expense is a decrease in owners' equity, it is increased with a debit.

    (c) *Record the transaction:*

CASH		UTILITY EXPENSE	
(1) 100,000	10,000 (6)	(7) 3,000	
(5) 5,000	3,000 (7)		

(8) Cash of $4,000 is collected from members for their January dues.

(a) *Analyze:* Cash is increased by the amount collected from the members. Another asset, Accounts Receivable, is decreased by the same amount. Glengarry has simply traded one asset for another.

(b) *Recall the rules of debits and credits:* An asset is increased with a debit and decreased with a credit. Thus, one asset is debited, and another is credited.

(c) *Record the transaction:*

CASH					ACCOUNTS RECEIVABLE	
(1)	100,000	10,000	(6)	(4) 15,000	**4,000**	**(8)**
(5)	5,000	3,000	(7)			
(8)	**4,000**					

(9) Dividends of $2,000 are distributed to the owners.

(a) *Analyze:* The asset account Cash is decreased by $2,000. At the same time, the owners' claim to the assets is decreased by this amount. Earlier in the chapter, we decreased Retained Earnings for dividends paid to the owners. Now we will use a separate account, Dividends, to record these distributions.

(b) *Recall the rules of debits and credits:* An asset is decreased with a credit. Retained earnings is decreased with a debit. Because dividends are a decrease in retained earnings, they are increased with a debit.

(c) *Record the transaction:*

CASH					DIVIDENDS	
(1)	100,000	10,000	(6)	**(9) 2,000**		
(5)	5,000	3,000	(7)			
(8)	4,000	**2,000**	**(9)**			

The Journal: The Firm's Chronological Record of Transactions

Each of the nine transactions was entered directly in the ledger accounts. By looking at the Cash account, we see that it increased by $5,000 in transaction (5). But what was the other side of this transaction? That is, what account was credited? To have a record of *each entry,* transactions are recorded first in a journal. A **journal** is a chronological record of transactions entered into by a business. Because a journal lists transactions in the order in which they took place, it is called the *book of original entry.* Transactions are recorded first in a journal and then are posted to the ledger accounts. **Posting** is the process of transferring a journal entry to the ledger accounts:

LO 6 Explain the purposes of a journal and the posting process.

Note that posting does not result in any change in the amounts recorded. It is simply a process of re-sorting the transactions from a chronological order to a topical arrangement.

A journal entry is recorded for each transaction. **Journalizing** is the process of recording entries in a journal. A standard format is normally used for recording journal entries. Consider the original investment by the owners of Glengarry Health Club. The format of the journal entry is as follows:

	DEBIT	CREDIT
Jan. xx Cash	100,000	
Capital Stock		100,000
To record the issuance of 10,000 shares of stock for cash.		

Each journal entry contains a date with columns for the amounts debited and credited. Accounts credited are indented to distinguish them from accounts debited. A brief explanation normally appears on the line below the entry.

Transactions are normally recorded in a **general journal.** Specialized journals may be used to record repetitive transactions. For example, a cash receipts journal may be used to record all transactions in which cash is received. Special journals accomplish the same purpose as a general journal, but they save time in recording similar transactions. In this chapter, we will use a general journal to record all transactions.

An excerpt from Glengarry Health Club's general journal appears in the top portion of Exhibit 3-5. One column needs further explanation. *Post. Ref.* is an abbreviation for *posting reference.* As part of the posting process explained below, the debit and credit amounts are posted to the appropriate accounts, and this column is filled in with the number assigned to the account.

Journal entries and ledger accounts are both *tools* used by the accountant. The end result, a set of financial statements, is the most important part of the process. Journalizing provides us with a chronological record of each transaction. So why not just prepare financial statements directly from the journal entries? Isn't it just extra work to *post* the entries to the ledger accounts? In our simple example of Glengarry Health Club, it would be possible to

---

EXHIBIT 3-5 Posting from the Journal to the Ledger

General Journal Page No. 1

Date		Account Titles and Explanation		Post Ref.	Debit	Credit
1998 Jan.	XX	Accounts Receivable		5	1 5 0 0 0	
		Membership Revenue		40		1 5 0 0 0
		Sold 300 memberships at $50 each.				
	XX	Cash		1	5 0 0 0	
		Court Fee Revenue		44		5 0 0 0
		Collected court fees.				

General Ledger
Cash Account No. 1

Date		Explanation		Post Ref.	Debit	Credit	Balance
1998 Jan.	XX			GJ1	1 0 0 0 0 0		1 0 0 0 0 0
	XX			GJ1	5 0 0 0		1 0 5 0 0 0

Court Fee Revenue Account No. 44

Date		Explanation		Post Ref.	Debit	Credit	Balance
1998 Jan.	XX			GJ1		5 0 0 0	5 0 0 0

prepare the statements directly from the journal entries. In real-world situations, however, the number of transactions in any given period is so large that it would be virtually impossible, if not terribly inefficient, to bypass the accounts. Accounts provide us with a convenient summary of the activity, as well as the balance, for a specific financial statement item.

The posting process for Glengarry Health Club is illustrated in Exhibit 3-5 for the health club's fifth transaction, in which cash is collected for court fees. Rather than a T-account format for the general ledger accounts, the *running balance form* is illustrated. A separate column indicates the balance in the ledger account after each transaction. The use of the explanation column in a ledger account is optional. Because an explanation of the entry in the account can be found by referring to the journal, this column is often left blank.

Note the cross-referencing between the journal and the ledger. As amounts are entered in the ledger accounts, the Posting Reference column is filled in with the page number of the journal. At the same time the Posting Reference column of the journal is filled in with the appropriate account number.

The frequency of posting differs among companies, partly based on the degree to which their accounting system is automated. For example, in some computerized systems, amounts are posted to the ledger accounts at the time an entry is recorded in the journal. In a manual system, posting is normally done periodically, for example, daily, weekly, or monthly. Regardless of when performed, the posting process changes nothing. It simply reorganizes the transactions by account.

ACCOUNTING FOR YOUR DECISIONS
You Are the Manager

You are the community relations manager for a company. You need to determine whether the company is spending its money wisely in promoting its image in the local community.

1. What types of accounts would you examine? Give examples of the possible names for some of these accounts.
2. Would a general journal or a general ledger be more useful to you in making your determination? Explain your answer.

ANS: **1.** Among the possible accounts that you want to examine are Entertainment, Travel, Promotions, Advertising, and Miscellaneous, in addition to any accounts that might contain expenditures related to community relations.

2. You want to examine the general ledger for each of the accounts listed in part 1. The ledger contains a record for each of the accounts and the activity in them during the period.

The Trial Balance

LO 7 Explain the purpose of a trial balance.

Accountants use one other tool to facilitate the preparation of a set of financial statements. A **trial balance** is a list of each account and its balance at a specific point in time. The trial balance is *not* itself a financial statement but merely a convenient device to prove the equality of the debit and credit balances in the accounts. It can be as informal as an adding-machine tape with the account titles penciled in next to the debit and credit amounts. A trial balance for Glengarry Health Club as of January 31, 1998, is shown in Exhibit 3-6 on page 121. The balance in each account was determined by adding the increases and subtracting the decreases for the account for the transactions detailed earlier.

Certain types of errors are detectable from a trial balance. For example, if the balance of an account is incorrectly computed, the total of the debits and credits in the trial balance will not equal. If a debit is posted to an account as a credit, or vice versa, the trial balance will be out of balance. The omission of part of a journal entry in the posting process will also be detected by the preparation of a trial balance.

Do not attribute more significance to a trial balance, however, than is warranted. It does provide a convenient summary of account balances for preparing financial statements. It also assures us that the balances of all the debit accounts equal the balances of all the credit accounts. But an equality of debits and credits does not necessarily mean that the *correct* accounts were debited and credited in an entry. For example, the entry to record the

FOCUS ON USERS

FINDING PROFITABLE NICHES IN THE CPA PROFESSION

As one of the top partners with the accounting firm of Clifton Gunderson LLC, Krista Kaland is constantly making business decisions based on financial information. The firm operates in cities throughout the country, and some offices are more profitable than others. "We're using accounting information all the time to determine what markets we should be in, what areas of services we should concentrate on, and in what industries we should focus," says Kaland, a CPA. "More and more, we're focusing on management and tax consulting, because it is more profitable than other accounting services."

Clients seem willing to pay for advice on how to lower their taxes and how to streamline their business operations, because the money spent on advice is typically a fraction of the cost savings realized from the advice. On the other hand, the traditional CPA services of accounting and auditing don't offer the same savings.

For one thing, the typical small business person can literally go into a computer software store and buy a powerful program that will allow him or her to produce a set of books—work that an accountant used to do. No wonder that accounting firms are moving away from the kind of work that can be more efficiently done by a machine.

For bigger businesses, "we're installing more computer systems and advising our clients on how to use that information in a more sophisticated way," says Kaland, who earned a bachelor's degree in accounting from the University of Illinois and has spent 20 years with Clifton Gunderson. Once the systems are installed, the client can produce accounting information more efficiently than before—

Name: Krista Kaland
Profession: CPA
College Major: Accounting

usually with fewer employees.

As director of audit and accounting for her firm, Kaland advises her colleagues and clients on technical matters having to do with accounting and auditing principles. Because of computer technology, she says that accounting firms are able to do much better audits than ten years ago. Since audits are based on sampling and testing of transactions, computers make that process much more precise. "We can now take a client's records, import them into our software, and search for unusual transactions," she says. "We have a much better ability to analyze data."

Even as computers make audits more efficient, other forces are making the process more burdensome. As the business world becomes more international and complex, and business managers come up with more complicated transactions, the time and expense required to audit financial statements lengthens. The people who rely on financial statements—primarily stockholders and creditors—still expect the statements to fairly present the company's financial results.

Yet clients often expect their accounting firms to do more work without a commensurate increase in fees. Successful CPA firms figure out ways to "leverage" their people in such a way that audit managers can supervise larger numbers of junior accountants, thus making the audit engagement profitable. After all, if an accounting firm can't figure out how to work efficiently, then who can?

purchase of land by signing a promissory note *should* result in a debit to Land and a credit to Notes Payable. If the accountant incorrectly debited Cash instead of Land, the trial balance would still show an equality of debits and credits. A trial balance can be prepared at any time; it is usually prepared as a preliminary step to the release of a set of financial statements.

ACCOUNTING FOR YOUR DECISIONS

You Are the Stockholder

You own 100 shares of stock in General Motors. Every year, you receive GM's annual report, which includes a chairman's letter, a description of new models, a financial section and footnotes to financial statements. Nowhere in the report do you see a general ledger or a trial balance. Is General Motors hiding something?

ANS: GM's balance sheet, income statement and statement of cash flows are derived from the company's journal entries, general ledgers, trial balances, and so on. These documents are the building blocks of the final statements. There could literally be millions of transactions during the year—which even the most diehard accounting fan would tire of reading.

EXHIBIT 3-6   Trial Balance for Glengarry Health Club

GLENGARRY HEALTH CLUB
TRIAL BALANCE
AT JANUARY 31, 1998

ACCOUNT TITLE	DEBITS	CREDITS
Cash	$ 94,000	
Accounts Receivable	11,000	
Building	150,000	
Land	50,000	
Equipment	20,000	
Accounts Payable		$ 20,000
Notes Payable		200,000
Capital Stock		100,000
Membership Revenue		15,000
Court Fee Revenue		5,000
Wage and Salary Expense	10,000	
Utility Expense	3,000	
Dividends	2,000	
Totals	$340,000	$340,000

Review Problem

The following transactions are entered into by Sparkle Car Wash during its first month of operations:

a. Articles of incorporation are filed with the state, and 20,000 shares of capital stock are issued. Cash of $40,000 is received from the new owners for the shares.

b. A five-year promissory note is signed at the local bank. The cash received from the loan is $120,000.

c. An existing car wash is purchased for $150,000 in cash. The values assigned to the land, building, and equipment are $25,000, $75,000, and $50,000, respectively.

d. Cleaning supplies are purchased on account for $2,500 from a distributor. All of the supplies are used in the first month.

e. During the first month, $1,500 is paid to the distributor for the cleaning supplies. The remaining $1,000 will be paid next month.

f. Gross receipts from car washes during the first month of operations amount to $7,000.

g. Wages and salaries paid in the first month amount to $2,000.

h. The utility bill of $800 for the month is paid.

i. A total of $1,000 in dividends is paid to the owners.

Required

1. Prepare a table to summarize the preceding transactions as they affect the accounting equation. Use the format in Exhibit 3-1. Identify each transaction by letter.

2. Prepare an income statement for the month.

3. Prepare a balance sheet at the end of the month.

Solution to Review Problem

1.

SPARKLE CAR WASH
TRANSACTIONS FOR THE MONTH

TRANS.	CASH	LAND	BUILDING	EQUIPMENT	ACCOUNTS PAYABLE	NOTES PAYABLE	CAPITAL STOCK	RETAINED EARNINGS
			Assets		=		**Liabilities + Owners' Equity**	
a.	$ 40,000						$40,000	
b.	120,000					$120,000		
Bal.	$160,000					$120,000	$40,000	
c.	−150,000	$25,000	$75,000	$50,000				
Bal.	$ 10,000	$25,000	$75,000	$50,000		$120,000	$40,000	
d.					$2,500			$−2,500
Bal.	$ 10,000	$25,000	$75,000	$50,000	$2,500	$120,000	$40,000	$−2,500
e.	−1,500				−1,500			
Bal.	$ 8,500	$25,000	$75,000	$50,000	$1,000	$120,000	$40,000	$−2,500
f.	7,000							7,000
Bal.	$ 15,500	$25,000	$75,000	$50,000	$1,000	$120,000	$40,000	$ 4,500
g.	−2,000							−2,000
Bal.	$ 13,500	$25,000	$75,000	$50,000	$1,000	$120,000	$40,000	$ 2,500
h.	−800							−800
Bal.	$ 12,700	$25,000	$75,000	$50,000	$1,000	$120,000	$40,000	$ 1,700
i.	−1,000							−1,000
Bal.	$ 11,700	$25,000	$75,000	$50,000	$1,000	$120,000	$40,000	$ 700

Total Assets: $161,700   Total Liabilities and Owners' Equity: $161,700

2.

SPARKLE CAR WASH
INCOME STATEMENT
FOR THE MONTH ENDED XX/XX/XX

Car wash revenue		$7,000
Expenses:		
Supplies	$2,500	
Wages and salaries	2,000	
Utilities	800	5,300
Net income		$1,700

3.

SPARKLE CAR WASH
BALANCE SHEET
XX/XX/XX

ASSETS		LIABILITIES AND OWNERS' EQUITY	
Cash	$ 11,700	Accounts payable	$ 1,000
Land	25,000	Notes payable	120,000
Building	75,000	Capital stock	40,000
Equipment	50,000	Retained earnings	700
		Total Liabilities	
Total Assets	$161,700	and Owners' Equity	$161,700

Chapter Highlights

1. **LO 1** Both internal and external events affect an entity. External events, such as the purchase of materials, involve the entity and its environment. Internal events, such as the placement of the materials into production, do not involve an outside entity. For any event to be recorded, it must be measurable.

2. **LO 2** Source documents are used as the basis for recording events as transactions. For certain repetitive transactions, a standard source document is used, such as a time card to document the payroll for the week. For other nonrepetitive transactions a source document has to be generated for the specific event.

3. **LO 3** Economic events are the basis for recording transactions. These transactions result in changes in the company's financial position. Transactions change the amount of individual items on the balance sheet, but the statement must balance after each transaction is recorded.

4. **LO 4** A separate account is used for each identifiable asset, liability, revenue, expense, and component of owners' equity. No standard set of accounts exists, and the types of accounts used depend to a certain extent on the nature of a company's business. A chart of accounts is a numerical list of all the accounts used by an entity. The general ledger in a manual system might consist of a set of cards, one for each account, in a file cabinet. In a computerized system, a magnetic tape or diskette might be used to store the accounts.

5. **LO 4** Accountants use T accounts as the basic form of analysis of transactions. The left side of an account is used for debits, and the right side is for credits. Transactions are recorded in the ledger in more formal accounts than the typical T account.

6. **LO 5** By convention, the left side of an asset account is used to record increases. Thus, an asset account is increased with a debit. Because liabilities are on the opposite side of the accounting equation, they are increased with a credit. Similarly, owners' equity accounts are increased with a credit. Because revenue is an increase in owners' equity, it is increased with a credit. Thus, an expense, as well as a dividend, is increased with a debit. According to the double entry system, there are two sides to every transaction. For each transaction, the debit or debits must equal the credit or credits.

7. **LO 6** Transactions are not recorded directly in the accounts but are recorded initially in a journal. A separate entry is recorded in the journal for each transaction. The account(s) debited appears first in the entry with the account(s) credited listed next and indented. Separate columns for debits and credits are used to indicate the amounts for each. A general journal is used in lieu of any specialized journals.

8. **LO 6** Amounts appearing in journal entries are posted to the ledger accounts. Posting can be done either at the time the entry is recorded or periodically. The Post. Ref. column in a journal indicates the account number to which the amount is posted, and a similar column in the account acts as a convenient reference back to the particular page number in the journal.

9. **LO 7** A trial balance proves the equality of the debits and credits in the accounts. If only one side of a transaction is posted to the accounts, the trial balance will not balance. Other types of errors are detectable from the process of preparing a trial balance. It cannot, however, detect all errors. A trial balance could be in balance even though the wrong asset account is debited in an entry.

Key Terms Quiz

Read each definition below and then write the number of the definition in the blank beside the appropriate term it defines. The solution appears at the end of the chapter.

___ Event	___ External event
___ Internal event	___ Transaction
___ Source document	___ Account
___ Chart of accounts	___ General ledger
___ Debit	___ Credit
___ Double entry system	___ Journal
___ Posting	___ Journalizing
___ General journal	___ Trial Balance

1. A numerical list of all the accounts used by a company.
2. A work sheet showing the balances in each account; used to prove the equality of debits and credits.
3. A happening of consequence to an entity.
4. An entry on the right side of an account.
5. An event occurring entirely within an entity.
6. A piece of paper, such as a sales invoice, that is used as the evidence to record a transaction.
7. The act of recording journal entries.
8. An entry on the left side of an account.
9. The process of transferring amounts from a journal to the appropriate ledger accounts.
10. An event involving interaction between an entity and its environment.
11. The record used to accumulate monetary amounts for each individual asset, liability, revenue, expense, and component of owners' equity.

12. A book, file, diskette, magnetic tape, or other device containing all of a company's accounts.

13. A chronological record of transactions, also known as the *book of original entry.*

14. Any event, external or internal, that is recognized in a set of financial statements.

15. The journal used in lieu of a specialized journal.

16. A system of accounting in which every transaction is recorded with equal debits and credits and the accounting equation is kept in balance.

Alternate Terms

Credit side of an account   Right side of an account.

Debit an account   Charge an account.

Debit side of an account   Left side of an account.

General ledger   Set of accounts.

Journal   Book of original entry.

Journalize an entry   Record an entry.

Posting an account   Transferring an amount from the journal to the ledger.

Questions

1. What are the two types of events that affect an entity? Describe each.

2. What is the significance of source documents to the recording process? Give two examples of source documents.

3. What are four different forms of cash?

4. How does an account receivable differ from a note receivable?

5. What is meant by the statement "One company's account receivable is another company's account payable"?

6. What do accountants mean when they refer to the "double entry system" of accounting?

7. Owners' equity represents the claim of the owners on the assets of the business. What is the distinction relative to the owners' claim between the Capital Stock account and the Retained Earnings account?

8. If an asset account is increased with a debit, what is the logic for increasing a liability account with a credit?

9. A friend comes to you with the following plight: "I'm confused. An asset is something positive, and it is increased with a debit. However, an expense is something negative, and it is also increased with a debit. I don't get it." How can you straighten your friend out?

10. The payment of dividends reduces cash. If the Cash account is reduced with a credit, why is the Dividends account debited when dividends are paid?

11. If Cash is increased with a debit, why does the bank credit your account when you make a deposit?

12. Your friend presents the following criticism of the accounting system: "Accounting involves so much duplication of effort. First, entries are recorded in a journal and then the same information is recorded in a ledger. No wonder accountants work such long hours!" Do you agree with this criticism?

13. How does the T account differ from the running balance form for an account? How are they similar?

14. What is the benefit of using a cross-referencing system between a ledger and a journal?

15. How often should a company post entries from the journal to the ledger?

16. What is the purpose of a trial balance?

Exercises

LO 1 **Exercise 3-1** Types of Events

For each of the following events, identify whether it is an external event that would be recorded as a transaction (E), an internal event that would be recorded as a transaction (I), or not recorded (NR):

_____ 1. A supplier of a company's raw material is paid an amount owed on account.

_____ 2. A customer pays its open account.

_____ 3. A new chief executive officer is hired.

_____ 4. The biweekly payroll is paid.

_____ 5. Raw materials are entered into production.

_____ 6. A new advertising agency is hired to develop a series of newspaper ads for the company.

_____ **7.** The advertising bill for the first month is paid.

_____ **8.** The accountant determines the federal income taxes owed based on the income earned during the period.

LO 2 **Exercise 3-2** Source Documents Matched with Transactions

Following are a list of source documents and a list of transactions. Indicate by letter next to each transaction the source document that would serve as evidence for the recording of the transaction.

Source Documents

a. Purchase invoice.

b. Sales invoice.

c. Cash register tape.

d. Time cards.

e. Promissory note.

f. Stock certificates.

g. Monthly statement from utility company.

h. No standard source document would normally be available.

Transactions

_____ **1.** Utilities expense for the month is recorded.

_____ **2.** A cash settlement is received from a pending lawsuit.

_____ **3.** Owners contribute cash to start a new corporation.

_____ **4.** The biweekly payroll is paid.

_____ **5.** Cash sales for the day are recorded.

_____ **6.** Equipment is acquired on a 30-day open account.

_____ **7.** A sale is made on open account.

_____ **8.** A building is acquired by signing an agreement to repay a stated amount plus interest in six months.

LO 3 **Exercise 3-3** The Effect of Transactions on the Accounting Equation

For each of the following transactions, indicate whether it increases (I), decreases (D), or has no effect (NE) on the total dollar amount of each of the elements of the accounting equation.

TRANSACTIONS	Assets	=	Liabilities	+	Owners' Equity
Example: Common stock is issued in exchange for cash.	I		NE		I

1. Equipment is purchased for cash.

2. Sales are made on account.

3. Cash sales are made.

4. An account payable is paid off.

5. Cash is collected on an account receivable.

6. Buildings are purchased in exchange for a three-year note payable.

7. Advertising bill for the month is paid.

8. Dividends are paid to stockholders.

9. Land is acquired by issuing shares of stock to the owner of the land.

LO 3 **Exercise 3-4** Types of Transactions

As you found out in reading the chapter, there are three elements to the accounting equation: assets, liabilities, and owners' equity. You also learned that every transaction affects at least two of these elements. Although other possibilities exist, five types of transactions are described below. For *each* of these five types, write out descriptions of at least *two* transactions that illustrate these types of transactions.

TYPE OF TRANSACTION	Assets	= Liabilities	+ Owners' Equity
1.	Increase	Increase	
2.	Increase		Increase
3.	Decrease	Decrease	
4.	Decrease		Decrease
5.	Increase Decrease		

LO 4   **Exercise 3-5** Balance Sheet Accounts and Their Use

Choose from the following list of account titles the one that most accurately fits the description of that account or is an example of that account. An account title may be used more than once or not at all.

Cash	**Accounts Receivable**	**Notes Receivable**
Prepaid Asset	**Land**	**Buildings**
Investments	**Accounts Payable**	**Notes Payable**
Taxes Payable	**Retained Earnings**	**Common Stock**
Preferred Stock		

_____   **1.** A written obligation to repay a fixed amount, with interest, at some time in the future.

_____   **2.** Twenty acres of land held for speculation.

_____   **3.** An amount owed by a customer.

_____   **4.** Corporate income taxes owed to the federal government.

_____   **5.** Ownership in a company that allows the owner to receive dividends before common shareholders receive any distributions.

_____   **6.** Five acres of land used as the site for a factory.

_____   **7.** Amounts owed on an open account to a supplier of raw materials, due in 90 days.

_____   **8.** A checking account at the bank.

_____   **9.** A warehouse used to store merchandise.

_____   **10.** Claims by the owners on the undistributed net income of a business.

_____   **11.** Rent paid on an office building in advance of use of the facility.

LO 5   **Exercise 3-6** Normal Account Balances

Each account has a normal balance. For the following list of accounts, indicate whether the normal balance of each is a debit or a credit.

ACCOUNT	NORMAL BALANCE
1. Cash.	_____
2. Prepaid Insurance.	_____
3. Retained Earnings.	_____
4. Bonds Payable.	_____
5. Investments.	_____
6. Capital Stock.	_____
7. Advertising Fees Earned.	_____
8. Wages and Salaries Expense.	_____
9. Wages and Salaries Payable.	_____
10. Office Supplies.	_____
11. Dividends.	_____

LO 5   **Exercise 3-7** Debits and Credits

The new bookkeeper for Darby Corporation is getting ready to mail the daily cash receipts to the bank for deposit. Because his previous job was at a bank, he is aware that the bank "credits" your account for all deposits and "debits" your account for all checks written. Therefore, he makes the following entry prior to sending the daily receipts to the bank:

June 5	Accounts Receivable	10,000	
	Sales Revenue	2,450	
	Cash		12,450
	To record cash received on June 5: $10,000 collections on account and $2,450 in cash sales.		

Required

Explain why this entry is wrong, and prepare the correct journal entry. Why does the bank refer to cash received from a customer as a *credit* to that customer's account?

LO 7   **Exercise 3-8** Trial Balance

The following list of accounts was taken from the general ledger of Spencer Corporation on December 31, 1998. The bookkeeper thought it would be helpful if the accounts were arranged in alphabetical order. Each account contains the balance normal for that type of account (for example, Cash normally has a debit balance). Prepare a trial balance as of this date, with the accounts arranged in the following order: (1) assets, (2) liabilities, (3) owners' equity, (4) revenues, (5) expenses, and (6) dividends.

ACCOUNT	BALANCE
Accounts Payable	$ 7,650
Accounts Receivable	5,325
Automobiles	9,200
Buildings	150,000
Capital Stock	100,000
Cash	10,500
Commissions Expense	2,600
Commissions Revenue	12,750
Dividends	2,000
Equipment	85,000
Heat, Light, and Water Expense	1,400
Income Tax Expense	1,700
Income Taxes Payable	2,500
Interest Revenue	1,300
Land	50,000
Notes Payable	90,000
Office Salaries Expense	6,000
Office Supplies	500
Retained Earnings	110,025

Multi-Concept Exercises

LO 3, 4, 5   **Exercise 3-9** Journal Entries Recorded Directly in T Accounts

Record each transaction shown below directly in T accounts, using the numbers preceding the transactions to identify them in the accounts. Each account involved needs a separate T account.

1. Received contribution of $6,500 from each of the three principal owners of the We-Go Delivery Service in exchange for shares of stock.
2. Purchased office supplies for cash of $130.
3. Purchased a van for $15,000 on an open account. The company has 25 days to pay for the van.

4. Provided delivery services to residential customers for cash of $125.

5. Billed a local business $200 for delivery services. The customer is to pay the bill within 15 days.

6. Paid the amount due on the van.

7. Received the amount due from the local business billed in transaction (5) above.

LO 7 **Exercise 3-10** Trial Balance

Refer to the transactions recorded directly in T accounts for the We-Go Delivery Service in Exercise 3-9. Assume that the transactions all took place during December 1998. Prepare a trial balance at December 31, 1998.

LO 3, 4, 5 **Exercise 3-11** Determining an Ending Account Balance

Jessie's Bead Shop was organized on June 1, 1998. The company received a contribution of $1,000 from each of the two principal owners. During the month, Jessie's Bead Shop had cash sales of $1,400, had sales on account of $450, received $250 from customers in payment of their accounts, purchased supplies on account for $600 and equipment on account for $1,350, received a utility bill for $250 which will not be paid until July, and paid the full amount due on the equipment. Use a T account to determine the company's Cash balance on June 30, 1998.

LO 3, 4, 5 **Exercise 3-12** Reconstructing a Beginning Account Balance

During the month, services performed for customers on account amounted to $7,500, and collections from customers in payment of their accounts totaled $6,000. At the end of the month, the Accounts Receivable account had a balance of $2,500. What was the Accounts Receivable balance at the beginning of the month?

General
Ledger

LO 3, 5, 6 **Exercise 3-13** Journal Entries

Prepare the journal entry to record each of the following independent transactions (use the number of the transaction in lieu of a date for identification purposes):

1. Sales on account of $1,530.

2. Purchases of supplies on account for $1,365.

3. Cash sales of $750.

4. Purchase of equipment for cash of $4,240.

5. Issuance of a promissory note for $2,500.

6. Collections on account for $890.

7. Sale of capital stock in exchange for a parcel of land. The land is appraised at $50,000.

8. Payment of $4,000 in salaries and wages.

9. Payment of open account in the amount of $500.

LO 3, 5, 6 **Exercise 3-14** Journal Entries

Following is a list of transactions entered into during the first month of operations of Gardener Corporation, a new landscape service. Prepare in journal form the entry to record each transaction.

April 1: Articles of incorporation are filed with the state, and 100,000 shares of common stock are issued for $100,000 in cash.

April 4: A six-month promissory note is signed at the bank. Interest at 9% per annum will be repaid in six months along with the principal amount of the loan of $50,000.

April 8: Land and a storage shed are acquired for a lump sum of $80,000. On the basis of an appraisal, 25% of the value is assigned to the land and the remainder to the building.

April 10: Mowing equipment is purchased from a supplier at a total cost of $25,000. A down payment of $10,000 is made, with the remainder due by the end of the month.

April 18: Customers are billed for services provided during the first half of the month. The total amount billed of $5,500 is due within 10 days.

April 27: The remaining balance due on the mowing equipment is paid to the supplier.

April 28: The total amount of $5,500 due from customers is received.

April 30: Customers are billed for services provided during the second half of the month. The total amount billed is $9,850.

April 30: Salaries and wages of $4,650 for the month of April are paid.

LO 5, 6 **Exercise 3-15** The Process of Posting Journal Entries to General Ledger Accounts

On June 1, Campbell Corporation purchased 10 acres of land in exchange for a promissory note in the amount of $50,000. Using the formats shown in Exhibit 3-5, prepare the journal entry to record this transaction in a general journal, and post it to the appropriate general ledger accounts. The entry will be recorded on page 7 of the general journal. Use whatever account numbers you would like in the general ledger. Assume that none of the accounts to be debited or credited currently contain a balance.

If at a later date you wanted to review this transaction, would you examine the general ledger or the general journal? Explain your answer.

Problems

LO 1 **Problem 3-1** Events to be Recorded in Accounts

The following events take place at Davidson's Drive-In:

1. Food is ordered from vendors, who will deliver the food within the week.
2. Vendors deliver food on account, payment due in 30 days.
3. Employees take frozen food from the freezers and prepare it for customers.
4. Food is served to customers, and sales are rung up on the cash register; sales will be totaled at the end of the day.
5. Trash is taken to dumpsters, and the floors are cleaned.
6. Cash registers are cleared at the end of the day.
7. Cash is deposited in the bank night depository.
8. Employees are paid weekly paychecks.
9. Vendors noted in item 2 are paid for the food delivered.

Required

Identify each event as internal (I) or external (E), and indicate whether each event would be recorded in the *accounts* of the company. For each event that is to be recorded, identify the names of at least two accounts that would be affected.

LO 3 **Problem 3-2** Transaction Analysis and Financial Statements

Just Rolling Along Inc. was organized on May 1, 1998, by two college students who recognized an opportunity to make money while spending their days at a beach along Lake Michigan. The two entrepreneurs plan to rent bicycles and in-line skates to weekend visitors to the lakefront. The following transactions occurred during the first month of operations:

May 1: Received contribution of $9,000 from each of the two principal owners of the new business in exchange for shares of stock.

May 1: Purchased 10 bicycles for $300 each on an open account. The company has 30 days to pay for the bicycles.

May 5: Registered as a vendor with the city and paid the $15 monthly fee.

May 9: Purchased 20 pairs of in-line skates at $125 per pair, 20 helmets at $50 each, and 20 sets of protective gear (knee and elbow pads and wrist guards) at $45 per set for cash.

May 10: Purchased $100 in miscellaneous supplies on account. The company has 30 days to pay for the supplies.

May 15: Paid $125 bill from local radio station for advertising for the last two weeks of May.

May 17: Customers rented in-line skates and bicycles for cash of $1,800.

May 24: Billed the local park district $1,200 for in-line skating lessons provided to neighborhood kids. The park district is to pay one-half of the bill within 5 working days and the rest within 30 days.

May 29: Received 50% of the amount billed to the park district.

May 30: Customers rented in-line skates and bicycles for cash of $3,000.

May 30: Paid wages of $160 to a friend who helped out over the weekend.

May 31: Paid the balance due on the bicycles.

Required

1. Prepare a table to summarize the preceding transactions as they affect the accounting equation. Use the format in Exhibit 3-1. Identify each transaction with the date.
2. Prepare an income statement for the month ended May 31, 1998.
3. Prepare a classified balance sheet at May 31, 1998.
4. Why do you think the two college students decided to incorporate their business rather than operate it as a partnership?

LO 3 | **Problem 3-3** Transaction Analysis and Financial Statements

Expert Consulting Services Inc. was organized on March 1, 1998, by two former college roommates. The corporation will provide computer consulting services to small businesses. The following transactions occurred during the first month of operations:

March 2: Received contributions of $20,000 from each of the two principal owners of the new business in exchange for shares of stock.

March 7: Signed a two-year promissory note at the bank and received cash of $15,000. Interest, along with the $15,000, will be repaid at the end of the two years.

March 12: Purchased $700 in miscellaneous supplies on account. The company has 30 days to pay for the supplies.

March 19: Billed a client $4,000 for services rendered by Expert in helping to install a new computer system. The client is to pay 25% of the bill upon its receipt and the remaining balance within 30 days.

March 20: Paid $1,300 bill from the local newspaper for advertising for the month of March.

March 22: Received 25% of the amount billed client on March 19.

March 26: Received cash of $2,800 for services provided in assisting a client in selecting software for its computer.

March 29: Purchased a computer system for $8,000 in cash.

March 30: Paid $3,300 of salaries and wages for March.

March 31: Received and paid $1,400 in gas, electric, and water bills.

Required

1. Prepare a table to summarize the preceding transactions as they affect the accounting equation. Use the format in Exhibit 3-1. Identify each transaction with the date.
2. Prepare an income statement for the month ended March 31, 1998.
3. Prepare a classified balance sheet at March 31, 1998.

4. From reading the balance sheet you prepared in part 3, what events would you expect to take place in April? Explain your answer.

LO 3 **Problem 3-4** Transactions Reconstructed From Financial Statements

The following financial statements are available for Elm Corporation for its first month of operations:

ELM CORPORATION
INCOME STATEMENT
FOR THE MONTH ENDED JUNE 30, 1998

Service revenue		$93,600
Expenses:		
Rent	$ 9,000	
Salaries and wages	27,900	
Utilities	13,800	50,700
Net income		$42,900

ELM CORPORATION
BALANCE SHEET
JUNE 30, 1998

ASSETS		LIABILITIES AND OWNERS' EQUITY	
Cash	$ 22,800	Accounts payable	$ 18,000
Accounts receivable	21,600	Notes payable	90,000
Equipment	18,000		
Building	90,000	Capital stock	30,000
Land	24,000	Retained earnings	38,400
Total	$176,400	Total	$176,400

Required

Using the format illustrated in Exhibit 3-1, prepare a table to summarize the transactions entered into by Elm Corporation during its first month of business. State any assumptions you believe are necessary in reconstructing the transactions.

Multi-Concept Problems

LO 1, 2 **Problem 3-5** Identification of Events With Source Documents

Many events are linked to a source document. The following is a list of events that occurred in an entity:

a. Paid a one-year insurance policy.

b. Paid employee payroll.

c. Sold merchandise to a customer on account.

d. Identified supplies in the storeroom destroyed by fire.

e. Received payment of bills from customers.

f. Purchased land for future expansion.

g. Calculated taxes due.

h. Entered into a car lease agreement and paid the tax, title, and license.

Required

For each item a through h, indicate whether the event should or should not be recorded in the entity's accounts. For each item that should be recorded in the entity's books:

1. Identify one or more source documents that are generated from the event.

2. Identify which source document would be used to record an event when it produces more than one source document.

3. For each document, identify the information that is most useful in recording the event in the accounts.

LO 3, 5 **Problem 3-6** Accounts Used to Record Transactions

A list of accounts, with an identifying number for each, is shown below. Following the list of accounts is a series of transactions entered into by a company during its first year of operations.

Required

For each transaction, indicate the account or accounts that should be debited and credited.

1. Cash
2. Accounts Receivable
3. Office Supplies
4. Buildings
5. Automobiles
6. Land
7. Accounts Payable
8. Income Tax Payable
9. Notes Payable
10. Capital Stock
11. Retained Earnings
12. Service Revenue
13. Wage and Salary Expense
14. Selling Expense
15. Utilities Expense
16. Income Tax Expense

TRANSACTIONS	ACCOUNTS DEBITED	CREDITED
Example: Purchased land and building in exchange for a three-year promissory note.	4, 6	9
a. Issued capital stock for cash.		
b. Purchased 10 automobiles; paid part in cash and signed a 60-day note for the balance.		
c. Purchased land in exchange for note due in six months.		
d. Purchased office supplies; agreed to pay total bill by the 10th of the following month.		
e. Billed clients for services performed during the month and gave them until the 15th of the following month to pay.		
f. Received cash on account from clients for services rendered to them in past months.		
g. Paid employees salaries and wages earned during the month.		
h. Paid newspaper for company ads appearing during the month.		
i. Received monthly gas and electric bill from the utility company; payment is due anytime within first 10 days of the following month.		
j. Computed amount of taxes due based on the income of the period; amount will be paid in the following month.		

LO 3, 4, 5 **Problem 3-7** Transaction Analysis and Journal Entries Recorded Directly in T Accounts

Four brothers organized Beverly Entertainment Enterprises on October 1, 1998. The following transactions occurred during the first month of operations:

October 1: Received contribution of $10,000 from each of the four principal owners of the new business in exchange for shares of stock.

October 2: Purchased the Arcada Theater for $125,000. The seller agreed to accept a down payment of $12,500 and a seven-year promissory note for the balance. The Arcada property consists of land valued at $35,000 and a building valued at $90,000.

October 3: Purchased new seats for the theater at a cost of $5,000, paying $2,500 down and agreeing to pay the remainder in 60 days.

October 12: Purchased candy, popcorn, cups, and napkins for $3,700 on an open account. The company has 30 days to pay for the concession supplies.

October 13: Sold tickets for the opening-night movie for cash of $1,800 and took in $2,400 at the concession stand.

October 17: Rented out the theater to a local community group for $1,500. The community group is to pay one-half of the bill within 5 working days and has 30 days to pay the remainder.

October 23: Received 50% of the amount billed to the community group.

October 24: Sold movie tickets for cash of $2,000 and took in $2,800 at the concession stand.

October 26: The four brothers, acting on behalf of Beverly Entertainment, paid a dividend of $750 on the shares of stock owned by each of them, or $3,000 in total.

October 27: Paid $500 for utilities.

October 30: Paid wages and salaries of $2,400 total to the ushers, the projectionist, concession stand workers, and the maintenance crew.

October 31: Sold movie tickets for cash of $1,800 and took in $2,500 at the concession stand.

Required

1. Prepare a table to summarize the preceding transactions as they affect the accounting equation. Use the format in Exhibit 3-1. Identify each transaction with a date.

2. Record each transaction directly in T accounts, using the dates preceding the transactions to identify them in the accounts. Each account involved in the problem needs a separate T account.

LO 7 **Problem 3-8** Trial Balance and Financial Statements
Refer to the table for Beverly Entertainment Enterprises in part (1) of Problem 3-7.

Required

1. Prepare a trial balance at October 31, 1998.
2. Prepare an income statement for the month ended October 31, 1998.
3. Prepare a statement of retained earnings for the month ended October 31, 1998.
4. Prepare a classified balance sheet at October 31, 1998.

LO 3, 5, 6 **Problem 3-9** Journal Entries
Atkins Advertising Agency began business on January 2, 1998. Listed below are the transactions entered into by Atkins during its first month of operations.

General
Ledger

a. Acquired its articles of incorporation from the state and issued 100,000 shares of capital stock in exchange for $200,000 in cash.

b. Purchased an office building for $150,000 in cash. The building is valued at $110,000, and the remainder of the value is assigned to the land.

c. Signed a three-year promissory note at the bank for $125,000.

d. Purchased office equipment at a cost of $50,000, paying $10,000 down and agreeing to pay the remainder in 10 days.

e. Paid wages and salaries of $13,000 for the first half of the month. Office employees are paid twice a month.

f. Paid the balance due on the office equipment.

g. Sold $24,000 of advertising during the first month. Customers have until the 15th of the following month to pay their bills.

h. Paid wages and salaries of $15,000 for the second half of the month.

i. Recorded $3,500 in commissions earned by the salespeople during the month. They will be paid on the fifth of the following month.

Required

Prepare in journal form the entry to record each transaction.

LO 3, 4, 5, 7 **Problem 3-10** Journal Entries Recorded Directly in T Accounts
Refer to the transactions for Atkins Advertising Agency in Problem 3-9.

Required

1. Record each transaction directly in T accounts, using the letters preceding the transactions to identify them in the accounts. Each account involved in the problem needs a separate T account.

2. Prepare a trial balance at January 31, 1998.

LO 3, 5, 7 **Problem 3-11** The Detection of Errors in a Trial Balance and Preparation of a Corrected Trial Balance
Malcolm Inc. was incorporated on January 1, 1998, with the issuance of capital stock in return for $90,000 of cash contributed by the owners. The only other transaction entered into prior to beginning operations was the issuance of a $75,300 note payable in exchange for building and equipment. The following trial balance was prepared at the end of the first month by the bookkeeper for Malcolm Inc.

MALCOLM INC.
TRIAL BALANCE
JANUARY 31, 1998

ACCOUNT TITLES	DEBITS	CREDITS
Cash	$ 9,980	
Accounts Receivable	8,640	
Land	80,000	
Building	50,000	
Equipment	23,500	
Notes Payable		$ 75,300
Capital Stock		90,000
Service Revenue		50,340
Wage and Salary Expense	23,700	
Advertising Expense	4,600	
Utilities Expense	8,420	
Dividends		5,000
Totals	$208,840	$220,640

Required

1. Identify the *two* errors in the trial balance.

2. Prepare a corrected trial balance.

General
Ledger

LO 3, 5, 6, 7 **Problem 3-12** Journal Entries, Trial Balance, and Financial Statements
Overnight Delivery Inc. is incorporated on January 2, 1998, and enters into the following transactions during its first month of operations:

January 2: Filed articles of incorporation with the state and issued 100,000 shares of capital stock. Cash of $100,000 is received from the new owners for the shares.

January 3: Purchased a warehouse and land for $80,000 in cash. An appraiser values the land at $20,000 and the warehouse at $60,000.

January 4: Signed a three-year promissory note at the Third State Bank in the amount of $50,000.

January 6: Purchased five new delivery trucks for a total of $45,000 in cash.

January 31:   Performed services on account during the month that amounted to
              $15,900. Cash amounting to $7,490 was received from customers on
              account during the month.

January 31:   Established an open account at a local service station at the beginning of
              the month. Purchases of gas and oil during January amounted to $3,230.
              Overnight has until the 10th of the following month to pay its bill.

Required

1. Prepare journal entries on the books of Overnight to record the transactions entered
   into during the month.
2. Prepare a trial balance at January 31, 1998.
3. Prepare an income statement for the month ended January 31, 1998.
4. Prepare a classified balance sheet at January 31, 1998.
5. Assume that you are considering buying stock in this company. Beginning with the
   transaction to record the purchase of the property on January 3, list any additional
   information you would like to have about each of the transactions during the remainder of the month.

LO 3, 5, 6, 7   **Problem 3-13** Journal Entries, Trial Balance, and Financial Statements

Neveranerror Inc. was organized on June 2, 1998, by a group of accountants to provide
accounting and tax services to small businesses. The following transactions occurred
during the first month of business:

General
Ledger

June 2:   Received contributions of $10,000 from each of the three owners of the
           business in exchange for shares of stock.

June 5:   Purchased a computer system for $12,000. The agreement with the vendor
           requires a down payment of $2,500 with the balance due in 60 days.

June 8:   Signed a two-year promissory note at the bank and received cash of $20,000.

June 15:   Billed $12,350 to clients for the first half of June. Clients are billed twice a
           month for services performed during the month, and the bills are payable
           within 10 days.

June 17:   Paid a $900 bill from the local newspaper for advertising for the month of
           June.

June 23:   Received the amounts billed to clients for services performed during the first
           half of the month.

June 28:   Received and paid gas, electric, and water bills. The total amount is $2,700.

June 29:   Received the landlord's bill for $2,200 for rent on the office space that
           Neveranerror leases. The bill is payable by the 10th of the following month.

June 30:   Paid salaries and wages for June. The total amount is $5,670.

June 30:   Billed $18,400 to clients for the second half of June.

June 30:   Declared and paid dividends in the amount of $6,000.

Required

1. Prepare journal entries on the books of Neveranerror Inc. to record the transactions
   entered into during the month.
2. Prepare a trial balance at June 30, 1998.
3. Prepare the following financial statements:
   a. Income statement for the month ended June 30, 1998.
   b. Statement of retained earnings for the month ended June 30, 1998.
   c. Classified balance sheet at June 30, 1998.

4. Assume that you have just graduated from college and have been approached to join this company as an accountant. From your reading of the financial statements for the first month, would you consider joining the company? Explain your answer. Limit your answer to financial considerations only.

Alternate Problems

LO 1 **Problem 3-1A** Events to Be Recorded in Accounts
The following events take place at Accurate Accountants Inc.:

1. Supplies are ordered from vendors, who will deliver the supplies within the week.
2. Vendors deliver supplies on account, payment due in 30 days.
3. New computer system is ordered.
4. Old computer system is sold for cash.
5. Services are rendered to customers on account. The invoices are mailed and due in 30 days.
6. Cash received from customer payments is deposited in the bank night depository.
7. Employees are paid weekly paychecks.
8. Vendors noted in item 2 are paid for the supplies delivered.

Required

Identify each event as internal (I) or external (E), and indicate whether each event would be recorded in the *accounts* of the company. For each event that is to be recorded, identify the names of at least two accounts that would be affected.

LO 3 **Problem 3-2A** Transaction Analysis and Financial Statements
Beachway Enterprises was organized on June 1, 1998, by two college students who recognized an opportunity to make money while spending their days at a beach in Florida. The two entrepreneurs plan to rent beach umbrellas. The following transactions occurred during the first month of operations:

June 1: Received contribution of $2,000 from each of the two principal owners of the new business in exchange for shares of stock.

June 1: Purchased 25 beach umbrellas for $250 each on account. The company has 30 days to pay for the beach umbrellas.

June 5. Registered as a vendor with the city and paid the $35 monthly fee.

June 10: Purchased $50 in miscellaneous supplies on an open account. The company has 30 days to pay for the supplies.

June 15: Paid $70 bill from a local radio station for advertising for the last two weeks of June.

June 17: Customers rented beach umbrellas for cash of $1,000.

June 24: Billed a local hotel $2,000 for beach umbrellas provided for use during a convention being held at the hotel. The hotel is to pay one-half of the bill in 5 days and the rest within 30 days.

June 29: Received 50% of the amount billed to the hotel.

June 30: Customers rented beach umbrellas for cash of $1,500.

June 30: Paid wages of $90 to a friend who helped out over the weekend.

June 30: Paid the balance due on the beach umbrellas.

Required

1. Prepare a table to summarize the preceding transactions as they affect the accounting equation. Use the format in Exhibit 3-1. Identify each transaction with a date.
2. Prepare an income statement for the month ended June 30, 1998.
3. Prepare a classified balance sheet at June 30, 1998.

LO 3   **Problem 3-3A** Transaction Analysis and Financial Statements

Dynamic Services Inc. was organized on March 1, 1998, by two former college roommates. The corporation will provide computer tax services to small businesses. The following transactions occurred during the first month of operations:

March 2:   Received contributions of $10,000 from each of the two principal owners in exchange for shares of stock.

March 7:   Signed a two-year promissory note at the bank and received cash of $7,500. Interest, along with the $7,500, will be repaid at the end of the two years.

March 12:   Purchased miscellaneous supplies on account for $350, payment due in 30 days.

March 19:   Billed a client $2,000 for tax-preparation services. According to an agreement between the two companies, the client is to pay 25% of the bill upon its receipt and the remaining balance within 30 days.

March 20:   Paid a $650 bill from the local newspaper for advertising for the month of March.

March 22:   Received 25% of the amount billed client on March 19.

March 26:   Received cash of $1,400 for services provided in assisting a client in preparing its tax return.

March 29:   Purchased a computer system for $4,000 in cash.

March 30:   Paid $1,650 in salaries and wages for March.

March 31:   Received and paid $700 of gas, electric, and water bills.

Required

1. Prepare a table to summarize the preceding transactions as they affect the accounting equation. Use the format in Exhibit 3-1. Identify each transaction with the date.
2. Prepare an income statement for the month ended March 31, 1998.
3. Prepare a classified balance sheet at March 31, 1998.
4. From reading the balance sheet you prepared in part 3, what events would you expect to take place in April? Explain your answer.

LO 3   **Problem 3-4A** Transactions Reconstructed From Financial Statements

The following financial statements are available for Oak Corporation for its first month of operations:

OAK CORPORATION
INCOME STATEMENT
FOR THE MONTH ENDED JULY 31, 1998

Service revenue		$75,400
Expenses:		
Rent	$ 6,000	
Salaries and wages	24,600	
Utilities	12,700	43,300
Net income		$32,100

OAK CORPORATION
BALANCE SHEET
JULY 31, 1998

ASSETS		LIABILITIES AND OWNERS' EQUITY	
Cash	$ 13,700	Wages payable	$ 6,000
Accounts receivable	25,700	Notes payable	50,000
Equipment	32,000	Unearned service revenue	4,500
Furniture	14,700	Capital stock	30,000
Land	24,000	Retained earnings	19,600
Total	$110,100	Total	$110,100

Required

Describe as many transactions as you can that were entered into by Oak Corporation during the first month of business.

Alternate Multi-Concept Problems

LO 1, 2 **Problem 3-5A** Identification of Events With Source Documents

Many events are linked to a source document. The following is a list of events that occurred in an entity:

a. Paid a security deposit and six months' rent on a building.

b. Hired three employees and agreed to pay them $400 per week.

c. Sold merchandise to a customer for cash.

d. Reported a fire that destroyed a billboard that is on the entity's property and is owned and maintained by another entity.

e. Received payment of bills from customers.

f. Purchased stock in another entity to gain some control over it.

g. Signed a note at the bank and received cash.

h. Contracted with a cleaning service to maintain the interior of the building in good repair. No money is paid at this time.

Required

For each item a through h, indicate whether the event should or should not be recorded in the entity's accounts. For each item that should be recorded in the entity's books:

1. Identify one or more source documents that are generated from the event.

2. Identify which source document would be used to record an event when it produces more than one source document.

3. For each document, identify the information that is most useful in recording the event in the accounts.

LO 3, 5 **Problem 3-6A** Accounts Used to Record Transactions

A list of accounts, with an identifying number for each, is shown below. Following the list of accounts is a series of transactions entered into by a company during its first year of operations.

Required

For each transaction, indicate the account or accounts that should be debited and credited.

1. Cash		**9.** Notes Payable	
2. Accounts Receivable		**10.** Capital Stock	
3. Prepaid Insurance		**11.** Retained Earnings	
4. Office Supplies		**12.** Service Revenue	
5. Automobiles		**13.** Wage and Salary Expense	
6. Land		**14.** Utilities Expense	
7. Accounts Payable		**15.** Income Tax Expense	
8. Income Tax Payable			

TRANSACTIONS	ACCOUNTS DEBITED	CREDITED
Example: Purchased office supplies for cash.	4	1
a. Issued capital stock for cash.		
b. Purchased an automobile and signed a 60-day note for the total amount.		
c. Acquired land in exchange for capital stock.		
d. Received cash from clients for services performed during the month.		
e. Paid employees salaries and wages earned during the month.		
f. Purchased flyers and signs from a printer, payment due in 10 days.		
g. Paid for the flyers and signs purchased in part f.		
h. Received monthly telephone bill; payment is due within 10 days of receipt.		
i. Paid for a six-month liability insurance policy.		
j. Paid monthly telephone bill.		
k. Computed amount of taxes due based on the income of the period and paid the amount.		

LO 3, 4, 5 **Problem 3-7A** Transaction Analysis and Journal Entries Recorded Directly in T Accounts

Three friends organized Rapid City Roller Rink on October 1, 1998. The following transactions occurred during the first month of operations:

October 1: Received contribution of $22,000 from each of the three principal owners of the new business in exchange for shares of stock.

October 2: Purchased land valued at $15,000 and a building valued at $75,000. The seller agreed to accept a down payment of $9,000 and a five-year promissory note for the balance.

October 3: Purchased new tables and chairs for the lounge at the roller rink at a cost of $25,000, paying $5,000 down and agreeing to pay for the remainder in 60 days.

October 9: Purchased 100 pairs of roller skates for cash at $35 per pair.

October 12: Purchased food and drinks for $2,500 on an open account. The company has 30 days to pay for the concession supplies.

October 13: Sold tickets for cash of $400 and took in $750 at the concession stand.

October 17: Rented out the roller rink to a local community group for $750. The community group is to pay one-half of the bill within 5 working days and has 30 days to pay the remainder.

October 23: Received 50% of the amount billed to the community group.

October 24: Sold tickets for cash of $500 and took in $1,200 at the concession stand.

October 26: The three friends, acting on behalf of Rapid City Roller Rink, paid a dividend of $250 on the shares of stock owned by each of them, or $750 in total.

October 27: Paid $1,275 for utilities.

October 30: Paid wages and salaries of $2,250.

October 31: Sold tickets for cash of $700 and took in $1,300 at the concession stand.

Required

1. Prepare a table to summarize the preceding transactions as they affect the accounting equation. Use the format in Exhibit 3-1. Identify each transaction with a date.

2. Record each transaction directly in T accounts, using the dates preceding the transactions to identify them in the accounts. Each account involved in the problem needs a separate T account.

LO 7 **Problem 3-8A** Trial Balance and Financial Statements
Refer to the table for Rapid City Roller Rink in part (1) of Problem 3-7A.

Required

1. Prepare a trial balance at October 31, 1998.
2. Prepare an income statement for the month ended October 31, 1998.
3. Prepare a statement of retained earnings for the month ended October 31, 1998.
4. Prepare a classified balance sheet at October 31, 1998.

General
Ledger

LO 3, 5, 6 **Problem 3-9A** Journal Entries
Castle Consulting Agency began business in February 1998. Listed below are the transactions entered into by Castle during its first month of operations.

a. Acquired articles of incorporation from the state and issued 10,000 shares of capital stock in exchange for $150,000 in cash.

b. Paid monthly rent of $400.

c. Signed a five-year promissory note for $100,000 at the bank.

d. Received $5,000 cash from a customer for services to be performed over the next two months.

e. Purchased software to be used on future jobs. The software costs $950 and is expected to be used on five to eight jobs over the next two years.

f. Billed customers $12,500 for work performed during the month.

g. Paid office personnel $3,000 for the month of February.

h. Received a utility bill of $100. The total amount is due in 30 days.

Required

Prepare in journal form the entry to record each transaction.

LO 3, 4, 5, 7 **Problem 3-10A** Journal Entries Recorded Directly in T Accounts
Refer to the transactions for Castle Consulting Agency in Problem 3-9A.

Required

1. Record each transaction directly in T accounts, using the letters preceding the transactions to identify them in the accounts. Each account involved in the problem needs a separate T account.

2. Prepare a trial balance at February 28, 1998.

LO 3, 4, 5, 7 **Problem 3-11A** Entries Prepared From a Trial Balance and Proof of the Cash Balance
Russell Company was incorporated on January 1, 1998, with the issuance of capital stock in return for $120,000 of cash contributed by the owners. The only other transaction entered into prior to beginning operations was the issuance of a $50,000 note payable in exchange for equipment and fixtures. The following trial balance was prepared at the end of the first month by the bookkeeper for Russell Company:

RUSSELL COMPANY
TRIAL BALANCE
JANUARY 31, 1998

ACCOUNT TITLES	DEBITS	CREDITS
Cash	$???	
Accounts Receivable	30,500	

Equipment and Fixtures	$ 50,000	
Wages Payable		$ 10,000
Notes Payable		50,000
Capital Stock		120,000
Service Revenue		60,500
Wage and Salary Expense	24,600	
Advertising Expense	12,500	
Rent Expense	5,200	

Required

1. Determine the balance in the Cash account.
2. Identify all of the transactions that affected the Cash account during the month. Use a T account to prove what the balance in Cash would be after all transactions are recorded.

General
Ledger

LO 3, 5, 6 **Problem 3-12A** Journal Entries

Overnight Delivery Inc. is incorporated on January 2, 1998, and enters into the following transactions during its second month of operations:

February 2: Paid $400 for wages earned by employees for the week ending January 31.

February 3: Paid $3,230 for gas and oil billed on an open account in January.

February 4: Declared and paid $2,000 cash dividends to stockholders.

February 15: Received $8,000 cash from customer accounts.

February 26: Provided $16,800 of services on account during the month.

February 27: Received a $3,400 bill from the local service station for gas and oil used during February.

Required

1. Prepare journal entries on the books of Overnight to record the transactions entered into during February.
2. For the transactions on February 2, 3, 4, and 27, indicate whether the amount is an expense of operating in the month of January or February or is not an expense in either month.

General
Ledger

LO 3, 5, 6 **Problem 3-13A** Journal Entries and a Balance Sheet

Krittersbegone Inc. was organized on July 1, 1998, by a group of technicians to provide termite inspections and treatment to homeowners and small businesses. The following transactions occurred during the first month of business:

July 2: Received contributions of $3,000 from each of the six owners in exchange for shares of stock.

July 3: Paid $1,000 rent for the month of July.

July 5: Purchased flashlights, tools, spray equipment, and ladders for $18,000, with a down payment of $5,000 and the balance due in 30 days.

July 17: Paid a $200 bill for the distribution of door-to-door advertising.

July 28: Paid August rent and July utilities to the landlord in the amounts of $1,000 and $450, respectively.

July 30: Received $8,000 in cash from homeowners for services performed during the month. In addition, billed $7,500 to other customers for services performed during the month. Billings are due in 30 days.

July 30: Paid commissions of $9,500 to the technicians for July.

July 31: Received $600 from a business client to perform services over the next two months.

Required

1. Prepare journal entries on the books of Krittersbegone to record the transactions entered into during the month.

2. Prepare a classified balance sheet dated July 31, 1998. From the balance sheet, what cash inflow and what cash outflow can you predict in the month of August? Who would be interested in the cash flow information and why?

Cases

Reading and Interpreting Financial Statements

LO 3, 5, 6 **Case 3-1** Reading and Interpreting Ben & Jerry's Statement of Cash Flows

Refer to Ben & Jerry's statement of cash flows for the year ended December 30, 1995.

Required

1. What amount did the company spend on additions to property, plant, and equipment during 1995? Prepare the journal entry to record these additions, assuming cash was paid.

2. What amount did the company receive from issuing common stock during 1995? Prepare the journal entry to record the issuance of stock. Do not be concerned at this point with the distinction between par value and additional paid-in capital on the balance sheet. This distinction will be explored in Chapter 11.

LO 1, 3, 5, 6 **Case 3-2** Reading and Interpreting United Airline's Balance Sheet

The following item appears in the current liabilities section of UAL Corporation's (the parent company for United Airlines) balance sheet at December 31, 1995:

Advance ticket sales $1,100 million

Required

1. What economic event caused United to incur this liability? Was it an external or an internal event?

2. Describe the effect on the accounting equation from the transaction to record advance ticket sales.

3. Assume that one customer purchases a $500 ticket in advance. Prepare the journal entry on United's books to record this transaction.

4. What economic event will cause United to reduce its liability for advance ticket sales? Is this an external or an internal event?

Making Financial Decisions

Decision
Making

LO 2, 3 **Case 3-3** Cash Flow Versus Net Income

Shelia Young started a real estate business in December of last year. After approval by the state for a charter to incorporate, she issued 1,000 shares of stock to herself and deposited $20,000 in a bank account under the name Young Properties. Because business was "booming," she spent all of her time during the first month selling properties rather than keeping financial records.

At the end of January, Shelia comes to you with the following plight:

I put $20,000 in to start this business last month. My January 31 bank statement shows a balance of $17,000. After all of my efforts, it appears as if I'm "in the hole" already! On the other hand, that seems impossible—we sold five properties for clients during the month. The total sales value of these properties was $600,000, and I receive a commission of 5% on each sale. Granted, one of the five sellers still owes me an $8,000 commission on the sale, but the other four have been collected in full. Three of the sales, totaling $400,000, were actually made by my assistants. I pay them 4% of the sales value of a property. Sure, I have a few office expenses for my car, utilities, and a secretary, but that's about it. How can I have possibly lost $3,000 this month?

You agree to help Shelia figure out how she really did this month. The bank statement is helpful. The total deposits during the month amount to $22,000. Shelia explains that this amount represents the commissions on the four sales collected so far. The canceled checks reveal the following expenditures:

CHECK NO.	PAYEE—MEMO AT BOTTOM OF CHECK	AMOUNT
101	Stevens Office Supply	$ 2,000
102	Why Walk, Let's Talk Motor Co.—new car	3,000
103	City of Westbrook—heat and lights	500
104	Alice Hill—secretary	2,200
105	Ace Property Management—office rent for month	1,200
106	Jerry Hayes (sales assistant)	10,000
107	Joan Harper (sales assistant)	6,000
108	Don's Fillitup - gas and oil for car	100

According to Shelia, the $2,000 check to Stevens Office Supply represents the down payment on a word processor and a copier for the office. The remaining balance is $3,000 and it must be paid to Stevens by February 15. Similarly, the $3,000 check is the down payment on a car for the business. A $12,000 note was given to the car dealer and is due along with interest in one year.

1. Prepare an income statement for the month of January for Young Properties.

2. Prepare a statement of cash flows for the month of January for Young Properties.

3. Draft a memorandum to Shelia Young explaining as simply and as clearly as possible why she *did* in fact have a profitable first month in business but experienced a decrease in her cash account. Support your explanation with any necessary figures.

4. The down payments on the car and the office equipment are reflected on the statement of cash flows. They are assets that will benefit the business for a number of years. Do you think that *any* of the cost associated with the acquisition of these assets should be recognized in some way on the income statement? Explain your answer.

LO 3, 5, 6, 7 **Case 3-4** Loan Request

Simon Fraser started a landscaping and lawn-care business in April 1998 by investing $20,000 cash in the business in exchange for capital stock. Because his business is in the Midwest, the season begins in April and concludes in September. He prepared the following trial balance (with accounts in alphabetical order) at the end of the first season in business.

Decision Making

FRASER LANDSCAPING
TRIAL BALANCE
SEPTEMBER 30, 1998

	DEBITS	CREDITS
Accounts Payable		$13,000
Accounts Receivable	$23,000	
Capital Stock		20,000
Cash	1,200	
Gas and Oil Expense	15,700	
Insurance Expense	2,500	
Landscaping Revenue		33,400
Lawn Care Revenue		24,000
Mowing Equipment	5,000	
Rent Expense	6,000	
Salaries Expense	22,000	
Truck	15,000	
Totals	$90,400	$90,400

Simon is pleased with his first year in business. "I paid myself a salary during the year of $22,000 and still have $1,200 in the bank. Sure, I have a few bills outstanding, but my accounts receivable will more than cover those." In fact, Simon is so happy with the first year, that he has come to you in your role as a lending officer at the local bank to ask for a $20,000 loan to allow him to add another truck and mowing equipment for the second season.

Required

1. From your reading of the trial balance, what does it appear to you that Simon did with the $20,000 in cash he originally contributed to the business? Reconstruct the journal entry to record the transaction you think took place.

2. Prepare an income statement for the six months ended September 30, 1998.

3. The mowing equipment and truck are assets that will benefit the business for a number of years. Do you think that any of the costs associated with the purchase of these assets should have been recognized as expenses in the first year? How would this have affected the income statement?

4. Prepare a classified balance sheet as of September 30, 1998. As a banker, what two items on the balance sheet concern you the most? Explain your answer.

5. As a banker, would you loan Simon $20,000 to expand his business during the second year? Draft a memo to respond to Simon's request for the loan, indicating whether you will make the loan.

Accounting and Ethics: What Would You Do?

LO 3, 5, 6 **Case 3-5** Delay in the Posting of a Journal Entry

As assistant controller for a small consulting firm, you are responsible for recording and posting the daily cash receipts and disbursements to the ledger accounts. After you have posted the entries, your boss, the controller, prepares a trial balance and the financial statements. You make the following entries on June 30, 1998:

1998			
June 30	Cash	1,430	
	Accounts Receivable	1,950	
	Service Revenue		3,380
	To record daily cash receipts.		
June 30	Advertising Expense	12,500	
	Utilities Expense	22,600	
	Rent Expense	24,000	
	Salary and Wage Expense	17,400	
	Cash		76,500
	To record daily cash disbursements.		

The daily cash disbursements are much larger on June 30 than any other day because many of the company's major bills are paid on the last day of the month. After you have recorded these two transactions and *before* you have posted them to the ledger accounts, your boss comes to you with the following request:

> As you are aware, the first half of the year has been a tough one for the consulting industry and for our business in particular. With first-half bonuses based on net income, I am concerned whether you or I will get any bonus this time around. However, I have a suggestion that should allow us to receive something for our hard work and at the same time will not hurt anyone. Go ahead and post the June 30 cash receipts to the ledger but don't bother to post that day's cash disbursements. Even though the treasurer writes the checks on the last day of the month and you normally journalize the transaction on the same day, it is pretty silly to bother posting the entry to the ledger since it takes at least a week for the checks to clear the bank.

Required

1. Explain *why* the controller's request will result in an increase in net income.

2. Do you agree with the controller that the omission of the entry on June 30 "will not hurt anyone"? If not, be explicit as to why you don't agree. Whom could it hurt?

3. What would you do? Whom should you talk to about this issue?

LO 5, 6 **Case 3-6** Debits and Credits

You are controller for an architectural firm whose accounting year ends on December 31. As part of the management team, your year-end bonus is directly related to the firm's earnings for the year. One of your duties is to review the journal entries recorded by the bookkeepers. A new bookkeeper prepared the following journal entry:

Dec. 3 Cash	10,000	
Service revenue		10,000
To record deposit from client.		

You notice that the explanation for the journal entry refers to the amount as a deposit and the bookkeeper explains to you that the firm plans to provide the services to the client in March of the following year.

1. Did the bookkeeper prepare the correct journal entry to account for the client's deposit? Explain your answer.

2. What would you do as controller for the firm? Do you have a responsibility to do anything to correct the books?

Research Case

Case 3-7 Ride Inc.

Snowboarding requires an ability to maneuver the slopes of mountains. Managing a snowboard company requires an ability to maneuver the ups and downs of economic conditions and changing consumer demand. Ride Inc., faces powerful marketplace forces on its revenues, expenses, product line, and company operations.

Conduct a search of the World Wide Web, obtain Ride's most recent annual report, or use library resources to obtain company financial data, and answer the following:

1. For the most recent year available, what is Ride Inc.'s, net income per share? How does this compare to the previous year?

2. What types of revenue and expense transactions might be part of Ride's operations that might not be typical in most other types of business? How might these transactions affect the company's net income per share?

3. Assume you are a manager for Ride Inc. What actions might be appropriate to address increased competition from other companies and other types of sports?

Optional Research. Conduct an interview of someone who participates in snowboarding, or seek out magazine advertisements for snowboarding products. Obtain information about Ride's product line, competitors, and methods to promote this sport. Does your research indicate that Ride maintains a unique edge in its markets?

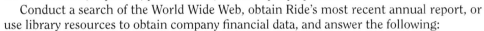

Solution to Key Terms Quiz

3 Event (p. 104)	**10** External event (p. 104)
5 Internal event (p. 104)	**14** Transaction (p. 104)
6 Source document (p. 104)	**11** Account (p. 110)
1 Chart of accounts (p. 110)	**12** General ledger (p. 111)
8 Debit (p. 113)	**4** Credit (p. 113)
16 Double entry system (p. 115)	**13** Journal (p. 117)
9 Posting (p. 117)	**7** Journalizing (p. 117)
15 General journal (p. 118)	**2** Trial Balance (p. 119)

Income Measurement and Accrual Accounting

STUDY LINKS

A Look at Previous Chapters

We focused our attention in Chapter 3 on how accounting information is processed. Debits and credits, journal entries, accounts, and trial balances were introduced as convenient tools to aid in the preparation of periodic financial statements.

A Look at This Chapter

We begin this chapter by considering the roles of recognition and measurement in the process of preparing financial statements. We explore in detail the accrual basis of accounting and its effect on the measurement of income. The recognition of revenues and expenses in an accrual system is examined, and we look at the role of adjusting entries in this process. In the appendix to this chapter, we see how the accountant uses work sheets to prepare financial statements.

A Look at Upcoming Chapters

Chapter 4 completes our overview of the accounting model. In the next section, we will examine accounting for the various types of assets. We begin by looking at accounting by merchandise companies in Chapter 5.

FOCUS ON FINANCIAL RESULTS

In its 1995 annual report, McDonald's Corporation calls itself the world's largest and best-known retailer in the food service industry. It boasts more than 18,000 restaurants in 89 countries and hopes to have 30,000 by the year 2000—not bad for a company that 40 years ago operated one drive-through restaurant.

Where does McDonald's get the revenues to fuel this growth? Its comparative income statements (excerpted here) show total revenues of approximately $9.8 billion in 1995 from two sources: sales by company-operated restaurants and revenues from franchised

McDonald's Corporation
Consolidated Statement of Income

(In millions of dollars, except per common share data)	Years ended December 31, 1995	1994	1993
Revenues			
Sales by Company-operated restaurants	**$6,863.5**	$5,792.6	$5,157.2
Revenues from franchised restaurants	**2,931.0**	2,528.2	2,250.9
Total revenues	**9,794.5**	8,320.8	7,408.1
Operating costs and expenses			
Company-operated restaurants			
Food and packaging	**2,319.4**	1,934.2	1,735.1
Payroll and other employee benefits	**1,730.9**	1,459.1	1,291.2
Occupancy and other operating expenses	**1,497.4**	1,251.7	1,138.3
	5,547.7	4,645.0	4,164.6
Franchised restaurants—occupancy expenses	**514.9**	435.5	380.4
General, administrative and selling expenses	**1,236.3**	1,083.0	941.1
Other operating (income) expense—net	**(105.7)**	(83.9)	(62.0)
Total operating costs and expenses	**7,193.2**	6,079.6	5,424.1
Operating income	**2,601.3**	2,241.2	1,984.0
Interest expense–net of capitalized interest of $22.5, $20.6 and $20.0	**340.2**	305.7	316.1
Nonoperating income (expense)—net	**(92.0)**	(48.9)	7.8
Income before provision for income taxes	**2,169.1**	1,886.6	1,675.7
Provision for income taxes	**741.8**	662.2	593.2
Net income	**$1,427.3**	$1,224.4	$1,082.5
Net income per common share	**$ 1.97**	$ 1.68	$ 1.45
Dividends per common share	**$ .26**	$ .23	$ .21

The accompanying Financial Comments are an integral part of the consolidated financial statements.

restaurants. Each type of restaurant contributes to corporate revenues differently.

At company-operated restaurants, revenues are generated directly by selling food. If you buy a hamburger, your payment increases the first line of the income statement. Two-thirds of McDonald's restaurants are franchised; their operators contract to pay McDonald's fees plus a share of their income for the right to operate as part of the chain. When you buy a hamburger at a franchise, that money adds to the revenues *of the franchise*. A designated portion of the franchisee's revenues is payable to McDonald's and increases the second line of its income statement.

Understanding how accountants measure income will help you to evaluate franchising as a source of income. How does franchising affect the timing of revenues and expenses? How does it affect profits? While studying this chapter, look for principles that suggest the answers.

SOURCE: *McDonald's Corporation Annual Report,* 1995.

After studying this chapter, you should be able to

LO 1 Explain the significance of recognition and measurement in the preparation and use of financial statements.

LO 2 Explain the differences between the cash and accrual bases of accounting.

LO 3 Describe the revenue recognition principle and explain its application in various situations.

LO 4 Describe the matching principle and the various methods for recognizing expenses.

LO 5 Identify the four major types of adjusting entries and prepare them for a variety of situations.

LO 6 Explain the steps in the accounting cycle and the significance of each step.

LO 7 Explain why and how closing entries are made at the end of an accounting period.

LO 8 Understand how to use a work sheet as a basis for preparing financial statements (Appendix 4A).

Recognition and Measurement in Financial Statements

LO 1 Explain the significance of recognition and measurement in the preparation and use of financial statements.

Accounting is a communication process. To successfully communicate information to the users of financial statements, accountants and managers must answer two questions: (1) What economic events should be communicated, or *recognized,* in the statements? and (2) How should the effects of these events be *measured* in the statements? The dual concepts of recognition and measurement are crucial to the success of accounting as a form of communication.

Recognition

"**Recognition** is the process of formally recording or incorporating an item into the financial statements of an entity as an asset, liability, revenue, expense, or the like. Recognition includes depiction of an item in both words and numbers, with the amount included in the totals of the financial statements."[1] We see in this definition the central idea behind general-purpose financial statements. They are a form of communication between the entity and external users. Stockholders, bankers, and other creditors have limited access to relevant information about a company. They depend on the periodic financial statements issued by management to provide the necessary information to make their decisions. Acting on behalf of management, accountants have a moral and ethical responsibility to provide users with financial information that will be useful in making their decisions. The process by which the accountant depicts, or describes, the effects of economic events on the entity is called *recognition.*

The items, such as assets, liabilities, revenues, and expenses, depicted in financial statements are *representations.* Simply stated, the accountant cannot show a stockholder or other user the company's assets, such as cash and buildings. What the user sees in a set of financial statements is a depiction of the real thing. That is, the accountant describes, with words and numbers, the various items in a set of financial statements. The system is imperfect at best and, for that reason, is always in the process of change. As society and the business environment have become more complex, the accounting profession has striven for ways to improve financial statements as a means of communicating with statement users.

Measurement

Accountants depict a financial statement item in both words and *numbers.* The accountant must *quantify* the effects of economic events on the entity. It is not enough to decide that an event is important and thus warrants recognition in the financial

---

[1]*Statement of Financial Accounting Concepts No. 5,* "Recognition and Measurement in Financial Statements of Business Enterprises" (Stamford, Conn.: Financial Accounting Standards Board, December 1984), par. 6.

statements. To be able to recognize it, the statement preparer must measure the financial effects of the event on the company.

Measurement of an item in financial statements requires that two choices be made. First, the accountant must decide on the *attribute* to be measured. Second, a scale of measurement, or *unit of measure,* must be chosen.

The Attribute to Be Measured Assume that a company holds a parcel of real estate as an investment. What attribute, or characteristic, of the property should be used to measure and thus recognize it as an asset on the balance sheet? The cost of the asset at the time it is acquired is the most logical choice. *Cost* is the amount of cash, or its equivalent, paid to acquire the asset. But how do we report the property on a balance sheet a year from now?

The simplest approach is to show the property on the balance sheet at its original cost, thus the designation historical cost. The use of historical cost is not only simple but also *verifiable.* Assume that two accountants are asked to independently measure the cost of the asset. After examining the sales contract for the land, they should arrive at the same amount.

An alternative to historical cost as the attribute to be measured is current value. Current value is the amount of cash, or its equivalent, that could be received currently from the sale of the asset. For the company's piece of property, current value is the *estimated* selling price of the land, reduced by any commissions or other fees involved in making the sale. But the amount is only an estimate, not an actual amount. If the company has not yet sold the property, how can we know for certain its selling price? We have to compare it to similar properties that *have* sold recently.

The choice between current value and historical cost as the attribute to be measured is a good example of the trade-off between *relevance* and *reliability.* As indicated earlier, historical cost is verifiable and is thus to a large extent a reliable measure. But is it as relevant to the needs of the decision makers as current value? Put yourself in the position of a banker trying to decide whether to lend money to the company. In evaluating the company's assets as collateral for the loan, is it more relevant to your decision to know what the firm paid for a piece of land 20 years ago or what it could be sold for today? But what *could* the property be sold for today? Two accountants might not necessarily arrive at the same current value for the land. Whereas value or selling price may be more relevant to your decision on the loan, the reliability of this amount is often questionable.

Because of its objective nature, historical cost is the attribute used to measure many of the assets recognized on the balance sheet. However, certain other attributes, such as current value, have increased in popularity in recent years. In other chapters of the book, we will discuss some of the alternatives to historical cost.

The Unit of Measure Regardless of the attribute of an item to be measured, it is still necessary to choose a yardstick or unit of measure. The yardstick we currently use is units of money. *Money* is something accepted as a medium of exchange or as a means of payment. The unit of money in the United States is the dollar. In Japan the medium of exchange is the yen, and in Great Britain it is the pound.

The use of the dollar as a unit of measure for financial transactions is widely accepted. The *stability* of the dollar as a yardstick is subject to considerable debate, however. Consider an example. You are thinking about buying a certain parcel of land. As part of your decision process, you measure the dimensions of the property and determine that the lot is 80 feet wide and 120 feet deep. Thus, the unit of measure used to determine the lot's size is the square foot. The company that owns the land offers to sell it for $10,000. Although the offer sounds attractive, you decide against the purchase today.

You return in one year to take a second look at the lot. You measure the lot again and, not surprisingly, find the width to still be 80 feet and the depth 120 feet. The owner is still willing to sell the lot for $10,000. This may appear to be the same price as last year. But the *purchasing power* of the unit of measure, the dollar, may very possibly have changed since last year. Even though the foot is a stable measuring unit, the dollar often is not. A *decline* in the purchasing power of the dollar is evidenced by a continuing *rise*

What events have economic consequences to a business? The destructive effects of a natural disaster, for example, will result in losses to buildings and other business assets. These losses will surely be reflected in the next year's financial statements of the affected companies—possibly in the income statement, as a downturn in revenues due to lost sales. What other financial statements would be affected by a big natural disaster?

in the general level of prices in an economy. For example, rather than paying $10,000 last year to buy the lot, you could have spent the $10,000 on other goods or services. However, a year later, the same $10,000 may very well not buy the same amount of goods and services.

Inflation, or a rise in the general level of prices in the economy, results in a decrease in purchasing power. In the past, the accounting profession has experimented with financial statements adjusted for the changing value of the dollar. As inflation has declined in recent years in the United States, the debate over the use of the dollar as a stable measuring unit has somewhat subsided.[2] It is still important to recognize the inherent weakness in the use of a measuring unit that is subject to change, however.

Summary of Recognition and Measurement in Financial Statements

The purpose of financial statements is to communicate various types of economic information about a company. The job of the accountant is to decide which information should be recognized in the financial statements and how the effects of that information on the entity should be measured. Exhibit 4-1 summarizes the role of recognition and measurement in the preparation of financial statements.

The Accrual Basis of Accounting

LO 2 Explain the differences between the cash and accrual bases of accounting.

The accrual basis of accounting is the foundation for the measurement of income in our modern system of accounting. The best way to understand the accrual basis is to compare it with the simpler cash approach.

Comparing the Cash and Accrual Bases of Accounting

The cash and accrual bases of accounting differ with respect to the *timing* of the recognition of revenues and expenses. For example, assume that on July 24, Barbara White, a salesperson for Spiffy House Painters, contracts with a homeowner to repaint a house for $1,000. A large crew comes in and paints the house the next day, July 25. The customer has 30 days from the day of completion of the job to pay and does, in fact, pay Spiffy on August 25. *When* should Spiffy recognize the $1,000 as revenue? As soon as the contract is signed on July 24? Or on July 25 when the work is done? Or on August 25 when the customer pays the bill?

In an income statement prepared on the **cash basis,** revenues are recognized when cash is *received.* Thus, on a cash basis, the $1,000 would not be recognized as revenue until the cash is collected, on August 25. On an **accrual basis,** revenue is recognized

EXHIBIT 4-1 Recognition and Measurement in Financial Statements

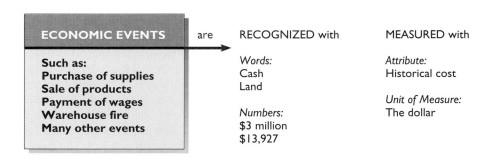

ECONOMIC EVENTS	are	RECOGNIZED with	MEASURED with
Such as:		*Words:*	*Attribute:*
Purchase of supplies		Cash	Historical cost
Sale of products		Land	
Payment of wages			*Unit of Measure:*
Warehouse fire		*Numbers:*	The dollar
Many other events		$3 million	
		$13,927	

[2]The rate of inflation in some countries, most noticeably those in South America, has far exceeded the rate in the United States. Companies operating in some of these countries with hyperinflationary economies are required to make adjustments to their statements.

when it is *earned.* On this basis, the $1,000 would be recognized as revenue on July 25, when the house is painted. This is the point at which the revenue is earned.

Recall from Chapter 3 the journal entry to recognize revenue before cash is received. Although cash has not yet been received, another account, Accounts Receivable, is recognized as an asset. This asset represents the right to receive cash in the future. The entry on completion of the job is as follows:

```
July 25   Accounts Receivable                    1,000
              Service Revenue                              1,000
          To recognize revenue from house painting.
```

Recall from Chapter 3 that the accounting equation must balance after each transaction is recorded. Throughout the remainder of the book, each time we record a journal entry, we illustrate the effect of the entry on the equation. The effect of the preceding entry on the equation is as follows:

Assets = **Liabilities** + **Owners' Equity**
+**1,000**   +**1,000**

At the time cash is collected, accounts receivable is reduced and cash is increased:

```
Aug. 25   Cash                                    1,000
              Accounts Receivable                          1,000
          To record cash received from house painting.
```

Assets = **Liabilities** + **Owners' Equity**
+**1,000**
−**1,000**

Assume that Barbara White is paid a 10% commission for all contracts and is paid on the 15th of the month following the month a house is painted. Thus, for this job, she will receive a $100 commission check on August 15. When should Spiffy recognize her commission of $100 as an expense? On July 24, when White gets the homeowner to sign a contract? When the work is completed, on July 25? Or on August 15, when she receives the commission check? Again, on a cash basis, commission expense would be recognized on August 15, when cash is *paid* to the salesperson. But on an accrual basis, expenses are recognized when they are *incurred.* In our example, the commission expense is incurred when the house is painted, on July 25.

Exhibit 4-2 summarizes the essential differences between recognition of revenues and expenses on a cash basis and recognition on an accrual basis.

What the Income Statement and the Statement of Cash Flows Reveal

Most business entities, other than the very smallest, use the accrual basis of accounting. Thus, the income statement reflects the accrual basis. Revenues are recognized when they are earned and expenses when they are incurred. At the same time, however, stockholders and creditors are also interested in information concerning the cash flows of an

EXHIBIT 4-2   Comparing the Cash and Accrual Bases of Accounting

	Cash Basis	Accrual Basis
Revenue is recognized	**When Received**	**When Earned**
Expense is recognized	**When Paid**	**When Incurred**

entity. The purpose of a statement of cash flows is to provide this information. Keep in mind that even though we present a statement of cash flows in a complete set of financial statements, the accrual basis is used for recording transactions and for preparing a balance sheet and an income statement.

Recall the example of Glengarry Health Club in Chapter 3. The club earned revenue from two sources, memberships and court fees. Both of these forms of revenue were recognized on the income statement presented in that chapter and reproduced in the top portion of Exhibit 4-3. Recall, however, that members have 30 days to pay and that, at the end of the first month of operation, only $4,000 of the membership fees of $15,000 had been collected.

Now consider the statement of cash flows for the first month of operation, partially reproduced in the bottom portion of Exhibit 4-3. Because we want to compare the income statement to the statement of cash flows, only the operating activities section of the statement is shown. (The investing and financing activities sections have been omitted from the statement.) Why is net income for the month a *positive* $7,000 but cash from operating activities a *negative* $4,000? Of the membership revenue of $15,000 reflected on the income statement, only $4,000 was collected in cash. Glengarry has accounts receivable for the other $11,000. Thus, cash from operating activities, as reflected on a statement of cash flows, is $11,000 *less* than net income of $7,000, or a negative $4,000. This is the reason that net income is adjusted downward by $11,000— to account for the fact that net income reflects $15,000 of sales but that only $4,000 of cash was collected, thus requiring an adjustment of $11,000.

The final portion of the exhibit provides a proof that cash from operating activities is a negative $4,000. Cash inflows and cash outflows are simply listed, with the result being an excess of cash outflows over inflows in the amount of $4,000. Note that the amount of cash listed as an inflow from membership fees is only $4,000, the amount collected.

Each of these two financial statements serves a useful purpose. The income statement reflects the revenues actually earned by the business, regardless of whether cash

---

EXHIBIT 4-3   Comparing the Income Statement and the Statement of Cash Flows

The **income statement** for Glengarry Health Club shows the following:

Revenues:		
Memberships	$15,000	
Court fees	5,000	$ 20,000
Expenses:		
Salaries and wages	$10,000	
Utilities	3,000	(13,000)
Net income		$ 7,000

A **partial statement of cash flows** for Glengarry Health Club shows the following:

Net income	$ 7,000
Adjustment to reconcile net income to net cash provided by operating activities:	
Increase in accounts receivable	(11,000)
Cash used by operating activities	$ (4,000)

Another way to look at the cash generated from operations:

Cash received from membership fees	$ 4,000	
Cash received from court fees	5,000	$ 9,000
Cash paid for:		
Salaries and wages	$10,000	
Utilities	3,000	(13,000)
Cash used by operating activities		$ (4,000)

has been collected. The statement of cash flows tells the reader about the actual cash inflows during a period of time. The need for the information provided by both statements is summarized by the Financial Accounting Standards Board as follows:

> Statements of cash flows commonly show a great deal about an entity's current cash receipts and payments, but a cash flow statement provides an incomplete basis for assessing prospects for future cash flows because it cannot show interperiod relationships. Many current cash receipts, especially from operations, stem from activities of earlier periods, and many current cash payments are intended or expected to result in future, not current, cash receipts. Statements of earnings and comprehensive income, especially if used in conjunction with statements of financial position, usually provide a better basis for assessing future cash flow prospects of an entity than do cash flow statements alone.[3]

Accrual Accounting and Time Periods

The *time period* assumption was introduced in Chapter 1. We assume that it is possible to prepare an income statement that fairly reflects the earnings of a business for a specific period of time, such as a month or a year. It is somewhat artificial to divide the operations of a business into periods of time as indicated on a calendar. The conflict arises because earning income is a *process* that takes place *over a period of time* rather than *at any one point in time*.

Consider an alternative to our present system of reporting on the operations of a business on a periodic basis. A new business begins operations with an investment of $50,000. The business operates for 10 years, during which time no records are kept other than a checkbook for the cash on deposit at the bank. At the end of the 10 years, the owners decide to go their separate ways and convert all of their assets to cash. They split among them the balance of $80,000 in the bank account. What is the profit of the business for the 10-year period? The answer is $30,000, the difference between the original cash of $50,000 contributed and the cash of $80,000 available at liquidation.

The point of this simple example is that we could be very precise and accurate in our measurement of the income of a business if it were not necessary to artificially divide operations according to a calendar. Stockholders, bankers, and other interested parties cannot wait until a business liquidates to make decisions, however. They need information on a periodic basis. Thus, the justification for the accrual basis of accounting lies in the needs of financial statement users for periodic information on the financial position as well as the profitability of the entity.

The Revenue Recognition Principle

"**Revenues** are inflows or other enhancements of assets of an entity or settlements of its liabilities (or a combination of both) from delivering or producing goods, rendering

LO 3 Describe the revenue recognition principle and explain its application in various situations.

ACCOUNTING FOR YOUR DECISIONS

You Are the Marketing Manager

The end of the year is fast approaching, and your department has not sold its quota of computers. As you understand the company's accounting policies, revenues are recorded when computers are ordered and shipped to customers. You know that if your department does not make its quota, then your job could be in jeopardy. So you get an idea. You call up some friends and tell them to order computers that they don't really need yet. In return, you'll get them a great price on the machines. Besides, if they don't want the computers, they can send them back in January and get a full refund. Meanwhile, you'll make your quota. Do you think there is anything wrong with this idea?

ANS: Yes, there is something wrong with the idea. For one thing, it is very poor business judgment to push products on customers if you believe they will be returned. Although many customers will say no to your idea, others will go along to get a lower price, only to later regret buying something they don't need. And if the computers are indeed returned in January, then the company's auditors will be obliged to indicate that the company has not followed generally accepted accounting, because the intent of the transaction was merely to boost sales in the current year. This short-cut is not only unethical but in violation of the revenue recognition principle.

---

[3]*SFAC No. 5*, par. 24c.

services, or other activities that constitute the entity's ongoing major or central operations."[4] Two points should be noted about this formal definition of revenues. First, an asset is not always involved when revenue is recognized. The recognition of revenue may result from the settlement of a liability rather than from the acquisition of an asset. Second, entities generate revenue in different ways: some companies produce goods, others distribute or deliver the goods to users, and still others provide some type of service.

On the accrual basis, revenues are recognized when earned. However, the **revenue recognition principle** involves two factors. Revenues are recognized in the income statement when they are both *realized* and *earned*.[5] Revenues are *realized* when goods or services are exchanged for cash or claims to cash.

Other Applications of the Revenue Recognition Principle

At what point are revenues realized and earned by an entity? As a practical rule, revenue is usually recognized at the time of sale. This is normally interpreted to mean at the time of delivery of the product or service to the customer. However, consider the following examples in which it is necessary either to modify or to interpret the meaning of the revenue recognition principle.

ACCOUNTING FOR YOUR DECISIONS
You Are the Stockholder

Assume that a construction company starts two projects during the year. One is a $5 million contract for a bridge. The other is a $4 million contract for a dam. Based on actual costs incurred to date and estimates of costs yet to be incurred, the contractor estimates that at the end of the year the bridge is 20% complete and the dam is 50% complete. Which would be more informative to you as a stockholder of the construction company: (1) an end-of-the-year report that indicates no revenue because no contracts are finished yet or (2) an end-of-the-year report that indicates revenue of $1 million on the bridge (20% of $5 million) and $2 million on the dam (50% of $4 million), both based on the extent of completion?

ANS: As a stockholder you need information on a timely basis to evaluate your various investments. The percentage-of-completion method will allow you to assess the profitability of your investment in the construction company on a regular basis rather than only at the point that projects are completed.

Long-Term Contracts The **percentage-of-completion method** allows a contractor to recognize revenue over the life of a project rather than at its completion. For long-term contracts in which the sales price is fixed by contract and in which the realization of revenue depends only on production, such as constructing the bridge or the dam (in the box above), the method is a reasonable alternative to deferring the recognition of revenue until the project is completed. The following excerpt from the 1995 annual report of CBI Industries Inc. is an example of how revenue is recognized by most companies in the construction industry:

> Revenues from Contracting Services are recognized on the percentage of completion method. Earned revenue is based on the percentage that incurred costs to date bear to total estimated costs after giving effect to the most recent estimates of total cost.

Franchises Over the last 30 years, franchising has achieved enormous popularity as a way to conduct business. It has been especially prevalent in retail sales, including the fast-food (McDonald's), motel (Holiday Inn), and car rental (Hertz) businesses. Typically, the franchisor grants the exclusive right to sell a product or service in a specific geographic area to the franchisee. As discussed in the chapter opener, a franchiser such as McDonald's generates revenues from one or both of two sources: (1) from the sale of the franchise and related services, such as help in selecting a site and hiring employees and

---

[4]*Statement of Financial Accounting Concepts No. 6*, "Elements of Financial Statements" (Stamford, Conn.: Financial Accounting Standards Board, December 1985), par. 78.

[5]An alternative is to recognize revenues when they are *realizable* and earned. *Realizable* has a slightly different meaning, which will be explained later when we look at commodities.

(2) from continuing fees based on performance, for example, a fixed percentage of sales by the franchisee. The following excerpt from the 1995 annual report of McDonald's Corp. indicates the typical arrangement the company has with its franchisees:

> Franchising is our most widely used and effective way to grow the business. About 66 percent of our restaurants are franchised to about 4,500 owner/operators around the world. We share the initial investment—the franchisee purchases the equipment, signs and seating, while the Company owns or controls the land and building. Over the term of the franchise agreement, the Company receives rent and service fee income based on a percentage of sales.

At what point should the revenue from the sale of a franchise be recognized? An FASB standard allows a franchisor to recognize initial franchise fees as revenue only when it has made "substantial performance" of its obligations and when collection of the fee is reasonably assured.[6] An excerpt from the 1995 annual report of Ben & Jerry's Homemade Inc. indicates how one company recognizes the initial franchise fee as revenue:

> *Revenue Recognition*
> The Company recognizes franchise fees as income for individual stores when services required by the franchise agreement have been substantially performed and the store opens for business. Franchise fees relating to area franchise agreements are recognized in proportion to the number of stores for which the required services have been substantially performed. Franchise fees recognized as income were approximately $166,000, $82,000, and $103,000 in 1995, 1994 and 1993, respectively. These amounts have been included in net sales.

Commodities Corn, wheat, gold, silver, and other agricultural and mining products trade on the open market at established prices. Readily convertible assets such as these are interchangeable and can be sold at a quoted price in an active market that can absorb the quantity being sold without significantly affecting the price.[7] Earlier we mentioned that to be recognized, revenues must be realized. An acceptable alternative is to recognize revenues when they are realizable. Revenues are *realizable* when assets received or held are readily convertible to known amounts of cash or claims to cash.

Assume that a company mines gold. Revenues are realizable by the company at the time the product is mined because each ounce of gold is interchangeable with another ounce of gold and the commodities market can absorb all of the gold the company sells without having an effect on the price. This is one of the few instances in which it is considered acceptable to recognize revenue *prior* to the point of sale. The exception is justified because the important event in the revenue-generation process is the *production* of the gold, not the sale of it. The **production method** of recognizing revenue is used for precious metals, as well as certain agricultural products and marketable securities.

Installment Sales Various consumer items, such as automobiles, appliances, and even vacation properties, are sold on an installment basis. A down payment is followed by a series of monthly payments over a period of years. Default on the payments and repossession of the item by the seller are more common in these types of sales than with most other arrangements. For this reason, it is considered acceptable, in limited circumstances, to defer the recognition of revenue on an installment sale until cash is actually collected. The **installment method,** which is essentially a cash basis of accounting, is acceptable only when the seller has no reasonable basis for estimating the degree of collectibility. Note that the production and installment methods are at opposite ends of the spectrum. Under the production method, revenue is recognized *before* a sale takes place; with the installment method, revenue is recognized *after* the sale.

Rent and Interest In some cases, revenue is earned *continuously* over time. In these cases, a product or service is not delivered at a specific point in time; instead, the earnings process takes place with the passage of time. Rent and interest are two examples. Interest is the cost associated with the use of someone else's money. When should a bank recognize the interest earned from granting a 90-day loan? Even though the

FROM CONCEPT TO PRACTICE 4.1
READING MCDONALD'S INCOME STATEMENT Refer to McDonald's comparative income statements for 1995, 1994 and 1993 in the chapter opener. What percentage of total revenues were derived from franchised restaurants? Has this percentage changed over the three year period?

[6]*Statement of Financial Accounting Standards No. 45,* "Accounting for Franchise Fee Revenue" (Stamford, Conn.: Financial Accounting Standards Board, December 1981), par. 5.
[7]*SFAC No. 5,* par. 83a.

interest may not be received until the loan itself is repaid, interest is earned every day the loan is outstanding. We will look at the process for recognizing interest earned but not yet received later in the chapter. The same procedure is used to recognize revenue from rent that is earned but uncollected.

Long-term contracts, franchises, commodities, installment sales, rent, and interest are not the only situations in which the revenue recognition principle must be interpreted. The intent in examining these particular examples was to help you think about the variety of ways in which businesses generate revenue and about the need to apply judgment in deciding when to recognize revenue. These examples should help you to realize the subjective nature of the work of an accountant and to understand that the discipline is not as precise as it may sometimes seem.

Expense Recognition and the Matching Principle

LO 4 Describe the matching principle and the various methods for recognizing expenses.

Companies incur a variety of costs. A new office building is constructed. Inventory is purchased. Employees perform services. The electric meter is read. In each of these situations, the company incurs a cost, regardless of when it pays cash. Conceptually, *any time a cost is incurred, an asset is acquired.* However, according to the definition in Chapter 1, an asset represents a future economic benefit. An asset ceases being an asset and becomes an expense when the economic benefits from having incurred the cost have expired. Assets are unexpired costs, and expenses are expired costs.

At what point do costs expire and become expenses? The expense recognition principle requires that we recognize expenses in different ways, depending on the nature of the cost. The ideal approach to recognizing expenses is to match them with revenues. Under the matching principle, the accountant attempts to associate revenues of a period with the costs necessary to generate those revenues. For certain types of expenses, a direct form of matching is possible; for others, it is necessary to associate costs with a particular period. The classic example of direct matching is cost of goods sold expense with sales revenue. Cost of goods sold is the cost of the inventory associated with a particular sale. A cost is incurred and an asset is recorded when the inventory is purchased. The asset, inventory, becomes an expense when it is sold. Another example of a cost that can be matched directly with revenue is commissions. The commission paid to a salesperson can be matched directly with the sale.

An indirect form of matching is used to recognize the benefits associated with certain types of costs, most noticeably long-term assets, such as buildings and equipment. These costs benefit many periods, but usually it is not possible to match them directly with a specific sale of a product. Instead, they are matched with the periods during which they will provide benefits. For example, an office building may be useful to a company for 30 years. *Depreciation* is the process of allocating the cost of a tangible long-term asset to its useful life. Depreciation Expense is the account used to recognize this type of expense.

The benefits associated with the incurrence of certain other costs are treated in accounting as expiring simultaneously with their acquisition. The justification for this treatment is that no future benefits from the incurrence of the cost are discernible. This is true of most selling and administrative costs. For example, the costs of heat and light in a building benefit only the current period and therefore are recognized as expenses as soon as the costs are incurred. Likewise, income taxes incurred during the period do not benefit any period other than the current period and are thus written off as an expense in the period incurred.

The relationships among costs, assets, and expenses are depicted in Exhibit 4-4 using three examples. First, costs incurred for purchases of merchandise result in an asset, Merchandise Inventory, and are eventually matched with revenue at the time the product is sold. Second, costs incurred for office space result in an asset, Office Building, which is recognized as Depreciation Expense over the useful life of the building. Third, the cost of heating and lighting benefits only the current period and is thus recognized immediately as Utilities Expense.

According to the FASB, expenses are "outflows or other using up of assets or incurrences of liabilities (or a combination of both) from delivering or producing goods, rendering services, or carrying out other activities that constitute the entity's ongoing major or central operations."[8] The key point to note about expenses is that they come about in two different ways: from the use of an asset or from the recognition of a liability. For example, when a retailer sells a product, the asset sacrificed is inventory. Cost of Goods Sold is the expense account that is debited when the Inventory account is credited. As we will see in the next section, the incurrence of an expense may result in a liability.

Accrual Accounting and Adjusting Entries

The accrual basis of accounting necessitates a number of adjusting entries at the end of a period. **Adjusting entries** are the journal entries the accountant makes at the end of a period for a company on the accrual basis of accounting. *Adjusting entries are not needed if a cash basis is used. It is the very nature of the accrual basis that results in the need for adjusting entries.* The frequency of the adjustment process depends on how often financial statements are prepared. Most businesses make adjustments at the end of each month.

LO 5 Identify the four major types of adjusting entries and prepare them for a variety of situations.

Types of Adjusting Entries

Why are there four basic types, or categories, of adjusting entries? The answer lies in the distinction between the cash and the accrual bases of accounting. On an accrual basis, *revenue* can be earned either *before* or *after* cash is received. *Expenses* can be incurred either *before* or *after* cash is paid. Each of these four distinct situations requires a different type of adjustment at the end of the period. We will consider each of the four categories and look at some examples of each.

(1) Cash Paid before Expense Is Incurred (Deferred Expense) Assets are often acquired before their actual use in the business. Insurance policies typically are prepaid, as often is rent. Office supplies are purchased in advance of their use, as are

---

EXHIBIT 4-4   Relationships Among Costs, Assets, and Expenses

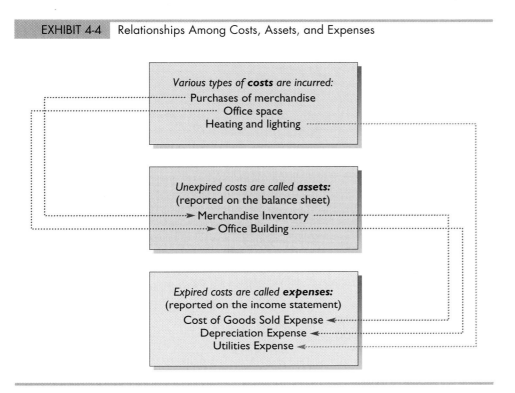

---

[8]*SFAC No. 6,* par. 80.

all types of property and equipment. Recall from our earlier discussion that unexpired costs are assets. As the costs expire and the benefits are used up, the asset must be written off and replaced with an expense.

Assume that on September 1 a company prepays $2,400 in rent on its office space for the next 12 months. The entry to record the prepayment follows:

Sept. 1   Prepaid Rent   2,400
            Cash   2,400
            To prepay the rent on office space for 12 months.

Assets = **Liabilities** + **Owners' Equity**
+2,400
−2,400

An asset account, Prepaid Rent, is recorded because the company will receive benefits over the next 12 months. Because the rent is for a 12-month period, $200 of benefits from the asset expires at the end of each month. The adjusting entry at the end of September to record this expiration accomplishes two purposes: (1) it recognizes the reduction in the asset Prepaid Rent and (2) it recognizes the expense associated with using up the benefits for one month. From the last chapter you should recall that an asset is decreased with a credit and that an expense is increased with a debit, as follows:

Sept. 30   Rent Expense   200
            Prepaid Rent   200
            To recognize $200 of rent expense for the month.

Assets = **Liabilities** + **Owners' Equity**
−200   **−200**

T accounts are an invaluable aid in understanding adjusting entries. They allow us to focus on the transactions and balances that will be included in the more formal general ledger accounts. The T accounts for Prepaid Rent and Rent Expense appear as follows after posting the original entry on September 1 and the adjusting entry on September 30:

PREPAID RENT				RENT EXPENSE	
9/1	2,400			9/30	200
		200	9/30		
Bal.	2,200				

The balance in Prepaid Rent represents the unexpired benefits from the prepayment of rent for the remaining 11 months: $200 × 11 = $2,200. The Rent Expense account reflects the expiration of benefits during the month of September.

As discussed earlier in the chapter, depreciation is the process of allocating the cost of a long-term tangible asset over its estimated useful life. The accountant does not attempt to measure the decline in *value* of the asset but simply tries to allocate its cost over its useful life. Thus, the adjustment for depreciation is similar to the one we made for rent expense. Assume that on January 1 a company buys a delivery truck, for which it pays $21,000. The entry to record the purchase is as follows:

Jan. 1   Delivery Truck   21,000
            Cash   21,000
            To record purchase of delivery truck for cash.

Assets = **Liabilities** + **Owners' Equity**
+21,000
−21,000

Two estimates must be made in depreciating the delivery truck: (1) the useful life of the asset and (2) the salvage value of the truck at the end of its useful life. Estimated salvage value is the amount a company expects to be able to receive when it sells an asset at the end of its estimated useful life. Assume a five-year estimated life for the truck and an estimated salvage value of $3,000 at the end of that time. Thus, the *depreciable cost* of the truck is $21,000 – $3,000, or $18,000. In a later chapter, we will consider alternative methods for allocating the depreciable cost over the useful life of an asset. For now, we will use the simplest approach, called the straight-line method, which assigns an equal amount of depreciation to each period. The monthly depreciation is found by dividing the depreciable cost of $18,000 over the estimated useful life of 60 months, which equals $300 per month.

The adjustment to recognize depreciation is conceptually the same as the adjustment to write off Prepaid Rent. That is, the asset account is reduced, and an expense is recognized. However, accountants normally use a contra account to reduce the total amount of long-term tangible assets by the amount of depreciation. A contra account has a balance that is the opposite of the balance in its related account. For example, Accumulated Depreciation is used to record the decrease in a long-term asset for depreciation and thus it carries a credit balance. An *increase* in Accumulated Depreciation is recorded with a *credit* because we want to *decrease* the amount of assets and assets are *decreased* by a *credit*. The entry to record depreciation at the end of January is as follows:

Jan. 31   Depreciation Expense   300
        Accumulated Depreciation   300
        To record depreciation on delivery truck.

Assets	**=**	**Liabilities**	**+**	**Owners' Equity**
–300				**–300**

Why do companies use a contra account for depreciation rather than simply reducing the long-term asset directly? If the asset account were reduced each time depreciation is recorded, its original cost would not be readily determinable from the accounting records. Businesses need to know the original cost of each asset, for various reasons. One of the most important of these reasons is the need to know historical cost for computation of depreciation for tax purposes.

The T accounts for Delivery Truck, Accumulated Depreciation, and Depreciation Expense show the following balances at the end of the first month:

DELIVERY TRUCK		**DEPRECIATION EXPENSE**	
1/1 21,000		1/31 300	

ACCUMULATED DEPRECIATION	
	300 1/31

On a balance sheet prepared on January 31, the contra account is shown as a reduction in the carrying value of the truck:

Delivery Truck	$21,000	
Less: Accumulated Depreciation	300	$20,700

(2) Cash Received before Revenue Is Earned (Deferred Revenue)   You
can benefit greatly in your study of accounting by recognizing its *symmetry*. By this we mean that one company's asset is another company's liability. In the earlier example

A gift certificate like this is a good example of a deferred revenue. Barnes & Noble has received the $20 in payment for the certificate but, because it must wait for the recipient of the gift to pick out a book, it considers the obligation to deliver the book in the future a liability.

involving the rental of office space, a second company, the landlord, received the cash paid by the first company, the tenant. At the time cash is received, the landlord has a liability because it has taken cash from the tenant but has not yet performed the service to earn the revenue. The revenue will be earned with the passage of time. This is the entry on the books of the landlord on September 1:

Sept. 1	Cash	2,400	
	Rent Collected in Advance		2,400
	To record receipt of rent on office space for 12 months.		

Assets	=	Liabilities	+	Owners' Equity
+2,400		+2,400		

The account Rent Collected in Advance is a liability. The landlord is obligated to provide the tenant uninterrupted use of the office facilities for the next 12 months. With the passage of time, the liability is satisfied as the tenant is provided the use of the space. The adjusting entry at the end of each month accomplishes two purposes: it recognizes (1) the reduction in the liability and (2) the revenue earned each month as the tenant occupies the space. Recall that we decrease a liability with a debit and increase revenue with a credit:

Sept. 30	Rent Collected in Advance	200	
	Rent Revenue		200
	To recognize rent earned for the month.		

Assets	=	Liabilities	+	Owners' Equity
		−200		+200

The balance in Rent Collected in Advance reflects the remaining liability, and the balance in the Rent Revenue account indicates the amount earned for the month:

RENT COLLECTED IN ADVANCE				RENT REVENUE		
		2,400	9/1		200	9/30
9/30	200					
		2,200	Bal.			

In another example, many magazine subscriptions require the customer to pay in advance. For example, you pay $12 for a one-year subscription to your favorite magazine, and the publisher in turn sends you 12 monthly issues. At the time you send money to the publisher, it incurs a liability. It has taken your money but has not yet done anything to earn it. The publisher has an obligation either to provide you with the magazine over the next 12 months or to refund your $12.

At what point should the publisher recognize revenue from magazine sales? The publisher receives cash at the time the subscription is sold. The revenue has not been *earned* until the company publishes the magazine and mails it to you, however. Thus, a publisher usually recognizes revenue at the time of delivery. An excerpt from the 1995 annual report of Time Warner Inc. (the publisher of such popular magazines as *Time, People,* and *Sports Illustrated*) reflects this policy:

> The unearned portion of subscriptions is deferred until magazines are delivered to subscribers. Upon each delivery, a proportionate share of the gross subscription price is included in revenues.

Assume that on March 1 Time Warner sells 500 one-year subscriptions to a monthly magazine at a price of $12 each. The entry to record the receipt of cash from the 500 subscribers is as follows:

Mar. 1   Cash   6,000
               Subscriptions Collected in Advance   6,000
               To record receipt of cash from sale of 500 one-year
               subscriptions at $12 each.

                  Assets = Liabilities + Owners' Equity
                  +6,000   +6,000

Assuming that each of the subscriptions starts with the March issue of the magazine, Time Warner accountants would make the following entry at the end of the month:

Mar. 31   Subscriptions Collected in Advance   500
                Subscription Revenue   500
                To recognize subscriptions earned for the month.

                  Assets = Liabilities + Owners' Equity
                                  -500   +500   Revenue of 500 × $1

The Subscriptions Collected in Advance and Subscription Revenue accounts appear as follows after posting the two entries:

SUBSCR. COLLECTED IN ADVANCE				SUBSCRIPTION REVENUE	
		6,000	3/1	500	3/31
3/31	500				
		5,500	Bal.		

As you know by now, accounting terminology differs among companies. The account title Subscriptions Collected in Advance is only one of any number of possible titles for the liability related to subscriptions. For example, this same account on Time Warner's balance sheet is called Unearned Portion of Paid Subscriptions.

ACCOUNTING FOR YOUR DECISIONS
You Are the Banker

A new midwestern publisher comes to you for a loan. Through an aggressive ad campaign, the company sold a phenomenal number of subscriptions to a new sports magazine in its first six months and needs additional money to go national. The first issue of the magazine is due out next month. The publisher presents you an income statement for its first six months and you notice that it includes all of the revenue from the initial subscriptions sold in the Midwest. What concerns do you have?

ANS: First, the accounting treatment for the magazine revenue is improper. Because the magazine has not yet been delivered to the customer, the subscriptions have not yet been earned, and therefore no revenue should be recognized. As a banker, you should be sufficiently concerned that a potential customer would present improper financial statements and deny the loan on that basis alone. That does not even take into account the fact that the company has yet to establish a sufficient track record to warrant the credit risk.

(3) Expense Incurred before Cash Is Paid (Accrued Liability)   This situation is just the opposite of (1). That is, cash is paid *after* an expense is actually incurred rather than *before* its incurrence, as was the case in (1). Many normal operating costs, such as payroll and utilities, fit this situation. The utility bill is received at the end of the

month, but the company has 10 days to pay it. Or consider the biweekly payroll for Jones Corporation. The company pays a total of $28,000 in wages on every other Friday. Assume that the last payday was Friday, May 31. The next two paydays will be Friday, June 14, and Friday, June 28. The journal entry will be the same on each of these paydays:

June 14	Wages Expense	28,000	
(and	Cash		28,000
June 28)	To pay the biweekly payroll.		

Assets	=	**Liabilities**	+	**Owners' Equity**
−28,000				**−28,000**

On a balance sheet prepared as of June 30, a liability must be recognized. Even though the next payment is not until July 12, Jones *owes* employees wages for the last two days of June and must recognize an expense for the wages earned by employees for these two days. We will assume that the company operates seven days a week and that the daily cost is 1/14th of the biweekly amount of $28,000, or $2,000. In addition to recognizing a liability on June 30, Jones must adjust the records to reflect an expense associated with the cost of wages for the last two days of the month:

June 30	Wages Expense	4,000	
	Wages Payable		4,000
	To record wages for last two days of the month.		

Assets	=	**Liabilities**	+	**Owners' Equity**
		+4,000		**−4,000**

What entry will be made on the next payday, July 12? Jones will need to eliminate the liability of $4,000 for the last two days of wages recorded on June 30 because the amount has now been paid. An additional $24,000 of expense has been incurred for the $2,000 cost per day associated with the first 12 days in July. Finally, cash is reduced for $28,000, which represents the biweekly payroll. The entry recorded is:

July 12	Wages Payable	4,000	
	Wages Expense	24,000	
	Cash		28,000
	To pay the biweekly payroll.		

Assets	=	**Liabilities**	+	**Owners' Equity**
−28,000		**−4,000**		**−24,000**

The following time line illustrates the amount of expense incurred in each of the two months, June and July, for the biweekly payroll:

2 days' expense in June: $4,000		12 days' expense in July: $24,000	
Friday, June 28: Last payday	Friday, June 30: End of accounting period	Friday, July 12: Next payday	

Another typical expense incurred before the payment of cash is interest. In many cases, the interest on a short-term loan is repaid with the amount of the loan, called the *principal,* on the maturity date. For example, Granger Company takes out a 9%, 90-day, $20,000 loan with its bank on March 1. The principal and interest will be repaid on May 30. The entry on Granger's books on March 1 follows:

Mar. 1	Cash	20,000	
	Notes Payable		20,000
	To record issuance of 9%, 90-day, $20,000 note.		

Assets	=	**Liabilities**	+	**Owners' Equity**
+20,000		**+20,000**		

The basic formula for computing interest follows:

$$I = P \times R \times T,$$

where I = The dollar amount of interest
P = The principal amount of the loan
R = The annual rate of interest as a percentage
T = Time in years (often stated as a fraction of a year).

The total interest on Granger's loan is as follows:

$$\$20,000 \times .09 \times 3/12 = \underline{\$450}$$

Therefore, the amount of interest that must be recognized as expense at the end of March is one-third of \$450 because one month of a total of three has passed. Alternatively, the formula for finding the total interest on the loan can be modified to compute the interest for one month:[9]

$$\$20,000 \times .09 \times 1/12 = \underline{\$150}$$

The adjusting entry for the month of March is as follows:

Mar. 31	Interest Expense	150	
	Interest Payable		150
	To record interest for one month on a 9%, $20,000 loan.		

Assets	=	**Liabilities**	+	**Owners' Equity**
		+150		**−150**

The same adjusting entry is also made at the end of April:

Apr. 30	Interest Expense	150	
	Interest Payable		150
	To record interest for one month on a 9%, $20,000 loan.		

Assets	=	**Liabilities**	+	**Owners' Equity**
		+150		**−150**

The entry on Granger's books on May 30 when it repays the principal and interest is as follows:

May 30	Interest Payable	300	
	Interest Expense	150	
	Notes Payable	20,000	
	Cash		20,450
	To record payment of 9%, 90-day, $20,000 loan with interest.		

Assets	=	**Liabilities**	+	**Owners' Equity**
−20,450		**−20,300**		**−150**

The reduction in Interest Payable eliminates the liability recorded at the end of March and April. The recognition of \$150 in Interest Expense is the cost associated with the month of May.[10] The reduction in Cash represents the \$20,000 of principal and the total interest of \$450 for three months.

(4) Revenue Earned before Cash Is Received (Accrued Asset)

Revenue is sometimes earned before the receipt of cash. Rent and interest are both earned with the passage of time and require an adjustment if cash has not yet been received. For

[9]In practice, interest is calculated on the basis of days rather than months. For example, the interest for March would be $20,000 × .09 × 30/365, or $147.95, to reflect 30 days in the month out of a total of 365 days in the year. The reason the number of days in March is 30 rather than 31 is because in computing interest, businesses normally count the day a note matures but not the day it is signed. To simplify the calculations, we will use months, even though the result is slightly inaccurate.

[10]This assumes that Granger did not make a separate entry prior to this to recognize interest expense for the month of May. If a separate entry had been made, a debit of $450 would be made to Interest Payable.

example, assume that Grand Management Company rents warehouse space to a number of tenants. Most of its contracts call for prepayment of rent for six months at a time. Its agreement with one tenant, however, allows the tenant to pay Grand $2,500 in monthly rent anytime within the first 10 days of the following month. The adjusting entry on Grand's books at the end of April, the first month of the agreement, is as follows:

Apr. 30	Rent Receivable	2,500	
	Rent Revenue		2,500
	To record rent earned for the month of April.		

Assets	=	Liabilities	+	Owners' Equity
+2,500				+2,500

When the tenant pays its rent on May 7, the effect on Grand's books is as follows:

May 7	Cash	2,500	
	Rent Receivable		2,500
	To record rent collected for the month of April.		

Assets	=	Liabilities	+	Owners' Equity
+2,500				
−2,500				

Although we used the example of rent to illustrate this category, the membership revenue of Glengarry Health Club in Chapter 3 also could be used as an example. Whenever a company records revenue before cash is received, some type of receivable is increased and revenue is also increased. In that chapter, the health club earned membership revenue even though members had until the following month to pay their dues.

Accruals and Deferrals

One of the challenges in learning accounting concepts is to gain an understanding of the terminology. Part of the difficulty stems from the alternative terms used by different accountants to mean the same thing. For example, the asset created when insurance is paid for in advance is termed a *prepaid asset* by some and a *prepaid expense* by others. Someone else might refer to it as a *deferred expense*.

We will use the term deferral to refer to a situation in which cash has been either paid or received but the expense or revenue has been deferred to a later time. A deferred expense indicates that cash has been paid but the recognition of expense has been deferred. Because a deferred expense represents a *future benefit* to a company, it is an *asset*. An alternative name for deferred expense is *prepaid expense*. Prepaid insurance and office supplies are deferred expenses. An adjusting entry is made periodically to record the portion of the deferred expense that has expired. A deferred revenue means that cash has been received, but the recognition of any revenue is deferred until a later time. Because a deferred revenue represents an *obligation* to a company, it is a *liability*. An alternative name for deferred revenue is *unearned revenue*. Rent collected in advance is deferred revenue. The periodic adjusting entry recognizes the portion of the deferred revenue that is earned in that period.

In this chapter, we have discussed in detail the accrual basis of accounting, which involves recognizing changes in resources and obligations as they occur, not simply when cash changes hands. More specifically, we will use the term accrual to refer to a situation in which no cash has been paid or received yet but it is necessary to recognize, or accrue, an expense or a revenue. An accrued liability is recognized at the end of the period in cases in which an expense has been incurred but cash has not yet been paid. Wages payable and interest payable are examples of accrued liabilities. An accrued asset is recorded when revenue has been earned but cash has not yet been collected. Rent receivable is an accrued asset.

Summary of Adjusting Entries

The four types of adjusting entries are summarized in Exhibit 4-5. Common examples of each are shown, along with the structure of the entries associated with the four

EXHIBIT 4-5 | Accruals and Deferrals

TYPE	SITUATION	EXAMPLES	ENTRY DURING PERIOD	ENTRY AT END OF PERIOD
Deferred expense	Cash paid before expense is incurred	Insurance policy Supplies Rent Buildings, equipment	Asset Cash	Expense Asset
Deferred revenue	Cash received before revenue is earned	Deposits, rent Subscriptions Gift certificates	Cash Liability	Liability Revenue
Accrued liability	Expense incurred before cash is paid	Salaries, wages Interest Taxes Rent	No Entry	Expense Liability
Accrued asset	Revenue earned before cash is received	Interest Rent	No Entry	Asset Revenue

categories. Finally, the following generalizations should help you in gaining a better understanding of adjusting entries and how they are used:

1. An adjusting entry is an internal transaction. It does not involve another entity.
2. Because it is an internal transaction, an adjusting entry *never* involves an increase or decrease in Cash.
3. At least one balance sheet account and one income statement account are involved in an adjusting entry. It is the nature of the adjustment process that an asset or liability account is adjusted with a corresponding change in either a revenue or an expense account.

Comprehensive Example of Adjusting Entries

We will now consider a comprehensive example involving the transactions for the first month of operations and the end-of-period adjusting entries for a hypothetical business, Duffy Transit Company. The trial balance in Exhibit 4-6 was prepared after posting to the accounts the transactions entered into during the first month of business. As discussed in Chapter 3, a trial balance can be prepared at any point in time. Because the trial balance is prepared *before* taking into account adjusting entries, it is called an *unadjusted* trial balance. This is the first month of operations for Duffy. Thus, the Retained Earnings account does not yet appear on the trial balance. After the first month, this account will have a balance and will appear on subsequent trial balances.

Duffy wants to prepare a balance sheet at the end of January and an income statement for its first month of operations. Use of the accrual basis necessitates a number of adjusting entries to update certain asset and liability accounts and to recognize the correct amounts for the various revenues and expenses.

Using a Trial Balance to Prepare Adjusting Entries

A trial balance is an important tool to use in preparing adjusting entries. The deferred expenses on Duffy's trial balance, such as Prepaid Insurance, must be reduced with a corresponding increase in expense. Similarly, any deferred revenues, such as Discount Tickets Sold in Advance, must be adjusted and a corresponding amount of revenue recognized. In addition, any accrued assets, such as Rent Receivable, and accrued liabilities, such as Interest Payable, which do not currently appear on the trial balance, must be recognized.

EXHIBIT 4-6   Unadjusted Trial Balance

DUFFY TRANSIT COMPANY
UNADJUSTED TRIAL BALANCE
JANUARY 31

	DEBIT	CREDIT
Cash	$ 50,000	
Prepaid Insurance	48,000	
Land	20,000	
Buildings—Garage	160,000	
Equipment—Buses	300,000	
Discount Tickets Sold in Advance		$ 25,000
Notes Payable		150,000
Capital Stock		400,000
Daily Ticket Revenue		30,000
Gas, Oil, and Maintenance Expense	12,000	
Wage and Salary Expense	10,000	
Dividends	5,000	
Totals	$605,000	$605,000

Adjusting Entries at the End of January

At the beginning of January, Duffy issued an 18-month, 12%, $150,000 promissory note for cash. Although interest will not be repaid until the loan's maturity date, Duffy must accrue interest for the first month. The calculation of interest for one month is $150,000 \times .12 \times 1/12$. The adjusting entry is as follows:

(a) Interest Expense   1,500
        Interest Payable   1,500
     To record interest for one month on 12%, $150,000
     promissory note.

Assets = Liabilities + Owners' Equity
                       +1,500   -1,500

liabilities increase as interest due adds up

The wages and salaries on the trial balance were paid in cash. At the end of the month, Duffy owes employees an additional $2,800 in salaries and wages:

(b) Wage and Salary Expense   2,800
        Wages and Salaries Payable   2,800
     To record wages and salaries owed.

Assets = Liabilities + Owners' Equity
                       +2,800   -2,800

At the beginning of January, Duffy acquired a garage to house the buses at a cost of $160,000. Land is not subject to depreciation. The cost of the land acquired in connection with the purchase of the building will remain on the books until the property is sold. The garage has an estimated useful life of 20 years and an estimated salvage value of $16,000 at the end of its life. The monthly depreciation is found by dividing the depreciable cost of $144,000 by the useful life of 240 months:

$$\frac{\$160,000 - \$16,000}{20 \text{ years} \times 12 \text{ months}} = \frac{\$144,000}{240 \text{ months}} = \$600 \text{ per month}$$

The entry to record the depreciation on the garage for January for a full month is as follows:

(c) Depreciation Expense—Garage   600
       Accumulated Depreciation—Garage   600
     To record depreciation for the month.

$$\text{Assets} = \text{Liabilities} + \text{Owners' Equity}$$
$$-600 \qquad\qquad\qquad\qquad -600$$

Duffy purchased 10 buses for $30,000 each at the beginning of January. The buses have an estimated useful life of five years, at which time the company plans to sell them for $6,000 each. The monthly depreciation on the 10 buses is

$$10 \times \frac{\$30,000 - \$6,000}{5 \text{ years} \times 12 \text{ months}} = 10 \times \frac{\$24,000}{60 \text{ months}} = \underline{\underline{\$4,000}} \text{ per month.}$$

The entry to recognize the depreciation on the buses for the first month is as follows:

(d) Depreciation Expense—Buses   4,000
       Accumulated Depreciation—Buses   4,000
     To record depreciation for the month.

$$\text{Assets} = \text{Liabilities} + \text{Owners' Equity}$$
$$-4,000 \qquad\qquad\qquad\qquad -4,000$$

Prepaid Insurance on the trial balance represents an insurance policy purchased for $48,000 on January 1. The policy provides property and liability protection for a 24-month period. The adjusting entry to allocate the cost to expense for the first month is as follows:

(e) Insurance Expense   2,000
       Prepaid Insurance   2,000
     To record expiration of insurance benefits.

$$\text{Assets} = \text{Liabilities} + \text{Owners' Equity}$$
$$-2,000 \qquad\qquad\qquad\qquad -2,000$$

In addition to selling tickets on the bus, Duffy sells discount tickets at the terminal. The tickets are good for a ride anytime within 12 months of purchase. Thus, as these tickets are sold, Duffy debits Cash and credits a liability account, Discount Tickets Sold in Advance. The sale of $25,000 worth of these tickets was recorded during January and is thus reflected on the trial balance. At the end of the first month, Duffy counts the number of tickets that have been redeemed. Because $20,400 worth of tickets has been turned in, this is the amount by which the company reduces its liability and recognizes revenue for the month:

(f) Discount Tickets Sold in Advance   20,400
       Discount Ticket Revenue   20,400
     To record redemption of discount tickets.

$$\text{Assets} = \text{Liabilities} + \text{Owners' Equity}$$
$$-20,400 \qquad +20,400$$

Duffy does not need all of the space in its garage and rents a section of it to another company for $2,500 per month. The tenant has until the 10th day of the following month to pay its rent. The adjusting entry on Duffy's books on the last day of the month is as follows:

(g) Rent Receivable   2,500
       Rent Revenue   2,500
     To record rent earned but not yet received.

$$\text{Assets} = \text{Liabilities} + \text{Owners' Equity}$$
$$+2,500 \qquad\qquad\qquad\qquad +2,500$$

Corporations pay estimated taxes on a quarterly basis. Because Duffy is preparing an income statement for the month of January, it must estimate its taxes for the month. We will assume a corporate tax rate of 34% on income before tax. The computation of Income Tax Expense is as follows (the amounts shown for the revenues and expenses reflect the effect of the adjusting entries):

Revenues:		
Daily Ticket Revenue	$30,000	
Discount Ticket Revenue	20,400	
Rent Revenue	2,500	$52,900
Expenses:		
Gas, Oil, and Maintenance Expense	$12,000	
Wage and Salary Expense	12,800	
Depreciation Expense	4,600	
Insurance Expense	2,000	
Interest Expense	1,500	32,900
Net Income before Tax		$20,000
Times the Corporate Tax Rate		× .34
Income Tax Expense		$ 6,800

Based on this estimate of taxes, the final adjusting entry recorded on Duffy's books for the month is

(h)	Income Tax Expense	6,800	
	Income Tax Payable		6,800
	To record estimated income taxes for the month.		

Assets = Liabilities + Owners' Equity
+6,800   −6,800

An *adjusted* trial balance, shown in Exhibit 4-7, indicates the equality of debits and credits after the adjusting entries have been recorded. Note the addition of a number of new accounts that did not appear on the unadjusted trial balance in Exhibit 4-6. The new trial balance includes the accounts that were added when adjusting entries were recorded.

Ethical Considerations for a Company on the Accrual Basis

As you have seen, the accrual basis requires the recognition of revenues when earned and expenses when incurred, regardless of when cash is received or paid. It was also noted earlier that adjusting entries are *internal* transactions in that they do not involve an exchange with an outside entity. Because adjustments do not involve another company, accountants may at times feel pressure from others within the organization to either speed or delay the recognition of certain adjustments.

Consider the following two examples for a construction company that is concerned about its "bottom line," that is, its net income. A number of jobs are in progress, but because of inclement weather, none of them are very far along. Management asks the accountant to recognize 50% of the revenue from a job in progress even though by the most liberal estimates it is only 25% complete. Further, the accountant has been asked to delay the recognition of various short-term accrued liabilities (and, of course, the accompanying expenses) until the beginning of the new year.

The "correct" response of the accountant to each of these requests may seem obvious: only 25% of the revenue on the one job should be recognized, and all accrued liabilities should be expensed at year-end. The pressures of the daily work environment make these decisions difficult for the accountant, however. The accountant must always remember that his or her primary responsibility in preparing financial statements is to accurately portray the affairs of the company to the various outside users. Bankers, stockholders, and others rely on the accountant to serve their best interests.

EXHIBIT 4-7   Adjusted Trial Balance

DUFFY TRANSIT COMPANY
ADJUSTED TRIAL BALANCE
JANUARY 31

	DEBIT	CREDIT
Cash	$ 50,000	
Prepaid Insurance	46,000	
Land	20,000	
Buildings—Garage	160,000	
Accumulated Depreciation—Garage		$ 600
Equipment—Buses	300,000	
Accumulated Depreciation—Buses		4,000
Gas, Oil, and Maintenance Expense	12,000	
Wage and Salary Expense	12,800	
Dividends	5,000	
Discount Tickets Sold in Advance		4,600
Notes Payable		150,000
Capital Stock		400,000
Daily Ticket Revenue		30,000
Rent Receivable	2,500	
Interest Expense	1,500	
Income Tax Expense	6,800	
Depreciation Expense—Garage	600	
Depreciation Expense—Buses	4,000	
Insurance Expense	2,000	
Interest Payable		1,500
Wages and Salaries Payable		2,800
Income Tax Payable		6,800
Discount Ticket Revenue		20,400
Rent Revenue		2,500
Totals	$623,200	$623,200

The Accounting Cycle

We have focused our attention in this chapter on accrual accounting and the adjusting entries it necessitates. Adjusting entries are one key component in the accounting cycle. The accountant for a business follows a series of steps each period. The objective is always the same: *collect the necessary information to prepare a set of financial statements.* Together, these steps make up the accounting cycle. The name comes from the fact that the steps are repeated each period.

LO 6 Explain the steps in the accounting cycle and the significance of each step.

The steps in the accounting cycle are shown in Exhibit 4-8. Note that step 1 involves not only *collecting* information but also *analyzing* it. Transaction analysis is probably the most challenging of all the steps in the accounting cycle. It requires the ability to think logically about an event and its effect on the financial position of the entity. Once the transaction is analyzed, it is recorded in the journal, as indicated by the second step in the exhibit. The first two steps in the cycle take place continuously.

Journal entries are posted to the accounts on a periodic basis. The frequency of posting to the accounts depends on two factors: the type of accounting system used by a company and the volume of transactions. In a manual system, entries might be posted daily, weekly, or even monthly, depending on the amount of activity. The larger the number of transactions a company records, the more often it posts. In an automated accounting system, posting is likely done automatically by the computer each time a transaction is recorded.

EXHIBIT 4-8 Steps in the Accounting Cycle

The Use of a Work Sheet

Step 4 in Exhibit 4-8 calls for the preparation of a work sheet. The end of an accounting period is a busy time. In addition to recording daily recurring transactions, the accountant must record adjusting entries as the basis for preparing financial statements. The time available to prepare the statements is usually very limited. The use of a **work sheet** allows the accountant to gather and organize the information required to adjust the accounts without actually recording and posting the adjusting entries to the accounts. Actually recording adjusting entries and posting them to the accounts can be done after the financial statements are prepared. *A work sheet itself is not a financial statement.* Instead, it is a useful device to *organize* the information needed to prepare the financial statements at the end of the period.

It is not essential that a work sheet be used before preparing financial statements. If it is not used, step 6, recording and posting adjusting entries, comes before step 5, preparing the financial statements. Appendix 4A illustrates how a work sheet is used to facilitate the preparation of financial statements.

The Closing Process

LO 7 Explain why and how closing entries are made at the end of an accounting period.

Two types of accounts appear on an adjusted trial balance. Balance sheet accounts are called **real accounts** because they are permanent in nature. For this reason, they are never closed. The balance in each of these accounts is carried over from one period to the next. In contrast, revenue, expense, and dividend accounts are *temporary* or *nominal accounts.* The balances in the income statement accounts and the Dividends account are *not* carried forward from one accounting period to the next. For this reason, these accounts are closed at the end of the period.

Closing entries serve two important purposes: (1) to return the balances in all temporary or nominal accounts to zero to start the next accounting period and (2) to transfer the net income (or net loss) and the dividends of the period to the Retained Earnings account.

An account with a debit balance is closed by crediting the account for the amount of the balance. An account with a credit balance is closed by debiting the account for the amount of the balance. Thus, revenue accounts are debited in the closing process. Expense accounts are credited to close them. In this way, the balance of each income statement account is restored to zero to start the next accounting period.

Various approaches are used to accomplish the same two purposes: restore the temporary accounts to zero and update the Retained Earnings account. We will use a holding account called Income Summary to facilitate the closing process. A single entry is made to close all of the revenue accounts. The total amount debited to the revenue accounts is credited to Income Summary. Similarly, a single entry is made to close all of the expense accounts, and the offsetting debit is made to Income Summary. This account acts as a temporary storage account. After closing the revenue and expense accounts, Income Summary has a *credit* balance *if revenues exceed expenses.* Finally, the credit balance in Income Summary is itself closed by debiting the account and crediting Retained Earnings for the same amount. The net result of the process is that all of the revenues less expenses, that is, net income, have been transferred to Retained Earnings.

The Dividends account is closed directly to Retained Earnings. Because dividends are *not* an expense, the Dividends account is not closed first to the Income Summary account as are expense accounts. A credit is made to close the Dividends account with an offsetting debit to Retained Earnings.

The closing process for Duffy Transit Company is illustrated with the use of T accounts in Exhibit 4-9. Rather than show each individual revenue and expense account, a single revenue account and a single expense account are used in the exhibit to illustrate the flow in the closing process.

The first closing entry results in a zero balance in each of the three revenue accounts, and the total of the three amounts, $52,900, which represents all of the revenue of the period, is transferred to the Income Summary account. The second entry closes each of the seven expense accounts and transfers the total expenses of $39,700 as a debit to the Income Summary account. At this point, the Income Summary account has a credit

EXHIBIT 4-9   The Closing Process

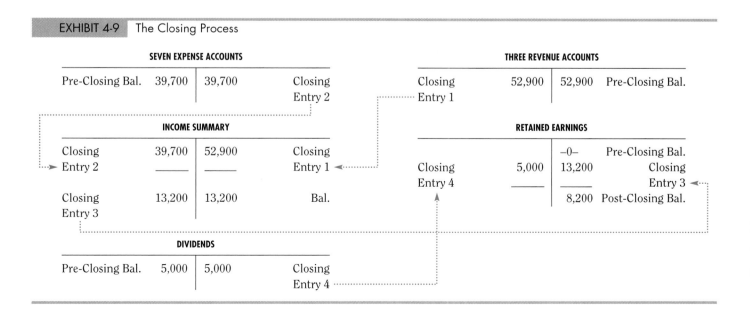

EXHIBIT 4-10 Closing Entries Recorded in the Journal

DATE		ACCOUNT TITLES AND EXPLANATION	POST. REF.	DEBIT	CREDIT
Jan.	31	Daily Ticket Revenue		30,000	
		Discount Ticket Revenue		20,400	
		Rent Revenue		2,500	
		Income Summary			52,900
		To close revenue accounts to Income Summary.			
	31	Income Summary		39,700	
		Gas, Oil, and Maintenance Expense			12,000
		Wage and Salary Expense			12,800
		Interest Expense			1,500
		Depreciation Expense—Garage			600
		Depreciation Expense—Buses			4,000
		Insurance Expense			2,000
		Income Tax Expense			6,800
		To close expense accounts to Income Summary.			
	31	Income Summary		13,200	
		Retained Earnings			13,200
		To close Income Summary to Retained Earnings.			
	31	Retained Earnings		5,000	
		Dividends			5,000
		To close Dividends account to Retained Earnings.			

balance of $13,200, which represents the net income of the period. The third entry closes this temporary holding account and transfers the net income to the Retained Earnings account. Finally, the fourth entry closes the Dividends account and transfers the $5,000 to the debit side of the Retained Earnings account. The Retained Earnings account is now updated to its correct ending balance of $8,200.

The four closing entries in journal form are shown in Exhibit 4-10. Note that each individual revenue and expense account is closed. Keep in mind that the Post. Ref. column will be filled in with the appropriate account numbers when the entries are posted to the ledger accounts.

Interim Financial Statements

We mentioned earlier in this chapter that certain steps in the accounting cycle are sometimes carried out only once a year rather than each month as in our example. For ease of illustration, we assumed a monthly accounting cycle. Many companies adjust and close the accounts only once a year, however. They use a work sheet more frequently than this as the basis for preparing interim statements. Statements prepared monthly, quarterly, or at other intervals less than a year in duration are called interim statements. Many companies prepare monthly financial statements for their own internal use. Similarly, corporations whose shares are publicly traded on one of the stock exchanges are required to file quarterly financial statements with the Securities and Exchange Commission.

Suppose that a company prepares monthly financial statements for internal use and completes the accounting cycle in its entirety only once a year. In this case, a work sheet is prepared each month as the basis for interim financial statements. Formal adjusting and closing entries are prepared only at the end of each year. The adjusting entries that appear on the monthly work sheet are not posted to the accounts. They are entered on the work sheet simply as a basis for preparing the monthly financial statements.

Review Problem

The trial balance of Northern Airlines at January 31 is shown below. It was prepared after posting the recurring transactions for the month of January, but it does not reflect any month-end adjustments.

NORTHERN AIRLINES
UNADJUSTED TRIAL BALANCE
JANUARY 31

Cash	$ 75,000	
Parts Inventory	45,000	
Land	80,000	
Buildings—Hangars	250,000	
Accumulated Depreciation—Hangars		$ 24,000
Equipment—Aircraft	650,000	
Accumulated Depreciation—Aircraft		120,000
Tickets Sold in Advance		85,000
Capital Stock		500,000
Retained Earnings		368,000
Ticket Revenue		52,000
Maintenance Expense	19,000	
Wage and Salary Expense	30,000	
Totals	$1,149,000	$1,149,000

The following additional information is available:

a. Airplane parts needed for repairs and maintenance are purchased regularly, and the amounts paid are added to the asset account Parts Inventory. At the end of each month, the inventory is counted. At the end of January, the amount of parts on hand is $36,100. *Hint:* What adjusting entry is needed to reduce the asset account to its proper carrying value? Any expense involved should be included in Maintenance Expense.

b. The estimated useful life of the hangar is 20 years with an estimated salvage value of $10,000 at the end of its life. The original cost of the hangar was $250,000.

c. The estimated useful life of the aircraft is 10 years with an estimated salvage value of $50,000. The original cost of the aircraft was $650,000.

d. As tickets are sold in advance, the amounts are added to Cash and to the liability account Tickets Sold in Advance. A count of the redeemed tickets reveals that $47,000 worth of tickets were used during January.

e. Wages and salaries owed to employees, but unpaid, at the end of January total $7,600.

f. Northern rents excess hangar space to other companies. The amount owed to Northern but unpaid at the end of January is $2,500.

g. Assume a corporate income tax rate of 34%.

Required

1. Set up T accounts for each of the accounts listed on the trial balance. Set up any other T accounts that will be needed to prepare adjusting entries.

2. Post the month-end adjusting entries directly to the T accounts; do not take the time to put the entries in journal format first. Use the letters (a) through (g) from the additional information to identify each entry.

3. Prepare a trial balance to prove the equality of debits and credits after posting the adjusting entries.

Solution to Review Problem

1. and 2.:

CASH				PARTS INVENTORY		
Bal.	75,000			Bal.	45,000	
						8,900 (a)
				Bal.	36,100	

LAND				TICKETS SOLD IN ADVANCE		
Bal.	80,000					85,000 Bal.
				(d)	47,000	
						38,000 Bal.

BUILDINGS—HANGARS			EQUIPMENT—AIRCRAFT	
Bal.	250,000		Bal. 650,000	

ACCUMULATED DEPRECIATION—HANGARS			ACCUMULATED DEPRECIATION—AIRCRAFT	
		24,000 Bal.		120,000 Bal.
		1,000 (b)		5,000 (c)
		25,000 Bal.		125,000 Bal.

CAPITAL STOCK		RETAINED EARNINGS	
	500,000 Bal.		368,000 Bal.

MAINTENANCE EXPENSE			TICKET REVENUE	
Bal.	19,000			52,000 Bal.
(a)	8,900			47,000 (d)
Bal.	27,900			99,000 Bal.

WAGE AND SALARY EXPENSE			WAGES AND SALARIES PAYABLE	
Bal.	30,000			7,600 (e)
(e)	7,600			
Bal.	37,600			

RENT RECEIVABLE		RENT REVENUE	
(f)	2,500		2,500 (f)

INCOME TAX EXPENSE		INCOME TAXES PAYABLE	
(g)	10,200		10,200 (g)

DEPRECIATION EXPENSE—HANGARS		DEPRECIATION EXPENSE—AIRCRAFT	
(b)	1,000	(c)	5,000

3.

NORTHERN AIRLINES
ADJUSTED TRIAL BALANCE
JANUARY 31

Cash	$ 75,000	
Parts Inventory	36,100	
Land	80,000	
Buildings—Hangars	250,000	
Accumulated Depreciation—Hangars		$ 25,000
Equipment—Aircraft	650,000	
Accumulated Depreciation—Aircraft		125,000
Tickets Sold in Advance		38,000
Capital Stock		500,000
Retained Earnings		368,000
Ticket Revenue		99,000

Maintenance Expense	$ 27,900	
Wage and Salary Expense	37,600	
Depreciation Expense—Hangars	1,000	
Depreciation Expense—Aircraft	5,000	
Rent Receivable	2,500	
Rent Revenue		$ 2,500
Wages and Salaries Payable		7,600
Income Tax Expense	10,200	
Income Taxes Payable		10,200
Totals	$1,175,300	$1,175,300

APPENDIX 4A

Accounting Tools: Work Sheets and Reversing Entries

Work sheets were introduced in the chapter as useful tools to aid the accountant. In this appendix we present a detailed discussion of these.

Work Sheets

A work sheet is used to organize the information needed to prepare financial statements without recording and posting formal adjusting entries. There is no one single format for a work sheet. We will illustrate a 10-column work sheet by using the information in the chapter for the Duffy Transit Company example. The format for a 10-column work sheet appears in Exhibit 4-11. We will concentrate on the *steps* to complete the work sheet, which has already been completed.

LO 8 Understand how to use a work sheet as a basis for preparing financial statements.

Step 1: The Unadjusted Trial Balance Columns

The starting point for the work sheet is the first two columns, which must be filled in with the appropriate amounts from the unadjusted trial balance of Duffy Transit Company as shown in Exhibit 4-6. The trial balance is labeled *unadjusted* because it does not reflect the adjusting entries at the end of the period.

At this point, only the accounts used during the period are entered on the work sheet. Any accounts that are used for the first time during the period because of the adjusting entries will be added in the next step. All but the first two columns of the work sheet should be ignored at this time. Three accounts are included on the work sheet even though they do not have a balance: Accumulated Depreciation—Garage, Accumulated Depreciation—Buses, and Retained Earnings. After this first month of operations, these accounts will always have a balance and will appear on an unadjusted trial balance.

Step 2: The Adjusting Entries Columns

The third and fourth columns of the work sheet have been completed in Exhibit 4-11. Rather than take the time now to prepare adjusting entries and post them to their respective accounts, the accountant makes the entries in these two columns of the work sheet. Formal entries can be made after the financial statements have been prepared. The addition of these two columns to the work sheet requires that we add the accounts used for the first time in the period because of the adjustment process. Letters are typically used on a work sheet to identify the adjusting entries and are therefore used here. In practice, the work sheet can be many pages long, and the use of identifying letters makes it easier to locate and match the debit and credit sides of each adjusting entry.

The two columns are totaled to ensure the equality of debits and credits for the adjusting entries. Keep in mind that the entries made in these two columns of the work sheet are *not* the actual adjusting entries; those will be recorded in the journal at a later time after the financial statements have been prepared.

EXHIBIT 4-11 The Work Sheet

DUFFY TRANSIT COMPANY
WORK SHEET
FOR THE MONTH ENDED JANUARY 31

ACCOUNT TITLES	UNADJUSTED TRIAL BALANCE DEBIT	CREDIT	ADJUSTING ENTRIES DEBIT	CREDIT	ADJUSTED TRIAL BALANCE DEBIT	CREDIT	INCOME STATEMENT DEBIT	CREDIT	BALANCE SHEET DEBIT	CREDIT
Cash	50,000				50,000				50,000	
Prepaid Insurance	48,000			(e) 2,000	46,000				46,000	
Land	20,000				20,000				20,000	
Buildings—Garage	160,000				160,000				160,000	
Accumulated Depreciation—Garage		–0–		(c) 600		600				600
Equipment—Buses	300,000				300,000				300,000	
Accumulated Depreciation—Buses		–0–		(d) 4,000		4,000				4,000
Discount Tickets Sold in Advance		25,000	(f) 20,400			4,600				4,600
Notes Payable		150,000				150,000				150,000
Capital Stock		400,000				400,000				400,000
Retained Earnings		–0–				–0–				–0–
Daily Ticket Revenue		30,000				30,000		30,000		
Gas, Oil, and Maintenance Expense	12,000				12,000		12,000			
Wage and Salary Expense	10,000		(b) 2,800		12,800		12,800			
Dividends	5,000				5,000				5,000	
	605,000	605,000								
Interest Expense			(a) 1,500		1,500		1,500			
Depreciation Expense—Garage			(c) 600		600		600			
Depreciation Expense—Buses			(d) 4,000		4,000		4,000			
Insurance Expense			(e) 2,000		2,000		2,000			
Discount Ticket Revenue				(f) 20,400		20,400		20,400		
Rent Receivable			(g) 2,500		2,500				2,500	
Rent Revenue				(g) 2,500		2,500		2,500		
Interest Payable				(a) 1,500		1,500				1,500
Wages and Salaries Payable				(b) 2,800		2,800				2,800
Income Tax Expense			(h) 6,800		6,800		6,800			
Income Tax Payable				(h) 6,800		6,800				6,800
			40,600	40,600	623,200	623,200	39,700	52,900	583,500	570,300
Net Income							13,200			13,200
							52,900	52,900	583,500	583,500

Step 3: The Adjusted Trial Balance Columns

Columns 5 and 6 of the work sheet represent an adjusted trial balance. The amounts entered in these two columns are found by adding or subtracting any debits or credits in the adjusting entries columns to or from the unadjusted balances. For example, Cash is not adjusted, and thus the $50,000 unadjusted amount is carried over to the Debit column of the adjusted trial balance. The $2,000 credit adjustment to Prepaid Insurance is subtracted from the unadjusted debit balance of $48,000, resulting in a debit balance of $46,000 on the adjusted trial balance. Finally, note the equality of the debits and credits on the new trial balance, $623,200.

Step 4: The Income Statement Columns

An adjusted trial balance is the basis for preparing the financial statements. The purpose of the last four columns of the work sheet is to separate the accounts into those that will appear on the income statement and those that will appear on the balance sheet. The income statement columns will be completed next.

The three revenue accounts appear in the credit column, and the seven expense accounts appear in the debit column. These amounts are simply carried over, or extended, from the adjusted trial balance. Because Duffy's revenues exceed its expenses, the total of the credit column, $52,900, exceeds the total of the debit column, $39,700. The difference between the two columns, the net income of the period of $13,200, is entered in the debit column. One purpose for showing the net income in this column is to balance the two columns. In addition, the entry in the debit column will be matched with an entry in the balance sheet credit column to represent the transfer of net income to retained earnings. If revenues were *less* than expenses, the *net loss* would be entered in the income statement *credit* column.

Step 5: The Balance Sheet Columns

Why do the income statement columns appear *before* the balance sheet columns on the work sheet? The income statement is in fact a *subset* of the balance sheet, and information from the income statement columns flows into the balance sheet columns. Recall that net income causes an increase in the owners' claim to the assets, that is, an increase in owners' equity, through the Retained Earnings account and, thus, is entered in the balance sheet credit column of the work sheet. In Exhibit 4-11, the amount of *net income,* $13,200, is carried over from the debit column of the income statement to the credit column of the balance sheet. If a company experiences a *net loss* for the period, the amount of the loss is entered in the credit column of the income statement and in the debit column of the balance sheet.

You will note that the Retained Earnings account has a zero balance in the last column of the work sheet, because this is the first month of operations for Duffy Transit Company. On future work sheets, the account will reflect the balance from the *end* of the *previous* month. Dividends appear in the debit column, and net income appears in the credit column. Thus, the ending balance of Retained Earnings can be found by taking its beginning balance, adding the net income of the period, and deducting the dividends. The completed work sheet provides all the necessary information to prepare an income statement, a statement of retained earnings, and a balance sheet.

Appendix Review Problem

Note to the Student: The following problem is based on the information for the Northern Airlines review problem at the end of this chapter. Try to prepare the work sheet without referring to the adjusting entries you prepared in solving that problem.

Required

Refer to the unadjusted trial balance and the additional information for Northern Airlines as presented on page 173. Prepare a 10-column work sheet for the month of January.

Solution to Review Problem

NORTHERN AIRLINES
WORK SHEET
FOR THE MONTH ENDED JANUARY 31

ACCOUNT TITLES	Unadjusted Trial Balance DEBIT	Unadjusted Trial Balance CREDIT	Adjusting Entries DEBIT	Adjusting Entries CREDIT	Adjusted Trial Balance DEBIT	Adjusted Trial Balance CREDIT	Income Statement DEBIT	Income Statement CREDIT	Balance Sheet DEBIT	Balance Sheet CREDIT
Cash	75,000				75,000				75,000	
Parts Inventory	45,000			(a) 8,900	36,100				36,100	
Land	80,000				80,000				80,000	
Buildings—Hangars	250,000				250,000				250,000	
Accumulated Depreciation—Hangars		24,000		(b) 1,000		25,000				25,000
Equipment—Aircraft	650,000				650,000				650,000	
Accumulated Depreciation—Aircraft		120,000		(c) 5,000		125,000				125,000
Tickets Sold in Advance		85,000	(d) 47,000			38,000				38,000
Capital Stock		500,000				500,000				500,000
Retained Earnings		368,000				368,000				368,000
Ticket Revenue		52,000		(d) 47,000		99,000		99,000		
Maintenance Expense	19,000		(a) 8,900		27,900		27,900			
Wage and Salary Expense	30,000		(e) 7,600		37,600		37,600			
	1,149,000	1,149,000								
Depreciation Expense—Hangars			(b) 1,000		1,000		1,000			
Depreciation Expense—Aircraft			(c) 5,000		5,000		5,000			
Rent Receivable			(f) 2,500		2,500				2,500	
Income Tax Expense			(g) 10,200		10,200		10,200			
Wages and Salaries Payable				(e) 7,600		7,600				7,600
Rent Revenue				(f) 2,500		2,500		2,500		
Income Taxes Payable				(g) 10,200		10,200				10,200
			82,200	82,200	1,175,300	1,175,300	81,700	101,500	1,093,600	1,073,800
Net Income							19,800			19,800
							101,500	101,500	1,093,600	1,093,600

Chapter Highlights

1. **LO 1** The success of accounting as a form of communication depends on two concepts: recognition and measurement. The items depicted in financial statements are representations. The accountant cannot show the reader an asset but instead depicts it with words and numbers.

2. **LO 1** Measurement in accounting requires choosing an attribute and a unit of measure. Historical cost is the attribute used for many of the assets included in financial statements. One alternative to historical cost is current value. The dollar as a unit of measure is subject to instability, depending on the level of inflation.

3. **LO 2** Under the accrual basis of accounting, revenues are recognized when earned and expenses when incurred. The income statement is prepared on an accrual basis, and the statement of cash flows complements it by providing valuable information about the operating, financing, and investing cash flows of a business.

4. **LO 3** According to the revenue recognition principle, revenues are recognized when they are realized or realizable and earned. On a practical basis, revenue is normally recognized at the time a product or service is delivered to the customer. Certain types of sales arrangements, such as long-term contracts and franchises, present special problems in applying the principle.

5. **LO 4** The matching principle attempts to associate with the revenue of the period all costs necessary to generate that revenue. A direct form of matching is possible for certain types of costs, such as cost of goods sold and commissions. Costs, such as depreciation, are recognized as expenses on an indirect basis. Depreciation is the allocation of the cost of a tangible, long-term asset over its useful life. The benefits from most selling and administrative expenses expire immediately and are recognized as expenses in the period the costs are incurred.

6. **LO 5** The accrual basis necessitates adjusting entries at the end of a period. The four types of adjusting entries result from differences between the recognition of revenues and expenses on an accrual basis and the receipt or payment of cash.

7. **LO 5** Cash paid before expense is incurred results in a deferred expense, which is recognized as an asset on the balance sheet. The adjusting entry reduces the asset and recognizes a corresponding amount of expense. Cash received before revenue is earned requires the recognition of a liability, a deferred revenue. The adjusting entry reduces the liability and recognizes a corresponding amount of revenue.

8. **LO 5** If cash is paid after an expense is incurred, an adjusting entry is needed to recognize the accrued liability and the related expense. Similarly, if cash is received after the revenue is earned, the adjusting entry recognizes the accrued asset and the corresponding revenue. The liability or asset is eliminated in a later period when cash is either paid or received.

9. **LO 5** Adjusting entries are prepared by reference to a trial balance and certain additional information. A trial balance prepared after posting the adjustments to the accounts ensures the equality of debits and credits in the ledger.

10. **LO 6** Steps in the accounting cycle are carried out each period as a basis for the preparation of financial statements. Some of the steps, such as journalizing transactions, are performed continuously, while others, such as recording adjusting entries, are performed only at the end of the period.

11. **LO 7** After adjusting entries are recorded and posted to the accounts, closing entries are made. They have two important purposes: (1) to return the balances in all revenue, expense, and dividend accounts to zero to start the following accounting period and (2) to transfer the net income (or net loss) and the dividends of the period to the Retained Earnings account.

12. **LO 7** A revenue account is closed by debiting it for the credit balance in the account and crediting Income Summary. An expense account is closed by crediting it and debiting Income Summary. If revenues exceed expenses, Income Summary will have a credit balance at this point, representing the net income of the period. Income Summary is closed by debiting it and crediting Retained Earnings. Finally, the Dividends account is closed with a credit and a corresponding debit to Retained Earnings.

13. **LO 8** A work sheet is not itself a financial statement. It is a useful device for organizing the necessary information to prepare financial statements without going through the formal process of recording and posting adjusting entries. The format for a 10-column work sheet includes two columns each (debits and credits) for the unadjusted trial balance, the adjustments, the adjusted trial balance, the income statement, and the balance sheet. (Appendix 4A)

Key Terms Quiz

Read each definition below and then write the number of the definition in the blank beside the appropriate term it defines. The solution appears at the end of the chapter.

___	Recognition	___	Historical cost
___	Current value	___	Cash basis
___	Accrual basis	___	Revenues
___	Revenue recognition principle	___	Percentage-of-completion method
___	Production method	___	Installment method
___	Matching principle	___	Expenses
___	Adjusting entries	___	Straight-line method
___	Contra account	___	Deferral
___	Deferred expense	___	Deferred revenue
___	Accrual	___	Accrued liability
___	Accrued asset	___	Accounting cycle
___	Work sheet	___	Real accounts
___	Nominal accounts	___	Closing entries
___	Interim statements		

1. A device used at the end of the period to gather the information needed to prepare financial statements without actually recording and posting adjusting entries.

2. Inflows or other enhancements of assets or settlements of liabilities from delivering or producing goods, rendering services, or other activities.

3. The method in which revenue is recognized when a commodity is produced rather than when it is sold.

4. Journal entries made at the end of a period by a company using the accrual basis of accounting.

5. Journal entries made at the end of the period to return the balance in all nominal accounts to zero and transfer the net income or loss and the dividends of the period to Retained Earnings.

6. The method used by contractors to recognize revenue before the completion of a long-term contract.

7. A liability resulting from the receipt of cash before the recognition of revenue.

8. The method in which revenue is recognized at the time cash is collected; used for various types of consumer items, such as automobiles and appliances.

9. The name given to balance sheet accounts because they are permanent and are not closed at the end of the period.

10. An asset resulting from the recognition of a revenue before the receipt of cash.

11. The amount of cash, or its equivalent, that could be received by selling an asset currently.

12. The assignment of an equal amount of depreciation to each period.

13. Cash has either been paid or received, but expense or revenue has not yet been recognized.

14. A system of accounting in which revenues are recognized when earned and expenses when incurred.

15. Cash has not yet been paid or received, but expense has been incurred or revenue earned.

16. Financial statements prepared monthly, quarterly, or at other intervals less than a year in duration.

17. Revenues are recognized in the income statement when they are realized, or realizable, and earned.

18. The process of recording an item in the financial statements as an asset, liability, revenue, expense, or the like.

19. An asset resulting from the payment of cash before the incurrence of expense.

20. The name given to revenue, expense, and dividend accounts because they are temporary and are closed at the end of the period.

21. A system of accounting in which revenues are recognized when cash is received and expenses when cash is paid.

22. A liability resulting from the recognition of an expense before the payment of cash.

23. The association of revenue of a period with all of the costs necessary to generate that revenue.

24. An account with a balance that is opposite that of a related account.

25. The amount that is paid for an asset and that is used as a basis for recognizing it on the balance sheet and carrying it on later balance sheets.

26. Outflows or other using up of assets or incurrences of liabilities resulting from delivering goods, rendering services, or carrying out other activities.

27. A series of steps performed each period and culminating with the preparation of a set of financial statements.

Alternate Terms

Historical cost   Original cost.

Asset   Unexpired cost.

Deferred expense   Prepaid expense, prepaid asset.

Deferred revenue   Unearned revenue.

Expense   Expired cost.

Nominal account   Temporary account.

Real account   Permanent account.

Questions

1. What is meant by the following statement? "The items depicted in financial statements are merely *representations* of the real thing."

2. What is the meaning of the following statement? "The choice between historical cost and current value is a good example of the trade-off in accounting between relevance and reliability."

3. A realtor earns a 10% commission on the sale of a $150,000 home. The realtor lists the home on June 5, the sale occurs on June 12, and the seller pays the realtor the $15,000 commission on July 8. When should the realtor recognize revenue from the sale, assuming (a) the cash basis of accounting and (b) the accrual basis of accounting?

4. What does the following statement mean? "If I want to assess the cash flow prospects for a company down the road, I look at the company's most recent statement of cash flows. An income statement prepared under the accrual basis of accounting is useless for this purpose."

5. What is the relationship between the time period assumption and accrual accounting?

6. Is it necessary for an asset to be acquired when revenue is recognized? Explain your answer.

7. What is the justification for recognizing revenue on a long-term contract by the percentage-of-completion method?

8. Illinois Fried Chicken sells franchises granting the franchisee in a specific geographic area the exclusive right to use the company name and sell chicken using its secret recipe. An initial franchise fee of $50,000 is charged by Illinois, along with a continuing fee of 3% of sales. The initial fee is for Illinois' assistance in selecting a site and training personnel. When should Illinois recognize the $50,000 as revenue?

9. When should a publisher of magazines recognize revenue?

10. What is the justification for recognizing revenue in certain industries at the time the product is *produced* rather than when it is *sold?*

11. A friend says to you: "I just don't get it. Assets cost money. Expenses reduce income. There must be some relationship among *assets, costs,* and *expenses*—I'm just not sure what it is!" What is the relationship? Can you give an example of it?

12. What is the meaning of *depreciation* to the accountant?

13. What are the four basic types of adjusting entries? Give an example of each.

14. What are the rules of debit and credit as they apply to the contra asset account Accumulated Depreciation?

15. Which of the following steps in the accounting cycle requires the most thought and judgment by the accountant: (a) preparing a trial balance, (b) posting adjusting and closing entries, or (c) analyzing and recording transactions? Explain your answer.

16. What is the difference between a real account and a nominal account?

17. What two purposes are served in making closing entries?

18. Why is the Dividends account closed directly to Retained Earnings rather than to the Income Summary account?

19. Assuming the use of a work sheet, are the formal adjusting entries recorded and posted to the accounts before or after the financial statements are prepared? Explain your answer. Would your answer change if a work sheet is not prepared? (Appendix 4A)

20. Some companies use an eight-column work sheet rather than the 10-column format illustrated in the chapter. Which two columns would you think are not used in the eight-column format? Why could these two columns be eliminated? (Appendix 4A)

21. Why do the income statement columns appear before the balance sheet columns on a work sheet? (Appendix 4A)

22. Does the Retained Earnings account that appears in the balance sheet credit column of a work sheet reflect the beginning or the ending balance in the account? Explain your answer. (Appendix 4A)

23. One asset account will always be carried over from the unadjusted trial balance columns of a work sheet to the balance sheet columns of the work sheet without any adjustment. What account is this? (Appendix 4A)

Exercises

LO 3   **Exercise 4-1** Revenue Recognition

The highway department contracted with a private company to collect tolls and maintain facilities on a turnpike. Users of the turnpike can pay cash as they approach the toll booth, or they can purchase a pass. The pass is equipped with an electronic sensor that subtracts the toll fee from the pass balance as the motorist slowly approaches a special toll booth. The passes are issued in $10 increments. Refunds are available to motorists who do not use the pass balance, but these are issued very infrequently. Last year $3,000,000 was collected at the traditional toll booths, $2,000,000 of passes were issued, and $1,700,000 of passes were used at the special toll booth. How much should the company recognize as revenue for the year? Explain how the revenue recognition rule should be applied in this case.

LO 4 **Exercise 4-2** The Matching Principle

Three methods of matching costs with revenue were described in the chapter: (a) directly match a specific form of revenue with a cost incurred in generating that revenue, (b) indirectly match a cost with the periods during which it will provide benefits or revenue, and (c) immediately recognize a cost incurred as an expense because no future benefits are expected. For each of the following costs, indicate how it is normally recognized as expense by indicating either *a, b,* or *c.* If you think there is more than one possible answer for any of the situations, explain why.

1. New office copier.
2. Monthly bill from the utility company for electricity.
3. Office supplies.
4. Biweekly payroll for office employees.
5. Commissions earned by salespeople.
6. Interest incurred on a six-month loan from the bank.
7. Cost of inventory sold during the current period.
8. Taxes owed on income earned during current period.
9. Cost of three-year insurance policy.

LO 5 **Exercise 4-3** Accruals and Deferrals

For the following situations, indicate whether each involves a deferred expense (DE), a deferred revenue (DR), an accrued liability (AL), or an accrued asset (AA).

Example: ___DE___ Office supplies purchased in advance of their use.

_____ 1. Wages earned by employees but not yet paid.
_____ 2. Cash collected from subscriptions in advance of publishing a magazine.
_____ 3. Interest earned on a customer loan for which principal and interest have not yet been collected.
_____ 4. One year's premium on life insurance policy paid in advance.
_____ 5. Office building purchased for cash.
_____ 6. Rent collected in advance from a tenant.
_____ 7. State income taxes owed at the end of the year.
_____ 8. Rent owed by a tenant but not yet collected.

LO 5 **Exercise 4-4** Office Supplies

Somerville Corp. purchases office supplies once a month and prepares monthly financial statements. The asset account Office Supplies on Hand has a balance of $1,450 on May 1. Purchases of supplies during May amount to $1,100. Supplies on hand at May 31 amount to $920. Prepare the necessary adjusting entry on Somerville's books on May 31. What would be the effect on net income for May if this entry is *not* recorded?

LO 5 **Exercise 4-5** Prepaid Rent—Quarterly Adjustments

On September 1, Northhampton Industries signed a six-month lease, effective September 16, for office space. Northhampton agreed to prepay the rent and mailed a check for $12,000 to the landlord on September 1. Assume that Northhampton prepares adjusting entries only four times a year, on March 31, June 30, September 30, and December 31.

Required

1. Compute the rental cost for each full month.
2. Prepare the journal entry to record the payment of rent on September 1.
3. Prepare the adjusting entry on September 30.
4. Assume that the accountant prepares the adjusting entry on September 30 but forgets to record an adjusting entry on December 31. Will net income for the year be understated or overstated? By what amount?

LO 5   **Exercise 4-6** Depreciation

On July 1, 1998, Red Gate Farm buys a combine for $100,000 in cash. Assume that the combine is expected to have a seven-year life and an estimated salvage value of $16,000 at the end of that time.

Required

1. Prepare the journal entry to record the purchase of the combine on July 1, 1998.
2. Compute the depreciable cost of the combine.
3. Using the straight-line method, compute the monthly depreciation.
4. Prepare the adjusting entry to record depreciation at the end of July 1998.
5. Compute the combine's carrying value that will be shown on Red Gate's balance sheet prepared on December 31, 1998.

LO 5   **Exercise 4-7** Prepaid Insurance—Annual Adjustments

On April 1, 1998, Briggs Corp. purchases a 24-month property insurance policy for $72,000. The policy is effective immediately. Assume that Briggs prepares adjusting entries only once a year, on December 31.

Required

1. Compute the monthly cost of the insurance policy.
2. Prepare the journal entry to record the purchase of the policy on April 1, 1998.
3. Prepare the adjusting entry on December 31, 1998.
4. Assume that the accountant forgets to record an adjusting entry on December 31, 1998. Will net income for the year ended December 31, 1998, be understated or overstated? Explain your answer.

LO 5   **Exercise 4-8** Subscriptions

Country Living publishes a monthly magazine for which a 12-month subscription costs $30. All subscriptions require payment of the full $30 in advance. On August 1, 1998, the balance in the Subscriptions Received in Advance account was $40,500. During the month of August, the company sold 900 yearly subscriptions. After the adjusting entry at the end of August, the balance in the Subscriptions Received in Advance account is $60,000.

Required

1. Prepare the journal entry to record the sale of the 900 yearly subscriptions during the month of August.
2. Prepare the adjusting journal entry on August 31.
3. Assume that the accountant made the correct entry during August to record the sale of the 900 subscriptions but forgot to make the adjusting entry on August 31. Would net income for August be overstated or understated? Explain your answer.

LO 5   **Exercise 4-9** Customer Deposits

Wolfe & Wolfe collected $9,000 from a customer on April 1 and agreed to provide legal services during the next three months. Wolfe & Wolfe expects to provide an equal amount of services each month.

Required

1. Prepare the journal entry for the receipt of the customer deposit on April 1.

2. Prepare the adjusting entry on April 30.

3. What would be the effect on net income for April if the entry in (2) is not recorded?

LO 5 **Exercise 4-10** Wages Payable

Denton Corporation employs 50 workers in its plant. Each employee is paid $10 per hour and works seven hours per day, Monday through Friday. Employees are paid every Friday. The last payday was Friday, October 20.

Required

1. Compute the dollar amount of the weekly payroll.

2. Prepare the journal entry on Friday, October 27, for the payment of the weekly payroll.

3. Denton prepares monthly financial statements. Prepare the adjusting journal entry on Tuesday, October 31, the last day of the month.

4. Prepare the journal entry on Friday, November 3, for the payment of the weekly payroll.

5. Would net income for the month of October be understated or overstated if Denton doesn't bother with an adjusting entry on October 31? Explain your answer.

LO 5 **Exercise 4-11** Interest Payable

Billings Company takes out a 12%, 90-day, $100,000 loan with First National Bank on March 1, 1998.

Required

1. Prepare the journal entry on March 1, 1998.

2. Prepare the adjusting entries for the months of March and April 1998.

3. Prepare the entry on May 30, 1998, when Billings repays the principal and interest to First National.

LO 5 **Exercise 4-12** Property Taxes Payable—Annual Adjustments

Lexington Builders owns property in Kaneland County. Lexington's 1997 property taxes amounted to $50,000. Kaneland County will send out the 1998 property tax bills to property owners during April 1999. Taxes must be paid by June 1, 1999. Assume that Lexington prepares adjusting entries only once a year, on December 31, and that property taxes for 1998 are expected to increase by 5% over those for 1997.

Required

1. Prepare the adjusting entry required to record the property taxes payable on December 31, 1998.

2. Prepare the journal entry to record the payment of the 1998 property taxes on June 1, 1999.

LO 5 **Exercise 4-13** Interest Receivable

On June 1, 1998, MicroTel Enterprises lends $60,000 to MaxiDriver Inc. The loan will be repaid in 60 days with interest at 10%.

Required

1. Prepare the journal entry on MicroTel's books on June 1, 1998.

2. Prepare the adjusting entry on MicroTel's books on June 30, 1998.

3. Prepare the entry on MicroTel's books on July 31, 1998, when MaxiDriver repays the principal and interest.

LO 5 **Exercise 4-14** Unbilled Accounts Receivable

Mike and Cary repair computers for small local businesses. Heavy thunderstorms during the last week of June resulted in a record number of service calls. Eager to review the results of operations for the month of June, Mike prepared an income statement and was puzzled by the lower-than-expected amount of revenues. Cary explained that he had not yet billed the company's customers for $40,000 of work performed during the last week of the month.

Required

1. Should revenue be recorded when services are performed or when customers are billed? Explain your answer.

2. Prepare the adjusting entry required on June 30.

LO 5 **Exercise 4-15** The Effect of Ignoring Adjusting Entries on Net Income
For each of the following independent situations, determine whether the effect of ignoring the required adjusting entry will result in an understatement (U), an overstatement (O), or no effect (NE) on net income for the period.

SITUATION	EFFECT ON NET INCOME
Example: Taxes owed but not yet paid are ignored.	O
1. A company fails to record depreciation on equipment.	
2. Sales made during the last week of the period are not recorded.	
3. A company neglects to record the expired portion of a prepaid insurance policy (its cost was originally debited to an asset account).	
4. Interest due but not yet paid on a long-term note payable is ignored.	
5. Commissions earned by salespeople but not payable until the 10th of the following month are ignored.	
6. A landlord receives cash on the date a lease is signed for the rent for the first six months and credits Unearned Rent Revenue. The landlord fails to make any adjustment at the end of the first month.	

LO 5 **Exercise 4-16** The Effect of Adjusting Entries on the Accounting Equation
Determine whether recording each of the following adjusting entries will increase (I), decrease (D), or have no effect (NE) on each of the three elements of the accounting equation.

	Assets = Liabilities + Owners' Equity		
Example: Wages earned during the period but not yet paid are accrued.	NE	I	D
1. Prepaid insurance is reduced for the portion of the policy that has expired during the period.			
2. Interest incurred during the period but not yet paid is accrued.			
3. Depreciation for the period is recorded.			
4. Revenue is recorded for the earned portion of a liability for amounts collected in advance from customers.			
5. Rent revenue is recorded for amounts owed by a tenant but not yet paid.			
6. Income taxes owed but not yet paid are accrued.			

LO 5 **Exercise 4-17** Reconstruction of Adjusting Entries from Unadjusted and Adjusted Trial Balances
Following are the unadjusted and adjusted trial balances for Power Corp. on May 31, 1998:

	UNADJUSTED TRIAL BALANCE		ADJUSTED TRIAL BALANCE	
	DEBIT	**CREDIT**	**DEBIT**	**CREDIT**
Cash	$ 3,160		$ 3,160	
Accounts Receivable	7,300		9,650	
Supplies on Hand	400		160	
Prepaid Rent	2,400		2,200	
Equipment	9,000		9,000	
Accumulated Depreciation		$ 2,800		$ 3,200
Accounts Payable		2,600		2,600
Capital Stock		5,000		5,000
Retained Earnings		8,990		8,990
Service Revenue		6,170		8,520
Promotions Expense	2,050		2,050	
Wage Expense	1,250		2,350	
Wages Payable				1,100
Supplies Expense			240	
Depreciation Expense			400	
Rent Expense			200	
Totals	$25,560	$25,560	$29,410	$29,410

Required

1. Reconstruct the adjusting entries that were made on Power's books at the end of May.

2. By how much would Power's net income for May have been overstated or understated (indicate which) if these adjusting entries had not been recorded?

LO 6   **Exercise 4-18** The Accounting Cycle

The steps in the accounting cycle are listed below in random order. Fill in the blank next to each step to indicate its *order* in the cycle. The first step in the cycle is filled in as an example.

ORDER	PROCEDURE
_____	Prepare a work sheet.
_____	Close the accounts.
___1___	Collect and analyze information from source documents.
_____	Prepare financial statements.
_____	Post transactions to accounts in the ledger.
_____	Record and post adjusting entries.
_____	Journalize daily transactions.

LO 6   **Exercise 4-19** Trial Balance

The following account titles, arranged in alphabetical order, are from the records of Hadley Realty Corporation. The balance in each account is the normal balance for that account. The balances are as of December 31, after adjusting entries have been made. Prepare an adjusted trial balance, listing the accounts in the following order: (1) assets, (2) liabilities, (3) owners' equity accounts, including dividends, (4) revenues, and (5) expenses.

Accounts Payable	$12,300
Accounts Receivable	21,230
Accumulated Depreciation—Automobiles	12,000
Accumulated Depreciation—Buildings	15,000
Automobiles	48,000
Buildings	60,000
Capital Stock	25,000
Cash	2,460
Commissions Earned	17,420

Commissions Expense	$ 2,300
Dividends Declared and Paid	1,500
Insurance Expense	300
Interest Expense	200
Interest Payable	200
Land	40,000
Notes Payable	20,000
Office Supplies	1,680
Office Supplies Expense	5,320
Prepaid Insurance	1,200
Rent Expense	2,400
Retained Earnings	85,445
Wages and Salaries Expense	1,245
Wages and Salaries Payable	470

LO 7   **Exercise 4-20** Closing Entries

At the end of the year, the adjusted trial balance for Devonshire Corporation contains the following amounts for the income statement accounts (the balance in each account is the normal balance for that type of account).

ACCOUNT	BALANCE
Advertising Fees Earned	$58,500
Interest Revenue	2,700
Wage and Salary Expense	14,300
Utilities Expense	12,500
Insurance Expense	7,300
Depreciation Expense	16,250
Interest Expense	2,600
Income Tax Expense	3,300
Dividends	2,000

Required

1. Prepare all necessary journal entries to close Devonshire Corporation's accounts at the end of the year.

2. Assume that the accountant for Devonshire forgets to record the closing entries. What will be the effect on net income for the following year? Explain your answer.

LO 7   **Exercise 4-21** Preparation of a Statement of Retained Earnings from Closing Entries

Fisher Corporation reported a Retained Earnings balance of $125,780 on January 1, 1998. Fisher Corporation made the following three closing entries on December 31, 1998 (the entry to transfer net income to Retained Earnings has been intentionally left out). Prepare a statement of retained earnings for Fisher for the year.

Dec. 31	Service Revenue	65,400	
	Interest Revenue	20,270	
	Income Summary		85,670
Dec. 31	Income Summary	62,345	
	Salary and Wage Expense		23,450
	Rent Expense		20,120
	Interest Expense		4,500
	Utilities Expense		10,900
	Insurance Expense		3,375
Dec. 31	Retained Earnings	6,400	
	Dividends		6,400

LO 7   **Exercise 4-22** Reconstruction of Closing Entries

The T accounts shown below summarize entries made to selected general ledger accounts of Cooper & Company. Certain entries, dated December 31, are closing entries. Prepare the closing entries that were made on December 31.

MAINTENANCE REVENUE			
12/31	90,000	64,000	12/1 bal.
		13,000	12/15
		13,000	12/30

WAGES EXPENSE			
12/1 bal.	11,000	12,000	12/31
12/15	500		
12/30	500		

SUPPLIES EXPENSE			
12/1 bal.	2,500	2,750	12/31
12/31	250		

RETAINED EARNINGS			
12/31	5,000	45,600	12/1 bal.
		75,250	12/31

DIVIDENDS			
12/1 bal.	5,000	5,000	12/31

INCOME SUMMARY			
12/31	14,750	90,000	12/31
12/31	75,250		

LO 7 **Exercise 4-23** Closing Entries for Ben & Jerry's

The following accounts appear on Ben & Jerry's 1995 income statement. The accounts are listed in alphabetical order, and the balance in each account is the normal balance for that account. Prepare closing entries for Ben & Jerry's for 1995.

Cost of Sales	$109,125,000
Income Tax Expense	3,457,000
Interest Expense	1,525,000
Interest Income	1,681,000
Net Sales	155,333,000
Other Expense	597,000
Selling, General and Administrative Expenses	36,362,000

LO 7 **Exercise 4-24** Closing Entries

Royston Realty reported the following accounts on its income statement:

Commissions Earned	$54,000
Real Estate Board Fees Paid	5,000
Computer Line Charge	864
Depreciation on Computer	450
Car Expenses	2,200
Travel and Entertainment	4,500
Insurance Expired	780
Advertising Expense	1,460
Office Supplies Used	940

Required

1. Prepare the necessary entries to close the temporary accounts.

2. Explain why the closing entries are necessary and when they should be recorded.

LO 8 **Exercise 4-25** The Difference Between a Financial Statement and a Work Sheet (Appendix 4A)

The balance sheet columns of the work sheet for Jones Corporation show total debits and total credits of $255,000 each. Dividends for the period are $3,000. Accumulated depreciation is $14,000 at the end of the period. Compute the amount that should appear on the balance sheet (i.e., the formal financial statement) for *total assets*. How do you explain the difference between this amount and the amount that appears as the total debits and total credits on the work sheet?

LO 8 **Exercise 4-26** Ten-Column Work Sheet (Appendix 4A)

Indicate whether amounts in each of the following accounts should be carried over from the adjusted trial balance columns of the work sheet to the income statement (IS) columns or to the balance sheet (BS) columns. Also indicate whether the account normally has a debit (D) balance or a credit (C) balance.

__BS-D__ **Example:** Cash

_____ **1.** Accumulated Depreciation—Trucks

_____ **2.** Subscriptions Sold in Advance

———— **3.** Accounts Receivable

———— **4.** Dividends

———— **5.** Capital Stock

———— **6.** Prepaid Insurance

———— **7.** Depreciation Expense—Trucks

———— **8.** Office Supplies

———— **9.** Office Supplies Expense

———— **10.** Subscription Revenue

———— **11.** Interest Receivable

———— **12.** Interest Revenue

———— **13.** Interest Expense

———— **14.** Interest Payable

———— **15.** Retained Earnings

Multi-Concept Exercises

LO 1, 2, 3 **Exercise 4-27** Revenue Recognition, Cash and Accrual Basis

Hathaway Health Club sold three-year memberships at a reduced rate during its opening promotion. One thousand three-year, nonrefundable memberships were sold for $366 each. The club expects to sell 100 additional three-year memberships for $900 each over each of the next two years. Membership fees are paid when clients sign up. The club's bookkeeper has prepared the following income statement for the first year of business and projected income statements for Years 2 and 3.

Cash-basis income statements:

	YEAR 1	YEAR 2	YEAR 3
Sales	$366,000	$90,000	$90,000
Equipment*	100,000	–0–	–0–
Salaries and Wages	50,000	50,000	50,000
Advertising	5,000	5,000	5,000
Rent and Utilities	36,000	36,000	36,000
Income (Loss)	$175,000	$ (1,000)	$ (1,000)

*Equipment was purchased at the beginning of Year 1 for $100,000 and is expected to last for three years and then to be worth $1,000.

Required

1. Convert the income statements for each of the three years to the accrual basis.

2. Describe how the revenue recognition principle applies. Do you believe that the cash-basis or the accrual-basis income statements are more useful to management? to investors? Why?

LO 1, 2, 3 **Exercise 4-28** The Effect of the Percentage-of-Completion Method on Financial Statements

Fox Valley Inc. is building a bridge. During the first year of the three-year project, Fox Valley incurred construction costs of $1.2 million. The company expects to spend an additional $600,000 in each of the next two years of the project. The state has agreed to pay Fox Valley $4 million for the bridge, $2 million in the first year and $2 million on completion. The company would like to use the percentage-of-completion method to report revenue and income.

Required

1. Complete the following table, comparing the percentage-of-completion method with the cash basis. Use the percentage of costs incurred to date to estimated total costs to determine the percentage of completion.

	INCOME RECOGNIZED UNDER	
YEAR	PERCENTAGE OF COMPLETION	CASH BASIS
1		
2		
3		
Total		

2. Explain how the revenue recognition principle applies to the percentage-of-completion method.

LO 4, 5 **Exercise 4-29** Depreciation Expense

During 1998, Carter Company acquired three assets, with the following costs, estimated useful lives, and estimated salvage values:

DATE	ASSET	COST	ESTIMATED USEFUL LIFE	ESTIMATED SALVAGE VALUE
March 28	Truck	$ 18,000	5 years	$ 3,000
June 22	Computer	55,000	10 years	5,000
October 3	Building	250,000	30 years	10,000

The company uses the straight-line method to depreciate all assets and computes depreciation to the nearest month. For example, the computer system will be depreciated for six months in 1998.

Required

1. Compute the depreciation expense that Carter will record on each of the three assets for 1998.

2. Comment on the following statement: "Accountants could save time and money by simply expensing the cost of long-term assets when they are purchased. In addition, this would be more accurate because depreciation requires estimates of useful life and salvage value."

LO 4, 5 **Exercise 4-30** Accrual of Interest on a Loan

On July 1, 1998, Paxson Corporation takes out a 12%, two-month, $50,000 loan at Friendly National Bank. Principal and interest are to be repaid on August 31.

Required

1. Prepare the journal entries for July 1 to record the borrowing, for July 31 to record the accrual of interest, and for August 31 to record repayment of the principal and interest.

2. Evaluate the following statement: "It would be much easier not to bother with an adjusting entry on July 31 and simply record interest expense on August 31 when the loan is repaid."

Problems

LO 3 **Problem 4-1** The Revenue Recognition Principle

Each of the following paragraphs describes a situation involving revenue recognition.

a. ABC Realty receives a 6% commission for every house it sells. It lists a house for a client on April 3 at a selling price of $150,000. ABC receives an offer from a buyer on April 28 to purchase the house at the asking price. The realtor's client accepts the offer on May 1. ABC will receive its 6% commission at a closing scheduled for May 16.

b. Chicken King is a fast-food franchisor on the West Coast. It charges all franchisees $10,000 to open an outlet in a designated city. In return for this fee, the franchisee receives the exclusive right to operate in the area, as well as assistance from Chicken King in selecting a site. On January 5, Chicken King signs an agreement with a franchisee and receives a down payment of $4,000, with the balance of $6,000 due in three months. On March 13, Chicken King meets with the new franchisee, and the two parties agree on a suitable site for the business. On April 5, the franchisee pays Chicken King the remaining $6,000.

c. Refer to part b. In addition to the initial fee, Chicken King charges a continuing fee equal to 2% of the franchisee's sales each month. Each month's fee is payable by the 10th of the following month. The franchisee opens for business on June 1. On July 3, Chicken King receives a report from the franchisee indicating its sales for the month of June amount to $60,000. On July 8, Chicken King receives its 2% fee for June sales.

d. Goldstar Mining Corporation mines and sells gold and other precious commodities on the open market. During August, the company mines 50 ounces of gold. The market price throughout August is $300 per ounce. The 50 ounces are eventually sold on the open market on September 5 for $310 per ounce.

e. Whatadeal Inc. sells used cars. Because of the uncertainties involved in collecting from customers, Whatadeal uses the installment basis of accounting. On December 2, Whatadeal sells a car for $10,000 with a 25% down payment and the balance due in 60 days. The company's accounting year ends on December 31. Whatadeal receives the balance of $7,500 on February 1.

Required

For each situation, indicate when revenue should be recognized, as well as the dollar amount. Give a brief explanation for each answer.

LO 5   **Problem 4-2** Adjusting Entries

Water Corporation prepares monthly financial statements and therefore adjusts its accounts at the end of every month. The following information is available for March 1998:

a. Water Corporation takes out a 90-day, 8%, $15,000 note on March 1, 1998, with interest and principal to be paid at maturity.

b. The asset account Office Supplies on Hand has a balance of $1,280 on March 1, 1998. During March, Water adds $750 to the account for the purchases of the period. A count of the supplies on hand at the end of March indicates a balance of $1,370.

c. The company purchased office equipment last year for $62,600. The equipment has an estimated useful life of six years and an estimated salvage value of $5,000.

d. The company's plant operates seven days per week with a daily payroll of $7,950. Wage earners are paid every Sunday. The last day of the month is Tuesday, March 31.

e. The company rented an idle warehouse to a neighboring business on February 1, 1998, at a rate of $2,500 per month. On this date, Water Corporation credited Rent Collected in Advance for six months' rent received in advance.

f. On March 1, 1998, Water Corporation credited a liability account, Customer Deposits, for $4,800. This sum represents an amount that a customer paid in advance and that will be earned evenly by Water over a four-month period.

g. Based on its income for the month, Water Corporation estimates that federal income taxes for March amount to $3,900.

Required

For each of the preceding situations, prepare in general journal form the appropriate adjusting entry to be recorded on March 31, 1998.

LO 5   **Problem 4-3** Effects of Adjusting Entries on the Accounting Equation

Refer to the information provided for Water Corporation in Problem 4-2.

Required

1. Prepare a table to summarize the required adjusting entries as they affect the accounting equation. Use the format in Exhibit 3-1. Identify each adjustment by letter.

2. Assume that Water reports income of $23,000 before any of the adjusting entries. What net income will Water report for March?

LO 5 **Problem 4-4** Adjusting Entries—Annual Adjustments

Palmer Industries prepares annual financial statements and adjusts its accounts only at the end of the year. The following information is available for the year ended December 1998:

a. Palmer purchased computer equipment two years ago for $15,000. The equipment has an estimated useful life of five years and an estimated salvage value of $250.

b. The Office Supplies account had a balance of $3,600 on January 1, 1998. During 1998, Palmer added $17,600 to the account for purchases of office supplies during the year. A count of the supplies on hand at the end of December 1998 indicates a balance of $1,850.

c. On August 1, 1998, Palmer credited a liability account, Customer Deposits, for $24,000. This sum represents an amount that a customer paid in advance and that will be earned evenly by Palmer over a six-month period.

d. Palmer rented some office space on November 1, 1998, at a rate of $2,700 per month. On that date, Palmer debited Prepaid Rent for three months' rent paid in advance.

e. Palmer took out a 120-day, 9%, $200,000 note on November 1, 1998, with interest and principal to be paid at maturity.

f. Palmer operates five days per week with an average daily payroll of $15,500. Palmer pays its employees every Friday. December 31, 1998, is a Thursday.

Required

1. For each of the preceding situations, prepare in general journal form the appropriate adjusting entry to be recorded on December 31, 1998.

2. Assume that Palmer's accountant forgets to record the adjusting entries on December 31, 1998. Will net income for the year be understated or overstated? By what amount? (Ignore the effect of income taxes.)

LO 5 **Problem 4-5** Recurring and Adjusting Entries

The following are Butler Realty Corporation's accounts, identified by number. The company has been in the real estate business for 10 years and prepares financial statements monthly. Following the list of accounts is a series of transactions entered into by Butler. For each transaction, enter the number(s) of the account(s) to be debited and credited.

ACCOUNTS

1. Cash
2. Accounts Receivable
3. Prepaid Rent
4. Office Supplies
5. Automobiles
6. Accumulated Depreciation
7. Land
8. Accounts Payable
9. Salaries and Wages Payable
10. Income Tax Payable

11. Notes Payable
12. Capital Stock, $10 par
13. Paid-in Capital in Excess of Par
14. Commissions Revenue
15. Office Supply Expense
16. Rent Expense
17. Salaries and Wages Expense
18. Depreciation Expense
19. Interest Expense
20. Income Tax Expense

TRANSACTION	DEBIT	CREDIT
a. **Example:** Issued additional shares of stock to owners at amount in excess of par.	1	12, 13
b. Purchased automobiles for cash.		
c. Purchased land; made cash down payment and signed a promissory note for the balance.		
d. Paid cash to landlord for rent for next 12 months.		

e. Purchased office supplies on account. _____ _____

f. Collected cash for commissions from clients for the properties sold during the month. _____ _____

g. Collected cash for commissions from clients for the properties sold in the prior month. _____ _____

h. During the month, sold properties for which cash for commissions will be collected from clients next month. _____ _____

i. Paid for office supplies purchased on account in an earlier month. _____ _____

j. Recorded an adjustment to recognize wages and salaries incurred but not yet paid. _____ _____

k. Recorded an adjustment for office supplies used during the month. _____ _____

l. Recorded an adjusting entry for the portion of prepaid rent that expired during the month. _____ _____

m. Made required month-end payment on note taken out in (c); payment is part principal and part interest. _____ _____

n. Recorded adjusting entry for monthly depreciation on the autos. _____ _____

o. Recorded adjusting entry for income taxes. _____ _____

LO 5 **Problem 4-6** Use of Account Balances as a Basis for Adjusting Entries—Annual Adjustments

The following account balances are taken from the records of Chauncey Company at December 31, 1998. The Prepaid Insurance account represents the cost of a three-year policy purchased on August 1, 1998. The Rent Collected in Advance account represents the cash received from a tenant on June 1, 1998, for 12 months' rent, beginning on that date. The Note Receivable represents a nine-month promissory note received from a customer on September 1, 1998. Principal and interest at an annual rate of 9% will be received on June 1, 1999.

Prepaid Insurance	$ 7,200 debit	
Rent Collected in Advance		$6,000 credit
Note Receivable	50,000 debit	

Required

1. Prepare the three necessary adjusting entries on the books of Chauncey on December 31, 1998. Assume that Chauncey prepares adjusting entries only once a year, on December 31.

2. Assume that adjusting entries are made at the end of each month rather than only at the end of the year. What would be the balance in Prepaid Insurance *before* the December adjusting entry is made? Explain your answer.

LO 5 **Problem 4-7** Use of a Trial Balance as a Basis for Adjusting Entries

Bob Reynolds operates a real estate business. A trial balance on April 30, 1998, *before* recording any adjusting entries, appears as follows:

General Ledger

REYNOLDS REALTY COMPANY
UNADJUSTED TRIAL BALANCE
APRIL 30, 1998

	DEBIT	CREDIT
Cash	$15,700	
Prepaid Insurance	450	
Office Supplies	250	
Office Equipment	50,000	
Accumulated Depreciation—Office Equipment		$ 5,000

Automobile	$12,000	
Accumulated Depreciation—Automobile		$ 1,400
Accounts Payable		6,500
Unearned Commissions		9,500
Notes Payable		2,000
Capital Stock		10,000
Retained Earnings		40,000
Dividends	2,500	
Commissions Earned		17,650
Utility Expense	2,300	
Salaries Expense	7,400	
Advertising Expense	1,450	
Totals	$92,050	$92,050

OTHER DATA

a. The monthly insurance cost is $50.

b. Office supplies on hand on April 30, 1998, amount to $180.

c. The office equipment was purchased on April 1, 1997. On that date, it had an estimated useful life of 10 years.

d. On September 1, 1997, the automobile was purchased; it had an estimated useful life of five years.

e. A deposit is received in advance of providing any services for first-time customers. Amounts received in advance are recorded initially in the account Unearned Commissions. Based on services provided to these first-time customers, the balance in this account at the end of April should be $5,000.

f. Repeat customers are allowed to pay for services one month after the date of the sale of their property. Services rendered during the month but not yet collected or billed to these customers amount to $1,500.

g. Interest owed on the note payable but not yet paid amounts to $20.

h. Salaries owed to employees but unpaid at the end of the month amount to $2,500.

Required

1. Prepare in general journal form the necessary adjusting entries at April 30, 1998. Label the entries a through h to correspond to the other data.

2. Note that the unadjusted trial balance reports a credit balance in Accumulated Depreciation—Office Equipment of $5,000. Explain *why* the account contains a balance of $5,000 on April 30, 1998.

LO 5 **Problem 4-8** Effects of Adjusting Entries on the Accounting Equation

Refer to the information provided for Reynolds Realty Company in Problem 4-7.

Required

1. Prepare a table to summarize the required adjusting entries as they affect the accounting equation. Use the format in Exhibit 3-1. Identify each adjustment by letter.

2. Compute the net increase or decrease in net income for the month from the recognition of the adjusting entries you prepared in part 1. (Ignore income taxes.)

LO 5 **Problem 4-9** Reconstruction of Adjusting Entries from Account Balances

Taggart Corp. records adjusting entries each month before preparing monthly financial statements. The following selected account balances are taken from its trial balances on June 30, 1998. The "unadjusted" columns set forth the general ledger balances before the adjusting entries were posted. The "adjusted" columns reflect the month-end adjusting entries.

ACCOUNT TITLE	UNADJUSTED DEBIT	UNADJUSTED CREDIT	ADJUSTED DEBIT	ADJUSTED CREDIT
Prepaid Insurance	$3,600		$3,450	
Equipment	9,600		9,600	
Accumulated Depreciation		$1,280		$1,360
Notes Payable		9,600		9,600
Interest Payable		2,304		2,448

Required

1. The company purchased a 36-month insurance policy on June 1, 1997. Reconstruct the adjusting journal entry for insurance on June 30, 1998.

2. What was the original cost of the insurance policy? Explain your answer.

3. The equipment was purchased on February 1, 1997, for $9,600. Taggart uses straight-line depreciation and estimates that the equipment will have no salvage value. Reconstruct the adjusting journal entry for depreciation on June 30, 1998.

4. What is the equipment's estimated useful life in months? Explain your answer.

5. Taggart signed a two-year note payable on February 1, 1997, for the purchase of the equipment. Interest on the note accrues on a monthly basis and will be paid at maturity along with the principal amount of $9,600. Reconstruct the adjusting journal entry for interest on June 30, 1998.

6. What is the *monthly* interest rate on the loan? Explain your answer.

LO 5 **Problem 4-10** Use of a Trial Balance to Record Adjusting Entries in T Accounts
Four Star Video has been in the video rental business for five years. An unadjusted trial balance at May 31, 1998, follows.

General
Ledger

FOUR STAR VIDEO
UNADJUSTED TRIAL BALANCE
MAY 31, 1998

	DEBIT	CREDIT
Cash	$ 4,000	
Prepaid Rent	6,600	
Video Inventory	25,600	
Display Stands	8,900	
Accumulated Depreciation		$ 5,180
Accounts Payable		3,260
Customer Subscriptions		4,450
Capital Stock		5,000
Retained Earnings		22,170
Rental Revenue		9,200
Wage and Salary Expense	2,320	
Utility Expense	1,240	
Advertising Expense	600	
Totals	$49,260	$49,260

The following additional information is available:

a. Four Star rents a store in a shopping mall and prepays the annual rent of $7,200 on April 1 of each year.

b. The asset account Video Inventory represents the cost of videos purchased from suppliers. When a new title is purchased from a supplier, its cost is debited to this account. When a title has served its useful life and can no longer be rented (even at a reduced price), it is removed from the inventory in the store. Based on the monthly count, the cost of titles on hand at the end of May is $23,140.

c. The display stands have an estimated useful life of five years and an estimated salvage value of $500.

d. Wages and salaries owed to employees but unpaid at the end of May amount to $1,450.

e. In addition to individual rentals, Four Star operates a popular discount subscription program. Customers pay an annual fee of $120 for an unlimited number of rentals. Based on the $10 per month earned on each of these subscriptions, the amount earned for the month of May is $2,440.

f. Four Star accrues income taxes using an estimated tax rate equal to 30% of the income for the month.

Required

1. Set up T accounts for each of the accounts listed in the trial balance. Based on the additional information given, set up any other T accounts that will be needed to prepare adjusting entries.

2. Post the month-end adjusting entries directly to the T accounts but do not bother to put the entries in journal format first. Use the letters a through f from the additional information to identify the entries.

3. Prepare a trial balance to prove the equality of debits and credits after posting the adjusting entries.

4. On the basis of the information you have, does Four Star appear to be a profitable business? Explain your answer.

LO 5 **Problem 4-11** Effects of Adjusting Entries on the Accounting Equation

Refer to the information provided for Four Star Video in Problem 4-10.

Required

Prepare a table to summarize the required adjusting entries as they affect the accounting equation. Use the format in Exhibit 3-1. Identify each adjustment by letter.

Multi-Concept Problems

LO 2, 3 **Problem 4-12** Cash and Accrual Income Statements for a Manufacturer

Drysdale Company was established to manufacture components for the auto industry. The components are shipped the same day they are produced. The following events took place during the first year of operations.

a. Issued common stock for a $50,000 cash investment.

b. Purchased delivery truck at the beginning of the year at a cost of $10,000 cash. The truck is expected to last five years and will be worthless at the end of that time.

c. Manufactured and sold 500,000 components the first year. The costs incurred to manufacture the components are (1) $1,000 monthly rent on a facility that included utilities and insurance, (2) $400,000 of raw materials purchased on account ($100,000 is still unpaid as of year-end, but all materials were used in manufacturing), and (3) $190,000 paid in salaries and wages to employees and supervisors.

d. Paid $100,000 to sales and office staff for salaries and wages.

e. Sold all components on account for $2 each. As of year-end, $150,000 is due from customers.

Required

1. How much revenue will Drysdale recognize under the cash basis and under the accrual basis?

2. Describe how Drysdale should apply the matching principle to recognize expenses.

3. Prepare an income statement under the accrual basis. Ignore income taxes.

LO 3, 4 **Problem 4-13** Revenue Recognition on Installment Sales and Commodities

John Deare, an Illinois corn farmer, retired in South Carolina. While retired, he volunteered his time at the Small Business Administration office. One day, Frances Hirise, a condominium builder, came in with a question about the amount of sales she should recognize on her income statement. She had constructed a complex of 200 units. Half of the units sell for $50,000 each, and the other half sell for $60,000. The developer agreed to finance the sale of all units, and by the end of the year, 40 units at $50,000 and 30 units at $60,000 had been sold. Each buyer made a down payment of 10% cash and agreed to pay the remainder in equal annual payments plus interest on the unpaid balance over the next nine years. No payments have been received other than the down payments. John advised Frances that she should recognize sales of $11 million (100 × $50,000) + (100 × $60,000).

Required

Do you agree with John? Why did he suggest this amount? What amount of revenue would you suggest that Frances recognize in the current and subsequent years as a result of these sales? When should the costs to build the condos (lumber, labor, etc.) be recognized as expenses?

LO 3, 4, 7 **Problem 4-14** Revenue and Expense Recognition and Closing Entries

Two years ago, Lu Wong opened a hair salon. Lu reports the following accounts on her income statement:

Sales	$69,000
Advertising expense	3,500
Salaries expense	39,000
Rent expense	10,000

These amounts represent two years of revenue and expenses. Lu has asked you how she can tell how much of the income is from the first year of business and how much is from the second year. She provides the following additional data:

a. Sales in the second year were double those of the first year.

b. Advertising expense is for a $500 opening promotion and weekly ads in the newspaper.

c. Salaries represent one employee for the first nine months and then two employees for the remainder of the time. Each is paid the same salary. No raises have been granted.

d. Rent has not changed since the salon opened.

Required

1. Prepare income statements for Years 1 and 2.

2. Prepare the closing entries for each year. Prepare a short explanation for Lu about the purpose of closing temporary accounts.

LO 5, 6, 8 **Problem 4-15** Ten-Column Work Sheet (Appendix 4A)

The following unadjusted trial balance is available for Ace Consulting Inc. on June 30, 1998.

General
Ledger

ACE CONSULTING INC.
UNADJUSTED TRIAL BALANCE
JUNE 30, 1998

Cash	$ 6,320	
Accounts Receivable	14,600	
Supplies on Hand	800	
Prepaid Rent	4,800	
Furniture and Fixtures	18,000	
Accumulated Depreciation		$ 5,625
Accounts Payable		5,200
Capital Stock		10,000
Retained Earnings		17,955
Consulting Revenue		12,340
Utility Expense	4,100	
Wage and Salary Expense	2,500	
Totals	$51,120	$51,120

Required

1. Enter the unadjusted trial balance in the first two columns of a 10-column work sheet.

2. Enter the necessary adjustments in the appropriate columns of the work sheet for each of the following:

   a. Wages and salaries earned by employees at the end of June but not yet paid amount to $2,380.

   b. Supplies on hand at the end of June amount to $550.

   c. Depreciation on furniture and fixtures for June is $375.

   d. Ace prepays the rent on its office space on June 1 of each year. The rent amounts to $400 per month.

   e. Consulting services rendered and billed for which cash has not yet been received amount to $4,600.

3. Complete the remaining columns of the work sheet.

General
Ledger

LO 5, 6, 8 **Problem 4-16** Monthly Transactions, 10-Column Work Sheet, and Financial Statements (Appendix 4A)

Moonlight Bay Inn is incorporated on January 2, 1998, by its three owners, each of whom contributes $20,000 in cash in exchange for shares of stock in the business. In addition to the sale of stock, the following transactions are entered into during the month of January:

January 2: A Victorian inn is purchased for $50,000 in cash. An appraisal performed on this date indicates that the land is worth $15,000 and the remaining balance of the purchase price is attributable to the house. The owners estimate that the house will have an estimated useful life of 25 years and an estimated salvage value of $5,000.

January 3: A two-year, 12%, $30,000 promissory note was signed at the Second State Bank. Interest and principal will be repaid on the maturity date of January 3, 2000.

January 4: New furniture for the inn is purchased at a cost of $15,000 in cash. The furniture has an estimated useful life of 10 years and no salvage value.

January 5: A 24-month property insurance policy is purchased for $6,000 in cash.

January 6: An advertisement for the inn is placed in the local newspaper. Moonlight Bay pays $450 cash for the ad, which will run in the paper throughout January.

January 7: Cleaning supplies are purchased on account for $950. The bill is payable within 30 days.

January 15: Wages of $4,230 for the first half of the month are paid in cash.

January 16: A guest mails the business $980 in cash as a deposit for a room to be rented for two weeks. The guest plans to stay at the inn during the last week of January and the first week of February.

January 31: Cash receipts from rentals of rooms for the month amount to $8,300.

January 31: Cash receipts from operation of the restaurant for the month amount to $6,600.

January 31: Each stockholder is paid $200 in cash dividends.

Required

1. Prepare journal entries to record each of the preceding transactions.

2. Post each of the journal entries to T accounts.

3. Place the balance in each of the T accounts in the unadjusted trial balance columns of a 10-column work sheet.

4. Enter the appropriate adjustments in the next two columns of the work sheet for each of the following:

a. Depreciation of the house.

b. Depreciation of the furniture.

c. Interest on the promissory note.

d. Recognition of the expired portion of the insurance.

e. Recognition of the earned portion of the guest's deposit.

f. Wages earned during the second half of January amount to $5,120 and will be paid on February 3.

g. Cleaning supplies on hand on January 31 amount to $230.

h. A gas and electric bill that is received from the city amounts to $740 and is payable by February 5.

i. Income taxes are to be accrued at a rate of 30% of income before taxes.

5. Complete the remaining columns of the work sheet.

6. Prepare in good form the following financial statements:

a. Income statement for the month ended January 31, 1998.

b. Statement of retained earnings for the month ended January 31, 1998.

c. Balance sheet at January 31, 1998.

7. Assume that you are the loan officer at Second State Bank (refer to the transaction on January 3). What are your reactions to Moonlight's first month of operations? Are you comfortable with the loan you made?

Alternate Problems

LO 3 **Problem 4-1A** The Revenue Recognition Principle
Each of the following paragraphs describes a situation involving revenue recognition.

a. Zee Zitter Inc. paints and decorates office buildings. On September 30, 1998, it received $5,750 for work to be completed over the next six months.

b. Tan Us is a tanning salon franchisor in the Midwest. It charges all franchisees a fee of $2,500 to open a salon and an ongoing fee equal to 5% of all revenue during the first five years. The $2,500 is for training and accounting systems to be used in each salon. During January 1998, Tan Us signed an agreement with five individuals to open salons over the next three months.

c. On June 1, 1998, Dan Diver Bridge Building Inc. entered into a contract with the county to renovate an old covered bridge. The county gives Dan an advance of $500,000 and agrees to pay Dan $75,000 each month for 20 months, at which time the project should be completed.

d. Joe Cropper, a wheat grower, harvested the current year's crop and delivered it to the elevator for storage on October 1, 1998, until it is sold to one of several foreign countries. The expected sales value of the wheat is $450,000.

e. Shop-n-Here, a convenience store chain, constructed a strip shopping center next to one of its stores. The spaces are being sold to individuals who will open auto parts and repair facilities. One person is planning to open a brake-repair shop, another will set up a transmission-repair shop, a third will do 10-minute oil changes, and so on. The store space sells for $25,000 each. There are six spaces, four of which are sold in May of 1998.

Required

For each of the preceding situations, indicate when in 1998 revenue should be recognized, as well as the dollar amount. Give a brief explanation for each answer.

LO 5 **Problem 4-2A** Adjusting Entries
Flood Relief Inc. prepares monthly financial statements and therefore adjusts its accounts at the end of every month. The following information is available for June 1998:

a. Flood received a $10,000, 4%, two-year note receivable from a customer for services rendered. The principal and interest are due on June 1, 2000. Flood expects to be able to collect the note and interest in full at that time.

b. Office supplies totaling $5,600 were purchased during the month. The asset account Supplies is debited whenever a purchase is made. A count in the storeroom on June 30, 1998, indicated that supplies on hand amount to $507. The supplies on hand at the beginning of the month total $475.

c. The company purchased machines last year for $170,000. The machines are expected to be used for four years and have an estimated salvage value of $2,000.

d. On June 1, the company paid $4,650 for rent for June, July, and August. The asset Prepaid Rent was debited; it did not have a balance on June 1.

e. The company operates seven days per week with a weekly payroll of $49,000. Wage earners are paid every Sunday. The last day of the month is Tuesday, June 30.

f. Based on its income for the month, Flood estimates that federal income taxes for June amount to $2,900.

Required

For each of the preceding situations, prepare in general journal form the appropriate adjusting entry to be recorded on June 30, 1998.

LO 5 **Problem 4-3A** Effects of Adjusting Entries on the Accounting Equation
Refer to the information provided for Flood Relief Inc. in Problem 4-2A.

Required

1. Prepare a table to summarize the required adjusting entries as they affect the accounting equation. Use the format in Exhibit 3-1. Identify each adjustment by letter.

2. Assume that Flood Relief reports income of $35,000 before any of the adjusting entries. What net income will Flood Relief report for June?

LO 5 **Problem 4-4A** Adjusting Entries—Annual Adjustments
Ogonquit Enterprises prepares annual financial statements and adjusts its accounts only at the end of the year. The following information is available for the year ended December 1998:

a. Ogonquit purchased office furniture last year for $25,000. The furniture has an estimated useful life of seven years and an estimated salvage value of $4,000.

b. The Supplies account had a balance of $1,200 on January 1, 1998. During 1998, Ogonquit added $12,900 to the account for purchases of supplies during the year. A count of the supplies on hand at the end of December 1998 indicates a balance of $900.

c. On July 1, 1998, Ogonquit credited a liability account, Customer Deposits, for $8,800. This sum represents an amount that a customer paid in advance and that will be earned evenly by Ogonquit over an eight-month period.

d. Ogonquit rented some warehouse space on September 1, 1998, at a rate of $4,000 per month. On that date, Ogonquit debited Prepaid Rent for six months' rent paid in advance.

e. Ogonquit took out a 90-day, 6%, $30,000 note on November 1, 1998, with interest and principal to be paid at maturity.

f. Ogonquit operates five days per week with an average weekly payroll of $17,250. Ogonquit pays its employees every Friday. December 31, 1998, is a Thursday.

Required

1. For each of the preceding situations, prepare in general journal form the appropriate adjusting entry to be recorded on December 31, 1998.

2. Assume that Ogonquit's accountant forgets to record the adjusting entries on December 31, 1998. Will net income for the year be understated or overstated? By what amount? (Ignore the effect of income taxes.)

LO 5   **Problem 4-5A** Recurring and Adjusting Entries

The following are the accounts of Dominique Inc., an interior decorator. The company has been in the decorating business for 10 years and prepares quarterly financial statements. Following the list of accounts is a series of transactions entered into by Dominique. For each transaction, enter the number(s) of the account(s) to be debited and credited.

ACCOUNTS

1. Cash	11. Capital Stock, $1 par
2. Accounts Receivable	12. Paid-in Capital in Excess of Par
3. Prepaid Rent	13. Consulting Revenue
4. Office Supplies	14. Office Supply Expense
5. Office Equipment	15. Rent Expense
6. Accumulated Depreciation	16. Salaries and Wages Expense
7. Accounts Payable	17. Depreciation Expense
8. Salaries and Wages Payable	18. Interest Expense
9. Income Tax Payable	19. Income Tax Expense
10. Interim Financing Notes Payable	

TRANSACTION	DEBIT	CREDIT
a. **Example:** Issued additional shares of stock to owners; shares issued at greater than par.	1	11, 12
b. Purchased office equipment for cash.	———	———
c. Collected open accounts receivable from customer.	———	———
d. Purchased office supplies on account.	———	———
e. Paid office rent for the next six months.	———	———
f. Paid interest on an interim financing note.	———	———
g. Paid salaries and wages.	———	———
h. Purchased office equipment; made a down payment in cash and signed an interim financing note.	———	———
i. Provided services on account.	———	———
j. Recorded depreciation on equipment.	———	———
k. Recorded income taxes due next month.	———	———
l. Recorded the used office supplies.	———	———
m. Recorded the used portion of prepaid rent.	———	———

LO 5   **Problem 4-6A** Use of Account Balances as a Basis for Adjusting Entries—Annual Adjustments

The following account balances are taken from the records of Laugherty Inc. at December 31, 1998. The Supplies account represents the cost of supplies on hand at the beginning of the year plus all purchases. A physical count on December 31, 1998, shows only $1,520 of supplies on hand. The Unearned Revenue account represents the cash received from a customer on May 1, 1998, for 12 months of service, beginning on that date. The Note Payable represents a six-month promissory note signed with a supplier on September 1, 1998. Principal and interest at an annual rate of 10% will be paid on March 1, 1999.

Supplies	$5,790 debit	
Unearned Revenue		$ 1,800 credit
Note Payable		60,000 credit

Required

1. Prepare the three necessary adjusting entries on the books of Laugherty on December 31, 1998. Assume that Laugherty prepares adjusting entries only once a year, on December 31.

2. Assume that adjusting entries are made at the end of each month rather than only at the end of the year. What would be the balance in Unearned Revenue *before* the December adjusting entry is made? Explain your answer.

General Ledger

LO 5 **Problem 4-7A** Use of a Trial Balance as a Basis for Adjusting Entries

Lori Matlock operates a graphic arts business. A trial balance on June 30, 1998, *before* recording any adjusting entries, appears as follows:

MATLOCK GRAPHIC ARTS STUDIO
UNADJUSTED TRIAL BALANCE
JUNE 30, 1998

	DEBIT	CREDIT
Cash	$ 7,000	
Prepaid Rent	18,000	
Supplies	15,210	
Office Equipment	46,120	
Accumulated Depreciation—Equipment		$4,000
Accounts Payable		1,800
Notes Payable		2,000
Capital Stock		50,000
Retained Earnings		24,350
Dividends	8,400	
Revenue		46,850
Utility Expense	2,850	
Salaries Expense	19,420	
Advertising Expense	12,000	
Totals	$129,000	$129,000

OTHER DATA

a. The monthly rent cost is $600.

b. Supplies on hand on June 30, 1998, amount to $1,290.

c. The office equipment was purchased on June 1, 1997. On that date, it had an estimated useful life of 10 years and a salvage value of $6,120.

d. Interest owed on the note payable but not yet paid amounts to $50.

e. Salaries of $620 are owed to employees but unpaid at the end of the month.

Required

1. Prepare in general journal form the necessary adjusting entries at June 30, 1998. Label the entries a through e to correspond to the other data.

2. Note that the unadjusted trial balance reports a credit balance in Accumulated Depreciation—Equipment of $4,000. Explain *why* the account contains a balance of $4,000 on June 30, 1998.

LO 5 **Problem 4-8A** Effects of Adjusting Entries on the Accounting Equation

Refer to the information provided for Matlock Graphic Arts Studio in Problem 4-7A.

Required

1. Prepare a table to summarize the required adjusting entries as they affect the accounting equation. Use the format in Exhibit 3-1. Identify each adjustment by letter.

2. Compute the net increase or decrease in net income for the month from the recognition of the adjusting entries you prepared in part 1 (ignore income taxes).

LO 5 **Problem 4-9A** Reconstruction of Adjusting Entries from Account Balances

Zola Corporation records adjusting entries each month before preparing monthly financial statements. The following selected account balances are taken from its trial balances on June 30, 1998. The "unadjusted" columns set forth the general ledger balances before the adjusting entries were posted. The "adjusted" columns reflect the month-end adjusting entries.

ACCOUNT TITLE	UNADJUSTED		ADJUSTED	
	DEBIT	CREDIT	DEBIT	CREDIT
Prepaid Rent	$4,000		$3,000	
Equipment	9,600		9,600	
Accumulated Depreciation		$ 800		$ 900
Notes Payable		9,600		9,600
Interest Payable		768		864

Required

1. The company paid for a six-month lease on April 1, 1998. Reconstruct the adjusting journal entry for rent on June 30, 1998.

2. What amount was prepaid on April 1, 1998? Explain your answer.

3. The equipment was purchased on September 30, 1997, for $9,600. Zola uses straight-line depreciation and estimates that the equipment will have no salvage value. Reconstruct the adjusting journal entry for depreciation on June 30, 1998.

4. What is the equipment's estimated useful life in months? Explain your answer.

5. Zola signed a two-year note on September 30, 1997, for the purchase of the equipment. Interest on the note accrues on a monthly basis and will be paid at maturity along with the principal amount of $9,600. Reconstruct the adjusting journal entry for interest expense on June 30, 1998.

6. What is the *monthly* interest rate on the loan? Explain your answer.

LO 5 **Problem 4-10A** Use of a Trial Balance to Record Adjusting Entries in T Accounts

Lewis and Associates has been in the termite inspection and treatment business for five years. An unadjusted trial balance at June 30, 1998, follows:

General Ledger

LEWIS AND ASSOCIATES
UNADJUSTED TRIAL BALANCE
JUNE 30, 1998

	DEBIT	CREDIT
Cash	$ 6,200	
Accounts Receivable	10,400	
Prepaid Rent	4,400	
Chemical Inventory	9,400	
Equipment	18,200	
Accumulated Depreciation		$ 1,050
Accounts Payable		1,180
Capital Stock		5,000
Retained Earnings		25,370
Treatment Revenue		40,600
Wages and Salary Expense	22,500	
Utility Expense	1,240	
Advertising Expense	860	
Totals	$73,200	$73,200

The following additional information is available:

a. Lewis rents a warehouse with office space and prepays the annual rent of $4,800 on May 1 of each year.

b. The asset account Equipment represents the cost of treatment equipment, which has an estimated useful life of 10 years and an estimated salvage value of $200.

c. Chemical inventory on hand equals $1,300.

   d. Wages and salaries owed to employees but unpaid at the end of the month amount to $1,080.

   e. Lewis accrues income taxes using an estimated tax rate equal to 30% of the income for the month.

Required

1. Set up T accounts for each of the accounts listed in the trial balance. Based on the additional information given, set up any other T accounts that will be needed to prepare adjusting entries.

2. Post the month-end adjusting entries directly to the T accounts but do not bother to put the entries in journal format first. Use the letters a through e from the additional information to identify the entries.

3. Prepare a trial balance to prove the equality of debits and credits after posting the adjusting entries.

4. On the basis of the information you have, does Lewis appear to be a profitable business? Explain your answer.

LO 5 **Problem 4-11A** Effects of Adjusting Entries on the Accounting Equation
Refer to the information provided for Lewis and Associates in Problem 4-10A.

Required

Prepare a table to summarize the required adjusting entries as they affect the accounting equation. Use the format in Exhibit 3-1. Identify each adjustment by letter.

Alternate Multi-Concept Problems

LO 2, 3 **Problem 4-12A** Cash and Accrual Income Statements for a Manufacturer
Marie's Catering makes sandwiches for vending machines. The sandwiches are delivered to the vendor on the same day that they are made. The following events took place during the first year of operations.

a. On the first day of the year, issued common stock for a $20,000 cash investment and a $10,000 investment of equipment. The equipment is expected to last 10 years and will be worthless at the end of that time.

b. Purchased a delivery truck at the beginning of the year at a cost of $14,000 cash. The truck is expected to last five years and will be worthless at the end of that time.

c. Made and sold 50,000 sandwiches during the first year of operations. The costs incurred to make the sandwiches are (1) $800 monthly rent on a facility that included utilities and insurance, (2) $25,000 of meat, cheese, bread, and condiments (all food was purchased on account, and $4,000 is still unpaid at year-end even though all of the food has been used), and (3) $35,000 paid in salaries and wages to employees and supervisors.

d. Paid $12,000 for part-time office staff salaries.

e. Sold all sandwiches on account for $2 each. As of year-end, $25,000 is still due from the vendors.

Required

1. How much revenue will Marie's Catering recognize under the cash basis and under the accrual basis?

2. Explain how accountants apply the revenue recognition principle to Marie's small business. What conditions would allow Marie's to use the cash method to recognize revenue?

3. Prepare an income statement according to the accrual method. Ignore income taxes.

LO 3, 4 **Problem 4-13A** Revenue Recognition on the Percentage-of-Completion and Commodities Methods
Judy Darling owns a diamond mine in South Africa. While vacationing on an island in the Caribbean, she discussed with Marty Jones a recent dig that yielded $1.5 million of raw diamonds. The product is stored with an agent until a buyer is located. The agent expects it to take about two and a half years to sell all of the diamonds. Judy's company

spent $1 million to extract the diamonds in 1998. Marty's company constructs airplane runways and hangars. He is in the process of building a runway for the island and expects to incur the following costs over the next two and one-half years:

1998	$400,000
1999	500,000
2000	100,000

Local residents and the government have already paid Marty $1 million in 1998 and will pay another $500,000 when the project is completed in 2000.

Required

Explain the difference between revenue and cash flow for Judy and Marty. How much revenue will each recognize in 1998, 1999, and 2000?

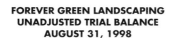 **Problem 4-14A** Revenue and Expense Recognition and Closing Entries

Two years ago, Sue Stern opened an audio book rental shop. Sue reports the following accounts on her income statement:

Sales	$84,000
Advertising expense	10,500
Salaries expense	12,000
Depreciation on tapes	5,000
Rent expense	18,000

These amounts represent two years of revenue and expenses. Sue has asked you how she can tell how much of the income is from the first year and how much is from the second year of business. She provides the following additional data:

a. Sales in the second year are triple those of the first year.

b. Advertising expense is for a $1,500 opening promotion and weekly ads in the newspaper.

c. Salaries represent one employee who was hired eight months ago. No raises have been granted.

d. Rent has not changed since the shop opened.

Required

1. Prepare income statements for Years 1 and 2.

2. Prepare the closing entries for each year. Prepare a short explanation for Sue about the purpose of closing temporary accounts.

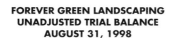 **Problem 4-15A** Ten-Column Work Sheet and Closing Entries (Appendix 4A)

The unadjusted trial balance for Forever Green Landscaping on August 31, 1998, follows:

General
Ledger

FOREVER GREEN LANDSCAPING
UNADJUSTED TRIAL BALANCE
AUGUST 31, 1998

Cash	$ 6,460	
Accounts Receivable	23,400	
Supplies on Hand	1,260	
Prepaid Insurance	3,675	
Equipment	28,800	
Accumulated Depreciation—Equipment		$ 9,200
Buildings	72,000	
Accumulated Depreciation—Buildings		16,800
Accounts Payable		10,500
Notes Payable		10,000
Capital Stock		40,000
Retained Earnings		42,100
Service Revenue		14,200

Advertising Expense	$ 1,200	
Gasoline and Oil Expense	1,775	
Wage and Salary Expense	4,230	
Totals	$142,800	$142,800

Required

1. Enter the unadjusted trial balance in the first two columns of a 10-column work sheet.

2. Enter the necessary adjustments in the appropriate columns of the work sheet for each of the following:

   a. A count of the supplies on hand at the end of August reveals a balance of $730.

   b. The company paid $4,200 in cash on May 1, 1998, for a two-year insurance policy.

   c. The equipment has a four-year estimated useful life and no salvage value.

   d. The buildings have an estimated useful life of 30 years and no salvage value.

   e. The company leases space in its building to another company. The agreement requires the tenant to pay Forever Green $700 on the 10th of each month for the previous month's rent.

   f. Wages and salaries earned by employees at the end of August but not yet paid amount to $3,320.

   g. The company signed a six-month promissory note on August 1, 1998. Interest at an annual rate of 12% and the principal amount of $10,000 are due on February 1, 1999.

3. Complete the remaining columns of the work sheet.

4. Assume that Forever Green closes its books at the end of each month before preparing financial statements. Prepare the necessary closing entries at August 31, 1998.

General
Ledger

LO 5, 6, 8 **Problem 4-16A** Ten-Column Work Sheet and Financial Statements (Appendix 4A)

The following unadjusted trial balance is available for Tenfour Trucking Company on January 31, 1998:

TENFOUR TRUCKING COMPANY
UNADJUSTED TRIAL BALANCE
JANUARY 31, 1998

Cash	$ 27,340	
Accounts Receivable	41,500	
Prepaid Insurance	18,000	
Warehouse	40,000	
Accumulated Depreciation—Warehouse		$ 21,600
Truck Fleet	240,000	
Accumulated Depreciation—Truck Fleet		112,500
Land	20,000	
Accounts Payable		32,880
Notes Payable		50,000
Interest Payable		4,500
Customer Deposits		6,000
Capital Stock		100,000
Retained Earnings		40,470
Freight Revenue		165,670
Gas and Oil Expense	57,330	
Maintenance Expense	26,400	
Wage and Salary Expense	43,050	
Dividends	20,000	
Totals	$533,620	$533,620

Required

1. Enter the unadjusted trial balance in the first two columns of a 10-column work sheet.

2. Enter the necessary adjustments in the appropriate columns of the work sheet for each of the following:

a. Prepaid insurance represents the cost of a 24-month policy purchased on January 1, 1998.

b. The warehouse has an estimated useful life of 20 years and an estimated salvage value of $4,000.

c. The truck fleet has an estimated useful life of six years and an estimated salvage value of $15,000.

d. The promissory note was signed on January 1, 1997. Interest at an annual rate of 9% and the principal of $50,000 are due on December 31, 1998.

e. The customer deposits represent amounts paid in advance by new customers. A total of $4,500 of the balance in Customer Deposits was earned during January 1998.

f. Wages and salaries earned by employees at the end of January but not yet paid amount to $8,200.

g. Income taxes are accrued at a rate of 30% at the end of each month.

3. Complete the remaining columns of the work sheet.

4. Prepare in good form the following financial statements:

  a. Income statement for the month ended January 31, 1998.

  b. Statement of retained earnings for the month ended January 31, 1998.

  c. Balance sheet at January 31, 1998.

5. Compute Tenfour's current ratio. What does this ratio tell you about the company's liquidity?

6. Explain why it is not possible to compute a gross profit ratio for Tenfour. Describe a ratio that you believe would be a meaningful measure of profitability for a trucking company. Feel free to "invent" a ratio if you think it would be a meaningful measure of profitability.

Cases

Reading and Interpreting Financial Statements

LO 3   **Case 4-1** Reading and Interpreting Ben & Jerry's Footnotes—Revenue Recognition

Refer to the footnote on page 155 where Ben & Jerry's explains how it recognizes initial franchise fees as revenue.

Required

1. Is the way in which Ben & Jerry's recognizes franchise fees for individual stores as revenue in accordance with the revenue recognition principle? Explain your answer.

2. Explain the logic behind the method Ben & Jerry's uses to recognize as revenue franchise fees relating to area franchise agreements.

3. Refer to Ben & Jerry's financial statements. How important are franchise fees as a form of revenue for the company? Support your answer with any necessary computations.

LO 3   **Case 4-2** Reading and Interpreting Sears, Roebuck's Footnotes—Revenue Recognition

The following excerpt is taken from Sears' 1995 annual report: "The Company sells extended service contracts with terms of coverage between 12 and 36 months. Revenue and incremental direct acquisition costs from the sale of these contracts are deferred and amortized on a straight-line basis over the lives of the contracts. Costs related to servicing the contracts are expensed as incurred."

Required

1. Why do retailers recognize the revenue over the life of the service contract even though cash is received at the time of the sale?

2. If a product is sold in Year 1 for $2,500, including a $180 service contract that will cover three years, how much revenue is recognized in Years 1, 2, and 3? What

corresponding account can you look for in the financial statements to determine the amount of service contract revenue that will be recognized in the future?

Making Financial Decisions

Decision
Making

LO 2, 3, 4 **Case 4-3** The Use of Net Income and Cash Flow to Evaluate a Company

After you have gained five years of experience with a large CPA firm, one of your clients, Duke Inc., asks you to take over as chief financial officer for the business. Duke advises its clients on the purchase of software products and assists them in installing the programs on their computer systems. Because the business is relatively new (it began servicing clients in January 1998), its accounting records are somewhat limited. In fact, the only statement available is an income statement for the first year:

DUKE INC.
STATEMENT OF INCOME
FOR THE YEAR ENDED DECEMBER 31, 1998

Revenues		$1,250,000
Expenses:		
Salaries and wages	$480,000	
Supplies	65,000	
Utilities	30,000	
Rent	120,000	
Depreciation	345,000	
Interest	138,000	
Total expenses		$1,178,000
Net income		$ 72,000

Based on its relatively modest profit margin of 5.76% (net income of $72,000 divided by revenues of $1,250,000), you are concerned about joining the new business. To alleviate your concerns, the president of the company is able to give you the following additional information:

a. Clients are given 90 days to pay their bills for consulting services provided by Duke. On December 31, 1998, $230,000 of the revenues is yet to be collected in cash.

b. Employees are paid on a monthly basis. Salaries and wages of $480,000 include the December payroll of $40,000, which will be paid on January 5, 1999.

c. The company purchased $100,000 of operating supplies when it began operations in January. The balance of supplies on hand at December 31 amounts to $35,000.

d. Office space is rented in a downtown high-rise building at a monthly rental of $10,000. When the company moved into the office in January, it prepaid its rent for the next 18 months, beginning January 1, 1998.

e. On January 1, 1998, Duke purchased its own computer system and related accessories at a cost of $1,725,000. The estimated useful life of the system is five years.

f. The computer system was purchased by signing a three-year, 8% note payable for $1,725,000 on the date of purchase. The principal amount of the note and interest for the three years are due on January 1, 2001.

Required

1. Based on the income statement and the additional information given, prepare a statement of cash flows for Duke for 1998 (*Hint:* Simply list all of the cash inflows and outflows that relate to operations).

2. On the basis of the income statement given and the statement of cash flows prepared in part 1, do you think it would be a wise decision on your part to join the company as its chief financial officer? Include in your response any additional questions that you believe are appropriate to ask before joining the company.

Decision
Making

LO 4 **Case 4-4** Depreciation

Jenner Inc., a graphic arts studio, is considering the purchase of computer equipment and software for a total cost of $18,000. Jenner can pay for the equipment and software over three years at the rate of $6,000 per year. The equipment is expected to last 10 to 20 years, but because of changing technology, Jenner believes it may need to replace the system as soon as three to five years. A three-year lease of similar equipment and software is available for $6,000 per year. Jenner's accountant has asked you to recommend whether the company should purchase or lease the equipment and software and to suggest the length of the period over which to depreciate the software and equipment if the company makes the purchase.

Required

Ignoring the effect of taxes, would you recommend the purchase or the lease? Why? Referring to the definition of *depreciation,* what is the appropriate useful life to use for the equipment and software?

Accounting and Ethics: What Would You Do?

LO 2, 3, 4, 5 **Case 4-5** Revenue Recognition and the Matching Principle

Listum & Sellum Inc. is a medium-size midwestern real estate company. It was founded five years ago by its two principal stockholders, Willie Listum and Dewey Sellum. Willie is president of the company, and Dewey is vice-president of sales. Listum & Sellum has enjoyed tremendous growth since its inception by aggressively seeking out listings for residential real estate and paying a very generous commission to the selling agent.

The company receives a 6% commission for selling a client's property and gives two-thirds of this, or 4% of the selling price, to the selling agent. For example, if a house sells for $100,000, Listum & Sellum receives $6,000 and pays $4,000 of this to the selling agent. At the time of the sale, the company records a debit of $6,000 to Accounts Receivable and a credit of $6,000 to Sales Revenue. The accounts receivable is normally collected within 30 days. Also at the time of sale, the company debits $4,000 to Commissions Expense and credits Commissions Payable for the same amount. Sales agents are paid by the 15th of the month following the month of the sale. In addition to the commissions expense, Listum & Sellum's other two major expenses are advertising of listings in local newspapers and depreciation of the company fleet of Cadillacs (Dewey has always believed that all of the sales agents should drive Cadillacs). The newspaper ads are taken for one month, and the company has until the 10th of the following month to pay that month's bill. The automobiles are depreciated over four years (Dewey doesn't believe that any salesperson should drive a car that is more than four years old).

Due to a downturn in the economy in the Midwest, sales have been sluggish for the first 11 months of the current year, which ends on June 30. Willie is very disturbed by the slow sales this particular year because a large note payable to the local bank is due in July and the company plans to ask the bank to renew the note for another three years. Dewey seems less concerned by the unfortunate timing of the recession and has some suggestions as to how they can "paint the rosiest possible picture for the banker" when they go for the loan extension in July. In fact, he has some very specific recommendations for you as to how to account for transactions during June, the last month in the fiscal year.

You are the controller for Listum & Sellum and have been treated very well by Willie and Dewey since joining the company two years ago. In fact, Dewey insists that you personally drive the top-of-the-line Cadillac. Following are his suggestions:

> First, for any sales made in June, we can record the 6% commission revenue immediately but delay recording the 4% commission expense until July, when the sales agent is paid. We record the sales at the same time we always have, the sales agents get paid when they always have, the bank sees how profitable we have been, we get our loan, and everybody is happy!
>
> Second, since we won't be paying our advertising bills for the month of June until July 10, we can just wait until then to record the expense. The timing seems perfect, given that we are to meet with the bank for the loan extension on July 8.

Third, since we will be depreciating the fleet of Caddys for the year ending June 30, how about just changing the estimated useful life on them to eight years instead of four years? We won't say anything to the sales agents; no need to rile them up about having to drive their cars for eight years. Anyhow, the change to eight years would just be for accounting purposes. In fact, we could even switch back to four years for accounting purposes next year. Likewise, the changes in recognizing commission expense and advertising expense don't need to be permanent either; these are just slight bookkeeping changes to help us get over the hump!

Required

1. Explain why each of the three proposed changes in accounting will result in an increase in net income for the year ending June 30.

2. Identify any concerns you have with each of the three proposed changes in accounting from the perspective of generally accepted accounting principles.

3. Identify any concerns you have with each of the three proposed changes in accounting from an ethical perspective.

4. What would you do? Draft your response to Willie and Dewey in the form of a business memo.

LO 4   **Case 4-6** Advice to a Potential Investor

Century Company was organized 15 months ago as a management consulting firm. At that time, the owners invested a total of $50,000 cash in exchange for stock. Century purchased equipment for $35,000 cash and supplies to be used in the business. The equipment is expected to last seven years with no salvage value. Supplies are purchased on account and paid for in the month after the purchase. Century normally has about $1,000 of supplies on hand. Its client base has increased so dramatically that the president and chief financial officer have approached an investor to provide additional cash for expansion. The balance sheet and income statement for the first year of business are presented below:

CENTURY COMPANY
BALANCE SHEET
DECEMBER 31, 1998

ASSETS		LIABILITIES AND OWNERS' EQUITY	
Cash	$10,100	Accounts payable	$ 2,300
Accounts receivable	1,200	Common stock	50,000
Supplies	16,500	Retained earnings	10,500
Equipment	35,000		
Total	$62,800	Total	$62,800

CENTURY COMPANY
INCOME STATEMENT
FOR THE YEAR ENDED DECEMBER 31, 1998

Revenues		$82,500
Wages and salaries	$60,000	
Utilities	12,000	72,000
Net income		$10,500

Required

The investor has asked you to look at these financial statements and give an opinion about Century's future profitability. Are the statements prepared in accordance with generally accepted accounting principles? If not, explain why. Based on only these two statements, what would you advise? What additional information would you need in order to give an educated opinion?

Research Case

Case 4-7 McDonald's

"Gas and a burger." "Shoes and a shake." These are just two of the ways McDonald's has attempted to expand sales. Smaller-size McDonald's restaurants have become a part of service stations, retail stores (such as Wal-Mart), hospitals, museums, and zoos.

Using the World Wide Web (http://www.mcdonalds.com), McDonald's most recent annual report, or library resources to obtain company financial data, answer the following:

1. Based on the latest accounting year available, what is the amount of McDonald's revenue from company-operated restaurants and franchised restaurants? How does this compare with the amounts for these items in the "Focus on Financial Results" in the opening vignette shown at the start of this chapter?

2. Locate the past 52-week high, low, and most current price for McDonald's stock. How might the company's revenue sources affect the stock price? If your investment club were considering McDonald's, would you recommend its stock to your fellow members? Discuss your reasons.

Optional Research. Based on restaurant visits and advertising, determine the menu items and pricing techniques used by McDonald's and other fast-food companies to attract customers. Do these techniques maximize McDonald's revenues?

Solution to Key Terms Quiz

__18__ Recognition (p. 148)

__11__ Current value (p. 149)

__14__ Accrual basis (p. 150)

__17__ Revenue recognition principle (p. 154)

__3__ Production method (p. 155)

__23__ Matching principle (p. 156)

__4__ Adjusting entries (p. 157)

__24__ Contra account (p. 159)

__19__ Deferred expense (p. 164)

__15__ Accrual (p. 164)

__10__ Accrued asset (p. 164)

__1__ Work sheet (p. 170)

__20__ Nominal accounts (p. 170)

__16__ Interim statements (p. 172)

__25__ Historical cost (p. 149)

__21__ Cash basis (p. 150)

__2__ Revenues (p. 153)

__6__ Percentage-of-completion method (p. 154)

__8__ Installment method (p. 155)

__26__ Expenses (p. 157)

__12__ Straight-line method (p. 159)

__13__ Deferral (p. 164)

__7__ Deferred revenue (p. 164)

__22__ Accrued liability (p. 164)

__27__ Accounting cycle (p. 169)

__9__ Real accounts (p. 170)

__5__ Closing entries (p. 171)

INTEGRATIVE PROBLEM

FOR

PART I

Completing Financial Statements, Computing Ratios, Comparing Accrual vs. Cash Income, and Evaluating the Company's Cash Needs

Mountain Home Health Inc. was formed in 1993 to provide home nursing services in the Great Smoky Mountains of Tennessee. When contacted by a client or referred by a physician, nurses visit with the patient and discuss needed services with the physician.

Mountain Home Health earns revenue from patient services. Most of the revenue comes from billing either insurance companies, the state of Tennessee, or the Medicare program. Amounts billed are recorded in the Billings Receivable account. Insurance companies, states, and the federal government do not fully fund all procedures. For example, the state of Tennessee pays an average 78% of billed amounts. Mountain Home Health has already removed the uncollectible amounts from the Billings Receivable account and reports it and Medical Services Revenue at the net amount. Services extended on Saturday, December 30, and Sunday, December 31, 2000, totaled $16,000, net of allowances for uncollectible amounts. The firm earns a minor portion of its total revenue directly from patients in the form of cash.

Employee salaries, medical supplies, depreciation, and gasoline are the major expenses. Employees are paid every Friday for work performed during the Saturday-to-Friday pay period. Salaries amount to $800 per day. In 2000, December 31 falls on a Sunday. Medical supplies (average use of $1,500 per week) are purchased periodically to support health care coverage. The inventory of supplies on hand on December 31 amounted to $8,653.

The firm owns five automobiles (all purchased at the same time) that average 50,000 miles per year and are replaced every 3 years. They typically have no residual value. The building has an expected life of 20 years with no residual value. Straight-line depreciation is used on all firm assets. Gasoline costs, which are a cash expenditure, average $375 per day. The firm purchases a 3-year, extended warranty contract to cover maintenance costs. The contract costs $9,000 (assume equal use each year).

On December 29, 2000, Mountain Home Health declared a dividend of $10,000, payable on January 15, 2001. The firm makes annual payments of principal and interest each June 30 on the mortgage. The interest rate on the mortgage is 6%.

The following unadjusted trial balance is available for Mountain Home Health on December 31, 2000.

MOUNTAIN HOME HEALTH
UNADJUSTED TRIAL BALANCE
DECEMBER 31, 2000

	DEBIT	CREDIT
Cash	$ 75,000	
Billings Receivable (net)	151,000	
Medical Supplies	73,000	
Extended Warranty	3,000	
Automobiles	90,000	
Accumulated Depreciation—Automobiles		$ 60,000
Building	200,000	
Accumulated Depreciation—Building		50,000
Accounts Payable		22,000
Dividend Payable		10,000
Mortgage Payable		100,000
Capital Stock		100,000
Additional Paid-in-Capital		50,000
Retained Earnings		99,900
Medical Services Revenue		550,000
Salary and Wages Expense	290,400	
Gasoline Expense	137,500	
Utilities Expense	12,000	
Dividends	10,000	
	$1,041,900	$1,041,900

Required

1. Set up T accounts for each of the accounts listed on the trial balance. Based on the information provided, set up any other T accounts that will be needed to prepare adjusting entries.

2. Post the year-end adjusting entries directly to the T accounts, but do not bother to put the entries in journal format first.

3. Prepare a statement of income and a statement of retained earnings for Mountain Home Health for the year ended December 31, 2000.

4. Prepare a balance sheet for Mountain Home Health as of December 31, 2000.

5. Compute the following as of December 31, 2000:

   a. Working capital

   b. Current ratio

6. Which of the adjusting entries might cause a difference between cash and accrual based income?

7. Mary Francis, controller of Mountain Home, became concerned about the company's cash flow after talking to a local bank loan officer. The firm tries to maintain a 7-week supply of cash to meet the demands of payroll, medical supply purchases, and gasoline. Determine the amount of cash Mountain Home needs to meet the 7-week supply.

A WORD TO STUDENTS ABOUT PART II

In Part I you learned how companies communicate their activities and financial results to users of financial information. You also discovered new ways of thinking about events as transactions, and how these business transactions culminate in a company's financial statements. You learned specialized terminology, used the accounting equation, and began to understand the basis for making financial decisions.

Part II tells what happens when assets flow into the business.

Chapter 5 introduces the effects of buying and selling merchandise on the financial statements, and the internal control necessary for keeping a business running smoothly. Chapter 6 expands on inventory issues and shows how inventory transactions affect the statement of cash flows. Chapter 7 covers the inflow of cash and receivables into the business. Chapter 8 recognizes that the business must invest its cash and receivables in operating assets.

Finally, you'll focus on how investors and other financial statement users evaluate companies with ratios and make decisions based on that information.

PART II

Accounting for Assets

Merchandise Accounting and Internal Control

STUDY LINKS

A Look at Previous Chapters

Chapter 4 completed our introduction to the accounting model. We examined the role of adjusting entries in an accrual accounting system.

A Look at This Chapter

In this chapter, we move beyond the basic accounting model to consider the accounting for the various elements on financial statements. We begin by looking at how merchandise companies—retailers and wholesalers—account for their inventory and the effects that buying and selling merchandise have on the income statement. The second part of the chapter introduces the concept of internal control and its applicability to merchandise inventory.

A Look at Upcoming Chapters

Chapter 6 continues the discussion begun in this chapter by focusing on valuation issues for inventory. In each of the remaining chapters in this part, we look at the accounting for other valuable assets of an entity.

FOCUS ON FINANCIAL RESULTS

Like all other successful specialty retailers, The Gap Inc. has grown by establishing a niche. The San Francisco–based company has built a reputation as an attractive source of khaki and denim clothing. The strategy, which has drawn both young customers and baby boomers, has benefited from the trend toward casual dress in the workplace. The Gap has established a GapKids division and an international division to deliver its style to a wider range of customers.

As a retailer, The Gap measures its success in terms of what it earns from buying and selling merchandise. Sales are, of course, a

The Gap Inc.

consolidated statements of earnings

($000 except per share amounts)	Fifty-three Weeks Ended February 3, 1996		Fifty-two Weeks Ended January 28, 1995		Fifty-two Weeks Ended January 29, 1994	
Net sales	$4,395,253	100.0%	$3,722,940	100.0%	$3,295,679	100.0%
Costs and expenses						
Cost of goods sold and occupancy expenses	2,821,455	64.2%	2,350,996	63.2%	2,121,789	64.4%
Operating expenses	1,004,396	22.9%	853,524	22.9%	748,193	22.7%
Net interest (income) expense	(15,797)	(0.4%)	(10,902)	(0.3%)	809	—
Earnings before income taxes	585,199	13.3%	529,322	14.2%	424,888	12.9%
Income taxes	231,160	5.2%	209,082	5.6%	166,464	5.1%
Net earnings	$ 354,039	8.1%	$ 320,240	8.6%	$ 258,424	7.8%
Weighted average number of shares[a]	288,062,430		291,141,076		289,682,274	
Earnings per share[a]	$ 1.23		$ 1.10		$ .89	

See notes to consolidated financial statements.
(a) Reflects the two-for-one split of common stock in the form of a stock dividend to stockholders of record on March 18, 1996.

fundamental measure, and The Gap's income statement (shown here) indicates that its 1995 sales increased by 18 percent from the previous year, to a record $4.4 billion. The Gap needs to create enough value for shoppers that they will pay more for the merchandise than the retailer's cost to acquire it. Thus, another important indicator is the income statement line "cost of goods sold and occupancy expenses." This line shows that nearly two-thirds of every sales dollar goes to these costs.

If you were a Gap manager, you would want the company—and each store—to maximize the difference between net sales and cost of goods sold. How would data on the square footage of each store help? Check a more recent annual report to see how this measure has changed.

SOURCE: *The Gap Inc. Annual Report,* 1995.

After studying this chapter, you should be able to

LO 1 Understand how wholesalers and retailers account for sales of merchandise.

LO 2 Explain the differences between periodic and perpetual inventory systems.

LO 3 Understand how wholesalers and retailers account for cost of goods sold.

LO 4 Explain the importance of internal control to a business.

LO 5 Describe the basic internal control procedures.

LO 6 Describe the various documents used in recording purchases of merchandise and their role in controlling cash disbursements (Appendix 5A).

The Income Statement for a Merchandiser

To this point, we have concentrated on the accounting for businesses that sell *services*. Banks, hotels, airlines, health clubs, real estate offices, law firms, and accounting firms are all examples of service companies. We turn our attention in this chapter to accounting by merchandisers. Both retailers and wholesalers are merchandisers. They purchase inventory in finished form and hold it for resale. This is in contrast to manufacturers' inventory, which takes three different forms: raw materials, work in process, and finished goods. Accounting for the three different forms of inventory for a manufacturer is more complex and is covered in a follow-up course to this one. We focus in this chapter on accounting for merchandise, that is, inventory held by either a wholesaler or a retailer.

A *condensed* multiple-step income statement for Tabor Hardware Stores is presented in Exhibit 5-1. First note the period covered by the statement: for the year ended December 31, 1998. Tabor ends its fiscal year on December 31; however, many merchandisers end their *fiscal year* on a date other than December 31. Retailers often choose a date toward the end of January because the busy holiday shopping season is over and time can be devoted to closing the records and preparing financial statements. For example, The Gap Inc. ends its fiscal year on the Saturday closest to January 31. Alternatively, Circuit City stores closes its books on February 28 each year.

We will concentrate our attention on the first two items on Tabor's statement: net sales and cost of goods sold. The major difference between this income statement and that for a service company is the inclusion of cost of goods sold. Because a service company does not sell a product, it does not report cost of goods sold. On the income statement of a merchandising company, cost of goods sold is deducted from net sales to arrive at gross margin or gross profit.

Gross margin as a percentage of net sales is a common analytical tool for merchandise companies. Analysts compare the gross margin percentages for various periods or

FROM CONCEPT TO PRACTICE 5.1

READING BEN & JERRY'S ANNUAL REPORT Is Ben & Jerry's a merchandiser? What items in the annual report can you cite to support your answer?

EXHIBIT 5-1 Condensed Income Statement for a Merchandiser

TABOR HARDWARE STORES
INCOME STATEMENT
FOR THE YEAR ENDED DECEMBER 31, 1998

Net sales	$100,000
Cost of goods sold	60,000
Gross margin	$ 40,000
Selling and administrative expenses	29,300
Net income before tax	$ 10,700
Income tax expense	4,280
Net income	$ 6,420

for several companies and express concern if a company's gross margin is dropping. Every industry in the retail sector has its average gross margin ratio, average overhead cost per square foot, and average sales per square foot of retail space. Analysts can use these facts to see how one company is performing in comparison with others in the same industry. If analysts looked at The Gap's ten-year summary in its annual report, they would find that sales per square foot have increased from $250 in 1986 to $425 in 1995.

Net Sales of Merchandise

The first section of Tabor's income statement is presented in Exhibit 5-2. Two deductions—for sales returns and allowances and sales discounts—are made from sales revenue to arrive at net sales. Sales revenue, or simply sales, as it is often called, is a *representation of the inflow of assets,* either cash or accounts receivable, from the sale of merchandise during the period. In a merchandising business, cash sales are recorded daily in the journal and are based on the total amount shown on the cash register tape. For example, suppose that the cash register tape in the paint department of Tabor Hardware Stores shows sales on March 31, 1998, of $350. The transaction is recorded in the journal as follows:

LO 1   Understand how wholesalers and retailers account for sales of merchandise.

Mar. 31	Cash	350
	Sales Revenue	350
	To record daily cash receipts in paint department.	

Assets = Liabilities + Owners' Equity
+350   +350

Sales on credit do not result in the immediate inflow of cash but in an increase in accounts receivable, a promise by the customer to pay cash at a later date. The entry to record a May 4 sale of tools on credit for $125 is recorded as follows:

May 4	Accounts Receivable	125
	Sales Revenue	125
	To record sale on credit in tools department.	

Assets = Liabilities + Owners' Equity
+125   +125

Sales Returns and Allowances

The cornerstone of marketing is to satisfy the customer. Most companies have standard policies that allow the customer to *return* merchandise within a stipulated period of time. Nordstrom, the Seattle-based retailer, has a very liberal policy regarding returns. That policy has, in large measure, fueled its growth. A company's policy might be that a customer who is not completely satisfied can return the merchandise anytime within 30 days of purchase for a full refund. Alternatively, the customer may be given an *allowance* for spoiled or damaged merchandise, that is, the customer keeps the merchandise but receives a credit for a certain amount in the account balance. Typically, a single account,

Merchandisers stock and sell products that other companies manufacture. Whether they are retail shops like this one, or wholesalers selling their merchandise to retail stores, merchandisers keep inventories of the different products they stock. They must track these items and their cost as they are delivered to their store, as they leave the store as sold—and sometimes as they come back as returned merchandise.

EXHIBIT 5-2   Net Sales Section of the Income Statement

TABOR HARDWARE STORES
PARTIAL INCOME STATEMENT
FOR THE YEAR ENDED DECEMBER 31, 1998

Sales revenue	$103,500
Less: Sales returns and allowances	2,000
Sales discounts	1,500
Net sales	$100,000

Sales Returns and Allowances, is used to account for both returns and allowances. If the customer has already paid for the merchandise, either a cash refund is given or the credit amount is applied to future purchases.

The accounting for a return or allowance depends on whether the customer is given a cash refund or credit on an account. Assume that Tabor's paint department gives a $25 cash refund on spoiled paint returned by a customer. The entry follows:

Apr. 25	Sales Returns and Allowances	25	
	Cash		25
	To record return of spoiled paint by customer for a cash refund.		

Assets	=	**Liabilities**	+	**Owners' Equity**
-25				-25

Sales Returns and Allowances is a *contra-revenue* account. A contra account has a balance opposite to its related account and is deducted from that account on the statement. Thus, the effect of the debit to this account is the same as if Sales Revenue had been reduced (debited) directly.

The purpose of this entry is to reduce the amount of previously recorded sales. So why didn't we simply reduce Sales Revenue for $25? The reason is that management needs to be able to *monitor* the amount of returns and allowances. If Sales Revenue is reduced for returns and at some point we need to determine the total dollars of returns for the period, we would need to add up all of the individual decreases to this account. A much more efficient method is to split the sales revenue into two accounts, one that includes only sales and another that includes only returns. In this way, the total amount of returns is readily available, and the decision-making process is more efficient and thus more effective.

The previous entry illustrates the accounting for a return of merchandise. The same account is normally used when a credit is given and the customer keeps the merchandise. Assume that on May 7 the customer that made the $125 purchase from Tabor on May 4 notifies it that one of the purchased tools is defective. Tabor agrees to reduce the customer's unpaid account by $10 because of the defect. The entry to record the allowance follows:

May 7	Sales Returns and Allowances	10	
	Accounts Receivable		10
	To record allowance given for defective merchandise.		

Assets	=	**Liabilities**	+	**Owners' Equity**
-10				-10

The Sales Returns and Allowances account gives management and stockholders an important piece of data: that merchandise is being returned or is not completely acceptable. It does not answer the following questions, however. Why is the merchandise being returned? Why are customers getting partial refunds? Is the merchandise shoddy? Are salespeople too aggressive? Should the store's liberal policy regarding returns be changed?

Trade Discounts and Quantity Discounts

Various types of discounts to the list price are given to customers. A trade discount is a selling price reduction offered to a special class of customers. For example, Tabor's plumbing department might offer a special price to building contractors. The difference between normal selling price and this special price is called a *trade discount*. A quantity discount is sometimes offered to customers who are willing to buy in large quantities.

Trade discounts and quantity discounts are *not* recorded in the accounts. Although a company might track the amount of these discounts for control purposes, the reason for ignoring the quantity and trade discounts in the accounting records is that the list price is not the actual selling price. The *net* amount is a more accurate reflection of the amount of a sale. For example, assume that Tabor gives a 20% discount from the normal selling price to any single customer who buys between 10 and 25 kitchen sinks and a 30% discount on purchases of more than 25 sinks. The list price for each unit is $200.

The selling price and the related journal entry for a customer's purchase of 40 sinks on July 2 are as follows:

List price	$ 200
Less: 30% quantity discount	60
Selling price	140
× Number of sinks sold	× 40
Sales revenue	$5,600

July 2	Accounts Receivable	5,600	
	Sales Revenue		5,600

To record sale of 40 kitchen sinks at list price less 30% quantity discount.

Assets	=	Liabilities	+	Owners' Equity
+5,600				+5,600

Credit Terms and Sales Discounts

Most companies have a standard credit policy. Special notation is normally used to indicate a particular firm's policy for granting credit. For example, credit terms of *n/30* mean that the *net* amount of the selling price, that is, the amount determined after deducting any returns or allowances, is due within 30 days of the date of the invoice. *Net, 10 EOM* means that the net amount is due anytime within 10 days after the end of the month in which the sale took place.

Another common element of the credit terms offered to customers is sales discounts, a reduction from the selling price given for early payment. For example, assume that Tabor offers a building contractor credit terms of *1/10, n/30*. This means that the customer may deduct 1% from the selling price if the bill is paid within 10 days of the date of the invoice. Normally the discount period begins with the day *after* the invoice date. If the customer does not pay within the first 10 days, the full invoice amount is due within 30 days. Finally, note that the use of *n* for *net* in this notation is really a misnomer. Although the amount due is net of any returns and allowances, it is the gross amount that is due within 30 days. That is, no discount is given if the customer does not pay early.

How valuable to the customer is a 1% discount for payment within the first 10 days? Assume that a $1,000 sale is made. If the customer pays at the end of 10 days, the cash paid will be $990, rather than $1,000, a net savings of $10. The customer has saved $10 by paying 20 days earlier than required by the 30-day term. If we assume 360 days in a year, there are 360/20 or 18 periods of 20 days each in a year. Thus, a savings of $10 for 20 days is equivalent to a savings of $10 times 18, or $180 for the year. An annual return of $180/$990, or 18.2%, would be difficult to match with any other type of investment. In fact, a company might want to consider borrowing the money to pay off the account early.

Some companies record sales *net* of any discounts for early payment; others record the *gross* amount of sales and then track sales discounts separately. Because the effect on the accounting equation does not differ between the two methods, we will concern ourselves only with the *gross method,* which assumes that customers will not necessarily take advantage of the discount offered for early payment. Sales discounts are rarely material, and companies do not normally disclose the method used on their financial statements.

Assume a sale on June 10 of $1,000 with credit terms of 2/10, net 30. The entry at the time of the sale is as follows:

June 10	Accounts Receivable	1,000	
	Sales Revenue		1,000

To record sale on account, terms 2/10, net 30.

Assets	=	Liabilities	+	Owners' Equity
+1,000				+1,000

If the customer pays after the discount period, the accountant simply makes an entry to record the receipt of $1,000 cash and the reduction of accounts receivable. However, assume the customer pays its account on June 20, within the discount period. The following entry would be made:

June 20	Cash	980	
	Sales Discounts	20	
	Accounts Receivable		1,000
	To record collection on account.		

Assets	=	**Liabilities**	+	**Owners' Equity**
+ 980				−20
−1,000				

The **Sales Discounts** account is a *contra-revenue* account and thus reduces owners' equity as shown in the accounting equation above. Also note in Exhibit 5-2 that sales discounts are deducted from sales on the income statement.

The Cost of Goods Sold

The cost of goods sold section of the income statement for Tabor is shown in Exhibit 5-3. We will soon turn our attention to each line item in this section. First let us take a look at the basic model for cost of goods sold.

The Cost of Goods Sold Model

The recognition of cost of goods sold as an expense is an excellent example of the *matching principle*. Sales revenue represents the *inflow* of assets, in the form of cash and accounts receivable, from the sale of products during the period. Likewise, cost of goods sold represents the *outflow* of an asset, inventory, from the sale of those same products. The company needs to match the revenue of the period with one of the most important costs necessary to generate the revenue, the *cost* of the merchandise sold.

It may be helpful in understanding cost of goods sold to realize what it is *not. Cost of goods sold is not necessarily equal to the cost of purchases of merchandise during the period.* Except in the case of a new business, a merchandiser starts the year with a certain stock of inventory on hand, called *beginning inventory.* For Tabor, beginning inventory is the dollar amount of merchandise on hand on January 1, 1998. During the year, Tabor purchases merchandise. When the cost of goods purchased is added to beginning inventory, the result is **cost of goods available for sale.** Just as the merchandiser starts the period with an inventory of merchandise on hand, a certain amount of *ending*

EXHIBIT 5-3 Cost of Goods Sold Section of the Income Statement

TABOR HARDWARE STORES
PARTIAL INCOME STATEMENT
FOR THE YEAR ENDED DECEMBER 31, 1998

Cost of goods sold:			
Inventory, January 1, 1998		$15,000	
Purchases	$65,000		
Less: Purchase returns and allowances	1,800		
Purchase discounts	3,700		
Net purchases	$59,500		
Add: Transportation-in	3,500		
Cost of goods purchased		63,000	
Costs of goods available for sale		$78,000	
Less: Inventory, December 31, 1998		18,000	
Cost of goods sold			$60,000

inventory is usually on hand at the end of the year. For Tabor, this is its inventory on December 31, 1998.

Think of cost of goods available for sale as a "pool" of costs to be distributed between what we sold and what we did not sell. If we subtract from the pool the cost of what we did *not* sell, the *ending inventory,* we will have the amount we *did* sell, the cost of goods sold. Cost of goods sold is simply the difference between the cost of goods available for sale and the ending inventory:

Beginning inventory	What is on hand to start the period
+ Purchases	What was acquired for resale during the period
= Cost of goods available for sale	The "pool" of costs to be distributed
− Ending inventory	What was not sold during the period and therefore is on hand to start the next period
= Cost of goods sold	What was sold during the period

The cost of goods sold model for a merchandiser is illustrated in Exhibit 5-4. The amounts used for the illustration are taken from the cost of goods sold section of Tabor's income statement as shown in Exhibit 5-3. Notice that ending inventory exceeds beginning inventory by $3,000. That means that the cost of goods purchased exceeded cost of goods sold by that same amount. Indeed, a key point for stockholders, bankers, and other users is whether inventory is building up, that is, whether a company is not selling as much inventory during the period as it is buying. A buildup may indicate that the company's products are becoming less desirable or that prices are becoming uncompetitive.

Inventory Systems: Perpetual and Periodic

Before we look at the journal entries to account for cost of goods sold, it is necessary to understand the difference between the periodic and the perpetual inventory systems. All businesses use one of these two distinct approaches to account for inventory. With the perpetual system, the Inventory account is updated *perpetually,* or after each sale or purchase of merchandise. Conversely, with the periodic system, the Inventory account is updated only at the end of the *period*.

In a perpetual system, every time goods are purchased, the Inventory account is increased, with a corresponding increase in Accounts Payable for a credit purchase or a decrease in the Cash account for a cash purchase. In addition to recognizing the increases in Accounts Receivable or Cash and in Sales Revenue when goods are sold, the accountant also records an entry to recognize the *cost* of the goods sold and the decrease in the cost of inventory on hand:

LO 2 Explain the differences between periodic and perpetual inventory systems.

EXHIBIT 5-4	The Cost of Goods Sold Model	
DESCRIPTION	**ITEM**	**AMOUNT**
Merchandise on hand to start the period	Beginning inventory	$15,000
Acquisitions of merchandise during the period	+ Cost of goods purchased	63,000
The pool of merchandise available for sale during the period	= Cost of goods available for sale	$78,000
Merchandise on hand at end of period	− Ending inventory	(18,000)
The expense recognized on the income statement	= Cost of goods sold	$60,000

Cost of Goods Sold	xxx	
Inventory		xxx
To record the sale of inventory under perpetual system.		

Assets = Liabilities + Owners' Equity
−xxx   **−xxx**

Thus, at any point during the period, the inventory account is up to date. It has been increased for the cost of purchases during the period and reduced for the cost of the sales.

Why don't all companies use the procedure we just described, the perpetual system? Depending on the volume of inventory transactions, that is, purchases and sales of merchandise, a perpetual system can be extremely costly to maintain. Historically, businesses that have a relatively small volume of sales at a high unit price have used perpetual systems. For example, dealers in automobiles, furniture, appliances, and jewelry normally use a perpetual system. Each purchase of a unit of merchandise, such as an automobile, can be easily identified and an increase recorded in the Inventory account. When the auto is sold, the dealer can easily determine the cost of the particular car sold by looking at a perpetual inventory record.

Can you imagine, however, a similar system for a supermarket or a hardware store? Consider a checkout stand in a grocery store. Through the use of a cash register tape, the sales revenue for that particular stand is recorded at the end of the day. Because of the tremendous volume of sales of various items of inventory, from cans of vegetables to boxes of soap, it may not be feasible to record the cost of goods sold every time a sale takes place. This illustrates a key point in financial information: the cost of the information should never exceed its benefit. If a store manager had to stop and update the records each time a can of Campbell's soup was sold, the retailer's business would obviously be disrupted.

To a certain extent, the ability of mass merchandisers to maintain perpetual inventory records has improved with the advent of point-of-sale terminals. When a cashier runs a can of corn over the sensing glass at the checkout stand and the bar code is read, the company's computer receives a message that a can of corn has been sold. In some companies, however, updating the inventory record is in units only and is used as a means to determine when a product needs to be reordered. The company still relies on a periodic system to maintain the *dollar* amount of inventory. In the remainder of this chapter, we limit our discussion to the periodic system. We discuss the perpetual system in detail in Chapter 6.

ACCOUNTING FOR YOUR DECISIONS
You Are the Entrepreneur

A year ago, you and your brother launched a running shoe company in your garage. You buy shoes from four of the major manufacturers and sell them over the phone. Your accountant suggests that you use a perpetual inventory system. Should you?

ANS: The periodic inventory system has the following advantages: The Inventory account is updated only once per year, not after every purchase; the inventory is physically counted on the last day of each period to determine ending inventory; and its cost is low. By operating out of your garage, you are focusing on keeping administrative costs down. A perpetual inventory system would be more costly and would not provide enough extra benefits at low volume. Your decision may change as your business grows.

Beginning and Ending Inventories in a Periodic System

In a periodic system, the Inventory account is *not* updated each time a sale or purchase is made. Throughout the year, the Inventory account contains the amount of merchandise on hand at the beginning of the year. The account is adjusted only at the end of the year. A company using the periodic system must physically *count* the units of inventory on hand at the end of the period. The number of units of each product is then multiplied by the cost per unit, to determine the dollar amount of ending inventory. Refer to Exhibit 5-3 for Tabor Hardware Stores. The procedure just described was used to determine its ending inventory of $18,000. Because one period's ending inventory is the next period's beginning inventory, the beginning inventory of $15,000 was based on the count at the end of the prior year.

In summary, the ending inventory in a periodic system is determined by counting the merchandise, not by looking at the Inventory account at the end of the period. The periodic system results in a trade-off. Use of the periodic system reduces record keeping but at the expense of a certain degree of control. Losses of merchandise due to theft, breakage, spoilage, or other reasons may go undetected in a periodic system because management may assume that all merchandise not on hand at the end of the year was sold. In a retail store, some of the merchandise may have been shoplifted rather than sold. In contrast, with a perpetual inventory system, a count of inventory at the end of the period serves as a *control device*. For example, if the Inventory account shows a balance of $45,000 at the end of the year but only $42,000 of merchandise is counted, management is able to investigate the discrepancy. No such control feature exists in a periodic system.

In addition to the loss of control, the use of a periodic system presents a dilemma when a company wants to prepare *interim* financial statements. Because most companies that use a periodic system find it cost-prohibitive to count the entire inventory more than once a year, they use estimation techniques to determine inventory for monthly or quarterly statements. These techniques are discussed in Chapter 6.

The Cost of Goods Purchased

The cost of goods purchased section of Tabor's income statement is shown in Exhibit 5-5. The company purchased $65,000 of merchandise during the period. Two amounts are deducted from purchases to arrive at net purchases: purchase returns and allowances of $1,800 and purchase discounts of $3,700. The cost of $3,500 incurred by Tabor to ship the goods to its place of business is called transportation-in and is added to net purchases of $59,500 to arrive at the cost of goods purchased of $63,000. Another name for transportation-in is *freight-in*.

LO 3 Understand how wholesalers and retailers account for cost of goods sold.

Purchases Assume that Tabor buys merchandise on account from one of its wholesalers at a cost of $4,000. Purchases is the temporary account used in a periodic inventory system to record acquisitions of merchandise. The journal entry to record the purchase follows:

Feb. 8	Purchases	4,000	
	Accounts Payable		4,000
	To record the purchase of merchandise on account.		

Assets	=	Liabilities	+	Owners' Equity
		+4,000		−4,000

EXHIBIT 5-5   Cost of Goods Purchased

TABOR HARDWARE STORES
PARTIAL INCOME STATEMENT
FOR THE YEAR ENDED DECEMBER 31, 1998

Purchases	$65,000	
Less: Purchase returns and allowances	1,800	
Purchase discounts	3,700	
Net purchases	$59,500	
Add: Transportation-in	3,500	
Cost of goods purchased		$63,000

It is important to understand that Purchases is *not* an asset account. It is included in the income statement as an integral part of the calculaion of cost of goods sold and is therefore shown as a reduction of owners' equity in the accounting equation. Because Purchases is a temporary account, it is closed at the end of the period.

Purchase Returns and Allowances   We discussed returns and allowances earlier in the chapter from the seller's point of view. From the standpoint of the buyer, purchase returns and allowances are reductions in the cost to purchase merchandise. Rather than record these reductions directly in the Purchases account, the accountant uses a separate account. The account, **Purchase Returns and Allowances,** is a *contra account* to Purchases. Because Purchases has a normal debit balance, the normal balance in Purchase Returns and Allowances is a credit balance. The use of a contra account allows management to monitor the amount of returns and allowances. For example, a large number of returns during the period relative to the amount purchased may signal that the purchasing department is not buying from reputable sources.

Suppose that Tabor returns $850 of merchandise to a wholesaler for credit on its account. The return decreases both liabilities and purchases. Note that because a return reduces purchases, it actually *increases* net income and thus also increases owners' equity. The journal entry follows:

Sept. 6	Accounts Payable	850	
	Purchase Returns and Allowances		850
	To record the return of merchandise for credit to account.		

Assets	=	Liabilities	+	Owners' Equity
		−850		+850

The entry to record an allowance for merchandise retained rather than returned is the same as the entry for a return.

ACCOUNTING FOR YOUR DECISIONS
You Are the President

You are the President of a mail-order computer business. Your company buys computers and related parts directly from manufacturers and sells them to consumers via direct mail. Recently, you have noticed an increase in the amount of purchase returns and allowances relative to the amount of purchases. What are some possible explanations for this increase?

ANS: Any number of explanations are possible. It is possible that the products are being damaged while in transit. Or it may be that the company has changed suppliers and the merchandise is not of the quality expected. Or it may be that the employees are becoming more demanding in what they accept than they used to be.

Purchase Discounts   Discounts were discussed earlier in the chapter from the seller's viewpoint. Merchandising companies often purchase inventory on terms that allow for a cash discount for early payment, such as 2/10, net 30. To the buyer, a cash discount is called a *purchase discount* and results in a reduction of the cost to purchase merchandise. The same two methods that are used to account for sales discounts are used to account for purchase discounts. Regardless of the method used, management must monitor the amount of purchase discounts taken as well as those opportunities missed by not taking advantage of the discounts for early payment. Because the effect on the accounting equation does not differ between the gross and the net methods, we will limit our discussion to the use of the *gross method*.

Assume a purchase of merchandise on March 13 for $500, with credit terms of 1/10, net 30. The entry at the time of the purchase is as follows:

Mar. 13	Purchases	500	
	Accounts Payable		500
	To record purchase on account, terms 1/10, net 30.		

Assets	=	Liabilities	+	Owners' Equity
+500		+500		−500

If the company does not pay within the discount period, the accountant simply makes an entry to record the payment of $500 cash and the reduction of accounts payable. However, assume the company does pay its account on March 23, within the discount period. The following entry would be made:

Mar. 23	Accounts Payable	500	
	Cash		495
	Purchase Discounts		5
	To record payment on account.		

Assets	=	**Liabilities**	+	**Owners' Equity**
−495		−500		+5

The **Purchase Discounts** account is contra to the Purchases account and thus increases owners' equity, as shown in the accounting equation above. Also note in Exhibit 5-5 that purchase discounts are deducted from Purchases on the income statement. Finally, note that the effect on the income statement is the same as illustrated earlier for a purchase return: because purchases are reduced, net income is increased.

Shipping Terms and Transportation Costs   The *cost principle* governs the recording of all assets. All costs necessary to prepare an asset for its intended use should be included in its cost. The cost of an item to a merchandising company is not necessarily limited to its invoice price. For example, any sales tax paid should be included in computing total cost. Any transportation costs incurred by the buyer should likewise be included in the cost of the merchandise.

The buyer does not always pay to ship the merchandise. This depends on the terms of shipment. Goods are normally shipped either **FOB destination point** or **FOB shipping point**; *FOB* stands for *free on board*. When merchandise is shipped FOB destination point, it is the responsibility of the seller to deliver the products to the buyer. Thus, the seller either delivers the product to the customer or pays a trucking firm, railroad, or other carrier to transport it. Alternatively, the agreement between the buyer and the seller may provide for the goods to be shipped FOB shipping point. In this case, the merchandise is the responsibility of the buyer as soon as it leaves the seller's premises. When the terms of shipment are FOB shipping point, the buyer incurs transportation costs.

Refer to Exhibit 5-5. Transportation-in represents the freight costs Tabor paid for inbound merchandise. These costs are added to net purchases, as shown in the exhibit, and increase the cost of goods purchased. Assume that on delivery of a shipment of goods, Tabor pays an invoice for $300 from the Chicago and Southwestern Railroad. The terms of shipment are FOB shipping point. The entry on the books of Tabor follows:

May 10	Transportation-in	300	
	Cash		300
	To record the payment of freight costs.		

Assets	=	**Liabilities**	+	**Owners' Equity**
−300				−300

The total of net purchases and transportation-in is called the *cost of goods purchased.* Transportation-in will be closed at the end of the period. In summary, cost of goods purchased consists of the following:

> Purchases
> Less: Purchase returns and allowances
>   Purchase discounts
> Equals: Net purchases
> Add: Transportation-in
> Equals: Cost of goods purchased

How should the *seller* account for the freight costs it pays when the goods are shipped FOB destination point? This cost, sometimes called *transportation-out,* is not an addition to the cost of purchases of the seller but is instead one of the costs necessary to *sell* the merchandise. Transportation-out is classified as a *selling expense* on the income statement.

Shipping Terms and Transfer of Title to Inventory   Terms of shipment take on additional significance at the end of an accounting period. It is essential that a company establish a proper cutoff at year-end. For example, what if Tabor purchases merchandise that is in transit at the end of the year? To whom does the inventory belong, Tabor or the seller? The answer depends on the terms of shipment. If goods are shipped FOB destination point, they remain the legal property of the seller until they reach their destination. Alternatively, legal title to goods shipped FOB shipping point passes to the buyer as soon as the seller turns the goods over to the carrier.

The example in Exhibit 5-6 is intended to summarize our discussion about shipping terms and ownership of merchandise. The example involves a shipment of merchandise in transit at the end of the year. Horton, the seller of the goods, pays the transportation charges if the terms are FOB destination point. Horton records a sale for goods in transit at year-end, however, only if the terms of shipment are FOB shipping point. If Horton does not record a sale, because the goods are shipped FOB destination point, the inventory appears on its December 31 balance sheet. Tabor, the buyer, pays freight costs if the goods are shipped FOB shipping point. Only in this situation does Tabor record a purchase of the merchandise and include it as an asset on its December 31 balance sheet.

ACCOUNTING FOR YOUR DECISIONS

You Are the Manager

You manage the student bookstore. To get ready for the Spring term, in December you order a large shipment of books from a publisher, with terms of FOB shipping point. Unfortunately, you learn in January the books were lost enroute. Should this shipment be included in the year-end inventory count even though it is not on hand to count? Assume a periodic inventory system.

ANS: Because the books were shipped FOB shipping point, they should be included in the year-end count even though they are not on hand to count. You should review the purchase invoice to determine the number of books ordered and the unit costs.

The Closing Process for a Merchandiser

The closing process serves two purposes. First, all income statement accounts are returned to a zero balance to start the next accounting period. Second, net income and dividends of the period are transferred to the Retained Earnings account. Many different procedural approaches may be used to close the accounts of a merchandising company. The list on page 229 indicates the normal balance in each of the accounts used in a periodic system and whether the account is closed with a debit or a credit:

EXHIBIT 5-6	Shipping Terms and Transfer of Title to Inventory

Facts On December 28, 1998, Horton Wholesale ships merchandise to Tabor Hardware Stores. The trucking company delivers the merchandise to Tabor on January 2, 1999. Tabor's fiscal year-end is December 31.

		IF MERCHANDISE IS SHIPPED FOB	
COMPANY		**DESTINATION POINT**	**SHIPPING POINT**
Horton	Pay freight costs?	Yes	No
(seller)	Record sale in 1998?	No	Yes
	Include inventory on balance sheet at December 31, 1998?	Yes	No
Tabor	Pay freight costs?	No	Yes
(buyer)	Record purchase in 1998?	No	Yes
	Include inventory on balance sheet at December 31, 1998?	No	Yes

ACCOUNT	NORMAL BALANCE	CLOSED WITH A
Sales Revenue	Credit	Debit
Sales Returns and Allowances	Debit	Credit
Sales Discounts	Debit	Credit
Purchases	Debit	Credit
Purchase Returns and Allowances	Credit	Debit
Purchase Discounts	Credit	Debit
Transportation-in	Debit	Credit

An Introduction to Internal Control

An employee of a large auto parts warehouse routinely takes spare parts home for personal use. A payroll clerk writes and signs two checks for an employee and then splits the amount of the second check with the worker. Through human error, an invoice is paid for merchandise never received from the supplier. These cases sound quite different from one another, but they share one important characteristic. They all point to a deficiency in a company's internal control system. An internal control system consists of the policies and procedures necessary to ensure the safeguarding of an entity's assets, the reliability of its accounting records, and the accomplishment of its overall objectives.

Three assets are especially critical to the operation of a merchandising company: cash, accounts receivable, and inventory. Activities related to these three assets compose the operating cycle of a business. Cash is used to buy inventory, the inventory is eventually sold, and assuming a sale on credit, the account receivable from the customer is collected. We turn now to the ways in which a company attempts to *control* the assets at its disposal. This section serves as an introduction to the important topic of internal control, which is explored further at appropriate points in the book. For example, controls to safeguard cash are discussed in Chapter 7.

LO 4 Explain the importance of internal control to a business.

The Report of Management: Showing Responsibility for Control

Modern business is characterized by absentee ownership. In most large corporations, it is impossible for the owners—the stockholders—to be actively involved in the daily affairs of the business. Professional managers have the primary responsibility for the business's smooth operation. They are also responsible for the content of the financial statements.

Most annual reports now include a report of management to the stockholders. A typical management report, in this case for The Gap Inc., is shown in Exhibit 5-7. The first paragraph of the report clearly spells out management's responsibility for the financial information presented in the annual report. The second paragraph refers to the system of internal controls within the company. One of the features of The Gap's internal control system is the use of an internal audit staff. Most large corporations today have a full-time staff of internal auditors who have the responsibility for evaluating the entity's internal control system.

The primary concern of the independent public accountants, or external auditors, is whether the financial statements have been presented fairly. Internal auditors focus more on the efficiency with which the organization is run. They are responsible for periodically reviewing both accounting and administrative controls, which we discuss later in this chapter. The internal audit staff also helps to ensure that the company's policies and procedures are followed.

The second paragraph of the report states that the company's independent public accountants have audited the company's financial statements. The management of most corporations would consider it cost-prohibitive for the auditors to verify the millions of transactions recorded in a single year. Instead, the auditors rely to a certain degree on

EXHIBIT 5-7   Report of Management—The Gap Inc.

management's report on financial information

Management is responsible for the integrity and consistency of all financial information presented in the Annual Report. The financial statements have been prepared in accordance with generally accepted accounting principles and necessarily include certain amounts based on Management's best estimates and judgements.

In fulfilling its responsibility for the reliability of financial information, Management has established and maintains accounting systems and procedures appropriately supported by internal accounting controls. Such controls include the selection and training of qualified personnel, an organizational structure providing for division of responsibility, communication of requirement for compliance with approved accounting control and business practices, and a program of internal audit. The extent of the Company's system of internal accounting control recognizes that the cost should not exceed the benefits derived and that the evaluation of those factors requires estimates and judgements by Management. Although no system can ensure that all errors or irregularities have been eliminated, Management believes that the internal accounting controls in use provide reasonable assurance, at reasonable cost, that assets are safeguarded against loss from unauthorized use or disposition, that transactions are executed in accordance with Management's authorization, and that the financial records are reliable for preparing financial statements and maintaining accountability for assets. The financial statements of the Company have been audited by Deloitte & Touche LLP, independent auditors. Their report, which appears in the Annual Report, is based upon their audits conducted in accordance with generally accepted auditing standards.

The Audit and Finance Committee of the Board of Directors is comprised solely of directors who are not officers or employees of the Company. The Committee is responsible for recommending to the Board of Directors the selection of independent auditors. It meets periodically with Management, the independent auditors, and the internal auditors to assure that they are carrying out their responsibilities. The Committee also reviews and monitors the financial, accounting, and auditing procedures of the Company in addition to reviewing the Company's financial reports. Deloitte & Touche LLP and the internal auditors have full and free access to the Audit and Finance Committee, with and without Management's presence.

the system of internal control as assurance that transactions are properly recorded and reported. The degree of reliance that they are able to place on the company's internal controls is a significant factor in determining the extent of their testing. The stronger the system of internal control, the less testing is necessary. A weak system of internal control requires that the auditors extend their tests of the records.

The board of directors of a corporation usually consists of key officers of the corporation as well as a number of directors whom it does not directly employ. For example, The Gap's board of 11 directors consists of 4 insiders and 7 outsiders. The outsiders often include presidents and key executive officers of other corporations and sometimes business school faculty. The board of directors is elected by the stockholders.

The audit committee of the board of directors provides direct contact between the stockholders and the independent accounting firm. Audit committees have assumed a much more active role since the passage of the Foreign Corrupt Practices Act in 1977. This legislation was passed in response to a growing concern over various types of improprieties by top management, such as kickbacks to politicians and bribes of foreign officials. The act includes a number of provisions intended to increase the accountability of management and the board of directors to stockholders. According to the act, management is responsible for keeping accurate records, and various provisions deal with the system of internal controls necessary to ensure the safeguarding of assets and the reliability of the financial statements. Audit committees have become much more involved in the oversight of the financial reporting system since the enactment of the act.

The Control Environment

The success of an internal control system begins with the competence of the people in charge of it. Management's operating style will have a determinable impact on the effectiveness of various policies. An autocratic style in which a few key officers tightly control operations will result in an environment different from that of a decentralized organization in which

---

FROM CONCEPT TO PRACTICE 5.2
READING THE GAP'S MANAGEMENT REPORT
Refer to the management's report for The Gap in Exhibit 5-7. What is the composition of its Audit and Finance Committee? Why do you think it is comprised the way it is?

departments have more freedom to make decisions. Personnel policies and practices form another factor in the internal control of a business. An appropriate system for hiring competent employees and firing incompetent ones is crucial to an efficient operation. After all, no internal control system will work very well if employees who are dishonest or poorly trained are on the payroll. On the other hand, too few people doing too many tasks defeats the purpose of an internal control system. Finally, the effectiveness of internal control in a business is influenced by the board of directors, particularly its audit committee.

The Accounting System

An **accounting system** consists of all the methods and records used to accurately report an entity's transactions and to maintain accountability for its assets and liabilities. Regardless of the degree of computer automation, the use of a journal to record transactions is an integral part of all accounting systems. Refinements are sometimes made to the basic components of the system, depending on the company's needs. For example, most companies use specialized journals to record recurring transactions, such as sales of merchandise on credit.

An accounting system can be completely manual, fully computerized, or as is often the case, a mixture of the two. Internal controls are important to all businesses, regardless of the degree of automation of the accounting system. The system must be capable of handling both the volume and the complexity of transactions entered into by a business. Most businesses use computers because of the sheer volume of transactions. The computer is ideally suited to the task of processing large numbers of repetitive transactions efficiently and quickly.

The cost of computing has dropped so substantially that virtually every business can now afford a system. Today some computer software programs that are designed for home-based businesses cost under $100 and are meant to run on machines that cost less than $1,000. Inexpensive software programs that categorize expenses and print checks, produce financial statements, and analyze financial ratios are available. Still, some people are uncomfortable with computers and are too busy working to spend the considerable amount of time it often takes to learn an automated system.

Internal Control Procedures

Management establishes policies and procedures on a number of different levels to ensure that corporate objectives will be met. Some procedures are formalized in writing. Others may not be written but are just as important. Certain **administrative controls** within a company are more concerned with the efficient operation of the business and adherence to managerial policies than with the accurate reporting of financial information. For example, a company policy that requires all prospective employees to be interviewed by the personnel department is an administrative control. Other **accounting controls** primarily concern safeguarding assets and ensuring the reliability of the financial statements. We now turn to a discussion of some of the most important internal control procedures:

Proper authorizations.

Segregation of duties.

Independent verification.

Safeguarding assets and records.

Independent review and appraisal of the system.

The design and use of business documents.

Proper Authorizations Management grants specific departments the authority to perform various activities. Along with the *authority* goes *responsibility*. Most large organizations give the authority to hire new employees to the personnel department. Management authorizes the purchasing department to order goods and services for the company and the credit department to establish specific policies for granting credit to customers. By specifically authorizing certain individuals to carry out specific tasks for the business, management is able to hold these same people responsible for the outcome of their actions.

This woman is using the paper source document in her hand as a reference for entering data into the accounting system. From the standpoint of internal control, should she be the one who is both ordering inventory, receiving it, and entering the information into the system? Is she authorized to make journal entries? If so, does her laptop have safeguards that prevent access by unauthorized personnel? These and other internal control procedures are part of the control environment within every company.

LO 5 Describe the basic internal control procedures.

The authorizations for some transactions are general in nature; others are specific. For example, a cashier authorizes the sale of a book in a bookstore by ringing up the transaction (a general authorization). It is likely, however, that the bookstore manager's approval is required before a book can be returned (a specific authorization).

Segregation of Duties   What might happen if one employee is given the authority both to prepare checks and to sign them? What could happen if a single employee is allowed to order inventory and receive it from the shipper? Or what if the cashier at a checkout stand also records the daily receipts in the journal? If the employee in each of these situations is both honest and never makes mistakes, nothing bad will happen. However, if the employee is dishonest or makes human errors, the company can experience losses. These situations all point to the need for the segregation of duties, which is one of the most fundamental of all internal control procedures. Without segregation of duties, an employee is able not only to perpetrate a fraud but also to conceal it. A good system of internal control requires that the *physical custody* of assets be separated from the *accounting* for those same assets.

Like most internal control principles, the concept of segregation of duties is an ideal that is not always completely attainable. For example, many smaller businesses simply do not have adequate personnel to achieve complete segregation of key functions. In certain instances, these businesses need to rely on the direct involvement of the owners in the business and on independent verification.

ACCOUNTING FOR YOUR DECISIONS

You Are the Chief Financial Officer

You have been hired by the owner of Mt. Rainier Broom Company to come in and replace the out-of-date accounting systems with a system that uses modern technology. The first thing you notice is that the company's bookkeeper, Mavis, is in charge of collecting receivables, recording payment, ordering and receiving inventory, preparing checks and signing them. When you suggest to her that she has too many duties, she gets angry and appeals to the owner. The owner backs up Mavis and tells you to focus entirely on new accounting technology. What should you do?

ANS: Ever so politely, you should inform the owner and Mavis in a three-way meeting that your suggestion that Mavis not do all the accounting functions is not meant as an insult but is simply good internal control. Even if Mavis is as honest as they come, there is a good chance that she will make errors which could result in losses to the company. By having at least two people involved in a transaction, the chances are excellent that an error will be caught by one or the other.

Independent Verification   Related to the principle of segregation of duties is the idea of independent verification. The work of one department should act as a check on the work of another. For example, the physical count of the inventory in a perpetual inventory system provides such a check. The accounting department maintains the general ledger card for inventory and updates it as sales and purchases are made. The physical count of the inventory by an independent department acts as a check on the work of the accounting department. As another example, consider a bank reconciliation as a control device. The reconciliation of a company's bank account with the bank statement by someone not responsible for either the physical custody of cash or the cash records acts as an independent check on the work of these parties. We will take a closer look at the use of a bank reconciliation as a control device in Chapter 7.

Safeguarding Assets and Records   Adequate safeguards must be in place to protect assets and the accounting records from losses of various kinds. Cash registers, safes, and lockboxes are important safeguards for cash. Secured storage areas with limited access are essential for the safekeeping of inventory. Protection of the accounting records against misuse is equally important. For example, access to a computerized accounting record should be limited to those employees authorized to prepare journal entries. This can be done with the use of a personal identification number and a password to access the system.

Independent Review and Appraisal   A well-designed system of internal control provides for periodic review and appraisal of the accounting system as well as the

ANALYZING MERCHANDISERS' MARGINS

William Bales is a portfolio manager for Janus Funds, a major mutual fund company based in Denver. Armed with accounting knowledge and degrees in marketing and finance, Mr. Bales follows a wide array of industries, including retailing, where the analysis of inventories and gross margins can be critical.

Driven by the booming stock market, the mutual fund industry is one of American's fastest growing enterprises. By the end of 1996, mutual fund assets exceeded $3 trillion, while the number of funds expanded from about 500 to 6,000 in the same 20-year time period. That growth has created tremendous employment opportunities for people with accounting knowledge. Mutual fund companies employ investment analysts and portfolio managers to study companies and make decisions about whether securities issued by these companies should be bought or sold on behalf of mutual fund customers. To qualify for such a position, a person needs to be comfortable around balance sheets, income statements and statements of cash flow.

But it's not enough to simply look at a retailer's gross margins in a vacuum. This statistic must also be compared to the company's historical performance, as well as to how it stacks up against competitors. If gross margins are shrinking over time, then investors need to be concerned about the possible inability of the company to maintain profitable pricing in the marketplace. A shrinking gross margin might also be due to spiraling raw material costs or burdensome labor costs.

Name: William Bales
Occupation: Portfolio manager, Janus Funds
Education: Master of science degree in marketing and finance, University of Colorado

It's also important to compare apples to apples—an investor shouldn't expect a grocery chain to have the same gross margin as an apparel retailer. Grocery stores may have gross margins of 10 percent or less, but they make up the thin profitability with tremendous volume. On the other hand, apparel companies might have gross margins of 40 percent or more, justifying high prices by selling whatever is in fashion.

Bales looks at other financial statistics such as unit and revenue growth on a "same-store" basis. That is, he's not as impressed if a 10-store apparel chain increases sales by 10 percent merely by acquiring an eleventh store. He would also be concerned if he saw excessive sales discounts and returns. When selecting stocks, "we prefer companies with predictable sales growth that are achieving economies of scale," he says. That is, if they can spread their costs over a larger volume, then the bottom line will grow. And stock prices are typically driven by earnings and the prospect of future growth in earnings.

However, you can only boost the bottom line for so long without growth in the top line—sales. With the U.S. economy growing at about three percent, sales growth is tough to come by in retailing.

---

people operating it. The group primarily responsible for review and appraisal of the system is the internal audit staff. Internal auditors provide management with periodic reports on the effectiveness of the control system and the efficiency of operations.

The Design and Use of Business Documents *Business documents* are the crucial link between economic transactions entered into by an entity and the accounting record of these events. They are often called *source documents*. Some source documents are manual; others are computer-generated. The source document for the recognition of the expense of an employee's wages is the time card. The source documents for a sale include the sales order, the sales invoice, and the related shipping document. Business documents must be designed so that they capture all relevant information about an economic event. They are also designed to ensure that related transactions are properly classified.

Business documents themselves must be properly controlled. For example, a key feature for documents is a *sequential numbering system* just like you have for your personal checks. This system results in a complete accounting for all documents in the series and negates the opportunity for an employee to misdirect one. Another key feature of well-designed business documents is the use of *multiple copies*. The various departments involved in a particular activity, such as sales or purchasing, are kept informed of the status of outstanding orders through the use of copies of documents. Appendix 5A provides an example of the use of business documents for a merchandiser.

Limitations on Internal Control

Internal control is a relative term. No system of internal control is totally foolproof. An entity's size affects the degree of control that it can obtain. In general, large organizations are able to devote a substantial amount of resources to safeguarding assets and records because these companies have the assets to justify the cost. Because the installation and maintenance of controls can be costly, an internal audit staff is a luxury that many small businesses cannot afford. The mere segregation of duties can result in added costs if two employees must be involved in a task previously performed by only one.

Segregation of duties can be effective in preventing collusion, but no system of internal control can ensure that it will not happen. It does no good to have one employee count the cash at the end of the day and another to record it if the two act in concert to steal from the company. Rotation of duties can help to lessen the likelihood for problems of this sort. An employee is less likely to collude with someone to steal if the assignment is a temporary one. Another control feature, a system of authorizations, is meaningless if management continually overrides it. Management must believe in a system of internal control enough to support it.

Intentional acts to misappropriate company assets are not the only problem. All sorts of human errors can weaken a system of internal control. Misunderstood instructions, carelessness, fatigue, and distraction can all lead to errors. A well-designed system of internal control should result in the best-possible people being hired to perform the various tasks, but no one is perfect.

Review Problem

Mickey's Marts, which operates a chain of department stores, uses the periodic inventory system. The cost of inventory on hand at January 1 amounts to $12,000, and on January 31, it is $9,500. The following transactions are entered into by Mickey's during January:

a. Purchased merchandise on account from various vendors for $25,000. All merchandise is bought with terms of 1/10, net 30. All purchases are recorded initially at the gross amount.

b. Reduced the total amount owed to vendors by $20,000. This is *not* the amount paid but the amount before taking the 1% discount. All accounts are paid within 10 days of the date of the invoice.

c. Recognized purchase returns and allowances of $1,900 during the month.

d. Recognized total sales of $42,000 for the month, of which $28,000 is cash sales and the remainder is on account.

e. Made collections on account of $17,000 for the month.

f. Applied $3,200 of sales returns and allowances for the month to customers' account balances.

g. Paid the freight cost of $2,700 on *incoming* purchases of merchandise.

Required

1. Prepare the necessary journal entries to record each of the transactions a through g.

2. Prepare a *partial* income statement for the month of January. The last line on the partial statement should be gross margin.

Solution to Review Problem

1. Journal entries:

a. Purchases 25,000

     Accounts Payable 25,000

    To record purchases on account.

Assets	=	Liabilities	+	Owners' Equity
		+25,000		−25,000

b. Accounts Payable ... 20,000

    Purchase Discounts ... 200

    Cash ... 19,800

To record payment of amounts owed on account, less 1% discount for early payment.

Assets	=	Liabilities	+	Owners' Equity
−19,800		−20,000		+200

c. Accounts Payable ... 1,900

    Purchase Returns and Allowances ... 1,900

To record purchase returns and allowances for the month.

Assets	=	Liabilities	+	Owners' Equity
		−1,900		+1,900

d. Cash ... 28,000

  Accounts Receivable ... 14,000

    Sales Revenue ... 42,000

To record sales for the month.

Assets	=	Liabilities	+	Owners' Equity
+28,000				+42,000
+14,000				

e. Cash ... 17,000

    Accounts Receivable ... 17,000

To record collections on account for the month.

Assets	=	Liabilities	+	Owners' Equity
+17,000				
−17,000				

f. Sales Returns and Allowances ... 3,200

    Accounts Receivable ... 3,200

To record sales returns and allowances for the month.

Assets	=	Liabilities	+	Owners' Equity
−3,200				−3,200

g. Transportation-in ... 2,700

    Cash ... 2,700

To record payment of freight bill on incoming merchandise.

Assets	=	Liabilities	+	Owners' Equity
−2,700				−2,700

2. Partial income statement:

MICKEY'S MARTS
PARTIAL INCOME STATEMENT
FOR THE MONTH OF JANUARY

Sales revenue			$42,000
Less: Sales returns and allowances			3,200
Net sales			$38,800
Cost of goods sold:			
Inventory, January 1		$12,000	
Purchases	$25,000		
Less: Purchase discounts	200		
Purchase returns and allowances	1,900		
Net purchases	$22,900		
Add: Transportation-in	2,700		
Cost of goods purchased		25,600	
Cost of goods available for sale		37,600	
Less: Inventory, January 31		9,500	
Cost of goods sold			28,100
Gross margin			$10,700

APPENDIX 5A

Internal Control for a Merchandising Company

Specific internal controls are necessary to control cash receipts and cash disbursements in a merchandising company. In addition to the separation of the custodianship of cash from the recording of it in the accounts, two other fundamental principles apply to its control. First, all cash receipts should be deposited *intact* in the bank on a *daily* basis. *Intact* means that no disbursements should be made from the cash received from customers. The second basic principle is related to the first: all cash disbursements should be made by check. The use of sequentially numbered checks results in a clear record of all disbursements. The only exception to this rule is the use of a petty cash fund to make cash disbursements for minor expenditures such as postage stamps and repairs. The use of such a fund is explained in Chapter 7.

Control over Cash Receipts

Most merchandisers receive checks and currency from customers in two distinct ways: (1) cash received over the counter, that is, from cash sales and (2) cash received in the mail, that is, cash collections from credit sales. Each of these types of cash receipts poses its own particular control problems.

Cash Received over the Counter   Several control mechanisms are used to handle these cash payments. First, cash registers allow the customer to see the display, which deters the salesclerk from ringing up a sale for less than the amount received from the customer and pocketing the difference. A locked-in cash register tape is another control feature. At various times during the day, an employee other than the clerk unlocks the register, removes the tape, and forwards it to the accounting department. At the end of the shift, the salesclerk remits the coin and currency from the register to a central cashier. Any difference between the amount of cash remitted to the cashier and the amount on the tape submitted to the accounting department is investigated.

Finally, prenumbered customer receipts, prepared in duplicate, are a useful control mechanism. The customer is given a copy, and the salesclerk retains another. The salesclerk is accountable for all numbers in a specific series of receipts and must be able to explain any differences between the amount of cash remitted to the cashier and the amount collected per the receipts.

Cash Received in the Mail   Most customers send checks rather than currency through the mail. Any form of cash received in the mail from customers should be applied to their account balances. The customer wants assurance that the account is appropriately reduced for the amount of the payment. The company must be assured that all cash received is deposited in the bank and that the account receivable is reduced accordingly.

To achieve a reasonable degree of control, two employees should be present when the mail is opened.[1] The first employee opens the mail in the presence of the second employee, counts the money received, and prepares a control list of the amount received on that particular day. The list is often called a *prelist* and is prepared in triplicate. The second employee takes the original to the cashier along with the total cash received on that day. The cashier is the person who makes the bank deposit. One copy of the prelist is forwarded to the accounting department to be used as the basis for recording the increase in Cash and the decrease in Accounts Receivable. The other copy is retained by one of the two persons opening the mail. A comparison of the prelist to the bank deposit slip is a timely way to detect receipts that do not make it to the bank. Because the two employees acting in concert could circumvent the control process, rotation of duties is important.

---

[1]In some companies this control procedure may be omitted because of the cost of having two employees present when the mail is opened.

Monthly customer statements act as an additional control device for customer payments received in the mail. Assume that the two employees responsible for opening the mail and remitting it to the cashier decide to pocket a check received from a customer. Checks made payable to a company *can* be stolen and cashed. The customer provides the control element. Because the check is not remitted to the cashier, the accounting department will not be notified to reduce the customer's account for the payment. The monthly statement, however, should alert the customer to the problem. The amount the customer thought was owed will be smaller than the balance due on the statement. At this point, the customer should ask the company to investigate the discrepancy. As evidence of its payment on account, the customer will be able to point to a canceled check—which was cashed by the unscrupulous employees.

Finally, keep in mind that the use of customer statements as a control device will be effective only if the employees responsible for the custody of cash received through the mail, for record keeping, and for authorization of adjustments to customers' accounts are not allowed to prepare and mail statements to customers. Employees allowed to do so are in a position to alter customers' statements.

Cash Discrepancies   Discrepancies occur occasionally due to theft by dishonest employees and to human error. For example, if a salesclerk either intentionally or unintentionally gives the wrong amount of change, the amount remitted to the cashier will not agree with the cash register tape. Any material differences should be investigated. Of particular significance are *recurring* differences between the amount remitted by any one cashier and the amount on the cash register tape.

The Role of Computerized Business Documents in Controlling Cash Disbursements

A company makes cash payments for a variety of purposes: to purchase merchandise, supplies, plant, and equipment; to pay operating expenditures; and to cover payroll expenses, to name a few. We will concentrate on the disbursement of cash to purchase goods for resale, focusing particularly on the role of business documents in the process. Merchandising companies rely on a smooth and orderly inflow of quality goods for resale to customers. It is imperative that suppliers be paid on time so that they will continue to make goods available.

LO 6   Describe the various documents used in recording purchases of merchandise and their role in controlling cash disbursements.

Business documents play a vital role in the purchasing function. The example that follows begins with a requisition for merchandise by the tool department of Tabor Hardware Stores. The example continues through the receipt of the goods and the eventual payment to the supplier. The entire process is summarized in Exhibit 5-8. You will want to refer to this exhibit throughout the remainder of the chapter.

Purchase Requisition   The tool department at Tabor Hardware Stores weekly reviews its stock to determine whether any items need replenishing. On the basis of its needs, the supervisor of the tool department fills out the **purchase requisition form** shown in Exhibit 5-9. The form indicates the preferred supplier or vendor, A-1 Tool.

The purchasing department has the responsibility for making the final decision on a vendor. Giving the purchasing department this responsibility means that it is held accountable for acquiring the goods at the lowest price, given certain standards for merchandise quality. Tabor assigns a separate item number to each of the thousands of individual items of merchandise it stocks. Note that the requisition also indicates the vendor's number for each item. The unit of measure for each item is indicated in the quantity column. For example, "24 ST" means 24 sets, and "12 CD" means 12 cards. The original and a copy of the purchase requisition are sent to the purchasing department. The tool department keeps one copy for its records.

Purchase Order   Like many other businesses, Tabor uses a computerized purchasing system. Most companies have either purchased software or developed software internally to perform such functions as purchasing, sales, and payroll. The software is capable not only of increasing the speed and accuracy of the process but also of generating the necessary documents.

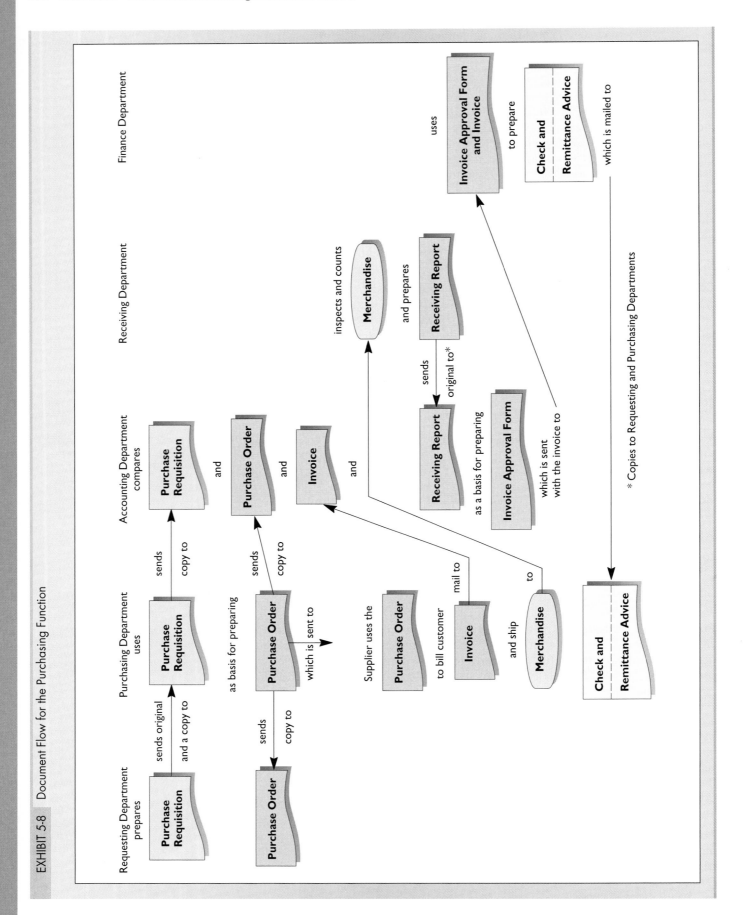

EXHIBIT 5-8 Document Flow for the Purchasing Function

EXHIBIT 5-9   Purchase Requisition

Tabor Hardware Stores
676 Glenwood St.
Chicago, IL

PURCHASE REQUISITION

Date __5/28/98__   **PR 75638**

Preferred vendor __A-1 Tool Co.__

Date needed by __6/5/98__

The following items are requested for __weekly dept. order__

Item No.	Quantity	Description/Vendor No.
314627	24 ST	Hobby tool set/5265
323515	12 CD	Hobby blades 5 pk/7512
323682	6 ST	Screwdriver set 5/PC/1589

Requested by _Joe Smith_   **Department** Tool department

A computer-generated **purchase order** is shown in Exhibit 5-10. Purchase orders are usually prenumbered; a company should periodically investigate any missing numbers. The purchasing department uses its copy of the purchase requisition as a basis for preparing the purchase order. An employee in the purchasing department keys in the relevant information from the purchase requisition and adds the unit cost for each item gathered from the vendor's price guide. The software program generates the purchase order as shown in Exhibit 5-10. You should trace all of the information for at least one of the three items ordered from the purchase requisition to the purchase order. The purchase order indicates the instructions for shipping, FOB destination point, and the terms for payment, 2/10, net 30.

The system generates the original purchase order and three copies. As indicated in Exhibit 5-8, the original is sent to the supplier after a supervisor in the purchasing department approves it. One copy is sent to the accounting department, where it will be matched with the original requisition. A second copy is sent to the tool department as confirmation that its request for the items has been attended to by the purchasing department. The purchasing department keeps the third copy for its records.

A purchase order is not the basis for recording a purchase and a liability. Legally, the order is merely an offer by the company to purchase goods from the supplier. Technically, the receipt of goods from the supplier is the basis for the purchaser's recognition of a liability. As a matter of practice, however, most companies record the payable upon receipt of the invoice.

Invoice   When A-1 Tool ships the merchandise, it also mails an invoice to Tabor, requesting payment according to the agreed-upon terms, in this case 2/10, net 30. The **invoice** may be mailed separately or included with the shipment of merchandise. A-1 Tool, the seller, calls this document a *sales invoice;* it is the basis for recording a sale and an account receivable. Tabor, the buyer, calls the same document a *purchase invoice,* which is the basis for recording a purchase and an account payable. The invoice that A-1 sent to Tabor's accounting department is shown in Exhibit 5-11.

EXHIBIT 5-10   Computer-Generated Purchase Order

Tabor Hardware Stores
676 Glenwood St.
Chicago, IL

PURCHASE ORDER

TO: PO 54296
A-1 Tool Co.
590 West St.
Milwaukee, WI
Date 5/30/98   Ship by Best Express   Instructions FOB destination point
Terms 2/10, net 30   Date required 6/5/98

Item No.	Quantity	Description/Vendor No.	Unit price	Amount
314627	24 ST	Hobby tool set/5265	$28.59	$686.16
323515	12 CD	Hobby blades 5 pk/7512	.69	8.28
323682	6 ST	Screwdriver set 5/PC/1589	4.49	26.94
				$721.38

Approved by _Mary Jones_

Receiving Report

The accounting department receives the invoice for the three items ordered. Within a few days before or after the receipt of the invoice, the merchandise arrives at Tabor's warehouse. As soon as the items are unpacked, the receiving department inspects and counts them. The same software program that generated the purchase order also generates a receiving report, as shown in Exhibit 5-12.

Tabor uses a blind receiving report. The column for the quantity received is left blank and is filled in by the receiving department. Rather than being able simply to indicate that the number ordered was received, an employee must count the items to determine that the number ordered is actually received. You should trace all of the relevant information for one of the three items ordered from the purchase order to the receiving report. The accounting system generates an original receiving report and three copies. The receiving department keeps one copy for its records and sends the original to the accounting department. One copy is sent to the purchasing department to be matched with the purchase order, and the other copy is sent to the tool department as verification that the items it originally requested have been received.

Invoice Approval Form

At this point, Tabor's accounting department has copies of the purchase requisition from the tool department, the purchase order from the purchasing department, the invoice from the supplier, and the receiving report from the warehouse. The accounting department uses an invoice approval form to document the accuracy of the information on each of these other forms. The invoice approval form for Tabor Hardware is shown in Exhibit 5-13.

The invoice is compared to the purchase requisition to ensure that the company is billed for goods that it requested. A comparison of the invoice with the purchase order ensures that the goods were in fact ordered. Finally, the receiving report is compared with the invoice to verify that all goods it is being billed for were received. An accounting department employee must also verify the mathematical accuracy of the amounts that appear on the invoice. The date the invoice must be paid to take advantage of the discount is noted so that the finance department will be sure to send the check by this date. At this point, the accounting department prepares the journal entry to increase

EXHIBIT 5-11   Invoice

NO. 427953

A-1 Tool Co.
590 West St.
Milwaukee, WI

INVOICE

Sold to Tabor Hardware Stores   **Date** 6/2/98
676 Glenwood St.   **Order No.** 54296
Chicago, IL   **Shipped via** Best Express
Ship to Same   **Date shipped** 6/2/98
Terms 2/10, net 30   **Ship terms** FOB destination

Quantity	Description/No.	Price	Amount
24 ST	Hobby tool set/5265	$28.59	$686.16
12 CD	Hobby blades 5 pk/7512	.69	8.28
6 ST	Screwdriver set 5 PC/1589	4.49	26.94
			$721.38

Purchases and Accounts Payable. The invoice approval form and the invoice are then sent to the finance department. Some businesses call the invoice approval form a *voucher;* it is used for all expenditures, not just for purchases of merchandise. Finally, it is worth noting that some businesses do not use a separate invoice approval form but simply note approval directly on the invoice itself.

EXHIBIT 5-12   Computer-Generated Receiving Report

Tabor Hardware Stores
676 Glenwood St.
Chicago, IL

Receiving Report

RR 23637

Purchase Order No. 54296   Date ordered 5/30/98
Vendor A-1 Tool Co.   Date required 6/5/98
Ship via Best Express   Instructions FOB Destination
Terms 2/10, net 30

Quantity received	Our Item No.	Description/Item No.	Remarks
24 ST	314627	Hobby tool set/5265	Box damaged but merchandise ok
12 CD	323515	Hobby blades 5 pk/7512	
6 ST	323682	Screwdriver set 5/PC/1589	

Received by Bob Reed   Date 6/4/98

EXHIBIT 5-13 Invoice Approval Form

Tabor Hardware Stores
676 Glenwood St.
Chicago, IL

Invoice Approval Form

	No.	Check
Purchase Requisition	PR 75638	✓
Purchase Order	PO 54296	✓
Receiving Report	RR 23637	✓

Invoice:

No.	427953
Date	6/2/98
Price	✓
Extensions	✓
Footings	✓

Last Day to Pay for Discount   6/12/98

Approved for Payment by   *Alice Johnson*

EXHIBIT 5-14 Check with Remittance Advice

3690

Tabor Hardware Stores
676 Glenwood St.
Chicago, IL

June 12 19 98

PAY TO THE
ORDER OF   A-1 Tool Co. $706.95

Seven hundred six and 95/100   DOLLARS

Second National Bank
Chicago, IL

3690 035932 9321

John B. Martin

- -

Purchase Order No.	Invoice No.	Invoice Date	Description	Amount
PO 54296	427953	6/2/98	24 ST Hobby tool set	$686.16
			12 CD Hobby blades 5pk	8.28
			6 ST Screwdriver set 5PC	26.94
			Total	721.38
			Less: 2% discount	14.43
			Net remitted	706.95

Check with Remittance Advice Tabor's finance department is responsible for issuing checks. This results from the need to segregate custody of cash (the signed check) from record keeping (the updating of the ledger). Upon receipt of the invoice approval form from the accounting department, a clerk in the finance department types a check with a remittance advice attached, as shown in Exhibit 5-14.[2]

Before the check is signed, the documents referred to on the invoice approval form are reviewed and canceled to prevent reuse. The clerk then forwards the check to one of the company officers authorized to sign checks. According to one of Tabor's internal control policies, only the treasurer and the assistant treasurer are authorized to sign checks. Both officers must sign check amounts above a specified dollar limit. To maintain separation of duties, the finance department should mail the check. The remittance advice informs the supplier as to the nature of the payment and is torn off by the supplier before cashing the check.

[2]In some companies an employee in the accounting department prepares checks and sends them to the finance department for review and signature. Also, many companies use computer-generated checks, rather than manually typed ones.

Chapter Highlights

1. **LO 1** Merchandise is inventory purchased in finished form and held for resale. Both wholesalers and retailers sell merchandise. Sales revenue is a representation of the inflow of assets from the sale of merchandise during the period. Two deductions are made from sales revenue on the income statement. Sales returns and allowances and sales discounts are both subtracted from sales revenue to arrive at net sales.

2. **LO 2** A perpetual inventory system requires the updating of the Inventory account at the time of each purchase and each sale of merchandise. With the periodic system, the Inventory account is updated only at the end of the year. Separate accounts are used during the period to record purchases, purchase returns and allowances, purchase discounts, and transportation-in. The periodic system relies on a count of the inventory on the last day of the period to determine ending inventory.

3. **LO 3** Cost of goods sold is recognized as an expense under the matching principle. It represents the cost associated with the merchandise sold during the period and is matched with the revenue of the period.

4. **LO 3** The purchases of the period are reduced by purchase returns and allowances and by purchase discounts. Any freight costs paid to acquire the merchandise, called *transportation-in,* are added. The result, cost of goods purchased, is added to the beginning inventory to determine cost of goods available for sale. Cost of goods sold is found by deducting ending inventory from cost of goods available for sale.

5. **LO 3** *FOB destination point* means that the seller is responsible for the cost of delivering the merchandise to the buyer. Title to the goods does not transfer to the buyer until the buyer receives the merchandise from the carrier. *FOB shipping point* means that the buyer pays shipping costs. Title to the goods transfers to the buyer as soon as the seller turns them over to the carrier.

6. **LO 4** The purpose of an internal control system is to provide assurance that overall company objectives are met. Specifically, accounting controls are designed to safeguard the entity's assets and provide the company with reliable accounting records. Management has the primary responsibility for the reliability of the financial statements. Many companies employ a full-time internal audit staff to monitor and evaluate the internal control system.

7. **LO 5** Segregation of duties is the most fundamental of all internal control procedures. Possession of assets must be kept separate from the record-keeping function. Other important control procedures include a system of independent verifications, proper authorizations, adequate safeguards for assets and their records, independent review and appraisal of the accounting system, and the design and use of business documents.

8. **LO 5** Control over cash requires that all receipts be deposited intact on a daily basis and that all disbursements be made by check. Control procedures are important for cash received over the counter as well as for cash received in the mail. Any material discrepancies between the cash actually on hand and the amount that should be on hand need to be investigated.

9. **LO 6** Business documents play a vital role in various business activities such as the purchase of merchandise. The requesting department fills out a purchase requisition form and sends it to the purchasing department. The purchasing department uses the requisition to complete a purchase order, which it sends to the supplier. The supplier mails an invoice to the buyer's accounting department. The accounting department also gets a receiving report from the warehouse to indicate the quantity and condition of the goods delivered. The accounting department fills out an invoice approval form, which it sends with the invoice to the finance department, which uses them as the basis for preparing and sending a check to the supplier. (Appendix 5A)

Key Terms Quiz

Because of the large number of terms introduced in this chapter, there are two key terms quizzes. Read each definition below and then write the number of the definition in the blank beside the appropriate term it defines. The solution appears at the end of the chapter.

Quiz 1: Merchandise Accounting

____ Net sales
____ Trade discount
____ Sales Discounts
____ Cost of goods sold
____ Periodic system
____ Purchases
____ Purchase Discounts
____ FOB shipping point

____ Sales Returns and Allowances
____ Quantity discount
____ Cost of goods available for sale
____ Perpetual system
____ Transportation-in
____ Purchase Returns and Allowances
____ FOB destination point

1. A reduction in selling price for buying a large number of units of a product.
2. The contra-revenue account used to record both refunds to customers and reductions of their accounts.
3. The adjunct account used to record freight costs paid by the buyer.
4. A selling price reduction offered to a special class of customers.
5. The system in which the Inventory account is increased at the time of each purchase of merchandise and decreased at the time of each sale.
6. The contra-purchases account used in a periodic inventory system when a refund is received from a supplier or a reduction given in the balance owed to the supplier.
7. The contra-revenue account used to record discounts given customers for early payment of their accounts.

8. Terms that require the seller to pay for the cost of shipping the merchandise to the buyer.
9. Terms that require the buyer to pay the shipping costs.
10. The system in which the Inventory account is updated only at the end of the period.
11. Beginning inventory plus cost of goods purchased.
12. The contra-purchases account used to record reductions in purchase price for early payment to the supplier.
13. The account used in a periodic inventory system to record acquisitions of merchandise.
14. Sales revenue less sales returns and allowances and sales discounts.
15. Cost of goods available for sale minus ending inventory.

Quiz 2: Internal Control

____ Internal control system
____ Internal audit staff
____ Audit committee
____ Accounting system
____ Accounting controls
____ Purchase order (Appendix 5A)
____ Blind receiving report (Appendix 5A)

____ Report of management
____ Board of directors
____ Foreign Corrupt Practices Act
____ Administrative controls
____ Purchase requisition form (Appendix 5A)
____ Invoice (Appendix 5A)
____ Invoice approval form (Appendix 5A)

1. The form sent by the seller to the buyer as evidence of a sale.
2. The group composed of key officers of a corporation and outside members responsible for the general oversight of the affairs of the entity.
3. The methods and records used to accurately report an entity's transactions and to maintain accountability for its assets and liabilities.

4. The board of directors subset that acts as a direct contact between the stockholders and the independent accounting firm.
5. Procedures concerned with safeguarding the assets or the reliability of the financial statements.
6. The form a department uses to initiate a request to order merchandise.

7. A form the accounting department uses before making payment to document the accuracy of all the information about a purchase.

8. A written statement in the annual report indicating the responsibility of management for the financial statements.

9. A form used by the receiving department to account for the quantity and condition of merchandise received from a supplier.

10. Legislation intended to increase the accountability of management for accurate records and reliable financial statements.

11. Procedures concerned with efficient operation of the business and adherence to managerial policies.

12. The form sent by the purchasing department to the supplier.

13. The department responsible for monitoring and evaluating the internal control system.

14. Policies and procedures necessary to ensure the safeguarding of an entity's assets, the reliability of its accounting records, and the accomplishment of overall company objectives.

Alternate Terms

Gross margin   Gross profit.

Invoice   Purchase invoice, sales invoice.

Invoice approval form   Voucher.

Merchandiser   Wholesaler, retailer.

Report of management   Management's report.

Sales revenue   Sales.

Transportation-in   Freight-in.

Questions

1. When a company gives a cash refund on returned merchandise, why doesn't it just reduce Sales Revenue instead of using a contra-revenue account?

2. Why are trade discounts and quantity discounts not accorded accounting recognition (the sale is simply recorded net of either of these types of discounts)?

3. What do credit terms of *3/20, n/60* mean? How valuable to the customer is the discount offered in these terms?

4. What is the difference between a periodic inventory system and a perpetual inventory system?

5. How have point-of-sale terminals improved the ability of mass merchandisers to use a perpetual inventory system?

6. In a periodic inventory system, what kind of account is Purchases? Is it an asset or an expense or neither?

7. Why are shipping terms, such as FOB shipping point or FOB destination point, important in deciding ownership of inventory at the end of the year?

8. How and why are transportation-in and transportation-out recorded differently?

9. How do the duties of an internal audit staff differ from those of the external auditors?

10. What is the typical composition of a board of directors of a publicly held corporation?

11. An order clerk fills out a purchase requisition for an expensive item of inventory and the receiving report when the merchandise arrives. The clerk takes the inventory home and then sends the invoice to the accounting department so that the supplier will be paid. What basic internal control procedure could have prevented this misuse of company assets?

12. What are some of the limitations on a company's effective system of internal control?

13. What two basic procedures are essential to an effective system of internal control over cash? (Appendix 5A)

14. How would you evaluate the following statement? "The only reason a company positions its cash register so that the customers can see the display is so that they feel comfortable they are being charged the correct amount for a purchase." (Appendix 5A)

15. Which document, a purchase order or an invoice, is the basis for recording a purchase and a corresponding liability? Explain your answer. (Appendix 5A)

16. What is a blind receiving report, and how does it act as a control device? (Appendix 5A)

17. What is the purpose in comparing a purchase invoice with a purchase order? In comparing a receiving report with a purchase invoice? (Appendix 5A)

Exercises

LO 1 **Exercise 5-1** Journal Entries to Record Sales

Prepare the journal entries to record the following transactions on the books of Ace Corporation for March 3, 1998:

a. Sold merchandise on credit for $500 with terms of 2/10, net 30. Ace records all sales at the gross amount.

b. Recorded cash sales for the day of $1,250 from the cash register tape.

c. Granted a cash refund of $135 to a customer for spoiled merchandise returned.

d. Granted a customer a credit of $190 on its outstanding bill and allowed the customer to keep a defective product.

e. Applied cash of $2,300, received through the mail, to customers' accounts. All amounts received qualify for the discount for early payment.

LO 1 **Exercise 5-2** Credit Terms

Ling Company sold merchandise on credit for $800 on September 10, 1998, to Letson Inc. For each of the following terms, indicate the last day Letson could take the discount, the amount Letson would pay if it took the discount, and the date full payment is due.

a. 2/10, n/30.

b. 3/15, n/45.

c. 1/7, n/21.

d. 5/15, n/30.

LO 1 **Exercise 5-3** Journal Entries for Sales Discounts

Prepare the journal entries on the books of Rambler Corporation for the following transactions, using the gross method to record sales discounts (all sales on credit are made with terms of 2/10, net 30).

June 2: Sold merchandise on credit to Huskie Corp. for $1,200.

June 4: Sold merchandise on credit to Hawkeye Company for $2,000.

June 13: Collected cash from Hawkeye Company.

June 30: Collected cash from Huskie Corp.

LO 1 **Exercise 5-4** L.A. Gear

In its 1995 annual report, L.A. Gear's principal business is described as "the design, development and marketing of quality athletic and lifestyle footwear." The company has not been profitable for a number of years and reported net losses of approximately $59.1 million and $29.7 million during the years ended November 30, 1995 and 1994, respectively. Net sales amounted to $296,551,000 and $415,966,000 during the years ended November 30, 1995 and 1994. The company's gross margin (gross profit) ratio (rounded to the nearest hundredth) increased slightly from 29.65% in 1994 to 29.93% in 1995.

Required

1. As part of its cost reduction efforts, L.A. Gear closed its seven retail outlet stores during fiscal 1995. Would L.A. Gear still be considered a merchandiser?

2. Estimate the company's cost of sales during fiscal 1995 and 1994.

LO 2 **Exercise 5-5** Perpetual and Periodic Inventory Systems

From the following list, identify whether the merchandisers described would most likely use a perpetual or periodic inventory system.

_____ Appliance store
_____ Car dealership
_____ Drug store
_____ Furniture store
_____ Grocery store
_____ Hardware store
_____ Jewelry store

How might changes in technology affect the ability of merchandisers to use perpetual inventory systems?

LO 3 **Exercise 5-6** Missing Amounts in Cost of Goods Sold Model

For each of the following independent cases, fill in the missing amounts:

	CASE 1	CASE 2	CASE 3
Beginning inventory	$ (a)	$2,350	$1,890
Purchases (gross)	6,230	5,720	(e)
Purchase returns and allowances	470	800	550
Purchase discounts	200	(c)	310
Transportation-in	150	500	420
Cost of goods available for sale	7,110	(d)	8,790
Ending inventory	(b)	1,750	1,200
Cost of goods sold	5,220	5,570	(f)

LO 3 **Exercise 5-7** Journal Entries for Purchase Discounts

Prepare the journal entries on the books of Buckeye Corporation for the following transactions, using the gross method to record purchase discounts (all purchases on credit are made with terms of 1/10, net 30, and Buckeye uses the periodic system of inventory):

July 3: Purchased merchandise on credit from Wildcat Corp. for $3,500.

July 6: Purchased merchandise on credit from Cyclone Company for $7,000.

July 12: Paid amount owed to Wildcat Corp.

August 5: Paid amount owed to Cyclone Company.

LO 3 **Exercise 5-8** Journal Entries for Purchases—Periodic System

Prepare journal entries for the following transactions entered into by Wolverine Corporation. The company uses the periodic system and the gross method to record purchase discounts.

March 3: Purchased merchandise from Spartan Corp. for $2,500 with terms of 2/10, net/30. Shipping costs of $250 were paid to Neverlate Transit Company.

March 7: Purchased merchandise from Boilermaker Company for $1,400 with terms of net/30.

March 12: Paid amount owed to Spartan Corp.

March 15: Received a credit of $500 on defective merchandise purchased from Boilermaker Company. The merchandise was kept.

March 18: Purchased merchandise from Gopher Corp. for $1,600 with terms of 2/10, net 30.

March 22: Received a credit of $400 from Gopher Corp. for spoiled merchandise returned to them. This is the amount of credit exclusive of any discount.

April 6: Paid amount owed to Boilermaker Company.

April 18: Paid amount owed to Gopher Corp.

LO 3 **Exercise 5-9** Shipping Terms and Transfer of Title

On December 23, 1998, Miller Wholesalers ships merchandise to Michael Retailers with terms of FOB destination point. The merchandise arrives at Michael's warehouse on January 3, 1999.

Required

1. Identify who pays to ship the merchandise.

2. Determine whether the inventory should be included as an asset on Michael's December 31, 1998, balance sheet. Should the sale be included on Miller's 1998 income statement?

3. Explain how your answers to part 2 would have been different if the terms of shipment had been FOB shipping point.

LO 3 **Exercise 5-10** Transfer of Title to Inventory

From the following list, identify whether the transactions described should be recorded by Cameron Companies during December 1998 or January 1999.

Purchases of merchandise that are in transit from vendors to Cameron Companies on December 31, 1998:

_____ Shipped FOB shipping point

_____ Shipped FOB destination point

Sales of merchandise that are in transit to customers of Cameron Companies on December 31, 1998:

_____ Shipped FOB shipping point
_____ Shipped FOB destination point

LO 5 **Exercise 5-11** Internal Control

The university drama club is planning a raffle. The president overheard you talking about internal control to another accounting student, so she has asked you to set up some guidelines to "be sure" that all money collected for the raffle is accounted for by the club.

Required

1. Describe guidelines that the club should follow to achieve an acceptable level of internal control.

2. Comment on the president's request that she "be sure" all money is collected and recorded.

LO 5 **Exercise 5-12** Segregation of Duties

The following tasks are performed by three employees, each of whom is capable of performing all of them. Do not concern yourself with the time required to perform the tasks but with the need to provide for segregation of duties. Assign the duties by using a check mark to indicate which employee should perform each task. Remember that you may assign any one of the tasks to any of the employees.

	EMPLOYEE		
TASK	MARY	SUE	JOHN
Prepare invoices			
Mail invoices			
Pick up mail from post office			
Open mail, separate checks			
List checks on deposit slip in triplicate			
Post payment to customer's account			
Deposit checks			
Prepare monthly schedule of accounts receivable			
Reconcile bank statements			

Multi-Concept Exercises

LO 1, 3 **Exercise 5-13** Income Statement for a Merchandiser

Fill in the missing amounts in the following income statement for Carpenters Department Store Inc.:

Sales revenue		$125,600	
Less: Sales returns and allowances		(a) ?	
Net sales			$122,040
Cost of goods sold:			
Beginning inventory		23,400	
Purchases	(b) ?		
Less: Purchase discounts	1,300		
Net purchases	(c) ?		
Add: Transportation-in	6,550		
Cost of goods purchased		81,150	
Cost of goods available for sale		104,550	
Less: Ending inventory		(e) ?	
Cost of goods sold			(d) ?
Gross margin			38,600

Operating expenses	$ (f) ?
Income before tax	26,300
Income tax expense	10,300
Net income	$ (g) ?

LO 1, 3 **Exercise 5-14** Partial Income Statement—Periodic System

LaPine Company has the following account balances as of December 31, 1998:

Purchases returns and allowances	$ 400
Inventory, January 1	4,000
Sales	80,000
Transportation-in	1,000
Sales returns and allowances	500
Purchases discounts	800
Inventory, December 31	3,800
Purchases	30,000
Sales discounts	1,200

Required

Prepare a partial income statement for LaPine Company for 1998 through gross margin. Calculate LaPine's gross margin (gross profit) ratio for 1998.

Problems

LO 1 **Problem 5-1** Trade Discounts

Keisling Inc. offers the following discounts to customers who purchase large quantities:

10% discount: 10–25 units.

20% discount: >25 units.

Mr. Keisling, the president, would like to record all sales at the list price and record the discount as an expense.

Required

1. Explain to Mr. Keisling why trade discounts do not enter into the accounting records.
2. Even though trade discounts do not enter into the accounting records, is it still important to have some record of these? Explain your answer.

LO 1 **Problem 5-2** Calculation of Gross Margins for Wal-Mart and Kmart

The following information was summarized from the consolidated statements of income of Wal-Mart Stores Inc. and Subsidiaries for the years ended January 31, 1995 and 1994 and the consolidated statements of operations of Kmart Corporation for the years ended January 31, 1996 and January 25, 1995:

	1995		1994	
(in millions)	SALES	COST OF SALES*	SALES	COST OF SALES*
Wal-Mart	$82,494	$65,586	$67,344	$53,444
Kmart	$34,389	$26,996	$32,514	$24,868

*Described as "cost of merchandise sold, including buying and occupancy costs" by Kmart Corporation.

Required

1. Calculate the gross margin (gross profit) ratios for Wal-Mart and Kmart for 1995 and 1994.
2. Which company appears to be performing better? What factors might cause the difference in the gross margin ratios of the two companies? What other information should you consider to determine how these companies are performing in this regard?

LO 5 **Problem 5-3** Internal Control Procedures

You are opening a summer business, a chain of three drive-thru snow cone stands. You have hired other college students to work and have purchased a cash register with locked-in tapes. You retain one key, and the other is available to the lead person on each shift.

Required

1. Write a list of the procedures for all employees to follow when ringing up sales and giving change.

2. Write a list of the procedures for the lead person to follow in closing out at the end of the day. Be as specific as you can so that employees will have few if any questions.

3. What is your main concern in the design of internal control for the snow cone stands? How did you address that concern? Be specific.

LO 6 **Problem 5-4** The Design of Internal Control Documents (Appendix 5A)

Motel $24.99 has purchased a large warehouse to store all supplies used by housekeeping departments in the company's expanding chain of motels. In the past, each motel bought supplies from local distributors and paid for the supplies from cash receipts.

Required

1. Name some potential problems with the old system.

2. Design a purchase requisition form and a receiving report to be used by the housekeeping departments and the warehouse. Indicate how many copies of each form should be used and who should receive each copy.

Multi-Concept Problems

General
Ledger

LO 1, 2, 3 **Problem 5-5** Journal Entries for a Merchandiser

The following transactions were entered into by North Coast Tires Inc. during the month of June:

June 2: Purchased 1,000 tires at a cost of $60 per tire. Terms of payment are 1/10, net 45.

June 4: Paid trucking firm $1,200 to ship the tires purchased on June 2.

June 5: Purchased 600 tires at a cost of $60 per tire. Terms of payment are 2/10, net 30.

June 6: Paid trucking firm $800 to ship the tires purchased on June 5.

June 7: Returned 150 of the tires purchased on June 2 because they were defective. Received a credit on open account from the seller.

June 11: Paid for tires purchased on June 2.

June 13: Sold 700 tires from those purchased on June 2. The selling price was $90 per tire. Terms are 1/10, net 30.

June 22: Received cash from sale of tires on June 13.

June 30: Paid for tires purchased on June 5.

Required

1. Prepare the journal entries to record these transactions on the books of North Coast Tires Inc. The company uses the gross method of recording purchase and sales discounts. North Coast uses a periodic inventory system.

2. Given the nature of its product, do you think it would be feasible for North Coast to use a perpetual inventory system? Why? If so, what advantages would accrue to the company by using a perpetual system?

LO 1, 2, 3 **Problem 5-6** Journal Entries for a Merchandiser

Leisure Time Furniture Store entered into the following transactions in the month of April:

April 3: Purchased 50 lounge chairs at $150 each with terms 2/10, net 45. The chairs were shipped FOB destination.

April 7: Sold 6 chairs for $320 each, terms 2/10, net 30.

April 8: Purchased 20 patio umbrella tables for $120 each, FOB shipping point, terms 1/10, net 30.

April 9: Due to defects, returned 5 lounge chairs purchased on April 3. Received a credit memorandum.

April 10: Paid the trucking firm $360 for delivery of the tables purchased on April 8.

April 13: Paid for the chairs purchased on April 3.

April 17: Received payment for the chairs sold on April 7.

April 20: Paid for the tables purchased on April 8.

Required

1. Prepare all journal entries needed to record these transactions for the furniture company. Leisure Time uses the gross method of recording purchase and sales discounts. The company uses a periodic inventory system.

2. Do you think Leisure Time should change to a perpetual inventory system, given the nature of their business? Why? What advantages would a company have using the perpetual system instead of the periodic system?

`LO 1, 3` **Problem 5-7** Trade and Cash Discounts

Kruizenga Inc. publishes books and offers trade discounts to customers who purchase in large quantities: 30% for purchases of more than 50 units. It also offers credit terms of 2/10, net 30 to induce early payment. The list price of one book is $60. Johnson Company purchased 100 of these books on September 12. Payment was made on September 21.

Required

1. Prepare the journal entries on Kruizenga's books to record the sale and the receipt of cash.

2. Prepare the journal entries on Johnson's books to record the purchase and the payment.

`LO 1, 3` **Problem 5-8** Journal Entries and Partial Income Statement for a Merchandiser

Weekend Wonders Inc. operates a chain of discount hardware stores. The company uses a periodic inventory system. Inventory on hand on June 1, 1998, amounts to $25,670; on June 30, 1998, it is $30,200. The company uses the gross method to record purchase and sales discounts. The following transactions take place during the month of June:

a. Purchased merchandise from suppliers at a cost of $80,000 with credit terms of 2/10, net 30.

b. Paid freight costs of $4,250 to the common carrier for merchandise purchased.

c. Returned defective merchandise to suppliers and received credits of $2,300, the amount of credit before taking into account any purchase discounts.

d. Realized $92,000 in sales for the month, of which $68,000 is on credit; the remainder was received in cash. The credit sales are made with terms of 2/10, net 45.

e. Gave sales returns and allowances on credit sales of $4,000 during the month.

f. Made cash payments of $62,000 to suppliers for earlier purchases on account. All amounts paid during the month are made within the discount period.

g. Received $56,000 in cash collections on account from customers. All amounts received during the month are within the discount period.

Required

1. Prepare the journal entries on the books of Weekend Wonders Inc. to record each transaction.

2. Prepare a partial income statement for the month of June. The last line on the statement should be gross margin.

3. Assume that Weekend Wonders decides as a matter of policy to forgo the discount for early payment on purchases (credit terms are 2/10, net 30). What return would Weekend Wonders need to earn on the money it invests by not paying early to justify this decision? Provide any necessary calculations to support your answer.

LO 1, 2, 3 **Problem 5-9** Purchases and Sales of Merchandise, Cash Flows

Two Wheeler, a bike shop, opened for business on April 1. It uses a periodic inventory system and records purchases at gross. The following transactions occurred during the first month of business:

April 1: Purchased five units from Duhan Co. for $500 total, with terms 3/10, net 30, FOB destination.

April 10: Paid for the April 1 purchase.

April 15: Sold one unit for $200 cash.

April 18: Purchased 10 units from Clinton Inc. for $900 total, with terms 3/10, net/30, FOB destination.

April 25: Sold three units for $200 each, cash.

April 28: Paid for the April 18 purchase.

Required

1. Prepare the journal entries to record the April transactions.

2. Determine net income for the month of April. Two Wheeler incurred and paid $100 for rent and $50 for miscellaneous expenses during April. Ending inventory is $967 (ignore income taxes).

3. Assuming that the only transactions during April are given (including rent and miscellaneous expenses), compute net cash flow from operating activities.

4. Explain why cash outflow is so much larger than expenses on the income statement.

LO 1, 3 **Problem 5-10** The Gap's Sales, Cost of Goods Sold and Gross Margin

The consolidated balance sheets of The Gap Inc. included merchandise inventory in the amount of $482,575,000 as of February 3, 1996 and $370,638,000 as of January 28, 1995. Refer also to the The Gap's consolidated statements of earnings for fiscal 1996 and 1995 which are set forth in the opening vignette of this chapter.

Required

1. Unlike the balance sheet of most merchandisers The Gap's doesn't include accounts receivable. Why doesn't The Gap's balance sheet include this account?

2. Prepare a summary journal entry for sales during the year ended February 3, 1996.

3. The Gap sets forth net sales but not gross sales on its income statement. What type(s) of deduction(s) would be made from gross sales to arrive at the amount of net sales reported? Why might the company decide not to report the amount(s) of the deduction(s) separately?

4. Reconstruct the cost of goods sold section of The Gap's 1996 income statement.

5. Calculate the gross margin (gross profit) ratios for The Gap for 1996, 1995, and 1994 and comment on the changes noted, if any. Is the company's performance improving? What factors might have caused the change in the gross margin ratio?

LO 4, 5 **Problem 5-11** Internal Control

At Morris Mart Inc. all sales are on account. Mary Morris-Manning is responsible for mailing invoices to customers, recording the amount billed, opening mail, and recording the payment. Mary is very devoted to the family business and never takes off more than one or two days for a long weekend. The customers know Mary and sometimes send personal notes with their payments. Another clerk handles all aspects of accounts payable. Mary's brother, who is president of Morris Mart, has hired an accountant to help with expansion.

Required

1. List some problems with the current accounts receivable system.

2. What suggestions would you make to improve internal control?

3. How would you explain to Mary that she personally is not the problem?

LO 1, 3 **Problem 5-12** Financial Statements

A list of accounts for Maple Inc. at 12/31/98, follows:

Accounts Receivable	$ 2,359
Advertising Expense	4,510
Buildings and Equipment, Net	55,550
Capital Stock	50,000
Cash	590
Depreciation Expense	2,300
Dividends	6,000
Income Tax Expense	3,200
Income Tax Payable	3,200
Interest Receivable	100
Inventory:	
January 1, 1998	6,400
December 31, 1998	7,500
Land	20,000
Purchase Discounts	800
Purchases	40,200
Retained Earnings, January 1, 1998	32,550
Salaries Expense	25,600
Salaries Payable	650
Sales	84,364
Sales Returns	780
Transportation-in	375
Utilities Expense	3,600

Required

1. Determine cost of goods sold for 1998.
2. Determine net income for 1998.
3. Prepare a balance sheet dated December 31, 1998.

Alternate Problems

LO 1 **Problem 5-1A** Discounts

Austin Inc., a recording distributor, would like to offer discounts to customers who purchase large quantities. Austin is unsure about the terms to use and how to account for discounts extended to customers. The company also wants to consider a cash discount for early payment by customers. Austin expects sales of about $3 million this year. All sales are on account to about 100 different outlets located within 500 miles of the warehouse. Deliveries are made by Austin's own trucks and cost about $25 per 100 miles driven. A full truck will hold 1,000 units.

Required

1. Explain the difference between a quantity discount and a discount for early payment. How is each accounted for in the accounting records? What are the reasons to extend the different discounts to customers?

2. Set up a quantity discount plan and a sales discount plan for Austin to extend to customers. Be able to explain why you chose your bases for the discounts and the amount of discounts.

LO 1 **Problem 5-2A** Calculation of Gross Margins for Sears and JCPenney

The following information was summarized from the 1995 and 1994 consolidated statements of income of Sears, Roebuck and Co. and JCPenney Company, Inc. and Subsidiaries:

	1995		1994	
(in millions)	SALES*	COST OF SALES**	SALES*	COST OF SALES**
Sears	$31,035	$22,866	$29,451	$21,568
JCPenney	$20,562	$14,333	$20,380	$13,970

*Described as "merchandise sales and services" by Sears and "retail sales" by JCPenney.
**Described as "cost of sales, buying and occupancy" by Sears and "cost of goods sold, occupancy, buying and warehousing costs" by JCPenney.

Required

1. Calculate the gross margin (gross profit) ratios for Sears and JCPenney for 1995 and 1994.

2. Which company appears to be performing better? What factors might cause the difference in the gross margin ratios of the two companies? What other information should you consider to determine how these companies are performing in this regard?

LO 5 **Problem 5-3A** Internal Control Procedures

The loan department in a bank is subject to regulation. Internal auditors work for the bank to ensure that the loan department complies with requirements. The internal auditors must verify that each car loan file has a note signed by the maker, verification of insurance, and a title issued by the state that names the bank as co-owner.

Required

1. Explain why the bank and the regulatory agency are concerned with these documents.

2. Describe the internal control procedures that should be in place to ensure that these documents are obtained and safeguarded.

LO 6 **Problem 5-4A** The Design of Internal Control Documents (Appendix 5A)

Tiger's Group is a newly formed company that produces and sells children's movies about an imaginary character. The movies are in such great demand that they are shipped to retail outlets as soon as they are produced. The company must pay a royalty to several actors for each movie that it sold to retail outlets.

Required

1. Describe some internal control features that should be in place to ensure that all royalties are paid to the actors.

2. Design the shipping form that Tiger's Group should use for the movies. Be sure to include authorizations and indicate the number of copies and the routing of the copies.

Alternate Multi-Concept Problems

General Ledger

LO 1, 3 **Problem 5-5A** Journal Entries for a Merchandiser

The following transactions were entered into by Maxwell Inc. during the month of July:

July 2: Purchased 1,000 pounds of sausage at a cost of $3 per pound. Terms of payment are 2/10, net 30.

July 4: Paid trucking firm $500 to ship the sausage purchased on July 2.

July 5: Purchased 600 pounds of sausage at a cost of $3 per pound. Terms of payment are 2/10, net 45.

July 6: Paid trucking firm $300 to ship the sausage purchased on July 5.

July 7: Due to expired dates on some packages, returned 100 pounds of the sausage purchased on July 2. Received a credit on open account from the seller.

July 11: Paid for sausage purchased on July 2.

July 13: Sold 1,200 pounds of sausage from those purchased on July 2 and July 5. The selling price was $7 per pound, cash.

July 30: Paid for sausage purchased on July 5.

Required

1. Prepare the journal entries to record these transactions on the books of Maxwell Inc. The company uses the gross method of recording purchase discounts. Maxwell uses a periodic inventory system.

2. Maxwell assumes a $3 per pound cost of inventory when planning profit and setting prices. Is this accurate? Explain.

LO 1, 2, 3 **Problem 5-6A** Journal Entries for a Merchandiser

Deckside Furniture Store entered into the following transactions in the month of April:

April 3: Purchased 50 lounge chairs at $120 each with terms 2/10, net 45. The chairs were shipped FOB destination.

April 7: Sold 6 chairs for $256 each, terms 2/10, net 30.

April 8: Purchased 20 patio umbrella tables for $96 each, FOB shipping point, terms 1/10, net 30.

April 9: Due to defects, returned 5 lounge chairs purchased on April 3. Received a credit memorandum.

April 10: Paid the trucking firm $288 for delivery of the tables purchased on April 8.

April 13: Paid for the chairs purchased on April 3.

April 17: Received payment for the chairs sold on April 7.

April 20: Paid for the tables purchased on April 8.

Required

1. Prepare all journal entries needed to record these transactions for the furniture company. Deckside uses the gross method of recording purchase and sales discounts. The company uses a periodic inventory system.

2. Do you think Deckside should change to a perpetual inventory system, given the nature of their business? Why? What advantages would a company have using the perpetual system instead of the periodic system?

LO 1, 3 **Problem 5-7A** Trade and Cash Discounts

Krittenger Inc. publishes books and offers trade discounts to customers who purchase in large quantities: 20% for purchases of more than 50 units. It also offers credit terms of 2/10, net 30 to induce early payment. The list price of one book is $50. Scholten Company purchased 100 of these books on September 12. Payment was made on September 21.

Required

1. Prepare the journal entries on Krittenger's books to record the sale and the receipt of cash.

2. Prepare the journal entries on Scholten's books to record the purchase and the payment.

LO 1, 3 **Problem 5-8A** Journal Entries and Partial Income Statement for a Merchandiser

Toppsie Turn Inc. operates a chain of T-shirt stores. The company uses a periodic inventory system. Inventories on hand on June 1 and June 30, 1998, amount to $12,840. The company uses the gross method to record purchase discounts. The following transactions take place during the month of June:

a. Purchased merchandise from suppliers at a cost of $62,000 with credit terms of 2/10, net 30.

b. Paid freight cost of $3,400 to the common carrier for merchandise purchased.

c. Realized $124,000 of sales for the month, all of which are cash sales.

d. Paid for merchandise purchased during the month within the discount period.

e. Accepted $500 in returned merchandise during the month.

Required

1. Prepare the journal entries on the books of Toppsie Turn Inc. to record each transaction.

2. Determine the gross margin that Toppsie Turn would report on the income statement for the month of June.

3. Toppsie is thinking about extending credit to some of its major customers to encourage credit customers to pay quickly. Toppsie expects existing sales will increase by 10% and that, at the new sales level, 60% of sales will be credit sales. Should Toppsie extend credit terms of 2/10, net 30? Explain your answer.

LO 1, 2, 3 **Problem 5-9A** Purchases and Sales of Merchandise, Cash Flows

Chestnut Corp., a ski shop, opened for business on October 1. It uses a periodic inventory system and the gross method to record purchase discounts. The following transactions occurred during the first month of business:

October 1: Purchased three units from Oshkosh Inc. for $249 total, terms 2/10, net 30, FOB destination.

October 10: Paid for the October 1 purchase.

October 15: Sold one unit for $200 cash.

October 18: Purchased 10 units from Wausau Company for $800 total, with terms 2/10, net/30, FOB destination.

October 25: Sold three units for $200 each, cash.

October 30: Paid for the October 18 purchase.

Required

1. Prepare the journal entries to record the October transactions.
2. Determine the number of units on hand on October 31.
3. If Chestnut started the month with $2,000, determine its balance in cash at the end of the month, assuming that these are the only transactions that occurred during October. Why has the cash balance decreased when the company reported net income?

LO 1, 3 **Problem 5-10A** Federated Department Stores' Sales, Cost of Goods Sold and Gross Margin

The following information was summarized from the consolidated balance sheets of Federated Department Stores, Inc. as of February 3, 1996 and January 28, 1995 (labeled as 1996 and 1995, respectively) and the consolidated statements of income for the 53 and 52 week periods then ended.

(in thousands)	1996	1995
Accounts receivable	$ 2,842,077	$2,265,651
Cost of sales	9,317,331	5,131,363
Merchandise inventories	3,094,848	2,380,621
Net sales	15,048,513	8,315,877

Required

1. Prepare summary journal entries related to the collection of accounts receivable and sales during 1996.
2. Federated sets forth net sales but not gross sales on its income statement. What type(s) of deduction(s) would be made from gross sales to arrive at the amount of net sales reported? Why might the company decide not to report the amount(s) of the deduction(s) separately?
3. Reconstruct the cost of goods sold section of Federated's 1996 income statement.
4. Calculate the gross margin (gross profit) ratios for Federated for 1996 and 1995 and comment on the change noted, if any. Is the company's performance improving? What factors might have caused the change in the gross margin ratio?

LO 4, 5 **Problem 5-11A** Internal Control

Abbott Inc. is expanding and needs to hire more personnel in the accounting office. Barbara Barker, the chief accounting clerk, knew that her cousin Cheryl was looking for a job. Barbara and Cheryl are also roommates. Barbara offered Cheryl a job as her assistant. Barbara will be responsible for Cheryl's performance reviews and training.

Required

1. List some problems with the proposed personnel situations in the accounting department.
2. Explain why accountants are concerned with the hiring of personnel. What suggestions would you make to improve internal control at Abbott?
3. How would you explain to Barbara and Cheryl that they personally are not the problem?

LO 1, 3 **Problem 5-12A** Financial Statements

A list of accounts for Lloyd Inc. at December 31, 1998, follows:

Accounts Receivable	$ 56,359
Advertising Expense	12,900
Capital Stock	50,000
Cash	22,340
Dividends	6,000
Income Tax Expense	1,450
Income Tax Payable	1,450
Inventory	
January 1, 1998	6,400
December 31, 1998	5,900
Purchase Discounts	1,237
Purchases	62,845
Retained Earnings, January 1, 1998	28,252
Salaries Payable	650
Sales	112,768
Sales Returns	1,008
Transportation-in	375
Utilities Expense	1,800
Wages and Salaries Expense	23,000
Wages Payable	120

Required

1. Determine cost of goods sold for 1998.
2. Determine net income for 1998.
3. Prepare a balance sheet dated December 31, 1998.

Cases

Reading and Interpreting Financial Statements

LO 3 **Case 5-1** Reading and Interpreting Ben & Jerry's Financial Statements
Refer to the 1995 financial statements included in Ben & Jerry's annual report.

Required

1. Determine the amount of cost of sales for 1995.
2. Is Ben & Jerry's a merchandiser, manufacturer, or service provider?
3. Compare and contrast the cost of sales for merchandisers and manufacturers.

LO 4 **Case 5-2** Reading and Interpreting Sears' Management Report
Sears, Roebuck and Co.'s 1995 annual report includes a management's report. Included in the report is the following:

Management maintains a system of internal controls which it believes provides reasonable assurance that, in all material respects, assets are maintained and accounted for in accordance with management's authorizations and transactions are recorded accurately in the books and records. The concept of reasonable assurance is based on the premise that the cost of internal controls should not exceed the benefits derived. To assure the effectiveness of the internal control system, the organizational structure provides for defined lines of responsibility and delegation of authority.

Required

1. Why did management include this report in the annual report?
2. What types of costs does Sears have in mind when it states that "the cost of internal controls should not exceed the benefits derived"?
3. Based on what you know about retail stores, and Sears stores in particular, list the kinds of accounting and system controls the company may have in place to safeguard assets.

Making Financial Decisions

Decision
Making

LO 1, 3 **Case 5-3** Gross Margin for a Merchandiser

Emblems For You sells specialty sweatshirts. The purchase price is $10 per unit, plus 10% tax and a shipping cost of 50¢ per unit. When the units arrive, they must be labeled, at an additional cost of 75¢ per unit. Emblems purchased, received, and labeled 1,500 units, of which 750 units were sold during the month for $20 each. The controller has prepared the following income statement:

Sales	$15,000
Cost of sales ($11 × 750)	8,250
Gross margin	$ 6,750
Shipping expense	750
Labeling expense	1,125
Net income	$ 4,875

Emblems is aware that a gross margin of 40% is standard for the industry. The marketing manager believes that Emblems should lower the price because the gross margin is higher than the industry average.

Required

1. Calculate Emblems' gross margin ratio.
2. Explain why you believe that Emblems should or should not lower its selling price.

Decision
Making

LO 1, 3 **Case 5-4** Pricing Decision

Caroline's Candy corner sells gourmet chocolates. The company buys chocolates, in bulk, for $5.00 per pound plus 5% sales tax. Credit terms are 2/10, net 25, and the company always pays promptly in order to take advantage of the discount. The chocolates are shipped to Caroline FOB shipping point. Shipping costs are $.05 per pound. When the chocolates arrive at the shop, Caroline's Candy repackages them into one-pound boxes labeled with the store name. Boxes cost $.70 each. The company pays its employees an hourly wage of $5.25 plus a commission of $.10 per pound.

Required

1. What is the cost per one-pound box of chocolates?
2. What price must Caroline's Candy charge in order to have a 40% gross margin?
3. Do you believe this is a sufficient margin for this kind of business? What other costs might the company still incur?

Decision
Making

LO 2 **Case 5-5** Use of a Perpetual Inventory System

Darrell Keith is starting a new business. He would like to keep a tight control over it. Therefore, he wants to know *exactly* how much gross profit he earns on each unit he sells. Darrell has set up an elaborate numbering system to identify each item as it is purchased and then to match the item with a sales price. Each unit is assigned a number as follows:

0000-000-00-000

a. The first four numbers represent the month and day an item was received.
b. The second three numbers are the last three numbers of the purchase order that authorized the purchase of the item.
c. The third set of two numbers is the department code assigned to different types of products.
d. The last three numbers are a chronological code assigned to units as they are received during a given day.

Required

1. Write a short memo to Darrell explaining the benefits and costs involved in a perpetual inventory system in conjunction with his quest to know exactly how much he will earn on each unit.
2. Comment on Darrell's inventory system, assuming that he is selling (a) automobiles or (b) trees, shrubs, and plants.

Accounting and Ethics: What Would You Do?

LO 1 **Case 5-6** Sales Returns and Allowances

You are the controller for a large chain of discount merchandise stores. You receive a memorandum from the sales manager for the midwestern region. He raises an issue regarding the proper treatment of sales returns. The manager urges you to discontinue the "silly practice" of recording Sales Returns and Allowances each time a customer returns a product. In the manager's mind, this is a waste of time and unduly complicates the financial statements. The manager recommends, "Things could be kept a lot simpler by just reducing Sales Revenue when a product is returned."

Required

1. What do you think the sales manager's *motivation* might be for writing you the memo? Is it that he believes the present practice is a waste of time and unduly complicates the financial statements?
2. Do you agree with the sales manager's recommendation? Explain why you agree or disagree.
3. Write a brief memo to the sales manager outlining your position on this matter.

LO 4, 5 **Case 5-7** Cash Receipts in a Bookstore

You were recently hired by a large retail bookstore chain. Your training involved spending a week at the largest and most profitable store in the district. The store manager assigned the head cashier to train you on the cash register and closing procedures required by the company's home office. In the process, the head cashier instructed you to keep an envelope for cash over and short that would include cash or IOUs equal to the net amount of overages or shortages in the cash drawer. "It is impossible to balance exactly, so just put extra cash in this envelope and use the cash when you are short." You studied accounting for one semester in college and remembered your professor saying that "all deposits should be made intact, daily."

Required

Draft a memorandum to the store manager detailing any problems you see with the current system.

Research Case

Case 5-8 The Gap Inc.

Despite expansion with Banana Republic and Old Navy stores, The Gap Inc., continues to face intense competition from discount retailers such as Target and Wal-Mart. The continually changing clothing marketplace has a strong impact on company's sales, cost of goods sold, net income, and other business activities.

Conduct a search of the World Wide Web, obtain The Gap's most recent annual report, or use library resources to obtain company financial data, and answer the following:

1. For the most recent year available, what is The Gap's net sales? How does this compare to the previous year?
2. Based on the latest accounting year available, what percentage of net sales goes for cost of goods sold and occupancy expenses? How does this compare with the amount in the "Focus on Financial Results" in the opening vignette shown at the start of this chapter?
3. As a manager, how might changes in the gross profit percentage influence future actions? What actions might be taken by management to maximize the difference between net sales and cost of goods sold?

Optional Research. Conduct a survey of students and other consumers about their clothes shopping habits and store preferences. Also, develop a brief description of The Gap's competitors such as The Limited, Structure, and Benetton. Does this research suggest that The Gap continues to have a unique advantage in its core markets?

Solutions to Key Terms Quiz

Quiz 1: Merchandise Accounting

14 Net sales (p. 219)
4 Trade discount (p. 220)
7 Sales Discounts (p. 222)
15 Cost of goods sold (p. 223)
10 Periodic system (p. 223)
13 Purchases (p. 225)
12 Purchase Discounts (p. 227)
9 FOB shipping point (p. 227)

2 Sales Returns and Allowances (p. 220)
1 Quantity discount (p. 220)
11 Cost of goods available for sale (p. 222)
5 Perpetual system (p. 223)
3 Transportation-in (p. 225)
6 Purchase Returns and Allowances (p. 226)
8 FOB destination point (p. 227)

Quiz 2: Internal Control

14 Internal control system (p. 229)
13 Internal audit staff (p. 229)
4 Audit committee (p. 230)
3 Accounting system (p. 231)
5 Accounting controls (p. 231)
12 Purchase order (Appendix 5A) (p. 239)
9 Blind receiving report (Appendix 5A) (p. 240)

8 Report of management (p. 229)
2 Board of directors (p. 230)
10 Foreign Corrupt Practices Act (p. 230)
11 Administrative controls (p. 231)
6 Purchase requisition form (Appendix 5A) (p. 237)
1 Invoice (Appendix 5A) (p. 239)
7 Invoice approval form (Appendix 5A) (p. 240)

CHAPTER

6

STUDY LINKS

A Look at Previous Chapters

In Chapter 5, we introduced inventory for merchandisers and examined how they account for purchases and sales of their products. We saw that companies track their inventory using one of two systems, periodic or perpetual.

A Look at This Chapter

In this chapter, we continue our examination of inventory by considering inventory costing methods. Specific identification, FIFO, LIFO, and weighted average are choices available to a company in assigning a value to inventory on the balance sheet and in determining cost of goods sold on the income statement. Other inventory topics discussed in the chapter include the lower of cost or market rule and methods of estimating inventory.

A Look at Upcoming Chapters

Chapter 7 concludes our look at accounting for current assets. When a company makes a sale of inventory on credit, it records an account receivable. The collection of the receivable adds to the company's cash balance. Chapter 7 looks at accounting issues for cash and receivables.

Inventories and Cost of Goods Sold

FOCUS ON FINANCIAL RESULTS

In the highly competitive consumer electronics business, Circuit City is a success story. The 1996 income statement, as seen here, reports record sales of over $7 billion. The company expects annual sales of approximately $15 billion by the end of the decade. A major factor in Circuit City's performance is consumers' insatiable appetite for electronic goods, from personal computers to stereo systems. Recognizing the competitive nature of selling these products, the company recently diversified with CarMax, its revolutionary used-car business.

Sales volume is important for any merchandiser, but so is getting the right mix of merchandise at the right price. Circuit City recognizes that its profitability depends on merchandise mix, inventory

CIRCUIT CITY

CONSOLIDATED STATEMENTS OF EARNINGS

				Years Ended February 29 or 28			
(AMOUNTS IN THOUSANDS EXCEPT PER SHARE DATA)	1996	%		1995	%	1994	%
NET SALES AND OPERATING REVENUES	$7,029,123	100.0		$5,582,947	100.0	$4,130,415	100.0
Cost of sales, buying and warehousing	5,394,293	76.7		4,197,947	75.2	3,024,759	73.2
GROSS PROFIT	1,634,830	23.3		1,385,000	24.8	1,105,656	26.8
Selling, general and administrative expenses [NOTE 8]	1,322,430	18.8		1,106,370	19.8	891,865	21.6
Interest expense [NOTE 3]	25,400	0.4		10,030	0.2	4,791	0.1
TOTAL EXPENSES	1,347,830	19.2		1,116,400	20.0	896,656	21.7
Earnings before income taxes	287,000	4.1		268,600	4.8	209,000	5.1
Provision for income taxes [NOTE 4]	107,625	1.5		100,725	1.8	76,600	1.9
NET EARNINGS	$ 179,375	2.6		$ 167,875	3.0	$ 132,400	3.2
Weighted average common shares and common share equivalents	98,546			97,369		97,391	
NET EARNINGS PER SHARE	$ 1.82			$ 1.72		$ 1.36	

CONSOLIDATED BALANCE SHEETS [Partial]

	At February 29 or 28	
(AMOUNTS IN THOUSANDS EXCEPT SHARE DATA)	1996	1995
ASSETS		
CURRENT ASSETS:		
Cash and cash equivalents	$ 43,704	$ 46,962
Net accounts and notes receivable [NOTE 9]	324,395	264,565
Merchandise inventory	1,323,183	1,035,776
Deferred income taxes [NOTE 4]	26,996	25,696
Prepaid expenses and other current assets	17,399	14,162
TOTAL CURRENT ASSETS	1,735,677	1,387,161
Property and equipment, net [NOTES 2 AND 3]	774,265	592,956
Deferred income taxes [NOTE 4]	–	5,947
Other assets	16,080	17,991
TOTAL ASSETS	$2,526,022	$2,004,055

See accompanying notes to consolidated financial statements.

management and efficient distribution of inventory. The company simply *must* focus on inventory issues because, as shown in the accompanying partial balance sheets, merchandise represents about half its investment in assets.

A key measure of inventory management at Circuit City is "inventory turns"—how often the retailer turns over its merchandise each year. What does a high number of inventory turns say about the company's effectiveness in choosing, pricing, and promoting its products? While studying this chapter, consider this question and also which items from the annual report you would use to approximate how often Circuit City turns over its merchandise each year.

SOURCE: Circuit City Stores Inc. Annual Report, 1996.

After studying this chapter, you should be able to

LO 1   Identify the forms of inventory held by different types of businesses and the types of costs incurred.

LO 2   Explain the relationship between the valuation of inventory and the measurement of income.

LO 3   Analyze the effects of an inventory error on various financial statement items.

LO 4   Apply the inventory costing methods of specific identification, weighted average, FIFO, and LIFO using a periodic system.

LO 5   Analyze the effects of the different costing methods on inventory, net income, income taxes, and cash flow.

LO 6   Apply the lower of cost or market rule to the valuation of inventory.

LO 7   Explain why and how the cost of inventory is estimated in certain situations.

LO 8   Analyze the management of inventory turnover.

LO 9   Explain the effects that inventory transactions have on the statement of cash flows.

LO 10   Explain the differences between a periodic and a perpetual inventory system (Appendix 6A).

LO 11   Apply the inventory costing methods using a perpetual system (Appendix 6A).

The Nature of Inventory

LO 1   Identify the forms of inventory held by different types of businesses and the types of costs incurred.

Inventory is an asset held for *resale* in the normal course of business. The distinction between inventory and an operating asset is the *intent* of the owner. For example, some of the computers that Circuit City owns are operating assets because they are used in various activities of the business such as the payroll and accounting functions. Many of the computers owned by Circuity City are inventory, however, because the company intends to sell them. This chapter is concerned with the proper valuation of inventory and the related effect on cost of goods sold.

It is important to distinguish between the *types* of inventory costs incurred and the *form* the inventory takes. Wholesalers and retailers incur a single type of cost, the *purchase price*, of the inventory they sell. On the balance sheet they use a single account for inventory, titled **Merchandise Inventory.** Wholesalers and retailers buy merchandise in finished form and offer it for resale without transforming the product in any way. Because they do not use factory buildings, assembly lines, or production equipment, merchandise companies have a relatively small dollar amount in operating assets and a large amount in inventory. For example, on its February 29, 1996, balance sheet, Circuit City reported merchandise inventories of approximately $1.3 billion and total assets of $2.5 billion. It is not unusual for inventories to account for one-half of the total assets of a merchandise company.

The cost of inventory to a *merchandiser* is limited to the product's purchase price, which may include such costs as taxes and transportation-in. Conversely, three distinct *types* of costs are incurred by a *manufacturer:* direct materials, direct labor, and manufacturing overhead. Direct materials, also called **raw materials,** are the ingredients used in making a product. The costs of direct materials used in manufacturing an automobile include the costs of steel, glass, and rubber. Direct labor consists of the amounts paid to workers to manufacture the product. The $20 per hour paid to an assembly line worker is a primary ingredient in the cost to manufacture the automobile. Manufacturing overhead includes all other costs that are related to the manufacturing process but cannot be directly matched to specific units of output. Depreciation of a factory building and the salary of a supervisor are two examples of overhead costs. Accountants have developed various allocation techniques to assign these manufacturing overhead costs to specific products.

In addition to the three types of costs incurred in a production process, the inventory of a manufacturer takes three distinct *forms.* The three forms or stages in the development of inventory are raw materials, work in process, and finished goods. Direct materials or raw materials enter a production process in which they are transformed into a

The inventory of a manufacturer consists of raw material, work in process, and finished goods. The electronic device being built here is part of a firm's work in process inventory. The direct materials probably consists of such items as the individual control knobs pruchased from another manufacturer. When the manufacturing process is complete, the inventory of finished goods is ready for sale.

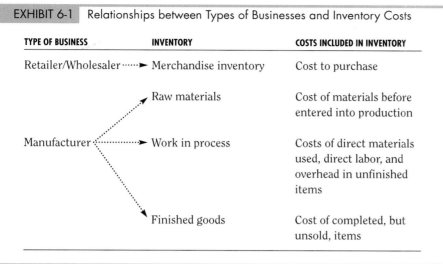

EXHIBIT 6-1   Relationships between Types of Businesses and Inventory Costs

TYPE OF BUSINESS	INVENTORY	COSTS INCLUDED IN INVENTORY
Retailer/Wholesaler ┈┈►	Merchandise inventory	Cost to purchase
Manufacturer	Raw materials	Cost of materials before entered into production
	Work in process	Costs of direct materials used, direct labor, and overhead in unfinished items
	Finished goods	Cost of completed, but unsold, items

finished product by the addition of direct labor and manufacturing overhead. At any point in time, including the end of an accounting period, some of the materials have entered the process and some labor costs have been incurred but the product is not finished. The cost of unfinished products is appropriately called **work in process** or *work in progress.* Inventory that has completed the production process and is available for sale is called **finished goods.** Manufacturers disclose the dollar amounts of each of the three forms of inventory in their annual report. For example, Nike disclosed in its 1995 annual report the following amounts, stated in thousands of dollars:

	THOUSANDS
Inventories:	
Finished goods	$618,521
Work in progress	9,064
Raw materials	2,157
	$629,742

Exhibit 6-1 summarizes the relationships between the types of costs incurred and the forms of inventory for different types of businesses.

Inventory Valuation and the Measurement of Income

Valuation is the major problem in accounting for inventories. Because of the additional complexities involved in valuing the inventory of a manufacturer, we will concentrate in this chapter on the valuation of *merchandise inventory.* Accounting for the inventory costs incurred by a manufacturing firm is covered in detail in management accounting textbooks.

One of the most fundamental concepts in accounting is the relationship between *asset valuation* and the *measurement of income.* Recall a point made in Chapter 4: assets are unexpired costs, and expenses are expired costs. Thus, the value assigned to an asset on the balance sheet determines the amount eventually recognized as an expense on the income statement. For example, the amount recorded as the cost of an item of plant and equipment will dictate the amount of depreciation expense recognized on the income statement over the life of the asset. Similarly, the amount recorded as the cost of inventory determines the amount recognized as cost of goods sold on the income statement when the asset is sold. An error in assigning the proper amount to inventory on

LO 2   Explain the relationship between the valuation of inventory and the measurement of income.

the balance sheet will affect the amount recognized as cost of goods sold on the income statement. The relationship between inventory as an asset and cost of goods sold can be understood by recalling the cost of goods sold section of the income statement. Assume the following example:

Beginning inventory	$ 500
Add: Purchases	1,200
Cost of goods available for sale	$1,700
Less: Ending inventory	(600)
Cost of goods sold	$1,100

The amount assigned to ending inventory is deducted from cost of goods available for sale to determine cost of goods sold. If the ending inventory amount is incorrect, cost of goods sold will be wrong, and thus the net income of the period will be in error as well.

Inventory Errors

LO 3   Analyze the effects of an inventory error on various financial statement items.

The importance of inventory valuation to the measurement of income can be illustrated by considering inventory errors. Many different types of inventory errors exist. Some errors are mathematical; for example, a bookkeeper may incorrectly add a column total. Other errors relate specifically to the physical count of inventory at year-end. For example, the count might inadvertently omit one section of a warehouse. Other errors arise from cutoff problems at year-end.

For example, assume that merchandise in transit at the end of the year is shipped FOB (free on board) shipping point. Under these shipment terms, the inventory belongs to the buyer at the time it is shipped. Because the shipment has not arrived at the end of the year, however, it cannot be included in the physical count. Unless some type of control is in place, the amount in transit may be erroneously omitted from the valuation of inventory at year-end.

Inventory errors sometimes occur when goods are held on consignment. A **consignment** is a legal arrangement in which inventory owned by one company, the consignor, is turned over to another company, the consignee, to sell. Most art galleries operate on a consignment basis. The artist agrees to split the profits with the gallery owner in exchange for having the art on display. Typically, a consignment arrangement relieves the gallery owner of taking a risk that the artwork will not be sold. During the consignment period, title to the goods remains with the consignor (in this case, the artist). The consignee acts as a selling agent for the consignor. Even though the consignor does not have physical possession of the goods at the end of the period, it must still include them in inventory on the balance sheet. Conversely, the consignee must be sure *not* to include any consigned goods in the physical count of its own merchandise at year-end.

To demonstrate the effect of an inventory error on the income statement, consider the following example. Through a scheduling error, two different inventory teams were assigned to count the inventory in the same warehouse on December 31, 1998. The correct amount of ending inventory is $250,000, but because two different teams counted the same inventory in one warehouse, the amount recorded is $300,000. The effect of this error on net income is analyzed in the left half of Exhibit 6-2.

The *overstatement* of *ending inventory* in 1998 leads to an *understatement* of the 1998 cost of goods sold *expense*. Because cost of goods sold is understated, *gross margin* for the year is *overstated*. Operating expenses are unaffected by an inventory error. Thus, *net income* is *overstated* by the same amount of overstatement of gross margin.[1] The most important conclusion from the exhibit is that an overstatement of ending inventory leads to a corresponding overstatement of net income.

Unfortunately, the effect of a misstatement of the year-end inventory is not limited to the net income for that year. As indicated in the right-hand portion of Exhibit 6-2, the error also affects the income statement for the following year. This happens simply

---

[1]An overstatement of gross margin also results in an overstatement of income tax expense. Thus, because tax expense is overstated, the overstatement of net income is not so large as the overstatement of gross margin. For now we will ignore the effect of taxes, however.

| EXHIBIT 6-2 | Effects of Inventory Error on the Income Statement |

	1998			1999		
	REPORTED	**CORRECTED**	**EFFECTS OF ERROR**	**REPORTED**	**CORRECTED**	**EFFECTS OF ERROR**
Sales	$1,000*	$1,000		$ 1,500	$ 1,500	
Costs of goods sold:						
Beginning inventory	200	200		**300**	**250**	$50 OS
Add: Purchases	700	700		1,100	1,100	
Cost of goods available for sale	$ 900	$ 900		**$1,400**	**$1,350**	50 OS
Less: Ending inventory	**300**	**250**	$50 OS†	350	350	
Cost of goods sold	**$ 600**	**$ 650**	50 US‡	**$1,050**	**$1,000**	50 OS
Gross margin	**$ 400**	**$ 350**	50 OS	**$ 450**	**$ 500**	50 US
Operating expenses	100	100		120	120	
Net income	**$ 300**	**$ 250**	50 OS	**$ 330**	**$ 380**	50 US

Note: Figures that differ as a result of the error are in bold.
*All amounts are in thousands of dollars.
†OS = Overstatement
‡US = Understatement

because *the ending inventory of one period is the beginning inventory of the following period.* The *overstatement* of the 1999 *beginning inventory* leads to an *overstatement* of *cost of goods available for sale.* Because cost of goods available for sale is overstated, *cost of goods sold* is also *overstated.* The *overstatement* of cost of goods sold *expense* results in an *understatement* of *gross margin* and thus an *understatement* of *net income.*

Exhibit 6-2 illustrates the nature of a *counterbalancing error.* The effect of the overstatement of net income in the first year, 1998, is offset or counterbalanced by the understatement of net income by the same dollar amount in the following year. If the net incomes of two successive years are misstated in the opposite direction by the same amount, what is the effect on retained earnings? Assume that retained earnings at the beginning of 1998 is correctly stated at $300,000. The counterbalancing nature of the error is seen by analyzing retained earnings. For 1998 the analysis would indicate the following (OS = overstated and US = understated):

	1998 REPORTED	1999 CORRECTED	EFFECT OF ERROR
Beginning retained earnings	$300,000	$300,000	Correct
Add: Net income	300,000	250,000	$50,000 OS
Ending retained earnings	$600,000	$550,000	$50,000 OS

An analysis for 1999 would show the following:

	1999 REPORTED	1999 CORRECTED	EFFECT OF ERROR
Beginning retained earnings	$600,000	$550,000	$50,000 OS
Add: Net income	330,000	380,000	$50,000 US
Ending retained earnings	$930,000	$930,000	Correct

Thus, even though retained earnings is overstated at the end of the first year, it is correctly stated at the end of the second year. This is the nature of a counterbalancing error.

The effect of the error on the balance sheet is shown in Exhibit 6-3. The only accounts affected by the error are Inventory and Retained Earnings. The overstatement of the 1998 ending inventory results in an overstatement of total assets at the end of the first year. Similarly, as our earlier analysis indicates, the overstatement of 1998 net

---

EXHIBIT 6-3   Effects of Inventory Error on the Balance Sheet

	1998		1999	
	REPORTED	**CORRECTED**	**REPORTED**	**CORRECTED**
Inventory	$ 300*	$ 250	$ 350	$ 350
All other assets	1,700	1,700	2,080	2,080
Total assets	$2,000	$1,950	$2,430	$2,430
Total liabilities	$ 400	$ 400	$ 500	$ 500
Capital stock	1,000	1,000	1,000	1,000
Retained earnings	**600**	**550**	930	930
Total liabilities and stockholders' equity	$2,000	$1,950	$2,430	$2,430

Note: Figures that differ as a result of the error are in bold.
*All amounts are in thousands of dollars.

---

income leads to an overstatement of retained earnings by the same amount. Because the error is counterbalancing, the 1999 year-end balance sheet is correct; that is, ending inventory is not affected by the error, and thus the amount for total assets at the end of 1999 is also correct. The effect of the error on retained earnings is limited to the first year because of the counterbalancing nature of the error.

The effects of inventory errors on various financial statement items are summarized in Exhibit 6-4. Our analysis focused on the effects of an overstatement of inventory. The effects of an understatement are just the opposite and are summarized in the bottom portion of the exhibit.

Not all errors are counterbalancing. For example, if a section of a warehouse *continues* to be omitted from the physical count every year, both the beginning and the ending inventory will be incorrect each year and the error will not counterbalance.

Part of the auditor's job is to perform the necessary tests to obtain reasonable assurance that inventory has not been overstated or understated. If there is an error and inventory is wrong, however, the balance sheet and the income statement will both be distorted. For example, if ending inventory is overstated, inflating total assets, then cost of goods sold will be understated, boosting profits. Thus, such an error overstates the financial health of the organization in two ways. A lender or an investor must make a decision based on the current year's statement and cannot wait until the next accounting cycle, when this error is reversed. This is one reason that investors and creditors insist on audited financial statements.

EXHIBIT 6-4   Summary of the Effects of Inventory Errors

	EFFECT OF OVERSTATEMENT OF ENDING INVENTORY ON	
	CURRENT YEAR	**FOLLOWING YEAR**
Cost of goods sold	Understated	Overstated
Gross margin	Overstated	Understated
Net income	Overstated	Understated
Retained earnings, end of year	Overstated	Correctly stated
Total assets, end of year	Overstated	Correctly stated

	EFFECT OF UNDERSTATEMENT OF ENDING INVENTORY ON	
	CURRENT YEAR	**FOLLOWING YEAR**
Cost of goods sold	Overstated	Understated
Gross margin	Understated	Overstated
Net income	Understated	Overstated
Retained earnings, end of year	Understated	Correctly stated
Total assets, end of year	Understated	Correctly stated

Inventory Costs: What Should Be Included?

All assets, including inventory, are recorded initially at cost. Cost is defined as "the price paid or consideration given to acquire an asset. As applied to inventories, cost means in principle the sum of the applicable expenditures and charges directly or indirectly incurred in bringing an article to its existing condition and location."[2]

Note the reference to the existing *condition* and *location*. For example, any freight costs incurred by the buyer in shipping inventory to its place of business should be included in the cost of the inventory. The cost of insurance taken out during the time that inventory is in transit should be added to the cost of the inventory. The cost of storing inventory before the time it is ready to be sold should be included in cost. Various types of taxes paid, such as excise and sales taxes, are other examples of costs necessary to put the inventory into a position to be able to sell it.

It is often very difficult, however, to allocate many of these incidental costs among the various items of inventory purchased. For example, consider a $500 freight bill that a supermarket paid on a merchandise shipment that includes 100 different items of inventory. To address the practical difficulty in assigning this type of cost to the different products, many companies have a policy by which transportation costs are charged to expense of the period if they are immaterial in amount. Thus, shipments of merchandise are simply recorded at the net invoice price, that is, after taking any cash discounts for early payment. It is a practical solution to a difficult allocation problem. Once again, the company must apply the cost/benefit test to accounting information.

Inventory Costing Methods with a Periodic System

LO 4 Apply the inventory costing methods of specific identification, weighted average, FIFO, and LIFO using a periodic system.

To this point, we have assumed that the cost to purchase an item of inventory is constant. For most merchandisers, however, the unit cost of inventory changes frequently. Consider a simple example. Everett Company purchases merchandise twice during the first year of business. The dates, the number of units purchased, and the costs are as follows:

February 4   200 units purchased at $1.00 per unit   = $200

October 13   200 units purchased at $1.50 per unit   = $300

Everett sells 200 units during the first year. Individual sales of the units take place relatively evenly throughout the year. The question is: *which* 200 units did the company sell, the $1.00 units or the $1.50 units or some combination of each? Recall the earlier discussion of the relationship between asset valuation and income measurement. The question is important because the answer determines not only the value assigned to the 200 units of ending inventory *but also* the amount allocated to cost of goods sold for the 200 units sold.

One possible method of assigning amounts to ending inventory and cost of goods sold is to *specifically identify* which 200 units were sold and which 200 units are on hand. This method is feasible for a few types of businesses in which units can be identified by serial numbers, but it is totally impractical in most situations. As an alternative to specific identification, we could make an *assumption* as to which units were sold and which are on hand. Three different answers are possible:

1. 200 units sold at $1.00 each   = $200 cost of goods sold
   and 200 units on hand at $1.50 each = $300 ending inventory

   or

2. 200 units sold at $1.50 each   = $300 cost of goods sold
   and 200 units on hand at $1.00 each = $200 ending inventory

   or

[2]*Accounting Research Bulletin No. 43,* "Inventory Pricing" (New York: American Institute of Certified Public Accountants, June 1953), ch. 4, statement 3.

3. 200 units sold at $1.25 each   = $250 cost of goods sold
   and 200 units on hand at $1.25 each = $250 ending inventory

The third alternative assumes an *average cost* for the 200 units on hand and the 200 units sold. The average cost is the cost of the two purchases of $200 and $300, or $500, divided by the 400 units available to sell, or $1.25 per unit.

If we are concerned with the actual *physical flow* of the units of inventory, all of the three methods illustrated may be incorrect. The only approach that will yield a "correct" answer in terms of the actual flow of *units* of inventory is the specific identification method. In the absence of a specific identification approach, it is impossible to say which particular units were *actually* sold. In fact, there may have been sales from each of the two purchases, that is, some of the $1.00 units may have been sold and some of the $1.50 units may have been sold. To solve the problem of assigning costs to identical units, accountants have developed inventory costing assumptions or methods. Each of these methods makes a specific *assumption* about the *flow of costs* rather than the physical flow of units. The only approach that uses the actual flow of the units in assigning costs is the specific identification method.

To take a closer look at specific identification as well as three alternative approaches to valuing inventory, we will use the following example:

	UNITS	UNIT COST	TOTAL COST
Beginning inventory			
January 1	500	$10	$ 5,000*
Purchases			
January 20	300	11	3,300
April 8	400	12	4,800
September 5	200	13	2,600
December 12	100	14	1,400
Total purchases	1,000 units		$12,100
Available for sale	1,500 units		$17,100
Units sold	900 units		?
Units in ending inventory	600 units		?

*Beginning inventory of $5,000 is carried over as the ending inventory from the prior period. It is highly unlikely that each of the four methods we will illustrate would result in the same dollar amount of inventory at any point in time. It is helpful when first learning the methods, however, to assume the same amount of beginning inventory.

The question marks indicate the dilemma. What portion of the cost of goods available for sale of $17,100 should be assigned to the 900 units sold? What portion should be assigned to the 600 units remaining in ending inventory? The purpose of an inventory costing method is to provide a reasonable answer to these two questions.

Specific Identification Method

It is not always necessary to make an assumption about the flow of costs. In certain situations, it may be possible to specifically identify which units are sold and which units are on hand. A serial number on an automobile allows a dealer to identify a car on hand and thus its unit cost. An appliance dealer with 15 refrigerators on hand at the end of the year can identify the unit cost of each by matching a tag number with the purchase records. To illustrate the use of the **specific identification method** for our example, assume that the merchandiser is able to identify the specific units in the inventory at the end of the year and their costs as follows:

DATE	UNITS	COST	TOTAL
January 20	100	$11	$1,100
April 8	300	12	3,600
September 5	200	13	2,600
Ending inventory	600		$7,300

One of two techniques can be used to find cost of goods sold. We can deduct ending inventory from the cost of goods available for sale:

Cost of goods available for sale	$17,100
Less:	Ending inventory	7,300
Equals:	Cost of goods sold	$ 9,800

Or we can calculate cost of goods sold independently by matching the units sold with their respective unit costs. By eliminating the units in ending inventory from the original acquisition schedule, the units sold and their costs are as follows:

DATE	UNITS	COST	TOTAL
January 1	500	$10	$5,000
January 20	200	11	2,200
April 8	100	12	1,200
December 12	100	14	1,400
Cost of goods sold	900		$9,800

The practical difficulty in keeping track of individual items of inventory sold is not the only problem with the use of this method. The method also allows management to *manipulate income.* For example, assume that a company is not having a particularly good year. Management may be tempted to do whatever it can to boost net income. One way it can do this is by selectively selling units with the lowest-possible unit cost. By doing so, the company can keep cost of goods sold down and net income up. Because of the potential for manipulation with the specific identification method, coupled with the practical difficulty of applying it in most situations, it is not widely used.

Weighted Average Cost Method

The weighted average cost method is a relatively easy approach to costing inventory. It assigns the same unit cost to all units available for sale during the period. The weighted average cost is calculated as follows for our example:

$$\frac{\text{Cost of Goods Available for Sale}}{\text{Units Available for Sale}} = \text{Weighted Average Cost}$$

$$\frac{\$17,100}{1,500} = \$11.40$$

Ending inventory is found by multiplying the weighted average unit cost by the number of units on hand:

Weighted Average Cost × Number of Units in Ending Inventory = Ending Inventory

$11.40 × 600 = $6,840

Cost of goods sold can be calculated in one of two ways:

Cost of goods available for sale	$17,100
Less:	Ending inventory	6,840
Equals:	Cost of goods sold	$10,260

or

Weighted Average Cost × Number of Units Sold = Cost of Goods Sold

$11.40 × 900 = $10,260

Note that the computation of the weighted average cost is based on the cost of *all* units available for sale during the period, not just the beginning inventory or purchases. Also note that the method is called the *weighted* average cost method. As the name indicates, each of the individual unit costs is multiplied by the number of units acquired at each price. The simple arithmetic average of the unit costs for the beginning inventory and the four purchases is ($10 + $11 + $12 + $13 + $14)/5 = $12. The weighted average cost is slightly less than $12 ($11.40), however, because more units were acquired at the lower prices than at the higher prices.

First-in, First-out Method (FIFO)

The FIFO method assumes that the first units in, or purchased, are the first units out, or sold. The first units sold during the period are assumed to come from the beginning inventory. After the beginning inventory is sold, the next units sold are assumed to come from the first purchase during the period and so forth. Thus, ending inventory consists of the most recent purchases of the period. In many businesses, this cost-flow assumption is a fairly accurate reflection of the *physical* flow of products. For example, to maintain a fresh stock of products, the physical flow in a grocery store is first-in, first-out.

To calculate *ending inventory*, we start with the *most recent* inventory acquired and work *backward*:

DATE	UNITS	COST	TOTAL
December 12	100	$14	$1,400
September 5	200	13	2,600
April 8	300	12	3,600
Ending inventory	600		$7,600

Cost of goods sold can then be found:

Cost of goods available for sale		$17,100
Less:	Ending inventory	7,600
Equals:	Cost of goods sold	$ 9,500

Or, because the FIFO method assumes that the first units in are the first ones sold, cost of goods sold can be calculated by starting with the *beginning inventory* and working *forward*:

DATE	UNITS	COST	TOTAL
January 1	500	$10	$5,000
January 20	300	11	3,300
April 8	100	12	1,200
Units sold	900	Cost of goods sold	$9,500

ACCOUNTING FOR YOUR DECISIONS

You Are the Controller

Your company, Princeton Systems, is a manufacturer of components for personal computers. The company uses the FIFO method to account for its inventory. The CEO, a stickler for accuracy, asks you why you can't identify each unit of inventory and place a cost on it, instead of making an assumption that the first unit of inventory is the first sold when that is not necessarily the case.

ANS: The CEO is suggesting the specific identification method, which works best when there are fewer pieces of unique inventory, not thousands of units of identical pieces. Because the company makes thousands of identical components each year, it would be impractical to assign specific costs to each unit of inventory. The FIFO method, on the other hand, assumes that the first units in are the first units sold, an appropriate assumption under these circumstances.

Last-in, First-out Method (LIFO)

The LIFO method assumes that the last units in, or purchased, are the first units out, or sold. The first units sold during the period are assumed to come from the latest purchase made during the period and so forth. Can you think of any businesses where the *physical* flow of products is last-in, first-out? Although this situation is not nearly so common as a first-in, first-out physical flow, a stockpiling operation, such as in a rock quarry, operates on this basis.

To calculate *ending inventory* using LIFO, we start with the *beginning inventory* and work *forward:*

DATE	UNITS	COST	TOTAL
Beginning inventory	500	$10	$5,000
January 20	100	11	1,100
Ending inventory	600		$6,100

Cost of goods sold can then be found:

Cost of goods available for sale	$17,100
Less:	Ending inventory	6,100
Equals:	Cost of goods sold	$11,000

Or, because the LIFO method assumes that the last units in are the first ones sold, *cost of goods sold* can be calculated by starting with the *most recent* inventory acquired and working *backward:*

DATE	UNITS	COST	TOTAL
December 12	100	$14	$ 1,400
September 5	200	13	2,600
April 8	400	12	4,800
January 20	200	11	2,200
Units sold	900	Cost of goods sold	$11,000

Selecting an Inventory Costing Method

The mechanics of each of the inventory costing methods are straightforward. But how does a company decide on the best method to use to value its inventory? According to the accounting profession, *the primary determinant in selecting an inventory costing method should be the ability of the method to accurately reflect the net income of the period.* But how and why does a particular costing method accurately reflect the net income of the period? Because there is no easy answer to this question, a number of arguments have been raised by accountants to justify the use of one method over the others. We turn now to some of these arguments.

LO 5 Analyze the effects of the different costing methods on inventory, net income, income taxes, and cash flow.

Costing Methods and Cash Flow

Comparative income statements for our example are presented in Exhibit 6-5. Note that with the use of the weighted average method, net income is between the amounts for FIFO and LIFO. Because the weighted average method normally yields results between the other two methods, we concentrate on the two extremes, LIFO and FIFO. The major advantage of using the weighted average method is its simplicity.

The original data for our example involved a situation in which prices were *rising* throughout the period: beginning inventory cost $10 per unit, and the last purchase during the year was at $14. With LIFO, the most recent costs are assigned to cost of goods sold; with FIFO, the older costs are assigned to expense. Thus, in a period of rising prices, the assignment of the *higher* prices to cost of goods sold under LIFO results in a *lower gross margin* under LIFO than under FIFO ($7,000 for LIFO and $8,500 for FIFO). Because operating expenses are not affected by the choice of inventory method, the lower gross margin under LIFO results in lower income before tax, which in turn leads to lower taxes. If we assume a 40% tax rate, income tax expense under LIFO is only

EXHIBIT 6-5 Income Statements for the Inventory Costing Methods

	WEIGHTED AVERAGE	FIFO	LIFO
Sales revenue—$20 each	$ 18,000	$18,000	$ 18,000
Beginning inventory	5,000	5,000	5,000
Purchases	12,100	12,100	12,100
Cost of goods available for sale	$ 17,100	$17,100	$ 17,100
Ending inventory	**6,840**	**7,600**	**6,100**
Cost of goods sold	**$10,260**	**$ 9,500**	**$11,000**
Gross margin	**$ 7,740**	**$ 8,500**	**$ 7,000**
Operating expenses	2,000	2,000	2,000
Net income before tax	**$ 5,740**	**$ 6,500**	**$ 5,000**
Income tax expense (40%)	**2,296**	**2,600**	**2,000**
Net income	**$ 3,444**	**$ 3,900**	**$ 3,000**

Note: Figures that differ among the three methods are in bold.

$2,000, compared with $2,600 under FIFO, a savings of $600 in taxes. Another way to look at the taxes saved by using LIFO is to focus on the difference in the expense under each method:

	LIFO cost of goods sold	$11,000
−	FIFO cost of goods sold	9,500
	Additional expense from use of LIFO	$ 1,500
×	Tax rate	.40
	Tax savings from the use of LIFO	$ 600

To summarize, *during a period of rising prices,* the two methods result in the following:

ITEM	LIFO	RELATIVE TO	FIFO
Cost of goods sold	Higher		Lower
Gross margin	Lower		Higher
Income before taxes	Lower		Higher
Taxes	Lower		Higher

In conclusion, lower taxes with the use of LIFO result in cash savings.

The tax savings available from the use of LIFO during a period of rising prices are largely responsible for its popularity. Keep in mind, however, that the cash saved from a lower tax bill with LIFO is only a temporary savings, or what is normally called a *tax deferral.* At some point in the life of the business, the inventory that is carried at the older, lower-priced amounts will be sold. This will result in a tax bill higher than that under FIFO. Yet even a tax deferral is beneficial; given the opportunity, it is better to pay less tax today and more in the future because today's tax savings can be invested.

LIFO Liquidation

Recall the assumption made about which costs remain in inventory when LIFO is used. The costs of the oldest units remains in inventory, and if prices are rising, the costs of these units will be lower than the costs of more recent purchases. Now assume that the company *sells more units than it buys during the period.* When a company using LIFO experiences a liquidation, some of the units assumed to be sold will come from the older layers, with a relatively low unit cost. This situation, called a LIFO liquidation, presents a dilemma for the company.

A partial or complete liquidation of the older, lower-priced units will result in a low cost of goods sold figure and a correspondingly high gross margin for the period. In turn, the company faces a large tax bill because of the relatively high gross margin. In fact, a liquidation causes the tax advantages of using LIFO to reverse on the company, which is faced with paying off some of the taxes that were deferred in earlier periods. Should a company facing this situation buy inventory at the end of the year to avoid the consequences of a liquidation? This is a difficult question to answer and depends on many factors, including the company's cash position. At the least, the accountant must be aware of the potential for a large tax bill if a liquidation occurs.

Of course, a LIFO liquidation also benefits—and may even distort—reported earnings if the liquidation is large enough. For this reason and the tax problem, many companies are reluctant to liquidate their LIFO inventory. The problem often festers, and companies find themselves with inventory costed at decade-old price levels.

The LIFO Conformity Rule

Would it be possible for a company to have the best of both worlds? That is, could it use FIFO to report its income to stockholders, thus maximizing the amount of net income reported to this group, and use LIFO to report to the IRS, minimizing its taxable income and the amount paid to the government? Unfortunately, the IRS says that if a company chooses LIFO for reporting cost of goods sold on its tax return, then it must also use LIFO on its books, that is, in preparing its income statement. This is called the **LIFO conformity rule.** Note that the rule applies only to the use of LIFO on the tax return. A company is free to use different methods in preparing its tax return and its income statement as long as the method used for the tax return is *not* LIFO.

The LIFO Reserve: Estimating LIFO's Effect on Income and on Taxes Paid for Whirlpool

If a company decides to use LIFO, an investor can still determine how much more income the company would have reported had it used FIFO. In addition, he or she can approximate the tax savings to the company from the use of LIFO. Consider the following footnote from the 1995 annual report for Whirlpool Corporation:

(4) Inventories

DECEMBER 31 (MILLIONS OF DOLLARS)	1995	1994
Finished products	$ 984	$ 832
Work in process	84	66
Raw materials	194	156
Total FIFO cost	$1,262	$1,054
Less excess of FIFO cost over LIFO cost	233	216
	$1,029	$ 838

LIFO inventories represent approximately 41% and 52% of total inventories at December 31, 1995 and 1994.

Note that Whirlpool uses more than one inventory method and that at the end of 1995, LIFO inventories accounted for only 41% of the total inventory. It is not unusual for companies to use more than one method to value inventories. For now it is important to understand that Whirlpool reported $1,029,000,000 as its total inventory on the December 31, 1995, balance sheet.

The following steps explain the logic for using the information in the inventory footnote to estimate LIFO's effect on income and on taxes:

1. The excess of the value of a company's inventory stated at FIFO over the value stated at LIFO is called the **LIFO reserve.** The *cumulative* excess of the value of Whirlpool's inventory on a FIFO basis over the value on a LIFO basis is $233 million at the end of 1995.

2. Because Whirlpool reports inventory at a lower value on its balance sheet using LIFO, it will report a higher cost of goods sold amount on the income statement.

Thus, the LIFO reserve not only represents the excess of the inventory balance on a FIFO basis over that on a LIFO basis but also *represents the cumulative amount by which cost of goods sold on a LIFO basis exceeds cost of goods sold on a FIFO basis.*

3. The increase in Whirlpool's LIFO reserve in 1995 was $17 million ($233 million − $216 million). This means that the increase in cost of goods sold for 1995 from using LIFO instead of FIFO was also this amount. Thus, income before tax for 1995 was $17 million lower because the company used LIFO.

4. If we assume a corporate tax rate of 35%, the tax savings to Whirlpool from using LIFO amounted to $17 million × .35, or $5.95 million.

Costing Methods and Inventory Profits

FIFO, LIFO, and weighted average are all cost-based methods to value inventory. They vary in terms of which costs are assigned to inventory and which to cost of goods sold, but all three assign *historical costs* to inventory. In our previous example, the unit cost for inventory purchases gradually increased during the year from $10 for the beginning inventory to a high of $14 on the date of the last purchase.

An alternative to assigning any of the historical costs incurred during the year to ending inventory and cost of goods sold would be to use **replacement cost** to value each of these. Assume that the cost to replace a unit of inventory at the end of the year is $15. Use of a replacement cost system results in the following:

Ending inventory   =   600 units   × $15 per unit   = $ 9,000
Cost of goods sold   =   900 units   × $15 per unit   = $13,500

A replacement cost approach is not acceptable under the profession's current standards, but many believe that it provides more relevant information to users. Inventory must be replaced if a company is to remain in business. Many accountants argue that the use of historical cost in valuing inventory leads to what is called **inventory profit,** particularly if FIFO is used in a period of rising prices. For example, cost of goods sold in our illustration was only $9,500 on a FIFO basis, compared with $13,500 if the replacement cost of $15 per unit is used. The $4,000 difference between the two cost of goods sold figures is a profit from holding the inventory during a period of rising prices and is called *inventory profit.* To look at this another way, assume that the units are sold for $20 each. The following analysis reconciles the difference between gross margin on a FIFO basis and on a replacement cost basis:

Sales revenue—900 units × $20 =		$18,000
Cost of goods sold—FIFO basis		9,500
Gross margin—FIFO basis		$ 8,500
Cost of goods sold—replacement		
cost basis	$13,500	
Cost of goods sold—FIFO basis	9,500	
Profit from holding inventory		
during a period of inflation		4,000
Gross margin on a replacement cost basis		$ 4,500

Those who argue in favor of a replacement cost approach would report only $4,500 of gross margin. They believe that the additional $4,000 of profit reported on a FIFO basis is simply due to holding the inventory during a period of rising prices. According to this viewpoint, if the 900 units sold during the period are to be replaced, a necessity if the company is to continue operating, the use of replacement cost in calculating cost of goods sold results in a better measure of gross margin than if it is calculated using FIFO.

Given that our current standards require the use of historical costs rather than replacement costs, does any one of the costing methods result in a better approximation of replacement cost of goods sold than the others? Because LIFO assigns the cost of the most recent purchases to cost of goods sold, it most nearly approximates the results with a replacement cost system. The other side of the argument, however, is that whereas LIFO results in the best approximation of *replacement cost of goods sold* on the *income statement,* FIFO most nearly approximates replacement cost of the *inventory* on the *balance sheet.* A comparison of the amounts from our example verifies this:

	ENDING INVENTORY	COST OF GOODS SOLD
Weighted average	$6,840	$10,260
FIFO	7,600	9,500
LIFO	6,100	11,000
Replacement cost	9,000	13,500

ACCOUNTING FOR YOUR DECISIONS

You Are a Student

The owner/manager of a dairy farm knows that you are an accounting student and has asked your advice about which inventory method to use to measure the cost of both the inventory and the cost of goods sold. Since the inventory of milk and milk byproducts spoils easily, does he have to use the FIFO inventory valuation method? Why or why not?

ANS: No, he does not have to use the FIFO method, just because his products are subject to spoilage. There is a difference between the actual physical flow of the product and the cost flow of that product. From a practical perspective, he would want to sell your milk and milk byproducts on a FIFO basis to minimize spoilage. However, he can keep track of your cost flows for inventory valuation and cost of goods sold purposes using the LIFO method or weighted average cost method.

Changing Inventory Methods

The purpose of each of the inventory costing methods is to match costs with revenues. If a company believes that a different method will result in a better matching than that being provided by the method currently being used, it should change methods. A company must be able to justify a change in methods, however. Taking advantage of the tax breaks offered by LIFO is not a valid justification for a change in methods.

It is very important for a company to *disclose* any change in accounting principle, including a change in the method of costing inventory. For example, some companies justify a change to LIFO on the basis of increasing prices, as illustrated by this excerpt from Chesapeake Corporation's 1994 annual report:

> Effective January 1, 1994, the Company changed the method of valuation of raw materials, work-in-process and finished goods of its Wisconsin Tissue Mills Inc. subsidiary from the average cost method to the LIFO method and expanded the use of the LIFO method to include all of the work-in-process and finished goods of its Chesapeake Packaging Co. subsidiary. The Company believes that, in periods of rapid cost increases, such as were experienced by the paper industry during 1994, use of the LIFO method will result in a better matching of current costs with current revenues. The effects of adopting the LIFO method at Wisconsin Tissue and expanding the use of the LIFO method at Chesapeake Packaging were to reduce consolidated year-end inventories by $4.4 million and to decrease net income for 1994 by $2.8 million ($.12 per share). The cumulative effect of this change to the LIFO method on the operating results as of the beginning of 1994 and the pro forma effects on the operating results of prior years have not been presented, as the effects are not readily determinable.

Popularity of the Costing Methods

An annual survey conducted by the AICPA indicates the relative popularity of the inventory costing methods. The inventory methods used by the 600 corporations in the survey are reported in Exhibit 6-6. Note that the number of companies each year totals more than 600. This happens because, as we saw for Whirlpool, many companies use more than one method to determine the total cost of inventory. The survey indicates the relatively equal popularity of LIFO and FIFO in practice.

FROM CONCEPT TO PRACTICE 6.1
READING BEN & JERRY'S ANNUAL REPORT Which inventory method does Ben & Jerry's use? Where did you find this information? Do you think the company is justified in using the method it does?

EXHIBIT 6-6	Inventory Cost Determination—AICPA Survey			
	NUMBER OF COMPANIES			
	1995	**1994**	**1993**	**1992**
METHODS				
First-in, first-out (FIFO)	411	417	417	415
Last-in, first-out (LIFO)	347	351	350	358
Average cost	185	192	189	193
Other	40	42	42	45
USE OF LIFO				
All inventories	14	17	17	23
50% or more of inventories	191	186	191	189
Less than 50% of inventories	88	98	92	91
Not determinable	54	50	50	55
Companies using LIFO	347	351	350	358

SOURCE: *Accounting Trends & Techniques,* 50th ed. (New York: American Institute of Certified Public Accountants, 1996).

Rather than increasing in popularity, as it had during more inflationary times, the use of LIFO appears to have stabilized, as indicated in Exhibit 6-6. Without significant inflation, a company has to be concerned about LIFO liquidation, LIFO reserves, and the complications that arise in the computation and disclosure of LIFO inventory.

Inventory Valuation in Other Countries

The acceptable methods of valuing inventory differ considerably around the world. Many countries prohibit the use of LIFO for either tax or financial reporting purposes. Countries in which LIFO is either prohibited or rarely used include the United Kingdom, Canada, New Zealand, Sweden, Denmark, and Brazil. On the other hand, Germany, France, Australia, and Japan allow LIFO for inventory valuation of foreign investments but not for domestic reports.

In Chapter 1 we mentioned the attempts by the International Accounting Standards Committee (IASC) to develop worldwide accounting standards. This group favors the use of either FIFO or weighted average when specific identification is not feasible. The IASC recognizes LIFO as an acceptable alternative if a company discloses information enabling users to reconcile LIFO inventory with either FIFO or weighted average (similar to the idea of a LIFO reserve discussed earlier in this chapter).

Two Inventory Systems: Periodic and Perpetual

In the examples presented so far in this chapter, we have assumed a periodic inventory system to concentrate our attention on the various cost-flow assumptions. Recall from Chapter 5 that with this system, a count of the inventory is necessary at the end of the period to determine the number of units sold and the number on hand. The reason is that the Inventory account is not updated each time a purchase is made and each time a sale is made.

For many years, the simplicity of the periodic system resulted in its widespread use. Because of the need in a perpetual system to record the cost of every individual sale when it occurs, use of the perpetual system was limited to businesses that sold products with a relatively high unit cost and low turnover, such as those of an automobile dealer. The ability to computerize the inventory system has resulted, however, in an increase in the use of the perpetual system in all types of businesses. A company can use any one of the costing methods with either a periodic or a perpetual inventory system. The application of the methods when a company maintains a perpetual inventory system is illustrated in Appendix 6A.

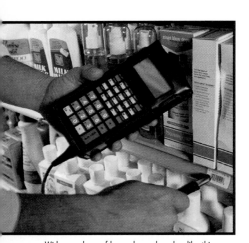

Widespread use of bar codes and readers like this one has made it possible for even small companies to track each item's inventory quantity, description, cost, current selling price, availability, and order information, among other possible data. This technology has popularized the use of what is called the perpetual inventory system, the focus of Appendix 6A.

Valuing Inventory at Lower of Cost or Market

One of the components sold by an electronics firm has become economically obsolete. A particular style of suit sold by a retailer is outdated and can no longer be sold at regular price. In each of these instances, it is likely that the retailer will have to sell the merchandise for less than the normal selling price. In these situations, a departure from the cost basis of accounting may be necessary because the *market value* of the inventory may be less than its *cost* to the company. The departure is called the lower of cost or market (LCM) rule.

LO 6 Apply the lower of cost or market rule to the valuation of inventory.

At the end of each accounting period, the original cost, as determined using one of the costing methods such as FIFO, is compared with the market price of the inventory. If market is less than cost, the inventory is written down to the lower amount.

For example, if cost is $100,000 and market value is $85,000, the accountant would make the following entry:

Dec. 31	Loss on Decline in Value of Inventory	15,000	
	Inventory		15,000
	To record decline in value of inventory.		

Assets	=	**Liabilities**	+	**Owners' Equity**
−15,000				−15,000

Note that the entry reduces both assets, in the form of inventory, and owners' equity. The reduction in owners' equity is the result of reporting the Loss on Decline in Value of Inventory on the income statement as an item of Other Expense.

Why Replacement Cost Is Used as a Measure of Market

A better name for the lower of cost or market rule would be the lower of cost or replacement cost rule because accountants define *market* as *replacement cost*.[3] To understand why replacement cost is used as a basis to compare with original cost, consider the following example. A clothier pays $150 for a man's double-breasted suit and normally sells it for $200. Thus, the normal markup on selling price is $50/$200, or 25%, as indicated in the column Before Price Change in Exhibit 6-7. Now assume that double-breasted suits fall out of favor with the fashion world. The retailer checks with the distributor and finds that because of the style change, the cost to the retailer to replace a double-breasted suit is now only $120. The retailer realizes that if double-breasted suits are to be sold at all, they will have to be offered at a reduced price. The selling price is dropped from $200 to $160. If the retailer now buys a suit for $120 and sells it for $160, the gross margin will be $40 and the gross margin percentage will be maintained at 25%, as indicated in the right-hand column of Exhibit 6-7.

EXHIBIT 6-7	Gross Margin Percentage before and after Price Change

	BEFORE PRICE CHANGE	AFTER PRICE CHANGE
Selling price	$200	$160
Cost	150	120
Gross margin	$ 50	$ 40
Gross margin percentage	25%	25%

[3]Technically, the use of replacement cost as a measure of market value is subject to two constraints. First, market cannot be more than the net realizable value of the inventory. Second, inventory should not be recorded at less than net realizable value less a normal profit margin. The rationale for these two constraints is covered in intermediate accounting texts. For our purposes, we assume that replacement cost falls between the two constraints.

To compare the results with and without the use of the LCM rule, assume that the facts are the same as before and that the retailer has 10 double-breasted suits in inventory on December 31, 1998. In addition, assume that all 10 suits are sold at a clearance sale in January 1999 at the reduced price of $160 each. If the lower of cost or market rule is not used, the results for the two years will be as follows:

LCM RULE NOT USED	1998	1999	TOTAL
Sales revenue ($160 per unit)	$–0–	$1,600	$1,600
Cost of goods sold			
(original cost of $150 per unit)	–0–	(1,500)	(1,500)
Gross margin	$–0–	$ 100	$ 100

If the LCM rule is not applied, the gross margin is distorted. Instead of the normal 25%, a gross margin percentage of $100/$1,600 or 6.25% is reported in 1999 when the 10 suits are sold. If the LCM rule is applied, however, the results for the two years are as follows:

LCM RULE USED	1998	1999	TOTAL
Sales revenue ($160 per unit)	$–0–	$1,600	$1,600
Cost of goods sold			
(replacement cost of $120 per unit)	–0–	(1,200)	(1,200)
Loss on decline in value of			
inventory: 10 units ×			
($150 – $120)	(300)	–0–	(300)
Gross margin	$(300)	$ 400	$ 100

The use of the LCM rule serves two important functions: (1) to report the loss in value of the inventory, $30 per suit or $300 in total, in the year the loss occurs and (2) to report in the year the suits are actually sold the normal gross margin of $400/$1,600, or 25%, which is not affected by a change in the selling price.

Conservatism Is the Basis for the Lower of Cost or Market Rule

The departure from the cost basis is normally justified on the basis of *conservatism*. According to the accounting profession, conservatism is "a prudent reaction to uncertainties to try to insure that uncertainties and risks inherent in business situations are adequately considered."[4] In our example, the future selling price of a suit is uncertain because of the style changes. The use of the LCM rule serves two purposes. First, the inventory of suits is written down from $150 to $120 each. Second, the decline in value of the inventory is recognized at the time it is first observed rather than waiting until the suits are sold. An investor in a company with deteriorating inventory has good reason to be alarmed. Merchandisers who do not make the proper adjustments to their product lines go out of business as they compete with the lower prices of warehouse clubs and the lower overhead of mail-order catalogs and home shopping networks.

You should realize that the write-down of the suits violates the historical cost principle, which says that assets should be carried on the balance sheet at their original cost. But the LCM rule is considered a valid exception to the principle because it is a prudent reaction to the uncertainty involved and, thus, an application of conservatism in accounting.

Application of the LCM Rule

We have yet to consider how the LCM rule is applied to the entire inventory of a company. Three different interpretations of the rule are possible: (1) the lower of total cost or total market value for the entire inventory could be reported, (2) the lower of cost or market value for each individual product or item could be reported, or (3) the lower of

[4]*Statement of Financial Accounting Concepts No. 2*, "Qualitative Characteristics of Accounting Information" (Stamford, Conn.: Financial Accounting Standards Board, May 1980), par. 95.

FROM CONCEPT TO PRACTICE 6.2

READING CIRCUIT CITY'S FINANCIAL STATEMENTS A footnote to Circuit City's financial statements indicates that "Inventory is stated at the lower of cost or market." Why do you think the application of the lower of cost or market rule would be important to a business like Circuit City?

cost or market value for groups of items could be reported. A company is free to choose any one of these approaches in applying the lower of cost or market rule. Three different answers are possible, depending on the approach selected.

The item-by-item approach is the most popular of the three approaches, for two reasons. First, it produces the most conservative result. The reason is that with either a group-by-group or a total approach, increases in the values of some items of inventory will offset declines in the values of other items. The item-by-item approach, however, ignores increases in value and recognizes all declines in value. Second, the item-by-item approach is the method required for tax purposes, although unlike LIFO, it is not required for book purposes merely because it is used for tax computations.

Consistency is important in deciding which of these approaches to use in applying the LCM rule. As is the case with the selection of one of the inventory costing methods discussed earlier in the chapter, the approach chosen to apply the rule should be used consistently from one period to the next.

Methods for Estimating Inventory Value

Situations arise in which it may not be practicable or even possible to measure inventory at cost. At times it may be necessary to *estimate* the amount of inventory. Two similar methods are used for very different purposes to estimate the amount of inventory. They are the gross profit method and the retail inventory method.

LO 7 Explain why and how the cost of inventory is estimated in certain situations.

Gross Profit Method

A company that uses a periodic inventory system may experience a problem if inventory is stolen or destroyed by fire, flooding, or some other type of damage. Without a perpetual inventory record, what is the cost of the inventory stolen or destroyed? The **gross profit method** is a useful technique to estimate the cost of inventory lost in these situations. The method relies *entirely* on the ability to reliably estimate the *ratio of gross profit to sales*.[5]

Exhibit 6-8 illustrates how the normal income statement model that we use to find cost of goods sold can be rearranged to estimate inventory. The model on the left shows the components of cost of goods sold as they appear on the income statement. Assuming a periodic system, the inventory on hand at the end of the period is counted and is subtracted from cost of goods available for sale to determine cost of goods sold. The model is rearranged on the right as a basis for estimating inventory under the gross profit method. The only difference in the two models is in the reversal of the last two components: ending inventory and cost of goods sold. Rather than attempting to estimate *ending* inventory, we are trying to estimate the amount of inventory that should be on hand at a specific date, such as the date of a fire or flood. The estimate of cost of goods sold is found by estimating gross profit and deducting this estimate from sales revenue.

---

[5]The terms *gross profit* and *gross margin* are synonymous in this context. Although we have used *gross margin* in referring to the excess of sales over cost of goods sold, the method is typically called the *gross profit method.*

| EXHIBIT 6-8 | The Gross Profit Method for Estimating Inventory |

INCOME STATEMENT MODEL	GROSS PROFIT METHOD MODEL
Beginning Inventory	Beginning Inventory
+ Purchases	+ Purchases
= Cost of Goods Available for Sale	= Cost of Goods Available for Sale
− Ending Inventory (per count)	− Estimated Cost of Goods Sold
= Cost of Goods Sold	= Estimated Inventory

To illustrate the method, assume that on March 12, 1998, a portion of Hardluck Company's inventory is destroyed in a fire. The company determines, by a physical count, that the cost of the merchandise not destroyed is $200. Hardluck needs to estimate the cost of the inventory lost for purposes of insurance reimbursement. If the insurance company pays Hardluck an amount equivalent to the cost of the inventory destroyed, no loss will be recognized. If the cost of the inventory destroyed exceeds the amount reimbursed by the insurance company, a loss will be recorded for the excess amount.

Assume that the insurance company agrees to pay Hardluck $250 as full settlement for the inventory lost in the fire. From its records, Hardluck is able to determine the following amounts for the period from January 1 to the date of the fire, March 12:

Net sales from January 1 to March 12	$6,000
Beginning inventory—January 1	1,200
Purchases from January 1 to March 12	3,500

Assume that based on recent years' experience, Hardluck estimates its gross profit ratio as 30% of net sales. The steps it will take to estimate the lost inventory follow:

1. Determine gross profit:
   Net Sales × Gross Profit Ratio = Gross Profit
   $6,000 × 30% = $1,800

2. Determine cost of goods sold:
   Net Sales − Gross Profit = Cost of Goods Sold
   $6,000 − $1,800 = $4,200

3. Determine cost of goods available for sale at time of fire:
   Beginning Inventory + Purchases = Cost of Goods Available for Sale
   $1,200 + $3,500 = $4,700

4. Determine inventory at time of the fire:
   Cost of Goods Available for Sale − Cost of Goods Sold = Inventory
   $4,700 − $4,200 = $500

5. Determine amount of inventory destroyed:
   Inventory at Time of Fire − Inventory not Destroyed = Inventory Destroyed
   $500 − $200 = $300

Hardluck would record the following journal entry to recognize a loss for the excess of the cost of the lost inventory over the amount of reimbursement from the insurance company:

Mar. 12	Loss on Insurance Settlement	50	
	Cash (from insurance company)	250	
	Inventory		300
	To record the insurance settlement from fire.		

Assets	=	Liabilities	+	Owners' Equity
+250				−50
−300				

Another situation in which the gross profit method is used is for *interim financial statements.* Most companies prepare financial statements at least once every three months. In fact, the Securities and Exchange Commission requires a quarterly report from corporations whose stock is publicly traded. Companies using the periodic inventory system, however, find it cost-prohibitive to count the inventory every three months. The gross profit method is used to estimate the cost of the inventory at these interim dates. A company is allowed to use the method only in interim reports. Inventory reported in the annual report must be based on actual, not estimated, cost.

Retail Inventory Method

The counting of inventory in most retail businesses is an enormous undertaking. Imagine the time involved to count all of the various items stocked in a hardware store. Because of the time and cost involved in counting inventory, most retail businesses take a physical inventory only once a year. The **retail inventory method** is used to estimate inventory for interim statements, typically prepared monthly.

The retail inventory method has another important use. Consider the year-end inventory count in a large supermarket. One employee counts the number of tubes of toothpaste on the shelf and relays the relevant information either to another employee or to a tape-recording device: "16 tubes of 8-ounce ABC brand toothpaste at $1.69." The key is that the price recorded is the *selling price* or *retail* price of the product, not its cost. It is much quicker to count the inventory at retail than it would be to trace the cost of each item to purchase invoices. The retail method can then be used to convert the inventory from retail to cost. The methodology used with the retail inventory method, whether for interim statements or at year-end, is similar to the approach used with the gross profit method and is covered in detail in intermediate accounting text books.

Analyzing the Management of Inventory Turnover

Managers must strike a balance between maintaining enough inventory to meet customers' needs and incurring the high cost of carrying inventory. The cost of storage and the lost income from the money tied up to own inventory make it very expensive to keep on hand. Investors are also concerned with a company's inventory management. They pay particular attention to a company's **inventory turnover ratio:**

LO 8 Analyze the management of inventory turnover.

$$\frac{\text{Inventory Turnover}}{\text{Ratio}} = \frac{\text{Cost of Goods Sold}}{\text{Average Inventory}}$$

Refer to Circuit City's financial statements as displayed in the chapter opener. From the information presented, we can compute the company's inventory turnover ratio for fiscal year 1996:

$$\frac{\text{Inventory Turnover}}{\text{Ratio}} = \frac{\text{Cost of Goods Sold}}{\text{Average Inventory}} = \frac{\$5,394,293}{(\$1,323,183 + \$1,035,776)/2}$$

(2/29/96 balance sheet) (2/28/95 balance sheet)

$$= \frac{\$5,394,293}{\$1,179,480}$$

$$= 4.6 \text{ times}$$

This ratio tells us that in fiscal year 1996, Circuit City turned over its inventory 4.6 times. An alternative way to look at a company's efficiency in managing inventory is to calculate the number of days, on average, that inventory is on hand before it is sold. This measure is called the **number of days' sales in inventory** and is calculated as follows (we will assume 360 days in a year):

$$\text{Number of Days' Sales in Inventory} = \frac{\text{Number of Days in the Period}}{\text{Inventory Turnover Ratio}}$$

$$= \frac{360}{4.6}$$

$$= 78 \text{ days}$$

How efficient was Circuit City in managing its inventory if it took an average of 78 days, or a little less than three months, to sell an item of inventory in fiscal year 1996? There are no easy answers to this question, but a starting point would be to compare this statistic with the same measure for prior years. Another basis for evaluation is to compare the measure with that for other companies in the same industry or business, in this case consumer electronics. As you can imagine, inventory turnover varies considerably from one industry to the next because of the differences in products. For example, consider Safeway, a large regional grocery chain. Safeway's average inventory turnover ratio in 1995 was approximately 10.3 times. This means that on average it takes Safeway only about 360/10.3, or 35 days, to sell its inventory. Given the perishable nature of its products, we would expect Safeway to turn over its inventory more rapidly than a consumer electronics company such as Circuit City. Exhibit 6-9 summarizes the differences in inventory turnover between the two companies.

FROM CONCEPT TO PRACTICE 6.3
READING BEN & JERRY'S FINANCIAL STATEMENTS
Compute Ben & Jerry's inventory turnover ratio for 1995. What is the average length of time it takes to sell its inventory? Does this seem reasonable for the type of business the company is in?

How Inventories Affect the Cash Flows Statement

LO 9 Explain the effects that inventory transactions have on the statement of cash flows.

The effects on the income statement and the statement of cash flows from inventory-related transactions differ significantly. We have focused our attention in the last two chapters on how the purchase and the sale of inventory are reported on the income statement. We found that the cost of the inventory sold during the period is deducted on the income statement as cost of goods sold.

The appropriate reporting on a statement of cash flows for inventory transactions depends on whether the direct or indirect method is used. If the direct method is used to prepare the Operating Activities category of the statement, the amount of cash paid to suppliers of inventory is shown as a deduction in this section of the statement.

If the more popular indirect method is used, it is necessary to make adjustments to net income for the changes in two accounts: Inventories and Accounts Payable. These adjustments are summarized in Exhibit 6-10. An increase in inventory is deducted because it indicates that the company is building up its stock of inventory and thus expending cash. A decrease in inventory is added to net income. An increase in accounts payable is added because it indicates that during the period, the company has increased the amount it owes suppliers and has therefore conserved its cash. A decrease in accounts payable is

	EXHIBIT 6-9	Inventory Turnover for Different Types of Companies	
COMPANY	**TYPES OF PRODUCTS SOLD**	**INVENTORY TURNOVER**	**NUMBER OF DAYS' SALES IN INVENTORY**
Circuity City	Televisions, VCRs, personal computers	4.6 times	78 days
Safeway	Grocery items	10.3 times	35 days

EXHIBIT 6-10 Inventories and the Statement of Cash Flows

deducted because the company actually reduced the amount owed suppliers during the period.

The Operating Activities category of the statement of cash flows for Circuit City is presented in Exhibit 6-11. Note that the company groups together merchandise inventory, prepaid expenses, and other current assets for purposes of presentation on the statement of cash flows. Similarly, accounts payable, accrued expenses and other current liabilities, and accrued income taxes are included as one item on the statement.

The increase in merchandise inventory, prepaid expenses, and other current assets in 1996 is deducted because the additional investments in these assets required an expenditure of cash by the company. On the other hand, a buildup of accounts payable, accrued expenses and other current liabilities, and accrued income taxes actually conserves Circuit City's cash. Thus, the increase in these items in 1996 is added to net earnings.

EXHIBIT 6-11 Partial Consolidated Statement of Cash Flows for Circuit City

CONSOLIDATED STATEMENTS OF CASH FLOWS

		Years Ended February 29 or 28	
(AMOUNTS IN THOUSANDS)	1996	1995	1994
OPERATING ACTIVITIES:			
Net earnings	$ 179,375	$ 167,875	$ 132,400
Adjustments to reconcile net earnings to net cash (used in) provided by operating activities:			
Depreciation and amortization	79,812	66,866	55,012
Loss on sales of property and equipment	5,600	2,199	1,910
Provision for deferred income taxes	22,411	73,745	(17,800)
(Decrease) increase in deferred revenue and other liabilities	(27,865)	(26,494)	36,306
Increase in net accounts and notes receivable	(59,830)	(75,575)	(68,542)
Increase in merchandise inventory, prepaid expenses and other current assets	(290,644)	(317,114)	(203,783)
Decrease (increase) in other assets	1,911	(3,819)	(522)
Increase in accounts payable, accrued expenses and other current liabilities, and accrued income taxes	33,910	159,297	173,300
NET CASH (USED IN) PROVIDED BY OPERATING ACTIVITIES	(55,320)	46,980	108,281

See accompanying notes to consolidated financial statements.

Review Problem

Stewart Distributing Company sells a single product for $2 per unit and uses a periodic inventory system. The following data are available for the year:

DATE	TRANSACTION	NUMBER OF UNITS	UNIT COST	TOTAL
1/1	Beginning inventory	500	$1.00	$500.00
2/5	Purchase	350	1.10	385.00
4/12	Sale	(550)		
7/17	Sale	(200)		
9/23	Purchase	400	1.30	520.00
11/5	Sale	(300)		

Required

1. Compute cost of goods sold, assuming the use of the weighted average costing method.
2. Compute the dollar amount of ending inventory, assuming the FIFO costing method.
3. Compute gross margin, assuming the LIFO costing method.
4. Assume a 40% tax rate. Compute the amount of taxes saved if Stewart uses the LIFO method rather than the FIFO method.

Solution to Review problem

1. Cost of goods sold, weighted average cost method:
   Cost of goods available for sale
   $500 + $385 + $520 = $1,405
   Divided by:
   Units available for sale:
   500 + 350 + 400 =   1,250   units
   Weighted average cost $1.124   per unit
   × Number of units sold:
   550 + 200 + 300 =   1,050   units
   Cost of goods sold $1,180.20

2. Ending inventory, FIFO cost method:
   Units available for sale   1,250
   − Units sold   1,050
   = Units in ending inventory   200
   × Most recent purchase price of $ 1.30
   = Ending inventory $ 260

3. Gross margin, LIFO cost method:
   Sales revenue: 1,050 units × $2 each $2,100
   Cost of goods sold
      400 units × $1.30 = $520
      350 units × $1.10 = 385
      300 units × $1.00 = 300   1,205
   Gross margin $ 895

4. Taxes saved from using LIFO instead of FIFO:
   LIFO Cost of goods sold $1,205
   − FIFO Cost of goods sold:
      Cost of goods available for sale $1,405
      Ending inventory from part 2   260
      Cost of goods sold   1,145
   Additional expense from use of LIFO $ 60
   × Tax rate   .40
   Tax savings from the use of LIFO $ 24

APPENDIX 6A

Accounting Tools: Inventory Costing Methods with the Use of a Perpetual Inventory System

The illustrations of the inventory costing methods in the chapter assumed the use of a periodic inventory system. In this appendix, we will see how the methods are applied when a company maintains a perpetual inventory system. Before doing so, however, it is useful to look closer at the differences between the two systems.

LO 10 Explain the differences between a periodic and a perpetual inventory system.

Journal Entries for the Two Systems

To highlight the differences between the two systems, consider the following three transactions:

1. Purchased on account 500 units at $8 each.
2. Returned for credit 100 units damaged in transit.
3. Sold on account 200 units at $10 each.

Exhibit 6-12 shows the journal entries for the three transactions under each of the two inventory systems. Because the inventory account is updated only *periodically* with the periodic system, the purchase of 500 units of merchandise is accumulated in the temporary account Purchases. The cost of the 100 units returned in the second transaction increases the contra-purchases account Purchase Returns and Allowances. The

EXHIBIT 6-12   Comparison of the Periodic and Perpetual Inventory Systems

PERIODIC SYSTEM	DR.	CR.	PERPETUAL SYSTEM	DR.	CR.
1. Purchases	4,000		Inventory	4,000	
Accounts Payable		4,000	Accounts Payable		4,000
To record purchase of 500 units.			To record purchase of 500 units.		
A = L + OE +4,000 −4,000			A = L + OE +4,000 +4,000		
2. Accounts Payable	800		Accounts Payable	800	
Purchase Returns and Allowances		800	Inventory		800
To record return of 100 damaged units.			To record return of 100 damaged units.		
A = L + OE −800 +800			A = L + OE −800 −800		
3. Accounts Receivable	2,000		Accounts Receivable	2,000	
Sales Revenue		2,000	Sales Revenue		2,000
To record sale of 200 units at $10 each.			To record sale of 200 units at $10 each.		
A = L + OE +2,000 +2,000			A = L + OE +2,000 +2,000		
			Cost of Goods Sold	1,600	
			Inventory		1,600
			To record 200 units sold at a cost of $8 each.		
			A = L + OE −1,600 −1,600		

only entry made at the time of a sale records the revenue earned. Because the inventory account has not been updated for purchases and sales during the period, a *physical count* of the merchandise is required at year-end. This establishes the amount to be shown on the balance sheet as the cost of the inventory and helps determine the amount to appear on the income statement for cost of goods sold. Cost of goods sold is in fact a calculated figure determined in the following way:

Beginning inventory	The inventory at the end of the prior period
+ Cost of goods purchased	The balance in the Purchases account, plus any freight-in, less any purchase returns and allowances and any purchase discounts
= Cost of goods available for sale	
− Ending inventory	Based on a physical count
= Cost of goods sold	

As you see in the right-hand side of Exhibit 6-12, in a perpetual system, purchases of merchandise increase the Inventory account directly, and any returns of merchandise reduce it. Unlike the periodic system, the perpetual system requires that *two* entries be made at the time of sale. The first entry is the same as the entry made under the periodic system: to record the sales revenue. Because the inventory account is kept *perpetually* up to date, however, a second entry is made to reduce the Inventory account, with a corresponding increase in expense for the cost of the merchandise sold. Finally, because the Inventory account has been updated for each purchase and sale of merchandise, a physical count is not the basis for valuing the inventory at the end of the period in a perpetual system. For control purposes, however, most businesses that use a perpetual system count the inventory once a year. Any differences between the amount on hand per the count and the amount appearing in the Inventory account require an adjusting entry in the records and should be investigated.

Inventory Costing Methods with a Perpetual System

LO 11 Apply the inventory costing methods using a perpetual system.

It is important to understand the difference between inventory *costing systems* and inventory *methods*. The two inventory systems differ in terms of how often the inventory account is updated: periodically or perpetually. However, when a company sells identical units of product and the cost to purchase each unit is subject to change, it also must choose an inventory costing method, such as FIFO, LIFO, or weighted average.

Earlier in the chapter, we illustrated the various costing methods with a periodic system. We now use the same data to illustrate how the methods differ when a perpetual system is used. Keep in mind that if a company uses specific identification, the results will be the same regardless of whether it uses the periodic or the perpetual system. To compare the periodic and perpetual systems for the other methods, one important piece of information, the date of each of the sales, must be added. The original data as well as number of units sold on the various dates are summarized below:

DATE	PURCHASES	SALES	BALANCE
Beginning inventory			500 units @ $10
January 20	300 units @ $11		800 units
February 18		450 units	350 units
April 8	400 units @ $12		750 units
June 19		300 units	450 units
September 5	200 units @ $13		650 units
October 20		150 units	500 units
December 12	100 units @ $14		600 units

FIFO Costing with a Perpetual System

Exhibit 6-13 illustrates the FIFO method on a perpetual basis. The basic premise of FIFO applies whether a periodic or a perpetual system is used: the first units purchased are assumed to be the first units sold. With a perpetual system, however, this concept is applied *at the time of each sale.* For example, note in the exhibit which 450 units are assumed to be sold on February 18. The 450 units sold are taken from the beginning inventory of 500 units with a unit cost of $10. Thus, the inventory or balance after this sale as shown in the last three columns is 50 units at $10 and 300 units at $11, for a total of $3,800. The purchase on April 8 of 400 units at $12 is added to the running balance. On a FIFO basis, the sale of 300 units on June 19 comes from the remainder of the beginning inventory of 50 units and another 250 units from the first purchase at $11 on January 20. The balance after this sale is 50 units at $11 and 400 units at $12. You should follow through the last three transactions in the exhibit to make sure that you understand the application of FIFO on a perpetual basis. An important point to note about the ending inventory of $7,600 is that it is the same amount that we calculated for FIFO periodic earlier in the chapter:

FIFO periodic (Exhibit 6-5)	$7,600
FIFO perpetual (Exhibit 6-13)	$7,600

Whether the method is applied each time a sale is made or only at the end of the period, the earliest units in are the first units out, and the two systems will yield the same ending inventory under FIFO.

EXHIBIT 6-13 Perpetual System: FIFO Cost-Flow Assumption

	PURCHASES				SALES				BALANCE		
DATE	UNITS	UNIT COST	TOTAL COST		UNITS	UNIT COST	TOTAL COST		UNITS	UNIT COST	BALANCE
1/1									500	$10	$5,000
1/20	300	$11	$3,300						500	10	
									300	11	8,300
2/18					450	$10	$4,500		50	10	
									300	11	3,800
4/8	400	12	4,800						50	10	
									300	11	
									400	12	8,600
6/19					50	10	500		50	11	
					250	11	2,750		400	12	5,350
9/5	200	13	2,600						50	11	
									400	12	
									200	13	7,950
10/20					50	11	550		300	12	
					100	12	1,200		200	13	6,200
12/12	100	14	1,400						300	12	
									200	13	
									100	14	7,600

LIFO Costing with a Perpetual System

A LIFO cost flow with the use of a perpetual system is illustrated in Exhibit 6-14. First, note which 450 units are assumed to be sold on February 18. The sale consists of the most recent units acquired, 300 units at $11, and then 150 units from the beginning inventory at $10. Thus, the balance after this sale is simply the remaining 350 units from the beginning inventory priced at $10. The purchase on April 8 results in a balance of 350 units at $10 and 400 units at $12.

Note what happens with LIFO when it is applied on a perpetual basis. In essence, a gap is created. Units acquired at the earliest price of $10 and units acquired at the most recent price of $12 are on hand, but none of those at the middle price of $11 remain. This situation arises because LIFO is applied every time a sale is made rather than only at the end of the year. Because of this difference, the amount of ending inventory differs, depending on which system is used:

LIFO periodic (Exhibit 6-5)	$6,100
LIFO perpetual (Exhibit 6-14)	$6,750

Moving Average with a Perpetual System

When a weighted average cost assumption is applied with a perpetual system, it is sometimes called a **moving average.** As indicated in Exhibit 6-15, each time a purchase is made, a new weighted average cost must be computed, thus the name *moving average.*

EXHIBIT 6-14 Perpetual System: LIFO Cost-Flow Assumption

	PURCHASES			SALES			BALANCE		
DATE	UNITS	UNIT COST	TOTAL COST	UNITS	UNIT COST	TOTAL COST	UNITS	UNIT COST	BALANCE
1/1							500	$10	$5,000
1/20	300	$11	$3,300				500	10	
							300	11	8,300
2/18				300	$11	$3,300			
				150	10	1,500	350	10	3,500
4/8	400	12	4,800				350	10	
							400	12	8,300
6/19				300	12	3,600	350	10	
							100	12	4,700
9/5	200	13	2,600				350	10	
							100	12	
							200	13	7,300
10/20				150	13	1,950	350	10	
							100	12	
							50	13	5,350
12/12	100	14	1,400				350	10	
							100	12	
							50	13	
							100	14	6,750

EXHIBIT 6-15   Perpetual System: Moving Average Cost-Flow Assumption

	PURCHASES				SALES				BALANCE		
DATE	UNITS	UNIT COST	TOTAL COST		UNITS	UNIT COST	TOTAL COST		UNITS	UNIT COST	BALANCE
1/1									500	$10	$5,000
1/20	300	$11	$3,300						800	10.38*	8,304
2/18					450	$10.38	$4,671		350	10.38	3,633
4/8	400	12	4,800						750	11.24†	8,430
6/19					300	11.24	3,372		450	11.24	5,058
9/5	200	13	2,600						650	11.78‡	7,657
10/20					150	11.78	1,767		500	11.78	5,890
12/12	100	14	1,400						600	12.15§	7,290

The moving average prices per unit are calculated as follows:
*($5,000 + $3,300) / 800 units = $10.38 (rounded to nearest cent)
†($3,633 + $4,800) / 750 units = $11.24
‡($5,058 + $2,600) / 650 units = $11.78
§($5,890 + $1,400) / 600 units = $12.15

For example, the goods available for sale after the January 20 purchase consist of 500 units at $10 and 300 units at $11, which results in an average cost of $10.38. This is the unit cost applied to the 450 units sold on February 18. The 400 units purchased on April 8 require the computation of a new unit cost, as indicated in the second footnote to the exhibit. As you might have suspected, the ending inventory with an average cost flow differs, depending on whether a periodic or a perpetual system is used:

Weighted average periodic (Exhibit 6-5) $6,840
Moving average perpetual (Exhibit 6-15) $7,290

Chapter Highlights

1. **LO 1** A manufacturer's inventory consists of raw materials, work in process, and finished goods. The inventory of a retailer or wholesaler is in a single form called *merchandise inventory.*

2. **LO 2, 3** The amount of cost of goods sold reported on the income statement is inherently tied to the value assigned to ending inventory on the balance sheet. Errors in valuing inventory affect cost of goods sold and thus affect the amount of income reported for the period. An understatement of ending inventory will result in an understatement of net income; an overstatement of ending inventory will result in an overstatement of net income.

3. **LO 3** All costs necessary to put inventory into a condition and location for sale should be included in its cost. Freight costs, storage costs, excise and sales taxes, and insurance during the time the merchandise is in transit are all candidates for inclusion in the cost of the asset. As a practical manner, however, some of these costs are very difficult to allocate to individual products and are therefore accounted for as expenses of the period.

4. **LO 4** The purchase of identical units of a product at varying prices necessitates the use of a costing method to assign a dollar amount to ending inventory and cost of goods sold. As alternatives to the use of a specific identification method, which is impractical in many instances as well as subject to manipulation, accountants have devised cost-flow assumptions.

5. **LO 4** The weighted average method assigns the same average unit cost to all units available for sale during the period. It is widely used because of its simplicity.

6. **LO 4** The FIFO method assigns the most recent costs to ending inventory. The older costs are assigned to cost of goods sold. A first-in, first-out approach does tend to parallel the physical flow of products in many businesses, although the actual flow is not our primary concern in choosing a costing method.

7. **LO 4** LIFO assigns the most recent costs to cost of goods sold, and the older costs remain in inventory. In a period of rising prices, this method results in a relatively higher amount assigned to cost of goods sold and, thus, a lower amount of reported net income. Lower net income results in a lower amount of taxes due, and the tax advantages have resulted in the widespread use of the LIFO method.

   A company that chooses to take advantage of the tax break from using LIFO on its tax return must also use the method in preparing the income statement. A concern with the use of LIFO is the possibility of a liquidation. If more units are sold than are bought in any one period, some of the units sold will come from the older, lower-priced units, resulting in a low cost of goods sold and a high gross margin. The high gross margin will necessitate a larger tax amount due.

8. **LO 5** Many accountants favor LIFO because it results in the nearest approximation to the current cost of goods sold. On the other hand, under LIFO, the inventory amount on the balance sheet is, in many cases, very outdated. FIFO gives a much closer approximation to current cost on the balance sheet. It leads, however, to what accountants describe as inventory profit: the portion of the gross margin that is due simply to holding the inventory during an inflationary period.

9. **LO 6** As used in the lower of cost or market rule, *market* means *replacement cost*. The purpose of valuing inventory at original cost or replacement cost, whichever is lower, is to anticipate declines in the selling price of goods subject to obsolescence, spoilage, and other types of loss. By being conservative and reducing the carrying value of the inventory at the end of the year, a company is more likely to report its normal gross margin when the units are sold at a reduced price in the next period. The rule can be applied to each item, to a group of items, or to the entire inventory.

10. **LO 7** The gross profit method is used to estimate the cost of inventory lost by theft, fire, flooding, and other types of damage. The method is also useful to estimate the amount of inventory on hand for interim reports, such as quarterly financial statements. It relies on a trustworthy estimate of the gross profit ratio.

11. **LO 7** Retailers use the retail inventory method to estimate the cost of inventory for interim financial statements and to convert the year-end inventory, per a physical count, from retail to cost.

12. **LO 8** Different measures are available to analyze how well a company is managing its inventory levels. The inventory turnover ratio indicates how many times during a period a company sells or turns over its inventory, and the number of days' sales in inventory indicates how long it takes, on average, to sell inventory.

13. **LO 9** The payment of cash to suppliers of inventory represents a cash outflow from operating activities on the statement of cash flows. If a company uses the indirect method, however, adjustments are made to net income for the increase or decrease in the Inventory and Accounts Payable accounts.

14. **LO 10** The periodic system relies on a count of inventory on hand at the end of the year to allocate costs between ending inventory and cost of goods sold. No entry is made in a periodic system to record the cost of inventory sold at the time of sale. Acquisitions of inventory during the period are recorded in the temporary account Purchases. (Appendix 6A)

15. **LO 10** In a perpetual system, the Inventory account is updated at the time of each sale and purchase of merchandise. The computer has made the perpetual system much more feasible for many businesses. (Appendix 6A)

16. **LO 11** Ending inventory costed at FIFO will be the same whether the periodic system or the perpetual system is used. This is not the case when the LIFO method is used: the results under the periodic and the perpetual systems differ. Likewise, ending inventory differs in the periodic system and the perpetual system when a weighted average approach is applied. The average method with a perpetual system is really a moving average approach. (Appendix 6A)

Key Terms Quiz

Read each definition below and then write the number of the definition in the blank beside the appropriate term it defines. The solution appears at the end of the chapter.

____ Merchandise Inventory	____ Raw materials
____ Work in process	____ Finished goods
____ Consignment	____ Specific identification method
____ Weighted average cost method	____ FIFO method
____ LIFO method	____ LIFO liquidation
____ LIFO conformity rule	____ LIFO reserve
____ Replacement cost	____ Inventory profit
____ Lower of cost or market (LCM) rule	____ Gross profit method
____ Retail inventory method	____ Inventory turnover ratio
____ Number of days' sales in inventory	____ Moving average (Appendix 6A)

1. The name given to an average cost method when it is used with a perpetual inventory system.

2. The cost of unfinished products in a manufacturing company.

3. An inventory costing method that assigns the same unit cost to all units available for sale during the period.

4. The account that wholesalers and retailers use to report inventory held for sale.

5. A conservative inventory valuation approach that is an attempt to anticipate declines in the value of inventory before its actual sale.

6. An inventory costing method that assigns the most recent costs to ending inventory.

7. The inventory of a manufacturer before the addition of any direct labor or manufacturing overhead.

8. The current cost of a unit of inventory.

9. An inventory costing method that assigns the most recent costs to cost of goods sold.

10. A measure of how long it takes to sell inventory.

11. A technique used to establish an estimate of the cost of inventory stolen, destroyed, or otherwise damaged or of the amount of inventory on hand at an interim date.

12. A manufacturer's inventory that is complete and ready for sale.

13. A technique used by retailers to convert the retail value of inventory to a cost basis.

14. The IRS requirement that if LIFO is used on the tax return, it must also be used in reporting income to stockholders.

15. An inventory costing method that relies on matching unit costs with the actual units sold.

16. A legal arrangement in which inventory owned by one company is turned over to another one for sale.

17. The portion of the gross profit that results from holding inventory during a period of rising prices.

18. The result of selling more units than are purchased during the period, which can have negative tax consequences if a company is using LIFO.

19. The excess of the value of a company's inventory stated at FIFO over the value stated at LIFO.

20. A measure of the number of times inventory is sold during a period.

Alternate Terms

Gross margin   Gross profit.

Interim statements   Quarterly or monthly statements.

Market (value for inventory)   Replacement cost.

Raw materials   Direct materials.

Retail price   Selling price.

Work in process   Work in progress.

Questions

1. What are three distinct types of costs that manufacturers incur? Describe each of them.

2. What is the relationship between the valuation of inventory as an asset on the balance sheet and the measurement of income?

3. Who owns consigned goods, and what is the significance of the ownership for accounting purposes?

4. Delevan Corp. uses a periodic inventory system and is counting its year-end inventory. Due to a lack of communication, two different teams count the same section of the warehouse. What effect will this error have on net income?

5. What is the justification for including freight costs incurred in acquiring incoming goods in the cost of the inventory rather than simply treating the cost as an expense of the period? What is the significance of this decision for accounting purposes?

6. What are the inventory characteristics that would allow a company to use the specific identification method? Give at least two examples of inventory for which the method is appropriate.

7. How can the specific identification method allow management to manipulate income?

8. What is the significance of the adjective *weighted* in the weighted average cost method? Use an example to illustrate your answer.

9. Which inventory method, FIFO or LIFO, more nearly approximates the physical flow of products in most businesses? Explain your answer.

10. York Inc. manufactures notebook computers and has experienced noticeable declines in the purchase price of many of the components it uses, including computer chips. Which inventory costing method should York use if it wants to maximize net income? Explain your answer.

11. Which inventory costing method should a company use if it wants to minimize taxes? Does your response depend on whether prices are rising or falling? Explain your answers.

12. The president of Ace Retail is commenting on the company's new controller: "The woman is brilliant! She has shown us how we can maximize our income and at the same time minimize the amount of taxes we have to pay

the government. Because the cost to purchase our inventory constantly goes up, we will use FIFO to calculate cost of goods sold on the income statement to minimize the amount charged to cost of goods sold and thus maximize net income. For tax purposes, however, we will use LIFO because this will minimize taxable income and thus minimize the amount we have to pay in taxes." Should the president be enthralled with the new controller? Explain your answer.

13. What does the term *LIFO liquidation* mean? How can it lead to poor buying habits?

14. Historical-based costing methods are sometimes criticized for leading to inventory profits. In a period of rising prices, which inventory costing method will lead to the most "inventory profit"? Explain your answer.

15. Is it acceptable for a company to disclose, in its annual report, that it is switching from some other inventory costing method to LIFO *to save on taxes?*

16. What is the rationale for valuing inventory at the lower of cost or market?

17. Why is it likely that the result from applying the lower of cost or market rule using a total approach, that is, by comparing total cost to total market value, and the result from applying the rule on an item-by-item basis will differ?

18. Patterson's controller makes the following suggestion: "I have a brilliant way to save us money. Because we are already using the gross profit method for our quarterly statements, we start using it to estimate the year-end inventory for the annual report and save the money normally spent to have the inventory counted on December 31." What do you think of his suggestion?

19. Why does a company save time and money by using the retail inventory method at the end of the year?

20. Ralston Corp.'s cost of sales has remained steady over the last two years. During this same time period, however, its inventory has increased considerably. What does this information tell you about the company's inventory turnover? Explain your answer.

21. In simple terms, how do the inventory costing methods, such as FIFO and LIFO, and the inventory systems, such as periodic and perpetual, differ? (Appendix 6A)

22. Why is the weighted average cost method called a *moving* average when a company uses a perpetual inventory system? (Appendix 6A)

Exercises

LO 1   **Exercise 6-1** Classification of Inventory Costs

Put an X in the appropriate column next to the inventory item to indicate its most likely classification on the books of a company that manufactures furniture and then sells it in retail company stores.

	CLASSIFICATION			
INVENTORY ITEM	RAW MATERIAL	WORK IN PROCESS	FINISHED GOODS	MERCHANDISE INVENTORY
Fabric				
Lumber				
Unvarnished tables				
Chairs on the showroom floor				
Cushions				
Decorative knobs				
Drawers				
Sofa frames				
Chairs in the plant warehouse				
Chairs in the retail storeroom				

LO 1   **Exercise 6-2** Inventoriable Costs

During the first month of operations, ABC Company incurred the following costs in ordering and receiving merchandise for resale. No inventory has been sold.

List price, $100, 200 units purchased.

Volume discount, 10% off list price.

Paid freight costs, $56.

Insurance cost while goods were in transit, $32.

Long-distance phone charge to place orders, $4.35.

Purchasing department salary, $1,000.

Supplies used to label goods at retail price, $9.75.

Interest paid to supplier, $46.

Required

What amount do you recommend the company record as merchandise inventory on its balance sheet? Explain your answer. For any items not to be included in inventory, indicate their appropriate treatment in the financial statements.

LO 2   **Exercise 6-3** Inventory and Income Manipulation

The president of SOS Inc. is concerned that the net income at year-end will not reach the expected figure. When the sales manager receives a large order on the last day of the fiscal year, the president tells the accountant to record the sale but to ignore any inventory adjustment because the physical inventory has already been taken. How will this affect the current year's net income? Next year's income? What would you do if you were the accountant? Assume that SOS uses a periodic inventory system.

LO 3   **Exercise 6-4** Inventory Errors

For each of the following independent situations, fill in the blanks to indicate the effect of the error on each of the various financial statement items. Indicate an understatement (U), an overstatement (O), or no effect (NE). Assume that each of the companies uses a periodic inventory system.

	BALANCE SHEET		INCOME STATEMENT	
ERROR	INVENTORY	RETAINED EARNINGS	COST OF GOODS SOLD	NET INCOME
1. A consignor doesn't include goods out on consignment in its ending inventory.	_____	_____	_____	_____
2. One section of a warehouse is counted twice during the year-end count of inventory.	_____	_____	_____	_____
3. A consignee includes goods held on consignment in its count of inventory at year-end.	_____	_____	_____	_____
4. During the count at year-end, the inventory sheets for one of the stores of a discount retailer are lost.	_____	_____	_____	_____

LO 3   **Exercise 6-5** Transfer of Title to Inventory

For each of the following transactions, indicate which company should include the inventory on its December 31, 1998 balance sheet:

1. Michelson Supplies Inc. shipped merchandise to PJ Sales on December 28, 1998, terms FOB destination. The merchandise arrives at PJ's on January 4, 1999.

2. Quarton Inc. shipped merchandise to Filbrandt on December 25, 1998, FOB destination. Fibrandt received the merchandise on December 31, 1998.

3. James Bros. Inc. shipped merchandise to Randall Company on December 27, 1998, FOB shipping point. Randall Company received the merchandise on January 3, 1999.

4. Hinz Company shipped merchandise to Barner Inc. on December 24, 1998, FOB shipping point. The merchandise arrived at Barner's on December 29, 1998.

5. Poortenga Company consigned merchandise to Brink Inc. on December 23, 1998. The merchandise was sold on December 30, 1998.

6. Wesbey Inc. consigned merchandise to Flannery Company on December 18, 1998. The merchandise was sold on January 4, 1999.

LO 4   **Exercise 6-6** Inventory Costing Methods

VanderMeer Inc. reported the following information for the month of February:

Inventory, February 1	65 units @ $20
Purchases:	
February 7	50 units @ $22
February 18	60 units @ $23
February 27	45 units @ $24

During February, VanderMeer sold 140 units. The company uses a periodic inventory system.

Required

What is the value of ending inventory and cost of goods sold for February under the following assumptions:

1. Of the 140 units sold, 55 cost $20, 35 cost $22, 45 cost $23, and 5 cost $24.
2. FIFO.
3. LIFO.
4. Weighted average.

LO 5 **Exercise 6-7** Evaluation of Inventory Costing Methods

Write the letter of the method that is most applicable to each statement.

a. Specific identification.
b. Average cost.
c. First-in, first-out (FIFO).
d. Last-in, first-out (LIFO).

_____ 1. Is the most realistic ending inventory.
_____ 2. Results in cost of goods sold being closest to current product costs.
_____ 3. Results in highest income during periods of inflation.
_____ 4. Results in highest ending inventory during periods of inflation.
_____ 5. Smooths out costs during periods of inflation.
_____ 6. Is not practical for most businesses.
_____ 7. Puts more weight on the cost of the larger number of units purchased.
_____ 8. Is an assumption that most closely reflects the physical flow of goods for most businesses.

LO 5 **Exercise 6-8** LIFO Liquidation—Owens Corning

The 1995 annual report of Owens Corning and Subsidiaries includes the following footnote:

> During 1995, 1994, and 1993, certain inventories were reduced, resulting in the liquidation of LIFO inventory layers carried at lower costs in prior years as compared with the current cost of inventory. The effect of these inventory reductions was to reduce 1995, 1994, and 1993 cost of sales by $7 million, $3 million, and $1 million, respectively.

Required

1. Why did the liquidation of LIFO inventory layers result in lower cost of sales figures? What was the effect on gross margin?
2. Was the LIFO liquidation advantageous to Owens Corning for tax purposes?

LO 7 **Exercise 6-9** Gross Profit Method

On February 12, a hurricane destroys the entire inventory of Suncoast Corporation. An estimate of the amount of inventory lost is needed for insurance purposes. The following information is available:

Inventory on January 1	$ 15,400
Net sales from January 1 to February 12	105,300
Purchases from January 1 to February 12	84,230

Suncoast estimates its gross profit ratio as 25% of net sales. The insurance company has agreed to pay Suncoast $10,000 as a settlement for the inventory destroyed.

Required

Prepare the journal entry on Suncoast's books to recognize the inventory lost and the insurance reimbursement.

LO 8 | **Exercise 6-10** Inventory Turnover for Sears

The following amounts are available from the 1995 annual report of Sears, Roebuck & Co. (all amounts are in millions of dollars):

Cost of sales, buying, and occupancy	$22,866
Merchandise inventories, December 30, 1995	4,033
Merchandise inventories, December 31, 1994	4,044

Required

1. Compute Sears' inventory turnover ratio for 1995.

2. What is the average length of time it takes to sell an item of inventory? Explain your answer.

3. Do you think the average length of time it took Sears to sell inventory in 1995 is reasonable? What other information do you need to fully answer this question?

LO 9 | **Exercise 6-11** Impact of Transactions Involving Inventories on Statement of Cash Flows

From the following list, identify whether the change in the account balance during the year would be added to (A) or deducted from (D) net income when the indirect method is used to determine cash flows from operating activities.

_____ Increase in accounts payable

_____ Decrease in accounts payable

_____ Increase in inventories

_____ Decrease in inventories

LO 9 | **Exercise 6-12** Effects of Transactions Involving Inventories on the Statement of Cash Flows—Direct Method

Masthead Company's comparative balance sheets included inventory of $180,400 at December 31, 1997 and $241,200 at December 31, 1998. Masthead's comparative balance sheets also included accounts payable of $85,400 at December 31, 1997 and $78,400 at December 31, 1998. Masthead's accounts payable balances are comprised solely of amounts due to suppliers for purchases of inventory on account. Cost of goods sold, as reported by Masthead on its 1998 income statement, amounted to $1,200,000.

Required

What is the amount of cash payments for inventory that Masthead will report in the Operating Activities category of its 1998 statement of cash flows assuming that the direct method is used?

LO 9 | **Exercise 6-13** Effects of Transactions Involving Inventories on the Statement of Cash Flows—Indirect Method

Refer to all of the facts in Exercise 6-12.

Required

Assume instead that Masthead uses the indirect method to prepare its statement of cash flows. Indicate how each item will be reflected as an adjustment to net income in the Operating Activities category of the statement of cash flows.

LO 10 | **Exercise 6-14** Periodic and Perpetual Journal Entries (Appendix 6A)

Record the journal entries to reflect the following transactions, assuming (a) a periodic system and (b) a perpetual system. Arrange your entries in parallel columns for comparison purposes.

October	1:	Purchased 100 units on account for $7 each.
October	3:	Returned 5 defective units for full credit.
October	8:	Paid $16 freight charges on the October 1 shipment.
October	20:	Sold 75 units on account for $10 each.

Multi-Concept Exercises

LO 4, 5 | **Exercise 6-15** Inventory Costing Methods—Periodic System

The following information is available concerning the inventory of Carter Inc.:

	UNITS	UNIT COST
Beginning inventory	200	$10
Purchases:		
March 5	300	11
June 12	400	12
August 23	250	13
October 2	150	15

During the year, Carter sold 1,000 units. It uses a periodic inventory system.

Required

1. Calculate ending inventory and cost of goods sold for each of the following three methods:
   a. Weighted average.
   b. FIFO.
   c. LIFO.
2. Assume an estimated tax rate of 30%. How much more or less (indicate which) will Carter pay in taxes by using FIFO instead of LIFO? Explain your answer.

LO 2, 6 **Exercise 6-16** Lower of Cost or Market Rule

Awards Etc. carries an inventory of trophies and ribbons for local sports teams and school clubs. The cost of trophies has dropped in the past year, which pleases the company except for the fact that it has on hand considerable inventory that was purchased at the higher prices. The president is not pleased with the lower profit margin the company is earning. "The lower profit margin will continue until we sell all of this old inventory," he grumbled to the new staff accountant. "Not really," replied the accountant. "Let's write down the inventory to the replacement cost this year, and then next year our profit margin will be in line with the competition."

Required

Explain why the inventory can be carried at an amount less than its cost. Which accounts will be affected by the write-down? What will be the effect on income in the current year and future years?

LO 5, 11 **Exercise 6-17** Inventory Costing Methods—Perpetual System (Appendix 6A)

The following information is available concerning Oshkosh Inc.:

	UNITS	UNIT COST
Beginning inventory	200	$10
Purchases:		
March 5	300	11
June 12	400	12
August 23	250	13
October 2	150	15

Oshkosh, which uses a perpetual system, sold 1,000 units for $22 each during the year. Sales occurred on the following dates:

	UNITS
February 12	150
April 30	200
July 7	200
September 6	300
December 3	150

Required

1. Calculate ending inventory and cost of goods sold for each of the following three methods:

a. Moving average.

b. FIFO.

c. LIFO.

2. For each of the three methods, compare the results with those for Carter in Exercise 6-15. Which of the methods gives a different answer depending on whether a company uses a periodic or a perpetual inventory system?

3. Assume the use of the perpetual system and an estimated tax rate of 30%. How much more or less (indicate which) will Oshkosh pay in taxes by using LIFO instead of FIFO? Explain your answer.

Problems

LO 1   **Problem 6-1** Inventory Costs in Various Businesses

Businesses incur various costs in selling goods and services. Each business must decide which costs are expenses of the period and which should be included in the cost of the inventory. Various types of businesses are listed below, along with certain types of costs they incur:

		ACCOUNTING TREATMENT		
		---	---	---
BUSINESS	TYPES OF COSTS	EXPENSE OF THE PERIOD	INVENTORY COST	OTHER TREATMENT
Retail shoe store	Shoes for sale			
	Shoe boxes			
	Advertising signs			
Grocery store	Canned goods on the shelves			
	Produce			
	Cleaning supplies			
	Cash registers			
Frame shop	Wooden frame supplies			
	Nails			
	Glass			
Walk-in print shop	Paper			
	Copy machines			
	Toner cartridges			
Restaurant	Frozen food			
	China and silverware			
	Prepared food			
	Spices			

Required

Fill in the table to indicate the correct accounting for each of these types of costs by placing an X in the appropriate column. For any costs that receive other treatment, explain what the appropriate treatment is for accounting purposes.

LO 3   **Problem 6-2** Inventory Error

The following highly condensed income statements and balance sheets are available for Budget Stores for a two-year period (all amounts are stated in thousands of dollars):

INCOME STATEMENTS	1998	1997
Revenues	$20,000	$15,000
Cost of goods sold	13,000	10,000
Gross profit	$ 7,000	$ 5,000
Operating expenses	3,000	2,000
Net income	$ 4,000	$ 3,000

BALANCE SHEETS	DECEMBER 31, 1998	DECEMBER 31, 1997
Cash	$ 1,700	$ 1,500
Inventory	4,200	3,500
Other current assets	2,500	2,000
Long-term assets	15,000	14,000
Total assets	$23,400	$21,000
Liabilities	$ 8,500	$ 7,000
Capital stock	5,000	5,000
Retained earnings	9,900	9,000
Total liabilities and owners' equity	$23,400	$21,000

Before releasing the 1998 annual report, Budget's controller learns that the inventory of one of the stores (amounting to $600,000) was inadvertently omitted from the count on December 31, 1997. The inventory of the store was correctly included in the December 31, 1998, count.

Required

1. Prepare revised income statements and balance sheets for Budget Stores for each of the two years. Ignore the effect of income taxes.

2. If Budget did not prepare revised statements before releasing the 1998 annual report, what would be the amount of overstatement or understatement of net income for the two-year period? What would be the overstatement or understatement of retained earnings at December 31, 1998, if revised statements were not prepared?

3. Given your answers in part 2, does it matter if Budget bothers to restate the financial statements of the two years to rectify the error? Explain your answer.

LO 5   **Problem 6-3** Evaluation of Inventory Costing Methods

Users of financial statements rely on the information available to them to decide whether to invest in a company or lend it money. As an investor, you are comparing three companies in the same industry. The cost to purchase inventory is rising in the industry. Assume that all expenses incurred by the three companies are the same except for cost of goods sold. The companies use the following methods to value ending inventory:

> Company A—weighted average cost.
> Company B—first-in, first-out (FIFO).
> Company C—last-in, first-out (LIFO).

Required

1. Which of the three companies will report the highest net income? Explain your answer.

2. Which of the three companies will pay the least in income taxes? Explain your answer.

3. Which method of inventory costing do you believe is superior to the others in providing information to potential investors? Explain.

4. Explain how your answers to 1, 2, and 3 would change if the costs to purchase inventory had been falling instead of rising.

LO 7   **Problem 6-4** Gross Profit Method of Estimating Inventory Losses

On August 1, an office supply store was destroyed by an explosion in its basement. A small amount of inventory valued at $4,500 was saved. An estimate of the amount of inventory lost is needed for insurance purposes. The following information is available:

Inventory, January 1	$ 3,200
Purchases, January–July	164,000
Sales, January–July	113,500

The normal gross profit ratio is 40%. The insurance company will pay the store $65,000.

Required

1. Using the gross profit method, estimate the amount of inventory lost in the explosion.
2. Prepare the journal entry to record the inventory loss and the insurance reimbursement.

LO 8   **Problem 6-5** Inventory Turnover for Compaq Computer and Digital Equipment

The following information was summarized from the 1995 annual report of Compaq Computer Corporation:

	(in millions)
Cost of sales for the year ended December 31:	
1995	$11,367
1994	8,139
Inventories, December 31:	
1995	2,156
1994	2,005
Sales for the year ended December 31:	
1995	14,755
1994	10,866

The following information was summarized from the fiscal year 1996 annual report of Digital Equipment Corporation:

	(in thousands)
Cost of product sales for the year ended:	
June 29, 1996	$5,541,792
July 1, 1995	5,397,723
Inventories:	
June 29, 1996	1,820,811
July 1, 1995	2,053,620
Product sales for the year ended:	
June 29, 1996	8,362,423
July 1, 1995	7,616,441

Required

1. Calculate the gross margin (gross profit) ratios for Compaq Computer and Digital Equipment for the most recent two fiscal years.
2. Calculate the inventory turnover ratios for both companies for the most recent fiscal year.
3. Which company appears to be performing better? What other information should you consider to determine how these companies are performing in this regard?

LO 9   **Problem 6-6** Effects of Changes in Inventory and Accounts Payable Balances on Statement of Cash Flows

Copeland Antiques reported a net loss of $33,200 for the year ended December 31, 1998. The following items were included on Copeland's balance sheets at December 31, 1998 and 1997:

	12/31/98	12/31/97
Cash	$ 65,300	$ 46,100
Trade accounts payable	123,900	93,700
Inventories	192,600	214,800

Copeland uses the indirect method to prepare its statement of cash flows. Copeland does not have any other current assets or current liabilities and did not enter into any investing or financing activities during 1998.

Required

1. Prepare Copeland's 1998 statement of cash flows.
2. Draft a brief memo to the president to explain why cash increased during such an unprofitable year.

Multi-Concept Problems

LO 2, 4, 5 **Problem 6-7** Comparison of Inventory Costing Methods—Periodic System

Bitten Company's inventory records show 600 units on hand on October 1 with a unit cost of $5 each. The following transactions occurred during the month of October:

DATE		UNIT PURCHASES	UNIT SALES
October	4		500 @ $10.00
	8	800 @ $5.40	
	9		700 @ $10.00
	18	700 @ $5.76	
	20		800 @ $11.00
	29	800 @ $5.90	

All expenses other than cost of goods sold amount to $3,000 for the month. The company uses an estimated tax rate of 30% to accrue monthly income taxes.

Required

1. Prepare a chart comparing cost of goods sold and ending inventory using the periodic system and the following costing methods:

	COST OF GOODS SOLD	ENDING INVENTORY	TOTAL
Weighted average			
FIFO			
LIFO			

2. What does the Total column represent?
3. Prepare income statements for each of the three methods.
4. Will the company pay more or less tax if it uses FIFO rather than LIFO? How much more or less?

LO 2, 5, 11 **Problem 6-8** Comparison of Inventory Costing Methods—Perpetual System (Appendix 6A)

Repeat Problem 6-7 using the perpetual system.

LO 2, 4, 5 **Problem 6-9** Inventory Costing Methods—Periodic System

Oxendine Company's inventory records for the month of November reveal the following:

Inventory, November 1	200 units @ $18.00
November 4, purchase	250 units @ $18.50
November 7, sale	300 units @ $42.00
November 13, purchase	220 units @ $18.90
November 18, purchase	150 units @ $19.00
November 22, sale	380 units @ $42.50
November 24, purchase	200 units @ $19.20
November 28, sale	110 units @ $43.00

Selling and administrative expenses for the month were $10,800. Depreciation expense was $4,000. Oxendine's tax rate is 35%.

Required

1. Calculate the cost of goods sold and ending inventory under each of the following three methods (assume a periodic inventory system): (a) FIFO, (b) LIFO, and (c) weighted average.
2. Calculate the gross margin and net income under each costing assumption.
3. Under which costing method will Oxendine pay the least taxes? Explain your answer.

LO 2, 4, 5 **Problem 6-10** Inventory Costing Methods—Periodic System

Following is an inventory acquisition schedule for Weaver Corp. for 1998:

	UNITS	UNIT COST
Beginning inventory	5,000	$10
Purchases:		
February 4	3,000	9
April 12	4,000	8
September 10	2,000	7
December 5	1,000	6

During the year, Weaver sold 12,500 units at $12 each. All expenses except cost of goods sold and taxes amounted to $20,000. The tax rate is 30%.

Required

1. Compute cost of goods sold and ending inventory under each of the following three methods (assume a periodic inventory system): (a) weighted average, (b) FIFO, and (c) LIFO.

2. Prepare income statements under each of the three methods.

3. Which method do you recommend so that Weaver pays the least amount of taxes during 1998? Explain your answer.

4. Weaver anticipates that unit costs for inventory will increase throughout 1999. Will it be able to switch from the method you recommended it use in 1998 to another method to take advantage for tax purposes of the increase in prices? Explain your answer.

LO 1, 5 **Problem 6-11** Interpreting Tribune Company's Inventory Accounting Policy

The 1995 annual report of Tribune Company and Subsidiaries includes the following in the footnote that summarizes its accounting policies:

Inventories Inventories are stated at the lower of cost or market. Cost is determined on the last-in, first-out (LIFO) basis for newsprint and on the first-in, first-out (FIFO) basis for all other inventories.

Required

1. What *types* of inventory cost does Tribune Company carry? What about newspapers? Are newspapers considered inventory?

2. Why would the company choose two different methods to value its inventory?

LO 4, 7 **Problem 6-12** Interpreting Sears' Inventory Accounting Policy

The 1995 annual report of Sears, Roebuck and Co. includes the following information in the footnote which describes its accounting policies relating to merchandise inventories:

Merchandise inventories of domestic operations are valued at the lower of cost (primarily using the last-in, first-out or LIFO method) or market using the retail method. To estimate the effects of inflation in inventories, the Company utilizes internally developed price indices.

The footnote also includes the following information about the company's international operations:

Merchandise inventories of international operations, Western Africa and Puerto Rico, which represent approximately 18% of merchandise inventories, are recorded based on the FIFO method.

Your grandfather knows you are studying accounting and asks you what this information means.

Required

1. Sears uses the last-in, first-out method for its domestic merchandise inventories and the first-in, first-out method for its international merchandise inventories. Does this mean it sells its newest merchandise first in the U.S. and its oldest merchandise first overseas? Explain your answer.

2. Does Sears report merchandise inventories on its balance sheet at their retail value? Explain your answer.

Alternate Problems

LO 1 **Problem 6-1A** Inventory Costs in Various Businesses

Sound Traxs Inc. sells and rents videos to retail customers. The accountant is aware that at the end of the year she must account for inventory but is unsure what videos are considered inventory and how to value them. Videos purchased by the company are placed on the shelf for rental. Every three weeks the company performs a detailed analysis of the rental income from each video and decides whether to keep it as a rental or to offer it for sale in the resale section of the store. Resale videos sell for $10 each regardless of the price Sound Traxs paid for the tape.

Required

1. How should Sound Traxs account for each of the two types of tapes—rentals and resales—on its balance sheet?
2. How would you suggest Sound Traxs account for the videos as they are transferred from one department to another?

LO 3 **Problem 6-2A** Inventory Error

The following condensed income statements and balance sheets are available for Planter Stores for a two-year period (all amounts are stated in thousands of dollars):

INCOME STATEMENTS	1998	1997
Revenues	$35,982	$26,890
Cost of goods sold	12,594	9,912
Gross profit	$23,388	$16,978
Operating expenses	13,488	10,578
Net income	$ 9,900	$ 6,400

BALANCE SHEETS	DECEMBER 31, 1998	DECEMBER 31, 1997
Cash	$ 9,400	$ 4,100
Inventory	4,500	5,400
Other current assets	1,600	1,250
Long-term assets, net	24,500	24,600
Total assets	$40,000	$35,350
Current liabilities	$ 9,380	$10,600
Capital stock	18,000	18,000
Retained earnings	12,620	6,750
Total liabilities and owners' equity	$40,000	$35,350

Before releasing the 1998 annual report, Planter's controller learns that the inventory of one of the stores (amounting to $500,000) was counted twice in the December 31, 1997, inventory. The inventory was correctly counted in the December 31, 1998, inventory count.

Required

1. Prepare revised income statements and balance sheets for Planter Stores for each of the two years. Ignore the effect of income taxes.
2. Compute the current ratio at December 31, 1997, before the statements are revised and then compute the current ratio at the same date after the statements are revised. If Planter applied for a loan in early 1998 and the lender required a current ratio of at least 1-to-1, would the error have affected the loan? Explain your answer.
3. If Planter did not prepare revised statements before releasing the 1998 annual report, what would be the amount of overstatement or understatement of net income for the two-year period? What would be the overstatement or understatement of retained earnings at December 31, 1998, if revised statements were not prepared?
4. Given your answers in parts 2 and 3, does it matter if Planter bothers to restate the financial statements of the two years to correct the error? Explain your answer.

LO 5 **Problem 6-3A** Evaluation of Inventory Costing Methods

Three large mass merchandisers use the following methods to value ending inventory:

Company X—weighted average cost.

Company Y—first-in, first-out (FIFO).

Company Z—last-in, first-out (LIFO).

The cost of inventory has steadily increased over the past 10 years of the product life. Recently, however, prices have started to decline slightly due to foreign competition.

Required

1. Will the effect on net income of the decline in cost of goods sold be the same for all three companies? Explain your answer?

2. Company Z would like to change its inventory costing method from LIFO to FIFO. Write an acceptable footnote for its annual report to justify the change.

LO 7 **Problem 6-4A** Gross Profit Method of Estimating Inventory Losses

On July 1, an explosion destroyed a fireworks supply company. A small amount of inventory valued at $4,500 was saved. An estimate of the amount of inventory lost is needed for insurance purposes. The following information is available:

Inventory, January 1	$14,200
Purchases, January–June	77,000
Sales, January–June	93,500

The normal gross profit ratio is 70%. The insurance company will pay the supply company $50,000.

Required

1. Using the gross profit method, estimate the amount of inventory lost in the explosion.

2. Prepare the journal entry to record the inventory loss and the insurance reimbursement.

LO 8 **Problem 6-5A** Inventory Turnover for Wal-Mart and Kmart

The following information was summarized from the 1995 annual report of Wal-Mart Stores, Inc.:

	(in millions)
Cost of sales for the year ended January 31:	
1995	$65,586
1994	53,444
Inventories, January 31:	
1995	14,064
1994	11,014

The following information was summarized from the fiscal year 1995 annual report of Kmart Corporation:

	(in millions)
Cost of merchandise sold for the year ended January 31:	
1995	$26,996
1994	24,868
Merchandise inventories, January 31:	
1995	6,635
1994	6,853

Required

1. Calculate the inventory turnover ratios for Wal-Mart and Kmart for 1995.

2. Which company appears to be performing better? What other information should you consider to determine how these companies are performing in this regard?

LO 9 **Problem 6-6A** Effects of Changes in Inventory and Accounts Payable Balances on Statement of Cash Flows

Carpetland City reported net income of $78,500 for the year ended December 31, 1998. The following items were included on Carpetland's balance sheet at December 31, 1998 and 1997:

	12/31/98	12/31/97
Cash	$ 14,400	$26,300
Trade accounts payable	23,900	93,700
Inventories	105,500	84,900

Carpetland uses the indirect method to prepare its statement of cash flows. Carpetland does not have any other current assets or current liabilities and did not enter into any investing or financing activities during 1998.

Required

1. Prepare Carpetland's 1998 statement of cash flows.
2. Draft a brief memo to the president to explain why cash decreased during a profitable year.

Alternate Multi-Concept Problems

LO 2, 4, 5 **Problem 6-7A** Comparison of Inventory Costing Methods—Periodic System

Stellar Inc.'s inventory records show 300 units on hand on November 1 with a unit cost of $4 each. The following transactions occurred during the month of November:

DATE	UNIT PURCHASES	UNIT SALES
November 4		200 @ $9.00
8	500 @ $4.50	
9		500 @ $9.00
18	700 @ $4.75	
20		400 @ $9.50
29	600 @ $5.00	

All expenses other than cost of goods sold amount to $2,000 for the month. The company uses an estimated tax rate of 25% to accrue monthly income taxes.

Required

1. Prepare a chart comparing cost of goods sold and ending inventory using the periodic system and the following costing methods:

	COST OF GOODS SOLD	ENDING INVENTORY	TOTAL
Weighted average			
FIFO			
LIFO			

2. What does the Total column represent?
3. Prepare income statements for each of the three methods.
4. Will the company pay more or less tax if it uses FIFO rather than LIFO? How much more or less?

LO 2, 5, 11 **Problem 6-8A** Comparison of Inventory Costing Methods—Perpetual System (Appendix 6A)

Repeat Problem 6-7A, using the perpetual system.

LO 2, 4, 5 **Problem 6-9A** Inventory Costing Methods—Periodic System

Story Company's inventory records for the month of November reveal the following:

Inventory, November 1	300 units @ $27.00
November 4, purchase	375 units @ $26.50
November 7, sale	450 units @ $63.00
November 13, purchase	330 units @ $26.00
November 18, purchase	225 units @ $25.40
November 22, sale	570 units @ $63.75
November 24, purchase	300 units @ $25.00
November 28, sale	165 units @ $64.50

Selling and administrative expenses for the month were $16,200. Depreciation expense was $6,000. Story's tax rate is 35%.

Required

1. Calculate the cost of goods sold and ending inventory under each of the following three methods (assume a periodic inventory system): (a) FIFO, (b) LIFO, and (c) weighted average.
2. Calculate the gross margin and net income under each costing assumption.
3. Under which costing method will Story pay the least taxes? Explain your answer.

LO 2, 4, 5 **Problem 6-10A** Inventory Costing Methods—Periodic System

Following is an inventory acquisition schedule for Fees Corp. for 1998:

	UNITS	UNIT COST
Beginning inventory	4,000	$20
Purchases:		
February 4	2,000	18
April 12	3,000	16
September 10	1,000	14
December 5	2,500	12

During the year, Fees sold 11,000 units at $30 each. All expenses except cost of goods sold and taxes amounted to $60,000. The tax rate is 30%.

Required

1. Compute cost of goods sold and ending inventory under each of the following three methods (assume a periodic inventory system): (a) weighted average, (b)FIFO, and (c) LIFO.
2. Prepare income statements under each of the three methods.
3. Which method do you recommend so that Fees pays the least amount of taxes during 1998? Explain your answer.
4. Fees anticipates that unit costs for inventory will increase throughout 1999. Will it be able to switch from the method you recommended it use in 1998 to another method to take advantage for tax purposes of the increase in prices? Explain your answer.

LO 1, 5 **Problem 6-11A** Interpreting Washington Post's Financial Statements

The 1995 annual report of The Washington Post Company includes the following note:

Inventories. Inventories are valued at the lower of cost or market. Cost of newsprint is determined by the first-in, first-out method and cost of magazine paper is determined by the specific-cost method.

Required

1. What *types* of inventory costs does The Washington Post Company have? What about newspapers? Aren't these considered inventory?
2. Why did the company choose two different methods to value its inventory?

LO 4, 7 **Problem 6-12A** Interpreting JCPenney's Financial Statements

The 1995 annual report for JCPenney includes the following in the footnote that summarizes its accounting policies:

> Merchandise inventory. Substantially all merchandise inventory is valued at the lower of cost (last-in, first-out) or market, determined by the retail method.

A friend knows that you are studying accounting and asks you what this note means.

Required

1. JCPenney uses the last-in, first-out method. Does this mean that it sells its newest merchandise first?

2. Does JCPenney report inventories on its balance sheet at their retail value?

Cases

Reading and Interpreting Financial Statements

LO 1, 4 **Case 6-1** Reading and Interpreting Ben & Jerry's Annual Report

Refer to Ben & Jerry's financial statements included in its annual report.

Required

1. Before you look at Ben & Jerry's annual report, what types of inventory accounts do you expect? What types of inventory accounts does Ben & Jerry's actually report (refer to the footnote on inventories)?

2. What inventory costing method does Ben & Jerry's use? Look in the footnotes to the financial statements.

3. What portion of total assets is represented by inventory at the end of 1994? at the end of 1995? Do these portions seem reasonable for a company in this business? Explain your answer.

4. Look at the statement of cash flows. Under the operating activities, you will find an adjustment for depreciation, yet there is no mention of depreciation on the income statement. Depreciation on equipment and buildings used in the manufacturing process is included in cost of sales. Make a list of other expenses that you would expect to be included in Ben & Jerry's cost of sales rather than listed separately on the income statement.

LO 9 **Case 6-2** Reading Ben & Jerry's Statement of Cash Flows

Refer to the statement of cash flows in Ben & Jerry's 1995 annual report and answer the following questions:

1. Did inventories increase or decrease during 1995? Why was the change in the Inventory account added to net income in the Operating Activities category of the statement?

2. Comment on the size of change in inventories over the last three years. Does the level of inventory at the end of 1995 seem appropriate?

3. Did accounts payable and accrued expenses increase or decrease during 1995? Why was the change in the account added to net income in the Operating Activities category of the statement?

LO 5 **Case 6-3** Reading and Interpreting Herman Miller's Inventory Footnote—the Lifo Reserve

The following disclosure is from the footnotes to the 1996 annual report for Herman Miller Inc., a manufacturer of office furniture:

INVENTORIES (in thousands)	1996	1995
Finished products	$24,787	$26,260
Work in process	10,896	8,074
Raw materials	30,047	36,742
	$65,730	$71,076

Inventories are valued at the lower of cost or market and include material, labor, and overhead. The inventories of Herman Miller, Inc., are valued using the last-in, first-out (LIFO) method. The inventories of the company's subsidiaries are valued using the first-in, first-out method. Inventories valued using the LIFO method amounted to $30.7 and $41.1 million at June 1, 1996, and June 3, 1995, respectively.

If all inventories had been valued using the first-in, first-out method, inventories would have been $16.4 and $18.1 million higher than reported at June 1, 1996, and June 3, 1995, respectively.

Required

1. Provide a possible justification for Herman Miller's use of LIFO for certain units of the business and FIFO for others (its subsidiaries).

2. What is the amount of the LIFO reserve on June 1, 1996? on June 3, 1995?

3. Explain the meaning of the increase or decrease in the LIFO reserve during the year ended June 1, 1996. What does this tell you about inventory costs for the company? Are they rising or falling? Explain your answer.

Making Financial Decisions

LO 4, 5 **Case 6-4** Inventory Costing Methods

You are the controller for Georgetown Company. At the end of its first year of operations, the company is experiencing cash flow problems. The following information has been accumulated during the year:

Decision
Making

PURCHASES	
January	1,000 units @ $8
March	1,200 units @ 8
October	1,500 units @ 9

During the year, Georgetown sold 3,000 units at $15 each. The expected tax rate is 35%. The president doesn't understand how to report inventory in the financial statements because no record of the cost of the units sold was kept as each sale was made.

Required

1. What inventory *system* must Georgetown use?

2. Determine the number of units on hand at the end of the year.

3. Explain cost-flow assumptions to the president and the method you recommend. Prepare income statements to justify your position, comparing your recommended method with at least one other method.

LO 3 **Case 6-5** Inventory Errors

You are the controller of a rapidly growing mass merchandiser. The company uses a periodic inventory system. As the company has grown and accounting systems have developed, errors have occurred in both the physical count of inventory and the valuation of inventory on the balance sheet. You have been able to identify the following errors as of December 1997:

Decision
Making

- In 1995 one section of the warehouse was counted twice. The error resulted in inventory overstated on December 31, 1995, by approximately $45,600.

- In 1996 the replacement cost of some inventory was less than the FIFO value used on the balance sheet. The inventory would have been $6,000 less on the balance sheet dated December 31, 1996.

- In 1997 the company used the gross profit method to estimate inventory for its quarterly financial statements. At the end of the second quarter, the controller made a math error and understated the inventory by $20,000 on the quarterly report. The error was not discovered until the end of the year.

Required

What, if anything, should you do to correct each of these errors? Explain your answers.

Accounting and Ethics: What Would You Do?

LO 6 **Case 6-6** Write-Down of Obsolete Inventory

As a newly hired staff accountant, you are assigned the responsibility of physically counting inventory at the end of the year. The inventory count proceeds in a timely fashion. The inventory is outdated, however. You suggest that the inventory could not be sold for the cost at which it is carried and that the inventory should be written down to a much lower level. The controller replies that experience has taught her how the market changes and she knows that the units in the warehouse will be more marketable again. The company plans to keep the goods until they are back in style.

Required

1. What effect will writing off the inventory have on the current year's income?

2. What effect does not writing off the inventory have on the year-end balance sheet?

3. What factors should you consider in deciding whether to persist in your argument that the inventory should be written down?

LO 5 **Case 6-7** Selection of an Inventory Method

As controller of a widely held public company, you are concerned with making the best decisions for the stockholders. At the end of its first year of operations, you are faced with the choice of method to value inventory. Specific identification is out of the question because the company sells a large quantity of diversified products. You are trying to decide between FIFO and LIFO. Inventory costs have increased 33% over the year. The chief executive officer has instructed you to do whatever it takes in all areas to report the highest income possible.

Required

1. Which method will satisfy the CEO?

2. Which method do you believe is in the best interest of the stockholders? Explain your answer.

3. Write a brief memo to the CEO to convince him that reporting the highest income is not always the best approach for the shareholders.

Research Case

Internet

Case 6-8 Circuit City

Personal computers, cellular phones, digital television, and virtual reality software are just a small part of the extensive merchandise mix found at Circuit City stores. New products from changing technology along with increased competition from other consumer electronic retailers have influenced the earnings, merchandise mix, inventory turnover, and operating activities of Circuit City.

Using Circuit City's Web site (http://www.circuitcity.com), its most recent annual report, or library resources, obtain company financial data and answer the following:

1. For the most recent year available, what amount is reported on the company balance sheet for merchandise inventory? What might be reasons for any changes compared to previous years?

2. Does Circuit City use LIFO, FIFO, or some other inventory costing method?

3. As a supplier, how might you assist Circuit City in reducing its carrying costs of merchandise.

Optional Research. Conduct an interview of someone who works in a consumer electronics or other retail store. Obtain information about the company's merchandise mix and procedures used to determine the size of inventory kept on hand to meet current consumer demand. How do you think these procedures contribute to Circuit City's efficiency in turning over its inventory?

Solution to Key Terms Quiz

4 Merchandise Inventory (p. 264)

2 Work in process (p. 265)

16 Consignment (p. 266)

3 Weighted average cost method (p. 271)

9 LIFO method (p. 272)

14 LIFO conformity rule (p. 275)

8 Replacement cost (p. 276)

5 Lower of cost or market (LCM) rule (p. 279)

13 Retail inventory method (p. 283)

10 Number of days' sales in inventory (p. 284)

7 Raw materials (p. 264)

12 Finished goods (p. 265)

15 Specific identification method (p. 270)

6 FIFO method (p. 272)

18 LIFO liquidation (p. 274)

19 LIFO reserve (p. 275)

17 Inventory profit (p. 276)

11 Gross profit method (p. 281)

20 Inventory turnover ratio (p. 283)

1 Moving average (Appendix 6A) (p. 290)

Cash and Receivables

STUDY LINKS

A Look at Previous Chapters

In the two preceding chapters, we discussed the accounting for inventories, a major asset for many companies. The emphasis in Chapter 5 was on merchandise inventory and the accounting for purchases and sales of inventory. In Chapter 6, we considered how inventory is valued in the accounts, using a costing method such as weighted average, FIFO, or LIFO.

A Look at This Chapter

We now turn our attention to assets, namely cash and receivables, that are increased when a company sells its inventory. We examine the composition of cash and the controls necessary to protect it. The second part of the chapter covers various valuation issues relative to both accounts receivable and notes receivable.

A look at Upcoming Chapters

Chapter 8 focuses attention on the long-term operational assets, such as property, plant, and equipment and intangibles, necessary to run a business. In Chapters 9 and 10 we explore the use of liabilities to finance the purchase of assets.

FOCUS ON FINANCIAL RESULTS

PepsiCo's 1995 annual report contains a letter to shareholders from Wayne Calloway, reflecting on his last full year as chief executive. Calloway states: "Looking at PepsiCo as a whole, I'd say that of all the things we did last year, nothing says more about the strength and vitality of this corporation than our cash flow. We generated $1.6 billion in cash from operations after capital spending, up 12% from 1994." This increase in cash is especially significant because the company has funded major growth—in fact, the fastest sales growth of *Fortune* 500 companies (America's largest industrial corporations) over the life of that listing.

Financial Highlights

PepsiCo, Inc. and Subsidiaries ($ in millions except per share amounts)	December 30, 1995 (a)	December 31, 1994 (a)	Percent Change
Statistics			
Year-end market price per share of PepsiCo capital stock	$ 55 7/8	36 1/4	+ 54
Annual return to shareholders (b)	% 56	(12)	
Cash dividends declared per share	$ 0.78	0.70	+ 11
Summary of Operations			
Net sales	$30,421	28,472	+ 7
Ongoing (c) (d)			
Operating profit	$ 3,507	3,201	+ 10
Income before cumulative effect of accounting changes	$ 1,990	1,767	+ 13
Per Share	$ 2.48	2.20	+ 13
Reported (d) (e)			
Operating profit	$ 2,987	3,201	- 7(g)
Income before cumulative effect of accounting changes	$ 1,606	1,784	- 10(g)
Per Share	$ 2.00	2.22	- 10(g)
Cumulative effect of accounting changes (f)	$ –	(32)	
Per Share	$ –	(0.04)	
Net income	$ 1,606	1,752	- 8(g)
Per Share	$ 2.00	2.18	- 8(g)
Cash Flows			
Provided by operating activities	$ 3,742	3,716	+ 1
Capital spending	$ 2,104	2,253	- 7
Purchases of treasury stock	$ 541	549	- 1
Dividends paid	$ 599	540	+ 11
Acquisitions and investments in unconsolidated affiliates	$ 466	316	+ 47

(a) Fiscal years 1995 and 1994 consisted of 52 and 53 weeks, respectively. The fifty-third week increased 1994 earnings by an estimated $54 ($35 after-tax or $0.04 per share).

(b) Represented stock appreciation plus cash dividends declared divided by the prior year-end market price per share of PepsiCo capital stock.

(c) Excluded the initial, noncash charge of $520 ($384 after-tax or $0.48 per share) in 1995 upon adoption of Statement of Financial Accounting Standards No. 121 (SFAS 121), "Accounting for the Impairment of Long-Lived Assets and for Long-Lived Assets to Be Disposed Of," at the beginning of the fourth quarter (see Note 2) and a $17 after-tax, noncash gain ($0.02 per share) in 1994 arising from a public share offering by BAESA, an unconsolidated franchised bottling affiliate in South America (see Note 16).

(d) Included a net gain in 1995 of $51 ($27 after-tax or $0.03 per share) from sales of restaurants to franchisees in excess of the cost of closing other restaurants.

(e) Included the initial, noncash charge upon adoption of SFAS 121 in 1995 and the 1994 BAESA noncash gain. See (c) above.

(f) Represented the cumulative effect of adopting a preferred method of accounting for pension assets (see Note 13) and Statement of Financial Accounting Standards No. 112, "Employers' Accounting for Postemployment Benefits," (see Note 14).

(g) These comparisons are not meaningful because of the adoption of SFAS 121 in 1995 (see (e) above) and two accounting changes in 1994 (see (f) above), as well as the 1994 BAESA gain (see (e) above).

A Word About The Year's Numbers...

Like a lot of companies, PepsiCo adopted a required new accounting rule in 1995, which caused our "reported" earnings to decline. It didn't involve cash and it didn't keep us from selling record amounts of Pepsi, pizza, tacos, chicken and chips. To understand what actually happened in the business, focus on "ongoing" earnings, which exclude the impact of accounting changes and onetime items.

■ Operating activities in 1995 generated $3.7 billion in cash, of which $2.1 billion went for capital spending.

Generating a lot of cash requires consistent selling. PepsiCo benefits from the strength of its brands, representing a variety of popular beverages and snacks, including Pepsi, Mountain Dew, Fritos, and Lay's. Calloway's letter comments that PepsiCo sells 10 pounds of Lay's potato chips every second! Also, a company like PepsiCo can generate cash through other activities, such as selling assets, earning interest on investments, or borrowing money.

To describe the "strength and vitality" of PepsiCo, Calloway refers to cash flow rather than profits. Why do you think he chose that measure? While studying this chapter, consider who might be especially interested in PepsiCo's ability to generate cash from operations.

SOURCE: *PepsiCo Inc. Annual Report,* 1995.

After studying this chapter, you should be able to

LO 1 Identify and describe the various forms of cash reported on a balance sheet.

LO 2 Understand the accounting for investments of idle cash in financial instruments such as certificates of deposit.

LO 3 Understand various techniques that companies use to control cash.

LO 4 Understand how to account for accounts receivable, including bad debts.

LO 5 Understand how to account for interest-bearing notes receivable.

LO 6 Understand how to account for non-interest-bearing notes receivable.

LO 7 Explain various techniques that companies use to accelerate the inflow of cash from sales.

LO 8 Explain the effects of transactions involving liquid assets on the statement of cash flows.

PepsiCo Inc., like all other businesses, relies on *liquid assets* to function smoothly. *Liquidity* is a relative term. It deals with a company's ability to pay its debts as they fall due. Most obligations must be paid in cash, and therefore cash is considered the most liquid of all assets. Accounts and notes receivable are not as liquid as cash. Their collection does result in an inflow of cash, however. Because cash in its purest form does not earn a return, most businesses invest in various types of securities as a way to use idle cash over the short term. The current asset section of PepsiCo's balance sheet, as shown in Exhibit 7-1, indicates three highly liquid assets: cash and cash equivalents, short-term investments, and accounts and notes receivable. Inventories are not considered as liquid as these three assets because they depend on a sale to be realized.

We begin the chapter by considering the various forms cash can take. We consider the use of various types of financial instruments, such as bank certificates of deposit, as a way to invest idle cash over the short term. We discuss two important cash control features, bank reconciliation and petty cash systems. The chapter concludes with a discussion of the accounting for both accounts receivable and notes receivable.

What Constitutes Cash?

LO 1 Identify and describe the various forms of cash reported on a balance sheet.

Cash takes many different forms. Coin and currency on hand and cash on deposit in the form of checking, savings, and money market accounts are the most obvious forms of cash. Also included in cash are various forms of checks, including undeposited checks from customers, cashier's checks, and certified checks. The proliferation of different types of financial instruments on the market today makes it very difficult to decide on the appropriate classification of these various items. The key to the classification of an amount as cash is that it be *readily available to pay debts*. Technically, a bank has the legal right to demand that a customer notify it before making withdrawals from savings accounts, or time deposits, as they are often called. Because this right is rarely exercised, however, savings accounts are normally classified as cash. In contrast, a certificate of deposit has a specific maturity date and carries a penalty for early withdrawal and is therefore not included in cash.

Cash Equivalents and the Statement of Cash Flows

Note that the first item on PepsiCo's balance sheet is titled Cash and Cash Equivalents. Examples of items normally classified as cash equivalents are commercial paper issued by corporations, Treasury bills issued by the federal government, and money market funds offered by financial institutions. According to current accounting standards, classification as a **cash equivalent** is limited to those investments that are readily convertible to known amounts of cash and that have an original maturity to the investor of

| EXHIBIT 7-1 | PepsiCo's Partial Balance Sheet |

(in millions except per share amount)
PepsiCo, Inc. and Subsidiaries
December 30, 1995 and December 31, 1994

	1995	1994
ASSETS		
Current Assets		
Cash and cash equivalents	$ 382	$ 331
Short-term investments, at cost	1,116	1,157
	1,498	1,488
Accounts and notes receivable, less allowance: $150 in 1995 and $151 in 1994	2,407	2,051
Inventories	1,051	970
Prepaid expenses, taxes and other current assets	590	563
Total Current Assets	5,546	5,072

three months or less. Note that according to this definition, a six-month bank certificate of deposit would *not* be classified as a cash equivalent.

The statement of cash flows that accompanies PepsiCo's balance sheet is shown in Exhibit 7-2. Note the direct tie between this statement and the balance sheet (refer to the current assets section of PepsiCo's balance sheet as shown in Exhibit 7-1). The cash and cash equivalents of $382 million at the end of 1995, as shown at the bottom of the statement of cash flows, is the same amount that appears as the first line on the balance sheet. The reason for this is that the statement of cash flows traces the flow of cash from the beginning balance of cash for the year—$331 million—to the year's ending balance, $382 million. Cash inflow from operating activities, $3,742 million, minus cash outflow from investing activities, $2,450 million, minus cash outflow from financing activities, $1,233 million, minus the effects of currency fluctuations, $8 million, equals a net increase in cash of $51 million. Add $51 million to the beginning cash balance to arrive at $382 million.

Note the fifth category listed under Cash Flows—Investing Activities on the statement of cash flows. The changes in short-term investments represent the net purchases or sales of short-term investments during the year. Any purchases or sales of items classified as short-term investments are considered significant and worthy of reporting on the statement of cash flows. Any purchases or sales of items classified as cash equivalents, however, are not considered significant activities. Instead, they are included with cash on the balance sheet and considered to be its "equivalent."

Investing Idle Cash

The seasonal nature of most businesses leads to the potential for a shortage of cash during certain times of the year and an excess of cash during other times. Companies typically deal with *cash shortages* by borrowing on a short-term basis, either from a bank in the form of notes or from other entities in the form of commercial paper. The maturities of the bank notes or the commercial paper generally range anywhere from 30 days to six months.

To highlight the need to deal with *excess cash* during certain times of the year, consider as an example the seasonal nature of the ice cream business. Ben & Jerry's 1995 annual report admits the obvious by stating, "The Company typically experiences more demand for

LO 2 Understand the accounting for investments of idle cash in financial instruments such as certificates of deposit.

EXHIBIT 7-2   PepsiCo's Statement of Cash Flows

Consolidated Statement of Cash Flows

(in millions)
PepsiCo, Inc. and Subsidiaries
Fiscal years ended December 30, 1995, December 31, 1994 and December 25, 1993

	1995 (52 Weeks)	1994 (53 Weeks)	1993 (52 Weeks)
Cash Flows – Operating Activities			
Income before cumulative effect of accounting changes	$ 1,606	$ 1,784	$ 1,588
Adjustments to reconcile income before cumulative effect of accounting			
changes to net cash provided by operating activities			
Depreciation and amortization	1,740	1,577	1,444
Impairment of long-lived assets	520	–	–
Deferred income taxes	(111)	(67)	83
Other noncash charges and credits, net	398	391	345
Changes in operating working capital, excluding effects of acquisitions			
Accounts and notes receivable	(434)	(112)	(161)
Inventories	(129)	(102)	(90)
Prepaid expenses, taxes and other current assets	76	1	3
Accounts payable	133	30	143
Income taxes payable	(97)	55	(125)
Other current liabilities	40	159	(96)
Net change in operating working capital	(411)	31	(326)
Net Cash Provided by Operating Activities	3,742	3,716	3,134
Cash Flows – Investing Activities			
Acquisitions and investments in unconsolidated affiliates	(466)	(316)	(1,011)
Capital spending	(2,104)	(2,253)	(1,982)
Sales of property, plant and equipment	138	55	73
Sales of restaurants	165	–	7
Short-term investments, by original maturity			
More than three months-purchases	(289)	(219)	(579)
More than three months-maturities	335	650	846
Three months or less, net	18	(10)	(8)
Other, net	(247)	(268)	(117)
Net Cash Used for Investing Activities	(2,450)	(2,361)	(2,771)
Cash Flows – Financing Activities			
Proceeds from issuances of long-term debt	2,030	1,285	711
Payments of long-term debt	(928)	(1,180)	(1,202)
Short-term borrowings, by original maturity			
More than three months-proceeds	2,053	1,304	3,034
More than three months-payments	(2,711)	(1,728)	(2,792)
Three months or less, net	(747)	114	839
Cash dividends paid	(599)	(540)	(462)
Purchases of treasury stock	(541)	(549)	(463)
Proceeds from exercises of stock options	252	97	69
Other, net	(42)	(43)	(37)
Net Cash Used for Financing Activities	(1,233)	(1,240)	(303)
Effect of Exchange Rate Changes on Cash and Cash Equivalents	(8)	(11)	(3)
Net Increase in Cash and Cash Equivalents	51	104	57
Cash and Cash Equivalents – Beginning of Year	331	227	170
Cash and Cash Equivalents – End of Year	$ 382	$ 331	$ 227
Supplemental Cash Flow Information			
Cash Flow Data			
Interest paid	$ 671	591	550
Income taxes paid	$ 790	663	676
Schedule of Noncash Investing and Financing Activities			
Liabilities assumed in connection with acquisitions	$ 66	224	897
Issuance of treasury stock and debt for acquisitions	$ 9	39	365
Book value of net assets exchanged for investments in unconsolidated affiliates	$ 39	–	61

See accompanying Notes to Consolidated Financial Statements.

■ Highlighted figure appears as the first line
of PepsiCo's balance sheet (Exhibit 7-1).

its products during the summer than during the winter." A footnote from the same report highlights the seasonality of the business (amounts are in thousands of dollars):

	FIRST QUARTER	SECOND QUARTER	THIRD QUARTER	FOURTH QUARTER
Net sales	$34,205	$42,936	$45,405	$32,787

Because sales in the third quarter of the year (the months of July, August, and September) were almost 140% of the sales of the fourth quarter of the year, it is natural that Ben & Jerry's had excess cash to invest at the end of the summer selling season. The company uses various financial instruments as a way to invest excess cash during the slower winter months, before using those funds to build up inventory during the busier summer months. According to the annual report, "Cash equivalents represent highly liquid investments with maturities of three months or less at date of purchase."

Accounting for an Investment in a Certificate of Deposit (CD)

Assume that on October 2, 1998, Ben & Jerry's invests $100,000 of excess cash in a 120-day certificate of deposit. The CD matures on January 30, 1999, at which time Ben & Jerry's receives the $100,000 invested and interest at an annual rate of 6%. The entry to record the purchase of the CD is as follows:

```
1998
Oct. 2   Short-Term Investments—CD                    100,000
             Cash                                                  100,000
         To record purchase of 6%, 120-day CD.
```

Assets	=	Liabilities	+	Owners' Equity
+100,000				
−100,000				

Assuming December 31 is the end of Ben & Jerry's fiscal year, an entry is needed on this date to record interest earned during 1998, even though no cash will be received until the CD matures in 1999:

```
1998
Dec. 31  Interest Receivable                            1,500
             Interest Revenue                                       1,500
         To record interest earned: $100,000 × .06 × 90/360
```

Assets	=	Liabilities	+	Owners' Equity
+1,500				**+1,500**

The basic formula to compute interest is as follows:

$$\text{Interest } (I) = \text{Principal } (P) \times \text{Interest Rate } (R) \times \text{Time } (T)$$

Because interest rates are normally stated on an annual basis, time is interpreted to mean the fraction of a year that the investment is outstanding. The amount of interest is based on the principal or amount invested ($100,000), times the rate of interest (6%), times the fraction of a year the CD was outstanding in 1998 (29 days in October + 30 days in November + 31 days in December = 90 days). To simplify calculations, it is easiest to assume 360 days in a year in computing interest. With the availability of computers to do the work, however, most businesses now use 365 days in a year to calculate interest. Throughout this book, we assume 360 days in a year to allow us to focus on concepts rather than detailed calculations. Thus, in our example, the fraction of a year that the CD is outstanding during 1998 is 90/360.

The entry on January 30 to record the receipt of the principal amount of the CD of $100,000 and interest for 120 days is as follows:

```
1999
Jan. 30  Cash                                          102,000
             Short-Term Investments—CD                            100,000
             Interest Receivable                                    1,500
             Interest Revenue                                         500
         To record the maturity of $100,000 CD.
```

Assets	= Liabilities	+ Owners' Equity
+102,000		+500
−100,000		
−1,500		

This combination journal entry results in the removal of both the CD and interest receivable from the records and the recognition of $500 in interest earned during the first 30 days of 1999: $100,000 × .06 × 30/360 = $500.

Classification of Short-Term Investments

Recall our earlier discussion in this chapter about cash equivalents. Accountants classify an item as a cash equivalent if it is convertible to a known amount of cash and has an original maturity to the investor of three months or less. For example, Ben & Jerry's would classify any certificates of deposit with a maturity of three months or less as cash equivalents. Those that mature in more than 90 days are classified as short-term investments. The same distinction holds true for all other liquid financial instruments, such as Treasury bills of the federal government and commercial paper issued by large corporations: if the original maturity is three months or less, the investments are classified as cash equivalents; otherwise, they are classified as short-term investments.

In addition to investments in highly liquid financial instruments, some companies invest in the stocks and bonds of other corporations, as well as bonds issued by various government agencies. Securities issued by corporations as a form of ownership in the business, such as common stock and preferred stock, are called **equity securities.** Because these securities are a form of ownership, they do not have a maturity date. Alternatively, bonds issued by corporations and governmental bodies as a form of borrowing are called **debt securities.** The term of a bond can be relatively short, such as 5 years, or much longer, such as 20 or 30 years.

Assume that Jacobsen Corporation buys 100 shares of General Motors common stock as an investment. Should the shares be classified as a short-term investment and thus included in the current asset section of the balance sheet, or should they be shown among the long-term assets? The answer depends on Jacobsen's *intent* and the *marketability* of the stock. Certainly shares of GM stock are marketable, that is, Jacobsen could sell them if it so desires. Thus, if the company intends to sell the 100 shares of GM stock within one year of the date of the balance sheet or within the operating cycle of the business, whichever is longer, the shares are classified as a short-term investment. Otherwise, they must be classified as long-term.

A company is not guaranteed a specific amount upon selling an investment just because it is "marketable." An investor reviewing his or her portfolio during the fourth quarter of 1987 could attest to that. The October 19, 1987, stock market crash cut the value of the Dow Jones Industrial Average by 508 points. The securities were marketable but at very depressed prices.

Current accounting standards recognize two distinct types of equity securities: trading securities and available-for-sale securities. *Trading securities* are purchased and held principally to sell in the near future and are therefore always classified as current assets. *Available-for-sale securities* are marketable, but the company's intent dictates whether they are classified as current or noncurrent. (The valuation of investments in equity securities as well as investments in debt securities is discussed in Chapter 13.)

One popular form of short-term investment is the certificate of deposit at banks. The federal government insures CDs up to $100,000 per account. Their chief drawback, however, is their lack of liquidity. That is, if the company needs the money right away, it may have to pay a penalty or forfeit interest to get cash. U.S. Treasury bonds, commercial paper (short-term notes issued by large industrial companies), and government and corporate bonds and stocks are more liquid but involve some degree of risk. Treasury bonds are backed by the "full faith and credit of the U.S. government," but they can trade at a discount if interest rates have risen. Commercial paper and corporate bonds also involve risk, and it's conceivable that the company issuing the debt could go out of business.

Control over Cash

In Chapter 5, we discussed the concept of internal control and the critical role it plays for an asset such as cash. Because cash is universally accepted as a medium of exchange, control over it is critical to the smooth functioning of any business, no matter how large or small.

LO 3 Understand various techniques that companies use to control cash.

Cash Management

In addition to the need to guard against theft and other abuses related to the physical custody of cash, management of this asset is also important. Cash management is necessary to ensure that at any point in time, a company has neither too little nor too much cash on hand. The need to have enough cash on hand is obvious: suppliers, employees, taxing agencies, banks, and all other creditors must be paid on time if an entity is to remain in business. It is equally important that a company not maintain cash on hand and on deposit in checking accounts beyond a minimal amount that is necessary to support ongoing operations, since cash is essentially a nonearning asset. Granted, some checking accounts pay a very meager rate of interest. However, the superior return that could be earned by investing idle cash in various forms of marketable securities dictates that companies carefully monitor the amount of cash on hand at all times.

An important tool in the management of cash, the cash flows statement, is discussed in detail in Chapter 14. Cash budgets, which are also critical to the management of cash, are discussed in management accounting and business finance texts. Cash management is just one important aspect of control over cash. Beyond cash management, companies often use two other cash control features: bank reconciliations and petty cash funds. Before we turn to these control devices, we need to review the basic features of a bank statement.

Reading a Bank Statement

Two fundamental principles of internal control discussed in Chapter 5 are worth repeating: all cash receipts should be deposited daily intact, and all cash payments should be made by check. Checking accounts at banks are critical in this regard. These accounts allow a company to carefully monitor and control cash receipts and cash payments. Control is aided further by the monthly **bank statement**. Most banks mail their customers a monthly bank statement for each account. The statement provides a detailed list of all activity for a particular account during the month. An example of a typical bank statement is shown in Exhibit 7-3. Note that the bank statement indicates the activity in one of the cash accounts maintained by Weber Products Inc. at the Mt. Etna State Bank.

Before we look at the various items that appear on a bank statement, it is important to understand the route a check takes after it is written. Assume that Weber writes a check on its account at the Mt. Etna State Bank. Weber mails the check to one of its suppliers, Keese Corp., which deposits the check in its account at the Second City Bank. At this point, Second City presents the check to Mt. Etna for payment, and Mt. Etna reduces the balance in Weber's account accordingly. The canceled check has now "cleared" the banking system. Either the canceled check itself or a copy of it is returned with Weber's next bank statement.

The following types of items appear on Weber's bank statement:

Canceled checks—Weber's checks that cleared the bank during the month of June are listed with the corresponding check number and the date paid. Keep in mind that some of these checks may have been written by Weber in a previous month but were not presented for payment to the bank until June. You also should realize that Weber may have written some checks during June that do not yet appear on the bank statement because they have not been presented for payment. A check

EXHIBIT 7-3	Bank Statement

MT. ETNA STATE BANK
CHICAGO, ILLINOIS
STATEMENT OF ACCOUNT

Weber Products Inc.
502 Dodge St.
Chicago, IL 66606

FOR THE MONTH ENDING   June 30, 1998
ACCOUNT   0371-22-514

DATE	DESCRIPTION	SUBTRACTIONS	ADDITIONS	BALANCE
6-01	Previous balance			3,236.41
6-01	Check 497	723.40		2,513.01
6-02	Check 495	125.60		2,387.41
6-06	Check 491	500.00		1,887.41
6-07	Deposit		1,423.16	3,310.57
6-10	Check 494	185.16		3,125.41
6-13	NSF check	245.72		2,879.69
6-15	Deposit		755.50	3,635.19
6-18	Check 499	623.17		3,012.02
6-20	Check 492	125.00		2,887.02
6-22	Deposit		1,875.62	4,762.64
6-23	Service charge	20.00		4,742.64
6-24	Check 493	875.75		3,866.89
6-24	Check 503	402.10		3,464.79
6-26	Customer note, interest		550.00	4,014.79
6-26	Service fee on note	16.50		3,998.29
6-27	Check 500	1,235.40		2,762.89
6-28	Deposit		947.50	3,710.39
6-30	Check 498	417.25		3,293.14
6-30	Interest earned		15.45	3,308.59
6-30	Statement Totals	5,495.05	5,567.23	

written by a company but not yet presented to the bank for payment is called an outstanding check.

Deposits—In keeping with the internal control principle calling for the deposit of all cash receipts intact, most companies deposit all checks, coin, and currency on a daily basis. For the sake of brevity, we have limited to four the number of deposits that Weber made during the month. Keep in mind that Weber also may have made a deposit on the last day or two of the month and that this deposit may not yet be reflected on the bank statement. This type of deposit is called a deposit in transit.

NSF check—NSF is an abbreviation for *not sufficient funds*. The NSF check listed on the bank statement on June 13 is a customer's check that Weber recorded on its books, deposited, and thus included in its cash account. When Mt. Etna State Bank learned that the check was not good because the customer did not have sufficient funds on hand in its bank account to cover the check, the bank deducted the amount from Weber's account. Weber needs to contact its customer to collect the amount due; ideally, the customer will issue a new check once it has sufficient funds in its account.

Service charge—Banks charge for various services they provide to customers. Among the most common bank service charges are monthly activity fees, fees charged for new checks, for the rental of a lockbox at the bank in which to store valuable company documents, and for the collection of customer notes by the bank.

Customer note and interest—It is often convenient to have customers pay amounts owed to a company directly to that company's bank. The bank simply acts as a collection agency for the company.

Interest earned—Most checking accounts pay interest on the average daily balance in the account. Rates paid on checking accounts are usually significantly less than could be earned on most other forms of investment.

The Bank Reconciliation

A bank reconciliation should be prepared for each individual bank account as soon as the bank statement is received. Ideally, the reconciliation should be performed or, at a minimum, thoroughly reviewed by someone independent of custody, record-keeping, and authorization responsibilities relating to cash. As the name implies, the purpose of a bank reconciliation is to *reconcile* the balance that the bank shows for an account with the balance that appears on the company's books. Differences between the two amounts are investigated, and if necessary, adjustments are made. The following are the steps in preparing a bank reconciliation:

1. Trace deposits listed on the bank statement to the books. Any deposits recorded on the books but not yet shown on the bank statement are deposits in transit. Prepare a list of the deposits in transit.

2. Arrange the canceled checks in numerical order, and trace each of them to the books. Any checks recorded on the books but not yet listed on the bank statement are outstanding. List the outstanding checks.

3. List all items, other than deposits, shown as additions on the bank statement, such as interest paid by the bank for the month and amounts collected by the bank from one of the company's customers. When the bank pays interest or collects an amount owed to a company by one of the company's customers, the bank increases or *credits* its liability to the company on its own books. For this reason, these items are called credit memoranda.

4. List all amounts, other than canceled checks, shown as subtractions on the bank statement, such as any NSF checks and the various service charges mentioned earlier. When a company deposits money in a bank, a liability is created on the books of the bank. Therefore, when the bank reduces the amount of its liability for these various items, it *debits* the liability on its own books. For this reason, these items are called debit memoranda.

5. Identify any errors made by the bank or by the company in recording the various cash transactions.

6. Use the information collected in steps 1 through 5 to prepare a bank reconciliation.

Companies use a number of different *formats* in preparing bank reconciliations. For example, some companies take the balance shown on the bank statement and reconcile this amount to the balance shown on the books. Another approach, which we will illustrate for Weber Products, involves reconciling the bank balance and the book balance to an adjusted balance, rather than one to the other. As we will see, the advantage of this approach is that it yields the correct balance and makes it easy for the company to make any necessary adjustments to its books. A bank reconciliation for Weber Products is shown in Exhibit 7-4. The following are explanations for the various items on the reconciliation:

1. The balance per bank statement of $3,308.59 is taken from the June statement as shown in Exhibit 7-3.

2. Weber's records showed a deposit for $642.30 made on June 30 that is not reflected on the bank statement. The deposit in transit is listed as an addition to the bank statement balance.

3. The accounting records indicate three checks written but not yet reflected on the bank statement. The three outstanding checks are as follows:

EXHIBIT 7-4   Bank Reconciliation

WEBER PRODUCTS
BANK RECONCILIATION
JUNE 30, 1998

Balance per bank statement, June 30			$3,308.59
Add:	Deposit in transit		642.30
Deduct:	Outstanding checks:		
	No. 496	$ 79.89	
	No. 501	213.20	
	No. 502	424.75	(717.84)
Adjusted balance, June 30			$3,233.05
Balance per books, June 30			$2,895.82
Add:	Customer note collected	$500.00	
	Interest on customer note	50.00	
	Interest earned during June	15.45	
	Error in recording check 498	54.00	619.45
Deduct:	NSF check	$245.72	
	Collection fee on note	16.50	
	Service charge for lockbox	20.00	(282.22)
Adjusted balance, June 30			$3,233.05

496	$ 79.89
501	$213.20
502	$424.75

Outstanding checks are the opposite of deposits in transit and therefore are deducted from the bank statement balance.

4. The adjusted balance of $3,233.05 is found by adding the deposit in transit and deducting the outstanding checks from the bank statement balance.

5. The $2,895.82 book balance on June 30 is taken from the company's records as of that date.

6. According to the bank statement, $550 was added to the account on June 26 for the collection of a note with interest. We assume that the repayment of the note itself accounted for $500 of this amount and that the other $50 was for interest. The bank statement notifies Weber that the note with interest has been collected. Therefore, Weber must add $550 to the book balance.

7. An entry on June 30 on the bank statement shows an increase of $15.45 for interest earned on the bank account during June. This amount is added to the book balance.

8. A review of the canceled checks returned with the bank statement detected an error made by Weber. The company records indicated that check 498 was recorded incorrectly as $471.25; the check was actually written for $417.25 and reflected as such on the bank statement. This error, referred to as a *transposition error,* resulted from transposing the 7 and the 1 in recording the check in the books. The error is the difference between the amount of $471.25 recorded and the amount of $417.25 that should have been recorded, or $54.00. Because Weber recorded the cash payment at too large an amount, $54.00 must be added back to the book balance.

9. In addition to canceled checks, three other deductions appear on the bank statement. Each of these must be deducted from the book balance:

a. A customer's NSF check for $245.72 (see June 13 entry on bank statement).

b. A $16.50 fee charged by the bank to collect the customer's note discussed in item 6 (see June 26 entry on bank statement).

c. A service fee of $20.00 charged by the bank for rental of a lockbox (see June 23 entry on bank statement).

10. The additions of $619.45 and deductions of $282.22 resulted in an adjusted cash balance of $3,233.05. Note that this adjusted balance agrees with the adjusted bank statement balance on the bank reconciliation (see item 4). Thus, all differences between the two balances have been explained.

The Bank Reconciliation and the Need for Adjustments to the Records

After it completes the bank reconciliation, Weber must prepare a number of adjustments to its records. In fact, all of the information for these adjustments will be from one section of the bank reconciliation. Do you think that the additions and deductions made to the bank balance or the ones made to the book balance are the basis for the adjustments? It is logical that the additions and deductions to the Cash account *on the books* should be the basis for the adjustments because these are items that Weber was unaware of before receiving the bank statement. Conversely, the additions and deductions to the bank's balance, that is, the deposits in transit and the outstanding checks, are items that Weber has already recorded on its books.

The first journal entry recognizes the bank's collection of customer's note, with interest:

June 30	Cash	550.00	
	Notes Receivable		500.00
	Interest Revenue		50.00
	To record the collection of note and interest.		

Assets	=	**Liabilities**	+	**Owners' Equity**
+550				+50
−500				

The next entry is needed to record interest earned and paid by the bank on the average daily balance maintained in the checking account during June:

June 30	Cash	15.45	
	Interest Revenue		15.45
	To record interest earned on checking account.		

Assets	=	**Liabilities**	+	**Owners' Equity**
+15.45				+15.45

Recall the error in recording check 498: it was actually written for $417.25, the amount paid by the bank. Weber recorded the cash disbursement on its books as $471.25, however. If we assume that the purpose of the cash payment was to buy supplies, the Cash account is understated and the Supplies account is overstated by the amount of the error. The entry needed to correct both accounts is as follows:

June 30	Cash	54.00	
	Supplies		54.00
	To correct for error in recording purchase of supplies.		

Assets	=	**Liabilities**	+	**Owners' Equity**
+54				
−54				

The customer's NSF check is handled by reducing the Cash account and reinstating the Account Receivable:

June 30	Accounts Receivable	245.72	
	Cash		245.72
	To record customer's NSF check.		

$$\begin{array}{ccc} \textbf{Assets} & \textbf{= Liabilities} & \textbf{+ Owners' Equity} \\ +\textbf{245.72} \\ -\textbf{245.72} \end{array}$$

Finally, two entries are needed to recognize the expenses incurred in connection with the fees charged by the bank for collecting the customer's note and for renting the lockbox:

June 30	Collection Fee Expense	16.50	
	Cash		16.50
	To record collection fee on note.		

$$\begin{array}{ccc} \textbf{Assets} & \textbf{= Liabilities} & \textbf{+ Owners' Equity} \\ -\textbf{16.50} & & -\textbf{16.50} \end{array}$$

June 30	Rent Expense—Lockbox	20.00	
	Cash		20.00
	To record rental charge on lockbox.		

$$\begin{array}{ccc} \textbf{Assets} & \textbf{= Liabilities} & \textbf{+ Owners' Equity} \\ -\textbf{20} & & -\textbf{20} \end{array}$$

Note that we made a separate entry to record each of the increases and decreases in the Cash account. Some companies combine all of the increases in Cash in a single journal entry and all of the decreases in a second entry. Finally, we should note that supervisory review and approval should take place before any of these entries are posted.

Establishing a Petty Cash Fund

Recall one of the fundamental rules in controlling cash: all disbursements should be made by check. Most businesses make an exception to this rule in the case of minor expenditures, for which they use a **petty cash fund.** This fund consists of coin and currency kept on hand to make minor disbursements. The necessary steps in setting up and maintaining a petty cash fund follow:

1. A check is written for a lump-sum amount, such as $100 or $500. The check is cashed, and the coin and currency are entrusted to a petty cash custodian.
2. A journal entry is made to record the establishment of the fund.
3. Upon presentation of the necessary documentation, employees receive minor disbursements from the fund. In essence, cash is traded from the fund in exchange for a receipt.
4. Periodically, the fund is replenished by writing and cashing a check in the amount necessary to bring the fund back to its original balance.
5. At the time the fund is replenished, an adjustment is made both to record its replenishment and to recognize the various expenses incurred.

The use of this fund is normally warranted on the basis of cost versus benefits. That is, the benefits in time saved in making minor disbursements from cash are thought to outweigh the cost associated with the risk of loss from decreased control over cash disbursements. The fund also serves a practical purpose for certain expenditures such as taxi fares and messengers which often must be paid in cash.

An Example of a Petty Cash Fund

Assume that on March 1, the treasurer of Keese Corporation cashes a check for $200 and remits the cash to the newly appointed petty cash custodian. On this date, the following journal entry is made:

Mar. 1	Petty Cash Fund	200.00	
	Cash		200.00
	To record establishment of petty cash fund.		

$$\begin{array}{ccc} \textbf{Assets} & \textbf{= Liabilities} & \textbf{+ Owners' Equity} \\ +\textbf{200} \\ -\textbf{200} \end{array}$$

ACCOUNTING FOR YOUR DECISIONS

You Are the Sorority Treasurer

You are in charge of the sorority's checking account and bank reconciliation. Each month, you are responsible for purchasing supplies, paying for parties, and paying rent and utilities on the sorority house. You also have a card for an automatic teller machine, which you use to draw out cash to pay for miscellaneous activities. Recently, the president of the sorority asked to see you because the sorority's expenses were exceeding revenues by a significant margin. After examining the checkbook and bank reconciliation, she wanted to know why you were spending roughly $200 per month in cash from an ATM. You told her that since there was no cancelled check for these expenditures, you had no record and couldn't answer her question. How could you have avoided this situation?

ANS: First, an important principle of internal control is that the person writing checks on an account should not be the same person who performs the bank reconciliation. Second, an ATM card confers special responsibilities on the user. Because there is no cancelled check, the person receiving cash from an ATM must document all expenses, obtaining receipts whenever possible or documenting the expenditures in a diary.

During March the custodian disburses coin and currency to various individuals who present receipts to the custodian for the following:

U.S. Post Office	$ 55.00
Overnight Delivery Service	69.50
Office Supply Express	45.30
Total expenditures	$169.80

At the end of March, the custodian counts the coin and currency on hand and determines the balance to be $26.50. Next, the treasurer writes and cashes a check in the amount of $173.50, which is the amount needed to return the balance in the account to $200.00. The treasurer remits the cash to the custodian. The following entry is made:

Mar. 31	Postage Expense	55.00	
	Delivery Expense	69.50	
	Office Expense	45.30	
	Cash Over and Short	3.70	
	Cash		173.50
	To record replenishment of petty cash fund.		

Assets	=	**Liabilities**	+	**Owners' Equity**
−173.50				−55.00
				−69.50
				−45.30
				−3.70

The Cash Over and Short account is necessary because the total expenditures for the month were only $169.80 but a check in the amount of $173.50 was necessary to restore the fund balance to $200.00. The discrepancy of $3.70 could be due to any number of factors, such as an error in making change. Any large discrepancies would be investigated, particularly if they recur. Assuming that the discrepancy is immaterial, a debit balance in the Cash Over and Short account is normally closed to Miscellaneous Expense. A credit balance in the account is closed to Other Income.

Accounts Receivable

To appreciate the significance of credit sales for many businesses, consider the case of Sears, Roebuck & Co. Sears operates retail outlets throughout the United States and around the world. The balance sheet of Sears reported total assets of approximately $33 billion at the end of 1995. Of this total amount, retail customer receivables accounted for over $20 billion, or 60%, of total assets. Sears or any other company would rather not sell on credit but would prefer to make all sales for cash. Selling on credit causes two

LO 4 Understand how to account for accounts receivable, including bad debts.

Delivering products such as Pepsi's new Frappuchino drink (made with Starbucks' coffee) to stores creates large receivables for PepsiCo. Indeed, receivables are a large and important part of the balance sheets of companies everywhere.

problems: it slows down the inflow of cash to the company, and it raises the possibility that the customer may not pay its bill on time or possibly ever. To remain competitive, however, Sears and most other businesses must sell their products and services on credit. Large retailers such as Sears often extend credit through the use of their own credit cards.

The types of receivables reported on a corporate balance sheet depend to some extent on a company's business. The "retail customer receivables" on the balance sheet of Sears represent the interest-bearing accounts it carries with its retail customers. Alternatively, consider the case of PepsiCo. The beverage and snack-food businesses usually sell their products to distributors. The asset resulting from a sale by Pepsi on credit, with an oral promise that the customer will pay within a specified period of time, is called an account receivable. This type of account does not bear interest and often gives the customer a discount for early payment. For example, the terms of sale might be 2/10, net 30, which means the customer can deduct 2% from the amount due if the bill is paid within 10 days of the date of sale; otherwise, payment in full is required within 30 days. In some instances, PepsiCo requires from a customer at the time of sale a written promise in the form of a promissory note. The asset resulting from a sale on credit, with a written promise that the customer will pay within a specified period of time, is called a note receivable. This type of account usually bears interest.

The Use of a Subsidiary Ledger

As mentioned earlier, PepsiCo sells its beverages and snack foods through distributors. Assume that it sells $25,000 of Fritos to ABC Distributors on an open account. The journal entry to record the sale would be as follows:

Accounts Receivable	25,000	
Sales Revenue		25,000
To record sale on open account.		

Assets	=	Liabilities	+	Owners' Equity
+25,000				+25,000

It is important for control purposes that PepsiCo keeps a record of *whom* the sale was to and includes this amount on a periodic statement or *bill* sent to the customer. What if a company has a hundred or a thousand different customers? Some mechanism is needed to track the balance owed by each of these customers. The mechanism companies use is called a subsidiary ledger.

A subsidiary ledger contains the necessary detail on each of a number of items that collectively make up a single general ledger account, called the control account. In theory, any one of the accounts in the general ledger could be supported by a subsidiary ledger. In addition to Accounts Receivable, two other common accounts supported by subsidiary ledgers are Plant and Equipment and Accounts Payable. An accounts payable subsidiary ledger contains a separate account for each of the suppliers or vendors from which a company purchases inventory. A plant and equipment subsidiary ledger consists of individual accounts, along with their balances, for each of the various long-term tangible assets the company owns.

It is important to understand that a subsidiary ledger does *not* take the place of the control account in the general ledger. Instead, at any point in time, the balances of the accounts that make up the subsidiary ledger should total to the single balance in the related control account. In the remainder of this chapter we will illustrate the use of only the control account. Whenever a specific customer's account is increased or decreased we will, however, note the name of the customer next to the control account in the journal entry.

The Valuation of Accounts Receivable

The following presentation of receivables is taken from PepsiCo's 1995 annual report:

	1995	1994
Accounts and notes receivable, less allowance: $150 in 1995 and $151 in 1994	$2,407	$2,051

You are the credit manager of USA Department Store, which offers its customers USA Department Store credit cards. An existing customer, Jane Doe, has requested a credit line increase. In processing her request, you must determine the current balance of her account. How would you use the accounting system to find her current balance? What other factors might you consider in granting Jane's request?

ANS: You would find Jane's current balance by looking for her account in the accounts receivable subsidiary ledger. The subsidiary ledger should have a current balance because daily postings are made to each customer's account. Other factors to consider in processing Jane's request can include researching her payment history to see if she paid on time not only for this credit card but for all debts, checking to see if her income is sufficient to cover her existing debt and the new credit line increase, and verifying employment to ensure income stability.

As you read this excerpt from the balance sheets, keep three points in mind. First, all amounts are stated in millions of dollars. Second, these are the balances at the *end* of each of the two years. Finally, note that PepsiCo combines its accounts receivable and notes receivable on the balance sheet. Apparently, the company sells its products to some customers on an open account while other customers are required to sign a note to repay the amount of products purchased on credit.

PepsiCo does not sell its products to distributors under the assumption that any particular customer will *not* pay its bill. In fact, the credit department of a business is responsible for performing a credit check on all potential customers before they are granted credit. Management of PepsiCo is not naive enough, however, to believe that all customers will be able to pay their accounts when due. This would be the case only if (1) all customers are completely trustworthy and (2) customers never experience unforeseen financial difficulties that make it impossible to pay on time.

The reduction in PepsiCo's receivables for an allowance is the way in which most companies deal with bad debts in their accounting records. Bad debts are unpaid customer accounts that a company gives up trying to collect. Some companies describe the allowance more fully as the allowance for doubtful accounts, and others call it the allowance for uncollectible accounts. Using the end of 1995 as an example, PepsiCo believes that the *net recoverable amount* of its receivables is $2,407 million, even though the *gross* amount of receivables is $150 million higher than this amount. The company has reduced the gross receivables for an amount that it believes is necessary to reflect the asset on the books at the *net recoverable amount* or *net realizable value*. We now take a closer look at how a company accounts for bad debts.

Two Methods to Account for Bad Debts

Assume that Roberts Corp. makes a $500 sale to Dexter Inc. on November 10, 1998, with credit terms of 2/10, net 60. Roberts makes the following entry on its books on this date:

```
1998
Nov. 10   Accounts Receivable—Dexter              500
               Sales Revenue                              500
          To record sale on credit, terms of 2/10, net 60.
```

Assets = Liabilities + Owners' Equity
+500   +500

Assume further that Dexter not only misses taking advantage of the discount for early payment but also is unable to pay within 60 days. After pursuing the account for four months into 1999, the credit department of Roberts informs the accounting department that it has given up on collecting the $500 from Dexter and advises that the account should be written off. To do so, the accounting department makes the following entry:

1999
May 1   Bad Debts Expense   500
              Accounts Receivable—Dexter   500
         To write off Dexter account.

                    Assets = Liabilities + Owners' Equity
                    −500   **−500**

This approach to accounting for bad debts is called the direct write-off method. Do you see any problems with its use? What about Roberts's balance sheet at the end of 1998? By ignoring the possibility that not all of its outstanding accounts receivable will be collected, Roberts is overstating the value of this asset at December 31, 1998. Also, what about the income statement for 1998? By ignoring the possibility of bad debts on sales made during 1998, Roberts has violated the *matching principle*. This principle requires that all costs associated with making sales in a period should be matched with the sales of that period. Roberts has overstated net income for 1998 by ignoring bad debts as an expense. The problem is one of *timing:* even though any one particular account may not prove to be uncollectible until a later period (e.g., the Dexter account), the cost associated with making sales on credit (bad debts) should be recognized in the period of sale.

Accountants use the allowance method to overcome the deficiencies of the direct write-off method. They *estimate* the amount of bad debts before these debts actually occur. For example, assume that Roberts's total sales during 1998 amount to $600,000 and that at the end of the year the outstanding accounts receivable total $250,000. Also assume that Roberts estimates that on the basis of past experience, 1% of the sales of the period, or $6,000, eventually will prove to be uncollectible. Under the allowance method, Roberts makes the following adjusting entry at the end of 1998:

1998
Dec. 31   Bad Debts Expense   6,000
              Allowance for Doubtful Accounts   6,000
         To record estimated bad debts for the year.

                    Assets = Liabilities + Owners' Equity
                    −6,000   **−6,000**

The debit recognizes the cost associated with the reduction in value of the asset Accounts Receivable. The cost is charged to the income statement, in the form of Bad Debts Expense. A contra-asset account is used to reduce the asset to its net realizable value. This is accomplished by crediting an allowance account, Allowance for Doubtful Accounts. Roberts presents accounts receivable as follows on its December 31, 1998, balance sheet:

Accounts receivable	$250,000
Less: Allowance for doubtful accounts	(6,000)
Net accounts receivable	$244,000

An alternative would be for Roberts to follow the form used by PepsiCo described earlier in the chapter:

Accounts receivable, less allowance for doubtful accounts of $6,000:	$244,000

Write-Offs of Uncollectible Accounts with the Allowance Method

Like the direct write-off method, the allowance method reduces Accounts Receivable to write off a specific customer's account. If the account receivable no longer exists, there is no need for the related allowance account and thus this account is reduced as well. For example, assume, as we did earlier, that Dexter's $500 account is written off on May 1, 1999. Under the allowance method, the following entry is recorded:

1999

May 1   Allowance for Doubtful Accounts   500
               Accounts Receivable—Dexter   500
           To record the write-off of Dexter account.

Assets = Liabilities + Owners' Equity
+**500**
−**500**

To summarize, whether the direct write-off method or the allowance method is used, the entry to write off a specific customer's account reduces Accounts Receivable. It is the debit that differs between the two methods: under the direct write-off method, an *expense* is increased, whereas under the allowance method, the *allowance* account is reduced.

Two Approaches to the Allowance Method of Accounting for Bad Debts

Because the allowance method results in a better *matching,* accounting standards require the use of this method rather than the direct write-off method, unless bad debts are immaterial in amount. Accountants use one of two different variations of the allowance method to estimate bad debts. One approach emphasizes matching bad debts expense with revenue on the income statement and bases bad debts on a percentage of the sales of the period. This was the method we illustrated earlier for Roberts Corp. The other approach emphasizes the net realizable amount (value) of accounts receivable on the balance sheet and bases bad debts on a percentage of the accounts receivable balance at the end of the period.

Percentage of Net Credit Sales Approach   If a company has been in business for enough years, it may be able to use the past relationship between bad debts and *net* credit sales to predict bad debt amounts. *Net* means that credit sales have been adjusted for sales discounts and returns and allowances. Assume that the accounting records for Bosco Corp. reveal the following:

YEAR	NET CREDIT SALES	BAD DEBTS
1993	$1,250,000	$ 26,400
1994	1,340,000	29,350
1995	1,200,000	23,100
1996	1,650,000	32,150
1997	2,120,000	42,700
	$7,560,000	$153,700

Although the exact percentage varied slightly over the five-year period, the average percentage of bad debts to net credit sales is very close to 2% ($153,700/$7,560,000 = .02033). Bosco needs to determine whether this estimate is realistic for the current period. For example, are current economic conditions considerably different from those in the prior years? Has the company made sales to any new customers with significantly different credit terms? If the answers to these types of questions are yes, Bosco should consider adjusting the 2% experience rate to estimate future bad debts. Otherwise, it should proceed with this estimate. Assuming that it uses the 2% rate and its net credit sales during 1998 are $2,340,000, Bosco makes the following entry:

1998

Dec. 31   Bad Debts Expense   46,800
               Allowance for Doubtful Accounts   46,800
           To record estimated bad debts: .02 × $2,340,000.

Assets = Liabilities + Owners' Equity
−**46,800**   −**46,800**

Thus, Bosco matches bad debt expense of $46,800 with sales revenue of $2,340,000.

[Handwritten margin notes, left side:]
Subtract
Bad debt from
(as an expense)
Expenses and
from ARS

Make sure to get
allowance back
at correct
ballance

① Difference
between %
of NCS and
% of AR

Assume you own a retail business that offers credit sales. To estimate bad debts, your business uses the percentage of net credit sales approach. For the new fiscal year, how would you decide what percentage to use to estimate your bad debts?

ANS: To determine the bad debt percentage for the new fiscal year, you can (1) review historical records to see what the actual percentages of bad debts were, (2) check to see if credit policies have substantially changed, (3) consider current and future economic conditions, and (4) consult with your managers and salespeople to see if they are aware of any changes in customers' paying habits.

Percentage of Accounts Receivable Approach

Some companies believe they can more accurately estimate bad debts by relating them to the balance in the Accounts Receivable account at the end of the period rather than to the sales of the period. The objective with both approaches is the same, however, namely to use past experience with bad debts to predict future amounts. Assume that the records for Cougar Corp. reveal the following:

YEAR	BALANCE IN ACCOUNTS RECEIVABLE DECEMBER 31	BAD DEBTS
1993	$ 650,000	$ 5,250
1994	785,000	6,230
1995	854,000	6,950
1996	824,000	6,450
1997	925,000	7,450
	$4,038,000	$32,330

The ratio of bad debts to the ending balance in Accounts Receivable over the past five years is $32,330/$4,038,000, or approximately .008 (.8%). Assuming balances in Accounts Receivable and the Allowance for Doubtful Accounts on December 31, 1998, of $865,000 (debit) and $2,100, (credit), respectively, Cougar records the following entry:

```
1998
Dec. 31   Bad Debts Expense                              4,820
              Allowance for Doubtful Accounts                      4,820
          To record estimated bad debts:
          Credit balance required in allowance
             account after adjustment
             ($865,000 × 0.8%)                                     $6,920
          Less: Credit balance in allowance
             account before adjustment                              2,100
          Amount for bad debt expense entry                        $4,820
```

Assets = Liabilities + Owners' Equity
−4,820   −4,820

[Handwritten margin notes, left-center:]
Figure out
what balance
you're starting
with; what you
need to end
up with; difference
is the
bad
debt
expense

[Handwritten margin notes, bottom left:]
(3000)
20000
─────
17000
(20000) = Expense
─────
3000 = Ending
       balance

Note the one major difference between this approach and the percentage of sales approach: *under the percentage of net credit sales approach, the balance in the allowance account is ignored, and the bad debts expense is simply a percentage of the sales of the period; under the percentage of accounts receivable approach, however, the balance in the allowance account must be considered.* A T account for Allowance for Doubtful Accounts with the balance before and after adjustment appears as follows:

ALLOWANCE FOR DOUBTFUL ACCOUNTS

2,100	Bal. before adjustment
4,820	Adjusting entry
6,920	Bal. after adjustment

| EXHIBIT 7-5 | Aging Schedule |

		NUMBER OF DAYS PAST DUE			
CUSTOMER	CURRENT	1–30	31–60	61–90	OVER 90
L. Ash	$ 4,400				
B. Budd	3,200				
C. Cox		$ 6,500			
E. Fudd					$6,300
G. Hoff			$ 900		
A. Matt	5,500				
......					
......					
......					
T. West				$ 3,100	
M. Young				4,200	
Totals*	$85,600	$31,200	$24,500	$18,000	$9,200

*Only a few of the customer accounts are illustrated; thus the column totals are higher than the amounts for the accounts illustrated.

[Handwritten margin note: Allowance = % of ending ARS]

[Handwritten margin note: If beginning allowance = ending allowance, expenses are amt of bad debt.]

In other words, making an adjustment for $4,820 results in a balance in the account of $6,920, which is .8% of the Accounts Receivable balance of $865,000. The net realizable value of Accounts Receivable is determined as follows:

Accounts receivable	$865,000
Less: Allowance for doubtful accounts	(6,920)
Net realizable value	$858,080

Aging of Accounts Receivable Some companies use a variation of the percentage of accounts receivable approach to estimate bad debts. This variation is actually a refinement of the approach because it considers the length of time that the receivables have been outstanding. It stands to reason that the older an account receivable is, the less likely that it is to be collected. An **aging schedule** categorizes the various accounts by length of time outstanding. An example of an aging schedule is shown in Exhibit 7-5. We assume that the company's policy is to allow 30 days for payment of an outstanding account. After that time, the account is past due. An alphabetical list of customers appears in the first column, with the balance in each account shown in the appropriate column to the right. The dotted lines after A. Matt's account indicate that many more accounts appear in the records; we have included just a few to show the format of the schedule. The totals on the aging schedule are used as the basis for estimating bad debts, as shown in Exhibit 7-6.

FROM CONCEPT TO PRACTICE 7.1
READING BEN & JERRY'S FINANCIAL STATEMENTS Does Ben & Jerry's disclose in its annual report which method it uses to estimate bad debts? In what line item on the income statement would you expect bad debts expense to be included?

| EXHIBIT 7-6 | Use of an Aging Schedule to Estimate Bad Debts |

CATEGORY	AMOUNT	ESTIMATED PERCENT UNCOLLECTIBLE	ESTIMATED AMOUNT UNCOLLECTIBLE
Current	$ 85,600	1%	$ 856
Past due:			
1–30 days	31,200	4%	1,248
31–60 days	24,500	10%	2,450
61–90 days	18,000	30%	5,400
Over 90 days	9,200	50%	4,600
Totals	$168,500		$14,554

Note that the estimated percentage of uncollectibles increases as the period of time the accounts have been outstanding lengthens. If we assume that the Allowance for Doubtful Accounts has a credit balance of $1,230 before adjustment, the adjusting entry is as follows:

1998			
Dec. 31	Bad Debts Expense	13,324	
	Allowance for Doubtful Accounts		13,324
	To record estimated bad debts:		
	Credit balance required in allowance		
	account after adjustment		$14,554
	Less: Credit balance in allowance		
	account before adjustment		1,230
	Amount for bad debt expense entry		$13,324

Assets	=	Liabilities	+	Owners' Equity
−13,324				−13,324

The net realizable value of accounts receivable would be determined as follows:

Accounts receivable	$168,500
Less: Allowance for doubtful accounts	14,554
Net realizable value	$153,946

Analyzing the Accounts Receivable Rate of Collection

Managers, investors, and creditors are keenly interested in how well a company manages its accounts receivable. One simple measure is to compare a company's sales to its accounts receivable. The result is the accounts receivable turnover ratio:

$$\text{Accounts Receivable Turnover} = \frac{\text{Net Credit Sales}}{\text{Average Accounts Receivable}}$$

Typically, the faster the turnover, the better. For example, if a company has sales of $10 million and an average accounts receivable of $1 million, it turns over its accounts receivable 10 times per year. If we assume 360 days in a year, that is once every 36 days. An observer would compare that figure with historical figures to see if the company is experiencing slower or faster collections. A comparison could also be made to other companies in the same industry. If receivables are turning over too slowly, that could mean that the company's credit department is not operating effectively and the company therefore is missing opportunities with the cash that isn't available. On the other hand, a turnover rate that is too fast might mean that the company's credit policies are too stringent and that sales are being lost as a result.

Notes Receivable

A **promissory note** is a written promise to repay a definite sum of money on demand or at a fixed or determinable date in the future. Promissory notes normally require the payment of interest for the use of someone else's money. The party that agrees to repay money is the **maker** of the note, and the party that receives money in the future is the **payee.** A company that holds a promissory note received from another company has an asset, called a **note receivable;** the company that makes or gives a promissory note to another company has a liability, a **note payable.** Over the life of the note, the maker incurs interest expense on its note payable, and the payee earns interest revenue on its note receivable. The following summarizes this relationship:

PARTY	RECOGNIZES ON BALANCE SHEET	RECOGNIZES ON INCOME STATEMENT
Maker	Note payable	Interest expense
Payee	Note receivable	Interest revenue

FROM CONCEPT TO PRACTICE 7.2

READING PEPSICO'S FINANCIAL STATEMENTS
Refer to p. 326 for the presentation of PepsiCo's accounts and notes receivable on its 1995 and 1994 year-end balance sheets. What was the amount of increase or decrease in the allowance account? What does the change in the account mean?

FROM CONCEPT TO PRACTICE 7.3

READING BEN & JERRY'S FINANCIAL STATEMENTS
Compute Ben & Jerry's accounts receivable turnover for 1995. What is the average length of time it takes to collect a receivable? Does this seem reasonable for the company's type of business?

Promissory notes are used for a variety of purposes. Banks normally require a company to sign a promissory note to borrow money. They are often used in the sale of consumer durables with relatively high purchase prices, such as appliances and automobiles. At times a promissory note is issued to replace an existing overdue account receivable.

Important Terms Connected with Promissory Notes

It is important to understand the following terms when dealing with promissory notes:

Principal The amount of cash received, or the fair value of the products or services received, by the maker when a promissory note is issued.

Maturity date The date that the promissory note is due.

Term The length of time a note is outstanding; that is, the period of time between the date it is issued and the date it matures.

Maturity value The amount of cash the maker is to pay the payee on the maturity date of the note.

Interest The difference between the principal amount of the note and its maturity value.

In some cases, the interest rate on a promissory note is stated explicitly on the face of the note. Even though the note's term may be less than a year, the interest rate is stated on an annual basis. In other cases, an interest rate does not appear on the face of the note. As we will see, however, there is *implicit* interest, because more is to be repaid at maturity than is owed at the time the note is signed. Notes in which an interest rate is explicitly stated are called **interest-bearing notes.** Notes in which interest is implicit in the agreement are called **non-interest-bearing notes.** We now look at the accounting for each of these types of notes.

Interest-Bearing Notes

Assume that on December 13, 1998, HighTec sells a computer to Baker Corp. at an invoice price of $15,000. Because Baker is short of cash, it gives HighTec a 90-day, 12% promissory note. The total amount of interest due on the maturity date is determined as follows:

LO 5 Understand how to account for interest-bearing notes receivable.

$$\$15,000 \times .12 \times 90/360 = \underline{\$450}$$

The entry to record receipt of the note by HighTec is as follows:

```
1998
Dec. 13   Notes Receivable                              15,000
              Sales Revenue                                       15,000
          To record sale of computer in exchange for promissory note.
```

Assets	=	Liabilities	+	Owners' Equity
+15,000				+15,000

If we assume that December 31 is the end of HighTec's accounting year, an adjustment is needed to recognize interest earned but not yet received. It is required when a company uses the accrual basis of accounting. The question is: how many days of interest have been earned during December? *It is normal practice to count the day a note matures, but not the day it is signed, in computing interest.* Thus, in our example, interest would be earned for 18 days (December 14 to December 31) during 1998 and for 72 days in 1999:

MONTH	NUMBER OF DAYS OUTSTANDING
December 1998	18 days
January 1999	31 days
February 1999	28 days
March 1999	13 days (matures on March 13, 1999)
Total days	90 days

An adjusting entry is made on December 31 to record interest earned during 1998:

1998:
Dec. 31   Interest Receivable   90
                   Interest Revenue   90
                   To record interest earned: $15,000 \times .12 \times 18/360.

Assets	**= Liabilities**	**+ Owners' Equity**
+90		+90

On March 13, 1999, HighTec collects the principal amount of the note and interest from Baker and records this entry:

1999
Mar. 13   Cash   15,450
                   Notes Receivable   15,000
                   Interest Revenue   360
                   Interest Receivable   90
                   To record collection of promissory note.

Assets	**= Liabilities**	**+ Owners' Equity**
+15,450		+360
−15,000		
−90		

This entry accomplishes a number of purposes. First, it removes the amount of $15,000 originally recorded in the Notes Receivable account. Second, it increases Interest Revenue for the interest earned during the 72 days in 1999 that the note was outstanding. The calculation of interest earned during 1999 is as follows:

$$\$15,000 \times .12 \times 72/360 \times = \underline{\$360}$$

Third, the entry decreases Interest Receivable by $90 to remove this account from the records now that the note has been collected. Finally, it increases Cash by $15,450, which represents the principal amount of the note, $15,000, plus interest of $450 for 90 days.

Non-Interest-Bearing Notes

LO 6 Understand how to account for non-interest-bearing notes receivable.

Assume that you walk in to an automobile dealership on November 1, 1998, and find the car of your dreams. After extensive negotiation, the dealer agrees to sell you the car outright for $10,000. Because you are short of cash, you give the dealer $1,000 as a down payment and sign a promissory note to pay $9,900 in six months. Even though interest is never mentioned, it is *implicitly* built into the transaction. You owe the car dealer $10,000 − $1,000, or $9,000, today, and you have agreed to pay $9,900 in six months. The $900 excess of the amount to be paid in six months over the amount owed today is *interest*. The note is called a non-interest-bearing note because no interest is *explicitly* stated. Anytime it is necessary to pay more in the future than is owed today, interest is involved. The *effective interest rate* can be found as follows:

1. The amount of interest implicit in the note: $9,900 − $9,000, or $900.
2. The length of the note: 6 months.
3. The number of 6-month periods in a year: $12/6 = 2$.
4. The amount of interest that would apply to a full year: 900×2, or $1,800.
5. The effective annual interest rate is $1,800/$9,000, or $\underline{\underline{20}}$%.

In essence, the car dealer has you sign a promissory note in the amount of $9,900 but gave you credit equivalent to only $9,000 in cash, that is, the difference between the value of the car today, $10,000, and the amount of your down payment, $1,000. The dealer deducted interest of $900 in advance and gave you the equivalent of a $9,000 loan. Another name for this non-interest-bearing note is a **discounted note.** On the date the note is signed, the car dealer makes this entry:

1998
Nov. 1   Cash   1,000
         Notes Receivable   9,900
            Discount on Notes Receivable   900
            Sales Revenue   10,000
         To record sale in exchange for note.

            Assets = Liabilities + Owners' Equity
            +1,000   +10,000
            +9,900
            −900

The debit to Cash represents the down payment. The debit to Notes Receivable is for $9,900, the maturity amount of the promissory note. The credit to Sales Revenue represents the amount the car could be sold for today. Discount on Notes Receivable is a contra account to the Notes Receivable account and represents the interest that the dealer will earn over the next six months. As interest is earned, this account will be reduced and Interest Revenue will be recognized. For example, at the end of the year, the dealer will make an adjustment to recognize that two months' interest of the total of six months' interest has been earned:

1998
Dec. 31 Discount on Notes Receivable   300
            Interest Revenue   300
         To record interest earned for two months: $900 × 2/6.

            Assets = Liabilities + Owners' Equity
            +300   +300

The current assets section of the dealer's balance sheet at December 31, 1998, includes the following:

         Notes receivable $9,900
         Less: Discount on notes receivable   (600) $9,300

The entry on April 30 to record collection of the maturity amount of the note and to recognize the remaining interest earned is as follows:

1999
Apr. 30 Cash   9,900
         Discount on Notes Receivable   600
            Notes Receivable   9,900
            Interest Revenue   600
         To record collection of note.

            Assets = Liabilities + Owners' Equity
            +9,900   +600
            +600
            −9,900

Accelerating the Inflow of Cash from Sales

Earlier in the chapter we pointed out why cash sales are preferable to credit sales: credit sales slow down the inflow of cash to the company and create the potential for bad debts. To remain competitive, most businesses find it necessary to grant credit to customers. That is, if one company won't grant credit to a customer, the customer may find another company willing to do so. Companies have found it possible, however, to circumvent the problems inherent in credit sales. In Chapter 5 we discussed the use of sales discounts to motivate timely repayment of accounts receivable. We now consider other approaches that companies use to speed up the flow of cash from sales.

LO 7 Explain various techniques that companies use to accelerate the inflow of cash from sales.

Credit Card Sales

Most retail establishments, as well as many service businesses, accept one or more major credit cards. Among the most common cards are MasterCard, VISA, American Express, Carte Blanche, Discover Card, and Diners Club. Most merchants believe that they must honor at least one or more of these credit cards to remain competitive. In return for a fee, the merchant passes the responsibility for collection on to the credit card company. Thus, the credit card issuer assumes the risk of nonpayment. The basic relationships among the three parties—the customer, the merchant, and the credit card company—are illustrated in Exhibit 7-7. Assume that Joe Smith entertains clients at Club Cafe and charges $100 in meals to his Diners Club credit card. When Joe is presented with his bill at the end of the evening he is asked to sign a multiple-copy credit card draft or invoice. Joe keeps one copy of the draft and leaves the other two copies at Club Cafe. The restaurant keeps one copy as the basis for recording its sales for the day and sends the other copy to Diners Club for payment. Diners Club uses the copy of the draft it gets for two purposes: to reimburse Club Cafe $95 (keeping $5 or 5% of the original sale as a collection fee) and to include Joe Smith's $100 purchase on the monthly bill it mails him.

Assume that total credit card sales on June 5 amount to $800. The entry on Club Cafe's books on that day is as follows:

June 5	Accounts Receivable—Diners Club	800	
	Sales Revenue		800
	To record daily credit card sales.		

Assets = Liabilities + Owners' Equity
+800   **+800**

Assume that Club Cafe remits the credit card drafts to Diners Club once a week and that the total sales for the week ending June 11 amount to $5,000. Further assume that on

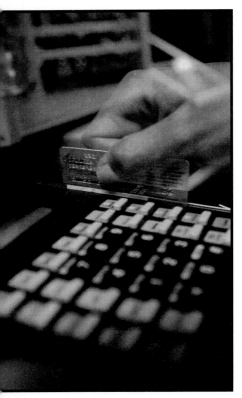

If credit card sales accelerate the inflow of cash from sales, then credit card scanners such as this one speed up the process even more.

EXHIBIT 7-7   Basic Relationships among Parties with Credit Card Sales

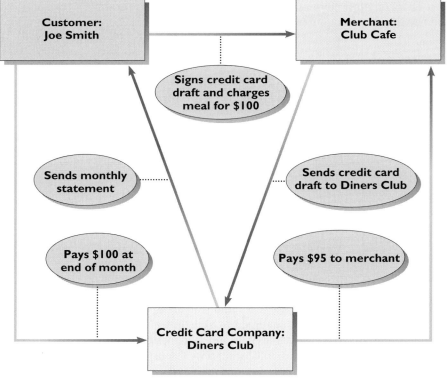

June 13 Diners Club pays the amount due to Club Cafe, after deducting a 5% collection fee. The entry on Club Cafe's books is as follows:

June 13	Cash	4,750	
	Collection Fee Expense	250	
	Accounts Receivable—Diners Club		5,000
	To record weekly receipts from credit card company.		

Assets	=	Liabilities	+	Owners' Equity
+4,750				−250
−5,000				

Some credit cards, such as MasterCard and VISA, allow a merchant to present a credit card draft directly for deposit in a bank account, in much the same way the merchant deposits checks, coins, and currency. Obviously, this type of arrangement is even more advantageous for the merchant because the funds are available as soon as the drafts are credited to the bank account. Assume that on July 9 Club Cafe presents VISA credit card drafts to its bank for payment in the amount of $2,000 and that the collection charge is 4%. The entry on its books on the date of deposit is as follows:

July 9	Cash	1,920	
	Collection Fee Expense	80	
	Sales Revenue		2,000
	To record credit card sales.		

Assets	=	Liabilities	+	Owners' Equity
+1,920				−80
				+2,000

Discounting Notes Receivable

Promissory notes are negotiable, which means that they can be endorsed and given to someone else for collection. In other words, a company can sign the back of a note, just as it would a check, sell it to a bank, and receive cash before the note's maturity date. This process is called discounting and is another way for companies to speed the collection of cash from receivables. A note can be sold immediately to a bank on the date it is issued, or it can be sold after it has been outstanding but before the due date.

When a note is discounted at a bank, it is normally done *with recourse*. This means that if the original customer fails to pay the bank the total amount due on the maturity date of the note, the company that transferred the note to the bank is liable for the full amount. Because there is *uncertainty* as to whether the company will have to make good on any particular note that it discounts at the bank, a *contingent liability* exists from the time the note is discounted until its maturity date. The accounting profession has adopted guidelines to decide whether a particular uncertainty requires that the company record a contingent liability on its balance sheet. Under these guidelines, the contingency created by the discounting of a note with recourse is not recorded as a liability. However, a *footnote* to the financial statements is used to inform the reader of the existing uncertainty.

How Liquid Assets Affect the Cash Flows Statement

As we discussed earlier in the chapter, cash equivalents are combined with cash on the balance sheet. These items are very near maturity and do not present any significant risk of collectibility. Because of this, any purchases or redemptions of cash equivalents are not considered significant activities to be reported on a statement of cash flows.

The purchase and the sale of short-term investments are considered significant activities and are therefore reported on the statement of cash flows. Under current accounting standards, however, the purchases and sales of certain types of these investments are

LO 8 Explain the effects of transactions involving liquid assets on the statement of cash flows.

INVESTING CASH IS THEIR BUSINESS

For most companies, investing cash and managing accounts receivable can have an important impact on the bottom line. Fortunately for AFLAC, a world leader in supplemental health insurance, the company has some special advantages in managing these two assets.

Because AFLAC sells insurance and not a product or service, it does not suffer as much when accounts receivable turn into bad debts. If the customer does not pay his or her premium, the policy is canceled after a warning notice and the insurance company keeps the premium paid in. Although this cancellation means a loss of future premiums flowing into the company that it can reinvest, this loss is not usually as crucial as a bad debt is for a merchant or a retailer.

As far as cash is concerned, insurance companies have expertise in this area that most industrial companies simply don't have. AFLAC's entire balance sheet is focused on investing cash from premiums in one way or another. Take a look at the company's balance sheet on the Internet (WWW.AFLAC.COM) and you'll see that these investments—more than $20 billion—dominate its total assets.

How the money is invested depends primarily on how the money is going to be used. The process of "matching" assets and liabilities is one of the jobs of Gary Stegman, the company's assistant CFO. "You'll find a lot of investments on one side of the balance sheet, and a lot of policy liabilities on the other side," says Stegman. "As long as we're able to find investments that yield more than our obligations, then we're covered," he says.

Name: Gary L. Stegman, CPA
Occupation: Assistant Chief Financial Officer
Education: Bachelor's degree in accounting, University of Cincinnati

So, if you were to purchase a life insurance policy from AFLAC, they would take your money and invest it in long-term bonds. The reason: the odds are that they won't be paying out any money to your heirs for many years to come. But if your grandfather were to purchase supplemental health insurance to fill the gaps in Medicare, then that money would be invested in shorter-term instruments since it would likely be paid out sooner. The same is true for a special cancer policy that the company sells—the world's first.

AFLAC's idle cash includes insurance premiums that have been collected while awaiting deployment in longer-term investments. The money is typically invested in very short-term U.S. Treasury bills or commercial paper—short-term obligations issued by blue-chip corporations. Most of these investments mature in 30 days or less. Because they are obligations of the U.S. government or the nation's leading corporations—and because they're due in such a short period of time—there is virtually no credit risk.

That suits Stegman just fine. "We're a very conservative company," he says.

---

classified as investing activities while others are categorized as operating activities. We will return to a full discussion of the various types of investments and their presentation on the statement of cash flows in Chapter 13.

The collection of either accounts receivable or notes receivable generates cash for a business and affects the Operating Activities section of the statement of cash flows. Most companies use the indirect method of reporting cash flows and begin the statement of cash flows with the net income of the period. Net income includes the sales revenue of the period. Therefore, a decrease in accounts or notes receivable during the period indicates that the company collected more cash than it recorded in sales revenue. Thus, *a decrease in accounts or notes receivable must be added back to net income because more cash was collected than is reflected in the sales revenue number.* Alternatively, an increase in accounts or notes receivable indicates that the company recorded more sales revenue than cash collected during the period. Therefore, *an increase in accounts or notes receivable requires a deduction from the net income of the period to arrive at cash flow from operating activities.* These adjustments are summarized in Exhibit 7-8.

Refer back to PepsiCo's statement of cash flows in Exhibit 7-2. Note in the Operating Activities section of the statement that accounts and notes receivable are combined. Does the combined change of $434 million in these two accounts during 1995 indicate an increase or a decrease in the receivables for the year? Because the amount is

EXHIBIT 7-8   How Liquid Assets Affect the Statement of Cash Flows

deducted in the Operating Activities section of the statement, we know that the receivables *increased* during 1995. An increase in receivables means that PepsiCo sold more products on open account and on notes than it actually collected in cash from customers. Thus, the increase is deducted from net income to arrive at the actual cash flow from operating activities.

Review Problem

The following items pertain to the current asset section of the balance sheet for Jackson Corp. at the end of its accounting year, December 31, 1998. Each item must be considered, and any necessary accounting entry on December 31 must be recorded. Additionally, the accountant for Jackson wants to develop the current asset section of the balance sheet as of the end of 1998.

a. Cash in a savings account at the Second State Bank amounts to $13,200.

b. Cash on hand in the petty cash fund amounts to $400.

c. A 9%, 120-day certificate of deposit was purchased on December 1, 1998, for $10,000.

d. The balance on the books for a checking account at the Second State Bank is $4,230. The bank statement indicates that one of Jackson's customers paid a $1,500 promissory note, along with $120 in interest, directly to the bank. The bank deducted a $25 collection fee from the amount it credited to Jackson's account. The statement also indicated that the bank had charged Jackson's account $50 to print new checks.

e. Gross accounts receivable at December 31, 1998, amount to $44,000. Before adjustment, the balance in the Allowance for Doubtful Accounts is $340. Based on past experience, the accountant estimates that 3% of the gross accounts receivable outstanding at December 31, 1998, will prove to be uncollectible.

f. A customer's 12%, 90-day promissory note in the amount of $6,000 is held at the end of the year. (*Note:* This is a different note than the one in item d.) The note has been held for 45 days during 1998.

Required

1. Record the accounting entries required in parts a–f.

2. Prepare the current asset section of Jackson's balance sheet as of December 31, 1998. In addition to items a–f, the balances in Inventory and Prepaid Insurance on this date are $65,000 and $4,800, respectively.

Solution to Review Problem

1. The following entries are recorded at December 31, 1998:

a. & b. No entries required.

c. Jackson needs an adjusting entry to record interest earned on the certificate of deposit at the Second State Bank. The CD has been outstanding for 30 days during 1998, and therefore the amount of interest earned is calculated as follows:

$$\$10,000 \times .09 \times 30/360 = \underline{\$75}$$

The adjusting entry follows:

```
1998
Dec. 31   Interest Receivable                          75
              Interest Revenue                              75
          To record interest earned during 1998.
```

Assets	=	Liabilities	+	Owners' Equity
+75				+75

d. Entries are needed to record the bank's collection of the promissory note and interest, the collection charge on the note, and the charge for the new checks:

```
1998
Dec. 31   Cash                                       1,620
              Notes Receivable                           1,500
              Interest Revenue                              120
          To record collection of note and interest.
```

Assets	=	Liabilities	+	Owners' Equity
+1,620				+120
−1,500				

```
1998
Dec. 31   Collection Fee Expense                       25
              Cash                                          25
          To record deduction from account for collection fee on note.
```

Assets	=	Liabilities	+	Owners' Equity
−25				−25

```
1998
Dec. 31   Miscellaneous Expense                        50
              Cash                                          50
          To record deduction from account for new checks.
```

Assets	=	Liabilities	+	Owners' Equity
−50				−50

e. Based on gross accounts receivable of $44,000 at year-end and an estimate that 3% of this amount will be uncollectible, the balance in the Allowance for Doubtful Accounts should be $1,320 ($44,000 × 3%). Given a current balance of $340, an adjusting entry for $980 ($1,320 − $340) is needed to bring the balance to the desired amount of $1,320:

```
1998
Dec. 31   Bad Debts Expense                           980
              Allowance for Doubtbul Accounts             980
          To record estimated bad debts for the year.
```

Assets	=	Liabilities	+	Owners' Equity
−980				−980

f. An adjusting entry is needed to accrue interest on the promissory note ($6,000 × .12 × 45/360 = $90):

1998
Dec. 31   Interest Receivable   90
                  Interest Revenue   90
                  To record interest earned on promissory note.

Assets   =   Liabilities   +   Owners' Equity
+90   **+90**

2. The current assets section of Jackson's balance sheet appears as follows:

JACKSON CORP.
PARTIAL BALANCE SHEET
DECEMBER 31, 1998

CURRENT ASSETS

Cash		$ 19,375*
Certificate of deposit		10,000
Accounts receivable	$44,000	
Less: Allowance for doubtful accounts	1,320	42,680
Notes receivable		6,000
Interest receivable		165§
Inventory		65,000
Prepaid insurance		4,800
Total current assets		$148,020

*Savings account	$13,200
Petty cash fund	400
Checking account ($4,230 + $1,620 − $25 − $50)	5,775
Total	$19,375

§$75 from CD and $90 from promissory note.

Chapter Highlights

1. **LO 1** The amount of cash reported on the balance sheet includes all items that are readily available to satisfy obligations. Items normally included in cash are coin and currency, petty cash funds, customers' undeposited checks, cashier's checks, certified checks, savings accounts, and checking accounts.

2. **LO 1** Cash equivalents include such items as commercial paper, money market funds, and treasury bills. They are included with cash on the balance sheet and are limited to those investments that are readily convertible to known amounts of cash and have original maturities of three months or less.

3. **LO 2** Companies classify an investment as short-term when it is readily marketable and the intent is to sell it within the next year or the operating cycle, whichever is longer. Included are stocks, bonds, and other types of financial instruments, such as certificates of deposit. Companies often use these financial instruments to invest idle cash during various times of the year.

4. **LO 3** A bank reconciliation is normally prepared monthly for all checking accounts to reconcile the amount of cash recorded on the books with the amount reported on the bank statement. One popular form for the reconciliation, and the one illustrated in the chapter, reconciles the balance on the bank statement and the balance on the books to the correct balance. Journal entries are made for all adjustments in the balance per books section of the reconciliation.

5. **LO 3** Many companies use a petty cash fund to disburse small amounts of cash that would otherwise require the use of a check and a more lengthy approval process. The fund is established by writing and cashing a check and placing the coin and currency in a secure place controlled by a custodian. At this point, a journal entry is made to record the establishment of the fund. On presentation of a supporting receipt to the custodian, employees receive disbursements from the fund. The fund is replenished periodically, and a journal entry is made to record the replenishment and to recognize the various expenses incurred.

6. **LO 4** The allowance method of accounting for bad debts matches the cost associated with uncollectible accounts to the revenue of the period in which the sale took place. One of two variations is used to estimate bad debts under the allowance method. Some companies base bad debts on a percentage of net credit sales. Others use an aging schedule as a basis for relating the amount of bad debts to the balance in Accounts Receivable at the end of the period.

7. **LO 5** A promissory note is a written promise to repay a definite sum of money on demand or at a fixed or determinable date in the future. Situations in which a promissory note is used include the purchase of consumer durables, the lending of money to another party, and the replacement of an existing account receivable. Interest earned but not yet collected should be accrued at the end of an accounting period.

8. **LO 6** The interest on certain promissory notes is implicitly included in the agreement instead of stated explicitly as a percentage of the principal amount of the note. Any difference between the cash purchase price of an item or, in the case of a loan, the amount borrowed and the amount to be repaid at maturity is interest. As is the case for interest-bearing notes, any interest earned but not yet collected is recognized as income at the end of an accounting period.

9. **LO 7** Many businesses accept credit cards in lieu of cash. In return for a fee, the credit card company assumes responsibility for collecting the customer charges. A credit card draft or invoice is the basis for recording a credit card sale and an account receivable. When the drafts are presented to the credit card company for payment, the excess of accounts receivable for these sales over the amount of cash received represents the expense associated with accepting credit cards. In some instances, companies do not have to wait to collect from the credit card company but can instead present the drafts for deposit to their bank account.

10. **LO 7** Because a promissory note is negotiable, it can be sold to another party, such as a bank. The sale of a note is called *discounting* and is a way for a company to accelerate the inflow of cash. If the note is sold or discounted with recourse, the company selling it is contingently liable until the maturity date of the loan. A footnote is used to report this contingency to financial statement readers.

11. **LO 8** Cash equivalents are included with cash on the balance sheet, and therefore changes in them do not appear as significant activities on a statement of cash flows. Purchases and sales of short-term investments do appear in the statement of cash flows. Under the indirect method of preparing the Operating Activities category of the statement of cash flows, an increase in accounts receivable is deducted from net income; a decrease is added back to net income.

Key Terms Quiz

Because of the large number of terms introduced in this chapter, it has two key terms quizzes. Read each definition below and then write the number of the definition in the blank beside the appropriate term it defines. The solution appears at the end of the chapter.

Quiz 1: Cash

___ Cash equivalent
___ Debt securities
___ Outstanding check
___ Bank reconciliation
___ Debit memoranda

___ Equity securities
___ Bank statement
___ Deposit in transit
___ Credit memoranda
___ Petty cash fund

1. Additions on a bank statement for such items as interest paid on the account and notes collected by the bank for the customer.

2. An investment that is readily convertible to a known amount of cash and has an original maturity to the investor of three months or less.

3. Deductions on a bank statement for such items as NSF checks and various service charges.

4. A deposit recorded on the books but not yet reflected on the bank statement.

5. Securities issued by corporations as a form of ownership in the business.

6. A check written by a company but not yet presented to the bank for payment.

7. Bonds issued by corporations and governmental bodies as a form of borrowing.

8. A detailed list, provided by the bank, of all the activity for a particular account during the month.

9. A form used by the accountant to reconcile the balance shown on the bank statement for a particular account with the balance shown in the accounting records.

10. Money kept on hand for making minor disbursements in coin and currency rather by writing checks.

Quiz 2: Receivables

___ Subsidiary ledger
___ Direct write-off method
___ Aging schedule
___ Maker

___ Control account
___ Allowance method
___ Promissory note
___ Payee

_____ Note receivable

_____ Principal

_____ Term

_____ Interest

_____ Non-interest-bearing note

_____ Credit card draft

_____ Note payable

_____ Maturity date

_____ Maturity value

_____ Interest-bearing note

_____ Discounted note

_____ Discounting

1. A method of estimating bad debts on the basis of either the net credit sales of the period or the amount of accounts receivable at the end of the period.

2. The party that will receive the money from a promissory note at some future date.

3. A written promise to repay a definite sum of money on demand or at a fixed or determinable date in the future.

4. A liability resulting from the signing of a promissory note.

5. The date that a promissory note is due.

6. A multiple-copy document used by a company that accepts a credit card for a sale.

7. An asset resulting from the acceptance of a promissory note from another company.

8. The length of time a promissory note is outstanding.

9. The process of selling a promissory note.

10. The party that agrees to repay the money for a promissory note at some future date.

11. A promissory note in which the interest rate is explicitly stated.

12. The amount of cash received, or the fair value of the products or services received, by the maker when a promissory note is issued.

13. A form used to categorize the various individual accounts receivable according to the length of time each has been outstanding.

14. The difference between the principal amount of a promissory note and its maturity value.

15. An alternative name for a non-interest-bearing promissory note.

16. The detail for a number of individual items that collectively make up a single general ledger account.

17. The amount of cash to be paid by the maker to the payee on the maturity date of a promissory note.

18. A promissory note in which interest is not explicitly stated but is implicit in the agreement.

19. The recognition of bad debts expense at the point an account is written off as uncollectible.

20. The general ledger account that is supported by a subsidiary ledger.

Alternate Terms

Allowance for doubtful accounts Allowance for Uncollectible Accounts.

Credit card draft Invoice.

Debit securities Bonds.

Equity securities Stocks.

Net realizable value Net recoverable amount.

Non-interest-bearing note Discounted note.

Short-term investments Marketable securities.

Questions

1. What is a cash equivalent? Why is it included with cash on the balance sheet?

2. Why does the purchase of an item classified as a cash equivalent _not_ appear on the statement of cash flows as an investing activity?

3. A friend says to you: "I understand why it is important to deposit all receipts intact and not keep coin and currency sitting around the business. Beyond this control feature, however, I believe that a company should strive to keep the maximum amount possible in checking accounts to always be able to pay bills on time." How would you evaluate your friend's statement?

4. A friend says to you: "I'm confused. I have a memo included with my bank statement indicating a $20 service charge for printing new checks. If the bank is deducting

this amount from my account, why do they call it a 'debit memorandum'? I thought a decrease in a cash account would be a credit, not a debit." How can you explain this?

5. Different formats for bank reconciliations are possible. What is the format for a bank reconciliation in which a service charge for a lockbox is _added_ to the balance per the bank statement? Explain your answer.

6. Why is a journal entry not made when a disbursement is made from a petty cash fund?

7. What conditions are necessary to classify an investment as short-term?

8. On December 31 Stockton Inc. invests idle cash in two different certificates of deposit. The first is an 8%, 90-day CD, and the second has an interest rate of 9% and

matures in 120 days. How is each of these CDs classified on the December 31 balance sheet?

9. What is the theoretical justification for the allowance method of accounting for bad debts?

10. In estimating bad debts, why is the balance in Allowance for Doubtful Accounts considered when the percentage of accounts receivable approach is used but not when the percentage of net credit sales approach is used?

11. When estimating bad debts on the basis of a percentage of accounts receivable, what is the advantage to using an aging schedule?

12. What is the distinction between an account receivable and a note receivable?

13. How would you evaluate the following statement? "Given the choice, it would always be better to require an interest-bearing note from a customer as opposed to a non-interest-bearing note. This is so because interest on a note receivable is a form of revenue and it is only in the case of an interest-bearing note that interest will be earned."

14. Why does the discounting of a note receivable with recourse result in a contingent liability? Should the liability be reported on the balance sheet?

Exercises

LO 2 **Exercise 7-1** Certificate of Deposit

On May 31, 1998, Elmer Corp. purchased a 120-day, 9% certificate of deposit for $50,000. The CD was redeemed on September 28, 1998. Prepare the journal entries on Elmer's books to account for the CD, including any entry on June 30, the end of the company's fiscal year. Assume 360 days in a year.

LO 3 **Exercise 7-2** Items on a Bank Reconciliation

Assume that a company is preparing a bank reconciliation for the month of June. It reconciles the bank balance and the book balance to the correct balance. For each of the following items, indicate whether the item is an addition to the bank balance (A-Bank), an addition to the book balance (A-Book), a deduction from the bank balance (D-Bank), a deduction from the book balance (D-Book), or would not appear on the June reconciliation (NA).

_____ 1. Check written in June but not yet returned to the bank for payment.

_____ 2. Customer's NSF check.

_____ 3. Customer's check written in the amount of $54 recorded on the books in the amount of $45.*

_____ 4. Service charge for new checks.

_____ 5. Principal and interest on a customer's note collected for the company by the bank.

_____ 6. Customer's check deposited on June 30 but not reflected on the bank statement.

_____ 7. Check written on the company's account, paid by the bank, and returned with the bank statement.

_____ 8. Check written on the company's account for $123 but recorded on the books as $132.*

_____ 9. Interest on the checking account for the month of June.

* Answer in terms of the adjustment needed to correct for the error.

LO 3 **Exercise 7-3** Petty Cash Fund

On January 2, 1998, Cleaver Video Stores decided to set up a petty cash fund. The treasurer established the fund by writing and cashing a $300 check and placing the coin and currency in a locked petty cash drawer. Edward Haskell was designated as the custodian for the fund. During January, the following receipts were given to Haskell in exchange for cash from the fund:

U. S. Post Office (stamps)	$76.00
Speedy Delivery Service	45.30
Cake N Cookies (party for retiring employee)	65.40
Office Supply Superstore (paper, pencils)	36.00

A count of the cash in the drawer on January 31 revealed a balance of $74.10. The treasurer wrote and cashed a check on the same day to restore the fund to its original balance of $300. Prepare the necessary journal entries, with explanations, for January. Assume that all stamps and office supplies were used during the month.

LO 4 **Exercise 7-4** Comparison of the Direct Write-Off and Allowance Methods of Accounting for Bad Debts
In its first year of business, Rideaway Bikes has net income of $145,000, exclusive of any adjustment for bad debt expense. The president of the company has asked you to calculate net income under each of two alternatives of accounting for bad debts: the direct write-off method and the allowance method. The president would like to use the method that will result in the higher net income. So far, no entries have been made to write off uncollectible accounts or to estimate bad debts. The relevant data are as follows:

Write-offs of uncollectible accounts during the year	$ 10,500
Net credit sales	$650,000
Estimated percentage of net credit sales that will be uncollectible	2%

Required

Compute net income under each of the two alternatives. Does Rideaway have a choice as to which method to use? Should it base its choice on which method will result in the higher net income? (Ignore income taxes.)

LO 4 **Exercise 7-5** Allowance Method of Accounting for Bad Debts—Comparison of the Two Approaches
Kandel Company had the following data available for 1998 (before making any adjustments):

Accounts receivable, 12/31/98	$320,100 (dr.)
Allowance for doubtful accounts	2,600 (cr.)
Net credit sales, 1998	834,000 (cr.)

Required

1. Prepare the journal entry to recognize bad debts under the following assumptions: (a) bad debt expense is expected to be 2% of net credit sales for the year and (b) Kandel expects it will not be able to collect 6% of the balance in accounts receivable at year-end.

2. Assume instead that the balance in the allowance account is a $2,600 debit. How will this affect your answers to part 1?

LO 4 **Exercise 7-6** Accounts Receivable Turnover for Quaker Oats
The 1996 annual report of Quaker Oats Company reported the following amounts (in millions of dollars). The accounts receivable balances are net of allowances for doubtful accounts.

Net sales	$5,199.0
Trade accounts receivable, December 31, 1996	294.9
Trade accounts receivable, December 31, 1995	398.3

Required

1. Compute Quaker's accounts receivable turnover ratio for 1996. (Assume that all sales are on credit.)

2. What is the average collection period, in days, for an account receivable? Explain your answer.

3. Give some examples of the types of customers you would expect Quaker Oats to have. Do you think the average collection period for sales to these customers is reasonable? What other information do you need to fully answer this question?

LO 5 **Exercise 7-7** Interest-Bearing Notes Receivable
On September 1, 1998, Dougherty Corp. accepted a six-month, 7%, $45,000 interest-bearing note from the Rozelle Company in payment of an accounts receivable. Doughtery's year-end is December 31. Rozelle paid the note and interest on the due date.

Required

1. Who is the maker and who is the payee of the note?
2. What is the maturity date of the note?
3. Prepare all journal entries Dougherty needs to make in connection with this note.

LO 6 **Exercise 7-8** Non-Interest-Bearing Note

On May 1, Radtke's Music Mart sold an electronic keyboard to Mary Reynolds. Reynolds made a $300 down payment and signed a 10-month note for $1,625. The normal selling price for the keyboard is $1,800 in cash. Radtke's fiscal year ends December 31. Reynolds paid Radtke in full on the maturity date.

Required

1. How much total interest did Radtke receive on this note?
2. Prepare the journal entries on Radtke's books on May 1, December 31, and the maturity date.
3. What is the effective interest rate on the note?

LO 7 **Exercise 7-9** Credit Card Sales

Darlene's Diner accepts American Express from its customers. Darlene's is closed on Sundays and on that day records the weekly sales and remits the credit card drafts to American Express. For the week ending on Sunday, June 12, cash sales totaled $2,430, and credit card sales amounted to $3,500. On June 15, Darlene's received $3,360 from American Express as payment for the credit card drafts. Prepare the necessary journal entries on Darlene's books on June 12 and June 15. As a percentage, what collection fee is American Express charging Darlene?

LO 8 **Exercise 7-10** Impact of Transactions Involving Receivables on Statement of Cash Flows

From the following list, identify whether the change in the account balance during the year would be added to or deducted from net income when the indirect method is used to determine cash flows from operating activities.

_____ Increase in accounts receivable
_____ Decrease in accounts receivable
_____ Increase in notes receivable
_____ Decrease in notes receivable

LO 8 **Exercise 7-11** Cash Collections—Direct Method

Emily Enterprises' comparative balance sheets included accounts receivable of $224,600 at December 31, 1997 and $205,700 at December 31, 1998. Sales reported on Emily's 1998 income statement amounted to $2,250,000. What is the amount of cash collections that Emily will report in the Operating Activities category of its 1998 statement of cash flows assuming that the direct method is used?

Multi-Concept Exercises

LO 1, 2 **Exercise 7-12** Composition of Cash

Using a Y for yes or an N for no, indicate whether each of the following items should be included in cash and cash equivalents on the balance sheet. If an item should not be included in cash and cash equivalents, indicate where it should appear on the balance sheet.

_____ 1. Checking account at Third County Bank.
_____ 2. Petty cash fund.
_____ 3. Coin and currency.
_____ 4. Postage stamps.
_____ 5. An IOU from an employee.
_____ 6. Savings account at the Ft. Worth Savings & Loan.
_____ 7. A six-month CD.
_____ 8. Undeposited customer checks.
_____ 9. A customer's check returned by the bank and marked NSF.
_____ 10. Sixty-day U.S. Treasury bills.
_____ 11. A cashier's check.

LO 1, 2 **Exercise 7-13** Classification of Cash Equivalents and Investments on a Balance Sheet
Classify each of the following items as either a cash equivalent (CE), a short-term investment (STI), or a long-term investment (LTI).

_____ **1.** A 120-day certificate of deposit.
_____ **2.** Three hundred shares of GM common stock. The company plans on selling the stock in six months.
_____ **3.** A six-month U.S. Treasury bill.
_____ **4.** A 60-day certificate of deposit.
_____ **5.** Ford Motor Co. bonds maturing in 15 years. The company intends to hold the bonds until maturity.
_____ **6.** Commercial paper issued by ABC Corp., maturing in four months.
_____ **7.** Five hundred shares of Chrysler common stock. The company plans to sell the stock in 60 days to help pay for a note due at that time at the bank.
_____ **8.** Two hundred shares of GE preferred stock. The company intends to hold the stock for 10 years and at that point sell it to help finance construction of a new factory.
_____ **9.** Ten-year U.S. Treasury bonds. The company plans to sell the bonds on the open market in six months.
_____ **10.** A 90-day U.S. Treasury bill.

LO 1, 2 **Exercise 7-14** Cash Equivalents
Systematic Enterprises invested its excess cash in the following instruments during December 1998:

Certificate of deposit, due January 31, 2001	$ 75,000
Certificate of deposit, due March 30, 1999	150,000
Commercial paper, original maturity date February 28, 1999	125,000
Deposit into a Money Market Fund	25,000
Investment in stock	65,000
90-day Treasury bills	100,000
Treasury note, due December 1, 2028	500,000

Required

Determine the amount of cash equivalents which should be combined with cash on the company's balance sheet at December 31, 1998 and for purposes of preparing a statement of cash flows for the year ended December 31, 1998.

LO 1, 8 **Exercise 7-15** Impact of Transactions Involving Cash and Receivables on Statement of Cash Flows
From the following list, identify each item as operating (O), investing (I), financing (F), or not separately reported on the statement of cash flows (N). Assume that the indirect method is used to determine the cash flows from operating activities.

_____ Purchase of cash equivalents
_____ Redemption of cash equivalents
_____ Purchase of short-term investments
_____ Sale of short-term investments
_____ Replenishment of the petty cash fund
_____ Write-off customer account (under the allowance method)

Problems

LO 3 **Problem 7-1** Bank Reconciliation and Journal Entries
The following information is available to assist you in preparing a bank reconciliation for Calico Corners on May 31, 1998:

a. The balance on the May 31, 1998, bank statement is $8,432.11.

b. Not included on the bank statement is a $1,250.00 deposit made by Calico Corners late on May 31.

c. A comparison between the canceled checks returned with the bank statement and the company records indicated that the following checks are outstanding at May 31:

No. 123	$ 23.40
No. 127	145.00
No. 128	210.80
No. 130	67.32

d. The Cash account on the company's books shows a balance of $9,965.34.

e. The bank acts as a collection agency for interest earned on some municipal bonds held by Calico Corners. The May bank statement indicates interest of $465.00 earned during the month.

f. Interest earned on the checking account and added to Calico Corners' account during May was $54.60. Miscellaneous bank service charges amounted to $50.00.

g. A customer's NSF check in the amount of $166.00 was returned with the May bank statement.

h. A comparison between the deposits listed on the bank statement and the company's books revealed that a customer's check in the amount of $123.45 was recorded on the books during May but was never added to the company's account. The bank erroneously added the check to the account of Calico Closet, which has an account at the same bank.

i. The comparison of deposits per the bank statement with those per the books revealed that another customer's check in the amount of $101.10 was correctly added to the company's account. In recording the check on the company's books, however, the accountant erroneously increased the Cash account $1,011.00.

Required

1. Prepare a bank reconciliation in good form.

2. Prepare the necessary journal entries on the books of Calico Corners.

3. A friend says to you: "I don't know why companies bother to prepare bank reconciliations—it seems a waste of time. Why don't they just do like I do and adjust the cash account for any difference between what the bank shows as a balance and what shows up in the books?" Explain to your friend *why* a bank reconciliation should be prepared as soon as a bank statement is received.

LO 3 **Problem 7-2** The Effect of Petty Cash on Cash and Income

ABC Company established a petty cash fund in the amount of $500. One month later, it replenished the fund based on the following receipts:

a. $40, postage due on computer supplies used in the administrative offices.

b. $5.80, postage stamps used by the president when she is on the road and without access to the postage meter.

c. $180, advertising fliers to be used by the marketing department and sent COD to the company.

d. $95, office supplies purchased at a local store for use in the administrative offices.

Required

1. Prepare the journal entry to establish the petty cash fund. Cash on hand at the end of the first month is $174. Do you believe that the $500 amount was an appropriate amount for ABC's petty cash fund? Explain.

2. Prepare the journal entry to replenish the petty cash fund at the end of the month. What is the effect of this entry on the total assets of the company? on income?

3. Explain why a petty cash fund is allowed even though proper accounting control over cash requires that all payments be made by check.

LO 4   **Problem 7-3** Allowance Method for Accounting for Bad Debts

At the beginning of 1998, EZ Tech Company's Accounts Receivable balance was $140,000, and the balance in the Allowance for Doubtful Accounts was $2,350 (cr.). EZ Tech's sales in 1998 were $1,050,000, 80% of which were on credit. Collections on account during the year were $670,000. The company wrote off $4,000 of uncollectible accounts during the year.

Required

1. Prepare summary journal entries related to the sales, collections, and write-offs of accounts receivable during 1998.

2. Prepare journal entries to recognize bad debts assuming (a) bad debt expense is 3% of credit sales and (b) amounts expected to be uncollectible are 6% of the year-end accounts receivable.

3. What is the net realizable value of accounts receivable on December 31, 1998 under each assumption (a and b) in part 2?

4. What effect does the recognition of bad debt expense have on the net realizable value? What effect does the write-off accounts have on the net realizable value?

LO 4   **Problem 7-4** Aging Schedule to Account for Bad Debts

Sparkle Jewels distributes fine stones. It sells on credit to retail jewelry stores and extends terms of 2/10, net 60. For accounts that are not overdue, Sparkle has found that there is a 95% probability of collection. For accounts up to one month past due, the likelihood of collection decreases to 80%. If accounts are between one and two months past due, the probability of collection is 60%, and if an account is more than two months past due, Sparkle Jewels estimates that there is only a 40% chance of collecting the receivable.

On December 31, 1998, the credit balance in Allowance for Doubtful Accounts is $12,300. The amounts of gross receivables, by age, on this date are as follows:

CATEGORY	AMOUNT
Current	$200,000
Past due:	
Less than one month	45,000
One to two months	25,000
More than two months	10,000

Required

1. Prepare a schedule to estimate the amount of uncollectible accounts at December 31, 1998.

2. On the basis of the schedule in part 1, prepare the journal entry on December 31, 1998, to estimate bad debts.

3. Show how accounts receivable would be presented on the December 31, 1998, balance sheet.

LO 4   **Problem 7-5** Accounts Receivable Turnover for Compaq Computer and Digital Equipment

The following information was summarized from the 1995 annual report of Compaq Computer Corporation:

	(in millions)
Accounts receivable, December 31:	
1995	$ 3,141
1994	2,287
Sales for the year ended December 31:	
1995	14,755
1994	10,866

The following information was summarized from the fiscal-year 1996 annual report of Digital Equipment Corporation:

	(in thousands)
Accounts receivable:	
June 29, 1996	$3,223,293
July 1, 1995	3,219,082
Product sales for the year ended:	
June 29, 1996	8,362,423
July 1, 1995	7,616,441

Required

1. Calculate the accounts receivable turnover ratios for Compaq Computer and Digital Equipment for the most recent fiscal year.

2. Calculate the average collection period, in days, for both companies for the most recent fiscal year. Comment on the reasonableness of the collection periods considering the types of companies that you would expect to be customers of Compaq Computer and Digital Equipment.

3. Which company appears to be performing better? What other information should you consider to determine how these companies are performing in this regard?

LO 6 **Problem 7-6** Non-Interest-Bearing Note Receivable

Northern Nursery sells a large stock of trees and shrubs to a landscaping business on May 31, 1998. The landscaper makes a down payment of $5,000 and signs a promissory note agreeing to pay $20,000 on August 29, 1998, the end of its busy season. The cash selling price of the nursery stock on May 31 was $24,000.

Required

1. Prepare the appropriate journal entry on Northern's books on each of the following dates:

   a. May 31, 1998, to record the receipt of the down payment and the promissory note.

   b. June 30, 1998, the end of Northern's fiscal year.

   c. August 29, 1998, to record collection of the note.

2. Compute the effective rate of interest earned by Northern on the note. Explain your answer.

LO 7 **Problem 7-7** Credit Card Sales

Gas stations often sell gasoline at a lower price to customers who pay cash than to customers who use a charge card. A local gas station owner pays 2% of the sales price to the credit card company when customers pay with a credit card. He pays $ .75 per gallon of gasoline and must earn at least $ .25 per gallon of gross margin to stay competitive.

Required

1. Determine the price the owner must charge credit card customers to maintain his gross margin.

2. How much discount could the owner offer to cash customers and still maintain the same gross margin?

LO 8 **Problem 7-8** Effects of Changes in Receivable Balances on Statement of Cash Flows

Stegner Inc. reported net income of $130,000 for the year ended December 31, 1998. The following items were included on Stegner's balance sheets at December 31, 1998 and 1997:

	12/31/98	12/31/97
Cash	$105,000	$110,000
Accounts receivable	223,000	83,000
Notes receivable	95,000	100,000

Stegner uses the indirect method to prepare its statement of cash flows. Stegner does not have any other current assets or current liabilities and did not enter into any investing or financing activities during 1998.

Required

1. Prepare Stegner's 1998 statement of cash flows.
2. Draft a brief memo to the owner to explain why cash decreased during a profitable year.

Multi-Concept Problems

LO 1, 2 **Problem 7-9** Cash and Liquid Assets on the Balance Sheet

The following accounts are listed in a company's general ledger. The accountant wants to place the items in order of liquidity on the balance sheet.

Accounts receivable
Certificates of deposit (six months)
Marketable securities
Prepaid rent
Money market fund
Cash in drawers

Required

Rank the accounts in terms of liquidity. Identify items to be included in the total of cash, and explain why the items not included in cash on the balance sheet are not as liquid as cash. Explain how these items should be classified.

LO 4, 5 **Problem 7-10** Accounts and Notes Receivable

Linus Corp. sold merchandise for $5,000 to C. Brown on May 15, 1998, with credit terms of net 30. Subsequent to this, Brown experienced cash flow problems and was unable to pay its debt. On August 10, 1998, Linus stopped trying to collect the outstanding receivable from Brown and wrote the account off as uncollectible. On December 1, 1998, Brown sent Linus a check for $1,000 and offered to sign a two-month, 9%, $4,000 promissory note to satisfy the remaining obligation. Brown paid the entire amount due Linus, with interest, on January 31, 1999. Linus ends its accounting year on December 31 each year, and uses the allowance method to account for bad debts.

Required

1. Prepare all of the necessary journal entries on the books of Linus Corp. from May 15, 1998, to January 31, 1999.
2. Why would Brown bother to send Linus a check for $1,000 on December 1 and agree to sign a note for the balance, given that such a long period of time had passed since the original purchase?

Alternate Problems

LO 3 **Problem 7-1A** Bank Reconciliation

The following information is available to assist you in preparing a bank reconciliation for Karen's Catering on March 31, 1998:

a. The balance on the March 31, 1998, bank statement is $6,506.10.

b. Not included on the bank statement is a deposit made by Karen's late on March 31 in the amount of $423.00.

c. A comparison between the canceled checks listed on the bank statement and the company records indicated that the following checks are outstanding at March 31:

No. 112	$ 42.92
No. 117	$307.00
No. 120	$ 10.58
No. 122	$ 75.67

d. The bank acts as a collection agency for checks returned for insufficient funds. The March bank statement indicates that one such check in the amount of $45.00 was collected and deposited and a collection fee of $4.50 was charged.

e. Interest earned on the checking account and credited to Karen's account during March was $4.30. Miscellaneous bank service charges amounted to $22.00.

f. A comparison between the deposits listed on the bank statement and the company's books revealed that a customer's check in the amount of $1,250.00 appears on the bank statement in March but was never credited to the customer's account on the company's books.

g. The comparison of checks cleared per the bank statement with those per the books revealed that the wrong amount was charged to the company's account for a check. The amount of the check was $990.00. The proof machine encoded the check in the amount of $909.00, the amount charged against the company's account.

Required

1. Determine the balance on the books before any adjustments as well as the corrected balance to be reported on the balance sheet.

2. What would you recommend Karen do as a result of the bank error in item g above? Why?

LO 3 **Problem 7-2A** The Effect of Petty Cash on Cash and Income

Arlington Inc. established a petty cash fund in the amount of $50. One month later, it replenished the fund based on the following receipts:

a. $4, postage due on computer supplies purchased for the administrative offices.

b. $5.80, postage stamps used by the receptionist so that he does not need to leave his desk to use the postage meter.

c. $18, a cake for the secretary's birthday.

d. $20, materials purchased at a local store for use by the sales staff.

Required

1. Prepare the journal entry to establish the petty cash fund. Cash on hand at the end of the month is $1.15. Do you believe that the $50 amount was an appropriate amount for Arlington's petty cash fund? Explain.

2. Prepare the journal entry to replenish the petty cash fund at the end of the month. What is the effect of this entry on the total assets of the company? on income?

3. Who should oversee the petty cash fund? Write a short description of how the process should be handled in the company.

LO 4 **Problem 7-3A** Allowance Method for Accounting for Bad Debts

At the beginning of 1998, Miyazaki Company's Accounts Receivable balance was $105,000 and the balance in the Allowance for Doubtful Accounts was $1,950 (cr.). Miyazaki's sales in 1998 were $787,500, 80% of which were on credit. Collections on account during the year were $502,500. The company wrote off $3,000 of uncollectible accounts during the year.

Required

1. Prepare summary journal entries related to the sales, collections, and write-offs of accounts receivable during 1998.

2. Prepare journal entries to recognize bad debts assuming (a) bad debt expense is 3% of credit sales or (b) amounts expected to be uncollectible are 6% of the year-end accounts receivable.

3. What is the net realizable value of accounts receivable on December 31, 1998 under each assumption (a and b) in part 2?

4. What effect does the recognition of bad debt expense have on the net realizable value? What effect does the write-off of accounts have on the net realizable value?

LO 4 **Problem 7-4A** Aging Schedule to Account for Bad Debts

Rough Stuff is a distributor of large rocks. It sells on credit to commercial landscaping companies and extends terms of 2/10, net 60. For accounts that are not overdue, Rough has found that there is a 90% probability of collection. For accounts up to one month past due, the likelihood of collection decreases to 75%. If accounts are between one and two months past due, the probability of collection is 65%, and if an account is more than two months past due, Rough estimates that there is only a 25% chance of collecting the receivable.

On December 31, 1998, the credit balance in Allowance for Doubtful Accounts is $34,590. The amounts of gross receivables, by age, on this date are as follows:

CATEGORY	AMOUNT
Current	$135,000
Past due:	
Less than one month	60,300
One to two months	35,000
More than two months	45,000

Required

1. Prepare a schedule to estimate the amount of uncollectible accounts at December 31, 1998.

2. Rough knows that $40,000 of the $45,000 amount that is more than two months overdue is due from one customer that is in severe financial trouble. It is rumored that the customer will be filing for bankruptcy in the near future. As controller for Rough Stuff, how would you handle this situation?

3. Show how accounts receivable would be presented on the December 31, 1998, balance sheet.

LO 4 **Problem 7-5A** Accounts Receivable Turnover for Boise Cascade and International Paper
The following information was summarized from the 1995 annual report of Boise Cascade Corporation and Subsidiaries:

	(in thousands)
Accounts receivable, December 31:	
1995	$ 457,608
1994	405,661
Sales for the year ended December 31:	
1995	5,074,230
1994	4,140,390

The following information was summarized from the 1995 annual report of International Paper Company:

	(in millions)
Accounts receivable, December 31:	
1995	$ 2,571
1994	2,241
Net sales for the year ended December 31:	
1995	19,797
1994	14,966

Required

1. Calculate the accounts receivable turnover ratios for Boise Cascade and International Paper for 1995.

2. Calculate the average collection period, in days, for both companies for 1995. Comment on the reasonableness of the collection periods considering the types of companies that you would expect to be customers of Boise Cascade and International Paper.

3. Which company appears to be performing better? What other information should you consider to determine how these companies are performing in this regard?

LO 6 **Problem 7-6A** Non-Interest-Bearing Note Receivable
Midwest Poultry sells a large stock of birds to a processor on May 31, 1998. The processor makes a $12,000 down payment and signs a $36,900 promissory note agreeing to pay

the remainder on August 29, 1998, the end of its busy season. The cash selling price of the birds on May 31 was $48,000.

1. Prepare the appropriate journal entry on Midwest's books on August 29, 1998, to record collection of the note. Midwest's accounting year ends on September 30.
2. Compute the effective rate of interest earned by Midwest on the note. Explain your answer.

LO 7   **Problem 7-7A** Credit Card Sales

A local fast-food store is considering the use of major credit cards in its outlets. Current annual sales are $800,000 per outlet. The company can purchase the equipment needed to handle credit cards and have an additional phone line installed in each outlet for approximately $800 per outlet. The equipment will be an expense in the year it is installed. The employee training time is minimal. The credit card company will charge a fee equal to 1.5% of sales for the use of credit cards. The company is unable to determine by how much, if any, sales will increase and whether cash customers will use a credit card rather than cash. No other fast-food stores in the local area accept credit cards for sales payment.

Required

1. Assuming only 5% of existing cash customers will use a credit card, what increase in sales is necessary to pay for the credit card equipment in the first year?
2. What other factors might the company consider in addition to an increase in sales dollars?

LO 8   **Problem 7-8A** Effects of Changes in Receivable Balances on Statement of Cash Flows

St. Charles Antique Market reported a net loss of $6,000 for the year ended December 31, 1998. The following items were included on St. Charles Antique Market's balance sheets at December 31, 1998 and 1997:

	12/31/98	12/31/97
Cash	$ 36,300	$ 3,100
Accounts receivable	79,000	126,000
Notes receivable	112,600	104,800

St. Charles Antique Market uses the indirect method to prepare its statement of cash flows. St. Charles Antique Market does not have any other current assets or current liabilities and did not enter into any investing or financing activities during 1998.

Required

1. Prepare St. Charles Antique Market's 1998 statement of cash flows.
2. Draft a brief memo to the owner to explain why cash increased during such an unprofitable year.

Alternate Multi-Concept Problems

LO 1, 2   **Problem 7-9A** Cash and Liquid Assets on the Balance Sheet

The following accounts are listed in a company's general ledger:

	DECEMBER 31, 1998	DECEMBER 31, 1997
Accounts receivable	$12,300	$10,000
Certificates of deposit (three months)	10,000	10,000
Marketable securities	4,500	4,000
Prepaid rent	1,200	1,500
Money market fund	25,800	28,000
Cash in checking account	6,000	6,000

Required

1. Which items are cash equivalents?
2. Explain where items that are not cash equivalents should be classified on the balance sheet.
3. What are the amount and the direction of change in cash and cash equivalents for 1998? Is the company as liquid at the end of 1998 as it was at the end of 1997? Explain your answer.

LO 4, 5 **Problem 7-10A** Accounts and Notes Receivable

Tweedy Inc. sold merchandise for $6,000 to P.D. Cat on July 31, 1998, with credit terms of net 30. Subsequent to this, Cat experienced cash flow problems and was unable to pay its debt. On December 24, 1998, Tweedy stopped trying to collect the outstanding receivable from Cat and wrote the account off as uncollectible. On January 15, 1999, Cat sent Tweedy a check for $1,500 and offered to sign a two-month, 8%, $4,500 promissory note to satisfy the remaining obligation. Cat paid the entire amount on the note due Tweedy, with interest, on March 15, 1999. Tweedy ends its accounting year on December 31 each year.

Required

1. Prepare all of the necessary journal entries on the books of Tweedy Inc. from July 31, 1998, to March 15, 1999.
2. Why would Cat bother to send Tweedy a check for $1,500 on January 15 and agree to sign a note for the balance, given that such a long period of time had passed since the original purchase?

Cases

Reading and Interpreting Financial Statements

LO 4 **Case 7-1** Reading and Interpreting Ben & Jerry's Financial Statements

Refer to the financial statements for 1995 included in Ben & Jerry's annual report.

Required

1. What is the balance in the Allowance for Doubtful Accounts at the end of each of the two years presented? What is the net realizable value at the end of each year?
2. Calculate the ratio of the Allowance for Doubtful Accounts to Gross Accounts Receivable at the end of each of the two years.
3. Why do you think the balance in the Allowance for Doubtful Accounts was increased at the end of 1995? Does this mean that the company expects a greater percentage of bad debts?

LO 8 **Case 7-2** Reading Ben & Jerry's Statement of Cash Flows

Refer to the financial statements for 1995 included in Ben & Jerry's annual report.

Required

1. Did the company buy or sell any investments during 1995? If so, what was the dollar amount?
2. Relate the change in investments on the statement of cash flows to a number on the balance sheet. How are investments categorized on the balance sheet?
3. What was the dollar amount of increase or decrease in accounts receivable for 1995? Why is this number deducted on the statement of cash flows?

Making Financial Decisions

LO 1, 2 **Case 7-3** Liquidity

R Montague and J Capulet both distribute films to movie theaters. The following are the current assets for each at the end of the year (all amounts are in millions of dollars):

Decision Making

	R MONTAGUE	J CAPULET
Cash	$10	$ 5
Six-month certificates of deposit	9	0
Short-term investments in stock	0	6
Accounts receivable	15	23
Allowance for doubtful accounts	(1)	(1)
Total current assets	$33	$33

Required

As a loan officer for the First National Bank of Verona Heights, assume that both companies have come to you asking for a $10 million, six-month loan. If you could lend money to only one of the two, which one would it be? Justify your answer by writing a brief memo to the president of the bank.

Decision
Making

LO 5, 6 **Case 7-4** Notes Receivable

Warren Land Development is considering two offers for a lot. Builder A has offered to pay $12,000 down and sign a 10%, $80,000 promissory note, with interest and principal due in one year. Builder B would make a down payment of $20,000 and sign a non-interest-bearing, one-year note for $80,000. The president believes that the deal with Builder A is better because it involves interest and the loan to Builder B does not. The vice president of marketing thinks the offer from Builder B is better because it involves more money "up front." The sales manager is indifferent, reasoning that both builders would eventually pay $100,000 in total and that because the lot was recently appraised at $75,000, both would be paying more than fair market value.

Required

1. Regardless of which offer it accepts, how much revenue should Warren recognize from the sale of the lot? Explain your answer.

2. Which offer do you think Warren should accept? Or is the sales manager correct that it doesn't matter which one is accepted? Explain your answer.

Accounting and Ethics: What Would You Do?

LO 4 **Case 7-5** Uncollectible Accounts

Ledermen Furniture Company has always experienced a problem collecting accounts. As of the end of 1998, Accounts Receivable was reported as follows:

Accounts receivable	$125,600
Allowance for bad debts	(32,800)
Accounts receivable, net	$ 92,800

During 1998 Ledermen wrote off $10,800 of accounts deemed to be uncollectible. The chief financial officer and the marketing vice president have an ongoing conflict regarding the credibility of customers. The financial officer believes that the marketing department is too generous in granting credit and that marketing has even overridden the finance department's credit rejections. The marketing vice president believes that the credit department does not understand the business and that without marketing's efforts, the company would not exist.

Required

What remedy could you recommend to resolve this conflict between the chief financial officer and the marketing vice president?

LO 6 **Case 7-6** Notes Receivable

Patterson Company is a large diversified business with a unit that sells commercial real estate. As a company, Patterson has been profitable in recent years with the exception of the real estate business, where economic conditions have resulted in weak sales. The vice president of the real estate division is aware of the poor performance of his group and needs to find ways to "show a profit."

During the current year the division is successful in selling a 100-acre tract of land for a new shopping center. The original cost of the property to Patterson was $4 million. The buyer has agreed to sign a $10 million note with payments of $2 million due at the end of each of the next five years. The property was appraised late last year at a market value of $7.5 million. The vice president has come to you, the controller, and asked that you record the sale as follows:

Notes Receivable	10,000,000	
Sales Revenue		10,000,000
To record sale of 100-acre tract.		

Required

1. Does the entry suggested by the vice president to record the sale violate any accounting principle? If so, explain the principle it violates.

2. What would you do? Write a brief memo to the vice president explaining the proper accounting for the sale.

Research Case

Case 7-7 PepsiCo

While PepsiCo is the number one snack-chip maker in the world with its Frito-Lay products, the company continues to finish second in the soft-drink cola wars. PepsiCo's strong promotion of its world-famous brand names in more than 100 countries results in revenue and cash flow for the company.

Internet

Using PepsiCo's World Wide Web site (http://www.pepsico.com), its most recent annual report, or library resources, obtain company financial data and answer the following:

1. For the most recent year available, what is the total of PepsiCo's cash, cash equivalents, and short-term investments? What types of transactions may have caused changes in these amounts from the previous accounting period?

2. What are some benefits of improved cash flows, even while profits may be growing at a slower rate?

3. Obtain the past 52-week high, low, and most current prices for PepsiCo's stock. How might the company's cash flow situation affect the stock price?

Optional Research. Based on store visits and a Web search, determine PepsiCo's snack-chip competitors. What ingredients, tastes, promotions, and pricing techniques are used by other snack-chip companies to attract customers?

Solutions to Key Terms Quiz

Quiz 1: Cash

2 Cash equivalent (p. 315)
7 Debt securities (p. 318)
6 Outstanding check (p. 320)
9 Bank reconciliation (p. 321)
3 Debit memoranda (p. 321)

5 Equity securities (p. 318)
8 Bank statement (p. 319)
4 Deposit in transit (p. 320)
1 Credit memoranda (p. 321)
10 Petty cash fund (p. 324)

Quiz 2: Receivables

16 Subsidiary ledger (p. 326)
19 Direct write-off method (p. 328)
13 Aging schedule (p. 331)
10 Maker (p. 332)
7 Note receivable (p. 332)
12 Principal (p. 333)
8 Term (p. 333)
14 Interest (p. 333)
18 Non-interest-bearing note (p. 333)
6 Credit card draft (p. 336)

20 Control account (p. 326)
1 Allowance method (p. 328)
3 Promissory note (p. 332)
2 Payee (p. 332)
4 Note payable (p. 332)
5 Maturity date (p. 333)
17 Maturity value (p. 333)
11 Interest-bearing note (p. 333)
15 Discounted note (p. 334)
9 Discounting (p. 337)

Operating Assets: Property, Plant, and Equipment, Natural Resources, and Intangibles

FOCUS ON FINANCIAL RESULTS

Time Warner markets information and entertainment in almost any format imaginable. Warner Brothers produces movies, publishes DC Comics, and operates Six Flags theme parks and Warner Bros. Worldwide Studio Stores. Warner Bros. Television produces prime-time programming, including *Friends* and *ER*. Warner Music Group markets recordings under the Warner Bros., Atlantic Group, Elektra, and Warner Music International labels. Time Inc. publishes popular magazines like *Time, Sports Illustrated,* and *People,* plus books under the imprints of Book-of-the-Month Club; Little, Brown; Warner Books; Time-Life Books;

Time Warner
Consolidated Balance Sheet

December 31, (millions, except per share amounts)	1995	1994
ASSETS		
Current assets		
Cash and equivalents	$ 628	$ 282
Receivables, less allowances of $786 and $768	1,755	1,439
Inventories	443	370
Prepaid expenses	894	726
Total current assets	3,720	2,817
Cash and equivalents segregated for redemption of long-term debt	557	–
Investments in and amounts due to and from Entertainment Group	5,734	5,350
Other investments	2,389	1,555
Land and buildings	431	412
Cable television equipment	361	–
Furniture, fixtures and other equipment	1,196	998
	1,988	1,410
Less accumulated depreciation	(869)	(657)
Property, plant and equipment	1,119	753
Music catalogues, contracts and copyrights	1,140	1,207
Cable television franchises	1,696	–
Goodwill	5,213	4,630
Other assets	564	404
Total assets	$22,132	$16,716

and more. Home Box Office offers a popular cable-television network. Time Warner Cable provides cable-TV systems to many communities.

To do all this, Time Warner relies on its operating assets. As shown on the asset portion of its balance sheet, these include land and buildings, equipment, and more. The company also relies heavily on intangible assets. Much of its growth and potential come from the images of its brands, from cartoon characters to magazine titles.

However, the balance sheet shows only the cost to acquire assets like copyrights and trademarks, not their potential value.

If you were a Time Warner manager, how would you establish the value of intangibles on the balance sheet? How would you communicate their potential to investors? While studying the chapter, compare the way organizations report tangible and intangible assets on the balance sheet.

SOURCE: *Time Warner Inc. Annual Report,* 1995.

LEARNING OBJECTIVES

After studying this chapter, you should be able to

LO 1 Understand balance sheet disclosures for operating assets.

LO 2 Determine the acquisition cost of an operating asset.

LO 3 Explain how to calculate the acquisition cost of assets purchased for a lump sum.

LO 4 Describe the impact of capitalizing interest as part of the acquisition cost of an asset.

LO 5 Compare depreciation methods and understand the factors affecting the choice of method.

LO 6 Understand the impact of a change in the estimate of the asset life or residual value.

LO 7 Determine which expenditures should be capitalized as asset costs and which should be treated as expenses.

LO 8 Analyze the effect of the disposal of an asset at a gain or loss.

LO 9 Understand the balance sheet presentation of intangible assets.

LO 10 Describe the proper amortization of intangible assets.

LO 11 Explain the impact that long-term assets have on the statement of cash flows.

Operating Assets: Property, Plant, and Equipment

Balance Sheet Presentation

LO 1 Understand balance sheet disclosures for operating assets.

Operating assets constitute the major productive assets of many companies. Current assets are important to a company's short-term liquidity; operating assets are absolutely essential to its long-term future. These assets must be used to produce the goods or services the company sells to customers. The dollar amount invested in operating assets may be very large, as is the case with most manufacturing companies. On the other hand, operating assets on the balance sheet may be insignificant to a company's value, as is the case with a computer software firm. Users of financial statements must assess the operating assets to make important decisions. For example, lenders are interested in the value of the operating assets as collateral when making lending decisions. Investors must evaluate whether the operating assets indicate long-term potential and can provide a return to the stockholders.

The terms used to describe the operating assets and the balance sheet presentation of those assets vary somewhat by company. Some firms refer to this category of assets as *fixed* or *plant assets*. Other firms prefer to present operating assets in two categories: *tangible assets* and *intangible assets*. The balance sheet of the toy company Mattel Inc. uses another way to classify operating assets. Mattel presents two classes of operating assets: *property, plant, and equipment* and *other noncurrent assets*. Because the latter term can encompass a variety of items, we will use the more descriptive term *intangible assets* for the second category. We begin by examining the accounting issues concerned with the first category: property, plant, and equipment.

The December 31, 1995, balance sheet of Mattel presents property, plant, and equipment as follows (in thousands):

Property, Plant, and Equipment	
Land	$ 25,724
Buildings	192,323
Machinery and equipment	354,469
Capitalized leases	24,271
Leasehold improvements	51,629
	$648,416
Less: Accumulated depreciation	265,885
	382,531
Tools, dies, and molds, net	116,783
Property, plant, and equipment, net	$499,314

You should note that the acquisition costs of the land, buildings, machinery and equipment, capitalized leases, and leasehold improvements are stated and the amount of accumulated depreciation is deducted to determine the net amount. Tools, dies, and molds are stated at the net amount, meaning that the amount of depreciation has been deducted before the number is presented on the balance sheet. Note that Mattel has assets acquired by capital lease arrangements. Capital leases are discussed in Chapter 10 and will not be addressed in this chapter. The account Leasehold Improvements indicates that the company has modified or improved leased assets in a manner that enhances their future service potential. The cost of the improvement is shown separately on the balance sheet.

Acquisition of Property, Plant, and Equipment

Assets classified as property, plant, and equipment are initially recorded at acquisition cost (also referred to as *historical cost*). As indicated on Mattel's balance sheet, these assets are normally presented on the balance sheet at original acquisition cost minus accumulated depreciation. It is important, however, to define the term *acquisition cost* (also known as original cost) in a more exact manner. What items should be included as part of the original acquisition? Acquisition cost should include all of the costs that are normal and necessary to acquire the asset and prepare it for its intended use. Items included in acquisition cost would generally include the following:

LO 2 Determine the acquisition cost of an operating asset.

> Purchase price.
>
> Taxes paid at time of purchase (for example, sales tax).
>
> Transportation charges.
>
> Installation costs.

An accountant must exercise careful judgment to determine which costs are "normal" and "necessary" and should be included in the calculation of the acquisition cost of operating assets. Acquisition cost should not include expenditures unrelated to the acquisition (for example, repair costs if an asset is damaged during installation) or costs incurred after the asset was installed and use begun.

ACCOUNTING FOR YOUR DECISIONS
You Are an Attorney

You are a newly licensed attorney who just opened a legal firm. As part of your office operations, you have purchased some "slightly used" computers. Should the cost of repairing the computers be considered as part of the acquisition cost?

ANS: If you were aware that the computers needed to be repaired when purchased, the repair costs are part of the cost of acquisition. If the computers were damaged after they were purchased, the costs should be treated as an expense on the income statement.

Group Purchase   Quite often a firm purchases several assets as a group and pays a lump-sum amount. This is most common when a company purchases land and a building situated on it and pays a lump-sum amount for both. It is important to measure separately the acquisition cost of the land and of the building. Land is not a depreciable asset, but the amount allocated to the building is subject to depreciation. In cases such as this, the purchase price should be allocated between land and building on the basis of the proportion of the *fair market values* of each.

LO 3 Explain how to calculate the acquisition cost of assets purchased for a lump sum.

   For example, assume that on January 1, Payton Company purchased a building and the land that it is situated on for $100,000. The accountant was able to establish that the fair market values of the two assets on January 1 were as follows:

Land	$ 30,000
Building	90,000
Total	$120,000

On the basis of the estimated market values, the purchase price should be allocated as follows:

To land: $100,000 \times $30,000/$120,000 = $25,000

To building: $100,000 \times $90,000/$120,000 = $75,000

The journal entry to record the purchase would be as follows:

Jan. 1	Land	25,000	
	Building	75,000	
	Cash		100,000

To record the purchase of land and building for a lump-sum amount.

Assets	**= Liabilities + Owners' Equity**
+25,000	
+75,000	
−100,000	

Market value is best established by an independent appraisal of the property. If such appraisal is not possible, the accountant must rely on the market value of other similar assets, on the value of the assets in tax records, or on other available evidence.

These efforts to allocate dollars between land and buildings will permit the appropriate allocation for depreciation. But when an investor or lender views the balance sheet, he or she is often more interested in the current market value. The best things that can be said about historical cost are that it is a verifiable number and that it is conservative. But it is still up to the lender or the investor to determine the appropriate value for these assets.

LO 4 Describe the impact of capitalizing interest as part of the acquisition cost of an asset.

Capitalization of Interest We have seen that acquisition cost may include several items. But should the acquisition cost of an asset include the interest cost necessary to finance the asset? That is, should interest be treated as an asset, or should it be treated as an expense of the period?

Generally, the interest on borrowed money should be treated as an expense of the period. If a company buys an asset and borrows money to finance the purchase, the interest on the borrowed money is not considered part of the asset's cost. Financial statements generally treat investing and financing as separate decisions. Purchase of an asset, an investing activity, is treated as a business decision that is separate from the decision concerning the financing of the asset. Therefore, interest is treated as a period cost and should appear on the income statement as interest expense in the period incurred.

There is one exception to this general guideline, however. If a company *constructs* an asset over a period of time and borrows money to finance the construction, the amount of interest incurred during the construction period is not treated as interest expense. Instead, the interest must be included as part of the acquisition cost of the asset. This is referred to as **capitalization of interest.** The amount of interest that is capitalized (treated as an asset) is based on the *average accumulated expenditures.* The logic of using the average accumulated expenditure is that this number represents an average amount of money tied up in the project over a year. If it takes $400,000 to construct a building, the interest should not be figured on the full $400,000 because there were times during the year when less than the full amount was being used.

When it costs $400,000 to build an asset and the amount of interest to be capitalized is $10,000, the acquisition cost of the asset is $410,000. The asset should appear on the balance sheet at that amount. Depreciation of the asset should be based on $410,000, less any residual value.

Land Improvements It is important to distinguish between land and other costs associated with it. The acquisition cost of land should be kept in a separate account because land has an unlimited life and is not subject to depreciation. Other costs associated with land should be recorded in an account such as Land Improvements. For example, the costs of paving a parking lot or landscaping costs are properly treated as land improvements, which have a limited life. Therefore, the acquisition costs of land improvements should be depreciated over their useful lives.

Use and Depreciation of Property, Plant, and Equipment

All property, plant, and equipment, except land, have a limited life and decline in usefulness over time. The accrual accounting process requires a proper *matching* of expenses and revenue to accurately measure income. Therefore, the accountant must estimate the decline in usefulness of operating assets and allocate the acquisition cost in a manner consistent with the decline in usefulness. This allocation is the process generally referred to as **depreciation.**

LO 5 Compare depreciation methods and understand the factors affecting the choice of method.

Unfortunately, proper matching for operating assets is not easy because of the many factors involved. An asset's decline in usefulness is related to *physical deterioration* factors such as wear and tear. In some cases, the physical deterioration results from heavy use of the asset in the production process, but it may also result from the passage of time or exposure to the elements.

The decline in an asset's usefulness is also related to *obsolescence* factors. Some operating assets, such as computers, decline in usefulness simply because they have been surpassed by a newer model or newer technology. Finally, the decline in an asset's usefulness is related to a company's *repair and maintenance* policy. A company with an aggressive and extensive repair and maintenance program will not experience a decline in usefulness of operating assets as rapidly as one without such a policy.

Because the decline in an asset's usefulness is related to a variety of factors, several depreciation methods have been developed. In theory, a company should use a depreciation method that allocates the original cost of the asset to the periods benefited and that allows the company to accurately match the expense to the revenue generated by the asset. We will present three methods of depreciation: *straight line, units of production,* and *double declining balance.*

All depreciation methods are based on the asset's original acquisition cost. In addition, all methods require an estimate of two additional factors: the asset's *life* and its *residual value.* The residual value (also referred to as *salvage value*) should represent the amount that could be obtained from selling or disposing of the asset at the end of its useful life. Often this may be a small amount or even zero.

Straight-Line Method   The **straight-line method** of depreciation allocates the cost of the asset evenly over time. This method calculates the annual depreciation as follows:

$$\text{Depreciation} = (\text{Acquisition Cost} - \text{Residual Value})/\text{Life}$$

For example, assume that on January 1, 1998, Kemp Company purchased a machine for $20,000. The company estimated that the machine's life would be five years and its residual value at the end of 2002 would be $2,000. The annual depreciation should be calculated as follows:

$$\text{Depreciation} = (\text{Acquisition Cost} - \text{Residual Value})/\text{Life}$$
$$\text{Depreciation} = (\$20,000 - \$2,000)/5$$
$$= \$3,600$$

An asset's **book value** is defined as its acquisition cost minus its total amount of accumulated depreciation. Thus, the book value of the machine in this example is $16,400 at the end of 1998:

$$\text{Book Value} = \text{Acquisition Cost} - \text{Accumulated Depreciation}$$
$$\text{Book Value} = \$20,000 - \$3,600$$
$$= \$16,400$$

The book value at the end of 1999 is $12,800:

$$\text{Book Value} = \text{Acquisition Cost} - \text{Accumulated Depreciation}$$
$$\text{Book Value} = \$20,000 - (2 \times \$3,600)$$
$$= \$12,800$$

The most attractive features of the straight-line method are its ease and simplicity. It is the most popular method for presenting depreciation in the annual report to stockholders.

Property, plant, and equipment (PP&E) constitute operating assets, which show up in the assets section of the balance sheet. For example, trucks and satellite equipment are essential for installing, maintaining, and operating cable service to customers and should be reported as property, plant, and equipment.

Units-of-Production Method In some cases, the decline in an asset's usefulness is directly related to wear and tear as a result of the number of units it produces. In those cases, depreciation should be calculated by the units-of-production method. With this method, the asset's life is expressed in terms of the number of units that the asset can produce. The depreciation *per unit* can be calculated as follows:

$$\text{Depreciation per Unit} = (\text{Acquisition Cost} - \text{Residual Value})/\text{Total Number of Units in Asset's Life}$$

The annual depreciation for a given year can be calculated based on the number of units produced during that year as follows:

$$\text{Annual Depreciation} = \text{Depreciation per Unit} \times \text{Units Produced in Current Year}$$

For example, assume that Kemp Company in the previous example wanted to use the units-of-production method for 1998. Also assume that Kemp has been able to estimate that the total number of units that will be produced during the asset's five-year life is 18,000. During 1998 Kemp produced 4,000 units. The depreciation per unit for Kemp's machine can be calculated as follows:

$$\text{Depreciation per Unit} = (\text{Acquisition Cost} - \text{Residual Value})/\text{Life in Units}$$

$$\text{Depreciation per Unit} = (\$20,000 - \$2,000)/18,000$$
$$= \$1 \text{ per Unit}$$

The amount of depreciation that should be recorded as an expense for 1998 is $4,000:

$$\text{Annual Depreciation} = \text{Depreciation per Unit} \times \text{Units Produced in 1998}$$

$$\text{Annual Depreciation} = \$1 \text{ per Unit} \times 4,000 \text{ Units}$$
$$= \$4,000$$

Depreciation will be recorded until the asset produces 18,000 units. The machine cannot be depreciated below its residual value of $2,000.

The units-of-production method is most appropriate when the accountant is able to estimate the total number of units that will be produced over the asset's life. For example, if a factory machine is used to produce a particular item, the life of the asset may be expressed in terms of the number of units produced. Further, the units produced must be related to particular time periods so that depreciation expense can be matched accurately with the related revenue.

Accelerated Depreciation Methods In some cases more cost should be allocated to the early years of an asset's use and less to the later years. For those assets, an accelerated method of depreciation is appropriate. The term accelerated depreciation refers to several depreciation methods by which a higher amount of depreciation is recorded in the early years than in later ones.

One form of accelerated depreciation is the double declining-balance method. Under this method, depreciation is calculated at double the straight-line rate but on a declining amount. The first step is to calculate the straight-line rate as a percentage. The straight-line rate for the Kemp asset with a five-year life is

$$100\%/5 \text{ Years} = 20\%.$$

The second step is to double the straight-line rate:

$$2 \times 20\% = 40\%$$

This rate will be applied in all years to the asset's book value at the beginning of each year. As depreciation is recorded, the book value declines. Thus, a constant rate is applied to a declining amount. This constant rate is applied to the full cost or initial book value, not to cost minus residual value as in the other methods. However, the machine cannot be depreciated below its residual value.

The amount of depreciation for 1998 would be calculated as follows:

$$\text{Depreciation} = \text{Beginning Book Value} \times \text{Rate}$$
$$\text{Depreciation} = \$20,000 \times 40\%$$
$$= \$8,000$$

The amount of depreciation for 1999 would be calculated as follows:

$$\text{Depreciation} = \text{Beginning Book Value} \times \text{Rate}$$
$$\text{Depreciation} = (\$20,000 - \$8,000) \times 40\%$$
$$= \$4,800$$

The complete depreciation schedule for Kemp Company for all five years of the machine's life would be as follows:

YEAR	RATE	BOOK VALUE AT BEGINNING OF YEAR	DEPRECIATION	BOOK VALUE AT END OF YEAR
1998	40%	$20,000	$ 8,000	$12,000
1999	40	12,000	4,800	7,200
2000	40	7,200	2,880	4,320
2001	40	4,320	1,728	2,592
2002	40	2,592	592	2,000
Total			$18,000	

[handwritten note: add up depreciation costs — watch out for adding up declining book values! That's wrong]

In the Kemp Company example, the depreciation for 2002 cannot be calculated as $2,592 × 40% because this would result in an accumulated depreciation amount more than $18,000. The total amount of depreciation recorded in Years 1 through 4 is $17,408. The accountant should record only $592 depreciation ($18,000 − $17,408) in 2002 so that the remaining value of the machine is $2,000 at the end of 2002.

The double declining-balance method of depreciation results in an accelerated depreciation pattern. It is most appropriate for assets subject to a rapid decline in usefulness as a result of technical or obsolescence factors. Double declining-balance depreciation is not widely used for financial statement purposes but may be appropriate for certain assets. As discussed earlier, most companies use straight-line depreciation for financial statement purposes because it generally produces the highest net income, especially in growing companies that have a stable or expanding base of assets.

Comparison of Depreciation Methods In this section, you have learned about several methods of depreciating operating assets. Exhibit 8-1 presents a comparison of the depreciation and book values of the Kemp Company asset for 1998–2002 using the straight-line and double declining-balance methods (we have excluded the units-of-production method). Note that both methods result in a depreciation total of $18,000 over the five-year time period. The amount of depreciation per year depends, however, on the method of depreciation chosen.

| EXHIBIT 8-1 | Comparison of Depreciation and Book Values of Straight-Line and Double Declining-Balance Methods |

	STRAIGHT LINE		DOUBLE DECLINING BALANCE	
YEAR	DEPRECIATION	BOOK VALUE	DEPRECIATION	BOOK VALUE
1998	$ 3,600	$16,400	$ 8,000	$12,000
1999	3,600	12,800	4,800	7,200
2000	3,600	9,200	2,880	4,320
2001	3,600	5,600	1,728	2,592
2002	3,600	2,000	592	2,000
Totals	$18,000		$18,000	

Nonaccountants often misunderstand the accountant's concept of depreciation. Accountants do not consider depreciation to be a process of *valuing* the asset. That is, depreciation does not describe the increase or decrease in the market value of the asset. Accountants consider depreciation to be a process of *cost allocation*. The purpose is to allocate the original acquisition cost to the periods benefited by the asset. The depreciation method chosen should be based on the decline in the asset's usefulness. A company can choose a different depreciation method for each individual fixed asset or for each class or category of fixed assets.

The choice of depreciation method can have a significant impact on the bottom line. If two companies are essentially identical in every other respect, a different depreciation method for fixed assets can make one company look more profitable than another. Or a company that uses accelerated depreciation for one year can find that its otherwise declining earnings are no longer declining if it switches to straight-line depreciation. Investors should pay some attention to depreciation methods when comparing companies. Statement users must be aware of the different depreciation methods to understand the calculation of income and to compare companies that may not use the same methods.

Some investors ignore depreciation altogether when evaluating a company, not because they do not know that assets depreciate but because they want to focus on cash flow instead of earnings. Depreciation is a "noncash" charge that reduces net income.

Depreciation and Income Taxes Financial accounting involves the presentation of financial statements to external users of accounting information, users such as investors and creditors. When depreciating an asset for financial accounting purposes, the accountant's goal should be to choose a depreciation method that is consistent with the asset's decline in usefulness and that properly allocates its cost to the periods that benefit from its use.

Depreciation is also deducted for income tax purposes. Sometimes depreciation is referred to as a *tax shield* because it reduces (as do other expenses) the amount of income tax that would otherwise have to be paid. When depreciating an asset for tax purposes, a company should generally choose a depreciation method that reduces the present value of its tax burden to the lowest-possible amount over the life of the asset. Normally, this is best accomplished with an accelerated depreciation method, which allows a company to save more income tax in the early years of the asset. This happens because the higher depreciation charges reduce taxable income more than the straight-line method does. The method allowed for tax purposes is referred to as MACRS, which stands for Modified Accelerated Cost Recovery System. As a form of accelerated depreciation, it results in a larger amount of depreciation in the early years of asset life and a smaller amount in later years.

Choice of Depreciation Method As we have stated, in theory a company should choose the depreciation method that best allocates the original cost of the asset to the periods benefited by the use of the asset. Theory aside, it is important to examine the other factors that affect a company's decision in choosing a depreciation method or methods. Exhibit 8–2 presents the factors that affect this decision and the likely choice that arises from each factor. Usually, the factors that are the most important are whether depreciation is calculated for presentation on the financial statements to stockholders or is calculated for income tax purposes.

When depreciation is calculated for financial statement purposes, a company generally wants to present the most favorable impression (the highest income) possible. Therefore, most companies choose the straight-line method of depreciation. Exhibit 8–3 indicates the results of a survey in which 600 companies were asked the depreciation method or methods used for their 1995 financial statements. The vast majority (572) used the straight-line method. Twenty-seven used the declining-balance method, 12 used the sum-of-the-years' digits method, 49 used accelerated depreciation but did not specify which form of accelerated depreciation, 38 used the units-of-production method, and 11 used other methods of depreciation. The number of companies does not total to 600 because many companies use different methods for different assets.

If the objective of the company's management is to minimize its income tax liability, then the company will generally not choose the straight-line method for tax purposes.

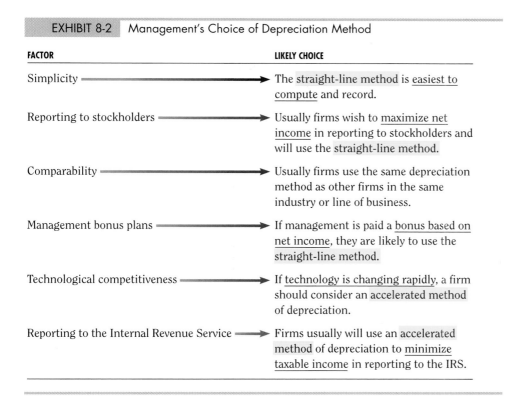

EXHIBIT 8-2   Management's Choice of Depreciation Method

FACTOR	LIKELY CHOICE
Simplicity	The straight-line method is easiest to compute and record.
Reporting to stockholders	Usually firms wish to maximize net income in reporting to stockholders and will use the straight-line method.
Comparability	Usually firms use the same depreciation method as other firms in the same industry or line of business.
Management bonus plans	If management is paid a bonus based on net income, they are likely to use the straight-line method.
Technological competitiveness	If technology is changing rapidly, a firm should consider an accelerated method of depreciation.
Reporting to the Internal Revenue Service	Firms usually will use an accelerated method of depreciation to minimize taxable income in reporting to the IRS.

As discussed in the preceding section, accelerated depreciation allows the company to save more on income taxes because depreciation is a tax shield. If we could construct an exhibit, similar to Exhibit 8–3, that indicated the methods of depreciation used for tax purposes, it would indicate that the vast majority of companies do, in fact, use accelerated depreciation for tax purposes.

Therefore, it is not unusual for a company to use *two* depreciation methods for the same asset, one for financial reporting purposes and another for tax purposes. This may seem somewhat confusing, but it is the direct result of the differing goals of financial and tax accounting. See Chapter 10 for more about this issue.

Change in Depreciation Estimate   An asset's acquisition cost is known at the time it is purchased, but its life and its residual value must be estimated. These estimates are then used as the basis for depreciating it. Occasionally, an estimate of the

LO 6   Understand the impact of a change in the estimate of the asset life or residual value.

EXHIBIT 8-3   Depreciation Methods Used for Financial Reporting Purposes

METHOD	NUMBER OF COMPANIES
Straight-line	572
Declining-Balance	27
Sum-of-the-years' digit	12
Other accelerated depreciation methods	49
Units of production	38
Other	11

SOURCE: *Accounting Trends & Techniques,* 50th ed. (New York: American Institute of Certified Public Accountants, 1996).

asset's life or residual value must be altered after the depreciation process has begun. This is an example of an accounting change that is referred to as a change in estimate.

Assume the same facts as in the Kemp Company example. The company purchased a machine on January 1, 1998, for $20,000. Kemp estimated that the machine's life would be five years and its residual value at the end of five years would be $2,000. Assume that Kemp has depreciated the machine using the straight-line method for two years. At the beginning of 2000, Kemp believes that the total machine life will be seven years, or another five years beyond the two years the machine has been used. Thus, depreciation must be adjusted to reflect the new estimate of the asset's life.

A change in estimate should be recorded *prospectively,* meaning that the depreciation recorded in prior years is not corrected or restated. Instead, the new estimate should affect the current year and future years. Kemp Company should depreciate the remaining depreciable amount during 2000 through 2004. The amount to be depreciated over that time period should be calculated as follows:

Acquisition Cost, Jan. 1, 1998	$20,000
Less: Accumulated Depreciation	
(2 years at $3,600 per year)	7,200
Book Value, Jan. 1, 2000	$12,800
Less: Residual Value	2,000
Remaining Depreciable Amount	$10,800

The remaining depreciable amount should be recorded as depreciation over the remaining life of the machine. In the Kemp Company case, the depreciation amount for 2000 and the following four years would be $2,160:

Depreciation = Remaining Depreciable Amount/Remaining Life
Depreciation = $10,800 / 5 Years
= $2,160

The journal entry to record depreciation for the year 2000 is as follows:

```
2000
Dec.31   Depreciation Expense                          2,160
             Accumulated Depreciation                         2,160
         To record depreciation for 2000 based on remaining
         life of five years.
```

Assets = Liabilities + Owners' Equity
−2,160   −2,160

If the change in estimate is a material amount, the company should disclose in the footnotes to the 2000 financial statements that depreciation has changed as a result of a change in estimate. The company's auditors have to be very careful that management's decision to change its estimate of the depreciable life of the asset is not simply an attempt to manipulate earnings. Particularly in capital-intensive manufacturing concerns, lengthening the useful life of equipment can have a material impact on earnings.

A change in estimate of an asset's residual value is treated in a manner similar to a change in an asset's life. There should be no attempt to correct or restate the income statements of past periods that were based on the original estimate. Instead, the accountant should use the new estimate of residual value to calculate depreciation for the current and future years.

A change in estimate is not treated the same way as a *change in principle*. If a company changes its *method* of depreciation, for example from accelerated depreciation to the straight-line method, this constitutes a change in accounting principle that must be disclosed separately on the income statement. A complete discussion of items treated as a change in accounting principle can be found in Chapter 12.

Capital versus Revenue Expenditures

Accountants must often decide whether certain expenditures related to operating assets should be treated as an addition to the cost of the asset or as an expense. One of the most common examples involving this decision concerns repairs to an asset. Should the repairs constitute capital expenditures or revenue expenditures? A capital expenditure is a cost that is added to the acquisition cost of the asset. A revenue expenditure is not treated as part of the cost of the asset but as an expense on the income statement. Thus, the company must decide whether to treat an item as an asset (balance sheet) and depreciate its cost over its life or to treat it as an expense (income statement) of a single period.

The distinction between capital and revenue expenditures is a matter of judgment. Generally, the guideline that should be followed is that if an expenditure increases the life of the asset or its productivity, it should be treated as a capital expenditure and added to the asset account. If an expenditure simply maintains an asset in its normal operating condition, however, it should be treated as an expense. The *materiality* of the expenditure must also be considered. Most companies establish a policy of treating an expenditure smaller than a specified amount as a revenue expenditure (an expense on the income statement).

It is very important that a company not improperly capitalize a material expenditure that should have been written off right away. The capitalization policies of companies are closely watched by Wall Street analysts who try to assess the value of these companies. When a company is capitalizing rather than expensing certain items to artificially boost earnings, that revelation can be very damaging to the stock price.

Expenditures related to operating assets may be classified in several categories. For each type of expenditure, its treatment as capital or revenue should be as follows:

LO 7 Determine which expenditures should be capitalized as asset costs and which should be treated as expenses.

CATEGORY	EXAMPLE	ASSET OR EXPENSE
Normal maintenance	Repainting	Expense
Minor repair	Replace spark plugs	Expense
Major repair	Replace a vehicle's engine	Asset, if life or productivity is enhanced
Addition	Add a wing to a building	Asset

ACCOUNTING FOR YOUR DECISIONS
You Are the Owner
You are a realtor whose business car has just had its transmission rebuilt for $400. Would you classify this "repair" as a capital expenditure or a revenue expenditure? Why is it important to properly classify the $400?

ANS: If the business car's life is not extended, then the repair should be treated as a revenue expenditure, in which the cost is expensed on the income statement. It is important to properly classify capital and revenue expenditures because capitalizing rather than expensing costs can artificially boost earnings. The opposite effect would occur if costs are expensed and not capitalized.

An item treated as a capital expenditure affects the amount of depreciation that should be recorded over the asset's remaining life. We return to the Kemp Company example to illustrate. Assume again that Kemp purchased a machine on January 1, 1998, for $20,000. Kemp estimated that its residual value at the end of five years would be $2,000 and has depreciated the machine using the straight-line method for 1998 and 1999. At the beginning of 2000, Kemp made a $3,000 overhaul to the machine, extending its life by three years. Because the expenditure qualifies as a capital expenditure, the cost of overhauling the machine should be added to the asset account. The journal entry to record the overhaul is as follows:

```
2000
Jan. 1   Machine                                              3,000
             Cash                                                      3,000
         To record the overhaul of an operating asset.
```

Assets   =   Liabilities   +   Owners' Equity
+3,000
−3,000

For the years 1998 and 1999, Kemp recorded depreciation of $3,600 per year:

Depreciation = (Acquisition Cost − Residual Value)/Life
Depreciation = ($20,000 − $2,000)/5
= $3,600

Beginning in 2000, Kemp should record depreciation of $2,300 per year, computed as follows:

Original Cost, Jan. 1, 1998	$20,000
Less: Accumulated Depreciation (2 years × $3,600)	7,200
Book Value, Jan. 1, 2000	$12,800
Plus: Major Overhaul	3,000
Less: Residual Value	(2,000)
Remaining Depreciable Amount	$13,800

Depreciation = Remaining Depreciable Amount/Remaining Life
Depreciation per year = $13,800/6 Years
= $2,300

The entry to record depreciation for the year 2000 follows:

```
2000
Dec. 31   Depreciation Expense                                2,300
              Accumulated Depreciation—Asset                        2,300
          To record annual depreciation on operating asset.
```

Assets   =   Liabilities   +   Owners' Equity
−2,300   −2,300

Environmental Aspects of Operating Assets

As the number of the government's environmental regulations has increased, businesses have been required to expend more money complying with them. A common example involves costs to comply with federal requirements to clean up contaminated soil surrounding plant facilities. In some cases the costs are very large and may exceed the value of the property. Should such costs be considered an expense and recorded entirely in one accounting period, or should they be treated as a capital expenditure and added to the cost of the asset? At the present time, there is little accounting guidance on such issues, and management must exercise careful judgment on a case-by-case basis. It is important, however, for companies at least to conduct a thorough investigation to determine the potential environmental considerations that may affect the value of operating assets and to ponder carefully the accounting implications of new environmental regulations.

Should the costs of cleaning up a contaminated factory be considered an expense of one period or a capital expenditure added to the cost of the plant asset? To make the best decision, management should gather all the facts about the extent of the proposed cleanup and its environmental impact.

Disposal of Operating Assets

An asset may be disposed of in any of several different ways. One common method is to sell the asset for cash. Sale of an asset involves two important considerations. First, depreciation must be recorded up to the date of sale. If the sale does not occur at the fiscal year-end, usually December 31, depreciation must be recorded for a partial period from the beginning of the year to the date of sale. Second, the company selling the asset must calculate and record the gain or loss on its sale.

Refer again to the Kemp Company example. Assume that Kemp purchased a machine on January 1, 1998, for $20,000, estimating its life to be five years and the residual value to be $2,000. Kemp used the straight-line method of depreciation. Assume that Kemp sold the machine on July 1, 2000, for $12,400. Depreciation for the six-month time period from January 1 to July 1, 2000, is $1,800 ($3,600 per year × 1/2 year = $1,800) and should be recorded as follows:

```
2000
July 1   Depreciation Expense                        1,800
              Accumulated Depreciation—Machine                1,800
         To record depreciation for a six-month time period.
```

Assets	=	Liabilities	+	Owners' Equity
−1,800				−1,800

After the July 1 entry, the balance of the Accumulated Depreciation—Machine account is $9,000, which reflects depreciation for the 2½ years from the date of purchase to the date of sale. The entry to record the sale follows:

```
2000
July 1   Accumulated Depreciation—Machine             9,000
         Cash                                        12,400
              Machine                                        20,000
              Gain on Sale of Asset                           1,400
         To record the sale of the machine.
```

Assets	=	Liabilities	+	Owners' Equity
+9,000				+1,400
+12,400				
−20,000				

When an asset is sold, all accounts related to it must be removed, In the preceding entry the Machine account is reduced (credited) to eliminate the account, and the Accumulated Depreciation—Machine account is reduced (debited) to eliminate it. The **Gain on Sale of Asset** indicates the amount by which the sale price of the machine *exceeds* the book value. Thus, the gain can be calculated as follows:

Asset cost	$20,000
Less: Accumulated depreciation	9,000
Book value	$11,000
Sale price	12,400
Gain on Sale of Asset	$ 1,400

The account Gain on Sale of Asset is an income statement account and should appear in the Other Income/Expense category of the statement. The Gain on Sale of Asset account is not treated as revenue because it does not constitute the company's ongoing or central activity. Instead, it appears as income but in a separate category to denote its incidental nature.

The calculation of a loss on the sale of an asset is similar to that of a gain. Assume in the above example that Kemp had sold the machine on July 1, 2000, for $10,000 cash. As in the previous example, depreciation must be recorded to the date of sale, July 1. The following is the entry to record the sale of the asset:

LO 8 Analyze the effect of the disposal of an asset at a gain or loss.

2000
July 1   Accumulated Depreciation—Machine   9,000
         Cash   10,000
         Loss on Sale of Asset   1,000
            Machine   20,000
         To record the sale of a machine.

Assets	=	Liabilities	+	Owners' Equity
+9,000				−1,000
+10,000				
−20,000				

The **Loss on Sale of Asset** indicates the amount by which the asset's sales price *is less than* its book value. Thus, the loss could be calculated as follows:

Asset cost	$20,000
Less: Accumulated depreciation	9,000
Book value	$11,000
Sale price	10,000
Loss on Sale of Asset	$ 1,000

The Loss on Sale of Asset account is an income statement account and should appear in the Other Income/Expense category of the income statement.

Operating Assets: Natural Resources

Balance Sheet Presentation

Important operating assets for some companies consists of natural resources such as coalfields, oil wells, other mineral deposits, and timberlands. Natural resources share one characteristic: the resource is consumed as it is used. For example, the coal a utility company uses to make electricity is consumed in the process. Most natural resources cannot be replenished in the foreseeable future. Coal and oil, for example, can be replenished only by nature over millions of years. Timberlands may be replenished in a shorter time period, but even trees must grow for many years to be usable for lumber.

Natural resources should be carried in the Property, Plant, and Equipment category of the balance sheet as an operating asset. Like other assets in the category, natural resources should initially be recorded at *acquisition cost*. Acquisition cost should include the cost of acquiring the natural resource and the costs necessary to prepare the asset for use. The preparation costs for natural resources may often be very large; for example, a utility may spend large sums to remove layers of dirt before the coal can be mined. These preparation costs should be added to the cost of the asset.

Depletion of Natural Resources

When a natural resource is used or consumed, it should be treated as an expense. The process of recording the expense is similar to the depreciation or amortization process but is usually referred to as *depletion*. The amount of depletion expense each period should reflect the portion of the natural resource that was used up during the current year.

Assume, for example, that Local Coal Company purchased a coalfield on January 1, 1998, for $1 million. The company employed a team of engineering experts who estimated the total coal in the field to be 200,000 tons and who determined that the field's residual value after removal of the coal would be zero. Local Coal should calculate the depletion per ton as follows:

$$\text{Depletion per Ton} = (\text{Acquisition Cost} - \text{Residual Value})/$$
$$\text{Total Number of Tons in Asset's Life}$$
$$= (\$1,000,000 - 0)/200,000 \text{ tons}$$
$$= \$5 \text{ per ton}$$

Depletion expense for each year should be calculated as follows:

Depletion Expense = Depletion per Ton × Tons Mined during Year

Assume that Local Coal Company mined 10,000 tons of coal during 1998. The depletion expense for 1998 for Local Coal follows:

$5 × 10,000 tons = $50,000

Local Coal should record the depletion in an Accumulated Depletion—Coalfield account that would appear as a contra-asset on the balance sheet. The company should record the following journal entry:

```
1998
Dec. 31   Depletion Expense                          50,000
               Accumulated Depletion—Coalfield                 50,000
          To record depletion for 1998.
```

Assets   =   Liabilities   +   Owners' Equity
−50,000   −50,000

Rather than using an accumulated depletion account, some companies may decrease (credit) the asset account directly.

There is an interesting parallel between depletion of natural resources and depreciation of plant and equipment. That is, depletion is very similar to depreciation using the units-of-production method. Both require an estimate of the useful life of the asset in terms of the total amount that can be produced (for units-of-production method) or consumed (for depletion) over the asset's life.

Natural resources may be important assets for some companies. For example, Exhibit 8-4 highlights the asset portion of the 1995 balance sheet and the accompanying

---

EXHIBIT 8-4 Georgia-Pacific Corporation and Subsidiaries 1995 Assets Section and Natural Resources Footnote

Balance Sheets
Georgia-Pacific Corporation and Subsidiaries

(Millions, except shares and per share amounts)	1995	1994
Timber and timberlands, net	1,374	1,363
Property, plant and equipment		
Land and improvements	305	246
Buildings	1,122	1,066
Machinery and equipment	10,551	9,881
Construction in progress	598	307
Total property, plant and equipment, at cost	12,576	11,500
Accumulated depreciation	(6,563)	(6,012)
Property, plant and equipment, net	6,013	5,488
Goodwill, net	1,714	1,773
Other assets	639	256
Total assets	$12,335	$10,864

December 31

Timber and Timberlands The Corporation depletes its investment in timber based on the total fiber that will be available during the estimated growth cycle. Timber carrying costs are expensed as incurred.

footnote of Georgia-Pacific Corporation. Georgia-Pacific had timber and timberlands, net of depletion, of $1,374 million as of December 31, 1995. The footnote indicates that the company records depletion based on the total fiber available during the estimated growth cycle of the timber.

Operating Assets: Intangible Assets

FROM CONCEPT TO PRACTICE 8.2
READING TIME-WARNER'S BALANCE SHEET Which items on Time-Warner's 1995 balance sheet should be considered intangible assets?

Intangible assets are long-term assets with no physical properties. Because one cannot see or touch most intangible assets, it is easy to overlook their importance. Intangibles are recorded as assets, however, because they provide future economic benefits to the company. In fact, an intangible asset may be the most important asset a company owns or controls. For example, a pharmaceutical company may own some property, plant, and equipment, but its most important asset may be its patent for a particular drug or process. Likewise, the company that publishes this textbook may consider the copyrights to textbooks to be among its most important revenue-producing assets.

The balance sheet includes the intangible assets that meet the accounting definition of assets. Patents, copyrights, and brand names are included because they are owned by the company and will produce a future benefit that can be identified and measured. The balance sheet, however, would indicate only the acquisition cost of those assets, not the value of the assets to the company or the sales value of the assets.

Of course, the balance sheet does not include all of the items that may produce future benefit to the company. A company's employees, its management team, its location, or the intellectual capital of a few key researchers may well provide important future benefits and value. They are not recorded on the balance sheet, however, because they do not meet the accountant's definition of assets and cannot be easily identified or measured.

Balance Sheet Presentation

LO 9 Understand the balance sheet presentation of intangible assets.

Intangible assets are long-term assets and should be shown separately from property, plant, and equipment. Some companies develop a separate category, Intangible Assets, for the various types of intangibles. For example, Exhibit 8-5 presents the Assets section and the accompanying footnote of the 1995 balance sheet of Quaker Oats Company. Note that intangibles account for nearly one-half of Quaker's total assets. Quaker presents only one line for intangible assets, but the footnote indicates that intangibles consist primarily of goodwill (see below), which is amortized on a straight-line basis. The presentation of intangible assets varies widely, however.

Exhibit 8-6 presents the Assets section and the accompanying footnote of the 1995 balance sheet of Alberto-Culver Company. Alberto-Culver presents the intangible assets of goodwill and trade names immediately after the Property, Plant, and Equipment category. Both accounts are presented net of the accumulated amortization. The footnote indicates that amortization was computed on the straight-line basis.

Exhibit 8-7 contains a list of the most common intangible assets. The nature of most intangible assets is fairly evident, but two of them are not so easily understood. Organization costs represent the costs incurred at the time a new corporation is formed. These costs include legal fees, registration fees, and other costs involved in starting the company. These costs are not treated as an expense when incurred because the benefit of incorporating occurs over a long time period. Instead, the costs are treated as an asset, Organization Costs, and are amortized over a future time period.

Goodwill represents the amount of the purchase price paid in excess of the market value of the individual net assets when a business is purchased. (See Chapter 13 for more details.) Goodwill is recorded only when a business is purchased. It is not recorded when a company engages in activities that do not involve the purchase of another business entity. For example, customer loyalty or a good management team may represent "goodwill," but neither meets the accountants' criteria to be recorded as an asset on a firm's financial statements.

EXHIBIT 8-5	The Quaker Oats Company and Subsidiaries 1995 Assets Section and Intangibles Footnote

THE QUAKER OATS COMPANY AND SUBSIDIARIES CONSOLIDATED BALANCE SHEET

June 30	1995
Assets	
Current Assets	
Cash and cash equivalents	$ 101.8
Trade accounts receivable — net of allowances	546.8
Inventories	
Finished goods	267.4
Grains and raw materials	94.4
Packaging materials and supplies	44.2
Total inventories	406.0
Other current assets	262.0
Total Current Assets	1,316.6
Property, Plant and Equipment	
Land	25.0
Buildings and improvements	376.0
Machinery and equipment	1,442.7
Property, plant and equipment	1,843.7
Less accumulated depreciation	730.3
Property — Net	1,113.4
Intangible Assets — Net of Amortization	2,311.1
Other Assets	85.8
Total Assets	$ 4,826.9

Intangibles – Intangible assets consist principally of excess purchase price over net tangible assets of businesses acquired (goodwill) and trademarks. Goodwill is amortized on a straight-line basis over periods not exceeding 40 years. The Company continually evaluates whether events or circumstances have occurred indicating that the remaining estimated useful life of goodwill may not be appropriate. When factors indicate that goodwill should be evaluated for possible impairment, the Company uses an estimate of the acquired business' undiscounted future cash flows compared to the carrying value of goodwill to determine if a write-off is necessary. Gross goodwill as of June 30, 1995, 1994 and 1993 was $1.87 billion, $615.2 million and $528.0 million, respectively. Accumulated goodwill amortization as of June 30, 1995, 1994 and 1993 was $122.1 million, $128.0 million and $113.3 million, respectively. Trademarks are amortized on a straight-line basis over periods not exceeding 40 years. Gross trademark cost and accumulated trademark amortization as of June 30, 1995 were $452.2 million and $8.0 million, respectively. Trademark cost as of June 30, 1994 and 1993 was not material. See Note 2 to the consolidated financial statements for further discussion of intangibles and amortization periods.

Some investors believe that goodwill is not an asset because it is difficult to determine the factors that caused this asset. They prefer to focus their attention on a company's tangible assets. These investors simply reduce the amount shown on the balance sheet by the amount of goodwill, deducting it from total assets and reducing stockholders' equity by the same amount. That is similar to the goodwill accounting that occurs in many foreign countries. International accounting standards allow firms *either* to present goodwill separately as an asset *or* to deduct it from stockholders' equity at the time of purchase. The result is that the presentation of goodwill on the financial statements of non-U.S. companies can look much different from that for U.S. companies.

EXHIBIT 8-6   Alberto-Culver Company and Subsidiaries 1995 Assets Section and Intangibles Footnote

ALBERTO-CULVER COMPANY AND SUBSIDIARIES
CONSOLIDATED BALANCE SHEETS

(Dollars in thousands, except per share data)	September 30,	
Assets	**1995**	**1994**
Current assets:		
Cash and cash equivalents	$142,585	41,833
Short-term investments	4,400	8,529
Receivables, less allowance for doubtful accounts of $5,663 in 1995 and $5,497 in 1994	128,482	108,877
Inventories:		
Raw materials	32,408	29,618
Work-in-process	4,897	5,868
Finished goods	211,224	195,633
Total inventories	248,529	231,119
Prepaid expenses	12,549	11,399
Total current assets	536,545	401,757
Property, plant and equipment (note 7):		
Land	8,396	7,328
Buildings	100,954	89,344
Machinery and equipment	176,684	146,560
Total property, plant and equipment	286,034	243,232
Accumulated depreciation	128,243	110,351
Property, plant and equipment, net	157,791	132,881
Goodwill, net	55,225	44,307
Trade names and other intangible assets, net	34,198	9,960
Other assets	31,327	21,303
	$815,086	610,208

> **Goodwill and Trade Names** The cost of goodwill and trade names is amortized on a straight-line basis over periods ranging from ten to forty years.

EXHIBIT 8-7   Most Common Intangible Assets

INTANGIBLE ASSET	DESCRIPTION
Patent	Right to use, manufacture, or sell a product; granted by the U.S. Patent Office. Patents have a legal life of 17 years.
Copyright	Right to reproduce or sell a published work. Copyrights are granted for 50 years plus the life of the creator.
Trademark	A symbol or name that allows a product or service to be identified; provides legal protection for 20 years plus an indefinite number of renewal periods.
Organization costs	Costs incurred at the time a new corporation is created. Costs include legal and registration fees.
Goodwill	The excess of the purchase price to acquire a business over the value of the individual net assets acquired.

Acquisition Cost of Intangible Assets

As was the case with property, plant, and equipment, the acquisition cost of an intangible asset includes all of the costs to acquire the asset and prepare it for its intended use. This should include all necessary costs such as legal costs incurred at the time of acquisition. Acquisition cost also should include those costs that are incurred after acquisition and that are necessary to the existence of the asset. For example, if a firm must pay legal fees to protect a patent from infringement, the costs should be considered part of the acquisition cost and should be included in the patent account.

You should also be aware of one item that is similar to intangible assets but is *not* on the balance sheet. Research and development costs are expenditures incurred in the discovery of new knowledge and the translation of research into a design or plan for a new product or service or in a significant improvement to an existing product or service. Firms that engage in research and development do so because they believe such activities provide future benefit to the company. In fact, many firms have become leaders in an industry by engaging in research and development and the discovery of new products or technology. It is often very difficult, however, to identify the amount of future benefits of research and development and to associate those benefits with specific time periods. Because of the difficulty in predicting future benefits, the FASB has ruled that firms are not allowed to treat research and development costs as an asset; all such expenditures must be treated as expenses in the period incurred. Many firms, especially high-technology ones, argue that this accounting rule results in seriously understated balance sheets. In their view, an important "asset" is not portrayed on their balance sheet. They also argue that they are at a competitive disadvantage when compared with foreign companies that are allowed to treat at least a portion of research and development as an asset. Users of financial statements somehow need to be aware of those "hidden assets" when analyzing the balance sheets of companies that must expense research and development costs.

It is important to distinguish between patent costs and research and development costs. Patent costs include legal and filing fees necessary to acquire a patent. Such costs are capitalized as an intangible asset, Patent. However, the Patent account should not include the costs of research and development of a new product. Those costs are not capitalized but are treated as an expense, Research and Development.

ACCOUNTING FOR YOUR DECISIONS
You Are the Student Intern

Your colleagues at the investment house where you are doing a summer internship insist that the intangible assets of the Quaker Oats and Alberto-Culver balance sheets are worthless and should be removed before any analysis can be completed on the two companies. Would you agree or disagree with their position?

ANS: Intangible assets are not worthless. Just because an asset is "intangible" and difficult to quantify doesn't mean it should be removed. Intangible assets such as goodwill and trademarks are frequently listed on balance sheets. They represent assets from an accounting viewpoint and may indeed be some of the most important assets of the company. The patents and trademarks of Quaker Oats and Alberto Culver are assets because they will provide future benefits in the form of sales of products.

Amortization of Intangibles

Intangibles should be reported on the balance sheet at acquisition cost less accumulated amortization. *Amortization* is very similar to depreciation of property, plant, and equipment. Amortization involves allocating the acquisition cost of the intangible asset to the period benefited by the use of the asset; and accounting standards state that the period may not exceed 40 years. In most cases, companies use the straight-line method of amortization. You may see instances of an accelerated form of amortization, however, if the decline in usefulness of the intangible asset does not occur evenly over time.

Assume that ML Company developed a patent for a new product on January 1, 1998. The costs involved with patent approval were $10,000, and the company wants to record

LO 10 Describe the proper amortization of intangible assets.

amortization on the straight-line basis over a five-year life with no residual value. The accounting entry to record the amortization for 1998 is as follows:

1998
Dec. 31 Patent Amortization Expense   2,000
              Accumulated Amortization—Patent   2,000
         To record amortization of patent for one year.

Assets = Liabilities + Owners' Equity
−2,000   −2,000

Rather than use an accumulated amortization account, some companies decrease (credit) the intangible asset account directly. In that case, the preceding transaction is recorded as follows:

1998
Dec. 31 Patent Amortization Expense   2,000
              Patent   2,000
         To record amortization of patent for one year.

Assets = Liabilities + Owners' Equity
−2,000   −2,000

No matter which of the two preceding entries is used, the asset should be reported on the balance sheet at acquisition cost ($10,000) less accumulated amortization ($2,000), or $8,000, as of December 31, 1998.

Some questions exist about the time period over which to amortize intangible assets. The general guideline is that an intangible should be amortized *over its legal life or useful life, whichever is shorter.* For example, a patent has a legal life of 17 years, but many are not useful for that long because new products and technology may surpass them. The patent should be amortized over the number of years in which the firm receives benefits, which may be a period shorter than its legal life.

Certain intangibles have no legal life, and their useful life is very difficult to determine. Goodwill is the primary example. Some accountants argue that goodwill has an unlimited life and should not be amortized. Others argue that the benefits of goodwill are too difficult to determine and this intangible asset should be written off as an expense in its entirety in the year of acquisition. The current accounting guideline takes a compromise approach. Goodwill must be amortized over a time period that cannot exceed 40 years. Thus, goodwill must be amortized in a manner similar to the amortization of other intangible assets: over its estimated useful life. But if it is not possible to determine the useful life, the maximum amortization period is 40 years.

Finally, it is important to monitor the usefulness of intangible assets as time passes. An intangible asset that will not produce future benefit should be written off as an expense. Assume in the ML example that ML learns on January 1, 1999, when accumulated amortization is $2,000 (or the book value of the patent is $8,000), that a competing company has developed a new product that renders ML's patent worthless. ML has a loss of $8,000 and should record an entry to write-off the asset as follows:

1999
Jan. 1 Loss on Patent   8,000
        Accumulated Amortization—Patent   2,000
             Patent   10,000
        To record the write-off of patent.

Assets = Liabilities + Owners' Equity
+2,000   −8,000
−10,000

This entry is consistent with the treatment of all assets. Assets existing on the balance sheet date represent future benefits or revenue. If an item does not have future usefulness, it must be removed from the balance sheet and treated as a loss or expense.

Analyzing Long-Term Assets for Average Life and Asset Turnover

Because long-term assets constitute the major productive assets of most companies, it is important to analyze the age and composition of these assets. We will analyze the assets of Ben & Jerry's in the following section. Analysis of the age of the assets can be accomplished fairly easily for those companies that use the straight-line method of depreciation. A rough measure of the *average life* of the assets can be calculated as follows:

Average Life = Property, Plant, and Equipment/Depreciation Expense

The *average age* of the assets can be calculated as follows:

Average Age = Accumulated Depreciation/Depreciation Expense

At the end of 1995, Ben & Jerry's had property, plant, and equipment of $84,360,000 and accumulated depreciation of $24,760,000. A careful reading of the annual report also indicates depreciation expense of $5,928,000 for 1995. Therefore, the average life of Ben & Jerry's assets is calculated as follows:

Average Life = Property, Plant, and Equipment/Depreciation Expense
Average Life = $84,360,000/$5,928,000
= 14.2 Years

This is a rough estimate because it assumes that the company has purchased assets fairly evenly over time. Because it is an average, it indicates that some assets have a life longer than 14.2 years and others shorter lives.

The average age of Ben & Jerry's assets is calculated as follows:

Average Age = Accumulated Depreciation/Depreciation Expense
Average Age = $24,760,000/$5,928,000
= 4.2 Years

This indicates that Ben & Jerry's assets are, on average, fairly new and should be productive for several more years.

The asset category of the balance sheet is also important in analyzing the company's *profitability.* The asset turnover ratio is a measure of the productivity of the assets and is measured as follows:

Asset Turnover = Net Sales/Average Total Assets

This ratio is a measure of how many dollars of assets are necessary for every dollar of sales. If a company is using its assets efficiently, each dollar of assets will create a high amount of sales. Technically, the ratio is based on average *total assets,* but long-term assets often constitute the largest portion of a company's total assets.

How Long-Term Assets Affect the Statement of Cash Flows

Determining the impact that acquisition, depreciation, and sale of long-term assets have on the statement of cash flows is important. Each of these business activities influences the statement of cash flows. Exhibit 8-8 illustrates the items discussed in this chapter and their effect on the statement of cash flows.

LO 11 Explain the impact that long-term assets have on the statement of cash flows.

The acquisition of a long-term asset is an investing activity and should be reflected in the Investing Activities category of the statement of cash flows. The acquisition should appear as a deduction or negative item in that section because it requires the use of cash to purchase the asset. This applies whether the long-term asset is property, plant, and equipment or an intangible asset.

The depreciation or amortization of a long-term asset is *not* a cash item. It was referred to earlier as a noncash charge to earnings. Nevertheless, it must be presented on

EXHIBIT 8-8   Long-Term Assets and the Statement of Cash Flows

Item	Cash Flow Statement
	Operating Activities
	Net income — xxx
Depreciation and Amortization	⟶ +
Gain on sale of asset	⟶ −
Loss on sale of asset	⟶ +
	Investing Activities
Purchase of asset	⟶ −
Sale of asset	⟶ +
	Financing Activities

the statement of cash flows (if the indirect method is used for the statement). The reason is that it was deducted from earnings in calculating the net income figure. Therefore, it must be eliminated or "added back" if the net income amount is used to indicate the amount of cash generated from operations. Thus, depreciation and amortization should be presented in the Operating Activities category of the statement of cash flows as an addition to net income.

The sale or disposition of long-term assets is an investing activity. When an asset is sold, the amount of cash received should be reflected as an addition or plus amount in the Investing Activities category of the statement of cash flows. If the asset was sold at a gain or loss, however, one additional aspect should be reflected. Because the gain or loss was reflected on the income statement, it should be eliminated from the net income amount presented in the Operating Activities category (if the indirect method is used). A sale of an asset is not an activity related to normal, ongoing operations, and all amounts involved with the sale should be removed from the Operating Activities category. For more detail on this issue, see Chapter 14. Exhibit 8-9 indicates the Operating and

EXHIBIT 8-9   Time Warner Partial Consolidated Statement of Cash Flows

Years Ended December 31, (millions)	1995
Operations	
Net loss	$ (166)
Adjustments for noncash and nonoperating items:	
Extraordinary loss on retirement of debt	42
One-time tax charge[a]	–
Depreciation and amortization	559
Noncash interest expense	176
Excess (deficiency) of distributions over equity in pretax income of Entertainment Group	807
Equity in income of other investee companies, net of distributions	(16)
Changes in operating assets and liabilities:	
Receivables	(68)
Inventories	(52)
Accounts payable and other liabilities	160
Other balance sheet changes	(391)
Cash provided by operations	1,051
Investing Activities	
Investments and acquisitions	(381)
Capital expenditures	(266)
Investment proceeds	376
Cash used by investing activities	(271)

Investing categories of the 1995 statement of cash flows of Time Warner. The company incurred a net loss during 1995; that loss, of $166 million, is the first line of the Operations category of the cash flow statement. Time Warner's performance is an excellent example of the difference between the net income or loss on the income statement and actual cash flow. Note that the company generated a positive cash flow from operations of $1,051 million. One of the primary reasons was that depreciation and amortization of $559 million affected the income statement but do not involve a cash outflow and are therefore added on the cash flow statement. Also note that the Investing Activities category indicates major outlays of cash for new assets: $381 million for investments and acquisitions and $266 million for capital expenditures which constitute additions to property, plant, and equipment.

Review Problem

The accountant for Becker Company wants to develop a balance sheet as of December 31, 1998. A review of the asset records has revealed the following information:

a. Asset A was purchased on July 1, 1996, for $40,000 and has been depreciated on the straight-line basis using an estimated life of six years and a residual value of $4,000.

b. Asset B was purchased on January 1, 1997, for $66,000. The straight-line method has been used for depreciation purposes. Originally, the estimated life of the asset was projected to be six years with a residual value of $6,000; however, at the beginning of 1998, the accountant learned that the remaining life of the asset was only three years with a residual value of $2,000.

c. Asset C was purchased on January 1, 1997, for $50,000. The double declining-balance method has been used for depreciation purposes, with a four-year life and a residual value estimate of $5,000.

Required

1. Assume that these assets represent pieces of equipment. Calculate the acquisition cost, accumulated depreciation, and book value of each asset as of December 31, 1998.

2. How would the assets appear on the balance sheet on December 31, 1998?

3. Assume that Becker Company sold Asset B on January 2, 1999, for $25,000. Calculate the amount of the resulting gain or loss and prepare the journal entry for the sale. Where would the gain or loss appear on the income statement?

Solution to Review Problem

1.

ASSET A

1996	Depreciation	($40,000 − $4,000)/6 × 1/2 Year	=	$ 3,000
1997		($40,000 − $4,000)/6	=	6,000
1998		($40,000 − $4,000)/6	=	6,000
	Accumulated Depreciation			$15,000

ASSET B

1997	Depreciation	($66,000 − $6,000)/6	=	$10,000
1998		($66,000 − $10,000 − $2,000)/3	=	18,000
	Accumulated Depreciation			$28,000

Note the impact of the change in estimate on 1998 depreciation.

ASSET C

1997	Depreciation	$50,000 × (25% × 2)	=	$25,000
1998		($50,000 − $25,000) × (25% × 2)	=	12,500
	Accumulated Depreciation			$37,500

BECKER COMPANY
SUMMARY OF ASSET COST AND ACCUMULATED DEPRECIATION
AS OF DECEMBER 31, 1998

ASSET	ACQUISITION COST	ACCUMULATED DEPRECIATION	BOOK VALUE
A	$ 40,000	$15,000	$25,000
B	66,000	28,000	38,000
C	50,000	37,500	12,500
Totals	$156,000	$80,500	$75,500

2. The assets would appear in the Long-Term Assets category of the balance sheet as follows:

Equipment	$156,000	
Less: Accumulated depreciation	80,500	
Equipment (net)		$75,500

3.

Asset B Book Value	$38,000
Selling Price	25,000
Loss on Sale of Asset	$13,000

The journal entry to record the sale is as follows:

1999
Jan. 2   Cash   25,000
           Accumulated Depreciation   28,000
           Loss on Sale of Asset   13,000
               Asset B   66,000
       To record the sale of asset B.

Assets = Liabilities + Owners' Equity
+25,000   −13,000
+28,000
−66,000

The Loss on Sale of Asset account should appear in the Other Income/Other Expense category of the income statement. It is similar to an expense but is not the company's major activity.

Chapter Highlights

1. **LO 1** Operating assets are normally presented on the balance sheet in one category for property, plant, and equipment and a second category for intangibles.

2. **LO 1** Operating assets should be presented at original acquisition cost less accumulated depreciation or amortization.

3. **LO 2** Acquisition cost should include all costs necessary to acquire the asset and prepare it for its intended use.

4. **LO 3** When assets are purchased for a lump sum, acquisition cost should be determined as the proportion of the market values of the assets purchased.

5. **LO 4** Interest on assets constructed over time should be capitalized. The amount of interest capitalized should be the average accumulated expenditures times an interest rate.

6. **LO 5** Several depreciation methods are available to describe the decline in usefulness of operating assets. The

straight-line method is the most commonly used and assigns the same amount of depreciation to each time period over the asset's life.

7. **LO 5** Accelerated depreciation allocates a greater expense to the earlier years of an asset's life and less to later years. The double declining-balance method is one form of accelerated depreciation.

8. **LO 6** Depreciation is based on an estimate of the life of the asset and the residual value. When it is necessary to change the estimate, the amount of depreciation expense is adjusted for the current year and future years. Past depreciation amounts are not restated.

9. **LO 7** Capital expenditures are costs that increase an asset's life or its productivity. Capital expenditures should be added to the cost of the asset. Revenue expenditures should be treated as an expense in the period in which they are incurred because they benefit only the current period.

10. **LO 8** The gain or loss on the disposal of an asset is the difference between the asset's book value and its selling price.

11. **LO 9** Intangible assets should be presented on the balance sheet at acquisition cost less accumulated amortization. Acquisition cost should include all costs necessary to acquire the asset.

12. **LO 10** Research and development costs are not treated as an intangible asset. Instead, they are treated as an expense in the year they are incurred.

13. **LO 10** Intangibles should be amortized over the shorter of their legal or useful life. All intangibles, including goodwill, should be amortized over a period not exceeding 40 years.

14. **LO 11** The acquisition of long-term assets should be reflected in the Investing Activities category of the statement of cash flows.

Key Terms Quiz

Read each definition below and then write the number of the definition in the blank beside the appropriate term it defines. The solution appears at the end of the chapter.

—— Acquisition cost
—— Land improvements
—— Straight-line method
—— Units-of-production method
—— Double declining-balance method
—— Capital expenditure
—— Gain on Sale of Asset
—— Natural resources
—— Organization costs
—— Research and development costs

—— Capitalization of interest
—— Depreciation
—— Book value
—— Accelerated depreciation
—— Change in estimate
—— Revenue expenditure
—— Loss on Sale of Asset
—— Intangible assets
—— Goodwill

1. This amount includes all of the costs normally necessary to acquire an asset and prepare it for its intended use.

2. Additions made to a piece of property such as paving or landscaping a parking lot. The costs are treated separately from land for purposes of recording depreciation.

3. A method by which the same dollar amount of depreciation is recorded in each year of asset use.

4. A method by which depreciation is determined as a function of the number of units the asset produces.

5. The process of treating the cost of interest on constructed assets as a part of the asset cost rather than as an expense.

6. A change in the life of an asset or in its expected residual value.

7. The allocation of the original acquisition cost of an asset to the periods benefited by its use.

8. A cost that improves an operating asset and is added to the asset account.

9. The original acquisition cost of an asset minus the amount of accumulated depreciation.

10. A cost that keeps an operating asset in its normal operating condition and is treated as an expense of the period.

11. An account whose amount indicates that the selling price received on an asset's disposal exceeds its book value.

12. An account whose amount indicates that the book value of an asset exceeds the selling price received on its disposal.

13. A term that refers to several methods by which a higher amount of depreciation is recorded in the early years of an asset's life and a lower amount is recorded in the later years.

14. Long-term assets that have no physical properties, for example patents, copyrights, and goodwill.

15. Costs that are incurred at the initial formation of a corporation and are treated as an intangible asset.

16. A method by which depreciation is recorded at twice the straight-line rate but the depreciable balance is reduced in each period.

17. The amount indicating that the purchase price of a business exceeded the total fair market values of the identifiable net assets at the time the business was acquired.

18. Expenditures incurred in the discovery of new knowledge and the translation of research into a design or plan for a new product.

19. Assets that are consumed during their use, for example coal or oil.

Alternate Terms

Accumulated depreciation Allowance for depreciation.

Acquisition cost Historical cost.

Capitalize Treat as asset.

Construction in progress Construction in process.

Goodwill Purchase price in excess of the market value of assets.

Hidden assets Unrecorded or off–balance sheet assets.

Property, Plant, and Equipment Fixed assets.

Prospective Current and future years.

Residual value Salvage value.

Revenue expenditure An expense of the period.

Questions

1. What are several examples of operating assets? Why are operating assets essential to a company's long-term future?

2. What is the meaning of the term *acquisition cost* of operating assets? Give some examples of costs that should be included in the acquisition cost.

3. When assets are purchased as a group, how should the acquisition cost of the individual assets be determined?

4. Why is it important to account separately for the cost of land and building, even when the two assets are purchased together?

5. Under what circumstances should interest be capitalized as part of the cost of an asset?

6. What factors may contribute to the decline in usefulness of operating assets? Should the choice of depreciation method be related to these factors? Must a company choose just one method of depreciation for all assets?

7. Why do you think that most companies use the straight-line method of depreciation?

8. How should the residual value of an operating asset be treated when using the straight-line method? How should it be treated when using the double declining-balance method?

9. Why do many companies use one method to calculate depreciation for the income statement developed for stockholders and another method for income tax purposes?

10. What should a company do if it finds that the original estimate of the life of an asset or the residual value of the asset must be changed?

11. What are the meanings of the terms *capital expenditures* and *revenue expenditures?* What determines whether an item is a capital or revenue expenditure?

12. How is the gain or loss on the sale of an operating asset calculated? Where would the Gain on Sale of Asset account appear on the financial statements?

13. What are several examples of items that constitute intangible assets? In what category of the balance sheet should intangible assets appear?

14. What is the meaning of the term *goodwill?* Give an example of a transaction that would result in the recording of goodwill on the balance sheet.

15. Do you agree with the FASB's ruling that all research and development costs should be treated as an expense on the income statement? Why or why not?

16. Do you agree with some accountants who argue that intangible assets have an unlimited life and therefore should not be subject to amortization?

17. When an intangible asset is amortized, should the asset's amortization occur over its legal life or over its useful life? Give an example in which the legal life exceeds the useful life.

18. Suppose that an intangible asset is being amortized over a 10-year time period but a competitor has just introduced a new product that will have a serious negative impact on the asset's value. Should the company continue to amortize the intangible asset over the 10-year life?

Exercises

LO 2 **Exercise 8-1** Acquisition Cost

Ruby Company purchased a piece of equipment with a list price of $40,000 on January 1, 1998. The following amounts were related to the equipment purchase:

- Terms of the purchase were 2/10, net 30. Ruby paid for the purchase on January 8.
- Freight costs of $1,000 were incurred.
- A state agency required that a pollution-control device be installed on the equipment at a cost of $2,500.
- During installation, the equipment was damaged and repair costs of $4,000 were incurred.
- Architect's fees of $6,000 were paid to redesign the work space to accommodate the new equipment.

- Ruby purchased liability insurance to cover possible damage to the asset. The three-year policy cost $8,000.

- Ruby financed the purchase with a bank loan. Interest of $3,000 was paid on the loan during 1998.

Required

Determine the acquisition cost of the equipment.

LO 3 **Exercise 8-2** Lump-Sum Purchase

To add to his growing chain of grocery stores, on January 1, 1998, Danny Marks bought a grocery store of a small competitor for $520,000. An appraiser was hired to assess the value of the assets acquired and determined that the land had a market value of $200,000, the building a market value of $150,000, and the equipment a market value of $250,000.

Required

1. What is the acquisition cost of each asset? Prepare a journal entry to record the acquisition.

2. Danny plans to depreciate the operating assets on a straight-line basis for 20 years. Determine the amount of depreciation expense for 1998 on these newly acquired assets.

3. How would the assets appear on the balance sheet as of December 31, 1998?

LO 5 **Exercise 8-3** Straight-Line and Units-of-Production Methods

Assume that Sample Company purchased factory equipment on January 1, 1998, for $50,000. The equipment has an estimated life of five years and an estimated residual value of $5,000. Sample's accountant is considering whether to use the straight-line or the units-of-production method to depreciate the asset. Because the company is beginning a new production process, the equipment will be used to produce 10,000 units in 1998, but production subsequent to 1998 will increase by 10,000 units each year.

Required

Calculate the depreciation expense, the accumulated depreciation, and the book value of the equipment under both methods for each of the five years of the asset's life. Do you think that the units-of-production method yields reasonable results in this situation?

LO 5 **Exercise 8-4** Accelerated Depreciation

Koffman's Warehouse purchased a forklift on January 1, 1998, for $5,000. It is expected to last for five years and have a residual value of $600. Koffman's uses the double declining-balance method for depreciation.

Required

1. Calculate the depreciation expense, the accumulated depreciation, and the book value for each year of the forklift's life.

2. Prepare the journal entry to record depreciation expense for 1999.

3. Refer to Exhibit 8-2. What factors may have influenced Koffman to use the double declining-balance method?

LO 6 **Exercise 8-5** Change in Estimate

Assume that Bloomer Company purchased a new machine on January 1, 1998, for $80,000. The machine has an estimated useful life of nine years and a residual value of $8,000. Bloomer has chosen to use the straight-line method of depreciation. On January 1, 2000, Bloomer discovered that the machine would not be useful beyond December 31, 2003, and estimated its value at that time to be $2,000.

Required

1. Calculate the depreciation expense, the accumulated depreciation, and the book value of the asset for each year, 1998 to 2003.

2. Was the depreciation recorded in 1998 and 1999 wrong? If so, why was it not corrected?

LO 8 **Exercise 8-6** Asset Disposal

Assume that Gonzalez Company purchased an asset on January 1, 1996, for $60,000. The asset had an estimated life of six years and an estimated residual value of $6,000. The company used the straight-line method to depreciate the asset. On July 1, 1998, the asset was sold for $40,000 cash.

Required

1. Make the journal entry to record depreciation for 1998. Also record all transactions necessary for the sale of the asset.
2. How should the gain or loss on the sale of the asset be presented on the income statement?

LO 8 **Exercise 8-7** Asset Disposal

Refer to Exercise 8-6. Assume that Gonzalez Company sold the asset on July 1, 1998, and received $15,000 cash and a note for an additional $15,000.

Required

1. Make the journal entry to record depreciation for 1998. Also record all transactions necessary for the sale of the asset.
2. How should the gain or loss on the sale of the asset be presented on the income statement?

LO 10 **Exercise 8-8** Amortization of Intangibles

For each of the following intangible assets, indicate the amount of amortization expense that should be recorded for the year 1998 and the amount of accumulated amortization on the balance sheet as of December 31, 1998.

	GOODWILL	PATENT	ORGANIZATION COSTS	TRADEMARK
Cost	$40,000	$50,000	$60,000	$80,000
Date of purchase	1/1/91	1/1/93	1/1/95	1/1/96
Useful life	50 yrs.	10 yrs.	10 yrs.	20 yrs.
Legal life	undefined	17 yrs.	undefined	20 yrs.
Method	SL*	SL	SL	SL

*Represents the straight-line method.

LO 11 **Exercise 8-9** Impact of Transactions Involving Operating Assets on Statement of Cash Flows

From the following list, identify each item as operating (O), investing (I), financing (F) or not separately reported on the statement of cash flows (N).

_____ Purchase of land

_____ Proceeds from sale of land

_____ Gain on sale of land

_____ Purchase of equipment

_____ Depreciation expense

_____ Proceeds from sale of equipment

_____ Loss on sale of equipment

LO 11 **Exercise 8-10** Impact of Transactions Involving Intangible Assets on Statement of Cash Flows

From the following list, identify each item as operating (O), investing (I), financing (F) or not separately reported on the statement of cash flows (N).

_____ Payment of costs involved in starting the company

_____ Cost incurred to acquire copyright

_____ Amortization of organization costs

_____ Amortization of goodwill

_____ Proceeds from sale of patent

_____ Gain on sale of patent

_____ Research and development costs

Multi-Concept Exercises

LO 1, 7 **Exercise 8-11** Capital Versus Revenue Expenditures

On January 1, 1996, Jose Company purchased a building for $100,000 and a delivery truck for $20,000. The following expenditures have been incurred during 1998 related to the building and the truck:

- The building was painted at a cost of $5,000.

- To prevent leaking, new windows were installed in the building at a cost of $10,000.

- To allow an improved flow of production, a new conveyor system was installed at a cost of $40,000.

- The delivery truck was repainted with a new company logo at a cost of $1,000.

- To allow better handling of large loads, a hydraulic lift system was installed on the truck at a cost of $5,000.

- The truck's engine was overhauled at a cost of $4,000.

Required

1. Determine which of these costs should be capitalized. Also record the journal entry for the capitalized costs. Assume that all costs were incurred on January 1, 1998.

2. Determine the amount of depreciation for the year 1998. The company uses the straight-line method and depreciates the building over 25 years and the truck over 6 years. Assume zero residual value for all assets.

3. How would the assets appear on the balance sheet of December 31, 1998?

LO 4, 5 **Exercise 8-12** Capitalization of Interest and Depreciation

During 1998, Mercator Company borrowed $80,000 from a local bank and, in addition, used $120,000 of cash to construct a new corporate office building. Based on average accumulated expenditures, the amount of interest capitalized during 1998 was $8,000. Construction was completed and the building was occupied on January 1, 1999.

Required

1. Determine the acquisition cost of the new building.

2. The building has an estimated useful life of 20 years and a $5,000 salvage value. Assuming that Mercator uses the straight-line basis to depreciate its operating assets, determine the amount of depreciation expense for 1998 and 1999.

LO 9, 10 **Exercise 8-13** Research and Development and Patents

Erin Company incurred the following costs during 1998.

a. Research and development costs of $20,000 were incurred. The research was conducted to discover a new product to sell to customers in future years. A product was successfully developed and a patent for the new product was granted during 1998. Erin is unsure of the period benefited by the research but believes the product will result in increased sales over the next five years.

b. Legal costs and application fees of $10,000 for the patent were incurred on January 1, 1998. The patent was granted for a life of 17 years.

c. A patent infringement suit was successfully defended at a cost of $8,000. Assume that all costs were incurred on January 1, 1999.

Required

Determine how the costs in parts a and b should be presented on Erin's financial statements as of December 31, 1998. Also determine the amount of amortization of intangible assets that Erin should record in 1998 and 1999.

Problems

LO 1   **Problem 8-1** Balance Sheet and Footnote Disclosures for Delta Airlines

The June 30, 1995, balance sheet of Delta Air Lines Inc. revealed the following information in the property and equipment category (in millions):

	1995	1994
Flight equipment	$9,288	$9,063
Less: Accumulated depreciation	4,209	3,880
	$5,079	$5,183
Ground property and equipment	$2,442	$2,398
Less: Accumulated depreciation	1,354	1,250
	$1,088	$1,148

The footnotes that accompany the financial statements revealed the following:

> Depreciation and Amortization—Prior to April 1, 1993, substantially all of the Company's flight equipment was being depreciated on a straight-line basis to residual values (10% of cost) over a 15-year period from the dates placed in service. As a result of a review of its fleet plan, effective April 1, 1993, the Company increased the estimated useful lives of substantially all of its flight equipment. Flight equipment that was not already fully depreciated is being depreciated on a straight-line basis to residual values (5% of cost) over a 20-year period from the dates placed in service. The effect of this change was a $34 million decrease in depreciation expense and a $22 million ($0.44 per common share) decrease in net loss for fiscal 1993. Ground property and equipment are depreciated on a straight-line basis over their estimated service lives, which range from three years to thirty years.

Required

1. Assume that Delta Air Lines did not dispose of any ground property and equipment during the fiscal year 1995. Calculate the amount of depreciation expense for the year.
2. What was the average life of the ground property and equipment as of 1995?
3. What was the average age of the ground property and equipment as of 1995?
4. What was the effect of Delta Air Lines' decision to change the depreciable lives and residual values of its flight equipment? On what line of the 1993 income statement would you find the impact disclosed?

LO 3   **Problem 8-2** Lump-Sum Purchase of Assets and Subsequent Events

Carter Development Company purchased, for cash, a large tract of land that was immediately platted and deeded into smaller sections:

> Section 1, retail development with highway frontage.
>
> Section 2, multifamily apartment development.
>
> Section 3, single-family homes in the largest section.

Based on recent sales of similar property, the fair market value of the three sections are as follows:

> Section 1, $630,000.
>
> Section 2, $378,000.
>
> Section 3, $252,000.

Required

1. What value is assigned to each section of land if the tract was purchased for (a) $1,260,000, (b) $1,560,000, or (c) $1,000,000?
2. How does the purchase of the tract affect the balance sheet?
3. Why would Carter be concerned with the value assigned to each individual section? Would Carter be more concerned with the values assigned if instead of purchasing three sections of land, it purchased land with buildings? Why or why not?

LO 5 **Problem 8-3** Depreciation as a Tax Shield

The term *tax shield* refers to the amount of income tax saved by deducting depreciation for income tax purposes. Assume that Supreme Company is considering the purchase of an asset as of January 1, 1998. The cost of an asset with a five-year life and zero residual value is $100,000. The company will use the straight-line method of depreciation.

Supreme's income for tax purposes before recording depreciation on the asset will be $50,000 per year for the next five years. The corporation is currently in the 35% tax bracket.

Required

Calculate the amount of income tax that Supreme must pay each year if the asset is not purchased. Calculate the amount of income tax that Supreme must pay each year if the asset is purchased. What is the amount of the depreciation tax shield?

LO 5 **Problem 8-4** Book Versus Tax Depreciation

Griffith Delivery Service purchased a delivery truck for $33,600. The truck has an estimated useful life of six years and no salvage value. For the purposes of preparing financial statements, Griffith is planning to use straight-line depreciation. For tax purposes, Griffith follows MACRS. Depreciation expense using MACRS is $6,720 in Year 1, $10,750 in Year 2, $6,450 in Year 3, $3,870 in each of Years 4 and 5, and $1,940 in Year 6.

Required

1. What is the difference in depreciation expense for each of the six years?

2. Griffith's president has asked why you have used one method for the books and another for calculating taxes. "Can you do this? Is it legal? Don't we take the same total depreciation either way?" he asked. Write a brief memo answering his questions and explaining the benefits of using two methods for depreciation.

LO 5 **Problem 8-5** Depreciation and Cash Flow

Ohare Company's only asset as of January 1, 1998, was a limousine. During 1998 only three transactions occurred:

> Provided services of $100,000 on account.
>
> Collected all accounts receivable.
>
> Depreciation on the limousine was $15,000.

Required

1. Develop an income statement for Ohare for 1998.

2. Determine the amount of the net cash inflow for Ohare for 1998.

3. Explain in one or more sentences why the amount of the net income on Ohare's income statement does not equal the amount of the net cash inflow.

4. If Ohare developed a cash flow statement for 1998 using the indirect method, what amount would appear in the category titled Cash Flow from Operating Activities?

LO 11 **Problem 8-6** Reconstruct Net Book Values using Statement of Cash Flows

Centralia Stores Inc. had property, plant, and equipment, net of accumulated depreciation of $4,459,000; and intangible assets, net of accumulated amortization, of $673,000 at December 31, 1998. The company's 1998 statement of cash flows, prepared using the indirect method, included the following items.

The cash flows from operating activities section included three additions to net income: (1) depreciation expense in the amount of $672,000, (2) amortization expense in the amount of $33,000, and (3) the loss on the sale of equipment in the amount of $35,000. The cash flows from operating activities section also included a subtraction from net income for the gain on the sale of a copyright of $55,000. The cash flows from investing activities section included outflows for the purchase of a building in the amount of $292,000 and $15,000 for the payment of legal fees to protect a patent from infringement. The cash flows from investing activities section also included inflows from the sale of equipment in the amount of $315,000 and the sale of a copyright in the amount of $75,000.

Required

1. Determine the book values of the assets that were sold during 1998.

2. Reconstruct the amount of property, plant, and equipment, net of accumulated depreciation, that was reported on the company's balance sheet at December 31, 1997.

3. Reconstruct the amount of intangibles, net of accumulated amortization, that was reported on the company's balance sheet at December 31, 1997.

Multi-Concept Problems

LO 1, 3, 5, 7, 8 **Problem 8-7** Cost of Assets, Subsequent Book Values, and Balance Sheet Presentation

The following events took place at Pete's Painting Company during 1998:

a. On January 1, Pete bought a used truck for $14,000. He added a tool chest and side racks for ladders for $4,800. The truck is expected to last four years and then be sold for $800. Pete uses straight-line depreciation.

b. On January 1, he purchased several items at an auction for $2,400. These items had fair market values as follows:

10 cases of paint trays and roller covers	$ 200
Storage cabinets	600
Ladders & scaffolding	2,400

Pete will use all the paint trays and roller covers this year. The storage cabinets are expected to last 9 years, and the ladders and scaffolding for four years.

c. On February 1, Pete paid the city $1,500 for a three-year license to operate the business.

d. On September 1, Pete sold an old truck for $4,800. The truck had cost $12,000 when it was purchased on September 1, 1993. It had been expected to last eight years and have a salvage value of $800.

Required

1. For each situation, explain the value assigned to the asset when it is purchased (or for part d, the book value when sold).

2. Determine the amount of depreciation or other expense to be recorded for each asset for 1998.

3. How would these assets appear on the balance sheet as of December 31, 1998?

LO 2, 5 **Problem 8-8** Cost of Assets and the Effect on Depreciation

Early in its first year of business, Toner Company, a fitness and training center, purchased new workout equipment. The acquisition included the following costs:

Purchase price	$150,000
Tax	15,000
Transportation	4,000
Setup*	25,000
Painting*	3,000

*The equipment was adjusted to Toner's specific needs and painted to match the other equipment in the gym.

The bookkeeper recorded an asset, Equipment, $165,000 (purchase price and tax). The remaining costs were expensed for the year. Toner used straight-line depreciation. The equipment was expected to last 10 years with zero salvage value.

Required

1. How much depreciation did Toner report on its income statement related to this equipment in Year 1? What do you believe is the correct amount of depreciation to report in Year 1 related to this equipment?

2. Income is $100,000, before costs related to the equipment are reported. How much income will Toner report in Year 1? What amount of income should it report? You may ignore income tax.

3. Using the equipment as an example, explain the difference between a cost and an expense.

LO 5, 7, 8 | **Problem 8-9** Capital Expenditures, Depreciation, and Disposal

Merton Company purchased an office building at a cost of $364,000 on January 1, 1997. Merton estimated that the building's life would be 25 years and the residual value at the end of 25 years would be $14,000.

On January 1, 1998, the company made several expenditures related to the building. The entire building was painted and floors were refinished at a cost of $21,000. A federal agency required Merton to install additional pollution-control devices in the building at a cost of $42,000. With the new devices, Merton believed it was possible to extend the life of the building by an additional six years.

In 1999 Merton altered its corporate strategy dramatically. The company sold the factory building on April 1, 1999, for $392,000 in cash and relocated all operations in another state.

Required

1. Determine the amount of depreciation that should be reflected on the income statement for 1997 and 1998.

2. Explain why the cost of the pollution-control equipment was not expensed in 1998. What conditions would have allowed Merton to expense the equipment? If Merton has a choice, would it prefer to expense or capitalize the equipment?

3. What amount of gain or loss did Merton record when it sold the building? What amount of gain or loss would have been reported if the pollution-control equipment had been expensed in 1998?

LO 6, 10 | **Problem 8-10** Amortization of Intangible, Revision of Rate

During 1993, Reynosa Inc.'s R & D department developed a new manufacturing process. R & D costs were $85,000. The process was patented on October 1, 1993. Legal costs to acquire the patent were $11,900. Reynosa decided to expense the patent over the maximum period of time allowed for a patent. Reynosa's fiscal year ends on September 30.

On October 1, 1998, Reynosa's competition announced that it had obtained a patent on a new process that would make Reynosa's patent obsolete in two years.

Required

1. How should Reynosa record the $85,000 and $11,900 costs?

2. How much amortization expense should Reynosa report in each year through the year ended September 30, 1998?

3. How much amortization expense should Reynosa report in the year ended September 30, 1999?

LO 8, 11 | **Problem 8-11** Purchase and Disposal of Operating Asset and Effects on Statement of Cash Flows

On January 1, 1998, Castlewood Company purchased some machinery for its production line for $104,000. Using an estimated useful life of eight years and a residual value of $8,000, the annual straight-line depreciation of the machinery was calculated to be $12,000. Castlewood used the machinery during 1998 and 1999, but then decided to automate its production process. On December 31, 1999, Castlewood sold the machinery at a loss of $5,000 and purchased new fully-automated machinery for $205,000.

Required

1. How would the transactions described above be presented on Castlewood's statements of cash flows for the years ended December 31, 1998 and 1999?

2. Why would Castlewood sell machinery that had a remaining useful life of six years at a loss and purchase new machinery with a cost almost twice that of the old?

LO 9, 10, 11 | **Problem 8-12** Amortization of Intangibles and Effects on Statement of Cash Flows

Tableleaf Inc. purchased a patent a number of years ago. The patent is being amortized on a straight-line basis over its estimated useful life. The company's comparative balance sheets as of December 31, 1998 and 1997, included the following line item:

	12/31/98	12/31/97
Patent, less accumulated amortization of $119,000 (1998) and $102,000 (1997)	$170,000	$187,000

Required

1. How much amortization expense was recorded during 1998?

2. What was the patent's acquisition cost? When was it acquired? What is its estimated useful life? How was the acquisition of the patent reported on that year's statement of cash flows?

3. Assume that Tableleaf uses the indirect method to prepare its statement of cash flows. How is the amortization of the patent reported annually on the statement of cash flows?

4. How would the sale of the patent on January 1, 1999, for $200,000 be reported on the 1999 statement of cash flows?

Alternate Problems

LO 1   **Problem 8-1A** Disclosures of Operating Assets for Quaker Oats

The footnotes to the June 30, 1994, financial statements of Quaker Oats Company included the following disclosures:

PROPERTY, PLANT AND EQUIPMENT (IN MILLIONS):

1994	BALANCE AT BEGINNING OF YEAR	ADDITIONS	RETIREMENTS AND SALES	OTHER CHANGES	BALANCE AT END OF YEAR
Land	$ 28.7	$ 0.5	$ (1.0)	$ 2.4	$ 30.6
Buildings and improvements	441.5	23.9	(10.2)	(0.2)	455.0
Machinery and equipment	1,589.0	161.0	(103.7)	(6.0)	1,640.3
Total	$2,059.2	$ 185.4	$(114.9)	$(3.8)	$2,125.9
Accumulated depreciation:					
Buildings and improvements	$ 120.3	$ 13.3	$ (1.3)	$(0.8)	$ 131.5
Machinery and equipment	710.7	124.0	(50.7)	(3.8)	780.2
Total	$ 831.0	$ 137.3	$ (52.0)	$(4.6)	$ 911.7

Software Costs—The Company defers significant software development project costs. Software costs of $5.3 million, $5.0 million and $13.2 million were deferred during fiscal 1994, 1993 and 1992, respectively, pending the projects' completion. Amounts deferred are amortized over a three-year period beginning with a project's completion.

Required

1. Based on the footnote disclosures, what was the amount of depreciation expense for fiscal year 1994 for buildings and improvements and for machinery and equipment? (You may ignore the Other Changes column when answering this question.)

2. What was the average life of the assets in the Buildings and Improvements and Machinery and Equipment categories?

3. What was the average age of the assets in the Buildings and Improvements and Machinery and Equipment categories?

4. Explain the meaning of the footnote that indicates that Quaker Oats defers and amortizes significant software costs.

LO 3   **Problem 8-2A** Lump-sum Purchase of Assets and Subsequent Events

Dixon Manufacturing purchased, for cash, three large pieces of equipment. Based on recent sales of similar equipment, the fair market values are as follows:

Piece 1	$200,000.
Piece 2	$200,000.
Piece 3	$440,000.

Required

1. What value is assigned to each piece of equipment if the equipment was purchased for (a) $960,000, (b) $680,000, or (c) $800,000?
2. How does the purchase of the equipment affect total assets?

LO 5 **Problem 8-3A** Depreciation as a Tax Shield

The term *tax shield* refers to the amount of income tax saved by deducting depreciation for income tax purposes. Assume that Rummy Company is considering the purchase of an asset as of January 1, 1998. The cost of the asset with a five-year life and zero residual value is $60,000. The company will use the double declining-balance method of depreciation.

Rummy's income for tax purposes before recording depreciation on the asset will be $62,000 per year for the next five years. The corporation is currently in the 28% tax bracket.

Required

Calculate the amount of income tax that Rummy must pay each year if the asset is not purchased and then the amount of income tax that Rummy must pay each year if the asset is purchased. What is the amount of tax shield over the life of the asset? What is the amount of tax shield for Rummy if it uses the straight-line method over the life of the asset? Why would Rummy choose to use the accelerated method?

LO 5 **Problem 8-4A** Book Versus Tax Depreciation

Payton Delivery Service purchased a delivery truck for $28,200. The truck will have a useful life of six years and zero salvage value. For the purposes of preparing financial statements, Payton is planning to use straight-line depreciation. For tax purposes, Payton follows MACRS. Depreciation expense using MACRS is $5,650 in Year 1, $9,025 in Year 2, $5,400 in Year 3, $3,250 in each of Years 4 and 5, and $1,625 in Year 6.

Required

1. What would be the difference in depreciation expense for each of the six years?
2. Payton's president has asked why you have used one method for the books and another for calculating taxes. "Can you do this? Is it legal? Don't we take the same total depreciation either way?" he asked. Write a brief memo answering his questions and explaining the benefits of using two methods for depreciation.

LO 10 **Problem 8-5A** Amortization and Cash Flow

Book Company's only asset as of January 1, 1998, was a copyright. During 1998, only three transactions occurred:

Royalties earned from copyright use, $500,000 in cash.

Cash paid for advertising and clerical services, $62,500.

Amortization of copyright, $50,000.

Required

1. What amount of income will Book report in 1998?
2. What is the amount of cash on hand at December 31, 1998?
3. Explain how the cash balance increased from zero at the beginning of the year to its end-of-year balance. Why does the increase in cash not equal the income?

LO 11 **Problem 8-6A** Reconstruct Net Book Values Using Statement of Cash Flows

E-Gen Enterprises Inc. had property, plant, and equipment, net of accumulated depreciation of $1,555,000; and intangible assets, net of accumulated amortization, of $34,000 at December 31, 1998. The company's 1998 statement of cash flows, prepared using the indirect method, included the following items.

The cash flows from operating activities section included three additions to net income: (1) depreciation expense in the amount of $205,000, (2) amortization expense in the amount of $3,000, and (3) the loss on the sale of land in the amount of $17,000. The cash flows from operating activities section also included a subtraction from net income for the gain on the sale of a trademark of $7,000. The cash flows from investing activities section included outflows for the purchase of equipment in the amount of $277,000 and $6,000 for the payment of legal fees to protect a copyright from infringement. The cash flows from investing activities section also included inflows from the sale of land in the amount of $187,000 and the sale of a trademark in the amount of $121,000.

Required

1. Determine the book values of the assets that were sold during 1998.

2. Reconstruct the amount of property, plant, and equipment, net of accumulated depreciation, that was reported on the company's balance sheet at December 31, 1997.

3. Reconstruct the amount of intangibles, net of accumulated amortization, that was reported on the company's balance sheet at December 31, 1997.

Alternate Multi-Concept Problems

LO 1, 5, 8, 9, 10 **Problem 8-7A** Cost of Assets, Subsequent Book Values, and Balance Sheet Presentation

The following events took place at Tasty-Toppins Inc., a pizza shop that specializes in home delivery, during 1998:

a. January 1, purchased a truck for $16,000 and added a cab and oven at a cost of $10,900. The truck is expected to last five years and be sold for $300 at the end of that time. The company uses straight-line depreciation for its trucks.

b. January 1, purchased equipment for $2,700 from a competitor who was retiring. The equipment is expected to last three years with zero salvage value. The company uses the double declining-balance method to depreciate its equipment.

c. April 1, sold a truck for $1,500. The truck had been purchased for $8,000 exactly five years earlier, had an expected salvage value of $1,000, and was depreciated over an eight-year life using the straight-line method.

d. July 1, purchased a $14,000 patent for a unique baking process to produce a new product. The patent is valid for 15 more years; however, the company expects to produce and market the product for only four years. The patent's value at the end of the four years is indeterminable.

Required

For each situation, explain the amount of depreciation or amortization recorded for each asset in the current year and the book value of each asset at the end of the year. For part c, indicate the accumulated depreciation and book value at the time of sale.

LO 2, 5 **Problem 8-8A** Cost of Assets and the Effect on Depreciation

Early in its first year of business, Key Inc., a locksmith and security consultant, purchased new equipment. The acquisition included the following costs:

Purchase price	$168,000
Tax	16,500
Transportation	4,400
Setup*	1,100
Operating Cost for First Year	26,400

*The equipment was adjusted to Key's specific needs.

The bookkeeper recorded the asset, Equipment, at $216,400. Key used straight-line depreciation. The equipment was expected to last 10 years with zero residual value.

Required

1. Was $216,400 the proper amount to record for the acquisition cost? If not, explain how each expenditure should be recorded.

2. How much depreciation did Key report on its income statement related to this equipment in Year 1? How much should have been reported?

3. If Key's income before the costs associated with the equipment is $55,000, what amount of income did Key report? What amount should it have reported? You may ignore income tax.

4. Explain how Key should determine the amount to capitalize when recording an asset. What is the effect on the income statement and balance sheet of Key's error?

LO 7, 8 **Problem 8-9A** Capital Expenditures, Depreciation, and Disposal

Wagner Company purchased a retail shopping center at a cost of $612,000 on January 1, 1997. Wagner estimated that the life of the building would be 25 years and the residual value at the end of 25 years would be $12,000.

On January 1, 1998, the company made several expenditures related to the building. The entire building was painted and floors were refinished at a cost of $115,200. A local zoning agency required Wagner to install additional fire-protection equipment, including sprinklers and built-in alarms, at a cost of $87,600. With the new protection, Wagner believed it was possible to increase the residual value of the building to $30,000.

In 1999 Wagner altered its corporate strategy dramatically. The company sold the retail shopping center on January 1, 1999, for $360,000 of cash.

Required

1. Determine the amount of depreciation that should be reflected on the income statement for 1997 and 1998.

2. Explain why the cost of the fire-protection equipment was not expensed in 1998. What conditions would have allowed Wagner to expense it? If Wagner has a choice, would it prefer to expense or capitalize the improvement?

3. What amount of gain or loss did Wagner record when it sold the building? What amount of gain or loss would have been reported if the fire-protection equipment had been expensed in 1998?

LO 6, 10 **Problem 8-10A** Amortization of Intangible, Revision of Rate

Dak Inc. purchased Under Company on January 1, 1998, for $500,000. To determine the value of the assets and liabilities purchased, Dak requested an appraisal of Under's assets and liabilities. The appraiser determined that the fair market values of the items purchased as of January 1, 1998, were as follows:

ASSETS	FAIR MARKET VALUE
Cash	$ 75,000
Receivables	125,000
Building	287,500
LIABILITIES	
Accounts payable	$125,000

Dak decided to amortize any goodwill in the transaction on a straight-line basis over the maximum possible time period.

On January 1, 1999, Dak's accountants determined that the goodwill should be amortized over a shorter period of time. Accordingly, Dak Inc. agreed to amortize all remaining goodwill for a period of 10 more years.

Required

1. Determine the amount of goodwill that resulted from the January 1, 1998, purchase of Under Company and the amount to be amortized in 1998.

2. Determine the amount of goodwill that should be amortized in 1999.

LO 8, 11 **Problem 8-11A** Purchase and Disposal of Operating Asset and Effects on Statement of Cash Flows

On January 1, 1998, Mansfield Inc. purchased a medium-sized delivery truck for $45,000. Using an estimated useful life of five years and a residual value of $5,000, the annual straight-line depreciation of the trucks was calculated to be $8,000. Mansfield used the truck during 1998 and 1999, but then decided to purchase a much larger delivery truck. On December 31, 1999, Mansfield sold the delivery truck at a loss of $12,000 and purchased a new, larger delivery truck for $80,000.

Required

1. How would the transactions described above be presented on Mansfield's statements of cash flows for the years ended December 31, 1998 and 1999?

2. Why would Mansfield sell a truck that had a remaining useful life of three years at a loss and purchase a new truck with a cost almost twice that of the old?

LO 9, 10, 11 **Problem 8-12A** Amortization of Intangibles and Effects on Statement of Cash Flows

Quickster Inc. acquired a single trademark a number of years ago. The trademark is being amortized on a straight-line basis over its estimated useful life. The company's comparative balance sheets as of December 31, 1998 and 1997, included the following line item:

	12/31/98	12/31/97
Trademark, less accumulated amortization of $1,661,000 (1998) and $1,510,000 (1997)	$1,357,000	$1,508,000

Required

1. How much amortization expense was recorded during 1998?

2. What was the trademark's acquisition cost? When was it acquired? What is its estimated useful life? How was the acquisition of the trademark reported on that year's statement of cash flows?

3. Assume that Quickster uses the indirect method to prepare its statement of cash flows. How is the amortization of the trademark reported annually on the statement of cash flows?

4. How would the sale of the trademark on January 1, 1999, for $1,700,000 be reported on the 1999 statement of cash flows?

Cases

Reading and Interpreting Financial Statements

LO 1, 9 **Case 8-1** Ben & Jerry's

Refer to the financial statements and footnotes included in the 1995 annual report of Ben & Jerry's.

Required

1. What items does Ben & Jerry's list in the Property, Plant, and Equipment category?

2. What method is used to depreciate the operating assets?

3. What is the estimated useful life of the operating assets?

4. What are the accumulated depreciation and book values of property, plant, and equipment for the most recent fiscal year?

5. Were any assets purchased or sold during the most recent fiscal year?

6. In what category of the balance sheet are intangible assets included?

7. Ben & Jerry's financial statements do not disclose the useful life for the account Land under Capital Lease. Why?

LO 1, 9, 10 **Case 8-2** JCPenney

The 1995 and 1994 consolidated balance sheets and notes for JCPenney Company Inc. included the following account balances and disclosures:

BALANCE SHEET ACCOUNT BALANCES

ASSETS	1995	1994
Property, net	$4,281,000,000	$3,954,000,000

Note:

PROPERTIES	1995	1994
Land	$ 216,000,000	$ 213,000,000
Buildings owned	2,410,000,000	2,178,000,000
Capital leases	182,000,000	186,000,000
Fixtures & equipment	2,978,000,000	2,763,000,000
Leasehold improvements	622,000,000	611,000,000
Accumulated depreciation	(2,127,000,000)	(1,997,000,000)
Properties, net	$4,281,000,000	$3,954,000,000

CAPITAL EXPENDITURES	1995
New stores	$399,000,000
Modernizations	134,000,000
Store improvements	54,000,000
Other	162,000,000
Total capital expenditures	$749,000,000

Required

1. What events could have affected the Properties account during 1995?

2. What events could have affected the Accumulated Depreciation account during 1995?

3. The footnote indicates that $749,000,000 was used for capital expenditures. Why did Property, Net increase only from $3,954,000,000 to $4,281,000,000?

4. Using the information given in the comparative balance sheets and the note, determine the amount of land that was purchased in 1995.

LO 11 **Case 8-3** Ben & Jerry's Statement of Cash Flows

Refer to the statement of cash flows in Ben & Jerry's 1995 annual report and answer the following questions:

1. What amount of cash was used to purchase property, plant, and equipment during 1995?

2. Did Ben & Jerry's sell any property, plant, and equipment during 1995? What amount of cash was received? Were the assets sold for a gain or loss?

3. What amount was reported for depreciation and amortization during 1995? Does the fact that depreciation and amortization are listed as a cash flow from operating activities mean that Ben & Jerry's created cash by reporting depreciation?

Making Financial Decisions

LO 1, 5 **Case 8-4** Comparing Companies

Assume that you are a financial analyst attempting to compare the financial results of two companies. The 1998 income statement of Straight Company is as follows:

Decision
Making

Sales		$720,000
Cost of goods sold		360,000
Gross profit		360,000
Administrative costs	$ 96,000	
Depreciation expense	120,000	216,000
Income before tax		144,000
Tax expense (40%)		57,600
Net income		$ 86,400

Straight Company depreciates all operating assets using the straight-line method for tax purposes and for the annual report provided to stockholders. All operating assets were purchased on the same date, and all assets had an estimated life of five years when purchased. Straight Company's balance sheet reveals that on December 31, 1998, the balance of the Accumulated Depreciation account was $240,000.

You want to compare the annual report of Straight Company to that of Accelerated Company. Both companies are in the same industry, and both have exactly the same assets, sales, and expenses except that Accelerated uses the double declining-balance method for depreciation for income tax purposes and for the annual report provided to stockholders.

Required

Develop Accelerated Company's 1998 income statement. As a financial analyst interested in investing in one of the companies, do you find Straight or Accelerated more attractive? Because depreciation is a "noncash" expense, should you be indifferent between the two companies? Explain your answer.

Decision Making

LO 5 **Case 8-5** Depreciation Alternatives

Medsupply Inc. produces supplies used in hospitals and nursing homes. Its sales, production, and costs to produce are expected to remain constant over the next five years. The corporate income tax rate is expected to increase over the next three years. The current rate, 15%, is expected to increase to 20% next year and then to 25% and continue at that rate indefinitely.

Medsupply is considering the purchase of new equipment that is expected to last for five years and to cost $150,000 with zero salvage value. As the controller, you are aware that the company can use one method of depreciation for accounting purposes and another method for tax purposes. You are trying to decide between the straight-line and the double declining-balance methods.

Required

Recommend which method to use for accounting purposes and which to use for tax purposes. Be able to justify your answer on both a numerical and a theoretical basis. How does a noncash adjustment to income, such as depreciation, affect cash flow?

Accounting and Ethics: What Would You Do?

LO 3 **Case 8-6** Valuing Assets

Dodger Company recently hired Val Fernando as an accountant. He was given responsibility for all accounting functions related to fixed asset accounting. Tammy Lasord, Val's boss, asked him to review all transactions involving the current year's acquisition of fixed assets and to take necessary action to ensure that acquired assets were recorded at proper values. Val is satisfied that all transactions are proper except for an April 15 purchase of an office building and the land on which it is situated. The purchase price of the acquisition was $200,000. Dodger Company has not separately reported the land and building, however.

Val hired an appraiser to determine the market values of the land and the building. The appraiser reported that his best estimates of the values were $150,000 for the building and $70,000 for the land. When Val proposed that these values be used to determine the acquisition cost of the assets, Ms. Lasord disagreed. She told Val to request another appraisal of the property and asked him to stress to the appraiser that the land component of the acquisition could not be depreciated for tax purposes. The second appraiser estimated that the values were $180,000 for the building and $40,000 for the land. Val and Ms. Lasord agreed that the second appraisal should be used to determine the acquisition cost of the assets.

Required

Did Val and Ms. Lasord act ethically in this situation? Explain your answer.

LO 5 **Case 8-7** Depreciation Estimates

Langsom's Mfg. is planning for a new project. Usually Langsom's depreciates long-term equipment for 10 years. The equipment for this project is specialized and will have no further use at the end of the project in three years. The manager of the project wants to depreciate the equipment over the usual 10 years and plans on writing off the remaining book value at the end of year 3 as a loss. You believe that the equipment should be depreciated over the three-year life.

Required

Which method do you think is conceptually better? What should you do if the manager insists on depreciating the equipment over 10 years?

Research Case

Case 8-7 Time Warner

Internet

Atlantic Records, Bugs Bunny, People Magazine, and the Courtroom Television Network are some of the revenue-generating tangible and intangible assets of Time Warner, Inc. These properties, along with many others, provide the company with potential for current income and long-term financial growth.

Conduct a search of the World Wide Web, obtain Time Warner's most recent annual report, or use library resources to obtain company financial data, and answer the following:

1. For the most recent year available, what types of operating assets (and amounts) are reported by Time Warner on its balance sheet?

2. What is the amount of accumulated depreciation reported by Time Warner for the latest accounting year available? How does this compare with the amount shown in the "Focus on Financial Results" in the opening vignette shown at the start of this chapter?

3. Obtain the past 52-week high, low, and most current prices for Time Warner common stock. Describe the trend for the company's common stock price over the past three to six months. Does this trend appear to be related to any recent management decisions to sell off operating assets, purchase new assets, or improve the performance of existing assets? An example might be the expansion of its music, cable, or news holdings into new markets.

Optional Research. Access the Time Warner Web site (http://www.pathfinder.com/Corp) to obtain current information about the company's products and business activities to prepare a brief description of the company's various product lines. In what businesses does Time Warner project its future growth?

Solutions to Key Terms Quiz

1	Acquisition cost (p. 363)	5	Capitalization of interest (p. 364)
2	Land improvements (p. 364)	7	Depreciation (p. 365)
3	Straight-line method (p. 365)	9	Book value (p. 365)
4	Units-of-production method (p. 366)	13	Accelerated depreciation (p. 366)
16	Double declining-balance method (p. 366)	6	Change in estimate (p. 370)
8	Capital expenditure (p. 371)	10	Revenue expenditure (p. 371)
11	Gain on Sale of Asset (p. 373)	12	Loss on Sale of Asset (p. 374)
19	Natural resources (p. 374)	14	Intangible assets (p. 376)
15	Organization costs (p. 376)	17	Goodwill (p. 376)
18	Research and development costs (p. 379)		

INTEGRATIVE PROBLEM

FOR
PART II

Correct an income statement and statement of cash flows and assess the impact of a change in inventory method; compute the effect of a bad debt recognition.

The following income statement, statement of cash flows, and additional information are available for PEK Company:

PEK COMPANY
INCOME STATEMENT
FOR THE YEAR ENDED DECEMBER 31, 1998

Sales revenue		$1,250,000
Cost of goods sold		636,500
Gross profit		$ 613,500
Depreciation on plant equipment	$58,400	
Depreciation on buildings	12,000	
Interest expense	33,800	
Other expenses	83,800	188,000
Income before taxes		$ 425,500
Income tax expense (30% rate)		127,650
Net income		$ 297,850

PEK COMPANY
STATEMENT OF CASH FLOWS
FOR THE YEAR ENDED DECEMBER 31, 1998

Cash flows from operating activities:	
Net income	$297,850
Adjustments to reconcile net income to net cash provided by operating activities (includes depreciation expense)	83,200
Net cash provided by operating activities	$381,050
Cash flows from financing activities:	
Dividends	(35,000)
Net increase in cash	$346,050

Additional information:

a. Beginning inventory and purchases for the one product the company sells are as follows:

	UNITS	UNIT COST
Beginning inventory	50,000	$2.00
Purchases:		
February 5	25,000	2.10
March 10	30,000	2.20
April 15	40,000	2.50
June 16	75,000	3.00
September 5	60,000	3.10
October 3	40,000	3.25

b. During the year the company sold 250,000 units at $5 each.

c. PEK uses the periodic FIFO method to value its inventory and the straight-line method to depreciate all of its long-term assets.

d. During the year-end audit, it was discovered that a January 3, 1998, transaction for the lump-sum purchase of a mixing machine and a boiler was not recorded. The fair market values of the mixing machine and the boiler were $200,000 and $100,000 respectively. Each asset has an estimated useful life of 10 years with no residual value expected. The purchase of the assets was financed by issuing a $270,000 five-year promissory note directly to the seller. Interest of 8% is paid annually on December 31.

Required

1. Prepare a revised income statement and a revised statement of cash flows to take into account the omission of the entry to record the purchase of the two assets. (*Hint:* you will need to take into account any change in income taxes as a result of changes in any income statement items. Assume that income taxes are paid on December 31 of each year.)

2. Assume the same facts as above, except that the company is considering the use of an accelerated method rather than the straight-line method for the assets purchased on January 3, 1998. All other assets would continue to be depreciated on a straight-line basis. Prepare a revised income statement and a revised statement of cash flows, assuming the company decides to use the accelerated method for these two assets rather than the straight-line method resulting in depreciation of $49,091 for 1998.

Treat the answers in requirements 3 and 4 as independent of the other parts.

3. Assume PEK decides to use the LIFO method rather than the FIFO method to value its inventory and recognize cost of goods sold for 1998. Compute the effect (amount of increase or decrease) this would have on

> Cost of goods sold
>
> Income tax expense
>
> Net income

4. Assume PEK failed to record an estimate of bad debts for 1998 (bad debt expense is normally included in "other expenses"). Before any adjustment, the balance in Allowance for Doubtful Accounts is $8,200. The credit manager estimates that 3% of the $800,000 of sales on account will prove to be uncollectible. Based on this information, compute the effect (amount of increase or decrease) of recognition of the bad debt estimate on

> Other expenses
>
> Income tax expense
>
> Net income

A WORD TO STUDENTS ABOUT PART III

By now it's clear that this book is organized along the lines of a balance sheet. That is, Part II covered assets; Part III will cover liabilities and equity. As we'll see, taking on liabilities to pay for assets is one way to provide financing for the future of the company; the other alternative is to issue stock.

Also, the chapters in Part III continue to discuss how the related transactions affect the statement of cash flows, which is key to understanding how companies' statements—and their activities—are interrelated.

PART III

Accounting for Liabilities and Owners' Equity

Current Liabilities, Contingent Liabilities, and the Time Value of Money

STUDY LINKS

A Look at Previous Chapters

Chapter 2 introduced classified balance sheets, which emphasize the distinction between current and noncurrent assets and liabilities. Current liabilities generally represent items to be paid within one year.

A Look at This Chapter

The first part of this chapter more closely examines the items that appear in the current liability category of the balance sheet. The second part examines whether contingent liabilities should be presented on the balance sheet, disclosed in the footnotes, or ignored altogether. The third part of the chapter presents the concept of the time value of money.

A Look at Upcoming Chapters

Chapter 10 presents the accounting for long-term liabilities. The time value of money concept developed in Chapter 9 will be applied to several long-term liability issues in Chapter 10.

FOCUS ON FINANCIAL RESULTS

JCPenney operates department stores in all 50 states plus Puerto Rico, Mexico, and Chile. Its other retail chains are Thrift Drug in the United States and JCPenney Collections in the Middle East, Indonesia, and the Philippines. Complementing these operations, the company offers insurance policies through JCPenney Insurance and a credit card through JCPenney National Bank.

Most of JCPenney's revenues come from selling clothing and home furnishings, a saturated and highly competitive industry with flat sales. JCPenney therefore must deliver exceptional value and operate very efficiently.

J.C. Penney Company, Inc. and Subsidiaries

ASSETS (In millions)	1995	1994	1993
Current assets			
Cash and short term investments of $173, $207, and $156	$ 173	$ 261	$ 173
Receivables, net	5,207	5,159	4,679
Merchandise inventory	3,935	3,876	3,545
Prepaid expenses	94	73	80
Total current assets	9,409	9,369	8,477
Properties, net	4,281	3,954	3,818
Investments, primarily insurance operations	1,651	1,359	1,182
Deferred insurance policy acquisition costs	582	482	426
Other assets	1,179	1,038	885
	$17,102	$16,202	$14,788

LIABILITIES AND STOCKHOLDERS' EQUITY (In millions)			
Current liabilities			
Accounts payable and accrued expenses	$ 2,404	$ 2,274	$ 2,139
Short term debt	1,509	2,092	1,284
Current maturities of long term debt	—	—	348
Deferred taxes	107	115	112
Total current liabilities	4,020	4,481	3,883
Long term debt	4,080	3,335	2,929
Deferred taxes	1,188	1,039	1,013
Bank deposits	767	702	581
Insurance policy and claims reserves	691	568	540
Other liabilities	472	462	477
Stockholders' equity			
Preferred stock, without par value:			
Authorized, 25 million shares — issued, 1 million shares			
of Series B LESOP convertible preferred	603	630	648
Guaranteed LESOP obligation	(228)	(307)	(379)
Common stock, par value 50¢:			
Authorized, 1,250 million shares — issued,			
224, 227, and 236 million shares	1,112	1,030	1,003
Reinvested earnings	4,397	4,262	4,093
Total stockholders' equity	5,884	5,615	5,365
	$17,102	$16,202	$14,788

JCPenney does this in ways requiring scrutiny of current liabilities (those requiring payment within one year). It speeds distribution with technology and close supplier relationships. JCPenney shares information with suppliers electronically, reordering automatically in an effort to meet the demands of consumers. To preserve supplier relationships, the company monitors accounts payable and keeps up with its bills.

Another goal is a strong balance sheet—enough current assets to pay current liabilities on time. At times, JCPenney must borrow money to pay suppliers, employees, lenders, and landlords. A strong balance sheet facilitates borrowing for such needs by supporting a favorable credit rating.

If you were a JCPenney manager concerned with the company's credit rating, what information would you want about current liabilities? While studying this chapter, consider which accounts on JCPenney's balance sheet are current liabilities and how they might influence its financial position.

SOURCE: *JCPenney Annual Report,* 1995.

After studying this chapter, you should be able to

LO 1 Identify the components of the current liability category of the balance sheet.

LO 2 Examine how accruals affect the current liability category.

LO 3 Understand how changes in current liabilities affect the statement of cash flows.

LO 4 Determine when contingent liabilities should be presented on the balance sheet or disclosed in footnotes and how to calculate their amounts.

LO 5 Explain the difference between simple and compound interest.

LO 6 Calculate amounts using the future value and present value concepts.

LO 7 Apply the compound interest concepts to some common accounting situations.

LO 8 Understand the deductions and expenses for payroll accounting (Appendix 9A).

LO 9 Determine when compensated absences must be accrued as a liability (Appendix 9A).

Current Liabilities

LO 1 Identify the components of the current liability category of the balance sheet.

A classified balance sheet presents financial statement items by category in order to provide more information to financial statement users. The balance sheet generally presents two categories of liabilities, current and long-term.

Current liabilities finance the working capital of the company. At any given time during the year, current liabilities may fluctuate substantially. It is important that the company generates sufficient cash flow to retire these debts as they come due. As long as the company's ratio of current assets to current liabilities stays fairly constant from quarter to quarter or year to year, financial statement users are not going to be too concerned.

The current liability portion of the 1995 balance sheet of McDonald's Corporation is highlighted in Exhibit 9-1. Some companies list the accounts in the current liability category in the order of payment due date. That is, the account that requires payment first is listed first, the account requiring payment next is listed second, and so forth. This allows users of the statement to assess the cash flow implications of each account. McDonald's uses a different approach and lists Notes Payable as the first account.

Current liabilities were first introduced to you in Chapter 2 of this text. In general, a *current liability* is an obligation that will be satisfied within one year. Although current liabilities are not due immediately, they are still recorded at face value; that is, the time until payment is not taken into account. If it were, current liabilities would be recorded at a slight discount to reflect interest that would be earned between now and the due date. The face value amount is generally used for all current liabilities because the time period involved is short enough that it is not necessary to record or calculate an interest factor. In addition, when interest rates are low, one need not worry about the interest that could be earned in this short period of time. In Chapter 10 we will find that many long-term liabilities must be stated at their present value on the balance sheet.

The current liability classification is important because it is closely tied to the concept of *liquidity*. Management of the firm must be prepared to pay current liabilities within a very short time period. Therefore, management must have access to liquid assets, cash, or other assets that can be converted to cash in amounts sufficient to pay the current liabilities. Firms that do not have sufficient resources to pay their current liabilities are often said to have a liquidity problem.

A handy ratio to help creditors or potential creditors determine a company's liquidity is the current ratio. A current ratio of current assets to current liabilities of 2:1 is usually a very comfortable margin. If the firm has a large amount of inventory, it is sometimes useful to exclude inventory when computing the ratio. That provides the "quick" ratio. Usually, one would want a quick ratio of at least 1.5:1 to feel secure that the company could pay its bills on time. Of course, the guidelines given for the current ratio, 2:1, and the quick ratio, 1.5:1, are only rules of thumb. The actual current and quick ratios of

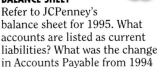

FROM CONCEPT TO PRACTICE 9.1
READING JCPENNEY'S BALANCE SHEET
Refer to JCPenney's balance sheet for 1995. What accounts are listed as current liabilities? What was the change in Accounts Payable from 1994 to 1995?

EXHIBIT 9-1   McDonald's Corporation 1995 Consolidated Balance Sheet

McDonald's Corporation
Consolidated Balance Sheet

(In millions of dollars)	December 31, 1995	1994
Assets		
Current assets		
Cash and equivalents	$ 334.8	$ 179.9
Accounts receivable	377.3	348.1
Notes receivable	36.3	31.2
Inventories, at cost, not in excess of market	58.0	50.5
Prepaid expenses and other current assets	149.4	131.0
Total current assets	955.8	740.7
Other assets and deferred charges		
Notes receivable due after one year	98.5	80.0
Investments in and advances to affiliates	656.9	579.3
Miscellaneous	357.3	380.4
Total other assets and deferred charges	1,112.7	1,039.7
Property and equipment		
Property and equipment, at cost	17,137.6	15,184.6
Accumulated depreciation and amortization	(4,326.3)	(3,856.2)
Net property and equipment	12,811.3	11,328.4
Intangible assets–net	534.8	483.1
Total assets	**$15,414.6**	**$13,591.9**
Liabilities and shareholders' equity		
Current liabilities		
Notes payable	$ 413.0	$ 1,046.9
Accounts payable	564.3	509.4
Income taxes	55.4	25.0
Other taxes	127.1	102.1
Accrued interest	117.4	107.7
Other accrued liabilities	352.5	291.9
Current maturities of long-term debt	165.2	368.3
Total current liabilities	1,794.9	2,451.3
Long-term debt	4,257.8	2,935.4
Other long-term liabilities and minority interests	664.7	422.8
Deferred income taxes	835.9	840.8
Common equity put options		56.2
Shareholders' equity		
Preferred stock, no par value; authorized–165.0 million shares; issued–7.2 thousand and 11.2 million	358.0	674.2
Common stock, no par value; authorized–1.25 billion shares; issued–830.3 million	92.3	92.3
Additional paid-in capital	387.4	286.0
Guarantee of ESOP Notes	(214.2)	(234.4)
Retained earnings	9,831.3	8,625.9
Foreign currency translation adjustment	(87.1)	(114.9)
	10,367.7	9,329.1
Common stock in treasury, at cost; 130.6 and 136.6 million shares	(2,506.4)	(2,443.7)
Total shareholders' equity	7,861.3	6,885.4
Total liabilities and shareholders' equity	**$15,414.6**	**$13,591.9**

■ Highlighted items will require payments within one year.

The accompanying Financial Comments are an integral part of the consolidated financial statements.

companies vary widely and depend on the company, the management policies, and the type of industry. Exhibit 9-2 presents the current and quick ratios for the companies that are used as examples in this chapter. The ratios do vary from company to company, yet all are solid companies without liquidity problems.

Accounting for current liabilities is an area in which U.S. accounting standards are very similar to those of most other countries. Nearly all countries encourage firms to provide a breakdown of liabilities into current and long-term in order to allow users to evaluate liquidity.

ACCOUNTING FOR YOUR DECISIONS

You Are a Student

What types of current liabilities could you, as a student, have? What makes them liabilities? What makes them current?

ANS: Your current liabilities might include the current payments due from (1) student loans, (2) car loans, (3) loans from family members, (4) rent or mortgage payments, (5) credit card charges, (6) cafeteria charges, and similar charges. These items are current liabilities because they are obligations that will be satisfied within a year.

Accounts Payable

Accounts payable represent amounts owed for the purchase of inventory, goods, or services acquired in the normal course of business. Often, Accounts Payable is the first account listed in the current liability category because it requires the payment of cash before other current liabilities. McDonald's is different from most other companies because it lists Notes Payable before Accounts Payable.

Normally, a firm has an established relationship with several suppliers, and formal contractual arrangements with those suppliers are unnecessary. Accounts payable usually do not require the payment of interest, but terms may be given to encourage early payment. For example, terms may be stated as 2/10, n30, which means that a 2% discount is available if payment occurs within the first 10 days and that if payment is not made within 10 days, the full amount must be paid within 30 days.

Timely payment of accounts payable is an important aspect of the management of cash flow. Generally, it is to the company's benefit to take advantage of discounts when they are available. After all, if your supplier is going to give you a 2% discount for paying on Day 10 instead of Day 30, that means you are earning 2% on your money over 20/360 of a year. If you took the 2% discount throughout the year, you would be getting a 36% annual return on your money, since there are 18 periods of 20 days each in a year. It is essential, therefore, that the accounts payable system be established in a manner that alerts management to take advantage of offered discounts.

Notes Payable

The first current liability on McDonald's balance sheet is notes payable of $413 million. How is a note payable different from an account payable? The most important difference is that an account payable is not a formal contractual arrangement, whereas a note

EXHIBIT 9-2	Current and Quick Ratios of Selected Companies for 1995		
COMPANY	**INDUSTRY**	**CURRENT RATIO**	**QUICK RATIO**
AMD	semiconductor	1.76	1.52
Ben & Jerry's	food	3.55	2.81
Georgia-Pacific	building products/lumber	1.47	.65
JCPenney	retailing	2.34	1.36
McDonald's	fast food	.53	.50
Quaker Oats	food and beverage	.73	.50

payable is represented by a formal agreement or note signed by the parties to the transaction. Notes payable may arise from dealing with a supplier or from acquiring a cash loan from a bank or creditor. Those notes that are expected to be paid within one year of the balance sheet date should be classified as current liabilities.

The accounting for notes payable depends on whether the interest is paid on the note's due date or is deducted before the borrower receives the loan proceeds. With the first type of note, the terms stipulate that the borrower receives a short-term loan and agrees to repay the principal and interest at the note's due date. For example, assume that Lamanski Company receives a one-year loan from First National Bank on January 1, 1998. The face amount of the note of $1,000 must be repaid on December 31 along with interest at the rate of 12%. Lamanski would make the following entries to record the loan and its repayment:

Jan. 1 Cash 1,000
    Notes Payable 1,000
    To record loan of $1,000.

Assets	=	**Liabilities**	+	**Owners' Equity**
+1,000		+1,000		

Dec. 31 Notes Payable 1,000
Interest Expense 120
    Cash 1,120
    To record the repayment of loan with interest.

Assets	=	**Liabilities**	+	**Owners' Equity**
−1,120		−1,000		−120

Banks also use another form of note, one in which the interest is deducted in advance. Suppose that on January 1, 1998, First National Bank granted to Lamanski a $1,000 loan, due on December 31, 1998, but deducted the interest in advance and gave Lamanski the remaining amount of $880 ($1,000 face amount of the note less interest of $120). This is sometimes referred to as *discounting a note;* the reason will become clear in the entries that are recorded. On January 1, Lamanski must make the following entry:

Jan. 1 Cash 880
Discount on Notes Paayable 120
    Notes Payable 1,000
    To record loan of $1,000 less interest deducted in advance.

Assets	=	**Liabilities**	+	**Owners' Equity**
+880		−120		
		+1,000		

The account titled **Discount on Notes Payable** should be treated as a reduction of Notes Payable (and should have a debit balance). If a balance sheet was developed immediately after the January 1 loan, the note would appear in the current liability category as follows:

Notes Payable	$1,000
Less: Discount on Notes Payable	120
Net Liability	$ 880

The original balance in the Discount on Notes Payable account represents interest that must be transferred to interest expense over the life of the note. Before Lamanski presents its year-end financial statements, it must make an adjustment to transfer the discount to interest expense. The effect of the adjustment on December 31 is as follows:

Dec. 31	Interest Expense	120	
	Discount on Notes Payable		120
	To record interest on note payable.		

Assets = Liabilities + Owners' Equity
+120   −120

Thus, the balance of the Discount on Notes Payable account is zero, and $120 has been transferred to interest expense. When the note is repaid on December 31, 1998, Lamanski must repay the full amount of the note as follows:

Dec. 31	Notes Payable	1,000	
	Cash		1,000
	To record payment of the note on its due date.		

Assets = Liabilities + Owners' Equity
−1,000   −1,000

It is important to compare the two types of notes payable. In the previous two examples, the stated interest rate on each note was 12%. The dollar amount of interest incurred in each case was $120. However, the interest *rate* on a discounted note, the second example, is always higher than it appears. Lamanski received the use of only $880, yet it was required to repay $1,000. Therefore, the interest rate incurred on the note was actually 120/880, or approximately 13.6%.

Current Maturities of Long-Term Debt

Another account that appears in the current liability category of McDonald's balance sheet is Current Maturities of Long-Term Debt. On other companies' balance sheets, this item may appear as Long-Term Debt, Current Portion. This account should appear when a firm has a liability and must make periodic payments. For example, assume that on January 1, 1998, your firm obtained a $10,000 loan from the bank. The terms of the loan require you to make payments in the amount of $1,000 per year for 10 years, payable each January 1, beginning January 1, 1999. On December 31, 1998, an entry should be made to classify a portion of the balance as a current liability as follows:

1998			
Dec. 31	Long-Term Liability	1,000	
	Current Portion of Liability		1,000
	To record the current portion of bank loan.		

Assets = Liabilities + Owners' Equity
−1,000
+1,000

The December 31, 1998, balance sheet should indicate that the liability for the note payable is classified into two portions: a $1,000 current liability that must be repaid within one year and a $9,000 long-term liability.

On January 1, 1999, the company must pay $1,000, and the entry should be recorded as follows:

1999			
Jan. 1	Current Portion of Liability	1,000	
	Cash		1,000
	To record payment of $1,000 on bank loan.		

Assets = Liabilities + Owners' Equity
−1,000   −1,000

On December 31, 1999, the company should again record the current portion of the liability. Therefore, the 1999 year-end balance sheet should indicate that the liability is classified into two portions: a $1,000 current liability and an $8,000 long-term liability. The process should be repeated each year until the bank loan has been fully paid. When an investor or creditor reads a balance sheet, he or she wants to distinguish between debt that is long-term and debt that is short-term. Therefore, it is important to segregate that portion of the debt that becomes due within one year.

The balance sheet category labeled Current Maturities of Long-Term Debt should include only the amount of principal to be paid. The amount of interest that has been incurred but is unpaid should be listed separately in an account such as Interest Payable.

Taxes Payable

Corporations pay a variety of taxes, including federal and state income taxes, property taxes, and other taxes. Usually, the largest dollar amount is incurred for state and federal income taxes. Taxes are an expense of the business and should be accrued in the same manner as any other business expense. A company that ends its accounting year on December 31 is not required to pay its tax amounts to the government until the following March 15 or April 15, depending on the type of business. Therefore, the business must make an accounting entry, usually as one of the year-end adjusting entries, to record the amount of tax that has been incurred but is unpaid. Normally, the entry would be recorded as follows:

LO 2 Examine how accruals affect the current liability category.

Dec. 31   Tax Expense   xxx
      Tax Payable   xxx
      To accrue income tax for the year.

Assets   =   Liabilities   +   Owners' Equity
        +xxx   **−xxx**

The calculation of the amount of tax a business owes is very complex. For now, the important point is that taxes are an expense when incurred (not when they are paid) and must be recorded as a liability as incurred.

Some analysts prefer to measure a company's profits before it pays taxes for several reasons. For one thing, tax rates change from year to year. A small change in the tax rate may drastically change a firm's profitability. Also, investors should realize that tax changes are not a recurring element of a business. Additionally, taxes are somewhat beyond the control of a company's management. For these reasons, it is important to consider a firm's operations *before* taxes to better evaluate management's ability to control operations.

Other Accrued Liabilities

McDonald's 1995 balance sheet listed an amount of $352.5 million as current liability under the category of Other Accrued Liabilities. What items might be included in this category?

In previous chapters, especially Chapter 4, we covered many examples of accrued liabilities. Accrued liabilities include any amount that has been incurred due to the passage of time but has not been paid as of the balance sheet date. A common example is salary or wages payable. Suppose that your firm has a payroll of $1,000 per day, Monday through Friday, and that employees are paid at the close of work each Friday. Also suppose that December 31 is the end of your accounting year and falls on a Tuesday. Your firm will then have to record the following entry as of December 31:

Dec. 31   Salary Expense   2,000
      Salary Payable   2,000
      To record two days' salary as expense.

Assets   =   Liabilities   +   Owners' Equity
        +2,000   **−2,000**

The amount of the salary payable would be classified as a current liability and could appear in a category such as Other Accrued Liabilities.

Interest is another item that often must be accrued at year-end. Assume that you received a one-year loan of $10,000 on December 1. The loan carries an interest rate of 12%. On December 31, an accounting entry must be made to record interest, even though the money may not actually be due:

Technology has changed how JCPenney operates as a retailer. New sales terminals allow sophisticated inventory tracking as well as scanning of inventory from other stores. How would such technology affect the amount of inventory on the financial statements?

Dec. 31 Interest Expense   100
         Interest Payable   100
        To record one month's interest as expense.

Assets = Liabilities + Owners' Equity
            +100   −100

The Interest Payable account should be classified as a current liability, assuming that it is to be paid within one year of the December 31 date.

Reading the Statement of Cash Flows for Changes in Current Liabilities

LO 3 Understand how changes in current liabilities affect the statement of cash flows.

It is important to understand the impact that current liabilities have on a company's cash flows. Exhibit 9-3 illustrates the placement of current liabilities on the statement of cash flows (using the indirect method) and their effect. Most current liabilities are directly related to a firm's ongoing operations. Therefore, the change in the balance of each current liability account should be reflected in the Operating Activities category of the statement of cash flows. A decrease in a current liability account indicates that cash has been used to pay the liability and should appear as a deduction on the cash flow statement. An increase in a current liability account indicates a recognized expense that has not yet been paid. Look for it as an increase in the Operating Activities category of the cash flow statement.

The cash flow statement of McDonald's Corporation is presented in Exhibit 9-4. Note that one of the items in the Operating Activities category is listed as Taxes and Other Liabilities of $158.3 million. This means that the balance of those current liabilities increased by $158.3 million, resulting in an increase of cash.

Almost all current liabilities appear in the Operating Activities category of the statement of cash flows, but there are exceptions. If a current liability is not directly related to operating activities, it should not appear in that category. For example, McDonald's uses some notes payable as a means of financing, distinct from operating activities. Therefore, note borrowings and repayments are reflected in the Financing Activities rather than the Operating Activities category (see Exhibit 9-3).

Contingent Liabilities

LO 4 Determine when contingent liabilities should be presented on the balance sheet or disclosed in footnotes and how to calculate their amounts.

We have seen that accountants must exercise a great deal of expertise and judgment in deciding what to record and in determining the amount to record. This is certainly true regarding contingent liabilities. A contingent liability is an obligation that involves an existing condition for which the outcome is not known with certainty and depends on some event that will occur in the future. The actual amount of the liability must be

EXHIBIT 9-3 Current Liabilities on the Statement of Cash Flows

Item	Cash Flow Statement
	Operating Activities
	Net income xxxx
Increase in current liability ⋯⋯⋯⋯	➤ +
Decrease in current liability ⋯⋯⋯⋯	➤ −
	Investing Activities
	Financing Activities
Increase in notes payable ⋯⋯⋯⋯	➤ +
Decrease in notes payable ⋯⋯⋯⋯	➤ −

EXHIBIT 9-4   McDonald's Corporation 1995 Consolidated Statement of Cash Flows

McDonald's Corporation
Consolidated Statement of Cash Flows

(In millions of dollars)	Years ended December 31, 1995	1994	1993
Operating activities			
Net income	$ 1,427.3	$ 1,224.4	$ 1,082.5
Adjustments to reconcile to cash provided by operations			
Depreciation and amortization	709.0	628.6	568.4
Deferred income taxes	(4.2)	(5.6)	52.4
Changes in operating working capital items			
Accounts receivable increase	(49.5)	(51.6)	(48.3)
Inventories, prepaid expenses and other current assets increase	(20.4)	(15.0)	(9.6)
Accounts payable increase	52.6	105.4	45.4
Accrued interest increase (decrease)	13.0	(25.5)	(5.1)
Taxes and other liabilities increase	158.3	95.2	26.5
Other–net	10.1	(29.7)	(32.4)
Cash provided by operations	2,296.2	1,926.2	1,679.8
Investing activities			
Property and equipment expenditures	(2,063.7)	(1,538.6)	(1,316.9)
Purchases of restaurant businesses	(110.1)	(133.8)	(64.2)
Sales of restaurant businesses	151.6	151.5	114.2
Property sales	66.2	66.0	61.6
Notes receivable additions	(33.4)	(15.1)	(33.1)
Notes receivable reductions	31.5	56.7	75.7
Other	(151.1)	(92.6)	(55.3)
Cash used for investing activities	(2,109.0)	(1,505.9)	(1,218.0)
Financing activities			
Net short-term borrowings (repayments)	(272.9)	521.7	(8.9)
Long-term financing issuances	1,250.2	260.9	1,241.0
Long-term financing repayments	(532.2)	(536.9)	(1,185.9)
Treasury stock purchases	(314.5)	(495.6)	(620.1)
Common and preferred stock dividends	(226.5)	(215.7)	(201.2)
Other	63.6	39.4	62.6
Cash used for financing activities	(32.3)	(426.2)	(712.5)
Cash and equivalents increase (decrease)	154.9	(5.9)	(250.7)
Cash and equivalents at beginning of year	179.9	185.8	436.5
Cash and equivalents at end of year	$ 334.8	$ 179.9	$ 185.8
Supplemental cash flow disclosures			
Interest paid	$ 331.0	$ 323.9	$ 312.2
Income taxes paid	$ 667.6	$ 621.8	$ 521.7

■ Notice the impact of current liabilities on cash flow.

The accompanying Financial Comments are an integral part of the consolidated financial statements.

estimated because we cannot clearly predict the future. The important accounting issues are whether contingent liabilities should be recorded and, if so, in what amounts.

This is a judgment call that is usually resolved through discussions among the company's management and its outside auditors. Management usually would rather not disclose contingent liabilities until they come due. The reason is that investors' and creditors' judgment of management is based on the company's earnings, and the recording of a contingent liability must be accompanied by a charge to (reduction in) earnings. Auditors, on the other hand, want management to disclose as much as possible because the auditors are essentially representing the interests of investors and creditors, who want to have as much information as possible.

Contingent Liabilities That Are Recorded

A contingent liability should be accrued and presented on the balance sheet if it is probable and if the amount can be reasonably estimated. But when is an event *probable* and what does *reasonably estimated* mean? The terms must be defined based on the facts of each situation. A financial statement user would want the company to err on the side of full disclosure. On the other hand, the company should not be required to disclose every remote possibility.

A common contingent liability that must be presented as a liability by firms involves product warranties or guarantees. Many firms sell products for which they provide the customer a warranty against defects that may develop in the products. If a product becomes defective within the warranty period, the selling firm ensures that it will repair or replace the item. This is an example of a contingent liability because the expense of fixing a product depends on some of the products becoming defective—an uncertain, although likely, event.

At the end of each period, the selling firm must estimate how many of the products sold in the current year will become defective in the future and the cost of repair or replacement. This type of contingent liability is often referred to as an **estimated liability** to emphasize that the costs are not known at year-end and must be estimated.

As an example, assume that Quickkey Computer sells a computer product for $5,000. When the customer buys the product, Quickkey provides a one-year warranty in case it must be repaired. Assume that in 1998 Quickkey sold 100 computers for a total sales revenue of $500,000. At the end of 1998, Quickkey must record an estimate of the warranty costs that will occur on 1998 sales. Using an analysis of past warranty records, Quickkey estimates that repairs will average 2% of total sales. Therefore, Quickkey should record the following transaction at the end of 1998:

Dec. 31	Warranty Expense	10,000	
	Estimated Liability		10,000
	To record estimated liability at 2% of sales.		

Assets	=	**Liabilities**	+	**Owners' Equity**
		+10,000		**−10,000**

The amount of warranty costs a company presents as an expense is of interest to investors and potential creditors. If the expense as a percentage of sales begins to rise, one might conclude that the product is becoming less reliable.

Warranties are an excellent example of the matching principle. In our Quickkey example, the warranty costs related to 1998 sales were estimated and recorded in 1998. This was done to match the 1998 sales with the expenses related to those sales. If actual repairs of the computers occurred in 1999, they do not result in an expense. The repair costs incurred in 1999 should be treated as a reduction in the liability that had previously been estimated.

Because items such as warranties involve estimation, you may wonder what happens if the amount estimated is not accurate. The company must analyze past warranty records carefully and incorporate any changes in customer buying habits, usage, technological changes, and other changes. Still, even with careful analysis, the actual amount of the expense is not likely to equal the estimated amount. Generally, firms do not change the amount of the expense recorded in past periods for such differences. They may adjust the amount recorded in future periods, however.

Warranties provide an example of a contingent liability that must be estimated and recorded. Another example is premium or coupon offers that accompany many products. Cereal boxes are an everyday example of premium offers. The boxes often allow customers to purchase a toy or game at a reduced price if the purchase is accompanied by cereal box tops or proof of purchase. The offer given to cereal customers represents a contingent liability. At the end of each year, the cereal company must estimate the number of premium offers that will be redeemed and the cost involved and must report a contingent liability for that amount.

Product warranties represent a *contingent liability* that must be presented on the balance sheet. This is because some amount of warranty work is *probable* and can be *estimated*. As the level of warranty expense rises, often so does the skepticism of investors toward these retailers.

A lawsuit that has been filed against a firm is also an example of a contingent liability. In today's business environment, lawsuits are a fact of life. They represent a contingent liability because an event has occurred but the outcome of that event, the resolution of the lawsuit, is not known. The defendant in the lawsuit must make a judgment about the outcome of the lawsuit in order to decide whether the item should be recorded on the balance sheet or should be disclosed in the footnotes. If an unfavorable outcome to the lawsuit is deemed to be probable, then the lawsuit should be recorded as a contingent liability on the balance sheet. Exhibit 9-5 provides a footnote disclosure that accompanied the 1995 financial statements of Quaker Oats Company; note 18 concerned litigation over the words *thirst-aid,* used to advertise the product Gatorade. The lawsuit had been ongoing since 1990 in various courts. In 1995 the company believed that an unfavorable outcome had become probable and, as a result, recorded a contingent liability of $29 million.

As you might imagine, firms are not usually eager to record contingent lawsuits as liabilities because the amount of loss is often difficult to estimate. Also, some may view the accountant's decision as an admission of guilt if a lawsuit is recorded as a liability before the courts have finalized a decision. Accountants must often consult with lawyers

EXHIBIT 9-5   Footnote Disclosure for Contingent Liability (Litigation) from Quaker Oats' 1995 Financial Statements

Note 18

Litigation

On December 18, 1990, Judge Prentice H. Marshall of the United States District Court for the Northern District of Illinois entered judgment against the Company in favor of Sands, Taylor & Wood Co., holding that the use of the words "thirst aid" in advertising *Gatorade* thirst quencher infringed the Plaintiff's rights in the trademark THIRST-AID. On July 9, 1991, Judge Marshall entered a judgment of $42.6 million, composed of $31.4 million in principal, prejudgment interest of $10.6 million, and fees, expenses and costs of $0.6 million. The order enjoined use of the phrase "THIRST-AID" in connection with the advertising or sale of *Gatorade* thirst quencher in the United States. The Company appealed the judgment. On September 2, 1992, the Court of Appeals for the Seventh Circuit affirmed the finding of infringement, but found that the monetary award was an inequitable "windfall" to the Plaintiff, and it therefore remanded the case to the District Court. On June 7, 1993, Judge Marshall issued a judgment on remand of $26.5 million, composed of $20.7 million in principal, prejudgment interest of $5.4 million, and fees, expenses and costs of $0.4 million. The Company appealed this judgment.

On September 13, 1994, the Court of Appeals affirmed the lower court's award of a reasonable royalty and prejudgment interest, but again remanded the case to allow the District Court to explain the enhancement of the royalty award. On April 11, 1995, Judge Marshall affirmed his prior ruling and the Company filed another appeal. Management, with advice from outside legal counsel, has determined that the Court of Appeals' opinion appears to indicate a range of exposure between $18 million and $30 million. The Company recorded a provision of $29.0 million for this litigation in fiscal 1995.

The Company is not a party to any other pending legal proceedings or environmental clean-up actions that it believes will have a material adverse effect on its financial position or results of operations.

or other legal experts to determine the probability of the loss of a lawsuit. In cases involving contingencies, it is especially important that the accountant make an independent judgment based on the facts and not be swayed by the desires of other parties.

Contingent Liabilities That Are Disclosed

FROM CONCEPT TO PRACTICE 9.2

READING BEN & JERRY'S ANNUAL REPORT Ben & Jerry's annual report contains a contingent liability. What is it? Do you think it has been properly disclosed? Was it recorded on the financial statements?

Any contingent liability that both is probable and can be reasonably estimated must be reported as a liability. We now must consider contingent liabilities that do not meet the probable criterion or cannot be reasonably estimated. In either case, a contingent liability must be disclosed in the footnotes but not reported on the balance sheet if the contingent liability is at least reasonably possible.

Although information in the footnotes to the financial statements contains very important data on which investors base decisions, some accountants believe that footnote disclosure does not have the same impact as does recording a contingent liability on the balance sheet. For one thing, footnote disclosure does not affect the important financial ratios that investors use to make decisions.

In the previous section we presented a lawsuit involving Quaker Oats as an example of a contingent liability that was probable and therefore was recorded on the balance sheet as a liability. Most lawsuits, however, are not recorded as liabilities either because the risk of loss is not considered probable or because the amount of the loss cannot be reasonably estimated. If a company does not record a lawsuit as a liability, it must still consider whether the lawsuit should be disclosed in the footnotes. If the risk of loss is at least *reasonably possible,* then the company should provide footnote disclosure. This is the course of action taken for most contingent liabilities involving lawsuits.

Exhibit 9-6 contains two excerpts from the footnotes of the 1995 financial statements of AMD Company, a large company in the semiconductor industry. The first portion of the exhibit indicates that the company became a defendant in a lawsuit involving a claim that they unfairly infringed on the patent of another firm. Patent disputes are a fairly common occurrence in the semiconductor industry because of the rapid rate of technological change. The second portion of the exhibit indictates that AMD has been involved in a series of ongoing disputes involving the costs of environmental contamination. In recent years, this has become an area of concern for many companies as society and governmental agencies have become more aware of the need to ensure that firms are responsible for any actions that adversely affect the environment. In AMD's case, the footnote indicates that their clean-up costs relate to activities that occurred many years ago, before 1979.

You should note that the two excerpts in Exhibit 9-6 are both examples of contingent liabilities that have been disclosed in the footnotes *but have not been recorded as liabilities on the balance sheet.* Readers of the financial statements, and analysts, must carefully read the footnotes to determine the impact of such contingent liabilities.

The amount and the timing of the cash outlays associated with contingent liabilities are especially difficult to determine. Lawsuits, for example, may extend several years into the future, and the dollar amount of possible loss may be subject to great uncertainty.

ACCOUNTING FOR YOUR DECISIONS
You Are the CEO

You run a high-technology company that grows fast some quarters and disappoints investors in other quarters. As a result, your company's stock price fluctuates widely, and you have attracted the unwanted attention of a law firm that filed a lawsuit on behalf of disgruntled shareholders. How do you reflect this lawsuit on your financial statements?

ANS: Your legal counsel should be consulted to determine whether the plaintiff's case has merit. If a loss is probable and the amount can be estimated, the lawsuit should be recorded as a liability. Unfortunately, lawsuits have become very common for many companies. In some cases, the lawsuits are totally without merit and are frivolous. If your attorneys agree that this case will not result in a loss, then no disclosure would be required.

EXHIBIT 9-6   Footnote Disclosures for Contingencies (Lawsuit and Environmental) from AMD Company's 1995 Annual Report

NOTE 16 *CONTINGENCIES*

I. LITIGATIONS

C. Thorn EMI North America, Inc. v. AMD. This litigation was filed in 1995 and alleges that AMD is infringing a patent owned by Thorn EMI North America, Inc. relating to the processes used by AMD to manufacture microprocessors. Based upon information presently known to management, the company does not believe that the ultimate resolution of this lawsuit will have a material adverse effect upon the financial condition or results of operations of the company.

III. ENVIRONMENTAL MATTERS

Clean-Up Orders. Since 1981, the company has discovered, investigated, and begun remediation of three sites where releases from underground chemical tanks at its facilities in Santa Clara County, California adversely affected the groundwater. The chemicals released into the groundwater were commonly in use in the semiconductor industry in the wafer fabrication process prior to 1979. At least one of the released chemicals (which is no longer used by the company) has been identified as a probable carcinogen.

In 1991, the company received four Final Site Cleanup Requirements Orders from the California Regional Water Quality Control Board, San Francisco Bay Region (RWQCB) relating to the three sites. One of the orders named the

company as well as TRW Microwave, Inc. and Philips Semiconductors Corporation. Another of the orders named the company as well as National Semiconductor Corporation.

The three sites in Santa Clara County are on the National Priorities List (Superfund). If the company fails to satisfy federal compliance requirements or inadequately performs the compliance measures, the government (a) can bring an action to enforce compliance, or (b) can undertake the desired response actions itself and later bring an action to recover its costs, and penalties, which is up to three times the costs of clean-up activities, if appropriate. With regard to certain claims related to this matter the statute of limitations has been tolled.

The company has computed and recorded the estimated environmental liability in accordance with applicable accounting rules and has not recorded any potential insurance recoveries in determining the estimated costs of the clean-up. The amount of environmental charges to earnings has not been material during the last three fiscal years. The company believes that the potential liability, if any, in excess of amounts already accrued with respect to the foregoing environmental matters will not have a material adverse effect on the financial condition or results of operations of the company.

Contingent Liabilities versus Contingent Assets

Contingent liabilities that are probable and can be reasonably estimated must be presented on the balance sheet before the outcome of the future events is known. This accounting rule applies only to contingent losses or liabilities. It does not apply to contingencies by which the firm may gain. Generally, contingent gains or contingent assets are not reported until the gain actually occurs. That is, contingent liabilities may be accrued, but contingent assets are not accrued. Exhibit 9-7 contains a portion of the footnotes from the 1995 financial statements of Georgia-Pacific Corporation. Like many other companies, Georgia-Pacific has had to pay rather large amounts for environmental remediation costs. The footnote indicates that Georgia-Pacific has filed suit against several insurance companies because it believes that their insurance policies should cover part of the costs. This is an example of a contingent asset because the company may receive some amounts at a future time. The financial statements reveal that Georgia-Pacific has recorded liabilities related to the remediation costs but has not recorded any of the potential recoveries from insurance even though it appears quite likely that some amount will be received. This may seem inconsistent—it is. Remember, however, that

EXHIBIT 9-7   Footnote Disclosure for Contingent Asset (Proceeds from Lawsuit) from Georgia-Pacific's 1995 Financial Statements

Georgia-Pacific Corporation and Subsidiaries

In the fourth quarter of 1992, the Corporation filed suit in the State of Washington against numerous insurance carriers for coverage under comprehensive general liability insurance policies issued by those carriers. The Corporation sought a declaratory judgment to the effect that past and future environmental remediation and other related costs with respect to certain of the sites are covered by such policies. The Corporation has now dismissed or settled its claims against all but one of those carriers for a total of approximately $54 million. Approximately $44 million of this amount has been received ($40 million of which was recorded as pretax income in 1995) and the remainder is payable, subject to certain contingencies, over approximately the next ten years. No amounts have been recorded for contingent payments.

accounting is a discipline based on a conservative set of principles. It is prudent and conservative to delay the recording of a gain until an asset is actually received but to record contingent liabilities in advance.

Of course, just because the contingent assets are not reported does not mean that they should not be considered. Wall Street analysts make their living trying to place a value on contingent assets that they believe will result in future benefits. By buying stock of a company that has unrecorded assets, or advising their clients to do so, investment analysts hope to make money when those assets become a reality.

Time Value of Money Concepts

In this section we will study the impact that interest has on decision making because of the time value of money. The **time value of money** concept means that people prefer a payment at the present time rather than in the future because of the interest factor. If an amount is received at the present time, it can be invested, and the resulting accumulation will be larger than if the same amount is received in the future. Thus, there is a *time value* to cash receipts and payments. This time value concept is important to every student for two reasons: it affects your personal financial decisions, and it affects accounting valuation decisions.

Exhibit 9-8 indicates some of the personal and accounting decisions affected by the time value of money concept. In your personal lives, you make decisions based on the time value of money concept nearly every day. When you invest money, you are interested in how much will be accumulated, and you must determine the *future value* based on the amount of interest that will be compounded. When you borrow money, you must determine the amount of the payments on the loan. You may not always realize it, but the amount of the loan payment is based on the *present value* of the loan, another time value of money concept.

Time value of money is also important because of its implications for accounting valuations. We will discover in Chapter 10 that the issue price of a bond is based on the present value of the cash flows that the bond will produce. The valuation of the bond and the recording of the bond on the balance sheet are based on this concept. Further, the amount that is considered interest expense on the financial statements is also based on time value of money concepts. The bottom portion of Exhibit 9-8 indicates that the valuations of many other accounts, including Notes Receivable and Leases, are based on compound interest calculations.

ACCOUNTING FOR YOUR DECISIONS
You Handle the Money in the Family

How many different personal financial situations can you think of in which the time value of money is relevant? How many in which it is irrelevant?

ANS: Relevant: Deciding whether to refinance your mortgage. Deciding how much money to put away every month for the kids' college fund. Deciding whether to lease or buy a car. Deciding whether you should go back to school to get retraining for a new career. Deciding whether to make a loan to your sister so that she can start a business. Irrelevant: Deciding whether to take a family vacation. Deciding whether to replace a broken refrigerator with a $1,500 model or a $3,000 model. Deciding whether to give $1,000 or $2,000 to charity this year.

The time value of money concept is used in virtually every advanced business course. Investment courses, marketing courses, and many other business courses will use the time value of money concept. *In fact, it is probably the most important decision-making tool to master in preparation for the business world.* This section of the text begins with an explanation of how simple interest and compound interest differ and then proceeds to the concepts of present values and future values.

Simple Interest

Simple interest is interest earned on the principal amount. If the amount of principal is unchanged from year to year, the interest per year will remain the same. Interest can be calculated by the following formula

LO 5 Explain the difference between simple and compound interest.

$$I = P \times R \times T,$$

EXHIBIT 9-8	Importance of the Time Value of Money

PERSONAL FINANCIAL DECISION	ACTION
■ How much money will accumulate if you invest in a CD or money market account?	→ Calculate the future value based on compound interest.
■ If you take out an auto loan, what will be the monthly loan payments?	→ Calculate the payments based on the present value of the loan.
■ If you invest in the bond market, what should you pay for a bond?	→ Calculate the present value of the bond based on compound interest.
■ If you win the lottery, should you take an immediate payment or payment over time?	→ Calculate the present value of the alternatives based on compound interest.

VALUATION DECISIONS ON THE FINANCIAL STATEMENTS	VALUATION
■ Long-term assets	→ Historical cost, but not higher than present value of the cash flows
■ Notes receivable	→ Present value of the cash flows
■ Loan payments	→ Based on the present value of the loan
■ Bond issue price	→ Present value of the cash flows
■ Leases	→ Present value of the cash flows

where

I = Dollar amount of interest per year

P = Principal

R = Interest rate as a percentage

T = Time in years.

For example, assume that our firm has signed a two-year note payable for $3,000. Interest and principal are to be paid at the due date with simple interest at the rate of 10% per year. The amount of interest on the note would be $600 calculated as $3,000 × .10 × 2. We would be required to pay $3,600 on the due date: $3,000 principal and $600 interest.

Compound Interest

Compound interest means that interest is calculated on the principal plus previous amounts of accumulated interest. Thus, interest is compounded, or we can say that there is interest on interest. For example, assume a $3,000 note payable for which interest and principal are due in two years with interest compounded annually at 10% per year. Interest would be calculated as follows:

YEAR	PRINCIPAL AMOUNT AT BEGINNING OF YEAR	INTEREST AT 10%	ACCUMULATED AT YEAR-END
1	$3,000	$300	$3,300
2	3,300	330	3,630

We would be required to pay $3,630 at the end of two years, $3,000 principal and $630 interest. A comparison of the note payable with 10% simple interest in the first example with the note payable with 10% compound interest in the second example clearly indicates that the amount accumulated with compound interest is always a higher amount because of the interest-on-interest feature.

Interest Compounding

LO 6 Calculate amounts using the future value and present value concepts.

For most accounting problems, we will assume that compound interest is compounded annually. In actual business practice, compounding usually occurs over much shorter intervals. This can be confusing because the interest rate is often stated as an annual rate even though it is compounded over a shorter period. If compounding is not done annually, you must adjust the interest rate by dividing the annual rate by the number of compounding periods per year.

For example, assume that the note payable from the previous example carried a 10% interest rate compounded semiannually for two years. The 10% annual rate should be converted to 5% per period for four semiannual periods. The amount of interest would be compounded, as in the previous example, but for four periods instead of two. The compounding process is as follows:

PERIOD	PRINCIPAL AMOUNT AT BEGINNING OF YEAR	INTEREST AT 5% PER PERIOD	ACCUMULATED AT END OF PERIOD
1	$3,000	$150	$3,150
2	3,150	158	3,308
3	3,308	165	3,473
4	3,473	174	3,647

The example illustrates that compounding more frequently results in a larger amount accumulated. In fact, many banks and financial institutions now compound interest on savings accounts on a daily basis.

In the remainder of this section, we will assume that compound interest is applicable. Four compound interest calculations must be understood:

ACCOUNTING FOR YOUR DECISIONS
You Invest Some Unexpected Cash

You want to invest some extra money you received from a long-lost uncle. You have narrowed your options down to two: (1) invest in a bond that offers 10% interest compounded semiannually, or (2) invest in a certificate of deposit that offers 10% interest compounded quarterly. Both options cover a one-year time period. Using the time value of money concepts you have learned in this accounting course, would you choose Option 1 or 2? Why?

ANS: You should choose Option 2, offering the same interest rate as the first option but compounding on a quarterly basis instead of a semiannual basis. More frequent compounding results in more interest, thus making Option 2's quarterly compounding more appealing than Option 1's semiannual compounding.

the longer you have to wait for a dollar, the less it is worth now

As interest rates get bigger, the present value of a future dollar gets smaller

1. Future value of a single amount
2. Present value of a single amount
3. Future value of an annuity
4. Present value of an annuity

Future Value of a Single Amount

We are often interested in the amount of interest plus principal that will be accumulated at a future time. This is called a *future amount* or *future value*. The future amount is always larger than the principal amount (payment) because of the interest that accumulates. The formula to calculate the future value of a single amount is

$$FV = p(1 + i)^n,$$

where

FV = Future value to be calculated
p = Payment or principal amount
i = Interest rate
n = Number of periods of compounding.

Money you end up with ÷ money you start with

Example: Grandpa Phil passed away and left your three-year-old son, Robert, $50,000 in cash and securities. If the funds were left in the bank and in the stock market and received an annual return of 10%, how much would be there in 15 years when Robert starts college?

Solution: FV = $50,000(1 + .10)^{15}$
= $50,000(4.177)
= $208,850

In some cases, we will use time diagrams to illustrate the relationships. A time diagram to illustrate a future value would be of the following form:

Payment ——————— Interest ——————— FV

Known Amount   Future Value = ?
of Payment

For example, consider a $2,000 note payable that carries interest at the rate of 10% compounded annually. The note is due in two years, and the principal and interest must be paid at that time. The amount that must be paid in two years is the future value. The future value can be calculated in the manner we have used in the previous examples:

YEAR	PRINCIPAL AMOUNT AT BEGINNING OF YEAR	INTEREST AT 10%	ACCUMULATED AT YEAR-END
1	$2,000	$200	$2,200
2	2,200	220	2,420

Assume you won the lottery and this check were yours. Which payment option would you take—a lump sum or an amount every year for 10 years? Only by understanding time value of money concepts would you make an intelligent choice.

The future value can also be calculated by using the following formula:

$$FV = \$2,000(1 + .10)^2$$
$$= \$2,000(1.21)$$
$$= \$2,420$$

Many calculators are capable of performing compound interest calculations. The future value formula is programmed into the calculator so that you do not see the calculations once you have entered the proper values.

Tables can also be constructed to assist in the calculations. Table 9-1 on page 432 indicates the future value of $1 at various interest rates and for various time periods. To find the future value of a two-year note at 10% compounded annually, you read across the line for two periods and down the 10% column and see an interest rate factor of 1.210. Because the table has been constructed for future values of $1, we would determine the future value of $2,000 as follows:

$$FV = \$2,000 \times 1.210$$
$$= \$2,420$$

We mentioned that compounding does not always occur annually. How does this affect the calculation of future value amounts? Suppose we want to find the future value of a $2,000 note payable due in two years. The note payable requires interest to be compounded quarterly at the rate of 12% per year. To calculate the future value, we must adjust the interest rate to a quarterly basis by dividing the 12% rate by the number of compounding periods per year, which in the case of quarterly compounding is four:

$$12\%/4 \text{ Quarters} = 3\% \text{ per Quarter}$$

Also, the number of compounding periods is eight, four per year times two years.

The future value of the note can be found in two ways. First, we can insert the proper values into the future value formula:

$$FV = \$2,000(1 + .03)^8$$
$$= \$2,000(1.267)$$
$$= \$2,534$$

We can arrive at the same future value amount with the use of Table 9-1. Refer to the interest factor in the table indicated for 8 periods and 3%. The future value would be calculated as follows:

$$FV = \$2,000(\text{interest factor})$$
$$= \$2,000(1.267)$$
$$= \$2,534$$

Present Value of a Single Amount

In many situations, we do not want to calculate how much will be accumulated at a future time. Rather, we want to determine the present amount that is equivalent to an amount at a future time. This is the present value concept. The present value of a single amount represents the value today of a single amount to be received or paid at a future time. This can be portrayed in a time diagram as follows:

The time diagram portrays discount, rather than interest, because we often speak of "discounting" the future payment back to the present time.

Suppose you know that you will receive $2,000 in two years. You also know that if you had the money now, it could be invested at 10% compounded annually. What is the present value of the $2,000? Another way to ask the same question is, What amount must be invested today at 10% compounded annually in order to have $2,000 accumulated in two years?

The formula used to calculate present value is

$$PV = \text{Payment} \times (1 + i)^{-n}$$

where

PV = Present value amount in dollars

Payment = Amount to be received in the future

i = Interest rate or discount rate

n = Number of periods.

We can use the present value formula to solve for the present value of the $2,000 note as follows:

$$PV = \$2,000 \times (1 + .10)^{-2}$$

$$= \$2,000 \times (.826)$$

$$= \$1,652$$

Example: A recent magazine article projects that it will cost $120,000 to attend a four-year college 10 years from now. If that is true, how much money would you have to put into an account today to fund that education, assuming a 5% rate of return?

Solution:

$$PV = \$120,000(1 + .05)^{-10}$$

$$= \$120,000(.614)$$

$$= \$73,680$$

[handwritten margin note: Present value should be smaller than future value, if interest rate is +]

Tables have also been developed to determine the present value of $1 at various interest rates and number of periods. Table 9-2 on page 433 presents the present value or discount factors for an amount of $1 to be received at a future time. To use the table for our two-year note example, you must read across the line for two periods and down the 10% column to the discount factor of .826. The present value of $2,000 would be calculated as follows:

$$PV = \$2,000(\text{discount factor})$$

$$= \$2,000(.826)$$

$$= \$1,652$$

Two other points are important. First, the example illustrates that the present value amount is always less than the future payment. This happens because of the discount factor. In other words, if we had a smaller amount at the present (the present value), we could invest it and earn interest that would accumulate to an amount equal to the larger amount (the future payment). Second, study of the present value and future value formulas indicates that each is the reciprocal of the other. When we want to calculate a present value amount, we normally use Table 9-2 and multiply a discount factor times the payment. However, we could also use Table 9-1 and divide by the interest factor. Thus, the present value of the $2,000 to be received in the future could also be calculated as follows:

$$PV = \$2,000/1.210$$

$$= \$1,652$$

Future Value of an Annuity

The present value and future value amounts are useful when a single amount is involved. Many accounting situations involve an annuity, however. Annuity means a series of payments of equal amounts. We will now consider the calculation of the future value when a series of payments is involved.

Suppose that you are to receive $3,000 per year at the end of each of the next four years. Also assume that each payment could be invested at an interest rate of 10% compounded annually. How much would be accumulated in principal and interest by the end of the fourth year? This is an example of an annuity of payments of equal amounts. A time diagram would portray the payments as follows:

$3,000 $3,000 $3,000 $3,000

| Interest | Interest | Interest |

$FV = ?$

Because we are interested in calculating the future value, we could use the future value of $1 concept and calculate the future value of each $3,000 payment using Table 9-1 as follows:

$3,000 × 1.331 Interest for 3 Periods	$ 3,993
3,000 × 1.210 Interest for 2 Periods	3,630
3,000 × 1.100 Interest for 1 Period	3,300
3,000 × 1.000 Interest for 0 Periods	3,000
Total Future Value	$13,923

It should be noted that four payments would be received but that only three of them would draw interest because the payments are received at the end of each period.

Fortunately, there is an easier method to calculate the *future value of an annuity*. Table 9-3 on page 434 has been constructed to indicate the future value of a series of payments of $1 per period at various interest rates and number of periods. The table can be used for the previous example by reading across the four-period line and down the 10% column to a table factor of 4.641. The future value of an annuity of $3,000 per year can be calculated as follows:

$$FV = \$3,000(\text{table factor})$$
$$= \$3,000(4.641)$$
$$= \$13,923$$

Example: You just had a baby girl two weeks ago and are already thinking about college. When she is 15, how much money would be in her college account if you deposit $2,000 into it on each of her 15 birthdays? The interest rate is 10%.

Solution:
$$FV = \$2,000(\text{table factor})$$
$$= \$2,000(31.772)$$
$$= \$63,544$$

When compounding occurs more frequently than annually, adjustments must be made to the interest rate and number of periods, adjustments similar to those discussed previously for single amounts. For example, how would the future value be calculated if the previous example was modified so that we deposited $1,000 semiannually and the interest rate was 10% compounded semiannually (or 5% per period) for 15 years? Table 9-3 could be used by reading across the line for 30 periods and down the column for 5% to obtain a table factor of 66.439. The future value would be calculated as follows:

$$FV = \$1,000(\text{table factor})$$
$$= \$1,000(66.439)$$
$$= \$66,439$$

Comparing the two examples illustrates once again that more frequent compounding results in larger accumulated amounts.

Present Value of an Annuity

Many accounting applications of the time value of money concept concern situations for which we want to know the present value of a series of payments that will occur in the future. This involves calculating the present value of an annuity.

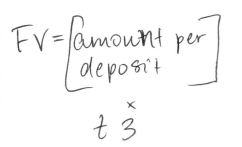
FV = [amount per deposit] × t3

An annuity is a series of payments of equal amounts. Suppose that you will receive an annuity of $4,000 per year for four years, with the first received one year from today. The amounts that are received can be invested at a rate of 10% compounded annually. What amount would we need at the present time to have an amount equivalent to the series of payments and interest in the future? To answer this question, we must calculate the **present value of an annuity.** A time diagram of the series of payments would appear as follows:

$4,000	$4,000	$4,000	$4,000
Discount	Discount	Discount	Discount

$PV = ?$

Because we are interested in calculating the present value, we could refer to the present value of $1 concept and discount each of the $4,000 payments individually using table factors from Table 9-2 as follows:

$4,000 × 0.683 Factor for Four Periods	$ 2,732
4,000 × 0.751 Factor for Three Periods	3,004
4,000 × 0.826 Factor for Two Periods	3,304
4,000 × 0.909 Factor for One Period	3,636
Total Present Value	$12,676

For a problem of any size, it is very cumbersome to calculate the present value of each payment individually. Therefore, tables have been constructed to ease the computational burden. Table 9-4 on page 435 provides table factors to calculate the present value of an annuity of $1 per year at various interest rates and number of periods. The previous example can be solved by reading across the four-year line and down the 10% column to obtain a table factor of 3.170. The present value would then be calculated as follows:

$$PV = \$4,000(\text{table factor})$$
$$= \$4,000(3.170)$$
$$= \$12,680$$

You should note that there is a $4 difference in the present value calculated by the first and second methods. This difference is caused by a small amount of rounding in the table factors that were used.

Example: You just won the lottery. You can take your $1 million in a lump sum today, or you can receive $100,000 per year over the next 12 years. Assuming a 5% interest rate, which would you prefer, ignoring tax considerations?

Solution: $$PV = \$100,000(\text{table factor})$$
$$= \$100,000(8.863)$$
$$= \$886,300$$

Because the present value of the payments over 12 years is less than the $1 million immediate payment, you should prefer the immediate payment.

Solving for Unknowns

In some cases, the present value or future value amounts will be known but the interest rate or the number of payments must be calculated. The formulas that have been presented thus far can be used for such calculations, but you must be careful to analyze each problem to be sure that you have chosen the correct relationship. We will use two examples to illustrate the power of the time value of money concepts.

Assume that you have just purchased a new automobile for $14,420 and must decide how to pay for it. Your local bank has graciously granted you a five-year loan. Because you are a good credit risk, the bank will allow you to make annual payments on the loan at the end of each year. The amount of the loan payments, which include principal and interest, is $4,000 per year. You are concerned that your total payments will be $20,000

LO 7 Apply the compound interest concepts to some common accounting situations.

($4,000 per year for five years) and want to calculate the interest rate that is being charged on the loan.

Because the market or present value of the car, as well as the loan, is $14,420, a time diagram of our example would appear as follows:

$4,000	$4,000	$4,000	$4,000	$4,000
Discount	Discount	Discount	Discount	Discount

$PV = 14,420$

The interest rate that we must solve for represents the discount rate that was applied to the $4,000 payments to result in a present value of $14,420. Therefore, the applicable formula is the following:

$$PV = \$4,000(\text{table factor})$$

In this case, PV is known, so the formula can be rearranged as follows:

$$\text{Table Factor} = PV/\$4,000$$
$$= \$14,420/\$4,000$$
$$= 3.605$$

The value of 3.605 represents a table factor in Table 9-4. We must read across the five-year line until we find a table factor of 3.605. In this case, that table factor is found in the 12% column. Therefore, the rate of interest being paid on the auto loan is 12%.

The second example involves solving for the number of interest periods. Assume that you want to accumulate $12,000 as a down payment on a home. You believe that you can save $1,000 per semiannual period, and your bank will pay interest of 8% per year, or 4% per semiannual period. How long will it take you to accumulate the desired amount?

The accumulated amount of $12,000 represents the future value of an annuity of $1,000 per semiannual period. Therefore, we can use the interest factors of Table 9-3 to assist in the solution. The applicable formula in this case is the following:

$$FV = \$1,000(\text{table factor})$$

The future value is known to be $12,000, and we must solve for the interest factor or table factor. Therefore, we can rearrange the formula as follows:

$$\text{Table factor} = FV/\$1,000$$
$$= \$12,000/\$1,000$$
$$= 12.00$$

Using Table 9-3, we must scan down the 4% column until we find a table value that is near 12.00. The closest table value we find is 12.006. That table value corresponds to 10 periods. Therefore, if we deposit $1,000 per semiannual period and invest the money at 4% per semiannual period, it will take 10 semiannual periods (five years) to accumulate $12,000.

Review Problem

Part A

The accountant for Lunn Express wants to develop a balance sheet as of December 31, 1998. The following items pertain to the liability category and must be considered in order to determine the items that should be reported in the current liability section of the balance sheet. You may assume that Lunn began business on January 1, 1998, and therefore the beginning balance of all accounts was zero.

a. During 1998 Lunn purchased $100,000 of inventory on account from suppliers. By year-end $40,000 of the balance has been eliminated as a result of payments. All items were purchased on terms of 2/10, n/30. Lunn uses the gross method of recording payables.

b. On April 1, 1998, Lunn borrowed $10,000 on a one-year note payable from Foss Bank. Terms of the loan indicate that Lunn must repay the principal and 12% interest at the due date of the note.

c. On October 1, 1998, Lunn also borrowed $8,000 from Dove Bank on a one-year note payable. Dove Bank deducted 10% interest in advance and gave to Lunn the net amount. At the due date, Lunn must repay the principal of $8,000.

d. On January 1, 1998, Lunn borrowed $20,000 from Owens Bank by signing a 10-year note payable. Terms of the note indicate that Lunn must make annual payments of principal each January 1 beginning in 1999 and also must pay interest each January 1 in the amount of 8% of the outstanding balance of the loan.

e. The accountant for Lunn has completed an income statement for 1998 that indicates that income before taxes was $10,000. Lunn must pay tax at the rate of 40% and must remit the tax to the Internal Revenue Service by April 15, 1999.

f. As of December 31, 1998, Lunn owes to employees salaries of $3,000 for work performed in 1998. The employees will be paid on the first payday of 1999.

g. During 1998 two lawsuits were filed against Lunn. In the first lawsuit, a customer sued for damages because of an injury that occurred on Lunn's premises. Lunn's legal counsel advised that it is probable that the lawsuit will be settled in 1999 at an amount of $7,000. The second lawsuit involves a patent infringement suit of $14,000 filed against Lunn by a competitor. The legal counsel has advised that there is some possibility that Lunn may be at fault but that loss does not appear probable at this time.

Part B

a. What amount will be accumulated by January 1, 2002, if $5,000 is invested on January 1, 1998, at 10% interest compounded semiannually?

b. Assume that we are to receive $5,000 on January 1, 2002. What amount at January 1, 1998, is equivalent to the $5,000 that is to be received in 2002? Assume that interest is compounded annually at 10%.

c. What amount will be accumulated by January 1, 2002, if $5,000 is invested each semiannual period for eight periods beginning with June 30, 1998, and ending December 31, 2001? Interest will accumulate at 10% compounded semiannually.

d. Assume that we are to receive $5,000 each semiannual period for eight periods beginning on June 30, 1998. What amount at January 1, 1998, is equivalent to the future series of payments? Assume that interest will accrue at 10% compounded semiannually.

e. Assume that a new bank has begun a promotional campaign to attract savings accounts. The bank advertisement indicates that customers who invest $1,000 will double their money in 10 years. Assuming annual compounding of interest, what rate of interest is the bank offering?

Required

1. Consider all items in part A. Develop the current liability section of Lunn's balance sheet as of December 31, 1998. To make investment decisions about this company, what additional data would you need? You do not need to consider the footnotes that accompany the balance sheet.

2. Answer the five questions in part B.

Solution to Part A

The accountant's decisions for items a through g of part A should be as follows:

a. The balance of the Accounts Payable account should be $60,000. The payables should be reported at the gross amount, and discounts would not be reported until the time of payment.

b. The note payable to Foss Bank of $10,000 should be included as a current liability. Also, interest payable of $900 ($10,000 × 12% × 9/12) should be considered a current liability.

c. The note payable to Dove Bank should be considered a current liability and listed at $8,000 minus the contra account Discount on Note Payable of $600 ($8,000 × 10% × 9/12 remaining).

d. The debt to Owens Bank should be split between current liability and long-term liability with the current portion shown as $2,000. Also, interest payable of $1,600 ($20,000 × 8% × 1 year) should be considered a current liability.

e. Income taxes payable of $4,000 ($10,000 × 40%) is a current liability.

f. Salaries payable of $3,000 represent a current liability.

g. The lawsuit involving the customer must be reported as a current liability of $7,000 because the possibility of loss is probable. The second lawsuit should not be reported but should be disclosed as a footnote to the balance sheet.

LUNN EXPRESS
PARTIAL BALANCE SHEET
AS OF DECEMBER 31, 1998

Current Liabilities

Accounts payable		$60,000
Interest payable ($900 + $1,600)		2,500
Salaries payable		3,000
Taxes payable		4,000
Note payable to Foss Bank		10,000
Note payable to Dove Bank	$8,000	
Less: Discount on note payable	(600)	7,400
Current maturity of long-term debt		2,000
Contingent liability for pending lawsuit		7,000
Total Current Liabilities		$95,900

Other data necessary to make an investment decision might include current assets, total assets, and current liabilities as of December 31, 1997 and 1998. If current assets are significantly larger than current liabilities, you can be comfortable that the company is capable of paying its short-term debt. The dollar amount of current assets and liabilities must be evaluated with regard to the size of the company. The larger the company, the less significant $95,900 in current liabilities would be. Knowing last year's current liabilities would give you an idea about the trend in current liabilities. If they are rising, you would want to know why.

Solution to Part B

a.
$$FV = \$5,000(\text{table factor}) \quad \text{using Table 9-1}$$
$$= \$5,000(1.477) \quad \text{where } i = 5\%, n = 8$$
$$= \$7,385$$

b.
$$PV = \$5,000(\text{table factor}) \quad \text{using Table 9-2}$$
$$= \$5,000(.683) \quad \text{where } i = 10\%, n = 4$$
$$= \$3,415$$

c.
$$FV \text{ annuity} = \$5,000(\text{table factor}) \quad \text{using Table 9-3}$$
$$= \$5,000(9.549) \quad \text{where } i = 5\%, n = 8$$
$$= \$47,745$$

d.
$$PV \text{ annuity} = \$5,000(\text{table factor}) \quad \text{using Table 9-4}$$
$$= \$5,000(6.463) \quad \text{where } i = 5\%, n = 8$$
$$= \$32,315$$

e.
$$FV = \$1,000(\text{table factor}) \quad \text{using Table 9-1}$$

Because the future value is known to be $2,000, the formula can be written as
$$\$2,000 = \$1,000(\text{table factor})$$
and rearranged as
$$\text{Table Factor} = \$2,000/\$1,000 = 2.0.$$
In Table 9-1, the table factor of 2.0 and 10 years corresponds with an interest rate of between 7% and 8%.

TABLE 9-1 Future Value of $1

(n) PERIODS	2	3	4	5	6	7	8	9	10	11	12	15
1	1.020	1.030	1.040	1.050	1.060	1.070	1.080	1.090	1.100	1.110	1.120	1.150
2	1.040	1.061	1.082	1.103	1.124	1.145	1.166	1.188	1.210	1.232	1.254	1.323
3	1.061	1.093	1.125	1.158	1.191	1.225	1.260	1.295	1.331	1.368	1.405	1.521
4	1.082	1.126	1.170	1.216	1.262	1.311	1.360	1.412	1.464	1.518	1.574	1.749
5	1.104	1.159	1.217	1.276	1.338	1.403	1.469	1.539	1.611	1.685	1.762	2.011
6	1.126	1.194	1.265	1.340	1.419	1.501	1.587	1.677	1.772	1.870	1.974	2.313
7	1.149	1.230	1.316	1.407	1.504	1.606	1.714	1.828	1.949	2.076	2.211	2.660
8	1.172	1.267	1.369	1.477	1.594	1.718	1.851	1.993	2.144	2.305	2.476	3.059
9	1.195	1.305	1.423	1.551	1.689	1.838	1.999	2.172	2.358	2.558	2.773	3.518
10	1.219	1.344	1.480	1.629	1.791	1.967	2.159	2.367	2.594	2.839	3.106	4.046
11	1.243	1.384	1.539	1.710	1.898	2.105	2.332	2.580	2.853	3.152	3.479	4.652
12	1.268	1.426	1.601	1.796	2.012	2.252	2.518	2.813	3.138	3.498	3.896	5.350
13	1.294	1.469	1.665	1.886	2.133	2.410	2.720	3.066	3.452	3.883	4.363	6.153
14	1.319	1.513	1.732	1.980	2.261	2.579	2.937	3.342	3.797	4.310	4.887	7.076
15	1.346	1.558	1.801	2.079	2.397	2.759	3.172	3.642	4.177	4.785	5.474	8.137
16	1.373	1.605	1.873	2.183	2.540	2.952	3.426	3.970	4.595	5.311	6.130	9.358
17	1.400	1.653	1.948	2.292	2.693	3.159	3.700	4.328	5.054	5.895	6.866	10.761
18	1.428	1.702	2.026	2.407	2.854	3.380	3.996	4.717	5.560	6.544	7.690	12.375
19	1.457	1.754	2.107	2.527	3.026	3.617	4.316	5.142	6.116	7.263	8.613	14.232
20	1.486	1.806	2.191	2.653	3.207	3.870	4.661	5.604	6.727	8.062	9.646	16.367
21	1.516	1.860	2.279	2.786	3.400	4.141	5.034	6.109	7.400	8.949	10.804	18.822
22	1.546	1.916	2.370	2.925	3.604	4.430	5.437	6.659	8.140	9.934	12.100	21.645
23	1.577	1.974	2.465	3.072	3.820	4.741	5.871	7.258	8.954	11.026	13.552	24.891
24	1.608	2.033	2.563	3.225	4.049	5.072	6.341	7.911	9.850	12.239	15.179	28.625
25	1.641	2.094	2.666	3.386	4.292	5.427	6.848	8.623	10.835	13.585	17.000	32.919
26	1.673	2.157	2.772	3.556	4.549	5.807	7.396	9.399	11.918	15.080	19.040	37.857
27	1.707	2.221	2.883	3.733	4.822	6.214	7.988	10.245	13.110	16.739	21.325	43.535
28	1.741	2.288	2.999	3.920	5.112	6.649	8.627	11.167	14.421	18.580	23.884	50.066
29	1.776	2.357	3.119	4.116	5.418	7.114	9.317	12.172	15.863	20.624	26.750	57.575
30	1.811	2.427	3.243	4.322	5.743	7.612	10.063	13.268	17.449	22.892	29.960	66.212

the future value of an
amount deposited today

money now · t1 = money later

FV = PV · t1

2 reciprocals →

TABLE 9-2   Present Value of $1

(n) PERIODS	RATE OF INTEREST IN %												
	2	3	4	5	6	7	8	9	10	11	12	15
1	0.980	0.971	0.962	0.952	0.943	0.935	0.926	0.917	0.909	0.901	0.893	0.870
2	0.961	0.943	0.925	0.907	0.890	0.873	0.857	0.842	0.826	0.812	0.797	0.756
3	0.942	0.915	0.889	0.864	0.840	0.816	0.794	0.772	0.751	0.731	0.712	0.658
4	0.924	0.888	0.855	0.823	0.792	0.763	0.735	0.708	0.683	0.659	0.636	0.572
5	0.906	0.863	0.822	0.784	0.747	0.713	0.681	0.650	0.621	0.593	0.567	0.497
6	0.888	0.837	0.790	0.746	0.705	0.666	0.630	0.596	0.564	0.535	0.507	0.432
7	0.871	0.813	0.760	0.711	0.665	0.623	0.583	0.547	0.513	0.482	0.452	0.376
8	0.853	0.789	0.731	0.677	0.627	0.582	0.540	0.502	0.467	0.434	0.404	0.327
9	0.837	0.766	0.703	0.645	0.592	0.544	0.500	0.460	0.424	0.391	0.361	0.284
10	0.820	0.744	0.676	0.614	0.558	0.508	0.463	0.422	0.386	0.352	0.322	0.247
11	0.804	0.722	0.650	0.585	0.527	0.475	0.429	0.388	0.350	0.317	0.287	0.215
12	0.788	0.701	0.625	0.557	0.497	0.444	0.397	0.356	0.319	0.286	0.257	0.187
13	0.773	0.681	0.601	0.530	0.469	0.415	0.368	0.326	0.290	0.258	0.229	0.163
14	0.758	0.661	0.577	0.505	0.442	0.388	0.340	0.299	0.263	0.232	0.205	0.141
15	0.743	0.642	0.555	0.481	0.417	0.362	0.315	0.275	0.239	0.209	0.183	0.123
16	0.728	0.623	0.534	0.458	0.394	0.339	0.292	0.252	0.218	0.188	0.163	0.107
17	0.714	0.605	0.513	0.436	0.371	0.317	0.270	0.231	0.198	0.170	0.146	0.093
18	0.700	0.587	0.494	0.416	0.350	0.296	0.250	0.212	0.180	0.153	0.130	0.081
19	0.686	0.570	0.475	0.396	0.331	0.277	0.232	0.194	0.164	0.138	0.116	0.070
20	0.673	0.554	0.456	0.377	0.312	0.258	0.215	0.178	0.149	0.124	0.104	0.061
21	0.660	0.538	0.439	0.359	0.294	0.242	0.199	0.164	0.135	0.112	0.093	0.053
22	0.647	0.522	0.422	0.342	0.278	0.226	0.184	0.150	0.123	0.101	0.083	0.046
23	0.634	0.507	0.406	0.326	0.262	0.211	0.170	0.138	0.112	0.091	0.074	0.040
24	0.622	0.492	0.390	0.310	0.247	0.197	0.158	0.126	0.102	0.082	0.066	0.035
25	0.610	0.478	0.375	0.295	0.233	0.184	0.146	0.116	0.092	0.074	0.059	0.030
26	0.598	0.464	0.361	0.281	0.220	0.172	0.135	0.106	0.084	0.066	0.053	0.026
27	0.586	0.450	0.347	0.268	0.207	0.161	0.125	0.098	0.076	0.060	0.047	0.023
28	0.574	0.437	0.333	0.255	0.196	0.150	0.116	0.090	0.069	0.054	0.042	0.020
29	0.563	0.424	0.321	0.243	0.185	0.141	0.107	0.082	0.063	0.048	0.037	0.017
30	0.552	0.412	0.308	0.231	0.174	0.131	0.099	0.075	0.057	0.044	0.033	0.015

The value today of an amount
to be paid later

money later · t_2 = money now

$$\begin{bmatrix} \text{what you} \\ \text{will end up} \\ \text{with} \end{bmatrix} \cdot t_2 = \begin{bmatrix} \text{what you} \\ \text{start} \\ \text{with} \end{bmatrix}$$

TABLE 9-3 Future Value of Annuity of $1

(n) PERIODS	RATE OF INTEREST IN %											
	2	3	4	5	6	7	8	9	10	11	12	15
1	1.000	1.000	1.000	1.000	1.000	1.000	1.000	1.000	1.000	1.000	1.000	1.000
2	2.020	2.030	2.040	2.050	2.060	2.070	2.080	2.090	2.100	2.110	2.120	2.150
3	3.060	3.091	3.122	3.153	3.184	3.215	3.246	3.278	3.310	3.342	3.374	3.473
4	4.122	4.184	4.246	4.310	4.375	4.440	4.506	4.573	4.641	4.710	4.779	4.993
5	5.204	5.309	5.416	5.526	5.637	5.751	5.867	5.985	6.105	6.228	6.353	6.742
6	6.308	6.468	6.633	6.802	6.975	7.153	7.336	7.523	7.716	7.913	8.115	8.754
7	7.434	7.662	7.898	8.142	8.394	8.654	8.923	9.200	9.487	9.783	10.089	11.067
8	8.583	8.892	9.214	9.549	9.897	10.260	10.637	11.028	11.436	11.859	12.300	13.727
9	9.755	10.159	10.583	11.027	11.491	11.978	12.488	13.021	13.579	14.164	14.776	16.786
10	10.950	11.464	12.006	12.578	13.181	13.816	14.487	15.193	15.937	16.722	17.549	20.304
11	12.169	12.808	13.486	14.207	14.972	15.784	16.645	17.560	18.531	19.561	20.655	24.349
12	13.412	14.192	15.026	15.917	16.870	17.888	18.977	20.141	21.384	22.713	24.133	29.002
13	14.680	15.618	16.627	17.713	18.882	20.141	21.495	22.953	24.523	26.212	28.029	34.352
14	15.974	17.086	18.292	19.599	21.015	22.550	24.215	26.019	27.975	30.095	32.393	40.505
15	17.293	18.599	20.024	21.579	23.276	25.129	27.152	29.361	31.772	34.405	37.280	47.580
16	18.639	20.157	21.825	23.657	25.673	27.888	30.324	33.003	35.950	39.190	42.753	55.717
17	20.012	21.762	23.698	25.840	28.213	30.840	33.750	36.974	40.545	44.501	48.884	65.075
18	21.412	23.414	25.645	28.132	30.906	33.999	37.450	41.301	45.599	50.396	55.750	75.836
19	22.841	25.117	27.671	30.539	33.760	37.379	41.446	46.018	51.159	56.939	63.440	88.212
20	24.297	26.870	29.778	33.066	36.786	40.995	45.762	51.160	57.275	64.203	72.052	102.444
21	25.783	28.676	31.969	35.719	39.993	44.865	50.423	56.765	64.002	72.265	81.699	118.810
22	27.299	30.537	34.248	38.505	43.392	49.006	55.457	62.873	71.403	81.214	92.503	137.632
23	28.845	32.453	36.618	41.430	46.996	53.436	60.893	69.532	79.543	91.148	104.603	159.276
24	30.422	34.426	39.083	44.502	50.816	58.177	66.765	76.790	88.497	102.174	118.155	184.168
25	32.030	36.459	41.646	47.727	54.865	63.249	73.106	84.701	98.347	114.413	133.334	212.793
26	33.671	38.553	44.312	51.113	59.156	68.676	79.954	93.324	109.182	127.999	150.334	245.712
27	35.344	40.710	47.084	54.669	63.706	74.484	87.351	102.723	121.100	143.079	169.374	283.569
28	37.051	42.931	49.968	58.403	68.528	80.698	95.339	112.968	134.210	159.817	190.699	327.104
29	38.792	45.219	52.966	62.323	73.640	87.347	103.966	124.135	148.631	178.397	214.583	377.170
30	40.568	47.575	56.085	66.439	79.058	94.461	113.283	136.308	164.494	199.021	241.333	434.745

get money now, and same amount for number of periods

Series of equal payments

periodic pmt x t3 = Ending balance (money you need in the future, ie save for college)

Make sure you are
looking at the correct column!

TABLE 9-4   Present Value of Annuity of $1

(*n*) PERIODS	RATE OF INTEREST IN %											
	2	3	4	5	6	7	8	9	10	11	12	15
1	0.980	0.971	0.962	0.952	0.943	0.935	0.926	0.917	0.909	0.901	0.893	0.870
2	1.942	1.913	1.886	1.859	1.833	1.808	1.783	1.759	1.736	1.713	1.690	1.626
3	2.884	2.829	2.775	2.723	2.673	2.624	2.577	2.531	2.487	2.444	2.402	2.283
4	3.808	3.717	3.630	3.546	3.465	3.387	3.312	3.240	3.170	3.102	3.037	2.855
5	4.713	4.580	4.452	4.329	4.212	4.100	3.993	3.890	3.791	3.696	3.605	3.352
6	5.601	5.417	5.242	5.076	4.917	4.767	4.623	4.486	4.355	4.231	4.111	3.784
7	6.472	6.230	6.002	5.786	5.582	5.389	5.206	5.033	4.868	4.712	4.564	4.160
8	7.325	7.020	6.733	6.463	6.210	5.971	5.747	5.535	5.335	5.146	4.968	4.487
9	8.162	7.786	7.435	7.108	6.802	6.515	6.247	5.995	5.759	5.537	5.328	4.772
10	8.983	8.530	8.111	7.722	7.360	7.024	6.710	6.418	6.145	5.889	5.650	5.019
11	9.787	9.253	8.760	8.306	7.887	7.499	7.139	6.805	6.495	6.207	5.938	5.234
12	10.575	9.954	9.385	8.863	8.384	7.943	7.536	7.161	6.814	6.492	6.194	5.421
13	11.348	10.635	9.986	9.394	8.853	8.358	7.904	7.487	7.103	6.750	6.424	5.583
14	12.106	11.296	10.563	9.899	9.295	8.745	8.244	7.786	7.367	6.982	6.628	5.724
15	12.849	11.938	11.118	10.380	9.712	9.108	8.559	8.061	7.606	7.191	6.811	5.847
16	13.578	12.561	11.652	10.838	10.106	9.447	8.851	8.313	7.824	7.379	6.974	5.954
17	14.292	13.166	12.166	11.274	10.477	9.763	9.122	8.544	8.022	7.549	7.120	6.047
18	14.992	13.754	12.659	11.690	10.828	10.059	9.372	8.756	8.201	7.702	7.250	6.128
19	15.678	14.324	13.134	12.085	11.158	10.336	9.604	8.950	8.365	7.839	7.366	6.198
20	16.351	14.877	13.590	12.462	11.470	10.594	9.818	9.129	8.514	7.963	7.469	6.259
21	17.011	15.415	14.029	12.821	11.764	10.836	10.017	9.292	8.649	8.075	7.562	6.312
22	17.658	15.937	14.451	13.163	12.042	11.061	10.201	9.442	8.772	8.176	7.645	6.359
23	18.292	16.444	14.857	13.489	12.303	11.272	10.371	9.580	8.883	8.266	7.718	6.399
24	18.914	16.936	15.247	13.799	12.550	11.469	10.529	9.707	8.985	8.348	7.784	6.434
25	19.523	17.413	15.622	14.094	12.783	11.654	10.675	9.823	9.077	8.422	7.843	6.464
26	20.121	17.877	15.983	14.375	13.003	11.826	10.810	9.929	9.161	8.488	7.896	6.491
27	20.707	18.327	16.330	14.643	13.211	11.987	10.935	10.027	9.237	8.548	7.943	6.514
28	21.281	18.764	16.663	14.898	13.406	12.137	11.051	10.116	9.307	8.602	7.984	6.534
29	21.844	19.188	16.984	15.141	13.591	12.278	11.158	10.198	9.370	8.650	8.022	6.551
30	22.396	19.600	17.292	15.372	13.765	12.409	11.258	10.274	9.427	8.694	8.055	6.566

Payments
@ end
of period

Periodic pmt × t4 = PV of all
pmts
(sale cost)   ie house
money you paid now mortgage

APPENDIX 9A
Accounting Tools: Payroll Accounting

LO 8 Understand the deductions and expenses for payroll accounting.

Salaries payable was one of the current liabilities discussed in Chapter 2. At the end of each accounting period, the accountant must accrue salaries that have been earned by the employees but have not yet been paid. To this point, we have not considered the accounting that must be done for payroll deductions and other payroll expenses.

Payroll deductions and expenses occur not only at year-end but every time, throughout the year, that employees are paid. The amount of cash paid for salaries and wages is the largest cash outflow for many firms. It is imperative that sufficient cash be available not only to meet the weekly or monthly payroll but also to remit the payroll taxes to the appropriate government agencies when required. The purpose of this appendix is to introduce the calculations and the accounting entries that are necessary when payroll is recorded.

The issue of payroll expenses is of great concern to businesses, particularly small entrepreneurial ones. One of the large issues facing companies is how to meet the increasing cost of hiring people. Salary is just one component. How are they going to pay salaries plus benefits such as health insurance, life insurance, disability, unemployment benefits, workers' compensation, and so on? More and more companies are trying to keep their payrolls as small as possible in order to avoid these costs. Unfortunately, this has been a contributing factor in the trends of using more part-time employees and of outsourcing some business functions. Outsourcing, or hiring independent contractors, allows the company to reduce salary expense and the expenses related to fringe benefits. However, it does not necessarily improve the company's profitability. The expenses that are increased as a result of hiring outside contractors must also be considered. A manager must carefully consider all of the costs that are affected before deciding whether to hire more employees or go with an independent contractor.

Calculation of Gross Wages

We will cover the payroll process by indicating the basic steps that must be performed. The first step is to calculate the **gross wages** of all employees. The gross wage represents the wage amount before deductions. Companies often have two general classes of employees, hourly and salaried. The gross wage of each hourly employee is calculated by multiplying the number of hours worked times his or her hourly wage rate. Salaried employees are not paid on a per-hour basis but at a flat rate per week, month, or year. For both hourly and salaried employees, the payroll accountant must also consider any overtime, bonus, or other salary supplement that may affect gross wages.

Calculation of Net Pay

The second step in the payroll process is to calculate the deductions from each employee's paycheck to determine **net pay.** Deductions from the employees' checks represent a current liability to the employer because the employer must remit the amounts at a future time to the proper agencies or government offices, for example to the Internal Revenue Service. The deductions that are made depend on the type of company and the employee. The most important deductions are indicated in the following sections.

Income Tax

The employer must withhold federal income tax from most employees' paychecks. The amount withheld depends on the employee's earnings and the number of *exemptions* claimed by that employee. An exemption reflects the number of dependents a taxpayer can claim. The more exemptions, the lower is the withholding amount required by the government. Tables are available from the Internal Revenue Service to calculate the proper amount that should be withheld. This amount must be remitted to the Internal Revenue Service periodically; the frequency depends on the company's size and its payroll. Income tax withheld represents a liability to the employer and is normally classified as a current liability.

Many states also have an income tax, and the employer must often withhold additional amounts for the state tax.

FICA—Employees' Share

FICA stands for Federal Insurance Contributions Act; it is commonly called the *social securities tax*. The FICA tax is assessed on both the employee and the employer. The employees' portion must be withheld from paychecks at the applicable rate. Currently, the tax is assessed at the rate of 7.65% on the first $62,700 paid to the employee each year. Other rates and special rules apply to certain types of workers and to self-employed individuals. The amounts withheld from the employees' checks must be remitted to the federal government periodically.

FICA taxes withheld from employees' checks represent a liability to the employer until remitted. It is important to remember that the employees' portion of the FICA tax does not represent an expense to the employer.

Voluntary Deductions

If you have ever received a paycheck, you are probably aware that a variety of items was deducted from the amount you earned. Many of these are voluntary deductions chosen by the employee. They may include health insurance, pension or retirement contributions, savings plans, contributions to charities, union dues, and others. Each of these items is deducted from the employees' paychecks, is held by the employer, and is remitted at a future time. Therefore, each represents a current liability to the employer until remitted.

Employer Payroll Taxes

The payroll items discussed thus far do not represent expenses to the employer because they are assessed on the employees and deducted from their paychecks. However, there are taxes that the employer must pay. The two most important are FICA and unemployment taxes.

FICA—Employer's Share

The FICA tax is assessed on both the employee and the employer. The employee amount is withheld from the employees' paychecks and represents a liability but is not an expense to the employer. Normally, an equal amount is assessed on the employer. Therefore, the employer must pay an additional 7.65% of employee wages to the federal government. The employer's portion represents an expense to the employer and should be reflected in a Payroll Tax Expense account or similar type of account. This portion is a liability to the employer until it is remitted.

Unemployment Tax

Most employers must also pay unemployment taxes. The state and federal governments jointly sponsor a program to collect unemployment tax from employers and to pay workers who lose their jobs. The maximum rate of unemployment taxes is 3.4%, of which 2.7% is the state portion and .7% the federal, on an employee's first $7,000 of wages earned each year. The rate is adjusted according to a company's employment history, however. If a company has been fairly stable and few of its employees have filed for unemployment benefits, the rate is adjusted downward.

Unemployment taxes are levied against the employer, not the employee. Therefore, the tax represents an expense to the employer and should be reflected in a Payroll Tax Expense account or similar type of account. The tax also represents a liability to the employer until it is remitted.

An Example

Assume that Kori Company has calculated the gross wages of all employees for the month of July to be $100,000. Also assume that the following amounts have been withheld from the employees' paychecks:

Income Tax	$20,000
FICA	7,650
United Way Contributions	5,000
Union Dues	3,000

In addition, assume that Kori's unemployment tax rate is 3%, that no employees have reached the $7,000 limit, and that Kori's portion of FICA matches the employees' share. Kori must make the following entries to record the payroll, to pay the employees, and to record the employer's payroll expenses.

July 31	Salary Expense	100,000	
	Salary Payable		64,350
	Income Tax Payable		20,000
	FICA Payable		7,650
	United Way Payable		5,000
	Union Dues Payable		3,000
	To record July salary and deductions.		

Assets	=	Liabilities	+	Owners' Equity
		+64,350		−100,000
		+20,000		
		+7,650		
		+5,000		
		+3,000		

July 31	Salary Payable	64,350	
	Cash		64,350
	To record payment of employee salaries.		

Assets	=	Liabilities	+	Owners' Equity
−64,350		−64,350		

July 31	Payroll Tax Expense	10,650	
	FICA Payable		7,650
	Unemployment Tax Payable		3,000
	To record employer's payroll taxes.		

Assets	=	Liabilities	+	Owners' Equity
		+7,650		−10,650
		+3,000		

Periodically, Kori must remit amounts to the appropriate government body or agency. The accounting entry to record remittance, assuming remittance at the end of July, is as follows:

July 31	Income Tax Payable	20,000	
	FICA Payable	15,300	
	United Way Payable	5,000	
	Union Dues Payable	3,000	
	Unemployment Tax Payable	3,000	
	Cash		46,300
	To record remittance of withheld amounts.		

Assets	=	Liabilities	+	Owners' Equity
−46,300		−20,000		
		−15,300		
		−5,000		
		−3,000		
		−3,000		

Compensated Absences

Most employers allow employees to accumulate a certain number of sick days and to take a certain number of paid vacation days each year. This causes an accounting question when recording payroll amounts. When should the sick days and vacation days be treated as an expense—in the period they are earned or in the period they are taken by the employee?

LO 9 Determine when compensated absences must be accrued as a liability.

The FASB has coined the term compensated absences. These are absences from employment, such as vacation, illness, and holidays, for which it is expected that employees will be paid. The FASB has ruled that an expense should be accrued if certain conditions are met: the services have been rendered, the rights (days) accumulate, and payment is probable and can be reasonably estimated. The result of the FASB ruling is that most employers are required to record a liability and expense for vacation days when earned, but sick days are not recorded until employees are actually absent.

Compensated absence is another example of the matching principle at work, and so it is consistent with good accounting theory. Unfortunately, it has also resulted in some complex calculations and additional work for payroll accountants. Part of the complexity is due to unresolved legal issues about compensated absences.

U.S. accounting standards on this issue are much more detailed and extensive than the standards of many foreign countries. The International Accounting Standards Committee has not issued a rule that parallels the FASB rule. As a result, U.S. companies may believe that they are subject to higher record-keeping costs than their foreign competitors.

Chapter Highlights

1. **LO 1** Balance sheets generally have two categories of liability: current liabilities and long-term liabilities. Current liabilities are obligations that will be satisfied within one year or within the next operating cycle.

2. **LO 2** Accruals are expenses that have been incurred, but not paid, by the balance sheet date. They increase current liabilities and should be valued at the face amount or the amount necessary to settle the obligation. They are not reported at the present value because of the short time span until payment.

3. **LO 2** Accounts payable represent amounts owed for the purchase of inventory, goods, or services. Accounts payable usually do not require the payment of interest, but a discount may be available to encourage prompt payment.

4. **LO 2** The accounting for notes payable depends on the terms of the note. Some notes payable require the payment of interest at the due date. If so, accounting entries must be made to accrue interest expense to the proper periods. Interest is an expense when incurred, not when paid. Alternatively, the terms of the note may require interest to be deducted in advance. The interest deducted should initially be recorded in a Discount on Notes Payable account and transferred to Interest Expense over the life of the note.

5. **LO 2** Accrued liabilities include any amount that is owed but not actually due as of the balance sheet date. These liabilities may be grouped together in an account such as Other Accrued Liabilities.

6. **LO 3** The changes in current liabilities affect the cash flow statement and, for most items, are reflected in the Operating Activities category. Decreases in current liabilities indicate a reduction of cash; increases in current liabilities indicate an increase in cash.

7. **LO 4** Contingent liabilities involve an existing condition whose outcome depends on some future event. If a contingent liability is probable and the amount of loss can be reasonably estimated, it should be reported on the balance sheet. If a contingent liability is reasonably possible, it must be disclosed but not reported.

8. **LO 5** Simple interest is interest earned on the principal amount. It is often calculated by the well-known formula of principal times rate times time. Compound interest is calculated on the principal plus previous amounts of interest accumulated.

9. **LO 6**   The future value of a single amount represents the amount of interest plus principal that will be accumulated at a future time. The future value of a single amount can be calculated by formula or by the use of Table 9-1.

10. **LO 6**   The present value of a single amount represents the amount at a present time that is equivalent to an amount at a future time. The present value of a single amount can be calculated by formula or by the use of Table 9-2.

11. **LO 6**   An annuity is a series of payments of equal amount. The future value of an annuity represents the amount that will be accumulated in principal and interest if a series of payments is invested for a specified time and for a specified rate. The future value of an annuity can be calculated by formula or by the use of Table 9-3.

12. **LO 6**   The present value of an annuity represents the amount at a present time that is equivalent to a series of payments in the future that will occur for a specified time and at a specified interest or discount rate. The present value of an annuity can be calculated by formula or by the use of Table 9-4.

13. **LO 7**   The compound interest concepts are also useful when solving for unknowns such as the number of interest periods or the interest rate on a series of payments using compound interest techniques.

14. **LO 8**   There are two types of payroll deductions and expenses. Deductions from the employee's check are made to determine net pay and represent a current liability to the employer. Employer's payroll taxes are also assessed directly on the employer and represent an expense. (Appendix 9A)

15. **LO 9**   Compensated absences such as sick pay and vacation pay are expenses and must be accrued by the employer if certain conditions are met. (Appendix 9A)

Key Terms Quiz

Read each definition below and then write the number of the definition in the blank beside the appropriate term it defines. The solution appears at the end of the chapter.

___Current liability

___Notes payable

___Current Maturities of Long-Term Debt

___Contingent liability

___Contingent asset

___Simple interest

___Future value of a single amount

___Annuity

___Present value of an annuity

___Net pay (Appendix 9A)

___Accounts payable

___Discount on Notes Payable

___Accrued liability

___Estimated liability

___Time value of money

___Compound interest

___Present value of a single amount

___Future value of an annuity

___Gross wages (Appendix 9A)

___Compensated absences (Appendix 9A)

1. Accounts that will be satisfied within one year or the next operating cycle.

2. The amount needed at the present time to be equivalent to a series of payments and interest in the future.

3. Amounts owed for the purchase of inventory, goods, or services acquired in the normal course of business.

4. A contra liability account that represents interest deducted from a loan or note in advance.

5. A series of payments of equal amount.

6. The portion of a long-term liability that will be paid within one year of the balance sheet date.

7. A liability that has been incurred but has not been paid as of the balance sheet date.

8. Amounts owed that are represented by a formal contractual agreement. These amounts usually require the payment of interest.

9. A liability that involves an existing condition for which the outcome is not known with certainty and depends on some future event.

10. Interest that is earned or paid on the principal amount only.

11. A contingent liability that is accrued and is reflected on the balance sheet. Common examples are warranties, guarantees, and premium offers.

12. An amount that involves an existing condition dependent on some future event by which the company stands to gain. These amounts are not normally reported.

13. Interest calculated on the principal plus previous amounts of interest accumulated.

14. The concept that indicates that people should prefer to receive an immediate amount at the present time over an equal amount in the future.

15. The amount that will be accumulated in the future when one amount is invested at the present time and accrues interest until the future time.

16. The amount that will be accumulated in the future when a series of payments is invested and accrues interest until the future time.

17. The present amount that is equivalent to an amount at a future time.

18. The amount of an employee's wages before deductions.

19. Employment absences, such as sick days and vacation days, for which it is expected that employees will be paid.

20. The amount of an employee's paycheck after deductions.

Alternate Terms

Accrued Interest   Interest payable.
Compensated Absences   Accrued vacation or sick pay.
Compound Interest   Interest on interest.
Contingent Asset   Contingent gain.
Contingent Liability   Contingent loss.
Current Liability   Short-term liability.
Current Maturities of Long-Term Debt   Long-term debt, current portion.

Discounting a Note   Interest in advance.
FICA   Social Security.
Future Value of an Annuity   Amount of an annuity.
Gross Wages   Gross pay.
Income Tax Liability   Income tax payable.
Warranties   Guarantees.

Questions

1. What is the definition of *current liabilities?* Why is it important to distinguish between current and long-term liabilities?

2. Most firms attempt to pay their accounts payable within the discount period to take advantage of the discount. Why is that normally a sound financial move?

3. Assume that your local bank gives you a $1,000 loan at 10% per year but deducts the interest in advance. Is 10% the "real" rate of interest that you will pay? How could the true interest rate be calculated?

4. Is the account Discount on Notes Payable an income statement or balance sheet account? Does it have a debit or credit balance?

5. A firm's year ends on December 31. Its tax is computed and submitted to the IRS on March 15 of the following year. When should the taxes be reported as a liability?

6. What is a contingent liability? Why are contingent liabilities accounted for differently than contingent assets?

7. Many firms believe that it is very difficult to estimate the amount of a possible future contingency. Should a contingent liability be reported even if the dollar amount of the loss is not known? Should it be disclosed in the footnotes?

8. Assume that a lawsuit has been filed against your firm. Your legal counsel has assured you that the likelihood of loss is not probable. How should the lawsuit be disclosed on the financial statements?

9. What is the difference between simple interest and compound interest? Would the amount of interest be higher or lower if the interest is simple rather than compound?

10. What is the effect if interest is compounded quarterly versus annually?

11. What is the meaning of the terms *present value* and *future value?* How can you determine whether to calculate the present value of an amount versus the future value?

12. What is the meaning of the word *annuity?* Could the present value of an annuity be calculated as a series of single amounts? If so, how?

13. Assume that you know the total dollar amount of a loan and the amount of the monthly payments on the loan. How could you determine the interest rate as a percentage of the loan?

14. The present value and future value concepts are applied to measure the amount of several accounts commonly encountered in accounting. What are some accounts that are valued in this manner?

15. Your employer withholds federal income tax from your paycheck and remits it to the IRS. How is the federal tax treated on the employer's financial statements? (Appendix 9A)

16. Unemployment tax is a tax on the employer rather than on the employee. How should unemployment taxes be treated on the employer's financial statements? (Appendix 9A)

17. What is the meaning of the term *compensated absences?* Give some examples. (Appendix 9A)

18. Do you agree or disagree with the following statement: "Vacation pay should be reported as an expense when the employee takes the vacation"? (Appendix 9A)

Exercises

LO 1   **Exercise 9-1** Current Liabilities

The items listed below are accounts on Smith's balance sheet of December 31, 1998.

Taxes Payable

Accounts Receivable

Notes Payable, 9%, due in 90 days

Investment in Bonds

Capital Stock

Accounts Payable

Estimated Warranty Payable in 1999

Retained Earnings

Trademark

Mortgage Payable ($10,000 due every year until 2015)

Required

Identify which of the above accounts should be classified as a current liability on Smith's balance sheet. For each item that is not a current liability, indicate the category of the balance sheet in which it would be classified.

LO 1   **Exercise 9-2** Current Liabilities

The following items all represent liabilities on a firm's balance sheet.

a. An amount of money owed to a supplier based on the terms 2/20, net 40, for which *no* note was executed.

b. An amount of money owed to a creditor on a note due April 30, 1999.

c. An amount of money owed to a creditor on a note due August 15, 2000.

d. An amount of money owed to employees for work performed during the last week in December.

e. An amount of money owed to a bank for the use of borrowed funds due on March 1, 1999.

f. An amount of money owed to a creditor as an annual installment payment on a 10-year note.

g. An amount of money owed to the federal government, based on the company's annual income.

Required

1. For each lettered item, state whether it should be classified as a current liability on the December 31, 1998, balance sheet. Assume that the operating cycle is shorter than one year. If the item should not be classified as a current liability, indicate where on the balance sheet it should be presented.

2. For each item identified as a current liability in part 1, state the account title that is normally used to report the item on the balance sheet.

3. Why would an investor or creditor be interested in whether an item is a current or a long-term liability?

LO 1   **Exercise 9-3** Current Liabilities Section

Jackie Company had the following accounts and balances on December 31, 1998:

Income Taxes Payable	$61,250
Allowance for Doubtful Accounts	17,800
Accounts Payable	24,400
Interest Receivable	5,000
Unearned Revenue	4,320

Wages Payable	$ 6,000
Notes Payable, 10%, due June 2, 1999	1,000
Accounts Receivable	67,500
Discount on Notes Payable	150
Current Maturities of Long-Term Debt	6,900
Interest Payable	3,010

Required

Prepare the current liabilities section of Jackie Company's balance sheet as of December 31, 1998.

LO 2 **Exercise 9-4** Transaction Analysis

Polly's Cards & Gifts Shop had the following transactions during the year:

General Ledger

a. Polly's purchased inventory on account from a supplier for $8,000. Assume that Polly's uses a periodic inventory system.

b. On May 1, land was purchased for $44,500. A 20% down payment was made, and an 18-month, 8% note was signed for the remainder.

c. Polly's returned $450 worth of inventory purchased in item a, which was found broken when the inventory was received.

d. Paid the balance due on the purchase of inventory.

e. On June 1, Polly signed a one-year $15,000 note to 1st State Bank and received $13,800.

f. Sold 200 gift certificates for $25 each for cash. Sales of gift certificates are recorded as a liability. At year-end, 35% of the gift certificates had been redeemed.

g. Sales for the year were $120,000, of which 90% were for cash. State sales tax of 6% applied to all sales and must be remitted to the state by January 31.

Required

1. Record all necessary journal entries relating to these transactions.

2. Assume that Polly's accounting year ends December 31. Prepare any necessary adjusting journal entries.

3. What is the total of the current liabilities at the end of the year?

LO 2 **Exercise 9-5** Current Liabilities and Ratios

Listed below are several accounts that appeared on Troytoy's 1998 balance sheet.

Accounts Payable	$ 55,000
Marketable Securities	40,000
Accounts Receivable	180,000
Notes Payable, 12%, due in 60 days	20,000
Capital Stock	1,150,000
Salaries Payable	10,000
Cash	15,000
Equipment	950,000
Taxes Payable	15,000
Retained Earnings	250,000
Inventory	85,000
Allowance for Doubtful Accounts	20,000
Land	600,000

Required

1. Prepare the current liabilities section of Troytoy's 1998 balance sheet.

2. Compute Troytoy's working capital.

3. Compute Troytoy's current ratio. What does this ratio indicate about Troytoy's condition?

LO 2 **Exercise 9-6** Discounts

Each of the following situations involves the use of discounts.

1. How much discount may Seals Inc. take in each of the following transactions? What was the annualized interest rate?
   a. Seals purchases inventory costing $450, 2/10, n/40.
   b. Seals purchases new office furniture costing $1,500, terms 1/10, n/30.
2. Calculate the discount rate Croft Co. received in each of these transactions.
   a. Croft purchased office supplies costing $200 and paid within the discount period with a check for $196.
   b. Croft purchased merchandise for $2,800. It paid within the discount period with a check for $2,674.

LO 2 **Exercise 9-7** Notes Payable and Interest

On July 1, 1998, Jo's Flower Shop borrowed $25,000 from the bank. Jo signed a 10-month, 8% promissory note for the entire amount. Jo's uses a calendar year-end.

Required

1. Prepare the journal entry on July 1 to record the issuance of the promissory note.
2. Prepare any adjusting entries needed at year-end.
3. Prepare the journal entry on May 1 to record the payment of principal and interest.

LO 2 **Exercise 9-8** Non-Interest-Bearing Notes Payable

On October 1, 1998, Ratkowski Inc. borrowed $18,000 from 2nd National Bank by issuing a 12-month note. The bank discounted the note at 9%.

Required

1. Prepare the journal entry needed to record the issuance of the note.
2. Prepare the journal entry needed at December 31, 1998, to accrue interest.
3. Prepare the journal entry to record the payment of the note on October 1, 1999.
4. What effective rate of interest did Ratkowski actually pay?

LO 3 **Exercise 9-9** Impact of Transactions Involving Current Liabilities on Statement of Cash Flows

From the following list, identify whether the change in the account balance during the year would be reported as an operating (O), investing (I), or financing (F) activity, or not separately reported on the statement of cash flows (N). Assume that the indirect method is used to determine the cash flows from operating activities.

_____ Accounts payable

_____ Current maturities of long-term debt

_____ Notes payable

_____ Other accrued liabilities

_____ Salaries and wages payable

_____ Taxes payable

LO 3 **Exercise 9-10** Impact of Transactions Involving Contingent Liabilities on Statement of Cash Flows

From the following list, identify whether the change in the account balance during the year would be reported as an operating (O), investing (I), or financing (F) activity, or not separately reported on the statement of cash flows (N). Assume that the indirect method is used to determine the cash flows from operating activities.

_____ Estimated liability for warranties

_____ Estimated liability for product premiums

_____ Estimated liability for probable loss relating to litigation

LO 3 **Exercise 9-11** Impact of Transactions Involving Payroll Liabilities on Statement of Cash Flows

From the following list, identify whether the change in the account balance during the year would be reported as an operating (O), investing (I), or financing (F) activity, or not separately reported on the statement of cash flows (N). Assume that the indirect method is used to determine the cash flows from operating activities.

_____ Accrued vacation days (compensated absences)

_____ Health insurance premiums payable

_____ FICA payable

_____ Union dues payable

_____ Salary payable

_____ Unemployment taxes payable

LO 4 **Exercise 9-12** Warranties

Clean Corporation manufactures and sells dishwashers. Clean provides all customers with a two-year warranty guaranteeing to repair, free of charge, any defects reported during this time period. During the year, it sold 100,000 dishwashers, for $325 each. Analysis of past warranty records indicates that 12% of all sales will be returned for repair within the warranty period. Clean expects to incur expenditures of $14 to repair each dishwasher. The account Estimated Liability for Warranties had a balance of $120,000 on January 1. Clean incurred $150,000 in actual expenditures during the year.

Required

Prepare all journal entries necessary to record the events related to the warranty transactions during the year. Determine the adjusted ending balance in the Estimated Liability for Warranties account.

LO 5 **Exercise 9-13** Simple Versus Compound Interest

Part 1. For each of the following notes, calculate the simple interest due at the end of the term.

NOTE	FACE VALUE (PRINCIPAL)	RATE	TERM
1	$20,000	4%	6 years
2	20,000	6%	4 years
3	20,000	8%	3 years

Part 2. Now assume that the interest on the notes is compounded annually. Calculate the amount of interest due at the end of the term for each note.

Part 3. Now assume that the interest on the notes is compounded semiannually. Calculate the amount of interest due at the end of the term for each note.

What conclusion can you draw from a comparison of your results in parts 1, 2, and 3?

LO 6 **Exercise 9-14** Present Value, Future Value

Brian Inc. estimates it will need $150,000 in 10 years to expand its manufacturing facilities. A bank has agreed to pay Brian 5% interest, compounded annually, if the company deposits the entire amount now needed to accumulate $150,000 in 10 years. How much money does Brian need to deposit now?

LO 6 **Exercise 9-15** Effect of Compounding Period

Kern Company deposited $1,000 in the bank on January 1, 1998, earning 8% interest. Kern Company withdraws the deposit plus accumulated interest on January 1, 2000. Compute the amount of money Kern withdraws from the bank, assuming that interest is compounded (a) annually, (b) semiannually, and (c) quarterly.

LO 6 **Exercise 9-16** Present Value, Future Value

The following situations involve time value of money calculations.

1. A deposit of $7,000 is made on January 1, 1998. The deposit will earn interest at a rate of 8%. How much will be accumulated on January 1, 2003, assuming that interest is compounded (a) annually, (b) semiannually, and (c) quarterly?

2. A deposit is made on January 1, 1998, to earn interest at an annual rate of 8%. The deposit will accumulate to $15,000 by January 1, 2003. How much money was

originally deposited, assuming that interest is compounded (a) annually, (b) semiannually, and (c) quarterly?

LO 6 **Exercise 9-17** Present Value, Future Value

The following are situations requiring the application of the time value of money.

1. On January 1, 1998, $16,000 is deposited. Assuming an 8% interest rate, calculate the amount accumulated on January 1, 2003, if interest is compounded (a) annually, (b) semiannually, and (c) quarterly.

2. Assume that a deposit made on January 1, 1998, earns 8% interest. The deposit plus interest accumulated to $20,000 on January 1, 2003. How much was invested on January 1, 1998, if interest was compounded (a) annually, (b) semiannually, and (c) quarterly?

LO 7 **Exercise 9-18** Annuity

Steve Jones has decided to start saving for his son's college education by depositing $2,000 at the end of every year for 15 years. A bank has agreed to pay interest at the rate of 4% compounded annually. How much will Steve have in the bank immediately after his 15th deposit?

LO 7 **Exercise 9-19** Calculation of Years

Kelly Seaver has decided to start saving for her daughter's college education. She wants to accumulate $41,000. The bank will pay interest at the rate of 4% compounded annually. If Kelly plans to make payments of $1,600 at the end of each year, how long will it take her to accumulate $41,000?

LO 7 **Exercise 9-20** Value of Payments

On graduation from college, Susana Lopez signed an agreement to buy a used car. Her annual payments, due at the end of each year for two years, are $1,480. The car dealer used a 12% rate compounded annually to determine the amount of the payments.

Required

1. What should Susana consider the value of the car to be?

2. If she had wanted to make quarterly payments, what would her payments have been, based on the value of the car as determined in part 1? How much less interest would she have had to pay if she had been making quarterly payments instead of annual payments? What do you think would happen to the amount of the payment and the interest if she had asked for monthly payments?

LO 8 **Exercise 9-21** Payroll Entries (APPENDIX 9A)

During the month of January, VanderSalm Company's employees earned $385,000. The following rates apply to VanderSalm's gross payroll:

Federal Income Tax Rate	28%
State Income Tax Rate	5%
FICA Tax Rate	7.65%
Federal Unemployment Tax Rate	.8%
State Unemployment Tax Rate	3.2%

In addition, employee deductions were $7,000 for health insurance and $980 for union dues.

Required

1. Prepare the journal entry the company made to record the January payroll.

2. Prepare the journal entry the company made to record the employer's portion of payroll taxes for January.

3. If the company paid fringe benefits, such as paying for employees' health insurance coverage, how would these contributions affect the payroll entries?

LO 8 **Exercise 9-22** Payroll, Employer's Portion (APPENDIX 9A)

Tasty Bakery Shop has six employees on its payroll. Payroll records include the following information on employee earnings for each employee:

NAME	EARNINGS FROM 1/1 TO 6/30/1998	EARNINGS FOR 3RD QUARTER, 1998
Dell	$ 23,490	$11,710
Fin	4,240	2,660
Hook	34,100	15,660
Patty	51,000	26,200
Tuss	30,050	19,350
Woo	6,300	3,900
Totals	$149,180	$79,480

FICA taxes are levied at 7.65% on the first $62,700 of each employee's current year's earnings. The unemployment tax rates are .8% for federal and 2.6% for state unemployment. Assume that unemployment taxes are levied on the first $7,000 of each employee's current year's earnings.

Required

1. Calculate the employer's portion of payroll taxes incurred by Tasty Bakery for each employee for the third quarter of 1998. Round your answers to the nearest dollar.

2. Prepare the journal entry that Tasty's should make to record the employer's portion of payroll taxes.

LO 9 **Exercise 9-23** Compensated Absences (APPENDIX 9A)

Wonder Inc. has a monthly payroll of $72,000 for its 24 employees. In addition to their salary, employees earn one day of vacation and one sick day for each month that they work. There are 20 workdays in a month. Prepare the end-of-the-month journal entry, if necessary, to record (a) vacation benefits and (b) sick days. From the owner's perspective, should the company offer the employees vacation and sick pay that accumulates year to year?

Multi-Concept Exercises

LO 6, 7 **Exercise 9-24** Compare Alternatives

Jane Bauer has won the lottery and has four options for receiving her winnings:

1. Receive $100,000 at the beginning of the current year.

2. Receive $108,000 at the end of the year.

3. Receive $20,000 at the end of each year for 8 years.

4. Receive $10,000 at the end of each year for 30 years.

Jane can invest her winnings at an interest rate of 8% compounded annually at a major bank. Which of the payment options should Jane choose?

LO 6, 7 **Exercise 9-25** Two Situations

The following situations involve the application of the time value of money concepts.

1. Sampson Company just purchased a piece of equipment with a value of $53,300. Sampson financed this purchase with a loan from the bank and must make annual loan payments of $13,000 at the end of each year for the next five years. Interest is compounded annually on the loan. What is the interest rate on the bank loan?

2. Simon Company needs to accumulate $200,000 to repay bonds due in six years. Simon estimates it can save $13,300 at the end of each semiannual period at a local bank offering an annual interest rate of 8% compounded semiannually. Will Simon have enough money saved at the end of six years to repay the bonds?

Problems

LO 2 **Problem 9-1** Notes and Interest

Glencoe Inc. operates with a June 30 year-end. During 1998, the following transactions occurred:

a. January 1: Signed a one-year, 10% loan for $25,000. Interest and principal are to be paid at maturity.

General Ledger

b. January 10: Signed a line of credit with the Little Local Bank to establish a $400,000 line of credit. Interest of 9% will be charged on all borrowed funds.

c. February 1: Issued a $20,000 non-interest-bearing, six-month note to pay for a new machine. Interest on the note, at 12%, was deducted in advance.

d. March 1: Borrowed $150,000 on the line of credit.

e. June 1: Repaid $100,000 on the line of credit, plus accrued interest.

f. June 30: Made all necessary adjusting entries.

g. August 1: Repaid the non-interest-bearing note.

h. September 1: Borrowed $200,000 on the line of credit.

i. November 1: Issued a three-month, 8%, $12,000 note in payment of an overdue open account.

j. December 31: Repaid the one-year loan (from item a) plus accrued interest.

Required

1. Record all journal entries necessary to report these transactions.

2. As of December 31, which notes are outstanding, and how much interest is due on each?

LO 3 **Problem 9-2** Effects of Sara Lee's Current Liabilities on Its Statement of Cash Flows

The following items are classified as current liabilities on Sara Lee Corporation's consolidated balance sheet at June 29, 1996 and July 1, 1995 (in millions):

	1996	1995
Notes payable	$ 319	$ 559
Accounts payable	1,592	1,436
Accrued liabilities:		
Payroll and employee benefits	702	693
Advertising and promotions	290	278
Taxes other than payroll and income	207	218
Income taxes	101	66
Other	1,296	1,373
Current maturities of long-term debt	135	221

Required

1. Sara Lee uses the indirect method to prepare its statement of cash flows. Prepare the operating activities section of the cash flow statement which indicates how each item will be reflected as an adjustment to net income. If you did not include any of the items set forth above, explain why not.

2. How would you decide whether Sara Lee has the ability to pay these liabilities as they become due?

LO 3 **Problem 9-3** Effects of Tommy Hilfiger's Changes in Current Assets and Liabilities on Statement of Cash Flows

The following items, listed in alphabetical order, are included in the current assets and liabilities categories on the consolidated balance sheet of Tommy Hilfiger Corporation at March 31, 1995 and 1994 (in thousands):

	1995	1994
Accounts payable	$ 2,098	$ 1,142
Accounts receivable	50,485	46,072
Accrued expenses and other liabilities	10,600	11,032
Cash and equivalents	35,817	38,145
Short-term borrowings	13,487	10,319
Income taxes payable	2,132	3,793
Inventories	52,009	34,814
Short-term investments	50,214	12,722
Prepaid expenses and other current assets	5,053	5,122

Required

1. Tommy Hilfiger uses the indirect method to prepare its statement of cash flows. Prepare the operating activities section of the cash flow statement which indicates how each item will be reflected as an adjustment to net income.

2. If you did not include any of the items set forth above in your answer to part 1, explain how these items would be reported on the statement of cash flows.

LO 3 **Problem 9-4** Reconstruction of Current Liability Balances Using Microsoft's Statement of Cash Flows

The following is an excerpt from the statement of cash flows of Microsoft Corporation for the year ended June 30, 1995 (in millions):

Cash flows from operations	
Net income	$1,453
Depreciation and amortization	269
Current liabilities	419
Accounts receivable	(91)
Inventories	15
Other current assets	(75)
Net cash from operations	$1,990

The adjustment for current liabilities in the reconciliation of net income to net cash from operations is made up of the following:

Accounts payable	$239
Accrued compensation	34
Income taxes payable	105
Other	56
Adjustment relating to current liabilities	$434

The following items were classified as current liabilities on Microsoft's consolidated balance sheet at June 30, 1994;

Accounts payable	$324
Accrued compensation	96
Income taxes payable	305
Other	188
Total current liabilities	$913

Required

1. Determine the balances of Microsoft's current liabilities as of June 30, 1995.
2. What types of liabilities might be included in the "other" category?
3. How would you decide whether Microsoft has the ability to pay its current liabilities as they become due?

LO 4 **Problem 9-5** Warranties

Clearview Company manufactures and sells high-quality television sets. The most popular line sells for $1,000 each and is accompanied by a three-year warranty to repair, free of charge, any defective unit. Average costs to repair each defective unit will be $90 for replacement parts and $60 for labor. Clearview estimates that warranty costs of $12,600 will be incurred during 1998. The company actually sold 600 television sets and incurred replacement part costs of $3,600 and labor costs of $5,400 during the year. The adjusted 1998 ending balance in the Estimated Liability for Warranties account is $10,200.

Required

1. How many defective units from this year's sales does Clearview Company estimate will be returned for repair?
2. What percentage of sales does Clearview Company estimate will be returned for repair?
3. What steps should Clearview take if actual warranty costs incurred during 1999 are significantly higher than the estimated liability recorded at the end of 1998?

LO 4 **Problem 9-6** Warranties

Bombeck Company sells a product for $1,500. When the customer buys it, Bombeck provides a one-year warranty. Bombeck sold 120 products during 1998. Based on analysis of past warranty records, Bombeck estimates that repairs will average 3% of total sales.

Required

1. Prepare the journal entry to record the estimated liability.
2. Assume that products under warranty must be repaired during 1998 using repair parts from inventory costing $4,950. Prepare the journal entry to record the repair of products.

LO 5 **Problem 9-7** Comparison of Simple and Compound Interest

On June 30, 1998, Rolf Inc. borrowed $25,000 from its bank, signing a 7%, two-year note.

Required

1. Assuming that the bank charges simple interest on the note, prepare the journal entry Rolf will record on each of the following dates:

   December 31, 1998

   December 31, 1999

   June 30, 2000

2. Assume instead that the bank charges 7% on the note, which is compounded semiannually. Prepare the necessary journal entries on the dates in part 1.
3. How much additional interest expense will Rolf have in part 2 over part 1?

LO 6 **Problem 9-8** Investment with Varying Interest Rate

Shari Thompson invested $1,000 in a financial institution on January 1, 1998. She leaves her investment in the institution until December 31, 2002. How much money does Shari accumulate if she earned interest, compounded annually, at the following rates?

1998	4%
1999	5%
2000	6%
2001	7%
2002	8%

LO 6 **Problem 9-9** Comparison of Alternatives

On January 1, 1998, Chen Yu's Office Supply Store plans to remodel the store and install new display cases. Chen has the following options of payment. Chen's interest rate is 8%.

a. Pay $180,000 on January 1, 1998.
b. Pay $196,200 on January 1, 1999.
c. Pay $220,500 on January 1, 2001.
d. Make four annual payments of $55,000 beginning on December 31, 1998.

Required

Which option should he choose? (*Hint:* Calculate the present value of each option as of January 1, 1998.)

LO 8 **Problem 9-10** Payroll Entries (APPENDIX 9A)

Vivian Company has calculated the gross wages of all employees for the month of August to be $210,000. The following amounts have been withheld from the employees' paychecks:

Income Tax	$42,500
FICA	16,000
Heart Fund Contributions	5,800
Union Dues	3,150

Vivian's unemployment tax rate is 3%, and its portion of FICA matches the employees' share.

Required

1. Prepare the journal entry to record the payroll as an amount payable to employees.
2. Prepare the journal entry that would be recorded to pay the employees.
3. Prepare the journal entry to record the employer's payroll costs.
4. Prepare the journal entry to remit the withholdings.

LO 9 **Problem 9-11** Compensated Absences (APPENDIX 9A)

Hetzel Inc. pays its employees every Friday. For every four weeks that employees work, they earn one vacation day. For every six weeks that they work without calling in sick, they earn one sick day. If employees quit or retire, they can receive a lump-sum payment for their unused vacation days and unused sick days.

Required

Write a short memo to the bookkeeper to explain how and when he should report vacation and sick days. Explain how the matching principle applies and why you believe that the timing you recommend is appropriate.

Multi-Concept Problems

LO 2, 5 **Problem 9-12** Interest in Advance Versus Interest Paid When Loan is Due

On July 1, 1998, Leach Company needs exactly $103,200 in cash to pay an existing obligation. Leach has decided to borrow from State Bank, which charges 14% interest on loans. The loan will be due in one year. Leach is unsure, however, whether to ask the bank for (a) an interest-bearing loan with interest and principal payable at the end of the year or (b) a loan due in one year but with interest deducted in advance.

Required

1. What will be the face value of the note assuming that
   a. interest is paid when the loan is due?
   b. interest is deducted in advance?
2. Calculate the effective interest rate on the note assuming that
   a. interest is paid when the loan is due.
   b. interest is deducted in advance.
3. Assume that Leach negotiates and signs the one-year note with the bank on July 1, 1998. Also assume that Leach's accounting year ends December 31. Prepare all the journal entries necessary to record the issuance of the note and the interest on the note, assuming that
   a. interest is paid when the loan is due.
   b. interest is deducted in advance.
4. Prepare the appropriate balance sheet presentation for July 1, 1998, immediately after the note has been issued, assuming that
   a. interest is paid when the loan is due.
   b. interest is deducted in advance.

LO 1, 4 **Problem 9-13** Contingent Liabilities

Listed below are several items for which the outcome of events is unknown at year-end.

a. A company offers a two-year warranty on sales of new computers. It believes that 4% of the computers will require repairs.
b. The company is involved in a trademark infringement suit. The company's legal experts believe an award of $500,000 in the company's favor will be made.
c. A company is involved in an environmental clean-up lawsuit. The company's legal counsel believes it is possible the outcome will be unfavorable and has not been able to estimate the costs of the possible loss.
d. A soap manufacturer has included a coupon offer in the Sunday newspaper supplements. The manufacturer estimates that 25% of the 50-cent coupons will be redeemed.

e. A company has been sued by the federal government for price fixing. The company's legal counsel believes there will be an unfavorable verdict and has made an estimate of the probable loss.

Required

1. Identify which of the items a through e should be recorded at year-end.

2. Identify which of the items a through e should not be recorded but should be disclosed on the year-end financial statements.

LO 6, 7 **Problem 9-14** Time Value of Money Concepts

The following situations involve the application of the time value of money concept.

1. Janelle Carter deposited $9,750 in the bank on January 1, 1981, at an interest rate of 11% compounded annually. How much has accumulated in the account by January 1, 1998?

2. Mike Smith deposited $21,600 in the bank on January 1, 1988. On January 2, 1998, this deposit has accumulated to $42,487. Interest is compounded annually on the account. What is the rate of interest that Mike earned on the deposit?

3. Lee Spony made a deposit in the bank on January 1, 1991. The bank pays interest at the rate of 8% compounded annually. On January 1, 1998, the deposit has accumulated to $15,000. How much money did Lee originally deposit on January 1, 1991?

4. Nancy Holmes deposited $5,800 in the bank on January 1 a few years ago. The bank pays an interest rate of 10% compounded annually, and the deposit is now worth $15,026. How many years has the deposit been invested?

LO 6, 7 **Problem 9-15** Comparison of Alternatives

Brian Imhoff's grandparents want to give him some money when he graduates from high school. They have offered Brian three choices:

a. Receive $15,000 immediately. Assume that interest is compounded annually.

b. Receive $2,250 at the end of each six months for four years. The first check will be received in six months.

c. Receive $4,350 at the end of each year for four years. Assume interest is compounded annually.

Required

Brian wants to have money for a new car when he graduates from college in four years. Assuming an interest rate of 8%, what option should he choose to have the most money in four years?

Alternate Problems

General
Ledger

LO 2 **Problem 9-1A** Notes and Interest

McLaughlin Inc. operates with a June 30 year-end. During 1998, the following transactions occurred:

a. January 1: Signed a one-year, 10% loan for $35,000. Interest and principal are to be paid at maturity.

b. January 10: Signed a line of credit with the Little Local Bank to establish a $560,000 line of credit. Interest of 9% will be charged on all borrowed funds.

c. February 1: Issued a $28,000 non-interest-bearing, six-month note to pay for a new machine. Interest on the note, at 12%, was deducted in advance.

d. March 1: Borrowed $210,000 on the line of credit.

e. June 1: Repaid $140,000 on the line of credit, plus accrued interest.

f. June 30: Made all necessary adjusting entries.

g. August 1: Repaid the non-interest-bearing note.

h. September 1: Borrowed $280,000 on the line of credit.

i. November 1: Issued a three-month, 8%, $16,800 note in payment of an overdue open account.

j. December 31: Repaid the one-year loan (from item a) plus accrued interest.

Required

1. Record all journal entries necessary to report these transactions.

2. As of December 31, which notes are outstanding, and how much interest is due on each?

LO 3   **Problem 9-2A** Effects of Boeing's Current Liabilities on Its Statement of Cash Flows

The following items are classified as current liabilities on The Boeing Company's consolidated statements of financial condition (or balance sheet) at December 31 (in millions):

	1995	1994
Accounts payable and other liabilities	$6,245	$6,267
Advances in excess of related costs	510	273
Income taxes payable	389	281
Current portion of long-term debt	271	6

Required

1. Boeing uses the indirect method to prepare its statement of cash flows. Prepare the operating activities section of the cash flow statement which indicates how each item will be reflected as an adjustment to net income. If you did not include any of the items set forth above, explain why not.

2. How would you decide whether Boeing has the ability to pay these liabilities as they become due?

LO 3   **Problem 9-3A** Effects of Nike's Changes in Current Assets and Liabilities on Its Statement of Cash Flows

The following items, listed in alphabetical order, are included in the current assets and liabilities categories on the consolidated balance sheet of Nike Inc. at May 31, 1995 and 1994 (in thousands):

	1995	1994
Accounts payable	$ 297,656	$210,576
Accounts receivable	1,053,237	703,682
Accrued liabilities	345,224	181,889
Cash and equivalents	216,071	518,816
Current portion of long-term debt	31,943	3,857
Deferred income taxes (a current asset)	72,657	37,603
Income taxes payable	35,612	38,287
Inventories	629,742	470,023
Notes payable	397,100	127,378
Prepaid expenses	74,221	40,307

Required

1. Nike uses the indirect method to prepare its statement of cash flows. Prepare the operating activities section of the cash flow statement which indicates how each item will be reflected as an adjustment to net income.

2. If you did not include any of the items set forth above in your answer to part 1, explain how these items would be reported on the statement of cash flows.

LO 3   **Problem 9-4A** Determine Current Liability Balances Using Walgreen's Statement of Cash Flows

The following is an excerpt from the consolidated statement of cash flows of Walgreen Co. and Subsidiaries for the year ended August 31, 1995 (in thousands):

Net earnings	$320,791
Adjustments to reconcile net earnings to net	
cash provided by operating activities:	
Depreciation and amortization	131,537
Cumulative effect of accounting changes	—
Deferred income taxes	(7,213)
Other	3,388
Changes in operating assets and liabilities:	
Inventories	(190,481)
Trade accounts payable	73,447
Accrued expenses and other liabilities	41,669
Accounts receivable, net	(36,265)
Insurance reserves	14,982
Other current assets	(7,807)
Income taxes	905
Net cash provided by operating activities	$344,953

The following items were classified as current liabilities on Walgreen's consolidated balance sheet at August 31, 1994:

Trade accounts payable	$532,816
Accrued expenses and other liabilities	390,683
Income taxes	22,375
Total current liabilities	$945,874

Required

1. Determine the balances of Walgreen's current liabilities as of August 31, 1995.

2. What types of liabilities might be included in accrued expenses and other liabilities?

3. How would you decide whether Walgreen's has the ability to pay its current liabilities as they become due?

LO 4 **Problem 9-5A** Warranties

Sound Company manufactures and sells high-quality stereo sets. The most popular line sells for $2,000 each and is accompanied by a three-year warranty to repair, free of charge, any defective unit. Average costs to repair each defective unit will be $180 for replacement parts and $120 for labor. Sound estimates that warranty costs of $25,200 will be incurred during 1998. The company actually sold 600 sets and incurred replacement part costs of $7,200 and labor costs of $10,800 during the year. The adjusted 1998 ending balance in the Estimated Liability for Warranties account is $20,400.

Required

1. How many defective units from this year's sales does Sound Company estimate will be returned for repair?

2. What percent of sales does Sound Company estimate will be returned for repair?

LO 4 **Problem 9-6A** Warranties

Beck Company sells a product for $3,200. When the customer buys it, Beck provides a one-year warranty. Beck sold 120 products during 1998. Based on analysis of past warranty records, Beck estimates that repairs will average 4% of total sales.

Required

1. Prepare the journal entry to record the estimated liability.

2. Assume that during 1998, products under warranty must be repaired using repair parts from inventory costing $10,200. Prepare the journal entry to record the repair of products.

3. Assume that the balance of the Estimated Liabilities for Warranties account as of the beginning of 1998 was $1,100. Calculate the balance of the account as of the end of 1998.

LO 5 **Problem 9-7A** Comparison of Simple and Compound Interest

On June 30, 1998, Rolloff Inc. borrowed $25,000 from its bank, signing a 6% note. Principal and interest are due at the end of two years.

Required

1. Assuming that the note earns simple interest for the bank, calculate the amount of interest accrued on each of the following dates:

    December 31, 1998

    December 31, 1999

    June 30, 2000

2. Assume instead that the note earns 6% for the bank but is compounded semiannually. Calculate the amount of interest accrued on the same dates as in part 1.

3. How much additional interest expense will Rolloff have to pay with semiannual interest?

LO 6 **Problem 9-8A** Investment With Varying Interest Rate

Trena Thompson invested $2,000 in a financial institution on January 1, 1998. She leaves her investment in the institution until December 31, 2002. How much money did Trena accumulate if she earned interest, compounded annually, at the following rates?

1998	4%
1999	5%
2000	6%
2001	7%
2002	8%

LO 6 **Problem 9-9A** Comparison of Alternatives

On January 1, 1998, Li Ping's Office Supply Store plans to remodel the store and install new display cases. Li Ping has the following options of payment. Li's interest rate is 8%.

a. Pay $270,000 on January 1, 1998.

b. Pay $294,300 on January 1, 1999.

c. Pay $334,750 on January 1, 2001.

d. Make four annual payments of $82,500 beginning on December 31, 1998.

Required

Which option should he choose? (*Hint:* Calculate the present value of each option as of January 1, 1998.)

LO 8 **Problem 9-10A** Payroll Entries (APPENDIX 9A)

Calvin Company has calculated the gross wages of all employees for the month of August to be $336,000. The following amounts have been withheld from the employees' paychecks:

Income Tax	$68,000
FICA	25,600
Heart Fund Contributions	9,280
Union Dues	5,040

Calvins' unemployment tax rate is 3%, and its portion of FICA matches the employees' share.

Required

1. Prepare the journal entry to record the payroll as an amount payable to employees.

2. Prepare the journal entry that would be recorded to pay the employees.

3. Prepare the journal entry to record the employer's payroll costs.

4. Prepare the journal entry to remit the withholdings, including FICA, and the unemployment tax.

LO 9 **Problem 9-11A** Compensated Absences (APPENDIX 9A)

Assume that you are the accountant for a large company with several divisions. The manager of Division B has contacted you with a concern. During 1998, several employees retired from Division B. The company's policy is that employees can be paid for days of sick leave accrued at the time they retire. Payment occurs in the year following retirement. The manager has been told by corporate headquarters that she cannot replace the employees in 1999 because the payment of the accrued sick pay will be deducted from Division B's budget in that year.

Required

In a memo to the manager of Division B, explain the proper accounting for accrued sick pay. Do you think that the policies of corporate headquarters should be revised?

Alternate Multi-Concept Problems

LO 2, 5 **Problem 9-12A** Interest in Advance Versus Interest Paid When Loan is Due

On July 1, 1998, Moton Company needs exactly $206,400 in cash to pay an existing obligation. Moton has decided to borrow from State Bank, which charges 14% interest on loans. The loan will be due in one year. Moton is unsure, however, whether to ask the bank for (a) an interest-bearing loan with interest and principal payable at the end of the year or (b) a non-interest-bearing loan due in one year but with interest deducted in advance.

Required

1. What will be the face value of the note, assuming that
   a. interest is paid when the loan is due?
   b. interest is deducted in advance?
2. Calculate the effective interest rate on the note, assuming that
   a. interest is paid when the loan is due.
   b. interest is deducted in advance.
3. Assume that Moton negotiates and signs the one-year note with the bank on July 1, 1998. Also assume that Moton's accounting year ends December 31. Prepare all the journal entries necessary to record the issuance of the note and the interest on it, assuming that
   a. interest is paid when the loan is due.
   b. interest is deducted in advance.
4. Prepare the appropriate balance sheet presentation for July 1, 1998, immediately after the note has been issued, assuming that
   a. interest is paid when the loan is due.
   b. interest is deducted in advance.

LO 1, 4 **Problem 9-13A** Contingent Liabilities

Listed below are several events for which the outcome is unknown at year-end.

a. A company has been sued by the federal government for price fixing. The company's legal counsel believes there will be an unfavorable verdict and has made an estimate of the probable loss.
b. A company is involved in an environmental clean-up lawsuit. The company's legal counsel believes it is possible the outcome will be unfavorable and has not been able to estimate the costs of the possible loss.
c. The company is involved in a trademark infringement suit. The company's legal experts believe an award of $750,000 in the company's favor will be made.
d. A company offers a three-year warranty on sales of new computers. It believes that 6% of the computers will require repairs.
e. A snack food manufacturer has included a coupon offer in the Sunday newspaper supplements. The manufacturer estimates that 30% of the 40-cent coupons will be redeemed.

Required

1. Identify which of the items a through e should be recorded at year-end.

2. Identify which of the items a through e should not be recorded but should be disclosed on the year-end financial statements.

LO 6, 7 **Problem 9-14A** Time Value of Money Concepts
The following situations involve the application of the time value of money concept.

1. Jan Cain deposited $19,500 in the bank on January 1, 1981, at an interest rate of 11% compounded annually. How much has been accumulated in the account by January 1, 1998?

2. Mark Schultz deposited $43,200 in the bank on January 1, 1988. On January 2, 1998, this deposit has accumulated to $84,974. Interest is compounded annually on the account. What is the rate of interest that Mark earned on the deposit?

3. Les Hinckle made a deposit in the bank on January 1, 1991. The bank pays interest at the rate of 8% compounded annually. On January 1, 1998, the deposit has accumulated to $30,000. How much money did Les originally deposit on January 1, 1991?

4. Val Hooper deposited $11,600 in the bank on January 1 a few years ago. The bank pays an interest rate of 10% compounded annually, and the deposit is now worth $30,052. For how many years has the deposit been invested?

LO 6, 7 **Problem 9-15A** Comparison of Alternatives
Darlene Page's grandparents want to give her some money when she graduates from high school. They have offered Darlene three choices.

a. Receive $16,000 immediately. Assume that interest is compounded annually.

b. Receive $2,400 at the end of each six months for four years. The first check will be received in six months.

c. Receive $4,640 at the end of each year for four years. Assume interest is compounded annually.

Required

Darlene wants to have money for a new car when she graduates from college in four years. Assuming an interest rate of 8%, what option should she choose to have the most money in four years?

Cases

Reading and Interpreting Financial Statements

LO 1, 2 **Case 9-1** Analysis of Current Liabilities
Refer to Ben & Jerry's annual report. Using Ben & Jerry's balance sheet, write a response to the following questions:

1. Ben & Jerry's total current liabilities increased from $14,468,000 in 1994 to $17,040,000 in 1995. What were the major factors that caused the increase in current liabilities during that time period?

2. Does the increase in Ben & Jerry's current liabilities indicate that the firm was experiencing liquidity problems? What numbers or ratios could be used to determine its liquidity?

3. Refer to footnote number 5. What amounts are included in the category Accounts Payable and Accrued Expenses?

4. The amount listed as Current Portion of Long-Term Debt and Obligations under Capital Lease decreased from $553,000 in 1994 to $448,000 in 1995. What do those amounts represent?

LO 3 **Case 9-2** Ben & Jerry's Cash Flow Statement

1. Ben & Jerry's balance sheet indicates that accounts payable and accrued expenses increased by $2,677,000. Where is this amount shown on the statement of cash flows? Does it represent an increase or decrease in cash?

2. In 1994, Ben & Jerry's borrowed $14,936,000 through long-term debt and also repaid $700,000. Which category of the statement of cash flows presents those amounts? For the purposes of the statement of cash flows, what category would include short-term borrowings?

3. Ben & Jerry's December 28, 1994, balance sheet indicated an amount as Deferred Taxes in the liabilities section. When this amount is paid, should it be disclosed in the Operating Activities category of the statement of cash flows?

LO 3, 4 **Case 9-3** Microsoft Corporation's Contingent Liabilities

Microsoft Corporation has a fiscal year ending on June 30 and uses the indirect method to prepare its statement of cash flows. The notes to its 1995 financial statements include the following which were set forth on pages 27 and 28 of the Proxy Statement and Form 10-K included with Microsoft Corporation's 1995 annual report:

NONCONTINUING ITEMS

In the fourth quarter of 1995, the Company paid a $46 million breakup fee to Intuit Inc. in connection with the termination of a planned merger.

In the third quarter of 1994, the Company recorded a $120 million charge to reflect the estimated impact of a jury verdict in the Stac Electronics patent litigation and related expenses. In June 1994, the Company reached an agreement with Stac to settle the litigation and adjusted its estimate accordingly, resulting in a credit of $30 million in the fourth quarter and a net pretax charge of $90 million for 1994.

CONTINGENCIES

On July 15, 1994, Microsoft and the U.S. Department of Justice (DOJ) entered into a consent decree resolving the DOJ's non-public investigation of Microsoft. In the consent decree, which involves no admission of wrongdoing on Microsoft's part, Microsoft agreed to make certain changes in its OEM licensing practices. Microsoft also agreed to employ a uniform duration in its nondisclosure agreement for precommercial versions of certain operating system products, and clarified the rights and responsibilities of those signing such nondisclosure agreements. The consent decree was approved by the U.S. District Court for the District of Columbia on August 21, 1995.

The Antitrust Division of the DOJ has stated that it is conducting an investigation concerning Microsoft's inclusion of client-access software for The Microsoft Network in Windows 95. Although there is no assurance that this matter will be resolved favorably and that Microsoft's future financial statements will not be adversely affected, Microsoft currently believes the resolution of this matter will not have a material adverse effect on its financial condition or results of operations.

Required

1. As discussed above, Microsoft reached an agreement with Stac to settle the patent litigation. Is disclosure of the settlement in the notes to the financial statements all that is required of Microsoft or is accrual required? If you decide that accrual is required, what amount should be accrued at June 30, 1994 (assuming that no payments were made to Stac during 1994) and how would this contingent liability be classified on Microsoft's balance sheet at June 30, 1994?

2. Assume that the settlement was paid to Stac sometime during the year ended June 30, 1995. How would the patent litigation settlement affect Microsoft's statement of cash flows for the years ended June 30, 1994 and 1995?

3. Interpret the meaning of the paragraph describing the investigation relating to the inclusion of client-access software for the Microsoft Network in Windows 95. Does it appear that Microsoft has accrued a contingent liability as a result of this litigation? Why or why not?

LO 4 **Case 9-4** Chrysler Corporation's Contingent Liabilities

The following is an excerpt from Chrysler's 1995 annual report:

Note 8. **Commitments,** **Contingencies and** **Concentrations**	**Litigation** Various claims and legal proceedings have been asserted or instituted against Chrysler, including some purporting to be class actions, and some which demand large monetary damages or other relief which could result in significant expenditures. Litigation is subject to many uncertainties, and the outcome of individual matters is not predictable with assurance. It is reasonably possible that the final resolution of some of these matters may require Chrysler to make expenditures, in excess of established reserves, over an extended period of time and in a range of amounts that cannot be reasonably estimated. The term "reasonably possible" is used herein to mean that the chance of a future transaction or event occurring is more than remote but less than likely. Although the final resolution of any such matters could have a material effect on Chrysler's consolidated operating results for the particular reporting period in which an adjustment of the estimated liability is recorded, Chrysler believes that any resulting liability should not materially affect its consolidated financial position.

Required

After reading this footnote to the financial statements, what accounts would you look for in the balance sheet? income statement? Explain the significance of the words in quotes in the excerpt. How did these words affect the way in which Chrysler reported its contingent liabilities?

Making Financial Decisions

LO 1, 2 **Case 9-5** Current Ratio Loan Provision

Assume that you are the controller of a small, growing sporting goods company. The prospects for your firm in the future are quite good, but like most other firms, it has been experiencing some cash flow difficulties because all available funds have been used to purchase inventory and finance start-up costs associated with a new business. At the beginning of the current year, your local bank advanced a loan to your company. Included in the loan is the following provision:

Decision
Making

> The company is obligated to pay interest payments each month for the next five years. Principal is due and must be paid at the end of Year 5. The company is further obligated to maintain a current assets to current liabilities ratio of 2 to 1 as indicated on quarterly statements to be submitted to the bank. If the company fails to meet any loan provisions, all amounts of interest and principal are due immediately upon notification by the bank.

You, as controller, have just gathered the following information as of the end of the first month of the current quarter:

Current Liabilities:	
Accounts payable	$400,000
Taxes payable	100,000
Accrued expenses	50,000
Total Current Liabilities	$550,000

You are concerned about the loan provision that requires a 2:1 ratio of current assets to current liabilities.

Required

1. Indicate what actions could be taken during the next two months to meet the loan provision. Which of the available actions should be recommended?

2. What is the meaning of the term *window-dressing* financial statements? What are the long-run implications of actions taken to window-dress financial statements?

Decision Making

LO 7 **Case 9-6** Alternative Payment Options

Kathy Clark owns a small company that makes ice machines for restaurants and food-service facilities. Kathy knows a lot about producing ice machines but is less familiar with the best terms to extend to her customers. One customer is opening a new business and has asked Kathy to consider any of the following options to pay for his new $20,000 ice machine.

a. Term 1: 10% down, the remainder paid at the end of the year plus 8% simple interest.

b. Term 2: 10% down, the remainder paid at the end of the year plus 8% interest, compounded quarterly.

c. Term 3: $0 down but $21,600 at the end of the year.

Required

Make a recommendation to Kathy. She believes that 8% is a fair return on her money at this time. Should she accept option a, b, or c, or take the $20,000 cash at the time of the sale? Justify your recommendation with calculations. What factors, other than the actual amount of cash received from the sale, should be considered?

Accounting and Ethics: What Would You Do?

LO 4 **Case 9-7** Warranty Cost Estimate

John Walton is an accountant for ABC Auto Dealers, a large auto dealership in a metropolitan area. ABC sells both new and used cars. New cars are sold with a five-year warranty, the cost of which is carried by the manufacturer. For several years, however, ABC has offered a two-year warranty on used cars. The cost of the warranty is an expense to ABC, and John has been asked by his boss, Mr. Sawyer, to review warranty costs and recommend the amount to accrue on the year-end financial statements.

For the past several years, ABC has recorded as warranty expense 5% of used car sales. John has analyzed past repair records and found that repairs, although fluctuating somewhat from year to year, have averaged near the 5% level. John is convinced, however, that 5% is inadequate for the coming year. He bases his judgment on industry reports of increased repair costs and on the fact that several cars that were recently sold on warranty have experienced very high repair costs. John believes that the current-year repair accrual will be at least 10%. He discussed the higher expense amount with Mr. Sawyer, who is the controller of ABC.

Mr. Sawyer was not happy with John's decision concerning warranty expense. He reminded John of the need to control expenses during the recent sales downturn. He also reminded John that ABC is seeking a large loan from the bank and that the bank loan officers may not be happy with recent operating results, especially if ABC begins to accrue larger amounts for future estimated amounts such as warranties. Finally, Mr. Sawyer reminded John that most of the employees of ABC, including Mr. Sawyer, were members of the company's profit-sharing plan and would not be happy with the reduced share of profits. Mr. Sawyer thanked John for his judgment concerning warranty cost but told him that the accrual for the current year would remain at 5%.

John left the meeting with Mr. Sawyer somewhat frustrated. He was convinced that his judgment concerning the warranty costs was correct. He knew that the owner of ABC would be visiting the office next week and wondered whether he should discuss the matter with him personally at that time. John also had met one of the loan officers from the bank several times and considered calling her to discuss his concern about the warranty expense amount on the year-end statements.

Required

Discuss the courses of action available to John. What should John do concerning his judgment of warranty costs?

LO 4 **Case 9-8** Retainer Fees As Sales

Bunch o' Balloons markets balloon arrangements to companies who want to thank clients and employees. Bunch o' Balloons has a unique style that has put it in high demand. Consequently, Bunch o' Balloons has asked clients to establish an account. Clients are asked to pay a retainer fee equal to about three months of client purchases. The fee will be used to cover the cost of arrangements delivered and will be reevaluated at the end of each month. At the end of the current month Bunch o' Balloons has $43,900 of retainer fees in its possession. The controller is eager to show this amount as sales because "it represents certain sales for the company."

Required

Do you agree with the controller? When should the sales be reported? Why would the controller be eager to report the cash receipts as sales?

Research Case

Case 9-7 JCPenny

JCPenney hopes a network of 1,200 stores will help the company maintain its market strength in response to intensive competition from other retailers. In recent years, JCPenney has expanded its emphasis on private label clothing (Original Arizona Jeans Company and St. John's Bay) in an effort to increase revenue and earnings.

Conduct a search of the World Wide Web, obtain JCPenney's most recent annual report, or use library resources to obtain company information to answer the following:

1. Based on the latest information available, determine the total current assets and total current liabilities for JCPenney Company. How do these amounts compare to the previous year?

2. Calculate JCPenney's current ratio based on the latest information available.

3. If you were a supplier of merchandise to JCPenney, how might its current ratio affect your willingness to extend credit to the company?

Optional Research. Conduct a survey of student and nonstudent consumers about store shopping preferences. What are the perceived strengths and weaknesses of JCPenney compared to other retailers?

Solution to Key Terms Quiz

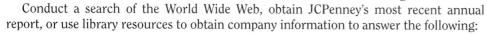

1 Current liability (p. 408)	**3** Accounts payable (p. 410)
8 Notes payable (p. 410)	**4** Discount on Notes Payable (p. 411)
6 Current Maturities of Long-Term Debt (p. 412)	**7** Accrued liability (p. 413)
9 Contingent liability (p. 414)	**11** Estimated liability (p. 416)
12 Contingent asset (p. 419)	**14** Time value of money (p. 420)
10 Simple interest (p. 421)	**13** Compound interest (p. 422)
15 Future value of a single amount (p. 423)	**17** Present value of a single amount (p. 424)
5 Annuity (p. 425)	**16** Future value of an annuity (p. 426)
2 Present value of an annuity (p. 427)	**18** Gross wages (p. 436)
20 Net pay (p. 436)	**19** Compensated absences (p. 439)

STUDY LINKS

A Look at Previous Chapters

The topic of long-term liabilities was introduced in Chapter 2 as an important aspect of a classified balance sheet, which segregates short-term and long-term assets and liabilities. Chapter 9 introduced compound interest and present value calculations as a method used to value long-term liabilities.

A Look at This Chapter

This chapter examines those items that typically appear in the long-term liability category of the balance sheet. The first section of the chapter will cover bonds, an important source of financing for many companies. The second section covers several other important long-term liabilities: leases, pensions, and deferred taxes. Although these liabilities are based on very complex financial arrangements, our primary purpose is to introduce these topics so that you are aware of their existence when reading financial statements.

A Look at Upcoming Chapters

Chapter 11 will examine the presentation of stockholders' equity, the other major category on the right-hand side of the balance sheet. Chapter 12 introduces other accounting issues related to liabilities and stockholders' equity.

Long-Term Liabilities

FOCUS ON FINANCIAL RESULTS

Thanks to global brand recognition, Coca-Cola Company's 1995 annual report indicated operating income of over $4 billion, with 82% generated outside the United States. Not content to stop there, Coca-Cola defines its market potential as the trillion gallons of liquid the world's people consume daily.

To expand profitably, Coca-Cola requires more money than it generates in profits. In 1995 the company invested $940 million in capital projects plus $3.8 billion in "aggressive marketing initiatives." It planned to spend still more in 1996. Therefore, Coca-Cola used a common financing tool: long-term debt. Its balance sheet (excerpted

The Coca-Cola Company and Subsidiaries

December 31,	1995	1994
Liabilities and Share-Owners' Equity		
Current		
Accounts payable and accrued expenses	$ **2,894**	$ 2,564
Loans and notes payable	**2,371**	2,048
Current maturities of long-term debt	**552**	35
Accrued taxes	**1,531**	1,530
Total Current Liabilities	**7,348**	6,177
Long-Term Debt	**1,141**	1,426
Other Liabilities	**966**	855
Deferred Income Taxes	**194**	180
Share-Owners' Equity		
Common stock, $.25 par value		
Authorized: 2,800,000,000 shares		
Issued: 1,711,839,497 shares in 1995; 1,707,627,955 shares in 1994	**428**	427
Capital surplus	**1,291**	1,173
Reinvested earnings	**12,882**	11,006
Unearned compensation related to outstanding restricted stock	**(68)**	(74)
Foreign currency translation adjustment	**(424)**	(272)
Unrealized gain on securities available for sale	**82**	48
	14,191	12,308
Less treasury stock, at cost (459,540,663 shares in 1995; 431,694,661 shares in 1994)	**8,799**	7,073
	5,392	5,235
	$ 15,041	$ 13,873

> Coca-Cola's long-term liabilities

See Notes to Consolidated Financial Statements.

8. Long-Term Debt

Long-term debt consists of the following (in millions):

December 31,	1995	1994
7¾% U.S. dollar notes due 1996	$ **250**	$ 250
5¾% Japanese yen notes due 1996	**292**	301
5¾% German mark notes due 1998[1]	**175**	161
7⅞% U.S. dollar notes due 1998	**250**	250
6% U.S. dollar notes due 2000	**252**	—
6⅝% U.S. dollar notes due 2002	**149**	149
6% U.S. dollar notes due 2003	**150**	150
7⅜% U.S. dollar notes due 2093	**116**	116
Other, due 1996 to 2013	**59**	84
	1,693	1,461
Less current portion	**552**	35
	$ 1,141	$ 1,426

[1]Portions of these notes have been swapped for liabilities denominated in other currencies.

here) reports that Coca-Cola ended 1995 with $1.141 billion in long-term debt. Huge as that sum is, management contends that expansion can generate enough earnings to provide an excellent return on the cost of the debt.

Coca-Cola's global presence and strong capital position open doors to financial markets around the world. The company can therefore get the world's "best buys" in financing. According to the balance sheet footnote, most of Coca-Cola's loans are in U.S. dollars, but some are in Japanese yen and others in German marks. As interest rates and currency exchange rates shift, management adjusts the composition of the debt to minimize the overall costs of borrowing.

What interest rate does Coca-Cola have to pay on long-term debt? How do accountants record the transactions involving long-term debt? Look for the answers as you study this chapter. Check Coca-Cola's most recent annual report to identify any changes.

SOURCE: *Coca-Cola Company Annual Report, 1995.*

After studying this chapter, you should be able to

LO 1 Identify the components of the long-term liability category of the balance sheet.

LO 2 Define the important characteristics of bonds payable.

LO 3 Determine the issue price of a bond using compound interest techniques.

LO 4 Understand the effect on the balance sheet of issuance of bonds.

LO 5 Find the amortization of premium or discount using effective interest amortization.

LO 6 Find the gain or loss on retirement of bonds.

LO 7 Determine whether a lease agreement must be reported as a liability on the balance sheet.

LO 8 Explain deferred taxes and calculate the deferred tax liability.

LO 9 Understand the meaning of a pension obligation and the effect of pensions on the long-term liability category of the balance sheet.

LO 10 Explain the effects that transactions involving long-term liabilities have on the statement of cash flows.

Balance Sheet Presentation

LO 1 Identify the components of the long-term liability category of the balance sheet.

FROM CONCEPT TO PRACTICE 10.1
READING COCA-COLA'S BALANCE SHEET Coca-Cola lists three items as long-term liabilities on its 1995 balance sheet. What are those items? Did they increase or decrease?

In general, **long-term liabilities** are obligations that will not be satisfied within one year. Essentially, all liabilities that are not classified as current liabilities are classified as long-term. We will concentrate on the long-term liabilities of bonds or notes, pension obligations, leases, and deferred taxes. On the balance sheet, the items are listed after current liabilities. For example, the noncurrent liabilities section of Sprint's balance sheet is highlighted in Exhibit 10-1. Sprint is a large, well-known company in the telephone communications industry. It has acquired financing through a combination of long-term debt, stock issuance, and internal growth or retained earnings. Exhibit 10-1 indicates that long-term debt is one portion of the long-term liability category of the balance sheet. But the balance sheet also reveals several other items that must be considered part of the long-term liability category, including deferred income taxes, postretirement benefits, and other liabilities. We will begin with an examination of a particular type of long-term debt, bonds payable.

Bonds Payable

Characteristics of Bonds

LO 2 Define the important characteristics of bonds payable.

A bond is a security or financial instrument that allows firms to borrow money and repay the loan over a long period of time. The bonds are sold, or *issued,* to investors who have amounts to invest and want a return on their investment. The *borrower* (issuing firm) promises to pay interest on specified dates, usually annually or semiannually. The borrower also promises to repay the principal on a specified date, the *due date* or maturity date.

A bond certificate, illustrated in Exhibit 10-2 on page 466, is issued at the time of purchase and indicates the *terms* of the bond. Generally, bonds are issued in denominations of $1,000. The denomination of the bond is usually referred to as the **face value** or par value. This is the amount that the firm must pay at the maturity date of the bond.

Firms issue bonds in very large amounts, often in millions in a single issue. After bonds are issued, they may be traded on a bond exchange in the same way that stocks are sold on the stock exchanges. Therefore, bonds are not always held until maturity by the initial investor but may change hands several times before their eventual due date. Because bond maturities are as long as 30 years, the "secondary" market in bonds—the market for bonds already issued—is a critical factor in a company's ability to raise money. Investors in bonds may want to sell them if interest rates paid by competing investments become more attractive or if the issuer becomes less creditworthy. Buyers of these bonds may be betting that interest rates will reverse course or that the company

Different from stock?

EXHIBIT 10-1 Sprint: Liability Section of the Balance Sheet

CONSOLIDATED BALANCE SHEETS

(in millions)
As of December 31,

	1995	1994
Assets		
Current assets		
Cash and equivalents	$ 124.2	$ 113.7
Accounts receivable, net of allowance for doubtful accounts of $222.5 million ($126.9 million in 1994)	1,523.7	1,387.9
Receivable from cellular division	1,400.0	—
Inventories	171.0	187.5
Deferred income taxes	45.5	54.2
Prepaid expenses	166.6	144.5
Other	188.4	155.4
Total current assets	3,619.4	2,043.2
Investments in equity securities	262.9	177.6
Property, plant and equipment		
Long distance communications services	6,773.7	6,056.3
Local communications services	12,603.1	11,827.4
Other	539.1	498.6
	19,915.9	18,382.3
Less accumulated depreciation	10,200.1	8,123.5
	9,715.8	10,258.8
Investments in affiliates	1,130.1	198.6
Receivable from cellular division	—	1,271.1
Net investment in cellular division	106.9	59.7
Other assets	360.8	538.5
	$15,195.9	$14,547.5
Liabilities and Shareholders' Equity		
Current liabilities		
Current maturities of long-term debt	$ 280.4	$ 332.4
Short-term borrowings	2,144.0	—
Accounts payable	938.9	927.8
Accrued interconnection costs	617.7	527.6
Accrued taxes	235.5	237.9
Other	925.6	817.4
Total current liabilities	5,142.1	2,843.1
Long-term debt	3,253.0	4,604.8
Deferred credits and other liabilities		
Deferred income taxes and investment tax credits	843.4	1,197.5
Postretirement and other benefit obligations	889.3	845.9
Other	393.0	494.3
	2,125.7	2,537.7
Redeemable preferred stock	32.5	37.1
Common stock and other shareholders' equity		
Common stock, par value $2.50 per share, authorized 500.0 million shares, issued 349.2 million (348.6 million in 1994), and outstanding 349.2 million (348.3 million in 1994)	872.9	871.4
Capital in excess of par or stated value	960.0	942.9
Retained earnings	2,766.5	2,730.9
Other	43.2	(20.4)
	4,642.6	4,524.8
	$15,195.9	$14,547.5

Sprint's long-term liabilities

will get back on its feet. Trading in the secondary market does not affect the financial statements of the issuing company.

We have described the general nature of bonds, but it should not be assumed that all bonds have the same terms and features. Following are some important features that often appear in the bond certificate.

Collateral The bond certificate should indicate the *collateral* of the loan. Collateral represents the assets that back the bonds in case the issuer cannot make the interest and principal payments and must default on the loan. **Debenture bonds** are not backed by specific collateral of the issuing company. Rather, the investor must examine the

EXHIBIT 10-2 Bond Certificate

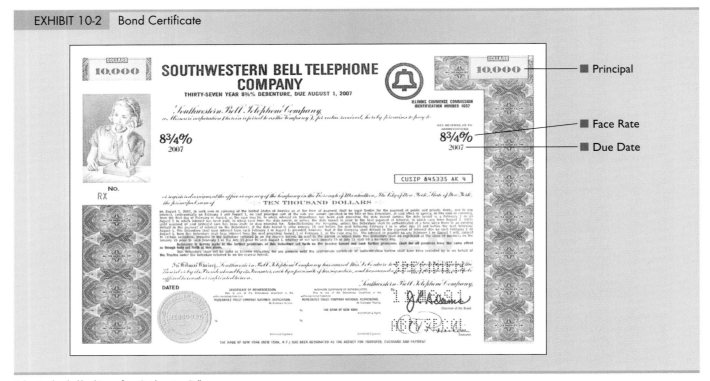

▪ Principal

▪ Face Rate

▪ Due Date

Debenture bonds, like this one from Southwestern Bell Telephone, are backed by the general creditworthiness of the issuing company, not by its assets as collateral. Buyers of such bonds should check the issuer's credit rating, should know how to read the firm's financial statements—and should learn as much as possible about its operations.

This bond trader assists investors on the secondary market in buying and selling bonds. On the board behind her, she tallies bond availability information including company name ("Dayton Hudson"), bond rates ("10" for 10%), maturity dates ("1-1-11" for January 1, 2011), and the issue price ("99.479" for 99.479% of face value).

general creditworthiness of the issuer. If a bond is a *secured bond,* the certificate indicates specific assets that serve as collateral in case of default.

Due Date The bond certificate specifies the date that the bond principal must be repaid. Normally, bonds are *term bonds,* meaning that the entire principal amount is due on a single date. Alternatively, bonds may be issued as **serial bonds,** meaning that not all of the principal is due on the same date. For example, a firm may issue serial bonds that have a portion of the principal due each year for the next 10 years. Issuing firms may prefer serial bonds because a firm does not need to accumulate the entire amount for principal repayment at one time.

Other Features Some bonds are issued as convertible or callable bonds. *Convertible bonds* can be converted into common stock at a future time. This feature allows the investor to buy a security that pays a fixed interest rate but that can be converted at a future date into an equity security (stock) if the issuing firm is growing and profitable. The conversion feature is also advantageous to the issuing firm because convertible bonds normally carry a lower rate of interest.

Callable bonds may be retired before their specified due date. *Callable* generally refers to the issuer's right to retire the bonds. If the buyer or investor has the right to retire the bonds, they are referred to as *redeemable bonds.* Usually, callable bonds stipulate the price to be paid at redemption; this price is referred to as the *redemption price* or the *reacquisition price.* The callable feature is like an insurance policy for the company. Say a bond pays 10% but interest rates plummet to 6%. Rather than continuing to pay 10%, the company is willing to offer a slight premium over face value for the right to retire those 10% bonds so that it can borrow at 6%. Of course, the investor is invariably disappointed when the company invokes its call privilege.

As you can see, a variety of terms and features is associated with bonds. Each firm seeks to structure the bond agreement in the manner that best meets its financial needs and will attract investors at the most favorable rates.

Bonds are a popular source of financing because of the tax advantages when compared with the issuance of stock. Interest paid on bonds is deductible for tax purposes, but dividends paid on stock are not. This may explain why the amount of debt on many firms' balance sheets has increased in recent years. Debt became popular in the 1980s to finance mergers and again in the early 1990s when interest rates reached 20-year lows. Still, investors and creditors tend to downgrade a company when the amount of debt it has on the balance sheet is deemed to be excessive.

Issuance of Bonds

When bonds are issued, the issuing firm must recognize the incurrence of a liability in exchange for cash. If bonds are issued at their face amount, the accounting entry is straightforward. For example, assume that on April 1 a firm issues bonds with a face amount of $10,000 and receives $10,000. In this case, the asset Cash and the liability Bonds Payable are both increased by $10,000. The accounting entry is as follows:

Apr. 1	Cash	10,000	
	Bonds Payable		10,000
	To record the issuance of bonds at face value.		

Assets	=	**Liabilities**	+	**Owners' Equity**
+10,000		**+10,000**		

Factors Affecting Bond Price

With bonds payable, two interest rates are always involved. The **face rate of interest** (also called the *stated rate, nominal rate, contract rate,* or *coupon rate*) is the rate specified on the bond certificate. It is the amount of interest that will be paid each interest period. For example, if $10,000 worth of bonds is issued with an 8% annual face rate of interest, then interest of $800 ($10,000 $\times$ 8% $\times$ 1 year) would be paid at the end of each annual period. Alternatively, bonds often require the payment of interest semiannually. If the bonds in our example required the 8% annual face rate to be paid semiannually (at 4%), then interest of $400 ($10,000 $\times$ 8% $\times$ 1/2 year) would be paid each semiannual period.

LO 3 Determine the issue price of a bond using compound interest techniques.

The second important interest rate is the **market rate of interest** (also called the *effective rate* or *bond yield*). The market rate of interest is the rate that bondholders could obtain by investing in other bonds that are similar to the issuing firm's bonds. The issuing firm does not set the market rate of interest. That rate is determined by the bond market on the basis of many transactions for similar bonds. The market rate incorporates all of the "market's" knowledge about economic conditions and all its expectations about future conditions. Normally, issuing firms try to set a face rate for their bonds that is equal to the market rate. However, because the market rate changes daily, there are almost always small differences between the face rate and the market rate at the time bonds are issued.

In addition to the number of interest payments and the maturity length of the bond, the face rate and the market rate of interest must both be known in order to calculate the issue price of a bond. The **bond issue price** equals the *present value* of the cash flows that the bond will produce. Bonds produce two types of cash flows for the investor, interest receipts and repayment of principal (face value). The interest receipts constitute an annuity of payments each interest period over the life of the bonds. The repayment of principal (face value) is a one-time receipt that occurs at the end of the term of the bonds. We must calculate the present value of the interest receipts (using Table 9-4) and the present value of the principal amount (using Table 9-2). The total of the two present-value calculations represents the issue price of the bond.

An Example   Suppose that on January 1, 1998, Discount Firm wants to issue bonds with a face value of $10,000. The face or coupon rate of interest has been set at 8%. The bonds will pay interest annually, and the principal amount is due in four years. Also suppose that the market rate of interest for other similar bonds is currently 10%. Because the market rate of interest exceeds the coupon rate, investors will not be willing to pay $10,000 but something less. We want to calculate the amount that will be obtained from the issuance of Discount Firm's bonds.

Discount's bond will produce two sets of cash flows for the investor, an annual interest payment of $800 ($10,000 $\times$ 8%) per year for four years and repayment of the principal of

ACCOUNTING FOR YOUR DECISIONS

You Rate the Bonds

One of the factors that determine the rate of interest on a bond is a rating by a rating agency such as Standard & Poor's or Moody's Investor Service. Bonds with a higher rating are considered less risky and can be issued for a lower rate of interest. You have been given an assignment to rate the bonds issued by Sprint Communications. What factors would you consider in your rating?

ANS: There are many factors that affect your evaluation of the riskiness of the company's bonds. One factor would be the amount of debt on Sprint's books, which can be found by examining the liability section of the balance sheet. It is important to relate the amount of debt to the total equity of the company; this is often done by computing the debt-to-equity ratio. Another important factor is the company's competitive position within the telecommunications industry. If Sprint can deliver service profitably, it will generate cash that can be used to pay the interest and principal on the bonds.

$10,000 at the end of the fourth year. To calculate the issue price, we must calculate the present value of the two sets of cash flows. A time diagram portrays the cash flows as follows:

Interest payments

Principal

We can calculate the issue price by using the compound-interest tables found in Chapter 9, as follows:

$800 × 3.170 (factor from Table 9-4 for 4 periods, 10%)	$2,536
$10,000 × .683 (factor from Table 9-2 for 4 periods, 10%)	6,830
Issue Price	$9,366

The table factors used represent four periods and 10% interest. This is a very key point. The issue price of a bond is always calculated using the market rate of interest. The face rate of interest determines the amount of the interest payments, but the market rate determines the present value of the payments and the present value of the principal (and therefore the issue price).

Our example of Discount Firm reveals that the bonds with a $10,000 face value amount would be issued for $9,366. The bond markets and the financial press often state the issue price as a percentage of the face amount. The percentage for Discount's bonds can be calculated as ($9,366/$10,000) × 100, or 93.66%.

Exhibit 10-3 illustrates how bonds are actually listed in the reporting of the bond markets. The exhibit lists two types of IBM bonds that were traded on a particular day.

EXHIBIT 10-3	Listing of Bonds on the Bond Market				
BONDS	**CUR YLD**	**VOL**	**CLOSE**	**NET CHG**
IBM 6⅜00	6.5	280	98¾	−¼
IBM 7¼02	7.1	68	101½	+¼

The portion immediately after the company name, for example "6 3/8 00," indicates that the face rate of interest is 6 3/8% and the due date of the bonds is the year 2000. The next column, for example "6.5," indicates that the bond investor who purchased the bonds on that day will receive a yield of 6.5%. The column labeled "vol" indicates the number of bonds, in thousands, that were bought and sold during the day. The column labeled "close" indicates the market price of the bonds at the end of the day. For example, the first issue of IBM bonds closed at 98 3/4, which means that the price was 98 3/4% of the face value of the bonds. These bonds were trading at a discount because the face rate (6 3/8%) is less than the market rate. The bonds in the second issue—"7 1/4 02"—have a face rate of 7 1/4%, will become due in the year 2002, and closed at 101 1/2, or at a premium. The net change column indicates the change in the bond price that occurred for the day's trading.

Premium or Discount on Bonds

Premium or discount represents the difference between the face value and the issue price of a bond. We may state the relationship as follows:

Premium = Issue Price − Face Value
Discount = Face Value − Issue Price

LO 4   Understand the effect on the balance sheet of issuance of bonds.

In other words, when issue price exceeds face value, the bonds have sold at a premium, and when the face value exceeds the issue price, the bonds have sold at a discount.

We will continue with the Discount Firm example to illustrate the accounting for bonds sold at a discount. Discount Firm's bonds sold at a discount calculated as follows:

Discount = $10,000 − $9,366
Discount = $634

Discount Firm would record both the discount and the issuance of the bonds in the following journal entry:

Jan. 1	Cash	9,366	
	Discount on Bonds Payable	634	
	Bonds Payable		10,000
	To record the issuance of bonds payable.		

Assets	=	**Liabilities**	+	**Owners' Equity**
+9,366		−634		
		+10,000		

The Discount on Bonds Payable account is shown as a contra liability on the balance sheet in conjunction with the Bonds Payable account and is a deduction from that account. If Discount Firm prepared a balance sheet immediately after the bond issuance, the following would appear in the long-term liability category of the balance sheet:

Long-Term Liabilities:	
Bonds Payable	$10,000
Less: Discount on Bonds Payable	634
	$ 9,366

The Discount Firm example has illustrated a situation in which the market rate of a bond issue is higher than the face rate. Now we will examine the opposite situation, when the face rate exceeds the market rate. Again, we are interested in calculating the issue price of the bonds.

Issuing at a Premium Suppose that on January 1, 1998, Premium Firm wants to issue the same bonds as in the previous example: $10,000 face value bonds, with an 8%

face rate of interest and with interest paid annually each year for four years. Assume, however, that the market rate of interest is 6% for similar bonds. The issue price is calculated as the present value of the annuity of interest payments plus the present value of the principal at the market rate of interest. The calculations are as follows:

$800 × 3.465 (factor from Table 9-4 for 4 periods, 6%)	$ 2,772
$10,000 × .792 (factor from Table 9-2 for 4 periods, 6%)	7,920
Issue price	$10,692

We have calculated that the bonds would be issued for $10,692. Because the bonds would be issued at an amount that is higher than the face value amount, they would be issued at a premium. The amount of the premium is calculated as follows:

Premium = $10,692 − $10,000
Premium = $692

The premium is recorded at the time of bond issuance in the following entry:

Jan. 1	Cash	10,692	
	Bonds Payable		10,000
	Premium on Bonds Payable		692
	To record the issuance of bonds payable.		

Assets = **Liabilities** + **Owners' Equity**
+10,692   **+10,000**
                +692

The account Premium on Bonds Payable is an addition to the Bonds Payable account. If Premium Firm presented a balance sheet immediately after the bond issuance, the long-term liability category of the balance sheet would appear as follows:

Long-Term Liabilities:	
Bonds Payable	$10,000
Plus: Premium on Bonds Payable	692
	$10,692

A company like Sprint, which operates a digital fiberoptic network to 8 million customers, must make huge investments in high-technology equipment it needs to grow its business. These investments can be reflected in the issuance of stock or the issuance of bonds or notes. By examining the financial statements of Sprint, you can see that Sprint does both.

You should learn two important points from the Discount Firm and Premium Firm examples. First, you should be able to determine whether a bond will sell at a premium or discount by the relationship that exists between the face rate and the market rate of interest. *Premium* and *discount* do not mean "good" and "bad." Premium or discount arises solely because of the difference that exists between the face rate and the market rate of interest for a bond issue. The same relationship always exists so that the following statements hold true:

If Market Rate = Face Rate THEN bonds are issued at
face value amount
If Market Rate > Face Rate THEN bonds are issued at
a discount
If Market Rate < Face Rate THEN bonds are issued at
a premium

The examples also illustrate a second important point. The relationship between interest rates and bond prices is always inverse. To understand the term *inverse relationship*, refer to the Discount Firm and Premium Firm examples. The bonds of the two firms are identical in all respects except for the market rate of interest. When the market rate was 10%, the bond issue price was $9,366 (the Discount Firm example). When the market rate was 6%, the bond issue price increased to $10,692 (the Premium Firm example). The examples illustrate that as interest rates decrease, prices on the bond markets increase and that as interest rates increase, bond prices decrease.

Many investors in the stock market perceive that they are taking a great deal of risk with their capital. In truth, bond investors are taking substantial risk too. The most obvious risk is that the company will fail and not be able to pay its debts. But another risk is that interest rates on comparable investments will rise. Interest rate risk can have a devastating impact on the current-market value of bonds. One way to minimize interest rate risk is to hold the bond to maturity, at which point the company must pay the face amount.

Bond Amortization

Purpose of Amortization The amount of interest expense that should be reflected on a firm's income statement for bonds payable is the true, or effective, interest. The effective interest should reflect the face rate of interest as well as interest that results from issuing the bond at a premium or discount. To reflect that interest component, the amount initially recorded in the Premium on Bonds Payable or the Discount on Bonds Payable account must be amortized or spread over the life of the bond.

Amortization refers to the process of transferring an amount from the discount or premium to interest expense each time period to adjust interest expense. One commonly used method of amortization is the effective interest method. We will illustrate how to amortize a discount amount and then how to amortize a premium amount.

To illustrate amortization of a discount, we need to return to our Discount Firm example introduced earlier. We have seen that the issue price of the bond could be calculated as $9,366, resulting in a contra-liability (debit) balance of $634 in the Discount on Bonds Payable account (see the entry on page 469). But what does the initial balance of the Discount account really represent? The discount should be thought of as additional interest that Discount Firm must pay over and above the 8% face rate. Remember that Discount received only $9,366 but must repay the full principal of $10,000 at the bond due date. For that reason, the $634 of discount is an additional interest cost that must be reflected as interest expense. It is reflected as interest expense by the process of amortization. In other words, interest expense is made up of two components: cash interest and amortization. We will now consider how to amortize premium or discount.

Effective Interest Method: Impact on Expense The effective interest method of amortization amortizes discount or premium in a manner that produces a constant effective interest rate from period to period. The *dollar amount* of interest expense will vary from period to period, but the *rate* of interest will be constant. This interest rate is referred to as the *effective interest rate* and is equal to the market rate of interest at the time the bonds are issued.

To illustrate this point, we introduce two new terms. The carrying value of bonds is represented by the following:

$$\text{Carrying Value} = \text{Face Value} - \text{Unamortized Discount}$$

For example, the carrying value of the bonds for our Discount Firm example, as of the date of issuance of January 1, 1998, could be calculated as follows:

$$\$10,000 - \$634 = \$9,366$$

In those situations in which there is a premium instead of a discount, carrying value is represented by the following:

$$\text{Carrying Value} = \text{Face Value} + \text{Unamortized Premium}$$

For example, the carrying value of the bonds for our Premium Firm example, as of the date of issuance of January 1, 1998, could be calculated as follows:

$$\$10,000 + \$692 = \$10,692$$

The second term has been suggested earlier. The *effective rate of interest* is represented by the following:

$$\text{Effective Rate} = \text{Annual Interest Expense/Carrying Value}$$

LO 5 Find the amortization of premium or discount using effective interest amortization.

Effective Interest Method: An Example   The amortization table in Exhibit 10-4 illustrates effective interest amortization of the bond discount for our Discount Firm example.

As illustrated in Exhibit 10-4, the effective interest method of amortization is based on several important concepts. The relationships can be stated in equation form as follows:

Cash Interest (in Column 1)   = Bond Face Value × Face Rate
Interest Expense (in Column 2)   = Carrying Value   × Effective Rate
Discount Amortized (in Column 3) = Interest Expense − Cash Interest

The first column of the exhibit indicates that the cash interest to be paid is $800 ($10,000 × 8%). The second column indicates the annual interest expense at the effective rate of interest (market rate at the time of issuance). This is a constant rate of interest (10% in our example) and is calculated by multiplying the carrying value *as of the beginning of the period* times the market rate of interest. In 1998 the interest expense is $937 ($9,366 × 10%). Note that the amount of interest expense changes each year because the carrying value changes as discount is amortized. The amount of discount amortized each year in Column 3 is the difference between the cash interest in Column 1 and the interest expense in Column 2. Again, note that the amount of discount amortized changes in each of the four years. Finally, the carrying value in Column 4 is the previous year's carrying value plus the discount amortized in Column 3. When bonds are issued at a discount, the carrying value starts at an amount less than face value and increases each period until it reaches the face value amount.

The amortization table in Exhibit 10-4 is the basis for the accounting entries that must be recorded. Discount Firm may record two entries for each period. The first entry at the end of 1998 is recorded to reflect the cash interest payment:

Dec. 31	Interest Expense	800	
	Cash		800
	To record annual payment on bonds payable.		

Assets   =   Liabilities   +   Owners' Equity
−800   −800

The second entry is recorded to amortize a portion of the discount and to reflect that amount as an adjustment of interest expense:

Dec. 31	Interest Expense	137	
	Discount on Bonds Payable		137
	To amortize annual portion of discount on bonds payable.		

Assets   =   Liabilities   +   Owners' Equity
**   +137   −137**

Instead of making two entries, firms often make one entry that combines the two. Thus, the entry for 1998 could also be recorded in the following manner:

EXHIBIT 10-4   Discount Amortization: Effective Interest Method of Amortization

DATE	COLUMN 1 CASH INTEREST	COLUMN 2 INTEREST EXPENSE	COLUMN 3 DISCOUNT AMORTIZED	COLUMN 4 CARRYING VALUE
	8%	10%	COL. 2 − COL. 1	
1/1/98	—	—	—	$ 9,366
12/31/98	$800	$937	$137	9,503
12/31/99	800	950	150	9,653
12/31/2000	800	965	165	9,818
12/31/2001	800	982	182	10,000

Dec. 31 Interest Expense   937
         Cash   800
         Discount on Bonds Payable   137
         To record annual interest payment and to amortize annual portion of
         discount on bonds payable.

Assets = Liabilities + Owners' Equity
−800   +137   −937

The T accounts of the issuing firm as of December 31, 1998, would appear as follows:

BONDS PAYABLE			DISCOUNT ON BONDS PAYABLE		
	10,000	1/1/98	1/1/98	634	
					137 12/31/98
			Bal.	497	

INTEREST EXPENSE		
12/31/98	800	
12/31/98	137	
Bal.	937	

The process of amortization would continue for four years, until the balance of the Discount on Bonds Payable account has been reduced to zero. By the end of 2001, all of the balance of the Discount on Bonds Payable account will have been transferred to the Interest Expense account and represents an increase in interest expense each period.

The amortization of a premium has an impact opposite that of the amortization of a discount. We will use our Premium Firm example to illustrate. Recall that on January 1, 1998, Premium Firm issued $10,000 face value bonds with a face rate of interest of 8%. At the time the bonds were issued, the market rate was 6%, resulting in an issue price of $10,692 and a credit balance in the Premium on Bonds Payable account of $692 (see page 470).

The amortization table in Exhibit 10-5 illustrates effective interest amortization of the bond premium for Premium Firm. As the exhibit illustrates, effective interest amortization of a premium is based on the same concepts as amortization of a discount. The following relationships still hold true:

Cash Interest (in Column 1)   = Bond Face Value × Face Rate
Interest Expense (in Column 2) = Carrying Value   × Effective Rate

The first column of the exhibit indicates that the cash interest to be paid is $800 ($10,000 × 8%). The second column indicates the annual interest expense at the effective rate. In 1998 the interest expense is $642 ($10,692 × 6%). Note, however, two differences between Exhibit 10-4 and Exhibit 10-5. In the amortization of a premium, the cash interest in Column 1 exceeds the interest expense in Column 2. Therefore, the premium amortized is defined as follows:

Premium Amortized (in Column 3) = Cash Interest − Interest Expense

EXHIBIT 10-5 Premium Amortization: Effective Interest Method of Amortization

DATE	COLUMN 1 CASH INTEREST	COLUMN 2 INTEREST EXPENSE	COLUMN 3 PREMIUM AMORTIZED	COLUMN 4 CARRYING VALUE
	8%	6%	COL. 1 − COL. 2	
1/1/98	—	—	—	$10,692
12/31/98	$800	$642	$158	10,534
12/31/99	800	632	168	10,366
12/31/2000	800	622	178	10,188
12/31/2001	800	612	188	10,000

Also note that the carrying value in Column 4 starts at an amount higher than the face value of $10,000 ($10,692) and is amortized downward until it reaches face value. Therefore, the carrying value at the end of each year is the carrying value at the beginning of the period minus the premium amortized for that year. For example, the carrying value in Exhibit 10-5 at the end of 1998 ($10,534) was calculated by subtracting the premium amortized for 1998 ($158 in Column 3) from the carrying value at the beginning of 1998 ($10,692).

The amortization table in Exhibit 10-5 again serves as the basis for the accounting entries that must be recorded. Premium Firm may record two entries for each period. The first entry at the end of 1998 is recorded to reflect the cash interest payment:

Dec. 31	Interest Expense	800
	Cash	800
	To record annual payment on bonds payable.	

Assets = Liabilities + Owners' Equity
−800   −800

The second entry is recorded to amortize a portion of the premium and to reflect that amount as an adjustment of interest expense:

Dec. 31	Premium on Bonds Payable	158
	Interest Expense	158
	To amortize annual portion of premium on bonds payable.	

Assets = Liabilities + Owners' Equity
**   −158   +158**

Of course, Premium Firm could combine the preceding two entries into one entry as follows:

Dec. 31	Interest Expense	642
	Premium on Bonds Payable	158
	Cash	800
	To record annual interest payment and to amortize annual portion of premium on bonds payable.	

Assets = Liabilities + Owners' Equity
−800   −158   −642

The T accounts of Premium Firm as of December 31, 1998, appear as follows:

BONDS PAYABLE		PREMIUM ON BONDS PAYABLE	
	10,000 1/1/98		692 1/1/98
		12/31/98 158	
			534 Bal.

INTEREST EXPENSE	
12/31/98 800	
	158 12/31/98
Bal. 642	

The process of amortization would continue for four years, until the balance of the Premium on Bonds Payable account has been reduced to zero. By the end of 2001, all of the balance of the Premium on Bonds Payable account will have been transferred to the Interest Expense account and represents a reduction of interest expense each period.

Redemption of Bonds

Redemption at Maturity   The term *redemption* refers to retirement of bonds by repayment of the principal. If bonds are retired on their due date, the accounting entry is not difficult. Refer again to the Discount Firm example. If Discount Firm retires its bonds on the due date of December 31, 2001, it must repay the principal of $10,000 and records the following entry:

Dec. 31 Bonds Payable   10,000
             Cash   10,000
            To record the retirement of bonds payable.

> **Assets** = **Liabilities** + **Owners' Equity**
> **−10,000**   **−10,000**

This assumes that the interest payment that was paid on December 31, 2001, and the discount amortization on that date have already been recorded. The balance of the Discount on Bonds Payable account is zero, since it has been fully amortized.

Retired Early at a Gain   A firm may want to retire bonds before their due date for several reasons. A firm may simply have excess cash and may determine that the best use of those funds is to repay outstanding bond obligations. Bonds may also be retired early because of changing interest rate conditions. If interest rates in the economy decline, firms may find it advantageous to retire bonds that have been issued at higher rates. Of course, what is advantageous to the issuer is not necessarily so for the investor. Early retirement of callable bonds is always a possibility that must be anticipated. Large institutional investors expect such a development and merely reinvest the money elsewhere. Many individual investors are more seriously inconvenienced when a bond issue is called.

LO 6 Find the gain or loss on retirement of bonds.

Bond terms generally specify that if bonds are retired before their due date, they are not retired at the face value amount but at a call price or redemption price indicated on the bond certificate. Also, the amount of unamortized premium or discount on the bonds must be considered when bonds are retired early. The retirement results in a **gain or loss on redemption** that must be calculated as follows:

> Gain = Carrying Value − Redemption Price
> Loss = Redemption Price − Carrying Value

In other words, the issuing firm must calculate the carrying value of the bonds at the time of redemption and compare it with the total redemption price. If the carrying value is higher than the redemption price, the issuing firm must record a gain. If the carrying value is lower than the redemption price, the issuing firm must record a loss.

We will use the Premium Firm example to illustrate the calculation of gain or loss. Assume that on December 31, 1998, Premium Firm wants to retire its bonds due in 2001. Assume, as in the previous section, that the bonds were issued at a premium of $692 at the beginning of 1998. Premium Firm has used the effective interest method of amortization and has recorded the interest and amortization entries for the year (see page 474). This has resulted in a balance of $534 in the Premium on Bonds Payable account as of December 31, 1998. Assume also that Premium Firm's bond certificates indicate that the bonds may be retired early at a call price of 102 (meaning 102% of face value). Thus, the redemption price is 102% of $10,000, or $10,200.

Premium Firm's retirement of bonds would result in a gain. The gain can be calculated using two steps. First, we must calculate the carrying value of the bonds as of the date they are retired. The carrying value of Premium Firm's bonds at that date is as follows:

> Carrying Value = Face Value + Unamortized Premium
>   = $10,000 + $534
>   = $10,534

Note that the carrying value we have calculated is the same amount indicated for December 31, 1998, in Column 4 of the effective interest amortization table of Exhibit 10-5.

The second step is to calculate the gain:

> Gain = Carrying Value − Redemption Price
>   = $10,534 − ($10,000 × 1.02)
>   = $10,534 − $10,200
>   = $334

It is important to remember that when bonds are retired, the balance of the Bonds Payable account and the remaining balance of the Premium on Bonds Payable account must be eliminated from the balance sheet.

Retired Early at a Loss   To illustrate retirement of bonds at a loss, assume that Premium Firm retires bonds at December 31, 1998, as in the previous section. However, assume that the call price for the bonds is 107 (or 107% of face value).

We can again perform the calculations in two steps. The first step is to calculate the carrying value:

$$\text{Carrying Value} = \text{Face Value} + \text{Unamortized Premium}$$
$$= \$10,000 + \$534$$
$$= \$10,534$$

The second step is to compare the carrying value with the redemption price to calculate the amount of the loss:

$$\text{Loss} = \text{Redemption Price} - \text{Carrying Value}$$
$$= (\$10,000 \times 1.07) - \$10,534$$
$$= \$10,700 - \$10,534$$
$$= \$166$$

In this case, a loss of $166 has resulted from the retirement of Premium Firm bonds. A loss means that the company paid more to retire the bonds than the amount at which the bonds were recorded on the balance sheet.

Financial Statement Presentation of Gain or Loss   The accounts Gain on Bond Redemption and Loss on Bond Redemption are income statement accounts. A gain on bond redemption increases Premium Firm's income; a loss decreases its income. In that respect, the accounts are similar to gains or losses that occur on the sale of equipment or other assets. There is an important difference, however. The FASB has ruled that gains and losses that occur on bond redemption merit separate recognition on the income statement. Such gains and losses are considered *extraordinary items* and must be shown in a separate section of the income statement.[1] This allows income statement readers to understand that bond redemption is not a part of the firm's "normal operating" activities. That is not to say that investors are not interested in such one-time gains or losses. Although redemptions on bonds are not part of normal operations, a large gain suggests that the company's financial managers are astute enough to take advantage of opportunities in the financial markets. (For a more complete discussion of the treatment of extraordinary items on the income statement, see Chapter 12.)

Other Long-Term Liabilities

Long-term bonds and notes payable are important sources of financing for many large corporations and are quite prominent in the long-term liability category of the balance sheet for many firms. But other important elements of that category of the balance sheet also represent long-term obligations. We will introduce you to three items: leases, deferred taxes, and pensions. In some cases, they are required to be reported on the financial statements and are important components of the long-term liability section of the balance sheet. In other cases, the items are not required to be presented in the financial statements and can be discerned only by a careful reading of the footnotes to the financial statements.

Leases

LO 7   Determine whether a lease agreement must be reported as a liability on the balance sheet.

A *lease,* a contractual arrangement between two parties, allows one party, the *lessee,* the right to use an asset in exchange for making payments to its owner, the *lessor.* A

---

[1]*Statement of Financial Accounting Standards No. 4,* "Reporting Gains and Losses from Extinguishment of Debt" (Stamford, Conn.: FASB, 1975).

common example of a lease arrangement is the rental of an apartment. The tenant is the lessee and the landlord is the lessor.

Lease agreements are a form of financing. In some cases, it is more advantageous to lease an asset than to borrow money to purchase it. The lessee can conserve cash because a lease does not require a large initial cash outlay. A wide variety of lease arrangements exists, ranging from simple agreements to complex ones that span a long time period. Lease arrangements are popular because of their flexibility. The terms of a lease can be structured in many ways to meet the needs of the lessee and lessor. This results in difficult accounting questions:

1. Should the right to use property be reported as an asset by the lessee?
2. Should the obligation to make payments be reported as a liability by the lessee?
3. Should all leases be accounted for in the same manner regardless of the terms of the lease agreement?

The answers are that some leases should be reported as an asset and liability by the lessee and some should not. The accountant must examine the terms of the lease agreement and compare those terms with an established set of criteria.

ACCOUNTING FOR YOUR DECISIONS

Should You Lease or Buy?

You want to acquire a new car and are considering leasing instead of buying. What factors should you consider to determine whether leasing is the better alternative?

ANS: To make this decision, answer the following questions: Do you have the cash to buy the car? If not, what is the cost of borrowing? How long will the car be used? Will another car be needed in the near future? What is the purpose of the car? How will the lease payments compare to the purchase payments? Will you own the car at the end of the lease?

Lease Criteria   From the viewpoint of the lessee, there are two types of lease agreements, operating and capital leases. In an operating lease, the lessee acquires the right to use an asset for a limited period of time. The lessee is *not* required to record the right to use the property as an asset or to record the obligation for payments as a liability. Therefore, the lessee is able to attain a form of *off-balance-sheet financing*. That is, the lessee has attained the right to use property but has not recorded that right, or the accompanying obligation, on the balance sheet. By escaping the balance sheet, the lease does not add to debt or impair the debt-to-equity ratio that investors usually calculate. Management has a responsibility to make sure that such off-balance-sheet financing is not in fact a long-term obligation. The company's auditors are supposed to analyze the terms of the lease carefully to make sure that management has exercised its responsibility.

The second type of lease agreement is a capital lease. In this type of lease, the lessee has acquired sufficient rights of ownership and control of the property to be considered its owner. The lease is called a *capital lease* because it is capitalized (recorded) on the balance sheet by the lessee.

A lease should be considered a capital lease by the lessee if *one or more* of the following criteria are met:[2]

1. The lease transfers ownership of the property to the lessee at the end of the lease term.
2. The lease contains a bargain purchase option to purchase the asset at an amount lower than its fair market value.
3. The lease term is 75% or more of the property's economic life.
4. The present value of the minimum lease payments is 90% or more of the fair market value of the property at the inception of the lease.

---

[2]*Statement of Financial Accounting Standards No. 13,* "Accounting for Leases" (Stamford, Conn.: FASB, 1976).

If none of the criteria are met, the lease agreement is accounted for as an operating lease. This is an area in which it is important for the accountant to exercise professional judgment. In some cases, firms may take elaborate measures to evade or manipulate the criteria that would require lease capitalization. The accountant should determine what is full and fair disclosure based on an unbiased evaluation of the substance of the transaction.

Operating Leases You have already accounted for operating leases in previous chapters when recording rent expense and prepaid rent. A rental agreement for a limited time period is also a lease agreement.

Suppose, for example, that Lessee Firm wants to lease a car for a new salesperson. A lease agreement is signed with Lessor Dealer on January 1, 1998, to lease a car for the year for $4,000, payable on December 31, 1998. Typically, a car lease does not transfer title at the end of the term, does not include a bargain purchase price, and does not last for more than 75% of the car's life. In addition, the present value of the lease payments is not 90% of the car's value. Because the lease does not meet any of the specified criteria, it should be presented as an operating lease. Lessee Firm would simply record lease expense, or rent expense, of $4,000 for the year.

Although operating leases are not recorded on the balance sheet by the lessee, they are mentioned in financial statement footnotes. The FASB requires footnote disclosure of the amount of future lease obligations for leases that are considered operating leases. Exhibit 10-6 provides a portion of the footnote from Tommy Hilfiger Corporation's 1995 annual report. The footnote reveals that Tommy Hilfiger has used operating leases as an important source of financing and has significant off-balance-sheet commitments in future periods as a result. An investor might want to add this off-balance-sheet item to the debt on the balance sheet to get a conservative view of the company's obligations.

Capital Leases Capital leases are presented as assets and liabilities by the lessee because they meet one or more of the lease criteria. Suppose that Lessee Firm in the previous example wanted to lease a car for a longer period of time. Assume that on January 1, 1998, Lessee signs a lease agreement with Lessor Dealer to lease a car. The terms of the agreement specify that Lessee will make annual lease payments of $4,000 per year for five years, payable each December 31. Assume also that the lease specifies that at the end of the lease agreement, the title to the car is transferred to Lessee Firm. Lessee must decide how to account for the lease agreement.

EXHIBIT 10-6 Tommy Hilfiger Corporation 1995 Footnote Disclosure of Leases

Commitments and Contingencies

(a) Leases
The Company leases office, warehouse and showroom space, retail stores and office equipment under operating leases which expire not later than 2007. Minimum annual rentals under noncancellable operating leases, excluding operating cost escalations and contingent rental amounts based upon retail sales, are payable as follows:

Fiscal Year Ending March 31,	(In thousands)
1996	$ 3,899
1997	4,571
1998	4,761
1999	4,890
2000	4,681
Thereafter	21,112

Rent expense was $2,282,000, $985,000 and $1,068,000 for the years ended March 31, 1995, 1994, and 1993, respectively.

The contractual arrangement between Lessee Firm and Lessor Dealer is called a lease agreement, but clearly the agreement is much different from a year-to-year lease arrangement. Essentially, Lessee Firm has acquired the right to use the asset for its entire life and does not need to return it to Lessor Dealer. You may call this agreement a lease, but it actually represents a purchase of the asset by Lessee with payments made over time.

The lease should be treated as a capital lease by Lessee because it meets at least one of the four criteria (it meets the first criteria concerning transfer of title). A capital lease must be recorded at its present value by Lessee as an asset and as an obligation. As of January 1, 1998, we must calculate the present value of the annual payments. If we assume an interest rate of 8%, the present value of the payments is $15,972 ($4,000 × an annuity factor of 3.993 from Table 9-4). The first entry is made on the basis of the present value as follows:

Jan. 1	Leased Asset	15,972	
	Lease Obligation		15,972
	To record a capital lease agreement.		

| **Assets** | = | **Liabilities** | + | **Owners' Equity** |
| +**15,972** | | +**15,972** | | |

The Leased Asset account is a long-term asset similar to plant and equipment and represents the fact that Lessee has acquired the right to use and retain the asset. Because the leased asset represents depreciable property, depreciation must be reported for each of the five years of asset use. On December 31, 1998, Lessee records depreciation of $3,194 ($15,972/5 years) as follows, assuming that the straight-line method is adopted:

Dec. 31	Depreciation Expense	3,194	
	Accumulated Depreciation—Leased Assets		3,194
	To record depreciation of leased assets.		

| **Assets** | = | **Liabilities** | + | **Owners' Equity** |
| −**3,194** | | | | −**3,194** |

Depreciation of leased assets is referred to as *amortization* by some firms.

On December 31, Lessee Firm also must make a payment of $4,000 to Lessor Dealer. A portion of each payment represents interest on the obligation (loan), and the remainder represents a reduction of the principal amount. Each payment must be separated into its principal and interest components. Generally, the effective interest method is used for that purpose. An effective interest table can be established using the same concepts as were used to amortize a premium or discount on bonds payable.

Exhibit 10-7 illustrates the effective interest method applied to the Lessee Firm example. Note that the table begins with an obligation amount equal to the present value of the payments of $15,972. Each payment is separated into principal and interest amounts so that the amount of the loan obligation at the end of the lease agreement equals zero. The amortization table is the basis for the accounting entries that are

EXHIBIT 10-7   Lease Amortization: Effective Interest Method of Amortization

DATE	COLUMN 1 LEASE PAYMENT	COLUMN 2 INTEREST EXPENSE	COLUMN 3 REDUCTION OF OBLIGATION	COLUMN 4 LEASE OBLIGATION
		8%	COL. 1 − COL. 2	
1/1/98	—	—	—	$15,972
12/31/98	$4,000	$1,278	$2,722	13,250
12/31/99	4,000	1,060	2,940	10,310
12/31/2000	4,000	825	3,175	7,135
12/31/2001	4,000	571	3,429	3,706
12/31/2002	4,000	294	3,706	−0−

recorded. Exhibit 10-7 indicates that the $4,000 payment in 1998 should be considered as interest of $1,278 (8% of $15,972) and reduction of principal of $2,722. On December 31, 1998, Lessee Firm records the following entry for the annual payment:

Dec. 31	Interest Expense	1,278	
	Lease Obligation	2,722	
	Cash		4,000
	To record annual lease payment.		

Assets	=	**Liabilities**	+	**Owners' Equity**
−4,000		**−2,722**		**−1,278**

Therefore, for a capital lease, Lessee Firm must record both an asset and a liability. The asset is reduced by the process of depreciation. The liability is reduced by reductions of principal using the effective interest method. According to Exhibit 10-7, the total lease obligation as of December 31, 1998, is $13,250. This amount must be separated into current and long-term categories. The portion of the liability that will be paid within one year of the balance sheet should be considered a current liability. Reference to Exhibit 10-7 indicates that the liability will be reduced by $2,940 in 1999, and that amount should be considered a current liability. The remaining amount of the liability, $10,310 ($13,250 − $2,940), should be considered long-term. On the balance sheet as of December 31, 1998, Lessee Firm reports the following balances related to the lease obligation:

Assets:		
Leased Assets	$15,972	
Less: Accumulated Depreciation	3,194	
		$12,778
Current Liabilities:		
Lease Obligation		$ 2,940
Long-Term Liabilities:		
Lease Obligation		$10,310

Notice that the depreciated asset does not equal the present value of the lease obligation. That is not unusual. For example, an automobile often may be completely depreciated but still have payments due on it.

The criteria used to determine whether a lease is an operating or a capital lease have provided a standard accounting treatment for all leases. The accounting for leases in foreign countries generally follows guidelines similar to those used in the United States. The criteria used in foreign countries to determine whether a lease is a capital lease are usually less detailed and less specific, however. As a result, capitalization of leases occurs less frequently in foreign countries than in the United States because of the increased use of judgment necessary in applying the accounting rules.

Deferred Tax

LO 8 Explain deferred taxes and calculate the deferred tax liability.

The financial statements of most major firms include an item titled Deferred Income Tax or Deferred Tax (see Sprint's deferred taxes in Exhibit 10-1 and Coca Cola's in the chapter opening). In most cases, the account appears in the long-term liability section of the balance sheet, and the dollar amount may be large enough to catch the user's attention. For another example, Exhibit 10-8 illustrates the presentation of deferred tax in the 1995 comparative balance sheets of PepsiCo Inc., one of Coca-Cola's chief rivals. The Deferred Income Taxes account is listed immediately after Other Liabilities and for PepsiCo should be considered a long-term liability. At the end of 1995, the firm had more than $1,885 million of deferred tax. The size of that account relative to the other liabilities should raise questions concerning its exact meaning. In fact, deferred income taxes represent one of the most misunderstood aspects of financial statements. In this section, we will attempt to address some of the questions concerning deferred taxes.

EXHIBIT 10-8   PepsiCo Inc. and Subsidiaries 1995 Consolidated Balance Sheets

Consolidated Balance Sheet

(in millions except per share amount)
PepsiCo, Inc. and Subsidiaries
December 30, 1995 and December 31, 1994

	1995	1994
ASSETS		
Current Assets		
Cash and cash equivalents	$ 382	$ 331
Short-term investments, at cost	1,116	1,157
	1,498	1,488
Accounts and notes receivable, less allowance: $150 in 1995 and $151 in 1994	2,407	2,051
Inventories	1,051	970
Prepaid expenses, taxes and other current assets	590	563
Total Current Assets	5,546	5,072
Investments in Unconsolidated Affiliates	1,635	1,295
Property, Plant and Equipment, net	9,870	9,883
Intangible Assets, net	7,584	7,842
Other Assets	797	700
Total Assets	$25,432	$24,792
LIABILITIES AND SHAREHOLDERS' EQUITY		
Current Liabilities		
Accounts payable	$ 1,556	$ 1,452
Accrued compensation and benefits	815	753
Short-term borrowings	706	678
Accrued marketing	469	546
Income taxes payable	387	672
Other current liabilities	1,297	1,169
Total Current Liabilities	5,230	5,270
Long-term Debt	8,509	8,841
Other Liabilities	2,495	1,852
Deferred Income Taxes	1,885	1,973
Shareholders' Equity		
Capital stock, par value 1⅔¢ per share: authorized 1,800 shares, issued 863 shares	14	14
Capital in excess of par value	1,060	935
Retained earnings	8,730	7,739
Currency translation adjustment and other	(808)	(471)
	8,996	8,217
Less: Treasury stock, at cost: 75 shares and 73 shares in 1995 and 1994, respectively	(1,683)	(1,361)
Total Shareholders' Equity	7,313	6,856
Total Liabilities and Shareholders' Equity	$25,432	$24,792

See accompanying Notes to Consolidated Financial Statements.

■ Deferred tax is a liability for PepsiCo.

Deferred tax is an amount that reconciles the differences between the accounting done for purposes of financial reporting to stockholders ("book" purposes) and the accounting done for tax purposes. It may surprise you that U.S. firms are allowed to use accounting methods for financial reporting that differ from those used for tax calculations. The reason is that the Internal Revenue Service defines income and expense differently than does the Financial Accounting Standards Board. As a result, companies tend to use accounting methods that minimize income for tax purposes but maximize income in the annual report to stockholders. This is not true in some foreign countries where financial accounting and tax accounting are more closely aligned. Firms in those countries do not report deferred tax because the difference between methods is not significant.

When differences between financial and tax reporting do occur, we can classify them into two types: permanent and temporary. **Permanent differences** occur when an item is included in the tax calculation and is never included for book purposes—or vice versa, when an item is included for book purposes but not for tax purposes.

For example, the tax laws allow taxpayers to exclude interest on certain investments, usually state and municipal bonds, from their income. These are generally called *tax-exempt bonds*. If a corporation buys tax-exempt bonds, it does not have to declare the interest as income for tax purposes. When the corporation develops its income statement for stockholders (book purposes), however, the interest is included and appears in the Interest Income account. Therefore, tax-exempt interest represents a permanent difference between tax and book calculations.

Temporary differences occur when an item affects both the book and the tax calculations but not in the same time period. A difference caused by depreciation methods is the most common type of temporary difference. In previous chapters you have learned that depreciation may be calculated using a straight-line method or an accelerated method such as the double declining-balance method. Most firms do not use the same depreciation method for book and tax purposes, however. Generally, straight-line depreciation is used for book purposes and an accelerated method is used for tax purposes because accelerated depreciation lowers taxable income—at least in early years—and therefore reduces the tax due. The IRS refers to this accelerated method as the *Modified Accelerated Cost Recovery System (MACRS)*. It is similar to other accelerated depreciation methods in that it allows the firm to take larger depreciation deductions for tax purposes in the early years of the asset and smaller deductions in the later years. Over the life of the depreciable asset, the total depreciation using straight-line is equal to that using MACRS. Therefore, this difference is an example of a temporary difference between book and tax reporting.

The Deferred Tax account is used to reconcile the differences between the accounting for book purposes and for tax purposes. It is important to distinguish between permanent and temporary differences because the FASB has ruled that not all differences should affect the Deferred Tax account. The Deferred Tax account should reflect temporary differences but not items that are permanent differences between book accounting and tax reporting.[3]

Example of Deferred Tax   Assume that Startup Firm begins business on January 1, 1998. During 1998 the firm has sales of $6,000 and has no expenses other than depreciation and income tax at the rate of 40%. Startup has depreciation on only one asset. That asset was purchased on January 1, 1998, for $10,000 and has a four-year life. Startup has decided to use the straight-line depreciation method for financial reporting purposes. Startup's accountants have chosen to use MACRS for tax purposes, however, resulting in $4,000 depreciation in 1998 and a decline of $1,000 per year thereafter.

The depreciation amounts for each of the four years for Startup's asset are as follows:

YEAR	TAX DEPRECIATION	BOOK DEPRECIATION	DIFFERENCE
1998	$ 4,000	$ 2,500	$1,500
1999	3,000	2,500	500
2000	2,000	2,500	(500)
2001	1,000	2,500	(1,500)
Totals	$10,000	$10,000	$ –0–

Startup's tax calculation for 1998 is based on the accelerated depreciation of $4,000, as follows:

[3]*Statement of Financial Accounting Standards No. 109,* "Accounting for Income Taxes" (Stamford, Conn.: FASB, 1992).

Sales	$6,000
Depreciation Expense	4,000
Taxable Income	$2,000
× Tax Rate	40%
Tax Payable to IRS	$ 800

For the year 1998, Startup owes $800 of tax to the Internal Revenue Service. This amount is ordinarily recorded as tax payable until the time it is remitted.

Startup wants also to develop an income statement to send to the stockholders. What amount should be shown as tax expense on the income statement? You may guess that the Tax Expense account on the income statement should reflect $800 because that is the amount to be paid to the IRS. That is not true in this case, however. Remember that the tax payable amount was calculated using the depreciation method that Startup chose for tax purposes. The income statement must be calculated using the straight-line method which Startup uses for book purposes. Therefore, Startup's income statement for 1998 appears as follows:

Sales	$6,000
Depreciation Expense	2,500
Income Before Tax	$3,500
Tax Expense (40%)	1,400
Net Income	$2,100

Startup must make the following accounting entry to record the amount of tax expense and tax payable for 1998:

Dec. 31	Tax Expense	1,400	
	Tax Payable		800
	Deferred Tax		600
	To record income tax for the year 1998.		

Assets	=	**Liabilities**	+	**Owners' Equity**
		+800		−1,400
		+600		

The Deferred Tax account is a balance sheet account. A credit balance in it reflects the fact that Startup has received a tax benefit by recording accelerated depreciation, in effect delaying the ultimate obligation to the IRS. To be sure, the amount of deferred tax still represents a liability of Startup. The Deferred Tax account balance of $600 represents the amount of the 1998 temporary difference of $1,500 times the tax rate of 40% ($1,500 × 40% = $600).

What can we learn from the Startup example? First, when you see a firm's income statement, the amount listed as tax expense does not represent the amount of cash paid to the government for taxes. Accrual accounting procedures require that the tax expense amount be calculated using the accounting methods chosen for book purposes.

Second, when you see a firm's balance sheet, the amount in the Deferred Tax account reflects all of the temporary differences between the accounting methods chosen for tax and book purposes. The accounting and financial communities are severely divided on whether the Deferred Tax account represents a "true" liability. For one thing, many investment analysts do not view it as a real liability because they have noticed that it continues to grow year after year. Others look at it as a bookkeeping item that is simply there to balance the books. The FASB has taken the stance that deferred tax is an amount that results in a future obligation and meets the definition of a liability. The controversy concerning deferred taxes is likely to continue for many years.

Pensions

Many large firms establish pension plans to provide income to employees after their retirement. These pension plans often cover a large number of employees and involve millions of dollars. The large amounts in pension funds have become a major force in our

LO 9 Understand the meaning of a pension obligation and the effect of pensions on the long-term liability category of the balance sheet.

economy, representing billions of dollars in stocks and bonds. In fact, pension funds are among the major "institutional investors" that have an enormous economic impact on our stock and bond exchanges.

Pensions are complex financial arrangements that involve difficult estimates and projections developed by specialists and actuaries. Pension plans also involve very difficult accounting issues requiring a wide range of estimates and assumptions about future cash flows.

We will concern ourselves with two accounting questions related to pensions. First, the employer must report the cost of the pension plan as an expense over some time period. How should that expense be reported? Second, the employer's financial statements should reflect a measure of the liability associated with a pension plan. What is the liability for future pension amounts, and how should it be recorded or disclosed? Our discussion will begin with the recording of pension expense.

ACCOUNTING FOR YOUR DECISIONS

You Are the Personnel Manager

A new employee comes to you and asks why your company does not offer a pension. You explain to her that instead of offering a pension, the company offers a 401(k) plan, which allows her to contribute 10 percent of her salary to a savings plan which the company matches. What is the difference between this 401(k) plan and a traditional pension?

ANS: In a traditional pension plan, the amount paid to the employee upon retirement is "defined" according to the employees' age, number of years the employee works for the company, or salary level. With a 401(k) plan, the amount that will be paid at retirement is not defined or guaranteed. The employee will receive whatever amounts are accumulated in the savings account at the time of retirement. Increasingly, companies are shifting to a plan such as a 401(k) and away from a traditional pension plan because they prefer not to be responsible for making fixed payments for life to retirees. Instead, they would rather help employees build their own nest eggs.

Pensions on the Income Statement   Most pension plans are of the following form:

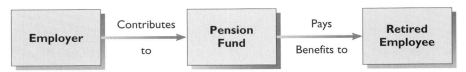

Normally, the employer must make payments to the pension fund at least annually, perhaps more frequently. This is often referred to as *funding the pension* or as the **funding payment**. *Funding* simply means that the employer has contributed cash to the pension fund. The pension fund is usually administered by a trustee, often a bank or other financial institution. The trustee must invest the employer's funds so that they earn interest and dividends sufficient to pay amounts owed to retired employees.

Our first accounting question concerns the amount that should be shown by the employer as pension expense. This is another example of the difference between cash-basis accounting and accrual accounting. The cash paid as the funding payment is not the same as the expense. When using the accrual basis of accounting, we must consider the amount of pension cost incurred, not the amount paid. Pension expense should be accrued in the period that the employee earns the benefits, regardless of the amount paid to the pension trustee. The amount expensed and the amount paid involve two separate decisions.

The FASB has specified the methods that should be used to calculate the amount of annual pension expense to record on the employer's income statement.[4] The accountant must determine the costs of the separate components of the pension and total them to arrive at the amount of pension expense. The components include the employee's service during the current year, the interest cost, the earnings on pension investments, and other factors. The details of those calculations are beyond our discussion.

[4]*Statement of Financial Accounting Standards No. 87,* "Employers' Accounting for Pension Plans" (Stamford, Conn.: FASB, 1985).

To illustrate, suppose that Employer Firm has calculated its annual pension expense to be $80,000 for 1998. Also suppose that Employer has determined that it will make a funding payment of $60,000 to the pension fund. On the basis of those decisions, Employer should make the following accounting entry for the year:

Dec. 31	Pension Expense	80,000	
	Cash		60,000
	Accrued Pension Cost		20,000
	To record annual pension expense and funding payment.		

Assets	=	Liabilities	+	Owners' Equity
−60,000		**+20,000**		**−80,000**

The Pension Expense account is an income statement account and is reflected on Employer's 1998 income statement.

Pensions on the Balance Sheet The Accrued Pension Cost account in the preceding example is a balance sheet account. The account could represent an asset or a liability, depending on whether the amount expensed is more or less than the amount of the funding payment. If the amount expensed is less than the amount paid, it is reported by Employer Firm as an asset and labeled as Prepaid Pension Cost. Normally, the amount expensed is greater than the amount paid, as in the example here. In that case, the Accrued Pension Cost is reported by Employer Firm as a long-term liability.

But what is the meaning of the Accrued Pension Cost account? Is it really a liability? It certainly is not a measure of the amount that is owed to employees at the time of retirement. In fact, the only true meaning that can be given to the account is to say that it is the difference between the amount expensed and the amount funded.[5] In that regard, the Accrued Pension Cost account is inadequate in determining a firm's liability to its employees for future retirement benefits. The FASB requires a great deal of footnote information for pension plans. This footnote section can be used to develop a clearer picture of the status of a firm's pension obligation.

Pension Footnote Information Readers of financial statements are often interested in the *funding status* of pension plans. This indicates whether sufficient assets are available in the pension fund to cover the amounts to be paid to employees as retirement benefits. We will use the footnote disclosures of an actual firm to illustrate the use of pension information.

Exhibit 10-9 presents portions of the 1995 pension footnote for Sprint. Sprint is a large company with thousands of employees who are covered by the company's pension

EXHIBIT 10-9 Sprint's Pension Footnote for 1995

The funded status and amounts recognized in the Consolidated Balance Sheets for the plan, as of December 31, are as follows:

(in millions)	1995	1994
Actuarial present value of benefit obligations		
Vested benefit obligation	$(1,705.1)	$(1,338.1)
Accumulated benefit obligation	(1,866.0)	(1,459.5)
Projected benefit obligation	(1,962.7)	(1,547.3)
Plan assets at fair value	2,331.3	1,950.2
Plan assets in excess of the projected benefit obligation	$ 368.6	$ 402.9

[5]Some pension plans that are underfunded may be required to report an additional amount as a liability. This is referred to as the *minimum liability provision*. Refer to *SFAS No. 87* for more detail.

plan. Analysts who follow the telecommunications industry must assess whether Sprint's pension is adequate for its employees. The amounts on the balance sheet (refer to Exhibit 10-1) give some indication about the status of the plan, but a more complete picture is provided in the company's footnotes. Several items in the footnote need to be defined. First, Sprint has disclosed the amount of *plan assets* at fair value. This is a measure of the total dollar amount of assets that has been accumulated in the pension fund. The footnote indicates that as of year-end 1995, Sprint had assets of $2,331.3 million. Second, there are two measures of the amount of pension benefits owed to employees at the time of retirement. One measure is referred to as the **accumulated benefit obligation (ABO).** This is a measure of the amount of pension benefits that would be payable to employees if they were to retire at their existing salary levels. The footnote indicates that as of year-end 1995, Sprint had an accumulated benefit obligation of $1,866.0 million.

Another measure provides a higher estimate of that obligation. The **projected benefit obligation (PBO)** is a measure of the amount of pension benefits payable to employees if an assumption is made concerning the future salary increases that will be earned by the employees. This is probably a more realistic view of the amount of the obligation to employees, but it is a less objective number because of the difficulty in estimating future salary increases for employees. The footnote indicates that as of year-end 1995, Sprint had a projected benefit obligation of $1,962.7 million.

To determine the funding status of the pension plan, we must compare the amount of plan assets with the ABO and PBO. At the end of 1995, Sprint had pension plan assets of $2,331.3 million, which was $368.6 million higher than the PBO and $465.3 million higher than the ABO. When the amount of assets exceeds the amount of the obligation, the plan is referred to as *overfunded,* indicating that the pension plan is healthy and well managed. Overfunding is also an example of an "off-balance-sheet" asset that investors use to assess the desirability of a company's stock.

Sprint's pension plans certainly appear to be quite healthy, but not all firms are as fortunate. There have been many press reports of firms whose pension plans are seriously *underfunded* and for which it is quite questionable whether sufficient assets are available to pay impending retirement benefits. Such underfunded plans must be considered an off-balance-sheet liability by investors or creditors in assessing the company's health.

Users of the financial statements of U.S. firms are somewhat fortunate because the disclosure of pensions on the balance sheet and in the footnotes is quite extensive. The accounting for pensions by firms outside the United States varies considerably. Many countries do not require firms to accrue pension costs, and the expense is reported only when paid to retirees. Furthermore, within the statements and footnotes, there is much less disclosure, making an assessment of the funding status of pensions much more difficult.

ACCOUNTING FOR YOUR DECISIONS
You Review Your Father's Pension Plan

Your father, after working for a small company for 20 years, is considering retirement. He has asked your help in reviewing the funding status of the company's pension plan. Why is this important? Where would you find the information?

ANS: The funding status shows whether enough assets are available to pay pension retirement benefits to your father. When the amount of the pension plan assets are greater than the amount of the pension plan liability, then the fund is considered "overfunded" and enough will be on hand to pay the pension benefits. The information about a pension' funding status is normally found in the pension footnote disclosures at the end of the company's annual report.

Postretirement Benefits

Pensions represent a benefit paid to employees after their retirement. In addition to pensions, other benefits may be paid to employees after their retirement. For example, many firms promise to pay a portion of retirees' health care costs. The accounting question is whether postretirement benefits should be considered an expense when paid or during the period that the employee worked for the firm.

A few years ago, most firms treated postretirement benefits as an expense when they were paid to the retiree. It was widely believed that costs such as those for health care after retirement were too uncertain to be accrued as an expense and that such costs did not meet the definition of a liability and thus did not merit recording. The result of this expense-as-you-pay accounting was that firms had an obligation that was not recorded as a liability. As health care costs began to escalate, this unrecorded—and often undisclosed—cost became a concern for many firms as well as for stockholders, analysts, and employees.

The FASB has modified the accounting for other postemployment benefits to be consistent with pension costs. Under the matching principle, postretirement costs must now be accrued as an expense during the period that the employee helps the firm generate revenues and thus *earns* the benefits. The accountant must determine the costs of the separate components of postretirement benefits and total them to calculate the amount of the expense. The amount of the expense is reflected on the income statement in the Postretirement Expense account. The balance sheet should normally reflect the Accrued Postretirement Cost account. That account should be classified as a liability in the long-term liability category; it indicates the employer's obligation to present and future retirees.

The dollar amount of the liability represented by postretirement obligations is very large for many companies. For example, in 1995 Sprint's obligation to its employees for these retirement costs was $759 million (in addition to its pension plan amounts, disclosed in Exhibit 10-9).

There is still much controversy concerning the accounting for postretirement costs. Many firms object to the accounting requirements because of the uncertainty involved in measuring an obligation that extends far into the future. They also object because the requirements result in reduced profits on the income statement and huge liabilities on the balance sheet. Interestingly, this accounting rule had little impact on the stock market because the investment community already knew the magnitude of the postretirement obligations.

Analyzing Debt to Assess a Firm's Solvency

Long-term liabilities are a component of the "capital structure" of the company and are included in the calculation of the debt-to-equity ratio:

$$\text{Debt-to-Equity Ratio} = \frac{\text{Total Liabilities}}{\text{Total Stockholders' Equity}}$$

For example, refer to the liability category of Sprint's balance sheet given in Exhibit 10-1. Sprint's total liabilities are $10,521 million (current liabilities of $5,142 + long-term debt of $3,253 + deferred credits and other liabilities of $2,126). Its total stockholders' equity is $4,642 million. Therefore, the debt-to-equity ratio is $10,521/$4,642 or 2.27, which means that Sprint has 2.27 times as much debt as equity, a situation that is not uncommon for companies in the telecommunications industry.

Most investors would prefer to see equity rather than debt on the balance sheet. Debt, and its interest charges, is a fixed obligation that must be repaid in a finite period of time. In contrast, equity never has to be repaid, and the dividends that are declared on it are optional. Stock investors view debt as a claim against the company that must be satisfied before they get a return on their money.

Other ratios used to measure the degree of debt obligation include the times interest earned ratio and the debt service coverage ratio:

$$\text{Times Interest Earned Ratio} = \frac{\text{Income before Interest and Tax}}{\text{Interest Expense}}$$

$$\text{Debt Service Coverage Ratio} = \frac{\text{Cash Flow from Operations before Interest and Tax}}{\text{Interest and Principal Payments}}$$

FROM CONCEPT TO PRACTICE 10.2

READING BEN & JERRY'S BALANCE SHEET   Calculate the 1994 and 1995 debt-to-equity ratios for Ben & Jerry's. Did 1995's debt-to-equity ratio go up or down from 1994's?

Lenders want to be sure that borrowers can pay the interest and repay the principal on a loan. Both of the preceding ratios reflect the degree to which a company can make its debt payments out of current cash flow.

How Long-Term Liabilities Affect the Statement of Cash Flows

LO 10 Explain the effects that transactions involving long-term liabilities have on the statement of cash flows.

Exhibit 10-10 indicates the impact that long-term liabilities have on a company's cash flow and their placement on the cash flow statement.

Most long-term liabilities are related to a firm's financing activities. Therefore, the change in the balance of each long-term liability account should be reflected in the Financing Activities category of the statement of cash flows. The decrease in a long-term liability account indicates that cash has been used to pay the liability. Therefore, in the cash flow statement, a decrease in a long-term liability account should appear as a subtraction or reduction. The increase in a long-term liability account indicates that the firm has obtained additional cash via a long-term obligation. Therefore, an increase in a long-term liability account should appear in the cash flow statement as an addition.

The cash flow statement of Coca-Cola Company is presented in Exhibit 10-11. Note that the Financing Activities category contains two large items related to long-term liabilities. In 1995 long-term debt was issued for $754 million and is an addition to cash. This indicates that Coca-Cola increased its cash position by borrowings. Second, the payment of debt is listed as a deduction of $212 million. This indicates that Coca-Cola paid long-term liabilities resulting in a reduction of cash.

Although most long-term liabilities are reflected in the financing category of the statement of cash flows, there are exceptions. The most notable exception involves the Deferred Tax account. The change in this account is reflected in the Operating Activities category of the statement of cash flows. This presentation is necessary because the Deferred Tax account is related to an operating item, income tax expense. For example, in Exhibit 10-11, Coca-Cola listed $157 million in the operating category of the 1995 statement of cash flows. This indicates that $157 million that was recorded as expense was not paid out in cash but was *deferred* to a future period. Therefore, the amount is a positive amount in or an addition to the operating category.

Review Problem

The following items pertain to the liabilities of Brent Foods. You may assume that Brent Foods began business on January 1, 1998, and therefore the beginning balance of all accounts was zero.

EXHIBIT 10-10	Long-Term Liabilities on the Statement of Cash Flows

Item	Statement of Cash Flows	
	Operating Activities	
	Net income	xxx
Increase in deferred tax		+
Decrease in deferred tax		−
	Investing Activities	
	Financing Activities	
Increase in liability		+
Decrease in liability		−

a. On January 1, 1998, Brent Foods issued bonds with a face value of $50,000. The bonds are due in five years and have a face interest rate of 10%. The market rate on January 1 for similar bonds was 12%. The bonds pay interest annually each December 31. Brent has chosen to use the effective interest method of amortization for any premium or discount on the bonds.

b. On December 31, Brent Foods signed a lease agreement with Cordova Leasing. The agreement requires Brent to make annual lease payments of $3,000 per year for four years, with the first payment due on December 31, 1999. The agreement stipulates that ownership of the property is transferred to Brent at the end of the four-year lease. Assume that an 8% interest rate is used for the leasing transaction.

c. Brent has calculated the amount of expense on its employee pension plan to be $40,000. The company wants to make a funding payment of $30,000 to the pension fund on December 31, 1998.

EXHIBIT 10-11	Coca-Cola Company and Subsidiaries 1995 Consolidated Statements of Cash Flows

The Coca-Cola Company and Subsidiaries

Consolidated Statements of Cash Flows

Year Ended December 31, (In millions)	1995	1994	1993
Operating Activities			
Net income	$ 2,986	$ 2,554	$ 2,176
Transition effect of change in accounting principle	—	—	12
Depreciation and amortization	454	411	360
Deferred income taxes	157	58	(62)
Equity income, net of dividends	(25)	(4)	(35)
Foreign currency adjustments	(23)	(6)	9
Gains on sales of assets	—	—	(84)
Other noncash items	(29)	41	78
Net change in operating assets and liabilities	(405)	129	54
Net cash provided by operating activities	3,115	3,183	2,508
Investing Activities			
Additions to finance subsidiary receivables	(144)	(94)	(177)
Collections of finance subsidiary receivables	46	50	44
Acquisitions and investments, principally bottling companies	(338)	(311)	(611)
Purchases of securities	(190)	(201)	(245)
Proceeds from disposals of investments and other assets	580	299	690
Purchases of property, plant and equipment	(937)	(878)	(800)
Proceeds from disposals of property, plant and equipment	44	109	312
Other investing activities	(74)	(11)	(98)
Net cash used in investing activities	(1,013)	(1,037)	(885)
Net cash provided by operations after reinvestment	2,102	2,146	1,623
Financing Activities			
Issuances of debt	754	491	445
Payments of debt	(212)	(154)	(567)
Issuances of stock	86	69	145
Purchases of stock for treasury	(1,796)	(1,192)	(680)
Dividends	(1,110)	(1,006)	(883)
Net cash used in financing activities	(2,278)	(1,792)	(1,540)
Effect of Exchange Rate Changes on Cash and Cash Equivalents	(43)	34	(41)
Cash and Cash Equivalents			
Net increase (decrease) during the year	(219)	388	42
Balance at beginning of year	1,386	998	956
Balance at end of year	$ 1,167	$ 1,386	$ 998

See Notes to Consolidated Financial Statements.

■ Changes in long-term debt generally affect the financing activities category.

d. Brent must calculate the correct amount of deferred tax for 1998. The only difference between the accounting methods chosen for tax purposes and the accounting methods used for financial reporting purposes concerns depreciation on an asset purchased January 1, 1998, for $120,000. For tax purposes, Brent is allowed to depreciate the asset on a straight-line basis over five years. For financial reporting purposes, Brent wants to use straight-line depreciation over eight years. You may assume that Brent pays income tax at the rate of 40%.

e. On January 1, 1999, Brent redeems its bonds payable at the specified redemption price of 101. Because this item occurs in 1999, it does not affect the balance sheet prepared for year-end 1998.

Required

1. Record the accounting entries necessary on December 31, 1998, to reflect the information in items a, b, and c.

2. For item d, calculate the amount of the Deferred Tax account on the year-end balance sheet. You do not need to develop an accounting entry.

3. Develop the long-term liability section of Brent Foods' balance sheet as of December 31, 1998, based on items a through d. You do not need to consider the footnotes that accompany the balance sheet.

4. Consider the following questions. Would the company prefer to treat the lease in item b as an operating lease? Why? Also, in item d why would the company prefer a shorter depreciation period for tax purposes than for financial reporting (book) purposes?

5. Calculate the gain or loss on the bond redemption for item e and indicate how it should be reported on the 1999 income statement.

Solution to Review Problem

1. a. The issue price of the bonds on January 1 must be calculated as the present value of the interest payments and the present value of the principal as follows:

$ 5,000 × 3.605	$18,025
$50,000 × 0.567	28,350
Issue price	$46,375

The amount of the discount is

$$\$50,000 - \$46,375 = \$3,625.$$

The following is the entry on December 31, 1998, to record interest and to amortize discount:

Dec. 31	Interest Expense	5,565	
	Cash		5,000
	Discount on Bonds Payable		565
	To record interest and amortize discount.		

Assets	=	**Liabilities**	+	**Owners' Equity**
−5,000		**+565**		**−5,565**

The interest expense is calculated using the effective interest method by multiplying the carrying value of the bonds times the market rate of interest ($46,375 × 12%).

Brent must show two accounts in the long-term liability category of the balance sheet: Bonds Payable of $50,000 and Discount on Bonds Payable of $3,060 ($3,625 less $565 amortized).

b. The lease meets the criteria to be a capital lease. Brent must report the lease as an asset and report the obligation for lease payments as a liability. The transaction should be reported at the present value of the lease payments, $9,936 (computed by multiplying $3,000 times the annuity factor of 3.312). The accounting entry should be as follows:

Dec. 31   Leased Asset   9,936
　　　　　　　　Lease Obligation   9,936
　　　　　　To record lease as a capital lease.

$$\textbf{Assets} \quad = \quad \textbf{Liabilities} \quad + \quad \textbf{Owners' Equity}$$
$$\textbf{+9,936} \qquad \textbf{+9,936}$$

Because the lease agreement was signed on December 31, 1998, it is not necessary to amortize the Lease Obligation account in 1998. The account should be stated in the long-term liability section of Brent's balance sheet at $9,936.

c. The difference between the amount of pension expense and the amount of pension funding should be considered as accrued pension cost. The following is Brent's accounting entry to record pension amounts:

Dec. 31   Pension Expense   40,000
　　　　　　　　Cash   30,000
　　　　　　　　Accrued Pension Cost   10,000
　　　　　　To record the annual pension expense and payment.

$$\textbf{Assets} \quad = \quad \textbf{Liabilities} \quad + \quad \textbf{Owners' Equity}$$
$$\textbf{-30,000} \qquad \textbf{+10,000} \qquad \textbf{-40,000}$$

The Accrued Pension Cost account should be stated in the long-term liability category of Brent's balance sheet.

2. The amount of deferred tax for 1998 is the difference between the amount of depreciation calculated for tax purposes ($120,000/5 years = $24,000) and the amount calculated for financial reporting purposes ($120,000/8 years = $15,000) times the tax rate of 40%. The Deferred Tax account balance therefore is

$$(\$24{,}000 - \$15{,}000) \times 40\% = \$3{,}600.$$

The Deferred Tax account should be reported in the long-term liability section of the balance sheet.

3. The long-term liability category of Brent's balance sheet for December 31, 1998, on the basis of items a to d is as follows:

BRENT FOODS
PARTIAL BALANCE SHEET
AS OF DECEMBER 31, 1998

Long-term liabilities:		
Bonds payable	$50,000	
Less: Unamortized discount on bonds payable	3,060	$46,940
Lease obligation		9,936
Deferred tax		3,600
Accrued pension cost		10,000
Total long-term liabilities		$70,476

4. The company would prefer that the lease be an operating lease because it would not have to report the asset or liability on the balance sheet. This off-balance-sheet financing may give a more favorable impression of the company.

　　The company would prefer a shorter life for tax purposes because this allows taxes to be reduced in the early years of the asset's life. At the same time, a longer life for book purposes allows the firm to report a higher income to the stockholders and investors in those years.

5. Brent must calculate the loss on the bond redemption as the difference between the carrying value of the bonds ($46,940) and the redemption price ($50,000 × 1.01). The amount of the loss is

$$\$50{,}500 - \$46{,}940 = \$3{,}560 \text{ loss on redemption.}$$

The loss should be reported as an extraordinary item on the 1999 income statement.

Chapter Highlights

1. **LO 1** Balance sheets generally have two categories of liabilities: current liabilities and long-term liabilities. Long-term liabilities are obligations that will not be satisfied within one year.

2. **LO 2** The terms of a bond payable are given in the bond certificate. The denomination of a bond is its face value. The interest rate stated in the bond certificate is referred to as the *face rate* or *stated rate of interest.* Term bonds all have the same due date. Serial bonds are not all due on the same date. Convertible bonds can be converted into common stock by the bondholders. Callable bonds may be redeemed or retired before their due date.

3. **LO 3** The issue price of a bond is the present value of the cash flows that the bond will provide to the investor. To determine the price, you must calculate the present values of the annuity of interest payments and of the principal amount. The present values must be calculated at the market rate of interest.

4. **LO 4** A bond sells at a discount or premium, depending on the relationship of the face rate to the market rate of interest. If the face rate exceeds the market rate, a bond is issued at a premium. If the face rate is less than the market rate, it will be issued at a discount.

5. **LO 5** Premiums or discounts must be amortized by transferring a portion of the premium or the discount each period to interest expense. The effective interest method of amortization reduces the balance of the premium or discount such that the effective interest rate on the bond is constant over its life.

6. **LO 5** The carrying value of the bond equals the face value plus unamortized premium or minus unamortized discount.

7. **LO 6** When bonds are redeemed before their due date, a gain or loss on redemption results. The gain or loss is the difference between the bond carrying value at the date of redemption and the redemption price. The gain or loss is treated as an extraordinary item on the income statement.

8. **LO 7** A lease, a contractual arrangement between two parties, allows the lessee the right to use property in exchange for making payments to the lessor.

9. **LO 7** There are two major categories of lease agreements: operating and capital. The lessee does not report an operating lease as an asset and does not present the

obligation to make payments as a liability. Capital leases are reported as assets and liabilities by the lessee. Leases are reported as capital leases if they meet one or more of four criteria.

10. **LO 7** Capital lease assets must be depreciated by the lessee over the life of the lease agreement. Capital lease payments must be separated into interest expense and reduction of principal using the effective interest method.

11. **LO 8** There are many differences between the accounting for tax purposes and for financial reporting purposes. Permanent differences occur when an item affects one calculation but never affects the other. Temporary differences affect both book and tax calculations but not in the same time period.

12. **LO 8** The amount of tax payable is calculated using the accounting method chosen for tax purposes. The amount of tax expense is calculated using the accounting method chosen for financial reporting purposes. The Deferred Tax account reconciles the differences between tax expense and tax payable. It reflects all of the temporary differences times the tax rate. Deferred taxes is a controversial item on the balance sheet, raising questions as to whether it is a true liability.

13. **LO 9** Pensions represent an obligation to compensate retired employees for service performed while employed.

14. **LO 9** Pension expense is presented on the income statement and is calculated on the basis of several complex components that have been specified by the FASB.

15. **LO 9** Pension expense does not represent the amount of cash paid by the employer to the pension fund. The cash payment is referred to as the *funding payment.* The Accrued Pension account is recorded as the difference between the amount of pension expense and the amount of the funding.

16. **LO 9** The required footnote information on pensions can be used to evaluate the funding status of a firm's pension plan. If the amount of assets in the pension fund exceeds the pension obligation, the fund is considered to be overfunded, generally indicating that it is healthy and well managed. An overfunded plan is an example of an "off-balance-sheet" asset that an investor can count toward the value of the company's stock.

17. **LO 10** Long-term liabilities represent methods of financing. Therefore, changes in the balances of long-term liability accounts should be reflected in the Financing Activities category of the statement of cash flows.

Key Terms Quiz

Read each definition below and then write the number of that definition in the blank beside the appropriate term it defines. The solution appears at the end of the chapter.

____	Long-term liability	____	Face value
____	Debenture bonds	____	Serial bonds
____	Callable bonds	____	Face rate of interest
____	Market rate of interest	____	Bond issue price
____	Premium on bonds	____	Discount on bonds
____	Effective interest method of amortization	____	Carrying value
____	Gain or loss on redemption	____	Operating lease
____	Capital lease	____	Deferred tax
____	Permanent difference	____	Temporary difference
____	Pension	____	Funding payment
____	Accrued pension cost	____	Accumulated benefit obligation (ABO)
____	Projected benefit obligation (PBO)		

1. The principal amount of the bond as stated on the bond certificate.

2. Bonds that do not all have the same due date. A portion of the bonds comes due each time period.

3. The interest rate stated on the bond certificate. It is also called the *nominal* or *coupon rate.*

4. The total of the present value of the cash flows produced by a bond. It is calculated as the present value of the annuity of interest payments plus the present value of the principal.

5. An obligation that will not be satisfied within one year.

6. The excess of the issue price over the face value of bonds. It occurs when the face rate on the bonds exceeds the market rate.

7. Bonds that are backed by the general creditworthiness of the issuer and are not backed by specific collateral.

8. The excess of the face value of bonds over the issue price. It occurs when the market rate on the bonds exceeds the face rate.

9. Bonds that may be redeemed or retired before their specified due date.

10. The process of transferring a portion of premium or discount to interest expense. This method transfers an amount resulting in a constant effective interest rate.

11. The face value of a bond plus the amount of unamortized premium or minus the amount of unamortized discount.

12. The interest rate that bondholders could obtain by investing in other bonds that are similar to the issuing firm's bonds.

13. The difference between the carrying value and the redemption price at the time bonds are redeemed. This amount is presented as an income statement account.

14. A measure of the amount owed to employees for pensions if estimates of future salary increases are incorporated.

15. A lease that does not meet any of four criteria and is not recorded by the lessee.

16. A payment made by the employer to the pension fund or its trustee.

17. A lease that meets one or more of four criteria and is recorded as an asset by the lessee.

18. A difference between the accounting for tax purposes and the accounting for financial reporting purposes. This type of difference affects both book and tax calculations but not in the same time period.

19. The account used to reconcile the difference between the amount recorded as income tax expense and the amount that is payable as income tax.

20. A difference between the accounting for tax purposes and the accounting for financial reporting purposes. This type of difference occurs when an item affects one set of calculations but never affects the other set.

21. An obligation to pay retired employees as compensation for service performed while employed.

22. An account that represents the difference between the amount of pension recorded as an expense and the amount of the funding payment made to the pension fund.

23. A measure of the amount owed to employees for pensions if the employees retired at their existing salary levels.

Alternate Terms

Accumulated Benefit Obligation ABO.

Bond Face Value Bond par value.

Bonds Payable Notes payable.

Bond Retirement Extinguishment of bonds.

Carrying Value of Bond Book value of bond.

Effective Interest Amortization Interest method of amortization.

Face Rate of Interest Stated rate or nominal rate or coupon rate of interest.

Long-Term Liabilities Noncurrent liabilities.

Market Rate of Interest Yield or effective rate of interest.

Postretirement Costs Other postemployment benefits.

Projected Benefit Obligation PBO.

Redemption Price Reacquisition price.

Temporary Difference Timing difference.

Questions

1. Which interest rate, the face rate or the market rate, should be used when calculating the issue price of a bond? Why?

2. What is the tax advantage that companies experience when bonds are issued instead of stock?

3. Does the issuance of bonds at a premium indicate that the face rate is higher or lower than the market rate of interest?

4. How does the effective interest method of amortization result in a constant rate of interest?

5. What is the meaning of the following sentence: "Amortization affects the amount of interest expense"? How does amortization of premium affect the amount of interest expense? How does amortization of discount affect the amount of interest expense?

6. Does amortization of a premium increase or decrease the bond carrying value? Does amortization of a discount increase or decrease the bond carrying value?

7. Is there always a gain or loss when bonds are redeemed? How is the gain or loss calculated?

8. Why is it important to show gains or losses on bond redemption separately on the income statement as an extraordinary item?

9. What are the reasons that not all leases are accounted for in the same manner? Do you think it would be possible to develop a new accounting rule that would treat all leases in the same manner?

10. What is the meaning of the term *off-balance-sheet financing?* Why do some firms want to engage in off-balance-sheet transactions?

11. What are the effects on the financial statements if a lease is considered an operating rather than a capital lease?

12. Should depreciation be reported on leased assets? If so, over what period of time should depreciation occur?

13. Why do firms have a Deferred Tax account? Where should that account be shown on the financial statements?

14. How can you determine whether an item should reflect a permanent or a temporary difference when calculating the deferred tax amount?

15. Does the amount of income tax expense presented on the income statement represent the amount of tax actually paid? Why or why not?

16. When an employer has a pension plan for employees, what information is shown on the financial statements concerning the pension plan?

17. How can you determine whether a pension plan is overfunded or underfunded?

18. What is the difference between the two measures of a pension plan's obligation, the projected benefit obligation and the accumulated benefit obligation?

19. Do you agree with this statement: "All liabilities could be legally enforced in a court of law"?

Exercises

LO 2 **Exercise 10-1** Relationships

The following components are computed annually when a bond is issued for other than its face value:

- Cash interest payment
- Interest expense
- Amortization of discount/premium
- Carrying value of bond

Required

State whether each component will increase (I), decrease (D), or remain constant (C) as the bond approaches maturity, given the following situations:

1. Issued at a discount.

2. Issued at a premium.

LO 3 **Exercise 10-2** Issue Price

Youngblood Inc. plans to issue $600,000 face value bonds with a stated interest rate of 8%. They will mature in 10 years. Interest will be paid semiannually. At the date of issuance, assume the market rate is (a) 8%, (b) 6%, and (c) 10%.

Required

For each market interest rate, answer the following questions:

1. What is the amount due at maturity?

2. How much cash interest will be paid every six months?

3. At what price will the bond be issued?

LO 3 **Exercise 10-3** Issue Price

The following terms relate to independent bond issues:

a. 500 bonds; $1,000 face value; 8% stated rate; 5 years; annual interest payments.

b. 500 bonds; $1,000 face value; 8% stated rate; 5 years; semiannual interest payments.

c. 800 bonds; $1,000 face value; 6% stated rate; 10 years; semiannual interest payments.

d. 2,000 bonds; $500 face value; 12% stated rate; 15 years; semiannual interest payments.

Required

Assuming the market rate of interest is 10%, calculate the selling price for each bond issue.

LO 4 **Exercise 10-4** Impact of Two Bond Alternatives

Yung Chong Company wants to issue 100 bonds, $1,000 face value, in January. The bonds will have a 10-year life and pay interest annually. The market rate of interest on January 1 will be 9%. Yung Chong is considering two alternative bond issues: (a) bonds with a face rate of 8% and (b) bonds with a face rate of 10%.

Required

1. Could the company save money by issuing bonds with an 8% face rate? If it chooses alternative (a), what would be the interest cost as a percentage?

2. Could the company benefit by issuing bonds with a 10% face rate? If it chooses alternative (b), what would be the interest cost as a percentage?

LO 6 **Exercise 10-5** Redemption of Bonds

Spelling Corporation issued $75,000 face value bonds at a discount of $2,500. The bonds contain a call price of 103. Spelling decides to redeem the bonds early when the unamortized discount is $1,750.

Required

1. Calculate Spelling Corporation's gain or loss on the early redemption of the bonds.

2. Describe how the gain or loss would be reported on the income statement and in the notes to the financial statements.

LO 6 **Exercise 10-6** Redemption of a Bond at Maturity

On March 31, 1998, Field's Inc. issued $250,000 face value bonds at a discount of $8,300. The bonds were retired at their maturity date, March 31, 2008.

Required

Assuming the last interest payment and amortization of discount have already been recorded, prepare the journal entry to record the redemption of the bonds on March 31, 2008.

LO 7 **Exercise 10-7** Leased Asset

Hopper Corporation signed a 10-year capital lease on January 1, 1998. The lease requires annual payments of $6,000 every December 31.

Required

1. Assuming an interest rate of 9 percent, calculate the present value of the minimum lease payments.
2. Explain why the value of the leased asset and the accompanying lease obligation is not initially reported on the balance sheet at $60,000.

LO 7 **Exercise 10-8** Financial Statement Impact of a Lease

Benjamin's Warehouse signed a six-year capital lease on January 1, 1998, with payments due every December 31. Interest is calculated annually at 10 percent, and the present value of the minimum lease payments is $13,065.

Required

1. Calculate the amount of the annual payment that Benjamin's must make every December 31.
2. Calculate the amount of the lease obligation that would be presented on the December 31, 1999, balance sheet (after two lease payments have been made).

LO 7 **Exercise 10-9** Leased Assets

Koffman and Sons signed a four-year lease for a forklift on January 1, 1998. Annual lease payments of $1,510, based on an interest rate of 8%, are to be made every December 31, beginning with December 31, 1998.

Required

1. Assume the lease is treated as an operating lease.
   a. Will the value of the forklift appear on Koffman's balance sheet?
   b. What account will indicate lease payments have been made?
2. Assume the lease is treated as a capital lease.
   a. Prepare any journal entries needed when the lease is signed. Explain why the value of the leased asset is not recorded at $6,040 ($1,510 × 4).
   b. Prepare the journal entry to record the first lease payment on December 31, 1998.
   c. Prepare the adjusting entry to record depreciation expense on December 31, 1998.
   d. At what amount would the lease obligation be presented on the balance sheet as of December 31, 1998?

LO 8 **Exercise 10-10** Temporary and Permanent Differences

Madden Corporation wants to determine the amount of deferred tax that should be reported on its 1998 financial statements. It has compiled a list of differences between the accounting conducted for tax purposes and the accounting used for financial reporting (book) purposes.

Required

For each of the following items, indicate whether the difference should be classified as a permanent or a temporary difference.

1. During 1998, Madden received interest on state bonds purchased as an investment. The interest can be treated as tax-exempt interest for tax purposes.
2. During 1998, Madden paid for a life insurance premium on two key executives. Madden's accountant has indicated that the amount of the premium cannot be deducted for income tax purposes.
3. During December 1998, Madden received money for renting a building to a tenant. Madden must report the rent as income on its 1998 tax form. For book purposes, however, the rent will be considered income on the 1999 income statement.

4. Madden owns several pieces of equipment that it depreciates using the straight-line method for book purposes. An accelerated method of depreciation is used for tax purposes, however.

5. Madden offers a warranty on the products it sells. The corporation records the expense of the warranty repair costs in the year the product is sold (the accrual method) for book purposes. For tax purposes, however, Madden is not allowed to deduct the expense until the period when the product is repaired.

6. During 1998, Madden was assessed a large fine by the federal government for polluting the environment. Madden's accountant has indicated that the fine cannot be deducted as an expense for income tax purposes.

LO 8 **Exercise 10-11** Deferred Tax

On January 1, 1998, Field Corporation purchased an asset for $16,000. Assume this is the only asset owned by the corporation. Field has decided to use the straight-line method to depreciate it. For tax purposes, it will be depreciated over three years. It will be depreciated over five years, however, for the financial statements provided to stockholders. Assume that Field Corporation is subject to a 40% tax rate.

Required

Calculate the balance that should be reflected in the Deferred Tax account for Field Corporation for each year 1998 through 2002.

LO 9 **Exercise 10-12** Pension Analysis

The following information was extracted from a footnote found in the 1998 annual report of a Fortune 500 company.

Plan Assets	$2.6 billion
Accumulated Benefit Obligation	$1.7 billion
Projected Benefit Obligation	$2.1 billion

Required

1. Determine whether the pension plan is overfunded or underfunded.

2. Explain what your response to part 1 implies about the ability of the plan to provide benefits to future retirees.

LO 10 **Exercise 10-13** Impact of Transactions Involving Bonds on Statement of Cash Flows

From the following list, identify each item as operating (O), investing (I), financing (F) or not separately reported on the statement of cash flows (N).

_____ Proceeds from issuance of bonds payable

_____ Interest expense

_____ Redemption of bonds payable at maturity

LO 10 **Exercise 10-14** Impact of Transactions Involving Capital Leases on Statement of Cash Flows

Assume that Vega Corporation signs a lease agreement with Myles Company to lease a piece of equipment and determines that the lease should be treated as a capital lease. Vega records a leased asset in the amount of $53,400 and a lease obligation in the same amount on its balance sheet.

Required

1. Indicate how this transaction would be reported on Vega's statement of cash flows.

2. From the following list of transactions relating to this lease, identify each item as operating (O), investing (I), financing (F) or not separately reported on the statement of cash flows (N).

_____ Reduction of lease obligation (principal portion of lease payment)

_____ Interest expense

_____ Depreciation expense—leased assets

LO 10 **Exercise 10-15** Impact of Transactions Involving Tax Liabilities on Statement of Cash Flows

From the following list, identify each item as operating (O), investing (I), financing (F) or not separately reported on the statement of cash flows (N). For items identified as operating, indicate whether the related amount would be added to or deducted from net income in determining the cash flows from operating activities.

_____ Decrease in taxes payable

_____ Increase in deferred taxes

Multi-Concept Exercises

LO 4, 5 **Exercise 10-16** Issuance of a Bond at Face Value

On January 1, 1998, Whitefeather Industries issued 300, $1,000 face value bonds. The bonds have a five-year life and pay interest at the rate of 10%. Interest is paid semiannually on July 1 and January 1. The market rate of interest on January 1 was 10%.

Required

1. Calculate the issue price of the bonds and record the issuance of the bonds on January 1, 1998.
2. Explain how the issue price would have been affected if the market rate of interest had been higher than 10%.
3. Prepare the journal entry to record the payment of interest on July 1, 1998.
4. Prepare the journal to record the accrual of interest on December 31, 1998.

LO 4, 5 **Exercise 10-17** Impact of a Discount

Berol Corporation sold 20-year bonds on January 1, 1998. The face value of the bonds was $100,000, and they carry a 9% stated rate of interest, which is paid on December 31 of every year. Berol received $91,526 in return for the issuance of the bonds when the market rate was 10%. Any premium or discount is amortized using the effective interest method.

Required

1. Prepare the journal entry to record the sale of the bonds on January 1, 1998, and the proper balance sheet presentation on this date.
2. Prepare the journal entry to record interest expense on December 31, 1998, and the proper balance sheet presentation on this date.
3. Explain why it was necessary for Berol to issue the bonds for only $91,526 rather than $100,000.

LO 4, 5 **Exercise 10-18** Impact of a Premium

Assume the same set of facts for Berol Corporation as in Exercise 10-17 except that it received $109,862 in return for the issuance of the bonds when the market rate was 8%.

Required

1. Prepare the journal entry to record the sale of the bonds on January 1, 1998, and the proper balance sheet presentation on this date.
2. Prepare the journal entry to record interest expense on December 31, 1998, and the proper balance sheet presentation on this date.
3. Explain why the company was able to issue the bonds for $109,862 rather than for the face amount.

Problems

LO 3 **Problem 10-1** Factors that Affect the Bond Issue Price

Fisher Company is considering the issue of $100,000 face value, five-year term bonds. The bonds will pay 6% interest each December 31. The current market rate is 6%; therefore the bonds will be issued at face value.

Required

1. For each of the following independent situations, indicate whether you believe that the company will receive a premium on the bonds or will issue them at a discount or at face value. Without using numbers, explain your position.

   a. Interest is paid semiannually instead of annually.

   b. Assume instead that the market rate of interest is 7%; the nominal rate is still 6%.

2. For each situation in part 1, prove your statement by determining the issue price of the bonds given the changes in parts a and b.

LO 5 **Problem 10-2** Amortization of Discount

Stacy Company issued five-year, 10% bonds with face value of $10,000 on January 1, 1998. Interest is paid annually on December 31. The market rate of interest on this date is 12%, and Stacy Company receives proceeds of $9,275 on the bond issuance.

Required

1. Prepare a five-year table (similar to Exhibit 10-4) to amortize the discount using the effective interest method.

2. What is the total interest expense over the life of the bonds? cash interest payment? discount amortization?

3. Prepare the journal entry to record interest expense on December 31, 2000 (the third year), and the balance sheet presentation of the bonds on that date.

LO 5 **Problem 10-3** Amortization of Premium

Assume the same set of facts for Stacy Company as in Problem 10-2 except that the market rate of interest of January 1, 1998, is 8% and the proceeds from the bond issuance equal $10,803.

Required

1. Prepare a five-year table (similar to Exhibit 10-5) to amortize the premium using the effective interest method.

2. What is the total interest expense over the life of the bonds? cash interest payment? premium amortization?

3. Prepare the journal entry to record interest expense on December 31, 2000 (the third year), and the balance sheet presentation of the bonds on that date.

LO 6 **Problem 10-4** Redemption of Bonds

McGee Company issued $200,000 face value bonds at a premium of $4,500. The bonds contain a call provision of 101. McGee decides to redeem the bonds, due to a significant decline in interest rates. On that date, McGee had amortized only $1,500 of the premium.

Required

1. Calculate the gain or loss on the early redemption of the bonds.

2. Calculate the gain or loss on the redemption, assuming that the call provision is 103 instead of 101.

3. Indicate where the gain or loss should be presented on the financial statements.

4. Why do you suppose the call price is normally higher than 100?

LO 7 **Problem 10-5** Financial Statement Impact of a Lease

On January 1, 1998, Muske Trucking Company leased a semitractor and trailer for five years. Annual payments of $28,300 are to be made every December 31, beginning December 31, 1998. Interest expense is based on a rate of 8%. The present value of the minimum lease payments is $113,000 and has been determined to be greater than 90% of the fair market value of the asset on January 1, 1998. Muske uses straight-line depreciation on all assets.

Required

1. Prepare a table similar to Exhibit 10-7 to show the five-year amortization of the lease obligation.

2. Prepare the journal entry to record the lease transaction on January 1, 1998.

3. Prepare all journal entries necessary on December 31, 1999 (the second year of the lease).

4. Prepare the balance sheet presentation as of December 31, 1999, for the leased asset and the lease obligation.

LO 8 **Problem 10-6** Deferred Tax

Kent Corporation has compiled its 1998 financial statements. Included in the long-term liability category of the balance sheet are the following amounts:

	1998	1997
Deferred Tax	$180	$100

Included in the income statement are the following amounts related to income taxes:

	1998	1997
Income before Tax	$500	$400
Tax Expense	$200	$160
Net Income	$300	$240

In the footnotes that accompany the 1998 statement are the following amounts:

	1998
Current Provision for Tax	$120
Deferred Portion	80

Required

1. Prepare the journal entry recorded in 1998 for income tax expense, deferred tax, and income tax payable.

2. Assume that a stockholder has inquired about the meaning of the numbers recorded and disclosed about deferred tax. Explain why the Deferred Tax liability account exists. Also, what do the terms *current provision* and *deferred portion* mean? Why is the deferred amount in the footnote $80 when the deferred amount on the 1998 balance sheet is $180?

LO 8 **Problem 10-7** Deferred Tax Calculations

Wyhowski Inc. reported income from operations, before taxes, for 1996–98 as follows:

1996	$210,000
1997	240,000
1998	280,000

When calculating income, Wyhowski deducted depreciation on plant equipment. The equipment was purchased January 1, 1996 at a cost of $88,000. The equipment is expected to last three years and have $8,000 salvage value. Wyhowski uses straight-line depreciation for book purposes. For tax purposes, depreciation on the equipment is $50,000 in 1996, $20,000 in 1997, and $10,000 in 1998. Wyhowski's tax rate is 35%.

Required

1. How much did Wyhowski pay in income tax each year?

2. How much income tax expense did Wyhowski record each year?

3. What is the balance in the Deferred Income Tax account at the end of 1996, 1997, and 1998?

LO 9 **Problem 10-8** Financial Statement Impact of a Pension

Smith Financial Corporation prepared the following schedule relating to its pension expense and pension funding payment for the years 1996 through 1998.

YEAR	EXPENSE	PAYMENT
1996	$100,000	$ 90,000
1997	85,000	105,000
1998	112,000	100,000

At the beginning of 1996, the Prepaid/Accrued Pension Cost account was reported on the balance sheet as an asset with a balance of $8,000.

Required

1. Prepare the journal entries to record Smith Financial Corporation's pension expense for 1996, 1997, and 1998.

2. Calculate the balance in the Prepaid/Accrued Pension Cost account at the end of 1998. Does this represent an asset or a liability?

3. Explain the effects that pension expense, the funding payment, and the balance in the Prepaid/Accrued Pension Cost account have on the 1998 income statement and balance sheet.

Multi-Concept Problems

LO 4, 6   **Problem 10-9** Entries for Bonds

Essink Company issued $1,000,000 face value, eight-year, 12% bonds on April 1, 1998, when the market rate of interest was 12%. Interest payments are due every October 1 and April 1. Essink uses a calendar year-end.

Required

1. Prepare the journal entry to record the issuance of the bonds on April 1, 1998.

2. Prepare the journal entry to record the interest payment on October 1, 1998.

3. Explain why additional interest must be recorded on December 31, 1998. What impact does this have on the amounts paid on April 1, 1999?

4. Determine the total cash inflows and outflows that occurred on the bonds over the eight-year life.

LO 1, 8, 9   **Problem 10-10** Partial Classified Balance Sheet for Tribune Company

The following items, listed alphabetically, appear on Tribune Company's consolidated balance sheet at December 31, 1995 (in thousands). The information in parentheses was added to aid in your understanding.

Accounts payable	$112,357
Accrued liabilities	91,571
Compensation and other obligations (due after 1996)	144,229
Contracts payable for broadcast rights (the related payments are due during 1996)	164,443
Contracts payable for broadcast rights (the related payments are due after 1996)	225,771
Deferred income	43,961
Deferred income taxes	223,756
Employee compensation and benefits	107,775
Income taxes	8,401
Long-term debt due within one year	28,665
Long-term debt (less portions due within one year)	747,437

Required

1. Prepare the current liability and long-term liability sections of Tribune Company's classified balance sheet at December 31, 1995.

2. Tribune Company had total liabilities of $1,452,845 and total shareholders' equity of $1,332,980 at December 31, 1994. Total stockholders' equity amounted to $1,379,909 at December 31, 1995. (All amounts are in thousands.) Compute the Tribune

Company's debt-to-equity ratio at December 31, 1995 and 1994. As an investor, how would you react to the change in this ratio?

3. What other related ratios would the company's lenders use to assess the company? What do these ratios measure?

Alternate Problems

LO 3 **Problem 10-1A** Factors That Affect the Bond Issue Price

Rivera Inc. is considering the issuance of $500,000 face value, 10-year term bonds. The bonds will pay 5% interest each December 31. The current market rate is 5%; therefore, the bonds will be issued at face value.

Required

1. For each of the following independent situations, indicate whether you believe that the company will receive a premium on the bonds or will issue them at a discount or at face value. Without using numbers, explain your position.
   a. Interest is paid semiannually instead of annually.
   b. Assume instead that the market rate of interest is 4%; the nominal rate is still 5%.
2. For each situation in part 1, prove your statement by determining the issue price of the bonds given the changes in parts a and b.

LO 5 **Problem 10-2A** Amortization of Discount

Griffith Company issued five-year, 5% bonds with face value of $50,000 on January 1, 1998. Interest is paid annually on December 31. The market rate of interest on this date is 8%, and Griffith Company receives proceeds of $44,011 on the bond issuance.

Required

1. Prepare a five-year table (similar to Exhibit 10-4) to amortize the discount using the effective interest method.
2. What is the total interest expense over the life of the bonds? cash interest payment? discount amortization?
3. Prepare the journal entry to record interest expense on December 31, 2000 (the third year), and the balance sheet presentation of the bonds on that date.

LO 5 **Problem 10-3A** Amortization of Premium

Assume the same set of facts for Griffith Company as in Problem 10-2A except that the market rate of interest of January 1, 1998, is 4% and the proceeds from the bond issuance equal $52,230.

Required

1. Prepare a five-year table (similar to Exhibit 10-5) to amortize the premium using the effective interest method.
2. What is the total interest expense over the life of the bonds? cash interest payment? premium amortization?
3. Prepare the journal entry to record interest expense on December 31, 2000 (the third year), and the balance sheet presentation of the bonds on that date.

LO 6 **Problem 10-4A** Redemption of Bonds

Elliot Company issued $100,000 face value bonds at a premium of $5,500. The bonds contain a call provision of 101. Elliot decides to redeem the bonds, due to a significant decline in interest rates. On that date, Elliot has amortized only $3,500 of the premium.

Required

1. Calculate the gain or loss on the early redemption of the bonds.
2. Calculate the gain or loss on the redemption, assuming that the call provision is 103 instead of 101.
3. Indicate how the gain or loss would be reported on the income statement and in the notes to the financial statements.

4. Why do you suppose that the call price of the bonds is normally an amount higher than 100?

LO 7 **Problem 10-5A** Financial Statement Impact of a Lease

On January 1, 1998, Kiger Manufacturing Company leased a factory machine for six years. Annual payments of $21,980 are to be made every December 31, beginning December 31, 1998. Interest expense is based on a rate of 9%. The present value of the minimum lease payments is $98,600 and has been determined to be greater than 90% of the fair market value of the machine on January 1, 1998. Kiger uses straight-line depreciation on all assets.

Required

1. Prepare a table similar to Exhibit 10-7 to show the six-year amortization of the lease obligation.

2. Prepare the journal entry to record the signing of the lease on January 1, 1998.

3. Prepare all journal entries necessary on December 31, 1999 (the second year of the lease).

4. Prepare the balance sheet presentation as of December 31, 1999, for the leased asset and the lease obligation.

LO 8 **Problem 10-6A** Deferred Tax

Tanner Corporation has compiled its 1998 financial statements. Included in the long-term liability category of the balance sheet are the following amounts:

	1998	1997
Deferred Tax	$180	$200

Included in the income statement are the following amounts related to income taxes:

	1998	1997
Income before Tax	$500	$400
Tax Expense	100	150
Net Income	$400	$250

Required

1. Prepare the journal entry recorded in 1998 for income tax expense, deferred tax, and income tax payable.

2. Assume that a stockholder has inquired about the meaning of the numbers recorded. Explain why the Deferred Tax liability account exists.

LO 8 **Problem 10-7A** Deferred Tax Calculations

Clemente Inc. has reported income for book purposes as follows for the past three years:

(IN THOUSANDS)	YEAR 1	YEAR 2	YEAR 3
Income before Taxes	$120	$120	$120

Clemente has identified two items that are treated differently in the financial records and in the tax records. The first one is interest income on municipal bonds, which is recognized on the financial reports to the extent of $5,000 each year but does not show up as a revenue item on the company's tax return. The other item is equipment that is depreciated using the straight-line method, at the rate of $20,000 each year, for financial accounting but is depreciated for tax purposes at the rate of $30,000 in Year 1, $20,000 in Year 2, and $10,000 in Year 3.

Required

1. Determine the amount of cash paid for income taxes each year by Clemente. Assume that a 50% tax rate applies to all three years.

2. Calculate the balance in the Deferred Tax account at the end of Years 1, 2, and 3. How does this account appear on the balance sheet?

LO 9 **Problem 10-8A** Financial Statement Impact of a Pension

Premier Consulting Corporation prepared the following schedule relating to its pension expense and pension funding payment for the years 1996 through 1998:

YEAR	EXPENSE	PAYMENT
1996	$100,000	$110,000
1997	85,000	80,000
1998	112,000	100,000

At the beginning of 1996, the Prepaid/Accrued Pension Cost account was reported on the balance sheet as an asset with a balance of $5,000.

Required

1. Prepare the journal entries to record Premier Consulting Corporation's pension expense for 1996, 1997, and 1998.

2. Calculate the balance in the Prepaid/Accrued Pension Cost account at the end of 1998.

3. Explain the effects that pension expense, the funding payment, and the balance in the Prepaid/Accrued Pension Cost account have on the 1998 income statement and balance sheet.

Alternate Multi-Concept Problems

LO 3, 4, 5, 6 **Problem 10-9A** Financial Statement Impact of a Bond

Worthington Company issued $1,000,000 face value, six-year, 10% bonds on July 1, 1998, when the market rate of interest was 12%. Interest payments are due every July 1 and January 1. Worthington uses a calendar year-end.

Required

1. Prepare the journal entry to record the issuance of the bonds on July 1, 1998.

2. Prepare the adjusting journal entry on December 31, 1998 to accrue interest expense.

3. Prepare the journal entry to record the interest payment on January 1, 1999.

4. Prepare the journal entry to record the retirement of the bonds on the maturity date.

LO 1, 8, 9 **Problem 10-10A** Partial Classified Balance Sheet for Allied Signal

The following items, listed alphabetically, appear on the consolidated balance sheet of Allied Signal Inc. at December 31, 1995 (in millions). The information in parentheses was added to aid in your understanding.

Accounts payable	$1,385
Accrued liabilities	1,775
Commercial paper (due during 1996)	58
Current maturities of long-term debt	189
Deferred income taxes	551
Long-term debt	1,366
Other liabilities (due after 1996)	1,288
Postretirement benefit obligations other than pensions	1,864
Short-term borrowings	397

Required

1. Prepare the current liability and long-term liability sections of Allied Signal's classified balance sheet at December 31, 1995.

2. Allied Signal had total liabilities of $8,339 and total shareholders' equity of $2,982 at December 31, 1994. Total stockholders' equity amounted to $3,592 at December 31, 1995. (All amounts are in millions.) Compute Allied Signal's debt-to-equity ratio at December 31, 1995 and 1994. As an investor, how would you react to the change in this ratio?

3. What other related ratios would the company's lenders use to assess the company? What do these ratios measure?

Cases

Reading and Interpreting Financial Statements

`LO 1, 7, 8` **Case 10-1** Reading and Interpreting Ben & Jerry's Balance Sheet

Refer to the financial statements included in Ben & Jerry's annual report.

Required

1. What is the total amount of long-term liabilities for Ben & Jerry's as of December 31, 1995?

2. Discuss whether deferred income taxes should be included when calculating the total amount of Ben & Jerry's liabilities.

3. Ben & Jerry's has an account titled Long-Term Debt and Obligation under Capital Leases. If that account is a long-term item, why is a portion shown in the current liability category?

4. Footnote 6 indicates that there are two notes payable in the long-term debt category. When are the principal and interest payments due, and what is the interest rate of each note? What other types of debt are included as long-term?

5. Assume that you are an analyst who must review Ben & Jerry's financial condition. Assume that Ben & Jerry's has indicated that it plans to issue debt of nearly $10 million. Your boss is concerned that the amount of long-term debt may be excessive and has asked you to review the financial statements. Prepare a memo to your boss with a response to her concerns. Include in the memo a discussion of the factors that you considered to determine whether the amount of long-term debt is too high.

6. Are any assets pledged as collateral for long-term debt? If so, how much has been pledged?

`LO 7, 8, 10` **Case 10-2** Reading Ben & Jerry's Statement of Cash Flows

Refer to the statement of cash flows in Ben & Jerry's 1995 annual report.

Required

1. Ben & Jerry's has leased assets using capital lease arrangements. When payments are made to reduce capital lease obligations, in which category of the cash flow statement are the payments disclosed?

2. In 1995, no long-term debt was issued. What changes occurred that helped Ben & Jerry's avoid issuing more debt?

3. Ben & Jerry's has a Deferred Tax account listed in the asset category of its balance sheet. Would an increase in that account result in an addition or a subtraction on the statement of cash flows? In which category?

Making Financial Decisions

`LO 1` **Case 10-3** Making a Loan Decision

Assume that you are a loan officer in charge of reviewing loan applications from potential new clients at a major bank. You are considering an application from Molitor Corporation, which is a fairly new company with a limited credit history. It has provided a balance sheet for its most recent fiscal year as follows:

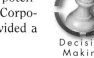

Decision
Making

MOLITOR CORPORATION
BALANCE SHEET
DECEMBER 31, 199X

ASSETS		LIABILITIES	
Cash	$ 10,000	Accounts payable	$100,000
Receivables	50,000	Notes payable	200,000
Inventory	100,000		
Equipment	500,000		
		STOCKHOLDERS' EQUITY	
		Common stock	80,000
		Retained earnings	280,000
Total assets	$660,000	Total liabilities and stockholders' equity	$660,000

Your bank has established certain guidelines that must be met before making a favorable loan recommendation. These include minimum levels for several financial ratios. You are particularly concerned about the bank's policy that loan applicants must have a total-assets-to-debt ratio of at least 2-to-1 to be acceptable. Your initial analysis of Molitor's balance sheet has indicated that the firm has met the minimum total-assets-to-debt ratio requirement. On reading the footnotes that accompany the financial statements, however, you discover the following statement:

> Molitor has engaged in a variety of innovative financial techniques resulting in the acquisition of $200,000 of assets at very favorable rates. The company is obligated to make a series of payments over the next five years to fulfill its commitments in conjunction with these financial instruments. Current generally accepted accounting principles do not require the assets acquired nor the related obligations to be reflected on the financial statements.

Required

1. How should this footnote affect your evaluation of Molitor's loan application? Calculate a revised total-assets-to-debt ratio for Molitor.

2. Do you believe that the bank's policy concerning a minimum total-assets-to-debt ratio can be modified to consider financing techniques that are not reflected on the financial statements? Write a statement that expresses your position on this issue.

Decision Making

LO 6 Case 10-4 Bond Redemption Decision

Armstrong Areo Ace, a flight training school, issued $100,000 of 20-year bonds at face value when the market rate was 10%. The bonds have been outstanding for 10 years. The company pays annual interest on January 1. The current rate for similar bonds is 4%. On January 1, the controller would like to purchase the bonds on the open market, retire the bonds, then issue $100,000 of 10-year bonds to pay 4% annual interest.

Required

Draft a memo to the controller advising him to retire the outstanding bonds and issue new debt. Ignore taxes. (*Hint:* find the selling price of bonds that pay 10% when the market rate is 4%.)

Accounting and Ethics: What Would You Do?

LO 7 Case 10-5 Determination of Asset Life

Jen Latke is an accountant for Hale's Manufacturing Company. Hale's has entered into an agreement to lease a piece of equipment from EZ Leasing. Jen must decide how to report the lease agreement on Hale's financial statements.

Jen has reviewed the lease contract carefully. She has also reviewed the four lease criteria specified in the accounting rules. She has been able to determine that the lease does not meet three of the criteria. However, she is concerned about the criterion that indicates that if the term of the lease is 75% or more of the life of the property, the lease should be classified as a capital lease. Jen is fully aware that Hale's does not want to record the lease agreement as a capital lease but prefers to show it as a type of off-balance-sheet financing.

Jen's reading of the lease contract indicates that the asset has been leased for seven years. She is unsure of the life of such assets, however, and has consulted two sources to determine it. One of them states that equipment similar to that owned by Hale's is depreciated over nine years. The other, a trade publication of the equipment industry, indicates that equipment of this type will usually last for 12 years.

Required

1. How should Jen report the lease agreement in the financial statements?

2. If Jen decides to present the lease as an off-balance-sheet arrangement, has she acted ethically?

LO 9 Case 10-6 Overfunded Pension Plan

Witty Company has sponsored a pension plan for employees for several years. Each year Witty has paid cash to the pension fund, and the pension trustee has used that cash to invest in stocks and bonds. Because the trustee has invested wisely, the amount of the pension assets exceeds the accumulated benefit obligation as of December 31, 1998.

The president of Witty Company wants to pay a dividend to the stockholders at the end of 1998. The president believes that it is important to maintain a stable dividend pattern. Unfortunately, the company, though profitable, does not have enough cash on hand to pay a dividend and must find a way to raise the necessary cash if the dividend is declared. Several executives of the company have recommended that assets be withdrawn from the pension fund. They have pointed out that the fund is currently "overfunded." Further, they have stated that a withdrawal of assets will not have an impact on the financial statements because the overfunding is an "off-balance-sheet item."

Required

Comment on the proposal to withdraw assets from the pension fund to pay a dividend to stockholders. Do you believe it is unethical?

Research Case

Case 10-7 Coca-Cola

Sold in over 200 countries, Coca-Cola is the most recognized brand name in the world. Sales of Classic Coke, diet Coke, and Sprite provide the company with the cash necessary to pay off debts.

Internet

Conduct a search of the World Wide Web, obtain Coca-Cola's most recent annual report, or use library resources to obtain company information to answer the following:

1. Based on the latest information available, what is the amount of Coca-Cola's long-term debt? How does this compare to the long-term debt in the "Focus on Financial Results" in the opening vignette shown at the start of this chapter?

2. What is the face rate on a Coca-Cola bond currently trading on the bond market? How does that rate compare with the current yield for the same bond?

3. During the past three to six months, has the yield for Coca-Cola's bonds increased or decreased?

Optional Research. Obtain information from the company's Web site (http://www. cocacola.com) to determine recent business activities and international expansion that may have affected the amount of long-term debt used by the company.

Solution to Key Terms Quiz

_5_	Long-term liability (p. 464)		_1_	Face value (p. 464)
_7_	Debenture bonds (p. 465)		_2_	Serial bonds (p. 466)
_9_	Callable bonds (p. 466)		_3_	Face rate of interest (p. 467)
_12_	Market rate of interest (p. 467)		_4_	Bond issue price (p. 467)
_6_	Premium on bonds (p. 469)		_8_	Discount on bonds (p. 469)
_10_	Effective interest method of amortization (p. 471)		_11_	Carrying value (p. 471)
			_15_	Operating lease (p. 477)
_13_	Gain or loss on redemption (p. 475)		_19_	Deferred tax (p. 481)
_17_	Capital lease (p. 477)		_18_	Temporary difference (p. 482)
_20_	Permanent difference (p. 482)		_16_	Funding payment (p. 484)
_21_	Pension (p. 484)		_23_	Accumulated benefit obligation (ABO) (p. 486)
_22_	Accrued pension cost (p. 485)			
_14_	Projected benefit obligation (PBO) (p. 486)			

STUDY LINKS

A Look at Previous Chapters

Chapters 9 and 10 covered the current and long-term liability portions of the balance sheet. Liabilities are one source of financing of business activities.

A Look at This Chapter

This chapter examines the other major source of financing available to companies: stock and stock transactions. The chapter begins with an overview of the stockholders' equity category of Ford's and Chrysler's balance sheets. The impact of stock issuance and repurchase is examined along with the declaration and payment of cash and stock dividends.

The discussion in this chapter centers on the corporate form of organization and the stockholders' equity of corporations. The accounts contained in the equity category of a sole proprietorship or partnership are presented in the appendix to this chapter.

A Look at Upcoming Chapters

Chapter 12 examines other company activities that affect stockholders' equity. It introduces the statement of stockholders' equity as a summary of all events affecting that section of the balance sheet.

Stockholders' Equity

FOCUS ON FINANCIAL RESULTS

Ford Motor Company, whose products range from the Fiesta subcompact car to the AeroMax heavy-duty truck, first sold stock to the public in 1956. As of 1995, as indicated in the excerpt from its consolidated balance sheet, Ford had issued over 1 billion shares of common stock and another 71 million shares of Class B stock.

The owners of the stock benefit from Ford's business success when they receive dividends and when their shares increase in value. Recognizing this, Ford's annual report supplements the financial statements with reports on the company's history of dividend payments and stock performance. Ford paid $1.6 billion in cash

Ford Motor Company and Subsidiaries
CONSOLIDATED BALANCE SHEET
(in millions)

	December 31, 1995	December 31, 1994
Stockholders' equity		
Capital stock (Notes 10 and 11)		
Preferred Stock, par value $1.00 per share (aggregate liquidation preference of $1 billion and $3.4 billion)	*	*
Common Stock, par value $1.00 per share (1,089 and 952 million shares issued)	**1,089**	952
Class B Stock, par value $1.00 per share (71 million shares issued)	**71**	71
Capital in excess of par value of stock	**5,105**	5,273
Foreign currency translation adjustments and other (Note 1)	**594**	189
Earnings retained for use in business	**17,688**	15,174
Total stockholders' equity	**24,547**	21,659

*Less than $1 million

Recent Dividend Rate Increases

Ford Common Stock Price Range (NYSE)

dividends during 1995; its fourth-quarter 1995 payment was 75 percent larger than the payment for the first quarter of 1994. Ford also has had several stock splits to make the stock affordable to a wider range of investors. The impacts of cash dividends and stock splits are described in this chapter. The market value of Ford's stock has generally grown during the period shown, from around $10 per share in 1986 to around $30 in 1995.

If you owned Ford stock, what information about the stock would you want to learn from Ford's balance sheet? What additional information would you want about Ford's stock? Use this chapter to help you answer those questions, and look up the latest Ford annual report to see how the stock has performed since 1995.

SOURCE: *Ford Motor Company Annual Report, 1995.*

After studying this chapter, you should be able to

LO 1 Identify the components of the stockholders' equity category of the balance sheet and the accounts found in each component.

LO 2 Understand the characteristics of common and preferred stock and the differences between the classes of stock.

LO 3 Determine the effect when stock is issued for cash or for other consideration.

LO 4 Describe the financial statement effect of stock treated as treasury stock.

LO 5 Compute the amount of cash dividends when a firm has issued both preferred and common stock.

LO 6 Understand the difference between cash and stock dividends and the effect of stock dividends.

LO 7 Determine the difference between stock dividends and stock splits.

LO 8 Understand how investors use ratios to evaluate owners' equity.

LO 9 Explain the effects that transactions involving stockholders' equity have on the statement of cash flows.

LO 10 Describe the important differences between the sole proprietorship and partnership forms of organization versus the corporate form (Appendix 11A).

An Overview of Stockholders' Equity

Equity as a Source of Financing

Whenever a company needs to raise money, it must choose from the alternative financing sources that are available. Financing can be divided into two general categories: debt (borrowing from banks or other creditors) and equity (issuing stock). The company's management must consider the advantages and disadvantages of each alternative. Exhibit 11-1 indicates a few of the factors that must be considered.

Issuing stock is a very popular method of financing because of its flexibility. It provides advantages for the issuing company and the investors (stockholders). Investors are primarily concerned with the return on their investment. With stock, the return may be in the form of dividends paid to the investors but may also be the price appreciation of the stock. Stock is popular because it generally provides a higher rate of return (but also a higher degree of risk) than can be obtained by creditors who receive interest from lending money. Stock is popular with issuing companies because dividends on stock can be adjusted according to the company's profitability; higher dividends can be paid when the firm is profitable and lower dividends when it is not. Interest on debt financing, on the other hand, is generally fixed and is a legal liability that cannot be adjusted when a company experiences lower profitability.

There are several disadvantages in issuing stock. Stock usually has voting rights, and issuing stock allows new investors to vote. Existing investors may not want to share the control of the company with new stockholders. From the issuing company's viewpoint, there is also a serious tax disadvantage to stock versus debt. As indicated in Chapter 10, interest on debt is tax deductible and results in lower taxes. Dividends on stock, on the

ACCOUNTING FOR YOUR DECISIONS

You Are the Investor

You have the opportunity to buy a company's bonds that pay 8 percent interest or the same company's stock. The stock has paid an 8 percent dividend rate for the last few years. The company is a large, reputable firm and has been profitable during recent times. Should you be indifferent between the two alternatives?

ANS: Interest on bonds is a fixed obligation. Unless the company goes out of business, you can count on receiving the 8 percent interest if you invest in the bonds. Dividends on stock are not fixed. There is no guarantee that the company will continue to pay 8 percent as the dividend on your investment. If the company is not profitable, it may decrease the size of the dividend. On the other hand, if the company becomes more profitable, it may pay a larger dividend.

EXHIBIT 11-1   Advantages and Disadvantages of Stock versus Debt Financing

ADVANTAGES OF FINANCING WITH STOCK

1. Flexibility → Dividends on stock can be increased in profitable years, reduced when the company is less profitable. Debt interest is fixed. (An advantage for issuing company)

2. Exchanges facilitate trading → Large companies have ready markets for stock through the stock exchanges. (An advantage for issuing company and investors) Sometimes debt is not as widely traded.

3. Return on investment → Stock generally provides a higher return in dividends and in growth, than interest on debt. (An advantage for investors)

DISADVANTAGES OF FINANCING WITH STOCK

1. Control → Issuing stock involves giving voting rights to new investors, less control of the company for existing stockholders. (A disadvantage for issuing company)

2. Tax consequences → Interest on debt is tax deductible for the issuing company, dividends on stock are not. (A disadvantage for issuing company)

3. Impact on ratios → Issuing stock decreases several important financial ratios, including earnings per share. (A disadvantage for issuing company)

other hand, are not tax deductible and do not result in tax savings to the issuing company. Finally, the following sections of this chapter indicate the impact that issuing stock has on the company's financial statements. Issuing stock decreases several important financial ratios, such as earnings per share. Issuing debt does not have a similar effect on the earnings per share ratio.

Management should consider many other factors in deciding between debt and equity financing. The company's goal should be financing the company in a manner that results in the lowest overall cost of capital to the firm. Usually, companies attain that goal by having a reasonable balance of both debt and equity financing.

Stockholders' Equity on the Balance Sheet

The basic accounting equation is often stated as follows:

$$Assets = Liabilities + Owners' Equity$$

Owners' equity is viewed as a residual amount. That is, the owners of a corporation have a claim to all assets after the claims represented by liabilities to creditors have been satisfied.

In this chapter, we concentrate on the corporate form of organization and refer to the owners' equity as *stockholders' equity*. Therefore, the basic accounting equation for a corporation can be restated as follows:

$$Assets = Liabilities + Stockholders' Equity$$

The stockholders are the owners of a corporation. They have a residual interest in its assets after the claims of all creditors have been satisfied.

The stockholders' equity category of all corporations has two major components or subcategories:

$$\text{Total Stockholders' Equity} = \text{Contributed Capital} + \text{Retained Earnings}$$

Contributed capital represents the amount the corporation has received from the sale of stock to stockholders. Retained earnings is the amount of net income that the corporation has earned but not paid as dividends. Instead, the corporation retains and reinvests the income.

Although all corporations maintain the two primary categories of contributed capital and retained earnings, within these categories they use a variety of accounts that have several alternative titles. The next section illustrates the stockholders' equity category with the use of an actual firm's balance sheet.

Identifying the Components of the Stockholders' Equity Section of the Balance Sheet

LO 1 Identify the components of the stockholders' equity category of the balance sheet and the accounts found in each component.

The 1995 balance sheet of Chrysler Corporation is provided in Exhibit 11-2. We will focus on the stockholders' (shareholders') equity category of the balance sheet. All corporations, including Chrysler, begin the stockholders' equity category with a list of the firm's contributed capital. Generally, there are two categories of stock: common stock and preferred stock (the latter is discussed later in this chapter). Common stock normally carries voting rights, and the common stockholders elect the officers of the corporation and establish its by-laws and governing rules. It is not unusual for corporations to have more than one type of common stock, each with different rights or terms. For example, General Motors, one of Chrysler's competitors, has four classes of preferred stock and three classes of common stock listed on its 1995 balance sheet.

Number of Shares It is important to determine the number of shares of stock for each stock account. Corporate balance sheets report the number of shares in three categories: authorized, issued, and outstanding shares.

To become incorporated, a business must develop articles of incorporation and apply to the proper state authorities for a corporate charter. The corporation must specify the maximum number of shares that it will be allowed to issue. This maximum number of shares is called the *authorized stock*. A corporation applies for authorization to issue many more shares than it will issue immediately, to allow for future growth and other events that may occur over its long life. For example, Chrysler indicates that it has 1,000.0 million shares of common stock authorized but that only 408.2 million shares had been issued as of December 31, 1995.

The number of shares *issued* indicates the number of shares that have been sold or transferred to stockholders. The number of shares issued does not necessarily mean, however, that those shares are currently outstanding. The term *outstanding* indicates shares actually in the hands of the stockholders. Shares that have been issued by the corporation and then repurchased are counted as shares issued but not as shares outstanding. Quite often corporations repurchase their own stock as treasury stock (explained in more detail later in this chapter). Treasury stock reduces the number of shares outstanding. The number of Chrysler's shares of common stock outstanding at December 31, 1995, could be calculated as follows:

Number of shares issued	408.2 million
Less: Treasury stock	29.9 million
Number of shares outstanding	378.3 million

Par Value: The Firm's "Legal Capital" The stockholders' equity category of many balance sheets refers to an amount as the *par value* of the stock. For example, Chrysler's common stock has a par value of $1 per share. Par value is an arbitrary

You Are the Entrepreneur

As an entrepreneur, you want to develop the articles of incorporation for your company's corporate charter. What are the decisions about stockholders' equity you have to make? Why are these decisions of value to the corporation?

ANS: Decisions include determining the types of stock (common or both common and preferred) to be issued, the number of authorized shares of each stock, the characteristics of each stock, and par values of each type of stock. These decisions are important to the corporation for several reasons: first, to do business in a certain state, the company must put these decisions in the state charter; second, these decisions affect the types of investors who are interested in the company; and third, the decisions are important because equity represents a major source of financing.

EXHIBIT 11-2   Chrysler Corporation's Consolidated Balance Sheet

CONSOLIDATED BALANCE SHEET

Chrysler Corporation and Consolidated Subsidiaries

	December 31	
In millions of dollars	1995	1994
Assets:		
Cash and cash equivalents (Note 1)	$ 5,543	$ 5,145
Marketable securities (Note 1)	2,582	3,226
Accounts receivable—trade and other (less allowance for doubtful accounts: $58 million in 1995 and 1994)	2,003	1,695
Inventories (Notes 1 and 2)	4,448	3,356
Prepaid taxes, pension and other expenses	985	1,330
Finance receivables and retained interests in sold receivables (Note 3)	13,623	12,433
Property and equipment (Note 4)	12,595	11,073
Special tools	3,566	3,643
Intangible assets (Note 1)	2,082	2,162
Deferred tax assets (Note 7)	490	395
Other assets (Note 11)	5,839	5,081
Total Assets	$53,756	$49,539
Liabilities:		
Accounts payable	$ 8,290	$ 7,826
Short-term debt (Note 6)	2,674	4,645
Payments due within one year on long-term debt (Note 6)	1,661	811
Accrued liabilities and expenses (Note 5)	7,032	5,582
Long-term debt (Note 6)	9,858	7,650
Accrued noncurrent employee benefits (Notes 1, 11 and 12)	9,217	8,595
Other noncurrent liabilities	4,065	3,736
Total Liabilities	42,797	38,845
Shareholders' Equity (Note 10): *(shares in millions)*		
Preferred stock—$1 per share par value; authorized 20.0 shares; Series A Convertible Preferred Stock; issued and outstanding: 1995 and 1994–0.1 and 1.7 shares, respectively (aggregate liquidation preference $68 million and $863 million, respectively)	*	2
Common stock—$1 per share par value; authorized 1,000.0 shares; issued: 1995 and 1994–408.2 and 364.1 shares, respectively	408	364
Additional paid-in capital	5,506	5,536
Retained earnings	6,280	5,006
Treasury stock—at cost: 1995–29.9 shares; 1994–9.0 shares	(1,235)	(214)
Total Shareholders' Equity	10,959	10,694
Total Liabilities and Shareholders' Equity	$53,756	$49,539

*Less than $1 million

See notes to consolidated financial statements.

amount stated on the face of the stock certificate and represents the legal capital of the corporation. Most corporations set the par value of the stock at very low amounts because there are legal difficulties if stock is sold at less than par. Therefore, par value does not indicate the stock's value or the amount that is obtained when it is sold on the stock exchange; it is simply an arbitrary amount that exists to fulfill legal requirements. A company's legal requirement depends on its state of incorporation. Some states do not require corporations to indicate a par value; others require them to designate the *stated value* of the stock. A stated value is accounted for in the same manner as a par value and appears in the stockholders' equity category in the same manner as a par value.

The amount of the par value is the amount that is presented in the stock account. That is, the dollar amount in a firm's stock account can be calculated as its par value per share times number of shares issued. For Chrysler, the dollar amount appearing in the common stock account can be calculated as follows:

$$\$1 \text{ Par Value per Share} \times 408.2 \text{ million Shares Issued} =$$
$$\$408 \text{ million (rounded) Balance in the Common Stock Account}$$

A prospective stockholder may purchase shares and receive certificates, like this one, either directly from the company or through a stockbroker. Usually, a broker purchases shares in its own name for the investor's account—and the investor never sees a certificate.

Additional Paid-in Capital The dollar amounts of the stock accounts in the stockholders' equity category do not indicate the amount that was received when the stock was sold to stockholders. The Common Stock and Preferred Stock accounts

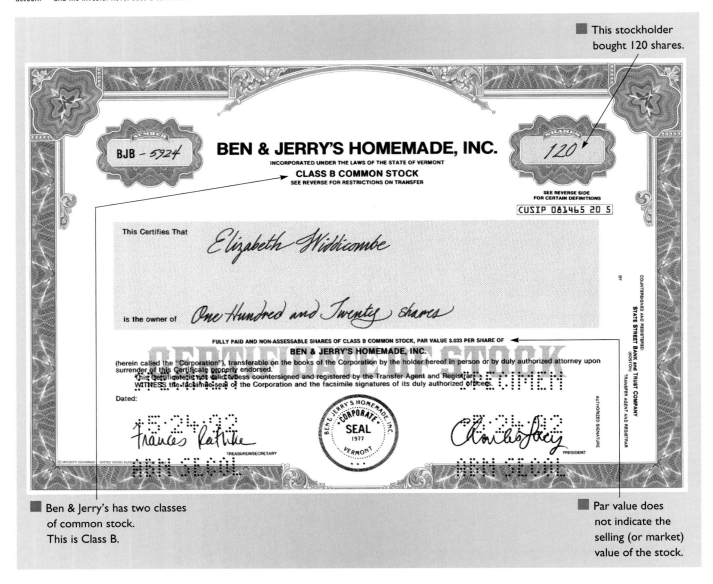

This stockholder bought 120 shares.

Ben & Jerry's has two classes of common stock. This is Class B.

Par value does not indicate the selling (or market) value of the stock.

indicate only the par value of the stock. When stock is issued for an amount higher than the par value, the excess is reported as additional paid-in capital. Several alternative titles are used for this account, including Paid-in Capital in Excess of Par, Capital Surplus (an old term that should no longer be used), and Premium on Stock. Regardless of the title, the account represents the amount received in excess of par when stock was issued.

Chrysler's balance sheet indicates additional paid-in capital of $5,506 million at December 31, 1995. Chrysler, as well as many other corporations, presents only one amount for additional paid-in capital for all stock transactions. Therefore, we are unable to determine whether the amount resulted from the issuance of common stock, preferred stock, or other stock transactions. As a result, it is often impossible to determine the issue price of each category of stock even with a careful analysis of the balance sheet and the accompanying footnotes.

Retained Earnings: The Amount *Not* Paid as Dividends   Retained earnings represents net income that the firm has earned but has *not* paid as dividends. Remember that retained earnings is an amount that is accumulated over the entire life of the corporation and does not represent the income or dividends for a specific year. For example, the balance of the Retained Earnings account on Chrysler's balance sheet at December 31, 1995, is $6,280 million. That does not mean that Chrysler had a net income of this amount in 1995; it simply means that over the life of the corporation, Chrysler has retained $6,280 million more net income than it paid out as dividends to stockholders.

It is also important to remember that the balance of the Retained Earnings account does not mean that liquid assets of that amount are available to the stockholders. Corporations decide to retain income because they have needs other than paying dividends to stockholders. The needs may include purchase of assets, retirement of debt, or other financial needs. Money spent for those needs usually benefits the stockholders in the long run, but liquid assets equal to the balance of the Retained Earnings account are not necessarily available to stockholders. In theory, income should be retained whenever the company can reinvest the money and get a better return within the business than the shareholders can get on their own. In summary, retained earnings is a stockholders' equity account. Although the company's assets have increased, retained earnings does not represent a pool of liquid assets.

What Is Preferred Stock?

Many companies have a class of stock called *preferred stock*. One of the advantages of preferred stock is the flexibility it provides because its terms and provisions can be tailored to meet the firm's needs. These terms and provisions are detailed in the stock certificate. Generally, preferred stock offers holders a preference to dividends declared by the corporation. That is, if dividends are declared, the preferred stockholders must receive dividends first, before the holders of common stock.

The dividend rate on preferred stock may be stated in two ways. First, it may be stated as a percentage of the stock's par value. For example, if a stock is presented in the balance sheet as $100 par, 7% preferred stock, its dividend rate is $7 per share ($100 times 7%). Second, the dividend may be stated as a per-share amount. For example, a stock may appear in the balance sheet as $100 par, $7 preferred stock, meaning that the dividend rate is $7 per share. Investors in common stock should note the dividend requirements of the preferred shareholder. The greater the obligation to the preferred shareholder, the less desirable the common stock becomes.

Several important provisions of preferred stock relate to the payment of dividends. Some preferred stock issues have a cumulative feature, which means that if a dividend is not declared to the preferred stockholders in one year, dividends are considered to be *in arrears*. Before a dividend can be declared to common stockholders in a subsequent period, the preferred stockholders must be paid all dividends in arrears as well as the current year's dividend. The cumulative feature ensures that the preferred stockholders will

LO 2   Understand the characteristics of common and preferred stock and the differences between the classes of stock.

FROM CONCEPT TO PRACTICE 11.1
READING FORD'S ANNUAL REPORT
Which financial statements could you look at to identify the different classes of stock issued by Ford? Which classes of stock are issued? How many shares of each class have been issued?

Various companies are often honored by being invited to ring the bell which begins trading at the New York Stock Exchange.

receive a dividend before one is paid to common stockholders. It does not guarantee a dividend to preferred stockholders, however. There is no legal requirement mandating that a corporation declare a dividend, and preferred stockholders have a legal right to receive a dividend only when it has been declared.

Some preferred stocks have a **participating feature.** Its purpose is to allow the preferred stockholders to receive a dividend in excess of the regular rate when a firm has been particularly profitable and declares an abnormally large dividend. When the participating feature is present and a firm declares a dividend, the preferred stockholders first have a right to the current year's dividend, and then the common stockholders must receive an equal portion (usually based on the par or stated value of the stocks) of the dividend. The participating feature then applies to any dividend declared in excess of the amounts in the first two steps. The preferred stockholders are allowed to share in the excess, normally on the basis of the total par value of the preferred and common stock. The participating feature is explained in more detail in the section of this chapter concerning dividends.

Preferred stock may also be convertible or callable. The **convertible feature** allows the preferred stockholders to convert their stockholdings to common stock. Convertible preferred stock offers stockholders the advantages of the low risk generally associated with preferred stock and the possibility of the higher return that is associated with common stock. The **callable feature** allows the issuing firm to retire the stock after it has been issued. Normally, the call price is specified as a fixed dollar amount. Firms may exercise the call option to eliminate a certain class of preferred stock so that control of the corporation is maintained in the hands of fewer stockholders. The call option also may be exercised when the dividend rate on the preferred stock is too high and other, more cost-effective financing alternatives are available.

Preferred stock is attractive to many investors because it offers a return in the form of a dividend at a level of risk that is lower than that of most common stocks. Usually, the dividend available on preferred stock is more stable from year to year, and as a result, the market price of the stock is also more stable. In fact, if preferred stock carries certain provisions, the stock is very similar to bonds or notes payable. Management must evaluate whether such securities really represent debt and should be presented in the liability category of the balance sheet or whether they represent equity and should be presented in the equity category. Such a decision involves the concept of *substance over form.* That is, a company must look not only at the legal form but also at the economic substance of the security to decide whether it is debt or equity.

Issuance of Stock

Stock Issued for Cash

LO 3 Determine the impact when stock is issued for cash or for other consideration.

Stock may be issued in several different ways. It may be issued for cash or for noncash assets. When stock is issued for cash, the amount of its par value should be reported in the stock account and the amount in excess of par should be reported in an additional paid-in capital account. For example, assume that on July 1 a firm issued 1,000 shares of $10 par common stock for $15 per share. The transaction is recorded as follows:

July 1	Cash	15,000	
	Common Stock		10,000
	Additional Paid-in Capital—		
	Common		5,000
	To record the issuance of 1,000 shares of common stock at $15 per share.		

Assets	=	**Liabilities**	+	**Owners' Equity**
+15,000				+10,000
				+ 5,000

As noted earlier, the Common Stock account and the Additional Paid-in Capital account are both presented in the stockholders' equity category of the balance sheet and represent the contributed capital component of the corporation.

If no-par stock is issued, the corporation does not distinguish between common stock and additional paid-in capital. If the firm in the previous example had issued no-par stock on July 1 for $15 per share, the transaction would be recorded as follows:

July 1	Cash	15,000	
	Common Stock		15,000
	To record the issuance of 1,000 shares of common stock at $15 per share.		

Assets	=	Liabilities	+	Owners' Equity
+15,000				+15,000

Stock Issued for Noncash Consideration

Occasionally, stock is issued in return for something other than cash. For example, a corporation may issue stock to obtain land or buildings. When such a transaction occurs, the company faces the difficult task of deciding what value to place on the transaction. This is especially difficult when the market values of the elements of the transaction are not known with complete certainty. According to the general guideline, the transaction should be reported at fair market value. Market value may be indicated by the value of the consideration given (stock) or the value of the consideration received (property), whichever can be most readily determined.

Assume that on July 1 a firm issued 500 shares of $10 par preferred stock to acquire a building. The stock is not widely traded, and the current market value of the stock is not evident. The building has recently been appraised by an independent firm as having a market value of $12,000. In this case, the issuance of the stock affects the balance sheet as follows:

July 1	Building	12,000	
	Preferred Stock		5,000
	Additional Paid-in Capital—		
	Preferred		7,000
	To record the issuance of preferred stock for building.		

Assets	=	Liabilities	+	Owners' Equity
+12,000				+5,000
				+7,000

In other situations, the market value of the stock may be more readily determined and should be used as the best measure of the value of the transaction. Market value may be represented by the current stock market quotation or by a recent cash sale of the stock. The company should attempt to develop the best estimate of the market value of the noncash transaction and should neither intentionally overstate nor understate the assets received by the issuance of stock.

What Is Treasury Stock?

The stockholders' equity category of Chrysler's balance sheet includes **treasury stock** in the amount of $1,235 million. The Treasury Stock account is created when a corporation buys its own stock sometime after issuing it. For an amount to be treated as treasury stock, (1) it must be the corporation's own stock, (2) it must have been issued to the stockholders at some point, (3) it must have been repurchased from the stockholders, and (4) it must not be retired but must be held for some purpose. Treasury stock is not considered outstanding stock and does not have voting rights.

LO 4 Describe the impact of stock treated as treasury stock.

A corporation may repurchase stock as treasury stock for several reasons. The most common is to have stock available to distribute to employees for bonuses or as part of an employee benefit plan. Firms also may buy treasury stock to maintain a favorable market price for the stock or to improve the appearance of the firm's financial ratios. More recently, firms have purchased their stock to maintain control of the ownership and to prevent unwanted takeover or buyout attempts. Of course, the lower the stock price, the more likely a company is to buy back its own stock and wait for the shares to rise in value before reissuing them.

The two methods to account for treasury stock transactions are the cost method and the par value method. We will present the more commonly used cost method. Assume that the stockholders' equity section of Rezin Company's balance sheet on December 31, 1997, appears as follows:

Common stock, $10 par value,	$10,000
1,000 shares issued and outstanding	
Additional paid-in capital—Common	12,000
Retained earnings	15,000
Total stockholders' equity	$37,000

Assume that on February 1, 1998, Rezin buys 100 of its shares as treasury stock at $25 per share. Rezin records the following transaction at that time:

Feb. 1	Treasury Stock	2,500	
	Cash		2,500
	To record the purchase of 100 shares of treasury stock.		

Assets	=	**Liabilities**	+	**Owners' Equity**
−2,500				**−2,500**

The purchase of treasury stock does not directly affect the Common Stock account itself. The Treasury Stock account is considered to be a contra account and is subtracted from the total of contributed capital and retained earnings in the stockholders' equity section. Treasury Stock is *not* an asset account. When a company buys its own stock, it is contracting its size and reducing the equity of the stockholders. Therefore, Treasury Stock is a contra-equity account, not an asset.

The stockholders' equity section of Rezin's balance sheet on February 1, 1998, after the purchase of the treasury stock, appears as follows:

Common stock, $10 par value,	$10,000
1,000 shares issued, 900 outstanding	
Additional paid-in capital—Common	12,000
Retained earnings	15,000
Total contributed capital and retained earnings	$37,000
Less: Treasury stock, 100 shares at cost	2,500
Total stockholders' equity	$34,500

Corporations may choose to reissue stock to investors after it has been held as treasury stock. When treasury stock is resold for more than it cost, the difference between the sales price and the cost appears in the Additional Paid-in Capital—Treasury Stock account. For example, if Rezin resold 100 shares of treasury stock on May 1, 1998, for $30 per share the Treasury Stock account would be reduced by $2,500 (100 shares times $25 per share), and the Additional Paid-in Capital—Treasury Stock account would be increased by $500 (100 shares times the difference between the purchase price of $25 and the reissue price of $30).

When treasury stock is resold for an amount less than its cost, the difference between the sales prices and the cost is deducted from the Additional Paid-in Capital—Treasury Stock account. If that account does not exist, the difference should be deducted from the Retained Earnings account. For example, assume that Rezin Company had resold 100 shares of treasury stock on May 1, 1998, for $20 per share, instead of $30 in the previous example. In this example, Rezin has had no other treasury stock transactions, and therefore, no balance existed in the Additional Paid-in Capital—Treasury Stock account. Rezin would then reduce the Treasury Stock account by $2,500 (100 shares times $25 per share) and would reduce Retained Earnings by $500 (100 shares times the difference between the purchase price of $25 and the reissue price of $20 per share). Thus, the Additional Paid-in Capital—Treasury Stock account may have a positive (credit) balance, but entries that result in a negative (debit) balance in the account should not be made.

Note that *income statement accounts are never involved* in treasury stock transactions. Regardless of whether treasury stock is reissued for more or less than its cost, the effect is reflected in the stockholders' equity accounts. It is simply not possible for a firm to engage in transactions involving its own stock and have the result affect the performance of the firm as reflected on the income statement.

Retirement of Stock

Retirement of stock occurs when a corporation buys back stock after it has been issued to investors and does not intend to reissue the stock. Retirement often occurs because the corporation wants to eliminate a particular class of stock or a particular group of stockholders. When stock is repurchased and retired, the balances of the stock account and the paid-in capital account that were created when the stock was issued must be eliminated. When the original issue price is higher than the repurchase price of the stock, the difference is reflected in the Paid-in Capital from Stock Retirement account. When the repurchase price of the stock is more than the original issue price, the difference reduces the Retained Earnings account. The general principle for retirement of stock is the same as for treasury stock transactions. No income statement accounts are affected by the retirement. The effect is reflected in the Cash account and the stockholders' equity accounts.

Dividends: Distribution of Income to Shareholders

Cash Dividends

Corporations may declare and issue several different types of dividends, the most common of which is a cash dividend to stockholders. Cash dividends may be declared quarterly, annually, or at other intervals. Normally, cash dividends are declared on one date, referred to as the *date of declaration,* and are paid out on a later date, referred to as the *payment date.* The dividend is paid to the stockholders that own the stock as of a particular date, the *date of record.*

Generally, two requirements must be met before the board of directors can declare a cash dividend. First, sufficient cash must be available by the payment date to pay to the stockholders. Second, the Retained Earnings account must have a sufficient positive balance. Dividends reduce the balance of the account, and therefore Retained Earnings must have a balance before the dividend declaration. Most firms have an established policy concerning the portion of income that will be declared as dividends. The **dividend payout ratio** is calculated as the annual dividend amount divided by the annual net income. The dividend payout ratios of the three largest members of the auto industry are given in Exhibit 11-3. The dividend payout ratio for many firms is 50% or 60% and seldom exceeds 70%. Typically, utilities pay a high proportion of their earnings. In contrast, fast-growing

EXHIBIT 11-3 — 1995 Dividend Payout Ratios to Common Stockholders in the Automotive Industry

companies in technology often pay nothing to shareholders. Some investors want and need the current income of a high-dividend payout, but others would rather not receive dividend income and prefer to gamble that the stock price will appreciate.

Cash dividends become a liability on the date they are declared. An accounting entry should be recorded on that date to acknowledge the liability and reduce the balance of the Retained Earnings account. For example, assume that on July 1 the board of directors of Grant Company declared a cash dividend of $7,000 to be paid on September 1. Grant records the declaration as follows:

July 1	Retained Earnings	7,000	
	Cash Dividend Payable		7,000
	To record the declaration of a cash dividend.		

Assets	=	**Liabilities**	+	**Owners' Equity**
		+7,000		−7,000

The Cash Dividend Payable account is a liability and is normally shown in the current liability section of the balance sheet.

Grant records the following accounting transaction on September 1 when the cash dividend is paid:

Sept. 1	Cash Dividend Payable	7,000	
	Cash		7,000
	To record the payment of a cash dividend.		

Assets	=	**Liabilities**	+	**Owners' Equity**
−7,000		−7,000		

The important point to remember is that dividends reduce the amount of retained earnings *when declared*. When dividends are paid, the company reduces the liability to stockholders reflected in the Cash Dividend Payable account.

Cash Dividends for Preferred and Common Stock

LO 5 Compute the amount of cash dividends when a firm has issued both preferred and common stock.

When cash dividends involving more than one class of stock are declared, the corporation must determine the proper amount to allocate to each class of stock. As indicated earlier, the amount of dividends that preferred stockholders have rights to depends on the terms and provisions of the preferred stock. We will illustrate the proper allocation of cash dividends with an example of a firm that has two classes of stock, preferred and common.

As a student, you have some extra cash that you would like to invest. Since your income is rather low, you decide to invest in stocks that pay "high" cash dividends, but you don't know which company to invest in. Which financial statement would help you make that decision, and which section of that financial statement shows the amount of dividends paid?

ANS: The statement of cash flows is the financial statement you would need. Since cash dividends represent a cost of financing the business with stock, they should appear in the Financing Activities section of the statement of cash flows, as a cash outflow.

Assume that on December 31, 1998, Stricker Company has outstanding 10,000 shares of $10 par, 8% preferred stock and 40,000 shares of $5 par common stock. Stricker was unable to declare a dividend in 1996 or 1997 but wants to declare a $70,000 dividend for 1998. The dividend is to be allocated to preferred and common stockholders in accordance with the terms of the stock agreements.

Noncumulative Preferred Stock If the terms of the stock agreement indicate that the preferred stock is not cumulative, the preferred stockholders do not have a right to dividends in arrears. The dividends that were not declared in 1996 and 1997 are simply lost and do not affect the distribution of the dividend in 1998. Therefore, the cash dividend declared in 1998 is allocated between preferred and common stockholders as follows:

	TO PREFERRED	TO COMMON
Step 1: Distribute current year dividend to preferred (10,000 shares × $10 par × 8% × 1 year)	$8,000	
Step 2: Distribute remaining dividend to common ($70,000 − $8,000)		$62,000
Total allocated	$8,000	$62,000
Dividend per share		
Preferred: $8,000/10,000 shares	$.80	
Common: $62,000/40,000 shares		$1.55

Cumulative Preferred Stock If the terms of the stock agreement indicate that the preferred stock is cumulative, the preferred stockholders have a right to dividends in arrears before the current year's dividend is distributed. Therefore, Stricker performs the following steps:

	TO PREFERRED	TO COMMON
Step 1: Distribute dividends in arrears to preferred (10,000 shares × $10 par × 8% × 2 years)	$16,000	
Step 2: Distribute current year dividend to preferred (10,000 shares × $10 par × 8% × 1 year)	8,000	
Step 3: Distribute remainder to common ($70,000 − $24,000)		$46,000
Total allocated	$24,000	$46,000
Dividend per share		
Preferred: $24,000/10,000 shares	$2.40	
Common: $46,000/40,000 shares		$1.15

Cumulative and Participating Preferred Stock If the terms of the stock agreement indicate that the preferred stock is both cumulative and participating, the preferred stockholders have a right to dividends in arrears (the cumulative feature) and to a portion of the current year's dividend that exceeds a specified amount (the participating feature). Assume that Stricker Company preferred stockholders participate in any dividend in excess of 8% of total par value and that the participation is based on the proportion of the total par value of the preferred and common stock. The 1998 dividend is distributed as follows:

	TO PREFERRED	TO COMMON
Step 1: Distribute dividend in arrears to preferred (10,000 shares × $10 par × 8% × 2 years)	$16,000	
Step 2: Distribute current year dividend to preferred (10,000 shares × $10 par × 8% × 1 year)	8,000	
Step 3: Distribute equal percentage to common (40,000 shares × $5 par × 8%)		$16,000
Step 4: Remainder to preferred and common on basis of total par value		
Preferred: ($70,000 − $40,000) × $100,000[a]/$300,000	10,000	
Common: ($70,000 − $40,000) × $200,000[b]/$300,000		20,000
Total allocated	$34,000	$36,000
Dividend per share		
Preferred: $34,000/10,000 shares	$3.40	
Common: $36,000/40,000 shares		$.90

[a]10,000 shares × $10 par   [b]40,000 shares × $5 par

The Stricker Company example illustrates the flexibility available with preferred stock. The provisions and terms of the preferred stock can be established to make the stock attractive to investors and to provide an effective form of financing for the corporation. The cumulative and participating features make the preferred stock more attractive. However, these features may make the *common stock* less attractive because more dividends for the preferred stockholders may mean less dividends for the common stockholders.

Stock Dividends

LO 6   Understand the difference between cash and stock dividends and the effect of stock dividends.

Cash dividends are the most popular and widely used form of dividend, but corporations may at times use stock dividends instead of, or in addition to, cash dividends. A **stock dividend** occurs when a corporation declares and issues additional shares of its own stock to its existing stockholders. Firms use stock dividends for several reasons. First, a corporation may simply not have sufficient cash available to declare a cash dividend. Stock dividends do not require the use of the corporation's resources and allow cash to be retained for other purposes. Second, stock dividends result in additional shares of stock outstanding and may decrease the market price per share of stock if the dividend is large (small stock dividends tend to have little effect on market price). The lower price may make the stock more attractive to a wider range of investors and allow enhanced financing opportunities. Finally, stock dividends normally do not represent taxable income to the recipients and may be attractive to some wealthy stockholders.

Similar to cash dividends, stock dividends are normally declared by the board of directors on a specific date, and the stock is distributed to the stockholders at a later date. The corporation recognizes the stock dividend on the date of declaration. Assume that Shah Company's stockholders' equity category of the balance sheet appears as follows as of January 1, 1998:

Common stock, $10 par,	
5,000 shares issued and outstanding	$ 50,000
Additional paid-in capital—Common	30,000
Retained earnings	70,000
Total stockholders' equity	$150,000

Assume that on January 2, 1998, Shah declares a 10% stock dividend to common stock-holders to be distributed on April 1, 1998. Small stock dividends (usually those of 20 to 25% or less) normally are recorded at the *market value* of the stock as of the date of de-claration. Assume that Shah's common stock is selling at $40 per share on that date. Therefore, the total market value of the stock dividend is $20,000 (10% of 5,000 shares outstanding, or 500 shares, times $40 per share). Shah records the transaction on the date of declaration as follows, with the par value per share recorded in the Common Stock Dividend Distributable account:

Jan. 2	Retained Earnings	20,000	
	Additional Paid-in Capital—Common		15,000
	Common Stock Dividend Distributable		5,000
	To record the declaration of a stock dividend.		

Assets	=	Liabilities	+	Owners' Equity
				−20,000
				+15,000
				+ 5,000

The Common Stock Dividend Distributable account represents shares of stock to be is-sued; it is not a liability account because no cash or assets are to be distributed to the stockholders. Thus, it should be treated as an account in the stockholders' equity sec-tion of the balance sheet and is a part of the contributed capital component of equity.

Note that the declaration of a stock dividend does not affect the total stockholders' equity of the corporation, although the retained earnings are reduced. That is, the stockholders' equity section of Shah's balance sheet on January 2, 1998, is as follows after the declaration of the dividend:

Common stock, $10 par,	
5,000 shares issued and outstanding	$ 50,000
Common stock dividend distributable, 500 shares	5,000
Additional paid-in capital—Common	45,000
Retained earnings	50,000
Total stockholders' equity	$150,000

The account balances are different, but total stockholders' equity is $150,000 both be-fore and after the declaration of the stock dividend. In effect, retained earnings has been capitalized (transferred permanently to the contributed capital accounts). When a cor-poration actually issues a stock dividend, it is necessary to transfer an amount from the Stock Dividend Distributable account to the appropriate stock account.

Our stock dividend example has illustrated the general rule that stock dividends should be reported at fair market value. That is, in the transaction to reflect the stock dividend, retained earnings is decreased (debited) in the amount of the fair market value per share of the stock times the number of shares to be distributed. When a large stock dividend is declared, however, accountants do not follow the general rule we have illus-trated. A large stock dividend is a stock dividend of more than 20% to 25% of the num-ber of shares of stock outstanding. In that case, the stock dividend is reported at *par value* rather than at fair market value. That is, Retained Earnings is decreased (debited) in the amount of the par value per share times the number of shares to be distributed.

Refer again to the Shah Company example. Assume that instead of a 10% dividend, on January 2, 1998, Shah declares and distributes a 100% stock dividend to be distrib-uted on April 1, 1998. The stock dividend results in 5,000 additional shares being issued and certainly meets the definition of a large stock dividend. Shah records the following transaction at the time of dividend declaration:

Jan. 2   Retained Earnings   50,000
                 Common Stock Dividend Distributable   50,000
                 To record the declaration of a large stock dividend.

Assets	=	Liabilities	+	Owners' Equity
				−50,000
				+50,000

The accounting transaction to be recorded when the stock is actually distributed is as follows:

Apr. 1   Common Stock Dividend Distributable   50,000
                 Common Stock   50,000
                 To record the distribution of a stock dividend.

Assets	=	Liabilities	+	Owners' Equity
				−50,000
				+50,000

The stockholders' equity category of Shah's balance sheet as of April 1 after the stock dividend is as follows:

Common stock, $10 par,	
10,000 shares issued and outstanding	$100,000
Additional paid-in capital—Common	30,000
Retained earnings	20,000
Total stockholders' equity	$150,000

Again, you should note that the stock dividend has not affected total stockholders' equity. Shah has $150,000 of stockholders' equity both before and after the stock dividend. The difference between large and small stock dividends is the amount transferred from retained earnings to the contributed capital portion of equity.

Stock Splits

LO 7 Determine the difference between stock dividends and stock splits.

A **stock split** is similar to a stock dividend in that it results in additional shares of stock outstanding and is nontaxable. In fact, firms may use a stock split for nearly the same reasons as a stock dividend: to increase the number of shares, reduce the market price per share, and make the stock more accessible to a wider range of investors. There is an important legal difference, however. Stock dividends do not affect the par value per share of the stock, whereas stock splits reduce the par value per share. There also is an important accounting difference. An accounting transaction is *not recorded* when a corporation declares and executes a stock split. None of the stockholders' equity accounts are affected by the split. Rather, the footnote information accompanying the balance sheet must disclose the additional shares and the reduction of the par value per share.

ACCOUNTING FOR YOUR DECISIONS
You Are the Stockbroker

Your firm recently recommended the shares of Intel Corp., a large semiconductor manufacturer based in northern California. The stock had been trading at about $100 per share when the company announced a 2:1 stock split. You have been receiving calls from your clients asking you why the company split its stock, even though there is no change in anyone's ownership interest as a result of the split. How would you answer your clients?

ANS: Although a stock split does not provide immediate income to current shareholders, it is an indication of the company's optimism about the future. To maintain interest from individual shareholders, many companies like to keep the price of their stock under $100. A stock split keeps the shares at an affordable price and allows a broader range of potential investors. From an investor's perspective, a stock split is usually a positive sign.

Return to the Shah Company example. Assume that on January 2, 1998, Shah issued a 2-for-1 stock split instead of a stock dividend. The split results in an additional 5,000 shares of stock outstanding but should not be recorded in a formal accounting transaction. Therefore, the stockholders' equity section of Shah Company immediately after the stock split on January 2, 1998, is as follows:

Common stock, $5 par,	
10,000 shares issued and outstanding	$ 50,000
Additional paid-in capital—Common	30,000
Retained earnings	70,000
Total stockholders' equity	$150,000

You should note that the par value per share has been reduced from $10 to $5 per share of stock as a result of the split. Like a stock dividend, the split does not affect total stockholders' equity because no assets have been transferred. Therefore, the split simply results in more shares of stock with claims to the same net assets of the firm.

Exhibit 11-4 presents the stockholders' equity category of Motorola Inc.'s 1995 and 1994 balance sheets. The exhibit indicates that in 1994 Motorola had 588 million shares of common stock issued and outstanding at year-end. The footnotes to the financial statements indicate that the company declared a 2-for-1 stock split during 1994. This doubled the number of shares of stock to the year-end level of 588 million shares. Thus, after the stock split, each stockholder had twice as many shares of stock but still had the same proportional ownership of the company. Although a stock split does not increase the wealth of the shareholder, it is usually a good sign. Companies with rising stock prices declare a stock split to make the stock more marketable to the small investor, who would be more likely to buy a stock at $50 per share than at $100.

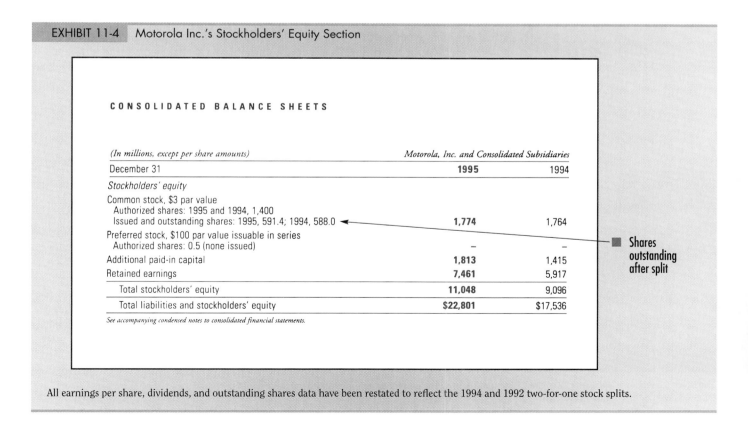

EXHIBIT 11-4   Motorola Inc.'s Stockholders' Equity Section

CONSOLIDATED BALANCE SHEETS

(In millions, except per share amounts)	Motorola, Inc. and Consolidated Subsidiaries	
December 31	**1995**	1994
Stockholders' equity		
Common stock, $3 par value		
Authorized shares: 1995 and 1994, 1,400		
Issued and outstanding shares: 1995, 591.4; 1994, 588.0	**1,774**	1,764
Preferred stock, $100 par value issuable in series		
Authorized shares: 0.5 (none issued)	–	–
Additional paid-in capital	**1,813**	1,415
Retained earnings	**7,461**	5,917
Total stockholders' equity	**11,048**	9,096
Total liabilities and stockholders' equity	**$22,801**	$17,536

See accompanying condensed notes to consolidated financial statements.

Shares outstanding after split

All earnings per share, dividends, and outstanding shares data have been restated to reflect the 1994 and 1992 two-for-one stock splits.

What Analyzing Owners' Equity Reveals about a Firm's Value

Book Value per Share

Users of financial statements are often interested in computing the value of a corporation's stock. This is a difficult task because *value* is not a well-defined term and means different things to different users. One measure of value is the book value of the stock. Book value per share of common stock represents the rights that each share of common stock has to the net assets of the corporation. The term *net assets* refers to the total assets of the firm minus total liabilities. In other words, net assets equal the total stockholders' equity of the corporation. Therefore, when only common stock is present, book value per share is measured as follows:

Book Value per Share =
Total Stockholders' Equity/Number of Shares of Stock Outstanding

The stockholders' equity of Motorola Inc. appears in Exhibit 11-4. As of December 31, 1995, the total stockholders' equity of Motorola is $11,048 million, and the number of outstanding shares of common stock is 591.4 million. Therefore, the book value per share for Motorola is $18.68, calculated as follows:

$$\$11,048/591.4 = \$18.68$$

This means that the company's common stockholders have the right to $18.68 per share of net assets in the corporation.

The book value per share indicates the recorded minimum value per share of the stock. In a sense, it indicates the rights of the common stockholders in the event that the company is liquidated. It does not indicate the market value of the common stock. That is, book value per share does not indicate the price that should be paid by those who want to buy or sell the stock on the stock exchange. Book value is also an incomplete measure of value because the corporation's net assets are normally measured on the balance sheet at the original historical cost, not at the current value of the assets. Thus, book value per share does not provide a very accurate measure of the price that a stockholder would be willing to pay for a share of stock. The book value of a stock is often thought to be the "floor" of a stock price. An investor's decision to pay less than book value for a share of stock suggests that he or she thinks that the company is going to continue to lose money, thus shrinking book value.

Calculating Book Value When Preferred Stock Is Present

The focus of the computation of book value per share is always on the value per share of the *common* stock. Therefore, the computation must be adjusted for corporations that have both preferred and common stock. The numerator of the fraction, total stockholders' equity, should be reduced by the rights that preferred stockholders have to the corporation's net assets. Normally, this can be accomplished by deducting the redemption value or liquidation value of the preferred stock along with any dividends in arrears on cumulative preferred stock. The denominator should not include the number of shares of preferred stock.

To illustrate the computation of book value per share when both common and preferred stock are present, we will refer to the stockholders' equity category of Chrysler, presented in Exhibit 11-5. When calculating book value per share, we want to consider only the *common* stockholders' equity. Exhibit 11-5 indicates (1) that Chrysler's total stockholders' equity in 1995 was $10,959 but also (2) that preferred stockholders had a right to $68 million in the event of liquidation. Therefore, $68 million must be deducted to calculate the rights of the common stockholders:

$$\$10,959 - \$68 = \$10,891 \text{ common stockholders' equity}$$

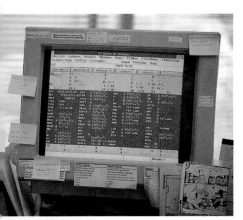

Stockbrokers use screens not only to keep track of the stocks, but also to match companies with investors, based on companies' numbers.

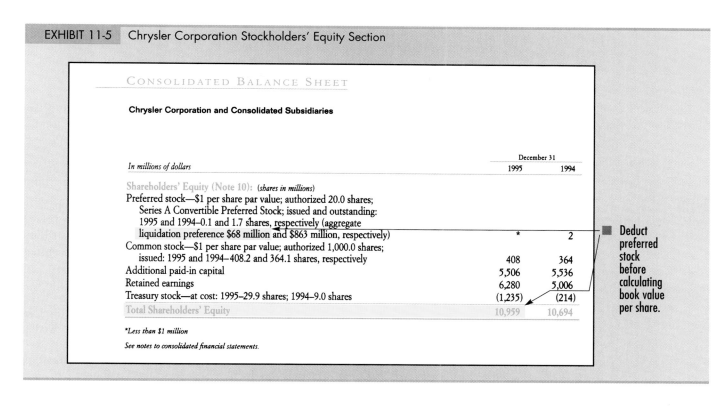

EXHIBIT 11-5   Chrysler Corporation Stockholders' Equity Section

CONSOLIDATED BALANCE SHEET

Chrysler Corporation and Consolidated Subsidiaries

	December 31	
In millions of dollars	1995	1994
Shareholders' Equity (Note 10): *(shares in millions)*		
Preferred stock—$1 per share par value; authorized 20.0 shares;		
Series A Convertible Preferred Stock; issued and outstanding:		
1995 and 1994–0.1 and 1.7 shares, respectively (aggregate		
liquidation preference $68 million and $863 million, respectively)	*	2
Common stock—$1 per share par value; authorized 1,000.0 shares;		
issued: 1995 and 1994–408.2 and 364.1 shares, respectively	408	364
Additional paid-in capital	5,506	5,536
Retained earnings	6,280	5,006
Treasury stock—at cost: 1995–29.9 shares; 1994–9.0 shares	(1,235)	(214)
Total Shareholders' Equity	10,959	10,694

Deduct preferred stock before calculating book value per share.

*Less than $1 million

See notes to consolidated financial statements.

The number of shares of common stock *outstanding* can be calculated from Exhibit 11-5 as follows:

$$
\begin{array}{r}
408.2 \text{ million shares issued} \\
-\ 29.9 \text{ million treasury shares} \\
\hline
378.3 \text{ million shares outstanding}
\end{array}
$$

Therefore, the computation of book value per share is as follows:

$$\$10,891/378.3 = \$28.79 \text{ Book Value per Share}$$

This indicates that if the company was liquidated and the assets were sold at their recorded values, the common stockholders would receive $28.79 per share. Of course, if the company went bankrupt and had to liquidate assets at distressed values, stockholders would receive something less than book value.

Market Value per Share

The market value of the stock is a more meaningful measure of the value of the stock to those financial statement users interested in buying or selling shares of stock. The **market value per share** is the price at which stock is currently selling. When stock is sold on a stock exchange, the price can be determined by its most recent selling price. For example, the listing for General Motors stock on the financial pages of a newspaper may indicate the following:

52-Week			Daily			
High	Low	Sym	High	Low	Last	Change
59⅜	45¾	GM	57⅝	56½	56½	−⅜

The two left-hand columns indicate the stock price for the last 52-week period. General Motors sold as high as $59⅜ and as low as $45¾ during that time period. The right-hand portion indicates the high and low for the previous day's trading and the closing price. General Motors sold as high as $57⅝ per share and as low as $56½ per share and closed at $56½. For the day, the stock decreased by ⅜ or $0.375 per share.

The market value of the stock depends on many factors. Stockholders must evaluate a corporation's earnings and liquidity as indicated in the financial statements. They must also consider a variety of economic factors and project all of the factors into the future to determine the proper market value per share of the stock. Many investors use sophisticated investment techniques, including large databases, to identify factors that affect a company's stock price.

How Changes in Stockholders' Equity Affect the Statement of Cash Flows

LO 9 Explain the effects that transactions involving stockholders' equity have on the statement of cash flows.

It is important to determine the effect that the issuance of stock, the repurchase of stock, and the payment of dividends have on the statement of cash flows. Each of these business activities' impact on cash must be reflected on the statement. Exhibit 11-6 indicates how these stockholders' equity transactions affect cash flow and where the items should be placed on the statement of cash flows.

The issuance of stock is a method to finance business. Therefore, the cash *inflow* from the sale of stock to stockholders should be reflected as an inflow in the Financing Activities section of the statement of cash flows. Generally, companies do not disclose separately the amount received for the par value of the stock and the amount received in excess of par. Rather, one amount is listed to indicate the total inflow of cash.

The repurchase or retirement of stock also represents a financing activity. Therefore, the cash *outflow* should be reflected as a reduction of cash in the Financing Activities section of the statement of cash flows. Again, companies do not distinguish between the amount paid for the par of the stock and the amount paid in excess of par. One amount is generally listed to indicate the total cash outflow to retire stock.

Dividends paid to stockholders represent a cost of financing the business with stock. Therefore, dividends paid should be reflected as a cash *outflow* in the Financing Activities section of the statement of cash flows. It is important to distinguish between the declaration of dividends and the payment of dividends. The cash outflow occurs at the time the dividend is paid and should be reflected on the statement of cash flows in that period.

The 1995 statement of cash flows for Ford Motor Company is given in Exhibit 11-7. Ford's statement is somewhat different because it indicates the activities of its two major divisions, automotive and financial services, in separate columns. Note the first two lines in the Financing Activities category of the statement of cash flows. First, Ford indicates a cash outflow of $1,559 million for cash dividends. On the second line, Ford indicates a cash inflow of $601 million from the issuance of common stock during 1995. Finally, note that the financial services division had a decrease in cash (outflow) of $1,875 million for the redemption of preferred stock.

EXHIBIT 11-6	The Effect of Stockholders' Equity Items on the Statement of Cash Flows

Item	Statement of Cash Flows
	Operating Activities Net income xxx
	Investing Activities
	Financing Activities
Issuance of stock	━━━━▶ +
Retirement or repurchase of stock	━━━━▶ −
Payment of dividends	━━━━▶ −

EXHIBIT 11-7   Ford Motor Company's 1995 Statement of Cash Flows

CONSOLIDATED STATEMENT OF CASH FLOWS
For the Years Ended December 31, 1995, 1994 and 1993 (in millions)

	1995 Automotive	1995 Financial Services
Cash and cash equivalents at January 1	$ 4,481	$ 1,739
Cash flows from operating activities (Note 16)	8,849	12,322
Cash flows from investing activities		
Capital expenditures	(8,676)	(321)
Proceeds from sale and leaseback of fixed assets	0	–
Acquisitions of other companies	0	0
Proceeds from sales of subsidiaries	0	0
Acquisitions of receivables and lease investments	–	(99,967)
Collections of receivables and lease investments	–	71,149
Net acquisitions of daily rental vehicles	–	(1,459)
Purchases of securities (Note 16)	(51)	(6,274)
Sales and maturities of securities (Note 16)	325	5,052
Proceeds from sales of receivables	–	4,360
Loans originated net of principal payments	–	(9)
Net investing activity with Financial Services	(19)	–
Other	558	(175)
Net cash used in investing activities	(7,863)	(27,644)
Cash flows from financing activities		
Cash dividends	(1,559)	–
Issuance of Common Stock	601	–
Changes in short–term debt	413	5,884
Proceeds from issuance of other debt	300	23,854
Principal payments on other debt	(177)	(11,489)
Net financing activity with Automotive	–	19
Changes in customers' deposits, excluding interest credited	–	–
Receipts from annuity contracts	–	283
Net (redemption)/issuance of subsidiary company preferred stock (Note 1)	–	(1,875)
Other	121	102
Net cash (used in)/provided by financing activities	(301)	16,778
Effect of exchange rate changes on cash	107	(28)
Net transactions with Automotive/ Financial Services	477	(477)
Net increase/(decrease) in cash and cash equivalents	1,269	951
Cash and cash equivalents at December 31	$ 5,750	$ 2,690

The accompanying notes are part of the financial statements.

■ Changes in stockholders' equity are shown in financing activities category.

Review Problem

Andrew Company was incorporated on January 1, 1998, under a corporate charter that authorized the issuance of 50,000 shares of $5 par common stock and 20,000 shares of $100 par, 8% preferred stock. The following events occurred during 1998. Andrew wants to record the events and develop financial statements on December 31, 1998.

a. Issued for cash 10,000 shares of common stock at $25 per share and 1,000 shares of preferred stock at $110 per share on January 15, 1998.

"HOT GROWTH COMPANY" BOOSTS EQUITY BY GOING PUBLIC

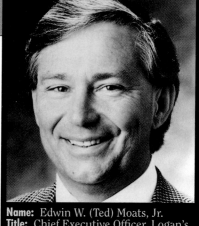

Name: Edwin W. (Ted) Moats, Jr.
Title: Chief Executive Officer, Logan's Roadhouse, Inc.

When Ted Moats was thinking about ways to grow his chain of country & western-themed restaurants, he could have borrowed money through a private placement of debt with big institutions, or he could have borrowed from the bank. After all, before he became CEO of this Nashville, Tennessee-based "Hot Growth Company," as *Business Week* magazine called it, he was a banker. The company financed its growth by partnering with another restaurant chain that leased its real estate and equipment. Although the relationship was a good one, Moats wanted independence from this other chain.

As a banker, he knew the limitations involved in borrowing money. As one of the owners, Mr. Moats and other top managers of the company would be forced to pay a large chunk of their cash flow to meet principal and interest payments on that debt. And he also knew that the bank would have veto power over his desire to build more restaurants. "We decided to go to the equity market first, and then add debt later if necessary," says Moats. By adding shareholders' equity first, the company would be able to go to the bank if need be with a solid capital base.

In July 1995, Logan's Roadhouse went public at $9 split adjusted per share, using the proceeds to retire debt and for future growth. Within a year, the stock more than doubled. Now, Moats can add debt to the balance sheet without feeling totally dependent on the bank or upsetting his stockholders. "Holders of restaurant stocks don't like to see a ratio of debt to stockholders' equity of more than 45%," he says.

Of course, being public has its disadvantages. The investors who buy stock expect the company to grow and the stock price to increase. There's scrutiny from the Securities and Exchange Commission, from Wall Street analysts, from the business press. And when you're a so-called "growth" stock that doesn't pay dividends, your stock price is going to be volatile, especially if you can't make your quarterly earnings expectations. But meeting or exceeding expectations is what business is all about.

In the restaurant business, "the key is getting good sales growth," says Moats. "If you've got that, then you can find managers who can control expenses to create a good bottom line." His strategy: provide an entertaining and relaxed environment, go for high volume and moderate prices, and offer a broad menu. "We want something in our restaurant to be appealing to everyone in the party."

---

b. Acquired a patent on April 1 in exchange for 2,000 shares of common stock. At the time of the exchange, the common stock was selling on the local stock exchange for $30 per share.

c. Repurchased 500 shares of common stock on May 1 at $20 per share. The corporation is holding the stock to be used for an employee bonus plan.

d. Declared a cash dividend of $1 per share to common stockholders and an 8% dividend to preferred stockholders on July 1. The preferred stock is noncumulative, nonparticipating. The dividend will be distributed on August 1.

e. Distributed the cash dividend on August 1.

f. Declared and distributed to preferred stockholders a 10% stock dividend on September 1. At the time of the dividend declaration, preferred stock was valued at $130 per share.

g. On December 31, calculated the annual net income for the year to be $200,000. Andrew wants to transfer the net income from the Income Summary account to the Retained Earnings account.

Required

1. Record the accounting entries in items a through g.

2. Develop the stockholders' equity section of Andrew Company's balance sheet at December 31, 1998. You do not need to consider the footnotes that accompany the balance sheet.

3. Determine the book value per share of the common stock. Assume that the preferred stock can be redeemed at par.

Solution to Review Problem

1. The following entries should be recorded:

   a. The entry to record the issuance of stock:

Jan. 15	Cash	360,000	
	Common Stock		50,000
	Additional Paid-in Capital—		
	Common		200,000
	Preferred Stock		100,000
	Additional Paid-in Capital—		
	Preferred		10,000
	To record the issuance of stock for cash.		

Assets	=	Liabilities	+	Owners' Equity
+360,000				+ 50,000
				+200,000
				+100,000
				+ 10,000

   b. The patent received for stock should be recorded at the value of the stock:

Apr. 1	Patent	60,000	
	Common Stock		10,000
	Additional Paid-in Capital—		
	Common		50,000
	To record the issuance of stock for patent.		

Assets	=	Liabilities	+	Owners' Equity
+60,000				+10,000
				+50,000

   c. Stock reacquired constitutes treasury stock and should be recorded as follows:

May 1	Treasury Stock	10,000	
	Cash		10,000
	To record the purchase of treasury stock.		

Assets	=	Liabilities	+	Owners' Equity
-10,000				-10,000

   d. A cash dividend should be declared on the number of shares of stock outstanding as of July 1. The dividend is recorded as follows:

July 1	Retained Earnings	19,500	
	Dividends Payable—Common		11,500
	Dividends Payable—Preferred		8,000
	To record the declaration of a cash dividend.		

Assets	=	Liabilities	+	Owners' Equity
		+11,500		-19,500
		+ 8,000		

   The number of shares of common stock outstanding should be calculated as the number of shares issued (12,000) less the number of shares of treasury stock (500). The preferred stock dividend should be calculated as 1,000 shares times $100 par times 8%.

   e. The entry to record the distribution of a cash dividend is recorded as follows:

Aug. 1	Dividends Payable—Common	11,500	
	Dividends Payable—Preferred	8,000	
	Cash		19,500
	To record the payment of cash dividend.		

Assets	=	Liabilities	+	Owners' Equity
-19,500		-11,500		
		- 8,000		

f. A stock dividend should be based on the number of shares of stock outstanding and should be declared and recorded at the market value of the stock as follows:

Sept. 1	Retained Earnings	13,000	
	Preferred Stock		10,000
	Additional Paid-in Capital—Preferred		3,000
	To record the declaration of a stock dividend.		

Assets	=	Liabilities	+	Owners' Equity
				−13,000
				+10,000
				+ 3,000

The amount of the debit to retained earnings should be calculated as the number of shares outstanding (1,000) times 10% times $130 per share.

g. The entry to close the Income Summary account to stockholders' equity should be recorded as follows:

Dec. 31	Income Summary	200,000	
	Retained Earnings		200,000
	To record the annual net income.		

Assets	=	Liabilities	+	Owners' Equity
				−200,000
				+200,000

2. The stockholders' equity for Andrew Company after completing these transactions appears as follows:

Preferred stock, $100 par, 8%,	
20,000 shares authorized, 1,100 issued	$110,000
Common stock, $5 par,	
50,000 shares authorized, 12,000 issued	60,000
Additional paid-in capital—Preferred	13,000
Additional paid-in capital—Common	250,000
Retained earnings	167,500*
Total contributed capital and retained	
earnings	$600,500
Less: Treasury stock, 500 shares, common	(10,000)
Total stockholders' equity	$590,500

*$200,000 − $19,500 − $13,000 = 167,500

3. The book value per share of the common stock is

($590,500 − $110,000)/11,500 shares = $41.78.

APPENDIX 11A

Accounting Tools: Unincorporated Businesses

The focus of Chapter 11 has been on the corporate form of organization. Most of the large, influential companies in the United States are organized as corporations. They have a legal and economic existence that is separate from that of the owners of the business, the stockholders. Yet many other companies in the economy are organized as

LO 10 Describe the important differences between the sole proprietorship and partnership forms of organization versus the corporate form.

sole proprietorships or partnerships. The purpose of this appendix is to show briefly how the characteristics of such organizations affect the accounting, particularly the accounting for the owners' equity category of the balance sheet.

Sole Proprietorships

A **sole proprietorship** is a business owned by one person. Most sole proprietorships are small in size, with the owner serving as the operator or manager of the company. The primary advantage of the sole proprietorship form of organization is its simplicity. The owners' equity category of the balance sheet consists of one account, the owner's capital account. The owner answers to no one but himself or herself. A disadvantage of the sole proprietorship is that all the responsibility for the success or failure of the venture attaches to the owner, who often has limited resources.

There are three important points to remember about this form of organization. First, a sole proprietorship is not a separate entity for legal purposes. This means that the law does not distinguish between the assets of the business and those of its owner. If an owner loses a lawsuit, for example, the law does not limit an owner's liability to the amount of assets of the business but extends liability to the owner's personal assets. Thus, the owner is said to have *unlimited liability*.

Second, accountants adhere to the *entity principle* and maintain a distinction between the owner's personal assets and the assets of the sole proprietorship. The balance sheet of a sole proprietorship should reflect only the "business" assets and liabilities, with the difference reflected as owner's capital.

Third, a sole proprietorship is not treated as a separate entity for federal income tax purposes. That is, the sole proprietorship does not pay tax on its income, Rather, the business income must be declared as income on the owner's personal tax return, and income tax is assessed at the personal tax rate rather than the rate that applies to companies organized as corporations. This may or may not be advantageous, depending on the amount of income involved and the owner's tax situation.

Typical Transactions   When the owners of a corporation, the stockholders, invest in the corporation, they normally do so by purchasing stock. When investing in a sole proprietorship, the owner simply contributes cash, or other assets, into the business. For example, assume that on January 1, 1998, Peter Tom began a new business by investing $10,000 cash. Peter Tom Company records the transaction as follows:

Jan. 1	Cash	10,000	
	Peter Tom, Capital		10,000
	To record the investment of cash in the business.		

Assets	=	**Liabilities**	+	**Owners' Equity**
+10,000				**+10,000**

The Peter Tom, Capital account is an owners' equity account and reflects the rights of the owner to the business assets.

An owner's withdrawal of assets from the business is recorded as a reduction of owners' equity. Assume that on July 1, 1998, Peter Tom took an auto valued at $6,000 from the business to use as his personal auto. The transaction is recorded as follows:

July 1	Peter Tom, Drawing	6,000	
	Equipment		6,000
	To record the withdrawal of an auto from the business.		

Assets	=	**Liabilities**	+	**Owners' Equity**
−6,000				**−6,000**

The Peter Tom, Drawing account is a contra-equity account. Sometimes a drawing account is referred to as a *withdrawals account,* as in Peter Tom, Withdrawal. An increase (debit) in the account reduces the owners' equity. At the end of the fiscal year, the drawing account should be closed to the capital account as follows:

Dec. 31   Peter Tom, Capital   6,000
          Peter Tom, Drawing   6,000
          To close the drawing account to capital.

Assets   =   Liabilities   +   Owners' Equity
                                   −6,000
                                   +6,000

The amount of the net income of the business should also be reflected in the capital account. Assume that all revenue and expense accounts of Peter Tom Company have been closed to the Income Summary account, resulting in a credit balance of $4,000, the net income for the year. The Income Summary account is closed to capital as follows:

Dec. 31   Income Summary   4,000
          Peter Tom, Capital   4,000
          To close income summary to the capital account.

Assets   =   Liabilities   +   Owners' Equity
                                   −4,000
                                   +4,000

The owners' equity section of the balance sheet for Peter Tom Company consists of one account, the capital account, calculated as follows:

Beginning balance, Jan. 1, 1998	$ –0–
Plus: Investments	10,000
Net income	4,000
Less: Withdrawals	(6,000)
Ending balance, Dec. 31, 1998	$ 8,000

Partnerships

A **partnership** is a company owned by two or more persons. Like sole proprietorships, most partnerships are fairly small businesses formed when individuals combine their capital and managerial talents for a common business purpose. Other partnerships are large, national organizations. For example, the major public accounting firms are very large, national companies but are organized in most states as partnerships.

Partnerships have characteristics similar to those of sole proprietorships. The following are the most important characteristics of partnerships:

1. *Unlimited liability.* Legally, the assets of the business are not separate from the partners' personal assets. Each partner is personally liable for the debts of the partnership. Creditors have a legal claim first to the assets of the partnership and then to the assets of the individual partners.

2. *Limited life.* Corporations have a separate legal existence and an unlimited life, but partnerships do not. The life of a partnership is limited; it exists as long as the contract between the partners is valid. The partnership ends when a partner withdraws or a new partner is added. A new partnership must be created for the business to continue.

3. *Not taxed as a separate entity.* Partnerships are subject to the same tax features as sole proprietorships. The partnership itself does not pay federal income tax. Rather, the income of the partnership is treated as personal income on each of the partner's individual tax returns and is taxed as personal income. All partnership income is subject to federal income tax on the individual partners' returns even if it is not distributed to the partners. A variety of other factors affects the tax consequences of partnerships versus the corporate form of organization. These aspects are quite complex and beyond the scope of this text.

A partnership is based on a **partnership agreement.** It is very important that the partners agree, in writing, about all aspects of the partnership. The agreement should detail items such as how much capital each partner is to invest, the time each is expected to devote to the business, the salary of each, and how income of the partnership is to be divided. If a partnership agreement is not present, the courts may be forced to settle disputes among partners. Therefore, the partners should develop a partnership agreement when the firm is first established and should review the agreement periodically to determine whether changes are necessary.

Investments and Withdrawals   In a partnership it is important to account separately for the capital of each of the partners. A capital account should be established in the owners' equity section of the balance sheet for each partner of the company. Investments into the company should be credited to the partner making the investment. For example, assume that on January 1, 1998, Page Thoms and Amy Rebec begin a partnership named AP Company. Page contributes $10,000 cash, and Amy contributes equipment valued at $5,000. The accounting transaction that should be recorded by AP Company follows:

Jan. 1	Cash	10,000	
	Equipment	5,000	
	Page Thoms, Capital		10,000
	Amy Rebec, Capital		5,000
	To record the contribution of assets to the business.		

Assets	=	Liabilities	+	Owners' Equity
+10,000				+10,000
+ 5,000				+ 5,000

A drawing account also should be established for each owner of the company to account for withdrawals of assets. Assume that on April 1, 1998, each owner withdraws $2,000 of cash from AP Company. The accounting entry is recorded:

Apr. 1	Page Thoms, Drawing	2,000	
	Amy Rebec, Drawing	2,000	
	Cash		4,000
	To record the withdrawal of assets from the business.		

Assets	=	Liabilities	+	Owners' Equity
−4,000				−2,000
				−2,000

Distribution of Income   The partnership agreement governs the manner in which income should be allocated to partners. The distribution may recognize the partners' relative investment in the business, their time and effort, their expertise and talents, or other factors. We will illustrate three methods of income allocation, but you should be aware that partnerships use many other allocation methods. Although these allocation methods are straightforward, partnerships dissolve often because one or more of the partners believes that the allocation is unfair. It is very difficult to devise a method that will make all partners happy.

One way to allocate income is to divide it evenly between or among the partners. In fact, when a partnership agreement is not present, the courts specify that an equal allocation must be applied, regardless of the relative contributions or efforts of the partners. For example, assume that AP Company has $30,000 net income for the period and has established an agreement that income should be allocated evenly between the two partners, Page and Amy. The accounting entry that AP Company records during the closing entry process is as follows:

Dec. 31	Income Summary	30,000	
	Page Thoms, Capital		15,000
	Amy Rebec, Capital		15,000
	To record the allocation of income between partners.		

Assets	=	Liabilities	+	Owners' Equity
				−30,000
				+15,000
				+15,000

An equal distribution of income to all partners is easy to apply but is not fair to those partners who have contributed more in money or time to the partnership.

Another way to allocate income is to specify in the partnership agreement that income be allocated according to a *stated ratio*. For example, Page and Amy may specify that all income of AP Company should be allocated on a 2-to-1 ratio, with Page receiving the larger portion. If that allocation method is applied to the preceding example, AP Company records the following transaction at year-end:

Dec. 31	Income Summary	30,000	
	Page Thoms, Capital		20,000
	Amy Rebec, Capital		10,000
	To record the allocation of income between partners.		

Assets = Liabilities + Owners' Equity
−30,000
+20,000
+10,000

Finally, we illustrate an allocation method that more accurately reflects the partners' input. It is based on salaries, interest on invested capital, and a stated ratio. Assume that the partnership agreement of AP Company specifies that Page and Amy be allowed a salary of $6,000 and $4,000, respectively, that each partner receive 10% on her capital balance, and that any remaining income be allocated equally. Assume that AP Company has been in operation for several years and the capital balances of the owners at the end of 1998, before the income distribution, are as follows:

Page Thoms, Capital	$40,000
Amy Rebec, Capital	50,000

If AP Company calculated that its 1998 net income (before partner salaries) was $30,000, income would be allocated between the partners as follows:

	PAGE	AMY
Distributed for salaries:	$ 6,000	$ 4,000
Distributed for interest:		
Page: ($40,000 × 10%)	4,000	
Amy: ($50,000 × 10%)		5,000
Remainder = $30,000 − $10,000 − $9,000 = $11,000		
Remainder distributed equally:		
Page: ($11,000/2)	5,500	
Amy: ($11,000/2)		5,500
Total distributed	$15,500	$14,500

The accounting transaction to transfer the income to the capital accounts is as follows:

Dec. 31	Income Summary	30,000	
	Page Thoms, Capital		15,500
	Amy Rebec, Capital		14,500
	To record the allocation of income to partners.		

Assets = Liabilities + Owners' Equity
−30,000
+15,500
+14,500

This indicates that the amounts of $15,500 and $14,500 were allocated to Page and Amy respectively. It does not indicate the amount actually paid to (or withdrawn by) the partners. However, for tax purposes, the income of the partnership is treated as personal income on the partners' individual tax returns regardless of whether or not the income is actually paid in cash to the partners. This aspect often encourages partners to withdraw income from the business and makes it difficult to retain sufficient capital for the business to operate profitably.

Chapter Highlights

1. **LO 1** The stockholders' equity category is composed of two parts. Contributed capital is the amount derived from stockholders and other external parties. Retained earnings is the amount of net income not paid as dividends.

2. **LO 1** The stockholders' equity category reveals the number of shares authorized, issued, and outstanding. Treasury stock is stock that the firm has issued and repurchased but not retired.

3. **LO 2** *Preferred stock* refers to a stock that has preference to dividends declared. If a dividend is declared, the preferred stockholders must receive a dividend before the common stockholders.

4. **LO 3** When stock is issued for cash, the par value of the stock should be reported in the stock account and the amount in excess of par should be reported in an additional paid-in capital account.

5. **LO 3** When stock is issued for a noncash asset, the transaction should reflect the value of the stock given or the value of the property received, whichever is more evident.

6. **LO 4** Treasury stock is accounted for as a reduction of stockholders' equity. When treasury stock is reissued and the cost is less than reissue price, the difference is reported in (credited to) additional paid-in capital. When cost exceeds reissue price, additional paid-in capital or retained earnings is reduced for the difference.

7. **LO 5** The amount of cash dividends to be paid to common and preferred stockholders depends on the terms of the preferred stock. If the stock is cumulative, preferred stockholders have the right to dividends in arrears before current-year dividends are paid. Participating preferred stock indicates that preferred stockholders can share in the amount of the dividend that exceeds a specified amount.

8. **LO 6** Stock dividends involve the issuance of additional shares of stock. The dividend should normally reflect the fair market value of the additional shares.

9. **LO 7** Stock splits are similar to stock dividends except that splits reduce the par value per share of the stock. No accounting transaction is necessary for splits.

10. **LO 8** Book value per share is calculated as net assets divided by the number of shares of common stock outstanding. It indicates the rights that stockholders have, based on recorded values, to the net assets in the event of liquidation and is therefore not a measure of the market value of the stock.

11. **LO 8** When a corporation has both common and preferred stock, the net assets attributed to the rights of the preferred stockholders must be deducted from the amount of net assets to determine the book value per share of the common stock.

12. **LO 9** Transactions involving stockholders' equity accounts should be reflected in the Financing Activities category of the statement of cash flows.

13. **LO 10** A sole proprietorship is a business owned by one person. It is not a separate entity for legal purposes and does not pay taxes on its income. However, a balance sheet should present the assets and liabilities of the business separate from those of the owner. (Appendix 11A)

14. **LO 10** A partnership is a company owned by two or more persons. Like sole proprietorships, partnerships are not a separate legal or tax entity. The balance sheet of the partnership should present the assets and liabilities of the business separate from those of the owners. (Appendix 11A)

Key Terms Quiz

Read each definition below and then write the number of the definition in the blank beside the appropriate term it defines. The solution appears at the end of the chapter.

___ Authorized shares
___ Outstanding shares
___ Additional paid-in capital
___ Cumulative feature
___ Convertible feature
___ Treasury stock
___ Dividend payout ratio
___ Stock split
___ Market value per share
___ Partnership (Appendix 11A)

___ Issued shares
___ Par value
___ Retained earnings
___ Participating feature
___ Callable feature
___ Retirement of stock
___ Stock dividend
___ Book value per share
___ Sole proprietorship (Appendix 11A)
___ Partnership agreement (Appendix 11A)

1. The number of shares sold or distributed to stockholders.

2. An arbitrary amount that is stated on the face of the stock certificate and that represents the legal capital of the firm.

3. Net income that has been made by the corporation but not paid out as dividends.

4. The holders of this stock have a right to dividends in arrears before the current year dividend is distributed.

5. Allows preferred stock to be returned to the corporation in exchange for common stock.

6. Stock issued by the firm and then repurchased but not retired.

7. The annual dividend amount divided by the annual net income.

8. A business with a single owner.

9. Creation of additional shares of stock and reduction of the par value of the stock.

10. Total stockholders' equity divided by the number of shares of common stock outstanding.

11. A business owned by two or more individuals and with the characteristic of unlimited liability.

12. The selling price of the stock as indicated by the most recent stock transactions on, for example, the stock exchange.

13. The maximum number of shares a corporation may issue as indicated in the corporate charter.

14. The number of shares issued less the number of shares held as treasury stock.

15. A document that specifies how much each owner should invest, the salary of each owner, and how profits are to be shared.

16. The amount received for the issuance of stock in excess of the par value of the stock.

17. A provision allowing the preferred stockholders to share, on a percentage basis, in the distribution of an abnormally large dividend.

18. Allows the issuing firm to eliminate a class of stock by paying the stockholders a fixed amount.

19. When the stock of a corporation is repurchased with no intention to reissue at a later date.

20. A corporation's declaration and issuance of additional shares of its own stock to existing stockholders.

Alternate Terms

Additional paid-in capital   Paid-in capital in excess of par value.

Additional paid-in capital—treasury stock   Paid-in capital from treasury stock transactions.

Callable   Redeemable.

Capital account   Owners' equity account.

Contributed capital   Paid-in capital.

Retained earnings   Retained income.

Small stock dividend   Stock dividend less than 20%.

Stockholders' equity   Owners' equity.

Drawing account   Withdrawal account.

Questions

1. What are the two major components of stockholders' equity? Which accounts generally appear in each component?

2. Corporations disclose the number of shares authorized, issued, and outstanding. What is the meaning of these terms? What causes a difference between the number of shares issued and the number outstanding?

3. Why do firms designate an amount as the par value of stock? Does par value indicate the selling price or market value of the stock?

4. If a firm has a net income for the year, will the balance in the Retained Earnings account equal the net income? What is the meaning of the balance of the account?

5. What is the meaning of the statement that preferred stock has a preference to dividends declared by the corporation? Do preferred stockholders have the right to dividends in arrears on preferred stock?

6. Why might some stockholders be inclined to buy preferred stock rather than common stock? What are the advantages of investing in preferred stock?

7. Why are common shareholders sometimes called *residual owners* when a company has both common and preferred stock outstanding?

8. When stock is issued in exchange for an asset, at what amount should the asset be reported? How could the fair market value be determined?

9. What is treasury stock? Why do firms use it? Where does it appear on a corporation's financial statements?

10. When treasury stock is bought and sold, the transactions do not result in gains or losses reported on the income statement. What account or accounts are used instead? Why are no income statement amounts recorded?

11. Many firms operate at a dividend payout ratio of less than 50%. Why do firms not pay a larger percentage of income as dividends?

12. What is a *stock dividend*? How should it be recorded?

13. Would you rather receive a cash dividend or a stock dividend from a company? Explain.

14. What is the difference between stock dividends and stock splits? How should stock splits be recorded?

15. How is the book value per share ratio calculated? Does the amount calculated as book value per share mean that stockholders will receive a dividend equal to the book value?

16. Can the market value per share of stock be determined by the information on the income statement?

17. What is an advantage of organizing a company as a corporation rather than a partnership? Why don't all companies incorporate? (Appendix 11A)

18. What are some ways that partnerships could share income among the partners? (Appendix 11A)

Exercises

LO 1 **Exercise 11-1** Stockholders' Equity Accounts

MJ Company has identified the following items. Indicate whether each item is included in an account in the stockholders' equity category of the balance sheet. Also indicate whether the normal balance of the account should be debit or credit.

1. Preferred stock issued by MJ.

2. Amount received by MJ in excess of par value when preferred stock was issued.

3. Dividends in arrears on MJ preferred stock.

4. Cash dividend declared but unpaid on MJ stock.

5. Stock dividend declared but unissued by MJ.

6. Treasury stock.

7. Amount received in excess of cost when treasury stock is reissued by MJ.

8. Retained earnings.

LO 1 **Exercise 11-2** Solve for Unknowns

The stockholders' equity category of Zache Company's balance sheet appears below.

Common stock, $10 par, 10,000 shares issued,	
9,200 outstanding	$??
Additional paid-in capital	??
Total contributed capital	$350,000
Retained earnings	100,000
Treasury stock, ?? shares at cost	10,000
Total stockholders' equity	??

Required

1. Determine the missing values that are indicated by question marks.

2. What was the cost per share of the treasury stock?

LO 3 **Exercise 11-3** Stock Issuance

Horace Company had the following transactions during 1998, its first year of business.

a. Issued 5,000 shares of $5 par common stock for cash at $15 per share.

b. Issued 7,000 shares of common stock on May 1 to acquire a factory building from Barkley Company. Barkley had acquired the building in 1994 at a price of $150,000. Horace estimated that the building was worth $175,000 on May 1, 1998.

c. Issued 2,000 shares of stock on June 1 to acquire a patent. The accountant has been unable to estimate the value of the patent but has determined that Horace's common stock was selling at $25 per share on June 1.

Required

1. Determine each event's impact on the accounting equation.

2. Determine the balance sheet amounts for common stock and additional paid-in capital.

LO 3 **Exercise 11-4** Stock Issuances

The following transactions are for Weber Corporation in 1998:

a. On March 1, the corporation was organized and received authorization to issue 5,000 shares of 8%, $100 par value preferred stock and 2,000,000 shares of $10 par value common stock.

b. On March 10, Weber issued 5,000 shares of common stock at $35 per share.

c. On March 18, Weber issued 100 shares of preferred stock at $120 per share.

d. On April 12, Weber issued another 10,000 shares of common stock at $45 per share.

Required

1. Prepare all journal entries needed for these transactions.

2. Prepare the stockholders' equity section of the balance sheet as of December 31, 1998.

3. Does the balance sheet indicate the market value of the stock at year-end? Explain.

LO 4 **Exercise 11-5** Treasury Stock

The stockholders' equity category of Bradford Company's balance sheet on January 1, 1998, appeared as follows:

Common stock, $10 par, 10,000 shares issued and outstanding	$100,000
Additional paid-in capital	50,000
Retained earnings	80,000
Total stockholders' equity	$230,000

The following transactions occurred during 1998.

a. Reacquired 2,000 shares of common stock at $20 per share on July 1.

b. Reacquired 400 shares of common stock at $18 per share on August 1.

Required

1. Record the entries in journal form.

2. Assume the company resold the shares of treasury stock at $28 per share on October 1. Did the company benefit from the treasury stock transaction? If so, where is the "gain" presented on the balance sheet?

LO 4 **Exercise 11-6** Treasury Stock Transactions

The stockholders' equity category of Little Joe's balance sheet on January 1, 1998, appeared as follows:

Common stock, $5 par, 40,000 shares issued and outstanding	$200,000
Additional paid-in capital	90,000
Retained earnings	100,000
Total stockholders' equity	$390,000

The following transactions occurred during 1998.

a. Reacquired 5,000 shares of common stock at $20 per share on February 1.

b. Reacquired 1,200 shares of common stock at $13 per share on March 1.

Required

1. Determine each event's impact on the accounting equation.

2. Assume that the treasury stock was reissued on October 1 at $12 per share. Did the company benefit from the treasury stock reissuance? Where is the "gain" or "loss" presented on the financial statements?

3. What effect did the two transactions to purchase treasury stock and the later reissuance of that stock have on the stockholders' equity section of the balance sheet?

LO 5 **Exercise 11-7** Cash Dividends

Kerry Company has 1,000 shares of $100 par value, 9% preferred stock and 10,000 shares of $10 par value common stock outstanding. The preferred stock is cumulative and nonparticipating. Dividends were paid in 1994. Since 1994, Kerry has declared and paid dividends as follows:

1995	$ 0
1996	10,000
1997	20,000
1998	25,000

Required

1. Determine the amount of the dividends to be allocated to preferred and common stockholders for each year, 1996 to 1998.

2. If the preferred stock had been noncumulative, how much would have been allocated to the preferred and common stockholders each year?

LO 5 **Exercise 11-8** Cash Dividends

The stockholders' equity category of Jackson Company's balance sheet as of January 1, 1998, appeared as follows:

Preferred stock, $100 par, 8%,	
2,000 shares issued and outstanding	$200,000
Common stock, $10 par,	
5,000 shares issued and outstanding	50,000
Additional paid-in capital	300,000
Total contributed capital	$550,000
Retained earnings	400,000
Total stockholders' equity	$950,000

The footnotes that accompany the financial statements indicate that Jackson has not paid dividends for the two years prior to 1998. On July 1, 1998, Jackson declares a dividend of $100,000 to be paid to preferred and common stockholders on August 1.

Required

1. Determine the amounts of the dividend to be allocated to preferred and common stockholders, assuming that the preferred stock is noncumulative, nonparticipating stock.

2. Record the appropriate journal transactions on July 1 and August 1, 1998.

3. Determine the amounts of the dividend to be allocated to preferred and common stockholders, assuming instead that the preferred stock is cumulative, nonparticipating stock.

LO 5 **Exercise 11-9** Cash Dividends—Participating Feature

Refer to Jackson Company's stockholders' equity category in Exercise 11-8. Assume that the footnotes to the financial statements indicate that Jackson has not paid dividends for the two years prior to 1998. On July 1, 1998, Jackson declares a dividend of $100,000 to be paid to preferred and common stockholders on August 1.

Required

1. Determine the amounts of the dividend to be allocated to preferred and common stock, assuming that the preferred stock is cumulative and participates in dividends in proportion to the total par value of preferred and common stock.

2. Record the appropriate journal transactions on July 1 and August 1, 1998.

LO 6 **Exercise 11-10** Stock Dividends

The stockholders' equity category of Worthy Company's balance sheet as of January 1, 1998, appeared as follows:

Common stock, $10 par,	
40,000 shares issued and outstanding	$400,000
Additional paid-in capital	100,000
Retained earnings	400,000
Total stockholders' equity	$900,000

The following transactions occurred during 1998:

a. Declared a 10% stock dividend to common stockholders on January 15. At the time of the dividend, the common stock was selling for $30 per share. The stock dividend was to be issued to stockholders on January 30, 1998.

b. Distributed the stock dividend to the stockholders on January 30, 1998.

Required

1. Record the 1998 transactions in journal entry form.

2. Develop the stockholders' equity category of Worthy Company's balance sheet as of January 31, 1998, after the stock dividend was issued. What effect did these transactions have on total stockholders' equity?

LO 7   **Exercise 11-11** Stock Dividends Versus Stock Splits

Campbell Company wants to increase the number of shares of its common stock outstanding and is considering a stock dividend versus a stock split. The stockholders' equity of the firm on its most recent balance sheet appeared as follows:

Common stock, $10 par,	
50,000 shares issued and outstanding	$ 500,000
Additional paid-in capital	750,000
Retained earnings	880,000
Total stockholders' equity	$2,130,000

If a stock dividend is chosen, the firm wants to declare a 100% stock dividend. Because the stock dividend qualifies as a "large stock dividend," it must be recorded at par value. If a stock split is chosen, Campbell will declare a 2-for-1 split.

Required

1. Compare the effects of the stock dividends and stock splits on the accounting equation.

2. Develop the stockholders' equity category of Campbell's balance sheet after (a) the stock dividend and (b) after the stock split.

LO 7   **Exercise 11-12** Stock Dividends and Stock Splits

Whitacre Company's stockholders' equity section of the balance sheet on December 31, 1997, was as follows:

Common stock, $10 par value,	
60,000 shares issued and outstanding	$ 600,000
Additional paid-in capital	480,000
Retained earnings	1,240,000
Total stockholders' equity	$2,320,000

On May 1, 1998, Whitacre declared and issued a 15% stock dividend, when the stock was selling for $20 per share. Then on November 1, it declared and issued a 2-for-1 stock split.

Required

1. How many shares of stock are outstanding at year-end?

2. What is the par value per share of these shares?

3. Develop the stockholders' equity category of Whitacre's balance sheet as of December 31, 1998.

LO 8   **Exercise 11-13** Payout Ratio and Book Value per Share

Divac Company has developed a statement of stockholders' equity for the year 1998 as follows:

	PREFERRED STOCK	PAID-IN CAPITAL— PREFERRED	COMMON STOCK	PAID-IN CAPITAL— COMMON	RETAINED EARNINGS
Balance Jan. 1	$100,000	$50,000	$400,000	$40,000	$200,000
Stock issued			100,000	10,000	
Net income					80,000
Cash dividend					− 45,000
Stock dividend	10,000	5,000			− 15,000
Balance Dec. 31	$110,000	$55,000	$500,000	$50,000	$220,000

Divac's preferred stock is $100 par, 8% stock. If the stock is liquidated or redeemed, stockholders are entitled to $120 per share. There are no dividends in arrears on the stock. The common stock has a par value of $5 per share.

Required

1. Determine the dividend payout ratio for the common stock.
2. Determine the book value per share of Divac's common stock.

LO 9 **Exercise 11-14** Impact of Transactions Involving Issuance of Stock on Statement of Cash Flows

From the following list, identify each item as operating (O), investing (I), financing (F), or not separately reported on the statement of cash flows (N).

_____ Issuance of common stock for cash

_____ Issuance of preferred stock for cash

_____ Issuance of common stock for equipment

_____ Issuance of preferred stock for land and building

_____ Conversion of preferred stock into common stock

LO 9 **Exercise 11-15** Impact of Transactions Involving Treasury Stock on Statement of Cash Flows

From the following list, identify each item as operating (O), investing (I), financing (F), or not separately reported on the statement of cash flows (N).

_____ Repurchase common stock as treasury stock

_____ Reissuance of common stock (held as treasury stock)

_____ Retirement of treasury stock

LO 9 **Exercise 11-16** Impact of Transactions Involving Dividends on Statement of Cash Flows

From the following list, identify each item as operating (O), investing (I), financing (F), or not separately reported on the statement of cash flows (N).

_____ Payment of cash dividend on common stock

_____ Payment of cash dividend on preferred stock

_____ Distribution of stock dividend

_____ Declaration of stock split

LO 9 **Exercise 11-17** Determining Dividends Paid on Statement of Cash Flows

Clifford Company's comparative balance sheet included dividends payable of $80,000 at December 31, 1997 and $100,000 at December 31, 1998. Dividends declared by Clifford during 1998 amounted to $400,000.

Required

1. Calculate the amount of dividends actually paid to stockholders during 1998.
2. How will Clifford report the dividend payments on its 1998 statement of cash flows?

LO 10 **Exercise 11-18** Sole Proprietorship (Appendix 11A)

Terry Woods opened Par Golf as a sole proprietor by investing $50,000 cash on January 1, 1998. Because the business was new, it operated at a net loss of $10,000 for 1998. During the year, Terry withdrew $20,000 from the business for living expenses. Terry also had $4,000 of interest income from sources unrelated to the business.

Required

1. Record all the necessary entries for 1998 on the books of Par Golf.
2. Present the owners' equity category of Par Golf's balance sheet as of December 31, 1998.

LO 10   **Exercise 11-19** Partnerships (Appendix 11A)

Sports Central is a sporting goods store owned by Lewis, Jamal, and Lapin in partnership. On January 1, 1998, their capital balances were as follows:

Lewis, Capital	$20,000
Jamal, Capital	50,000
Lapin, Capital	30,000

During 1998, Lewis withdrew $5,000; Jamal, $12,000; and Lapin, $9,000. Income for the partnership for 1998 was $50,000.

Required

If the partners agreed to allocate income equally, what was the ending balance in each of their capital accounts on December 31, 1998?

Problems

LO 1   **Problem 11-1** Stockholders' Equity Category

Peeler Company was incorporated as a new business on January 1, 1998. The corporate charter approved on that date authorized the issuance of 1,000 shares of $100 par, 7% cumulative, nonparticipating preferred stock and 10,000 shares of $5 par common stock. On January 10, Peeler issued for cash 500 shares of preferred stock at $120 per share and 4,000 shares of common at $80 per share. On January 20, it issued 1,000 shares of common stock to acquire a building site, at a time when the stock was selling for $70 per share.

During 1998 Peeler established an employee benefit plan and acquired 500 shares of common stock at $60 per share as treasury stock for that purpose. Later in 1998, it resold 100 shares of the stock at $65 per share.

On December 31, 1998, Peeler determined its net income for the year to be $40,000. The firm declared the annual cash dividend to preferred stockholders and a cash dividend of $5 per share to the common stockholders. The dividends will be paid in 1999.

Required

Develop the stockholders' equity category of Peeler's balance sheet as of December 31, 1998. Indicate on the statement the number of shares authorized, issued, and outstanding for both preferred and common stock.

Decision
Making

LO 2   **Problem 11-2** Evaluating Alternative Investments

Ellen Hays received a windfall from one of her investments. She would like to invest $100,000 of the money in Linwood Inc., which is offering common stock, preferred stock, and bonds on the open market. The common stock has paid $8 per share in dividends for the past three years and the company expects to be able to perform as well in the current year. The current market price of the common stock is $100 per share. The preferred stock has an 8% dividend rate, cumulative and nonparticipating. The bonds are selling at par with an 8% stated rate.

1. What are the advantages and disadvantages of each type of investment?
2. Recommend one type of investment over the others to Ellen, and justify your reason.

LO 5   **Problem 11-3** Dividends for Preferred and Common Stock

The stockholders' equity category of Greenbaum Company's balance sheet as of December 31, 1998, appeared as follows:

Preferred stock, $100 par, 8%,	
1,000 shares issued and outstanding	$ 100,000
Common stock, $10 par,	
20,000 shares issued and outstanding	200,000
Additional paid-in capital	250,000
Total contributed capital	$ 550,000
Retained earnings	450,000
Total stockholders' equity	$1,000,000

The footnotes to the financial statements indicate that dividends were not declared or paid for 1996 or 1997. Greenbaum wants to declare a dividend of $59,000 for 1998.

Required

Determine the total and the per-share amounts that should be declared to the preferred and common stockholders under the following assumptions:

1. The preferred stock is noncumulative, nonparticipating.
2. The preferred stock is cumulative, nonparticipating.
3. The preferred stock is cumulative and participating on the basis of the proportion of the total par values of the preferred and common stock.

LO 6   **Problem 11-4** Effect of Stock Dividend

Favre Company has a history of paying cash dividends on its common stock. The firm did not have a particularly profitable year, however, in 1998. At the end of the year, Favre found itself without the necessary cash for a dividend and therefore declared a stock dividend to its common stockholders. A 50% stock dividend was declared to stockholders on December 31, 1998. The board of directors is unclear about a stock dividend's effect on Favre's balance sheet and has requested your assistance.

Required

1 Write a statement to indicate the effect that the stock dividend has on the financial statements of Favre Company.
2. A group of common stockholders has contacted the firm to express its concern about the effect of the stock dividend and to question the effect the stock dividend may have on the market price of the stock. Write a statement to address the stockholders' concerns.

LO 7   **Problem 11-5** Dividends and Stock Splits

On January 1, 1998, Frederiksen's Inc.'s stockholders' equity category appeared as follows:

Preferred stock, $80 par value, 7%,	
3,000 shares issued and outstanding	$ 240,000
Common stock, $10 par value,	
15,000 shares issued and outstanding	150,000
Additional paid-in capital—	
Preferred	60,000
Additional paid-in capital—	
Common	225,000
Total contributed capital	675,000
Retained earnings	2,100,000
Total stockholders' equity	$2,775,000

The preferred stock is noncumulative and nonparticipating. During 1998, the following transactions occurred:

a. On March 1, declared a cash dividend of $16,800 on preferred stock. Paid the dividend on April 1.
b. On June 1, declared a 5% stock dividend on common stock. The current market price of the common stock was $18. The stock was issued on July 1.
c. On September 1, declared a cash dividend of $.50 per share on the common stock; paid the dividend on October 1.

d. On December 1, issued a 2-for-1 stock split of common stock, when the stock was selling for $50 per share.

Required

1. Explain each transaction's effect on the stockholders' equity accounts and the total stockholders' equity.
2. Develop the stockholders' equity category of the December 31, 1998, balance sheet. Assume the net income for the year was $650,000.
3. Write a paragraph that explains the difference between a stock dividend and a stock split.

LO 9 | **Problem 11-6** Effects of Stockholders' Equity Transactions on Statement of Cash Flows

Refer to all the facts in Problem 11-1.

Required

Indicate how each of the transactions described affects the cash flows of Peeler Company by preparing the financing activities section of the 1998 statement of cash flows. Provide an explanation for the exclusion of any of these transactions from the financing activities section of the statement.

LO 10 | **Problem 11-7** Income Distribution of a Partnership (Appendix 11A)

Louise Abbott and Buddie Costello are partners in a comedy club business. The partnership agreement specifies the manner in which income of the business is to be distributed. Louise is to receive a salary of $20,000 for managing the club, and Buddie is to receive interest at the rate of 10% on her capital balance of $300,000. Remaining income is to be distributed on a 2-to-1 ratio.

Required

Determine the amount that should be distributed to each partner, assuming the following business net incomes:

1. $15,000
2. $50,000
3. $80,000

LO 10 | **Problem 11-8** Sole Proprietorships (Appendix 11A)

On May 1, Chong Yu deposited $120,000 of his own savings in a separate bank account to start a printing business. He purchased copy machines for $42,000. Expenses for the year, including depreciation on the copy machines, were $84,000. Sales for the year, all in cash, were $108,000. Chong withdrew $12,000 during the year.

Required

1. Prepare the journal entries for the following transactions: the May 1 initial investment, Chong's withdrawal of cash, and the December 31 closing entries. Chong closes revenues and expenses to an Income Summary account.
2. What is the balance in Chong's capital account at the end of the year?
3. Explain why the balance in Chong's capital account is different than the amount of cash on hand.

LO 10 | **Problem 11-9** Partnerships (Appendix 11A)

Kirin Nerise and Milt O'Brien agreed to form a partnership to operate a sandwich shop. Kirin contributed $25,000 cash and will manage the store. Milt contributed computer equipment worth $8,000 and $92,000 cash. Milt will keep the financial records. During the year, sales were $90,000 and expenses were $76,000. Kirin withdrew $500 per month. Milt withdrew $4,000 (total). Their partnership agreement specified that Kirin would receive a salary of $7,200 for the year. Milt would receive 6% interest on his initial capital investment. All remaining income or loss would be equally divided.

Required

Calculate the ending balance in the equity account of each of the partners.

Multi-Concept Problems

LO 1, 4 **Problem 11-10** Analysis of Stockholders' Equity

The stockholders' equity section of the December 31, 1998, balance sheet of Eldon Company appeared as follows:

Preferred stock, $30 par value,	
5,000 shares authorized, ? shares issued	$120,000
Common stock, ? par,	
10,000 shares authorized, 7,000 shares issued	70,000
Additional paid-in capital——Preferred	6,000
Additional paid-in capital—Common	560,000
Additional paid-in capital—Treasury stock	1,000
Total contributed capital	$757,000
Retained earnings	40,000
Less: Treasury stock, preferred, 100 shares	(3,200)
Total stockholders' equity	??

Required

Determine the following items based on Eldon's balance sheet.

1. The number of shares of preferred stock issued.
2. The number of shares of preferred stock outstanding.
3. The average per-share sales price of the preferred stock when issued.
4. The par value of the common stock.
5. The average per-share sales price of the common stock when issued.
6. The cost of the treasury stock per share.
7. The total stockholders' equity.
8. The per-share book value of the common stock, assuming that there are no dividends in arrears and that the preferred stock can be redeemed at its par value.

LO 3, 4, 7 **Problem 11-11** Effects of Stockholders' Equity Transactions on The Balance Sheet

The following transactions occurred at Horton Inc. during its first year of operation:

a. Issued 100,000 shares of common stock at $5 each; 1,000,000 shares are authorized at $1 par value.

b. Issued 10,000 shares of common stock for a building and land. The building was appraised for $20,000, but the value of the land is undeterminable. The stock is selling for $10 on the open market.

c. Purchased 1,000 shares of its own common stock on the open market for $16 per share.

d. Declared a dividend of $.10 per share on outstanding common stock. The dividend is to be paid after the end of the first year of operations. Market value of the stock is $26.

e. Declared a 2-for-1 stock split. The market value of the stock was $37 before the stock split.

f. Reported $180,000 of income for the year.

Required

1. Indicate each transaction's effect on the assets, liabilities, and owners' equity of Horton Inc.
2. Prepare the owners' equity section of the balance sheet.
3. Write a paragraph that explains the number of shares of stock issued and outstanding at the end of the year.

LO 2, 4 **Problem 11-12** Owner's Equity Section of The Balance Sheet

The newly hired accountant at Ives Inc. prepared the following balance sheet.

ASSETS	
Cash	$ 3,500
Accounts receivable	5,000
Treasury stock	500
Plant, property, and equipment	108,000
Retained earnings	1,000
Total assets	$118,000
LIABILITIES	
Accounts payable	$ 5,500
Dividends payable	1,500
OWNERS' EQUITY	
Common stock, $1 par,	
100,000 shares issued	100,000
Additional paid-in capital	11,000
Total liabilities and owners' equity	$118,000

Required

1. Prepare a corrected balance sheet. Write a short explanation for each correction.
2. Why does the Retained Earnings account have a negative balance?

LO 8, 9 **Problem 11-13** Effects of Stockholders' Equity Transactions on Nike's Statement of Cash Flows and Calculation of Book Value Per Share

Nike Inc. describes the three types of stock that are outstanding in the notes to its consolidated financial statements in its 1995 annual report:

- All of its preferred stock is owned by Nissho Iwai American Corporation (NIAC). The preferred stock is redeemable at the option of NIAC at par value aggregating $300,000.
- Each share of Nike's Class A common stock (no par value) is convertible into one share of its Class B common stock.
- Nike adopted a stock incentive plan in 1980. This plan expired when a new stock incentive plan was adopted in 1990. Eligible employees may purchase shares of the company's Class B stock at prices determined by the terms of the stock incentive plans. In addition, the company also has several stock option agreements outside of these plans with certain directors, endorsers and employees. Total proceeds from the exercise of stock options during 1995 amounted to $6,154,000.

Nike's 1995 consoloidated statement of shareholders' equity appears below:

NIKE, INC. CONSOLIDATED STATEMENT OF SHAREHOLDERS' EQUITY
(IN THOUSANDS)

	COMMON STOCK				CAPITAL IN EXCESS OF STATED VALUE	FOREIGN CURRENCY TRANSLATION ADJUSTMENT	RETAINED EARNINGS	TOTAL
	CLASS A		CLASS B					
	SHARES	AMOUNT	SHARES	AMOUNTS				
Balance at May 31, 1994	26,679	$159	46,521	$2,704	$108,284	$(15,123)	$1,644,925	$1,740,949
Stock options exercised			241	2	8,954			8,956
Conversion to Class B Common Stock	(784)	(4)	784	4				—
Repurchase of Class B Common Stock			(2,130)	(13)	(4,801)		(138,106)	(142,920)
Stock issued pursuant to contractual obligations			134	1	9,999			10,000
Translation of statements of international operations						16,708		16,708
Net income							399,664	399,664
Dividends on Redeemable Preferred Stock							(30)	(30)
Dividends on Common Stock							(68,638)	(68,638)
Balance at May 31, 1995	25,895	$155	45,550	$2,698	$122,436	$ 1,585	$1,837,815	$1,964,689

Required

1. With the exception of the transaction appearing under the Foreign Currency Translation Adjustment column, indicate how each of the transactions described affected the cash flows of Nike, Inc. by preparing the financing activities section of its 1995 statement of cash flows. Provide an explanation for the exclusion of any of these transactions from the financing activities section of the statement. You may assume that dividends declared were paid in the same year.

2. What were the book values per share of Nike's common stock at May 31, 1995 and 1994?

3. As a common stockholder, how would you react to the change in book value? What are the limitations of the use of book value as a ratio used to evaluate owners' equity?

Alternate Problems

LO 1 **Problem 11-1A** Stockholders' Equity Category

Kebler Company was incorporated as a new business on January 1, 1998. The corporate charter approved on that date authorized the issuance of 2,000 shares of $100 par 7% cumulative, nonparticipating preferred stock and 20,000 shares of $5 par common stock. On January 10, Kebler issued for cash 1,000 shares of preferred stock at $120 per share and 8,000 shares of common at $80 per share. On January 20, it issued 2,000 shares of common stock to acquire a building site, at a time when the stock was selling for $70 per share.

During 1998 Kebler established an employee benefit plan and acquired 1,000 shares of common stock at $60 per share as treasury stock for that purpose. Later in 1998, it resold 100 shares of the stock at $65 per share.

On December 31, 1998, Kebler determined its net income for the year to be $80,000. The firm declared the annual cash dividend to preferred stockholders and a cash dividend of $5 per share to the common stockholders. The dividend will be paid in 1999.

Required

Develop the stockholders' equity category of Kebler's balance sheet as of December 31, 1998. Indicate on the statement the number of shares authorized, issued, and outstanding for both preferred and common stock.

LO 2 **Problem 11-2A** Evaluating Alternative Investments

Rob Lowe would like to invest $100,000 in Franklin Inc., which is offering common stock, preferred stock, and bonds on the open market. The common stock has paid $1 per share in dividends for the past three years, and the company expects to be able to double the dividend in the current year. The current market price of the common stock is $10 per share. The preferred stock has an 8% dividend rate. The bonds are selling at par with a 5% stated rate.

Decision
Making

Required

1. Explain Franklin's obligation to pay dividends or interest on each instrument.

2. Recommend one type of investment over the others to Rob, and justify your reason.

LO 5 **Problem 11-3A** Dividends for Preferred and Common Stock

The stockholders' equity category of Rausch Company's balance sheet as of December 31, 1998, appeared as follows:

Preferred stock, $100 par, 8%,	
2,000 shares issued and outstanding	$ 200,000
Common stock, $10 par,	
40,000 shares issued and outstanding	400,000
Additional paid-in capital	500,000
Total contributed capital	$1,100,000
Retained earnings	900,000
Total stockholders' equity	$2,000,000

The footnotes to the financial statements indicate that dividends were not declared or paid for 1996 or 1997. Rausch wants to declare a dividend of $118,000 for 1998.

Required

Determine the total and the per-share amounts that should be declared to the preferred and common stockholders under the following assumptions:

1. The preferred stock is noncumulative, nonparticipating.
2. The preferred stock is cumulative, nonparticipating.
3. The preferred stock is cumulative and participating on the basis of the proportion of the total par values of the preferred and common stock.

LO 6 **Problem 11-4A** Effect of Stock Dividend

Travanti Company has a history of paying cash dividends on its common stock. Although the firm has been profitable this year, the board of directors has been planning construction of a second manufacturing plant. To reduce the amount that they must borrow to finance the expansion, the directors are contemplating replacing their usual cash dividend with a 40% stock dividend. The board is unsure what the effect of a stock dividend will be on the company's balance sheet and has requested your assistance.

Required

1. Write a statement to indicate the effect that the stock dividend has on the financial statements of Travanti Company.
2. A group of common stockholders has contacted the firm to express its concern about the effect of the stock dividend and to question the effect that the stock dividend may have on the market price of the stock. Write a statement to address the stockholders' concerns.

LO 7 **Problem 11-5A** Dividends and Stock Splits

On January 1, 1998, Svenberg Inc.'s stockholders' equity category appeared as follows:

Preferred stock, $80 par value, 8%,	
1,000 shares issued and outstanding	$ 80,000
Common stock, $10 par value,	
10,000 shares issued and outstanding	100,000
Additional paid-in capital—	
Preferred	60,000
Additional paid-in capital—	
Common	225,000
Total contributed capital	465,000
Retained earnings	1,980,000
Total stockholders' equity	$2,445,000

The preferred stock is noncumulative and nonparticipating. During 1998, the following transactions occurred:

a. On March 1, declared a cash dividend of $6,400 on preferred stock. Paid the dividend on April 1.

b. On June 1, declared an 8% stock dividend on common stock. The current market price of the common stock was $26. The stock was issued on July 1.

c. On September 1, declared a cash dividend of $.70 per share on the common stock; paid the dividend on October 1.

d. On December 1, issued a 3-for-1 stock split of common stock, when the stock was selling for $30 per share.

Required

1. Explain each transaction's effect on the stockholders' equity accounts and the total stockholders' equity.

2. Develop the stockholders' equity category of the balance sheet. Assume the net income for the year was $720,000.

3. Write a paragraph that explains the difference between a stock dividend and a stock split.

LO 9   **Problem 11-6A** Effects of Stockholders' Equity Transactions on Statement of Cash Flows
Refer to all the facts in Problem 11-1A.

Required

Indicate how each of the transactions described affects the cash flows of Kebler Company by preparing the financing activities section of the 1998 statement of cash flows. Provide an explanation for the exclusion of any of these transactions from the financing activities section of the statement.

LO 10   **Problem 11-7A** Income Distribution of a Partnership (Appendix 11A)
Kay Katz and Doris Kan are partners in a dry-cleaning business. The partnership agreement specifies the manner in which income of the business is to be distributed. Kay is to receive a salary of $40,000 for managing the business. Doris is to receive interest at the rate of 10% on her capital balance of $600,000. Remaining income is to be distributed on a 2-to-1 ratio.

Required

Determine the amount that should be distributed to each partner, assuming the following business net incomes:

1. $30,000
2. $100,000
3. $160,000

LO 10   **Problem 11-8A** Sole Proprietorships (Appendix 11A)
On May 1, Chen Chien Lao deposited $150,000 of her own savings in a separate bank account to start a printing business. She purchased copy machines for $52,500. Expenses for the year, including depreciation on the copy machines, were $105,000. Sales for the year, all in cash, were $135,000. Chen withdrew $15,000 during the year.

Required

1. Prepare the journal entries for the following transactions: the May 1 initial investment, Chen's withdrawal of cash, and the December 31 closing entries. Chen closes revenues and expenses to an Income Summary account.
2. What is the balance in Chen's capital account at the end of the year?
3. Explain why the balance in Chen's capital account is different than the amount of cash on hand.

LO 10   **Problem 11-9A** Partnerrships (Appendix 11A)
Karen Locke and Gina Keyes agreed to form a partnership to operate a sandwich shop. Karen contributed $35,000 cash and will manage the store. Gina contributed computer equipment worth $11,200 and $128,800 cash. Gina will keep the financial records. During the year, sales were $126,000 and expenses were $106,400. Karen withdrew $700 per month. Gina withdrew $5,600 (total). Their partnership agreement specified that Karen would receive a salary of $10,800 for the year. Gina would receive 6% interest on her initial capital investment. All remaining income or loss would be equally divided.

Required

Calculate the ending balance in the equity account of each of the partners.

Alternate Multi-Concept Problems

LO 1, 4   **Problem 11-10A** Aanalysis of Stockholders' Equity
The stockholders' equity section of the December 31, 1998, balance sheet of Carter Company appeared as follows:

Preferred stock, $50 par value,	
10,000 shares authorized, ? shares issued	$ 400,000
Common stock, ? par value,	
20,000 shares authorized, 14,000 shares issued	280,000
Additional paid-in capital—Preferred	12,000
Additional paid-in capital—Common	980,000
Additional paid-in capital—Treasury stock	2,000
Total contributed capital	$1,674,000
Retained earnings	80,000
Less: Treasury stock, preferred, 200 shares	(12,800)
Total stockholders' equity	$?

Determine the following items based on Carter's balance sheet.

1. The number of shares of preferred stock issued.
2. The number of shares of preferred stock outstanding.
3. The average per-share sales price of the preferred stock when issued.
4. The par value of the common stock.
5. The average per-share sales price of the common stock when issued.
6. The cost of the treasury stock per share.
7. The total stockholders' equity.
8. The per-share book value of the common stock, assuming that there are no dividends in arrears and that the preferred stock can be redeemed at its par value.

LO 3, 4 **Problem 11-11A** Effects of Stockholders' Equity Transactions on Balance Sheet

The following transactions occurred at Hilton Inc. during its first year of operation:

a. Issued 10,000 shares of common stock at $10 each; 100,000 shares are authorized at $1 par value.
b. Issued 10,000 shares of common stock for a patent, which is expected to be effective for the next 15 years. The value of the patent is undeterminable. The stock is selling for $10 on the open market.
c. Purchased 1,000 shares of its own common stock on the open market for $10 per share.
d. Declared a dividend of $.50 per share of outstanding common stock. The dividend is to be paid after the end of the first year of operations. Market value of the stock is $10.
e. Income for the year is reported as $340,000.

Required

1. Indicate each transaction's effect on the assets, liabilities, and owners' equity of Hilton Inc.
2. Hilton's president has asked you to explain the difference between contributed capital and retained earnings. Discuss these terms as they relate to Hilton.
3. Determine the book value per share of the stock at the end of the year.

LO 2, 4 **Problem 11-12A** Equity Section of the Balance Sheet

The newly hired accountant at Grainfield Inc. is considering the following list of accounts as he prepares the balance sheet. All of the accounts have positive balances. The company is authorized to issue 1,000,000 shares of common stock and 10,000 shares of preferred stock. The treasury stock was purchased at $5 per share.

Treasury stock (common)	$ 15,000
Retained earnings	54,900
Dividends payable	1,500
Common stock, $1 par	100,000
Additional paid-in capital	68,400
Preferred stock, $10 par, 5%	50,000

Required

1. Prepare the owners' equity section of the balance sheet for Grainfield.

2. Explain why some of the listed accounts are not shown in the owners' equity section.

LO 8, 9   **Problem 11-13A** Effects of Stockholders' Equity Transactions on Wells Fargo's Statement of Cash Flows and Calculation of Book Value Per Share

Wells Fargo & Company had 46,973,319 shares of common stock issued and outstanding at December 31, 1995 and 51,251,648 issued and outstanding at December 31, 1994. Wells Fargo describes liquidation preferences of each of the three types of preferred stock that were issued and outstanding at December 31, 1995 and 1994, in the notes to its consolidated financial statements in its 1995 annual report:

Adjustable Rate—Cumulative, Series B	
(Liquidation preference $50)	$1,500,000
Adjustable Rate—Cumulative, Series C	
(Liquidation preference $50)	$ 477,500
Adjustable Rate—Cumulative, Series D	
(Liquidation preference $50)	$ 350,000

Wells Fargo's 1995 consolidated statement of changes in stockholders' equity appears below:

CONSOLIDATED STATEMENT OF CHANGES IN STOCKHOLDERS' EQUITY
(IN MILLIONS)

	PREFERRED STOCK	COMMON STOCK	ADDITIONAL PAID-IN CAPITAL	RETAINED EARNINGS	FOREIGN CURRENCY TRANSLATION ADJUSTMENTS	INVESTMENT SECURITIES VALUATION ALLOWANCE	TOTAL STOCK-HOLDERS' EQUITY
Balance December 31, 1994	$489	$256	$ 871	$2,409	$(4)	$(110)	$3,911
Net income—1995				1,032			1,032
Common stock issued under employee benefit and dividend reinvestment plans		4	86				90
Common stock repurchased		(25)	(822)				(847)
Preferred stock dividends				(42)			(42)
Common stock dividends				(225)			(225)
Change in unrealized net losses, after applicable taxes						136	136
Transfer			1,000	(1,000)			–
Net change	–	(21)	264	(235)	–	136	144
Balance December 31, 1995	$489	$235	$1,135	$2,174	$(4)	$ 26	$4,055

Required

1. With the exception of the transaction appearing under the "investment securities valuation allowance" column, indicate how each of the transactions described affected the cash flows of Wells Fargo by preparing the financing activities section of its 1995 statement of cash flows. Provide an explanation for the exclusion of any of these transactions from the financing activities section of the statement. You may assume that dividends declared were paid in the same year.

2. What were the book values per share of Wells Fargo's common stock at December 31, 1995 and 1994?

3. As a common stockholder, how would you react to the change in book value? What are the limitations of the use of book value as a ratio used to evaluate owners' equity?

Cases

Reading and Interpreting Financial Statements

LO 1, 2 **Case 11-1** Ben & Jerry's Stockholders' Equity Category
Refer to Ben & Jerry's 1995 annual report.

Required

1. What are the numbers of shares of preferred stock authorized, issued, and outstanding as of the balance sheet date?
2. The preferred stock indicates an "aggregate preference on voluntary or involuntary liquidation." What does that provision of the preferred stock mean?
3. Calculate the book value per share of the common stock.
4. The balance of the Retained Earnings account increased during the year. What are the possible factors that affect its balance?
5. The total stockholders' equity as of December 30, 1995, is $78,531,000. Does that mean that stockholders would receive that amount if the company were liquidated?

LO 3 **Case 11-2** Stock-Purchase Plans
Refer to note 9 of Ben & Jerry's 1995 annual report. Ben and Jerry's authorizes eligible employees to purchase Class A common stock through payroll accumulations.

Required

At what price may the employees purchase stock? How many shares have been issued, and how many are still available? In which statement could you find out how many shares had been issued under the stock-purchase plan? Why would Ben & Jerry's be willing to issue stock to their employees for less than the current market price?

LO 9 **Case 11-3** Reading Ben & Jerry's Statement of Cash Flows
Refer to the 1995 statement of cash flows in Ben & Jerry's annual report.

Required

1. During 1995 Ben & Jerry's issued common stock. What amount of cash was received? What category of the statement of cash flows reflects this amount?
2. If Ben & Jerry's had paid a dividend in 1995, where would it appear on the statement of cash flows?
3. Why do you think investors are willing to purchase stock in Ben & Jerry's when the company does not pay a dividend on the stock?

Making Financial Decisions

Decision
Making

LO 1, 2 **Case 11-4** Debt Versus Preferred Stock
Assume that you are an analyst attempting to compare the financial structure of two companies. In particular, you must analyze the debt and equity categories of the two firms and calculate a debt-to-equity ratio for each firm. The liability and equity categories of First Company at year-end appeared as follows:

LIABILITIES	
Accounts payable	$ 500,000
Loan payable	800,000
STOCKHOLDERS' EQUITY	
Common stock	300,000
Retained earnings	600,000
Total debt and equity	$2,200,000

First Company's loan payable bears interest at 8%, which is paid annually. The principal is due in five years.

The liability and equity categories of Second Company at year-end appeared as follows:

LIABILITIES	
Accounts payable	$ 500,000
STOCKHOLDERS' EQUITY	
Common stock	300,000
Preferred stock	800,000
Retained earnings	600,000
Total debt and equity	$2,200,000

Second Company's preferred stock is 8%, cumulative stock. A provision of the stock agreement specifies that the stock must be redeemed at face value in five years.

Required

1. It appears that the loan payable of First Company and the preferred stock of Second Company are very similar. What are the differences between the two securities?

2. When calculating the debt-to-equity ratio, do you believe that the Second Company preferred stock should be treated as debt or as stockholders' equity? Write a statement expressing your position on this issue.

LO 2 **Case 11-5** Preferred Versus Common Stock

Rohnan Inc. needs to raise $500,000. It is considering two options.

Decision
Making

a. Issue preferred stock, $100 par, 8%, cumulative, nonparticipating, callable at $110. The stock could be issued at par.

b. Issue common stock, $1 par, market $10. Currently, the company has 400,000 shares outstanding equally in the hands of five owners. The company has never paid a dividend.

Required

Rohnan has asked you to consider both options and make a recommendation. It is equally concerned with cash flow and company control. Write your recommendations.

Accounting and Ethics: What Would You Do?

LO 8 **Case 11-6** Inside Information

Jim Brock was an accountant with Hubbard Inc., a large corporation with stock that was publicly traded on the New York Stock Exchange. One of Jim's duties was to manage the corporate reporting department, which was responsible for developing and issuing Hubbard's annual report. At the end of 1998, Hubbard closed its accounting records, and initial calculations indicated a very profitable year. In fact, the net income exceeded the amount that had been projected during the year by the financial analysts who followed Hubbard's stock.

Jim was very pleased with the company's financial performance. In January 1999, he suggested that his father buy Hubbard's stock because he was sure the stock price would increase when the company announced its 1998 results. Jim's father followed the advice and bought a block of stock at $25 per share.

On February 15, 1999, Hubbard announced its 1998 results and issued the annual report. The company received favorable press coverage about its performance, and the stock price on the stock exchange increased to $32 per share.

What was Jim's professional responsibility to Hubbard Inc. concerning the issuance of the 1998 annual report? Did Jim act ethically in this situation?

LO 5 **Case 11-7** Dividend Policy

Hancock Inc. is owned by nearly 100 shareholders. Judith Stitch owns 48% of the stock. She needs cash to fulfill her commitment to donate the funds to construct a new art gallery. Some of her friends have agreed to vote for Hancock to pay a larger-than-normal dividend to shareholders. Judith has asked you to vote for the large dividend because she knows that you also support the arts. When informed that the dividend may create a working capital hardship on Hancock, Judith responded: "There is plenty of money in Retained Earnings. The dividend will not affect the cash of the company." Respond to her comment. What ethical questions do you and Judith face? How would you vote?

Research Case

Internet

Case 11-8 Ford Motor Co.

From 1992 to 1995, the Ford Taurus was the top selling automobile in the United States. Since then, consumer demand has changed and Ford Motor Company has increased its promotional efforts on trucks and on sales of motor vehicles in foreign markets.

Conduct a search of the World Wide Web, obtain Ford's most recent annual report, or use library resources to obtain company information to answer the following:

1. Based on the latest information available, what is Ford's (a) authorized number of common stock shares, (b) issued number of shares, (c) outstanding number of shares, and (d) the average issue price for those shares?

2. For the most recent year available, what dividend per common share did Ford Motor Company pay its stockholders?

3. Locate the past 52-week high, low, and most current market price for Ford Motor Company common stock. What financial factors may have affected the company's stock price over the past three to six months? Would you buy Ford stock at this time? Explain your response.

Optional Research. Interview a salesperson or other employee of an auto dealership. Obtain information about changing consumer preferences for motor vehicles. How do Ford's products try to meet those preferences?

Solution to Key Terms Quiz

13	Authorized shares (p. 512)	**1**	Issued shares (p. 512)
14	Outstanding shares (p. 512)	**2**	Par value (p. 512)
16	Additional paid-in capital (p. 515)	**3**	Retained earnings (p. 515)
4	Cumulative feature (p. 515)	**17**	Participating feature (p. 516)
5	Convertible feature (p. 516)	**18**	Callable feature (p. 516)
6	Treasury stock (p. 517)	**19**	Retirement of stock (p. 519)
7	Dividend payout ratio (p. 519)	**20**	Stock dividend (p. 522)
9	Stock split (p. 524)	**10**	Book value per share (p. 526)
12	Market value per share (p. 527)	**8**	Sole proprietorship (p. 533)
11	Partnership (p. 534)	**15**	Partnership agreement (p. 534)

STUDY LINKS

A Look at Previous Chapters

In previous chapters, you studied the basic concepts of income statement presentation. Chapter 2 introduced the multi-step income statement for corporations.

A Look at This Chapter

This chapter develops the corporate income statement in more detail. The first section presents the proper classification and income statement presentation for a multi-step income statement.

The second section of the chapter examines the retained earnings statement. The section also reviews the elements of stockholders' equity and presents a statement of stockholders' equity that many large corporations use.

The final sections of the chapter develop ratio analysis of profitability with the earnings per share ratio and the impact that various transactions have on the statement of cash flows.

A Look at Upcoming Chapters

Chapter 13 will examine gains and losses on investment securities in more detail, Chapter 14 takes a closer look at the statement of cash flows, and Chapter 15 will present a more complete discussion of ratio analysis of profitability.

Analysis of Retained Earnings and Stockholders' Equity

FOCUS ON FINANCIAL RESULTS

Sprint operates the only totally digital, fiber-optic telecommunications network, which transmits voice, video, and data, in the United States. It provides telephone services in 19 states and publishes telephone directories for 20. It sells business communications equipment and security systems. Through its Global One joint venture, Sprint provides international voice and data services. In partnership with three cable companies, it is building a nationwide network for wireless personal communications.

The diverse product mix is a strategic adaptation to radical change in the telecommunications industry. Most notable is deregulation,

SPRINT
CONSOLIDATED STATEMENTS OF INCOME

(in millions, except per share data)
For the years ended December 31,

	1995	1994	1993
Net Operating Revenues	$12,765.1	$11,986.6	$10,914.7
Operating Expenses			
Costs of services and products	6,504.9	6,154.5	5,591.9
Selling, general and administrative	2,871.9	2,755.4	2,532.5
Depreciation and amortization	1,466.4	1,386.0	1,283.7
Merger, integration and restructuring costs	87.6	—	292.5
Total operating expenses	10,930.8	10,295.9	9,700.6
Operating Income	1,834.3	1,690.7	1,214.1
Interest expense	(260.7)	(300.7)	(367.0)
Other expense, net	(93.2)	(2.1)	(34.0)
Income from continuing operations before income taxes	1,480.4	1,387.9	813.1
Income tax provision	(534.3)	(488.7)	(296.0)
Income from Continuing Operations	946.1	899.2	517.1
Discontinued operations, net			
Cellular division	14.5	(15.5)	(38.1)
Other	—	7.0	(12.3)
Extraordinary items, net	(565.3)	—	(29.2)
Cumulative effect of changes in accounting principles, net	—	—	(382.6)
Net income	395.3	890.7	54.9
Preferred stock dividends	(2.6)	(2.7)	(2.8)
Earnings applicable to common stock	$ 392.7	$ 888.0	$ 52.1
Earnings per Common Share			
Continuing operations	$ 2.69	$ 2.57	$ 1.50
Discontinued operations	0.04	(0.02)	(0.15)
Extraordinary items	(1.61)	—	(0.08)
Cumulative effect of changes in accounting principles	—	—	(1.12)
Total	$ 1.12	$ 2.55	$ 0.15
Weighted average number of common shares	350.1	348.7	343.7
Dividends per common share	$ 1.00	$ 1.00	$ 1.00

See accompanying Notes to Consolidated Financial Statements.

---

including a recent U.S. law allowing companies to compete in providing local telephone services.

Because of industry revolution and more routine reasons, Sprint reports its results in several different categories. Sprint's 1995 income statement includes operating income ($1.834 billion), income from continuing operations ($946 million), and net income ($395 million). Its net income is much less than income from continuing operations because Sprint took a charge of $565.3 million for "extraordinary

items" (adjustments made so that Sprint's statement would conform with the accounting principles followed by most businesses, instead of just those businesses in regulated industries).

Which income measure would interest you most if you were a stockholder? If you were a banker considering a loan to Sprint? A news reporter? While studying this chapter, consider the importance of including different income measures on an income statement.

SOURCE: *Sprint Annual Report,* 1995.

After studying this chapter, you should be able to

LO 1 Understand a multi-step corporate income statement and its categories.

LO 2 Describe the appropriate presentation and disclosure of discontinued operations.

LO 3 Determine when items should be considered extraordinary and develop the income statement presentation when such items are present.

LO 4 Analyze accounting changes and determine their effect on the income statement.

LO 5 Use the earnings per share ratio as a measure of a company's profitability.

LO 6 Identify the proper way to present corrections of errors on the retained earnings statement.

LO 7 Understand the effect that appropriations and other restrictions have on retained earnings.

LO 8 Prepare a statement of stockholders' equity.

LO 9 Understand the meaning and importance of comprehensive income.

LO 10 Explain the effects that income statement events have on the statement of cash flows.

Reading a Corporate Income Statement

Categories on the Multi-Step Income Statement

LO 1 Understand a multi-step corporate income statement and its categories.

The purpose of the income statement is to report the amount of net income for the corporation for a given time period. It is an expression of the basic accounting equation:

$$\text{Revenue} - \text{Expenses} = \text{Net Income}$$

Most corporations do not report all revenue in one category and all expense in another. Rather, they have found that it is more meaningful to provide categories of revenues and expenses. This is referred to as a **multi-step income statement.**

Cisco Systems, a major technology company, uses a multi-step statement; its 1995 statement is included as Exhibit 12-1. Cisco Systems' income statement has four main categories of income. The purpose of the first category is to determine the amount of the gross profit or gross margin. **Gross profit** is expressed as follows:

$$\text{Net Sales} - \text{Cost of Sales} = \text{Gross Profit}$$

For the year 1995, Cisco Systems had net sales of $1,978,916,000 and cost of sales (often referred to as *cost of goods sold*) of $644,152,000 resulting in gross profit of $1,334,764,000. A gross profit, as opposed to a gross loss, means that Cisco Systems is selling its products for more than it costs to buy or produce them. This is a favorable indication of the company's profitability, but the amount of the gross profit should be compared with that of similar firms to determine whether it is adequate. For such comparison, a **gross profit percentage** is often computed:

$$\text{Gross Profit} / \text{Net Sales} = \text{Gross Profit Percentage}$$

This determination allows companies of different sizes to be compared on the basis of the percentage, rather than the dollar amount, of gross profit. Cisco Systems' gross profit percentage for 1995 was approximately 67.4% ($1,334,764,000/$1,978,916,000) and appears to be adequate when compared with that of other companies in the same line of business. Sufficient gross profit must be available to cover all of the firm's other expenses for it to be profitable. An analysis of the gross profit percentage over time also indicates the company's ability to pass higher costs to customers or to survive price-cutting competitors. Remember, however, that gross profit is only an initial measure of profitability and considers only one revenue, sales revenue, and one expense, cost of goods sold.

The second category of income on Cisco Systems' income statement is the operating income. **Operating income** is expressed as follows:

$$\text{Gross Profit} - \text{Operating Expenses} = \text{Operating Income}$$

EXHIBIT 12-1   Cisco Systems: Multi-Step Income Statement

Consolidated Statements of Operations
(in thousands, except per-share amounts)

YEARS ENDED	July 30, 1995	July 31, 1994	July 25, 1993
Net sales	$1,978,916	$1,242,975	$ 649,035
Cost of sales	644,152	412,824	210,528
Gross margin	1,334,764	830,151	438,507
Expenses:			
Research and development	164,819	88,753	44,254
Sales and marketing	354,722	205,797	109,717
General and administrative	76,524	47,485	20,965
Purchased research and development	95,760		
Total operating expenses	691,825	342,035	174,936
Operating income	642,939	488,116	263,571
Interest and other income, net	36,107	21,377	11,557
Income before provision for income taxes	679,046	509,493	275,128
Provision for income taxes	258,038	194,626	103,173
Net income	$ 421,008	$ 314,867	$ 171,955
Net income per common share	$ 1.52	$ 1.19	$ .67
Shares used in per-share calculation	277,298	265,051	258,133

The accompanying notes are an integral part of these financial statements.

Most firms disclose several categories of operating expenses. Cisco Systems has four types: research and development, sales and marketing, general and administrative, and purchased research and development. The importance of research in the technology industry is evident when you examine this category of the income statement. For the year 1995, these four expenses totaled $691,825,000. When that amount is deducted from the amount of the gross profit, an operating income of $642,939,000 resulted for 1995:

$$\$1,334,764,000 - \$691,825,000 = \$642,939,000$$

Operating income is a measure of the amount of income derived from the firm's primary or central activities. Cisco Systems is the world's largest supplier of computer networking solutions, so its main source of income must come from such activities if it is to be profitable.

The third category of income on Cisco Systems' income statement includes those items that enter into the computation of income before income taxes. This amount for Cisco Systems can be expressed as follows:

Operating Income + Interest and Other Income = Income before Income Taxes

The items listed in this category of the income statement involve income and expense items that are *not* the firm's primary or central activities. Interest expense and interest

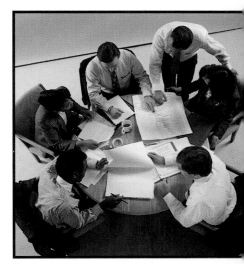

Cisco Systems workers get together for a systems integration session. Cisco is a high-tech supplier of computer network solutions.

revenue reflect the decisions the firm has made concerning how to finance its operations and invest its excess funds. The financing decision is extremely important, but it is separate from the operating decisions of the firm and is therefore listed with other expenses and losses on the income statement. In this category Cisco Systems has only one line, labeled "Interest and other income, net." This line combines the company's interest income, interest expense, and other income and expenses. The term "net" here means that the company has aggregated all of the amounts into one line on the income statement. The amount of income before income taxes can be calculated as $679,046,000:

$$\$642,939,000 + \$36,107,000 = \$679,046,000$$

The fourth category of income involves the computation of *net income*. Because income tax is a very important item, most firms separate that expense from the other expenses. Therefore, a line titled *income before tax* is presented, and income tax expense or provision for income taxes is deducted to arrive at net income. The relationship can be expressed as follows:

$$\text{Income before Income Tax} - \text{Income Tax} = \text{Net Income}$$

For 1995 Cisco Systems had income before income taxes of $679,046,000, but after the income tax expense was deducted, the net income was $421,008,000:

$$\$679,046,000 - \$258,038,000 = \$421,008,000$$

Note that the term *net income* is reserved for the bottom line of the income statement. It is a measure of profit after all revenues and all expenses, including income tax expense, have been considered.

Analysts may disagree about which income figure is most important. Ask a banker, and he or she might tell you that cash flow is the most critical factor in determining whether a loan is repaid. A Wall Street analyst might tell you that operating income is the most important figure because it excludes nonrecurring items. An industry analyst might focus on gross profit because statistics regarding materials and labor are available across companies and thus are comparable. The public, however, puts more faith in the bottom line than in any other number. That's the figure that the press quotes when a company releases its earnings.

Three other items also must be displayed on the income statement. These items occur infrequently and are not included in normal business operations. They usually are material when they do occur, however, and should be reported after income from continuing or normal operations. These items are income (loss) from discontinued operations, extraordinary gains or losses, and the cumulative effect of changes in accounting principles. They are discussed in the following sections.

Discontinued Operations

LO 2 Describe the appropriate presentation and disclosure of discontinued operations.

Users of financial statements desire income statements that help them predict the income and cash flow that will occur for a firm in the future. Normally, the current-year income statement provides a good indication of those activities that will continue in future periods. Revenues, cost of goods sold, and administrative expenses, viewed over several years, usually exhibit a trend. Problems arise, however, if a company sells major segments or divisions during a year. In that case, it is necessary to separate the results of activities that will continue in the future from the results of activities that were conducted by the portion of the business that has been sold or discontinued.

The **discontinued operations** section should be presented when a company sells a major division or segment. For a transaction to qualify as a discontinued operation, it must be a separate, identifiable portion of the business. Further, the sale must change the nature of the company's operations in a way that affects the financial statement user's ability to predict future activities. For example, assume that a large auto firm has two divisions, one that manufactures and sells autos and another that finances and leases them. If the company decides to sell the financing and leasing division, the transaction should be reported as a discontinued operation on the income statement.

When a transaction meets the criteria to be classified as a discontinued operation, it should appear in a separate category of the income statement. For example, assume that Wirtz Company decided on December 31, 1998, to sell one of its major divisions and on that date received as the selling price an amount that was $1,000 less than the book value of the assets. During 1998 the division that was sold had sales to customers of $12,000 and operating expenses of $15,000, resulting in a loss before tax of $3,000. Wirtz pays income tax at the rate of 30%. The transaction should be portrayed on the income statement as follows:

Income from continuing operations	$XXXXX
Discontinued operations:	
Loss from operations ($3,000 less tax effect of $900)	(2,100)
Loss from disposal of assets ($1,000 less tax effect of $300)	(700)
Net income	$XXXXX

The first item indicates the loss from *operating* the division during 1998. The second item indicates the loss from *selling* the division. Note that both items should be shown *net* of the tax effect involved. The tax effect may be confusing and should be analyzed carefully. Essentially, a loss results in a tax savings. For example, the company had a $3,000 loss from operating the division in 1998, reducing the firm's income by $3,000. As a result, the firm paid $900 less tax than it would have paid if the loss had not occurred. Therefore, the $900 is a tax savings or tax benefit and reduces the amount of the loss net of taxes to $2,100.

The consolidated income statement of Unisys Corporation for the year 1995 is presented in Exhibit 12-2. Unisys is a large company that, before 1995, had been in the mainframe computer business and also in the defense electronics business. Over time, it had seen the information services portion of its business grow and its prospects in the defense electronics segment diminish. The company had become unprofitable, and action was necessary. The 1995 income statement indicates that Unisys had a loss from continuing operations of $627.3 million and income from discontinued operations of $2.7 million, resulting in a net loss of $624.6 million:

$$(\$627.3) + \$2.7 = (\$624.6)$$

The footnotes to the annual report indicate that Unisys sold its defense business during 1995. The results of the defense operations are presented separately on the income statement as "income from discontinued operations." The income statements presented for 1994 and 1993 also have a line for income from discontinued operations so that the reader of the statement can compare the results from those years.

Unisys Corporation's net loss figure is a good indication of the firm's overall performance or activity for the year. Because the defense business was discontinued, however, the loss is probably not a good indication of future income. Users of the statement should place primary importance on the amount of *income or loss from continuing operations* to indicate future activities. Of course, it would be easier to predict future income if the changes in "income (loss) from continuing operations before extraordinary items and changes in accounting principles" were not so dramatic. In 1993, the total is $286.3 million; it falls to $12.1 million in 1994 and then falls to a loss of $627.3 million in 1995. That makes it difficult to forecast 1996 results.

Extraordinary Items

When developing an income statement, management makes a variety of judgments concerning the proper presentation and communication of results. An example of the application of judgment concerns the determination of extraordinary items. The accountant classifies extraordinary items separately so that the statement user can easily determine the nature of the item and consider whether such items should be expected in future periods. This requires careful judgment on the part of the company's accountant and management.

LO 3 Determine when items should be considered extraordinary and develop the income statement presentation when such items are present.

EXHIBIT 12-2	Unisys Corporation's 1995 Consolidated Income Statement

CONSOLIDATED STATEMENT OF INCOME

Unisys Corporation

Year Ended December 31 (Millions, except per share data)	1995	1994	1993
Revenue			
Sales	$2,646.3	$2,877.1	$ 3,178.6
Services	2,198.1	1,759.4	1,358.2
Equipment maintenance	1,357.9	1,341.7	1,444.0
	6,202.3	5,978.2	5,980.8
Costs and expenses			
Cost of sales	1,611.0	1,568.7	1,563.8
Cost of services	2,030.4	1,374.0	1,018.6
Cost of equipment maintenance	965.7	872.7	820.4
Selling, general and administrative expenses	1,883.8	1,544.8	1,516.3
Research and development expenses	409.5	463.6	489.3
	6,900.4	5,823.8	5,408.4
Operating income (loss)	(698.1)	154.4	572.4
Interest expense	202.1	203.7	241.7
Other income, net	119.1	63.9	40.2
Income (loss) from continuing operations before income taxes	(781.1)	14.6	370.9
Estimated income taxes (benefit)	(153.8)	2.5	84.6
Income (loss) from continuing operations before extraordinary items and changes in accounting principles	(627.3)	12.1	286.3
Income from discontinued operations	2.7	96.1	75.3
Extraordinary items		(7.7)	(26.4)
Effect of changes in accounting principles			230.2
Net income (loss)	(624.6)	100.5	565.4
Dividends on preferred shares	120.3	120.1	121.6
Earnings (loss) on common shares	$ (744.9)	$ (19.6)	$ 443.8
Earnings (loss) per common share			
Primary			
Continuing operations	$ (4.37)	$ (.63)	$ 1.00
Discontinued operations	.02	.56	.46
Extraordinary items		(.04)	(.16)
Effect of changes in accounting principles			1.39
Total	$ (4.35)	$ (.11)	$ 2.69
Fully diluted			
Continuing operations	$ (4.37)	$ (.63)	$ 1.17
Discontinued operations	.02	.56	.31
Extraordinary items		(.04)	(.11)
Effect of changes in accounting principles			.94
Total	$ (4.35)	$ (.11)	$ 2.31

See notes to consolidated financial statements.

An item should be treated as an **extraordinary item** if it is both *unusual* and *infrequent*. The accountant must judge what constitutes unusual and infrequent with regard to the environment of each individual firm. Thus, an occurrence may be unusual and infrequent to one firm but not to another. For example, if a tornado destroys a firm's assets, the loss probably should be considered extraordinary. If the firm is located in a geographic area known for tornadoes or if it has experienced tornado losses several times in past years, however, the loss is not considered extraordinary.

ACCOUNTING FOR YOUR DECISIONS
You Are the CFO

You are one of a new breed of Internet companies. Because you are located in northern California, you were unable to buy earthquake insurance for your corporate headquarters. During the year, northern California experienced a major earthquake that damaged your office building. You wish to record the loss as extraordinary, because you believe the investment community will not count the loss against you. Your auditors disagree, saying that you are located on the San Andreas fault. Who's right?

ANS: What is extraordinary is always a matter of judgment. What is "unusual and infrequent" for one company is not for another. In this case, your auditors are probably right that the loss is not extraordinary. Earthquakes in your environment are not considered to be unusual and infrequent. The fact that you could not buy earthquake insurance is an indication that earthquakes are common in your area and insurance companies do not want the risk exposure. You should communicate to the investment community that this loss is not extraordinary according to accounting standards, but hopefully, will not occur very often and will not alter the company's future profitability.

Typically, management prefers that a major *loss* be categorized as extraordinary because the investment community tends to ignore extraordinary events when predicting future income levels. A loss that is part of continuing operations will probably hurt the company's stock price. On the other hand, management would rather not categorize an unusual *gain* as extraordinary because it wants investors to believe that such a gain was part of continuing operations. Accountants must develop a careful, professional judgment based on all the facts available concerning the transaction and the environment of the firm to determine whether an item is extraordinary.

An item or transaction that is deemed to be extraordinary should be presented in a separate category of the income statement. For example, assume that Lily Company had a large fire loss of $6,000 and pays income tax at the rate of 30%. The fire loss should be presented as follows:

Income before extraordinary item	$XXXXX
Extraordinary loss	
($6,000 less tax effect of $1,800)	(4,200)
Net income	$XXXXX

Like discontinued items, extraordinary items should always be presented net of tax. Thus, the $6,000 loss in the preceding example is reduced by $1,800, the amount of the *taxes saved* as a result of the loss. The amount of $4,200 is reported on the income statement. If the extraordinary item results in a gain, the amount should be reduced by the amount of *additional taxes* that result from the gain to obtain the net-of-tax amount.

Chapter 10 referred to gains and losses on the redemption of bonds payable as extraordinary items. Gains and losses on bond redemption are a special type of extraordinary item. The accountant is not required to determine whether the items are "unusual and infrequent." The FASB has ruled that *all* gains and losses on the redemption of bonds should be classified as extraordinary items by the firm that issued the bonds. This is one of the most frequent types of extraordinary items, and you will see these gains or losses reflected on the financial statements of many companies.

Exhibit 12-3 reports the frequency of extraordinary items among 600 companies included in an annual survey. In 1995, debt extinguishment was the most frequently cited item included as extraordinary, and in 1994 it was the *only* item treated as extraordinary by the surveyed companies.

On January 17, 1994, a major earthquake hit the Northridge area near Los Angeles and affected homes and businesses in a wide area of southern California, including Anaheim Stadium (shown here). Can such damage be considered an extraordinary loss for *any* company in the Los Angeles area, which is prone to quakes?

EXHIBIT 12-3	Extraordinary Items Reported by Surveyed Companies		
		NUMBER OF ITEMS REPORTED	
NATURE OF ITEM		1995	1994
Debt of extinguishments		53	59
Operating loss carry-forwards		—	—
Litigation settlements		—	—
Other		3	—
Total Extraordinary Items		56	59
Total Number of Companies		600	600

SOURCE: *Accounting Trends & Techniques,* 50th ed. (New York: American Institute of Certified Public Accountants, 1996).

The opening of this chapter presented the income statement of Sprint. The 1995 income statement contains a rather large extraordinary loss that was the result of Sprint's decision to follow generally accepted accounting procedures in its new, deregulated environment. For a second example of extraordinary items, refer to the 1994 column of Unisys Corporation's income statement in Exhibit 12-2. The income statement indicates that an extraordinary loss of $7.7 million occurred in 1994. The footnotes to the financial statements explained, "In 1994, the company recorded an extraordinary charge for the repurchases of debt of $7.7 million, net of $5.1 million of income tax benefits." Thus the loss before taxes was $12.8 million ($7.7 + $5.1). Unisys deducted the net amount to arrive at its 1994 net income of $100.5 million.

Unisys was required to treat the item as an extraordinary loss, regardless of whether it was unusual and infrequent. Still, the bond redemption should be considered a one-time occurrence that is unlikely to happen again for Unisys. Therefore, although the net income of Unisys may be a good measure of the overall performance of the firm, it is probably not a good indication of the activities that will continue in the future. Users should consider the company's earnings *before* the extraordinary item as a more accurate reflection of future activities.

ACCOUNTING FOR YOUR DECISIONS
You Are the Analyst

You have reviewed the financial statements of Unisys for the years 1993–1995 as a starting point for your analysis. You are concerned because the income statement reveals several different measures of income—income from continuing operations, income from discontinued operations, and net income or loss. Which income should you emphasize in your analysis?

ANS: All of the income measures are important and indicate aspects of the company's performance for the period. If you want an indication of how the company will perform in the future, it is best to use income from continuing operations. The other income measures include one-time charges that may be unrelated to future activity. Unfortunately, analysts and other users often pick the net income figure since it's the "bottom line."

Change in Accounting Principle

LO 4 Analyze accounting changes and determine their effect on the income statement.

One of the important concepts of accounting information is consistency. The consistency principle states that firms should normally use the same accounting methods from year to year to allow users of the financial statements to accurately evaluate the firm's performance. It is necessary on some occasions, however, for a firm to change its accounting methods. The accountant must then evaluate the effect of the change and determine the proper way to present the change on the financial statements.

A **change in accounting principle** occurs when a firm changes from one generally accepted accounting method to another method that is also generally accepted. A common example is a firm's change to the straight-line method of depreciation from an accelerated method. Another example is a change from the first-in, first-out inventory method to the weighted average method. When a change in accounting principle occurs, the company must present the **cumulative effect** of the change in a separate category of the income statement in the year of the change. The cumulative effect is the total difference in income as a result of applying the previous accounting method instead of the adopted method for all years prior to the current year.

Assume that Zielinski Company was formed in 1996 and adopted an accelerated method to depreciate all assets. In 1998 Zielinski finds it appropriate to change to the straight-line method. Also assume that the company pays income tax at the rate of 30%. To calculate the cumulative effect of the change in depreciation, the company must first determine the amount of depreciation for each method for the previous years, 1996 and 1997. Assume that the following depreciation schedules have been developed:

YEAR	STRAIGHT-LINE	ACCELERATED	DIFFERENCE
1996	$50,000	$100,000	$50,000
1997	50,000	80,000	30,000
Total			$80,000

In this example, the cumulative effect of the change in accounting principle is $80,000 before tax. It should be presented on the 1998 income statement, net of tax, as follows:

Income before cumulative effect	$XXXXX
Plus: Cumulative effect of a change in principle ($80,000 less tax effect of $24,000)	56,000
Net income	$XXXXX

If the straight-line method had been used in 1996 and 1997, less depreciation would have been taken, and income would have been higher. Therefore, the cumulative effect must be added to income. Other accounting changes may require an amount to be *deducted* from income. For example, if Zielinski Company had changed from straight-line depreciation to an accelerated method, it would have been necessary to deduct the cumulative effect of the change in principle.

Refer again to the income statement of Unisys Corporation in Exhibit 12-2. The 1993 column of the statement contains a figure in the line labeled "effect of changes in accounting principles." The footnotes to the financial statements reveal that in 1993, the company changed its method of accounting for postretirement benefits. Previously, the firm had recorded the costs as an expense when paid, but the FASB issued a new accounting rule that required firms to accrue the retirement costs as an expense over the period that the employee worked for the company. Because of the new accounting rule, Unisys changed its accounting for retirement costs in 1993. Unisys also changed its accounting for income taxes in 1993 as a result of a new accounting rule issued by the FASB. The cumulative effect of both changes was shown on the 1993 income statement. Because the combined effect was positive, Unisys increased its income by a rather large amount, $230.2 million, before arriving at the net income amount. The cumulative effect amount on the income statement of Unisys represents a one-time charge and is unlikely to occur in the future.

Unfortunately, some companies change accounting principles because their results will look better under the new method, not because the new principle better reflects business reality. Companies that change accounting methods must justify the change and should not be attempting merely to increase their income as a result. When a change in accounting principle does occur, the income *before* the cumulative effect of a change in accounting principle is a better measure of the activities that will continue in the future.

Analyzing Profitability Using Earnings Per Share

LO 5 Use the earnings per share ratio as a measure of a company's profitability.

Ratios are often helpful to evaluate the profitability of a firm and to compare the performance of one firm with that of another. The most common ratio to evaluate a firm's profitability is **earnings per share.** All public companies are required to disclose this important ratio on their income statement. Earnings per share is calculated as follows:

$$\frac{\text{Net Income} - \text{Preferred Dividends}}{\text{Weighted Average Number of Shares of Common Stock}}$$

The purpose of the earnings per share calculation is to determine the amount of earnings of the *common* stockholder. When a firm has both preferred and common stock, the preferred stockholders have a claim to earnings in the amount of the preferred stock dividend. Therefore, preferred stock dividends must be deducted in the numerator; the remaining amount represents the earnings of the common stockholder.

The denominator represents the number of shares of *common* stock outstanding for the firm. The income number, the numerator of the fraction, measures income of a specific time period, in this case a year. Therefore, it is necessary that the denominator of the fraction, the number of shares, also be measured over a time period. For that reason, a **weighted average of shares** is used as the denominator in the earnings per share calculation. The weighted average is calculated by weighting the number of shares by the time that those shares were outstanding during the period.

The following example illustrates the calculation of a weighted average. Assume that a firm had 1,000 shares of common stock issued as of the beginning of 1998. On September 1, 1998, the firm issued an additional 600 shares of common stock. The September 1 transaction was the only transaction during the year affecting the number of shares. On December 31, 1998, the firm had 1,600 shares of common stock outstanding, but this is not the number that is used as the denominator when calculating earnings per share. The weighted average number of shares is calculated as follows:

$$\text{Beginning Shares} + (\text{Increase in Shares} \times \text{Time Factor}) = \text{Weighted Average Shares}$$
$$1,000 + (600 \times 4/12) = 1,200$$

The shares must be weighted by the time period the shares were outstanding, so the 600 shares are weighted by 4/12 (4 months divided by 12 months).

Companies must compute earnings per share for the bottom-line net income figure and for other categories of income on the income statement. For example, if a firm's income statement has an extraordinary item, earnings per share for income before extraordinary items is calculated as follows:

$$\frac{\text{Income before Extraordinary Items} - \text{Preferred Dividends}}{\text{Weighted Average Number of Shares of Common Stock}}$$

Thus, the income statements of most corporations reveal several earnings per share numbers corresponding to the income categories disclosed on the income statement.

The income statement of Cisco Systems in Exhibit 12-1 is an excellent example of the presentation of earnings per share. Note that toward the bottom of the statement, the company has indicated that the "shares used in per-share calculation" for 1995 were 277,298,000. This represents the weighted average number of shares of common stock and was used as the denominator for calculating earnings per share. Because Cisco Systems did not have any extraordinary items or changes in accounting principle, the income statement presents only one earnings per share amount, which the company has labeled "net income per common share." Thus the amount for 1995 of $1.52 per share can be calculated as net income divided by the weighted average number of shares of common stock:

$$\$421,008,000/277,298,000 \text{ shares} = \$1.52 \text{ per share}$$

FROM CONCEPT TO PRACTICE 12.1

READING SPRINT'S INCOME STATEMENT

Refer to Sprint's 1995 income statement. Why was more than one earnings per share number presented? Sprint calculated earnings per share for which lines of the statement?

The earnings per share ratio is a very important measure of a firm's profitability. Investors commonly use it to determine the proper market price of a firm's stock. A company's management is expected to meet the earnings per share predicted for the company by analysts and investors. If a company does not meet such goals, the stock price often falls in response.

The earnings per share ratio represents the *earnings* per share of the firm, however, not the *dividend* that the stockholders will receive. A firm's disclosure of earnings per share of $1.52 does not mean that stockholders will receive a dividend of $1.52 per share. Most firms pay only a portion of their earnings to stockholders as dividends. Others, such as Ben & Jerry's, do not pay any dividends. The amounts not paid as dividends are retained by the firm to finance its future growth.

Events Affecting Stockholders' Equity

In this section we will examine in more detail those events that affect the stockholders' equity section of the balance sheet. Initially, we will focus on two important events, income and dividends, and on their impact on one particular account in stockholders' equity, the Retained Earnings account.

How Income and Dividends Affect Retained Earnings

The Retained Earnings account plays an important role because it serves as a link between the income statement and the balance sheet. The term *articulated statements* refers to the fact that the information on the income statement is related to the information on the balance sheet. The bridge (or link) between the two statements is the Retained Earnings account. Exhibit 12-4 presents this relationship graphically. As the exhibit indicates, the income statement is used to calculate a company's net income for a given period of time. The amount of the net income is transferred to the statement of retained earnings and is added to the beginning balance of retained earnings (with dividends deducted) to calculate the ending balance of retained earnings. The ending balance of retained earnings is the amount that is portrayed on the balance sheet in the stockholders' equity category. That is why you must always prepare the income statement before you prepare the balance sheet, as you have discovered when developing financial statements in previous chapters of the text.

EXHIBIT 12-4	Retained Earnings Connects the Income Statement and the Balance Sheet

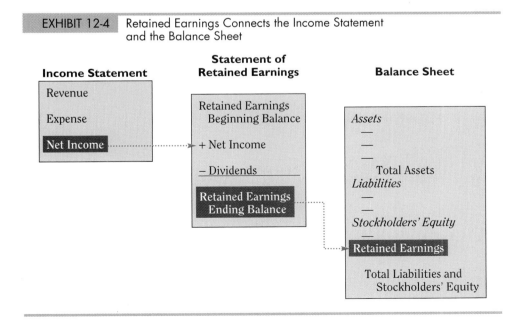

Exhibit 12-4 indicates that income and dividends are important events that affect stockholders' equity. In the sections that follow we present several other events that also have an impact on the stockholders' equity category. Some of the items affect the Retained Earnings account, and some are portrayed in other stockholders' equity accounts.

ACCOUNTING FOR YOUR DECISIONS
You Have a Class Project

You are researching a company for a class project. You want to determine the company's net income for the most recent year. Unfortunately, you have been unable to find the company's income statement, but have found their balance sheet for the two most recent years. How can you determine their net income?

ANS: Usually net income is determined on the income statement by deducting expenses from revenue. It may also be possible to find net income by using the balance sheet for two years. You first must calculate the change in the balance of Retained Earnings that occurred during the year. You then must eliminate other items that affected Retained Earnings such as dividends. The remaining amount should represent the company's net income for the current year.

Prior Period Adjustments

LO 6 Identify the proper way to present corrections of errors on the retained earnings statement.

A **prior period adjustment** is an adjustment to the income of previous years. Because the income of each period affects the Retained Earnings account, a prior period adjustment is reported directly in the Retained Earnings account rather than on the income statement. The most common example of a prior period adjustment is a correction of an error in a previous period. For example, assume that Heidi Company purchased a $10,000 asset on January 1, 1996. The asset has a 10-year life, and Heidi had planned to use straight-line depreciation. In 1998, however, the accountant for Heidi discovers that the company has neglected to report depreciation on the asset since the time of purchase.

This situation is an example of the need for an error correction that should be treated as a prior period adjustment. The accountant for Heidi should first determine the amount of the error for the prior periods, as follows:

$$\$10,000/10 \text{ Years} = \$1,000 \text{ Depreciation per Year} \times 2 \text{ Years}$$
$$\text{Error before Tax} = \underline{\$2,000}$$

Note that the error in Retained Earnings is the amount of the error for *prior* periods, 1996 and 1997 in this example. Depreciation expense for 1996 and 1997 cannot be corrected, however, by changing the Depreciation Expense account. Depreciation Expense is a temporary account that was closed each year. The result was that net income was overstated each year. Net income is closed to the Retained Earnings account at year-end; therefore, Retained Earnings is overstated. To correct for the error, the accountant must decrease the beginning balance of Retained Earnings as of January 1, 1998.

Prior period adjustments must be presented *net* of the tax effect of the item. Assume that the tax rate for Heidi Company is 40%. The error, net of taxes, would be computed as follows:

Error before tax	$2,000
Tax effect at 40%	(800)
Error net of tax	$1,200

The prior period adjustment would appear on the 1998 statement of retained earnings as follows:

Retained earnings, January 1, 1998	$XXXXX
Less: Correction of error (net of $800 tax effect)	($1,200)
Corrected balance, January 1, 1998	$XXXXX

When an error occurs and a prior period adjustment item is presented, it should be presented as the first item after the beginning balance on the retained earnings statement.

The beginning balance of the Retained Earnings account should be shown as previously reported. The correction of error should then be presented to arrive at a corrected beginning balance. After the corrected beginning balance, the other items on the retained earnings statement, such as net income and dividends, should be handled as we have indicated in previous chapters.

Although adjustments due to prior errors occur with some frequency on the unaudited financial statements of privately held companies, such an adjustment is rarely seen on the audited financial statements of publicly held companies.

ACCOUNTING FOR YOUR DECISIONS

You Advise Your Boss

You have just taken a part-time accounting job to help pay your college expenses. In reviewing the company's records you discover several expenses that were not recorded by the company on last year's financial statements. Your boss has suggested that the company should have recorded the expenses during the current year. How should you respond?

ANS: If the expenses are a material amount, the company should correct last year's financial statements. The correction should be treated as a prior period adjustment and previous statements should be corrected and reissued. It is not correct accounting procedure to simply record the overlooked expenses in the current year.

Appropriations of Retained Earnings

Another example of an item that does not affect the income of the company but does affect retained earnings is appropriations of retained earnings. An **appropriation of retained earnings** occurs when a company designates a portion of the balance of retained earnings for a specific purpose, thereby making that amount unavailable for dividends. The amount can be presented in a separate account or reported in a footnote. Appropriations of retained earnings are today used less frequently than in past years and are usually reported in a footnote.

LO 7 Understand the effect that appropriations and other restrictions have on retained earnings.

Assume, for example, that the board of directors of Dran Company has voted to engage in a plant expansion program. As part of the program, the directors voted on January 1, 1998, to appropriate $10,000 of retained earnings for plant expansion to a separate account. The effect of the appropriation is simply to transfer $10,000 from one account, Retained Earnings, to another account, Retained Earnings Appropriated for Plant Expansion. Dran Company now has two accounts within the retained earnings category. The first account, Retained Earnings, represents the amount that is available for dividend purposes. The second account, Retained Earnings Appropriated for Plant Expansion, represents the amount designated for a specific purpose.

What is the purpose of appropriating retained earnings? It may serve at least two purposes. First, appropriating retained earnings reduces the company's ability to pay dividends to stockholders. Dividends are declared from the Retained Earnings account, which is reduced when the entry to appropriate is recorded. Second, appropriating retained earnings serves a signaling effect. Stockholders and other statement users are made aware that the firm has future plans and needs to retain funds for those plans. Many firms disclose such intentions in a footnote or a parenthetical disclosure attached to the Retained Earnings account in lieu of a Retained Earnings Appropriated account.

Other Events

Thus far in this section, we have presented two examples of items that are not recorded on the income statement but are reported directly in the Retained Earnings account. Additional items are also not reported on the income statement but are recorded in the stockholders' equity category. We mention these briefly because you may see these items on the financial statements of many large corporations. First, the stockholders' equity category of some firms reveals the account **Unrealized Gain/Loss—Available-for-Sale Securities,** which occurs when a firm adjusts its investments in securities for changes in the market values of the securities. For example, if a company buys stock in another company and the value of that stock changes, it may be necessary to write the stock up or down to market value. (See Chapter 13 for more detail.) The adjustment of available-for-sale investments is not considered a gain or loss on the income statement. Instead, the adjustment on these items is reported directly in the stockholders' equity category; the Unrealized Gain/Loss—Available-for-Sale Securities account is reflected on the balance sheet after retained earnings.

A second item that may appear in the stockholders' equity category is the account Foreign Currency Translation Adjustments. Most large corporations operate in several countries, and their assets may be held in the currency of several denominations, such as U.S. dollars and Japanese yen. Generally, when these international companies present their financial statements, they are required to present all of their assets in one currency. For example, U.S. companies must state their financial statements in U.S. dollars, requiring restatement of all their assets to U.S. dollars. When assets of another currency are restated to U.S. dollars, a gain or loss on restatement occurs. The gain or loss is not the result of selling the assets but results from differences in the values of the two currencies involved.

This gain or loss is not presented on the income statement. Instead, it is presented as an account in the stockholders' equity category of the balance sheet. If a loss has resulted from the translation, the balance of the account is subtracted from stockholders' equity; if a gain has resulted, its balance is added to stockholders' equity.

You should note that there is considerable controversy about the importance of translation adjustment amounts on companies' annual reports. Companies consider the translation adjustments to be "paper" gains or losses because they are unrealized and do not directly result in any cash inflows or outflows. The gains or losses are realized only if foreign assets are transferred to U.S. dollars. Most international firms do not actually intend to engage in such transactions; they calculate the translation adjustments only for the purpose of presenting financial statements.

Statement of Stockholders' Equity

LO 8 Prepare a statement of stockholders' equity.

In addition to a balance sheet, an income statement, and a cash flows statement, many annual reports contain a **statement of stockholders' equity.** The purpose of this statement is to explain all of the reasons for the difference between the beginning and the ending balances of each of the accounts in the stockholders' equity category of the balance sheet. Of course, if the only changes are the result of dividends, a statement of retained earnings is sufficient. When other changes have occurred in stockholders' equity accounts, this more complete statement is necessary.

The statement of stockholders' equity of Starbucks Corporation is presented in Exhibit 12-5 for the year 1995. The statement starts with the beginning balances of each of the accounts as of October 2, 1994. Starbucks' stockholders' equity is presented in three categories (the columns on the statement) as of October 2, 1994, as follows:

Common stock	$89,861,000
Retained earnings	20,037,000
Treasury stock	0

Starbucks' statement of stockholders' equity indicates the items or events that affected stockholders' equity during 1995. The four most important items or events were as follows:

FROM CONCEPT TO PRACTICE 12.2

READING BEN & JERRY'S ANNUAL REPORT Refer to Ben & Jerry's statement of stockholders' equity. What were the major reasons for the difference between the 1994 year-end stockholders' equity amount of $72,502,000 and the 1995 year-end amount of $78,531,000?

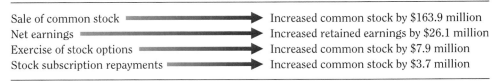

ITEM OR EVENT		EFFECT ON STOCKHOLDERS' EQUITY
Sale of common stock	➡	Increased common stock by $163.9 million
Net earnings	➡	Increased retained earnings by $26.1 million
Exercise of stock options	➡	Increased common stock by $7.9 million
Stock subscription repayments	➡	Increased common stock by $3.7 million

EXHIBIT 12-5	Starbucks' Statement of Stockholders' Equity, 1995

[Consolidated Statements of Shareholders' Equity]
in thousands, except share data

	Common stock		Retained earnings	Treasury stock		Total
	Shares	Amount		Shares	Amount	
Balance, October 2, 1994	57,936,988	89,861	20,037	—	—	109,898
Exercise of stock options including tax benefit of $4,754	945,780	7,911	—	—	—	7,911
Sale of common stock	12,050,000	163,873	—	—	—	163,873
Stock subscription notes repayments	—	3,671	—	—	—	3,671
Conversion of convertible debentures, net	6,798	100	—	—	—	100
Sale of common stock under employee stock purchase plan	17,424	263	—	—	—	263
Net earnings	—	—	26,102	—	—	26,102
Unrealized holding gains, net	—	—	141	—	—	141
Translation adjustment	—	—	272	—	—	272
Balance, October 1, 1995	70,956,990	$265,679	$ 46,552	—	$ —	$312,231

See notes to consolidated financial statements.

Several other items of smaller amounts affected stockholders' equity during 1995. The last line of the statement of stockholders' equity indicates the ending balances of the stockholders' equity accounts as of the balance sheet date, October 1, 1995. You should note that total stockholders' equity has increased substantially during 1995, to $312.2 million at year-end. The statement of stockholders' equity is useful in explaining the reasons for the changes that occurred.

What Is Comprehensive Income?

There has always been some question about which items or transactions should be shown on the income statement and should be included in the calculation of net income. Generally, the accounting rule-making bodies have held that the income statement should reflect an *all-inclusive* approach. That is, all events and transactions that affect income should be shown on the income statement. This approach prevents the manipulation of the income figure by those who would like to show "good news" on the income statement and "bad news" directly on the retained earnings statement or the statement of stockholders' equity. The result of the all-inclusive approach is that the income statement includes items that are not necessarily under management's control, such as losses from natural disasters, and thus the income statement may not be a true reflection of a company's future potential.

LO 9 Understand the meaning and importance of comprehensive income.

The FASB has accepted certain exceptions to the all-inclusive approach and has allowed items to be recorded directly to the stockholders' equity category. This chapter has presented several examples of such items: prior period adjustments, foreign currency translation adjustments, and unrealized gains and losses on some investment securities. Items such as these have been excluded from the income statement for various reasons. Quite often, the justification is a concern for the volatility of the net income number. The items we have cited are often large dollar amounts; if included in the income statement, they would cause income to fluctuate widely from period to period. Therefore, the income statement is deemed to be more useful if the items are excluded.

EXHIBIT 12-6	The Relationship of the Income Statement and Statement of Comprehensive Income

INCOME STATEMENT
FOR YEAR ENDED DECEMBER 31, 19XX

Revenues	XXXX
Expenses	XXXX
Other gains and losses	XXXX
Income before tax	XXXX
Income tax expense	XXXX
Income before extraordinary item	XXXX
Extraordinary item, net of tax	XXXX
Income before cumulative effect	XXXX
Cumulative effect, net of tax	XXXX
Net Income	XXXX

STATEMENT OF COMPREHENSIVE INCOME
FOR YEAR ENDED DECEMBER 31,19XX

Net income	XXXX
Foreign currency translation adjustment	XXXX
Unrealized holding gains/losses	XXXX
Minimum pension liability adjustment	XXXX
Other comprehensive income	XXXX
Comprehensive Income	XXXX

A new term has been coined to incorporate the "income-type" items that escape the income statement. **Comprehensive income** is the net assets increase resulting from all transactions during a time period (except for investments by owners and distributions to owners). Exhibit 12-6 presents the statement of comprehensive income and its relationship to the traditional income statement. It illustrates that comprehensive income encompasses all the revenues and expenses that are presented on the income statement to calculate net income and also includes items that are not presented on the income statement but affect total stockholders' equity.[1] The comprehensive income measure is truly all-inclusive because it includes transactions such as unrealized gains and prior period adjustments that affect stockholders' equity. Firms are required to disclose comprehensive income, because it provides a more complete measure of performance.

How Income Statement Events Affect the Statement of Cash Flows

LO 10 Explain the effects that income statement events have on the statement of cash flows.

In this chapter, we have reviewed several accounting issues and their impact on the income statement. In this section, we concentrate on events involving extraordinary items and changes in accounting principle to determine their cash flow impact and the proper way to disclose such items on the statement of cash flows. Exhibit 12-7 indicates how such items should be treated.

Some extraordinary items do not have a cash flow impact. For example, assume that a company's plant, with a book value of $600,000, is destroyed by a fire. If the company

---

[1]The format of Exhibit 12-6 is suggested by the FASB. The FASB also allows other possible formats of the statement of comprehensive income.

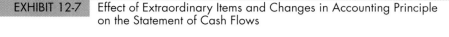

EXHIBIT 12-7   Effect of Extraordinary Items and Changes in Accounting Principle on the Statement of Cash Flows

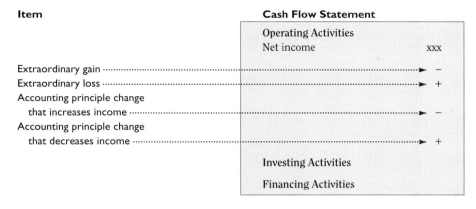

Item   **Cash Flow Statement**

Operating Activities
Net income   XXX

Extraordinary gain ··► –
Extraordinary loss ··► +
Accounting principle change
   that increases income ···► –
Accounting principle change
   that decreases income ···► +

Investing Activities

Financing Activities

did not have fire insurance, the result would be an extraordinary loss of $600,000 on the income statement (assuming no tax effect). Because no cash was received, the event has no cash flow impact. If the indirect method is used for the statement of cash flows, the loss should be disclosed by *adding back* the amount to the net income in the Operating Activities category of the statement. Adding back the item *does not* mean that it was a source of cash. Because the loss was deducted in calculating net income, however, it must be added back to indicate that it did not involve cash, in the same way that depreciation and other noncash items are added back in the Operating Activities category.

Extraordinary gains must also be disclosed on the statement of cash flows. A gain increases net income, so the item must be *deducted* on the statement of cash flows to remove the effect from the Operating Activities category of the statement.

When a company makes a change in accounting principle, the cumulative effect of the change should appear on the income statement in the year of the change. The company does not pay cash or receive cash, however, as a result of making a change in its accounting methods. It is a bookkeeping change that affects net income but does not involve cash. Changes in accounting principle should be reflected on the statement of cash flows in a manner similar to that described for extraordinary items. If a change in principle resulted in a cumulative effect that was deducted on the income statement, the change should be *added back* on the statement of cash flows. The item should appear in the Operating Activities category to show that changes in accounting principle are not a part of normal operating activities.

If a change in principle resulted in a cumulative effect that was added on the income statement, the change should be *deducted* on the statement of cash flows. Again, the item should be deducted from the Operating Activities category to indicate that changes in principle do not result in cash and are not part of normal operating activities.

The 1995 statement of cash flows of Sprint is given in Exhibit 12-8. Earlier we noted that Sprint reported an extraordinary loss of $565.3 million on its 1995 income statement because it changed its accounting methods as it began to operate in a deregulated environment. The loss, however, is not a cash item and so must be eliminated from income in determining the company's cash flow. The 1995 cash flows statement indicates that $565.3 million was *added* in the Operating Activities section of the cash flows statement to remove the effect of the extraordinary loss.

You should also note the 1993 column of Sprint's statement of cash flows. In that year Sprint had a large deduction ($382.6 million) in income as a result of a change in accounting principle. Since this was also a noncash item, it was *added* on the cash flows statement in the Operating Activities category.

EXHIBIT 12-8   Sprint's 1995 Statement of Cash Flows

CONSOLIDATED STATEMENTS OF CASH FLOWS

(in millions) *For the years ended December 31,*	1995	1994	1993
Operating Activities			
Net income	$ 395.3	$ 890.7	$ 54.9
Adjustments to reconcile net income to net cash provided			
by operating activities:			
(Income) Loss from cellular division	(14.5)	15.5	38.1
Extraordinary items	565.3	—	20.4
Cumulative effect of changes in accounting principles	—	—	382.6
Depreciation and amortization	1,466.4	1,386.0	1,283.7
Deferred income taxes and investment tax credits	5.8	53.2	(39.1)
Changes in operating assets and liabilities			
Accounts receivable, net	(135.8)	(226.5)	(166.4)
Inventories and other current assets	(38.6)	(56.1)	(9.9)
Accounts payable and other current liabilities	178.5	120.2	315.3
Noncurrent assets and liabilities, net	124.0	128.5	33.3
Other, net	20.0	34.5	94.9
Net cash provided by continuing operations	2,566.4	2,346.0	2,007.8
Net cash provided by cellular division	162.5	172.9	197.7
Net cash provided by operating activities	2,728.9	2,518.9	2,205.5
Investing Activities			
Capital expenditures	(1,857.3)	(1,751.6)	(1,429.8)
Proceeds from sale of investment in equity securities	—	117.7	—
Investments in affiliates	(948.7)	(74.1)	(31.2)
Other, net	(10.4)	(44.4)	(9.3)
Net cash used by continuing operations	(2,816.4)	(1,752.4)	(1,470.3)
Net cash used by cellular division	(324.6)	(272.4)	(169.9)
Net cash used by investing activities	(3,141.0)	(2,024.8)	(1,640.2)
Financing Activities			
Proceeds from long-term debt	260.7	107.9	840.4
Retirements of long-term debt	(630.0)	(597.0)	(1,589.0)
Net increase in notes payable and commercial paper	1,109.5	321.5	393.5
Proceeds from common stock issued	16.9	42.7	70.8
Proceeds from employee stock purchase installments	38.8	33.1	28.3
Dividends paid	(351.5)	(349.4)	(347.1)
Other, net	(21.8)	(15.7)	(11.5)
Net cash provided (used) by financing activities	422.6	(456.9)	(614.6)
Increase (Decrease) in Cash and Equivalents	10.5	37.2	(49.3)
Cash and Equivalents at Beginning of Year	113.7	76.5	125.8
Cash and Equivalents at End of Year	$ 124.2	$ 113.7	$ 76.5
Supplemental Cash Flows Information			
Cash paid for interest—continuing operations	$ 263.5	$ 320.8	$ 368.2
Cash paid for interest—cellular division	$ 124.0	$ 97.3	$ 85.4
Cash paid for income taxes	$ 532.8	$ 435.1	$ 292.4
Noncash Activities			
Common stock contributed to employee savings plans, at market	$ —	$ 31.0	$ 39.0

See accompanying Notes to Consolidated Financial Statements.

Review Problem

The accountant for Jalen Company wants to develop an income statement for 1998. The following preliminary amounts have been calculated at year-end:

Gross profit	$500,000
Selling and administrative expense	100,000
Interest expense	20,000
Other income and expense	–0–
Income tax rate	40%

These amounts were calculated before several items and transactions were considered. The following items must be considered before Jalen can prepare an income statement:

a. Jalen determined that it was holding some obsolete inventory. The goods in inventory had been purchased in 1997 for $8,000 and were now considered to be worthless.

b. On December 31, 1998, Jalen decided to drastically change the nature of its business. The board of directors voted to sell a major division of the company in 1999. It was estimated that the loss on the division would amount to $10,000 when sold in 1999. (*Hint:* This item should be reported on the 1998 income statement.)

c. During 1998 a fire caused $40,000 of damage to one of Jalen's plants. Jalen had a long history of safe operating conditions and had never experienced a fire loss to its property before 1998. The fire loss is uninsured.

d. On January 1, 1998, Jalen changed its method of recording inventory from the first-in, first-out method to a weighted average method. Jalen has calculated that if the new inventory method had been used in past periods, income would have been higher by $20,000 before considering the tax effect of the change.

e. During 1998 Jalen discovered that the company had neglected to report an expense of $9,000 in 1996. It must make the proper corrections on the 1998 financial statements.

f. During 1998 Jalen's board of directors voted to appropriate $20,000 of retained earnings for possible inventory losses. The amount of the inventory loss for the year was $8,000, as indicated in item a.

g. Jalen must present the necessary earnings per share figures to accompany the income statement. Its capital structure consists of one class of stock. On January 1, 1998, 5,000 shares of stock were outstanding; an additional 2,000 shares were issued on July 1, 1998; no other stock transactions occurred during the year.

Required

1. Indicate the income statement category where each of the items a through f should be presented and the dollar amount for that category. Develop a revised 1998 income statement for Jalen Company beginning with gross profit, as given.

2. At the bottom of the income statement, present the necessary earnings per share figures for Jalen's income statement.

3. Which line of the income statement would be the most useful for predicting Jalen's future income?

Solution to Review Problem

1. The items should be treated as follows:

a. A loss on obsolete inventory is *not* considered to be an extraordinary item. The loss of $8,000 should be presented in the "other expense" category of the income statement. Because the item in this case is a loss, it should be deducted in arriving at Jalen's income.

b. A company's sale of a major division should be presented as a discontinued operation. The amount of $10,000 is before the tax effect. The amount net of the tax effect is $6,000, or $10,000 × 60% (100% − 40%). Note that this estimated loss is presented on the 1998 income statement even though the division will not be sold until 1999.

c. The fire loss appears to meet the criteria to be classified as an extraordinary item. The loss of $40,000 does not consider the tax benefit of the loss. The amount net of the tax effect is $24,000, or $40,000 × 60% (100% − 40%).

d. The change in inventory methods represents a change in accounting principle and should be presented in a separate category of the income statement. The cumulative effect of the change was an increase in income of $20,000 before tax. The amount net of the tax effect is $12,000, or $20,000 × 60% (100% − 40%).

e. The failure to record an expense in 1996, discovered in 1998, is an error that must be corrected. The correction is *not* presented on the income statement. Rather, the error correction is presented on the retained earnings statement, net of its tax effect, as an adjustment to the beginning balance of retained earnings.

f. An appropriation of retained earnings is *not* presented on the income statement. It represents a reduction of the Retained Earnings account and the creation of a separate Appropriated Retained Earnings account. Note that the income statement impact is the amount of the actual loss that occurred, as reflected in item a. The appropriation of retained earnings does not have an impact on the income statement.

The revised income statement appears as follows:

JALEN COMPANY
PARTIAL INCOME STATEMENT
FOR THE YEAR ENDED DECEMBER 31, 1998

Gross profit		$500,000
Selling and administrative expenses		(100,000)
Income from operations		$400,000
Other income and expense:		
Interest expense	($20,000)	
Loss on obsolete inventory	(8,000)	(28,000)
Income from continuing operations before tax		$372,000
Income tax expense		(148,800)
Income from continuing operations		$223,200
Discontinued operations—expected loss on disposal of division,		
$10,000, less tax effect of $4,000		(6,000)
Income before extraordinary item		$217,200
Extraordinary loss—loss from fire,		
$40,000, less tax effect of $16,000		(24,000)
Income before cumulative effect		$193,200
Cumulative effect of change in inventory method,		
$20,000, less tax effect of $8,000		12,000
Net income		$205,200

2. For purposes of calculating earnings per share, the weighted average number of shares is computed as 6,000 shares:

$$5,000 + 2,000\ (6/12) = 6,000 \text{ shares}$$

Earnings per share should be presented as follows:

Income from continuing operations	$223,200/6,000 = $37.20
Discontinued operations—expected loss on disposal of division	(6,000)/6,000 = (1.00)
Income before extraordinary item	217,200/6,000 = $36.20

Extraordinary loss—loss from fire	(24,000)/6,000 = (4.00)
Income before cumulative effect	193,200/6,000 = $32.20
Cumulative effect of change in inventory method	12,000/6,000 = 2.00
Net income	$205,200/6,000 = $34.20

3. The income statement line labeled "Income from continuing operations" is the best indication of Jalen's future income potential.

Chapter Highlights

1. **LO 1** Most corporations present the revenues and expenses of the period on the income statement in a multi-step, rather than single-step, format to provide more relevant information to users of the statement.

2. **LO 1** Operating income is a measure of the amount of income derived from the firm's primary or central activities. It does not include other income and expenses such as interest.

3. **LO 2** A discontinued operations category indicates that a company has taken action to sell a major segment of the company. The amount of the gain or loss on disposal should be presented separately on the income statement, net of the income tax effect of the transaction.

4. **LO 3** An item should be considered extraordinary if it is both unusual and infrequent. Management must consider the criteria with regard to the company's environment. If an item is considered extraordinary, the amount of the gain or loss should be presented separately on the income statement, net of the income tax effect of the transaction.

5. **LO 3** Gains or losses on the redemption of bonds payable should always be considered extraordinary and are not required to be judged as unusual and infrequent.

6. **LO 4** A change in accounting principle occurs when a company changes its method of accounting for an item from one year to the next. The cumulative effect of the change in accounting principle should be presented on the income statement in the year of the change, net of the income tax effect of the transaction.

7. **LO 4** The cumulative effect of a change in accounting principle is the total difference, for all years prior to the current year, between income calculated using the previous accounting method and the income figured under the adopted method.

8. **LO 5** Earnings per share is a measure of the right of the common stockholder to the income of the company.

It is generally calculated by subtracting preferred stock dividends from the net income and dividing by the weighted average number of shares of common stock outstanding.

9. **LO 6** Corrections of errors of prior periods are not presented on the income statement. They are presented as an adjustment to the beginning balance of the Retained Earnings account.

10. **LO 7** An appropriation of retained earnings occurs when a company designates a portion of the balance of retained earnings and creates a separate Appropriated Retained Earnings account within the stockholders' equity category of the balance sheet.

11. **LO 7** Several items that are reported as part of stockholders' equity do not affect net income. These items include the adjustments for changes in the market value of available-for-sale securities and for foreign currency translation.

12. **LO 8** A statement of stockholders' equity explains the changes in the balances of all stockholders' equity accounts. It is similar to a statement of retained earnings except that it explains the changes in all stockholders' equity accounts.

13. **LO 9** Comprehensive income is the net assets increase resulting from all transactions during a time period except for investments by owners and distributions to owners. It is the broadest measure of income available and provides a more complete measure of a company's performance.

14. **LO 10** When the indirect method is used to prepare the statement of cash flows, adjustments are necessary in the Operating Activities section for extraordinary items and cumulative effects. Those items that were deductions on the income statement must be added back, and those that were additions on the income statement must be deducted.

Key Terms Quiz

Read each definition below and then write the number of that definition in the blank beside the appropriate term it defines. The solution appears at the end of the chapter.

____ Multi-step income statement
____ Gross profit percentage
____ Income before income taxes
____ Extraordinary item
____ Cumulative effect
____ Weighted average of shares
____ Appropriation of retained earnings
____ Statement of stockholders' equity
____ Comprehensive income

____ Gross profit
____ Operating income
____ Discontinued operations
____ Change in accounting principle
____ Earnings per share
____ Prior period adjustment
____ Unrealized Gain/Loss—Available-for-Sale Securities

1. A ratio calculated as the gross profit divided by the net sales.
2. An income statement subtotal calculated as operating income plus other income items, such as interest, minus other expense items.
3. The amount of net sales minus the amount of cost of sales.
4. An income statement category indicating that a major segment or division of the company has been or will be sold.
5. An income statement subtotal calculated as gross profit minus operating expenses.
6. An income statement item that occurs when a company changes from one accounting method to another.
7. A correction that is not reported on the income statement but is presented as an adjustment to the balance of the Retained Earnings account.
8. An item that is considered both unusual and infrequent and is presented in a separate category of the income statement.
9. An income statement that presents revenues and expenses by category.

10. A statement that indicates the differences between beginning and ending balances for all accounts in the stockholders' equity category.
11. The total effect of a change in accounting principle for all years prior to the current year.
12. A stockholders' equity account that reflects that the investment in certain securities was adjusted to market value.
13. The number of shares of stock weighted by the time period that the stock was outstanding.
14. The amount that reflects the total change in net assets from all sources except investments or withdrawals by the owners of the company.
15. An account that indicates that a company has designated a portion of the balance of Retained Earnings for a specific purpose.
16. A number that represents the rights of the common stockholders to the income of the company; calculated as net income minus preferred dividends divided by the number of shares of common stock outstanding.

Alternate Terms

Change in principle Change in accounting method.
Discontinued operations Disposal of a segment.
Earnings per share Net income per share.
Extraordinary items Unusual and infrequent items.
Gross Profit Gross margin.
Income Tax Expense Provision for income tax.

Operating income Income from operations.
Operating expenses Selling, general, and administrative expenses.
Prior period adjustment Correction of error.
Stockholders' equity Shareholders' equity.

Questions

1. Why do most firms consider a multi-step income statement to be better than a single-step statement?
2. How is gross profit calculated? What does the gross profit amount tell financial statement users about a company?
3. How is the gross profit percentage calculated? How would you determine whether a company's gross profit percentage was at an acceptable level?

4. Where does the term *net income* appear on the income statement? Is net income calculated before or after income tax is deducted on the income statement?

5. If you see an income statement that has a discontinued operations category, what does it indicate about the company's operations? Is the discontinued operations amount calculated before or after the tax effect of the transaction?

6. If a company has a gain on a transaction, will the tax effect increase or reduce the gain? If a company has a loss on a transaction, will the income tax effect increase or reduce the loss?

7. What are the two criteria that must be met for an item to be considered an extraordinary item?

8. How are extraordinary items presented on the income statement? How should the tax effect of the transaction be presented?

9. How are gains and losses on the redemption of bonds payable presented on the income statement?

10. When a company changes from one accounting method to another, how should the effect of the change be presented on the income statement? Give an example of a change in accounting principle.

11. What does the *cumulative effect* of a change in accounting principle mean? How is the amount calculated?

12. When calculating earnings per share, why should you deduct preferred stock dividends? Does the amount of earnings per share indicate the amount of dividend that will be paid?

13. How is the weighted average number of shares of stock figured when calculating earnings per share?

14. When a company discovers that an error has occurred, how should it present the correction on the financial statements? Give an example of a prior period adjustment.

15. What is an appropriation of retained earnings, and why would it be used?

16. What is an example of an item that is not recorded on the income statement but is recorded directly in the stockholders' equity category? What are possible reasons that such items are not reported on the income statement?

17. What is the difference between a statement of stockholders' equity and a retained earnings statement?

18. What is meant by the term *comprehensive income?* How does comprehensive income differ from the net income figure presented on the traditional income statement?

Exercises

LO 1 **Exercise 12-1** Multi-Step Income Statement

FCL Company has compiled the following single-step income statement for 1998:

Revenues:		
Sales revenue	$130,000	
Interest revenue	19,500	
Total revenue		$149,500
Expenses:		
Cost of goods sold	$ 78,000	
Selling and administrative expense	26,000	
Interest expense	13,000	
Income taxes	19,500	
Total expenses		$136,500
Net income		$ 13,000

Required

1. Develop a multi-step income statement for FCL Company for 1998.

2. Calculate the gross profit percentage. Explain what this ratio means for FCL Company.

LO 2 **Exercise 12-2** Discontinued Operations

Nagle Inc. has several operating divisions. On August 1, 1998, it sold the snack foods division. During 1998, before the sale, the snack food division reported revenues of $20,000 and expenses (other than income tax) of $8,000. The division was sold at a gain of $80,000. Nagle's tax rate is 35%.

Required

1. In what part(s) of the income statement should Nagle report the income from operating the division and the gain on the sale?

2. Prepare the income statement section that reports the sale of the snack foods division.

LO 3 **Exercise 12-3** Extraordinary Items

Easley Company has developed the following preliminary income statement for the year 1998:

Revenues	$100,000
Cost of goods sold	60,000
Gross profit	$ 40,000
Selling and administrative expenses	20,000
Income before tax	$ 20,000
Income tax	8,000
Net income	$ 12,000

The preliminary income statement does not include the impact of one additional event. During 1998 a fire destroyed a building that had a book value of $30,000; the loss was not covered by insurance. Assume that the tax rate applicable to the loss was the same as the rate on other transactions for Easley.

Required

1. Develop a revised 1998 income statement for Easley Company to reflect the fire loss. You do not need to include the earnings per share calculations.

2. How would Easley's income statement differ if the fire was not treated as an extraordinary item?

LO 3 **Exercise 12-4** Extraordinary Items

Assume that Easley Company has developed the same preliminary income statement as in Exercise 12-3. One additional event (rather than the fire loss in Exercise 12-3) has not been reflected on the 1998 income statement. During 1998 Easley retired bonds payable at a gain of $30,000. Assume that the gain is taxed at the same rate as the gain on other transactions.

Required

1. Develop a revised income statement for 1998 for Easley Company to reflect the bond retirement. You do not need to include the earnings per share calculations.

2. Compare the tax effect on the extraordinary items in Exercises 12-3 and 12-4. Why is the tax effect positive in one case and negative in the other?

LO 3 **Exercise 12-5** Extraordinary Items

Consider the following items independently:

a. Loss on inventory as a result of obsolescence.

b. Write-off of receivables because a customer was unsatisfied with the product purchased.

c. Client notification of bankruptcy and the inability to pay its accounts receivable. The client is a major customer that has constituted at least 50% of the firm's sales each year for several years.

d. A gain or loss on the sale of equipment.

e. An equipment loss recorded as the result of a flood.

f. A California company's loss due to structural damage resulting from an earthquake.

g. A loss on the redemption of bonds payable, which were retired before the due date because of changing interest rate conditions.

h. A gain on the redemption of bonds payable, which were retired before the due date because of changing interest rate conditions.

i. The discovery that a piece of the company's equipment purchased three years ago has not been depreciated.

j. The decision by a company during the current year to change its method of inventory from the FIFO method to the weighted average method. Because of the composition of the inventory, the change had a very large impact on current-year income.

Required

Indicate whether each of the above items should be treated as extraordinary on the income statement. If the situation does not qualify as an extraordinary item, indicate the section or category of the statement in which it should be reported.

LO 4 **Exercise 12-6** Change in Accounting Principle

Assume that on January 1, 1995, Tarpley Company purchased a $150,000 asset. Tarpley chose to depreciate the asset over five years using an accelerated method resulting in depreciation of $50,000, $40,000, and $30,000 in 1995, 1996, and 1997 respectively. For depreciation purposes, Tarpley assumed a zero salvage value. On January 1, 1998, Tarpley changed to the straight-line method of depreciation. The company continued to assume a zero salvage value and did not revise its estimate of the life of the asset.

Required

1. Calculate the amount that should be reflected on Tarpley's 1998 income statement as the cumulative effect of the change in accounting principle. Assume that a 40% tax rate applies to the transaction.

2. Calculate the amount that should be reported as depreciation expense by Tarpley on the 1998 income statement. Compare the 1997 depreciation to that recorded in 1998.

LO 5 **Exercise 12-7** Earnings Per Share

Einset Company calculated its net income for the year ended December 31, 1998, as $50,000. The stockholders' equity category of Einset's December 31, 1998, balance sheet contains the following:

Preferred stock, $10 par, 8%, cumulative,	
5,000 shares issued and outstanding	$50,000
Common stock, $1 par,	
10,000 shares issued and outstanding	10,000

Two stock transactions occurred during 1998. On April 1, 3,000 shares of common stock were issued for cash. On October 1, an additional 1,500 shares were issued for cash.

Required

Calculate the earnings per share amount that should be disclosed on Einset's 1998 income statement.

LO 6 **Exercise 12-8** Error Correction

Benson Company has begun to prepare its 1998 financial statements. The following two situations involve errors that occurred in reporting Benson Company transactions in years prior to 1998:

a. In 1997 Benson Company understated ending inventory by $40,000; the error was discovered during 1998. The ending inventory for 1998 was calculated and recorded correctly.

b. In 1995 Benson purchased a new delivery truck for $8,000 and reported the purchase correctly. During 1998, however, Benson discovered that the company had failed to depreciate the delivery truck in all past periods. Assume that the asset has a five-year life and no salvage value and that the company wants to record depreciation using the straight-line method.

Required

1. For each situation, record a transaction in journal form to correct the error. You may assume that tax does not apply to these transactions.

2. Describe how the two items should be presented on Benson's financial statements.

LO 7 **Exercise 12-9** Appropriations of Retained Earnings

On January 1, 1998, McAdams Company had a positive balance in the Retained Earnings account of $400,000. The following transactions occurred in 1998:

a. On March 1, McAdams's board of directors voted to appropriate $100,000 of retained earnings for possible future fire losses.

b. On June 1, a fire completely destroyed one of McAdams's buildings. The building originally cost $100,000; the accumulated depreciation on June 1 was $60,000. There was no insurance to cover the loss.

c. On December 15, 1998, McAdams's board of directors voted to eliminate the appropriation of retained earnings and to return the amount to the Retained Earnings account.

d. On December 31, 1998, McAdams's recorded closing entries and calculated the net income for the year as $80,000.

Required

1. Determine the total amount of retained earnings after each transaction.

2. Determine the amount that is available for dividend purposes after each transaction.

LO 8 **Exercise 12-10** Reporting Changes in Stockholders' Equity Items

On May 1, 1997, Ryde Inc. had common stock of $345,000, additional paid-in capital of $1,298,000 and retained earnings of $3,013,000. Ryde did not purchase or sell any common stock during the year. The company reported net income of $556,000 and declared dividends in the amount of $78,000 during the year ended April 30, 1998.

Required

Prepare a financial statement which explains all of the reasons for the differences between the beginning and ending balances for the accounts in the stockholders' equity category of the balance sheet.

LO 9 **Exercise 12-11** Comprehensive Income

Assume that you are the accountant for Ellis Corporation, which has issued its 1998 annual report. You have received an inquiry from a stockholder who has questions about several items in the annual report, including why Ellis has not shown certain transactions on the income statement. In particular, Ellis's 1998 balance sheet revealed two accounts in stockholders' equity (Unrealized Gain/Loss—Available-for-Sale Securities and Loss on Foreign Currency Translation Adjustments) for which the dollar amounts involved had not been reported on the income statement.

Required

Draft a written response to the stockholder's inquiry that explains the nature of the two accounts and the reason that the amounts involved were not recorded on the 1998 income statement. Do you think the concept of comprehensive income would be useful to explain the impact of all events for Ellis Corporation?

LO 10 **Exercise 12-12** Impact of Discontinued Operations and Extraordinary and Other Items on Statement of Cash Flows

From the following list, identify each item as operating (O), investing (I), financing (F) or not separately reported on the statement of cash flows (N). Briefly explain your classifications. Also, indicate whether the item should be added or subtracted on the statement of cash flows.

_____ Cumulative effect of a change in principle (decrease in net income)

_____ Cumulative effect of a change in principle (increase in net income)

_____ Extraordinary loss

_____ Extraordinary gain

_____ Foreign currency translation adjustment

LO 10 **Exercise 12-13** Impact of Discontinued Operations and Extraordinary and Other Items on Statement of Cash Flows

Mystical Enterprises uses the indirect method to determine its cash flow from operating activities. Mystical reported net income of $1,445,600 during the year ended June 30, 1998. During the year, Mystical recognized an extraordinary loss resulting from uninsured damage from a hurricane in the amount of $150,000. In addition, Mystical changed one of its accounting principles during the year. The cumulative effect of the change in principles caused 1998 net income to increase by $35,000. A foreign currency translation adjustment in the amount of $13,000 was charged directly to stockholders' equity during the year.

Required

What is Mystical's net cash flow from operating activities for the year ended June 30, 1998? (Assume that no other adjustments are necessary.)

Multi-Concept Exercises

`LO 1, 2` **Exercise 12-14** Discontinued Operations

King Company has developed the following preliminary income statement for the year 1998:

Revenues	$100,000
Cost of goods sold	60,000
Gross profit	$ 40,000
Selling and administrative expenses	20,000
Income before tax	$ 20,000
Income tax	8,000
Net income	$ 12,000

King Company is composed of two major divisions, A and B. On December 31, 1998, King agreed to sell or eliminate Division A. Assume that all of Division A's assets will be sold at book value, resulting in zero gain or loss. The preliminary income statement must be altered, however, to reflect the discontinued operations of Division A. All of the division's revenues and expenses must appear on a separate line, "income or loss from discontinued operations." Assume that when the income statement is altered, the income from continuing operations line is $8,400. During 1998 the results of Division A were as follows:

Revenue	$30,000
Expenses (except tax)	24,000
Tax	40%

Required

Develop a revised income statement for King Company for 1998, beginning with income from continuing operations. You do not need to include the earnings per share calculations on the income statement.

`LO 1, 5` **Exercise 12-15** Multi-Step Income Statement and Earnings Per Share

Ellis Company's account balances at December 31, 1998 are as follows:

Salaries and wages expense	$ 31,000
Interest expense	12,000
Rent expense	12,000
Cost of goods sold	82,000
Income taxes	7,000
Insurance expense	3,600
Sales revenue	150,000
Dividends	5,000
Interest revenue	9,000
Gain on sale of equipment	4,500
Miscellaneous expense	2,800

Required

1. Prepare a multi-step income statement for Ellis Company.
2. Calculate the gross profit percentage. Is the company's gross profit percentage a favorable indication of the company's profitability? What other information would you need to make this decision?

3. Calculate earnings per share. The company had 5,000 shares of common stock outstanding at all times during the year. What percent of earnings per share were given out as dividends?

LO 2, 3, 4, 6   **Exercise 12-16**   Infrequent Events

Consider each of the following independent items:

a. Loss on redemption of bonds, retired early due to a change in interest rates.

b. Loss of orange crop in Florida due to late freeze.

c. Sale of manufacturing plant in one location to consolidate operations in home state.

d. Gain on sale of building.

e. Accrued expected costs for postretirement benefits following a new FASB ruling.

f. Discovered that merchandise on consignment from another business had been included in last year's inventory.

g. Changed the estimate of the expected remaining life of a depreciable asset.

h. Loss from sale of all office supply stores to concentrate efforts on hardware store line.

i. Discovered that the entry to record the current year's depreciation for a machine had not been made.

j. Change in depreciation method from double declining-balance to straight-line method.

Required

For each item, indicate whether it is a discontinued operation, an extraordinary item, a change in accounting principle, or a prior period adjustment. If it doesn't qualify as any of these, indicate how it should be classified.

Problems

LO 2   **Problem 12-1**   Sale of Segments

Los Cruces Company, a New Mexico dairy producer, owns more than 3,000 head of cattle as well as land, buildings, and equipment. Included in the assets are a fleet of trucks and a chain of convenience stores. During 1998 Los Cruces sold 500 head of cattle and purchased 700 more. The company sold all of its trucks at a $10,000 gain and entered into a long-term agreement with a trucking firm to transport milk. The convenience stores reported losses for the past three years, so Los Cruces decided on December 31, 1998, to sell them. The amount of loss from convenience store operations during 1998 was $40,000, and the company estimated that future losses related to the segment would be $30,000. The company sold an investment in stock, resulting in a $1,200 loss. Los Cruces's tax rate is 28%.

Required

1 Explain which, if any, of these transactions should be reported as a separate item on the income statement after income from continuing operations.

2. Assume that the income from continuing operations in 1998 has been calculated correctly as $624,500. Present the items that would appear on the income statement after the income from continuing operations line. You may ignore earnings per share calculations.

LO 4   **Problem 12-2**   Change in Accounting Principle

Temmrick Company purchased equipment on January 1, 1995, for $600,000. It was estimated, at that time, to have a 10-year life with zero salvage value. The company depreciated the equipment using the double declining-balance method. On January 1, 1998, it decided to switch to the straight-line method of depreciation. Temmrick's tax rate is 40%.

Required

1. How should Temmrick treat this change in depreciation method in 1998? Prepare the appropriate 1998 financial statement section to report the depreciation expense for 1998 and the change (if necessary).

2. Assume that instead of changing depreciation methods on January 1, 1998, the company discovered that no depreciation was recorded for this asset for 1997. By what amount will the 1998 retained earnings statement be affected by the omission?

`LO 5` **Problem 12-3** Earnings Per Share

Mirasol Company had 10,000 shares of common stock outstanding on January 1, 1998. During 1998 the following common stock transactions occurred:

On March 1, issued 2,000 shares of stock for cash.

On April 1, purchased 1,000 shares as treasury stock.

On July 1, reissued 1,000 shares of stock held as treasury stock.

On October 1, issued 3,000 shares of stock for cash.

Mirasol also had 200 shares of $100 par, 9% cumulative preferred stock outstanding as of January 1, 1998. No preferred stock transactions occurred during 1998.

Required

1. Assume that the net income of Mirasol Company for 1998 was $100,000. Compute the earnings per share amount that should accompany the 1998 income statement.

2. Does the amount calculated as earnings per share indicate the dividend the stockholders can expect to receive? Explain.

`LO 7` **Problem 12-4** Appropriations of Retained Earnings

Gridley Company's stockholders' equity section includes the following items on December 31, 1998:

Common stock, $1 par, 100,000 shares issued	$ 100,000
Additional paid-in capital	500,000
Retained earnings, unappropriated	462,300
Retained earnings, appropriated for expansion	200,000
Treasury stock, at cost, 5,000 shares	(75,000)
Total stockholders' equity	$1,187,300

At the annual meeting, the chief financial officer is asked to explain the nature of the items in the stockholders' equity section. A group of stockholders is pushing for a $4 per share dividend.

Required

1. Write a brief summary to be used by the CFO to explain the meaning of each of the items in the stockholders' equity section. The CFO will be speaking to a group of shareholders who are not trained in accounting.

2. Answer the following questions from stockholders:

"Why is treasury stock subtracted from the total? Doesn't the company actually own the stock?"

"In which bank is the $200,000 for the expansion, and is it earning interest?"

"Why can't we have the $4 per share dividend? Why should we leave the money in retained earnings when we could put it in the bank to earn interest?"

`LO 8` **Problem 12-5** Statement of Stockholders' Equity

Peeler Company was incorporated as a new business on January 1, 1998. The corporate charter approved on that date authorized the issuance of 1,000 shares of $100 par, 7% cumulative, nonparticipating preferred stock and 10,000 shares of $5 par common stock. On January 10, Peeler issued for cash 500 shares of preferred at $120 per share and 4,000 shares of common at $80 per share. On January 20, Peeler issued 1,000 shares of common stock to acquire a building site at a time when the stock was selling for $70 per share.

During 1998 Peeler established an employee benefit plan and acquired 500 shares of common stock at $60 per share as treasury stock for that purpose. One hundred shares of the stock were later resold during 1998 at $65 per share.

On December 31, 1998, Peeler determined that its net income for the year was $40,000. The firm declared the annual cash dividend to preferred stockholders and a cash dividend of $5 per share to the common stockholders. The dividend will be paid in 1999.

Required

Develop a statement of stockholders' equity for Peeler Company for 1998. The statement should start with the beginning balance of each stockholders' equity account and explain the changes that occurred in each account to arrive at the 1998 ending balances.

LO 9 **Problem 12-6** American Brands' Comprehensive Income

The consolidated statement of common stockholders' equity of American Brands, Inc. and subsidiaries for the year ended December 31, 1995 appears below:

CONSOLIDATED STATEMENT OF COMMON STOCKHOLDERS' EQUITY
AMERICAN BRANDS, INC. AND SUBSIDIARIES

(IN MILLIONS)	COMMON STOCK	PAID-IN CAPITAL	FOREIGN CURRENCY ADJUSTMENTS	RETAINED EARNINGS	TREASURY STOCK, AT COST
Balance at January 31, 1994	$717.4	$174.6	$(249.0)	$4,724.4	$ (745.6)
Net income	–	–	–	540.4	–
Cash dividends	–	–	–	(377.5)	–
Translation adjustments	–	–	14.4	–	–
Purchases	–	–	–	–	(981.1)
Conversion of securities and delivery of stock plan shares	–	(3.0)	–	–	48.1
Balance at December 31, 1995	$717.4	$171.6	$(234.6)	$4,887.3	$(1,678.6)

Required

1. Determine the company's comprehensive income for the year ended December 31, 1995.

2. Do you think that the concept of comprehensive income would be useful to explain the impact of all of the events that took place during 1995 to the stockholders of American Brands?

Multi-Concept Problems

LO 1, 5 **Problem 12-7** Multi-Step Income Statement and Earnings Per Share

The Robinson Group, LTD's December 31, 1998 trial balance included the following accounts:

Cost of goods sold	$ 80,000
Dividend revenue	4,000
Extraordinary loss	5,000
Gain on discontinued operations	6,000
Interest expense	18,000
Interest income	20,000
Loss on sale of machine	4,000
Sales	150,000
Selling and administrative expenses	45,000

The company has 25,000 shares of common stock outstanding.

Required

1. Prepare a multi-step income statement for 1998. Assume that a 35% tax rate applies to all transactions. Include the appropriate earnings per share calculations to accompany the 1998 income statement.

2. Does the earnings per share amount indicate stockholders will receive a dividend of that amount?

LO 3, 4 **Problem 12-8** Extraordinary Items and Changes in Accounting Principle

Grinde Company has developed the following preliminary income statement for the year 1998:

Revenues	$200,000
Cost of goods sold	120,000
Gross profit	$ 80,000
Selling and administrative expenses	40,000
Income before tax	$ 40,000
Income tax	16,000
Net income	$ 24,000

The preliminary income statement does not reflect two additional transactions that occurred in 1998. First, Grinde experienced a tornado loss of $50,000 during the year. You may assume that tornado losses are rare where Grinde is located. Second, on January 1, 1998, Grinde changed the depreciation method used for its only depreciable asset, which was originally purchased on January 1, 1996, for $150,000. Grinde depreciated the asset using an estimated life of five years and an accelerated method of depreciation resulting in depreciation of $50,000 and $40,000 for 1996 and 1997. Beginning in 1988, Grinde changed to the straight-line method and depreciated the asset over a five-year life. The 1998 depreciation is reflected in the Selling and Administrative Expenses account.

Required

Prepare a revised 1998 income statement for Grinde Company to reflect the two additional transactions. Also present the earnings per share amounts to accompany the income statement. Grinde had 1,000 shares of common stock outstanding at all times during 1998. Assume a 40% tax rate applies to additional transactions.

LO 1, 6, 10 **Problem 12-9** Errors and Retained Earnings Presentation

The preliminary income statement of Weaver Company for 1998 is as follows:

Revenues	$200,000
Cost of goods sold	120,000
Gross profit	$ 80,000
Selling and administrative expenses	40,000
Income before tax	$ 40,000
Income tax	16,000
Net income	$ 24,000

The preliminary income statement does not reflect one additional event. On January 1, 1996, Weaver appropriately reported goodwill of $15,000 as a result of the purchase of another company. Weaver has discovered, however, that the goodwill was not amortized in 1996 or any subsequent period.

Required

1. Record any entry or entries to correct for the failure to amortize goodwill. Weaver wants to amortize the goodwill over a five-year period using the straight-line method. You may assume that there is no tax impact of the correction.

2. Prepare a revised income statement for Weaver for 1998. You may omit the required earnings per share calculations.

3. Prepare a statement of retained earnings for Weaver for 1998. The balance of the Retained Earnings account on January 1, 1998, was $50,000. During 1998 Weaver declared dividends of $20,000 to stockholders.

4. Explain how the amortization of goodwill should appear on the cash flows statement.

LO 1, 3, 4 **Problem 12-10** Unusual Events and Errors

Schaefer Company's preliminary income statement for 1998 is as follows:

Sales	$300,000
Cost of goods sold	185,000
Gross margin	115,000
Selling and administrative expenses	70,000
Income before taxes	45,000
Income taxes (at 40%)	18,000
Net income	$ 27,000

The preliminary statement does not include the following transactions:

a. On January 1, Schaefer sold its restaurant operations at a pretax gain of $15,000.

b. In June, the company experienced severe flood damage. It did not have flood insurance because floods are extremely rare in the area. The loss was $20,000.

c. In 1997, the company purchased equipment for $60,000. At that time it was estimated to last five years and have zero salvage value. Schaefer used the double declining-balance method in 1997, resulting in $24,000 of depreciation being taken. In 1998, it decided to change to the straight-line method to calculate depreciation expense (included in selling and administrative expenses).

Schaefer's retained earnings as of January 1, 1998, were $40,000. Schaefer had 10,000 shares of common stock outstanding all year. The company paid dividends of $.50 per share in 1998.

Required

1. Prepare a revised income statement for 1998 reflecting the additional information.

2. If you were asked to predict the company's income for 1999, which 1998 income statement number would you use?

3. Prepare a statement of retained earnings for 1998.

Alternate Problems

LO 2 **Problem 12-1A** Sale of Segments

Carolina Company, a furniture manufacturer, owns more than 30,000 acres of forests, buildings, and equipment. Included in the assets are a fleet of trucks, a lumber-processing facility, and a chain of office supply stores. During 1998 Carolina sold lumber to its customers at its processing facility and purchased other specialty lumber from outside suppliers. An unusual fire destroyed several acres of timber, resulting in a $5,600 loss. Fires are infrequent in this area. A new furniture warehouse was constructed in 1998. During construction, Carolina rented warehouse space at a cost of $7,800. All the trucks were sold because the company entered into a long-term agreement with a trucking firm to transport finished pieces of furniture across the country. Three office supply stores were sold at a $12,000 loss because they were not as profitable as the average stores. The company purchased additional land in seven cities for expansion of profitable office supply stores. The company sold an investment in stock, resulting in a $3,400 loss. Carolina's tax rate is 28%.

Required

1. Explain which, if any, of these transactions should be reported as a separate item on the income statement after income from continuing operations.

2. Assume that 1998 income from continuing operations has been correctly calculated as $590,500. Prepare the sections of the income statement that follow the income from continuing operations line. You may ignore earnings per share calculations.

LO 4 **Problem 12-2A** Change in Accounting Principle

Carter Company purchased equipment on January 1, 1995, for $480,000. It was estimated, at that time, to have a 10-year life with zero salvage value. The company depreciated the equipment using the double declining-balance method. On January 1, 1998, it decided to switch to the straight-line method of depreciation. Carter's tax rate is 40%.

Required

1. How should Carter treat this change in depreciation method in 1998? Prepare the appropriate 1998 financial statement section to report the depreciation expense for 1998 and the change (if necessary).

2. Assume that instead of changing depreciation methods on January 1, 1998, the company discovered that no depreciation was recorded for this asset for 1997. By what amount will the 1998 statement of retained earnings be affected by the omission?

LO 5 **Problem 12-3A** Earnings per Share

Brigham Company had 100,000 shares of common stock outstanding on January 1, 1998. During 1998 the following common stock transactions occurred:

On March 1, issued 12,000 shares of stock for cash.

On April 1, purchased 8,000 shares as treasury stock.

On October 1, issued 16,000 shares of stock for land.

Brigham Company also had 1,000 shares of $100 par, 8% cumulative preferred stock outstanding as of January 1, 1998. No preferred stock transactions occurred during 1998.

Required

1. Assume that the net income of Brigham Company for 1998 was $116,000. Compute the earnings per share amount that should accompany the 1998 income statement.

2. Do Brigham's preferred stockholders have a right to a dividend? If so, what are those rights?

LO 7 **Problem 12-4A** Appropriations of Retained Earnings

Wyhowski Company's stockholders' equity section includes the following items on December 31, 1998:

Common stock, $1 par, 500,000 shares issued	$ 500,000
Additional paid-in capital	890,000
Retained earnings, unappropriated	1,483,900
Retained earnings, appropriated for buildings	300,000
Treasury stock, at cost, 5,000 shares	(75,000)
Total stockholders' equity	$3,098,900

At the annual board meeting, the chief financial officer asked the board to appropriate $1,000,000 for future expansion of the manufacturing facilities that have become inefficient. The CFO also plans to recommend that the board approve the issuance of $1,000,000 of bonds to finance the construction of the new facilities. One stockholder asks why the bonds are needed if the company is already using the retained earnings to build new facilities.

Required

1. Write a response to the stockholder's question about the need for bonds.

2. Answer the following questions from other stockholders:

"How is the amount of retained earnings calculated?"

"How does the company report a gain or loss when it sells its treasury stock?"

"Does the company report a gain or loss if it issues stock at an amount greater than the par value? Why? Why not?"

LO 8 **Problem 12-5A** Statement of Stockholders' Equity

Kreits Company was incorporated as a new business on January 1, 1998. The corporate charter approved on that date authorized the issuance of 2,000 shares of $100 par, 7% cumulative, nonparticipating preferred stock and 20,000 shares of $5 par common stock. On January 10, Kreits issued for cash 1,000 shares of preferred at $120 per share and 8,000 shares of common at $80 per share. On January 20, Kreits issued 2,000 shares of common stock to acquire a building site at a time when the stock was selling for $70 per share.

During 1998 Kreits established an employee benefit plan and acquired 1,000 shares of common stock at $60 per share as treasury stock for that purpose. Later in 1998 it resold 100 shares of the stock at $65 per share.

On December 31, 1998, Kreits determined that its net income for the year was $80,000. The firm declared the annual cash dividend to preferred stockholders and a cash dividend of $5 per share to the common stockholders. The dividend will be paid in 1999.

Required

Develop the statement of stockholders' equity for Kreits for the year ended December 31, 1998. The statement should start with the beginning balance of each account and explain the changes that occurred in each account to result in the ending balances.

LO 9 **Problem 12-6A** Chevron's Comprehensive Income

The consolidated statement of common stockholders' equity of Chevron Corporation for the year ended December 31, 1995 appears below:

	NUMBER OF SHARES		MILLIONS OF DOLLARS					
	COMMON STOCK ISSUED	COMMON STOCK IN TREASURY	COMMON STOCK	CAPITAL IN EXCESS OF PAR VALUE	DEFERRED COMPENSA-TION-ESOP	CURRENCY TRANSLATION ADJUSTMENT AND OTHER	RETAINED EARNINGS	TREASURY STOCK
Balance at January 1, 1995	712,487,068	(60,736,435)	$1,069	$1,858	$(900)	$175	$14,457	$(2,063)
Net income	–	–	–	–	–	–	930	–
Cash dividends— $1.925 per share	–	–	–	–	–	–	(1,255)	–
Tax benefit from dividends paid on unallocated ESOP shares	–	–	–	–	–	–	14	–
Market value adjustments on investments	–	–	–	–	–	23	–	–
Foreign currency translation adjustment	–	–	–	–	–	(28)	–	–
Pension plan minimum liability	–	–	–	–	–	4	–	–
Reduction of ESOP debt	–	–	–	–	50	–	–	–
Purchase of treasury shares	–	(83,028)	–	–	–	–	–	(4)
Reissuance of treasury shares	–	659,406	–	5	–	–	–	20
Balance at December 31, 1995	712,487,068	(60,160,057)	$1,069	$1,863	$(850)	$174	$14,146	$(2,047)

Required

1. Determine the company's comprehensive income for the year ended December 31, 1995.

2. Do you think that the concept of comprehensive income would be useful to explain the impact of all of the events that took place during 1995 to the stockholders of Chevron?

Alternate Multi-Concept Problems

LO 1, 5 **Problem 12-7A** Multi-Step Income Statement and Earnings Per Share

The Griffith Group's December 31, 1998 trial balance included the following accounts:

Cost of goods sold	$100,000
Dividend revenue	5,000
Extraordinary loss	6,250
Gain on discontinued operations	7,500
Interest expense	22,500

Interest income	$ 25,000
Loss on sale of machine	5,000
Sales	187,500
Selling and administrative expenses	56,250

The company has 25,000 shares of common stock and 800 shares of $125 par, 8% preferred stock outstanding.

Required

1. Prepare a multi-step income statement for 1998. Assume that a 35% tax rate applies to all transactions. Include the appropriate earnings per share calculations to accompany the 1998 income statement.

2. Why is the amount of the earnings per share different from the amount of the dividends that Griffith may declare?

LO 3, 4, 10 **Problem 12-8A** Extraordinary Items and Changes in Accounting Principle
Smoother Company has developed the following preliminary income statement for the year 1998.

Revenues	$340,000
Cost of goods sold	170,000
Gross profit	$170,000
Selling and administrative expenses	125,000
Income from continuing operations	$ 45,000
Income tax	13,500
Net income	$ 31,500

The preliminary income statement does not reflect two additional transactions that occurred in 1998. First, Smoother experienced a freeze loss of $12,000 during the year. You may assume that freeze losses are rare where Smoother is located. Second, on January 1, 1998, Smoother changed its method for recognizing exploration costs. Exploration costs of $150,000 had been incurred on January 1, 1996. The company used to capitalize these costs and amortize them over five years. After the change, the company will expense all costs. Exploration costs incurred in 1998 were correctly included in Selling and Administrative Expenses.

Required

1. Prepare a revised 1998 income statement for Smoother Company to reflect the freeze loss and exploration costs. Also present the earnings per share amounts to accompany the income statement. Smoother had 10,000 shares of common stock outstanding at all times during 1998. Assume that a 30% tax rate applies to the two additional transactions.

2. What is the effect of the two transactions on Smoother's 1998 cash flow? How should the items appear on the statement of cash flows?

LO 1, 6, 10 **Problem 12-9A** Errors and Retained Earnings Presentation
The preliminary income statement of Looman Company for 1998 is as follows:

Revenues	$350,000
Selling and administrative expenses	301,000
Income before tax	$ 49,000
Income tax	14,700
Net income	$ 34,300

The preliminary income statement does not reflect one additional event. On January 1, 1996, Looman failed to report depreciation of $6,900. Depreciation was reported correctly in 1997 and 1998.

Required

1. Record an entry, if needed, to correct for the failure to depreciate. You may ignore income taxes.

2. Prepare a statement of retained earnings for Looman for 1998. The balance of the Retained Earnings account on January 1, 1998, was $35,000. During 1998 Looman declared dividends to stockholders of $14,000.

3. Explain how the depreciation should be shown on the statement of cash flows.

LO 1, 3, 4, 6 **Problem 12-10A** Unusual Events and Errors

Penninger Company's preliminary income statement for 1998 is as follows:

Sales	$400,000
Cost of goods sold	227,500
Gross margin	172,500
Selling and administrative expenses	105,000
Income before taxes	67,500
Income taxes (at 40%)	27,000
Net income	$ 40,500

The preliminary statement does not include the following transactions:

a. On January 1, Penninger sold its restaurant operations at a pretax gain of $22,500.

b. In June, the company experienced severe flood damage. It did not have flood insurance because floods are extremely rare in the area. The loss was $30,000.

c. In 1997, the company purchased equipment for $90,000. At that time it was estimated to last five years and have zero salvage value. Penninger used the double declining-balance method in 1997, resulting in $36,000 of depreciation being taken. In 1998, it decided to change to the straight-line method to calculate depreciation expense (included in selling and administrative expenses).

Penninger's retained earnings as of January 1, 1998, were $40,000. Penninger had 10,000 shares of common stock outstanding all year. The company paid dividends of $.50 per share in 1998.

Required

1. Prepare a revised income statement for 1998 reflecting the additional information.

2. If you were asked to predict the company's income for 1999, which 1998 income statement number would you use?

3. Prepare a statement of retained earnings for 1998.

4. How will items a, b, and c affect the balance sheet accounts?

Cases

Reading and Interpreting Financial Statements

LO 1, 5 **Case 12-1** Reading Ben & Jerry's Income Statement

Refer to the financial statements included in Ben & Jerry's annual report.

Required

1. Calculate the gross profit percentage for each of the three years of the financial statements. Has the percentage increased or decreased over time? What are the reasons for the trend in the percentage?

2. What are the possible reasons that Ben & Jerry's has not paid a dividend in recent years?

3. From the income statement and balance sheet, determine the number of shares of common stock outstanding as of the balance sheet date for each year and the weighted average number of shares outstanding each year. Why do these numbers differ? What were the earnings per share amounts for all three years?

4. What are the items contained in the other income (expense) category of Ben & Jerry's income statement? Why are those items separated from operating income?

LO 10 **Case 12-2** Reading Quicksilver's Cash Flow Statement

A summary of the information contained in the operating category of Quicksilver Inc.'s statement of cash flows for 1995 is presented below:

Cash Flow from Operating Activities:	
Net income	$10,012,000
Items in income not affecting cash:	
Depreciation	2,314,000
Provision for losses on accounts receivable	923,000
Loss on sale of fixed assets	99,000
Deferred taxes	(380,000)
Increase in operating assets and liabilities:	
Trade accounts receivable	(9,257,000)
Inventories	(6,746,000)
Accounts payable	4,100,000
Accrued liabilities	3,810,000
Income taxes payable	(860,000)
Other	(309,000)
Net Cash Provided by Operating Activities	$ 3,706,000

Required

1. Write a paragraph explaining why the company had $10.0 million in net income but generated $3.7 million in cash from operating activities.

2. Was the loss on sale of fixed assets a positive or negative amount on the income statement? Why is the item displayed as a positive amount on the statement of cash flows?

Making Financial Decisions

LO 2, 3, 10 **Case 12-3** Comparing Two Companies

Assume that you are a financial analyst who must compare two companies. You are particularly concerned about the amount of income tax expense reported by Companies A and B. The 1998 income statement of Company A is as follows:

Decision
Making

Revenues	$200,000
Cost of goods sold	120,000
Gross profit	$ 80,000
Selling and administrative expenses	40,000
Income before tax	$ 40,000
Income tax	16,000
Net income	$ 24,000

The 1998 income statement of Company B is as follows:

Revenues	$150,000
Cost of goods sold	90,000
Gross profit	$ 60,000
Selling and administrative expenses	30,000
Income before tax	$ 30,000
Income tax expense	12,000
Income from continuing operations	$ 18,000
Loss from discontinued operations (net of 40% tax)	9,000
Income before extraordinary item	$ 9,000
Extraordinary gain (net of 40% tax)	15,000
Net income	$ 24,000

Required

1. Compare the amount of income tax reported by Company A and Company B.

2. Does the amount of income tax expense on the income statement represent the amount of income tax paid to the Internal Revenue Service? What other factors need to be considered to determine the amount of cash actually paid for income taxes?

Decision Making

LO 2 **Case 12-4** Sale of Segment

A diverse company owns a chain of barbecue restaurants. It is probable that the city in which most of the restaurants are located will pass an ordinance to ban smoking in all public places. Sales are expected to drop if the ordinance passes because most of the restaurants' customers are smokers. The company has an opportunity to sell all of its restaurants to an investor, who plans to open health food stores. The president does not want to sell the segment, which will result in a loss that will affect current-year income. He proposes to keep the segment and "bury" the annual operating losses evenly over the next few years and then to sell. The sales price of the restaurants at a future date is undeterminable.

Required

How would the sale be disclosed on the income statement? Is it better to keep the restaurants and spread the loss over the next few years?

Accounting and Ethics: What Would You Do?

LO 6 **Case 12-5** Change in Estimate

Regina Lewis is an accountant for Ajax, a large industrial company. In the process of preparing the 1998 financial statements, she has become concerned about the accounting for the company's warranty costs. Ajax sells a product with a one-year warranty. Analysis of information indicates that the cost of warranty repairs has averaged approximately 5% of sales price. Ajax uses the accrual method and reports the warranty costs as an expense in the year that the product is sold.

Ms. Lewis has discovered that the accrual of warranty costs for 1997 was estimated at 1% of sales. When she questioned the individuals who made the estimate, she learned that the estimate was below the historical average because Ajax was under pressure to meet certain performance measures. Specifically, Ajax creditors had become concerned about the company's sagging profit and had required Ajax to be more profitable in 1997.

Ms. Lewis reported the matter to her superior, Mr. Russell, who agreed that the warranty accrual in 1997 had been too low. He suggested that this matter was an example of a "change in estimate" and should be recorded on the 1998 income statement. He recommended a 7% accrual to compensate for 1997. Mr. Russell reminded Ms. Lewis that accruals are always estimates and that corrections or adjustments are not unusual.

Required

Based on the information Ms. Lewis has gathered, what action should she take concerning the warranty accrual for 1997 and 1998?

LO 6 **Case 12-6** Change in Estimate

Refer to Case 12-5. Would your answer be the same if the 1997 accrual had been overstated (at 8%) rather than understated (at 1%)?

Research Case

Case 12-7 Sprint

Sprint's goal for the 21st century is to become a global telecommunications network combining cable television with cellular, local, and long-distance telephone service. Sprint believes this vision will provide the company with the expanded operating revenues needed for long-term financial growth.

Conduct a search of the World Wide Web, obtain Sprint's most recent annual report, or use library resources to obtain company financial data, and answer the following:

1. What is the gross profit percentage for Sprint for the latest accounting year available? How does this compare with the previous year?

2. What is the amount of "earnings applicable to common stock" for the most recent year available? How does this compare to the amount shown in the "Focus on Financial Results" in the opening vignette shown at the start of this chapter?

3. Describe the trend for the company's stock price over the past three to six months. Did earnings per share increase or decrease in each of the last two quarters? How might the company's earnings per share have affected recent changes in Sprint's stock price?

Optional Research. Access the Sprint World Wide Web site to obtain current information about the company's latest efforts related to telecommunications services. (Sprint's company profile and its financial information are also available through the Employment page.) In what ways is the company positioned for growth?

Solution to Key Terms Quiz

9 Multi-step income statement (p. 560)

1 Gross profit percentage (p. 560)

2 Income before income taxes (p. 561)

8 Extraordinary item (p. 565)

11 Cumulative effect (p. 567)

13 Weighted average of shares (p. 568)

15 Appropriation of retained earnings (p. 571)

10 Statement of stockholders' equity (p. 572)

3 Gross profit (p. 560)

5 Operating income (p. 560)

4 Discontinued operations (p. 562)

6 Change in accounting principle (p. 567)

16 Earnings per share (p. 568)

7 Prior period adjustment (p. 570)

12 Unrealized Gain/Loss—Available-for-Sale Securities (p. 571)

14 Comprehensive income (p. 574)

INTEGRATIVE PROBLEM

FOR

PART III

Evaluating financing options for asset acquisition and their impact on financial statements

Following are the financial statements for Griffin Inc. for the year 1998:

GRIFFIN INC.
BALANCE SHEET
AS OF DECEMBER 31, 1998
(IN MILLIONS)

ASSETS		LIABILITIES	
Cash	$ 1.6	Current portion of lease	
Other current assets	6.4	obligation	$ 1.0
Leased assets (net of		Other current liabilities	3.0
accumulated depreciation)	7.0	Lease obligation—Long-term	6.0
Other long-term assets	45.0	Other long-term liabilities	6.0
		Total liabilites	$16.0
		Stockholders' Equity	
		Preferred stock	$ 1.0
		Additional paid-in capital	
		on preferred stock	2.0
		Common stock	4.0
		Additional paid-in capital	
		on common stock	16.0
		Retained earnings	21.0
		Total stockholders' equity	$44.0
		Total liabilties and	
Total assets	$60.0	stockholders' equity	$60.0

GRIFFIN INC.
INCOME STATEMENT
FOR THE YEAR ENDED DECEMBER 31, 1998
(IN MILLIONS)

Revenues		$50.0
Expenses:		
Depreciation of leased asset	$ 1.0	
Depreciation—Other assets	3.2	
Interest on leased asset	.5	
Other expenses	27.4	
Income tax (30% rate)	5.4	
Total expenses		(37.5)
Income before extraordinary loss		$12.5
Extraordinary loss (net of		
$.9 taxes)		(2.1)
Net income		$10.4
EPS before extraordinary loss		$3.10
EPS extraordinary loss		(.53)
EPS—Net income		$2.57

Additional information:

Griffin Inc. has authorized 500,000 shares of 10%, $10 par value cumulative preferred stock. There were 100,000 shares issued and outstanding at all times during 1998. The firm has also authorized 5 million shares of $1 par common stock, with 4 million shares issued and outstanding.

On January 1, 1998, Griffin Inc. acquired an asset, a piece of specialized heavy equipment, for $8 million with a capital lease. The lease contract indicates that the term of the lease is eight years. Payments of $1.5 million are to be made each December 31. The first lease payment was made December 31, 1998 and consisted of $1 million principal and $.5 million of interest expense. The capital lease is depreciated using the straight-line method over eight years with zero salvage value.

Required

1. Assuming the acquisition of the equipment using a capital lease, provide the entries for the acquisition, depreciation, and lease payment.

2. The management of Griffin Inc. is considering the financial statement impact of methods of financing, other than the capital lease, that could have been used to acquire the equipment. For each alternative a, b, and c, provide all necessary entries, each entry's impact on the accounting equation, and revised 1998 financial statements and calculate, as revised, the following amounts or ratios:

> Current ratio
>
> Debt-to-equity ratio
>
> Net income
>
> EPS—Net income

Assume that the following alternative actions would have taken place on January 1, 1998.

a. Instead of acquiring the equipment with a capital lease, the company negotiated an operating lease to use the asset. The lease requires annual year-end payments of $1.5 million and results in "off–balance sheet" financing. (*Hint:* The $1.5 million should be treated as rental expense.)

b. Instead of acquiring the equipment with a capital lease, Griffin Inc. issued bonds for $8 million and purchased the equipment with the proceeds of the bond issue. Assume the bond interest of $.5 million was accrued and paid on December 31, 1998. A portion of the principal also is paid each year for eight years. On December 31, 1998, the company paid $1 million of principal and anticipated another $1 million of principal to be paid in 1999. Assume the equipment would have an eight-year life and would be depreciated on a straight-line basis with zero salvage value.

c. Instead of acquiring the equipment with a capital lease, Griffin Inc. issued 200,000 additional shares of 10% preferred stock to raise $8 million and purchased the equipment for $8 million with the proceeds from the stock issue. Dividends on the stock are declared and paid annually. Assume that a dividend payment was made on December 31, 1998. Assume the equipment would have an eight-year life and would be depreciated on a straight-line basis with zero salvage value.

A WORD TO STUDENTS ABOUT PART IV

Part IV will be fascinating and even fun—as long as you *keep practicing the concepts and reading the links from chapter to chapter.* **How does an international corporation report its earnings?** Chapter 13 uses Whirlpool Inc., a major international company, to show how.

How does the corporation report cash flows? See Chapter 14 to learn how to evaluate a company based on its cash flows. **Can you find the trends in a company's performance?** Use any set of financial statements you can find to practice the analysis concepts and skills presented in Chapter 15.

PART IV

Additional Topics in Financial Reporting

Additional Reporting Issues: Intercompany Investments and Foreign Currency

STUDY LINKS

A Look at Previous Chapters

In the previous three chapters, we considered accounting for various types of securities issued by corporations. Specifically, in Chapter 10 we looked at how companies account for the issuance of bonds, notes, and other forms of borrowing on a long-term basis. Chapters 11 and 12 focused on permanent types of financing in the form of capital stock.

A Look at This Chapter

In this chapter, we look at the "other side of the fence." That is, we explore the accounting by companies that invest in the stocks and bonds of other corporations, using Whirlpool Corporation as an example.

A Look at Upcoming Chapters

Many of the topics discussed in Chapter 13 have cash flow implications. In Chapter 14 we turn our attention to an expanded consideration of the preparation and use of the statement of cash flows. The analysis of this statement, as well as the other financial statements, is the focus of Chapter 15.

FOCUS ON FINANCIAL RESULTS

Whirlpool Corporation, which markets major home appliances, has adopted what many investors consider the success formula for American business: a global strategy. Like other successful businesses, Whirlpool has recognized tremendous opportunities in the emerging markets of Eastern Europe, the Far East, and Latin America. To tap these opportunities, Whirlpool enters foreign markets by building factories, establishing sales offices, entering joint ventures, and investing in foreign-based companies.

Whirlpool's 1995 annual report shows the impact of those international ventures. Whirlpool divides its global activities into five

Whirlpool Corporation

- Management's Discussion & Analysis -

Net Sales by Business Unit

(millions of dollars)	– 1995 –	– 1994 –	Increase/(Decrease)	
North America	$ 5,093	$ 5,048	$ 45	1%
Europe	2,428	2,373	55	2
Asia	376	205	171	83
Latin America	271	329	(58)	(18)
Other	(5)	(6)	1	–
Total Appliance Business	$ 8,163	$ 7,949	$ 214	3%

About Our Company :

Whirlpool Corporation is the world's leading manufacturer and marketer of major home appliances. The company manufacturers in 12 countries and markets products in approximately 140 countries under major brand names such as *Whirlpool, Kitchen Aid, Roper, Estate, Bauknecht, Ignis, Laden and Inglis.* Whirlpool is also the principal supplier to Sears Roebuck and Co. of many home appliances marketed under the *Kenmore* brand name.

business units: North America, Europe, Asia, Latin America, and Other. The "Chairman's Letter" discusses factors influencing these units and managements's expectations for future growth.

The company's greatest revenues come from North America. The North American Free Trade Agreement encouraged greater sales to Canada and Mexico by lowering trade barriers between the United States and those countries. However, the largest rate of growth (83%) comes from Whirlpool's Asian operations. Given Asia's sizable population and economic growth, Whirlpool forecasts that by the end of the decade, Asians will each year buy twice the 60 million appliances purchased in 1995 and that the Asian market will become twice the size of the North American or European market.

Along with growth potential, global operations bring significant risks. While studying this chapter, identify sources of risk and opportunity that are unique to international businesses.

SOURCE: *Whirlpool Corporation Annual Report,* 1995.

After studying this chapter, you should be able to

LO 1   Explain the various reasons that one company might invest in another company.

LO 2   Understand the accounting and reporting requirements for held-to-maturity securities.

LO 3   Understand the accounting and reporting requirements for trading securities.

LO 4   Understand the accounting and reporting requirements for available-for-sale securities.

LO 5   Understand the accounting and reporting requirements for equity investees.

LO 6   Explain the different forms of business combinations and how to account for a merger using the purchase method.

LO 7   Explain when, why, and how consolidated financial statements are prepared.

LO 8   Understand how to account for foreign currency transactions.

LO 9   Understand how to translate foreign financial statements into U.S. dollars.

LO 10   Describe the reporting requirements for segments of a business.

Operating in a Global Environment

Whirlpool Corporation is a typical corporation of the 1990s. Its core business is major home appliances, of which it is the world's leading manufacturer and marketer. In addition, it operates Whirlpool Financial Corporation (WFC), which provides financing services for dealers, distributors, and consumers. This unit makes loans for the purchase of Whirlpool products and in this respect is similar to General Motors Acceptance Corporation (GMAC), the financing arm of General Motors.

In addition to the complexities of operating a manufacturing business and a financing business, Whirlpool must deal with other challenges. It generates a significant portion of its revenues from sales to Sears, Roebuck & Co. Whirlpool is the principal supplier to Sears of many appliances marketed under the Kenmore brand name. Thus, Sears's success in selling its products directly affects Whirlpool's success.

Until the late 1980s, Whirlpool sold its washers, dryers, refrigerators, ranges, and other appliances almost exclusively in the United States. The competitive nature of the U.S. business climate led to a corporate decision in 1988 to dramatically increase its presence in foreign markets. By the end of 1995, Whirlpool manufactured in 12 countries and sold products in approximately 140 countries.

Exhibit 13-1 illustrates the global nature of Whirlpool's business. The company operates in four major world markets: North America (the United States, Canada, and Mexico), Europe, Latin America (Central and South America and the Caribbean), and Asia. To accomplish its global goals, the business is organized into a number of units. Operations in North America are carried out by the parent, Whirlpool Corporation. A subsidiary, Whirlpool Europe B.V., is responsible for European operations. Other subsidiaries manage the company's businesses in Latin America and Asia. Only recently, Whirlpool set up two separate global business units to manufacture and distribute microwave ovens and air conditioners on a worldwide basis.

As we discuss in the chapter, a **subsidiary** is a separate legal entity that is controlled by another entity, the **parent.** Normally, control over another entity results from ownership of a majority of that company's stock. In many cases, the parent owns all of the stock of a subsidiary, thus making it a **wholly owned subsidiary.**

In addition to subsidiaries, Whirlpool has investments in a number of affiliates. Although Whirlpool doesn't control the **affiliate,** it owns enough of the other company to exercise significant influence over it. For example, Whirlpool has direct voting rights, ranging from 30% to 49%, in two Brazilian companies, a Mexican manufacturer, and several other international companies.

EXHIBIT 13-1   Organization of Whirlpool Corporation

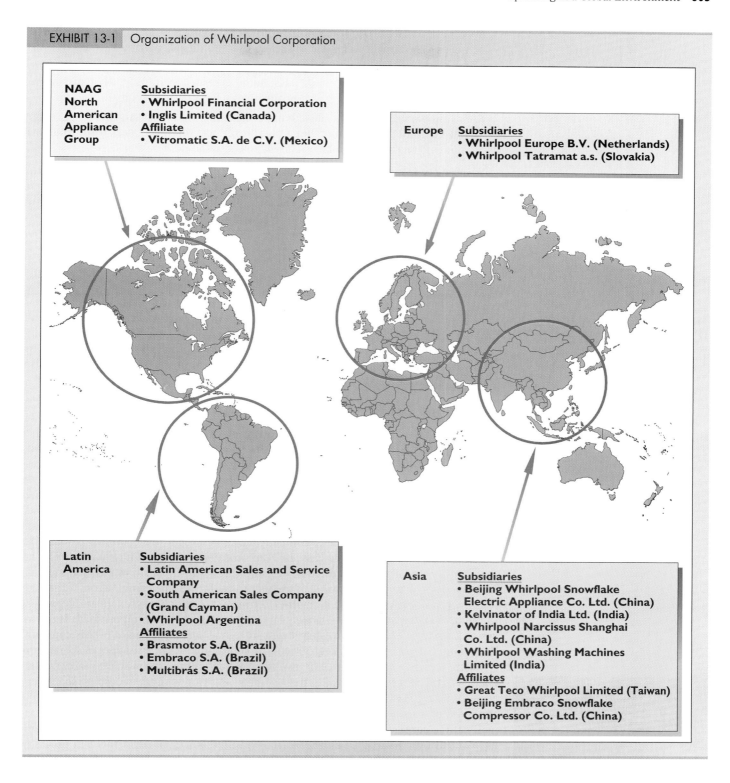

NAAG
North American Appliance Group

Subsidiaries
• **Whirlpool Financial Corporation**
• **Inglis Limited (Canada)**
Affiliate
• **Vitromatic S.A. de C.V. (Mexico)**

Europe   Subsidiaries
• **Whirlpool Europe B.V. (Netherlands)**
• **Whirlpool Tatramat a.s. (Slovakia)**

Latin America

Subsidiaries
• **Latin American Sales and Service Company**
• **South American Sales Company (Grand Cayman)**
• **Whirlpool Argentina**
Affiliates
• **Brasmotor S.A. (Brazil)**
• **Embraco S.A. (Brazil)**
• **Multibrás S.A. (Brazil)**

Asia   Subsidiaries
• **Beijing Whirlpool Snowflake Electric Appliance Co. Ltd. (China)**
• **Kelvinator of India Ltd. (India)**
• **Whirlpool Narcissus Shanghai Co. Ltd. (China)**
• **Whirlpool Washing Machines Limited (India)**
Affiliates
• **Great Teco Whirlpool Limited (Taiwan)**
• **Beijing Embraco Snowflake Compressor Co. Ltd. (China)**

This introduction to the business of Whirlpool raises a number of questions:

1. What is the appropriate accounting for the acquisition of another business? How should a company account for a significant investment in another business?

2. How should a subsidiary be reported in the financial statements of a parent corporation? Does it matter if the subsidiary is engaged in a line of business entirely different from that of the parent?

3. How should a corporation report on an affiliate in its financial statements?

4. What if a subsidiary or an affiliate keeps its books in a foreign currency? What needs to be done to *translate* the relevant amounts into dollars?

5. If a company operates in more than one industry, what supplementary disclosures would be useful to the financial statement reader? Similarly, what disclosures would be useful regarding a company's various geographic segments?

6. Is it important for financial statement readers to know if a company relies on any one customer or customers for a significant portion of its sales? If so, what specific information should be disclosed, and how should it be disclosed?

We first try to provide general answers to each of these questions in the context of current accounting standards. We begin by looking at various types of investments in stocks and bonds, some of which give the investor influence over the company and some of which do not. Then we will return to consider how Whirlpool actually addresses these issues in its annual report.

Intercompany Investments

LO 1 Explain the various reasons that one company might invest in another company.

Corporations frequently invest in the securities of other businesses. These investments take two forms: debt securities and equity securities. A **debt security** results when one company loans money to another company; an **equity security** represents one company's ownership interest in another entity. The most common type of debt security is a bond; equity securities are usually in the form of either common or preferred stock.

Why One Company Invests in Another Company

Corporations have varying motivations for investing in the stocks and bonds of other companies. We will refer to the company that invests as the *investor* and the company whose stocks or bonds are purchased as the *investee*. At times, companies invest excess funds in stocks and bonds over the short run. The seasonality of certain businesses may result in otherwise idle cash being available during certain times of the year. In other cases, stocks and bonds are purchased as a way to invest cash over the long run. Often these types of investments are made in anticipation of a need for cash at some distant point in the future. For example, a company may invest today in a combination of stocks and bonds because it will need cash 10 years from today to build a new plant. The investor may be primarily interested in periodic income in the form of interest and dividends, in appreciation in the value of the securities, or in some combination of the two.

Sometimes shares of stock in another company are bought with a different purpose in mind. If a company buys a relatively large percentage of the common stock of the investee, it may be able to secure significant influence over the policies of this company. For example, a company may buy 30% of the common stock of a supplier of its raw materials to ensure a steady source of inventory. When an investor is able to secure influence over the investee, the **equity method** of accounting is used. According to current accounting standards, this method is appropriate when an investor owns at least 20% of the common stock of the investee.

Finally, a corporation may buy stock in another company with the purpose of obtaining control over that other entity. Normally, this requires an investment in excess of 50% of the common stock of the investee. When an investor owns more than half of the stock of another company, accountants normally prepare a set of **consolidated financial statements.** This involves combining the financial statements of the individual entities into a single set of statements. As we noted earlier, an investor with an interest of more than 50% in another company is called the *parent,* and the investee in these situations is called the *subsidiary.*

In the next section of this chapter, we consider how companies account for investments that do *not* give them any significant influence over the other company. After that, we discuss how to account for investments in which there is significant influence, that is, when the equity method is used. Finally, we turn to the accounting for

Whirlpool is one company that has dramatically increased its presence in foreign markets, operating in Asia, Europe, and Latin America along with North America.

investments that give the investor control over the other company and require the use of consolidated statements. As we will see, how a company accounts for each of these types of investments varies considerably. The following chart summarizes the accounting by an investor for investments in the common stock of another company:

Investor's Percentage Ownership in the Common Stock of Another Company

Investments without Significant Influence

Companies face a number of major issues in deciding how to account for and report on investments in the stocks and bonds of other companies:

1. What should be the basis for the recognition of periodic income from an investment? That is, what event causes income to be recognized?

2. How should an investment be valued and thus reported at the end of an accounting period? At original cost? At fair value?

3. How should an investment be classified on a balance sheet? As a current asset? As a noncurrent asset?

The answer to each of these questions depends on the type of investment. Accountants classify investments in the securities of other companies into one of three categories:[1]

Held-to-maturity securities are investments in the bonds of other companies when the investor has the positive intent and the ability to hold the securities to maturity. *Note that only bonds can qualify as held-to-maturity securities because shares of stock do not have a maturity date.*

Trading securities are stocks and bonds that are bought and held for the purpose of selling them in the near term. These securities are usually held for only a short period of time with the objective of generating profits on short-term appreciation in the market price of the stocks and bonds.

Available-for-sale securities are stocks and bonds that are not classified as either held-to-maturity or trading securities.

Investments in Held-to-Maturity Securities

By their nature, only bonds, not stock, can qualify as held-to-maturity securities. A bond is categorized as a held-to-maturity security if the investor plans to hold it until it matures. In Chapter 10, we looked at the accounting by an *issuer* of bonds. Accounting by an *investor* in bonds parallels this accounting. An investor may buy the bonds either on the original issuance date or later. If the investor buys them on the date they are originally issued, the purchase is from the issuer. It is also possible, however, for an investor to buy bonds on the *open market* after they have been outstanding for a period of time.

To understand an open-market purchase of bonds, consider the following example. On January 1, 1998, Homer buys $100,000 in face value of Simpson bonds at 103. This means that the bonds are currently selling in the market at 103% of face value. The

LO 2 Understand the accounting and reporting requirements for held-to-maturity securities.

---

[1]*Statement of Financial Accounting Standards No. 115,* "Accounting for Certain Investments in Debt and Equity Securities" (Stamford, Conn.: Financial Accounting Standards Board, May 1993), par 7–12.

coupon rate is 10%, with interest payable semiannually on June 30 and December 31. The original term of the bonds was 20 years; they were issued on January 1, 1993. Thus, at the time of Homer's purchase, the bonds have a remaining life of 15 years. The entry on Homer's books to record the purchase of the bonds is as follows:

1998
Jan. 1   Investment in Bonds   103,000
              Cash   103,000
          To record purchase of Simpson bonds at 103.

Assets	=	Liabilities	+	Owners' Equity
+103,000				
−103,000				

Two points are worth noting. First, the premium of $3,000 paid for the bonds is not recorded separately, as it is by issuers of bonds. Although it is possible to use a separate premium account, the premium is often simply included in the Investment in Bonds account.[2] Second, recall what the premium paid by Homer indicates: the stated rate or coupon rate of 10% must be higher than the effective or market rate of interest at this time because an investor is willing to pay more than face value for the bonds.

On June 30, Homer must record the receipt of semiannual interest and recognize amortization of the premium. In Chapter 10 we illustrated the effective interest method of bond amortization. If the results are not materially different, a company may use the less desirable straight-line method. To keep our calculations simple, we assume that Homer elects to use the straight-line method of amortization. The entry on June 30 is as follows:

1998
June 30   Cash   5,000
              Investment in Bonds   100
              Interest Income   4,900
          To record interest income on Simpson bonds.

Assets	=	Liabilities	+	Owners' Equity
+5,000				**+4,900**
−100				

The amount of cash received is equal to the semiannual stated rate of interest of 5% times the face value of the bonds of $100,000. Straight-line amortization of the premium is computed as follows:

Amount of premium	$3,000
Divided by:	
Number of six-month periods in remaining life of bonds of 15 years	30
Premium amortized for six months	= $ 100

Under the straight-line method, the amount of interest income recognized is the difference between the amount of cash received of $5,000 and the amount of premium amortized of $100. The fact that the actual income earned for the six-month period is less than cash received is logical given the nature of a *premium*. Because Homer paid more for the bonds, $103,000, than it will receive when they mature, $100,000, interest income is less than the cash received in interest each six months.

The approach just illustrated to account for an investment in held-to-maturity bonds is the amortized cost method. The investment was recorded initially at cost, including any premium paid or less any discount. The basis for recognition of income on the bonds was the receipt of interest (if interest was not received at the end of an accounting period, a company should accrue interest earned but not yet received). Because a

[2]Recall from Chapter 10 that bonds can be issued at either a premium or a discount. As is the case for a premium, most investors do not record a discount separately. Instead, the discount is netted against the investment account.

premium paid reduces the amount of interest earned, it is amortized over the remaining life of the bonds. Similarly, a discount increases the interest earned, and it is amortized in the same way that a premium is amortized. Finally, an investment in held-to-maturity bonds is normally classified as a *noncurrent asset*. Any held-to-maturity bonds that are one year or less from maturity, however, are classified in the current assets section of a balance sheet.

Assume that before the maturity date, Homer needs cash and decides to sell the bonds. Keep in mind that this is a definite change in Homer's plans, since the bonds were initially categorized as held-to-maturity securities. The principles that were applied in Chapter 10 in accounting for the retirement of bonds early by the issuer apply here. Any difference between the proceeds received from the sale of the bonds and their carrying value on the date of the sale is recognized as either a gain or a loss.

Assume that on January 1, 2001, Homer sells all of its Simpson bonds at 99. This means that the amount of cash received is .99 × $100,000, or $99,000. The carrying value of the bonds on this date is calculated as follows:

Amount paid for bonds on 1/1/1998	$103,000
Less: Three years of amortization at $200 per year ($100 each six months)	600
Carrying value of bonds on 1/1/2001	$102,400

The entry on January 1 is as follows:

2001			
Jan. 1	Cash	99,000	
	Loss on Sale of Bonds	3,400	
	Investment in Bonds		102,400
	To record sale of Simpson bonds.		

Assets	=	**Liabilities**	+	**Owners' Equity**
+99,000				**−3,400**
−102,400				

The $3,400 loss on the sale is the excess of the carrying value of $102,400 over the cash proceeds of $99,000. The loss is reported in the other income and expenses section on the 2001 income statement.

Investments in Trading Securities

A company invests in trading securities as a way to profit from increases in the market prices of these securities over the short term. Because the intent is to hold them for the short term, trading securities are classified as current assets. All trading securities are recorded initially at cost, including any brokerage fees, commissions, or other fees paid to acquire the shares. Assume that Dexter Corp. invests in the following securities on November 30, 1998:

LO 3 Understand the accounting and reporting requirements for trading securities.

SECURITY	COST
Stuart common stock	$50,000
Menlo preferred stock	25,000
Total cost	$75,000

The entry on Dexter's books on the date of purchase is as follows:

1998
Nov. 30   Investment in Stuart Common Stock   50,000
          Investment in Menlo Preferred Stock   25,000
             Cash   75,000
         To record purchase of trading securities for cash.

Assets = Liabilities + Owners' Equity
+**50,000**
+**25,000**
−**75,000**

Many companies attempt to pay dividends every year as a signal of overall financial strength and profitability.[3] Assume that on December 10, 1998, Dexter received dividends of $1,000 from Stuart and $600 from Menlo. The dividends received from trading securities are recognized as income as shown in the following entry on Dexter's books:

1998
Dec. 10   Cash   1,600
         Dividend Income   1,600
         To record receipt of dividends on trading securities.

Assets = Liabilities + Owners' Equity
+**1,600**   +**1,600**

Unlike interest on a bond or a note, dividends do not accrue over time. In fact, a company does not have a legal obligation to pay dividends until its board of directors declares them. Up to that point, the investor has no guarantee that dividends will ever be paid.

As noted earlier, trading securities are purchased with the intention of holding them for a short period of time. Assume that Dexter sells the Stuart stock on December 15, 1998, for $53,000. In this case, Dexter recognizes a gain for the excess of the cash proceeds, $53,000, over the amount recorded on the books, $50,000:

1998
Dec. 15   Cash   53,000
         Investment in Stuart Common Stock   50,000
         Gain on Sale of Stock   3,000
         To record sale of Stuart common stock.

Assets = Liabilities + Owners' Equity
+**53,000**   +**3,000**
−**50,000**

For accounting purposes, the gain is considered realized and is classified on the income statement as other income. For tax purposes, this gain is referred to as a *capital gain* and is taxed at a rate of 28%, as opposed to the 35% rate for regular income and dividends. The tax rate on capital gains has historically been less than that on ordinary income to provide an incentive to invest in the economy.

Assume that on December 22, 1998, Dexter replaces the Stuart stock in its portfolio by purchasing Canby common stock for $40,000. The entry on this date follows:

[3]IBM's March 1997 dividend of $.35 per share was the computer company's 328th consecutive quarterly dividend, an uninterrupted string of 82 years in which it paid dividends.

1998
Dec. 22 Investment in Canby Common Stock   40,000
         Cash   40,000
        To record purchase of trading securities for cash.

Assets = **Liabilities** + **Owners' Equity**
+**40,000**
−**40,000**

Now assume that Dexter ends its accounting period on December 31. Should it adjust the carrying value of its investments to reflect their fair values on this date? According to the accounting profession, fair values should be used to report investments in trading securities on a balance sheet. The fair values are thought to be relevant information to the various users of financial statements. Assume the following information for Dexter on December 31, 1998:

SECURITY	TOTAL COST	TOTAL FAIR VALUE ON DECEMBER 31, 1998	GAIN (LOSS)
Menlo preferred stock	$25,000	$27,500	$2,500
Canby common stock	40,000	39,000	(1,000)
Totals	$65,000	$66,500	$1,500

The entry on Dexter's books on this date follows:

1998
Dec. 31 Investment in Menlo Preferred Stock   2,500
          Investment in Canby Common Stock   1,000
          Unrealized Gain—Trading Securities   1,500
           (Income Statement)
        To adjust trading securities to fair value.

Assets = **Liabilities** + **Owners' Equity**
+**2,500**   +**1,500**
−**1,000**

Note that this entry results in each security being written up or down so that it will appear on the December 31 balance sheet at its market or fair value. This type of fair value accounting for trading securities is often referred to as a *mark to market* approach because at the end of each period, the value of each security is adjusted to its current market value. Also, it is important to realize that for trading securities, the changes in value are recognized on the income statement. The difference of $1,500 between the original cost of the two securities, $65,000, and their fair value, $66,500, is recorded in the account Unrealized Gain—Trading Securities to call attention to the fact that the securities have not been sold. Even though the gain or loss is *unrealized,* it is recognized on the income statement as a form of other income or loss.

Assume one final transaction in our Dexter example. On January 20, 1999, Dexter sells the Menlo stock for $27,000. The entry on Dexter's books on this date follows:

1999
Jan. 20 Loss on Sale of Stock (Income Statement)   500
        Cash   27,000
          Investment in Menlo Preferred Stock   27,500
        To record sale of Menlo preferred stock.

Assets = **Liabilities** + **Owners' Equity**
+**27,000**   −**500**
−**27,500**

The important point to note about this entry is that the $500 loss represents the difference between the cash proceeds of $27,000 and the *fair value of the stock at the most recent reporting date,* $27,500. Because the Menlo stock was adjusted to a fair value of

$27,500 on December 31, the excess of this amount over the cash proceeds of $27,000 results in a loss of $500. Keep in mind that a gain of $2,500 was recognized last year when the stock was adjusted to its fair value at the end of the year.

Investments in Available-for-Sale Securities

Stocks and bonds that do not qualify as trading securities and bonds that are not intended to be held to maturity are categorized as available-for-sale securities. The accounting for these securities is similar to the accounting for trading securities, with one major exception: *even though fair value accounting is used to report available-for-sale securities at the end of an accounting period, any gains or losses resulting from marking to market are not reported on the income statement but instead are accumulated in a stockholders' equity account.* This inconsistency is justified by the accounting profession on the grounds that the inclusion in income of fluctuations in the value of securities that are available for sale but that are not necessarily being actively traded could lead to volatility in reported earnings. Regardless, reporting gains and losses on the income statement for one class of securities but not for others is a subject of considerable debate.

To understand the use of fair value accounting for available-for-sale securities, assume that Lenox Corp. purchases two different stocks late in 1998. The costs and fair values at the end of 1998 are as follows:

SECURITY	TOTAL COST	FAIR VALUE ON DECEMBER 31, 1998	GAIN (LOSS)
Adair preferred stock	$15,000	$16,000	$ 1,000
Casey common stock	35,000	32,500	(2,500)
Totals	$50,000	$48,500	$(1,500)

The entry on Lenox's books on this date is as follows:

```
1998
Dec. 31   Unrealized Gain/Loss—Available-for-Sale
                 Securities (Stockholders' Equity)           1,500
          Investment in Adair Preferred Stock                1,000
             Investment in Casey Common Stock                          2,500
          To adjust available-for-sale securities to fair value.
```

Assets	=	Liabilities	+	Owners' Equity
+1,000				−1,500
−2,500				

Note the similarity between this entry and the one we made at the end of the period in the example for trading securities. In both instances, the individual investments are adjusted to their fair values for purposes of presenting them on the year-end balance sheet. The unrealized loss of $1,500 does not, however, affect income in this case. Instead, the loss is shown as a reduction of stockholders' equity on the balance sheet.

Now assume that Lenox sells its Casey stock for $34,500 on June 30, 1999. The entry on this date is as follows:

```
1999
June 30   Cash                                              34,500
          Loss on Sale of Stock (Income Statement)             500
             Investment in Casey Common Stock                         32,500
             Unrealized Gain/Loss—Available-for-Sale
                 Securities (Stockholders' Equity)                     2,500
          To record sale of Casey common stock.
```

Assets	=	Liabilities	+	Owners' Equity
+34,500				− 500
−32,500				+2,500

Lenox recognizes a loss on the income statement of $500, which represents the excess of the cost of the stock of $35,000 over the cash proceeds of $34,500. Note, however, that the Investment in Casey Common Stock is removed from the books at $32,500, the fair value at the end of the prior period. Thus, it is also necessary to adjust the Unrealized Gain/Loss account for the difference between the original cost of $35,000 and the fair value at the end of 1998 of $32,500.

Finally, assume that Lenox does not buy any additional securities during the remainder of 1999 and that the fair value of the one investment it holds, the Adair preferred stock, is $19,000 on December 31, 1999. The entry to adjust the Adair stock to fair value on this date is as follows:

1999

Dec. 31	Investment in Adair Preferred Stock	3,000	
	Unrealized Gain/Loss—Available-for-Sale		
	Securities (Stockholders' Equity)		3,000
	To adjust available-for-sale securities to fair value.		

Assets = Liabilities + Owners' Equity
+3,000   +3,000

The increase in the Investment in Adair Preferred Stock account results in a balance of $19,000 in this account, the fair value of the stock. The stockholders' equity account now has a *credit* balance of $4,000 as reflected in the following T account:

UNREALIZED GAIN/LOSS—AVAILABLE-FOR-SALE SECURITIES

12/31/98 bal.	1,500		
		2,500	6/30/99 entry
		1,000	6/30/99 bal.
		3,000	12/31/99 entry
		4,000	12/31/99 bal.

The balance of $4,000 in this account represents the excess of the $19,000 fair value of the one security now held over its original cost of $15,000.

Where Investments Appear on the Statement of Cash Flows

Purchases of stocks and bonds in other companies require the use of cash, and the sales of these investments result in the inflow of cash to the business. The classification of these activities on the statement of cash flows depends on the type of investment. Cash flows from purchases, sales, and maturities of held-to-maturity securities and available-for-sale securities are classified as *investing* activities. On the other hand, these same types of cash flows for trading securities are classified as *operating* activities. We present a complete discussion of the statement of cash flows, including the reporting of investments, in Chapter 14.

The following excerpt from the 1995 statement of cash flows for the microprocessor company Intel illustrates how it reports its investments in available-for-sale securities:

Cash flows provided by (used for) investing activities:	
Additions to property, plant, and equipment	$(3,550)
Purchases of long-term, available-for-sale investments	(129)
Sales of long-term, available-for-sale investments	114
Maturities and other changes in available-for-sale	
investments, net	878
Net cash (used for) investing activities	**$(2,687)**

EXHIBIT 13-2	Accounting for Investments without Significant Influence				
CATEGORIES	**TYPES**	**CLASSIFIED ON BALANCE SHEET AS**	**RECOGNIZE AS INCOME**	**REPORT ON BALANCE SHEET AT**	**REPORT CHANGES IN FAIR VALUE ON**
Held-to-maturity	Bonds	Noncurrent*	Interest	Amortized cost	Not applicable
Trading	Bonds, stock	Current	Interest, dividends	Fair value	Income statement
Available-for-sale	Bonds, stock	Current or noncurrent	Interest, dividends	Fair value	Balance sheet (in stockholders' equity)

*Reclassified as current if they mature within one year of the balance sheet date.

Summary of Accounting and Reporting Requirements

A summary of the accounting and reporting requirements for each of the three categories of investments is shown in Exhibit 13-2. Periodic income from each of these types of investments is recognized in the form of interest and dividends. Held-to-maturity bonds are reported on the balance sheet at *amortized cost*. Both trading securities and available-for-sale securities are reported on the balance sheet at fair value. Unrealized gains and losses from holding trading securities are recognized on the income statement, whereas these same gains and losses for available-for-sale securities are accumulated in a stockholders' equity account.

The Controversy over Fair Value Accounting

Only recently have accounting standards changed to require that certain investments be reported at fair value. Before the change, the lower of cost or market rule was followed when accounting for these investments. The use of market or fair values is clearly an exception to the cost principle as first introduced in Chapter 1. Whether the exception is justified has been, and will continue to be, a matter of debate.

One concern of financial statement users is the hybrid system now used to report assets on a balance sheet. Consider the following types of assets and how we report them on the balance sheet:

ASSET	REPORTED ON THE BALANCE SHEET AT
Inventories	Lower of cost or market
Investments	Either amortized cost or fair value
Property, plant, and equipment	Original cost, less accumulated depreciation

It is difficult to justify so many different valuation methods to report the assets of a single company. Recall that the lower of cost or market approach to valuing inventory is based on conservatism. Why should it be used for inventories while fair value is used for investments? Proponents of fair values believe that the information provided to the reader of the statements is more relevant, and they argue that the subjectivity inherent in valuing other types of assets is not an issue when dealing with securities that have a ready market. The controversy surrounding the valuation of assets on a balance sheet is likely to continue.

Investments in Stock Using the Equity Method

LO 5 Understand the accounting and reporting requirements for equity investees.

The accounting profession has set 20% as the minimum investment that one company can make in the common stock of another company to be able to exercise significant influence over the policies of that other company. These policies include key decisions related to the investee's operating, investing, and financing activities. For example, an equity investor normally has a significant voice in such decisions as the amount of dividends to be paid by the investee, whether the investee should expand its plant, and whether it should borrow more funds. The 20% rule is somewhat arbitrary, and there are exceptions to it; however, it provides a useful reference for determining how a company should account for an investment in common stock.

Assume that on January 2, 1998, Marlin Corp. buys as a form of long-term investment 3,000 of the 10,000 outstanding shares of Cougar Inc. at a price of $25 per share, plus commissions of $1,000. An investee such as Cougar is usually referred to by the investor, Marlin, as an *affiliate*. Marlin records the investment in its new affiliate:

1998
Jan. 2   Investment in Stock   76,000
            Cash   76,000
          To record purchase of 3,000 shares of Cougar stock
          at $25 per share, plus commissions of $1,000.

Assets	=	Liabilities	+	Owners' Equity
+76,000				
-76,000				

Assume that during 1998 Cougar reports net income of $50,000 and declares and pays dividends of $30,000. *The equity method gets its name from the fact that the investor increases the investment account for its proportionate share of the increase in the investee's stockholders' equity.* For example, what effect did the recognition of net income have on Cougar's stockholders' equity? The net income *increases* Cougar's stockholders' equity by $50,000. Thus, Marlin will increase its investment account by 30% of $50,000, or $15,000. The other side of the adjustment is an increase in income. That is, *income reported under the equity method is based on the investor's proportionate share of the income reported by the investee.* The entry on Marlin's books to record its share of the investee's income is as follows:

1998
Dec. 31   Investment in Stock   15,000
              Equity Income   15,000
          To record 30% share of Cougar's reported income
          of $50,000.

Assets	=	Liabilities	+	Owners' Equity
+15,000				+15,000

Note that the basis for recognition of income under the equity method differs from the basis used for investments without significant influence. In those cases, dividends received were recognized as income. Under the equity method, income is based not on dividends but on the investor's proportionate share of the investee's income. Equity income is usually reported as a separate line item on the investor's income statement.

Turning to dividends, what is the effect on Cougar's stockholders' equity from declaring and paying dividends? The 1998 dividends *reduce* Cougar's equity by $30,000. Thus, under the equity method, Marlin reduces its long-term investment account for the dividends it receives from Cougar with the following entry:

1998
Dec. 31   Cash   9,000
              Investment in Stock   9,000
          To record dividends received from Cougar:
          .30 × $30,000.

Assets	=	Liabilities	+	Owners' Equity
+9,000				
-9,000				

A T account for Marlin's investment account is helpful to understand why these two entries are made:

INVESTMENT IN STOCK			
1/1/98 bal.	76,000	9,000	Dividends
Income	15,000		
12/31/98 bal.	82,000		

Thus, we see that the increase in Marlin's investment account during 1998 was $6,000. According to the concept behind the equity method, this should represent 30% of the increase in the investee's stockholders' equity:

Investee's reported net income	$50,000
Less: Investee's dividends	(30,000)
Increase in investee's stockholders' equity	$20,000
× Investor's percentage ownership	.30
Increase in Investment in Stock account	$ 6,000

The rationale for recognizing income based on a percentage of the income of the investee rather than on dividends received is related to the concept of significant influence. Think of the potential for manipulation if an investor were in a position to influence the amount of dividends paid by an investee. Recognizing income based on the amount of dividends received would allow the investor to increase its income simply by voting for higher dividends.

Two final points can be made about the use of the equity method. First, if an investor sells an investment accounted for under the equity method, a gain or loss normally results. The gain or loss, however, is not the difference between the cash proceeds and the *historical cost*. Because the investment account has been adjusted upward for a share of the investee's income and downward for the dividends received, the gain or loss is the difference between the cash proceeds and this adjusted balance. The second point concerns the valuation at the end of the period of an investment accounted for under the equity method. Unlike trading securities and available-for-sale securities, equity investments are *not* periodically adjusted to fair value. Instead, the investment is adjusted to reflect the investor's share of increases in the investee's equity.

Business Combinations and Consolidated Financial Statements

Mergers and acquisitions are a way of life in American business. Their popularity has varied over time, depending on the overall state of the economy and numerous other factors. Sometimes they work; at other times they are doomed to failure from the beginning, as in the case of the 1994 acquisition of Snapple Beverage Corp. by Quaker Oats for a price of $1.7 billion. Within three years, Quaker sold Snapple at a substantial loss. In some situations, only time will tell, as in the case of the recent merger of Time Warner and Turner Broadcasting System. What would prompt the marriage of these two media giants? We begin our study of business combinations and consolidations by considering why companies combine.

Why Corporations Combine

Sometimes *competitors* combine. This is called a horizontal combination because it involves companies operating on the same level. The combination of Jeep in the late 1980s with Chrysler Corp. was an example of a horizontal combination. In 1992, Marvel Entertainment Group Inc., the famous comic book company, acquired Fleer, the trading card company. Marvel saw Fleer as a good fit as it continued to compete for the youth entertainment market. Certainly the combination of Time Warner and Turner could be described as a horizontal combination, given the interests both companies have in the entertainment and cable television industries.

On other occasions, a company may combine with either one of its *suppliers* or one of its *customers.* For example, a combination with a supplier may be viewed as a way to ensure a reliable source of raw material for a product. A company also might combine with one of its customers to guarantee a steady market for its products. Because the company is reaching either down in terms of the product chain to combine with a supplier or up to combine with a customer, this is called a vertical combination.

Finally, some business combinations involve companies without any obvious tie to each other. For example, at one time Sears, Roebuck & Co. owned Allstate, an insurance company, Dean Witter, a brokerage firm, and Coldwell Banker, a real estate company. This type of corporation, with widely varying business interests, is termed a conglomerate. Normally these types of combinations are justified as a way to spread the various risks of doing business over a number of different industries.

Legal Forms of Business Combinations

Before we consider how to account for a business combination, it is important to understand the different *legal forms* for business combinations. Assume that two competitors, A and B, decide to combine their operations. In a statutory merger, A acquires all of the assets of B and assumes all of its liabilities, and B ceases to exist. In effect, B is merged into A and goes out of business as a separate legal entity. In a statutory consolidation, A and B combine, but instead of B being merged into A, a new corporation, C, is created to continue the business of the two former entities. It is important to understand that in both of these instances, a *single* entity survives: one of the two combining companies or a new entity.

In contrast, in a stock acquisition, two companies combine, but after the combination, both entities maintain their legal identities. Both entities survive in this type of business combination because of the structure of the transaction. Instead of A acquiring B's *assets and liabilities,* as in a merger, A acquires the *stock* of B. The three legal forms for business combinations are summarized in Exhibit 13-3.

Methods of Accounting for Business Combinations

Regardless of the legal form a business combination takes, one of two methods is used to account for it. Unlike depreciation or inventory methods, a company is not free to choose between the two methods. One or the other should be used, based on the facts in a particular combination. One is called the purchase method and is used when one company acquires another through the transfer of a significant amount of cash, other assets, or debt. For example, the Quaker Oats acquisition of Snapple was accounted for as a purchase. The other method is the pooling of interests method and is used in limited situations in which shares of stock in the two companies are exchanged. For example, in June 1994 Novell Inc. merged with WordPerfect in a transaction accounted for as a pooling of interests. Approximately 51 million shares of Novell common stock were exchanged for all of the common stock of WordPerfect. Because the pooling of interests method is used less frequently, we focus our attention on the purchase method. Both methods are covered in detail in advanced accounting textbooks.

LO 6 Explain the different forms of business combinations and how to account for a merger using the purchase method.

EXHIBIT 13-3 Legal Forms for Business Combinations

LEGAL FORM	WHAT HAPPENS	AFTER THE COMBINATION
Statutory merger	A acquires net assets of B.	A is surviving entity. B goes out of existence.
Statutory consolidation	A and B combine net assets.	A and B go out of existence. New entity, C, is created.
Stock acquisition	A acquires the stock of B.	A and B continue to exist.

Use of the Purchase Method to Record a Merger

As we have seen in previous chapters, any asset acquired by a company should be recorded initially at its cost. Under the purchase method, the same idea holds true. The investor company is simply buying a "basket" of assets. Thus, the individual assets should be recorded on the investor's books at their market value, which represents cost at the time of purchase.

Assume that on January 1, 1998, Alan Corp. purchases the assets and agrees to assume the liabilities of Jackson Inc. for $40 million in cash. Thus, the legal form is a statutory merger. Condensed balance sheets for each of the two companies before the purchase are shown in Exhibit 13-4.

Three amounts are relevant in a business combination accounted for as a purchase:

1. The *cost* or *purchase price*.
2. The *book value* of the net assets (assets minus liabilities) acquired.
3. The *fair value* of the net assets acquired.

In our example, the *purchase price* is $40 million. One of two approaches can be used to find the *book value* of the net assets acquired by Alan. One way is to compute the book value of Jackson's assets minus its liabilities as shown on its balance sheet:

Book value of assets, $10 + $10 + $15	$35
Less: Book value of liabilities, $3 + $7	10
Book value of net assets acquired	$25

According to the accounting equation, assets minus liabilities equal stockholders' equity. Thus, another way to find the book value of a company's net assets is to add the components of Jackson's stockholders' equity on its balance sheet:

Capital stock, $1 par	$ 5
Additional paid-in capital	10
Retained earnings	10
Book value of stockholders' equity	$25

Why did Alan pay $40 million, or $15 million *more* than the book value of $25 million, to acquire the net assets of Jackson? Two explanations are possible. First, the book value of Jackson's assets and liabilities may not be equal to their fair values. Second, not

---

EXHIBIT 13-4	Pre-Merger Balance Sheets for Two Companies

ALAN CORP. AND JACKSON INC.
BALANCE SHEETS
JANUARY 1, 1998
(IN MILLIONS OF DOLLARS)

	ALAN CORP.	JACKSON INC.
Current assets	$300	$10
Land	200	10
Buildings, net of depreciation	300	15
Total assets	$800	$35
Current liabilities	$ 50	$ 3
Bonds payable	200	7
Capital stock, $1 par	100	5
Additional paid-in capital	300	10
Retained earnings	150	10
Total equities	$800	$35

all of Jackson's value as a company may be currently recognized on the balance sheet in the form of assets. Jackson may have some unrecorded assets—such as its reputation, number of years in business, and location—that are valuable assets but are not currently recorded on the books. In addition, the high price could be the result of an old-fashioned bidding war. Accountants refer to the excess of the purchase price for a business over the fair value of its net assets as goodwill.

Recall from Chapter 8 that goodwill exists in most businesses but is normally not recorded because of the difficulty in valuing it. In fact, goodwill is recorded as an asset only when it is purchased, that is, when one company buys another company. In this instance, the accountant records goodwill for the excess of the purchase price of a business over the fair value of the net assets acquired.

As part of the negotiation process, an acquiring company often hires an appraiser to value the assets of the acquired firm. Assume that on the basis of an appraisal, the accountant prepares the following analysis to compare the cost of the net assets purchased from Jackson with the *fair value* of those net assets:

Cost (purchase price)		$40
Fair value of net assets acquired:		
Current assets	10	
Land	15	
Buildings	18	
Current liabilities	(3)	
Bonds payable	(10)*	30
Excess of cost over fair value of net assets acquired (goodwill)		$10

*The bonds' market or fair value differs from their book value because of changes in interest rates. In this case, market rates of interest have gone down since Jackson issued its bonds, making the Jackson bonds relatively more valuable.

According to this analysis, the net assets now recognized on Jackson's books are worth $30 million, even though they are currently recorded on the books at only $25 million. Thus, an excess of fair value over book value explains $5 million of the excess purchase price. The other $10 million is attributable to unrecorded assets, that is, goodwill. The following summarizes these points:

Excess of cost over book value of net assets acquired: $40 − $25	$15
Excess of fair value of net assets over book value: $30 − $25	5
Excess of cost over fair value of net assets acquired (goodwill): $40 − $30	$10

At this point, we will record a journal entry on Alan's books to record the purchase of the other company. The entry is similar to one made to record the acquisition of any asset, although it involves a number of assets, as well as the recognition of the liabilities:

```
1998
Jan. 1   Current Assets                    10 ⎤
         Land                              15 ⎥ 53
         Buildings                         18 ⎥
         Goodwill                          10 ⎦
             Current Liabilities                  3 ⎤ 13
             Bonds Payable                       10 ⎦
             Cash                                40
         To record purchase of Jackson Inc.
```

Assets = Liabilities + Owners' Equity
+53   +13
−40

Note that the assets and liabilities are recorded on Alan's books at their individual fair values. Because the amount of cash paid exceeded the fair value of the net assets acquired, a new intangible asset, labeled Goodwill, is recorded. Goodwill, like other intangible assets, should be amortized over its useful life. According to current accounting standards in the U.S., the maximum amortization period for goodwill is 40 years. Thus, if Alan chooses the maximum write-off period for its goodwill and the method most often used for intangibles, straight-line amortization, it will recognize amortization expense beginning in 1998 equal to $10 million divided by 40 years, or $250,000 per year.

Many analysts and lenders ignore goodwill. They add back the amortization on the income statement to remove its effect. Even though accountants recognize it, these other groups do not because goodwill does not have value as collateral. That is, if a loan goes bad, a lender cannot repossess goodwill.

A balance sheet prepared immediately after the purchase of Jackson by Alan is presented in Exhibit 13-5. Keep in mind that the only surviving entity is Alan. Jackson has gone out of existence and has effectively been merged with Alan. The balance sheet is prepared by posting each of the amounts in the journal entry directly to Alan's accounts. The calculation of the amount of current assets deserves special attention. The balance of $270 million is found by adding Jackson's current assets of $10 million to Alan's current assets of $300 million and deducting the cash of $40 million paid to acquire Jackson. Finally, note the recognition of $10 million of goodwill.

Consolidated Financial Statements

LO 7 Explain when, why, and how consolidated financial statements are prepared.

Many of the financial statements that you use in your career will be consolidated. We now turn our attention to understanding when, why, and how consolidated financial statements are prepared.

When Are Consolidated Financial Statements Prepared?

Consolidated financial statements are prepared when one company *controls* another company. The two companies are legally separate but under common control. Recall our earlier discussion of the three types of business combinations: statutory merger, statutory consolidation, and stock acquisition. Which of these three types of combinations results in the need for consolidated financial statements? The answer is that *only when a business combination is effected as a stock acquisition is there a need for consolidated*

EXHIBIT 13-5 Post-Merger Balance Sheet

ALAN CORP.
BALANCE SHEET
JANUARY 1, 1998
(IN MILLIONS OF DOLLARS)

Current assets	$270
Land	215
Buildings, net of depreciation	318
Goodwill	10
Total assets	$813
Current liabilities	$ 53
Bonds payable	210
Capital stock, $1 par	100
Additional paid-in capital	300
Retained earnings	150
Total equities	$813

statements, because it is the only case in which the two combining entities survive. The two companies continue their separate legal identities, but through ownership of a majority of the stock, one company controls the affairs of the other.

As we described earlier, the company that owns the majority of the stock in another company is called the *parent company.* The company that has a majority of its stock held by another entity is called a *subsidiary.* In today's global environment, many companies have foreign subsidiaries. With national boundaries no longer a constraint, it is not uncommon for a parent to control more than 100 subsidiaries. Although exceptions exist, the normal rule that accountants follow to decide whether a company controls another and should therefore prepare consolidated statements is ownership of more than 50% of the common stock of the other company. Many times the parent owns 100% of the subsidiary's stock, in which case the subsidiary is referred to as a *wholly owned subsidiary.*

Why Are Consolidated Statements Prepared?

Two important accounting concepts justify the preparation of consolidated statements: substance over form and the economic entity concept. Consolidated statements are an example in accounting of *substance over form.* In form, a parent and its subsidiary are separate legal entities. This is the very nature of a stock acquisition. Recall that if a company buys the assets of another company, a merger takes place and only a single entity survives. In a stock acquisition, however, the two companies continue their legal identities. For our purposes, it is equally important to recognize that the two companies continue to keep their own sets of records. That is, for accounting purposes, the companies are kept separate, but in *substance,* the companies are controlled by a single entity, the parent company.

Recall from Chapter 1 the *economic entity concept.* This concept requires that an identifiable, specific entity be the subject of a set of financial statements. In the case of consolidated statements, the parent corporation and its subsidiaries form one identifiable entity under common control.

What Happens in a Stock Acquisition?

To understand a stock acquisition and, eventually, consolidated financial statements, we return to the example of Alan Corp. Assume the same facts in the Alan and Jackson example with one exception: *instead of paying $40 million to buy the assets and assume the liabilities of Jackson, Alan buys all of the shares of Jackson's stock.* As noted in Jackson's balance sheet in Exhibit 13-4, it has $5 million of $1 par value per share stock outstanding for a total of 5 million shares. Thus, if Alan paid $40 million for all of the shares, the purchase price was $8 per share.

Exhibit 13-6 illustrates what happens in a stock acquisition. The key to understanding what happens is understanding who buys the shares and what happens to the prior stockholders. Assume that before the acquisition, three stockholders, A, B, and C, own all of Alan's stock. Similarly, three stockholders, D, E, and F, own all of Jackson's stock. Alan's management, acting on behalf of the corporation's stockholders, goes directly to D, E, and F and buys their 5 million shares of Jackson's stock for $40 million. *The owners of the Jackson stock sell their ownership interests to Alan, and Jackson now has a single stockholder: Alan.* Stockholders D, E, and F have been bought out and are no longer associated with Jackson.

Balance sheets for the two entities immediately *after* the stock acquisition are presented in Exhibit 13-7. Compare these balance sheets with those in Exhibit 13-4, which reflected the financial positions of the two companies before any combination. Alan took $40 million of cash and used it to buy shares of stock in Jackson. Thus, it's balance sheet in Exhibit 13-7 shows a reduction in current assets from $300 million to $260 million and a new asset, Investment in Jackson, for $40 million. Note that Jackson's balance sheets are identical in the two exhibits because the stock acquisition does not directly affect Jackson as an entity. The transaction was between Alan and the stockholders of Jackson.

EXHIBIT 13-6   What Happens in a Stock Acquisition

BEFORE STOCK ACQUISITION:

CORPORATIONS:

Alan Corp.
100 million shares
held by:

Jackson Inc.
5 million shares
held by:

STOCKHOLDERS: A   B   C   D   E   F

STOCK ACQUISITION:
   Alan pays $40 million to stockholders D, E, and F to acquire their stock.

AFTER STOCK ACQUISITION:

CORPORATIONS:

Alan Corp.
100 million shares
held by:

Jackson Inc.
5 million shares
held by:

STOCKHOLDERS: A   B   C   Alan Corp.

Consolidated Balance Sheet

A consolidated balance sheet for Alan Inc. is shown in Exhibit 13-8. Compare this balance sheet to the one shown in Exhibit 13-5. Why are these two balance sheets identical? You will recall that the balance sheet in Exhibit 13-5 reported the financial position of Alan immediately after Jackson had been merged into Alan. *Whether one company is legally merged into the other, as in Exhibit 13-5, or one company controls the other through ownership of its stock, as in Exhibit 13-8, the combined financial position of the two should be the same.*

EXHIBIT 13-7   Post-Stock Acquisition Balance Sheets for Two Companies

ALAN CORP. AND JACKSON INC.
BALANCE SHEETS
JANUARY 1, 1998
(IN MILLIONS OF DOLLARS)

	ALAN CORP.	JACKSON INC.
Current assets	$260	$10
Investment in Jackson	40	0
Land	200	10
Buildings, net of depreciation	300	15
Total assets	$800	$35
Current liabilities	$ 50	$ 3
Bonds payable	200	7
Capital stock, $1 par	100	5
Additional paid-in capital	300	10
Retained earnings	150	10
Total equities	$800	$35

EXHIBIT 13-8   Consolidated Balance Sheet

ALAN CORP. AND SUBSIDIARY
CONSOLIDATED BALANCE SHEET
JANUARY 1, 1998
(IN MILLIONS OF DOLLARS)

Current assets	$270
Land	215
Buildings, net of depreciation	318
Goodwill	10
Total assets	$813
Current liabilities	$ 53
Bonds payable	210
Capital stock, $1 par	100
Additional paid-in capital	300
Retained earnings	150
Total equities	$813

Consolidation involves two steps: aggregation and elimination. *Aggregation* means that similar accounts on the balance sheets of the two companies are added together. For example, Alan's current assets of $260 million are added to Jackson's current assets of $10 million with a result of $270 million on the consolidated balance sheet. Note, however, that land on the consolidated balance sheet in Exhibit 13-8 amounts to $215 million; the individual amounts were $200 million on Alan's books and $10 million on Jackson's books. The additional $5 million is due to the excess of the fair value of Jackson's land over its book value. The same is true of buildings and bonds payable. The amounts on the consolidated balance sheet for Jackson represent fair values rather than book values. Like the post-merger balance sheet, the consolidated balance sheet reflects goodwill of $10 million. This is the excess of the purchase price paid for Jackson over the fair value of its net assets.

In the preparation of consolidated financial statements, *elimination* means that to avoid *double counting,* one must eliminate any *reciprocal* accounts. Reciprocal accounts are opposite but related accounts. In our example, there is one set of reciprocal accounts. The Investment in Jackson account on Alan's books is related to the stockholders' equity accounts on Jackson's books because it represents Alan's interest in the equity of Jackson. Note that neither the investment account from Alan's books nor the stockholders' equity accounts from Jackson's books have been included on the consolidated balance sheet. The investment account is eliminated and replaced with the individual assets and liabilities of Jackson. The stockholders' equity accounts of Jackson are eliminated. Because the owners of Alan own Jackson, only the stockholders' equity accounts for Alan remain on the consolidated balance sheet.

Consolidated work sheets typically contain a number of other types of eliminations. For example, assume that a parent company that manufactures athletic shoes owns a subsidiary that supplies it with rubber for the soles of the shoes. At any point in time, it is likely that the parent company will owe money to the subsidiary on open account. That is, the parent will report Accounts Payable on its separate balance sheet and the subsidiary will report Accounts Receivable. On a consolidated balance sheet, however, neither of these accounts is reported. The reason is that the debt is "in the family." On the consolidated work papers, the intercompany accounts, Accounts Payable and Accounts Receivable, are eliminated.

Consolidated Income Statement

The rationale for all consolidated statements is the same: to report on legally separate entities as if they were one because they are under common control. Thus, the purpose of a consolidated income statement is to report the results of operations for a period of time for a parent and its subsidiaries. The work paper procedures used by the accountant to prepare a consolidated income statement are beyond the scope of this text and are the subject of advanced accounting courses.

For our purposes, it is important to understand that a consolidated income statement combines the revenues and the expenses of the parent and its subsidiaries. For example, sales revenues for the two or more entities are combined and reported as a single amount on the consolidated income statement. Likewise, purchases are added together as one of the components to arrive at cost of goods sold for the two entities. However, recall our example of the athletic shoe manufacturer. The amount bought from the rubber subsidiary is included in the shoemaker's purchases for any one period. Similarly, the subsidiary reports on its own income statement the sales that it made to the parent. For purposes of preparing a consolidated income statement, the purchases from the records of the parent and the sales from the books of the subsidiary must be eliminated. Any other intercompany revenue and expense items are also subject to elimination in the preparation of a consolidated income statement.

What Is Minority Interest?

In certain situations, a parent company may own less than 100% of the stock of a subsidiary. When this is the case, a minority interest exists. Minority interest is that portion of the subsidiary's stockholders' equity that is owned by stockholders other than the parent corporation. For example, assume that a parent company owns 90% of a subsidiary. This means there is a 10% minority interest. Even when a minority interest exists, a consolidated balance sheet reports *all* of the assets under the control of the parent entity. That is, even if only 90% of a subsidiary is owned, 100% of its assets are included on the consolidated balance sheet. It would be artificial to split the assets of the subsidiary as if only part of them were controlled. All of the assets are under the control of the parent.

Turning to the right side of the balance sheet, recall that in preparing a consolidated balance sheet, the accountant eliminates the stockholders' equity of the subsidiary. However, what about that portion of the subsidiary's stockholders' equity that is *not* attributable to the parent but represents the claim of the minority shareholders? This portion of stockholders' equity is not eliminated.

How should minority interest be reported on the right side of a consolidated balance sheet? Some accountants, arguing that minority shareholders are truly outsiders, report minority interest in the liabilities section of the consolidated balance sheet. The difficulty with this argument is that there is no legal obligation or due date for the minority interest. Others, arguing that minority interest represents equity in a portion of the consolidated entity, report it as an element of stockholders' equity. Interestingly, in published financial statements, the theoretical issue of the proper treatment of minority interest is normally avoided by placing it *between* liabilities and stockholders' equity on the consolidated balance sheet. This approach sidesteps the question of whether it is debt or equity.

Many family businesses that go public have minority interests—often it is the public that is in the minority. That is, the family owns most of the stock. Many investors question whether it is a good idea to buy stock in a company that is controlled by a family. Management is more likely to act in the best interests of the family shareholders, and minority shareholders often find it difficult to sell their stock because of the lack of an active market for it.

FROM CONCEPT TO PRACTICE 13.1
READING BEN & JERRY'S FOOTNOTES
Locate the footnote in which the company describes its consolidation policies. What percentage of the stock does Ben & Jerry's own in its subsidiaries? Given the nature of its business, what kinds of subsidiaries would you expect Ben & Jerry's to own?

Accounting for the Global Corporation

U.S. corporations are increasingly looking abroad to expand their business opportunities. In 1995, only 29% of Coca-Cola's revenues were attributable to its U.S. operations. Exhibit 13-9 highlights the importance of foreign markets for a number of companies in the food and beverage business, including Coca-Cola. Note from the exhibit how reliant

| EXHIBIT 13-9 | Reliance of U.S. Companies on Foreign Markets | | |

COMPANY	FOREIGN SALES AS % OF TOTAL SALES	% GROWTH IN FOREIGN SALES	% GROWTH IN U.S. SALES
Coca-Cola Co.	71%	14%	7%
CPC International	66	9	5
Heinz	43	9	8
McDonald's Corp.	54	15	5
Ralston Purina	40	6	–4
Sara Lee	40	16	6

SOURCE: *Standard & Poor's Investment Review and Forecast,* December 1996, p. 2.

each of these companies is on foreign markets for its sales. For all six companies, the growth in foreign sales exceeds the growth in U.S. sales. Certainly the dramatic political changes in Eastern Europe and the former Soviet Union, along with the passage of the North American Free Trade Agreement, have only added to the opportunities abroad for American businesses.

When a company does business internationally, the currency of the local country often becomes an issue. For example, assume that a company purchases inventory from a supplier in Mexico. The agreement is that the U.S. company will pay the Mexican supplier 10,000 pesos for the purchase. How does the U.S. company account for this *foreign currency transaction?* As another example, assume that a U.S. parent owns a subsidiary in France. The French subsidiary keeps its books in the currency of that country, the franc. How does the parent *translate the foreign financial statements* into U.S. dollars before consolidating them with the parent's statements? We now turn to a brief consideration of each of these issues.

Foreign Currency Transactions

To understand how foreign currency transactions are accounted for, you must first understand the meaning of an exchange rate. An exchange rate measures the relative worth of two *different currencies.* Refer to Exhibit 13-10 for the exchange rates published in a recent issue of the *Chicago Tribune.*

As you can see in this excerpt from the newspaper, exchange rates can be stated in one of two ways. The first column—titled "U.S."—represents the number of U.S. dollars, or the fraction of a U.S. dollar, required to buy a particular foreign currency unit. For example, according to the table, on this particular date it would take $.6541 to purchase a

LO 8 Understand how to account for foreign currency transactions.

| EXHIBIT 13-10 | Foreign Exchange Rates |

Foreign exchange Dollar vs. — Yen 111.55 — Pound .63351 — Mark 1.5289

	U.S.	Foreign		U.S.	Foreign
Argentina (Peso)	1.0012	.9988	Israel (Shekel)	.3132	3.1926
Australia (Dollar)	.7909	1.2644	Italy (Lira)	.0007	1520.50
Austria (Schilling)	.0930	10.755	Japan (Yen)	.0090	111.55
Belgium (Franc)	.0317	31.53	Mexico (Peso)	.1294	7.7250
Brazil (Real)	.9751	1.0255	Netherlands (Guilder)	.5827	1.7161
Britain (Pound)	1.5785	.6335	Norway (Krone)	.1540	6.4928
Canada (Dollar)	.7396	1.3521	Poland (Zloty)	.3559	2.81
Denmark (Krone)	.1704	5.8681	Portugal (Escudo)	.0065	154.56
Finland (Mark)	.2191	4.5651	Saudi Arabia (Riyal)	.2667	3.7500
France (Franc)	.1932	5.1770	South Africa (Rand)	.2206	4.5330
Germany (Mark)	.6541	1.5289	Spain (Peseta)	.0078	128.56
Greece (Drachma)	.0042	239.06	Sweden (Krona)	.1519	6.5824
India (Rupee)	.0281	35.650	Switzerland (Franc)	.7984	1.2525
Ireland (Pound)	1.6109	.6208	Venezuela (Bolivar)	.0021	470.000

German mark. Conversely, the second column—titled "Foreign"—represents the number of a particular foreign currency unit required to buy a U.S. dollar. For example, according to the table, it would take 1.5289 German marks to buy a U.S. dollar.

To better understand the meaning of exchange rates, consider the following example. Your rich uncle has just left you $50,000, and you have decided to use the money to purchase a Porsche automobile. A dealer in your hometown will sell you the model you want for $50,000. However, another option is to purchase the car from a dealer in Germany who will sell you the same model for 70,000 German marks. Using the appropriate exchange rate in Exhibit 13-10, should you buy the car locally or buy it from the German dealer?

If you buy the car from the foreign dealer, you will need to go to a bank and buy 70,000 German marks because the German dealer requires that you pay in marks. Assuming an exchange rate of $.6541 per German mark, you will pay $.6541 × 70,000, or $45,787, to buy the required number of marks. However, before you conclude that this is less costly than buying the car locally for $50,000, consider the cost to ship the car from Germany. If the car can be shipped for less than $50,000 − $45,787, or $4,213, it would be to your advantage to buy the car from the German dealer.

ACCOUNTING FOR YOUR DECISIONS

You Are the Purchasing Agent

It is your job to purchase everything from pencils to automobiles for your company. You are getting ready to purchase 100 cars for your comapny's salesforce. You have been watching the relationship of the yen to the dollar lately, and you have noticed that the yen has moved from 100 to 120 to the dollar. Does this make you more or less likely to buy 100 Hondas instead of 100 Fords?

ANS: The yen has weakened in relation to the dollar; more yen are now needed (120) to buy what 100 yen could buy recently. As a result, your dollar has greater purchasing power in Japan. All other things being equal, you may find that you can get a better deal on the Hondas at this time. But the dollar's strength is not necessarily permanent. In four years, when you replace these cars, it could very well be the case that the dollar has weakened, making Japanese cars less desirable.

A foreign currency transaction occurs when a company agrees to either accept payment or make payment in a foreign currency. In other words, if Coca-Cola sells $10,000 of products to a wholesaler in Norway and requires payment in U.S. dollars, there is no foreign currency transaction. Foreign currency transactions arise from a decision to deal in foreign currency. As we will see, this can subject a company to risks.

Consider the following example. On October 15, 1996, a U.S. steel manufacturer, Sturdy Steel, makes a sale to a German automaker. The selling price is 1,000,000 marks, and the terms are net 30. Based on the exchange rate quoted in Exhibit 13-10 for German marks, the entry on Sturdy Steel's books on the date of the sale is as follows:

1996
Oct. 15   Accounts Receivable   654,100
    Sales Revenue   654,100
   To record sale: 1,000,000 marks × .6541

Assets	=	Liabilities	+	Owners' Equity
+654,100				+654,100

Because each mark on this date is worth $.6541, Sturdy records the sale at 1,000,000 marks times $.6541, or a total of $654,100. Now assume that the German automaker pays Sturdy on November 15, 1996. It will be up to Sturdy to take the 1,000,000 marks to a bank or other financial institution that deals in foreign currencies and exchange them for U.S. dollars. Assume that the exchange rate on November 15 has dropped to $.6125. The drop in the rate means that Sturdy will receive only 1,000,000 × $.6125, or $612,500. Because the original sale was recorded at an amount that reflected the higher exchange rate, Sturdy recognizes a loss at the time it collects from the German customer. The entry on Sturdy's books on this date is as follows:

Whereas Whirlpool is constantly striving to build foreign operations, so is The Gap.

1996
Nov. 15   Cash   612,500
   Foreign Exchange Loss   41,600
    Accounts Receivable   654,100
   To record collection on account.

Assets	=	Liabilities	+	Owners' Equity
+612,500				−41,600
−654,100				

The loss represents the decline in value of the asset Accounts Receivable from $654,100 on October 15 to $612,500 when it was collected on November 15. Sturdy has incurred a loss because it was willing to accept foreign currency at a later date. This is one of many different risks faced by companies dealing across national boundaries. Another way to look at the loss is that it represents the decline in value of the mark over the month:

Value of one mark on 10/15/96	$ .6541
Value of one mark on 11/15/96	.6125
Decline in value of the mark	.0416
× Number of marks	1,000,000
Foreign exchange loss	$ 41,600

What if the value of the German mark rose between the time of the sale and the time of collection? In this case, Sturdy records a gain. Foreign exchange gains and losses are normally presented as other revenues and expenses on the income statement.

ACCOUNTING FOR YOUR DECISIONS
Your Business Ships Goods to London

You are the owner of a bookstore and you have received an order to ship books to a customer in London. The customer insists that it be allowed to pay the bill in British pounds and you agree to sell the books for 1,000 pounds. The exchange rate on the date you make the sale is $1.60 per British pound and it rises to $1.65 on the date the customer pays you. What is the amount of your gain or loss from dealing in foreign currency? Explain your answer.

ANS: The rise in the exchange rate results in a gain to you of $50. You would record a receivable on the date of the sale for 1,000 × $1.60 or $1,600. When the customer pays you, however, you are able to receive 1,000 × $1.65 or $1,650 from exchanging the British pounds for dollars. The result is a $50 gain from dealing in foreign currency.

Translation of Foreign Financial Statements

LO 9 Understand how to translate foreign financial statements into U.S. dollars.

Two major issues arise in the translation of foreign financial statements. First, it may be necessary to restate various accounts on the statements of a foreign subsidiary or affiliate to conform with U.S. accounting standards. For example, it is common in other English-speaking countries of the world, such as England, Australia, South Africa, and Canada, to report plant and equipment at an amount in excess of historical cost on the balance sheet. If a U.S. company operates a subsidiary in London, it may need to restate the subsidiary's plant and equipment accounts in historical cost terms if they have been adjusted to reflect current values. This is done before the consolidation of the subsidiary with the U.S. parent.

The second issue concerns the translation of the *amounts* on the other statements. The British subsidiary most likely keeps its records in pounds, not U.S. dollars. Thus, it is necessary to *translate* those statements into U.S. dollars before consolidating them with the statements of the parent. Foreign currency translation is the process of restating the financial statements of a company from one currency to another.

Assume that at the beginning of the year, Mel's Motor City Manufacturing in Detroit opens a wholly owned subsidiary, Windsor Wheels, in Windsor, Canada. Windsor Wheels begins operations with an investment of 250,000 Canadian dollars (CD) from Motor City. All of the capital stock is held by the parent, Motor City, because the subsidiary is wholly owned. After the initial investment, Windsor Wheels buys a new plant for one million CD by signing a five-year, 10% note with a Toronto bank. The plant will be depreciated on a straight-line basis over 20 years. The relevant exchange rates are as follows:

DATE	EXCHANGE RATE PER CANADIAN DOLLAR
Beginning of year	$.80
End of year	$.70
Average for year	$.75

One critical question must be answered before we translate the income statement for the year and the balance sheet at the end of the first year into U.S. dollars: What exchange rate should be used to translate? The answer to this question depends on the functional currency, the currency of the primary economic environment in which the foreign entity operates. For example, if Windsor sells most of its wheels in the United States and remits most of its cash to its parent, Motor City, the U.S. dollar might be designated as the functional currency. It is more common, however, that the functional currency is the local currency of the foreign country. Because this is the case, we focus on situations in which the local currency is the functional currency. The appropriate treatment for situations in which the reporting currency, that is, the U.S. dollar, is the functional currency and for situations in which the foreign entity operates in a highly inflationary economy is covered in advanced accounting courses.

If we assume that the Canadian dollar is the functional currency, the translation process is very straightforward. All *income statement items* are translated using the *average* exchange rate for the year. The rationale for this treatment is that most revenues are earned and most expenses are incurred evenly over the period. An income statement for Windsor Wheels is shown in Exhibit 13-11, in Canadian dollars and translated into U.S. dollars. Note that each item on the income statement is translated using the average exchange rate for the year, $.75 per Canadian dollar. The amounts in U.S. dollars are found by simply multiplying the amount of Canadian dollars times the exchange rate. For example, sales in U.S. dollars of $750,000 are calculated by multiplying 1,000,000 CD times the average exchange rate of $.75 per CD.

The translation of items on a balance sheet is also easy when the local currency of the subsidiary is the functional currency. All *assets and liabilities* are translated using the current rate, meaning the *rate at the end of the year*. A balance sheet for Windsor Wheels, first in Canadian dollars and then translated into U.S. dollars, is presented in Exhibit 13-12. Note that all of the assets and liabilities are translated using the exchange rate at the end of the year. However, common stock is translated to U.S. dollars using the rate at the beginning of the year, when the stock was issued. Measurement of the

---

EXHIBIT 13-11   Translation of a Foreign Income Statement

WINDSOR WHEELS
INCOME STATEMENT
FOR THE FIRST YEAR

ITEMS	CANADIAN DOLLARS	EXCHANGE RATE	U.S. DOLLARS
Sales	1,000,000 CD	.75 per CD	$750,000
Cost of sales	(600,000)	.75	(450,000)
Depreciation	(50,000)	.75	(37,500)
Interest expense	(40,000)	.75	(30,000)
Other expenses	(60,000)	.75	(45,000)
Net income	250,000 CD		$187,500

EXHIBIT 13-12 Translation of a Foreign Balance Sheet

WINDSOR WHEELS
BALANCE SHEET
AT THE END OF THE FIRST YEAR

ITEMS	CANADIAN DOLLARS	EXCHANGE RATE	U.S. DOLLARS
Cash	200,000 CD	$.70 per CD	$ 140,000
Accounts receivable	450,000	.70	315,000
Inventory	200,000	.70	140,000
Plant, net	950,000	.70	665,000
Totals	1,800,000 CD		$1,260,000
Current liabilities	300,000 CD	$.70	$ 210,000
Notes payable	1,000,000	.70	700,000
Common stock	250,000	.80	200,000
Retained earnings	250,000		187,500
Totals	1,800,000 CD		
Translation adjustment			(37,500)
Totals			$1,260,000

original contributed capital of the foreign entity using the rate when the stock was first issued, that is, the historical exchange rate, provides a base, and this rate is used in the translation of all subsequent balance sheets. Also, note that an exchange rate is not used to translate retained earnings. Because this is a new business and because the subsidiary paid no dividends in the first year, retained earnings at year-end in U.S. dollars is simply the net income for the first year, $187,500.

How should the reader of the financial statements interpret the **translation adjustment?** The translation adjustment is the amount needed to balance the two sides of the balance sheet. For Windsor Wheels, it is calculated as follows:

Assets	$1,260,000
Liabilities, common stock, and retained earnings	$1,297,500
Negative translation adjustment	$ (37,500)

In this particular case, the adjustment is a negative amount because the value of the Canadian dollar relative to the value of the U.S. dollar decreased during the period from $.80 at the beginning of the year to $.70 at the end of the year. The amount is not considered to be realized in any sense, however. The investment in the subsidiary is not being sold. There are presently no *cash flow* implications from the decrease in the exchange rate during the period. Thus, the negative translation adjustment appears in stockholders' equity as a contra account. Note that a positive translation adjustment would appear at the end of the first year if the exchange rate had gone up during the period instead of down.

Reporting Requirements for Segments of a Business

Earlier in the chapter, we focused on the need for consolidated financial statements when two or more entities are under common control. We described the process of preparing consolidated statements as being one of *aggregation*. The problem with aggregation, however, is that it can make judging the performance and financial position of the various segments of the business difficult. Users of financial statements,

LO 10 Describe the reporting requirements for segments of a business.

particularly investors and creditors, find it useful at times to assess the individual *segments* of the business. Current accounting standards require a company to present *supplementary* information about its segments in the company's footnotes. Essentially, the reporting requirements require a reverse process from consolidation, that is, a *disaggregation* of the operations and financial position of a business.

Accounting standards require four areas of disclosure, related to the following elements of a company:

1. Operations in different industries.
2. Operations in foreign countries.
3. Major customers.
4. Export sales.

The accounting standards in this area are quite detailed. If certain criteria are met that deal with how significant an industry, a foreign segment, a major customer, or export sales are to a business, certain disclosures are required. For example, the following disclosures appear in the footnotes or in a separate schedule for a company that has significant operations in more than one *industry*. For each reportable industry, the following segment disclosures are required:

1. Revenues.
2. Operating profit or loss.
3. Carrying value of the assets.
4. Depreciation, depletion, and amortization.
5. Capital expenditures.

In addition to disclosures about industry segments, *geographic* segmentation may be required. Companies with significant foreign operations are required to disclose the first three items noted above: revenues, operating profit or loss, and carrying value of assets, each by geographic segment. The grouping of foreign operations by countries is left to the accountant's discretion. For example, it is common to report on operations by continents: Europe, Asia, South America, and so forth. In addition, a company with a significant amount of export sales (sales generated in this country, with the product shipped outside the United States) is required to disclose the amount of these sales.

Finally, disclosures are required when a company relies on any one or a number of its customers to a significant extent. The accounting standards require a disclosure if 10% or more of revenue is derived from sales to any single customer. The amount of revenue from each such customer must also be disclosed. The need for this type of information is obvious; it is important for investors and creditors to be aware of an entity's reliance on any single customer in the event that the customer experiences financial difficulties.

Many analysts find segment information to be among the most useful in the financial statements. Many companies would rather not disclose details about their various divisions because they don't want their competition to find out key information about them. Nonetheless, many investors prefer to place values on parts of the enterprise, and the fate of the stock price is affected if one of these parts is sold or discontinued.

FROM CONCEPT TO PRACTICE 13.2
READING BEN & JERRY'S FOOTNOTES
Who does Ben & Jerry's disclose as a significant customer? How reliant is Ben & Jerry's on this customer for business? Would this concern you as a Ben & Jerry's stockholder?

ACCOUNTING FOR YOUR DECISIONS
Your Investment Club Looks to You

You belong to an investment club and the group is considering buying stock in a contractor that builds highways around the United States. Which of the four areas of segment disclosure would be of most interest to you and why?

ANS: You would be most interested in the major customer disclosures. A reading of this information would give you an understanding of how reliant the company is on contracts with any one customer such as a state agency or an agency of the federal government. The more reliant the contractor is on any one customer the riskier will be your investment.

At the beginning of this chapter, we introduced Whirlpool Corporation. We asked a number of questions about how it should account for and report on its global operations. We now look at the answers to these questions by reviewing the company's 1995 annual report.

Business Acquisitions

The second footnote in Whirlpool's annual report is entitled "Business Acquisitions and Dispositions." This footnote describes all significant acquisitions and dispositions of other businesses in recent years. One paragraph is devoted to a description of the way Whirlpool acquired its original interest in one of its Chinese subsidiaries:

> In November 1995, the Company acquired a majority interest in Raybo Air Conditioner Manufacturing Company, a Chinese manufacturer and marketer of air conditioners, for about $22 million in cash. Raybo annual sales were about $20 million for its fiscal year 1994.[4]

The following points can be made by relating this footnote to items discussed in the chapter:

1. Because Whirlpool acquired Raybo Air by a payment of cash, the combination was accounted for as a *purchase* rather than a pooling of interests. This fact is referred to later in the same footnote: "The acquisitions have been accounted for as purchases and their operating results have been consolidated with the Company's results since the date of acquisition."[5]

2. Goodwill is included on Whirlpool's consolidated balance sheet in Exhibit 13-13 under the account title Intangibles, net. Included in the footnotes is a description of how the company amortizes its goodwill that arises from paying for other businesses in amounts that exceed the value of the net assets acquired:

> Intangibles: The cost of business acquisitions in excess of net tangible assets acquired is amortized on a straight-line basis principally over 40 years. Non-compete agreements are amortized on a straight-line basis over the terms of the agreement. Accumulated amortization aggregated $162 million at December 31, 1995 and $124 million at December 31, 1994.[6]

Thus, we see that Whirlpool uses a *straight-line* approach to writing off goodwill and that it uses the maximum write-off period allowed by accounting rules, 40 years.

Consolidations

Whirlpool's first footnote describes its consolidation policies:

> *Principles of Consolidation:* The consolidated financial statements include all majority-owned subsidiaries. Investments in affiliated companies are accounted for by the equity method. Intercompany transactions and amounts between Whirlpool Corporation and WFC included in the supplemental consolidating data have been eliminated in the consolidated financial statements. The eliminations relate primarily to intercompany financing, interest and leasing transactions.[7]

Before 1988, companies had more latitude than they have now in deciding which subsidiaries to report on a consolidated basis. For example, many companies chose not to consolidate subsidiaries that were in a completely different type of business.

[4]*Whirlpool Corporation Annual Report,* 1995, p. 43.
[5]*Whirlpool Corporation Annual Report,* 1995, p. 43.
[6]*Whirlpool Corporation Annual Report,* 1995, p. 42.
[7]*Whirlpool Corporation Annual Report,* 1995, p. 42.

EXHIBIT 13-13 Whirlpool's Balance Sheets

1995 | CONSOLIDATED BALANCE SHEETS

■ Supplemental data allows reader to look at two types of businesses separately

Supplemental Consolidating Data

December 31 (millions of dollars)	Whirlpool Corporation (Consolidated)		Whirlpool with WFC on an Equity Basis		Whirlpool Financial Corporation (WFC)	
	– 1995 –	– 1994 –	– 1995 –	– 1994 –	– 1995 –	– 1994 –
ASSETS						
Current Assets						
Cash and equivalents	$ 149	$ 72	$ 125	$ 51	$ 24	$ 21
Trade receivables, less allowances of $39 in 1995 and $38 in 1994	1,031	1,001	1,031	1,001	–	–
Financing receivables and leases, less allowances	1,086	866	–	–	1,086	866
Inventories	1,029	838	1,029	838	–	–
Prepaid expenses and other	152	197	141	183	11	14
Deferred income taxes	94	104	94	104	–	–
Total Current Assets	3,541	3,078	2,420	2,177	1,121	901
Other Assets						
Investment in affiliated companies	425	370	425	370	–	–
Investment in WFC	–	–	269	253	–	–
Financing receivables and leases, less allowances	772	717	–	–	772	717
Intangibles, net	931	730	931	730	–	–
Deferred income taxes	153	171	153	171	–	–
Other	199	149	199	149	–	–
	2,480	2,137	1,977	1,673	772	717
Property, Plant and Equipment						
Land	97	73	97	73	–	–
Buildings	710	610	710	610	–	–
Machinery and equipment	2,855	2,418	2,831	2,392	24	26
Accumulated depreciation	(1,883)	(1,661)	(1,867)	(1,645)	(16)	(16)
	1,779	1,440	1,771	1,430	8	10
Total Assets	$7,800	$6,655	$6,168	$5,280	$1,901	$1,628

Whirlpool Financial Corporation (WFC) is a good example. Its primary business is loaning money. The main business of the parent, of course, is making and selling appliances. Beginning in 1988, however, the accounting profession ruled that virtually all subsidiaries should be consolidated, regardless of the industry in which they operate.

This change in accounting rules to require consolidation of virtually all subsidiaries has been controversial. A company such as Whirlpool or General Motors, with relatively low debt, is forced to add the liabilities of a financial subsidiary, which has huge "liabilities" but in a different sense of the word. Think of a bank's deposits. Those are liabilities under this definition, as are similar obligations of finance companies. As we will see, the change in accounting rules has led Whirlpool and many other companies to add additional disclosures.

Refer back to Whirlpool's two-year comparative balance sheets in Exhibit 13-13. You will see that in addition to the first two columns, which show the consolidated financial position of the company at the end of the two years, two additional sets of columns appear. The heading over both of these sets of columns indicates that this information is "supplemental consolidating data." Management's Discussion and Analysis provides an explanation for this additional information:

EXHIBIT 13-13   continued

■ **Supplemental data allows reader to look at two types of businesses separately**

Supplemental Consolidating Data

December 31 (millions of dollars)	Whirlpool Corporation (Consolidated)		Whirlpool with WFC on an Equity Basis		Whirlpool Financial Corporation (WFC)	
	– 1995 –	– 1994 –	– 1995 –	– 1994 –	– 1995 –	– 1994 –
LIABILITIES AND STOCKHOLDERS' EQUITY						
<ins>Current Liabilities</ins>						
Notes payable	$ 1,939	$ 1,162	$ 709	$ 226	$ 1,230	$ 936
Accounts payable	977	843	896	795	81	48
Employee compensation	232	201	222	192	10	9
Accrued expenses	552	629	552	620	–	9
Restructuring costs	70	114	70	112	–	2
Current maturities of long-term debt	59	39	56	36	3	3
Total Current Liabilities	**3,829**	**2,988**	**2,505**	**1,981**	**1,324**	**1,007**
<ins>Other Liabilities</ins>						
Deferred income taxes	234	221	114	110	120	111
Postemployment benefits	517	481	517	481	–	–
Other liabilities	181	262	181	262	–	–
Long-term debt	983	885	870	703	113	182
	1,915	1,849	1,682	1,556	233	293
<ins>Minority Interests</ins>	179	95	104	20	75	75
<ins>Stockholders' Equity</ins>						
Common stock, $1 par value: 250 million shares authorized, 81 million and 80 million shares issued in 1995 and 1994	81	80	81	80	8	8
Paid-in capital	229	214	229	214	26	26
Retained earnings	1,863	1,754	1,863	1,754	234	220
Unearned restricted stock	(8)	(8)	(8)	(8)	–	–
Cumulative translation adjustments	(53)	(93)	(53)	(93)	1	(1)
Treasury stock – 6 million shares at cost in 1995 and 1994	(235)	(224)	(235)	(224)	–	–
	1,877	1,723	1,877	1,723	269	253
Total Liabilities and Stockholders' Equity	**$7,800**	**$6,655**	**$6,168**	**$5,280**	**$1,901**	**$1,628**

See notes to consolidated financial statements

The accompanying consolidated financial statements include supplemental consolidating data reflecting the Company's investment in Whirlpool Financial Corporation ("WFC") on an equity basis rather than as a consolidated subsidiary. Management believes this presentation provides more meaningful information about the major home appliance and financial services businesses.[8]

Whirlpool believes that it is more meaningful to look at the financial statements for its home appliance business separately from those for its finance subsidiary. *Thus, it has complied with the accounting rules by including all subsidiaries on a consolidated basis in the first set of columns but has added the other two sets of columns to allow the reader to look at the two types of businesses separately.*

Whirlpool with WFC on an Equity Basis   The purpose of this balance sheet is to show the financial position of the parent and all subsidiaries on a consolidated basis, with the exception of the financial subsidiary. This allows the reader to focus attention on the part of the business that makes and sells appliances. Note that this results in the need to report Investment in WFC as an asset ($269 million at the end of 1995). This

[8]*Whirlpool Corporation Annual Report,* 1995, p. 30.

asset appears when WFC is reported on the equity basis (the middle columns) but not when it is consolidated (the first set of columns). In this case, the investment account has been eliminated.

Whirlpool Financial Corporation (WFC) The purpose of the last two columns is to report the financial position of the financial services subsidiary. Note the *types* of assets and liabilities that both appear and do not appear:

Financing Receivables and Leases When Whirlpool sells an appliance, it often allows the customer to pay for the purchase over time. The amounts due from customers within the next year are classified as current assets, and all other amounts are classified as other assets. Note that financing receivables and leases relate entirely to Whirlpool Financial Corporation. When the financing subsidiary is put on an equity basis in the middle columns, nothing appears on the line for financing receivables and leases because the parent corporation itself does not have any of these assets.

Property, Plant, and Equipment Note in the last two columns that WFC has no land or buildings and that the amount of net machinery and equipment is insignificant ($8 million compared with total assets of $1,901 million).

Notes Payable In contrast, a majority of the consolidated notes payable shown as the first item under current liabilities is attributable to the financing subsidiary. In fact, at the end of 1995, of the consolidated notes payable of $1,939 million, $1,230 million was owed by WFC.

Consolidated Income Statement As it did for the balance sheets, Whirlpool presents three different income statements for each of the two years, as shown in Exhibit 13-14. The advantages to the reader of this presentation are apparent by focusing on the revenues. Note on the first line of the income statements that *all* of the corporation's net sales are attributable to the parent and subsidiaries other than WFC. Conversely, all of the company's revenues from financial services on the second line were earned by the financial subsidiary. The revenue for WFC of $219 million in 1995 is higher than the consolidated revenue of $184 million because a small portion of WFC's revenue was intercompany. As we saw earlier, in the consolidation footnote, intercompany amounts have been eliminated in the consolidated data.

It is also informative to note the treatment given to the operations of the financing subsidiary when it is reported on an equity basis (the middle columns of Exhibit 13-14). As we saw earlier, WFC's specific revenues and expenses are not reported individually when it is reported on an equity basis. This allows the reader to focus attention instead on the revenues and expenses related to making and selling appliances. Instead, the profitability of the subsidiary is summarized on a single line, Equity in WFC. Finally, note that this same amount, $14 million of equity in WFC in 1995, can be traced back to the income statement of the subsidiary in the third set of columns.

FROM CONCEPT TO PRACTICE 13.3
READING WHIRLPOOL'S BALANCE SHEET
Refer to Whirlpool's 1995 consolidated balance sheet in Exhibit 13-13. How does Whirlpool classify its minority interests? What is the amount of minority interests at December 31, 1995?

Investments in Affiliates

As mentioned in the consolidation footnote, Whirlpool uses the equity method to account for investments in affiliates. These are the domestic and foreign companies in which Whirlpool holds between 20% and 50% of the common stock and thus exerts significant influence. Referring back to the consolidated balance sheets in Exhibit 13-13, you will note that Whirlpool reports an investment in affiliated companies of $425 million at the end of 1995. Why did this investment increase from a balance of $370 million at the end of 1994? The increase represents Whirlpool's share of the income reported by its affiliates, less any dividends declared by the affiliates.

Translation Adjustments

Many of Whirlpool's subsidiaries and affiliates are located in foreign countries. Whirlpool has to translate the statements for the subsidiaries from the local currency into U.S. dollars before consolidation. As we noted earlier, translation adjustments result from the

EXHIBIT 13-14 | Whirlpool's Income Statements

1995 | CONSOLIDATED STATEMENTS OF EARNINGS

	Whirlpool Corporation (Consolidated)			Whirlpool with WFC on an Equity Basis			Whirlpool Financial Corporation (WFC)		
Year ended December 31 (millions of dollars except per share data)	– 1995 –	– 1994 –	– 1993 –	– 1995 –	– 1994 –	– 1993 –	– 1995 –	– 1994 –	–1993 –
Revenues									
Net sales	$8,163	$7,949	$7,368	$8,163	$7,949	$7,368	$ –	$ –	$ –
Financial services	184	155	165	–	–	–	219	184	193
	8,347	8,104	7,533	8,163	7,949	7,368	219	184	193
Expenses									
Cost of products sold	6,245	5,952	5,503	6,245	5,952	5,503	–	–	–
Selling and administrative	1,609	1,490	1,433	1,521	1,415	1,305	123	104	155
Financial services interest	66	51	59	–	–	–	79	63	72
Intangible amortization	31	24	25	31	24	25	–	–	–
Gain on dispositions	–	(60)	–	–	(60)	–	–	–	–
Restructuring costs	–	250	31	–	248	31	–	2	–
	7,951	7,707	7,051	7,797	7,579	6,864	202	169	227
Operating Profit (Loss)	396	397	482	366	370	504	17	15	(34)
Other Income (Expense)									
Interest and sundry	(13)	9	6	(23)	3	19	11	8	(9)
Interest expense	(141)	(114)	(113)	(129)	(104)	(105)	–	–	–
Earnings (Loss) Before Income Taxes, Other Items and Accounting Change	242	292	375	214	269	418	28	23	(43)
Income taxes	100	176	148	90	169	167	10	7	(19)
Earnings (Loss) Before Equity Earnings, Minority Interests and Accounting Change	142	116	227	124	100	251	18	16	(24)
Equity in WFC	–	–	–	14	11	(28)	–	–	–
Equity in affiliated companies	72	59	16	72	59	16	–	–	–
Minority interests	(5)	(17)	(12)	(1)	(12)	(10)	(4)	(5)	(2)
Net Earnings (Loss) Before Cumulative Effect of Accounting Change	209	158	231	209	158	229	14	11	(26)
Cumulative effect of accounting change for postretirement benefits	–	–	(180)	–	–	(178)	–	–	(2)
Net Earnings (Loss)	$ 209	$ 158	$ 51	$ 209	$ 158	$ 51	$ 14	$ 11	$ (28)
Per share of common stock:									
Primary earnings before accounting change	$ 2.80	$ 2.10	$ 3.19						
Primary earnings	$ 2.80	$ 2.10	$ 0.67						
Fully diluted earnings before accounting change	$ 2.76	$ 2.09	$ 3.11						
Fully diluted earnings	$ 2.76	$ 2.09	$ 0.67						
Cash dividends	$ 1.36	$ 1.22	$ 1.19						
Average number of common shares outstanding (millions)	74.8	75.5	72.3						

See notes to consolidated financial statements

translation of the various assets and liabilities at current exchange rates and the stockholders' equity at historical exchange rates. Because these adjustments result merely from the translation process, they are not included on the income statement but instead are reported in the stockholders' equity section of the balance sheet.

Note on the consolidated balance sheets in Exhibit 13-13 that the *negative* cumulative translation adjustment decreased from $93 million at the end of 1994 to $53 million at the end of 1995. Recall the negative amount for the translation adjustment in our earlier example in the chapter for Windsor Wheels. A negative adjustment indicates that over time the value of the foreign currency units has *decreased* relative to the value of the dollar. The negative translation adjustment for Whirlpool indicates a decrease over time in the value of the foreign currency. The decrease in this account during 1995, however, tells the reader that the foreign currency units have actually increased in value relative to the dollar during the year. Although the translation adjustment is not reflected on the income statement, it is still important information. Recall from our earlier discussion that any cash flow implications from the translation adjustment arise only if the foreign entity is sold.

EXHIBIT 13-15   Whirlpool's Geographic Segment Disclosures

(15) BUSINESS SEGMENT INFORMATION

Geographic Segments - Major Home Appliances

(millions of dollars)	North America	Europe	Other and (Eliminations)	Major Home Appliances
Net sales				
1995	$5,093	$2,502	$ 568	$8,163
1994	$5,048	$2,451	$ 450	$7,949
1993	$4,547	$2,410	$ 411	$7,368
Operating profit				
1995	$ 314	$ 90	$ (38)	$ 366
1994	$ 311	$ 43	$ 16	$ 370
1993	$ 341	$ 129	$ 34	$ 504
Identifiable assets				
1995	$2,031	$2,104	$2,033	$6,168
1994	$2,046	$1,824	$1,410	$5,280
1993	$1,742	$1,758	$1,154	$4,654
Depreciation expense				
1995	$ 140	$ 105	$ 8	$ 253
1994	$ 141	$ 98	$ 4	$ 243
1993	$ 137	$ 101	$ 1	$ 239
Net capital expenditures				
1995	$ 262	$ 186	$ 29	$ 477
1994	$ 269	$ 135	$ 12	$ 416
1993	$ 188	$ 116	$ 3	$ 307

Segmental Disclosures

Whirlpool reports on its geographic segments in a footnote to the financial statements. (Because financial services are insignificant relative to Whirlpool's primary, home appliance business, it is not required to disclose details on an industry basis.) The schedule for this presentation is shown in Exhibit 13-15. Whirlpool reports on two major geographic markets: North America and Europe. The geographic information tells the reader that Whirlpool relies on its European operations for a very significant share of its sales and operating profits.

Whirlpool operates in two primary industry segments: major home appliances and financial services. Information concerning the two segments can be found by referring to the consolidated balance sheets and income statements in Exhibits 13-13 and 13-14, respectively. Financial services generates a very insignificant amount of the consolidated revenues and operating profits, but the identifiable assets of this segment are more significant, due mainly to the large amounts of receivables on the balance sheet of Whirlpool Financial Corporation. Many investment analysts do not look at the consolidated totals because they believe that the finance subsidiary's receivables and payables are a distortion. That is why the company has chosen to present the finance subsidiary using the equity method in addition to the required method.

Finally, recall the accounting rule that requires a company to disclose information about any customer that it relies on for a significant amount of its sales. The same footnote that provides Whirlpool's information on geographic segments includes the following statement:

ISSUES FOR THE GLOBAL CORPORATION: WENDY'S GOES GLOBAL

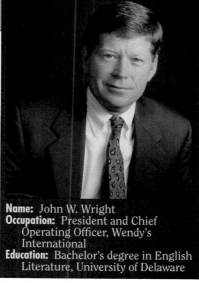

Name: John W. Wright
Occupation: President and Chief Operating Officer, Wendy's International
Education: Bachelor's degree in English Literature, University of Delaware

As the head of Wendy's international division, John Wright spends a good deal of his time on airplanes and poring over financial information from the company's restaurants all over the world. By and large, American fast food is pretty much accepted worldwide. Wendy's can thank archrival McDonald's for that. But competing with McDonald's anywhere is tough, considering that Wendy's total size and financial resources are just a fraction as large. For Wendy's, international sales are still only 10% of the total. But that's where the growth opportunities are, particularly in the emerging markets of Latin America and Asia. Wright's goal is to open 150 restaurants per year outside the United States, and to get into new countries such as Australia and Malaysia. He reviews the weekly sales report by restaurant, by country, in U.S. dollar terms and in local currency terms. He also sees a report that emphasizes sales and earnings growth by country. How is Mexico performing this week? What about Argentina, or New Zealand? "We do a lot of acquisitions of individual restaurants, so I spend a lot of my time on balance sheet analysis," says Wright, who spent 13 years with PepsiCo. On the cost side, Wright is constantly examining food costs, labor staffing or leasing arrangements. "We look at every element of the income statement to see if we need to take some sort of action."

For Wright, focusing on international performance means making sure the accounting data from each location can be made comparable. "Each restaurant is free to use whatever financial reporting system is appropriate for their local countries," says Wright, whose staff converts the data into a format that makes it easier to analyze.

Each country presents unique challenges. In Argentina, the government levies a 21% "valued-added tax," a form of sales tax on manufactured items. "When we're building a new restaurant, the equipment alone could cost $300,000. A 21% tax on top of that is a cash flow drain," says Wright. Another restriction: In Argentina, leases are limited to ten years, "so we can't depreciate an item for any longer than that, which knocks down net income. . . . If sales are flat in a particular country, then we might take another look at their marketing strategy," he says. That examination might include the advertising plan. Or perhaps the restaurant's pricing isn't aggressive enough to compete. For instance, he's noticed that customers are much more price sensitive in the Philippines than they are in Argentina. It is Wright's role to make sure Wendy's responds to these global challenges while maintaining its growth goals.

Sales activity with Sears, Roebuck and Co., a North American major home appliance retailer, represented 20% of consolidated net sales in 1995 and 19% in 1994 and 1993. Related receivables were 14% and 16% of consolidated trade receivables at December 31, 1995 and 1994.[9]

[9]Whirlpool Corporation Annual Report, 1995, p. 55.

Review Problem

Cubs Corp. is a large, diversified company. On January 1, 1998, Cubs entered into two transactions:

a. Cubs paid $750,000 to acquire all of the assets and assume all of the debts of Cardinals Inc. After the purchase, Cardinals will cease to exist as an entity. The following condensed balance sheet was available for Cardinals on this date:

Current assets	$150,000	Current liabilities	$ 50,000
Land	100,000	Long-term debt	250,000
Plant and equipment	350,000	Capital stock	100,000
		Retained earnings	200,000
Total	$600,000	Total	$600,000

All of these amounts represent fair values with the exception of the land and the plant and equipment, which were appraised at $200,000 and $500,000, respectively, on January 1, 1998.

b. Cubs paid the market price to acquire 3,000 shares of the common stock of Mets Inc. On this date Mets had 10,000 shares of stock outstanding, trading on the market at $25 per share. During 1998 Mets reported net income of $90,000 and declared and paid dividends of $40,000.

Required

1. What is the legal form of the business combination with Cardinals Inc.? Explain your answer.

2. Compute the amount of goodwill arising from the purchase of Cardinals.

3. Prepare the entry on Cubs' books on January 1, 1998, to record the purchase of Cardinals.

4. Prepare the entry on Cubs' books on January 1, 1998, to record the purchase of shares of stock of Mets Inc.

5. Prepare the entries on Cubs' books at the end of 1998 to account for its investment in Mets.

Solution to Review Problem

1. The business combination with Cardinals is a statutory merger because Cubs is purchasing the assets and assuming the debts of the other company. Cardinals will cease to exist and thus is being merged into Cubs.

2. Computation of goodwill:

Cost		$750,000
Fair value of net assets acquired:		
Current assets	$150,000	
Land	200,000	
Plant and equipment	500,000	
Current liabilities	(50,000)	
Long-term debt	(250,000)	550,000
Excess of cost over fair value of net assets acquired (goodwill)		$200,000

3. Entry on Cubs' books to record merger of Cardinals:

1998			
Jan. 1	Current Assets	150,000	
	Land	200,000	
	Plant and Equipment	500,000	
	Goodwill	200,000	
	Current Liabilities		50,000
	Long-Term Debt		250,000
	Cash		750,000
	To record purchase of Cardinals Inc.		

(1,050,000 debit total grouped for Current Assets, Land, Plant and Equipment, Goodwill; 300,000 grouped for Current Liabilities and Long-Term Debt)

Assets	=	**Liabilities**	+	**Owners' Equity**
+1,050,000		+300,000		
−750,000				

4. Entry to record purchase of shares of stock of Mets:

1998			
Jan. 1	Long-Term Investment	75,000	
	Cash		75,000
	To record purchase of 3,000 shares of stock at $25 per share.		

```
Assets   =  Liabilities  +  Owners' Equity
+75,000
−75,000
```

5. Entries at the end of the first year:

1998
Dec. 31   Long-Term Investment   27,000
              Equity Income   27,000
              To record share of income of investee:
                 (3,000/10,000) × $90,000 = .3 × $90,000

```
Assets   =  Liabilities  +  Owners' Equity
+27,000                        +27,000
```

1998
Dec. 31   Cash   12,000
              Long-Term Investment   12,000
              To record share of dividends paid by investee:
                 .3 × $40,000

```
Assets   =  Liabilities  +  Owners' Equity
+12,000
−12,000
```

Chapter Highlights

1. [LO 1] Corporations invest for various reasons in the debt and equity securities of other companies. Some investments are made without the intention of influencing or controlling the other company. Accountants classify these investments as either held-to-maturity securities, trading securities, or available-for-sale securities. Other investments are made to exert significant influence over the policies of the other companies. The equity method is used in these instances. Finally, companies may buy enough of the common stock of another company to control it. This situation normally results in the presentation of consolidated financial statements.

2. [LO 2] Held-to-maturity securities are bonds that are purchased with the intention of holding them until they mature. The principles that govern the accounting by the issuer of bonds apply as well to an investor in bonds. The amortized cost method results in the recognition of periodic interest income and the amortization of any premium or discount over the remaining life of the bonds.

3. [LO 3] Trading securities are stocks and bonds held for the short term with the intention of profiting from appreciation in their trading price. Dividends received are recognized as income. Trading securities are adjusted to their fair value at the end of each period, and any increase or decrease in value is reported on the income statement.

4. [LO 4] Available-for-sale securities are investments that are not classified as either held-to-maturity or trading securities. The accounting and reporting requirements for this category are similar to the rules for trading securities. The primary difference is that unrealized gains and losses from holding available-for-sale securities (changes in fair value from one period to the next) are not recognized on the income statement. Instead, these amounts are reported as a separate component of stockholders' equity.

5. [LO 5] The equity method of accounting is used when an investment in the common stock of another company allows the investor to exert significant influence over the investee. The general rule is that the method should be used when the investor owns at least 20% of the common stock of the investee. Under the equity method, the investor recognizes as income its proportionate share of the income of the investee. Dividends received from the investee reduce the investment account.

6. [LO 6] Corporations combine for many reasons. Three different legal forms of combination are possible. In a statutory merger, one company goes out of existence, and in a statutory consolidation, both combining entities cease to exist and are replaced by a new entity. In a stock acquisition, one company buys the stock of the other, and both entities survive. Regardless of the legal form, one of two different accounting methods is used to record a business combination. A pooling of interests is used in limited situations in which shares of stock in the two companies are exchanged. The purchase method is used when one company acquires another through cash, other assets, or debt. In a purchase, all assets and liabilities are recorded at their fair values. Goodwill is recognized for the excess of the purchase price over the fair value of the net assets acquired.

7. **LO 7** When two companies combine by means of a stock acquisition, both survive the combination even though one company controls the other. Because of this control, consolidated statements are prepared to report on the two entities as if they were one. Consolidated financial statements are prepared to reflect the combined position and results of operations for a parent and its subsidiaries. Any intercompany transactions are eliminated in the consolidation process.

8. **LO 8** A foreign currency transaction is one that is billed in a foreign currency. When a company agrees either to accept or to make payment in a foreign currency at a later date, it will recognize a gain or a loss if the exchange rate changes between the time of the original transaction and the settlement date.

9. **LO 9** Before consolidation, financial statements for a foreign subsidiary must be restated to conform to accounting standards in the United States if any differences exist. After this, the statements must be translated from the local currency into the reporting currency, the U.S. dollar. Assuming that the local currency is the functional currency, income statement items are translated using the average exchange rate for the period. Assets and liabilities are translated using the exchange rate at the end of the period. A translation adjustment results from this process and is reported in stockholders' equity.

10. **LO 10** Many companies are required to disclose supplementary information in their annual report for their operations in different industries and in different geographic markets. The purpose of these disclosures is to allow the user of consolidated financial statements to analyze the various segments of the business on a disaggregated basis. Disclosures about major customers and significant export sales are also required.

Key Terms Quiz

Read each definition below and then write the number of that definition in the blank beside the appropriate term it defines. The solution appears at the end of the chapter.

___ Subsidiary
___ Wholly owned subsidiary
___ Debt security
___ Equity method
___ Held-to-maturity securities
___ Available-for-sale securities
___ Horizontal combination
___ Conglomerate
___ Statutory consolidation
___ Purchase method
___ Goodwill
___ Exchange rate
___ Foreign currency translation
___ Translation adjustment

___ Parent
___ Affiliate
___ Equity security
___ Consolidated financial statements
___ Trading securities
___ Amortized cost method
___ Vertical combination
___ Statutory merger
___ Stock acquisition
___ Pooling of interests method
___ Minority interest
___ Foreign currency transaction
___ Functional currency

1. A combination of a company and either a supplier or a customer.

2. In recording a business combination, an accounting approach that is used when one company uses cash, other assets, or debt to acquire the other company.

3. A business combination in which a new entity is created to carry on the activities of the entities involved in the combination.

4. A security issued by a corporation as a form of borrowing.

5. A method of accounting for investments in which income is recognized as a proportionate share of the income of the investee.

6. A combination of companies with operations in different industries.

7. A security that represents a form of ownership in a corporation.

8. A separate legal entity controlled by another entity.

9. A company that has enough of its stock held by another company to give the other entity significant influence over it.

10. A business combination in which only one of the two entities survives.

11. A subsidiary in which the parent owns all of the common stock.

12. A business combination in which one company acquires a majority of the common stock of the other company.

13. The amount needed to balance the two sides of a balance sheet when financial statements are translated from one currency into another currency.

14. The process of restating the financial statements of a company from one currency to another.

15. In recording a business combination, an accounting approach that is sometimes used when shares of stock in the two companies are exchanged.

16. A method of accounting for investments in bonds in which the investment account is adjusted periodically to recognize the amortization of premium or discount.

17. A subsidiary's owners' equity not attributable to the interest of the parent.

18. An entity that controls another entity by ownership of a majority of the other company's common stock.

19. Other companies' stocks and bonds bought and held for the purpose of selling them in the near term to generate profits on the appreciation in their price.

20. A measure of the relative worth of two different currencies.

21. Stocks and bonds that are not classified as either held-to-maturity or trading securities.

22. Statements that report on the parent corporation and any separate legal entities called *subsidiaries*.

23. A transaction in which a company agrees to receive or make payment in a foreign currency.

24. The currency of the primary economic environment in which an entity operates.

25. Investments in other companies' bonds that the investor has the positive intent and the ability to hold to maturity.

26. An intangible asset that represents the excess of the purchase price for a business over the fair value of the net assets acquired.

27. A combination of businesses that are in competition with each other.

Alternate Terms

Affiliate   Equity investee.
Debt securities   Bonds.

Equity securities   Common stock, preferred stock.
Mergers and acquisitions   Business combinations.

Questions

1. Stanzel Corp. purchased 1,000 shares of IBM common stock. What will determine whether the shares are classified as trading securities or available-for-sale securities?

2. How does a company decide when to use the amortized cost method to account for an investment in bonds? What is the amortized cost method?

3. A company buys $10,000 face value of Ace Corp. bonds at 98. In addition, it incurs $300 of brokerage fees in making the purchase. What amount should the company report as the cost of the investment?

4. Basset Inc. purchases 5,000 shares of the 20,000 shares of common stock of Beagle Corp. What method of accounting should Basset use? What is the justification for this method?

5. What is the theoretical justification for preparing consolidated financial statements?

6. What is the primary difference in the accounting requirements for trading securities and available-for-sale securities? How is the primary difference justified?

7. Why are changes in the fair value of trading securities reported in the account *Unrealized* Gains/Losses—Trading Securities even though the gains and losses are reported on the income statement?

8. Why should dividends received from an investee that is accounted for using the equity method be treated as a reduction in the investment account? Why aren't the dividends recognized as income?

9. Can you give an example of a horizontal combination that would occur by the combination of two real-world companies? a vertical combination?

10. What is the difference between a statutory merger and a statutory consolidation?

11. Which is the only one of the three legal forms of business combination that requires the preparation of periodic consolidated financial statements? Explain your answer.

12. Why do accountants report goodwill only when a business is purchased?

13. Why would one company pay more than the fair market value for the net assets of another company?

14. A parent buys raw materials on account from one of its subsidiaries. Why would any accounts payable on the books of the parent and any accounts receivable on the books of the subsidiary be eliminated when preparing consolidated financial statements?

15. Should minority interest be classified on a consolidated balance sheet as a liability or as a component of stockholders' equity? Explain your answer.

16. Do all sales by U.S. companies to foreign companies result in foreign currency transactions? Explain your answer.

17. A U.S. corporation sells on account to a London firm, with payment in British pounds. The exchange rate at the time of the sale was $1.50 per pound and at the time of collection of the account was $1.60. Will the U.S. corporation report a foreign exchange gain or loss when it collects the receivable? Explain your answer.

18. Assuming that the local currency is the functional currency, what exchange rate is used to translate income statement items? What is the rationale for using this rate?

19. Assuming that the local currency is the functional currency, what exchange rate is used to translate balance sheet items? Are all items on the balance sheet translated at the same rate? Explain your answer.

20. What is the purpose of requiring disclosure of a significant amount of sales a company makes to a single customer?

21. What inherent weakness in consolidated financial statements is addressed by supplemental disclosure of segmental information for a company?

Exercises

LO 2 **Exercise 13-1** Purchase and Sale of Bonds

Starship Enterprises enters into the following transactions during 1998 and 1999:

1998
Jan. 1   Purchased $100,000 face value of Northern Lights Inc. bonds at 100. The newly issued bonds have a coupon rate of 8% paid semiannually on June 30 and December 31. The bonds mature in five years.
June 30   Received interest on the Northern Lights bonds.
Dec. 31   Received interest on the Northern Lights bonds.

1999
Jan. 1   Sold the Northern Lights Inc. bonds at 102.

Assume Starship classifies all bonds as held to maturity.

Required

1. Prepare all necessary journal entries on Starship's records to account for its investment in the Northern Lights bonds.

2. Why was Starship able to sell its Northern Lights bonds at 102?

LO 2 **Exercise 13-2** Investment in Bonds—Straight-Line Amortization

On January 1, 1998, Advantage Corp. purchased $50,000 face value of the bonds of Georgetown Inc. The bonds are dated January 1, 1998, and have a term of 20 years. They were purchased for $41,506, which reflects an effective rate of interest of 10%. Interest of 8% is paid annually on December 31. Advantage uses the straight-line method to amortize any discount or premium and classifies all bonds as held to maturity.

Required

1. Prepare the journal entry on Advantage's records on January 1, 1998, to account for the purchase of the bonds.

2. Prepare the journal entry, or entries, on Advantage's records on December 31, 1998, to account for the receipt of interest and the amortization of any discount or premium.

3. Why was Advantage able to buy the bonds for less than it will receive when they mature?

LO 2 **Exercise 13-3** Investment in Bonds—Effective Interest Amortization

Assume the same facts as in Exercise 13-2, except that Advantage uses the effective interest method to amortize any discount or premium.

Required

1. Prepare the journal entry on Advantage's records on January 1, 1998, to account for the purchase of the bonds.

2. Prepare the journal entry, or entries, on Advantage's records on December 31, 1998, to account for the receipt of interest and the amortization of any discount or premium.

3. Why was Advantage able to buy the bonds for less than it will receive when they mature?

LO 2 **Exercise 13-4** Investment in Bonds—Straight-Line Amortization

On January 2, 1998, Competitive Corp. purchased $100,000 face value of the bonds of Fordham Inc. The bonds are dated January 2, 1998, and have a term of 10 years. The bonds were purchased for $113,400, which reflects an effective rate of interest of 8%.

Interest of 10% is paid annually on December 31. Competitive uses the straight-line method to amortize any discount or premium and classifies all bonds as held to maturity.

Required

1. Prepare the journal entry on Competitive's records on January 2, 1998, to account for the purchase of the bonds.

2. Prepare the journal entry, or entries, on Competitive's records on December 31, 1998, to account for the receipt of interest and the amortization of any discount or premium.

3. Why was Competitive willing to pay more for the bonds than it will receive when they mature?

LO 2 **Exercise 13-5** Investment in Bonds—Effective Interest Amortization

Assume the same facts as in Exercise 13-4, except that Competitive uses the effective interest method to amortize any discount or premium.

Required

1. Prepare the journal entry on Competitive's records on January 2, 1998, to account for the purchase of the bonds.

2. Prepare the journal entry, or entries, on Competitive's records on December 31, 1998, to account for the receipt of interest and the amortization of any discount or premium.

3. Why was Competitive willing to pay more for the bonds than it will receive when they mature?

LO 2 **Exercise 13-6** Investment in Bonds—Straight-Line Amortization

On January 2, 1998, Interface Inc. purchased $100,000 face value of the bonds of Systems Enterprises. The bonds are dated January 2, 1998, and have a term of five years. The bonds were purchased for $92,639, which reflects an effective rate of interest of 12%. Interest of 10% is paid semiannually on June 30 and December 31. Interface uses the straight-line method to amortize any discount or premium and classifies all bonds as held to maturity.

Required

1. Calculate the carrying value of the bonds on July 1, 1998, after the first interest payment.

2. Calculate the carrying value of the bonds on December 31, 1999, after the fourth interest payment.

LO 2 **Exercise 13-7** Investment in Bonds—Effective Interest Amortization

Assume the same facts as in Exercise 13-6, except that Interface uses the effective interest method to amortize any discount or premium.

Required

1. Calculate the carrying value of the bonds on June 30, 1998, after the first interest payment.

2. Calculate the carrying value of the bonds on December 31, 1999, after the fourth interest payment.

LO 3 **Exercise 13-8** Investment in Stock

On December 1, 1998, Chicago Corp. purchased 1,000 shares of the preferred stock of Denver Corp. for $40 per share. Chicago expected the price of the stock to increase over the next few months and plans to sell it for a profit. On December 20, 1998, Denver declares a dividend of $1 per share to be paid on January 15, 1999. On December 31, 1998, Chicago's accounting year-end, the Denver stock is trading on the market at $42 per share. Chicago sells the stock on February 12, 1999, at a price of $45 per share.

Required

1. Should Chicago classify its investment as held-to-maturity, trading, or available-for-sale securities? Explain your answer.

2. Prepare all necessary entries on Chicago's books in connection with its investment, beginning with the purchase on December 1, 1998, and ending with the sale on

February 12, 1999. Indicate next to each account title in your entries whether the account appears on the balance sheet (BS) or the income statement (IS).

3. How should Chicago classify its investment on its December 31, 1998, balance sheet?

LO 4 **Exercise 13-9** Investment in Stock

On August 15, 1998, Cubs Corp. purchases 5,000 shares of common stock in Sox Inc. at a market price of $15 per share. In addition, Cubs pays brokerage fees of $1,000. Cubs plans to hold the stock indefinitely rather than as a part of its active trading portfolio. The market value of the stock is $13 per share on December 31, 1998, the end of Cubs' accounting year. On July 8, 1999, Cubs sells the Sox stock for $10 per share.

Required

1. Should Cubs classify its investment as held-to-maturity, trading, or available-for-sale securities? Explain your answer.

2. Prepare all necessary entries on Cubs' books in connection with the investment, beginning with the purchase on August 15, 1998, and ending with the sale on July 8, 1999. Indicate next to each account title in your entries whether the account appears on the balance sheet (BS) or the income statement (IS).

3. How should Cubs classify its investment on its December 31, 1998, balance sheet?

LO 5 **Exercise 13-10** Equity Method

On January 1, 1998, Beaman buys on the open market 3,000 shares of common stock in Roberts at $15 per share. Beaman incurs $1,000 in various fees to make the purchase. Roberts has 10,000 shares of stock outstanding on this date. Roberts declares a dividend of $1 per share each quarter in 1998 and reports net income for the year of $60,000.

Required

1. What amount should Beaman report on its December 31, 1998, balance sheet for its investment in Roberts? Explain your answer.

2. Compute the amount of gain or loss Beaman would have if it sold all of its Roberts shares on January 10, 1999, for $20 per share. Explain your answer.

LO 6 **Exercise 13-11** Business Combinations and Goodwill

On June 13, 1998, Mystic Rock Company merged with Synthetic Stone Enterprises by purchasing Synthetic's net assets for $75,000 in cash. Before the acquisition, the cash balances of the two companies were $350,000 and $25,000, respectively. The book value of Synthetic's stockholders' equity was $57,000 on June 13, 1998. The fair value of Synthetic's net assets was estimated at $70,000 as of June 13, 1998.

Required

1. How much cash would be reported on a post-merger balance sheet prepared for Mystic on June 13, 1998?

2. What is the amount of goodwill that resulted from Mystic's purchase of Synthetic?

LO 6 **Exercise 13-12** Business Combinations and Goodwill

On January 1, 1998, Keller Corp. purchases all of the assets and assumes all of the liabilities of Newton Inc., for $400,000 in cash. After this date, Newton ceases to exist as an entity. On this date, Newton's balance sheet reported total assets of $500,000 and total liabilities of $200,000. According to an appraisal performed on this date, all assets are recorded at their fair values except for a parcel of real estate. It is included on the balance sheet at a cost of $100,000, but an appraisal indicates that it is worth $140,000.

Required

1. What type of business combination is this legally? Explain your answer.

2. Determine the amount at which Keller should record the real estate on its books.

3. Compute the amount of goodwill Keller should recognize in connection with this business combination.

4. Why would Keller pay more than fair market value to acquire the net assets of Newton?

LO 8 **Exercise 13-13** Foreign Exchange Gains and Losses

For each of the following situations, determine the dollar amount of foreign exchange gain or loss that the U.S. company would recognize on the settlement date of each of the foreign currency transactions. Also indicate whether it is a foreign exchange gain (G) or a foreign exchange loss (L).

_____ 1. On August 8, Boston sells merchandise to a London firm. The buyer agrees to pay Boston 10,000 British pounds on September 30. The exchange rate on August 8 is $1.50 per British pound and then falls to $1.40 on September 30.

_____ 2. On May 3, San Diego sells inventory to a Tokyo company. The buyer agrees to pay 100,000 Japanese yen on June 15. The exchange rate on May 3 is $.008 per Japanese yen and then rises to $.009 on June 15.

_____ 3. On March 5, St. Louis buys supplies from a Mexican vendor. The seller agrees to accept 50,000 pesos on March 31. The exchange rate on March 5 is $.30 per Mexican peso and then rises to $.35 per peso on March 31.

_____ 4. On October 7, Seattle buys inventory from a company in Germany. The German company agrees to accept 20,000 German marks on November 15. The exchange rate on October 7 is $.60 per German mark; it falls to $.50 per mark on November 15.

LO 9 **Exercise 13-14** Translation of a Foreign Subsidiary

Carson Corp. opened a new subsidiary in France at the beginning of the year with an investment of 200,000 French francs. Capital stock in the same amount was issued. At the time, this was equivalent to $36,000 (that is, the exchange rate at this time was $.18 per French franc). The functional currency for the subsidiary is the local currency, the French franc. The exchange rate at the end of the year had risen to $.20. At the end of the year, the subsidiary's balance sheet reported assets of 400,000 francs and liabilities of 80,000 francs. The subsidiary's net income for the year amounted to the equivalent of $10,000.

Required

1. What dollar amount should appear for total assets on a balance sheet for the subsidiary at the end of the year translated from French francs to U.S. dollars?

2. What dollar amount should appear on the same balance sheet for the translation adjustment?

3. Interpret the translation adjustment. How does it affect the subsidiary's net income and its cash flow?

Multi-Concept Exercises

LO 1, 3, 4, 5, 7 **Exercise 13-15** Classification of Investments

Red Oak makes the following investments in the stock of other companies during 1998. For each investment, indicate how it would be accounted for and reported on; use the following designations: trading security (T), available-for-sale security (AS), equity investee (E), or a subsidiary included in consolidated statements (S).

_____ 1. 500 shares of ABC common stock to be held for short-term share appreciation.

_____ 2. 20,000 shares of the 50,000 shares of Ace common stock to be held for the long term.

_____ 3. 100 shares of Creston preferred stock to be held for an indefinite period of time.

_____ 4. 80,000 of the 100,000 shares of Orient common stock.

_____ 5. 10,000 of the 40,000 shares of Omaha preferred stock to be held for the long term.

LO 2, 3, 4 **Exercise 13-16** Classification of Investments

Fill in the blanks below to indicate whether each of the following investments should be classified as a held-to-maturity security (HM), a trading security (T), or an available-for-sale security (AS):

_____ 1. Shares of IBM stock to be held indefinitely.

_____ 2. GM bonds due in 10 years. The intent is to hold them until they mature.

_____ 3. Shares of Motorola stock. Plans are to hold the stock until the price goes up by 10% and then sell it.

_____ 4. Ford Motor Company bonds due in 15 years. The bonds are part of a portfolio that turns over on the average of every 60 days.

_____ 5. Chrysler bonds due in ten years. Plans are to hold them indefinitely.

Problems

LO 6 **Problem 13-1** Business Combination

On March 1, 1998, Mantle Inc., a software developer, paid $2,700,000 to acquire all of the assets and assume all of the liabilities of Maris Corp., a regional competitor. After the acquisition, Maris ceased to exist as a separate entity. The balance sheets of the two companies before the merger were as follows:

	MANTLE INC.	MARIS CORP.
Cash	$2,900,000	$ 500,000
Accounts receivable	2,200,000	750,000
Prepayments	210,000	120,000
Furniture and fixtures	1,000,000	250,000
Copyrights	3,500,000	1,200,000
Total assets	$9,810,000	$2,820,000
Accounts payable	$ 200,000	$ 120,000
Long-term notes payable	2,400,000	1,200,000
Common stock, $1 par	1,000,000	500,000
Retained earnings	6,210,000	1,000,000
Total equities	$9,810,000	$2,820,000

Mantle is able to determine that all of Maris's assets and liabilities are on its books at their fair values with the exception of the copyrights. Mantle estimates that these are worth $2,000,000.

Required

1. What type of business combination is this from a legal perspective? Explain your answer.

2. Compute the amount of goodwill that Mantle should record in connection with the combination.

3. Prepare the journal entry on Mantle's books to record the combination.

4. How does the estimate of the fair value assigned to the copyrights of Maris affect the amount of goodwill that is recognized? Why is it important for Mantle to have reliable estimates of the values of each of these assets?

LO 7 **Problem 13-2** Consolidated Financial Statements

On June 30, 1998, Lacey Inc. buys all of the outstanding stock of Larson Corp. for $300 million in cash. Before the acquisition, balance sheets for the two companies appeared as follows (amounts are in millions of dollars):

| | JUNE 30, 1998 | |
	LACEY	LARSON
Cash	$350	$ 30
Accounts receivable	100	50
Inventory	80	60
Land	200	100
Buildings, net	250	150
Total assets	$980	$390
Accounts payable	$ 80	$ 20
Long-term debt	200	100
Capital stock, $10 par	100	50
Additional paid-in capital	400	150
Retained earnings	200	70
Total equities	$980	$390

All of the recorded values for Larson's assets are equivalent to their fair market values, with the exception of the land. It has an estimated fair value of $120 million.

Required

1. From a legal perspective, what type of business combination is this? Explain your answer.

2. Prepare the journal entry on Lacey's books to record its purchase of the Larson stock.

3. Compute the amount of goodwill that should be recognized on a consolidated balance sheet prepared immediately after the combination.

4. Prepare a consolidated balance sheet for Lacey and Larson.

LO 7 **Problem 13-3** Consolidated Financial Statements
On January 1, 1998, Hemisphere Inc. acquires all of the outstanding common stock of Red River Corp. at a price of $45 per share. The fair values of Red River's current assets and its liabilities are equal to their book values. However, Red River's land, buildings, and intangibles were appraised at $200 million, $350 million, and $150 million, respectively. Before the acquisition, the condensed balance sheets for the two companies appeared as follows (all amounts are in millions of dollars):

	HEMISPHERE INC.	RED RIVER CORP.
Current assets	$ 600	$ 50
Land	400	150
Buildings, net of depreciation	800	300
Intangibles	500	100
Total assets	$2,300	$600
Current liabilities	$ 400	$100
Long-term notes payable	700	250
Common stock, $10 par	500	100
Retained earnings	700	150
Total equities	$2,300	$600

Required

1. What type of business combination is this from a legal perspective? Explain your answer.

2. Prepare the journal entry on Hemisphere's books to record the acquisition of the Red River stock.

3. Prepare balance sheets for each of the two companies as they would appear immediately after the acquisition.

4. Prepare a consolidated balance sheet as it would appear immediately after the acquisition.

5. For purposes of a consolidated income statement, what is the proper accounting treatment for any goodwill arising from the combination?

General
Ledger

LO 8   **Problem 13-4** Foreign Currency Transactions

During January 1998, Premiere Inc. entered into the following transactions with foreign companies:

Jan. 5   Purchased inventory from a company in Toronto. Premiere agrees to pay the supplier 20,000 Canadian dollars by the end of the month. The exchange rate on January 5 is $.90 per Canadian dollar.

Jan. 12   Sold inventory to a company in Mexico. The company agrees to pay Premiere 50,000 pesos by the end of the month. The exchange rate on January 12 is $.25 per Mexican peso.

Jan. 15   Sold inventory to a company in London. The firm agrees to pay Premiere $15,000 by January 25. The exchange rate on January 15 is $1.30 per British pound.

Jan. 18   Purchased inventory from a company in France for 15,000 French francs and immediately made payment. The exchange rate on this date was $.20 per French franc.

Jan. 25   Received payment for inventory sold on January 15. The exchange rate on January 25 is $1.40 per British pound.

Jan. 30   Paid for inventory purchased on January 5. The exchange rate on January 30 is $.95 per Canadian dollar.

Jan. 31   Received payment for inventory sold on January 12. The exchange rate on January 31 is $.30 per Mexican peso.

Required

1. Prepare all necessary journal entries on Premiere's books during the month of January to record these transactions. Assume Premiere uses a periodic inventory system.

2. Compute the net amount of foreign exchange gain or loss Premiere would report on an income statement for the month of January 1998.

3. How can a company do business with foreign suppliers and customers but avoid the risks associated with dealing in foreign currency?

LO 9   **Problem 13-5** Translation of a Foreign Subsidiary

On January 1, 1998, Smith Enterprises, a large New York–based conglomerate, opened a new subsidiary in Germany by issuing common stock for a total of 1,000,000 German marks. The subsidiary, Thomas Inc., will produce parts for one of Smith's products. Thomas's income statement for 1998 and a balance sheet prepared as of December 31, 1998, are as follows:

THOMAS INC.
INCOME STATEMENT
FOR THE YEAR ENDED DECEMBER 31, 1998
(ALL AMOUNTS IN GERMAN MARKS)

Sales revenue	6,000,000
Cost of goods sold	3,200,000
Gross profit	2,800,000
Selling and administrative expenses	(1,700,000)
Interest expense	(200,000)
Net income	900,000

THOMAS INC.
BALANCE SHEET
AS OF DECEMBER 31, 1998
(ALL AMOUNTS IN GERMAN MARKS)

Cash	600,000	Accounts payable	500,000
Accounts receivable	900,000	Notes payable	1,600,000
Inventories	800,000	Common stock	1,000,000
Plant, net	1,700,000	Retained earnings	900,000
Total	4,000,000	Total	4,000,000

At the beginning of 1998, the exchange rate was $.60 per German mark, and at the end of the year, it was $.40. The average exchange rate for the year was $.50. Assume that the German mark is the functional currency.

Required

1. Prepare an income statement for Thomas translated from German marks into U.S. dollars.

2. Prepare a balance sheet as of December 31, 1998, for Thomas, translated from German marks into U.S. dollars.

3. Why is it necessary to create the account Translation Adjustment? Is it an addition to or a deduction from stockholders' equity? What are the cash flow implications to the parent, Smith, from this adjustment?

Multi-Concept Problems

LO 2, 3 **Problem 13-6** Investments in Bonds and Stock

Swartz Inc. enters into the following transactions during 1998:

General
Ledger

July 1 — Paid $9,450 to acquire on the open market $10,000 face value of Gallatin bonds. The bonds have a stated annual interest rate of 6% with interest paid semiannually on June 30 and December 31. The remaining life of the bonds on the date of purchase is 5½ years.

Oct. 23 — Purchased 600 shares of Eagle Rock common stock at $20 per share.

Nov. 21 — Purchased 200 shares of Montana preferred stock at $30 per share.

Dec. 10 — Received dividends of $1.50 per share on the Eagle Rock stock and $2.00 per share on the Montana stock.

Dec. 28 — Sold 400 shares of Eagle Rock common stock at $25 per share.

Dec. 31 — Received interest from the Gallatin bonds.

Dec. 31 — Noted market price of $29 per share for the Eagle Rock stock and $26 per share for the Montana stock.

Required

1. Prepare all necessary journal entries on Swartz's records to account for its investments during 1998. Swartz classifies the bonds as held-to-maturity securities and all stock investments as trading securities. The straight-line method is used to amortize any bond discount or premium.

2. Prepare a partial balance sheet as of December 31, 1998, to indicate the proper presentation of the investments.

3. Indicate the items, and the amount of each, that will appear on the 1998 income statement relative to the investments.

LO 3, 4 **Problem 13-7** Investments in Stock

Atlas Superstores occasionally finds itself with excess cash to invest and consequently entered into the following transactions during 1998:

Jan. 15 — Purchased 200 shares of Sears common stock at $50 per share, plus $500 in commissions.

May 23   Received dividends of $2 per share on the Sears stock.

June 1   Purchased 100 shares of Ford Motor Co. stock at $74 per share, plus $300 in commissions.

Oct. 20   Sold all of the Sears stock at $42 per share, less commissions of $400.

Dec. 15   Received notification from Ford Motor Co. that a $1.50 per share dividend had been declared. The checks will be mailed to stockholders on January 10, 1999.

Dec. 31   Noted that the Ford Motor Co. stock was quoted on the stock exchange at $85 per share.

Required

1. Prepare journal entries on the books of Atlas Superstores during 1998 to record these transactions, including any necessary entry on December 15 when the dividend was declared and at the end of the year. Assume that Atlas categorizes all investments as available-for-sale securities.

2. What is the total amount of income that Atlas should recognize from its investments during 1998?

3. Assume all of the same facts except that Atlas categorizes all investments as trading securities. How would your answer to part 2 change? Explain why your answer would change.

LO 5, 9 **Problem 13-8** Foreign Equity Investee

Edgar Enterprises holds 30% of the common stock of Kyoto Corp., an affiliate in Japan. The Investment in Kyoto account was reported on Edgar's December 31, 1997, balance sheet at $5 million. Edgar's 30% investment gives it the ability to exert significant influence over Kyoto. The affiliate presents the following income statement for the year ended December 31, 1998 (all amounts are stated in millions of Japanese yen):

KYOTO CORP.
INCOME STATEMENT
FOR THE YEAR ENDED DECEMBER 31, 1998

Revenues	2,500
Operating expenses	(1,500)
Interest expense	(400)
Net income	600

On June 1, 1998, Kyoto declared and paid a dividend of 200 million yen. On December 31, 1998, it declared and paid another dividend of 150 million yen. The Japanese yen is the functional currency. The following exchange rates are available:

DATE	EXCHANGE RATE PER JAPANESE YEN
January 1	$.0100
June 1	.0095
December 31	.0080
Average for the year	.0090

Required

1. Translate Kyoto's income statement from Japanese yen into U.S. dollars. Why is it necessary for Edgar to translate the statement?

2. What amount of income, in dollars, should Edgar recognize from its investment in Kyoto for 1998?

3. At what amount should Edgar report the Investment in Kyoto account on its balance sheet as of December 31, 1998? Support your answer with any necessary computations. (*Hint:* Dividends should be translated at the exchange rate in effect when they were paid.)

LO 2, 3, 4, 5 **Problem 13-9** Partial Classified Balance Sheet

Shown below, in alphabetical order, are items taken from the records of Royal European Industries at December 31, 1998:

Accounts receivable	$165,700
Accumulated depreciation	14,800
Allowance for doubtful accounts	16,900
Cash	13,300
Dividends receivable	11,000
Goodwill	150,000
Interest receivable	5,500
Inventory	145,000
Investment in Golden common stock (a trading security):	
Cost	45,600
Market value	48,000
Investment in Hemisphere bonds: (held-to-maturity, due 12/31/2005)	
Carrying value	165,100
Market value	150,000
Investment in InterTel preferred stock (a trading security):	
Cost	133,300
Market value	135,000
Investment in TrueBlue common stock, at equity	215,900
Prepaid expenses	3,500
Property, plant, and equipment	148,000

Required

Prepare the assets section of a classified balance sheet at December 31, 1998.

Alternate Problems

LO 6 **Problem 13-1A** A Business Combination

On March 1, 1998, Mays Inc., a software developer, paid $5,400,000 to acquire all of the assets and assume all of the liabilities of Aaron Corp., a regional competitor. After the acquisition, Aaron ceased to exist as a separate entity. The balance sheets of the two companies before the merger were as follows:

	MAYS INC.	AARON CORP.
Cash	$ 5,800,000	$1,000,000
Accounts receivable	4,400,000	1,500,000
Prepayments	420,000	240,000
Furniture and fixtures	2,000,000	500,000
Copyrights	7,000,000	2,400,000
Total assets	$19,620,000	$5,640,000
Accounts payable	$ 400,000	$ 240,000
Long-term notes payable	4,800,000	2,400,000
Common stock, $1 par	2,000,000	1,000,000
Retained earnings	12,420,000	2,000,000
Total equities	$19,620,000	$5,640,000

Mays is able to determine that all of Aaron's assets and liabilities are on its books at their fair values with the exception of the copyrights. Mays estimates that they are worth $4,000,000.

Required

1. What type of business combination is this from a legal perspective? Explain your answer.
2. Compute the amount of goodwill that Mays should record in connection with the combination.
3. Prepare the journal entry on Mays's books to record the combination.
4. How does the estimate of the fair value assigned to the copyrights of Aaron affect the amount of goodwill that is recognized? Why is it important for Mays to have reliable estimates of the values of each of these assets?

LO 7 **Problem 13-2A** Consolidated Financial Statements

On January 1, 1998, Market Place Inc. buys all of the outstanding stock of Immedia Corp. for $490 million in cash. Before the acquisition, balance sheets for the two companies appeared as follows (amounts are in millions of dollars):

	JANUARY 1, 1998	
	MARKET PLACE	IMMEDIA
Cash	$ 550	$ 60
Accounts receivable	120	80
Inventory	200	90
Land	300	150
Buildings, net	450	250
Total assets	$1,620	$630
Accounts payable	$ 90	$ 60
Long-term debt	500	150
Capital stock, $10 par	200	100
Additional paid-in capital	400	200
Retained earnings	430	120
Total equities	$1,620	$630

All of the recorded values for Immedia's assets are equivalent to their fair market values, with the exception of the land. It has an estimated fair value of $180 million.

Required

1. From a legal perspective, what type of business combination is this? Explain your answer.
2. Prepare the journal entry on Market Place's books to record its purchase of the Immedia stock.
3. Compute the amount of goodwill that should be recognized on a consolidated balance sheet prepared immediately after the combination.
4. Prepare a consolidated balance sheet for Market Place and Immedia.

LO 7 **Problem 13-3A** Consolidated Financial Statements

On January 1, 1998, Taurus Inc. acquires all of the outstanding common stock of Gemini Corp. at a price of $50 per share. The fair values of Gemini's current assets and its liabilities are equal to their book values. However, Gemini's land, buildings, and intangibles were appraised at $400 million, $700 million, and $300 million, respectively. Before the acquisition, the condensed balance sheets for the two companies appeared as follows (all amounts are in millions of dollars):

	TAURUS INC.	GEMINI CORP.
Current assets	$1,200	$ 100
Land	800	300
Buildings, net of depreciation	1,600	600
Intangibles	1,000	200
Total assets	$4,600	$1,200

	TAURUS INC.	GEMINI CORP.
Current liabilities	$ 800	$ 200
Long-term notes payable	1,400	500
Common stock, $10 par	1,000	200
Retained earnings	1,400	300
Total equities	$4,600	$1,200

Required

1. What type of business combination is this from a legal perspective? Explain your answer.

2. Prepare the journal entry on Taurus's books to record the acquisition of the Gemini stock.

3. Prepare balance sheets for each of the two companies as they would appear immediately after the acquisition.

4. Prepare a consolidated balance sheet as it would appear immediately after the acquisition.

5. For purposes of a consolidated income statement, what is the proper accounting treatment for any goodwill arising from the combination?

LO 8 **Problem 13-4A** Foreign Currency Transactions

During January 1998, Arbor Inc. entered into the following transactions with foreign companies:

General
Ledger

Jan. 5   Purchased inventory from a company in Toronto. Arbor agrees to pay the supplier 10,000 Canadian dollars by the end of the month. The exchange rate on January 5 is $.95 per Canadian dollar.

Jan. 12   Sold inventory to a company in Mexico. The company agrees to pay Arbor 60,000 pesos by the end of the month. The exchange rate on January 12 is $.30 per Mexican peso.

Jan. 15   Sold inventory to a company in London. The firm agrees to pay Arbor $25,000 by January 25. The exchange rate on January 15 is $1.30 per British pound.

Jan. 18   Purchased inventory from a company in France for 20,000 French francs and immediately made payment. The exchange rate on this date was $.25 per French franc.

Jan. 25   Received payment for inventory sold on January 15. The exchange rate on January 25 is $1.40 per British pound.

Jan. 30   Paid for inventory purchased on January 5. The exchange rate on January 30 is $.90 per Canadian dollar.

Jan. 31   Received payment for inventory sold on January 12. The exchange rate on January 31 is $.40 per Mexican peso.

Required

1. Prepare all necessary journal entries on Arbor's books during the month of January to record these transactions. Assume Arbor uses a periodic inventory system.

2. Compute the net amount of foreign exchange gain or loss Arbor would report on an income statement for the month of January 1998.

3. How can a company do business with foreign suppliers and customers but avoid the risks associated with dealing in foreign currency?

LO 9 **Problem 13-5A** Translation of a Foreign Subsidiary

On January 1, 1998, Aikman Enterprises, a large Chicago-based conglomerate, opened a new subsidiary in London by issuing common stock for a total of 500,000 British pounds. The subsidiary, Kelly Ltd., will produce parts for one of Aikman's products. Kelly's income statement for 1998 and a balance sheet prepared as of December 31, 1998, are as follows:

KELLY LTD.
INCOME STATEMENT
FOR THE YEAR ENDED DECEMBER 31, 1998
(ALL AMOUNTS IN BRITISH POUNDS)

Sales revenue	3,000,000
Cost of goods sold	1,600,000
Gross profit	1,400,000
Selling and administrative expenses	(850,000)
Interest expense	(100,000)
Net income	450,000

KELLY LTD.
BALANCE SHEET
AS OF DECEMBER 31, 1998
(ALL AMOUNTS IN BRITISH POUNDS)

Cash	300,000	Accounts payable	250,000
Accounts receivable	450,000	Notes payable	800,000
Inventories	400,000	Common stock	500,000
Plant, net	850,000	Retained earnings	450,000
Totals	2,000,000	Totals	2,000,000

At the beginning of 1998, the exchange rate was $1.40 per British pound, and at the end of the year, it was $1.60. The average exchange rate for the year was $1.50. Assume that the British pound is the functional currency.

Required

1. Prepare an income statement for Kelly, translated from British pounds into U.S. dollars.

2. Prepare a balance sheet as of December 31, 1998, for Kelly, translated from British pounds into U.S. dollars.

3. Why is it necessary to create the account Translation Adjustment? Is it an addition to or a deduction from stockholders' equity? What are the cash flow implications to the parent, Aikman, from this adjustment?

Alternate Multi-Concept Problems

General
Ledger

LO 2, 3 **Problem 13-6A** Investments in Bonds and Stock

Vermont Corp. enters into the following transactions during 1998:

July 1   Paid $10,700 to acquire on the open market $10,000 face value of Maine bonds. The bonds have a stated annual interest rate of 8% with interest paid semiannually on June 30 and December 31. The remaining life of the bonds on the date of purchase is 3½ years.

Oct. 23   Purchased 1,000 shares of Virginia common stock at $15 per share.

Nov. 21   Purchased 600 shares of Carolina preferred stock at $8 per share.

Dec. 10   Received dividends of $.50 per share on the Virginia stock and $1.00 per share on the Carolina stock.

Dec. 28   Sold 700 shares of Virginia common stock at $19 per share.

Dec. 31   Received interest from the Maine bonds.

Dec. 31   The Virginia stock and the Carolina stock have market prices of $20 per share and $11 per share, respectively.

Required:

1. Prepare all necessary journal entries on Vermont's records to account for its investments during 1998. Vermont classifies the bonds as held-to-maturity securities and all stock investments as trading securities. The straight-line method is used to amortize any bond discount or premium.

2. Prepare a partial balance sheet as of December 31, 1998, to indicate the proper presentation of the investments.

3. Indicate the items, and the amount of each, that will appear on the 1998 income statement relative to the investments.

LO 3, 4 **Problem 13-7A** Investments in Stock

Trendy Supercenter occasionally finds itself with excess cash to invest and consequently entered into the following transactions during 1998:

Jan. 15   Purchased 100 shares of IBM common stock at $50 per share, plus $250 in commissions.

May 23   Received dividends of $1 per share on the IBM stock.

June 1   Purchased 200 shares of General Motors stock at $60 per share, plus $300 in commissions.

Oct. 20   Sold all of the IBM stock at $65 per share, less commissions of $400.

Dec. 15   Received notification from General Motors that a $.75 per share dividend had been declared. The checks will be mailed to stockholders on January 10, 1999.

Dec. 31   Noted that the General Motors stock was quoted on the stock exchange at $45 per share.

Required

1. Prepare journal entries on the books of Trendy Supercenter during 1998 to record these transactions, including any necessary entry on December 15 when the dividend was declared and at the end of the year. Assume that Trendy categorizes all investments as available-for-sale securities.

2. What is the total amount of income that Trendy should recognize from its investments during 1998?

3. Assume all of the same facts except that Trendy categorizes all investments as trading securities. How would your answer to part 2 change? Explain why your answer would change.

LO 5, 9 **Problem 13-8A** Foreign Equity Investee

Elston Enterprises holds 40% of the common stock of Norris Ltd., an affiliate in Canada. The Investment in Norris account was reported on Elston's December 31, 1997, balance sheet at $210 million. Elston's 40% investment gives it the ability to exert significant influence over Norris. The affiliate presents the following income statement for the year ended December 31, 1998 (all amounts are stated in millions of Canadian dollars):

NORRIS LTD.
INCOME STATEMENT
FOR THE YEAR ENDED DECEMBER 31, 1998

Revenues	500
Operating expenses	(300)
Interest expense	(50)
Net income	150

On June 1, 1998, Norris declared and paid a dividend of 50 million Canadian dollars. On December 31, 1998, it declared and paid another dividend of 30 million Canadian dollars. The Canadian dollar is the functional currency. The following exchange rates are available:

DATE	EXCHANGE RATE PER CANADIAN DOLLAR
January 1	$.80
June 1	.75
December 31	.60
Average for the year	.70

Required

1. Translate Norris's income statement from Canadian dollars into U.S. dollars. Why is it necessary for Elston to translate the statement?

2. What amount of income, in dollars, should Elston recognize from its investment in Norris for 1998?

3. At what amount should Elston report the Investment in Norris account on its balance sheet as of December 31, 1998? Support your answer with any necessary computations. (*Hint:* Dividends should be translated at the exchange rate in effect when they were paid.)

LO 2, 3, 4, 5 **Problem 13-9A** Partial Classified Balance Sheet

Shown below, in alphabetical order, are items taken from the records of Regal Asian Enterprises at June 30, 1998:

Accounts receivable	$313,500
Accumulated depreciation	167,000
Allowance for doubtful accounts	31,500
Cash	3,100
Dividends receivable	25,600
Goodwill	215,800
Interest receivable	21,400
Inventory	290,000
Investment in Azure common stock (a trading security):	
Cost	88,300
Market value	89,000
Investment in Bronze bonds: (held-to-maturity, due 12/31/2005)	
Carrying value	45,600
Market value	43,000
Investment in Lindall preferred stock (a trading security):	
Cost	91,200
Market value	99,000
Investment in Sage common stock, at equity	66,700
Prepaid expenses	13,200
Property, plant, and equipment	334,000

Required

Prepare the assets section of a classified balance sheet at June 30, 1998.

Cases

Reading and Interpreting Financial Statements

LO 6 **Case 13-1** Acquisitions by Time Warner

Time Warner described its telecommunications strategy in its "Management's Discussion and Analysis of Results of Operations and Financial Condition" section on page 50 of its 1995 annual report:

> In 1994, Time Warner embarked on a strategy to expand its cable television business, leading to agreements to combine with or acquire cable television systems serving approximately 3.7 million subscribers. This strategy was based on management's expectation that there would be a significant increase in the value of cable television systems related, in part, to a future convergence of the cable and telephone industries which would provide cable companies with an opportunity to operate large geographic clusters

of cable television systems for purposes of maximizing the devleopment and distribution of new and improved services on a cost efficient basis, such as increased channel capacity, high speed data transmission and telephone services.

This strategy continued into 1995. On May 2, 1995, Time Warner acquired Summit Communications Group. Time Warner's acquisition of Summit Communications Group is described in the following footnote from page 76 of Time Warner's 1995 annual report:

> On May 2, 1995, Time Warner acquired Summit Communications Group, Inc. ("Summit"), which owned cable television systems serving approximately 162,000 subscribers, in exchange for the issuance of approximately 1.6 million shares of common stock and approximately 3.3 million shares of a new convertible preferred stock ("Series C Preferred Stock") and the assumption of $140 million of indebtedness. The acquisition was accounted for by the purchase method of accounting for business combinations; accordingly, the cost to acquire Summit of approximately $351 million was allocated to the net assets acquired in proportion to estimates of their respective fair values, as follows: cable television franchises—$372 million; goodwill—$146 million; other current and noncurrent assets—$144 million; long-term debt—$140 million; deferred income taxes—$166 million; and other current liabilities—$5 million.

Required

1. Why was the acquisition of Summit accounted for using the purchase method of accounting rather than the pooling of interests method?
2. What was the fair value of the net assets acquired?
3. Why did Time Warner pay $351 million to acquire Summit?
4. Time Warner's consolidated balance sheet reported goodwill of approximately $4,630 million at the beginning of 1995 and $5,213 million at the end of the year. As described above, goodwill in the amount of $146 million arose from the acquisition of Summit. In addition, goodwill in the amount of $586 million arose from Time Warner's acquisition of KBLCOM. Taking into account these increases, what caused a *reduction* in goodwill during the year?

LO 6 **Case 13-2** Rockwell's Acquisition of Reliance Electric

In January 1995, Rockwell International Corporation acquired Reliance Electric Company. Rockwell's acquisition of Reliance is described in footnote 2 of Rockwell's 1995 annual report:

> In January 1995, the company completed its acquisition of Reliance Electric Company (Reliance), a major manufacturer of industrial products and telecommunications equipment for $1,586 million. The purchase price was financed through $311 million of short-term borrowings, $800 million of long-term debt, and the $475 million of proceeds from the August 1995 sale of Reliance's telecommunications business. The company's results of operations do not include the results of Reliance's telecommunications business or the interest expense related to the short-term borrowings that were repaid with the sale proceeds.
>
> The acquisition of Reliance was accounted for as a purchase as of December 31, 1994 and the results of operations of Reliance have been included since that date. The purchase price exceeded the fair value of net assets acquired by $880 million, which is recognized as goodwill and is being amortized over 40 years.

Required

1. Why did Rockwell account for its acquisition of Reliance using the purchase method of accounting rather than the pooling of interests method?
2. What was the fair value of Reliance's net assets that were acquired by Rockwell?
3. Why did Rockwell pay $1,586 million to acquire Reliance?
4. Rockwell's consolidated balance sheet reported intangible assets of approximately $777 million at the beginning of 1995 and $2,016 million at the end of the year. What caused the large net increase in intangible assets during the year? Aside from the net increase, what caused a reduction in goodwill during the year?

5. Considering the information set forth in this case, what large cash outflow would you expect to find on Rockwell's 1995 statement of cash flows? In which section of the statement would this large cash flow apprear?

LO 9 **Case 13-3** Johnson & Johnson Foreign Operations

The 1995 Johnson & Johnson annual report includes the following footnote:

> In consolidating international subsidiaries, balance sheet currency effects are recorded as a separate component of stockholders' equity. This equity account includes the results of translating all balance sheet assets and liabilities at current exchange rates, except for those located in highly inflationary economies, principally Latin America, which are reflected in operating results.
>
> An analysis of the changes during 1995 and 1994 in the separate component of stockholders' equity for cumulative currency translation adjustments follows:

(DOLLARS IN MILLIONS)	1995	1994
Beginning of year	$ (35)	$(338)
Translation adjustments	183	303
End of year	$148	$ (35)

Required

1. Over the two-year period shown, the translation adjustment has gone from a debit balance of $338 million to a credit balance of $148 million. What does this tell you about the value of the U.S. dollar relative to the functional currencies of those countries in which Johnson & Johnson has operations? Explain your answer.

2. Should Johnson & Johnson be pleased by the large increase in this component of stockholders' equity? Explain your answer.

Making Financial Decisions

Decision Making

LO 10 **Case 13-4** Segment Information

Carburetor Corp. started in business 25 years ago as a manufacturer of auto parts that it sells to the Big Three auto manufacturers and to auto parts wholesalers. Ten years ago, the company decided that it should diversify and began a business to distribute sporting goods to retail outlets. The following segment information is included in Carburetor's footnotes to its 1998 annual report (amounts in millions of dollars):

	AUTO PARTS	SPORTING GOODS
Sales revenue	$375	$250
Operating profit	20	75
Carrying value of assets	800	450
Depreciation expense	225	50
Capital expenditures	100	10

Sales to Ford, GM, and Chrysler during 1998 amounted to $120 million, $160 million, and $60 million respectively.

Required

1. Which segment of the business appears to you to be doing better? Justify your response with any computations or ratios you believe are relevant.

2. What percentage of the revenues of the auto parts division is from each of the Big Three? What percentage of the revenues of this segment do the Big Three account for on a combined basis?

3. Assume that the chief financial officer of Carburetor has come to you for a $100 million loan. Carburetor wants to spend $80 million to build a new plant to manufacture auto parts and another $20 million to add another warehouse to its sporting goods distribution operation. Will you make the loan? Explain why or why not.

Decision
Making

LO 10 **Case 13-5** Reading and Interpreting Segment Information for RJR Nabisco

RJR Nabisco Holdings Corp. (RJRN) is the parent company of RJR Nabisco Inc. The following footnote from pages 69 and 70 of the 1995 annual report of RJRN sets forth industry and geographic segment data about the company (all amounts are in millions of dollars):

SEGMENT INFORMATION

Industry Segment Data

RJRN is engaged principally in the manufacture, distribution and sale of tobacco products, cookies, crackers and other food products. Cigarettes are manufactured in the United States by RJRT and in over 40 foreign countries and territories by Reynolds International and subsidiaries or licensees of RJRT and are sold throughout the United States and in more than 170 markets around the world including Western Europe, the Middle East, Africa, Asia and Canada. RJRN, through its 80.5% owned subsidiary Nabisco Holdings, also manufactures and markets cookies, crackers, non-chocolate candy and gum products, nuts and snacks, various margarines and spreads and other specialty products under several brand names in the United States, Canada, Europe, Asia and Latin America. See the Management's Discussion and Analysis of Financial Condition and Results of Operations, appearing elsewhere herein, for further discussion of RJRN's operations. Summarized financial information for these operations is shown in the following tables.

YEAR ENDED DECEMBER 31	1995	1994	1993
Net sales:			
Tobacco	$ 7,714	$ 7,667	$ 8,079
Food	8,294	7,699	7,025
Consolidated net sales	$16,008	$15,366	$15,104
Operating income:			
Tobacco[1][2]	$ 1,500	$ 1,801	$ 866
Food[1][2]	902	887	578
Headquarters[2]	(64)	(138)	(66)
Consolidated operating income	$ 2,338	$ 2,550	$ 1,378
Capital expenditures:			
Tobacco	$ 231	$ 215	$ 224
Food	513	455	391
Consolidated capital expenditures	$ 744	$ 670	$ 615
Depreciation expense:			
Tobacco	$ 236	$ 228	$ 237
Food	244	218	206
Headquarters	2	8	5
Consolidated depreciation expense	$ 482	$ 454	$ 448

DECEMBER 31	1995	1994
Assets:		
Tobacco	$19,226	$19,420
Food	12,239	11,803
Headquarters[3]	53	185
Consolidated assets	$31,518	$31,408

(1) Includes amortization of trademarks and goodwill for Tobacco and Food for the year ended December 31, 1995, of $409 million and $227 million, respectively; for the year ended December 31, 1994, of $404 million and $225 million, respectively; and for the year ended December 31, 1993, of $407 million and $218 million, respectively.

(2) The 1995 and 1993 amounts include the effects of a restructuring expense at Tobacco (1995—$154 million; 1993—$544 million), Food (1993—$153 million) and Headquarters (1993—$33 million) (See Note 2 to the Consolidated Financial Statements).

(3) Cash and cash equivalents for the domestic tobacco operations are included in Headquarters' assets.

Geographic Data

The following tables show certain financial information relating to RJRN's continuing operations in various geographic areas.

YEAR ENDED DECEMBER 31	1995	1994	1993
Net sales:			
United States (including U.S. export sales)	$11,295	$11,144	$11,570
Europe	2,184	1,934	1,671
Other geographic areas	3,261	3,039	2,794
Less transfers between geographic areas[1]	(732)	(751)	(931)
Consolidated net sales	$16,008	$15,366	$15,104
Operating income:[2]			
United States	$ 1,749	$ 2,090	$ 1,211
Europe	299	272	40
Other geographic areas	354	326	193
Headquarters	(64)	(138)	(66)
Consolidated operating income[3]	$ 2,338	$ 2,550	$ 1,378

DECEMBER 31	1995	1994
Assets:		
United States	$25,606	$26,447
Europe	2,663	2,141
Other geographic areas	3,171	2,749
Headquarters	78	71
Consolidated assets	$31,518	$31,408
Liabilities of RJRN Holdings' operations located in foreign countries	$ 2,100	$ 1,725

(1)Transfers between geographic areas (which consist principally of tobacco transferred principally from the United States to Europe) are generally made at fair market value.

(2)The 1995 and 1993 amounts include the effects of restructuring expenses of $154 million and $730 million, respectively (see Note 2 to the Consolidated Financial Statements).

(3)Includes amortization of trademarks and goodwill of $636 million, $629 million and $625 million for the 1995, 1994 and 1993 periods, respectively.

Required

1. In general, for companies meeting the requirements for segment reporting, what are the four possible segments for which information must be disclosed? What kind of information must be disclosed for each of these segments?

2. What are the major geographic segments in which RJR Nabisco operates? Compare each geographic segment's net sales with total consolidated net sales for 1993, 1994, and 1995. Comment on trends, if any, in the percentage amounts.

3. What are the major industry segments in which RJR Nabisco operates? Compare each industry segment's net sales with total consolidated net sales for 1993, 1994, and 1995. Comment on trends, if any, in the percentage amounts.

Accounting and Ethics: What Would You Do?

LO 3, 4 **Case 13-6** Fair Market Values for Investments

Kennedy Corp. operates a chain of discount stores. The company regularly holds stock of various companies in a trading securities portfolio. One of these investments is 10,000 shares of Clean Air Inc., stock purchased for $100 per share during December 1998.

Clean Air manufactures highly specialized equipment used to test automobile emissions. Unfortunately, the market price of Clean Air's stock dropped during December 1998 and closed the year trading at $75 per share. Kennedy expects the Clean Air stock to experience a turnaround, however, as states pass legislation to require an emissions test on all automobiles.

As controller for Kennedy, you have followed the fortunes of Clean Air with particular interest. You and the company's treasurer are both concerned by the negative impact that a write-down of the stock to fair value would have on Kennedy's earnings for 1998. You have calculated net income for 1998 to be $400,000, exclusive of the recognition of any loss on the stock.

The treasurer comes to you on January 31, 1999, with the following idea:

> Since you haven't closed the books yet for 1998 and we haven't yet released the 1998 financials, let's think carefully about how Clean Air should be classified. I realize that we normally treat these types of investments as trading securities, but if we categorize the Clean Air stock on the balance sheet as available-for-sale rather than a trading security, we won't need to report the adjustment to fair value on the income statement. I don't see anything wrong with this since we would still report the stock at its fair value on the balance sheet.

Required

1. Compute Kennedy's net income for 1998, under two different assumptions: (a) the stock is classified as a trading security and (b) the stock is classified as an available-for-sale security.

2. Which classification do you believe is appropriate, according to accounting standards? Explain your answer.

3. Would you have any ethical concerns in following the treasurer's advice? Explain your answer.

LO 5 **Case 13-7** Equity Method

Pizza Express is a nationwide pizza-delivery company. A few years ago, the company purchased 20% of the common stock of Top Tomato, a supplier of tomato sauce and other fresh vegetables. Because Pizza Express has significant influence over the operations of Top Tomato, it uses the equity method to account for its investment. Recently, Top Tomato has experienced considerable volatility in its earnings, due in large part to the unpredictable weather in locales where its products are grown. In fact, the supplier reported a net loss of $20 million for 1998. Top Tomato paid dividends of $5 million in 1998, the same amount it has paid for many years.

Pizza Express had a good year in 1998. Exclusive of any adjustment for its share of Top Tomato's loss, Pizza Express's net income amounted to $6 million. You are the controller for Pizza Express and are approached by its president in January 1999, before the release of the 1998 financial statements. He is concerned that the recognition of a share of Top Tomato's net loss will put a serious damper on an otherwise successful year for Pizza Express. After all, he reasons, "My bonus, your bonus, and our ability to attract new capital from banks and other lenders hinge on our profitability."

He goes on to offer the following remedy:

> I understand that accounting rules require you to use the equity method, given our 20% stake in Top Tomato. I believe we should instruct the treasurer to sell 1% of our holdings in this company. This would relieve you of the responsibility to use this peculiar accounting method that requires us to share in their profits and losses. Instead of picking up a share of their net loss, we can recognize as income the dividends they paid us. This approach to recognizing income on an investment makes much more sense to me anyhow. Besides, divesting ourselves of such a minor percentage of Top Tomato's stock shouldn't jeopardize at all our ability to continue to have a strong voice in their strategic decisions.

Required

1. Compute Pizza Express's net income for 1998 under two different assumptions: (a) the use of the equity method to account for the investment in Top Tomato and (b) the use of the method proposed by the president. Assume that the market value of Top Tomato's stock did not change over the year.

2. Does the president's proposal violate generally accepted accounting principles? Explain your answer.

3. Does the president's proposal present you with an ethical dilemma in your role as controller of the company? Explain your answer.

Research Case

Internet

Case 13-8 Whirlpool Corporation

Pesos, pounds, and yen. Whether recording sales in Mexico, Britain, or Japan, these currencies are familiar to the accountants and financial managers at Whirlpool Corporation. This global company hopes its international business activities will generate sales growth to increase earnings.

Conduct a search of the World Wide Web, obtain Whirlpool's most recent annual report, or use library resources to obtain company financial data, and answer the following:

1. For the most recent year available, locate Whirlpool's net sales for North America, Europe, Asia, and Latin America. How do these figures compare with the amount shown in the "Focus on Financial Results" in the opening vignette shown at the start of this chapter? Which geographic segment is growing most rapidly?

2. As a financial planner, would you recommend Whirlpool's stock to those who desire to invest in a growth-oriented company? Why?

Optional Research. Access Whirlpool's Web site and other sites to obtain information about current and planned international growth of the company. Are management's plans and company growth philosophy supported by its financial trends?

Solution to Key Terms Quiz

8	Subsidiary (p. 604)	18	Parent (p. 604)
11	Wholly owned subsidiary (p. 604)	9	Affiliate (p. 604)
4	Debt security (p. 606)	7	Equity security (p. 606)
5	Equity method (p. 606)	22	Consolidated financial statements (p. 606)
25	Held-to-maturity securities (p. 607)		
21	Available-for-sale securities (p. 607)	19	Trading securities (p. 607)
27	Horizontal combination (p. 616)	16	Amortized cost method (p. 608)
6	Conglomerate (p. 617)	1	Vertical combination (p. 617)
3	Statutory consolidation (p. 617)	10	Statutory merger (p. 617)
2	Purchase method (p. 617)	12	Stock acquisition (p. 617)
26	Goodwill (p. 619)	15	Pooling of interests method (p. 617)
20	Exchange rate (p. 625)	17	Minority interest (p. 624)
14	Foreign currency translation (p. 627)	23	Foreign currency transaction (p. 626)
13	Translation adjustment (p. 629)	24	Functional currency (p. 628)

The Statement of Cash Flows

STUDY LINKS

A Look at Previous Chapters

In previous chapters we have seen that assets and liabilities involve important cash flows to a business at one time or another. In Chapters 1 and 2, we introduced the statement of cash flows along with the other financial statements.

Chapter 13 completed our examination of the accounting and reporting issues for a company's various assets and liabilities. Specifically, in that chapter, we considered how companies account for investments in other entities. In addition, we looked at issues related to the consolidation of a group of entities under common control and issues related to foreign currency.

A Look at This Chapter

Now that we have a fuller appreciation of how to account for the various assets and liabilities of a business, we turn our attention in this chapter to an in-depth examination of the statement of cash flows.

A Look at the Upcoming Chapter

Stockholders, creditors, and other groups use financial statements, including the statement of cash flows, to analyze a company. We called attention in earlier chapters to various ratios often used to aid in these analyses. In the final chapter, we discuss the use of ratios and other types of analysis to better understand the financial strength and health of companies.

FOCUS ON FINANCIAL RESULTS

Many people think of IBM as a powerhouse in the computer industry, but in 1993 the company suffered a net loss of over $8 billion. Then, just two years later, it earned more than $4 billion. How? The story is in IBM's comparative statement of cash flows, shown here.

Each statement of cash flows begins with the year's profit or loss, then adds back expenses that do not have cash flow effects. In 1993 a sizable part of the loss came from restructuring charges. At a cost of

(DOLLARS IN MILLIONS)

For the year ended December 31:	1995	1994	1993
Cash flow from operating activities:			
Net earnings (loss)	$ 4,178	$ 3,021	$ (8,101)
Adjustments to reconcile net earnings (loss) to cash provided from operating activities:			
Effect of change in accounting principle	–	–	114
Effect of restructuring charges	(2,119)	(2,772)	5,230
Depreciation	3,955	4,197	4,710
Deferred income taxes	1,392	825	(1,335)
Amortization of software	1,647	2,098	1,951
Purchased in-process research and development	1,840	–	–
(Gain) loss on disposition of fixed and other assets	(339)	(11)	151
Other changes that provided (used) cash:			
Receivables	(530)	653	1,185
Inventories	107	1,518	583
Other assets	(1,100)	187	1,865
Accounts payable	659	305	359
Other liabilities	1,018	1,772	1,615
Net cash provided from operating activities	10,708	11,793	8,327
Cash flow from investing activities:			
Payments for plant, rental machines and other property	(4,744)	(3,078)	(3,154)
Proceeds from disposition of plant, rental machines and other property	1,561	900	793
Acquisition of Lotus Development Corporation – net	(2,880)	–	–
Investment in software	(823)	(1,361)	(1,507)
Purchases of marketable securities and other investments	(1,315)	(3,866)	(2,721)
Proceeds from marketable securities and other investments	3,149	2,476	2,387
Proceeds from the sale of Federal Systems Company	–	1,503	–
Net cash used in investing activities	(5,052)	(3,426)	(4,202)
Cash flow from financing activities:			
Proceeds from new debt	6,636	5,335	11,794
Short-term borrowings less than 90 days – net	2,557	(1,948)	(5,247)
Payments to settle debt	(9,460)	(9,445)	(8,741)
Preferred stock transactions – net	(870)	(10)	1,091
Common stock transactions – net	(4,656)	318	122
Cash dividends paid	(591)	(662)	(933)
Net cash used in financing activities	(6,384)	(6,412)	(1,914)
Effect of exchange rate changes on cash and cash equivalents	65	106	(796)
Net change in cash and cash equivalents	(663)	2,061	1,415
Cash and cash equivalents at January 1	7,922	5,861	4,446
Cash and cash equivalents at December 31	$ 7,259	$ 7,922	$ 5,861
Supplemental data:			
Cash paid during the year for:			
Income taxes*	$ 1,453	$ 649	$ 813
Interest	$ 1,720	$ 2,132	$ 2,410

*Prior years restated to include withholding taxes paid on repatriation of dividends and royalties from foreign subsidiaries.

The notes on pages 54 through 78 are an integral part of this statement.

$5.23 billion, IBM had reorganized the business from top to bottom—a change that created a leaner, more competitive company.

One benefit of the change was that it helped IBM increase its total cash from $5.861 billion at the end of 1993 to $7.922 billion a year later. That healthy cash position made IBM's 1995 purchase of software producer Lotus Development Corporation readily affordable. With Lotus in the fold, IBM sold $12.7 billion in software, making the company the world leader in sales of software as well as hardware.

If you were an IBM stockholder, what evidence from the statements of cash flows would help you determine whether IBM's restructuring and the purchase of Lotus will generate long-term benefits? What additional information would you want? Look up IBM's most recent annual report; how well has the company generated and used cash since 1995?

SOURCE: *IBM Annual Report,* 1995.

LEARNING OBJECTIVES

After studying this chapter, you should be able to

LO 1 Explain the purpose of a statement of cash flows.

LO 2 Explain what cash equivalents are and how they are treated on the statement of cash flows.

LO 3 Describe operating, investing, and financing activities, and give examples of each.

LO 4 Describe the difference between the direct and the indirect methods of computing cash flow from operating activities.

LO 5 Use T accounts to prepare a statement of cash flows, using the direct method to determine cash flow from operating activities.

LO 6 Use T accounts to prepare a statement of cash flows, using the indirect method to determine cash flow from operating activities.

LO 7 Use a work sheet to prepare a statement of cash flows, using the indirect method to determine cash flow from operating activities (Appendix 14A).

Cash Flows and Accrual Accounting

The *bottom line* is a phrase used in many different ways in today's society. "I wish politicians would cut out all of the rhetoric and get to the bottom line." "The bottom line is that the manager was fired because the team wasn't winning." "Our company's bottom line is twice what it was last year." This last use of the phrase, in reference to a company's net income, is probably the way in which *bottom line* was first used. In recent years, managers, stockholders, creditors, analysts, and other users of financial statements have become more and more wary of focusing on any one number as an indicator of a company's overall performance. Most experts now agree that there has been a tendency to rely far too heavily on net income and its companion, earnings per share, and in many cases to ignore a company's cash flows. As you know by now from your study of accounting, you can't pay bills with net income; you need cash!

To understand the difference between a company's bottom line and its cash flow, consider the case of Unisys Corporation in 1995. The computer and information services company suffered a net loss of nearly $625 million, after reporting earnings of over $100 million a year earlier. During the same 12-month period, however, Unisys's cash position actually improved by over 28%, from $868 million at the beginning of the year to $1,114 million at year-end. How is this possible? First, net income is computed on an accrual basis, not a cash basis. Second, the income statement primarily reflects events related to the operating activities of a business, that is, selling products or providing services.

If you think about it, any one of four combinations is possible. That is, a company's cash position can increase or decrease during a period, and it can report a net profit or a net loss. Exhibit 14-1 illustrates this point by showing the performance of four well-known computer companies, including Unisys and IBM, during 1995. Dell Computer Corporation is the only one of the four companies that both improved its cash position in 1995 and reported a net profit. As discussed in the chapter opener, IBM reported a net profit; nevertheless, it experienced a net decrease in cash during 1995. Both Data General and Unysys reported net losses in 1995. As we saw earlier, Unisys improved its cash position, but Data General's cash actually declined during the year. To summarize, a

	EXHIBIT 14-1	Cash Flows and Net Income for Four Computer Companies in 1995 (all amounts in millions of dollars)			

COMPANY	BEGINNING BALANCE IN CASH	ENDING BALANCE IN CASH	INCREASE (DECREASE) IN CASH	NET INCOME (LOSS)
Dell Computer	$ 3	$ 43	$ 40	$ 149
IBM	7,922	7,259	(663)	4,178
Data General	142	117	(25)	(47)
Unisys	868	1,114	246	(625)

The Quaker Oats Company and Subsidiaries

Dollars in Millions

Consolidated Statements of Cash Flows

Year Ended June 30	1995	1994	1993
Cash Flows from Operating Activities:			
Net income	$ 802.0	$ 231.5	$ 171.3
Adjustments to reconcile net income to net cash provided by operating activities:			
Cumulative effect of accounting changes	4.1	—	115.5
Depreciation and amortization	191.4	171.2	156.9
Deferred income taxes	17.8	(7.7)	(46.4)
Gains on divestitures — net of tax of $476.2 in 1995	(694.6)	(9.8)	(27.8)
Restructuring charges	76.5	118.4	48.3
Loss on disposition of property and equipment	22.0	15.0	23.8
(Increase) decrease in trade accounts receivable	(70.8)	(77.7)	59.1
(Increase) decrease in inventories	(56.5)	(67.6)	41.9
(Increase) in other current assets	(53.4)	(56.3)	(25.8)
Increase (decrease) in trade accounts payable	83.9	44.1	(7.6)
Increase (decrease) in other current liabilities	52.1	6.6	(6.4)
Change in deferred compensation	17.2	15.6	11.0
Other items	83.8	67.5	44.4
Net Cash Provided by Operating Activities	475.5	450.8	558.2
Cash Flows from Investing Activities:			
Additions to property, plant and equipment	(275.5)	(175.1)	(172.3)
Business acquisitions	(1,876.5)	(96.3)	(40.4)
Business divestitures — net of tax of $476.2 in 1995	1,253.4	14.2	41.6
Change in other assets	(4.0)	(6.4)	(25.6)
Net Cash Used in Investing Activities	(902.6)	(263.6)	(196.7)
Cash Flows from Financing Activities:			
Cash dividends	(154.8)	(144.6)	(140.3)
Change in short-term debt	216.4	83.3	67.0
Proceeds from long-term debt	213.3	222.2	0.5
Reduction of long-term debt	(89.3)	(100.6)	(59.0)
Proceeds from short-term debt to be refinanced	188.0	—	—
Issuance of common treasury stock	23.0	11.8	23.3
Repurchases of common stock	(22.5)	(214.9)	(323.1)
Repurchases of preferred stock	(2.4)	(1.2)	(1.1)
Net Cash Provided by (Used) in Financing Activities	371.7	(144.0)	(432.7)
Effect of Exchange Rate Changes on Cash and Cash Equivalents	16.8	36.2	37.0
Net (Decrease) Increase in Cash and Cash Equivalents	(38.6)	79.4	(34.2)
Cash and Cash Equivalents — Beginning of Year	140.4	61.0	95.2
Cash and Cash Equivalents — End of Year	$ 101.8	$ 140.4	$ 61.0

See accompanying notes to the consolidated financial statements.

company with a profitable year does not necessarily increase its cash position, nor does a company with an unprofitable year always experience a decrease in cash.

Purpose of the Statement of Cash Flows

The **statement of cash flows** is an important complement to the other major financial statements. It summarizes the operating, investing, and financing activities of a business over a period of time. The balance sheet summarizes the cash on hand and the balances in other assets, liabilities, and owners' equity accounts, providing a snapshot at a specific point in time. The statement of cash flows reports the changes in cash over a period of time and, most important, *explains these changes.*

The income statement summarizes performance on an accrual basis. As you have learned in your study of accrual accounting, income on this basis is considered a better indicator of *future* cash inflows and outflows than is a statement limited to current cash flows. The statement of cash flows complements the accrual-based income statement by allowing users to assess a company's performance on a cash basis. As we will see in the following simple example, however, it also goes beyond presenting data related to operating performance and looks at other activities that affect a company's cash position.

An Example

Consider the following discussion between the owner of Fox River Realty and the company accountant. After a successful first year in business in 1997 in which it earned a profit of $100,000, the owner reviews the income statement for the second year, as presented in Exhibit 14-2.

As seen in the Quaker Oats 1995 statement of cash flows, the company's cash decreased during the year even though the company more than tripled its earnings from the prior year. How could this be? One need look no further than the Investing Activities section to find that Quaker spent $1,876.5 million to acquire other businesses during 1995, with most of this ($1,700 million) going to pay for the purchase of Snapple.

LO 1 Explain the purpose of a statement of cash flows.

EXHIBIT 14-2   Income Statement for Fox River Realty

FOX RIVER REALTY
INCOME STATEMENT
FOR THE YEAR ENDED DECEMBER 31, 1998

Revenues	$400,000
Depreciation expense	$ 50,000
All other expenses	100,000
Total expenses	$150,000
Net income	$250,000

The owner is pleased with the results and asks to see the balance sheet. Comparative balance sheets for the first two years are presented in Exhibit 14-3.

Where Did the Cash Go?   At first glance, the owner is surprised to see the significant decline in the Cash account. She immediately presses the accountant for answers. With such a profitable year, where has the cash gone? Specifically, why has cash decreased from $150,000 to $50,000, even though income rose from $100,000 in the first year to $250,000 in the second year?

The accountant begins his explanation to the owner by pointing out that income on a cash basis is even *higher* than the reported $250,000. Because depreciation expense is an expense that does not use cash (cash is used when the plant and equipment are purchased, not when they are depreciated), cash provided from operating activities is calculated as follows:

Net income	$250,000
Add back: Depreciation expense	50,000
Cash provided by operating activities	$300,000

Further, the accountant reminds the owner of the additional $50,000 that she invested in the business during the year. Now the owner is even more bewildered: with cash from operations of $300,000 and her own infusion of $50,000, why did cash *decrease* by $100,000? The accountant refreshes the owner's memory on three major outflows of cash during the year. First, even though the business earned $250,000, she withdrew $150,000 in dividends during the year. Second, the comparative balance sheets indicate that notes payable with the bank were reduced from $150,000 to

EXHIBIT 14-3   Balance Sheets for Fox River Realty

FOX RIVER REALTY
COMPARATIVE BALANCE SHEETS
DECEMBER 31

	DECEMBER 31	
	1998	1997
Cash	$ 50,000	$ 150,000
Plant and equipment	600,000	350,000
Accumulated depreciation	(150,000)	(100,000)
Total assets	$ 500,000	$ 400,000
Notes payable	$ 100,000	$ 150,000
Common stock	250,000	200,000
Retained earnings	150,000	50,000
Total equities	$ 500,000	$ 400,000

$100,000, requiring the use of $50,000 in cash. Finally, the comparative balance sheets show an increase in plant and equipment for the year from $350,000 to $600,000—a sizable investment of $250,000 in new long-term assets.

Statement of Cash Flows   To summarize what happened to the cash, the accountant prepares a statement of cash flows as shown in Exhibit 14-4. Although the owner is not particularly happy with the decrease in cash for the year, she is at least satisfied with the statement as an explanation of where the cash came from and how it was used. The statement summarizes the important cash activities for the year and fills a void created with the presentation of just an income statement and a balance sheet.

Reporting Requirements for a Statement of Cash Flows

Accountants have prepared variations of the statement of cash flows for many years. Names for these statements included *statement of sources and uses of funds, funds statement,* and *statement of changes in financial position.* For most companies, the definition of *funds* was broader than cash and included all working capital (current asset and current liability) accounts. Most often, the top of the statement merely listed all sources of funds; all uses of funds were listed below them. In 1987 the accounting profession decided that more standardization was necessary in the preparation of the statement, and it mandated two important changes.[1] First, the statement must be prepared on a cash basis. Second, the cash flows must be classified into three categories: operating, investing, and financing activities. We now take a closer look at each of these important requirements in preparing a statement of cash flows.

The Definition of Cash: Cash and Cash Equivalents

The purpose of the statement of cash flows is to provide information about a company's cash inflows and outflows. Thus, it is essential to have a clear understanding of what the definition of *cash* includes. According to accounting standards, certain items are

LO 2 Explain what cash equivalents are and how they are treated on the statement of cash flows.

EXHIBIT 14-4   Statement of Cash Flows for Fox River Realty

FOX RIVER REALTY
STATEMENT OF CASH FLOWS
FOR THE YEAR ENDED DECEMBER 31, 1998

Cash provided (used) by operating activities:	
Net income	$ 250,000
Add back: Depreciation expense	50,000
Net cash provided (used) by operating activities	$ 300,000
Cash provided (used) by investing activities:	
Purchase of new plant and equipment	$(250,000)
Cash provided (used) by financing activities:	
Additional investment by owner	$ 50,000
Cash dividends paid to owner	(150,000)
Repayment of notes payable to bank	(50,000)
Net cash provided (used) by financing activities	$(150,000)
Net increase (decrease) in cash	$(100,000)
Cash balance at beginning of year	150,000
Cash balance at end of year	$ 50,000

---

[1]*Statement of Financial Accounting Standards No. 95,* "Statement of Cash Flows" (Stamford, Conn.: Financial Accounting Standards Board, November 1987).

recognized as being equivalent to cash and are combined with cash on the balance sheet and the statement of cash flows.

Commercial paper (short-term notes issued by corporations), money market funds, and Treasury bills are examples of cash equivalents. To be classified as a **cash equivalent,** an item must be readily convertible to a known amount of cash and have an original maturity *to the investor* of three months or less. For example, a three-year Treasury note purchased two months before its maturity is classified as a cash equivalent. The same note purchased two years before maturity is not classified as a cash equivalent but as an investment.

To understand why cash equivalents are combined with cash when preparing a statement of cash flows, assume that a company has a cash balance of $10,000 and no assets that qualify as cash equivalents. Further assume that the $10,000 is used to purchase 90-day Treasury bills and is recorded by the following entry:

Investment in Treasury Bills	10,000	
Cash		10,000
To record purchase of 90-day Treasury bills.		

Assets	=	**Liabilities**	+	**Owners' Equity**
+10,000				
−10,000				

For record-keeping purposes, it is important to recognize this transaction as a transfer between cash in the bank and an investment in a government security. In the strictest sense, the investment represents an outflow of cash. The purchase of a security with such a short maturity does not, however, involve any significant degree of risk in terms of price changes and thus is not reported on the statement of cash flows as an outflow. Instead, for purposes of classification on the balance sheet and the statement of cash flows, this is merely a transfer *within* the cash and cash equivalents category. The important point is that before the purchase of the Treasury bills the company had $10,000 in cash and cash equivalents and that after the purchase it still had $10,000 in cash and cash equivalents. Because nothing changed, the transaction is not reported on the statement of cash flows.

Consider a different transaction involving the $10,000 and the following entry:

Investment in GM Common Stock	10,000	
Cash		10,000
To record the purchase of GM common stock.		

Assets	=	**Liabilities**	+	**Owners' Equity**
+10,000				
−10,000				

This purchase involves a certain amount of risk for the company making the investment. The GM stock is not convertible to a known amount of cash because its market value is subject to change. Thus, for balance sheet purposes, the investment is not considered a cash equivalent and is not therefore combined with cash but is classified as either a trading security or an available-for-sale security, depending on the company's intent in holding the stock (the distinction between these two types was discussed in Chapter 13). In the preparation of a statement of cash flows, the investment in stock of another company is considered a significant activity and thus is reported on the statement of cash flows.

Classification of Cash Flows

LO 3 Describe operating, investing, and financing activities, and give examples of each.

For the statement of cash flows, companies are required to classify activities into three categories: operating, investing, or financing. These categories represent the major functions of an entity, and classifying activities in this way allows users to look at important relationships. For example, one important financing activity for many businesses is borrowing money. Grouping the cash inflows from borrowing money during the period with the cash outflows from repayments of loans during the period makes it easier for analysts and other users of the statements to evaluate the company.

Each of the three types of activities can result in both cash inflows and cash outflows to the company. Thus, the general format for the statement is as shown in Exhibit 14-5. Note the direct tie between the bottom portion of this statement and the balance sheet. The beginning and ending balances in cash and cash equivalents shown as the last two lines on the statement of cash flows are taken directly from the comparative balance sheets. Some companies end their statement of cash flows with the figure for the net increase or decrease in cash and cash equivalents and do not report the beginning and ending balances in cash and cash equivalents directly on the statement of cash flows. Instead, the reader must turn to the balance sheet for these amounts. We now take a closer look at the types of activities that appear in each of the three categories on the statement of cash flows.

Operating Activities   Operating activities involve acquiring and selling products and services. The specific activities of a business depend on its type. For example, the purchase of raw materials is an important operating activity for a manufacturer. For a retailer, the purchase of inventory from a distributor constitutes an operating activity. For a realty company, the payment of a commission to a salesperson is an operating activity. All three types of businesses sell either products or services, and their sales are important operating activities.

A statement of cash flows reflects the cash effects, either inflows or outflows, associated with each of these activities. For example, the manufacturer's payment for purchases of raw materials results in a cash outflow. The receipt of cash from collecting an account receivable results in a cash inflow. The income statement reports operating activities on an accrual basis. The statement of cash flows reflects a company's operating activities on a cash basis.

Investing Activities   Investing activities involve acquiring and disposing of long-term assets. Replacing worn-out plant and equipment and expanding the existing base of long-term assets are essential to all businesses. In fact, cash paid for these acquisitions, often called *capital expenditures,* is usually the largest single item in the Investing Activities section of the statement. The following excerpt from IBM's 1995 statement of cash flows indicates that the company spent over $4.7 billion for plant, rental machines, and other property during 1995 (all amounts are in millions of dollars):

EXHIBIT 14-5   Format for the Statement of Cash Flows

THE SMITH CORPORATION
STATEMENT OF CASH FLOWS
FOR THE YEAR ENDED DECEMBER 31, 1998

Cash flows from operating activities:		
Inflows	$ xxx	
Outflows	(xxx)	
Net cash provided (used) by operating activities		$xxx
Cash flows from investing activities:		
Inflows	xxx	
Outflows	(xxx)	
Net cash provided (used) by investing activities		xxx
Cash flows from financing activities:		
Inflows	xxx	
Outflows	(xxx)	
Net cash provided (used) by financing activities		xxx
Net increase (decrease) in cash and cash equivalents		$xxx
Cash and cash equivalents at beginning of year		xxx
Cash and cash equivalents at end of year		$xxx

Cash flow from investing activities:

Payments for plant, rental machines and other property	(4,744)
Proceeds from disposition of plant, rental machines and other property	1,561
Acquisition of Lotus Development Corporation—net	(2,880)
Investment in software	(823)
Purchases of marketable securities and other investments	(1,315)
Proceeds from marketable securities and other investments	3,149
Net cash used in investing activities	(5,052)

Sales of long-term assets, such as plant and equipment, are not generally a significant source of cash. These assets are acquired to be used in producing goods and services, or to support this function, rather than to be resold, as is true for inventory. Occasionally, however, plant and equipment may wear out or no longer be needed and are offered for sale. In fact, the excerpt from IBM's report indicates that it generated over $1.5 billion of cash in 1995 from disposals of plant, rental machines, and other property.

In Chapter 13 we explained why companies sometimes invest in the stocks and bonds of other companies. The classification of these investments on the statement of cash flows depends on the type of investment. The acquisition of one company by another, whether in the form of a merger or a stock acquisition, is an important *investing* activity to bring to the attention of statement readers. We see that IBM spent $2,880 million in 1995 to acquire Lotus. Note that it spent another $1,315 to buy marketable securities and other investments and generated $3,149 million from selling these investments. According to a footnote to IBM's statements, the company classifies marketable securities and other investments as available for sale.

Cash flows from purchases, sales, and maturities of held-to-maturity securities (bonds) and available-for-sale securities (stocks and bonds) are classified as *investing* activities. On the other hand, these same types of cash flows for trading securities are classified as *operating* activities. This apparent inconsistency in the accounting rules is based on the idea that trading securities are held for the express purpose of generating short-term profits and thus are operating in nature.

Financing Activities   All businesses rely on internal financing, external financing, or a combination of the two in meeting their needs for cash. Initially, a new business must have a certain amount of investment by the owners to begin operations. After this, many companies use notes, bonds, and other forms of debt to provide financing.[2] Issuing stock and various forms of debt results in cash inflows that appear as **financing activities** on the statement of cash flows. On the other side, the repurchase of a company's own stock and the repayment of borrowings are important cash outflows to be reported in the financing section of the statement. Another important activity listed in the financing section of the statement is the payment of dividends to stockholders. IBM's 1995 statement of cash flows lists most of the common cash inflows and outflows from financing activities (amounts in millions of dollars):

Cash flow from financing activities:

Proceeds from new debt	6,636
Short-term borrowings less than 90 days—net	2,557
Payments to settle debt	(9,460)
Preferred stock transactions—net	(870)
Common stock transactions—net	(4,656)
Cash dividends paid	(591)
Net cash used in financing activities	(6,384)

In 1995 IBM received over $6.6 billion from issuing new debt and paid over $9.4 billion to retire old debt. In analyzing IBM, your next step would probably be to read the

---

[2]Wm. Wrigley Jr. Company is unusual is this regard in that it relies almost solely on funds generated from stockholders, in the form of common stock, for financing. The company had no short-term notes payable at December 31, 1995, and total long-term liabilities accounted for barely over 8% of the total liabilities and stockholders' equity on the balance sheet on that date.

long-term debt footnote to see whether the company essentially refinanced the old debt with new debt at a lower interest rate and, if it did, what the interest saving is, because this will continue to be a benefit for many years.

Summary of the Three Types of Activities   To summarize the categorization of the activities of a business as operating, investing, and financing, refer to Exhibit 14-6. The exhibit lists examples of each of the three activities along with the related accounts on the balance sheet and the account classifications on the balance sheet.

In the exhibit, operating activities center on the acquisition and sale of products and services and related costs, such as wages and taxes. Two important observations can be made about the cash flow effects from the operating activities of a business. *First, the cash flows from these activities are the cash effects of transactions that enter into the determination of net income.* For example, the sale of a product enters into the calculation of net income. The cash effect of this transaction, that is, the collection of the account receivable, results in a cash inflow from operating activities. *Second, cash flows from operating activities usually relate to an increase or decrease in either a current asset or a current liability.* For example, the payment of taxes to the government results in a decrease in taxes payable, which is a current liability on the balance sheet.

Note that investing activities normally relate to long-term assets on the balance sheet. For example, the purchase of new plant and equipment increases long-term assets, and the sale of these same assets reduces long-term assets on the balance sheet.

Finally, *note that financing activities usually relate to either long-term liabilities or stockholders' equity accounts.* There are exceptions to these observations about the type of balance sheet account involved with each of the three types of activities, but these rules of thumb are useful as we begin to analyze transactions and attempt to determine their classification on the statement of cash flows.

Two Methods of Reporting Cash Flow from Operating Activities

Companies use one of two different methods to report the amount of cash flow from operating activities. The first approach, called the direct method, involves reporting major classes of gross cash receipts and cash payments. For example, cash collected from customers is reported separately from any interest and dividends received. Each of the

LO 4 Describe the difference between the direct and the indirect methods of computing cash flow from operating activities.

EXHIBIT 14-6   Classification of Items on the Statement of Cash Flows

ACTIVITY	EXAMPLES	EFFECT ON CASH	RELATED BALANCE SHEET ACCOUNT	CLASSIFICATION ON BALANCE SHEET
Operating	Collection of customer accounts	Inflow	Accounts receivable	Current asset
	Payment to suppliers for inventory	Outflow	Accounts payable Inventory	Current liability Current asset
	Payment of wages	Outflow	Wages payable	Current liability
	Payment of taxes	Outflow	Taxes payable	Current liability
Investing	Capital expenditures	Outflow	Plant and equipment	Long-term asset
	Purchase of another company	Outflow	Long-term investment	Long-term asset
	Sale of plant and equipment	Inflow	Plant and equipment	Long-term asset
	Sale of another company	Inflow	Long-term investment	Long-term asset
Financing	Issuance of capital stock	Inflow	Capital stock	Stockholders' equity
	Issuance of bonds	Inflow	Bonds payable	Long-term liability
	Issuance of bank note	Inflow	Notes payable	Long-term liability
	Repurchase of stock	Outflow	Treasury stock	Stockholders' equity
	Retirement of bonds	Outflow	Bonds payable	Long-term liability
	Repayment of notes	Outflow	Notes payable	Long-term liability
	Payment of dividends	Outflow	Retained earnings	Stockholders' equity

---

EXHIBIT 14-7   Boulder Company Income Statement

BOULDER COMPANY
INCOME STATEMENT
FOR THE YEAR ENDED DECEMBER 31, 1998

Revenues	$80,000
Operating expenses	(64,000)
Income before tax	$16,000
Income tax expense	(4,000)
Net income	$12,000

---

major types of cash payments related to the company's operations follows, such as cash paid for inventory, for salaries and wages, for interest, and for taxes. An acceptable alternative to this approach is the indirect method. Under the indirect method, net cash flow from operating activities is computed by adjusting net income to remove the effect of all deferrals of past operating cash receipts and payments, and all accruals of future operating cash receipts and payments.

Although the direct method is preferred by the Financial Accounting Standards Board, it is used much less frequently than the indirect method in practice. In fact, an annual survey of 600 companies reported that 585 companies used the indirect method and only 15 companies used the direct method.[3]

To compare and contrast the two methods, assume that Boulder Company begins operations on January 1, 1998, with the owners' investment of $10,000 in cash. An income statement for 1998 and a balance sheet as of December 31, 1998, are presented in Exhibits 14-7 and 14-8, respectively.

Direct Method   To report cash flow from operating activities under the direct method, we look at each of the items on the income statement and determine how much cash each of these activities either generated or used. For example, revenues for the period were $80,000. Since the balance sheet at the end of the period shows a balance in Accounts Receivable of $13,000, however, Boulder collected only $80,000 – $13,000, or $67,000, from its sales of the period. Thus, the first line on the statement of cash flows in Exhibit 14-9 reports $67,000 in cash collected from customers. Remember that the *net increase* in Accounts Receivable must be deducted from sales to find cash collected. For a new company, this is the same as the ending balance because the company starts the year without a balance in Accounts Receivable.

The same logic can be applied to determine the amount of cash expended for operating purposes. Operating expenses on the income statement are reported at $64,000.

EXHIBIT 14-8   Boulder Company Balance Sheet

BOULDER COMPANY
BALANCE SHEET
AS OF DECEMBER 31, 1998

ASSETS		LIABILITIES AND STOCKHOLDERS' EQUITY	
Cash	$15,000	Accounts payable	$ 6,000
Accounts receivable	13,000	Capital stock	10,000
		Retained earnings	12,000
Total	$28,000	Total	$28,000

---

[3]*Accounting Trends & Techniques,* 50th ed. (New York: American Institute of Certified Public Accountants, 1996).

EXHIBIT 14-9   Statement of Cash Flows Using the Direct Method

BOULDER COMPANY
STATEMENT OF CASH FLOWS
FOR THE YEAR ENDED DECEMBER 31, 1998

CASH FLOWS FROM OPERATING ACTIVITIES

Cash collected from customers	$ 67,000
Cash payments for operating purposes	(58,000)
Cash payments for taxes	(4,000)
Net cash inflow from operating activities	$ 5,000

CASH FLOWS FROM FINANCING ACTIVITIES

Issuance of capital stock	$ 10,000
Net increase in cash	$ 15,000
Cash balance, beginning of period	–0–
Cash balance, end of period	$ 15,000

According to the balance sheet, however, $6,000 of the expense is unpaid at the end of the period as evidenced by the balance in Accounts Payable. Thus, the amount of cash expended for operating purposes as reported on the statement of cash flows in Exhibit 14-9 is $64,000 – $6,000, or $58,000. The other cash payment in the Operating Activities section of the statement is $4,000 for income taxes. Because no liability for income taxes is reported on the balance sheet, we know that $4,000 represents both the income tax expense of the period and the amount paid to the government. The only other item on the statement of cash flows in Exhibit 14-9 is the cash inflow from financing activities for the amount of cash invested by the owner in return for capital stock.

Indirect Method   When the indirect method is used, the first line in the Operating Activities section of the statement of cash flows as shown in Exhibit 14-10 is the net income of the period. Net income is then adjusted to reconcile it to the amount of cash provided by operating activities. As reported on the income statement, this net income figure includes the sales of $80,000 for the period. As we know, however, the amount of cash collected was $13,000 less than this because not all customers paid Boulder the

EXHIBIT 14-10   Statement of Cash Flows Using the Indirect Method

BOULDER COMPANY
STATEMENT OF CASH FLOWS
FOR THE YEAR ENDED DECEMBER 31, 1998

CASH FLOWS FROM OPERATING ACTIVITIES

Net income	$ 12,000
Adjustments to reconcile net income to net cash from operating activities:	
Increase in accounts receivable	(13,000)
Increase in accounts payable	6,000
Net cash inflow from operating activities	$ 5,000

CASH FLOWS FROM FINANCING ACTIVITIES

Issuance of capital stock	$ 10,000
Net increase in cash	$ 15,000
Cash balance, beginning of period	–0–
Cash balance, end of period	$ 15,000

amount due. *The increase in Accounts Receivable for the period is deducted from net income on the statement because the increase indicates that the company sold more during the period than it collected in cash.*

The logic for the addition of the increase in Accounts Payable is similar, although the effect is the opposite. The amount of operating expenses deducted on the income statement was $64,000. We know, however, that the amount of cash paid was $6,000 less than this, as the balance in Accounts Payable indicates. *The increase in Accounts Payable for the period is added back to net income on the statement because the increase indicates that the company paid less during the period than it recognized in expense on the income statement.* One observation can be noted about this example. Because this is the first year of operations for Boulder, we wouldn't be too concerned that accounts receivable is increasing faster than accounts payable. If this becomes a trend, however, we would try to improve the accounts receivable collections process.

Two important observations should be made in comparing the two methods illustrated in Exhibits 14-9 and 14-10. First, the amount of cash provided by operating activities is the same under the two methods; the two methods are simply different computational approaches to arrive at the cash generated from operations. Second, the remainder of the statement of cash flows is the same, regardless of which method is used. The only difference between the two methods is in the Operating Activities section of the statement.

Noncash Investing and Financing Activities

Occasionally, companies engage in important investing and financing activities that do not affect cash. For example, assume that at the end of the year Wolk Corp. issues capital stock to an inventor in return for the exclusive rights to a patent. Although the patent has no ready market value, the stock could have been sold on the open market for $25,000. Thus, the following entry is made on Wolk's books:

Patent	25,000	
Capital Stock		25,000
To record issuance of stock in exchange for patent.		

Assets	=	**Liabilities**	+	**Owners' Equity**
+25,000				**+25,000**

This transaction does not involve cash and is therefore not reported on the statement of cash flows. However, what if we changed the scenario slightly? Assume that Wolk wants the patent but the inventor is not willing to accept stock in return for it. So instead Wolk sells stock on the open market for $25,000 and then pays this amount in cash to the inventor for the rights to the patent. Now Wolk records two journal entries. The first is as follows:

Cash	25,000	
Capital Stock		25,000
To record issuance of capital stock for cash.		

Assets	=	**Liabilities**	+	**Owners' Equity**
+25,000				**+25,000**

It next records this entry:

Patent	25,000	
Cash		25,000
To record acquisition of patent for cash.		

Assets	=	**Liabilities**	+	**Owners' Equity**
+25,000				
−25,000				

How would each of these two transactions be reported on a statement of cash flows? The first transaction appears as a cash inflow in the Financing Activities section of the statement; the second is reported as a cash outflow in the Investing Activities section.

FROM CONCEPT TO PRACTICE 14.1

READING IBM'S STATEMENT OF CASH FLOWS Does IBM use the direct or the indirect method in the Operating Activities section of its statement of cash flows? How can you tell which it is?

The point is that even though the *form* of this arrangement (with stock sold for cash and then the cash paid to the inventor) differs from the form of the first arrangement (with stock exchanged directly for the patent), the *substance* of the two arrangements is the same. That is, both involve a significant financing activity, the issuance of stock, and an important investing activity, the acquisition of a patent. Because the substance is what matters, accounting standards require that any significant noncash transactions be reported either in a separate schedule or in a footnote to the financial statements. For our transaction in which stock was issued directly to the inventor, presentation in a schedule is as follows:

SUPPLEMENTAL SCHEDULE OF NONCASH INVESTING AND FINANCING ACTIVITIES
Acquisition of patent in exchange for capital stock $25,000

To this point, we have concentrated on the purpose of a statement of cash flows and the major reporting requirements related to it. We turn our attention next to a methodology to use in actually preparing the statement.

How the Statement of Cash Flows Is Put Together

Two interesting observations can be made about the statement of cash flows. First, the "answer" to a statement of cash flows is known before we start to prepare it. That is, the change in cash for the period is known by comparing two successive balance sheets. Thus, it is not the change in cash itself that is emphasized on the statement of cash flows but the *explanations* for the change in cash. That is, each item on a statement of cash flows helps to explain why cash changed by the amount it did during the period. The second important observation about the statement of cash flows relates even more specifically to how we prepare it. Both an income statement and a balance sheet are prepared simply by taking the balances in each of the various accounts in the general ledger and putting them in the right place on the right statement. This is not true for the statement of cash flows, however. Instead, it is necessary to analyze the transactions during the period and attempt to (1) determine which of these affected cash and (2) classify each of the cash effects into one of the three categories.

In the simple examples presented so far in the chapter, we prepared the statement of cash flows without the use of any special tools. In more complex situations, however, some type of methodology is needed. We first will review the basic accounting equation and then illustrate a T-account approach for preparing the statement. Appendix 14A presents a work-sheet approach to the preparation of the statement of cash flows.

The Accounting Equation and the Statement of Cash Flows

The basic accounting equation is as follows:

$$Assets = Liabilities + Owners'\ Equity$$

Next, consider this refinement of the equation:

$$Cash + NCCA + LTA = CL + LTL + CS + RE$$

where

$$NCCA = \text{noncash current assets}$$
$$LTA = \text{long-term assets}$$
$$CL = \text{current liabilities}$$
$$LTL = \text{long-term liabilities}$$
$$CS = \text{capital stock}$$
$$RE = \text{retained earnings}$$

The equation can be rearranged so that cash is on the left side and all other items are on the right side:

$$\text{Cash} = CL + LTL + CS + RE - NCCA - LTA$$

Finally, it stands to reason that any changes in cash must be accompanied by a corresponding change in the right side of the equation. For example, an increase or inflow of cash could result from an *increase* in long-term liabilities in the form of issuing bonds payable, an important financing activity for many companies. Or an increase in cash could come from a *decrease* in long-term assets in the form of a sale of fixed assets. The various possibilities for inflows and outflows of cash can be summarized by activity as follows:

ACTIVITY	LEFT SIDE	RIGHT SIDE	EXAMPLE
Operating	+ Cash	− NCCA	Collect accounts receivable
	− Cash	+ NCCA	Prepay insurance
	+ Cash	+ CL	Collect customer's deposit
	− Cash	− CL	Pay suppliers
	+ Cash	+ RE	Make a cash sale
Investing	+ Cash	− LTA	Sell equipment
	− Cash	+ LTA	Buy equipment
Financing	+ Cash	+ LTL	Issue bonds
	− Cash	− LTL	Retire bonds
	+ Cash	+ CS	Issue capital stock
	− Cash	− CS	Buy treasury stock
	− Cash	− RE	Pay dividends

What becomes clear by considering these examples is that inflows and outflows of cash relate to increases and decreases in the various balance sheet accounts. We now turn our attention to a methodology for analyzing these accounts as a way to assemble a statement of cash flows.

A Master T-Account Approach to Preparing the Statement of Cash Flows: Direct Method

LO 5 Use T accounts to prepare a statement of cash flows, using the direct method to determine cash flow from operating activities.

The following steps can be used to prepare a statement of cash flows:

1. **Set up three master T accounts with the following headings:**

   a. Cash Flows from Operating Activities

   b. Cash Flows from Investing Activities

   c. Cash Flows from Financing Activities

   These master T accounts take the place of the Cash account. As we analyze the transactions that affect each of the noncash balance sheet accounts, any cash effects are entered on the appropriate master account. When completed, the three master accounts contain all of the information needed to prepare a statement of cash flows.

2. **Determine the cash flows from operating activities.** Generally, this requires analyzing each item on the *income statement* and the *current asset* and *current liability* accounts. Draft journal entries for each transaction, using a lettering system for identification purposes, and post them to the appropriate balance sheet accounts. In many instances, these will be summary entries for the entire period. For example, we make one entry for all credit sales for the period, one entry for all collections on account, and so forth. Enter any increases in cash on the left side of the Cash Flow from Operating Activities master T account and any decreases on the right side.

3. **Determine the cash flows from investing activities.** Generally, this requires analyzing the *long-term asset* accounts and any additional information provided. Draft journal entries for each transaction and post them to the appropriate balance sheet accounts. Enter any increases in cash on the left side of the Cash Flow from Investing Activities master T account and any decreases on the right side. Enter any significant noncash activities on a supplemental schedule.

4. **Determine the cash flows from financing activities.** Generally, this requires analyzing the *long-term liability* and *stockholders' equity* accounts and any additional information provided. Draft journal entries for each transaction. Enter any increases in cash on the left side of the Cash Flow from Financing Activities master T account and any decreases on the right side of the T account. Enter any significant noncash activities on a supplemental schedule.

Remember that these are general rules that the cash effects of changes in current accounts are reported in the operating section, those relating to long-term asset accounts in the investing section, and those relating to long-term liabilities and stockholders' equity in the financing section. The general rules for classification of activities have a few exceptions, but we will not concern ourselves with them.

To illustrate this approach, we will refer to the income statement in Exhibit 14-11 and to the comparative balance sheets and the additional information provided for Julian Corp. in Exhibit 14-12.

Determine the Cash Flows from Operating Activities   To do this, we need to consider each of the items on the income statement and any related current assets or liabilities from the balance sheet.

Sales Revenue and Accounts Receivable   Sales as reported on the income statement in Exhibit 14-11 amounted to $670,000. The journal entry was as follows:

(a)   Accounts Receivable   670,000
     Sales Revenue   670,000
    To record sales on account.

Assets   =   **Liabilities**   +   **Owners' Equity**
+**670,000**   +**670,000**

EXHIBIT 14-11   Julian Corp. Income Statement

JULIAN CORP.
INCOME STATEMENT
FOR THE YEAR ENDED DECEMBER 31, 1998

Revenues and gains:		
Sales revenue	$670,000	
Interest revenue	15,000	
Gain on sale of machine	5,000	
Total revenues and gains		$690,000
Expenses and losses:		
Cost of goods sold	$390,000	
Salaries and wages	60,000	
Depreciation	40,000	
Insurance	12,000	
Interest	15,000	
Income taxes	50,000	
Loss on retirement of bonds	3,000	
Total expenses and losses		570,000
Net income		$120,000

EXHIBIT 14-12 Julian Corp. Comparative Balance Sheets

JULIAN CORP.
COMPARATIVE BALANCE SHEETS

| | DECEMBER 31 | |
	1998	1997
Cash	$ 35,000	$ 46,000
Accounts receivable	63,000	57,000
Inventory	84,000	92,000
Prepaid insurance	12,000	18,000
Total current assets	$ 194,000	$213,000
Long-term investments	$ 120,000	$ 90,000
Land	150,000	100,000
Property and equipment	320,000	280,000
Accumulated depreciation	(100,000)	(75,000)
Total long-term assets	$ 490,000	$395,000
Total assets	$ 684,000	$608,000
Accounts payable	$ 38,000	$ 31,000
Salaries and wages payable	7,000	9,000
Income taxes payable	8,000	5,000
Total current liabilities	$ 53,000	$ 45,000
Notes payable	$ 85,000	$ 35,000
Bonds payable	200,000	260,000
Total long-term liabilities	$ 285,000	$295,000
Capital stock	$ 100,000	$ 75,000
Retained earnings	246,000	193,000
Total stockholders' equity	$ 346,000	$268,000
Total liabilities and stockholders' equity	$ 684,000	$608,000

Additional Information

1. Long-term investments were purchased for $30,000. The securities are classified as available for sale.
2. Land was purchased by issuing a $50,000 note payable.
3. Equipment was purchased for $75,000.
4. A machine with an original cost of $35,000 and a book value of $20,000 was sold for $25,000.
5. Bonds with a face value of $60,000 were retired by paying $63,000 in cash.
6. Capital stock was issued in exchange for $25,000 in cash.
7. Dividends of $67,000 were paid.

Based on the beginning and ending balances in Exhibit 14-12, a T account for Accounts Receivable appears as follows after posting the debit for the sales of the period:

ACCOUNTS RECEIVABLE			
Bal. Jan. 1	57,000		
(a) Sales on account	670,000	?	Cash collections (b)
Bal. Dec. 31	63,000		

Accounts Receivable increased by $6,000 for the period. *This indicates that Julian had $6,000 more in sales to its customers than it collected in cash from them* (assuming that all sales are on credit). Thus, cash collections must have been $670,000 − $6,000, or $664,000. Another way to look at this is as follows:

Beginning accounts receivable	$ 57,000
+ Sales revenue	670,000
− Cash collections	(X)
= Ending accounts receivable	$ 63,000

Solving for X, we can find cash collections:

$$57,000 + 670,000 - X = 63,000$$
$$X = \underline{664,000}$$

The journal entry to record cash collections was as follows:

(b) Cash   664,000
          Accounts Receivable   664,000
          To record cash collected on account.

Assets	=	**Liabilities**	+	**Owners' Equity**
+**664,000**				
−**664,000**				

At this point, note the debit to Cash for $664,000 as shown in the master T account Cash Flows from Operating Activities, in Exhibit 14-13.

Interest Revenue Julian reported interest revenue on the income statement of $15,000. Did the company actually receive this amount of cash, or was it merely an accrual of revenue earned but not yet received? The answer can be found by examining the current asset section of the balance sheet. *Because there is no Interest Receivable account, the amount of interest earned was the amount of cash received:*

(c) Cash   15,000
          Interest Revenue   15,000
          To record interest earned and received.

| **Assets** | = | **Liabilities** | + | **Owners' Equity** |
| +**15,000** | | | | +**15,000** |

The debit should be entered in the master T account Cash Flows from Operating Activities, as shown in Exhibit 14-13.

Gain on Sale of Machine A gain on the sale of machine of $5,000 is reported as the next line on the income statement. Any cash received from the sale of a long-term asset is reported in the Investing Activities section of the statement of cash flows. Thus, we ignore the gain when reporting cash flows from operating activities under the direct method.

Cost of Goods Sold, Inventory, and Accounts Payable Cost of goods sold, as reported on the income statement, amounts to $390,000 and was recorded with this entry:

(d) Cost of Goods Sold   390,000
          Inventory   390,000
          To record cost of goods sold.

| **Assets** | = | **Liabilities** | + | **Owners' Equity** |
| −**390,000** | | | | −**390,000** |

EXHIBIT 14-13 Master T Account for Cash Flows from Operating Activities

CASH FLOWS FROM OPERATING ACTIVITIES

Cash receipts from:		Cash payments for:	
(b) Sales on account	664,000	(f) Inventory purchases	375,000
(c) Interest	15,000	(h) Salaries and wages	62,000
		(k) Insurance	6,000
		(l) Interest	15,000
		(n) Taxes	47,000

We see that $390,000 is not the amount of cash expended to pay suppliers of inventory. First, cost of goods sold represents the cost of the inventory sold during the period, not the amount purchased. Thus, we must analyze the Inventory account to determine the purchases of the period. Second, the amount of purchases is not the same as the cash paid to suppliers because purchases are normally on account. Thus, we must analyze the Accounts Payable account to determine the cash payments.

Based on the beginning and ending balances from Exhibit 14-12, a T account for Inventory appears as follows after posting the reduction in the account for cost of goods sold:

INVENTORY			
Bal. Jan. 1	92,000		
(e) Purchases on account	?	390,000	Cost of goods sold (d)
Bal. Dec. 31	84,000		

Note the $8,000 net decrease in Inventory. *This means that the cost of inventory sold was $8,000 more than the purchases of the period.* Thus, purchases must have been $390,000 − $8,000, or $382,000. Another way to look at this is as follows:

Beginning inventory	$ 92,000
+ Purchases	X
− Cost of goods sold	(390,000)
= Ending inventory	$ 84,000

Solving for X, we can find purchases:

$$92,000 + X - 390,000 = 84,000$$
$$X = \underline{382,000}$$

The journal entry to record purchases was as follows:

(e) Inventory	382,000	
Accounts Payable		382,000
To record purchases on account.		

Assets	**=**	**Liabilities**	**+**	**Owners' Equity**
+382,000		**+382,000**		

From Exhibit 14-12, a T account for Accounts Payable, after posting the credit for purchases of the period, is as follows:

ACCOUNTS PAYABLE			
		31,000	Bal. Jan. 1
(f) Cash payments	?	382,000	Purchases (e)
		38,000	Bal. Dec. 31

Note the $7,000 net increase in Accounts Payable. *This means that Julian's purchases were $7,000 more during the period than its cash payments.* Thus, cash payments must have been $382,000 − $7,000, or $375,000. Another way to look at this is as follows:

Beginning accounts payable	$ 31,000
+ Purchases	382,000
− Cash payments	(X)
= Ending accounts payable	$ 38,000

Solving for X, we can find cash payments:

$$31,000 + 382,000 - X = 38,000$$
$$X = \underline{375,000}$$

The journal entry to record payments on account was as follows:

(f) Accounts Payable   375,000
        Cash   375,000
     To record cash payments on account.

                    Assets   = Liabilities + Owners' Equity
                   −375,000   −375,000

At this point, the credit to cash should be entered in the master T account Cash Flows from Operating Activities, as shown in Exhibit 14-13.

Salaries and Wages Expense and Salaries and Wages Payable   The entry to record salaries and wages expense was as follows:

(g) Salaries and Wages Expense   60,000
        Salaries and Wages Payable   60,000
     To record salaries and wages.

                    Assets   = Liabilities + Owners' Equity
                                  +60,000   −60,000

After this entry is posted to Salaries and Wages Payable, note the $2,000 net decrease in the account for the period:

	SALARIES AND WAGES PAYABLE		
		9,000	Bal. Jan. 1
(h) Cash payments	?	60,000	Expense (g)
		7,000	Bal. Dec. 31

This means that the amount of cash paid to employees was $2,000 more than the amount of expense accrued. Another way to look at the cash payments of $60,000 + $2,000, or $62,000, is as follows:

	Beginning salaries and wages payable	$ 9,000
+	Salaries and wages expense	60,000
−	Cash payments to employees	(X)
=	Ending accounts payable	$ 7,000

Solving for X, we can find cash payments:

$$9{,}000 + 60{,}000 - X = 7{,}000$$
$$X = \underline{62{,}000}$$

The journal entry to record the cash paid was as follows:

(h) Salaries and Wages Payable   62,000
        Cash   62,000
     To record cash paid to employees.

                    Assets   = Liabilities + Owners' Equity
                   −62,000   −62,000

As you see in Exhibit 14-13, the credit of $62,000 in this entry appears in the T account for Cash Flows from Operating Activities.

Depreciation Expense   The next item on the income statement is depreciation of $40,000. The entry to record depreciation was as follows:

(i) Depreciation Expense   40,000
        Accumulated Depreciation   40,000
     To record depreciation.

                    Assets   = Liabilities + Owners' Equity
                   −40,000   −40,000

Depreciation of tangible long-term assets, amortization of intangible assets, and depletion of natural resources are different from most other expenses in that they have no effect on cash flow. The only related cash flows are from the purchase and the sale of these long-term assets, and these are reported in the Investing Activities section of the statement of cash flows.

ACCOUNTING FOR YOUR DECISIONS
You Are an Entrepreneur

You operate a coffee cart in the lobby of an office building. You started the business this year by investing $5,000 of your own money to buy the coffee cart. Even though you think the cart will last for five years, a friend who has studied accounting has advised you to recognize the entire cost of the cart as an expense the first year. He reasons that "the first year is very crucial to any business and since depreciation is added back in the operating activities section of the statement of cash flows why not add back the maximum amount so that you will maximize the cash flow from operations." Is your friend's reasoning sound?

ANS: Your friend is correct in stating that depreciation is added back in the operating activities section, assuming use of the indirect method. The only reason that depreciation is added back, however, is because it was deducted as an expense on the income statement but does not use any cash. Depreciation is not a cash flow and any manipulation of the amount of depreciation expensed in any one year will not affect the amount of cash generated from operations.

Insurance Expense and Prepaid Insurance   According to the income statement in Exhibit 14-11, Julian recorded Insurance Expense of $12,000 during 1998. This amount is not the cash payments for insurance, however, because Julian has a Prepaid Insurance account on the balance sheet. The entry to record expense involves a reduction in the Prepaid Insurance account as follows:

(j)   Insurance Expense   12,000
          Prepaid Insurance   12,000
       To record expiration of insurance.

Assets   =   Liabilities   +   Owners' Equity
-12,000   -12,000

When the credit to Prepaid Insurance is posted, note the $6,000 net decrease in the account for the period:

PREPAID INSURANCE

Bal. Jan. 1	18,000		
(k) Cash payments	?	12,000	Expense (j)
Bal. Dec. 31	12,000		

This means that the amount of cash paid for insurance was $6,000 less than the amount of expense recognized. Thus, the cash payments must have been $12,000 − $6,000, or $6,000. Another way to look at the cash payments is as follows:

Beginning prepaid insurance	$18,000
+ Cash payments for insurance	X
− Insurance expense	(12,000)
= Ending prepaid insurance	$12,000

Solving for X, we can find the amount of cash paid:

$$18,000 + X - 12,000 = 12,000$$
$$X = \underline{6,000}$$

The journal entry to record the cash paid was as follows:

(k)   Prepaid Insurance   6,000
          Cash   6,000
       To record cash paid to employees.

Assets	=	Liabilities	+	Owners' Equity
+6,000				
−6,000				

Note that the credit to Cash is entered in Exhibit 14-13 in the T account for Cash Flows from Operating Activities.

Interest Expense The amount of interest expense reported on the income statement is $15,000. Because the balance sheet does not report an accrual of interest owed but not yet paid (an Interest Payable account), we know that $15,000 is also the amount of cash paid:

(l) Interest Expense	15,000	
Cash		15,000
To record interest expense.		

Assets	=	Liabilities	+	Owners' Equity
−15,000				−15,000

The entry is recorded as as cash outflow in Exhibit 14-13. Whether interest paid is properly classified as an operating activity is subject to considerable debate. The Financial Accounting Standards Board decided in favor of classification of *interest* as an *operating* activity because, unlike dividends, it appears on the income statement. This, it was argued, provides a direct link between the statement of cash flows and the income statement. Many argue, however, that it is inconsistent to classify dividends paid as a financing activity but interest paid as an operating activity. After all, both represent returns paid to providers of capital: interest to creditors and dividends to stockholders.

Income Tax Expense and Income Taxes Payable The entry to record Income Tax Expense was as follows:

(m) Income Taxes Expense	50,000	
Income Taxes Payable		50,000
To record income taxes.		

Assets	=	Liabilities	+	Owners' Equity
		+50,000		−50,000

When the credit to Income Taxes Payable is posted, note the $3,000 net increase in the account for the period:

INCOME TAXES PAYABLE			
		5,000	Bal. Jan. 1
(n) Cash payments	?	50,000	Expense (m)
		8,000	Bal. Dec. 31

This means that the amount of cash paid to the government in taxes was $3,000 less than the amount of expense accrued. Another way to look at the cash payments of $50,000 − $3,000, or $47,000, is as follows:

	Beginning income taxes payable	$ 5,000
+	Income tax expense	50,000
−	Cash payments for taxes	(X)
=	Ending income taxes payable	$ 8,000

Solving for X, we can find the amount of cash paid:

$$5,000 + 50,000 - X = 8,000$$
$$X = \underline{47,000}$$

The journal entry to record cash paid was as follows:

(n) Income Taxes Payable	47,000	
Cash		47,000
To record cash paid in taxes.		

$$\begin{array}{ccc} \textbf{Assets} & = & \textbf{Liabilities} & + & \textbf{Owners' Equity} \\ \textbf{--47,000} & & \textbf{--47,000} \end{array}$$

As you see by examining Exhibit 14-13, the cash payments for taxes is the last item in the T account for Cash Flows from Operating Activities.

Loss on Retirement of Bonds   A $3,000 loss on the retirement of bonds is reported as the last item under expenses and losses on the income statement in Exhibit 14-11. Any cash paid to retire a long-term liability is reported in the Financing Activities section of the statement of cash flows. Thus, we ignore the loss when reporting cash flows from operating activities under the direct method.

Compare Net Income with Net Cash Flow from Operating Activities.
At this point, all of the items on the income statement have been analyzed (with the exception of the gain and the loss), as have all of the current asset and current liability accounts. All of the information needed to prepare the Operating Activities section of your statement of cash flows has been gathered.

To summarize, the preparation of the Operating Activities section of the statement of cash flows requires the conversion of each item on the income statement to a cash basis. The current asset and current liability accounts are analyzed to discover the cash effects of each item on the income statement. Exhibit 14-14 summarizes this conversion process.

Note in the exhibit the various adjustments made to put each income statement item on a cash basis. For example, the $6,000 increase in accounts receivable for the period is deducted from sales revenue of $670,000 to arrive at cash collected from customers. Similar adjustments are made to each of the other income statement items with the exception of depreciation, the gain, and the loss. Depreciation is ignored because it does not have an effect on cash flow. The gain relates to the sale of a long-term asset, and any cash effect is reflected in the Investing Activities section of the statement of cash flows. Similarly, the loss resulted from the retirement of bonds, and any cash flow effect is reported in the Financing Activities section. The bottom of the exhibit highlights an important point: Julian reported net income of $120,000 but actually generated $174,000 in cash from operations.

Determine the Cash Flows from Investing Activities   At this point, we turn our attention to the long-term asset accounts and any additional information available about these accounts. Julian has three long-term assets on its balance sheet: Long-Term Investments, Land, and Property and Equipment.

Long-Term Investments   Item 1 in the additional information in Exhibit 14-12 indicates that Julian purchased $30,000 of investments during the year. The $30,000 net increase in the Long-Term Investments account confirms this (no mention is made of the sale of any investments during 1998):

LONG-TERM INVESTMENTS		
Bal. Jan. 1	90,000	
(o) Purchases	?	
Bal. Dec. 31	120,000	

The entry to record the purchase was as follows:

(o)	Long-Term Investments	30,000	
	Cash		30,000
	To record purchase of investments.		

$$\begin{array}{ccc} \textbf{Assets} & = & \textbf{Liabilities} & + & \textbf{Owners' Equity} \\ \textbf{+30,000} \\ \textbf{--30,000} \end{array}$$

The credit in this entry is the first cash outflow in the master T account Cash Flows from Investing Activities, as shown in Exhibit 14-15.

EXHIBIT 14-14   Conversion of Income Statement Items to Cash Basis

INCOME STATEMENT	AMOUNT	ADJUSTMENTS	CASH FLOWS
Sales revenue	$670,000		$670,000
		+ Decreases in accounts receivable	–0–
		− Increases in accounts receivable	(6,000)
		Cash collected from customers	$664,000
Interest revenue	15,000		$ 15,000
		+ Decreases in interest receivable	–0–
		− Increases in interest receivable	–0–
		Cash collected in interest	$ 15,000
Gain on sale of machine	5,000	*Not an operating activity*	$ –0–
Cost of goods sold	390,000		$390,000
		+ Increases in inventory	–0–
		− Decreases in inventory	(8,000)
		+ Decreases in accounts payable	–0–
		− Increases in accounts payable	(7,000)
		Cash paid to suppliers	$375,000
Salaries and wages	60,000		$ 60,000
		+ Decreases in salaries/wages payable	2,000
		− Increases in salaries/wages payable	–0–
		Cash paid to employees	$ 62,000
Depreciation	40,000	*No cash flow effect*	$ –0–
Insurance	12,000		$ 12,000
		+ Increases in prepaid insurance	–0–
		− Decreases in prepaid insurance	(6,000)
		Cash paid for insurance	$ 6,000
Interest	15,000		$ 15,000
		+ Decreases in interest payable	–0–
		− Increases in interest payable	–0–
		Cash paid for interest	$ 15,000
Income taxes	50,000		$ 50,000
		+ Decreases in income taxes payable	–0–
		− Increases in income taxes payable	(3,000)
		Cash paid for taxes	$ 47,000
Loss on retirement of bonds	3,000	*Not an operating activity*	$ –0–
Net income	$120,000	Net cash flow from operating activities	$174,000

Land   Note the $50,000 net increase in land:

LAND	
Bal. Jan. 1	100,000
(p) Acquisitions	?
Bal. Dec. 31	150,000

Item 2 in the additional information indicates that Julian purchased land by issuing a $50,000 note payable. The entry to record the purchase was as follows:

(p)	Land	50,000	
	Notes Payable		50,000

To record acquisition of land in exchange for note.

EXHIBIT 14-15 Master T Account for Cash Flows from Investing Activities

CASH FLOWS FROM INVESTING ACTIVITIES

Cash inflows from:		Cash outflows for:	
(r) Sale of machine	25,000	(o) Purchase of investments	30,000
		(q) Purchase of plant and	
		equipment	75,000

Assets = **Liabilities** + **Owners' Equity**
+50,000   **+50,000**

This entry obviously does not involve cash. The transaction has both an important financing element and an investing component, however. The issuance of the note is a financing activity, and the acquisition of land is an investing activity. Because no cash was involved, the transaction is reported in a separate schedule instead of directly on the statement of cash flows:

SUPPLEMENTAL SCHEDULE OF NONCASH INVESTING AND FINANCING ACTIVITIES
Acquisition of land in exchange for note payable $50,000

Property and Equipment   Property and equipment increased by $40,000 during 1998. However, Julian both acquired equipment and sold a machine (items 3 and 4 in the additional information). The acquisition of the equipment for $75,000 resulted in this journal entry:

(q) Property and Equipment   75,000
     Cash   75,000
     To record acquisition of equipment for cash.

Assets = **Liabilities** + **Owners' Equity**
+75,000
−75,000

As we discussed earlier in the chapter, acquisitions of new plant and equipment are important investing activities for most businesses. Thus, the credit to Cash appears in the master T account Cash Flows from Investing Activities in Exhibit 14-15.

After this entry is posted to the Property and Equipment account, it appears as follows:

PROPERTY AND EQUIPMENT

Bal. Jan. 1	280,000		
(q) Acquisitions	75,000	?	Disposals (r)
Bal. Dec. 31	320,000		

Julian obviously disposed of fixed assets during the period. In fact, item 4 in the additional information in Exhibit 14-12 reports the sale of a machine with an original cost of $35,000. An analysis of the Property and Equipment account at this point confirms this amount:

Beginning property and equipment	$280,000
+ Acquisitions	75,000
− Disposals	(X)
= Ending property and equipment	$320,000

Solving for X, we can find the *cost* of the fixed assets sold during the year:

$$280,000 + 75,000 - X = 320,000$$
$$X = \underline{\$35,000}$$

A T account for Accumulated Depreciation appears as follows after posting Depreciation Expense in entry (i).

ACCUMULATED DEPRECIATION			
		75,000	Bal. Jan. 1
(r) Disposals	?	40,000	Depreciation expense (i)
		100,000	Bal. Dec. 31

The additional information also indicates that the book value of the machine sold was $20,000. This means that if the original cost was $35,000 and the book value was $20,000, the Accumulated Depreciation on the machine sold must have been $35,000 − $20,000, or $15,000. An analysis similar to the one we just looked at for Property and Equipment confirms this amount:

Beginning accumulated depreciation	$ 75,000
+ Depreciation expense (entry i)	40,000
− Accumulated depreciation on assets sold	(X)
= Ending accumulated depreciation	$100,000

Solving for X, we can find the accumulated depreciation on the assets disposed of during the year:

$$75,000 + 40,000 - X = 100,000$$
$$X = \underline{\$15,000}$$

Finally, we are told in the additional information that the machine was sold for $25,000. *If the selling price was $25,000 and the book value was $20,000, Julian reports a gain on sale of $5,000, an amount that is confirmed on the income statement in Exhibit 14-11.* The journal entry to record the sale of the machine was as follows:

(r) Cash	25,000	
Accumulated Depreciation	15,000	
Property and Equipment		35,000
Gain on Sale of Machine (Retained Earnings)		5,000
To record sale of machine.		

Assets	=	Liabilities	+	Owners' Equity
+25,000				+5,000
+15,000				
−35,000				

To summarize, the machine was sold for $25,000, an amount that exceeded its book value of $20,000, thus generating a gain of $5,000. The debit to Cash is entered in the master T account for Cash Flows from Investing Activities in Exhibit 14-15.

Determine the Cash Flows from Financing Activities These activities generally involve long-term liabilities and stockholders' equity. We first consider Julian's two long-term liabilities, Notes Payable and Bonds Payable, and then the two stockholders' equity accounts: Capital Stock and Retained Earnings.

Notes Payable Recall that item 2 in the additional information reported that Julian purchased land in exchange for a $50,000 note payable. The T account for Notes Payable confirms this amount:

NOTES PAYABLE		
	35,000	Bal. Jan. 1
	?	Additional issuances (p)
	85,000	Bal. Dec. 31

In our discussion of investing activities, we recorded entry (p) to account for this exchange and entered the transaction on a supplemental schedule of noncash activities because it was a significant financing activity but did not involve cash.

Bonds Payable A T account for Bonds Payable appears as follows:

	BONDS PAYABLE	
	260,000	Bal. Jan. 1
(s) Retirement ?		
	200,000	Bal. Dec. 31

Item 5 in the additional information in Exhibit 14-12 indicates that bonds with a face value of $60,000 were retired by paying $63,000 in cash. The book value of the bonds retired is the same as the face value of $60,000 because there is no unamortized discount or premium on the records. *When a company has to pay more in cash ($63,000) to settle a debt than the book value of the debt ($60,000), it reports a loss.* Recall the $3,000 loss reported on the income statement in Exhibit 14-11. The entry to record the retirement of the bonds was as follows:

(s) Loss on Retirement of Bonds (Retained Earnings)   3,000
    Bonds Payable   60,000
      Cash   63,000
To record retirement of bonds.

Assets = Liabilities + Owners' Equity
−63,000   −60,000   −3,000

The credit to Cash in this entry is presented in the master T account Cash Flows from Financing Activities, as shown in Exhibit 14-16.

Capital Stock The Capital Stock account indicates a $25,000 net increase during 1998:

	CAPITAL STOCK	
	75,000	Bal. Jan. 1
	?	Stock issued (t)
	100,000	Bal. Dec. 31

Julian issued capital stock in exchange for $25,000 in cash, according to item 6 in the additional information in Exhibit 14-12. Some companies issue additional stock after the initial formation of a corporation to raise needed capital. The entry was as follows:

(t) Cash   25,000
    Capital Stock   25,000
To record issuance of stock in exchange for cash.

Assets = Liabilities + Owners' Equity
+25,000   +25,000

The debit to Cash in this entry is presented as a cash inflow in the master T account Cash Flows from Financing Activities, as shown in Exhibit 14-16.

EXHIBIT 14-16 Master T Account for Cash Flows from Financing Activities

CASH FLOWS FROM FINANCING ACTIVITIES			
Cash inflows from:		Cash outflows for:	
(t) Issuance of stock	25,000	(s) Retirement of bonds	63,000
		(u) Payment of cash dividends	67,000

ACCOUNTING FOR YOUR DECISIONS
You Decide for Your Investment Club

You are a member of an investment club and have been given the assignment of analyzing the statements of cash flows for the Norfolk Corp. for the last three years. The company has neither issued nor retired any stock during this time period. You notice that the company's cash balance has increased steadily during this period but that a majority of the increase is due to a large net inflow of cash from financing activities in each of the three years. Should you be concerned?

ANS: The net inflow of cash from financing activities indicates that the company is borrowing more than it is repaying. Certainly borrowing can be an attractive means of financing the purchase of new plant and equipment. At some point, however, the debt along with interest, will need to be repaid. The company must be able to generate sufficient cash from its operations to make these payments.

Retained Earnings   An analysis of the Retained Earnings account indicates the following:

RETAINED EARNINGS			
		193,000	Bal. Jan. 1
(u) Cash dividends	?	120,000	Net income for 1998
		246,000	Bal. Dec. 31

We can determine the amount of cash dividends for 1998 in the following manner:

Beginning retained earnings	$193,000
+ Net income	120,000
− Cash dividends	(X)
= Ending retained earnings	$246,000

Solving for X, we can find the amount of cash dividends paid during the year:[4]

$$193,000 + 120,000 - X = 246,000$$
$$X = \underline{\$67,000}$$

Item 7 in the additional information confirms that this was in fact the amount of dividends paid during the year. The final entry was as follows:

(u) Retained Earnings	67,000	
Cash		67,000
To record cash dividends paid.		

Assets	=	**Liabilities**	+	**Owners' Equity**
−67,000				**−67,000**

The credit to Cash in this entry appears in the master T account Cash Flows from Financing Activities, as presented in Exhibit 14-16.

Using the Master T Accounts to Prepare a Statement of Cash Flows
All of the information needed to prepare a statement of cash flows is now available in the three master T accounts, along with the supplemental schedule prepared earlier. From the information gathered in Exhibits 14-13, 14-15, and 14-16, a completed statement of cash flows appears in Exhibit 14-17.

What does Julian's statement of cash flows tell us? Cash flow from operations totaled $174,000. Cash used to acquire investments and equipment amounted to $80,000, after receiving $25,000 from the sale of a machine. A net amount of $105,000 was used for

---

[4]Any decrease in Retained Earnings represents the dividends *declared* during the period rather than the amount paid. If there had been a Dividends Payable account, we would analyze it to find the amount of dividends paid. The lack of a balance in such an account at either the beginning or the end of the period tells us that Julian paid the same amount of dividends that it declared during the period.

EXHIBIT 14-17 Completed Statement of Cash Flows for Julian Corp.

JULIAN CORP.
STATEMENT OF CASH FLOWS
FOR THE YEAR ENDED DECEMBER 31, 1998

CASH FLOWS FROM OPERATING ACTIVITIES

Cash receipts from:		
Sales on account		$ 664,000
Interest		15,000
Total cash receipts		$ 679,000
Cash payments for:		
Inventory purchases		$(375,000)
Salaries and wages		(62,000)
Insurance		(6,000)
Interest		(15,000)
Taxes		(47,000)
Total cash payments		$(505,000)
Net cash provided by operating activities		$ 174,000

CASH FLOWS FROM INVESTING ACTIVITIES

Purchase of investments	$ (30,000)
Purchase of plant and equipment	(75,000)
Sale of machine	25,000
Net cash used by investing activities	$ (80,000)

CASH FLOWS FROM FINANCING ACTIVITIES

Retirement of bonds	$ (63,000)
Issuance of stock	25,000
Payment of cash dividends	(67,000)
Net cash used by financing activities	$(105,000)
Net decrease in cash	$ (11,000)
Cash balance, December 31, 1997	46,000
Cash balance, December 31, 1998	$ 35,000

SUPPLEMENTAL SCHEDULE OF NONCASH INVESTING AND FINANCING ACTIVITIES

Acquisition of land in exchange for note payable	$ 50,000

financing activities. Thus, Julian used more cash than it generated, and that's why the cash balance declined. That's okay for a year or two, but if this continues, the company won't be able to pay its bills.

A Master T-Account Approach to Preparing the Statement of Cash Flows: Indirect Method

LO 6 Use T accounts to prepare a statement of cash flows, using the indirect method to determine cash flow from operating activities.

The purpose of the Operating Activities section of the statement changes when we use the indirect method. Instead of reporting cash receipts and cash payments, *the objective is to reconcile net income to net cash flow from operating activities.* The other two sections of the completed statement in Exhibit 14-17, the investing and financing sections, are unchanged. The use of the indirect or the direct method for presenting cash flow from operating activities does not affect these two sections.

A T-account methodology, similar to that used for the direct method, can be used to prepare the Operating Activities section of the statement of cash flows under the indirect method.

Net Income Recall that the first line in the Operating Activities section of the statement under the indirect method is net income. That is, we start with the assumptions that all revenues and gains reported on the income statement increase cash flow and that all expenses and losses decrease cash flow. Julian's net income of $120,000, as reported on its income statement in Exhibit 14-11, is reported as the first item in the Operating Activities section of the statement of cash flows as shown in Exhibit 14-18.

Accounts Receivable   The net increase in Accounts Receivable, as shown below in T-account form, indicates that Julian recorded more sales than cash collections during the period:

ACCOUNTS RECEIVABLE		
Bal. Jan. 1	57,000	
Net increase	6,000	
Bal. Dec. 31	63,000	

Because net income includes sales, as opposed to cash collections, the $6,000 *net increase* must be *deducted* to adjust net income to cash from operations. To help you remember to deduct the net increase in accounts receivable in the Operating Activities section of the statement, consider the following. The $6,000 net increase appears in the preceding T account as a *debit*. Think of the deduction on the statement of cash flows as the equivalent of a *credit*. That is, the debit is to Accounts Receivable, and the credit is recorded as a bracketed amount (i.e., as a deduction) on the statement of cash flows.

Gain on Sale of Machine   The gain itself did not generate any cash, but the *sale* of the machine did. And as we found earlier, the cash generated by selling the machine was reported in the Investing Activities section of the statement. The cash proceeds included the gain. Because the gain is included in the net income figure, it must be *deducted* to determine cash from operations. Also note that the gain is included twice in cash inflows if it is not deducted from the net income figure in the Operating Activities section. Note the deduction of $5,000 in Exhibit 14-18.

Inventory   As the $8,000 net decrease in the Inventory account indicates, Julian liquidated a portion of its stock of inventory during the year:

INVENTORY			
Bal. Jan. 1	92,000		
		8,000	Net decrease
Bal. Dec. 31	84,000		

> **FROM CONCEPT TO PRACTICE 14.2**
>
> **READING BEN & JERRY'S STATEMENT OF CASH FLOWS**   Did Accounts Receivable increase or decrease during 1995? Why is the change in this account deducted on the statement of cash flows?

EXHIBIT 14-18   Indirect Method for Reporting Cash Flows from Operating Activities

JULIAN CORP.
PARTIAL STATEMENT OF CASH FLOWS
FOR THE YEAR ENDED DECEMBER 31, 1998

NET CASH FLOWS FROM OPERATING ACTIVITIES

Net income	$120,000
Adjustments to reconcile net income to net cash provided by operating activities:	
Increase in accounts receivable	(6,000)
Gain on sale of machine	(5,000)
Decrease in inventory	8,000
Increase in accounts payable	7,000
Decrease in salaries and wages payable	(2,000)
Depreciation expense	40,000
Decrease in prepaid insurance	6,000
Increase in income taxes payable	3,000
Loss on retirement of bonds	3,000
Net cash provided by operating activities	$174,000

A net decrease in this account indicates that the company sold more products than it purchased during the year. As shown in Exhibit 14-18, the *net decrease* of $8,000 is *added back* to net income. As discussed for Accounts Receivable, note the debit and credit logic for this adjustment. Because Inventory is credited in the T account for the decrease, the statement of cash flows shows an increase, which is equivalent to a debit to Cash.

Accounts Payable Julian owed suppliers $31,000 at the start of the year. By the end of the year, the balance had grown to $38,000. A T account for Accounts Payable follows:

	ACCOUNTS PAYABLE	
	31,000	Bal. Jan. 1
	7,000	Net increase
	38,000	Bal. Dec. 31

Effectively, the company saved cash by delaying the payment of some of its outstanding accounts payable. The *net increase* of $7,000 in this account is *added back* to net income, as shown in Exhibit 14-18.

Salaries and Wages Payable A T account for Salaries and Wages Payable indicates a net decrease of $2,000:

	SALARIES AND WAGES PAYABLE		
		9,000	Bal. Jan. 1
Net decrease	2,000		
		7,000	Bal. Dec. 31

The rationale for *deducting* the $2,000 *net decrease* in this liability in Exhibit 14-18 follows from what we just said about an increase in Accounts Payable. The payment to employees of $2,000 more than the amount included in expense on the income statement requires an additional deduction under the indirect method.

Depreciation Expense Depreciation is a noncash expense. Because it was deducted to arrive at net income, we must *add back* $40,000, the amount of depreciation, to find cash from operations. The same holds true for amortization of intangible assets and depletion of natural resources.

Prepaid Insurance This account decreased by $6,000, according to the T account:

	PREPAID INSURANCE		
Bal. Jan. 1	18,000		
		6,000	Net decrease
Bal. Dec. 31	12,000		

A decrease in this account indicates that Julian deducted more on the income statement for the insurance expense of the period than it paid in cash for new policies. That is, the cash outlay for insurance protection was not as large as the amount of expense reported on the income statement. Thus, the *net decrease* in the account is *added back* to net income in Exhibit 14-18.

Income Taxes Payable A T account for Income Taxes Payable indicates a net increase of $3,000:

	INCOME TAXES PAYABLE	
	5,000	Bal. Jan. 1
	3,000	Net increase
	8,000	Bal. Dec. 31

The *net increase* of $3,000 in this liability is *added back* to net income in Exhibit 14-18 because the payments to the government were $3,000 less than the amount included on the income statement.

Loss on Retirement of Bonds   The $3,000 loss from retiring bonds was reported on the income statement as a deduction. There are two parts to the explanation for *adding back* the loss to net income to eliminate its effect in the Operating Activities section of the statement. First, any cash outflow from retiring bonds is properly classified as a financing activity, not an operating activity. The entire cash outflow should be reported in one classification rather than being allocated between two classifications. Second, the amount of the cash outflow is $63,000, not $3,000. To summarize, to convert net income to a cash basis, the loss is added back in the Operating Activities section to eliminate its effect. The actual use of cash to retire the bonds is shown in the financing section of the statement.

Summary of Adjustments to Net Income under the Indirect Method   The following is a list of the most common adjustments to net income when the indirect method is used to prepare the Operating Activities section of the statement of cash flows:

ADDITIONS TO NET INCOME	DEDUCTIONS FROM NET INCOME
Decrease in accounts receivable	Increase in accounts receivable
Decrease in inventory	Increase in inventory
Decrease in prepayments	Increase in prepayments
Increase in accounts payable	Decrease in accounts payable
Increase in accrued liabilities	Decrease in accrued liabilities
Losses on sales of long-term assets	Gains on sales of long-term assets
Losses on retirements of bonds	Gains on retirements of bonds
Depreciation, amortization, and depletion	

Comparison of the Indirect and Direct Methods

Earlier in the chapter we pointed out that the amount of cash provided by operating activities is the same under the direct and the indirect methods. The relative merits of the two methods, however, have stirred considerable debate in the accounting profession. The Financial Accounting Standards Board has expressed a strong preference for the direct method but allows companies to use the indirect method.

If a company uses the indirect method, it must separately disclose two important cash payments: income taxes paid and interest paid. Thus, if Julian uses the indirect method, it reports the following either at the bottom of the statement of cash flows or in a footnote:[5]

Income taxes paid	$47,000
Interest paid	$15,000

Advocates of the direct method believe that the information provided with this approach is valuable in evaluating a company's operating efficiency. For example, the use of the direct method allows the analyst to follow any trends in cash receipts from customers and compare them with cash payments to suppliers. The information presented in the Operating Activities section of the statement under the direct method is certainly user-friendly. Someone without a technical background in accounting can easily tell where cash came from and where it went during the period.

Advocates of the indirect method argue two major points. Many companies believe that the use of the direct method reveals too much about their business by telling readers exactly the amount of cash receipts and cash payments from operations. Whether

---

[5]The same *Accounting Trends & Techniques* survey referred to earlier in the chapter indicated that of those companies using the indirect method, approximately 60% disclose interest and taxes paid in notes to the financial statements and approximately 40% report these amounts at the bottom of the statement of cash flows.

the use of the direct method tells the competition too much about a company is subject to debate. The other argument made for the indirect method is that it focuses attention on the differences between income on an accrual basis and a cash basis. In fact, this reconciliation of net income and cash provided by operating activities is considered to be important enough that *if a company uses the direct method, it must present a separate schedule to reconcile net income to net cash from operating activities.* This schedule, in effect, is the same as the Operating Activities section for the indirect method.

The Use of Cash Flow Information

The statement of cash flows is a critical disclosure to a company's investors and creditors. Many investors focus on cash flow from operations, rather than net income, as their key statistic. Similarly, many bankers are as concerned with cash flow from operations as they are with net income because they care about a company's ability to pay its bills. There is the concern that accrual accounting can mask cash flow problems. For example, a company with smooth earnings could be building up accounts receivable and inventory. This may not become evident until the company is in deep trouble.

The statement of cash flows provides investors, analysts, bankers, and other users with a valuable starting point as they attempt to evaluate a company's financial health. From this point, these groups must decide *how* to use the information presented on the statement. They pay particular attention to the *relationships* among various items on the statement, as well as to other financial statement items. In fact, many large banks have their own cash flow models, which typically involve a rearrangement of the items on the statement of cash flows to suit their needs. We now turn our attention to two examples of how various groups use cash flow information.

Creditors and Cash Flow Adequacy

Bankers and other creditors are especially concerned with a company's ability to meet its principal and interest obligations. *Cash flow adequacy* is a measure intended to help in this regard.[6] It gauges the cash available to meet future debt obligations after paying taxes and interest costs and making capital expenditures. Because capital expenditures on new plant and equipment are a necessity for most companies, analysts are concerned with the cash available to repay debt *after* the company has replaced and updated its existing base of long-term assets.

Cash flow adequacy can be computed as follows:

$$\text{Cash Flow Adequacy} = \frac{\text{Cash Flow from Operating Activities } - \text{ Capital Expenditures}}{\text{Average Amount of Debt Maturing over Next Five Years}}$$

How could you use the information in an annual report to measure a company's cash flow adequacy? First, whether a company uses the direct or indirect method to report cash flow from operating activities, this number represents cash flow *after* paying interest and taxes. The numerator of the ratio is determined by deducting capital expenditures, as they appear in the Investing Activities section of the statement, from cash flow from operating activities. A disclosure required by the Securities and Exchange Commission provides the information needed to calculate the denominator of the ratio. This regulatory body requires companies to report the annual amount of long-term debt maturing over each of the next five years.

Managers, investors, and brokers gauge the relative strengths of retailers by observing which stores are the most popular. But they also study the financial statements, particularly the statement of cash flows and its indicators of cash flow adequacy, as the most fundamental way to measure a firm's strength.

---

[6]An article appearing in the January 10, 1994, edition of *The Wall Street Journal* reported that Fitch Investors Service Inc. has published a rating system to compare the cash flow adequacy of companies that it rates single-A in its credit ratings. The rating system is intended to help corporate bond investors assess the ability of these companies to meet their maturing debt obligations. Lee Berton, "Investors Have a New Tool for Judging Issuers' Health: 'Cash-Flow Adequacy,'" p. C1.

IBM's Cash Flow Adequacy   As an example of the calculation of this ratio, consider the following amounts from IBM's statement of cash flows for the year ended December 31, 1995 (amounts in millions of dollars):

Net cash provided by operating activities	$10,708
Payments for plant, rental machines, and other property	$ 4,744

Note G in IBM's 1995 annual report provides the following information:

Annual maturity and sinking fund requirements in millions of dollars on long-term debt outstanding at December 31, 1995, are as follows: 1996, $2,881; 1997, $3,197; 1998, $1,500; 1999, $440; 2000, $1,783; 2001 and beyond, $3,163.

We can now compute IBM's cash flow adequacy for the year ended December 31, 1995, as follows:

$$\text{Cash Flow Adequacy} = \frac{\$10,708 - \$4,744}{(\$2,881 + \$3,197 + \$1,500 + \$440 + \$1,783)/5} = \frac{\$5,964}{\$1,960.2} = 3.0$$

Would you feel comfortable lending to IBM if you knew that its ratio of cash flow from operations, after making necessary capital expenditures, to average maturities of debt over the next five years was 3 to 1? Before answering this question, you would want to compare the ratio with the ratios for prior years as well as with the ratio for companies of similar size and in lines of business similar to those of IBM. As a starting point, however, IBM's ratio of 3 to 1 indicates that its 1995 cash flow was certainly sufficient to repay its average annual debt over the next five years.

Stockholders and Cash Flow per Share

As we will see in Chapter 15, one measure of the relative worth of an investment in a company is the ratio of the stock's market price per share to the company's earnings per share (that is, the price/earnings ratio). But many stockholders and Wall Street analysts are even more interested in the price of the stock in relation to the company's cash flow per share. Cash flow for purposes of this ratio is normally limited to cash flow from operating activities. This ratio has been used by these groups to evaluate investments even though the accounting profession has expressly forbidden the reporting of cash flow per share information in the financial statements. The belief is that this type of information is not an acceptable alternative to earnings per share as an indicator of company performance. Obviously, differences of opinion exist among various groups as to the usefulness of cash flow per share information.

ACCOUNTING FOR YOUR DECISIONS
You Are the Banker

You and your old college roommate are having an argument. You say that cash flow is all that matters when looking at a company's prospects. Your roommate says that the most important number is earnings per share. Who's right?

ANS: You're both wrong. True, bankers are interested in cash flow to make sure that a company can pay back its loans. But earnings per share is important also because it is less easily manipulated. After all, companies can decide when they want to finance expansion, pay down debt or invest in new businesses. A company with strong earnings can appear weak from a cash flow perspective if it invests too much in new operating assets or other businesses. On the other hand, a company that wishes to appear cash rich can avoid making all of the investments that it ought to be making. Although companies can manipulate earnings to some extent, the matching principle ensures that revenues and expenses relating to those revenues take place during the same period.

Review Problem

An income statement and comparative balance sheets for Dexter Company are shown below:

DEXTER COMPANY
INCOME STATEMENT
FOR THE YEAR ENDED DECEMBER 31, 1998

Sales revenue	$89,000
Cost of goods sold	57,000
Gross margin	$32,000
Depreciation expense	6,500
Advertising expense	3,200
Salaries expense	12,000
Total operating expenses	$21,700
Operating income	$10,300
Loss on sale of land	2,500
Income before tax	$ 7,800
Income tax expense	2,600
Net income	$ 5,200

DEXTER COMPANY
COMPARATIVE BALANCE SHEETS

	DECEMBER 31	
	1998	**1997**
Cash	$ 12,000	$ 9,500
Accounts receivable	22,000	18,400
Inventory	25,400	20,500
Prepaid advertising	10,000	8,600
Total current assets	$ 69,400	$ 57,000
Land	120,000	80,000
Equipment	190,000	130,000
Accumulated depreciation	(70,000)	(63,500)
Total long-term assets	$240,000	$146,500
Total assets	$309,400	$203,500
Accounts payable	$ 15,300	$ 12,100
Salaries payable	14,000	16,400
Income taxes payable	1,200	700
Total current liabilities	$ 30,500	$ 29,200
Capital stock	$200,000	$100,000
Retained earnings	78,900	74,300
Total stockholders' equity	$278,900	$174,300
Total liabilities and stockholders' equity	$309,400	$203,500

ADDITIONAL INFORMATION

1. Land was acquired during the year for $70,000.
2. An unimproved parcel of land was sold during the year for $27,500. Its original cost to Dexter was $30,000.
3. A specialized piece of equipment was acquired in exchange for capital stock in the company. The value of the capital stock was $60,000.
4. In addition to the capital stock issued in item 3, stock was sold for $40,000.
5. Dividends of $600 were paid.

Required

Prepare a statement of cash flows for 1998 using the direct method in the Operating Activities section of the statement. Include supplemental schedules to report any noncash investing and financing activities and to reconcile net income to net cash provided by operating activities.

Solution to Review Problem

**DEXTER COMPANY
STATEMENT OF CASH FLOWS
FOR THE YEAR ENDED DECEMBER 31, 1998**

CASH FLOWS FROM OPERATING ACTIVITIES

Cash collections from customers	$ 85,400
Cash payments:	
To suppliers	$(58,700)
For advertising	(4,600)
To employees	(14,400)
For income taxes	(2,100)
Total cash payments	$(79,800)
Net cash provided by operating activities	$ 5,600

CASH FLOWS FROM INVESTING ACTIVITIES

Purchase of land	$(70,000)
Sale of land	27,500
Net cash used by investing activities	$(42,500)

CASH FLOWS FROM FINANCING ACTIVITIES

Issuance of capital stock	$ 40,000
Payment of cash dividends	(600)
Net cash provided by financing activities	$ 39,400
Net increase in cash	$ 2,500
Cash balance, December 31, 1997	9,500
Cash balance, December 31, 1998	$ 12,000

SUPPLEMENTAL SCHEDULE OF NONCASH INVESTING AND FINANCING ACTIVITIES

Acquisition of specialized equipment in exchange for capital stock	$ 60,000

RECONCILIATION OF NET INCOME TO NET CASH PROVIDED BY OPERATING ACTIVITIES

Net income	$ 5,200
Adjustments to reconcile net income to net cash provided by operating activities:	
Increase in accounts receivable	(3,600)
Increase in inventory	(4,900)
Increase in prepaid advertising	(1,400)
Increase in accounts payable	3,200
Decrease in salaries payable	(2,400)
Increase in income taxes payable	500
Depreciation expense	6,500
Loss on sale of land	2,500
Net cash provided by operating activities	$ 5,600

APPENDIX 14A

Accounting Tools: A Work-Sheet Approach to the Statement of Cash Flows

LO 7 Use a work sheet to prepare a statement of cash flows, using the indirect method to determine cash flow from operating activities.

In the chapter, we illustrated the use of T accounts to aid in the preparation of a statement of cash flows. We pointed out that T accounts are simply tools to help in analyzing the transactions of the period. We now consider the use of a work sheet as an alternative tool to organize the information needed to prepare the statement. We will use the information given in the chapter for Julian Corp. (refer to Exhibits 14-11 and 14-12 for the income statements and comparative balance sheets). Although it is possible to use a work sheet to prepare the statement when the Operating Activities section is prepared under the direct method, we illustrate the use of a work sheet using the more popular *indirect* method.

A work sheet for Julian Corp. is presented in Exhibit 14-19. The following steps were followed in preparing the work sheet:

Step 1: The balances in each account at the end and at the beginning of the period are entered in the first two columns of the work sheet. For Julian, these balances can be found in its comparative balance sheets in Exhibit 14-12. Note that credit balances are bracketed on the work sheet. Because the work sheet lists all balance sheet accounts, the total of the debit balances must equal the total of the credit balances, and thus, the totals at the bottom for these first two columns equal $0.

Step 2: The additional information listed at the bottom of Exhibit 14-12 is used to record the various investing and financing activities on the work sheet (the item numbers discussed below correspond to the superscript numbers on the work sheet in Exhibit 14-19):

1. Long-term investments were purchased for $30,000. Because this transaction required the use of cash, it is entered as a bracketed amount in the Investing column and as an addition to the Long-term Investments account in the Changes column.

2. Land was acquired by issuing a $50,000 note payable. This transaction is entered on two lines on the work sheet. First, $50,000 is added to the Changes column for Land and as a corresponding deduction in the Noncash column (the last column on the work sheet). Likewise, $50,000 is added for Notes Payable to the Changes column and to the Noncash column.

3. Item 3 in the additional information indicates the acquisition of equipment for $75,000. This amount appears on the work sheet as an addition to Property and Equipment in the Changes column and as a deduction (cash outflow) in the Investing column.

4. A machine with an original cost of $35,000 and a book value of $20,000 was sold for $25,000, resulting in four entries on the work sheet. First, the amount of cash received, $25,000, is entered as an addition in the Investing column on the line for property and equipment. On the same line, the cost of the machine, $35,000, is entered as a deduction in the Changes column. The difference between the cost of the machine, $35,000, and its book value, $20,000, is its accumulated depreciation of $15,000. This amount is shown as a deduction from this account in the Changes column. Because the gain of $5,000 is included in net income, it is deducted in the Operating column (on the Retained Earnings line).

5. Bonds with a face value of $60,000 were retired by paying $63,000 in cash, resulting in the entry of three amounts on the work sheet. The face value of the bonds, $60,000, is entered as a reduction of Bonds Payable in the Changes column. The amount paid to retire the bonds, $63,000, is entered on the same line in the Financing column. The loss of $3,000 is added in the Operating column because it was a deduction to arrive at net income.

EXHIBIT 14-19 Julian Corp. Statement of Cash Flows Work Sheet

JULIAN CORP.
STATEMENT OF CASH FLOWS WORK SHEET (INDIRECT METHOD)
(ALL AMOUNTS IN THOUSANDS OF DOLLARS)

| | BALANCES | | | CASH INFLOWS (OUTFLOWS) | | | NONCASH |
ACCOUNTS	12/31/98	12/31/97	CHANGES	OPERATING	INVESTING	FINANCING	ACTIVITIES
Cash	35	46	$(11)^{16}$				
Accounts receivable	63	57	6^{10}	$(6)^{10}$			
Inventory	84	92	$(8)^{11}$	8^{11}			
Prepaid insurance	12	18	$(6)^{12}$	6^{12}			
Long-term investments	120	90	30^1		$(30)^1$		
Land	150	100	50^2				$(50)^2$
Property and equipment	320	280	75^3		$(75)^3$		
			$(35)^4$		25^4		
Accumulated depreciation	(100)	(75)	15^4				
			$(40)^9$	40^9			
Accounts payable	(38)	(31)	$(7)^{13}$	7^{13}			
Salaries and wages payable	(7)	(9)	2^{14}	$(2)^{14}$			
Income taxes payable	(8)	(5)	$(3)^{15}$	3^{15}			
Notes payable	(85)	(35)	$(50)^2$				50^2
Bonds payable	(200)	(260)	60^5			$(63)^5$	
Capital stock	(100)	(75)	$(25)^6$			25^6	
Retained earnings	(246)	(193)	67^7	$(5)^4$		$(67)^7$	
				3^5			
			$(120)^8$	120^8			
Totals	–0–	–0–	–0–	174	(80)	(105)	–0–
Net decrease in cash				$(11)^{16}$			

SOURCE: The authors are grateful to Jeannie Folk for the development of this work sheet.

6. Capital stock was issued for $25,000. This amount is entered on the Capital Stock line under the Changes column (as an increase in the account) and under the Financing column as an inflow.

7. Dividends of $67,000 were paid. This amount is entered as a reduction in Retained Earnings in the Changes column and as a cash outflow in the Financing Activities column.

Step 3: Because the indirect method is being used, net income of $120,000 for the period is entered as an addition to Retained Earnings in the Operating column of the work sheet (entry 8). The amount is also entered as an increase (bracketed) in the Changes column.

Step 4: Any noncash revenues or expenses are entered on the work sheet on the appropriate lines. For Julian, depreciation expense of $40,000 is added (bracketed) to Accumulated Depreciation in the Changes column and in the Operating column. This entry is identified on the work sheet as entry 9.

Step 5: Each of the changes in the noncash current asset and current liability accounts is entered in the Changes column and in the Operating column. These entries are identified on the work sheet as entries 10 through 15.

Step 6: Totals are determined for the Operating, Investing, and Financing columns and entered at the bottom of the work sheet. The total for the final column, Noncash Activities, of $0, is also entered.

Step 7: The net cash inflow (outflow) for the period is determined by adding the totals of the operating, investing, and financing columns. For Julian, the net cash *outflow* is $11,000, shown as entry 16 at the bottom of the statement. This same amount is then transferred to the line for Cash in the Changes column. Finally, the total of the Changes column at this point should net to $0.

Chapter Highlights

1. **LO 1** The purpose of a statement of cash flows is to summarize the cash flows of an entity during a period of time. The cash inflows and outflows are categorized into three activities: operating, investing, and financing.

2. **LO 2** Cash equivalents are convertible to a known amount of cash and are therefore included with cash on the balance sheet. Because such items as commercial paper, money market funds, and Treasury bills do not involve any significant risk, neither their purchase nor their sale is shown as an investing activity on the statement of cash flows.

3. **LO 3** Operating activities are generally the effects of items that enter into the determination of net income, such as the effects of buying and selling products and services. Other operating activities include payments of compensation to employees, taxes to the government, and interest to creditors. Preparation of the Operating Activities section of the statement of cash flows requires an analysis of the current assets and current liabilities.

4. **LO 3** Investing activities are critical to the success of a business because they involve the replacement of existing productive assets and the addition of new ones. Capital expenditures are normally the single largest cash outflow for most businesses. Occasionally, companies generate cash from the sale of existing plant and equipment. The information needed to prepare the Investing Activities section of the statement of cash flows is found by analyzing the long-term asset accounts.

5. **LO 3** All businesses rely on financing in one form or another. At least initially, all corporations sell stock to raise funds. Many turn to external sources as well, generating cash from the issuance of promissory notes and bonds. The repayment of debt and the reacquisition of capital stock are important uses of cash for some companies. Given the nature of financing activities, long-term liability and stockholders' equity accounts must be examined in preparing this section of the statement of cash flows.

6. **LO 4** Two different methods are acceptable to report cash flow from operating activities. Under the direct method, cash receipts and cash payments related to operations are reported. Under the indirect method, net income is reconciled to net cash flow from operating activities. Regardless of which method is used, the amount of cash generated from operations is the same.

7. **LO 5** Preparation of the Operating Activities section under the direct method requires the conversion of income statement items from an accrual basis to a cash basis. Certain items, such as depreciation, do not have a cash effect and are not included on the statement. Gains and losses typically relate to either investing or financing activities and are not included in the Operating Activities section of the statement. When the direct method is used to present cash flow from operating activities, a separate schedule is required to reconcile net income to net cash flow from operating activities. This schedule is the same as the Operating Activities section under the indirect method. Some type of methodology, such as a T-account approach, can be helpful in preparing the statement for more complex situations.

8. **LO 6** When the indirect method is used, the reconciliation of net income to net cash flow from operating activities appears on the face of the statement. Adjustments are made for the changes in each of the operating-related current asset and current liability accounts, as well as adjustments for noncash items, such as depreciation. The effects of gains and losses on net income must also be removed to convert to a cash basis. If the indirect method is used, a company must separately disclose the amount of cash paid for taxes and for interest.

9. **LO 7** A work sheet is sometimes used in preparing a statement of cash flows. Similar to T accounts, the work sheet acts as a tool to aid in the preparation of the statement. (Appendix 14A)

Key Terms Quiz

Read each definition below and then write the number of that definition in the blank beside the appropriate term it defines. The solution appears at the end of the chapter.

___ Statement of cash flows
___ Operating activities
___ Financing activities
___ Indirect method
___ Cash equivalent
___ Investing activities
___ Direct method

1. Activities concerned with the acquisition and sale of products and services.

2. For preparing the Operating Activities section of the statement of cash flows, the approach in which net income is reconciled to net cash flow from operations.

3. The financial statement that summarizes an entity's cash receipts and cash payments during the period from operating, investing, and financing activities.

4. An item readily convertible to a known amount of cash and with an original maturity to the investor of three months or less.

5. Activities concerned with the acquisition and disposal of long-term assets.

6. For preparing the Operating Activities section of the statement of cash flows, the approach in which cash receipts and cash payments are reported.

7. Activities concerned with the raising and repayment of funds in the form of debt and equity.

Alternate Terms

Bottom line   Net income.

Cash flow from operating activities   Cash flow from operations.

Statement of cash flows   Cash flows statement.

Questions

1. What is the purpose of the statement of cash flows? As a flows statement, explain how it differs from the income statement.

2. What is a cash equivalent? Why is it included with cash for purposes of preparing a statement of cash flows?

3. Preston Corp. acquires a piece of land by signing a $60,000 promissory note and making a down payment of $20,000. How should this transaction be reported on the statement of cash flows?

4. Hansen Inc. made two purchases during December. One was a $10,000 Treasury bill that matures in 60 days from the date of purchase. The other was a $20,000 investment in Motorola common stock that will be held indefinitely. How should each of these be treated for purposes of preparing a statement of cash flows?

5. Companies are required to classify cash flows as either operating, investing, or financing. Which of these three categories do you think will most likely have a net cash *outflow* over a number of years? Explain your answer.

6. A fellow student says to you: "The statement of cash flows is the easiest of the basic financial statements to prepare because you know the answer before you start. You compare the beginning and ending balances in cash on the balance sheet and compute the net inflow or outflow of cash. What could be easier!" Do you agree? Explain your answer.

7. What is your evaluation of the following statement? "Depreciation is responsible for providing some of the highest amounts of cash for capital-intensive businesses. This is obvious by examining the Operating Activities section of the statement of cash flows. Other than the net income of the period, depreciation is often the largest amount reported in this section of the statement."

8. Which method for preparing the Operating Activities section of the statement of cash flows, the direct or the indirect method, do you believe provides the most information to users of the statement? Explain your answer.

9. Assume that a company uses the indirect method to prepare the Operating Activities section of the statement of cash flows. Why would a decrease in accounts receivable during the period be added back to net income?

10. Why is it necessary to analyze both inventory and accounts payable in trying to determine cash payments to suppliers when the direct method is used?

11. A company has a very profitable year. What explanations might there be for a decrease in cash?

12. A company reports a net loss for the year. Is it possible that cash could increase during the year? Explain your answer.

13. What effect does a decrease in income taxes payable for the period have on cash generated from operating activities? Does it matter whether the direct or the indirect method is used?

14. Why do accounting standards require a company to separately disclose income taxes paid and interest paid if it uses the indirect method?

15. Is it logical that interest paid is classified as a cash outflow in the *Operating* Activities section of the statement of cash flows but that dividends paid are included in the *Financing* Activities section? Explain your answer.

16. Jackson Company prepays the rent on various office facilities. The beginning balance in Prepaid Rent was $9,600, and the ending balance was $7,300. The income statement reports Rent Expense of $45,900. Under the direct method, what amount would appear for cash paid in rent in the Operating Activities section of the statement of cash flows?

17. Baxter Inc. buys 2,000 shares of its own common stock at $20 per share as treasury stock. How is this transaction reported on the statement of cash flows?

18. Duke Corp. sold a delivery truck for $9,000. Its original cost was $25,000, and the book value at the time of the

sale was $11,000. How does the transaction to record the sale appear on a statement of cash flows prepared under the indirect method?

19. Billings Company has a patent on its books with a balance at the beginning of the year of $24,000. The ending balance for the asset was $20,000. The company neither bought nor sold any patents during the year, nor does it use an Accumulated Amortization account. Assuming that the company uses the indirect method in preparing a statement of cash flows, how is the decrease in the Patents account reported on the statement?

20. Ace Inc. declared and distributed a 10% stock dividend during the year. Explain how, if at all, you think this transaction should be reported on a statement of cash flows.

Exercises

LO 2 **Exercise 14-1** Cash Equivalents

Metropolis Industries invested its excess cash in the following instruments during December 1998:

Certicicate of deposit, due January 31, 1999	$ 35,000
Certificate of deposit, due June 30, 1999	95,000
Investment in City of Elgin bonds, due May 1, 2000	15,000
Investment in Quantum Data stock	66,000
Kemper Money Market Fund	105,000
90-day Treasury bills	75,000
Treasury note, due December 1, 1999	200,000

Required

Determine the amount of cash equivalents that should be combined with cash on the company's balance sheet at December 31, 1998, and for purposes of preparing a statement of cash flows for the year ended December 31, 1998.

LO 3 **Exercise 14-2** Classification of Activities

For each of the following transactions reported on a statement of cash flows, fill in the blank to indicate if it would appear in the Operating Activities section (O), in the Investing Activities section (I), or in the Financing Activities section (F). Put an S in the blank if the transaction does not affect cash but is reported in a supplemental schedule of noncash activities. Assume the company uses the direct method in the Operating Activities section.

_____ 1. A company purchases its own common stock in the open market and immediately retires it.
_____ 2. A company issues preferred stock in exchange for land.
_____ 3. A six-month bank loan is obtained.
_____ 4. Twenty-year bonds are issued.
_____ 5. A customer's open account is collected.
_____ 6. Income taxes are paid.
_____ 7. Cash sales for the day are recorded.
_____ 8. Cash dividends are declared and paid.
_____ 9. A creditor is given shares of common stock in the company in return for cancellation of a long-term loan.
_____ 10. A new piece of machinery is acquired for cash.
_____ 11. Stock of another company is acquired as an investment.
_____ 12. Interest is paid on a bank loan.
_____ 13. Factory workers are paid.

LO 3 **Exercise 14-3** Retirement of Bonds Payable on the Statement of Cash Flows—Indirect Method

Carolee Inc. has the following debt outstanding on December 31, 1998:

10% bonds payable, due 12/31/02	$500,000	
Discount on bonds payable	(40,000)	$460,000

On this date, Carolee retired the entire bond issue by paying cash of $510,000.

Required

1. Prepare the journal entry to record the bond retirement.
2. Describe how the bond retirement would be reported on the statement of cash flows, assuming that Carolee uses the indirect method.

LO 5   **Exercise 14-4** Cash Collections—Direct Method

Stanley Company's comparative balance sheets included accounts receivable of $80,800 at December 31, 1997, and $101,100 at December 31, 1998. Sales reported by Stanley on its 1998 income statement amounted to $1,450,000. What is the amount of cash collections that Stanley will report in the Operating Activities section of its 1998 statement of cash flows assuming that the direct method is used?

LO 5   **Exercise 14-5** Cash Payments—Direct Method

Lester Enterprises' comparative balance sheets included inventory of $90,200 at December 31, 1997, and $70,600 at December 31, 1998. Lester's comparative balance sheets also included accounts payable of $57,700 at December 31, 1997, and $39,200 at December 31, 1998. Lester's accounts payable balances are comprised solely of amounts due to suppliers for purchases of inventory on account. Cost of goods sold, as reported by Lester on its 1998 income statement, amounted to $770,900. What is the amount of cash payments for inventory that Lester will report in the Operating Activities section of its 1998 statement of cash flows assuming that the direct method is used?

LO 5   **Exercise 14-6** Operating Activities Section—Direct Method

The following account balances for the noncash current assets and current liabilities of Labrador Company are available:

	DECEMBER 31	
	1998	1997
Accounts receivable	$ 4,000	$ 6,000
Inventory	32,000	25,000
Office supplies	7,000	10,000
Accounts payable	7,500	4,500
Salaries and wages payable	1,500	2,500
Interest payable	500	1,000
Income taxes payable	4,500	3,000

In addition, the income statement for 1998 is as follows:

	1998
Sales revenue	$100,000
Cost of goods sold	75,000
Gross profit	$ 25,000
General and administrative expense	$ 8,000
Depreciation expense	3,000
Total operating expenses	$ 11,000
Income before interest and taxes	$ 14,000
Interest expense	3,000
Income before tax	$ 11,000
Income tax expense	5,000
Net income	$ 6,000

Required

1. Prepare the Operating Activities section of the statement of cash flows using the direct method.
2. What does the use of the direct method reveal about a company that the indirect method does not?

LO 5 **Exercise 14-7** Determination of Missing Amounts—Cash Flow From Operating Activities

The computation of cash provided by operating activities requires analysis of the non-cash current asset and current liability accounts. Using T accounts, determine the missing amounts for each of the following independent cases:

CASE 1

Accounts receivable, beginning of year	$150,000
Accounts receivable, end of year	100,000
Credit sales for the year	175,000
Cash sales for the year	60,000
Write-offs of uncollectible accounts	35,000
Total cash collections for the year (from cash sales and collections on account)	?

CASE 2

Inventory, beginning of year	$ 80,000
Inventory, end of year	55,000
Accounts payable, beginning of year	25,000
Accounts payable, end of year	15,000
Cost of goods sold	175,000
Cash payments for inventory (assume all purchases of inventory are on account)	?

CASE 3

Prepaid insurance, beginning of year	$ 17,000
Prepaid insurance, end of year	20,000
Insurance expense	15,000
Cash paid for new insurance policies	?

CASE 4

Income taxes payable, beginning of year	$ 95,000
Income taxes payable, end of year	115,000
Income tax expense	300,000
Cash payments for taxes	?

LO 5 **Exercise 14-8** Dividends on the Statement of Cash Flows

The following selected account balances are available from the records of Truesdale Company:

	DECEMBER 31	
	1998	**1997**
Dividends payable	$ 30,000	$ 20,000
Retained earnings	375,000	250,000

Other information available for 1998 follows:

a. Truesdale reported $285,000 net income for the year.

b. It declared and distributed a stock dividend of $50,000 during the year.

c. It declared cash dividends at the end of each quarter and paid them within the next 30 days of the following quarter.

Required

1. With the use of T accounts, determine the amount of cash dividends *paid* during the year for presentation in the Financing Activities section of the statement of cash flows.

2. Should the stock dividend described in part b appear on a statement of cash flows? Explain your answer.

LO 6 **Exercise 14-9** Adjustments to Net Income with the Indirect Method

Assume that a company uses the indirect method to prepare the Operating Activities section of the statement of cash flows. For each of the following items, fill in the blank to indicate whether it would be added to net income (A), deducted from net income (D), or not reported in this section of the statement under the indirect method (NR).

_____ 1. Depreciation expense.

_____ 2. Gain on sale of used delivery truck.

_____ 3. Bad debts expense.

_____ 4. Increase in accounts payable.

_____ 5. Purchase of new delivery truck.

_____ 6. Loss on retirement of bonds.

_____ 7. Increase in prepaid rent.

_____ 8. Decrease in inventory.

_____ 9. Increase in short-term investments (classified as available-for-sale securities).

_____ 10. Amortization of patents.

LO 6 **Exercise 14-10** Operating Activities Section—Indirect Method

The following account balances for the noncash current assets and current liabilities of Salvatore Company are available:

	DECEMBER 31	
	1998	1997
Accounts receivable	$43,000	$35,000
Inventory	30,000	40,000
Prepaid rent	17,000	15,000
Totals	$90,000	$90,000
Accounts payable	$26,000	$19,000
Income taxes payable	6,000	10,000
Interest payable	15,000	12,000
Totals	$47,000	$41,000

Net income for 1998 is $40,000. Depreciation expense is $20,000. Assume that all sales and all purchases are on account.

Required

1. Prepare the Operating Activities section of the statement of cash flows using the indirect method.

2. Provide a brief explanation as to why cash flow from operating activities is more or less than the net income of the period.

Multi-Concept Exercises

LO 2, 3 **Exercise 14-11** Classification of Activities

Use the following legend to indicate how each of the following transactions would be reported on the statement of cash flows (assume that the stocks and bonds of other companies are classified as available-for-sale securities):

II = Inflow from investing activities

OI = Outflow from investing activities

IF = Inflow from financing activities

OF = Outflow from financing activities

CE = Classified as a cash equivalent and included with cash for purposes of preparing the statement of cash flows

————   **1.** Purchased a six-month certificate of deposit.

————   **2.** Purchased a 60-day Treasury bill.

————   **3.** Issued 1,000 shares of common stock.

————   **4.** Purchased 1,000 shares of stock in another company.

————   **5.** Purchased 1,000 shares of its own stock to be held in the treasury.

————   **6.** Invested $1,000 in a money market fund.

————   **7.** Sold 500 shares of stock of another company.

————   **8.** Purchased 20-year bonds of another company.

————   **9.** Issued 30-year bonds.

————   **10.** Repaid a six-month bank loan.

LO 3, 5   **Exercise 14-12** Classification of Activities

Use the following legend to indicate how each of the following transactions would be reported on the statement of cash flows (assume that the company uses the direct method in the Operating Activities section):

IO = Inflow from operating activities

OO = Outflow from operating activities

II = Inflow from investing activities

OI = Outflow from investing activities

IF = Inflow from financing activities

OF = Outflow from financing activities

NR = Not reported in the body of the statement of cash flows, but in a supplemental schedule.

————   **1.** Collected $10,000 in cash from customers' open accounts for the period.

————   **2.** Paid one of the company's inventory suppliers $500 in settlement of an open account.

————   **3.** Purchased a new copier for $6,000; signed a 90-day note payable.

————   **4.** Issued bonds at face value of $100,000.

————   **5.** Made $23,200 in cash sales for the week.

————   **6.** Purchased an empty lot adjacent to the factory for $50,000. The seller of the land agrees to accept a five-year promissory note as consideration.

————   **7.** Renewed the property insurance policy for another six months. Cash of $1,000 is paid for the renewal.

————   **8.** Purchased a machine for $10,000.

————   **9.** Paid cash dividends of $2,500.

————   **10.** Reclassified as short-term a long-term note payable of $5,000 that is due within the next year.

————   **11.** Purchased 500 shares of the company's own stock on the open market for $4,000.

————   **12.** Sold 500 shares of Nike stock for book value of $10,000 (they had been classified as available-for-sale securities).

LO 3, 6   **Exercise 14-13** Long-Term Assets on the Statement of Cash Flows—Indirect Method

The following account balances are taken from the records of Martin Corp. for the past two years (credit balances are in parentheses):

	DECEMBER 31	
	1998	1997
Plant and equipment	$750,000	$500,000
Accumulated depreciation	(160,000)	(200,000)
Patents	92,000	80,000
Retained earnings	(825,000)	(675,000)

Other information available for 1998 follows:

a. Net income for the year was $200,000.

b. Depreciation expense on plant and equipment was $50,000.

c. Plant and equipment with an original cost of $150,000 were sold for $64,000 (you will need to determine the book value of the assets sold).

d. Amortization expense on patents was $8,000.

e. Both new plant and equipment and patents were purchased for cash during the year.

Required

Indicate, with amounts, how all items related to these long-term assets would be reported in the 1998 statement of cash flows, including any adjustments in the Operating Activities section of the statement. Assume that Martin uses the indirect method.

LO 1, 5   Exercise 14-14 Income Statement, Statement of Cash Flows (Direct Method), and Balance Sheet
The following events occurred at Handsome Hounds Grooming Company during its first year of business:

a. To establish the company, the two owners contributed a total of $50,000 in exchange for common stock.

b. Grooming service revenue for the first year amounted to $150,000, of which $40,000 was on account.

c. Customers owe $10,000 at the end of the year from the services provided on account.

d. At the beginning of the year a storage building was rented. The company was required to sign a three-year lease for $12,000 per year and make a $2,000 refundable security deposit. The first year's lease payment and the security deposit were paid at the beginning of the year.

e. At the beginning of the year the company purchased a patent at a cost of $100,000 for a revolutionary system to be used for dog grooming. The patent is expected to be useful for 10 years. The company paid 20% down in cash and signed a four-year note at the bank for the remainder.

f. Operating expenses, including amortization of the patent and rent on the storage building, totaled $80,000 for the first year. No expenses were accrued or unpaid at the end of the year.

g. The company declared and paid a $20,000 cash dividend at the end of the first year.

Required

1. Prepare an income statement for the first year.

2. Prepare a statement of cash flows for the first year, using the direct method in the Operating Activities section.

3. Did the company generate more or less cash flow from operations than it earned in net income? Explain why there is a difference.

4. Prepare a balance sheet as of the end of the first year.

Problems

LO 6 **Problem 14-1** Statement of Cash Flows—Indirect Method

The following balances are available for Chrisman Company:

	DECEMBER 31	
	1998	**1997**
Cash	$ 8,000	$ 10,000
Accounts receivable	20,000	15,000
Inventory	15,000	25,000
Prepaid rent	9,000	6,000
Land	75,000	75,000
Plant and equipment	400,000	300,000
Accumulated depreciation	(65,000)	(30,000)
Totals	$462,000	$401,000
Accounts payable	$ 12,000	$ 10,000
Income taxes payable	3,000	5,000
Short-term notes payable	35,000	25,000
Bonds payable	75,000	100,000
Common stock	200,000	150,000
Retained earnings	137,000	111,000
Totals	$462,000	$401,000

Bonds were retired during 1998 at face value, plant and equipment were acquired for cash, and common stock was issued for cash. Depreciation expense for the year was $35,000. Net income was reported at $26,000.

Required

1. Prepare a statement of cash flows for 1998, using the indirect method in the Operating Activities section.
2. Did Chrisman generate sufficient cash from operations to pay for its investing activities? How did it generate cash other than from operations? Explain your answers.

LO 7 **Problem 14-2** Statement of Cash Flows Using a Work Sheet—Indirect Method (Appendix 14A)

Refer to all of the facts in Problem 14-1.

Required

1. Using the format in Appendix 14A, prepare a statement of cash flows work sheet.
2. Prepare a statement of cash flows for 1998, using the indirect method in the Operating Activities section.
3. Did Chrisman generate sufficient cash from operations to pay for its investing activities? How did it generate cash other than from operations? Explain your answers.

LO 5 **Problem 14-3** Statement of Cash Flows—Direct Method

Peoria Corp. has just completed another very successful year, as indicated by the following income statement:

	FOR THE YEAR ENDED DECEMBER 31, 1998
Sales revenue	$1,250,000
Cost of goods sold	700,000
Gross profit	$ 550,000
Operating expenses	150,000
Income before interest and taxes	$ 400,000
Interest expense	25,000
Income before taxes	$ 375,000
Income tax expense	150,000
Net income	$ 225,000

Presented below are comparative balance sheets:

	DECEMBER 31	
	1998	1997
Cash	$ 52,000	$ 90,000
Accounts receivable	180,000	130,000
Inventory	230,000	200,000
Prepayments	15,000	25,000
Total current assets	$ 477,000	$ 445,000
Land	$ 750,000	$ 600,000
Plant and equipment	700,000	500,000
Accumulated depreciation	(250,000)	(200,000)
Total long-term assets	$1,200,000	$ 900,000
Total assets	$1,677,000	$1,345,000
Accounts payable	$ 130,000	$ 148,000
Other accrued liabilities	68,000	63,000
Income taxes payable	90,000	110,000
Total current liabilities	$ 288,000	$ 321,000
Long-term bank loan payable	$ 350,000	$ 300,000
Common stock	$ 550,000	$ 400,000
Retained earnings	489,000	324,000
Total stockholders' equity	$1,039,000	$ 724,000
Total liabilities and stockholders' equity	$1,677,000	$1,345,000

Other information follows:

a. Dividends of $60,000 were declared and paid during the year.

b. Operating expenses include $50,000 of depreciation.

c. Land and plant and equipment were acquired for cash, and additional stock was issued for cash. Cash was also received from additional bank loans.

The president has asked you some questions about the year's results. She is very impressed with the profit margin of 18% (net income divided by sales revenue). She is bothered, however, by the decline in the cash balance during the year. One of the conditions of the existing bank loan is that the company maintain a minimum cash balance of $50,000.

Required

1. Prepare a statement of cash flows for 1998, using the direct method in the Operating Activities section.

2. On the basis of your statement in requirement 1, draft a brief memo to the president to explain why cash decreased during such a profitable year. Include in your explanation any recommendations for improving the company's cash flow in future years.

LO 6   **Problem 14-4** Statement of Cash Flows—Indirect Method
Refer to all of the facts in Problem 14-3.

Required

1. Prepare a statement of cash flows for 1998, using the indirect method in the Operating Activities section.

2. On the basis of your statement in requirement 1, draft a brief memo to the president to explain why cash decreased during such a profitable year. Include in your explanation any recommendations for improving the company's cash flow in future years.

LO 7   **Problem 14-5** Statement of Cash Flows Using a Work Sheet—Indirect Method (Appendix 14A)
Refer to all of the facts in Problem 14-3.

Required

1. Using the format in Appendix 14A, prepare a statement of cash flows work sheet.
2. Prepare a statement of cash flows for 1998, using the indirect method in the Operating Activities section.
3. On the basis of your statement in requirement 2, draft a brief memo to the president to explain why cash decreased during such a profitable year. Include in your explanation any recommendations for improving the company's cash flow in future years.

LO 5   **Problem 14-6** Statement of Cash Flows—Direct Method

The income statement for Astro Inc. for 1998 follows:

	FOR THE YEAR ENDED DECEMBER 31, 1998
Sales revenue	$ 500,000
Cost of goods sold	400,000
Gross profit	$ 100,000
Operating expenses	180,000
Loss before interest and taxes	$ (80,000)
Interest expense	20,000
Net loss	$(100,000)

Presented below are comparative balance sheets:

	DECEMBER 31	
	1998	1997
Cash	$ 95,000	$ 80,000
Accounts receivable	50,000	75,000
Inventory	100,000	150,000
Prepayments	55,000	45,000
Total current assets	$ 300,000	$ 350,000
Land	475,000	400,000
Plant and equipment	870,000	800,000
Accumulated depreciation	(370,000)	(300,000)
Total long-term assets	$ 975,000	$ 900,000
Total assets	$1,275,000	$1,250,000
Accounts payable	$ 125,000	$ 100,000
Other accrued liabilities	35,000	45,000
Interest payable	15,000	10,000
Total current liabilities	$ 175,000	$ 155,000
Long-term bank loan payable	$ 340,000	$ 250,000
Common stock	450,000	400,000
Retained earnings	310,000	445,000
Total stockholders' equity	$ 760,000	$ 845,000
Total liabilities and stockholders' equity	$1,275,000	$1,250,000

Other information follows:

a. Dividends of $35,000 were declared and paid during the year.
b. Operating expenses include $70,000 of depreciation.
c. Land and plant and equipment were acquired for cash, and additional stock was issued for cash. Cash was also received from additional bank loans.

The president has asked you some questions about the year's results. He is disturbed with the $100,000 net loss for the year. He notes, however, that the cash position at the end of the year is improved. He is confused about what appear to be conflicting signals: "How could we have possibly added to our bank accounts during such a terrible year of operations?"

Required

1. Prepare a statement of cash flows for 1998, using the direct method in the Operating Activities section.

2. On the basis of your statement in requirement 1, draft a brief memo to the president to explain why cash increased during such an unprofitable year. Include in your memo your recommendations for improving the company's bottom line.

`LO 6` **Problem 14-7** Statement of Cash Flows—Indirect Method

Refer to all of the facts in Problem 14-6.

Required

1. Prepare a statement of cash flows for 1998, using the indirect method in the Operating Activities section.

2. On the basis of your statement in requirement 1, draft a brief memo to the president to explain why cash increased during such an unprofitable year. Include in your memo your recommendations for improving the company's bottom line.

`LO 7` **Problem 14-8** Statement of Cash Flows Using a Work Sheet—Indirect Method (Appendix 14A)

Refer to all of the facts in Problem 14-6.

Required

1. Using the format in Appendix 14A, prepare a statement of cash flows work sheet.

2. Prepare a statement of cash flows for 1998, using the indirect method in the Operating Activities section.

3. On the basis of your statement in requirement 2, draft a brief memo to the president to explain why cash increased during such an unprofitable year. Include in your memo your recommendations for improving the company's bottom line.

`LO 6` **Problem 14-9** Year-end Balance Sheet and Statement of Cash Flows—Indirect Method

The balance sheet of Terrier Company at the end of 1997 is presented below, along with certain other information for 1998:

	DECEMBER 31, 1997
Cash	$ 140,000
Accounts receivable	155,000
Total current assets	$ 295,000
Land	$ 300,000
Plant and equipment	500,000
Accumulated depreciation	(150,000)
Investments	100,000
Total long-term assets	$ 750,000
Total assets	$1,045,000
Current liabilities	$ 205,000
Bonds payable	$ 300,000
Common stock	400,000
Retained earnings	140,000
Total stockholders' equity	$ 540,000
Total liabilities and stockholders' equity	$1,045,000

Other information follows:

a. Net income for 1998 was $70,000.

b. Included in operating expenses was $20,000 in depreciation.

c. Cash dividends of $25,000 were declared and paid.

d. An additional $150,000 of bonds was issued for cash.

e. Common stock of $50,000 was purchased for cash and retired.

f. Cash purchases of plant and equipment during the year were $200,000.

g. An additional $100,000 of bonds was issued in exchange for land.

h Sales exceeded cash collections on account during the year by $10,000. All sales are on account.

i. The amount of current liabilities remained unchanged during the year.

Required

1. Prepare a statement of cash flows for 1998, using the indirect method in the Operating Activities section. Include a supplemental schedule for noncash activities.

2. Prepare a balance sheet at December 31, 1998.

3. Provide a possible explanation as to why Terrier decided to issue additional bonds for cash during 1998.

LO 7 **Problem 14-10** Statement of Cash Flows Using a Work Sheet—Indirect Method (Appendix 14A)
Refer to all of the facts in Problem 14-9.

Required

1. Prepare a balance sheet at December 31, 1998.

2. Using the format in Appendix 14A, prepare a statement of cash flows work sheet.

3. Prepare a statement of cash flows for 1998, using the indirect method in the Operating Activities section.

4. Provide a possible explanation as to why Terrier decided to issue additional bonds for cash during 1998.

Multi-Concept Problems

LO 4, 5 **Problem 14-11** Statement of Cash Flows—Direct Method
Satisfax Corp. is in the process of preparing its statement of cash flows for the year ended June 30, 1998. An income statement for the year and comparative balance sheets follow:

	FOR THE YEAR ENDED JUNE 30, 1998
Sales revenue	$550,000
Cost of goods sold	350,000
Gross profit	$200,000
General and administrative expenses	$ 55,000
Depreciation expense	75,000
Loss on sale of plant assets	5,000
Total expenses and losses	$135,000
Income before interest and taxes	$ 65,000
Interest expense	15,000
Income before taxes	$ 50,000
Income tax expense	17,000
Net income	$ 33,000

	JUNE 30	
	1998	1997
Cash	$ 31,000	$ 40,000
Accounts receivable	90,000	75,000
Inventory	80,000	95,000
Prepaid rent	12,000	16,000
Total current assets	$213,000	$226,000
Land	$250,000	$170,000
Plant and equipment	750,000	600,000
Accumulated depreciation	(310,000)	(250,000)
Total long-term assets	$690,000	$520,000
Total assets	$903,000	$746,000
Accounts payable	$155,000	$148,000
Other accrued liabilities	32,000	26,000
Income taxes payable	8,000	10,000
Total current liabilities	$195,000	$184,000
Long-term bank loan payable	$100,000	$130,000
Common stock	$350,000	$200,000
Retained earnings	258,000	232,000
Total stockholders' equity	$608,000	$432,000
Total liabilities and stockholders' equity	$903,000	$746,000

Dividends of $7,000 were declared and paid during the year. New plant assets were purchased for $195,000 in cash during the year. Also, land was purchased for cash. Plant assets were sold during 1998 for $25,000 in cash. The original cost of the assets sold was $45,000, and their book value was $30,000. Additional stock was issued for cash, and a portion of the bank loan was repaid.

Required

1. Prepare a statement of cash flows, using the direct method in the Operating Activities section.
2. Evaluate the following statement: "Whether a company uses the direct or the indirect method to report cash flows from operations is irrelevant because the amount of cash flow from operating activities is the same regardless of which method is used."

LO 4, 6 **Problem 14-12** Statement of Cash Flows—Indirect Method
Refer to all of the facts in Problem 14-11.

Required

1. Prepare a statement of cash flows for 1998, using the indirect method in the Operating Activities section.
2. Evaluate the following statement: "Whether a company uses the direct or indirect method to report cash flows from operations is irrelevant because the amount of cash flow from operating activities is the same regardless of which method is used."

LO 2, 5 **Problem 14-13** Statement of Cash Flows—Direct Method
Lang Company has not yet prepared a formal statement of cash flows for 1998. Comparative balance sheets as of December 31, 1998 and 1997, and a statement of income and retained earnings for the year ended December 31, 1998, follow:

LANG COMPANY
BALANCE SHEET
DECEMBER 31
(THOUSANDS OMITTED)

ASSETS	1998	1997
Current assets:		
Cash	$ 60	$ 100
U.S. Treasury bills (six-month)	–0–	50
Accounts receivable	610	500
Inventory	720	600
Total current assets	$1,390	$1,250
Long-term assets:		
Land	$ 80	$ 70
Buildings and equipment	710	600
Accumulated depreciation	(180)	(120)
Patents (less amortization)	105	130
Total long-term assets	$ 715	$ 680
Total assets	$2,105	$1,930
LIABILITIES AND OWNERS' EQUITY		
Current liabilities:		
Accounts payable	$ 360	$ 300
Taxes payable	25	20
Notes payable	400	400
Total current liabilities	$ 785	$ 720
Term notes payable—due 2002	200	200
Total liabilities	$ 985	$ 920
Owners' equity:		
Common stock outstanding	$ 830	$ 700
Retained earnings	290	310
Total owners' equity	$1,120	$1,010
Total liabilities and owners' equity	$2,105	$1,930

LANG COMPANY
STATEMENT OF INCOME AND RETAINED EARNINGS
FOR THE YEAR ENDED DECEMBER 31, 1998
(THOUSANDS OMITTED)

Sales		$2,408
Less expenses and interest:		
Cost of goods sold	$1,100	
Salaries and benefits	850	
Heat, light, and power	75	
Depreciation	60	
Property taxes	18	
Patent amortization	25	
Miscellaneous expense	10	
Interest	55	2,193
Net income before income taxes		$ 215
Income taxes		105
Net income		$ 110
Retained earnings—January 1, 1998		310
		$ 420
Stock dividend distributed		130
Retained earnings—December 31, 1998		$ 290

Required

1. For purposes of a statement of cash flows, are the U.S. Treasury bills cash equivalents? If not, how should they be classified? Explain your answers.

2. Prepare a statement of cash flows for 1998, using the direct method in the Operating Activities section. (CMA adapted)

Alternate Problems

LO 6 **Problem 14-1A** Statement of Cash Flows—Indirect Method
The following balances are available for Madison Company:

	DECEMBER 31	
	1998	1997
Cash	$ 12,000	$ 10,000
Accounts receivable	10,000	12,000
Inventory	8,000	7,000
Prepaid rent	1,200	1,000
Land	75,000	75,000
Plant and equipment	200,000	150,000
Accumulated depreciation	(75,000)	(25,000)
Totals	$231,200	$230,000
Accounts payable	$ 15,000	$ 15,000
Income taxes payable	2,500	2,000
Short-term notes payable	20,000	22,500
Bonds payable	75,000	50,000
Common stock	100,000	100,000
Retained earnings	18,700	40,500
Totals	$231,200	$230,000

Bonds were issued during 1998 at face value, and plant and equipment were acquired for cash. Depreciation expense for the year was $50,000. A net loss of $21,800 was reported.

Required

1. Prepare a statement of cash flows for 1998, using the indirect method in the Operating Activities section.

2. Explain briefly how Madison was able to increase its cash balance during a year in which it incurred a net loss.

LO 7 **Problem 14-2A** Statement of Cash Flows Using a Work Sheet—Indirect Method (Appendix 14A)
Refer to all of the facts in Problem 14-1A.

Required

1. Using the format in Appendix 14A, prepare a statement of cash flows work sheet.

2. Prepare a statement of cash flows for 1998, using the indirect method in the Operating Activities section.

3. Explain briefly how Madison was able to increase its cash balance during a year in which it incurred a net loss.

LO 5 **Problem 14-3A** Statement of Cash Flows—Direct Method
Wabash Corp. has just completed another very successful year, as indicated by the following income statement:

	FOR THE YEAR ENDED DECEMBER 31, 1998
Sales revenue	$2,460,000
Cost of goods sold	1,400,000
Gross profit	$1,060,000
Operating expenses	460,000
Income before interest and taxes	$ 600,000
Interest expense	100,000
Income before taxes	$ 500,000
Income tax expense	150,000
Net income	$ 350,000

The following are comparative balance sheets:

	DECEMBER 31	
	1998	1997
Cash	$ 140,000	$ 210,000
Accounts receivable	60,000	145,000
Inventory	200,000	180,000
Prepayments	15,000	25,000
Total current assets	$ 415,000	$ 560,000
Land	$ 600,000	$ 700,000
Plant and equipment	850,000	600,000
Accumulated depreciation	(225,000)	(200,000)
Total long-term assets	$1,225,000	$1,100,000
Total assets	$1,640,000	$1,660,000
Accounts payable	$ 140,000	$ 120,000
Other accrued liabilities	50,000	55,000
Income taxes payable	80,000	115,000
Total current liabilities	$ 270,000	$ 290,000
Long-term bank loan payable	$ 200,000	$ 250,000
Common stock	$ 450,000	$ 400,000
Retained earnings	720,000	720,000
Total stockholders' equity	$1,170,000	$1,120,000
Total liabilities and stockholders' equity	$1,640,000	$1,660,000

Other information follows:

a. Dividends of $350,000 were declared and paid during the year.

b. Operating expenses include $25,000 of depreciation.

c. Land was sold for its book value, and new plant and equipment was acquired for cash.

d. Part of the bank loan was repaid, and additional common stock was issued for cash.

The president has asked you some questions about the year's results. She is very impressed with the profit margin of 14% (net income divided by sales revenue). She is bothered, however, by the decline in the company's cash balance during the year. One of the conditions of the existing bank loan is that the company maintain a minimum cash balance of $100,000.

Required

1. Prepare a statement of cash flows for 1998, using the direct method in the Operating Activities section.

2. On the basis of your statement in requirement 1, draft a brief memo to the president to explain why cash decreased during such a profitable year. Include in your explanation any recommendations for improving the company's cash flow in future years.

LO 6 **Problem 14-4A** Statement of Cash Flows—Indirect Method
Refer to all of the facts in Problem 14-3A.

Required

1. Prepare a statement of cash flows for 1998, using the indirect method in the Operating Activities section.

2. On the basis of your statement in requirement 1, draft a brief memo to the president to explain why cash decreased during such a profitable year. Include in your explanation any recommendations for improving the company's cash flow in future years.

LO 7 **Problem 14-5A** Statement of Cash Flows Using a Work Sheet—Indirect Method (Appendix 14A)
Refer to all of the facts in Problem 14-3A.

Required

1. Using the format in Appendix 14A, prepare a statement of cash flows work sheet.

2. Prepare a statement of cash flows for 1998, using the indirect method in the Operating Activities section.

3. On the basis of your statement in requirement 2, draft a brief memo to the president to explain why cash decreased during such a profitable year. Include in your explanation any recommendations for improving the company's cash flow in future years.

LO 5 **Problem 14-6A** Statement of Cash Flows—Direct Method
The income statement for Pluto Inc. for 1998 follows:

	FOR THE YEAR ENDED DECEMBER 31, 1998
Sales revenue	$350,000
Cost of goods sold	150,000
Gross profit	$200,000
Operating expenses	250,000
Loss before interest and taxes	$ (50,000)
Interest expense	10,000
Net loss	$ (60,000)

Presented below are comparative balance sheets:

	DECEMBER 31	
	1998	1997
Cash	$ 25,000	$ 10,000
Accounts receivable	30,000	80,000
Inventory	100,000	100,000
Prepayments	36,000	35,000
Total current assets	$191,000	$225,000
Land	$300,000	$200,000
Plant and equipment	500,000	250,000
Accumulated depreciation	(90,000)	(50,000)
Total long-term assets	$710,000	$400,000
Total assets	$901,000	$625,000
Accounts payable	$ 50,000	$ 10,000
Other accrued liabilities	40,000	20,000
Interest payable	22,000	12,000
Total current liabilities	$112,000	$ 42,000
Long-term bank loan payable	$450,000	$100,000
Common stock	$300,000	$300,000
Retained earnings	39,000	183,000
Total stockholders' equity	$339,000	$483,000
Total liabilities and stockholders' equity	$901,000	$625,000

Other information follows:

a. Dividends of $84,000 were declared and paid during the year.

b. Operating expenses include $40,000 of depreciation.

c. Land and plant and equipment were acquired for cash. Cash was received from additional bank loans.

The president has asked you some questions about the year's results. He is disturbed with the net loss of $60,000 for the year. He notes, however, that the cash position at the end of the year is improved. He is confused about what appear to be conflicting signals: "How could we have possibly added to our bank accounts during such a terrible year of operations?"

Required

1. Prepare a statement of cash flows for 1998, using the direct method in the Operating Activities section.

2. On the basis of your statement in requirement 1, draft a brief memo to the president to explain why cash increased during such an unprofitable year. Include in your memo your recommendations for improving the company's bottom line.

LO 6 **Problem 14-7A** Statement of Cash Flows—Indirect Method
Refer to all of the facts in Problem 14-6A.

Required

1. Prepare a statement of cash flows for 1998, using the indirect method in the Operating Activities section.

2. On the basis of your statement in requirement 1, draft a brief memo to the president to explain why cash increased during such an unprofitable year. Include in your memo your recommendations for improving the company's bottom line.

LO 7 **Problem 14-8A** Statement of Cash Flows Using a Work Sheet—Indirect Method (Appendix 14A)
Refer to all of the facts in Problem 14-6A.

Required

1. Using the format in Appendix 14A, prepare a statement of cash flows work sheet.
2. Prepare a statement of cash flows for 1998, using the indirect method in the Operating Activities section.
3. On the basis of your statement in requirement 2, draft a brief memo to the president to explain why cash increased during such an unprofitable year. Include in your memo your recommendations for improving the company's bottom line.

LO 6 **Problem 14-9A** Year-end Balance Sheet and Statement of Cash Flows—Indirect Method

The balance sheet of Poodle Company at the end of 1997 is presented below along with certain other information for 1998:

	DECEMBER 31, 1997
Cash	$ 155,000
Accounts receivable	140,000
Total current assets	$ 295,000
Land	$ 100,000
Plant and equipment	700,000
Accumulated depreciation	(175,000)
Investments	125,000
Total long-term assets	$ 750,000
Total assets	$1,045,000
Current liabilities	$ 325,000
Bonds payable	$ 100,000
Common stock	$ 500,000
Retained earnings	120,000
Total stockholders' equity	$ 620,000
Total liabilities and stockholders' equity	$1,045,000

Other information follows:

a. Net income for 1998 was $50,000.
b. Included in operating expenses was $25,000 in depreciation.
c. Cash dividends of $40,000 were declared and paid.
d. An additional $50,000 of common stock was issued for cash.
e. Bonds payable of $100,000 were purchased for cash and retired at no gain or loss.
f. Cash purchases of plant and equipment during the year were $60,000.
g. An additional $200,000 of land was acquired in exchange for a long-term note payable.
h. Sales exceeded cash collections on account during the year by $15,000. All sales are on account.
i. The amount of current liabilities decreased by $20,000 during the year.

Required

1. Prepare a statement of cash flows for 1998, using the indirect method in the Operating Activities section. Include a supplemental schedule for noncash activities.
2. Prepare a balance sheet at December 31, 1998.
3. What primary uses did Poodle make of the cash it generated from operating activities?

LO 7 **Problem 14-10A** Statement of Cash Flows Using a Work Sheet—Indirect Method (Appendix 14A)

Refer to all of the facts in Problem 14-9A.

Required

1. Prepare a balance sheet at December 31, 1998.
2. Using the format in Appendix 14A, prepare a statement of cash flows work sheet.

3. Prepare a statement of cash flows for 1998, using the indirect method in the Operating Activities section.

4. Provide a possible explanation as to why Poodle decided to purchase and retire bonds during 1998.

Alternate Multi-Concept Problems

LO 4, 5 **Problem 14-11A** Statement of Cash Flows—Direct Method

World Wide Corp. is in the process of preparing its statement of cash flows for the year ended June 30, 1998. An income statement for the year and comparative balance sheets follow:

	FOR THE YEAR ENDED JUNE 30, 1998
Sales revenue	$400,000
Cost of goods sold	240,000
Gross profit	$160,000
General and administrative expenses	$ 40,000
Depreciation expense	80,000
Loss on sale of plant assets	10,000
Total expenses and losses	$130,000
Income before interest and taxes	$ 30,000
Interest expense	15,000
Income before taxes	$ 15,000
Income tax expense	5,000
Net income	$ 10,000

	JUNE 30	
	1998	1997
Cash	$ 25,000	$ 40,000
Accounts receivable	80,000	69,000
Inventory	75,000	50,000
Prepaid rent	2,000	18,000
Total current assets	$ 182,000	$ 177,000
Land	$ 60,000	$ 150,000
Plant and equipment	575,000	500,000
Accumulated depreciation	(310,000)	(250,000)
Total long-term assets	$ 325,000	$ 400,000
Total assets	$ 507,000	$ 577,000
Accounts payable	$ 145,000	$ 140,000
Other accrued liabilities	50,000	45,000
Income taxes payable	5,000	15,000
Total current liabilities	$ 200,000	$ 200,000
Long-term bank loan payable	$ 75,000	$ 150,000
Common stock	$ 100,000	$ 100,000
Retained earnings	132,000	127,000
Total stockholders' equity	$ 232,000	$ 227,000
Total liabilities and stockholders' equity	$ 507,000	$ 577,000

Dividends of $5,000 were declared and paid during the year. New plant assets were purchased for $125,000 in cash during the year. Also, land was sold for cash at its book value. Plant assets were sold during 1998 for $20,000 in cash. The original cost of the assets sold was $50,000, and their book value was $30,000. A portion of the bank loan was repaid.

Required

1. Prepare a statement of cash flows for 1998, using the direct method in the Operating Activities section.
2. Evaluate the following statement: "Whether a company uses the direct or the indirect method to report cash flows from operations is irrelevant because the amount of cash flow from operating activities is the same regardless of which method is used."

LO 4, 6 **Problem 14-12A** Statement of Cash Flows—Indirect Method
Refer to all of the facts in Problem 14-11A

Required

1. Prepare a statement of cash flows for 1998, using the indirect method in the Operating Activities section.
2. Evaluate the following statement: "Whether a company uses the direct or indirect method to report cash flows from operations is irrelevant because the amount of cash flow from operating activities is the same regardless of which method is used."

LO 2, 5 **Problem 14-13A** Statement of Cash Flows—Direct Method
Shepard Company has not yet prepared a formal statement of cash flows for 1998. Comparative balance sheets as of December 31, 1998 and 1997, and a statement of income and retained earnings for the year ended December 31, 1998, follow:

SHEPARD COMPANY
BALANCE SHEET
DECEMBER 31
(THOUSANDS OMITTED)

ASSETS	1998	1997
Current assets:		
Cash	$ 50	$ 75
U.S. Treasury bills (six-month)	25	–0–
Accounts receivable	125	200
Inventory	525	500
Total current assets	$ 725	$ 775
Long-term assets:		
Land	$ 100	$ 80
Buildings and equipment	510	450
Accumulated depreciation	(190)	(150)
Patents (less amortization)	90	110
Total long-term assets	$ 510	$ 490
Total assets	$1,235	$1,265
LIABILITIES AND OWNERS' EQUITY		
Current liabilities:		
Accounts payable	$ 370	$ 330
Taxes payable	10	20
Notes payable	300	400
Total current liabilities	$ 680	$ 750
Term notes payable—due 2002	200	200
Total liabilities	$ 880	$ 950
Owners' equity:		
Common stock outstanding	$ 220	$ 200
Retained earnings	135	115
Total owners' equity	$ 355	$ 315
Total liabilities and owners' equity	$1,235	$1,265

SHEPARD COMPANY
STATEMENT OF INCOME AND RETAINED EARNINGS
YEAR ENDED DECEMBER 31, 1998
(THOUSANDS OMITTED)

Sales		$1,416
Less expenses and interest:		
Cost of goods sold	$990	
Salaries and benefits	195	
Heat, light, and power	70	
Depreciation	40	
Property taxes	2	
Patent amortization	20	
Miscellaneous expense	2	
Interest	45	1,364
Net income before income taxes		$ 52
Income taxes		12
Net income		$ 40
Retained earnings—January 1, 1998		115
		$ 155
Stock dividend distributed		20
Retained earnings—December 31, 1998		$ 135

Required

1. For purposes of a statement of cash flows, are the U.S. Treasury bills cash equivalents? If not, how should they be classified? Explain your answers.

2. Prepare a statement of cash flows for 1998, using the direct method in the Operating Activities section.

(CMA adapted)

Cases

Reading and Interpreting Financial Statements

LO 2, 3 **Case 14-1** Reading and Interpreting Ben & Jerry's Statement of Cash Flows

Refer to Ben & Jerry's statement of cash flows for 1995 and any other pertinent information in its annual report.

Required

1. According to a footnote in the annual report, how does the company define cash equivalents?

2. According to the statement of cash flows, did inventories increase or decrease during the most recent year? Explain your answer.

3. What are the major reasons for the difference between net income and net cash provided by operating activities?

4. Excluding operations, what was Ben & Jerry's largest source of cash during the most recent year? the largest use of cash?

5. What common type of cash outflow from financing activities is missing from Ben & Jerry's statement?

LO 4 **Case 14-2** Reading and Interpreting the American Institute of Certified Public Accountants'
Statement of Cash Flows

As you know, the American Institute of Certified Public Accountants (the "Institute") is the national professional organization for all Certified Public Accountants. The Institute prepares "combined" financial statements. That is, the financial statements of the Institute also include the accounts of the following related organizations: the Division for CPA Firms, the Accounting Research Association Inc., the AICPA Benevolent Fund Inc., and the American Institute of Certified Public Accountants Foundation.

The Institute is a not-for-profit organization. As such, the excess of its assets over liabilities is described as "net assets" rather than stockholders' equity. For the most part, these net assets are unrestricted as to use; however, certain net assets are permanently restricted as to use. Also, instead of reporting net income for the year, the Institute reports the change in its unrestricted net assets.

Presented below is a combined statement of cash flows for the Institute and these related organizations for the year ended July 31, 1996 (thousands omitted).

INCREASE (DECREASE) IN CASH:

Operating Activities:

Cash received from members and customers	$128,455
Interest and dividends received	2,965
Cash paid to suppliers, employees and other	(117,789)
Interest paid	(139)
Income taxes paid	(280)
Net cash provided by operating activities	13,212

Investing Activities:

Payments for purchase of equipment	(4,320)
Payments for purchase of marketable securities	(142,050)
Proceeds from sale of marketable securities	136,423
Net cash used in investing activities	(9,947)
Financing Activities—payments of long-term borrowings	(2,800)
Net increase in cash	465
Cash, beginning of year	165
Cash, end of year	$ 630

RECONCILIATION OF INCREASE IN UNRESTRICTED NET ASSETS TO NET CASH PROVIDED BY OPERATING ACTIVITIES:

Increase in unrestricted net assets	$ 1,911

Adjustments to reconcile increase in unrestricted net assets to net cash provided by operating activities:

Depreciation and amortization:

Furniture, equipment and leasehold improvements	3,389
Internal computer systems	975
Gain on sale of marketable securities	(3,826)
Amortization of subscription revenue	(246)
Unrealized loss on marketable securities	$ 1,565
Cumulative effect of changes in accounting principles	4,148

Provision for:

Losses on accounts and notes receivable	322
Obsolete inventories	575
Deferred rent	1,259
Deferred employee benefits	1,790

Changes in operating assets and liabilities:

Accounts and notes receivable	(872)
Inventories	(677)
Deferred costs and prepaid expenses	(248)
Accounts payable and other liabilities	(922)
Advance dues	2,377
Unearned revenue	1,656
Deferred rent	290
Deferred employee benefits	(254)
Total adjustments	11,301
Net cash provided by operating activities	$ 13,212

Required

1. Which method, direct or indirect, does the Institute use in preparing the Operating Activities section of its combined statement of cash flows? Explain.

2. What was the Institute's largest source of cash during the year?

3. Furniture, equipment, and leasehold improvements, net of accumulated depreciation and amortization, in the amount of $22,850 (thousands omitted) were reported on the Institute's combined statement of financial position (balance sheet) at July 31, 1996. Using the information set forth in the 1996 combined statement of cash flows, what amount of furniture, equipment, and leasehold improvements, net of accumulated depreciation and amortization, appeared on the Institute's combined statement of financial position (balance sheet) at July 31, 1995?

LO 4 **Case 14-3** Reading and Interpreting Time Warner's Statement of Cash Flows

Presented below is the first section of Time Warner's 1995 statement of cash flows (in millions of dollars):

OPERATIONS	
Net loss	$ (166)
Adjustments for noncash and nonoperating items:	
Extraordinary loss on retirement of debt	42
Depreciation and amortization	559
Noncash interest expense	176
Excess of distributions over equity in pretax income	
of Entertainment Group	807
Equity in income of other investee companies,	
net of distributions	(16)
Changes in operating assets and liabilities:	
Receivables	(68)
Inventories	(52)
Accounts payable and other liabilities	160
Other balance sheet changes	(391)
Cash provided by operations	$1,051

Required

1. Which method, direct or indirect, does Time Warner use in preparing this section of the statement? Explain.

2. Based on your review of this section of Time Warner's 1995 statement of cash flows, what are the primary reasons the company reported a large net loss but was able to generate significant cash from operations?

Making Financial Decisions

Decision
Making

LO 1, 5 **Case 14-4** Dividend Decision and the Statement of Cash Flows—Direct Method

Bailey Corp. just completed the most profitable year in its 25-year history. Reported earnings of $1,020,000 on sales of $8,000,000 resulted in a very healthy profit margin of 12.75%. Each year before releasing the financial statements, the board of directors meets to decide on the amount of dividends to declare for the year. For each of the past nine years, the company has declared a dividend of $1 per share of common stock, which has been paid on January 15 of the following year.

Presented below are the income statement for the year and comparative balance sheets as of the end of the last two years.

	FOR THE YEAR ENDED DECEMBER 31, 1998
Sales revenue	$8,000,000
Cost of goods sold	4,500,000
Gross profit	$3,500,000
Operating expenses	1,450,000
Income before interest and taxes	$2,050,000
Interest expense	350,000
Income before taxes	$1,700,000
Income tax expense 40%	680,000
Net income	$1,020,000

	DECEMBER 31	
	1998	1997
Cash	$ 480,000	$ 450,000
Accounts receivable	250,000	200,000
Inventory	750,000	600,000
Prepayments	60,000	75,000
Total current assets	$ 1,540,000	$ 1,325,000
Land	$ 3,255,000	$ 2,200,000
Plant and equipment	4,200,000	2,500,000
Accumulated depreciation	(1,250,000)	(1,000,000)
Long-term investments	500,000	900,000
Patents	650,000	750,000
Total long-term assets	$ 7,355,000	$ 5,350,000
Total assets	$ 8,895,000	$ 6,675,000
Accounts payable	$ 350,000	$ 280,000
Other accrued liabilities	285,000	225,000
Income taxes payable	170,000	100,000
Dividends payable	–0–	200,000
Notes payable due within next year	200,000	–0–
Total current liabilities	$ 1,005,000	$ 805,000
Long-term notes payable	$ 300,000	$ 500,000
Bonds payable	2,200,000	1,500,000
Total long-term liabilities	$ 2,500,000	$ 2,000,000
Common stock, $10 par	$ 2,500,000	$ 2,000,000
Retained earnings	2,890,000	1,870,000
Total stockholders' equity	$ 5,390,000	$ 3,870,000
Total liabilities and stockholders' equity	$ 8,895,000	$ 6,675,000

Additional information follows:

a. All sales are on account, as are all purchases.

b. Land was purchased through the issuance of bonds. Additional land (beyond the amount purchased through the issuance of bonds) was purchased for cash.

c. New plant and equipment were acquired during the year for cash. No plant assets were retired during the year. Depreciation expense is included in operating expenses.

d. Long-term investments were sold for cash during the year.

e. No new patents were acquired, and none were disposed of during the year. Amortization expense is included in operating expenses.

f. Notes payable due within the next year represents the amount reclassified from long-term to short-term.

g. Fifty thousand shares of common stock were issued during the year at par value.

As Bailey's controller, you have been asked to recommend to the board whether to declare a dividend this year and, if so, whether the precedent of paying a $1 per share dividend can be maintained. The president is eager to keep the dividend at $1 in view of the successful year just completed. He is also concerned, however, about the effect of a dividend on the company's cash position. He is particularly concerned about the large amount of notes payable that comes due next year. He further notes the aggressive growth pattern in recent years, as evidenced this year by large increases in land and plant and equipment.

Required

1. Using the format in Exhibit 14-14, convert the income statement from an accrual basis to a cash basis.

2. Prepare a statement of cash flows, using the direct method in the Operating Activities section.

3. What do you recommend to the board of directors concerning the declaration of a cash dividend? Should the $1 per share dividend be declared? Should a smaller amount be declared? Should no dividend be declared? Support your answer with any necessary computations. Include in your response your concerns, from a cash flow perspective, about the following year.

Decision Making

LO 1, 6 **Case 14-5** Equipment Replacement Decision and Cash Flows From Operations

Auberge Company has been in operation for four years. The company is pleased with the continued improvement in net income but is concerned about a lack of cash available to replace existing equipment. Land, buildings, and equipment were purchased at the beginning of Year 1. No subsequent fixed asset purchases have been made, but the president believes that equipment will need to be replaced in the near future. The following information is available (all amounts are in millions of dollars):

	YEAR OF OPERATION			
	YEAR 1	YEAR 2	YEAR 3	YEAR 4
Net income (loss)	$(10)	$ (2)	$15	$20
Depreciation expense	30	25	15	14
Increase (decrease) in:				
Accounts receivable	32	5	12	20
Inventories	26	8	5	9
Prepayments	0	0	10	5
Accounts payable	15	3	(5)	(4)

Required

1. Compute the cash flow from operations for each of Auberge's first four years of operation.

2. Write a memo to the president explaining why the company is not generating sufficient cash from operations to pay for the replacement of equipment.

Accounting and Ethics: What Would You Do?

LO 1, 6 **Case 14-6** Loan Decision and the Statement of Cash Flows—Indirect Method

Mega Enterprises is in the process of negotiating an extension of its existing loan agreements with a major bank. The bank is particularly concerned with Mega's ability to generate sufficient cash flow from operating activities to meet the periodic principal and interest payments. In conjunction with the negotiations, the controller prepared the following statement of cash flows to present to the bank:

MEGA ENTERPRISES
STATEMENT OF CASH FLOWS
FOR THE YEAR ENDED DECEMBER 31, 1998
(ALL AMOUNTS IN MILLIONS OF DOLLARS)

CASH FLOWS FROM OPERATING ACTIVITIES

Net income	$ 65
Adjustments to reconcile net income to net cash provided by operating activities:	
Depreciation and amortization	56
Increase in accounts receivable	(19)
Decrease in inventory	27
Decrease in accounts payable	(42)
Increase in other accrued liabilities	18
Net cash provided by operating activities	$ 105

CASH FLOWS FROM INVESTING ACTIVITIES

Acquisitions of other businesses	$(234)
Acquisitions of plant and equipment	(125)
Sale of other businesses	300
Net cash used by investing activities	$ (59)

CASH FLOWS FROM FINANCING ACTIVITIES

Additional borrowings	$ 150
Repayments of borrowings	(180)
Cash dividends paid	(50)
Net cash used by financing activities	$ (80)
Net decrease in cash	$ (34)
Cash balance, January 1, 1998	42
Cash balance, December 31, 1998	$ 8

During 1998 Mega sold one of its businesses in California. A gain of $150 million was included in 1998 income as the difference between the proceeds from the sale of $450 million and the book value of the business of $300 million. The entry to record the sale is as follows:

Cash	450	
California Properties		300
Gain on Sale of Business		150
To record sale of a business.		

Required

1. Comment on the presentation of the sale of the California business on the statement of cash flows. Does the way in which the sale was reported violate generally accepted accounting principles? Regardless of whether it violates GAAP, does the way in which the transaction was reported on the statement result in a misstatement of the net decrease in cash for the period? Explain your answers.

2. Prepare a revised statement of cash flows for 1998, with the proper presentation of the sale of the California business.

3. Has the controller acted in an unethical manner in the way the sale was reported on the statement of cash flows? Explain your answer.

LO 2, 3   **Case 14-7** Cash Equivalents and the Statement of Cash Flows

In December 1998, Rangers Inc. invested $100,000 of idle cash in U.S. Treasury notes. The notes mature on October 1, 1999, at which time Rangers expects to redeem them at face value of $100,000. The treasurer believes that the notes should be classified as cash equivalents because of the plans to hold them to maturity and receive face value. He would also like to avoid presentation of the purchase as an investing activity because the company has made sizable capital expenditures during the year. The treasurer realizes that the decision about classification of the Treasury notes rests with you, as controller.

Required

1. According to generally accepted accounting principles, how should the investment in U.S. Treasury notes be classified for purposes of preparing a statement of cash flows? Explain your answer.

2. As controller for Rangers, what would you do in this situation? What would you tell the treasurer?

Research Case

Internet

Case 14-8 IBM

By providing business and consumer hardware, software, and technical support, IBM continues to find ways to serve both its global business customers and families with a home computer. IBM believes that its past ability to adapt to changing customer needs will continue to generate substantial cash flows for the company.

Conduct a search of the World Wide Web, obtain IBM's most recent annual report, or use library resources to obtain company financial data, and answer the following:

1. Based on the latest financial information, what is the amount of IBM's (a) cash flows from operating activities, (b) cash flows from investing activities, and (c) cash flows from financing activities? How do these compare to the corresponding numbers from 1995 in the "Focus on Financial Results" vignette at the start of the chapter? What is the trend?

2. Using current bond market information, how does the current yield for an IBM bond coming due in the next couple of years compare with the average current yield for the market as a whole? What are some of the internal and external factors that would affect the current yields of IBM's bonds?

3. As an information systems manager, what financial data and other company information would you find useful when deciding between IBM or another company as your supplier of computer products?

Optional Research. Interview a person who sells or works with computers. Obtain information about the technology affecting new computer hardware and software. Also obtain information from the company's Web site to determine IBM's recent actions to enhance company revenue. Then determine whether IBM discloses revenue by classes of similar products or services. What class or classes have grown the fastest? Why do you think that is the case?

Solution to Key Terms Quiz

3	Statement of cash flows (p. 667)	4	Cash equivalent (p. 670)
1	Operating activities (p. 671)	5	Investing activities (p. 671)
7	Financing activities (p. 672)	6	Direct method (p. 673)
2	Indirect method (p. 674)		

Financial Statement Analysis

STUDY LINKS

A Look at Previous Chapters

In Chapter 2, we introduced a few key financial ratios and saw the way that investors and creditors use them to better understand a company's financial statements. In many of the subsequent chapters, we introduced ratios relevant to the particular topic being discussed.

A Look at This Chapter

Ratio analysis is one important type of analysis used to interpret financial statements. In this chapter, we expand our discussion of ratio analysis and introduce other valuable techniques used by investors, creditors, and analysts in reaching informed decisions. We will find that ratios and other forms of analyses can provide additional insight beyond that available from merely reading the financial statements.

FOCUS ON FINANCIAL RESULTS

Wm. Wrigley Jr. Company has enjoyed a long and successful run in the chewing-gum business. From a small family operation, it has grown to a large publicly owned corporation with annual sales exceeding $1.7 billion. The company once owned the Chicago Cubs baseball team but sold it a few years ago to another Chicago-based business, The Tribune Company. Wrigley now concentrates on a single industry: making chewing gum and selling it in over 120 countries.

Basic data for assessing the success of this strategy appear in the "Highlights of Operations" section of the company's annual report.

HIGHLIGHTS OF OPERATIONS

WM. WRIGLEY JR. COMPANY AND ASSOCIATED COMPANIES

	1995	1994
	In thousands of dollars except for per share amounts	
Net Sales	$1,754,931	1,596,551
Earnings before nonrecurring gain on sale of Singapore property in 1994	223,739	205,767
—Per Share of Common Stock	1.93	1.77
Net Earnings	223,739	230,533
—Per Share of Common Stock	1.93	1.98
Dividends Paid	111,401	104,694
—Per Share of Common Stock	.96	.90
Property Additions	102,759	87,013
Stockholders' Equity	796,852	688,470
Return on Average Equity	30.1%	36.5%
Stockholders at Close of Year	28,959	24,078
Average Shares Outstanding (000)	116,066	116,358

For additional historical financial data, see page 22.

The highlights, shown here, indicate an overall pattern of success. The company's net earnings, excluding a gain from selling Singapore property in 1994, increased 9 percent from 1994 to 1995, reaching a record level of over $223 million. About half of those earnings ($111 million) were paid in dividends to shareholders. However, the company has to make some trade-offs. The more of its earnings it pays in dividends, the less it has to invest in its future growth. Most companies would be envious of the robust return on average equity of over 30% in each of the last two years.

If you were a potential investor in Wrigley, you would want to compare its stock with alternative investments in terms of the ability to generate income and pay dividends. If you were to buy Wrigley stock today, which measures of financial performance would be most important to you? Find the company's most recent annual report, and determine whether those measures have improved since 1995.

SOURCE: *Wm. Wrigley Jr. Company Annual Report, 1995.*

LEARNING OBJECTIVES

After studying this chapter, you should be able to

LO 1 Explain the various limitations and considerations in financial statement analysis.

LO 2 Use comparative financial statements to analyze a company over time (horizontal analysis).

LO 3 Use common-size financial statements to compare various financial statement items (vertical analysis).

LO 4 Compute and use various ratios to assess liquidity.

LO 5 Compute and use various ratios to assess solvency.

LO 6 Compute and use various ratios to assess profitability.

Precautions in Statement Analysis

Various groups have different purposes for analyzing a company's financial statements. For example, a banker is primarily interested in the likelihood that a loan will be repaid. Certain ratios, as we will see, indicate the ability to repay principal and interest. A stockholder, on the other hand, is concerned with a fair return on the amount invested in the company. Again, certain ratios are helpful in assessing the return to the stockholder. The management of a business is also interested in the tools of financial statement analysis because various outside groups judge management on the basis of its performance as measured by certain key ratios. Publicly held corporations are required to include in their annual reports a section that reviews the past year, with management's comments on its performance as measured by selected ratios and other forms of analysis.

Before we turn our attention to various techniques commonly used in the financial analysis of a company, it is important to understand some of the limitations and other considerations in statement analysis.

Watch for Alternative Accounting Principles

LO 1 Explain the various limitations and considerations in financial statement analysis.

Every set of financial statements is based on various assumptions. For example, a cost-flow method must be assumed in valuing inventory and recognizing cost of goods sold. The accountant chooses FIFO, LIFO, or one of the other acceptable methods. The analyst or other user finds this type of information in the footnotes to the financial statements. The selection of a particular inventory valuation method has a significant effect on certain key ratios. Recognition of the acceptable alternatives is especially important in comparing two or more companies. Finally, as we saw in Chapter 12, *changes* in accounting methods, such as a change in the depreciation method, also make comparing results for a given company over time more difficult. Again, the reader must turn to the footnotes for information regarding these changes.

Take Care When Making Comparisons

Users of financial statements often place too much emphasis on summary indicators and key ratios, such as the current ratio and the earnings per share amount. No single ratio is capable of telling the user everything there is to know about a particular company. The calculation of various ratios for a company is only a starting point. One technique we discuss is the comparison of ratios for different periods of time. Has the ratio gone up or down from last year? What is the percentage of increase or decrease in the ratio over the last five years? Recognizing trends in ratios is important in analyzing any company.

The potential investor must also recognize the need to compare one company with others in the same industry. For example, a particular measure of performance may cause an investor to conclude that the company is not operating efficiently. Comparison with an industry standard, however, might indicate that the ratio is normal for companies in that industry. Various organizations publish summaries of selected ratios for a sample of companies in the United States. The ratios are usually organized by industry.

Dun & Bradstreet's *Industry Norms and Key Business Ratios,* for example, is an annual review that organizes companies into five major industries and approximately 800 specific lines of business.

Although industry comparisons are useful, caution is necessary in interpreting the results of such analyses. Few companies in today's economy operate in a single industry. Exceptions exist (Wrigley is almost exclusively in the business of making and selling chewing gum), but most companies cross the boundaries of a single industry. *Conglomerates,* companies operating in more than one industry, present a special challenge to the analyst. Keep in mind also the point made earlier about alternative accounting methods. It is not unusual to find companies in the same industry using different inventory valuation techniques or depreciation methods.

Finally, many corporate income statements contain nonoperating items, such as extraordinary items, cumulative effects from accounting changes, and gains and losses from discontinued operations. When these items exist, the reader must exercise extra caution in making comparisons. To assess the future prospects of a group of companies, you may want to compare income statements *before* taking into account the effects these items have on income.

Understand the Possible Effects of Inflation

Inflation, or an increase in the level of prices, is another important consideration in analyzing financial statements. The statements, to be used by outsiders, are based on historical costs and are not adjusted for the effects of increasing prices. For example, consider the following trend in a company's sales for the past three years:

	1998	1997	1996
Net sales	$121,000	$110,000	$100,000

As measured by the actual dollars of sales, sales have increased by 10% each year. Caution is necessary in concluding that the company is better off in each succeeding year because of the increase in sales *dollars.* Assume, for example, that 1996 sales of $100,000 are the result of selling 100,000 units at $1 each. Are 1997 sales of $110,000 the result of selling 110,000 units at $1 each or of selling 100,000 units at $1.10 each? Although on the surface it may seem unimportant which result accounts for the sales increase, the answer can have significant ramifications. If the company found it necessary to increase selling price to $1.10 in the face of increasing *costs,* it may be no better off than it was in 1996 in terms of gross profit. On the other hand, if the company is able to increase sales revenue by 10% primarily based on growth in unit sales, then its performance is usually considered stronger than if the increase is merely due to a price increase. The point to be made is one of caution: published financial statements are stated in historical costs and therefore have not been adjusted for the effects of inflation.

Fortunately, inflation has been relatively subdued in the past several years. During the late 1970s, the FASB actually required a separate footnote in the financial statements to calculate the effects of inflation. The requirement was abandoned in the mid-1980s when inflation had subsided and the profession decided that the cost of providing inflation-adjusted information exceeded the benefits to the users.

Analysis of Comparative and Common-Size Statements

We are now ready to analyze a set of financial statements. We will begin by looking at the comparative statements of a company for a two-year period. The analysis of the statements over a series of years is often called horizontal analysis. We will then see how the statements can be recast in what are referred to as *common-size statements*. The analysis of common-size statements is called vertical analysis. Finally, we will consider the use of a variety of ratios to analyze a company.

EXHIBIT 15-1 Comparative Balance Sheets—Horizontal Analysis

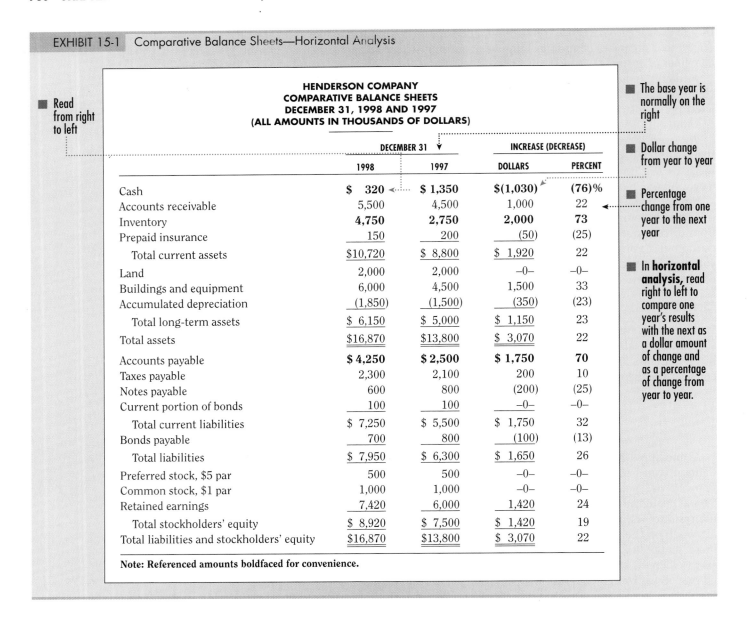

■ Read from right to left

HENDERSON COMPANY
COMPARATIVE BALANCE SHEETS
DECEMBER 31, 1998 AND 1997
(ALL AMOUNTS IN THOUSANDS OF DOLLARS)

	DECEMBER 31		INCREASE (DECREASE)	
	1998	1997	DOLLARS	PERCENT
Cash	$ 320	$ 1,350	$(1,030)	(76)%
Accounts receivable	5,500	4,500	1,000	22
Inventory	**4,750**	**2,750**	**2,000**	**73**
Prepaid insurance	150	200	(50)	(25)
Total current assets	$10,720	$ 8,800	$ 1,920	22
Land	2,000	2,000	–0–	–0–
Buildings and equipment	6,000	4,500	1,500	33
Accumulated depreciation	(1,850)	(1,500)	(350)	(23)
Total long-term assets	$ 6,150	$ 5,000	$ 1,150	23
Total assets	$16,870	$13,800	$ 3,070	22
Accounts payable	**$ 4,250**	**$ 2,500**	**$ 1,750**	**70**
Taxes payable	2,300	2,100	200	10
Notes payable	600	800	(200)	(25)
Current portion of bonds	100	100	–0–	–0–
Total current liabilities	$ 7,250	$ 5,500	$ 1,750	32
Bonds payable	700	800	(100)	(13)
Total liabilities	$ 7,950	$ 6,300	$ 1,650	26
Preferred stock, $5 par	500	500	–0–	–0–
Common stock, $1 par	1,000	1,000	–0–	–0–
Retained earnings	7,420	6,000	1,420	24
Total stockholders' equity	$ 8,920	$ 7,500	$ 1,420	19
Total liabilities and stockholders' equity	$16,870	$13,800	$ 3,070	22

Note: Referenced amounts boldfaced for convenience.

■ The base year is normally on the right

■ Dollar change from year to year

■ Percentage change from one year to the next year

■ In **horizontal analysis,** read right to left to compare one year's results with the next as a dollar amount of change and as a percentage of change from year to year.

Horizontal Analysis

LO 2 Use comparative financial statements to analyze a company over time (horizontal analysis).

Comparative balance sheets for a hypothetical entity, Henderson Company, are presented in Exhibit 15-1. The increase or decrease in each of the major accounts on the balance sheet is shown in both absolute dollars and as a percentage. The base year for computing the percentage increase or decrease in each account is the first year, 1997, and is normally shown on the right side. By reading across from right to left (thus the term *horizontal analysis*), the analyst can quickly spot any unusual changes in accounts from the previous year. Three accounts stand out: Cash decreased by 76%, Inventory increased by 73%, and Accounts Payable increased by 70%. (These lines are boldfaced for convenience.) Individually, each of these large changes is a red flag. Taken together, these changes send the financial statement user the warning that the business may be deteriorating. Each of these large changes should be investigated further.

Exhibit 15-2 shows comparative statements of income and retained earnings for Henderson for 1998 and 1997. At first glance, the 20% increase in sales to $24 million appears promising, but management was not able to limit the increase in either cost of goods sold or selling, general, and administrative expense to 20%. The analysis indicates that cost of goods sold increased by 29% and selling, general, and administrative

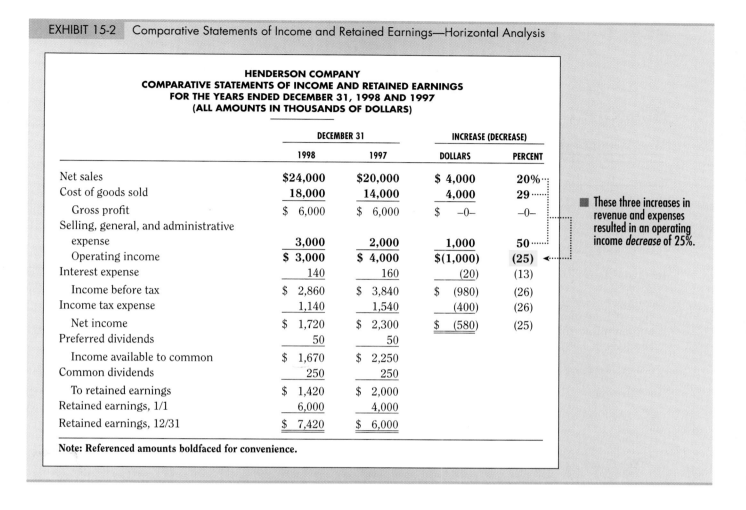

EXHIBIT 15-2   Comparative Statements of Income and Retained Earnings—Horizontal Analysis

HENDERSON COMPANY
COMPARATIVE STATEMENTS OF INCOME AND RETAINED EARNINGS
FOR THE YEARS ENDED DECEMBER 31, 1998 AND 1997
(ALL AMOUNTS IN THOUSANDS OF DOLLARS)

	DECEMBER 31 1998	1997	INCREASE (DECREASE) DOLLARS	PERCENT
Net sales	$24,000	$20,000	$ 4,000	20%
Cost of goods sold	18,000	14,000	4,000	29
Gross profit	$ 6,000	$ 6,000	$ –0–	–0–
Selling, general, and administrative expense	3,000	2,000	1,000	50
Operating income	$ 3,000	$ 4,000	$(1,000)	(25)
Interest expense	140	160	(20)	(13)
Income before tax	$ 2,860	$ 3,840	$ (980)	(26)
Income tax expense	1,140	1,540	(400)	(26)
Net income	$ 1,720	$ 2,300	$ (580)	(25)
Preferred dividends	50	50		
Income available to common	$ 1,670	$ 2,250		
Common dividends	250	250		
To retained earnings	$ 1,420	$ 2,000		
Retained earnings, 1/1	6,000	4,000		
Retained earnings, 12/31	$ 7,420	$ 6,000		

Note: Referenced amounts boldfaced for convenience.

■ These three increases in revenue and expenses resulted in an operating income *decrease* of 25%.

expense increased by 50%. The increases in these two expenses more than offset the increase in sales and resulted in a decrease in operating income of 25%.

Companies that experience sales growth often become lax about controlling expenses. Their managements sometimes forget that it is the bottom line that counts, not the top line. Perhaps the salespeople are given incentives to increase sales without considering the costs of the sales. Maybe management is spending too much on overhead, including its own salaries. The owners of the business will have to address these concerns if they want to get a reasonable return on their investment.

Horizontal analysis can be extended to include more than two years of results. At a minimum, publicly held companies are required to include income statements and statements of cash flows for the three most recent years and balance sheets as of the end of the two most recent years. Many annual reports include, as supplementary information, financial summaries of operations for extended periods of time. As illustrated in Exhibit 15-3, for example, Wrigley includes an 11-year summary of selected financial data, such as net sales, dividends paid, return on average equity, and total assets. Note the increase in net sales in every year over the 11-year period. Also note, however, that Wrigley does not include in the summary the gross profit ratio (gross profit divided by net sales). A comparison of the trend in this ratio would help to determine whether the company has effectively controlled the cost to manufacture its products. The summary does show that Wrigley has reported an increase in net earnings before any nonrecurring gains and accounting changes for 10 consecutive years, an enviable record for any company.

Tracking items over a series of years, a practice called *trend analysis,* can be a very powerful tool for the analyst. Advanced statistical techniques are available for analyzing trends in financial data and, most important, for projecting those trends to future

FROM CONCEPT TO PRACTICE 15.1
READING BEN & JERRY'S ANNUAL REPORT   Where does Ben & Jerry's annual report provide a financial summary? How many years does it include? In terms of a trend over time, which item on the summary do you think is the most significant?

EXHIBIT 15-3	Wrigley Financial Summary

SELECTED FINANCIAL DATA

WM. WRIGLEY JR. COMPANY AND ASSOCIATED COMPANIES

	1995	1994	1993	1992
OPERATING DATA				
Net Sales	$1,754,931	1,596,551	1,428,504	1,286,921
Cost of Sales	778,019	697,442	617,156	572,468
Income Taxes	126,492	122,746	103,944	83,730
Earnings before nonrecurring gain on sale of Singapore property in 1994 and cumulative effect of accounting changes in 1992	223,739	205,767	174,891	148,573
—Per Share of Common Stock	1.93	1.77	1.50	1.27
Net Earnings	223,739	230,533	174,891	141,295
—Per Share of Common Stock	1.93	1.98	1.50	1.21
Dividends Paid	111,401	104,694	87,344	72,511
—Per Share of Common Stock	.96	.90	.75	.62
—As a Percent of Net Earnings	50%	45%	50%	51%
Dividends Declared Per Share of Common Stock	.99	.94	.75	.63
Average Shares Outstanding	116,066	116,358	116,511	117,055
OTHER FINANCIAL DATA				
Total Property, Plant and Equipment (Net)	$ 347,491	289,420	239,868	222,137
Total Assets	1,099,219	978,834	815,324	711,372
Working Capital	458,683	413,414	343,132	299,149
Stockholders' Equity	796,852	688,470	575,182	498,935
Return on Average Equity	30.1%	36.5%	32.6%	29.4%
Stockholders at Close of Year	28,959	24,078	18,567	14,546
Employees at Close of Year	7,300	7,000	6,700	6,400
Market Price of Stock—High	54.000	53.875	46.125	39.875
—Low	42.875	38.125	29.500	22.125

EXHIBIT 15-3   (continued)

					In thousands of dollars and shares except for per share amounts	
1991	1990	1989	1988	1987	1986	1985
1,148,875	1,110,639	992,853	891,392	781,059	698,982	620,267
507,795	508,957	451,773	392,460	338,081	318,280	295,430
79,362	70,897	64,277	53,491	52,863	49,840	36,963
128,652	117,362	106,149	87,236	70,145	53,818	43,498
1.09	1.00	.90	.73	.56	.42	.34
128,652	117,362	106,149	87,236	70,145	53,818	43,498
1.09	1.00	.90	.73	.56	.42	.34
64,609	58,060	53,506	43,591	35,080	27,056	21,819
.55	.49	.45	.36	.28	.21	.17
50%	49%	50%	50%	50%	50%	50%
.55	.51	.47	.37	.29	.22	.17
117,517	117,743	118,035	120,308	125,006	126,817	126,697
201,386	188,959	171,951	155,260	151,425	134,383	129,194
625,074	563,665	498,624	440,400	407,350	394,352	351,512
276,047	229,735	186,588	165,430	149,154	168,754	131,839
463,399	401,386	342,994	308,538	288,965	292,962	258,809
29.8%	31.5%	32.6%	29.2%	24.1%	19.5%	17.8%
11,086	10,497	10,218	9,440	9,351	8,956	8,344
6,250	5,850	5,750	5,500	5,500	5,500	5,600
27.000	19.750	17.917	13.750	11.833	8.667	5.271
16.375	14.583	11.833	10.667	6.500	4.583	3.188

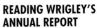

FROM CONCEPT TO PRACTICE 15.2
READING WRIGLEY'S ANNUAL REPORT
Refer to Wrigley's Financial Highlights in Exhibit 15-3. Compute the company's gross profit ratio for each of the 11 years. Is there a noticeable upward or downward trend in the ratio over this time period?

periods. Some of the techniques, such as time series analysis, have been used extensively in forecasting sales trends.

Historically, attention has focused on the balance sheet and income statement in analyzing a company's position and results of operation. Only recently have analysts and other users begun to appreciate the value in incorporating the statement of cash flows into their analyses.

Comparative statements of cash flows for Henderson appear in Exhibit 15-4. Henderson's financing activities remained constant over the two-year period, as indicated in that section of the statements. Each year the company paid $200,000 on notes, another $100,000 to retire bonds, and $300,000 to stockholders in dividends. Cash outflow from investing activities slowed down somewhat in 1998, with the purchase of $1,500,000 in new buildings, compared with $2,000,000 the year before.

The most noticeable difference between Henderson's statements of cash flows for the two years is in the Operating Activities section. Operations generated almost $2 million

---

EXHIBIT 15-4   Comparative Statements of Cash Flow—Horizontal Analysis

HENDERSON COMPANY
COMPARATIVE STATEMENTS OF CASH FLOW
FOR THE YEARS ENDED DECEMBER 31, 1998 AND 1997
(ALL AMOUNTS IN THOUSANDS OF DOLLARS)

		1998	1997	INCREASE (DECREASE) DOLLARS	INCREASE (DECREASE) PERCENT
NET CASH FLOWS FROM OPERATING ACTIVITIES					
Net income		$1,720	$2,300	$ (580)	(25)%
Adjustments:					
Depreciation expense		350	300		
Changes in:					
Accounts receivable		(1,000)	500		
Inventory		(2,000)	(300)		
Prepaid insurance		50	50		
Accounts payable		1,750	(200)		
Taxes payable		200	300		
Net cash provided by operating activities	Unfavorable	$1,070	$2,950	$(1,880)	(64)%
NET CASH FLOWS FROM INVESTING ACTIVITIES					
Purchase of buildings		$(1,500)	$(2,000)	$ (500)	(25)%
NET CASH FLOWS FROM FINANCING ACTIVITIES					
Repayment of notes		$ (200)	$ (200)	–0–	–0–
Retirement of bonds		(100)	(100)	–0–	–0–
Cash dividends—preferred		(50)	(50)	–0–	–0–
Cash dividends—common		(250)	(250)	–0–	–0–
Net cash used by financing activities		$ (600)	$ (600)	–0–	–0–
Net increase (decrease) in cash		$ (1,030)	$ 350		
Beginning cash balance		1,350	1,000		
Ending cash balance		$ 320	$ 1,350		
SUPPLEMENTAL INFORMATION					
Interest paid		$ 140	$ 160		
Income taxes paid		$ 940	$ 1,440		

Note: Referenced amounts boldfaced for convenience.

less in cash in 1998 than in 1997 ($1.07 million in 1998 versus $2.95 million in 1997). The decrease in net income, as presented in the exhibit, was partially responsible for this reduction in cash from operations. However, the increases in accounts receivable and inventories in 1998 had a significant impact on the decrease in cash generated from operating activities.

Vertical Analysis

Often it is easier to examine comparative financial statements if they have been standardized. *Common-size statements* recast all items on the statement as a percentage of a selected item on the statement. This excludes size as a relevant variable in the analysis. One could use this type of analysis to compare General Motors with the smaller Chrysler or to compare IBM with the much smaller Apple Computer. It is also a convenient way to compare the same company from year to year.

LO 3 Use common-size financial statements to compare various financial statement items (vertical analysis).

Vertical analysis involves looking at the relative size and composition of various items on a particular financial statement. Common-size comparative balance sheets for Henderson Company are presented in Exhibit 15-5. Note that all asset accounts are stated as a percentage of total assets. Similarly, all liability and stockholders' equity accounts are

EXHIBIT 15-5 Common-Size Comparative Balance Sheets—Vertical Analysis

HENDERSON COMPANY
COMMON-SIZE COMPARATIVE BALANCE SHEETS
DECEMBER 31, 1998 AND 1997
(ALL AMOUNTS IN THOUSANDS OF DOLLARS)

	DECEMBER 31, 1998		DECEMBER 31, 1997	
	DOLLARS	PERCENT	DOLLARS	PERCENT
Cash	$ 320	1.9%	$ 1,350	9.8%
Accounts receivable	5,500	32.6	4,500	32.6
Inventory	**4,750**	**28.1**	**2,750**	**19.9**
Prepaid insurance	150	0.9	200	1.5
Total current assets	**$10,720**	**63.5%**	**$ 8,800**	**63.8%**
Land	2,000	11.9	2,000	14.5
Buildings and equipment, net	4,150	24.6	3,000	21.7
Total long-term assets	$ 6,150	36.5	$ 5,000	36.2
Total assets	$ 16,870	100.0%	$13,800	100.0%
Accounts payable	$ 4,250	25.2%	$ 2,500	18.1%
Taxes payable	2,300	13.6	2,100	15.2
Notes payable	600	3.6	800	5.8
Current portion of bonds	100	0.6	100	0.7
Total current liabilities	**$ 7,250**	**43.0%**	**$ 5,500**	**39.8%**
Bonds payable	700	4.1	800	5.8
Total liabilities	$ 7,950	47.1%	$ 6,300	45.6%
Preferred stock, $5 par	500	3.0	500	3.6
Common stock, $1 par	1,000	5.9	1,000	7.3
Retained earnings	7,420	44.0	6,000	43.5
Total stockholders' equity	**$ 8,920**	**52.9%**	**$ 7,500**	**54.4%**
Total liabilities and stockholders' equity	$ 16,870	100.0%	$13,800	100.0%

Note: Referenced amounts boldfaced for convenience.

■ In **vertical analysis,** compare each line item as a percent of total (100%) to highlight company's overall condition.

■ Compare percentages across years to spot year-to-year trends.

stated as a percentage of total liabilities and stockholders' equity. The combination of the comparative balance sheets for the two years and the common-size feature allows the analyst to spot critical changes in the composition of the assets. We noted in Exhibit 15-1 that cash had decreased by 76% over the two years. The decrease of cash from 9.8% of total assets to only 1.9% is highlighted in Exhibit 15-5.

One can also observe in the exhibit that total current assets have continued to represent just under two-thirds (63.5%) of total assets. If cash has decreased significantly in terms of the percentage of total assets, what accounts have increased to maintain current assets at two-thirds of total assets? We can quickly determine from the data in Exhibit 15-5 that although inventory represented 19.9% of total assets at the end of 1997, the percentage is up to 28.1% at the end of 1998. This change in the relative composition of current assets between cash and inventory may have important implications. The change, for instance, may signal that the company is having trouble selling inventory.

Total current liabilities represent a slightly higher percentage of total liabilities and stockholders' equity at the end of 1998 than at the end of 1997. The increase is balanced by a slight decrease in the relative percentages of long-term debt (the bonds) and of stockholders' equity. We will return later to further analysis of the composition of both the current and the noncurrent accounts.

Common-size comparative income statements for Henderson are presented in Exhibit 15-6. The *base,* or benchmark, on which all other items in the income statement are compared is net sales. Again, observations from the comparative statements alone are further confirmed by examining the common-size statements. Although the gross profit ratio—gross profit as a percentage of sales—was 30% in 1997, the same ratio for 1998 is only 25%. Recall the earlier observation that although sales increased by 20% from one year to the next, cost of goods sold increased by 29%.

In addition to the gross profit ratio, an important relationship from Exhibit 15-6 is the *ratio of net income to net sales,* or profit margin ratio. The ratio, an overall indicator of management's ability to control expenses, reflects the amount of income for each dollar of sales. Some analysts prefer to look at income before tax, rather than final net income, because taxes are not typically an expense that can be controlled. Further, if the

---

EXHIBIT 15-6 Common-Size Comparative Income Statements—Vertical Analysis

HENDERSON COMPANY
COMMON-SIZE COMPARATIVE INCOME STATEMENTS
FOR THE YEARS ENDED DECEMBER 31, 1998 AND 1997
(ALL AMOUNTS IN THOUSANDS OF DOLLARS)

	1998		1997	
	DOLLARS	PERCENT	DOLLARS	PERCENT
Net sales	$24,000	100.0%	$20,000	100.0%
Cost of goods sold	18,000	75.0	14,000	70.0
Gross profit	$ 6,000	25.0%	$ 6,000	30.0%
Selling, general, and administrative expense	3,000	12.5	2,000	10.0
Operating income	$ 3,000	12.5%	$ 4,000	20.0%
Interest expense	140	0.6	160	0.8
Income before tax	$ 2,860	11.9%	$ 3,840	19.2%
Income tax expense	1,140	4.8	1,540	7.7
Net income	$ 1,720	7.1%	$ 2,300	11.5%

■ Gross profit as a percentage of sales is the **gross profit ratio.**

■ The ratio of net income to net sales is the **profit margin ratio.**

Note: Referenced amounts boldfaced for convenience.

company does not earn a profit before tax, it will incur no tax expense. Note the decrease in Henderson's profit margin: from 11.5% in 1997 to 7.1% in 1998 (or from 19.2% to 11.9% on a before-tax basis).

Liquidity Analysis and the Management of Working Capital

Two ratios were discussed in the last section: the *gross profit ratio* and the *profit margin ratio.* A ratio is simply the relationship, normally stated as a percentage, between two financial statement amounts. In this section, we consider a wide range of ratios used by management, analysts, and others for a variety of purposes. We classify the ratios in three main categories according to their use in performing (1) liquidity analysis, (2) solvency analysis, and (3) profitability analysis.

> **LO 4** Compute and use various ratios to assess liquidity.

Liquidity is a relative measure of the nearness to cash of the assets and liabilities of a company. Nearness to cash deals with the length of time before cash is realized. Various ratios are used to measure liquidity, and they basically concern the company's ability to pay its debts as they come due. Recall the distinction between the current and long-term classifications on the balance sheet. Current assets are assets that will be either converted into cash or consumed within one year or the operating cycle, if the cycle is longer than one year. The operating cycle for a manufacturing company is the length of time between the purchase of raw materials and the eventual collection of any outstanding account receivable from the sale of the product. Current liabilities are a company's obligations that require the use of current assets or the creation of other current liabilities to satisfy them.

The nearness to cash of the current assets is indicated by their placement on the balance sheet. Current assets are listed on the balance sheet in descending order of their nearness to cash. Liquidity is, of course, a matter of degree, with cash being the most liquid of all assets. With few exceptions, such as prepaid insurance, most current assets are convertible into cash. However, accounts receivable is closer to being converted into cash than is inventory. An account receivable need only be collected to be converted to cash. An item of inventory must first be sold, and then, assuming that sales of inventory are on account, the account must be collected before cash is realized.

Working Capital

Working capital is the excess of current assets over current liabilities at a point in time:

$$\text{Working Capital} = \text{Current Assets} - \text{Current Liabilities}$$

Reference to Henderson's comparative balance sheets in Exhibit 15-1 indicates the following:

	DECEMBER 31	
	1998	**1997**
Current assets	$10,720,000	$8,800,000
Current liabilities	7,250,000	5,500,000
Working capital	$ 3,470,000	$3,300,000

The management of working capital is an extremely important task for any business. A comparison of Henderson's working capital at the end of each of the two years indicates a slight increase in the degree of protection for short-term creditors of the company. Management must always strive for the ideal balance of current assets and current liabilities. The amount of working capital is limited in its informational value, however. For example, it tells us nothing about the composition of the current accounts. Also, the dollar amount of working capital may not be useful to compare other companies of different sizes in the same industry. Working capital of $3,470,000 may be adequate for Henderson Company, but it might signal impending bankruptcy for a company much larger than Henderson.

Current Ratio

The current ratio is one of the most widely used of all financial statement ratios and is calculated as follows:

$$\text{Current Ratio} = \frac{\text{Current Assets}}{\text{Current Liabilities}}$$

For Henderson Company, the ratio at each year-end is as follows:

DECEMBER 31	
1998	**1997**
$\dfrac{\$10,720,000}{\$7,250,000} = 1.48 \text{ to } 1$	$\dfrac{\$8,800,000}{\$5,500,000} = 1.60 \text{ to } 1$

At the end of 1998, Henderson had $1.48 of current assets for every $1 of current liabilities. Is this current ratio adequate? Or is it a sign of impending financial difficulties? There is no definitive answer to either of these questions. Some analysts use a general rule of thumb of 2:1 for the current ratio as a sign of short-term financial health. The answer depends first on the industry. Companies in certain industries have historically operated with current ratios much less than 2:1.

A second concern in interpreting the current ratio involves the composition of the current assets. Cash is usually the only acceptable means of payment for most liabilities. Therefore, it is important to consider the makeup, or *composition,* of the current assets. Refer to Exhibit 15-5 and Henderson's common-size balance sheets. Not only did the current ratio decline during 1998 but also the proportion of the total current assets made up by inventory increased whereas the proportion made up by accounts receivable remained the same. Recall that accounts receivable is only one step removed from cash, whereas inventory requires both sale and collection of the subsequent account.

Acid-Test Ratio

The acid-test or quick ratio is a stricter test of a company's ability to pay its current debts as they are due. Specifically, it is intended to deal with the composition problem because it *excludes* inventories and prepaid assets from the numerator of the fraction:

$$\text{Acid-Test or Quick Ratio} = \frac{\text{Quick Assets}}{\text{Current Liabilities}}$$

where

$$\text{Quick Assets} = \text{Cash} + \text{Marketable Securities} + \text{Current Receivables}$$

Henderson's quick assets consist of only cash and accounts receivable, and its quick ratios are as follows:

DECEMBER 31	
1998	**1997**
$\dfrac{\$320,000 + \$5,500,000}{\$7,250,000} = 0.80 \text{ to } 1$	$\dfrac{\$1,350,000 + \$4,500,000}{\$5,500,000} = 1.06 \text{ to } 1$

Does the quick ratio of less than 1:1 at the end of 1998 mean that Henderson will be unable to pay creditors on time? *For many companies, an acid-test ratio below 1 is not desirable because it may signal the need to liquidate marketable securities to pay bills, regardless of the current trading price of the securities.* Although the quick ratio is a better indication of short-term debt-paying ability than the current ratio, it is still not perfect. For example, we would want to know the normal credit terms that Henderson extends to its customers, as well as the credit terms that the company receives from its suppliers.

Assume that Henderson requires its customers to pay their accounts within 30 days and that the normal credit terms extended by Henderson's suppliers allow payment anytime within 60 days. The relatively longer credit terms extended by Henderson's suppliers gives it some cushion in meeting its obligations. The due date of the $2,300,000 in taxes payable could also have a significant effect on the company's ability to remain in business.

Cash Flow from Operations to Current Liabilities

Two limitations exist with either the current ratio or the quick ratio as a measure of liquidity. First, almost all debts require the payment of cash. Thus, a ratio that focuses on cash is more useful. Second, both ratios focus on liquid assets at a *point in time.* Cash flow from operating activities, as reported on the statement of cash flows, can be used to indicate the flow of cash during the year to cover the debts due.[1] The cash flow from operations to current liabilities ratio is computed as follows:

$$\text{Cash Flow from Operations to Current Liabilities Ratio} = \frac{\text{Net Cash Provided by Operating Activities}}{\text{Average Current Liabilities}}$$

Note the use of *average* current liabilities in the denominator. This results in a denominator that is consistent with the numerator, which reports the cash flow over a period of time. Because we need to calculate the *average* current liabilities for both years, it is necessary to add the ending balance sheet for 1996 for use in the analysis. The balance sheet for Henderson on December 31, 1996, is given in Exhibit 15-7. The ratio for Henderson for each year is as follows:

1998	**1997**
$\dfrac{\$1,070,000}{(\$7,250,000 + \$5,500,000)/2} = 16.8\%$	$\dfrac{\$2,950,000}{(\$5,500,000 + \$5,600,000)/2} = 53.2\%$

Two factors are responsible for the large decrease in this ratio from 1997 to 1998. First, cash generated from operations during 1998 was less than half what it was during 1997 (the numerator). Second, average current liabilities were smaller in 1997 than in 1998 (the denominator). In examining the health of the company in terms of its liquidity, an analyst would concentrate on the reason for these decreases.

Accounts Receivable Analysis

The analysis of accounts receivable is an important component in the management of working capital. A company must be willing to extend credit terms that are liberal enough to attract and maintain customers, but at the same time, management must continually monitor the accounts to ensure collection on a timely basis. One measure of the efficiency of the collection process is the accounts receivable turnover ratio:

$$\text{Accounts Receivable Turnover Ratio} = \frac{\text{Net Credit Sales}}{\text{Average Accounts Receivable}}$$

Note an important distinction between this ratio and either the current or the quick ratio. Although both of those ratios measure liquidity at a point in time and all numbers come from the balance sheet, a turnover ratio is an *activity* ratio and consists of an activity (sales, in this case) divided by a base to which it is naturally related (accounts receivable). Because an activity such as sales is for a period of time (a year, in this case), the base should be stated as an average for that same period of time.

---

[1]For a detailed discussion on the use of information contained in the statement of cash flows in performing ratio analysis, see Charles A. Carslaw and John R. Mills, "Developing Ratios for Effective Cash Flow Statement Analysis," *Journal of Accountancy* (November 1991), pp. 63–70.

EXHIBIT 15-7	Henderson's Balance Sheet, End of 1996

HENDERSON COMPANY
BALANCE SHEET
DECEMBER 31, 1996
(ALL AMOUNTS IN THOUSANDS OF DOLLARS)

Cash	$ 1,000
Accounts receivable	5,000
Inventory	2,450
Prepaid insurance	250
Total current assets	$ 8,700
Land	2,000
Buildings and equipment, net	1,300
Total long-term assets	$ 3,300
Total assets	$12,000
Accounts payable	$ 2,700
Taxes payable	1,800
Notes payable	1,000
Current portion of bonds	100
Total current liabilities	$ 5,600
Bonds payable	900
Total liabilities	$ 6,500
Preferred stock, $5 par	500
Common stock, $1 par	1,000
Retained earnings	4,000
Total stockholders' equity	$ 5,500
Total liabilities and stockholders' equity	$12,000

The accounts receivable turnover ratios for both years can now be calculated (we assume that all sales are on account):

1998	1997
$\dfrac{\$24,000,000}{(\$5,500,000 + \$4,500,000)/2} = 4.8 \text{ times}$	$\dfrac{\$20,000,000}{(\$4,500,000 + \$5,000,000)/2} = 4.2 \text{ times}$

Accounts turned over, on average, 4.2 times in 1997, compared with 4.8 times in 1998. This means that the average number of times accounts were collected during each year was between four and five times. What does this mean about the average length of time that an account was outstanding? Another way to measure efficiency in the collection process is to calculate the **number of days' sales in receivables:**

$$\text{Number of Days' Sales in Receivables} = \frac{\text{Number of Days in the Period}}{\text{Accounts Receivable Turnover}}$$

For simplicity, we assume 360 days in a year:

1998	1997
$\dfrac{360 \text{ Days}}{4.8 \text{ Times}} = 75 \text{ Days}$	$\dfrac{360 \text{ Days}}{4.2 \text{ Times}} = 86 \text{ Days}$

The average number of days an account is outstanding, or the average collection period, is 75 days in 1998, down from 86 days in 1997. Is this acceptable? The answer depends on the company's credit policy. If Henderson's normal credit terms require payment within 60 days, further investigation is needed, even though the number of days outstanding has decreased from the previous year.

Management needs to be concerned with both the collectibility of an account as it ages and the cost of funds tied up in receivables. For example, a $1 million average receivable balance that requires an additional month to collect suggests that the company is forgoing $10,000 in lost profits if we assume that the money could be reinvested in the business to earn 1% per month, or 12% per year.

ACCOUNTING FOR YOUR DECISIONS
You Examine Your Business's Trends

You are a small business owner and have noticed that over the past two years sales have increased but the accounts receivable turnover ratio has decreased. Should you be concerned?

ANS: You should certainly be pleased with an increase in sales but a decrease in accounts receivable turnover should concern you. A decline in this ratio indicates that the average time to collect an open account is increasing. Regardless of the specific reason for this change (e.g., more liberal credit terms, change in creditworthiness of customers, lack of follow up on overdue accounts), the increase in the time to collect may result in cash flow problems for you.

Inventory Analysis

A similar set of ratios can be calculated to analyze the efficiency in managing inventory. The inventory turnover ratio is as follows:

$$\text{Inventory Turnover Ratio} = \frac{\text{Cost of Goods Sold}}{\text{Average Inventory}}$$

The ratio for each of the two years follows:

1998	1997
$\dfrac{\$18,000,000}{(\$4,750,000 + \$2,750,000)/2} = 4.8$ times	$\dfrac{\$14,000,000}{(\$2,750,000 + \$2,450,000)/2} = 5.4$ times

Henderson was slightly more efficient in 1997 in moving its inventory. The number of "turns" each year varies widely for different industries. For example, a wholesaler of perishable fruits and vegetables may turn over inventory at least 50 times per year. An airplane manufacturer, however, may turn over its inventory once or twice a year. What does the number of turns per year tell us about the average length of time it takes to sell an item of inventory? The number of days' sales in inventory is an alternative measure of the company's efficiency in managing inventory. It is the number of days between the date an item of inventory is purchased and the date it is sold:

$$\text{Number of Days' Sales in Inventory} = \frac{\text{Number of Days in the Period}}{\text{Inventory Turnover}}$$

The number of days' sales in inventory for Henderson is as follows:

1998	1997
$\dfrac{360 \text{ Days}}{4.8 \text{ Times}} = 75$ Days	$\dfrac{360 \text{ Days}}{5.4 \text{ Times}} = 67$ Days

This measure can reveal a great deal about inventory management. For example, an unusually low turnover (and, of course, high number of days in inventory) may signal a large amount of obsolete inventory or problems in the sales department. Or, it may indicate that the company is pricing its products too high and the market is reacting by reducing demand for the company's products.

You have been presented with two companies—Boeing and Safeway. Boeing, a commercial aircraft company, has a very slow inventory turnover, while Safeway, a grocery chain, has a very fast inventory turnover. Would it be correct to conclude that Safeway is a better investment because its inventory turns over faster?

ANS: Not at all. These industries are completely different and not comparable. On the contrary, comparing Safeway's inventory turnover with Albertson's, another grocery chain, might be useful, just as comparing Boeing with Lockheed Martin Marietta might make sense. Ratios can be used when comparing companies in the same industry, but not companies in different industries.

Cash Operating Cycle

The **cash to cash operating cycle** is the length of time between the purchase of merchandise for sale, assuming a retailer or wholesaler, and the eventual collection of the cash from the sale. One method to approximate the number of days in a company's operating cycle involves combining two measures:

Cash to Cash Operating Cycle = Number of Days' Sales in Inventory
+ Number of Days' Sales in Receivables

Henderson's operating cycles for 1998 and 1997 are as follows:

1998	1997
75 Days + 75 Days = 150 Days	67 Days + 86 Days = 153 Days

The average length of time between the purchase of inventory and the collection of cash from sale of the inventory was 150 days in 1998. Note that although the length of the operating cycle did not change significantly from 1997 to 1998, the composition did change: the increase in the average number of days in inventory was offset by the decrease in the average number of days in receivables.

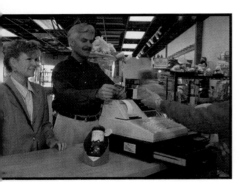

Due to the perishable nature of their products, grocery chains have high inventory turnovers and short cash-to-cash cycles. Firms in other segments have relatively longer cycles.

Solvency Analysis

LO 5 Compute and use various ratios to assess solvency.

Solvency refers to a company's ability to remain in business over the long term. It is related to liquidity but differs in time. Although liquidity relates to the firm's ability to pay next year's debts as they come due, solvency concerns the ability of the firm to stay financially healthy over the period of time that existing debt (short- and long-term) will be outstanding.

Debt-to-Equity Ratio

Capital structure is the focal point in solvency analysis. This refers to the composition of the right side of the balance sheet and the mix between debt and stockholders' equity. The composition of debt and equity in the capital structure is an important determinant of the cost of capital to a company. We will have more to say later about the effects that the mix of debt and equity has on profitability. For now, consider the **debt-to-equity ratio:**

$$\text{Debt-to-Equity Ratio} = \frac{\text{Total Liabilities}}{\text{Total Stockholders' Equity}}$$

Henderson's debt-to-equity ratio at each year-end is as follows:

DECEMBER 31	
1998	1997
$\dfrac{\$7,950,000}{\$8,920,000} = 0.89 \text{ to } 1$	$\dfrac{\$6,300,000}{\$7,500,000} = 0.84 \text{ to } 1$

The 1998 ratio indicates that for every $1 of capital that stockholders provided, creditors provided $.89. Variations of the debt-to-equity ratio are sometimes used to assess solvency. For example, an analyst might calculate the ratio of total liabilities to the sum of total liabilities and stockholders' equity. This results in a ratio that differs from the debt-to-equity ratio, but the objective of the measure is the same—to determine the degree to which the company relies on outsiders for funds.

What is an *acceptable* ratio of debt to equity? As with all ratios, the answer depends on the company, the industry, and many other factors. You should not assume that a lower debt-to-equity ratio is better. Certainly taking on additional debt is risky. Many companies are able to benefit from borrowing money, however, by putting the cash raised to good uses in their businesses. Later in the chapter we discuss the concept of leverage: using borrowed money to benefit the company and its stockholders.

In the 1980s, investors and creditors tolerated a much higher debt-to-equity ratio than is considered prudent today. The savings and loan crisis in the 1980s prompted the federal government to enact regulations requiring financial institutions to have a lower proportion of debt-to-equity. By the mid-1990s, investors and creditors were demanding that all types of companies display lower debt-to-equity ratios.

Times Interest Earned

The debt-to-equity ratio is a measure of the company's overall long-term financial health. Management must also be aware of its ability to meet current interest payments to creditors. The times interest earned ratio indicates the company's ability to meet current-year interest payments out of current-year earnings:

$$\text{Times Interest Earned Ratio} = \frac{\text{Net Income} + \text{Interest Expense} + \text{Income Tax Expense}}{\text{Interest Expense}}$$

Both interest expense and income tax expense are added back to net income in the numerator because interest is a deduction in arriving at the amount of income subject to tax. Stated slightly differently, if a company had just enough income to cover the payment of interest, tax expense would be zero. The greater is the interest coverage, the better, as far as lenders are concerned. Bankers often place more importance on the times interest earned ratio than even on earnings per share. The ratio for Henderson for each of the two years indicates a great deal of protection in this regard:

1998	1997
$\dfrac{\$1,720,000 + \$140,000 + \$1,140,000}{\$140,000}$	$\dfrac{\$2,300,000 + \$160,000 + \$1,540,000}{\$160,000}$
$= 21.4 \text{ to } 1$	$= 25 \text{ to } 1$

Debt Service Coverage

Two problems exist with the times interest earned ratio as a measure of the ability to pay creditors. First, the denominator of the fraction considers only *interest*. Management must also be concerned with the *principal* amount of loans maturing in the next year. The second problem deals with the difference between the cash and the accrual bases of accounting. The numerator of the times interest earned ratio is not a measure of the *cash* available to repay loans. Keep in mind the various noncash adjustments, such as depreciation, that enter into the determination of net income. Also, recall that the denominator of the times interest earned ratio is a measure of interest expense, not interest payments. The debt service coverage ratio is a measure of the amount of cash that is generated from operating activities during the year and that is available to repay interest due and any maturing principal amounts (that is, the amount available to "service" the debt):

$$\frac{\text{Debt Service}}{\text{Coverage Ratio}} = \frac{\text{Cash Flow from Operations before Interest and Tax Payments}}{\text{Interest and Principal Payments}}$$

Some analysts use an alternative measure in the numerator of this ratio, as well as for other purposes. The alternative is referred to as EBITDA, which stands for earnings before interest, taxes, depreciation, and amortization. Whether EBITDA is a good substitute for cash flow from operations before interest and tax payments depends on whether there were significant changes in current assets and current liabilities during the period. If significant changes in these accounts occurred during the period, cash flow from operations before interest and tax payments is a better measure of a company's ability to cover interest and debt payments.

Cash flow from operations is available on the comparative statement of cash flows in Exhibit 15-4. As was the case with the times interest earned ratio, the net cash provided by operating activities is adjusted to reflect the amount available *before* paying interest and taxes.

Keep in mind that the income statement in Exhibit 15-2 reflects the *expense* for interest and taxes each year. The amounts of interest and taxes *paid* each year are shown as supplemental information at the bottom of the statement of cash flows in Exhibit 15-4 and are relevant in computing the debt service coverage ratio.

We must include any principal payments with interest paid in the denominator of the debt service coverage ratio. According to the financing activities section of the statements of cash flows in Exhibit 15-4, Henderson repaid $200,000 each year on the notes payable and $100,000 each year on the bonds. The debt service coverage ratios for the two years are calculated as follows:

1998

$$\frac{\$1,070,000 + \$140,000 + \$940,000}{\$140,000 + \$200,000 + \$100,000} = 4.89 \text{ times}$$

1997

$$\frac{\$2,950,000 + \$160,000 + \$1,440,000}{\$160,000 + \$200,000 + \$100,000} = 9.89 \text{ times}$$

Like Henderson's times interest earned ratio, its debt service coverage ratio decreased during 1998. According to the calculations, however, Henderson still generated almost $5 of cash from operations during 1998 to "cover" every $1 of required interest and principal payments.

Cash Flow from Operations to Capital Expenditures Ratio

One final measure is useful in assessing the solvency of a business. The cash flow from operations to capital expenditures ratio measures a company's ability to use operations to finance its acquisitions of productive assets. To the extent that a company is able to do this, it should rely less on external financing or additional contributions by the owners to replace and add to the existing capital base. The ratio is computed as follows:

$$\frac{\text{Cash Flow from Operations}}{\text{to Capital Expenditures Ratio}} = \frac{\text{Cash Flow from Operations} - \text{Total Dividends Paid}}{\text{Cash Paid for Acquisitions}}$$

Note that the numerator of the ratio measures the cash flow *after* meeting all dividend payments.[2] The calculation of the ratios for Henderson follows:

1998	**1997**
$\dfrac{\$1{,}070{,}000 - \$300{,}000}{\$1{,}500{,}000} = 51.3\%$	$\dfrac{\$2{,}950{,}000 - \$300{,}000}{\$2{,}000{,}000} = 132.5\%$

Although the amount of capital expenditures was less in 1998 than in 1997, the company generated considerably less cash from operations in 1998 to cover these acquisitions. In fact, the ratio of less than 100% in 1998 indicates that Henderson was not able to finance all of its capital expenditures from operations *and* cover its dividend payments.

Profitability Analysis

Liquidity analysis and solvency analysis deal with management's ability to repay short- and long-term creditors. Creditors are concerned with a company's profitability because a profitable company is more likely to be able to make principal and interest payments. Of course, stockholders care about a company's profitability because it affects the market price of the stock and the ability of the company to pay dividends. Various measures of **profitability** indicate how well management is using the resources at its disposal to earn a return on the funds invested by various groups.

LO 6 Compute and use various ratios to assess profitability.

Rate of Return on Assets

Before computing the rate of return, we must answer an important question: *return to whom? Every return ratio is a measure of the relationship between the income earned by the company and the investment made in the company by various groups.* The broadest rate of return ratio is the **return on assets ratio** because it considers the investment made by *all* providers of capital, from short-term creditors to bondholders to stockholders. Therefore, the denominator, or base, for the return on assets ratio is average total liabilities and stockholders' equity—which of course is the same as average total assets.

The numerator of a return ratio will be some measure of the company's income for the period. The income selected for the numerator must match the investment or base in the denominator. For example, if average total assets is the base in the denominator, it is necessary to use an income number that is applicable to all providers of capital. Therefore, the income number used in the rate of return on assets is income *after* adding back interest expense. This adjustment considers creditors as one of the groups that have provided funds to the company. In other words, we want the amount of income before either creditors or stockholders have been given any distributions (that is, interest to creditors or dividends to stockholders). Interest expense must be added back on a net-of-tax basis. Because net income is on an after-tax basis, for consistency purposes interest must also be placed on a net, or after-tax, basis.

The return on assets ratio is as follows:

$$\text{Return on Assets Ratio} = \frac{\text{Net Income} + \text{Interest Expense, Net of Tax}}{\text{Average Total Assets}}$$

If we assume a 40% tax rate (which *is* the actual ratio of income tax expense to income before tax for Henderson), its return on assets ratios are as follows:

---

[2]Dividends paid are reported on the statement of cash flows in the Financing Activities section. The amount *paid* should be used for this calculation rather than the amount declared, which appears on the statement of retained earnings.

	1998		1997	
Net income		$ 1,720,000		$ 2,300,000
Add back:				
Interest expense	$140,000		$160,000	
× (1 − tax rate)	0.6	84,000	0.6	96,000
Numerator		$ 1,804,000		$ 2,396,000
Assets, beginning of year		$13,800,000		$12,000,000
Assets, end of year		16,870,000		13,800,000
Total		$30,670,000		$25,800,000
Denominator:				
Average total assets		$15,335,000		$12,900,000
(total above divided by 2)				
Return on assets ratio		$ 1,804,000		$ 2,396,000
		$15,335,000		$12,900,000
		= 11.76%		= 18.57%

Components of Return on Assets

What caused Henderson's return on assets to decrease so dramatically from the previous year? The answer can be found by considering the two individual components that make up the return on assets ratio. The first of these components is the **return on sales ratio** and is calculated as follows:

$$\text{Return on Sales Ratio} = \frac{\text{Net Income} + \text{Interest Expense, Net of Tax}}{\text{Net Sales}}$$

The return on sales ratios for Henderson for the two years follow:

1998	1997
$\dfrac{\$1,720,000 + \$84,000}{\$24,000,000} = 7.52\%$	$\dfrac{\$2,300,000 + \$96,000}{\$20,000,000} = 11.98\%$

The ratio for 1998 indicates that for every $1 of sales, the company was able to earn a profit, before the payment of interest, of between 7 and 8 cents, as compared with a return of almost 12 cents on the dollar in 1997.

The other component of the rate of return on assets is the **asset turnover ratio.** The ratio is similar to both the inventory turnover and the accounts receivable turnover ratios because it is a measure of the relationship between some activity (net sales, in this case) and some investment base (average total assets):

$$\text{Asset Turnover Ratio} = \frac{\text{Net Sales}}{\text{Average Total Assets}}$$

For Henderson, the ratio for each of the two years follows:

1998	1997
$\dfrac{\$24,000,000}{\$15,335,000} = 1.57 \text{ times}$	$\dfrac{\$20,000,000}{\$12,900,000} = 1.55 \text{ times}$

It now becomes evident that the explanation for the decrease in Henderson's return on assets lies in the drop in the return on sales, since the asset turnover ratio was almost the same. To summarize, note the relationship among the three ratios:

$$\text{Return on Assets} = \text{Return on Sales} \times \text{Asset Turnover}$$

For 1998 Henderson's return on assets consists of the following:

$$\frac{\$1,804,000}{\$24,000,000} \times \frac{\$24,000,000}{\$15,335,000} = 7.52\% \times 1.57 = 11.8\%$$

Finally, notice that net sales cancels out of both ratios, leaving the net income adjusted for interest divided by average assets as the return on assets ratio.

Return on Common Stockholders' Equity

Reasoning similar to that used to calculate return on assets can be used to calculate the return on capital provided by the common stockholder. Because we are interested in the return to the common stockholder, our base is no longer average total assets but average common stockholders' equity. Similarly, the appropriate income figure for the numerator is net income less preferred dividends because we are interested in the return to the common stockholder after all claims have been settled. Income taxes and interest expense have already been deducted in arriving at net income, but preferred dividends have not been because dividends are a distribution of profits, not an expense.

The **return on common stockholders' equity ratio** is computed as follows:

Return on Common Stockholders' Equity Ratio =

$$\frac{\text{Net Income} - \text{Preferred Dividends}}{\text{Average Common Stockholders' Equity}}$$

The average common stockholders' equity is calculated using information from Exhibits 15-1 and 15-7:

	ACCOUNT BALANCES AT DECEMBER 31		
	1998	1997	1996
Common stock, $1 par	$1,000,000	$1,000,000	$1,000,000
Retained earnings	7,420,000	6,000,000	4,000,000
Total common equity	$8,420,000	$7,000,000	$5,000,000

Average common equity:
1997: ($7,000,000 + $5,000,000)/2 = $6,000,000
1998: ($8,420,000 + $7,000,000)/2 = $7,710,000

Net income less preferred dividends—or "income available to common," as it is called—can be found by referring to net income on the income statement and preferred dividends on the statement of retained earnings. The combined statement of income and retained earnings in Exhibit 15-2 gives the relevant amounts for the numerator. The return on equity for the two years is as follows:

1998	1997
$\dfrac{\$1,720,000 - \$50,000}{\$7,710,000} = 21.66\%$	$\dfrac{\$2,300,000 - \$50,000}{\$6,000,000} = 37.50\%$

Even though Henderson's return on stockholders' equity ratio decreased significantly from one year to the next, most stockholders would be very happy to achieve these returns on their money. Very few investments offer much more than 10% return unless substantial risk is involved. This is particularly true in the low-interest-rate environment of the late-1990s.

Return on Assets, Return on Equity, and Leverage

The return on assets for 1998 was 11.8%. But the return to the common stockholders was much higher: 21.7%. How do you explain this phenomenon? Why are the stockholders receiving a higher return on their money than all of the providers of money combined are getting? A partial answer to these questions can be found by reviewing the cost to Henderson of the various sources of capital.

Exhibit 15-1 indicates that notes, bonds, and preferred stock are the primary sources of capital other than common stock (accounts payable and taxes payable are *not* included because they represent interest-free loans to the company from suppliers and the government). These sources and the average amount of each outstanding during 1998 follow:

	ACCOUNT BALANCES AT DECEMBER 31		
	1998	1997	AVERAGE
Notes payable	$ 600,000	$ 800,000	$ 700,000
Current portion of bonds	100,000	100,000	100,000
Bonds payable—Long-term	700,000	800,000	750,000
Total liabilities	$1,400,000	$1,700,000	$1,550,000
Preferred stock	$ 500,000	$ 500,000	$ 500,000

What was the cost to Henderson of each of these sources? The cost of the money provided by the preferred stockholders is clearly the amount of dividends of $50,000. The cost as a percentage is $50,000/$500,000, or 10%. The average cost of the borrowed money can be approximated by dividing the 1998 interest expense of $140,000 by the average of the notes payable and bonds payable of $1,550,000. The result is an average cost of these two sources of $140,000/$1,550,000, or approximately 9%.

The concept of leverage refers to the practice of using borrowed funds and amounts received from preferred stockholders in an attempt to earn an overall return that is higher than the cost of these funds. Recall the rate of return on assets for 1998: 11.8%. Because this return is on an after-tax basis, it is necessary, for comparative purposes, to convert the average cost of borrowed funds to an after-tax basis. Although we computed an average cost for borrowed money of 9%, the actual cost of the borrowed money is 5.4% [9% × (100% − 40%)] after taxes. Because dividends are *not* tax-deductible, the cost of the money provided by preferred stockholders is 10%, as calculated earlier.

Has Henderson successfully employed favorable leverage? That is, has it been able to earn an overall rate of return on assets that is higher than the amounts that it must pay creditors and preferred stockholders? Henderson has been successful in using outside money: neither of the sources must be paid a rate in excess of the 11.8% overall rate on assets used. Also keep in mind that Henderson has been able to borrow some amounts on an interest-free basis. As mentioned earlier, the accounts payable and taxes payable represent interest-free loans from suppliers and the government, although the loans are typically for a short period of time, such as 30 days.

In summary, the excess of the 21.7% return on equity over the 11.8% return on assets indicates that the Henderson management has been successful in employing leverage; that is, there is favorable leverage. Is it possible to be unsuccessful in this pursuit; that is, can there be unfavorable leverage? If the company must pay more for the amounts provided by creditors and preferred stockholders than it can earn overall, as indicated by the return on assets, there will, in fact, be unfavorable leverage. This may occur when interest requirements are high and net income is low. A company likely would have a high debt-to-equity ratio as well when there is unfavorable leverage.

Earnings per Share

Earnings per share is one of the most quoted statistics for publicly traded companies. Stockholders and potential investors want to know what their share of profits is, not just the total dollar amount. Presentation of profits on a per-share basis also allows the stockholder to relate earnings to what he or she paid for a share of stock or to the current trading price of a share of stock.

In simple situations, such as our Henderson Company example, earnings per share (EPS) is calculated as follows:

$$\text{Earnings per Share} = \frac{\text{Net Income} - \text{Preferred Dividends}}{\text{Weighted Average Number of Common Shares Outstanding}}$$

Because Henderson had 1,000,000 shares of common stock outstanding throughout both 1997 and 1998, its EPS for each of the two years is as follows:

1998	1997
$\dfrac{\$1,720,000 - \$50,000}{1,000,000 \text{ shares}} = \$1.67 \text{ per share}$	$\dfrac{\$2,300,000 - \$50,000}{1,000,000 \text{ shares}} = \$2.25 \text{ per share}$

A number of complications can arise in the computation of EPS, and the calculations can become exceedingly complex for a company with many different types of securities in its capital structure. Some of these complications, as well as the calculation of the weighted average number of shares, were discussed in Chapter 12; others are beyond the scope of this book and are discussed in more advanced accounting courses.

Price-Earnings Ratio

Earnings per share is an important ratio for an investor because of its relationship to dividends and market price. Stockholders hope to earn a return by receiving periodic dividends or eventually selling the stock for more than they paid for it or both. Although earnings are related to dividends and market price, the latter two are of primary interest to the stockholder.

We mentioned earlier the desire of investors to relate the earnings of the company to the market price of the stock. Now that we have stated Henderson's earnings on a per-share basis, we can calculate the price/earnings (P/E) ratio. What market price is relevant? Should we use the market price that the investor paid for a share of stock, or should we use the current market price? Because earnings are based on the most recent evaluation of the company for accounting purposes, it seems logical to use current market price, which is based on the stock market's current assessment of the company. Therefore, the ratio is computed as follows:

$$\text{Price/Earnings Ratio} = \frac{\text{Current Market Price}}{\text{Earnings per Share}}$$

Assume that the current market price for Henderson's common stock is $15 per share at the end of 1998 and $18 per share at the end of 1997. The price/earnings ratio for each of the two years is as follows:

1998	1997
$\dfrac{\$15 \text{ per Share}}{\$1.67 \text{ per Share}} = 9 \text{ to } 1$	$\dfrac{\$18 \text{ per Share}}{\$2.25 \text{ per Share}} = 8 \text{ to } 1$

What is normal for a P/E ratio? As is the case for all other ratios, it is difficult to generalize as to what is good or bad. The P/E ratio compares the stock market's assessment of a company's performance with its success as reflected on the income statement. A relatively high P/E ratio may indicate that a stock is overpriced by the market; one that is relatively low could indicate that it is underpriced.

The P/E ratio is often thought to indicate the "quality" of a company's earnings. For example, assume that two companies have identical EPS ratios of $2 per share. Why should investors be willing to pay $20 per share (or 10 times earnings) for the stock of one company but only $14 per share (or 7 times earnings) for the stock of the other company? First, we must realize that many factors in addition to the reported earnings of the company affect market prices. General economic conditions, the outlook for the particular industry, and pending lawsuits are just three examples of the various factors that can affect the trading price of a company's stock. The difference in P/E ratios for the two companies may reflect the market's assessment of the accounting practices of the companies, however. Assume that the company with a market price of $20 per share uses LIFO in valuing inventory and that the company trading at $14 per share uses FIFO. The difference in prices may indicate that investors believe that even though the companies have the same EPS, the LIFO company is "better off" because it will have a

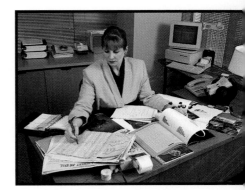

Making financial decisions requires having the right tools at hand, including the annual reports of companies under consideration and recent stock market quotations, printed in most large newspapers.

lower amount of taxes to pay. (Recall that in a period of inflation, the use of LIFO results in more cost of goods sold, less income, and therefore less income taxes.) Finally, aside from the way investors view the accounting practices of different companies, they also consider the fact that, to a large extent, earnings reflect the use of historical costs, as opposed to fair market values, in assigning values to assets. Investors must consider the extent to which a company's assets are worth more than what was paid for them.

ACCOUNTING FOR YOUR DECISIONS
You Are the CEO

You have just been promoted to the chief executive officer of Orange Computer, a company that has recently fallen on hard times. Sales and earnings have been sluggish. Part of the reason that the prior CEO was dismissed by the board was the lagging stock price. Although the typical computer company stock price is roughly 25 times earnings, Orange Computer is languishing at just 8 times earnings. What can you do to restore the company's stock price?

ANS: The best way to boost your company's stock price is to restore earnings to levels comparable to other companies in the industry. If investors see that you are cutting costs, boosting sales, and restoring earnings, then they may see a future earnings and dividends stream from Orange Computer that matches other competing investments. Consider the case of Lou Gerstner, IBM's CEO. Since Gerstner joined the company, IBM's earnings have experienced a dramatic turnaround, from a loss of $5 billion in 1992, to a profit of $5 billion in 1996. By May of 1997, IBM's common stock was trading at an all-time high.

Dividend Ratios

Two ratios are used to evaluate a company's dividend policies: the **dividend payout ratio** and the **dividend yield ratio.** The dividend payout ratio is the ratio of the common dividends per share to the earnings per share:

$$\text{Dividend Payout Ratio} = \frac{\text{Common Dividends per Share}}{\text{Earnings per Share}}$$

Exhibit 15-2 indicates that Henderson paid $250,000 in common dividends each year, or with 1 million shares outstanding, $.25 per share. The two payout ratios are as follows:

1998	1997
$\dfrac{\$.25}{\$1.67} = 15.0\%$	$\dfrac{\$.25}{\$2.25} = 11.1\%$

Henderson management was faced with an important financial policy decision in 1998. Should the company maintain the same dividend of $.25 per share, even though EPS dropped significantly? Many companies prefer to maintain a level dividend pattern, hoping that a drop in earnings is only temporary.

The second dividend ratio of interest to stockholders is the dividend yield ratio:

$$\text{Dividend Yield Ratio} = \frac{\text{Common Dividends per Share}}{\text{Market Price per Share}}$$

The yield to Henderson's stockholders would be calculated as follows:

1998	1997
$\dfrac{\$.25}{\$15} = 1.7\%$	$\dfrac{\$.25}{\$18} = 1.4\%$

As we see, Henderson common stock does not provide a high yield to its investors. The relationship between the dividends and the market price indicates that investors buy the stock for reasons other than the periodic dividend return.

The dividend yield is very important to investors who depend on dividend checks to pay their living expenses. Utility stocks are popular among retirees because these shares

FROM CONCEPT TO PRACTICE 15.3

READING WRIGLEY'S ANNUAL REPORT
Refer back to the financial highlights for Wrigley in the chapter opener. Compute Wrigley's dividend payout ratio for both 1995 and 1994 (use earnings before the nonrecurring gain). Why do you think dividends per share were increased to $.96 in 1995?

PREPARING FOR OPPORTUNITY TO STRIKE, THIS MONEY MANAGER RELIES ON RATIOS

Virtually every investment firm uses financial ratios to a greater or lesser extent. "We use them a great deal in the process of analyzing companies for inclusion in our portfolios," says Maceo Sloan, CEO of Sloan Financial Group, an international financial services company based in Durham, N.C.

In the past few years, Mr. Sloan has built Sloan Financial Group into a huge enterprise with several divisions. New Africa Advisers (NAA) is a subsidiary that provides investors access to African-related investment opportunities, particularly in post-apartheid South Africa. In 1996, NAA was selected by the Overseas Private Investment Corporation, a U.S. government agency, to manage a $120 million private equity fund—the New Africa Opportunity Fund. The Fund, which provides investors the guarantee of the full faith and credit of the U.S. government, brings the first sizable pool of private capital to the southern region of Africa. The largest subsidiary is NCM Capital Management Group, which is an investment advisor that manages funds for institutional clients such as corporations, municipalities, and unions. Total money under management: over $4 billion in 1996, up from $600 million in 1991.

Somehow, NCM Capital has to narrow down the world of stocks. One way to do that is to use computers to screen out companies that are unattractive based upon certain ratios. For example, a screen could filter out companies that are selling at more than 40 times earnings. Another variable might be that the

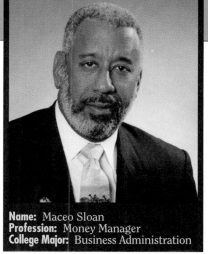

Name: Maceo Sloan
Profession: Money Manager
College Major: Business Administration

stock have a minimum market capitalization of $200 million to insure liquidity.

One of the firm's big success stories was a company called Micron Technology. In 1991, the stock was selling at $30 per share. By 1994, the stock was selling in the mid $80s. A tipoff: the company had a high ratio of cash flow to earnings—$2.47 to $1. "Although the price-earnings ratio is 32, which may look rather high, the price-cash flow is actually much more modest than that," says Mr. Sloan, a Morehouse College graduate who holds an MBA from Georgia State University and a law degree from the North Carolina Central School of Law.

Another important ratio Mr. Sloan uses is return on equity, or ROE. "It's a judge of how good the management is," he says. "When you look at the return on equity number and compare it to ROE for other firms in the same industry, you can tell whether the management team is reaching its potential for that industry."

Speaking of reaching one's potential, what advice would he give to college students seeking to follow in his footsteps? "It would probably be a motto that I've lived by all my life: luck is when opportunity meets preparation. Some people are very fortunate to get many opportunities, but it doesn't mean anything if you're not prepared."

---

have dividend yields as high as 5%. That is considered a good investment with relatively low risk and some opportunity for gains in the stock price. On the other hand, investors who want to put money into growing companies are willing to forgo dividends if it means the potential for greater price appreciation.

52 Weeks		Stock	Sym	Div	Yld %	PE	Vol 100s	Hi	Lo	Close	Net Chg
Hi	Lo										
30⅜	20½	WestpacBk	WBK	1.30e	4.7	...	114	27⅞	27⅞	27⅞	...
33⅛	25⅜	Westvaco	W	.88	2.9	14	1302	30⅛	29¾	30	...
50⅝	39½	Weyerhsr	WY	1.60	3.2	16	4830	50½	49¼	49½	−1
17⅛	13⅞	WheelbrTch	WTI	.12f	.8	21	416	15⅞	15⅝	15¾	−⅛
61⅜	44¼	Whirlpool	WHR	1.36	2.7	29	1281	49⅝	49⅜	49⅝	−⅛
44¼	27½	Whitehall	WHT			32	114	45¼	43⅜	44½	+1½
25¾	21¾	WhitmanCp	WH	.42	1.9	16	1716	22½	22¼	22⅜	...
26⅜	12¼	Whittaker	WKR			dd	340	12¾	12¼	12⅜	−¼

Each company's price/earnings ratio (here "PE") and dividend yield ratio ("Yld %") are two of the statistics listed in daily stock quotations available from on-line services such as CompuServe and America Online as well as in most major newspapers.

Summary of Selected Financial Ratios

We have now completed our review of the various ratios used to assess a company's liquidity, solvency, and profitability. For ease of reference, Exhibit 15-8 summarizes the ratios

EXHIBIT 15-8   Summary of Selected Financial Ratios

LIQUIDITY ANALYSIS

Working capital

$$\text{Current Assets} - \text{Current Liabilities}$$

Current ratio

$$\frac{\text{Current Assets}}{\text{Current Liabilities}}$$

Acid-test ratio (quick ratio)

$$\frac{\text{Cash} + \text{Marketable Securities} + \text{Current Receivables}}{\text{Current Liabilities}}$$

Cash flow from operations to current liabilities ratio

$$\frac{\text{Net Cash Provided by Operating Activities}}{\text{Average Current Liabilities}}$$

Accounts receivable turnover ratio

$$\frac{\text{Net Credit Sales}}{\text{Average Accounts Receivable}}$$

Number of days' sales in receivables

$$\frac{\text{Numbers of Days in the Period}}{\text{Accounts Receivable Turnover}}$$

Inventory turnover ratio

$$\frac{\text{Cost of Goods Sold}}{\text{Average Inventory}}$$

Number of days' sales in inventory

$$\frac{\text{Number of Days in the Period}}{\text{Inventory Turnover}}$$

Cash to cash operating cycle

$$\text{Number of Days' Sales in Inventory} + \text{Number of Days' Sales in Receivables}$$

SOLVENCY ANALYSIS

Debt-to-equity ratio

$$\frac{\text{Total Liabilities}}{\text{Total Stockholders' Equity}}$$

Times interest earned ratio

$$\frac{\text{Net Income} + \text{Interest Expense} + \text{Income Tax Expense}}{\text{Interest Expense}}$$

Debt service coverage ratio

$$\frac{\text{Cash Flow from Operations before Interest and Tax Payments}}{\text{Interest and Principal Payments}}$$

ACCOUNTING FOR YOUR DECISIONS
You Decide on a Stock Purchase

You are starting college and your parents have agreed to help pay your tuition. They will put money into a stock fund for four years and allow you to use the dividends from the fund to pay your quarterly tuition. Should you advise your parents to find a stock with a relatively low dividend yield ratio if it has an above average return on stockholders' equity?

ANS: Regardless of how attractive a company's return on equity ratio might be, you need cash on a regular basis to pay tuition. You should advise your parents to find a stock with a relatively high dividend yield ratio.

---

discussed in this chapter. Keep in mind that this list is not all-inclusive and that certain ratios used by analysts and others may be specific to a particular industry or type of business.

Review Problem

On the following pages are the comparative financial statements for Wm. Wrigley Jr. Company, the chewing gum manufacturer, as shown in its 1995 annual report.

EXHIBIT 15-8   (continued)

Cash flow from operations to capital expenditures ratio

$$\frac{\text{Cash Flow from Operations} - \text{Total Dividends Paid}}{\text{Cash Paid for Acquisitions}}$$

PROFITABILITY ANALYSIS

Gross profit ratio

$$\frac{\text{Gross Profit}}{\text{Net Sales}}$$

Profit margin ratio

$$\frac{\text{Net Income}}{\text{Net Sales}}$$

Return on assets ratio

$$\frac{\text{Net Income} + \text{Interest Expense, Net of Tax}}{\text{Average Total Assets}}$$

Return on sales ratio

$$\frac{\text{Net Income} + \text{Interest Expense, Net of Tax}}{\text{Net Sales}}$$

Asset turnover ratio

$$\frac{\text{Net Sales}}{\text{Average Total Assets}}$$

Return on common stockholders' equity ratio

$$\frac{\text{Net Income} - \text{Preferred Dividends}}{\text{Average Common Stockholders' Equity}}$$

Earnings per share

$$\frac{\text{Net Income} - \text{Preferred Dividends}}{\text{Weighted Average Number of Common Shares Outstanding}}$$

Price/earnings ratio

$$\frac{\text{Current Market Price}}{\text{Earnings per Share}}$$

Dividend payout ratio

$$\frac{\text{Common Dividends per Share}}{\text{Earnings per Share}}$$

Dividend yield ratio

$$\frac{\text{Common Dividends per Share}}{\text{Market Price per Share}}$$

Required

1. Compute the following ratios for the two years 1995 and 1994, either for each year or as of the end of each of the years, as appropriate. Beginning balances for 1994 are not available; that is, you do not have a balance sheet as of the end of 1993. Therefore, to be consistent, use year-end balances for both years where you would normally use average amounts for the year. To compute the return on assets ratio, you will need to find the tax rate. Use the relationship between income taxes and earnings before taxes and cumulative effects to find the rate for each year.

   a. Current ratio.
   b. Quick ratio.
   c. Cash flow from operations to current liabilities ratio.
   d. Number of days' sales in receivables.
   e. Number of days' sales in inventory.
   f. Debt-to-equity ratio.
   g. Debt service coverage ratio.
   h. Cash flow from operations to capital expenditures ratio.

      i. Return on assets ratio.

      j. Return on common stockholders' equity ratio.

2. Comment on Wrigley's liquidity. Has it improved or declined over the two-year period?

3. Does Wrigley appear to be solvent to you? Does there appear to be anything unusual about its capital structure?

4. Comment on Wrigley's profitability. Would you buy stock in the company?

Solution to Review Problem

1. Ratios:

    a. 1995: $672,096/$213,413 = <u>3.15</u>
       1994: $623,312/$209,898 = <u>2.97</u>

    b. 1995: ($125,725 + $105,947 + $170,803)/$213,413 = <u>1.89</u>
       1994: ($127,569 + $102,679 + $138,547)/$209,898 = <u>1.76</u>

CONSOLIDATED STATEMENT OF EARNINGS AND RETAINED EARNINGS

WM. WRIGLEY JR. COMPANY AND ASSOCIATED COMPANIES

YEAR ENDED DECEMBER 31	1995	1994	1993
	In thousands of dollars except for per share amounts		
EARNINGS			
Revenues:			
Net sales	$1,754,931	1,596,551	1,428,504
Investment and other income	14,811	26,597	11,938
Nonrecurring gain on sale of Singapore property	—	38,102	—
Total revenues	1,769,742	1,661,250	1,440,442
Costs and expenses:			
Cost of sales	778,019	697,442	617,156
Selling, distribution and general administrative	639,537	609,039	542,944
Interest	1,955	1,490	1,507
Total costs and expenses	1,419,511	1,307,971	1,161,607
Earnings before income taxes	350,231	353,279	278,835
Income taxes	126,492	122,746	103,944
Net earnings	223,739	230,533	174,891
RETAINED EARNINGS			
Retained earnings at beginning of year	685,850	564,640	491,481
Dividends declared			
(per share: **1995—$.99**; 1994—$.94; 1993—$.75)	(114,852)	(109,323)	(87,301)
Treasury stock retirement	(8,194)	—	(14,431)
Retained earnings at end of year	$ 786,543	685,850	564,640
PER SHARE AMOUNTS			
Net earnings per average share of common stock	$ 1.93	1.98	1.50
Dividends paid per share of common stock	$ .96	.90	.75

See accompanying accounting policies and notes.

c. 1995: $222,551/$213,413 = <u><u>1.04</u></u>

1994: $203,536/$209,898 = <u><u>.97</u></u>

d. 1995: 360 days/[($1,754,931/$170,803)] = 360/10.27 = <u>35 days</u>

1994: 360 days/[($1,596,551/$138,547)] = 360/11.52 = <u>31 days</u>

CONSOLIDATED STATEMENT
OF CASH FLOWS

WM. WRIGLEY JR. COMPANY AND ASSOCIATED COMPANIES

YEAR ENDED DECEMBER 31	1995	1994	1993
	In thousands of dollars		
CASH FLOWS—OPERATING ACTIVITIES			
Net earnings	$ 223,739	230,533	174,891
Adjustments to reconcile net earnings to net cash flows from operating activities:			
Depreciation	43,773	41,057	34,565
Gain on sales of property, plant and equipment	(1,090)	(38,762)	(806)
(Increase) decrease in:			
Accounts receivable	(28,619)	(13,608)	(26,754)
Inventories	(11,422)	(38,086)	(24,771)
Other current assets	2,164	(13,578)	(1,551)
Other assets and deferred charges	(6,297)	461	(3,929)
Increase (decrease) in:			
Accounts payable	6,427	3,086	10,298
Accrued expenses	(3,657)	(525)	18,157
Income and other taxes payable	(6,889)	35,774	(14,241)
Deferred income taxes	720	(7,894)	(3,834)
Other noncurrent liabilities	3,702	5,078	9,345
Net cash flows—operating activities	222,551	203,536	171,370
CASH FLOWS—INVESTING ACTIVITIES			
Additions to property, plant and equipment	(102,759)	(87,013)	(63,095)
Proceeds from property retirements	3,690	40,855	4,042
Purchases of short-term investments	(281,065)	(232,591)	(140,186)
Maturities of short-term investments	277,913	234,092	135,204
Net cash flows—investing activities	(102,221)	(44,657)	(64,035)
CASH FLOWS—FINANCING ACTIVITIES			
Dividends paid	(111,401)	(104,694)	(87,344)
Common stock purchased	(11,811)	(13,225)	(15,077)
Net cash flows—financing activities	(123,212)	(117,919)	(102,421)
Effect of exchange rate changes on cash and cash equivalents	1,038	319	(2,768)
Net increase (decrease) in cash and cash equivalents	(1,844)	41,279	2,146
Cash and cash equivalents at beginning of year	127,569	86,290	84,144
Cash and cash equivalents at end of year	$ 125,725	127,569	86,290
SUPPLEMENTAL CASH FLOW INFORMATION			
Income taxes paid	$ 133,494	94,576	124,127
Interest paid	$ 1,957	1,508	1,491
Interest and dividends received	$ 14,639	12,135	12,164

See accompanying accounting policies and notes.

e. 1995: 360 days/[($778,019/$235,347)] = 360/3.31 = <u>109 days</u>
1994: 360 days/[($697,442/$221,109)] = 360/3.15 = <u>114 days</u>

f. 1995: ($213,413 + $19,536 + $69,418)/796,852 = <u>0.38</u>
1994: ($209,898 + $15,760 + $64,706)/688,470 = <u>0.42</u>

g. 1995: ($222,551 + $133,494 + $1,957)/$1,957 = <u>183</u>
1994: ($203,536 + $94,576 + $1,508)/$1,508 = <u>199</u>

h. 1995: ($222,551 − $111,401)/$102,759 = <u>1.08</u>
1994: ($203,536 − $104,694)/$87,013 = <u>1.14</u>

CONSOLIDATED BALANCE SHEET

WM. WRIGLEY JR. COMPANY AND ASSOCIATED COMPANIES

AS OF DECEMBER 31	1995	1994
	In thousands of dollars	
ASSETS		
Current assets:		
Cash and cash equivalents	$ 125,725	127,569
Short-term investments, at amortized cost	105,947	102,679
Accounts receivable (less allowance for doubtful accounts: **1995—$9,060**; 1994—$6,645)	170,803	138,547
Inventories—		
Finished goods	54,231	59,205
Raw materials and supplies	181,116	161,904
	235,347	221,109
Other current assets	24,683	25,924
Deferred income taxes—current	9,591	7,484
Total current assets	672,096	623,312
Marketable equity securities, at fair value	19,827	14,687
Deferred charges and other assets	39,696	30,581
Deferred income taxes—noncurrent	20,109	20,834
Property, plant and equipment, at cost:		
Land	24,478	23,281
Buildings and building equipment	230,065	204,877
Machinery and equipment	475,955	410,305
	730,498	638,463
Less accumulated depreciation	383,007	349,043
	347,491	289,420
Total assets	$1,099,219	978,834

i. 1995: {\$223,739 + [\$1,955(1 − .36*)]}/\$1,099,219 = <u>20.5%</u>

1994: {\$230,533 + [\$1,490(1 − .35*)]}/\$978,834 = <u>23.7%</u>

j. 1995: \$223,739/(\$796,852[†]) = <u>28.1%</u>

1994: \$230,533/(\$688,470[†]) = <u>33.5%</u>

*Tax rate for each of the two years:
1995: \$126,492/\$350,231 = 0.36
1994: \$122,746/\$353,279 = 0.35

†In addition to its common stock, Wrigley has outstanding Class B common stock. Because this is a second class of stock (similar in many respects to preferred stock), the contributed capital attributable to it should be deducted from total stockholders' equity in the denominator. Similarly, any dividends paid on the Class B common stock should be deducted from net income in the numerator to find the return to the regular common stockholders. We have ignored the difficulties involved in determining these adjustments in our calculations of return on equity.

As of December 31	1995	1994
	In thousands of dollars and shares	
LIABILITIES AND STOCKHOLDERS' EQUITY		
Current liabilities:		
Accounts payable	\$ **75,815**	68,097
Accrued expenses	**67,958**	69,716
Dividends payable	**19,720**	16,269
Income and other taxes payable	**49,152**	55,178
Deferred income taxes—current	**768**	638
Total current liabilities	**213,413**	209,898
Deferred income taxes—noncurrent	**19,536**	15,760
Other noncurrent liabilities	**69,418**	64,706
Stockholders' equity:		
Preferred stock—no par value		
Authorized: 20,000 shares		
Issued: None		
Common stock—no par value		
Common stock		
Authorized: 400,000 shares		
Issued: **1995—91,541 shares**; 1994—91,326 shares	**12,205**	12,177
Class B common stock—convertible		
Authorized: 80,000 shares		
Issued and outstanding: **1995—24,680 shares**; 1994—25,075 shares	**3,291**	3,343
Additional paid-in capital	**1,625**	1,781
Retained earnings	**786,543**	685,850
Foreign currency translation adjustment	**(8,038)**	(13,502)
Unrealized holding gains on marketable equity securities	**11,404**	7,855
Common stock in treasury, at cost		
(**1995—219 shares**; 1994—192 shares)	**(10,178)**	(9,034)
Total stockholders' equity	**796,852**	688,470
Total liabilities and stockholders' equity	**\$1,099,219**	978,834

See accompanying accounting policies and notes.

2. Both the current ratio and the quick ratio improved during 1995. In addition, the amount of cash flow from operations was up in 1995, as was the ratio of cash flow from operations to current liabilities. Wrigley appears to be quite liquid and should have no problems meeting its short-term obligations.

3. Wrigley is extremely solvent. Its capital structure reveals that it does not rely in any significant way on long-term debt to finance its business. The amount of noncurrent liabilities is less than 9% of total liabilities and stockholders' equity at the end of each year. In fact, a majority of Wrigley's debt is in the form of interest-free current liabilities. Most revealing is the debt service coverage ratio of 183 times in 1995 and 199 times in 1994. The total interest expense each year is insignificant.

4. The return on assets for 1995 is 20.5%, and the return on common stockholders' equity is 28.1%. Although these return ratios are down from the prior year, they indicate a very profitable company. It should be noted that the company paid nearly half of its 1995 earnings in dividends. Wrigley appears to be a very sound investment, but many other factors, including information on the current market price of the stock, should be considered before making a decision.

Chapter Highlights

1. **LO 1** Various parties, including management, creditors, stockholders, and others, perform financial statement analysis. Care must be exercised, however, in all types of financial analysis. For example, the existence of alternative accounting principles can make comparing different companies difficult. Published financial statements are not adjusted for the effects of inflation, and thus comparisons over time must be made with caution.

2. **LO 2** Horizontal analysis uses comparative financial statements to examine the increases and decreases in items from one period to the next. The analysis can look at the change in items over an extended period of time. Many companies present a summary of selected financial items for a 5- or 10-year period.

3. **LO 3** Vertical analysis involves stating all items on a particular financial statement as a percentage of one item on the statement. For example, all expenses on a common-size income statement are stated as a percentage of net sales. This technique, along with horizontal analysis, can be useful in spotting problem areas within a company.

4. **LO 4** Ratios can be categorized according to their primary purpose. Liquidity ratios indicate the company's ability to pay its debts as they are due. The focus of liquidity analysis is on a company's current assets and current liabilities.

5. **LO 5** Solvency ratios deal with a company's long-term financial health, that is, its ability to repay long-term creditors. The right side of the balance sheet is informative in this respect because it reports on the various sources of capital to the business.

6. **LO 6** Profitability ratios measure how well management has used the assets at its disposal to earn a return for the various providers of capital. Return on assets indicates the return to all providers; return on common stockholders' equity measures the return to the residual owners of the business. Certain other ratios are used to relate a company's performance according to the financial statements with its performance in the stock market.

Key Terms Quiz

Because of the number of terms introduced in this chapter, there are two key term quizzes. For each quiz, read each definition below and then write the number of that definition in the blank beside the appropriate term it defines. The solution appears at the end of the chapter.

Quiz 1:

___ Horizontal analysis

___ Gross profit ratio

___ Liquidity

___ Current ratio

___ Cash flow from operations to current liabilities ratio

___ Number of days' sales in receivables

___ Cash to cash operating cycle

___ Vertical analysis

___ Profit margin ratio

___ Working capital

___ Acid-test or quick ratio

___ Accounts receivable turnover ratio

___ Inventory turnover ratio

___ Number of days' sales in inventory

1. A stricter test of liquidity than the current ratio, this ratio excludes inventory and prepayments from the numerator.
2. Current assets minus current liabilities.
3. The ratio of current assets to current liabilities.
4. A measure of the average age of accounts receivable.
5. A measure of the ability to pay current debts from operating cash flows.
6. A measure of the number of times accounts receivable are collected in a period.
7. A measure of how long it takes to sell inventory.

8. The length of time from the purchase of inventory to the collection of any receivable from the sale.
9. A measure of the number of times inventory is sold during a period.
10. Gross profit to net sales.
11. A comparison of various financial statement items within a single period with the use of common-size statements.
12. Net income to net sales.
13. The nearness to cash of the assets and liabilities.
14. A comparison of financial statement items over a period of time.

Quiz 2:
___ Solvency
___ Times interest earned ratio
___ Cash flow from operations to capital expenditures ratio
___ Return on assets ratio
___ Asset turnover ratio
___ Leverage
___ Price/earnings (P/E) ratio
___ Dividend yield ratio

___ Debt-to-equity ratio
___ Debt service coverage ratio
___ Profitability
___ Return on sales ratio
___ Return on common stockholders' equity ratio
___ Earnings per share
___ Dividend payout ratio

1. A measure of a company's success in earning a return for the common stockholders.
2. The relationship between a company's performance according to the income statement and its performance in the stock market.
3. The ability of a company to remain in business over the long term.
4. A variation of the profit margin ratio, this ratio measures earnings before payments to creditors.
5. A company's bottom line stated on a per-share basis.
6. The percentage of earnings paid out as dividends.
7. The ratio of total liabilities to total stockholders' equity.
8. A measure of the ability of a company to finance long-term asset acquisitions from cash from operations.

9. A measure of a company's success in earning a return for all providers of capital.
10. The relationship between net sales and total assets.
11. The relationship between dividends and the market price of a company's stock.
12. The use of borrowed funds and amounts contributed by preferred stockholders to earn an overall return higher than the cost of these funds.
13. An income statement measure of the ability of a company to meet its interest payments.
14. A statement of cash flows measure of the ability of a company to meet its interest and principal payments.
15. How well management is using company resources to earn a return on the funds invested by the various groups.

Alternate Terms

Acid-test ratio   Quick ratio.
Horizontal analysis   Trend analysis.

Number of days' sales in receivables   Average collection period.
Price/earnings ratio   P/E ratio.

Questions

1. Two companies are in the same industry. Company A uses the LIFO method of inventory valuation, and Company B uses FIFO. What difficulties does this present when comparing the two companies?
2. You are told to compare the company's results for the year, as measured by various ratios, with one of the pub-

lished surveys that arranges information by industry classification. What are some of the difficulties you may encounter when making comparisons using industry standards?
3. What types of problems does inflation cause in analyzing financial statements?

4. Distinguish between horizontal and vertical analysis. Why is the analysis of common-size statements called *vertical* analysis? Why is horizontal analysis sometimes called *trend* analysis?

5. A company experiences a 15% increase in sales over the previous year. However, gross profit actually decreased by 5% from the previous year. What are some of the possible causes for an increase in sales but a decline in gross profit?

6. A company's total current assets have increased by 5% over the prior year. Management is concerned, however, about the composition of the current assets. Why is the composition of current assets important?

7. Ratios were categorized in the chapter according to their use in performing three different types of analysis. What are the three types of ratios?

8. Describe the operating cycle for a manufacturing company. How would the cycle differ for a retailer?

9. What accounts for the order in which current assets are presented on a balance sheet?

10. A company has a current ratio of 1.25 but an acid-test or quick ratio of only 0.65. How can this difference in the two ratios be explained? What are some concerns that you would have about this company?

11. Explain the basic concept underlying all turnover ratios. Why is it advisable in computing a turnover ratio to use an average in the denominator (for example, average inventory)?

12. Sanders Company's accounts receivable turned over nine times during the year. The credit department extends terms of 2/10, net 30. Does the turnover ratio indicate any problems that management should investigate?

13. The turnover of inventory for Ace Company has slowed from 6.0 times per year to 4.5 times. What are some of the possible explanations for this decrease?

14. How does the operating cycle for a manufacturer differ from the operating cycle for a service company, for example, an airline?

15. What is the difference between liquidity analysis and solvency analysis?

16. Why is the debt service coverage ratio a better measure of solvency than the times interest earned ratio?

17. A friend tells you that the best way to assess solvency is by comparing total debt to total assets. Another friend says that solvency is measured by comparing total debt to total stockholders' equity. Which one is right?

18. A company is in the process of negotiating with a bank for an additional loan. Why will the bank be very interested in the company's debt service coverage ratio?

19. What is the rationale for deducting dividends when computing the ratio of cash flow from operations to capital expenditures?

20. The rate of return on assets ratio is computed by dividing net income and interest expense, net of tax, by average total assets. Why is the numerator net income and interest expense, net of tax, rather than just net income?

21. A company has a return on assets of 14% and a return on common stockholders' equity of 11%. The president of the company has asked you to explain the reason for this difference. What causes the difference? How is the concept of financial leverage involved?

22. What is meant by the "quality" of a company's earnings? Explain why the price/earnings ratio for a company may indicate the quality of earnings.

23. Some ratios are more useful for management, whereas others are better suited to the needs of outsiders, such as stockholders and bankers. What is an example of a ratio that is primarily suited to management use? What is one that is more suited to use by outsiders?

24. The needs of service-oriented companies in analyzing financial statements differ from those of product-oriented companies. Why is this true? Give an example of a ratio that is meaningless to a service business.

Exercises

LO 4 **Exercise 15-1** Accounts Receivable Analysis

The following account balances are taken from the records of the Faraway Travel Agency:

	DECEMBER 31		
	1998	1997	1996
Accounts receivable	$150,000	$100,000	$80,000

	1998	1997
Net credit sales	$600,000	$540,000

Faraway extends credit terms requiring full payment in 60 days, with no discount for early payment.

Required

1. Compute Faraway's accounts receivable turnover ratio for 1998 and 1997.

2. Compute the number of days' sales in receivables for 1998 and 1997. Assume 360 days in a year.

3. Comment on the efficiency of Faraway's collection efforts over the two-year period.

LO 4 **Exercise 15-2** Inventory Analysis

The following account balances are taken from the records of Lewis Inc., a wholesaler of fresh fruits and vegetables:

	DECEMBER 31		
	1998	1997	1996
Merchandise inventory	$ 200,000	$ 150,000	$120,000

	1998	1997
Cost of goods sold	$7,100,000	$8,100,000

Required

1. Compute Lewis's inventory turnover ratio for 1998 and 1997.

2. Compute the number of days' sales in inventory for 1998 and 1997. Assume 360 days in a year.

3. Comment on your answers in parts 1 and 2 relative to the company's management of inventory over the two years. What problems do you see in its inventory management?

LO 4 **Exercise 15-3** Accounts Receivable and Inventory Analyses for General Motors, Ford, and Chrysler

The following information was obtained from the 1995 and 1994 financial statements of General Motors, Ford Motor Company, and Chrysler Corporation:

(in millions)		GENERAL MOTORS	FORD	CHRYSLER
Accounts receivable	12/21/95	$ 9,988.4	$ 3,321	$ 2,003
	12/31/94	8,977.8	2,548	1,695
Inventories	12/31/95	11,529.5	7,162	4,448
	12/31/94	10,127.8	6,487	3,356
Net Sales (Revenues)	1995	168,828.6	110,496	53,195
	1994	154,951.2	107,137	52,235
Cost of Sales*	1995	126,535.3	101,171	41,304
	1994	117,220.5	95,887	38,032

*Described as "cost of sales and other operating charges, exclusive of items listed below" by General Motors, "cost of sales" by Ford and "costs, other than items below" by Chrysler.

Required

1. Using the information provided above, compute the following for each company for 1995:

   a. Accounts receivable turnover ratio.

   b. Number of days' sales in receivables.

   c. Inventory turnover ratio.

   d. Number of days' sales in inventory.

   e. Cash to cash operating cycle.

2. Comment briefly on the liquidity of each of these three companies.

LO 4 **Exercise 15-4** Liquidity Analyses for Coca-Cola and Pepsi

The following information was summarized from the balance sheets of the Coca-Cola Company and Subsidiaries and PepsiCo Inc. and Subsidiaries at December 31, 1995:

(in millions)	COCA-COLA	PEPSI
Cash and cash equivalents	$1,167	$ 382
Short-term investments/ marketable securities	148	1,116
Accounts, notes, and other receivables, net	1,750	2,407
Inventories	1,117	1,051
Other current assets	1,268	590
Total current assets	$5,450	$ 5,546
Current liabilities	$7,348	$ 5,230
Other liabilities	$2,301	$12,889
Stockholders' equity	$5,392	$ 7,313

Required

1. Using the information provided above, compute the following for each company at December 31, 1995:

   a. Current ratio.

   b. Quick ratio.

2. Comment briefly on the liquidity of each of these two companies. Which appears to be the most liquid?

3. What other ratios would help you to more fully assess the liquidity of these companies?

LO 4 **Exercise 15-5** Liquidity Analyses for McDonald's and Wendy's

The following information was summarized from the balance sheets of McDonald's Corporation and Wendy's International Inc. at December 31, 1995:

(in thousands)	MCDONALD'S	WENDY'S
Current Assets:		
Cash and cash equivalents	$ 334,800	$206,127
Short-term investments	—	7,682
Accounts receivable, net	377,300	49,555
Notes receivable, net	36,300	12,272
Other current assets	207,400	45,643
Total current assets	$ 955,800	$321,279
Current liabilities	$1,794,900	$295,869
Other liabilities	$5,758,400	$394,513
Stockholders' equity	$7,861,300	$818,779

Required

1. Using the information provided above, compute the following for each company at December 31, 1995:

   a. Working capital.

   b. Current ratio.

   b. Quick ratio.

2. Comment briefly on the liquidity of each of these two companies. Which appears to be the most liquid?

3. McDonald's reported cash flows from operations of $2,296,200 during 1995. Wendy's reported cash flows from operations of $164,897. Current liabilities reported by McDonald's and Wendy's at December 31, 1994, were $2,451,300 and $286,110, respectively. (All amounts are stated in thousands.) Calculate the cash flow from operations to current liabilities ratio for each company. Does the information provided by this ratio change your opinion as to the relative liquidity of each of these two companies?

4. What steps might be taken by McDonald's to cover its short-term cash requirements?

LO 5 **Exercise 15-6** Solvency Analyses for Tommy Hilfiger

Tommy Hilfiger Corporation is a wholesaler of high-quality designer sportswear. During fiscal 1995, the company expanded its wholesale sportswear business by adding over 225 men's in-store shops and installing more than 110 boys' fixtured areas in department stores, increased the number of products offered through licensing relationships with premier apparel and accessories companies, and entered into an arrangement with the Estée Lauder Company to produce and market the first Tommy Hilfiger fragrance.

The following information was obtained from the comparative financial statements included in the company's 1995 annual report (all amounts are in thousands of dollars):

	MARCH 31, 1995	MARCH 31, 1994
Total liabilities	$ 30,469	$ 28,663
Total shareholders' equity	209,024	161,715

	FOR THE FISCAL YEARS ENDED MARCH 31	
	1995	1994
Interest expense	$ 207	$ 317
Provision for income taxes	22,742	16,422
Net income	40,715	25,344
Net cash provided by operating activities	31,435	4,326
Total dividends paid	—	—
Cash used to purchase property and equipment	20,042	18,655
Payments on long-term debt	277	130

Required

1. Using the information provided above, compute the following for 1995 and 1994:
   a. Debt-to-equity ratio (at each year-end).
   b. Times interest earned ratio.
   c. Debt service coverage ratio.
   d. Cash flow from operations to capital expenditures ratio.
2. Comment briefly on the company's solvency.

LO 5 **Exercise 15-7** Solvency Analysis

The following information is available from the balance sheets at the ends of the two most recent years and the income statement for the most recent year of Impact Company:

	DECEMBER 31	
	1998	1997
Accounts payable	$ 65,000	$ 50,000
Accrued liabilities	25,000	35,000
Taxes payable	60,000	45,000
Short-term notes payable	–0–	75,000
Bonds payable due within next year	200,000	200,000
Total current liabilities	$ 350,000	$ 405,000
Bonds payable	$ 600,000	$ 800,000
Common stock, $10 par	$1,000,000	$1,000,000
Retained earnings	650,000	500,000
Total stockholders' equity	$1,650,000	$1,500,000
Total liabilities and stockholders' equity	$2,600,000	$2,705,000

	1998
Sales revenue	$1,600,000
Cost of goods sold	950,000
Gross profit	$ 650,000
Selling and administrative expense	300,000
Operating income	$ 350,000
Interest expense	89,000
Income before tax	$ 261,000
Income tax expense	111,000
Net income	$ 150,000

Other Information

a. Short-term notes payable represents a 12-month loan that matured in November 1998. Interest of 12% was paid at maturity.

b. One million dollars of serial bonds had been issued 10 years earlier. The first series of $200,000 matured at the end of 1998, with interest of 8% payable annually.

c. Cash flow from operations was $185,000 in 1998. The amounts of interest and taxes paid during 1998 were $89,000 and $96,000, respectively.

Required

1. Compute the following for Impact Company:

   a. The debt-to-equity ratio at December 31, 1998, and December 31, 1997.

   b. The times interest earned ratio for 1998.

   c. The debt service coverage ratio for 1998.

2. Comment on Impact's solvency at the end of 1998. Do the times interest earned ratio and the debt service coverage ratio differ in terms of their indication of Impact's ability to pay its debts?

LO 6 **Exercise 15-8** Return Ratios and Leverage

The following selected data are taken from the financial statements of Evergreen Company:

Sales revenue	$ 650,000
Cost of goods sold	400,000
Gross profit	$ 250,000
Selling and administrative expense	100,000
Operating income	$ 150,000
Interest expense	50,000
Income before tax	$ 100,000
Income tax expense (40%)	40,000
Net income	$ 60,000
Accounts payable	$ 45,000
Accrued liabilities	70,000
Income taxes payable	10,000
Interest payable	25,000
Short-term loans payable	150,000
Total current liabilities	$ 300,000
Long-term bonds payable	$ 500,000
Preferred stock, 10%, $100 par	$ 250,000
Common stock, no par	600,000
Retained earnings	350,000
Total stockholders' equity	$1,200,000
Total liabilities and stockholders' equity	$2,000,000

Required

1. Compute the following ratios for Evergreen Company:

   a. Return on sales.

   b. Asset turnover (assume that total assets at the beginning of the year were $1,600,000).

   c. Return on assets.

   d. Return on common stockholders' equity (assume that the only changes in stockholders' equity during the year were from the net income for the year and dividends on the preferred stock).

2. Comment on Evergreen's use of leverage. Has it successfully employed leverage? Explain your answer.

LO 6 | **Exercise 15-9** Relationships among Return on Assets, Return on Sales, and Asset Turnover

A company's return on assets is a function of its ability to turn over its investment (asset turnover) and earn a profit on each dollar of sales (return on sales). For each of the *independent* cases below, determine the missing amounts. (*Note:* Assume in each case that the company has no interest expense; that is, net income is used as the definition of income in all calculations.)

CASE 1

Net income	$ 10,000
Net sales	$ 80,000
Average total assets	$ 60,000
Return on assets	?

CASE 2

Net income	$ 25,000
Average total assets	$ 250,000
Return on sales	2%
Net sales	?

CASE 3

Average total assets	$ 80,000
Asset turnover	1.5 times
Return on sales	6%
Return on assets	?

CASE 4

Return on assets	10%
Net sales	$ 50,000
Asset turnover	1.25 times
Net income	?

CASE 5

Return on assets	15%
Net income	$ 20,000
Return on sales	5%
Average total assets	?

LO 6 **Exercise 15-10** EPS, P/E Ratio, and Dividend Ratios

The stockholders' equity section of the balance sheet for Cooperstown Corp. at the end of 1998 appears as follows:

8%, $100 par, cumulative preferred stock, 200,000 shares authorized, 50,000 shares issued and outstanding	$ 5,000,000
Additional paid-in capital on preferred	2,500,000
Common stock, $5 par, 500,000 shares authorized, 400,000 shares issued and outstanding	$ 2,000,000
Additional paid-in capital on common	18,000,000
Retained earnings	37,500,000
Total stockholders' equity	$65,000,000

Net income for the year was $1,300,000. Dividends were declared and paid on the preferred shares during the year, and a quarterly dividend of $.40 per share was declared and paid each quarter on the common shares. The closing market price for the common shares on December 31, 1998, was $24.75 per share.

Required

1. Compute the following ratios for the common stock:

   a. Earnings per share.

   b. Price/earnings ratio.

   c. Dividend payout ratio.

   d. Dividend yield ratio.

2. Assume that you are an investment adviser. What other information would you want to have before advising a client regarding the purchase of Cooperstown stock?

LO 6 **Exercise 15-11** Earnings Per Share and Extraordinary Items

The stockholders' equity section of the balance sheet for Lahey Construction Company at the end of 1998 follows:

9%, $10 par, cumulative preferred stock, 500,000 shares authorized, 200,000 shares issued and outstanding	$ 2,000,000
Additional paid-in capital on preferred	7,500,000
Common stock, $1 par, 2,500,000 shares authorized, 1,500,000 shares issued and outstanding	1,500,000
Additional paid-in capital on common	21,000,000
Retained earnings	25,500,000
Total stockholders' equity	$57,500,000

The lower portion of the 1998 income statement indicates the following:

Net income before tax		$ 9,750,000
Income tax expense (40%)		(3,900,000)
Income before extraordinary items		$ 5,850,000
Extraordinary loss from flood	$(6,200,000)	
Less: related tax effect (40%)	2,480,000	(3,720,000)
Net income		$ 2,130,000

Assume the number of shares outstanding did not change during the year.

Required

1. Compute earnings per share *before* extraordinary items.

2. Compute earnings per share *after* the extraordinary loss.

3. Which of the two EPS ratios is more useful to management? Explain your answer. Would your answer be different if the ratios were to be used by an outsider, for example, by a potential stockholder? Why?

Multi-Concept Exercises

LO 2, 3 **Exercise 15-12** Common-Size Balance Sheets and Horizontal Analysis

Comparative balance sheets for Farinet Company for the past two years are as follows:

	DECEMBER 31	
	1998	1997
Cash	$ 16,000	$ 20,000
Accounts receivable	40,000	30,000
Inventory	30,000	50,000
Prepaid rent	18,000	12,000
Total current assets	$104,000	$112,000
Land	$150,000	$150,000
Plant and equipment	800,000	600,000
Accumulated depreciation	(130,000)	(60,000)
Total long-term assets	$820,000	$690,000
Total assets	$924,000	$802,000
Accounts payable	$ 24,000	$ 20,000
Income taxes payable	6,000	10,000
Short-term notes payable	70,000	50,000
Total current liabilities	$100,000	$ 80,000
Bonds payable	$150,000	$200,000
Common stock	$400,000	$300,000
Retained earnings	274,000	222,000
Total stockholders' equity	$674,000	$522,000
Total liabilities and stockholders' equity	$924,000	$802,000

Required

1. Using the format in Exhibit 15-5, prepare common-size comparative balance sheets for the two years for Farinet Company.

2. What observations can you make about the changes in the relative composition of Farinet's accounts from the common-size balance sheets? List at least five observations.

3. Using the format in Exhibit 15-1, prepare comparative balance sheets for Farinet Company, including columns for both the dollars and percentage increase or decrease in each item on the statement.

4. Identify the four items on the balance sheet that experienced the largest change from one year to the next. For each of these, explain where you would look to find additional information about the change.

LO 2, 3 **Exercise 15-13** Common-Size Income Statements and Horizontal Analysis

Income statements for Mariners Corp. for the past two years follow:

	(AMOUNTS IN THOUSANDS OF DOLLARS)	
	1998	1997
Sales revenue	$60,000	$50,000
Cost of goods sold	42,000	30,000
Gross profit	$18,000	$20,000
Selling and administrative expense	9,000	5,000
Operating income	$ 9,000	$15,000
Interest expense	2,000	2,000
Income before tax	$ 7,000	$13,000
Income tax expense	2,000	4,000
Net income	$ 5,000	$ 9,000

Required

1. Using the format in Exhibit 15-6, prepare common-size comparative income statements for the two years for Mariners Corp.

2. What observations can you make about the common-size statements? List at least four observations.

3. Using the format in Exhibit 15-2, prepare comparative income statements for Mariners Corp., including columns for both the dollars and percentage increase or decrease in each item on the statement.

4. Identify the two items on the income statement that experienced the largest change from one year to the next. For each of these, explain where you would look to find additional information about the change.

Problems

LO 4 **Problem 15-1** Effect of Transactions on Working Capital, Current Ratio, and Quick Ratio

(*Note:* Consider completing Problem 15-2 after this problem to ensure that you obtain a clear understanding of the effect of various transactions on these measures of liquidity.)

The following account balances are taken from the records of Liquiform Inc.:

Cash	$ 70,000
Trading securities (short-term)	60,000
Accounts receivable	80,000
Inventory	100,000
Prepaid insurance	10,000
Accounts payable	75,000
Taxes payable	25,000
Salaries and wages payable	40,000
Short-term loans payable	60,000

Required

1. Use the information provided above to compute the amount of working capital and Liquiform's current and quick ratios (round to three decimal points).

2. Determine the effect that each of the following transactions will have on Liquiform's working capital, current ratio, and quick ratio by recalculating each and then indicating whether the measure is increased, decreased, or not affected by the transaction. (For the ratios, round to three decimal points.) Consider each transaction independently; that is, assume that it is the *only* transaction that takes place.

	EFFECT OF TRANSACTION ON:		
TRANSACTION	**WORKING CAPITAL**	**CURRENT RATIO**	**QUICK RATIO**
a. Purchased inventory on account for $20,000.			
b. Purchased inventory for cash, $15,000.			
c. Paid suppliers on account, $30,000.			
d. Received cash on account, $40,000.			
e. Paid insurance for next year, $20,000.			
f. Made sales on account, $60,000.			
g. Repaid short-term loans at bank, $25,000.			
h. Borrowed $40,000 at bank for 90 days.			
i. Declared and paid $45,000 cash dividend.			
j. Purchased $20,000 of trading securities (classified as current assets).			
k. Paid $30,000 in salaries.			
l. Accrued additional $15,000 in taxes.			

LO 4   **Problem 15-2** Effect of Transactions on Working Capital, Current Ratio, and Quick Ratio

(*Note:* Consider completing this problem after Problem 15-1 to ensure that you obtain a clear understanding of the effect of various transactions on these measures of liquidity.)

The following account balances are taken from the records of Veriform Inc.:

Cash	$ 70,000
Trading securities (short-term)	60,000
Accounts receivable	80,000
Inventory	100,000
Prepaid insurance	10,000
Accounts payable	75,000
Taxes payable	25,000
Salaries and wages payable	40,000
Short-term loans payable	210,000

Required

1. Use the information provided above to compute the amount of working capital and Veriform's current and quick ratios (round to three decimal points).

2. Determine the effect that each of the following transactions will have on Veriform's working capital, current ratio, and quick ratio by recalculating each and then indicating whether the measure is increased, decreased, or not affected by the transaction. (For the ratios, round to three decimal points.) Consider each transaction independently; that is, assume that it is the *only* transaction that takes place.

	EFFECT OF TRANSACTION ON:		
TRANSACTION	**WORKING CAPITAL**	**CURRENT RATIO**	**QUICK RATIO**
a. Purchased inventory on account for $20,000.			
b. Purchased inventory for cash, $15,000.			
c. Paid suppliers on account, $30,000.			
d. Received cash on account, $40,000.			
e. Paid insurance for next year, $20,000.			
f. Made sales on account, $60,000.			
g. Repaid short-term loans at bank, $25,000.			
h. Borrowed $40,000 at bank for 90 days.			
i. Declared and paid $45,000 cash dividend.			

j. Purchased $20,000 of trading securities (classified as current assets).

k. Paid $30,000 in salaries.

l. Accrued additional $15,000 in taxes.

LO 6 **Problem 15-3** Goals for Sales and Return on Assets

The president of Blue Skies Corp. is reviewing with his vice presidents the operating results of the year just completed. Sales increased by 15% from the previous year to $60,000,000. Average total assets for the year were $40,000,000. Net income, after adding back interest expense, net of tax, was $5,000,000.

The president is happy with the performance over the past year but is never satisfied with the status quo. He has set two specific goals for next year: (1) a 20% growth in sales and (2) a return on assets of 15%.

To achieve the second goal, the president has stated his intention to increase the total asset base by 12.5% over the base for the year just completed.

Required

1. For the year just completed, compute the following ratios:

    a. Return on sales.

    b. Asset turnover.

    c. Return on assets.

2. Compute the necessary asset turnover for next year to achieve the president's goal of a 20% increase in sales.

3. Calculate the income needed next year to achieve the goal of a 15% return on total assets. (*Note:* Assume that *income* is defined as net income plus interest, net of tax.)

4. Based on your answers to parts 2 and 3, comment on the reasonableness of the president's goals. What must the company focus on to attain these goals?

LO 6 **Problem 15-4** Goals for Sales and Income Growth

Sunrise Corp. is a major regional retailer. The chief executive officer (CEO) is concerned with the slow growth of both sales and net income and the subsequent effect on the trading price of the common stock. Selected financial data for the past three years follow.

SUNRISE CORP.
(IN MILLIONS)

	1998	1997	1996
1. Sales	$200.0	$192.5	$187.0
2. Net income	6.0	5.8	5.6
3. Dividends declared and paid	2.5	2.5	2.5
DECEMBER 31 BALANCES:			
4. Owners' equity	70.0	66.5	63.2
5. Debt	30.0	29.8	30.3
SELECTED YEAR-END FINANCIAL RATIOS			
Net income to sales	3.0%	3.0%	3.0%
Asset turnover	2 times	2 times	2 times
6. Return on owners' equity*	8.6%	8.7%	8.9%
7. Debt to total assets	30.0%	30.9%	32.4%

*Based on year-end balances in owners' equity.

The CEO believes that the price of the stock has been adversely affected by the downward trend of the return on equity, the relatively low dividend payout ratio, and the lack of dividend increases. To improve the price of the stock, she wants to improve the return on equity and dividends. She believes that the company should be able to meet these objectives by (1) increasing sales and net income at an annual rate of 10% a year and (2) establishing a new dividend policy that calls for a dividend payout of 50% of earnings or $3,000,000, whichever is larger.

The 10% annual sales increase will be accomplished through a new promotional program. The president believes that the present net income to sales ratio of 3% will be unchanged by the cost of this new program and any interest paid on new debt. She expects that the company can accomplish this sales and income growth while maintaining the current relationship of total assets to sales. Any capital that is needed to maintain this relationship and that is not generated internally would be acquired through long-term debt financing. The CEO hopes that debt would not exceed 35% of total liabilities and owners' equity.

Required

1. Using the CEO's program, prepare a schedule that shows the appropriate data for the years 1999, 2000, and 2001 for the items numbered 1 through 7 on the preceding schedule.

2. Can the CEO meet all of her requirements if a 10% per year growth in income and sales is achieved? Explain your answer.

3. What alternative actions should the CEO consider to improve the return on equity and to support increased dividend payments?

4. Explain the reasons that the CEO might have for wanting to limit debt to 35% of total liabilities and owners' equity.   (CMA adapted)

Multi-Concept Problems

LO 4, 5, 6 | **Problem 15-5** Basic Financial Ratios

The accounting staff of CCB Enterprises has completed the financial statements for the 1998 calendar year. The statement of income for the current year and the comparative statements of financial position for 1998 and 1997 follow.

CCB ENTERPRISES
STATEMENT OF INCOME
FOR THE YEAR ENDED DECEMBER 31, 1998
(THOUSANDS OMITTED)

Revenue:	
Net sales	$800,000
Other	60,000
Total revenue	$860,000
Expenses:	
Cost of goods sold	$540,000
Research and development	25,000
Selling and administrative	155,000
Interest	20,000
Total expenses	$740,000
Income before income taxes	$120,000
Income taxes	48,000
Net income	$ 72,000

CCB ENTERPRISES
COMPARATIVE STATEMENTS OF FINANCIAL POSITION
DECEMBER 31, 1998 AND 1997
(THOUSANDS OMITTED)

	1998	1997
ASSETS		
Current assets:		
Cash and short-term investments	$ 26,000	$ 21,000
Receivables, less allowance for doubtful accounts ($1,100 in 1998 and $1,400 in 1997)	48,000	50,000
Inventories, at lower of FIFO cost or market	65,000	62,000
Prepaid items and other current assets	5,000	3,000
Total current assets	$144,000	$136,000
Other assets:		
Investments, at cost	$106,000	$106,000
Deposits	10,000	8,000
Total other assets	$116,000	$114,000
Property, plant, and equipment:		
Land	$ 12,000	$ 12,000
Buildings and equipment, less accumulated depreciation ($126,000 in 1998 and $122,000 in 1997)	268,000	248,000
Total property, plant, and equipment	$280,000	$260,000
Total assets	$540,000	$510,000
LIABILITIES AND STOCKHOLDERS' EQUITY		
Current liabilities:		
Short-term loans	$ 22,000	$ 24,000
Accounts payable	72,000	71,000
Salaries, wages, and other	26,000	27,000
Total current liabilities	$120,000	$122,000
Long-term debt	$160,000	$171,000
Total liabilities	$280,000	$293,000
Stockholders' equity:		
Common stock, at par	$ 44,000	$ 42,000
Paid-in capital in excess of par	64,000	61,000
Total paid-in capital	$108,000	$103,000
Retained earnings	152,000	114,000
Total stockholders' equity	$260,000	$217,000
Total liabilities and stockholders' equity	$540,000	$510,000

Required:

1. Calculate the following financial ratios for 1998 for CCB Enterprises:

    a. Times interest earned.

    b. Return on total assets.

    c. Return on common stockholders' equity.

    d. Debt-equity ratio (at December 31, 1998).

    e. Current ratio (at December 31, 1998).

    f. Quick (acid-test) ratio (at December 31, 1998).

    g. Accounts receivable turnover ratio (assume that all sales are on credit).

h. Number of days' sales in receivables.

i. Inventory turnover ratio (assume that all purchases are on credit).

j. Number of days' sales in inventory.

k. Number of days in cash operating cycle.

2. Prepare a few brief comments on the overall financial health of CCB Enterprises. For each comment, indicate any information that is not provided in the problem and that you would need to fully evaluate the company's financial health.

(CMA adapted)

LO 5, 6 **Problem 15-6** Projected Results to Meet Corporate Objectives

Tablon Inc. is a wholly owned subsidiary of Marbel Co. The philosophy of Marbel's management is to allow the subsidiaries to operate as independent units. Corporate control is exercised through the establishment of minimum objectives for each subsidiary, accompanied by substantial rewards for success and penalties for failure. The time period for performance review is long enough for competent managers to display their abilities.

Each quarter the subsidiary is required to submit financial statements. The statements are accompanied by a letter from the subsidiary president explaining the results to date, a forecast for the remainder of the year, and the actions to be taken to achieve the objectives if the forecast indicates that the objectives will not be met.

Marbel management, in conjunction with Tablon management, had set the objectives listed below for the year ending May 31, 1999. These objectives are similar to those set in previous years.

Sales growth of 20%.

Return on stockholders' equity of 15%.

A long-term debt-to-equity ratio of not more than 1.0.

Payment of a cash dividend of 50% of net income, with a minimum payment of at least $400,000.

Tablon's controller has just completed the financial statements for the six months ended November 30, 1998, and the forecast for the year ending May 31, 1999. The statements are presented below and on the following page.

After a cursory glance at the financial statements, Tablon's president concluded that not all objectives would be met. At a staff meeting of the Tablon management, the president asked the controller to review the projected results and recommend possible actions that could be taken during the remainder of the year so that Tablon would be more likely to meet the objectives.

TABLON INC.
INCOME STATEMENT
(THOUSANDS OMITTED)

	YEAR ENDED MAY 31, 1998	SIX MONTHS ENDED NOVEMBER 30, 1998	FORECAST FOR YEAR ENDING MAY 31, 1999
Sales	$25,000	$15,000	$30,000
Cost of goods sold	$13,000	$ 8,000	$16,000
Selling expenses	5,000	3,500	7,000
Administrative expenses and interest	4,000	2,500	5,000
Income taxes (40%)	1,200	400	800
Total expenses and taxes	$23,200	$14,400	$28,800
Net income	$ 1,800	$ 600	$ 1,200
Dividends declared and paid	600	0	600
Income retained	$ 1,200	$ 600	$ 600

TABLON INC.
STATEMENT OF FINANCIAL POSITION
(THOUSANDS OMITTED)

	MAY 31, 1998	NOVEMBER 30, 1998	FORECAST FOR MAY 31, 1999
ASSETS			
Cash	$ 400	$ 500	$ 500
Accounts receivable (net)	4,100	6,500	7,100
Inventory	7,000	8,500	8,600
Plant and equipment (net)	6,500	7,000	7,300
Total assets	$18,000	$22,500	$23,500
LIABILITIES AND EQUITIES			
Accounts payable	$ 3,000	$ 4,000	$ 4,000
Accrued taxes	300	200	200
Long-term borrowing	6,000	9,000	10,000
Common stock	5,000	5,000	5,000
Retained earnings	3,700	4,300	4,300
Total liabilities and equities	$18,000	$22,500	$23,500

Required

1. Calculate the projected results for each of the four objectives established for Tablon Inc. State which results will not meet the objectives by year-end.

2. From the data presented, identify the factors that seem to contribute to the failure of Tablon Inc. to meet all of its objectives.

3. Explain the possible actions that the controller could recommend in response to the president's request.   (CMA adapted)

LO 4, 5, 6 **Problem 15-7** Comparison With Industry Averages

Heartland Inc. is a medium-size company that has been in business for 20 years. The industry has become very competitive in the last few years, and Heartland has decided that it must grow if it is going to survive. It has approached the bank for a sizable five-year loan, and the bank has requested its most recent financial statements as part of the loan package.

The industry in which Heartland operates consists of approximately 20 companies relatively equal in size. The trade association to which all of the competitors belong publishes an annual survey of the industry, including industry averages for selected ratios for the competitors. All companies voluntarily submit their statements to the association for this purpose.

Heartland's controller is aware that the bank has access to this survey and is very concerned about how the company fared this past year compared with the rest of the industry. The ratios included in the publication, and the averages for the past year, are as follows:

RATIO	INDUSTRY AVERAGE
Current ratio	1.23
Acid-test (quick) ratio	0.75
Accounts receivable turnover	33 times
Inventory turnover	29 times
Debt-to-equity ratio	0.53
Times interest earned	8.65 times
Return on sales	6.57%
Asset turnover	1.95 times
Return on assets	12.81%
Return on common stockholders' equity	17.67%

The financial statements to be submitted to the bank in connection with the loan follow:

HEARTLAND INC.
STATEMENT OF INCOME AND RETAINED EARNINGS
FOR THE YEAR ENDED DECEMBER 31, 1998
(THOUSANDS OMITTED)

Sales revenue	$ 542,750
Cost of goods sold	(435,650)
Gross margin	$ 107,100
Selling, general, and administrative expense	$ (65,780)
Loss on sales of securities	(220)
Income before interest and taxes	$ 41,100
Interest expense	(9,275)
Income before taxes	$ 31,825
Income tax expense	(12,730)
Net income	$ 19,095
Retained earnings, January 1, 1998	58,485
	$ 77,580
Dividends paid on common stock	(12,000)
Retained earnings, December 31, 1998	$ 65,580

HEARTLAND INC.
COMPARATIVE STATEMENTS OF FINANCIAL POSITION
(THOUSANDS OMITTED)

	DECEMBER 31, 1998	DECEMBER 31, 1997
ASSETS		
Current assets:		
Cash	$ 1,135	$ 750
Marketable securities	1,250	2,250
Accounts receivable, net of allowances	15,650	12,380
Inventories	12,680	15,870
Prepaid items	385	420
Total current assets	$ 31,100	$ 31,670
Long-term investments	$ 425	$ 425
Property, plant, and equipment:		
Land	$ 32,000	$ 32,000
Buildings and equipment, net of accumulated depreciation	216,000	206,000
Total property, plant, and equipment	$248,000	$238,000
Total assets	$279,525	$270,095
LIABILITIES AND STOCKHOLDERS' EQUITY		
Current liabilities:		
Short-term notes	$ 8,750	$ 12,750
Accounts payable	20,090	14,380
Salaries and wages payable	1,975	2,430
Income taxes payable	3,130	2,050
Total current liabilities	$ 33,945	$ 31,610
Long-term bonds payable	$ 80,000	$ 80,000
Stockholders' equity:		
Common stock, no par	$100,000	$100,000
Retained earnings	65,580	58,485
Total stockholders' equity	$165,580	$158,485
Total liabilities and stockholders' equity	$279,525	$270,095

Required

1. Prepare a columnar report for the controller of Heartland Inc., comparing the industry averages for the ratios published by the trade association with the comparable ratios for Heartland. For Heartland, compute the ratios as of December 31, 1998, or for the year ending December 31, 1998, whichever is appropriate.

2. Briefly evaluate Heartland's ratios relative to the industry.

3. Do you think that the bank will approve the loan? Explain your answer.

Alternate Problems

LO 5 **Problem 15-1A** Effect of Transactions on Debt-To-Equity Ratio

(*Note:* Consider completing Problem 15-2A after this problem to ensure that you obtain a clear understanding of the effect of various transactions on this measure of solvency.)

The following account balances are taken from the records of Monet's Garden Inc.:

Current liabilities	$150,000
Long-term liabilities	375,000
Stockholders' equity	400,000

Required

1. Use the information provided above to compute Monet's debt-to-equity ratio (round to three decimal points).

2. Determine the effect that each of the following transactions will have on Monet's debt-to-equity ratio by recalculating the ratio and then indicating whether the ratio is increased, decreased, or not affected by the transaction. (Round to three decimal points.) Consider each transaction independently; that is, assume that it is the *only* transaction that takes place.

TRANSACTION	EFFECT OF TRANSACTION ON DEBT-TO-EQUITY RATIO
a. Purchased inventory on account for $20,000.	
b. Purchased inventory for cash, $15,000.	
c. Paid suppliers on account, $30,000.	
d. Received cash on account, $40,000.	
e. Paid insurance for next year, $20,000.	
f. Made sales on account, $60,000.	
g. Repaid short-term loans at bank, $25,000.	
h. Borrowed $40,000 at bank for 90 days.	
i. Declared and paid $45,000 cash dividend.	
j. Purchased $20,000 of trading securities (classified as current assets).	
k. Paid $30,000 in salaries.	
l. Accrued additional $15,000 in taxes.	

LO 5 **Problem 15-2A** Effect of Transactions on Debt-To-Equity Ratio

(*Note:* Consider completing this problem after Problem 15-1A to ensure that you obtain a clear understanding of the effect of various transactions on this measure of solvency.)

The following account balances are taken from the records of Degas Inc.:

Current liabilities	$ 25,000
Long-term liabilities	125,000
Stockholders' equity	400,000

Required

1. Use the information provided above to compute Degas' debt-to-equity ratio (round to three decimal points).

2. Determine the effect that each of the following transactions will have on Degas's debt-to-equity ratio by recalculating the ratio and then indicating whether the ratio is increased, decreased, or not affected by the transaction. (Round to three decimal points.) Consider each transaction independently; that is, assume that it is the *only* transaction that takes place.

TRANSACTION	EFFECT OF TRANSACTION ON DEBT-TO-EQUITY RATIO
a. Purchased inventory on account for $20,000.	
b. Purchased inventory for cash, $15,000.	
c. Paid suppliers on account, $30,000.	
d. Received cash on account, $40,000.	
e. Paid insurance for next year, $20,000.	
f. Made sales on account, $60,000.	
g. Repaid short-term loans at bank, $25,000.	
h. Borrowed $40,000 at bank for 90 days.	
i. Declared and paid $45,000 cash dividend.	
j. Purchased $20,000 of trading securities (classified as current assets).	
k. Paid $30,000 in salaries.	
l. Accrued additional $15,000 in taxes.	

LO 6 **Problem 15-3A** Goals for Sales and Return on Assets

The president of Blue Moon Corp. is reviewing with her department managers the operating results of the year just completed . Sales increased by 12% from the previous year to $750,000. Average total assets for the year were $400,000. Net income, after adding back interest expense, net of tax, was $60,000.

The president is happy with the performance over the past year but is never satisfied with the status quo. She has set two specific goals for next year: (1) a 15% growth in sales and (2) a return on assets of 20%.

To achieve the second goal, the president has stated her intention to increase the total asset base by 10% over the base for the year just completed.

Required

1. For the year just completed, compute the following ratios:
   a. Return on sales.
   b. Asset turnover.
   c. Return on assets.

2. Compute the necessary asset turnover for next year to achieve the president's goal of a 15% increase in sales.

3. Calculate the income needed next year to achieve the goal of a 20% return on total assets. (*Note:* Assume that *income* is defined as net income plus interest, net of tax.)

4. Based on your answers to parts 2 and 3, comment on the reasonableness of the president's goals. What must the company focus on to attain these goals?

LO 6 **Problem 15-4A** Goals for Sales and Income Growth

Sunset Corp. is a major regional retailer. The chief executive officer (CEO) is concerned with the slow growth of both sales and net income and the subsequent effect on the trading price of the common stock. Selected financial data for the past three years follow.

SUNSET CORP.
(IN MILLIONS)

	1998	1997	1996
1. Sales	$100.0	$96.7	$93.3
2. Net income	3.0	2.9	2.8
3. Dividends declared and paid	1.2	1.2	1.2
DECEMBER 31 BALANCES:			
4. Owners' equity	40.0	38.2	36.5
5. Debt	10.0	10.2	10.2
SELECTED YEAR-END FINANCIAL RATIOS			
Net income to sales	3.0%	3.0%	3.0%
Asset turnover	2 times	2 times	2 times
6. Return on owners' equity*	7.5%	7.6%	7.7%
7. Debt to total assets	20.0%	21.1%	21.8%

*Based on year-end balances in owners' equity.

The CEO believes that the price of the stock has been adversely affected by the downward trend of the return on equity, the relatively low dividend payout ratio, and the lack of dividend increases. To improve the price of the stock, he wants to improve the return on equity and dividends.

He believes that the company should be able to meet these objectives by (1) increasing sales and net income at an annual rate of 10% a year and (2) establishing a new dividend policy that calls for a dividend payout of 60% of earnings or $2,000,000, whichever is larger.

The 10% annual sales increase will be accomplished through a product enhancement program. The president believes that the present net income to sales ratio of 3% will be unchanged by the cost of this new program and any interest paid on new debt. He expects that the company can accomplish this sales and income growth while maintaining the current relationship of total assets to sales. Any capital that is needed to maintain this relationship and that is not generated internally would be acquired through long-term debt financing. The CEO hopes that debt would not exceed 25% of total liabilities and owners' equity.

Required

1. Using the CEO's program, prepare a schedule that shows the appropriate data for the years 1999, 2000, and 2001 for the items numbered 1 through 7 on the preceding schedule.

2. Can the CEO meet all of his requirements if a 10% per year growth in income and sales is achieved? Explain your answers.

3. What alternative actions should the CEO consider to improve the return on equity and to support increased dividend payments? (CMA adapted)

Alternate Multi-Concept Problems

LO 4, 5, 6 **Problem 15-5A** Basic Financial Ratios

The accounting staff of SST Enterprises has completed the financial statements for the 1998 calendar year. The statement of income for the current year and the comparative statements of financial position for 1998 and 1997 follow.

SST ENTERPRISES
STATEMENT OF INCOME
YEAR ENDED DECEMBER 31, 1998
(THOUSANDS OMITTED)

Revenue:

Net sales	$600,000
Other	45,000
Total revenue	$645,000

Expenses:

Cost of goods sold	$405,000
Research and development	18,000
Selling and administrative	120,000
Interest	15,000
Total expenses	$558,000
Income before income taxes	$ 87,000
Income taxes	27,000
Net income	$ 60,000

SST ENTERPRISES
COMPARATIVE STATEMENTS OF FINANCIAL POSITION
DECEMBER 31, 1998 AND 1997
(THOUSANDS OMITTED)

	1998	1997
ASSETS		
Current assets:		
Cash and short-term investments	$ 27,000	$ 20,000
Receivables, less allowance for doubtful accounts ($1,100 in 1998 and $1,400 in 1997)	36,000	37,000
Inventories, at lower of FIFO cost or market	35,000	42,000
Prepaid items and other current assets	2,000	1,000
Total current assets	$100,000	$100,000
Property, plant, and equipment:		
Land	$ 9,000	$ 9,000
Buildings and equipment, less accumulated depreciation ($74,000 in 1998 and $62,000 in 1997)	191,000	186,000
Total property, plant, and equipment	$200,000	$195,000
Total assets	$300,000	$295,000
LIABILITIES AND STOCKHOLDERS' EQUITY		
Current liabilities:		
Short-term loans	$ 20,000	$ 15,000
Accounts payable	80,000	68,000
Salaries, wages, and other	5,000	7,000
Total current liabilities	$105,000	$ 90,000
Long-term debt	15,000	40,000
Total liabilities	$120,000	$130,000
Stockholders' equity:		
Common stock, at par	$ 50,000	$ 50,000
Paid-in capital in excess of par	25,000	25,000
Total paid-in capital	$ 75,000	$ 75,000
Retained earnings	105,000	90,000
Total stockholders' equity	$180,000	$165,000
Total liabilities and stockholders' equity	$300,000	$295,000

Required

1. Calculate the following financial ratios for 1998 for SST Enterprises:

   a. Times interest earned.

   b. Return on total assets.

   c. Return on common stockholders' equity.

   d. Debt-equity ratio (at December 31, 1998).

   e. Current ratio (at December 31, 1998).

   f. Quick (acid-test) ratio (at December 31, 1998).

   g. Accounts receivable turnover ratio (assume that all sales are on credit).

   h. Number of days' sales in receivables.

   i. Inventory turnover ratio (assume that all purchases are on credit).

   j. Number of days' sales in inventory.

   k. Number of days in cash operating cycle.

2. Prepare a few brief comments on the overall financial health of SST Enterprises. For each comment, indicate any information that is not provided in the problem and that you would need to fully evaluate the company's financial health.

(CMA adapted)

LO 5, 6 | **Problem 15-6A** Projected Results to Meet Corporate Objectives

Grout Inc. is a wholly owned subsidiary of Slait Co. The philosophy of Slait's management is to allow the subsidiaries to operate as independent units. Corporate control is exercised through the establishment of minimum objectives for each subsidiary, accompanied by substantial rewards for success and penalties for failure. The time period for performance review is long enough for competent managers to display their abilities.

Each quarter the subsidiary is required to submit financial statements. The statements are accompanied by a letter from the subsidiary president explaining the results to date, a forecast for the remainder of the year, and the actions to be taken to achieve the objectives if the forecast indicates that the objectives will not be met.

Slait management, in conjunction with Grout management, had set the objectives listed below for the year ending September 30, 1999. These objectives are similar to those set in previous years.

> Sales growth of 10%.
>
> Return on stockholders' equity of 20%.
>
> A long-term debt-to-equity ratio of not more than 1.0.
>
> Payment of a cash dividend of 50% of net income, with a minimum payment of at least $500,000.

Grout's controller has just completed preparing the financial statements for the six months ended March 31, 1999, and the forecast for the year ending September 30, 1999. The statements are presented on the following page.

After a cursory glance at the financial statements, Grout's president concluded that not all objectives would be met. At a staff meeting of the Grout management, the president asked the controller to review the projected results and recommend possible actions that could be taken during the remainder of the year so that Grout would be more likely to meet the objectives.

GROUT INC.
INCOME STATEMENT
(THOUSANDS OMITTED)

	YEAR ENDED SEPTEMBER 30, 1998	SIX MONTHS ENDED MARCH 31, 1999	FORECAST FOR YEAR ENDING SEPTEMBER 30, 1999
Sales	$10,000	$6,000	$12,000
Cost of goods sold	$ 6,000	$4,000	$ 8,000
Selling expenses	1,500	900	1,800
Administrative expenses and interest	1,000	600	1,200
Income taxes	500	300	600
Total expenses and taxes	$ 9,000	$5,800	$11,600
Net income	$ 1,000	$ 200	$ 400
Dividends declared and paid	500	0	400
Income retained	$ 500	$ 200	$ 0

GROUT INC.
STATEMENT OF FINANCIAL POSITION
(THOUSANDS OMITTED)

	SEPTEMBER 30, 1998	MARCH 31, 1999	FORECAST FOR SEPTEMBER 30, 1999
ASSETS			
Cash	$ 400	$ 500	$ 500
Accounts receivable (net)	2,100	3,400	2,600
Inventory	7,000	8,500	8,400
Plant and equipment (net)	2,800	2,500	3,200
Total assets	$12,300	$14,900	$14,700
LIABILITIES AND EQUITIES			
Accounts payable	$ 3,000	$ 4,000	$ 4,000
Accrued taxes	300	200	200
Long-term borrowing	4,000	5,500	5,500
Common stock	4,000	4,000	4,000
Retained earnings	1,000	1,200	1,000
Total liabilities and equities	$12,300	$14,900	$14,700

Required

1. Calculate the projected results for each of the four objectives established for Grout Inc. State which results will not meet the objectives by year-end.

2. From the data presented, identify the factors that seem to contribute to the failure of Grout Inc. to meet all of its objectives.

3. Explain the possible actions that the controller could recommend in response to the president's request. (CMA adapted)

LO 4, 5, 6 **Problem 15-7A** A Comparison with Industry Averages

Midwest Inc. is a medium-size company that has been in business for 20 years. The industry has become very competitive in the last few years, and Midwest has decided that it must grow if it is going to survive. It has approached the bank for a sizable five-year loan, and the bank has requested its most recent financial statements as part of the loan package.

The industry in which Midwest operates consists of approximately 20 companies relatively equal in size. The trade association to which all of the competitors belong publishes an annual survey of the industry, including industry averages for selected ratios for the competitors. All companies voluntarily submit their statements to the association for this purpose.

Midwest's controller is aware that the bank has access to this survey and is very concerned about how the company fared this past year compared with the rest of the industry. The ratios included in the publication, and the averages for the past year, are as follows:

RATIO	INDUSTRY AVERAGE
Current ratio	1.20
Acid-test (quick) ratio	0.50
Inventory turnover	35 times
Debt-to-equity ratio	0.50
Times interest earned	25 times
Return on sales	3%
Asset turnover	3.5 times
Return on common stockholders' equity	20%

The financial statements to be submitted to the bank in connection with the loan follow:

MIDWEST INC.
STATEMENT OF INCOME AND RETAINED EARNINGS
FOR THE YEAR ENDED DECEMBER 31, 1998
(THOUSANDS OMITTED)

Sales revenue	$ 420,500
Cost of goods sold	(300,000)
Gross margin	$ 120,500
Selling, general, and administrative expense	$ (85,000)
Income before interest and taxes	$ 35,500
Interest expense	(8,600)
Income before taxes	$ 26,900
Income tax expense	(12,000)
Net income	$ 14,900
Retained earnings, January 1, 1998	12,400
	$ 27,300
Dividends paid on common stock	(11,200)
Retained earnings, December 31, 1998	$ 16,100

MIDWEST INC.
COMPARATIVE STATEMENTS OF FINANCIAL POSITION
(THOUSANDS OMITTED)

	DECEMBER 31, 1998	DECEMBER 31, 1997
ASSETS		
Current assets:		
Cash	$ 1,790	$ 2,600
Marketable securities	1,200	1,700
Accounts receivable, net of allowances	400	600
Inventories	8,700	7,400
Prepaid items	350	400
Total current assets	$ 12,440	$ 12,700
Long-term investments	$ 560	$ 400
Property, plant, and equipment:		
Land	$ 12,000	$ 12,000
Buildings and equipment, net of accumulated depreciation	87,000	82,900
Total property, plant, and equipment	$ 99,000	$ 94,900
Total assets	$112,000	$108,000

LIABILITIES AND STOCKHOLDERS' EQUITY

Current liabilities:		
Short-term notes	$ 800	$ 600
Accounts payable	6,040	6,775
Salaries and wages payable	1,500	1,200
Income taxes payable	1,560	1,025
Total current liabilities	$ 9,900	$ 9,600
Long-term bonds payable	$ 36,000	$ 36,000
Stockholders' equity:		
Common stock, no par	$ 50,000	$ 50,000
Retained earnings	16,100	12,400
Total stockholders' equity	$ 66,100	$ 62,400
Total liabilities and stockholders' equity	$112,000	$108,000

Required

1. Prepare a columnar report for the controller of Midwest Inc., comparing the industry averages for the ratios published by the trade association with the comparable ratios for Midwest. For Midwest, compute the ratios as of December 31, 1998, or for the year ending December 31, 1998, whichever is appropriate.
2. Briefly evaluate Midwest's ratios relative to the industry.
3. Do you think that the bank will approve the loan? Explain your answer.

Cases

Reading and Interpreting Financial Statements

LO 2 **Case 15-1** Horizontal Analysis for Ben & Jerry's

Refer to Ben & Jerry's comparative income statements included in its annual report.

Required

1. Prepare a work sheet with the following headings:

	INCREASE (DECREASE) FROM			
	1994 TO 1995		1993 TO 1994	
INCOME STATEMENT ACCOUNTS	DOLLARS	PERCENT	DOLLARS	PERCENT

2. Complete the work sheet using each of the account titles on Ben & Jerry's income statement. Round dollar amounts to the nearest one-tenth of $1 million and percentages to the nearest one-tenth of a percent.
3. What observations can you make from this horizontal analysis? What is your overall analysis of operations? Has the company's operations improved over the three-year period?

LO 3 **Case 15-2** Vertical Analysis for Ben & Jerry's

Refer to Ben & Jerry's financial statements included in its annual report.

Required

1. Using the format in Exhibit 15-6, prepare common-size comparative income statements for the years ended December 30, 1995, and December 31, 1994. Round dollar amounts to the nearest one-tenth of $1 million and percentages to the nearest one-tenth of a percent.
2. What changes do you detect in the income statement relationships from 1994 to 1995?
3. Using the format in Exhibit 15-5, prepare common-size comparative balance sheets at December 30, 1995, and December 31, 1994. Round dollar amounts to the nearest one-tenth of $1 million and percentages to the nearest one-tenth of a percent.

4. What observations can you make about the relative composition of Ben & Jerry's assets from the common-size statements? What observations can be made about the changes in the relative composition of liabilities and owners' equity accounts?

LO 4, 5, 6 **Case 15-3** Ratio Analysis for Ben & Jerry's

Refer to Ben & Jerry's financial statements included in its annual report.

Required

1. Compute the following ratios and other amounts for each of the two years, 1995 and 1994. Because only two years of data are given on the balance sheets, to be consistent you should use year-end balances for each year in lieu of average balances. Assume a 40% tax rate and 360 days to a year. State any other necessary assumptions in making the calculations. Round all ratios to the nearest one-tenth of a percent.

  a. Working capital.
  b. Current ratio.
  c. Acid-test ratio.
  d. Cash flow from operations to current liabilities.
  e. Number of days' sales in receivables.
  f. Number of days' sales in inventory.
  g. Debt-to-equity ratio.
  h. Times interest earned.
  i. Debt service coverage.
  j. Cash flow from operations to capital expenditures.
  k. Asset turnover.
  l. Return on sales.
  m. Return on assets.
  n. Return on common stockholders' equity.

2. What is your overall analysis of the financial health of Ben & Jerry's? What do you believe are the company's strengths and weaknesses?

Making Financial Decisions

Decision Making

LO 4, 5, 6 **Case 15-4** Acquisition Decision

Diversified Industries is a large conglomerate and is continually in the market for new acquisitions. The company has grown rapidly over the last 10 years through buyouts of medium-size companies. Diversified does not limit itself to companies in any one industry but looks for firms with a sound financial base and the ability to stand on their own financially.

The president of Diversified recently told a meeting of the company's officers: "I want to impress two points on all of you. First, we are not in the business of looking for bargains. Diversified has achieved success in the past by acquiring companies with the ability to be a permanent member of the corporate family. We don't want companies that may appear to be a bargain on paper but can't survive in the long run. Second, a new member of our family must be able to come in and make it on its own—the parent is not organized to be a funding agency for struggling subsidiaries."

Ron Dixon is the vice president of acquisitions for Diversified, a position he has held for five years. He is responsible for making recommendations to the board of directors on potential acquisitions. Because you are one of his assistants, he recently brought you a set of financials for a manufacturer, Heavy Duty Tractors. Dixon believes that Heavy Duty is a "can't-miss" opportunity for Diversified and asks you to confirm his hunch by performing basic financial statement analysis on the company. The most recent income statement and comparative balance sheets for the company follow:

HEAVY DUTY TRACTORS INC.
STATEMENT OF INCOME AND RETAINED EARNINGS
FOR THE YEAR ENDED DECEMBER 31, 1998
(THOUSANDS OMITTED)

Sales revenue	$875,250
Cost of goods sold	542,750
Gross margin	$332,500
Selling, general, and administrative expenses	264,360
Operating income	$ 68,140
Interest expense	45,000
Net income before taxes and extraordinary items	$ 23,140
Income tax expense	9,250
Income before extraordinary items	$ 13,890
Extraordinary gain, less taxes of $6,000	9,000
Net income	$ 22,890
Retained earnings, January 1, 1998	169,820
	$192,710
Dividends paid on common stock	10,000
Retained earnings, December 31, 1998	$182,710

HEAVY DUTY TRACTORS INC.
COMPARATIVE STATEMENTS OF FINANCIAL POSITION
(THOUSANDS OMITTED)

	DECEMBER 31, 1998	DECEMBER 31, 1997
ASSETS		
Current assets:		
Cash	$ 48,500	$ 24,980
Marketable securities	3,750	–0–
Accounts receivable, net of allowances	128,420	84,120
Inventories	135,850	96,780
Prepaid items	7,600	9,300
Total current assets	$324,120	$215,180
Long-term investments	$ 55,890	$ 55,890
Property, plant, and equipment:		
Land	$ 45,000	$ 45,000
Buildings and equipment, less accumulated depreciation of $385,000 in 1998 and $325,000 in 1997	545,000	605,000
Total property, plant, and equipment	$590,000	$650,000
Total assets	$970,010	$921,070
LIABILITIES AND STOCKHOLDERS' EQUITY		
Current liabilities:		
Short-term notes	$ 80,000	$ 60,000
Accounts payable	65,350	48,760
Salaries and wages payable	14,360	13,840
Income taxes payable	2,590	3,650
Total current liabilities	$162,300	$126,250
Long-term bonds payable, due 2005	$275,000	$275,000
Stockholders' equity:		
Common stock, no par	$350,000	$350,000
Retained earnings	182,710	169,820
Total stockholders' equity	$532,710	$519,820
Total liabilities and stockholders' equity	$970,010	$921,070

Required

1. How liquid is Heavy Duty Tractors? Support your answer with any ratios that you believe are necessary to justify your conclusion. Also indicate any other information that you would want to have in making a final determination on its liquidity.

2. In light of the president's comments, should you be concerned about the solvency of Heavy Duty Tractors? Support your answer with the necessary ratios. How does the maturity date of the outstanding debt affect your answer?

3. Has Heavy Duty demonstrated the ability to be a profitable member of the Diversified family? Support your answer with the necessary ratios.

4. What will you tell your boss? Should he recommend to the board of directors that Diversified put in a bid for Heavy Duty Tractors?

Decision Making

LO 3 **Case 15-5** Pricing Decision

BPO's management believes that the company has been successful at increasing sales because it has not increased the selling price of the products, even though its competition has increased prices and costs have increased. Price and cost relationships in Year 1 were established because they represented industry averages. The following income statements are available for BPO's first three years of operation:

	YEAR 3	YEAR 2	YEAR 1
Sales	$125,000	$110,000	$100,000
Cost of goods sold	62,000	49,000	40,000
Gross profit	$ 63,000	$ 61,000	$ 60,000
Operating expenses	53,000	49,000	45,000
Net income	$ 10,000	$ 12,000	$ 15,000

Required

1. Using the format in Exhibit 15-6, prepare common-size comparative income statements for the three years.

2. Explain why net income has decreased while sales have increased.

3. Prepare an income statement for Year 4. Sales volume in units is expected to increase by 10% and costs are expected to increase by 8%.

4. Do you think BPO should raise its prices or maintain the same selling prices? Explain your answer.

Accounting and Ethics: What Would You Do?

LO 4, 5 **Case 15-6** Provisions in a Loan Agreement

As controller of Midwest Construction Company, you are reviewing with your assistant, Dave Jackson, the financial statements for the year just ended. During the review, Jackson reminds you of an existing loan agreement with Southern National Bank. Midwest has agreed to the following conditions:

■ The current ratio will be maintained at a minimum level of 1.5 to 1.0 at all times.

■ The debt-to-equity ratio will not exceed .5 to 1.0 at any time.

Jackson has drawn up the following preliminary, condensed balance sheet for the year just ended:

MIDWEST CONSTRUCTION COMPANY
BALANCE SHEET
DECEMBER 31
(IN MILLIONS OF DOLLARS)

Current assets	$16	Current liabilities	$10
Long-term assets	64	Long-term debt	15
		Stockholders' equity	55
Total	$80	Total	$80

Jackson wants to discuss two items with you: First, long-term debt currently includes a $5 million note payable, to Eastern State Bank, that is due in six months. The plan is to go to Eastern before the note is due and ask it to extend the maturity date of the note for five years. Jackson doesn't believe that Midwest needs to include the $5 million in current liabilities because the plan is to roll over the note.

Second, in December of this year, Midwest received a $2 million deposit from the state for a major road project. The contract calls for the work to be performed over the next 18 months. Jackson recorded the $2 million as revenue this year because the contract is with the state; there shouldn't be any question about being able to collect.

Required

1. Based on the balance sheet Jackson prepared, is Midwest in compliance with its loan agreement with Southern? Support your answer with any necessary computations.

2. What would you do with the two items in question? Do you see anything wrong with the way Jackson has handled each of them? Explain your answer.

3. Prepare a revised balance sheet based on your answer to part 2. Also, compute a revised current ratio and debt-to-equity ratio. Based on the revised ratios, is Midwest in compliance with its loan agreement?

LO 4 **Case 15-7** Inventory Turnover

Garden Fresh Inc. is a wholesaler of fresh fruits and vegetables. Each year it submits a set of financial ratios to a trade association. Even though the association doesn't publish the individual ratios for each company, the president of Garden Fresh thinks it is important for public relations that his company look as good as possible. Due to the nature of the fresh fruits and vegetables business, one of the major ratios tracked by the association is inventory turnover. Garden Fresh's inventory stated at FIFO cost was as follows:

	YEAR ENDING DECEMBER 31	
	1998	1997
Fruits	$10,000	$ 9,000
Vegetables	30,000	33,000
Totals	$40,000	$42,000

Sales revenue for the year ending December 31, 1998, is $3,690,000. The company's gross profit ratio is normally 40%.

Based on these data, the president thinks the company should report an inventory turnover ratio of 90 times per year.

Required

1. Explain, using the necessary calculations, how the president came up with an inventory turnover ratio of 90 times.

2. Do you think the company should report a turnover ratio of 90 times? If not, explain why you disagree and explain, with calculations, what you think the ratio should be.

3. Assume you are the controller for Garden Fresh. What will you tell the president?

Research Case

Case 15-8 Wm. Wrigley Jr. Company

For Wrigley's Doublemint gum to get to customers in China, several forms of transportation are required, including a rusting freighter, a thousand-mile trip by truck, a tricycle cart, and a bicycle. These determined efforts by the company to meet consumer demand in over 120 countries provides Wrigley with the potential for strong financial performance.

Conduct a search of the World Wide Web, obtain Wrigley's most recent annual report, or use library resources to obtain company financial data, and answer the following:

1. Based on the latest information available, what is Wrigley's price-earnings ratio? How does this compare to the average price-earnings ratio for the market as a whole?

2. For the most recent annual accounting information available, what is Wrigley's working capital? What actions do you think management could take to improve its working capital? If you were a manager for Wrigley, how would working capital affect your day-to-day decisions?

3. Locate the past 52-week high, low, and most current market price for the Wm. Wrigley Jr. Company. What recent financial performance results may have affected the company's stock price over the past three to six months?

Optional Research. Based on store visits and other research, list Wrigley's competitors in the gum and candy markets. What companies make these competing brands? Are these companies growing revenues at a faster or slower rate than Wrigley? How is Wrigley responding to this competition?

Solutions to Key Terms Quiz

Quiz 1:
- _14_ Horizontal analysis (p. 735)
- _10_ Gross profit ratio (p. 742)
- _13_ Liquidity (p. 743)
- _3_ Current ratio (p. 744)
- _5_ Cash flow from operations to current liabilities ratio (p. 745)
- _4_ Number of days' sales in receivables (p. 746)
- _8_ Cash to cash operating cycle (p. 748)
- _11_ Vertical analysis (p. 735)
- _12_ Profit margin ratio (p. 742)
- _2_ Working capital (p. 743)
- _1_ Acid-test or quick ratio (p. 744)
- _6_ Accounts receivable turnover ratio (p. 745)
- _9_ Inventory turnover ratio (p. 747)
- _7_ Number of days' sales in inventory (p. 747)

Quiz 2:
- _3_ Solvency (p. 748)
- _13_ Times interest earned ratio (p. 749)
- _8_ Cash flow from operations to capital expenditures ratio (p. 750)
- _9_ Return on assets ratio (p. 751)
- _10_ Asset turnover ratio (p. 752)
- _12_ Leverage (p. 754)
- _2_ Price/earnings (P/E) ratio (p. 755)
- _11_ Dividend yield ratio (p. 756)
- _7_ Debt-to-equity ratio (p. 748)
- _14_ Debt service coverage ratio (p. 750)
- _15_ Profitability (p. 751)
- _4_ Return on sales ratio (p. 752)
- _1_ Return on common stockholders' equity ratio (p. 753)
- _5_ Earnings per share (p. 754)
- _6_ Dividend payout ratio (p. 756)

INTEGRATIVE PROBLEM
FOR
PART IV

Computing and comparing ratios for consolidation in U.S. and British companies, translating foreign financial statements, preparing purchase entry and revised statements to reflect a consolidation, and recommending for or against the purchase.

The following condensed financial statements and additional information are available for Felknor Inc. and Rimmer Ltd., a British firm. Felknor is considering the acquisition of Rimmer but has asked your consulting firm for advice. The financial statements for Rimmer Ltd. are presently stated in British pounds.

FELKNOR INC.
BALANCE SHEET
AS OF DECEMBER 31, 1998
(IN MILLIONS OF DOLLARS)

ASSETS

Quick assets	$205
Other current assets	243
Total current assets	$448
Long-term assets	222
Total assets	$670

LIABILITIES

Current liabilities	$149
Long-term liabilities	63
Total liabilities	$212

STOCKHOLDERS' EQUITY

Common stock, $1 par	$ 10
Additional paid-in capital	140
Retained earnings	308
Total stockholders' equity	$458
Total liabilities and stockholders' equity	$670

FELKNOR INC.
INCOME STATEMENT
FOR THE YEAR ENDED DECEMBER 31, 1998
(IN MILLIONS OF DOLLARS)

Net revenue	$130
Expenses:	
Cost of sales	57
Other expenses	50
Operating income	$ 23

Additional information for Felknor Inc.:

1. Interest expense and income tax expense are not reflected on this income statement. Interest equals $1.4 million for 1998.

2. Income taxes amount to $6.5 million for 1998. The amount reflects a 30% rate of tax on income before taxes.

3. The market price of Felknor's common stock was $25 per share at the end of 1998.

RIMMER LTD.
BALANCE SHEET
AS OF DECEMBER 31, 1998
(IN MILLIONS OF POUNDS £)

ASSETS

Quick assets	£19
Other current assets	17
Total current assets	£36
Long-term assets	52
Total assets	£88

LIABILITIES

Current liabilities	£18
Long-term liabilities	2
Total liabilities	£20

STOCKHOLDERS' EQUITY

Common stock, $10 par	£38
Additional paid-in capital	26.2
Retained earnings	3.8
Total stockholders' equity	£68
Total liabilities and stockholders' equity	£88

RIMMER LTD.
INCOME STATEMENT
FOR THE YEAR ENDED DECEMBER 31, 1998
(IN MILLIONS OF POUNDS £)

Net revenue	£132
Expenses:	
Cost of sales	94
Other expenses	31
Operating income	£ 7

Additional information for Rimmer Ltd.:

1. This is Rimmer's first year of operation. Rimmer opened the facility at the beginning of 1998.

2. Interest expense and income tax expense are not reflected on this income statement. Interest equals £.7 million for 1998.

3. Income taxes amount to £2.5 million for 1998. This amount reflects a 40% rate of tax on income before taxes.

4. The market price of Rimmer's common stock was £10 per share at the end of 1998 (this was the equivalent of $16 per share in U.S. dollars).

5. Rimmer originally sold its stock at the beginning of 1998.

6. The following exchange rates are available:

	EXCHANGE RATE PER BRITISH POUND
Beginning of year	$1.5
End of year	1.6
Average for the year	1.5

The following industry-wide ratios are available for both Felknor and Rimmer.

	FELKNOR INC.	RIMMER LTD.
Current ratio	3.00	2.00
Acid-test ratio	1.50	1.00
Debt-to-equity ratio	0.30	0.65
Times interest earned	2 times	3 times
Return on assets	8.0%	15.0%
Return on stockholders' equity	10.0%	15.0%
Earnings per share	2.00	3.00
Price/earnings ratio	10.50	5.60

Required

1. For each of the industry-wide ratios listed above, compute the corresponding ratios for 1998 for the following:

   a. Felknor Inc. before the possible acquisition of Rimmer Ltd.

   b. Rimmer Ltd., with all ratios based on British pounds.

2. Using the exchange rates provided, translate Rimmer's December 31, 1998, balance sheet and its 1998 income statement from British pounds into U.S. dollars.

3. For each of the industry-wide ratios, compute the corresponding ratios for 1998 for Rimmer Ltd., with all ratios based on U.S. dollar amounts. Based on a comparison of these ratios to those calculated in part 1 (b), which of the ratios are affected by the translation process?

4. Assume that on December 31, 1998, Felknor Inc. purchased all of the assets and assumed all of the liabilities of Rimmer Ltd. for $110 million in cash. The fair values for all of Rimmer's assets and liabilities were equal to their book values on this date. Prepare the journal entry that would appear on Felknor's books to record the purchase of Rimmer.

5. Prepare a revised December 31, 1998, balance sheet and a revised 1998 income statement for Felknor to reflect the purchase of Rimmer.

6. For each of the industry-wide ratios, compute the corresponding ratios for 1998 for Felknor Inc., assuming it purchases Rimmer Ltd. on December 31, 1998. Based on a comparison of these ratios to those calculated in part 1(a), which of the ratios are improved and which of the ratios are adversely affected by the purchase of Rimmer?

7. As a consultant to Felknor, would you recommend that it purchase Rimmer? What other factors would be relevant to your recommendation? Explain your answers.

APPENDIX

Financial Statements of Ben & Jerry's

The following pages reprinted from pages 29–48 of the 1995 Annual Report of Ben & Jerry's Homemade, Inc., are a handy introduction to the company's financial information. Use them to answer the questions posed in the "From Concepts to Practice" marginal assignment boxes throughout the book. Also consult them when doing the "Reading and Interpreting Financial Statements" cases relating to Ben & Jerry's at the back of each chapter.

One of the two "Concept to Practice" boxes in each chapter are based on Ben & Jerry's 1995 financial statements and notes. The other is based on the company used as the chapter-opening focus for each chapter. For a convenient list of these assignment boxes, see the Index to "From Concept to Practice Assignments" following this Appendix.

For a fuller understanding of Ben & Jerry's as a company and its mission and strategic goals, read its 1995 Annual Report shrinkwrapped with each copy of the textbook.

Internet

For the most recent financial information about Ben & Jerry's, access its site on the World Wide Web (http://www/benjerry.com).

Market Information

The Company's Class A Common Stock is traded on the NASDAQ National Market System under the symbol BJICA. The following table sets forth for the period January 1, 1994 through March 8, 1996 the high and low closing sales prices of the Company's Class A Common Stock for the periods indicated.

1994	High	Low
First Quarter	$20	$14 3/4
Second Quarter	18 1/2	14
Third Quarter	16 3/4	13
Fourth Quarter	14	9 1/2

1995	High	Low
First Quarter	$14	$ 9 5/8
Second Quarter	15 1/2	11 3/4
Third Quarter	20	13 5/8
Fourth Quarter	19	14 1/2

1996	High	Low
First Quarter (through March 8)	17 1/4	13 1/2

The Class B Common Stock is generally non-transferable, and there is no trading market for the Class B Common Stock. The Class B Common Stock is freely convertible into Class A Common Stock on a share-for-share basis, and transferable thereafter.

The Company has never declared a cash dividend on its Class A Common Stock or the Class B Common Stock and the current policy of its Board of Directors is to retain earnings for expansion and development of the Company's business. Accordingly, the Board of Directors does not anticipate declaring any cash dividends on the Class A or Class B Common Stock in the foreseeable future.

As of March 8, 1996 there were 11,168 holders of record of the Company's Class A Common Stock and 2,508 holders of record of the Company's Class B Common Stock.

5-Year Financial Highlights

The following table contains selected financial information for the Company's fiscal years 1991 through 1995. (In thousands except per share data)

Summary of Operations:	12/30/95	12/31/94	Year Ended 12/25/93	12/26/92	12/28/91
Net sales	$ 155,333	$ 148,802	$ 140,328	$ 131,969	$ 96,997
Cost of sales	109,125	109,760	100,210	94,389	68,500
Gross profit	46,208	39,042	40,118	37,580	28,497
Selling, general and administrative expenses	36,362	36,253	28,270	26,243	21,264
Asset write-down		6,779			
Other income (expense)–net	(441)	228	197	(23)	(729)
Income (loss) before income taxes	9,405	(3,762)	12,045	11,314	6,504
Income tax expense (benefit)	3,457	(1,893)	4,844	4,639	2,765
Net income (loss)	5,948	(1,869)	7,201	6,675	3,739
Net income (loss) per common share[1]	$ 0.83	$ (0.26)	$ 1.01	$ 1.07	$ 0.67
Weighted average common and common equivalent shares outstanding[1]	7,222	7,148	7,138	6,254	5,572

Balance Sheet Data:	12/30/95	12/31/94	Year Ended 12/25/93	12/26/92	12/28/91
Working capital	$ 51,023	$ 37,456	$ 29,292	$ 18,053	$ 11,035
Total assets	131,074	120,296	106,361	88,207	43,056
Long-term debt	31,977	32,419	18,002	2,641	2,787
Stockholders' equity[2]	78,531	72,502	74,262	66,760	26,269

[1] The per share amounts and average shares outstanding have been adjusted for the effects of all stock splits, including stock splits in the form of stock dividends.

[2] No cash dividends have been declared or paid by the Company on its capital stock since the Company's organization. The Company intends to reinvest earnings for use in its business and to finance future growth. Accordingly, the Board of Directors does not anticipate declaring any cash dividends in the foreseeable future.

Management's Discussion & Analysis of Financial Condition & Results of Operations

Results of Operations

The following table shows certain items as a percentage of net sales which are included in the Company's Statement of Operations.

	Percentage of Net Sales Year Ended		
	12/30/95	12/31/94	12/25/93
Net sales	100.0 %	100.0 %	100.0 %
Cost of sales	70.2	73.8	71.4
Gross profit	29.8	26.2	28.6
Selling, general and administrative expense	23.4	24.4	20.2
Asset write-down		(4.6)	
Other income (expenses)	(0.4)	0.2	0.2
Income (loss) before income taxes	6.0	(2.6)	8.6
Income tax expense (benefit)	2.2	(1.3)	3.5
Net income (loss)	3.8 %	(1.3) %	5.1 %

Sales

Net sales in the fourth quarter of 1995 increased 5% from the fourth quarter of 1994, and net sales in 1995 overall increased 4.4% to $155 million from $149 million in 1994. Pint volume decreased 1.5% compared to 1994. The Company believes this decrease in pint volume is consistent with the recent performance in the super premium category overall, excluding sorbet which the Company did not introduce until 1996. This volume decrease was offset by a 3.7% price increase of pints sold to distributors that went into effect in March 1995. Net sales of both novelties and 2¹/₂ gallon bulk containers product categories had modest increases in 1995.

Pint sales represented approximately 85% of total net sales in 1995, 1994 and 1993. Net sales of 2¹/₂ gallon bulk containers represented approximately 7% of total net sales in 1995 and 1994, and 8% in 1993. Net sales of novelties accounted for approximately

6% of total net sales in 1995 and 5% in 1994 and 1993. Net sales from the Company's retail stores represented 2% of total net sales in 1995, 3% in 1994 and 2% in 1993.

Net sales in 1994 overall increased 6.0% to $149 million from $140 million in 1993. This was primarily the result of a 7% increase in net sales of packaged pints. The increase in pint sales was primarily due to sales of the Company's new "Smooth, No Chunks!™" line which was introduced nationally during the months of March through May 1994. Sales of the Company's reformulated and repackaged Peace Pops™ resulted in an increase in Peace Pop™ sales. However this was offset by the absence of sales of the Brownie Bar which the Company discontinued manufacturing in May 1993, resulting in approximately the same level of net sales of novelties overall in 1994 as in 1993.

Cost of Sales

Cost of sales in 1995 decreased approximately $0.6 million or 0.6% over the same period in 1994 and overall gross profit as a percentage of net sales increased from 26.2% in 1994 to 29.8% in 1995. The higher gross profit as a percentage of sales in 1995 is due to the price increase effective in March 1995 combined with improved inventory management and production efficiencies, as compared with 1994. In addition, the improved gross margin reflects less product manufactured for the Company by Edy's Grand Ice Cream, a subsidiary of Dreyer's Grand Ice Cream, resulting from the transfer of production to the Company's new manufacturing facility in St. Albans, Vermont. During 1995 approximately 16% of the packaged pints manufactured by the Company were produced by Edy's, compared to 40% in 1994.

Cost of sales in 1994 increased approximately $9.6 million, or 9.5% over the same period in 1993 and overall gross profit as a percentage of net sales decreased from 28.6% in 1993 to 26.2% in 1994. Overall gross profit in 1994 was impacted by inventory management problems and production inefficiencies, as well as by 1994 start-up costs associated with certain flavors of the new "Smooth, No Chunks!™" ice cream line in packaged pints. The significant increase in the number and complexity of some of the pint flavors being produced requires a higher level of production planning, purchasing, inventory management, and operational systems than were then in place in the Company.

During 1994 the lower gross profit as a percentage of sales also reflected higher manufacturing costs due to more product being produced for the Company by Edy's, with approximately 40% of the packaged pints manufactured by the Company produced by Edy's in 1994 as compared to 37% in 1993.

Selling, General & Administrative Expenses

Selling, general and administrative expenses increased 0.3% to $36.4 million in 1995 from $36.3 million in 1994 but decreased as a percentage of net sales to 23.4% in 1995 from 24.4% in 1994. This increase in dollar spending primarily reflects strengthening of the Company's infrastructure in order to prepare for increased growth, offset by the lower level of marketing and sales spending compared to 1994, when the launch of the new "Smooth, No Chunks!™" line occurred.

Selling, general and administrative expenses had increased 28% to $36.3 million in 1994 from $28.3 million in 1993 and increased as a percentage of net sales to 24.4% in 1994 from 20.2% in 1993. This increase was due principally to increased marketing and selling expenses including higher than anticipated coupon redemption expenses associated with promoting the then new "Smooth, No Chunks!™" line as well as the Company's taking over the distribution arrangements to the smaller classes of trade in the New York market, and one-time costs asso-

ciated with changes in distribution arrangements in the United Kingdom.

Asset Write-Down

1994 results included a pretax charge of $6.8 million, representing a write-down of certain assets of the Company's new St. Albans, Vermont plant, including a portion of the previously incurred capitalized interest and project management costs. The impact of this charge on both the 1994 fourth quarter and full year 1994 results was $4.1 million or $0.57 per share. Following substantial delays with the implementation and completion of certain automated handling processes and refrigeration hardening equipment of the new plant and after receipt of a report from an outside engineering firm experienced in the refrigerated food industry, the Company decided to replace certain of the software and equipment installed at the new plant.

The Company began manufacturing at the new St. Albans plant in March 1995, utilizing a temporary set-up on one production line. The two currently planned manufacturing lines were fully operational in December 1995 and it is expected that the rate of production on these lines will be increased in 1996.

Other Income (Expense)

Interest income increased $0.6 million during 1995 compared to 1994. This increase was primarily due to higher interest rates on investments. Interest expense increased $1.2 million in 1995 compared to 1994. This increase was due primarily to the capitalization of interest in the prior year as part of the cost of the new plant in St. Albans, Vermont as compared with capitalization of only a small amount of interest in 1995 before the plant became operational.

Interest income increased $0.3 million during 1994 compared to 1993 reflecting interest earned on investments. Interest expense increased $0.2 million reflecting the issuance of the $30 million Series A and B Notes bearing interest at a weighted average rate of 5.84%. Interest expense was

reduced during 1994 by capitalization of interest as part of the cost of the new plant.

Income Taxes

The Company's effective income tax rate increased from (50.3%) in 1994 to 36.8% in 1995 primarily reflecting the profit in 1995, as compared to the loss in 1994, combined with lower income tax credits and tax-exempt interest income in 1995 as compared to 1994. In 1993, the Company's effective income tax rate was 40.2% reflecting lower income tax credits and tax-exempt interest income. Management expects 1996's effective income tax rate to increase to approximately 38%.

Net Income

As a result of the foregoing, net income increased $7.8 million to $5.9 million in 1995 compared to a net loss of $1.9 million in 1994, and net income of $7.2 million in 1993. Net income (loss) as a percentage of net sales was 3.8% in 1995, (1.3%) in 1994 and 5.1% in 1993.

Seasonality

The Company typically experiences more demand for its products during the summer than during the winter.

Inflation

Inflation has not had a material effect on the Company's business to date. Management believes that the effects of inflation and changing prices were successfully managed in 1995, with both margins and earnings being protected through a combination of pricing adjustments, cost control programs and productivity gains.

Liquidity & Capital Resources

The Company's working capital at December 30, 1995 was approximately $51.0 million as compared to $37.5 million at December 31, 1994. This $13.5 million increase was primarily due to increases of $14.6 million in cash and cash equivalents.

Net cash provided by operations in 1995 was approximately $15.9 million. Approximately $7.5 million was used for net additions to property, plant and equipment, primarily for the new plant in St. Albans, Vermont that began production in 1995. At December 30, 1995 cash and cash equivalents were $35.4 million.

Inventories have decreased slightly since the end of December 1994 from $13.5 million to $12.6 million at December 30, 1995. Accounts receivable has increased $1.8 million since December 31, 1994 from $9.9 million to $11.7 million at December 30, 1995. This increase is due to increased sales for the month of December, 1995 as compared with December, 1994 as well as increased international sales which have a longer collection cycle than domestic sales.

During the second quarter of 1989, the Company entered into a manufacturing and warehouse agreement with Edy's Grand Ice Cream, a subsidiary of Dreyer's Grand Ice Cream, Inc., to manufacture product at Edy's plant in Fort Wayne, Indiana in accordance with specifications and quality control provided by the Company and using dairy products from Vermont. This agreement expired in September 1995. This agreement assisted the Company in meeting its demand prior to and during the construction period of the Company's new plant in St. Albans, Vermont. Because per unit manufacturing costs were higher under this agreement than at the Company's plants, this agreement had an adverse impact on the Company's gross profit as a percentage of net sales throughout its term.

In October 1992, the Company began construction of a new third plant in St. Albans, Vermont. At December 30, 1995, the Company has spent approximately $38.2 million to date, net of the 1994 $6.8 million write-down of certain assets, on building and equipping the new plant ($6.2 million in 1995 of which $1.2 million was transferred from the temporary facility at the St. Albans Cooperative) and anticipates additional capital costs for the St. Albans plant of approximately $1.9 million in 1996. The cost of building and equipping the new plant, net of the 1994 $6.8 million write-down of certain assets is currently estimated to be approximately $40.1 million.

In addition to the $6.2 million construction expenditures for the new plant, other capital expenditures in 1995 totaled $2.5 million. These projects included equipment upgrades at the Waterbury and Springfield plants.

In addition to $1.9 million of capital expenditures to complete the new plant at St. Albans, the Company anticipates other capital expenditures in 1996 of approximately $10.6 million. Substantially all of these additional projected capital expenditures relate to equipment upgrades in Waterbury and Springfield, leasehold improvements at the Company's headquarters offices in South Burlington, Vermont, and computer-related expenditures, with a small proportion for equipment enhancements at the St. Albans plant.

The Company's long-term debt includes $30 million aggregate principal amount of Senior Notes issued in 1993 and 1994, which are held in cash equivalents pending their use in the business.

On December 29, 1995, the Company extended two line of credit agreements, for an aggregate of $20 million, with The First National Bank of Boston and Key Bank of Vermont. These are unsecured agreements providing for borrowings from time to time, expiring September 29, 1998 and December 29, 1998, respectively. The agreements specify interest at either the banks' Base Rate or the Eurodollar rate plus a maximum of 1.25%. As of March 28,1996 there have been no borrowings under these lines of credit.

Management believes that internally generated funds, cash currently on hand, investments held in cash equivalents (pending their use in the business), and equipment lease financing and/or borrowings under the Company's two unsecured bank lines of credit will be adequate to meet anticipated operating and capital requirements.

Forward-Looking Statements

This section, as well as other portions of this document, includes certain forward-looking statements about the

Company's business and new products, sales and expenses, effective tax rate, and operating and capital requirements. In addition, forward-looking statements may be included in various other Company documents to be issued in the future and in various oral statements by Company representatives to security analysts and investors from time to time. Any such statements are subject to risks that could cause the actual results or needs to vary materially. These risks are discussed below in "Risk Factors" in this document.

Risk Factors
Dependence on Independent Ice Cream Distributors

The Company is dependent on maintaining satisfactory relationships with independent ice cream distributors that now generally ac⁺ ⁻ the Company's exclusive or mast⸱ distributor in their assigned territories. While the Company believes its relationships with Dreyer's and its other distributors generally have been satisfactory and have been instrumental in the Company's growth, the Company has at times experienced difficulty in maintaining such relationships. Available distribution alternatives are limited. Accordingly, there can be no assurance that difficulties in maintaining relationships with distributors, which may be related to actions by the Company's competitors or by one or more of the Company's distributors themselves (or their controlling persons), will not have a material adverse effect on the Company's business. The loss of one or more of the Company's principal distributors or termination of one or more of the related distribution agreements could have a material adverse effect on the Company's business.

Growth in Sales and Earnings

In 1995, net sales of the Company increased 4.4% to $155 million from $149 million in 1994. Pint volume decreased 1.5% compared to 1994. The Company believes this decrease is consistent with the recent performance in the super premium category overall excluding sorbet, which contributed more growth than the total increase in the super premium category from 1994 to 1995. Given these overall domestic super premium industry trends, the successful introduction of innovative flavors on a periodic basis has become increasingly important to any sales growth by the Company. Accordingly, the future degree of market acceptance of the Company's Sorbet line, which is being introduced February through May 1996, and which will be accompanied by a significant increase in promotional expenditures, is likely to have an important impact on the Company's 1996 and future financial results.

Competitive Environment

The super premium frozen dessert market is highly competitive with the distinctions between the super premium category, and the "adjoining" premium category less marked than in the past and with the domestic super premium frozen dessert category showing a recent decline in industry sales, except for sorbet. And, as noted above, the ability to successfully introduce innovative flavors on a periodic basis that are accepted by the marketplace is a significant competitive factor. In addition, the Company's principal competitors are large, diversified companies with resources significantly greater than the Company's. The Company expects strong competition to continue, including competition for adequate distribution and competition for the limited shelf space for the frozen dessert category in supermarkets and other retail food outlets.

Reliance on a Limited Number of Key Personnel

The success of the Company is significantly dependent on the services of Robert Holland, Jr., the Chief Executive Officer and a limited number of executive managers working under Mr. Holland, as well as certain continued services of Ben Cohen, the Chairperson of the Board and co-founder of the Company; and Jerry Greenfield, Vice Chairperson and co-founder of the Company. Loss of the services of any of these persons could have a material adverse effect on the Company's business.

The Company's Social Mission

The Company's basic business philosophy is embodied in a three-part "mission statement," which includes a "social mission" to "operate the Company...[to] improve the quality of life of our employees and a broad community: local, national and international." The Company believes that implementation of its social mission, which is integrated into the Company's business, has been beneficial to the Company's overall financial performance. However, it is possible that at some future date the amount of the Company's energies and resources devoted to its social mission could have a material adverse financial effect on the Company's business.

Control of the Company

The Company has two classes of common stock - the Class A Common Stock, entitled to one vote per share, and the Class B Common Stock, entitled, except to the extent otherwise provided by law, to ten votes per share. Ben Cohen, Jerry Greenfield, Fred Lager and Jeffrey Furman (collectively, the "Principal Stockholders") hold shares representing 48.0% of the aggregate voting power in elections for directors, permitting them as a practical matter to elect all members of the Board of Directors and thereby effectively control the business, policies and management of the Company. Because of their significant holdings of Class B Common Stock, the Principal Stockholders may continue to exercise this control even if they were to sell substantial portions of their Class A Common Stock.

In addition, the Company has issued all of the Class A Preferred Stock to the Foundation. All current directors of the Foundation are directors and/or employees of the Company. The Preferred Stock gives the Foundation a special class voting right to act with respect to certain Business Combinations (as defined in the Company's charter) and effectively limits the voting rights that holders of the Class A Common Stock and Class B Common Stock, the owners of virtually all of the equity in the Company, would otherwise have with respect to such Business Combinations.

While the Board of Directors believes that the Class B Common Stock and the Preferred Stock are important elements in keeping Ben & Jerry's an independent Vermont-based business, the Class B Common Stock and the Preferred Stock may be deemed to be "anti-takeover" devices (and thus may be deemed to have the potential for adverse consequences on the business) in that the Board of Directors believes the existence of these securities will make it difficult for a third party to acquire control of the Company on terms opposed by the holders of the Class B Common Stock, including primarily the Principal Stockholders, or the Foundation, or for incumbent management and the Board of Directors to be removed.

International

The Company's principal competitors have substantial market shares in various countries outside the United States, principally Europe and Japan. The Company has limited international sales to date but is investigating the possibility of international expansion. However, there can be no assurance that the Company will be successful in entering, on a long-term profitable basis, such international markets as it selects.

Consolidated Balance Sheets

(In thousands except share data)

	December 30, 1995	December 31, 1994
Assets		
Current assets:		
Cash and cash equivalents	$ 35,406	$ 20,778
Accounts receivable		
Trade (less allowance of $802 in 1995 and $504 in 1994		
for doubtful accounts)	11,660	9,902
Other	854	2,003
Inventories	12,616	13,463
Deferred income taxes	3,599	3,146
Income taxes receivable	2,831	2,098
Prepaid expenses	1,097	534
Total current assets	68,063	51,924
Property, plant and equipment, net	59,600	57,981
Investments	1,000	8,000
Other assets	2,411	2,391
	$ 131,074	$ 120,296
Liabilities & Stockholders' Equity		
Current liabilities:		
Accounts payable and accrued expenses	$ 16,592	$ 13,915
Current portion of long-term debt and		
capital lease obligations	448	553
Total current liabilities	17,040	14,468
Long-term debt and capital lease obligations	31,977	32,419
Deferred income taxes	3,526	907
Commitments and contingencies		
Stockholders' equity:		
$1.20 noncumulative Class A preferred stock -		
$1.00 par value, redeemable at the Company's option		
at $12.00 per share; 900 shares authorized,		
issued and outstanding, aggregate preference		
on voluntary or involuntary liquidation - $9	1	1
Class A common stock - $.033 par value; authorized		
20,000,000 shares; issued: 6,330,302 shares at		
December 30, 1995 and 6,290,580 shares at		
December 31, 1994	209	208
Class B common stock - $.033 par value; authorized		
3,000,000 shares; issued: 914,325 shares at		
December 30, 1995 and 932,448 shares at		
December 31, 1994	30	31
Additional paid-in capital	48,521	48,366
Retained earnings	31,264	25,316
Cumulative translation adjustment	(114)	
Treasury stock, at cost: 67,032 Class A and 1,092		
Class B shares at December 30, 1995 and 69,032		
Class A and 1,092 Class B shares at		
December 31, 1994	(1,380)	(1,420)
Total stockholders' equity	78,531	72,502
	$ 131,074	$ 120,296

See accompanying notes.

Consolidated Statements of Operations

(In thousands except per share data)

	Dec. 30, 1995	Years Ended Dec. 31, 1994	Dec. 25, 1993
Net sales	$ 155,333	$ 148,802	$ 140,328
Cost of sales	109,125	109,760	100,210
Gross profit	46,208	39,042	40,118
Selling, general and administrative expenses	36,362	36,253	28,270
Asset write-down		6,779	
Other income (expense):			
Interest income	1,681	1,034	757
Interest expense	(1,525)	(295)	(104)
Other	(597)	(511)	(456)
	(441)	228	197
Income (loss) before income taxes	9,405	(3,762)	12,045
Income tax expense (benefit)	3,457	(1,893)	4,844
Net income (loss)	$ 5,948	$ (1,869)	$ 7,201
Net income (loss) per common share	$ 0.83	$ (0.26)	$ 1.01
Weighted average common and common equivalent shares outstanding.	7,222	7,148	7,138

See accompanying notes.

Consolidated Statements of

(In thousands except share data)

	Preferred Stock Par Value	Common Stock		Additional Paid-in Capital
		Class A Par Value	Class B Par Value	
Balance at December 26, 1992	$1	$ 206	$ 33	$47,941
Net income				
Common stock issued under stock purchase plan (12,826 Class A shares)				280
Common stock issued under restricted stock plan (100 Class A shares)				1
Conversion of Class B shares to Class A shares (14,371 shares)		1	(1)	
Amortization of unearned compensation				
Balance at December 25, 1993	1	207	32	48,222
Net income (loss)				
Common stock issued under stock purchase plan (8,619 Class A shares)				139
Conversion of Class B shares to Class A shares (15,189 shares)		1	(1)	
Termination of stock award (Class A shares)				5
Balance at December 31, 1994	1	208	31	48,366
Net income				
Common stock issued under stock purchase plan (21,599 Class A shares)				174
Conversion of Class B shares to Class A shares (18,123 shares)		1	(1)	
Common stock issued under restricted stock plan (2,000 Class A shares)				(19)
Foreign currency translation adjustment				
Balance at December 30, 1995	$1	$ 209	$30	$ 48,521

See accompanying notes.

Stockholders' Equity

Retained Earnings	Unearned Compensation	Cumulative Translation Adjustment	Treasury Stock Class A Cost	Class B Cost
$19,984	$ (38)	$0	$(1,362)	$(5)
7,201				
			2	
	18			
27,185	(20)	0	(1,360)	(5)
(1,869)				
	20		(55)	
25,316	0	0	(1,415)	(5)
5,948				
			40	
		(114)		
$ 31,264	$0	$ (114)	$ (1,375)	$(5)

Consolidated Statements of Cash Flows

(In thousands)

	December 30, 1995	Years Ended December 31, 1994	December 25, 1993
Cash flows from operating activities:			
Net income (loss)	$ 5,948	$ (1,869)	$ 7,201
Adjustments to reconcile net income (loss) to net cash provided by operating activities:			
Depreciation and amortization	5,928	4,707	4,303
Deferred income taxes	2,166	(1,564)	(264)
Provision for doubtful accounts	400	311	58
Amortization of unearned compensation			18
Loss on asset write-down		6,779	
Loss (gain) on disposition of assets	171	69	(10)
Stock awards	21		3
Changes in assets and liabilities			
Accounts receivable	(1,009)	(536)	(2,888)
Income taxes receivable/payable	(733)	(2,442)	650
Inventories	847	(10)	3,637
Prepaid expenses and other assets	(563)	313	(639)
Accounts payable and accrued expenses	2,677	(1,159)	(4,790)
Net cash provided by operating activities	15,853	4,599	7,279
Cash flows from investing activities:			
Additions to property, plant and equipment	(7,532)	(26,213)	(17,796)
Proceeds from sale of property, plant and equipment	96	194	48
Decrease in investments	7,000	14,000	3,200
Changes in other assets	(303)	(882)	(57)
Net cash used for investing activities	(739)	(12,901)	(14,605)
Cash flows from financing activities:			
Net proceeds from long-term debt		14,936	15,145
Repayments of long-term debt and capital leases	(547)	(700)	(751)
Net proceeds from issuance of common stock	174	139	281
Net cash (used for) provided by financing activities	(373)	14,375	14,675
Effect of exchange rate changes on cash	(113)		
Increase in cash and cash equivalents	14,628	6,073	7,349
Cash and cash equivalents at beginning of year	20,778	14,705	7,356
Cash and cash equivalents at end of year	$ 35,406	$ 20,778	$ 14,705

See accompanying notes.

Notes to Consolidated Financial Statements

1. Significant Accounting Policies

Business

Ben & Jerry's Homemade, Inc. (the Company) makes and sells super premium ice cream and other frozen dessert products through distributors and directly to retail outlets, including Company-owned and franchised ice cream scoop shops.

Principles of Consolidation

The consolidated financial statements include the accounts of the Company and all its wholly-owned subsidiaries. Intercompany accounts and transactions have been eliminated.

Use of Estimates

The preparation of the financial statements in accordance with generally accepted accounting principles requires management to make estimates and assumptions that affect the amounts reported in the financial statements and accompanying notes. Actual results could differ from those estimates.

Fiscal Year

The Company's fiscal year is a fifty-two or fifty-three week period ending on the last Saturday in December. 1995 was fifty-two weeks, 1994 was fifty-three weeks and 1993 was fifty-two weeks. The effect of the additional week on 1994's results of operations was not material.

Inventories

Inventories are stated at the lower of cost or market. Cost is determined by the first-in, first-out method.

Cash Equivalents

Cash equivalents represent highly liquid investments with maturities of three months or less at date of purchase.

Investments

Management determines the appropriate classification of debt securities at the time of purchase and reevaluates such designation as of each balance sheet date. Marketable equity securities and debt securities not classified as held-to-maturity are classified as available-for-sale. Available-for-sale securities are carried at fair value, with the unrealized gains and losses, net of tax, reported in a separate component of shareholders' equity. The amortized cost of debt securities in this category is adjusted for amortization of premiums and accretion of discounts to maturity. Such amortization is included in interest income. Realized gains and losses and declines in value judged to be other-than-temporary on available-for-sale securities are included in income. The cost of securities sold is based on the specific identification method. Interest and dividends on securities classified as available-for-sale are included in investment income.

Concentration of Credit Risk

Financial instruments, which potentially subject the Company to significant concentration of credit risk, consist of cash, investments and trade accounts receivable. The Company places its investments in highly rated financial institutions around the country, obligations of the United States Government and investment grade short-term instruments. No more than 20% of the total investment portfolio shall be in any one issuer or guarantor other than United States Government instruments which limits the amount of credit exposure. The Company sells its products primarily to well established frozen dessert distribution companies throughout the United States and the United Kingdom. The Company performs ongoing credit evaluations of its customers and maintains reserves for potential credit losses. Historically,

the Company has not experienced significant losses related to investments or trade receivables.

Property, Plant & Equipment

Property, plant and equipment are carried at cost. Depreciation, including amortization of leasehold improvements, is computed using the straight-line method over the estimated useful lives of the related assets. Amortization of assets under capital leases is computed on the straight-line method over the lease term and is included in depreciation expense.

Translation of Foreign Currencies

Assets and liabilities of the Company's foreign operations are translated into United States dollars at exchange rates in effect on the balance sheet date. Income and expense items are translated at average exchange rates prevailing during the year. Translation adjustments are accumulated as a separate component of stockholders' equity. Transaction gains or losses are recognized as other income or expense in the period incurred. Transaction gains or losses have been immaterial for all periods presented.

Revenue Recognition

The Company recognizes revenue and the related costs when product is shipped. The Company recognizes franchise fees as income for individual stores when services required by the franchise agreement have been substantially performed and the store opens for business. Franchise fees relating to area franchise agreements are recognized in proportion to the number of stores for which the required services have been substantially performed. Franchise fees recognized as income were approximately $166,000, $82,000 and

$103,000 in 1995, 1994 and 1993, respectively. These amounts have been included in net sales.

Advertising

Advertising costs are expensed as incurred. Advertising expense (excluding cooperative advertising with distribution companies) amounted to approximately $4.3 million, $5.0 million, and $1.6 million for the years ended December 30, 1995, December 31, 1994 and December 25, 1993.

Income Taxes

The Company accounts for income taxes under the liability method in accordance with Statement of Financial Accounting Standards No. 109, "Accounting for Income Taxes" (SFAS 109). Under the liability method, deferred tax liabilities and assets are recognized for the tax consequences of temporary differences between the financial reporting and tax bases of assets and liabilities.

Stock Based Compensation

The Company grants stock options for a fixed number of shares with an exercise price equal to the fair value of the shares at the date of the grant. The Company accounts for stock option grants in accordance with APB Opinion No. 25, "Accounting for Stock Issued to Employees" and intends to continue to do so. Accordingly, no compensation expense for stock option grants is recognized.

Earnings Per Share

Primary earnings per common share is computed based on the weighted average number of shares of Class A and Class B Common Stock outstanding during the period, and for incremental shares assumed issued for dilutive common stock equivalents. Fully diluted earnings per share did not differ materially from primary earnings per share.

Impact of Recently Issued Accounting Standards

In March 1995, the FASB issued Statement No. 121, "Accounting for the Impairment of Long-Lived Assets and for Long-Lived Assets to Be Disposed Of" which requires impairment losses to be recorded on long-lived assets used in operations when indicators of impairment are present and the undiscounted cash flows estimated to be generated by those assets are less than the assets' carrying amount. Statement 121 also addresses the accounting for long-lived assets that are expected to be disposed of. The Company will adopt Statement 121 in the first quarter of 1996 and, based on current circumstances, does not believe the effect of the adoption will be material.

(Dollars in tables in thousands except share data)

2. Inventories

	1995	1994
Ice cream and ingredients	$ 11,480	$12,395
Paper goods	674	486
Food, beverages, and gift items	462	582
	$12,616	$13,463

The Company purchases certain ingredients (approximately $1,500,000 annually) from a company owned by the Company's Chairperson and a member of the Board of Directors.

3. Property, Plant & Equipment

	1995	1994	Estimated Useful Lives/ Lease Term
Land and improvements	$3,575	$2,456	15-25 years
Land under capital lease	866	866	
Buildings	35,644	13,234	25 years
Equipment and furniture	41,324	26,771	3-20 years
Equipment under capital lease	934	934	5 years
Leasehold improvements	1,277	2,002	3-10 years
Construction in progress	740	32,269	
	84,360	78,532	
Less accumulated depreciation	24,760	20,551	
	$59,600	$57,981	

Accumulated depreciation at December 30, 1995 and December 31, 1994, included accumulated amortization of $902,000 and $874,000 respectively, related to assets under capital lease.

4. Cash & Investments

In May 1993, the Financial Accounting Standards Board issued Statement of Financial Accounting Standards No. 115, "Accounting for Certain Investments in Debt and Equity Securities." As required under the Statement, the Company adopted the provisions of the new standards as of the beginning of 1994. In accordance with the Statement, prior period financial statements have not been restated to reflect the change in accounting principle. The cumulative effect of adopting Statement 115 did not have a material effect on the Company's financial statements.

The Company's cash and investments in debt securities available-for-sale are carried at fair value, which approximates cost, as summarized below:

	1995	1994
Municipal bonds	$16,507	$9,003
U.S. corporate securities	14,139	10,000
Total debt securities available-for-sale	30,646	19,003
Cash, cash equivalents and money market accounts	5,760	9,775
Total cash, cash equivalents and investments	$36,406	$28,778

All debt securities at December 30, 1995 have maturities of less than twelve months. Certain debt securities have been classified as long-term to reflect their intended use to finance capital projects.

Investments in debt securities mature at par in thirty to forty-five day intervals, at which time the stated interest rates are reset at the then market rate. Gross purchases and maturities aggregated $94,500,000 and $83,525,000 in 1995, and $81,400,000 and $91,960,000 respectively in 1994.

(Dollars in tables in thousands except share data)

5. Accounts Payable & Accrued Expenses

	1995	1994
Trade accounts payable	$7,283	$5,075
Accrued expenses	6,071	2,627
Accrued construction costs	51	2,975
Accrued payroll and related costs	1,749	1,607
Accrued promotional costs	1,313	1,580
Other	125	51
	$16,592	$13,915

6. Long-Term Debt & Capital Lease Obligations

	1995	1994
Senior Notes - Series A payable in annual installments beginning in 1998 through 2003 with interest payable semiannually at 5.9%	$20,000	$20,000
Senior Notes - Series B payable in annual installments beginning in 1998 through 2003 with interest payable semiannually at 5.73%	10,000	10,000
Industrial Revenue Bonds (IRB), payable in monthly installments of $12,500 plus interest at 75% of the prime rate (6.375% at December 30, 1995 and 6.375% at December 31, 1994) through June 2000	613	766
Urban Development Action Grant, payable in quarterly installments of $22,130 including interest at 9% through April 2000	310	367
Capital lease obligations	771	827
Other long-term obligations	731	1,012
	32,425	32,972
Less current portion	448	553
	$31,977	$32,419

Property, plant and equipment having a net book value of approximately $18,872,000 at December 30, 1995 is pledged as collateral for certain long-term debt.

Long-term debt & capital lease obligations at December 30, 1995 maturing in each of the next five years and thereafter are as follows:

	Capital lease obligations	Long-term debt
1996	$ 114	$ 382
1997	581	343
1998	15	5,411
1999	15	5,295
2000	15	5,229
Thereafter	245	14,994
Total minimum payments	985	31,654
Less amounts representing interest	214	
Present value of minimum payments	$ 771	$ 31,654

Interest of approximately $497,000, $1,288,000 and $295,000 was capitalized in 1995, 1994 and 1993, respectively, as part of the acquisition cost of property, plant and equipment. Interest paid, including interest capitalized, amounted to $2,023,000, $1,755,000 and $239,000 for 1995, 1994 and 1993, respectively.

(Dollars in tables in thousands except share data)

The Company has available two $10,000,000 unsecured working capital line of credit agreements with two banks. Interest on borrowings under the agreements is set at the banks' Base Rate or at the Eurodollar Rate plus a maximum of up to 1.25%. The agreements expire December 29, 1998 and September 29, 1998, respectively, and any outstanding borrowings are due at that time. No amounts were borrowed under these or any prior bank agreements during 1995, 1994, and 1993.

Certain of the debt agreements contain certain restrictive covenants requiring maintenance of minimum levels of working capital, net worth and debt to capitalization ratios. As of December 30, 1995 the Company was in compliance with the provisions of these agreements. Under the most restrictive of these covenants requiring maintenance of a minimum consolidated tangible net worth of $55,000,000, approximately $23,000,000 of retained earnings at December 30, 1995 was available for payment of dividends.

7. Income Taxes

The provision (benefit) for income taxes consists of the following:

	1995	1994	1993
Federal:			
Current	$ 873	$ (314)	$ 4,086
Deferred	1,695	(1,263)	(211)
	2,568	(1,577)	3,875
State:			
Current	418	(15)	1,022
Deferred	471	(301)	(53)
	889	(316)	969
	$ 3,457	$ (1,893)	$ 4,844

Income taxes computed at the federal statutory rate differ from amounts provided as follows:

	1995	1994	1993
Tax at statutory rate	34.0%	(34.0)%	35.0%
State tax, less federal tax effect	4.5	(5.6)	5.3
Income tax credits	(2.9)	(6.7)	
Municipal bond interest	(1.1)	(5.0)	(1.8)
Other, net	2.3	1.0	1.7
Provision (benefit) for income taxes	36.8%	(50.3)%	40.2%

Deferred income taxes reflect the net tax effects of temporary differences between the carrying amounts of assets and liabilities for financial reporting purposes and the amounts used for income tax purposes and are attributable to the following:

	1995	1994
Deferred tax assets:		
Accrued liabilities	$1,514	$2,057
Inventories	1,106	703
Accounts receivable	386	254
Other	695	245
Total deferred tax assets	3,701	3,259
Deferred tax liabilities:		
Depreciation	3,628	1,003
Other		17
Total deferred tax liabilities	3,628	1,020
Net deferred tax assets	$ 73	$2,239

Income taxes paid amounted to $1,918,000, $2,111,000 and $4,477,000 during 1995, 1994 and 1993, respectively.

(Dollars in tables in thousands except share data)

8. The Ben & Jerry's Foundation, Inc.

In October 1985, the Company issued Class A Preferred Stock to The Ben & Jerry's Foundation, Inc. (the Foundation), a non-profit corporation qualified under section 501(c)(3) of the Internal Revenue Code. The primary purpose of the Foundation is to be a principal recipient of cash contributions from the Company which are then donated to various community organizations and other charitable institutions. Amounts expensed for contributions to the Foundation and directly to other charitable organizations, at the rate of approximately 7.5% of income before income taxes amounted to approximately $768,000 and $977,000 for 1995 and 1993, respectively. In 1994 there were no amounts expensed for contributions to the Foundation.

The Preferred Stock is entitled to vote as a separate class in certain business combinations, such that approval of two-thirds of the class is required for such business combinations. Two directors, including one of the founders of the Company, are members of the Board of Directors of the Foundation.

9. Stock Plans

The Company maintains an Employee Stock Purchase Plan which authorizes the issuance of up to 300,000 shares of common stock. All employees with six months of continuous service are eligible to participate in this plan. Participants in the plan are entitled to purchase Class A Common Stock during specified semi-annual periods through the accumulation of payroll, at the lower of 85% of market value of the stock at the beginning or end of the offering period. At December 30, 1995, 96,664 shares had been issued under the plan and 203,336 shares were available for future issuance.

The Company maintains two Stock Option Plans:

The 1985 Option Plan provides for the grant of incentive and non-incentive stock options to employees or consultants. The 1985 Option Plan provides that options granted are exercisable at the market value on the date of grant. On March 31, 1994 stock options were granted under the Plan to approximately 500 employees across all levels of the Company. Additional options were granted under the Plan during 1995. While the Company may grant options which may become exercisable at different times or within different periods, the Company has generally granted options to employees of which 50% vest at two years from the date of grant and 100% vest within four years. At December 30, 1995, no shares of Class A Common Stock were available under the 1985 Option Plan for additional grants as the plan had expired.

	Number of Options	Option Price Per Share		
A summary of the 1985 Option Plan activity is as follows:				
Outstanding at December 25, 1993	0	$ 0.00	-	$ 0.00
Granted	177,927	16.75	-	16.75
Exercised	0	0.00	-	0.00
Forfeited	(15,619)	16.75	-	16.75
Outstanding at December 31, 1994	162,308	16.75	-	16.75
Granted	215,000	10.63	-	14.00
Exercised	0	0.00	-	0.00
Forfeited	(19,871)	16.75	-	16.75
Outstanding at December 30, 1995	357,437	$ 10.63	-	$ 16.75
Options vested at December 30, 1995	25,000	$ 10.63	-	$ 10.81

The 1995 Equity Incentive Plan provides for the grant to employees and consultants of incentive and non-incentive stock options, stock appreciation rights, restricted stock, unrestricted stock awards, deferred stock awards, cash or stock performance awards, loans or supplemental grants, or combinations thereof. At December 30, 1995, 475,000 shares of Class A Common Stock were available under the 1995 Equity Incentive Plan for additional grants.

	Number of Options	Option Price Per Share		
A summary of the 1995 Equity Incentive Plan activity is as follows:				
Outstanding at December 31, 1994	0	$ 0.00	-	$ 0.00
Granted	25,000	19.00	-	19.00
Exercised	0	0.00	-	0.00
Forfeited	0	0.00	-	0.00
Outstanding at December 30, 1995	25,000	$ 19.00	-	$ 19.00
Options vested at December 30, 1995	0	$ 0.00	-	$ 0.00

(Dollars in tables in thousands except share data)

The Company has three restricted stock plans (the 1986, 1991, and 1992 Plans) which provide that employees, consultants or non-employee directors, on becoming eligible, may be awarded shares of Class A Common Stock by the Compensation Committee of the Board of Directors. Shares issued under the plans become vested over periods of up to five years. The Company has also adopted the 1995 Plan, which provides that non-employee directors can elect to receive stock in lieu of a Director's cash retainer. These shares are vested immediately. At December 30, 1995, a total of 71,000 shares had been awarded under these plans, of which 57,955 were fully vested and 13,045 had been forfeited. 33,000 shares were available for future awards. No further shares may be awarded under the 1986 or 1991 Plans. Restricted shares may also be issued under the 1995 Equity Incentive Plan. Unearned compensation on unvested shares is recorded as of the award date and is amortized over the vesting period.

As of December 30, 1995, a total of 711,336 shares are reserved for future grant under all of the Company's stock plans.

10. Employee Benefit Plans

The Company maintains profit sharing and savings plans for all eligible employees. Contributions to the profit sharing plan are allocated among all current full-time and regular part-time employees (other than the Co-founders, CEO and the Senior Director of Operations) based upon length of service with the Company. The profit sharing plan is informal and discretionary. The savings plan is maintained in accordance with the provisions of Section 401(k) of the Internal Revenue Code and allows all employees with at least twelve months of service to make annual tax-deferred voluntary contributions up to fifteen percent of their salary. The Company may match the contribution up to two percent of the employee's gross annual salary. Total contributions by the Company to the profit sharing and savings plans were approximately $769,000, $508,000 and $894,000 for 1995, 1994 and 1993, respectively.

11. Common Stock

In June 1987, the Company's shareholders adopted an amendment to the Company's Articles of Association that authorized 3,000,000 shares of a new Class B Common Stock and redesignated the Company's existing Common Stock as Class A Common Stock. The Class B Common Stock has 10 votes per share on all matters, is generally non-transferable and is convertible into Class A Common Stock on a one-for-one basis.

12. Write-Down of Assets in 1994

In 1994, following substantial delays with the implementation and completion of certain automated handling processes and refrigeration hardening equipment of the Company's St. Albans, Vermont plant and after receipt of a report from an outside engineering firm experienced in the refrigerated food industry, the Company decided to replace certain of the software and equipment installed at the new plant. The loss from the write-down of the related assets (including a portion of the previously incurred capitalized interest and project management costs), recorded in the Company's fourth quarter, amounted to $6,779,000 (approximately $4.1 million after tax or $0.57 per share). Of this amount, $3,804,000 was offset against the balance in construction in progress while $2,975,000 was accrued for additional anticipated costs, which were paid during 1995.

13. Legal Matters

On December 14, 1995, the Company was served with a class action complaint filed in federal court in Burlington, Vermont. The complaint, captioned *Henry G. Jakobe, Jr. v. Ben & Jerry's Inc., et al.*, was filed by a Ben & Jerry's shareholder on behalf of himself and purportedly on behalf of all other Ben & Jerry's shareholders who purchased the common stock of the Company during the period from March 25, 1994 through December 19, 1994. Plaintiff alleges that the Company violated the federal securities laws by making, in 1994, untrue statements of material facts and omitting to state material facts primarily concerning the Company's construction and start-up of its new manufacturing facility in St. Albans, Vermont. Also named as defendants in the Complaint are certain present and former officers and directors of the Company, Ben Cohen, Chairperson of the Board; Jerry Greenfield, Vice Chairperson of the Board; Frances Rathke, Chief Financial Officer; and Charles Lacy, former President. Plaintiff is seeking an unspecified amount of monetary damages.

While this action is in its preliminary stages management believes, based on an initial review, the allegations made in the lawsuit are without merit and the Company intends to defend the lawsuit vigorously.

14. Commitments

The Company leases certain property and equipment under operating leases. Minimum payments for operating leases having initial or remaining noncancelable terms in excess of one year are as follows:

Year	Amount
1996	$454
1997	316
1998	206
1999	131
2000	37

Rent expense for operating leases amounted to approximately $662,000, $516,000 and $425,000 in 1995, 1994 and 1993, respectively.

15. Significant Customers

The Company's most significant customer, Dreyer's Grand Ice Cream, Inc., accounted for 44%, 49% or 54% of net sales in 1995, 1994 and 1993, respectively.

(Dollars in tables in thousands except share data)

16. Fair Value of Financial Instruments

The following methods and assumptions were used by the Company in estimating its fair value disclosures for financial instruments:

Cash and cash equivalents: The carrying amount reported in the balance sheet for cash and cash equivalents approximates its fair value.

Investments: The fair values for marketable securities are based on quoted market prices.

Long and short-term debt: The fair values of the Company's long-term debt are estimated using discounted cash flow analyses, based on the Company's current incremental borrowing rates for similar types of borrowing arrangements.

The carrying amounts and fair values of the Company's financial instruments are as follows:

	1995		1994	
	Carrying Amount	Fair Value	Carrying Amount	Fair Value
Cash & cash equivalents	$35,406	$35,406	$20,778	$20,778
Investments	1,000	1,000	8,000	8,000
Long-term debt	(32,425)	(29,815)	(32,972)	(29,917)

17. Selected Quarterly Financial Information (Unaudited)

	First Quarter	Second Quarter	Third Quarter	Fourth Quarter
1995				
Net sales	$34,205	$42,936	$45,405	$32,787
Gross profit	$ 9,702	$13,496	$14,076	$ 8,934
Net income	$ 911	$ 1,653	$ 2,525	$ 859
Net income per common share	$ 0.13	$ 0.23	$ 0.35	$ 0.12
1994¹				
Net sales	$32,191	$40,657	$44,761	$31,193
Gross profit	$ 7,983	$11,064	$12,921	$ 7,074
Net income (loss)	$ 902	$ 714	$ 1,415	$(4,900)
Net income (loss) per common share	$ 0.13	$ 0.10	$ 0.20	$ (0.69)

¹Fourth quarter 1994 results include an after-tax charge of $4.1 million or $.57 per share, representing a write-down of certain assets at the Company's new plant as described in Note 12.

Report of Ernst & Young LLP, Independent Auditors

The Board of Directors and Stockholders
Ben & Jerry's Homemade, Inc.

We have audited the accompanying consolidated balance sheets of Ben & Jerry's Homemade, Inc. as of December 30, 1995 and December 31, 1994, and the related consolidated statements of operations, stockholders' equity, and cash flows for each of the three years in the period ended December 30, 1995. These financial statements are the responsibility of the Company's management. Our responsibility is to express an opinion on these financial statements based on our audits.

We conducted our audits in accordance with generally accepted auditing standards. Those standards require that we plan and perform the audit to obtain reasonable assurance about whether the financial statements are free of material misstatement. An audit includes examining, on a test basis, evidence supporting the amounts and disclosures in the financial statements. An audit also includes assessing the accounting principles used and significant estimates made by management, as well as evaluating the overall financial statement presentation. We believe that our audits provide a reasonable basis for our opinion.

In our opinion, the consolidated financial statements referred to above present fairly, in all material respects, the consolidated financial position of Ben & Jerry's Homemade, Inc. at December 30, 1995 and December 31, 1994 and the consolidated results of its operations and its cash flows for each of the three years in the period ended December 30,1995 in conformity with generally accepted accounting principles.

Boston, Massachusetts
January 26, 1996

Ernst & Young LLP

An Invitation

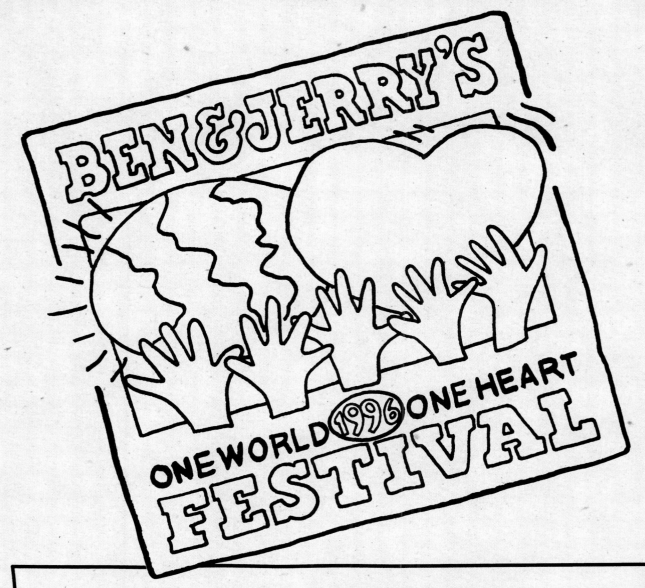

The Annual Meeting of Stockholders will be held on
Saturday, June 22, 1996, at 10:00 am
Mt. Ellen (Sugarbush North) in Warren, Vermont.

In conjunction with the Annual Shareholders' Meeting, Ben & Jerry's will host the annual
One World, One Heart Festival
Lincoln Peak (Sugarbush South) in Warren, Vermont, from 11:00 am until 7:00 pm.

For further information about Festival events and performers,
Call 1-800-BJ-FESTS
For lodging information in the Sugarbush area for the Annual Meeting
and Festival weekend, please call 1-800-53-SUGAR.

INDEX FOR "FROM CONCEPT TO PRACTICE" ASSIGNMENTS

"From Concept to Practice" assignments, printed in the margins throughout the book, are based on annual reports from Ben & Jerry's and other companies profiled in the opening vignette of each chapter. This Index is a convenient list of these financial statement assignments, which can be used in conjunction with the chapter or as cumulative problems at key points in the course.

Chapter 1

1.1 Reading Ben & Jerry's **Income Statement**   p. 14
Note the large amount of cost of sales—$109,125,000—in relation to the selling, general, and administrative expenses on Ben & Jerry's 1995 income statement (consolidated statement of operations). What types of costs would fall into the cost of sales category for Ben & Jerry's?

1.2 Reading Ben & Jerry's **Auditors' Report**   p. 25
Note the date at the bottom of the report. Why do you think it takes one month after the end of the year to release this report?

Chapter 2

2.1 Reading Ben & Jerry's **Income Statement**   p. 71
Which income statement format does Ben & Jerry's use: single-step or multiple-step? Calculate Ben & Jerry's 1995 and 1994 gross profit ratio. Explain what happened from 1994 to 1995.

2.2 Reading Starbucks' **Income Statement**   p. 72
Compute Starbucks' profit margin for the past two years. Did it go up or down from the prior year to the current year?

Chapter 3

3.1 Reading Ride's **Financial Statements**   p. 104
Ride Inc. purchases wood to use in making snowboards. Is this an internal or an external event? The company subsequently uses the wood in the production process. Is this an internal or an external event?

3.2 Reading Ben & Jerry's **Balance Sheet and Footnotes**   p. 110
How many liability accounts does the company report on its balance sheet? How are these liability accounts broken down in the accompanying notes?

Chapter 4

4.1 Reading McDonald's **Income Statement**   p. 155
Refer to McDonald's comparative income statements for 1995, 1994, and 1993 in the chapter opener. What percentage of total revenues were derived from franchised restaurants? Has this percentage changed over the three year period?

4.2 Reading Ben & Jerry's **Balance Sheet**   p. 158
Refer to the balance sheet in Ben & Jerry's annual report. How does Ben & Jerry's classify prepaid expenses? What types of prepaid expenses would you expect the company to have?

Chapter 5

5.1   Reading Ben & Jerry's **Annual Report**   p. 218
Is Ben & Jerry's a merchandiser? What items in the annual report can you cite to support your answer?

5.2   Reading The Gap's **Management Report**   p. 230
Refer to the management's report for The Gap in Exhibit 5-7. What is the composition of its Audit and Finance Committee? Why do you think it is comprised the way it is?

Chapter 6

6.1   Reading Ben & Jerry's **Annual Report**   p. 277
Which inventory method does Ben & Jerry's use? Where did you find this information? Do you think the company is justified in using the method it does?

6.2   Reading Circuit City's **Financial Statements**   p. 280
A footnote to Circuit City's financial statements indicates that "Inventory is stated at the lower of cost or market." Why do you think the application of the lower of cost or market rule would be important to a business like Circuit City?

6.3   Reading Ben & Jerry's **Financial Statements**   p. 284
Compute Ben & Jerry's inventory turnover ratio for 1995. What is the average length of time it takes to sell its inventory? Does this seem reasonable for the type of business the company is in?

Chapter 7

7.1   Reading Ben & Jerry's **Financial Statements**   p. 331
Does Ben & Jerry's disclose in its annual report which method it uses to estimate bad debts? In what line item on the income statement would you expect bad debts expense to be included?

7.2   Reading PepsiCo's **Financial Statements**   p. 332
Refer to p. 326 for the presentation of PepsiCo's accounts and notes receivable on its 1995 and 1994 year-end balance sheets. What was the amount of increase or decrease in the allowance account? What does the change in the account mean?

7.3   Reading Ben & Jerry's **Financial Statements**   p. 332
Compute Ben & Jerry's accounts receivable turnover for 1995. What is the average length of time it takes to collect a receivable? Does this seem reasonable for the company's type of business?

Chapter 8

8.1   Reading Ben & Jerry's **Annual Report**   p. 365
What amount did Ben & Jerry's report as depreciation in 1995? Where is it disclosed? What depreciation method was used?

8.2   Reading Time-Warner's **Balance Sheet**   p. 376
Which items on Time-Warner's 1995 balance sheet should be considered intangible assets?

Chapter 9

9.1   Reading JCPenney's **Balance Sheet**   p. 408
Refer to JCPenney's balance sheet for 1995. What accounts are listed as current liabilities? What was the change in Accounts Payable from 1994 to 1995?

9.2   Reading Ben & Jerry's **Annual Report**   p. 418
Ben & Jerry's annual report contains a contingent liability. What is it? Do you think it has been properly disclosed? Was it recorded on the financial statements?

Chapter 10

10.1   Reading Coca-Cola's **Balance Sheet**   p. 464
Coca-Cola lists three items as long-term liabilities on its 1995 balance sheet. What are those items? Did they increase or decrease?

10.2   Reading Ben & Jerry's **Balance Sheet**   p. 487
Calculate the 1994 and 1995 debt-to-equity ratios for Ben & Jerry's. Did 1995's debt-to-equity ratio go up or down from 1994's?

Chapter 11

11.1   Reading Ford's **Annual Report**   p. 515
Which financial statements could you look at to identify the different classes of stock issued by Ford? Which classes of stock are issued? How many shares of each class have been issued?

11.2   Reading Ben & Jerry's **Annual Report**   p. 526
Refer to Ben & Jerry's 1995 report. What was the book value per share of the common stock? How did that relate to the market value of the stock?

Chapter 12

12.1   Reading Sprint's **Income Statement**   p. 568
Refer to Sprint's 1995 income statement. Why was more than one earnings per share number presented? Sprint calculated earnings per share for which lines of the statement?

12.2   Reading Ben & Jerry's **Annual Report**   p. 572
Refer to Ben & Jerry's statement of stockholders' equity. What were the major reasons for the difference between the 1994 year-end stockholders' equity amount of $72,502,000 and the 1995 year-end amount of $78,531,000?

Chapter 13

13.1   Reading Ben & Jerry's **Footnotes**   p. 624
Locate the footnote in which the company describes its consolidation policies. What percentage of the stock does Ben & Jerry's own in its subsidiaries? Given the nature of its business, what kinds of subsidiaries would you expect Ben & Jerry's to own?

13.2   Reading Ben & Jerry's **Footnotes**   p. 630
Who does Ben & Jerry's disclose as a significant customer? How reliant is Ben & Jerry's on this customer for business? Would this concern you as a Ben & Jerry's stockholder?

13.3   Reading Whirlpool's **Balance Sheet**   p. 634
Refer to Whirlpool's 1995 consolidated balance sheet in Exhibit 13-13. How does Whirlpool classify its minority interests? What is the amount of minority interests at December 31, 1995?

Chapter 14

14.1   Reading IBM's **Statement of Cash Flows**   p. 676
Does IBM use the direct or indirect method in the Operating Activities section of its statement of cash flows? How can you tell which it is?

14.2   Reading Ben & Jerry's **Statement of Cash Flows**   p. 693
Did Accounts Receivable increase or decrease during 1995? Why is the change in this account deducted on the statement of cash flows?

Chapter 15

15.1   Reading Ben & Jerry's **Annual Report**   p. 737
Where does Ben & Jerry's annual report provide a financial summary? How many years does it include? In terms of a trend over time, which item on the summary do you think is the most significant?

15.2   Reading Wrigley's **Annual Report**   p. 740
Refer to Wrigley's Financial Highlights in Exhibit 15-3. Compute the company's gross profit ratio for each of the 11 years. Is there a noticeable upward or downward trend in the ratio over this time period?

15.3   Reading Wrigley's **Annual Report**   p. 756
Refer back to the financial highlights for Wrigley in the chapter opener. Compute Wrigley's dividend payout ratio for both 1995 and 1994 (use earnings before the nonrecurring gain). Why do you think dividends per share were increased to $.96 in 1995?

GLOSSARY

ABO   *See* Accumulated benefit obligation.

Accelerated depreciation   A term that refers to several methods by which a higher amount of depreciation is recorded in the early years of an asset's life and a lower amount is recorded in the later years. (p. 366)

Account   The record used to accumulate monetary amounts for each individual asset, liability, revenue, expense, and component of owners' equity. (p. 110)

Accounting controls   Procedures concerned with safeguarding the assets or the reliability of the financial statements. (p. 231)

Accounting cycle   A series of steps performed each period and culminating with the preparation of a set of financial statements. (p. 169)

Accounting system   The methods and records used to accurately report an entity's transactions and to maintain accountability for its assets and liabilities. (p. 231)

Accounting   The process of identifying, measuring, and communicating economic information to various users. (p. 9)

Accounts payable   Amounts owed for the purchase of inventory, goods, or services acquired in the normal course of business. (p. 410)

Accounts receivable turnover ratio   A measure of the number of times accounts receivable are collected in a period. (p. 745)

Accrual basis   A system of accounting in which revenues are recognized when earned and expenses when incurred. (p. 150)

Accrual   Cash has not yet been paid or received, but expense has been incurred or revenue earned. (p. 164)

Accrued asset   An asset resulting from the recognition of a revenue before the receipt of cash. (p. 164)

Accrued liability   A liability resulting from the recognition of an expense before the payment of cash. (p. 164)

Accrued pension cost   An account that represents the difference between the amount of pension recorded as an expense and the amount of the funding payment made to the pension fund. (p. 485)

Accrued vacation or sick pay   *See* Compensated Absences.

Accumulated benefit obligation (ABO)   A measure of the amount owed to employees for pensions if the employees retired at their existing salary levels. (p. 486)

Acid-test or quick ratio   A stricter test of liquidity than the current ratio, this ratio excludes inventory and prepayments from the numerator. (p. 744)

Acquisition cost   This amount includes all of the costs normally necessary to acquire an asset and prepare it for its intended use. (p. 363)

Additional paid-in capital   The amount received for the issuance of stock in excess of the par value of the stock. (p. 515)

Adjusting entries   Journal entries made at the end of a period by a company using the accrual basis of accounting. (p. 157)

Administrative controls   Procedures concerned with efficient operation of the business and adherence to managerial policies. (p. 231)

Affiliate   A company that has enough of its stock held by another company to give the other entity significant influence over it. (p. 604)

Aging schedule   A form used to categorize the various individual accounts receivable according to the length of time each has been outstanding. (p. 331)

Allowance method   A method of estimating bad debts on the basis of either the net credit sales of the period or the amount of accounts receivable at the end of the period. (p. 328)

American Accounting Association   The professional organization for accounting educators. (p. 26)

American Institute of Certified Public Accountants (AICPA)   The professional organization for certified public accountants. (p. 23)

Amortized cost method   A bond investment accounting method in which the investment account is adjusted periodically to recognize the amortization of premium or discount. (p. 608)

Amount of an annuity   *See* Future Value of an Annuity.

An expense of the period   *See* Revenue expenditure.

Annuity   A series of payments of equal amount. (p. 425)

Appropriation of retained earnings   An account that indicates that a company has designated a portion of the balance of Retained Earnings for a specific purpose. (p. 571)

Asset turnover ratio   The relationship between net sales and total assets. (p. 752)

Asset   A future economic benefit. (p. 8)

Audit committee   The board of directors subset that acts as a direct contact between the stockholders and the independent accounting firm. (p. 230)

Auditing   The process of examining the financial statements and the underlying records of a company in order to render an opinion as to whether the statements are fairly presented. (p. 25)

Auditors' report   The opinion rendered by a public accounting firm concerning the fairness of the presentation of the financial statements. (p. 25)

Authorized shares   The maximum number of shares a corporation may issue as indicated in the corporate charter. (p. 512)

Available-for-sale securities   Stocks and bonds that are not classified as either held-to-maturity or trading securities. (p. 607)

Average collection period   *See* Number of days' sales in receivables.

Balance sheet The financial statement that summarizes the assets, liabilities, and owners' equity at a specific point in time. (p. 12)

Bank reconciliation A form used by the accountant to reconcile the balance shown on the bank statement for a particular account with the balance shown in the accounting records. (p. 321)

Bank statement A detailed list, provided by the bank, of all the activity for a particular account during the month. (p. 319)

Blind receiving report A form used by the receiving department to account for the quantity and condition of merchandise received from a supplier. (p. 240)

Board of directors The group composed of key officers of a corporation and outside members responsible for the general oversight of the affairs of the entity. (p. 230)

Bond issue price The total of the present value of the cash flows produced by a bond. It is calculated as the present value of the annuity of interest payments plus the present value of the principal. (p. 467)

Bond par value *See* Face Value.

Bond A certificate that represents a corporation's promise to repay a certain amount of money and interest in the future. (p. 6)

Bonds *See* Debt securities.

Book of original entry *See* Journal.

Book value of bond *See* Carrying Value.

Book value per share Total stockholders' equity divided by the number of shares of common stock outstanding. (p. 526)

Book value The original acquisition cost of an asset minus the amount of accumulated depreciation. (p. 365)

Callable bonds Bonds that may be redeemed or retired before their specified due date. (p. 466)

Callable feature Allows the issuing firm to eliminate a class of stock by paying the stockholders a fixed amount. (p. 516)

Capital expenditure A cost that improves an operating asset and is added to the asset account. (p. 371)

Capital lease A lease that meets one or more of four criteria and is recorded as an asset by the lessee. (p. 477)

Capital stock A category on the balance sheet to indicate the owners' contributions to a corporation. (p. 8)

Capitalization of interest The process of treating the cost of interest on constructed assets as a part of the asset cost rather than as an expense. (p. 364)

Carrying value The face value of a bond plus the amount of unamortized premium or minus the amount of unamortized discount. (p. 471)

Cash basis A system of accounting in which revenues are recognized when cash is received and expenses when cash is paid. (p. 150)

Cash equivalent An investment that is readily convertible to a known amount of cash and has an original maturity to the investor of three months or less. (p. 315)

Cash flow from operations to capital expenditures ratio A measure of the ability of a company to finance long-term asset acquisitions from cash from operations. (p. 750)

Cash flow from operations to current liabilities ratio A measure of the ability to pay current debts from operating cash flows. (p. 745)

Cash flows statement *See* Statement of cash flows.

Cash to cash operating cycle The length of time from the purchase of inventory to the collection of any receivable from the sale. (p. 748)

Certified Public Accountant (CPA) The professional designation for public accountants who have passed a rigorous exam and met certain requirements determined by the state. (p. 23)

Change in accounting method *See* Change in accounting principle.

Change in accounting principle An income statement item that occurs when a company changes from one accounting method to another. (p. 567)

Change in estimate A change in the life of an asset or in its expected residual value. (p. 371)

Chart of accounts A numerical list of all the accounts used by a company. (p. 110)

Closing entries Journal entries made at the end of the period to return the balance in all nominal accounts to zero and transfer the net income or loss and the dividends of the period to Retained Earnings. (p. 171)

Common stock, preferred stock *See* Equity securities.

Comparability The quality of accounting information that allows a user to analyze two or more companies and look for similarities and differences. (p. 57)

Compensated absences Employment absences, such as sick days and vacation days, for which it is expected that employees will be paid. (p. 439)

Compound interest Interest calculated on the principal plus previous amounts of interest accumulated. (p. 422)

Comprehensive income The amount that reflects the total change in net assets from all sources except investments or withdrawals by the owners of the company. (p. 574)

Conglomerate A combination of companies with operations in different industries. (p. 617)

Conservatism The practice of using the least optimistic estimate when two estimates of amounts are about equally likely. (p. 59)

Consignment A legal arrangement in which inventory owned by one company is turned over to another one for sale. (p. 266)

Consistency The quality of accounting information that allows a user to compare two or more accounting periods for a single company. (p. 58)

Consolidated financial statements Statements that report on the parent corporation and any separate legal entities called *subsidiaries.* (p. 606)

Contingent asset An amount that involves an existing condition dependent on some future event by which the company stands to gain. These amounts are not normally reported. (p. 419)

Contingent gain *See* Contingent Asset.

Contingent liability A liability that involves an existing condition for which the outcome is not known with certainty and depends on some future event. (p. 414)

Contingent loss *See* Contingent Liability.

Contra account An account with a balance that is opposite that of a related account. (p. 159)

Contributed capital *See* Capital stock.

Control account The general ledger account that is supported by a subsidiary ledger. (p. 326)

Controller The chief accounting officer for a company. (p. 24)

Convertible feature Allows preferred stock to be returned to the corporation in exchange for common stock. (p. 516)

Corporation A form of entity organized under the laws of a particular state; ownership evidenced by shares of stock. (p. 6)

Correction of error *See* Prior period adjustment.

Cost of goods available for sale Beginning inventory plus cost of goods purchased. (p. 222)

Cost of goods sold Cost of goods available for sale minus ending inventory. (p. 223)

Cost of sales *See* Cost of goods sold.

Cost principle Assets recorded at the cost to acquire them. (p. 21)

Credit card draft A multiple-copy document used by a company that accepts a credit card for a sale. (p. 336)

Credit memoranda Additions on a bank statement for such items as interest paid on the account and notes collected by the bank for the customer. (p. 321)

Credit An entry on the right side of an account. (p. 113)

Creditor Someone to whom a company has a debt. (p. 8)

Cumulative effect The total effect of a change in accounting principle for all years prior to the current year. (p. 567)

Cumulative feature The holders of this stock have a right to dividends in arrears before the current year dividend is distributed. (p. 515)

Current asset An asset that is expected to be realized in cash or sold or consumed during the operating cycle or within one year if the cycle is shorter than one year. (p. 61)

Current liability An obligation that will be satisfied within the next operating cycle or within one year if the cycle is shorter than one year. (p. 408)

Current maturities of long-term debt The portion of a long-term liability that will be paid within one year of the balance sheet date. (p. 412)

Current ratio Current assets divided by current liabilities. (p. 65)

Current value The amount of cash, or its equivalent, that could be received by selling an asset currently. (p. 149)

Debenture bonds Bonds that are backed by the general creditworthiness of the issuer and are not backed by specific collateral. (p. 465)

Debit memoranda Deductions on a bank statement for such items as NSF checks and various service charges. (p. 321)

Debit An entry on the left side of an account. (p. 113)

Debt securities Bonds issued by corporations and governmental bodies as a form of borrowing. (p. 318)

Debt service coverage ratio A statement of cash flows measure of the ability of a company to meet its interest and principal payments. (p. 750)

Debt-to-equity ratio Total liabilities to total stockholders' equity. (p. 66)

Debt-to-total-assets ratio Total liabilities divided by total assets. (p. 66)

Deferral Cash has either been paid or received, but expense or revenue has not yet been recognized. (p. 164)

Deferred expense An asset resulting from the payment of cash before the incurrence of expense. (p. 164)

Deferred revenue A liability resulting from the receipt of cash before the recognition of revenue. (p. 164)

Deferred tax The account used to reconcile the difference between the amount recorded as income tax expense and the amount that is payable as income tax. (p. 481)

Deposit in transit A deposit recorded on the books but not yet reflected on the bank statement. (p. 320)

Depreciation The allocation of the cost of a tangible, long-term asset over its useful life. (p. 57)

Direct method For preparing the Operating Activities section of the statement of cash flows, the approach in which cash receipts and cash payments are reported. (p. 673)

Direct write-off method The recognition of bad debts expense at the point an account is written off as uncollectible. (p. 328)

Discontinued operations An income statement category indicating that a major segment or division of the company has been or will be sold. (p. 562)

Discount on bonds The excess of the face value of bonds over the issue price. It occurs when the market rate on the bonds exceeds the face rate. (p. 469)

Discount on notes payable A contra liability account that represents interest deducted from a loan or note in advance. (p. 411)

Discounted note An alternative name for a non-interest-bearing promissory note. (p. 334)

Discounting The process of selling a promissory note. (p. 337)

Disposal of a segment *See* Discontinued operations.

Dividend payout ratio The annual dividend amount divided by the annual net income. (p. 519)

Dividend yield ratio The relationship between dividends and the market price of a company's stock. (p. 756)

Dividends A distribution of the net income of a business to its owners. (p. 14)

Double declining-balance method A method by which depreciation is recorded at twice the straight-line rate but the depreciable balance is reduced in each period. (p. 366)

Double entry system A system of accounting in which every transaction is recorded with equal debits and credits and the accounting equation is kept in balance. (p. 115)

Earned capital *See* Retained earnings.

Earnings per share A number that represents the rights of the common stockholders to the income of the company; calculated as net income minus preferred dividends divided by the number of shares of common stock outstanding. (p. 568)

Economic entity concept The assumption that a single, identifiable unit must be accounted for in all situations. (p. 5)

Effective interest method of amortization The process of transferring a portion of premium or discount to interest expense. This method transfers an amount resulting in a constant effective interest rate. (p. 471)

Equity investee *See* Affiliate.

Equity method An investment accounting method in which income is recognized as a proportionate share of the income of the investee. (p. 606)

Equity securities Securities issued by corporations as a form of ownership in the business. (p. 318)

Estimated liability A contingent liability that is accrued and is reflected on the balance sheet. Common examples are warranties, guarantees, and premium offers. (p. 416)

Event A happening of consequence to an entity. (p. 104)

Exchange rate A measure of the relative worth of two different currencies. (p. 625)

Expenses Outflows or other using up of assets or incurrences of liabilities resulting from delivering goods, rendering services, or carrying out other activities. (p. 157)

Expired costs *See* Expenses.

External event An event involving interaction between an entity and its environment. (p. 104)

Extinguishment of bonds *See* Bond Retirement.

Extraordinary item An item that is considered both unusual and infrequent and is presented in a separate category of the income statement. (p. 565)

Face rate of interest The interest rate stated on the bond certificate. It is also called the *nominal or coupon rate*. (p. 467)

Face value The principal amount of the bond as stated on the bond certificate. (p. 464)

FIFO method An inventory costing method that assigns the most recent costs to ending inventory. (p. 272)

Financial Accounting Standards Board (FASB) The group in the private sector with authority to set accounting standards. (p. 23)

Financial accounting The branch of accounting concerned with the preparation of general-purpose financial statements for both management and outsider use. (p. 11)

Financing activities Activities concerned with the raising and repayment of funds in the form of debt and equity. (p. 672)

Finished goods A manufacturer's inventory that is complete and ready for sale. (p. 265)

FOB destination point Terms that require the seller to pay for the cost of shipping the merchandise to the buyer. (p. 227)

FOB shipping point Terms that require the buyer to pay the shipping costs. (p. 227)

Foreign Corrupt Practices Act Legislation intended to increase the accountability of management for accurate records and reliable financial statements. (p. 230)

Foreign currency transaction A transaction in which a company agrees to receive or make payment in a foreign currency. (p. 626)

Foreign currency translation The process of restating the financial statements of a company from one currency to another. (p. 627)

Freight-in *See* Transportation-in.

Functional currency The currency of the primary economic environment in which an entity operates. (p. 628)

Funding payment A payment made by the employer to the pension fund or its trustee. (p. 484)

Future value of a single amount The amount that will be accumulated in the future when one amount is invested at the present time and accrues interest until the future time. (p. 423)

Future value of an annuity The amount that will be accumulated in the future when a series of payments is invested and accrues interest until the future time. (p. 426)

Gain on sale of asset An account whose amount indicates that the selling price received on an asset's disposal exceeds its book value. (p. 373)

Gain or loss on redemption The difference between the carrying value and the redemption price at the time bonds are redeemed. This amount is presented as an income statement account. (p. 475)

General journal The journal used in lieu of a specialized journal. (p. 118)

General ledger A book, file, diskette, magnetic tape, or other device containing all of a company's accounts. (p. 111)

Generally accepted accounting principles (GAAP) The various methods, rules, practices, and other procedures that have evolved over time in response to the need to regulate the preparation of financial statements. (p. 22)

Going concern The assumption that an entity is not in the process of liquidation and that it will continue indefinitely. (p. 21)

Goodwill An intangible asset that represents the excess of the purchase price for a business over the fair value of the net assets acquired. (p. 376)

Gross margin *See* Gross profit.

Gross pay *See* Gross wages.

Gross profit method A technique used to establish an estimate of the cost of inventory stolen, destroyed, or otherwise damaged or of the amount of inventory on hand at an interim date. (p. 281)

Gross profit ratio Gross profit to net sales. (p. 742)

Gross profit The amount of net sales minus the amount of cost of sales. (p. 560)

Gross wages The amount of an employee's wages before deductions. (p. 436)

Held-to-maturity securities Investments in other companies' bonds that the investor has the positive intent and the ability to hold to maturity. (p. 607)

Historical cost The amount that is paid for an asset and that is used as a basis for recognizing it on the balance sheet and carrying it on later balance sheets. (p. 149)

Horizontal analysis A comparison of financial statement items over a period of time. (p. 735)

Horizontal combination A combination of businesses that are in competition with each other. (p. 616)

Income before income taxes An income statement subtotal calculated as operating income plus other income items, such as interest, minus other expense items. (p. 561)

Income from operations *See* Operating income.

Income statement A statement that summarizes revenues and expenses. (p. 12)

Indirect method For preparing the Operating Activities section of the statement of cash flows, the approach in which net income is reconciled to net cash flow from operations. (p. 674)

Installment method The method in which revenue is recognized at the time cash is collected; used for various types of consumer items, such as automobiles and appliances. (p. 155)

Intangible assets Long-term assets that have no physical properties, for example patents, copyrights, and goodwill. (p. 376)

Interest method of amortization *See* Effective Interest Method of Amortization.

Interest on interest *See* Compound Interest.

Interest-bearing note A promissory note in which the interest rate is explicitly stated. (p. 333)

Interest The difference between the principal amount of a promissory note and its maturity value. (p. 333)

Interim statements Financial statements prepared monthly, quarterly, or at other intervals less than a year in duration. (p. 172)

Internal audit staff The department responsible for monitoring and evaluating the internal control system. (p. 229)

Internal auditing The department in a company responsible for the review and appraisal of a company's accounting and administrative controls. (p. 24)

Internal control system Policies and procedures necessary to ensure the safeguarding of an entity's assets, the reliability of its accounting records, and the accomplishment of overall company objectives. (p. 229)

Internal event An event occurring entirely within an entity. (p. 104)

International Accounting Standards Committee (IASC) The organization formed to develop worldwide accounting standards. (p. 23)

Inventory profit The portion of the gross profit that results from holding inventory during a period of rising prices. (p. 276)

Inventory turnover ratio A measure of the number of times inventory is sold during a period. (p. 283)

Investing activities Activities concerned with the acquisition and disposal of long-term assets. (p. 671)

Invoice The form sent by the seller to the buyer as evidence of a sale. (p. 239)

Invoice approval form A form the accounting department uses before making payment to document the accuracy of all the information about a purchase. (p. 240)

Issued shares The number of shares sold or distributed to stockholders. (p. 512)

Journal A chronological record of transactions, also known as the *book of original entry*. (p. 117)

Journalizing The act of recording journal entries. (p. 117)

Land improvements Additions made to a piece of property such as paving or landscaping a parking lot. The costs are treated separately from land for purposes of recording depreciation. (p. 364)

Lender *See* Creditor.

Leverage The use of borrowed funds and amounts contributed by preferred stockholders to earn an overall return higher than the cost of these funds. (p. 754)

Liability An obligation of a business. (p. 8)

LIFO conformity rule The IRS requirement that if LIFO is used on the tax return, it must also be used in reporting income to stockholders. (p. 275)

LIFO liquidation The result of selling more units than are purchased during the period, which can have negative tax consequences if a company is using LIFO. (p. 274)

LIFO method An inventory costing method that assigns the most recent costs to cost of goods sold. (p. 272)

LIFO reserve   The excess of the value of a company's inventory stated at FIFO over the value stated at LIFO. (p. 275)

Liquidity   The ability of a company to pay its debts as they come due. (p. 63)

Long-term debt, current portion   *See* Current Maturities of Long-Term Debt.

Long-term liability   An obligation that will not be satisfied within one year. (p. 464)

Loss on sale of asset   An account whose amount indicates that the book value of an asset exceeds the selling price received on its disposal. (p. 374)

Lower of cost or market (LCM) rule   A conservative inventory valuation approach that is an attempt to anticipate declines in the value of inventory before its actual sale. (p. 279)

Maker   The party that agrees to repay the money for a promissory note at some future date. (p. 332)

Management accounting   The branch of accounting concerned with providing management with information to facilitate the planning and control functions. (p. 10)

Management's report   *See* Report of management.

Market rate of interest   The interest rate that bondholders could obtain by investing in other bonds that are similar to the issuing firm's bonds. (p. 467)

Market value per share   The selling price of the stock as indicated by the most recent stock transactions on, for example, the stock exchange. (p. 527)

Matching principle   The association of revenue of a period with all of the costs necessary to generate that revenue. (p. 156)

Materiality   The magnitude of an omission or misstatement in accounting information that will affect the judgment of someone relying on the information. (p. 58)

Maturity date   The date that a promissory note is due. (p. 333)

Maturity value   The amount of cash to be paid by the maker to the payee on the maturity date of a promissory note. (p. 333)

Merchandise inventory   The account that wholesalers and retailers use to report inventory held for sale. (p. 264)

Minority interest   A subsidiary's owners' equity not attributable to the interest of the parent. (p. 624)

Monetary unit   The yardstick used to measure amounts in financial statements; the dollar in the United States. (p. 21)

Moving average   The name given to an average cost method when it is used with a perpetual inventory system. (p. 290)

Multiple-step income statement   An income statement that provides the reader with classifications of revenues and expenses as well as with important subtotals. (p. 69)

Natural resources   An asset that is consumed during its use, for example coal or oil. (p. 374)

Net income per share   *See* Earnings per share.

Net pay   The amount of an employee's paycheck after deductions. (p. 436)

Net sales   Sales revenue less sales returns and allowances and sales discounts. (p. 219)

Nominal accounts   The name given to revenue, expense, and dividend accounts because they are temporary and are closed at the end of the period. (p. 170)

Non-interest-bearing note   A promissory note in which interest is not explicitly stated but is implicit in the agreement. (p. 333)

Nonbusiness entity   Organization operated for some purpose other than to earn a profit. (p. 6)

Noncurrent liability   *See* Long-Term Liability.

Note receivable   An asset resulting from the acceptance of a promissory note from another company. (p. 332)

Notes payable   Amounts owed that are represented by a formal contractual agreement. These amounts usually require the payment of interest. (p. 410)

Number of days' sales in inventory   A measure of how long it takes to sell inventory. (p. 284)

Number of days' sales in receivables   A measure of the average age of accounts receivable. (p. 746)

Operating activities   Activities concerned with the acquisition and sale of products and services. (p. 671)

Operating cycle   The period of time between the purchase of inventory and the collection of any receivable from the sale of the inventory. (p. 60)

Operating income   An income statement subtotal calculated as gross profit minus operating expenses. (p. 560)

Operating lease   A lease that does not meet any of four criteria and is not recorded by the lessee. (p. 477)

Organization costs   Costs that are incurred at the initial formation of a corporation and are treated as an intangible asset. (p. 376)

Original cost   *See* Historical cost.

Outstanding check   A check written by a company but not yet presented to the bank for payment. (p. 320)

Outstanding shares   The number of shares issued less the number of shares held as treasury stock. (p. 512)

Owners' equity   The owners' claim on the assets of an entity. (p. 12) *See also* Stockholders' equity.

P/E ratio   *See* Price/earnings ratio.

Paid-in capital in excess of par value   *See* Additional paid-in capital.

Paid-in capital   *See* Capital stock.

Par value   An arbitrary amount that is stated on the face of the stock certificate and that represents the legal capital of the firm. (p. 512)

Parent   An entity that controls another entity by ownership of a majority of the other company's common stock. (p. 604)

Participating feature Stock that has a provision allowing the stockholders to share, on a percentage basis, in the distribution of an abnormally large dividend. (p. 516)

Partnership agreement A document that specifies how much each owner should invest, the salary of each owner, and how profits are to be shared. (p. 534)

Partnership A business owned by two or more individuals and with the characteristic of unlimited liability. (p. 6)

Payee The party that will receive the money from a promissory note at some future date. (p. 332)

PBO *See* Projected benefit obligation.

Pension An obligation to pay retired employees as compensation for service performed while employed. (p. 484)

Percentage-of-completion method The method used by contractors to recognize revenue before the completion of a long-term contract. (p. 154)

Periodic system The system in which the Inventory account is updated only at the end of the period. (p. 223)

Permanent accounts *See* Real accounts.

Permanent difference A difference between the accounting for tax purposes and the accounting for financial reporting purposes. This type of difference occurs when an item affects one set of calculations but never affects the other set. (p. 482)

Perpetual system The system in which the Inventory account is increased at the time of each purchase of merchandise and decreased at the time of each sale. (p. 223)

Petty cash fund Money kept on hand for making minor disbursements using coin and currency rather than writing checks. (p. 324)

Pooling of interests method In recording a business combination, an accounting approach that is sometimes used when shares of stock in the two companies are exchanged. (p. 617)

Posting The process of transferring amounts from a journal to the appropriate ledger accounts. (p. 117)

Premium on bonds The excess of the issue price over the face value of bonds. It occurs when the face rate on the bonds exceeds the market rate. (p. 469)

Prepaid expense, prepaid asset *See* Deferred expense.

Present value of a single amount The present amount that is equivalent to an amount at a future time. (p. 424)

Present value of an annuity The amount needed at the present time to be equivalent to a series of payments and interest in the future. (p. 427)

Price/earnings (P/E) ratio The relationship between a company's performance according to the income statement and its performance in the stock market. (p. 755)

Principal The amount of cash received, or the fair value of the products or services received, by the maker when a promissory note is issued. (p. 333)

Prior period adjustment A correction that is not reported on the income statement but is presented as an adjustment to the balance of the Retained Earnings account. (p. 570)

Production method The method in which revenue is recognized when a commodity is produced rather than when it is sold. (p. 155)

Profit margin ratio Net income to net sales. (p. 472)

Profitability How well management is using company resources to earn a return on the funds invested by the various groups. (p. 751)

Profits or earnings *See* Net income.

Projected benefit obligation (PBO) A measure of the amount owed to employees for pensions if estimates of future salary increases are incorporated. (p. 486)

Promissory note A written promise to repay a definite sum of money on demand or at a fixed or determinable date in the future. (p. 332)

Purchase discounts The contra-purchases account used to record reductions in purchase price for early payment to the supplier. (p. 227)

Purchase invoice, sales invoice *See* Invoice.

Purchase method In recording a business combination, an accounting approach that is used when one company uses cash, other assets, or debt to acquire the other company. (p. 617)

Purchase order The form sent by the purchasing department to the supplier. (p. 239)

Purchase price in excess of the market value of assets *See* Goodwill.

Purchase requisition form The form a department uses to initiate a request to order merchandise. (p. 237)

Purchase returns and allowances The contra-purchases account used in a periodic inventory system when a refund is received from a supplier or a reduction given in the balance owed to the supplier. (p. 226)

Purchases The account used in a periodic inventory system to record acquisitions of merchandise. (p. 225)

Quantity discount A reduction in selling price for buying a large number of units of a product. (p. 220)

Quick ratio *See* Acid-test ratio.

Raw materials The inventory of a manufacturer before the addition of any direct labor or manufacturing overhead. (p. 264)

Real accounts The name given to balance sheet accounts because they are permanent and are not closed at the end of the period. (p. 170)

Recognition The process of recording an item in the financial statements as an asset, liability, revenue, expense, or the like. (p. 148)

Relevance The capacity of information to make a difference in a decision. (p. 56)

Reliability The quality of accounting information that makes it dependable in representing the events that it purports to represent. (p. 57)

Replacement cost The current cost of a unit of inventory. (p. 276)

Report of independent accountants *See* Auditors' report.

Report of management A written statement in the annual report indicating the responsibility of management for the financial statements. (p. 229)

Research and development costs Expenditures incurred in the discovery of new knowledge and the translation of research into a design or plan for a new product. (p. 379)

Retail inventory method A technique used by retailers to convert the retail value of inventory to a cost basis. (p. 283)

Retained earnings The part of owners' equity that represents the income earned less dividends paid over the life of an entity. (p. 12)

Retained income *See* Retained earnings.

Retirement of stock When the stock of a corporation is repurchased with no intention to reissue at a later date. (p. 519)

Return on assets ratio A measure of a company's success in earning a return for all providers of capital. (p. 751)

Return on common stockholders' equity ratio A measure of a company's success in earning a return for the common stockholders. (p. 753)

Return on sales ratio A variation of the profit margin ratio, this measures earnings before payments to creditors. (p. 752)

Return on stockholders' equity Net income divided by average stockholders' equity. (p. 72)

Revenue expenditure A cost that keeps an operating asset in its normal operating condition and is treated as an expense of the period. (p. 371)

Revenue recognition principle Revenues are recognized in the income statement when they are realized, or realizable, and earned. (p. 154)

Revenues Inflows or other enhancements of assets or settlements of liabilities from delivering or producing goods, rendering services, or other activities. (p. 153)

Sales discounts The contra-revenue account used to record discounts given customers for early payment of their accounts. (p. 222)

Sales returns and allowances The contra-revenue account used to record both refunds to customers and reductions of their accounts. (p. 220)

Securities and Exchange Commission (SEC) The federal agency with ultimate authority to determine the rules in preparing statements for companies whose stock is sold to the public. (p. 22)

Serial bonds Bonds that do not all have the same due date. A portion of the bonds comes due each time period. (p. 466)

Set of accounts *See* General ledger.

Share of stock A certificate that acts as ownership in a corporation. (p. 6)

Shareholder *See* Stockholder.

Shareholders' equity *See* Stockholders' equity.

Short-term liability *See* Current Liability.

Simple interest Interest that is earned or paid on the principal amount only. (p. 421)

Single-step income statement An income statement in which all expenses are added together and subtracted from all revenues. (p. 69)

Sole proprietorship Form of organization with a single owner. (p. 5)

Solvency The ability of a company to remain in business over the long term. (p. 748)

Source document A piece of paper, such as a sales invoice, that is used as the evidence to record a transaction. (p. 104)

Specific identification method An inventory costing method that relies on matching unit costs with the actual units sold. (p. 270)

Stated rate or nominal rate or coupon rate of interest *See* Face Rate of Interest.

Statement of cash flows The statement that summarizes the cash effects of the operating, investing, and financing activities for a period of time. (p. 667)

Statement of financial position or condition *See* Balance sheet.

Statement of income *See* Income statement.

Statement of retained earnings The statement that summarizes the income earned and dividends paid over the life of a business. (p. 14)

Statement of stockholders' equity A statement that indicates the differences between beginning and ending balances for all accounts in the stockholders' equity category. (p. 572)

Statutory consolidation A business combination in which a new entity is created to carry on the activities of the entities involved in the combination. (p. 617)

Statutory merger A business combination in which only one of the two entities survives. (p. 617)

Stock acquisition A business combination in which one company acquires a majority of the common stock of the other company. (p. 617)

Stock dividend A corporation's declaration and issuance of additional shares of its own stock to existing stockholders. (p. 522)

Stock split Creation of additional shares of stock and reduction of the par value of the stock. (p. 524)

Stockholder One of the owners of a corporation. (p. 8)

Stockholders' equity The owners' equity in a corporation. (p. 12)

Stocks *See* Equity securities.

Straight-line method A method by which the same dollar amount of depreciation is recorded in each year of asset use. (p. 159)

Subsidiary ledger The detail for a number of individual items that collectively make up a single general ledger account. (p. 326)

Subsidiary A separate legal entity controlled by another entity. (p. 604)

Temporary accounts *See* Nominal accounts.

Temporary difference A difference between the accounting for tax purposes and the accounting for financial reporting purposes. This type of difference affects both book and tax calculations but not in the same time period. (p. 482)

Term The length of time a promissory note is outstanding. (p. 333)

Time period Artificial segment on the calendar used as the basis for preparing financial statements. (p. 22)

Time value of money The concept that indicates that people should prefer to receive an immediate amount at the present time over an equal amount in the future. (p. 420)

Times interest earned ratio An income statement measure of the ability of a company to meet its interest payments. (p. 749)

Timing difference *See* Temporary difference.

Trade discount A selling price reduction offered to a special class of customers. (p. 220)

Trading securities Other companies' stocks and bonds bought and held for the purpose of selling them in the near term to generate profits on the appreciation in their price. (p. 607)

Transaction Any event, external or internal, that is recognized in a set of financial statements. (p. 104)

Translation adjustment The amount needed to balance the two sides of a balance sheet when financial statements are translated from one currency into another currency. (p. 629)

Transportation-in The adjunct account used to record freight costs paid by the buyer. (p. 225)

Treasurer The officer of an organization responsible for the safeguarding and efficient use of a company's liquid assets. (p. 24)

Treasury stock Stock issued by the firm and then repurchased but not retired. (p. 517)

Trend analysis *See* Horizontal analysis.

Trial balance A work sheet showing the balances in each account; used to prove the equality of debits and credits. (p. 119)

Understandability The quality of accounting information that makes it comprehensible to those willing to spend the necessary time. (p. 56)

Unearned revenue *See* Deferred revenue.

Unexpired cost *See* Asset.

Units-of-production method A method by which depreciation is determined as a function of the number of units the asset produces. (p. 366)

Unrealized gain/loss—available-for-sale securities A stockholders' equity account that reflects that the investment in certain securities was adjusted to market value. (p. 571)

Unusual and infrequent items *See* Extraordinary item.

Vertical analysis A comparison of various financial statement items within a single period with the use of common-size statements. (p. 735)

Vertical combination A combination of a company and either a supplier or a customer. (p. 617)

Voucher *See* Invoice approval form.

Weighted average cost method An inventory costing method that assigns the same unit cost to all units available for sale during the period. (p. 271)

Weighted average of shares The number of shares of stock weighted by the time period that the stock was outstanding. (p. 568)

Wholly owned subsidiary A subsidiary in which the parent owns all of the common stock. (p. 604)

Work in process The cost of unfinished products in a manufacturing company. (p. 265)

Work in progress *See* Work in process.

Work sheet A device used at the end of the period to gather the information needed to prepare financial statements without actually recording and posting adjusting entries. (p. 170)

Working capital Current assets minus current liabilities. (p. 743)

Yield or effective rate of interest *See* Market rate of interest.

PHOTO CREDITS

Chapter 1: page 2, Ben & Jerry's; page 4, Courtesy of Ben & Jerry's; page 21, © The Stock Yard; page 28, Stuart Weiss. **Chapter 2:** page 52, PhotoDisc; page 58, © Steve Lunetta/StockUp; page 61, PhotoDisc. **Chapter 3:** page 102, Photo courtesy of Ride Snowboards/Sean Sullivan; page 105, © 1997 Don Couch Photography; page 109, PhotoDisc; page 120, Stuart Weiss. **Chapter 4:** page 146, © 1997 Don Couch Photography; page 149, AP/Wide World Photos; page 160, © The Stock Yard. **Chapter 5:** page 216, The Gap Inc.; page 219, PhotoDisc; page 231, PhotoDisc. **Chapter 6:** page 262, PhotoDisc; page 264, Digital Stock; page 278, PhotoDisc. **Chapter 7:** page 312, Courtesy of Pepsi-Cola Company © 1995 Photo-Tech Inc.; page 326, Courtesy of Pepsi-Cola Company; page 336, PhotoDisc. **Chapter 8:** page 360, © 1997 Don Couch Photography; page 365, © 1997 Don Couch Photography; page 372, © Christian Bassu-Picca/Tony Stone Images. **Chapter 9:** page 406, Courtesy of JCPenney; page 413, Courtesy of JCPenney; page 416, Courtesy of the Tandy Corporation; page 423, Texas Lottery Commission; page 428, Stuart Weiss. **Chapter 10:** page 462, © 1997 Don Couch Photography; page 466, © Bill Varie/Image Bank; page 470, Sprint. **Chapter 11:** page 508, Ford Motor Company; page 516, Ford Motor Company; page 526, © The Stock Yard; page 530, © The Stock Yard. **Chapter 12:** page 558, PhotoDisc; page 561, Photo courtesy of Unisys Corporation; page 565, AP/World Wide Photos. **Chapter 13:** page 602, Courtesy of Whirlpool Corporation; page 606, Courtesy of Whirlpool Corporation; page 626, The Gap Inc.; page 637, Stuart Weiss; **Chapter 14:** page 664, Courtesy of International Business Machines Corporation. Unauthorized use not permitted; page 696, PhotoDisc. **Chapter 15:** page 732, Photograph reprinted courtesy of the Wm. Wrigley Jr. Company; page 748, PhotoDisc; page 755, © The Stock Yard.

Accounting for Your Decisions box photos © 1997 Don Couch Photography

Part Opener photo Steve Bardens © Tony Stone Images

Ben & Jerry's annual report material is reprinted by permission of Ben & Jerry's Homemade Inc. All rights reserved.

COMPANY INDEX

SUBJECT INDEX

Excess cash, 315
Exchange rate, 625–626
Expenditures. *See* Capital expenditure;
    Revenue expenditure
Expenses
  debits and credits for, 113–114
  deferred expenses, 158–160, 164–165
  definition, **157**
  recognition of, 156–157
External event, 104
External users, of accounting, 10–11
Extraordinary items
  on financial statement, 476
  on income statement, 563, **565**–566
  on statement of cash flows, 575

F

Face rate of interest, on bonds payable,
    467
Fair value accounting, 612, 614
FASB. *See* Financial Accounting Standards
    Board (FASB)
Federal Trade Commission, 11
FICA, 437
FIFO (first-in, first-out) method
  for inventory costs, 272
  with perpetual system, 289
**Financial Accounting Standards Board
    (FASB), 23**, 54–57, 439, 478, 567,
    573, 674
Financial activities. *See* Business activities
Financial decisions, need for, 4–5, 54, 55
Financial highlights, 2–3, A2
Financial information. *See* Accounting
    information
Financial ratios. *See* Ratios
Financial reporting
  cash flow, 55
  decision making information, 54
  Financial Accounting Standards Board
    (FASB) rules, 54
  by global company, 629–637
  international perspective, 59–60
  for investors and creditors, 54–55
  objectives, 54–56
  permanent differences with tax
    reporting, 482
  resources and claims to resources, 55
  temporary differences with tax
    reporting, 482
Financial statements. *See also* Annual
    reports; and headings
    beginning with Consolidated, such as
    Consolidated financial
    statements; and headings beginning
    with Statement, such as
    Statement of cash flows
  accounting equation, 12
  alternative accounting principles used
    in, 734
  analysis of comparative and
    common-size statements, 735–743
  comparisons between, 734–735
  conceptual framework, 21–22
  horizontal analysis, 735–741
  inflation effects on, 735

interim financial statements, 172
liquidity analysis and management of
  working capital, 743– 748, 758
precautions for analysis of, 734–735
profitability analysis, 751–757, 759
recognition and measurement in,
  148–150
relationships among, 18–20
solvency analysis, 748–751, 758
time period assumption, 22
translation of foreign financial
  statements, 627–629
types of, 11–20
vertical analysis, 735, 741–742
Financing activities
  determining cash flows from, 689,
    689–691
  noncash investing and, 676–677
  on statement of cash flows, **672**–673
  start up, 8
First-in, first-out. *See* FIFO (first-in,
    first-out) method
Fiscal year, 66
Five-year financial highlights, 2–3, A2
Fixed assets, 362
FOB destination point, 227
FOB shipping point, 227
Footings, 112
Foreign Corrupt Practices Act, 230
Foreign currency transactions, 625–627,
    626
Foreign Currency Translation
    Adjustments, 572
Foreign currency translations, 627
Foreign exchange rates, 625
Foreign financial statements, translation
    of, 627–629
Foreign markets, for U.S. corporations, 625
Franchises, 154–155
Freight-in, 225
Functional currency, 628
Fund accounting, 7
Future value of a single amount, 423–424
Future value of an annuity, 425–**426**

G

GAAP. *See* Generally accepted accounting
    principles (GAAP)
Gain on bond redemption, 476
Gain on sale of asset, 373, 681
General ledger, 111–112
**Generally accepted accounting principles
    (GAAP), 22**
Gift certificates, 156
Global corporations
  accounting for, 624–629
  business acquisitions, 631
  challenges for, 637
  consolidations, 631–634
  foreign currency transactions, 625–627
  investments in affiliates, 634
  operating in global environment,
    604–605
  reporting by, 629–637
  segmental disclosures, 629–630,
    636–637

  subsidiaries, 604–605
  translation adjustments, 634–635
  translation of foreign financial
    statements, 627–629
Goodwill
  definition, **376**
  legal life of, 380
  purchase of business and, 619
Government agencies, 11
Great Depression, 11
Gross method, of recording sales, 221
Gross profit, 70, **560**
Gross profit method, of valuing inventory,
    281–283
Gross profit percentage, 560
Gross profit ratio, 742
Gross wages, 436

H

Held-to-maturity bonds, 609
Held-to-maturity securities, 607–609
Historical cost, 21, 149. *See also*
    Acquisition cost
Horizontal analysis, 735–741
Horizontal combination, of business
    competitors, **616**

I

IASC. *See* International Accounting
    Standards Committee (IASC)
Income. *See also* Income statements
  comprehensive income, 573–574
  impact on retained earnings, 569–570
  operating income, 560–561
Income before income taxes, 561–562
Income measurement
  attribute to be measured, 149
  definition, 148–149
  inventory valuation and, 265–269
  unit of measure, 149–150
Income statements
  change in accounting principle and,
    566–567
  compared with statement of cash flows,
    152
  condensed income statement, 218
  conversion to cash basis, 687
  cost of goods purchased, 225
  cost of goods sold, 222, 681–683
  definition, 12, 14, 68
  discontinued operations on, 562–563
  examples, 72–73, 109, 668, 674
  extraordinary items on, 563, 565–566
  format, 69–71
  information revealed in, 151–153
  for merchandiser, 218–219
  multiple-step income statement, 69–72,
    560–562
  net sales, 219
  pensions on, 484–485
  reading a corporate income statement,
    560–567
  relationship with statement of
    comprehensive income, 574
  single-step format, 69

Bonds

FV = Amount on paper
    Stated interest rate

Market Rate = What people could
get if they invest elsewhere

Table 2 value for market rate
= PV of Principal

Table 4 value for market rate
= PV of interest payment

Add together to get proceeds
of bond issue

If this is less than FV, you are
selling at a discount.

If this is more, you are selling
at a premium

ex.

FV 100,000 @ 8%. $n = 10$
  mkt value = 9%.

   Principal = 100,000
   annual pmt = 8,000

  PV of principal = 42,241
  PV of interest = 51,341
                     ‾‾‾‾‾‾‾
   you can sell for 93,582, which is
   a discount off face value of 100,000

Bonds and Discounts

Bond of $1,000,000 @ 10%

Market value = 11%

∴ we must issue at a discount

Proceeds = $940,248

Discount = $59,752

As we pay off the interest on the bond,
we must _amortize_ the discount,
so that after bond is up we will be even

Amortization = Interest Expense - Cash interest

In the balance sheet,
Record amount of bond
    and subtract   (discount)
    but add back   amt of amortized discount

   ie   1,000,000   amt. bond
            (59,752)   discount
             3522   amortized so far